66.00

HAYDN:
CHRONICLE AND WORKS

HAYDN: CHRONICLE AND WORKS
in five volumes by
H. C. ROBBINS LANDON

Haydn: the Early Years 1732–1765
(in preparation)
Haydn at Eszterháza 1766–1790
Haydn in England 1791–1795
Haydn: the Years of 'The Creation' 1796–1800
Haydn: the Late Years 1801–1809

HAYDN
AT ESZTERHÁZA
1766–1790

For
Else Radant Landon
with love

Haydn: Chronicle and Works

VOLUME II

HAYDN
AT ESZTERHÁZA
1766–1790

H. C. ROBBINS LANDON

INDIANA UNIVERSITY PRESS

BLOOMINGTON   LONDON

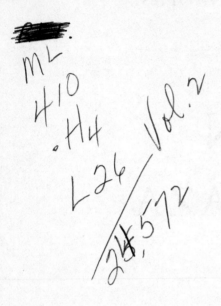
First American edition 1978 by Indiana University Press

Copyright © 1978 by H. C. Robbins Landon

Library of Congress Cataloging in Publication Data

Landon, Howard Chandler Robbins, 1926–
    Haydn: chronicle and works.

    Includes bibliographies and indexes.
    CONTENTS
  v. 2. Haydn at Eszterháza 1766–1790
    1. Haydn, Joseph, 1732–1809.
ML410.H4L26   780'.92'4[B]   76–14630
ISBN 0–253–37002–7   1 2 3 4 5 82 81 80 79 78

Printed in Great Britain

Contents

LIST OF ILLUSTRATIONS

Preface

As the reader will soon perceive, the documentation for this volume is dauntingly large. Twenty-five years ago, most of the Esterházy documents were not only unpublished but their existence unknown. They come from the Esterházy Archives, which are now housed basically in three places: in Budapest (Országos Széchényi Könyvtár [National Széchényi Library] and the Magyar Országos Levétár [Hungarian National Archives], where the former library may be subdivided in two further sections, the actual music being now in the Music Section and the documents – the so-called Acta Musicalia and Acta Theatralia – in the Theatre Section); in the Esterházy Castle of Forchtenstein (Burgenland, Austria); and in the Esterházy Castle of Eisenstadt. As a result of these data we are, for the first time, in a position to reconstruct life at Eszterháza, and Haydn's position there, in considerable detail. Nothing comparable, in fact, exists for the other major composers of the eighteenth century: apart from the autographs that Mozart and Michael Haydn (and their respective families) preserved, all the music, and almost all the documents, of the Archiepiscopal Court in Salzburg from 1750 to its demise in the Napoleonic Wars, have disappeared.

New documents from the Esterházy Archives keep coming to light: this is because, apart from the Acta Musicalia and the Acta Theatralia, most of the other material is as yet uncatalogued; in particular, new and important documents from Forchtenstein Castle appeared while this book was in progress and could be incorporated into the text. It is clear that the search for such documents is not yet over, though it is hardly likely that any more actual music will appear: the catalogue of 1806 by Haydn's successor, *Konzertmeister* J. N. Hummel, shows that only a small percentage of the music then known has since disappeared. Probably a great deal was lost when Eszterháza was abandoned in 1790, and (for example) the whole wind-band music repertoire of the Princely Grenadiers from the years 1761–90 is entirely lost.

I could not possibly include every document of this period: to have done so would have produced a volume of 10,000 pages. I have, however, tried to include all the important material about Haydn, his repertoire, his singers and his orchestra, based on those documents known up to the Autumn of 1977. Nor could I attempt to include all the contemporary criticisms of Haydn's music found principally in German-language newspapers and periodicals, many of which are – especially in the 1780s – laudatory but uninteresting: the reader will, however, find a generous selection here. Since it is important for the student to know the kind of thing I omitted, here are several typical specimens:

(1) Not only Haydn but several other members of the Esterházy operatic troupe at Eszterháza ordered opera scores for study and for possible performance. On 8 January 1788 Nunziato Porta, the Director of the Italian Opera, submitted a bill 'for

the Opera *La Bellinda fedele* [G. Tritto] as agreed, 4 fl. 30 xr.' The low price shows that the score was not new: it has survived (Esterházy Archives, Budapest, Ms. Mus. OE–95) and indeed shows traces of a pre-Eszterháza performance.[1] Haydn, however, never conducted the work. It seemed to me, therefore, that I might omit documentation of this sort, especially since such unperformed Esterházy scores are listed in detail in Bartha-Somfai.

(2) In the *Preßburger Zeitung*, we find in issue No. 56 of 14 July 1787, a long report about the origins of the 'Farewell' Symphony. Although the *PZ* is an invaluable source of information about musical life at Eszterháza – there was a regular correspondent there who sent in reports about operatic and theatrical activities – in this case, the story is obviously second-hand and could be omitted. (The *PZ* version, incidentally, has some relation to that told in Framery's *Notice sur Joseph Haydn*, about which more anon.)[2]

(3) There are many contemporary reports about Eszterháza Castle: I have included several *in extenso* and several more in extracts. I have not thought it necessary, for example, to include the whole of G. F. von R.[otenstein]'s 'Esterhaz' from Johann Bernouilli's *Sammlung kurzer Reisebeschreibungen* (Jahrgang 1783, IX. Band, pp. 250–98), but only those sections which were of direct interest to our story. It will be seen that in the part included there is a report of a *Fest* at the Esterházy Castle of Kittsee in 1770 in which we know, from documents in the Esterházy Archives, that Haydn and his band participated 'in their new summer uniforms' (*infra*, pp. 162f.). This whole *Fest* was totally unknown to Haydn scholarship hitherto (except for the fact that it had taken place).

(4) Haydn intended to make a trip to London as early as 1782, but was prevented from so doing. The British Press carried a series of stories about this non-appearance, and echoes of it were reprinted in German periodicals. In Cramer's *Magazin der Musik*, often cited in this volume, we find a report from Vienna in June 1784 (p. 194), stating that the English have decided to erect a monument to Haydn in Westminster Abbey, the actual unveiling of which has been postponed till Haydn himself arrives on British soil. I have mentioned this tale (*infra*, p. 597), but not quoted the document.

I have attempted to give as complete an account as is at present possible of the theatrical repertoire at Eszterháza, and this includes reports of the *Wandertruppen* (strolling players) which were engaged regularly. Since the publication of M. Horányi's brilliant book, *The Magnificence of Eszterháza* (English translation 1962), some Viennese periodicals have been discovered that enable us to amplify many details of repertoire in the middle 1770s. As far as the operatic repertoire is concerned, in 1954 I began studying photographs, made before the Second World War for the Library of Congress in Washington, of the non-Haydn Eszterháza operas. Later, in 1958–60, I was able to study the originals in Budapest. When in 1961 D. Bartha and L. Somfai published their monumental work, *Haydn als Opernkapellmeister*, I naturally abandoned my own research on the subject; but in the intervening years, a number of important Esterházy libretti – such as the pivotal pasticcio *La Circe* of 1789, for which Haydn contributed so much original music of his own – has come to light, and also my own studies of the non-Haydn operatic scores and parts in Budapest led to conclusions which were in some respects slightly different to those reached by my distinguished Hungarian colleagues (e.g. the identification of a false Haydn Cantata, 'Oime, dove m'ascondo' [XXIVa:Es 1] as part of Giuseppe Sarti's *Fra i due litiganti il terzo gode*,

---

1 Bartha-Somfai, 149f., 378.
2 *PZ* report reprinted in *HJB* VIII, pp. 189f.

conducted by Haydn at Eszterháza in 1783). Thus, if I have seemed to retraverse Bartha-Somfai's steps, it was primarily to amplify and clarify.

Of dire necessity I have been forced to ignore, for the most part, the musical value of these non-Haydn operas. Most of them are scarcely even names, except to a handful of experts; but although the average present-day music-lover can hardly see any great difference between the music, say, of Paisiello and Cimarosa, there was a vast difference to *settecento* ears, even to unmusical ones such as those of Catherine the Great. When Paisiello's *Gli astrologi immaginari* (which Haydn later conducted under its alternative title *I filosofi immaginari*) was first given at St Petersburg in 1779, the Empress, a few months afterwards, writes to Melchior Grimm:

> Il faut en passant que vous sachiez que dans tout cet opéra, il n'y a pas un air que je ne sache par cœur, et que depuis sti-là je crois que Paisiello peut faire rire, pleurer et donner à l'âme, à l'esprit et au cœur tel sentiment qu'il voudra, et que c'est un sorcier.... [St Petersburg, 23 August 1779]

whereas later she speaks witheringly of Cimarosa:

> ... Cimarosa a fait ici le Messe des morts pour la duchesse de Serra Capriola et un opéra comique dont je ne donnerais pas dix sous.... [St Petersburg, 21 April 1788]

The same opinion, curiously, was held by Napoleon, who adored Paisiello and particularly detested Cimarosa. I mention this as a warning to all of us not to fall into the same trap as our Victorian ancestors: they tended to place Haydn and Mozart together as worthy predecessors of Beethoven, and we tend to group Gazzaniga, Sarti, Paisiello and Cimarosa as rather unworthy precursors of Mozart. We err, and one day all these highly interesting composers of *settecento* Italian opera will be given their rightful place in music history.

***

Haydn was far away from the centre of Austrian politics for most of the period under consideration, but a few words about the general situation may not be amiss. Our volume begins in January 1766: Empress Maria Theresa's beloved husband, Franz (Francis) Stephan of Lorraine, had died in August 1765, so that, *mutatis mutandis*, a new life began not only for Haydn in Hungary but for the Empress in Schönbrunn. The story of her careful reforms belong to an earlier chapter of history, and the remaining years of her life – she died in 1780 – do not shine with the lustre of her previous reign when, aided by capable ministers (foremost among them Chancellor Kaunitz) she faced a bankrupt state as well as the devious statesmanship and formidable armies of Frederick the Great. Her son, Joseph II, who became her co-regent after Franz Stephan's death, turned out to be the most interesting and controversial monarch ever to sit on the Habsburg throne. To judge him solely from Haydn's standpoint – as of necessity was done in this volume – would be grossly to underestimate Joseph's many abilities. I have attempted briefly to show that even his knowledge of music was not restricted to disliking Haydn's and mistrusting Mozart's. Apart from that, we may turn to a recent work by Karl A. Roider, Jr., for an admirable summary of Joseph II's brief reign:

> ... Upon her death, Maria Theresa was succeeded by her son, Joseph II, who immediately implemented the sweeping reforms he had tried to persuade his mother to accept. Within a year after her death, he issued both an Edict of Toleration, allowing Protestants and Greek Orthodox a measure of religious

freedom, and a Patent to Abolish Serfdom, guaranteeing freedom of person to every peasant. Joseph then instituted a thorough centralization of the monarchy by obliterating all traditional and provincial divisions, introduced extensive changes in law and judicial procedure, abolished all monasteries and convents that failed to serve social needs, and decreed equal taxation for all citizens. During the ten years of his reign, he issued over 6,000 edicts, covering virtually every matter of concern to himself and his subjects. To Joseph II, the state existed to ensure "the greatest good for the greatest number," and no customs, institutions, or sentiments were going to prevent him from achieving that goal.

Unfortunately for Joseph, however, his wholesale changes did not create a state of satisfied citizens but elicited instead an outburst of protest against him. Upon embarking on a war with the Ottoman Empire in 1788, Joseph found himself confronted by threatened revolution in Hungary and open rebellion in Belgium. Stunned by these outbursts and warned of seething discontent elsewhere in the monarchy, Joseph revoked many of his reforms. In February, 1790, he died, convinced that he had utterly failed.

[*Maria Theresa*, Englewood Cliffs, N.J., 1973, p. 177]

Of Maria Theresa's children, we shall frequently encounter Maria Christina (Marie Christine), who was allowed to marry the man of her choice in April 1766: Albert, Duke von Sachsen-Teschen. One of the most attractive and gifted of the Habsburg princesses, this clear-headed, handsome woman and her husband (who was Governor of the Hungarian Lands, 1765–80, and *Generalstatthalter* of the Austrian Netherlands, 1780–90) resided in Pressburg, then the capital of Hungary, and had at their permanent disposal a suite of rooms at Eszterháza Castle. Haydn's relationship with Maria Antonia (Marie Antoinette) was probably slight, but the Parisians named Symphony No. 85 after her ('La Reine de France') and the unfortunate Queen had a macabre encounter with the Symphony during her imprisonment (*infra*, p. 595).

Of the many sources about Haydn's life in Hungary, one of the most interesting series is that provided – mostly, alas, at second hand – by his most promising pupil, Ignaz Pleyel, who came to Eszterháza in 1772. Some of these documents are quoted in the main text. The longest and perhaps the most important are the quotations from Framery's *Notice sur Joseph Haydn* (Paris, 1810), where we are given a wholly new and not entirely implausible account of the 'Farewell' Symphony; although Pleyel's version differs from those of the 'authentic' biographies (Dies, Griesinger), I have nevertheless included it, and all relevant extracts from Framery, in the Appendix.

The central figure of our book, apart from Haydn, is his extraordinary patron, Prince Nicolaus I (about whose character we also learn some curious details from Framery *via* Pleyel): a man as complicated in his way as Joseph II, with the same dark side to his nature (see Pleyel's account of Nicolaus, glowering in the back of his box during a Haydn symphony; it rings true, even if it is not the usual picture). One of the great Hungarian magnates who was friendly to and with the Habsburgs – although he cordially disliked Vienna and went there only to pay his obligatory respects to the court at Christmas – Esterházy's wealth was almost incredible, his powers enormous within his vast domains (he even had his own executioner).

Hungary itself, with its stately castles, endless plains and toiling peasants emerges fitfully and incompletely from the contemporary documents. It was something of a mystery to many eighteenth-century observers. Johann Kaspar Riesbeck's *Briefe eines reisenden Franzosen über Deutschland,*[1] whose notes on Eszterháza have been quoted

---

1 Just reprinted in a handsome new edition by Jochen Golz, Berlin, 1976, pp. 259f.; Eszterháza: pp. 260ff.

below (*infra*, pp. 99f.), was surprised to see wolves in the woods, and disconcerted to observe, side by side, magnificent palaces next to wild country

> where the people live like animals in underground caves or like the Mongols in tents ... The clearest proof that a country is unhappy is the confrontation between the greatest magnificence and the most wretched poverty, and the greater the confrontation, the unhappier the country. A people can be quite poor but happy; however, when one glimpses, among the clusters of straw huts which hardly protect their dwellers from wind and weather, soaring marble palaces rising to Heaven out of this incredible wilderness, on which swarms of skeleton-like men look for roots to still their hunger; when in their midst, one sees gardens with fountains, grottos, parterres, terraces, statues and costly paintings; then one has the proof that one part of the population lives from robbing the other.
>
> Not long after my arrival here I made an excursion to the resident Castle of Prince Esterházy. . . .

Behind the delicate Rococo façade of Eszterháza were starving peasants and roving wolves. Behind the façade of Haydn's elegant and wiry music lay another kind of demon. It has been called by various names, and often associated with the German literary movement called *Sturm und Drang*, which it preceded by some years. Riesbeck (pp. 41ff.) speaks exasperatedly of the *Theaterwut* which engulfed Germany as a direct result of the *Sturm und Drang* movement: of sentences that end with !!! and ???; of words massacred and paragraphs that end in ...; in short, all the paraphernalia of the pre-Romantic movement. Actually the trend began, in slightly altered fashion ('Gothic horror'), with Walpole's *The Castle of Otranto* (London, 1765). Certainly, this dark thread may be traced throughout the literature of the eighteenth century and well into the Byronic beginnings of the next: Mary Shelley's monster in *Frankenstein* reads *Paradise Lost*, a volume of Plutarch's *Lives* – and that cornerstone of the *Sturm und Drang* movement, Goethe's *Werther* (Shelley's novel was published in London in 1818: see chapter 15). It will be seen that the same demonic strain runs through Austrian music, beginning with Haydn and his school *c.* 1766, finding a superb flowering in the 'dark' side of Mozart and reaching a culmination in Beethoven.

When did Haydn meet Mozart? I have suggested that their friendship began in 1784 (*infra*, Chapter Six), but since their first 'official' meeting was of crucial importance for the history of Western music, here are the relevant documents. In 1775, Haydn had first given his Oratorio, *Il ritorno di Tobia*, at the Tonkünstler-Societät. In 1783, at their second pair of annual concerts in the Burgtheater, the Society gave the following programmes on 22 and 23 December, when Haydn was in Vienna for the Christmas holidays, the opera season at Eszterháza having closed at the end of November (slightly earlier than usual).[1]

Symphony [Overture] and Chorus   Haydn [possibly the Overture and Opening Chorus from *Il ritorno di Tobia*?]
Arias by Sacchini (sung by Sig. Mandini and Mlle. Cavalieri)
Concerto for Forte-Piano & Orchestra, composed & played by Herr Mozart [only 22 Dec.; on 23 Dec. a violin concerto played by Schlesinger; Mozart's work: K.413, 414, 415?]
Symphony by Kozeluch
A new Rondo by Mozart (sung by Adamberger) [the original Belmonte in *Entführung*; probably 'Misero! o sogno!' K.431; see *Mozart – Köchel-Verzeichnis*, 5th ed., Einstein, where listed as K.425b., pp. 546f.; only 23 Dec.]

1 Harich in *HJB* I, 48. Pohl *Denkschrift*, 60f.

Terzetto by Sarti (Cavalieri, Adamberger, Mandini)
Choruses by Hasse, Sacchini, Dittersdorf.
Conductor: Joseph Starzer.

Haydn can have heard one of Mozart's greatest vocal pieces, in which the intensity, passion and personal involvement with the text clearly distinguish his treatment of libretto as compared to Haydn's more objective and sometimes more cynical approach. 'Misero! o sogno!' must have been a breathtaking revelation not only for Haydn but for the other *Capellmeister* in the audience. As to the piano concerto, perhaps it was the brilliant and martial K.415, suited to a large hall, a large audience and the large orchestra of 180 for which the Tonkünstler-Societät was renowned.

The end of Haydn's long stay in Hungary was marked by the beginning of the French Revolution. We have no documents that even suggest Haydn's reaction, or that of anyone else at Eszterháza, including Prince Nicolaus. Soon Haydn was to leave Austria and to experience the results of the Revolution at much closer hand, in London. He also lived long enough to see the failure of the *sans-culottes*, the general popular disillusionment, and the rise of the Napoleonic government (which may have been democratic in that talents, from whichever social stratum, were welcomed and could rise to astronomic heights, but which could hardly be called a government 'of' or 'for' the people, at least in its later stages). Haydn would even live to experience, at least from second-hand tales, that which an English traveller to France in 1803–4 described as follows:

> I met a paysanne working in a vynyard [*sic*] who lamented bitterly their past infatuation and told me their poverty was infinitely greater now than before the Revolution... 'Ah Madame[,] Dieu n'a pas permys une seule bonne vendange depuis la Revolution[,] il est en colère et tout a changé jusqu'au climat'...[1]

I do not presume to trespass here on the great historical work of Richard Cobb, whose publications of the Revolutionary period have changed the whole method of history; but I have followed him gladly in writing 'Lyon' for 'Lyons'. The whole problem of foreign names and places requires a short note here. The Empress of Austria's name was 'Maria Theresia' (not 'Theresa'), but we have (with regret) succumbed to general English usage here. The other 'Theresias' have been left as they themselves wrote their name: one 'Theresa' is bad enough. Perhaps there is an English rendering 'Pressburg' (Bratislava) for the German 'Preßburg', but I have retained '*Preßburger Zeitung*'. Similarly, I have used 'Regensburg' for 'Ratisbon' (one day we may, I hope, have 'Livorno' for that particularly fatuous 'Leghorn'). French, Italian and German quotations – also English, when they appear – have as usual been given in their original spelling and punctuation: I can see no merit in 'improving' the occasional oversight (or old spelling, the '-oit' ending, for instance) of Joseph II (French), Count Zinzendorf (French) – or Haydn himself. Thus the incredible mixture of abbreviations in German for Gulden and Kreuzer (fl., f., xr., k., kr., etc.) has been left unchanged. Sometimes Haydn signed his name 'Joseph', sometimes 'Josephus': we have not always the original document (especially the many letters to Artaria, his publishers, which are now dispersed, many in unlocated private collections).

1 Autograph Journal of Phillida Call, daughter of Sir John Call of Cornwall, 1803 and 1804. Sold at Sotheby's, 6 December 1977, lot 430.

I Joseph Haydn, anonymous
miniature on ivory, *c.* 1780.

II Prince Nicolaus I Esterházy in
the uniform of an Austrian
officer; anonymous miniature on
ivory.

III Joseph Haydn, portrait in oils on panel by Ludwig Guttenbrunn, *c.* 1791–2 (revised version of a portrait first painted *c.* 1770); this painting was the original on which the well-known engraving by L. Schiavonetti (published in London in 1792) was based.

IV Ludwig Guttenbrunn, self-portrait, painted in 1782. The artist was engaged by Prince Nicolaus I Esterházy and painted portraits of both the Prince and Haydn (cf. pl. III), as well as working on frescoes and decorative schemes at Eszterháza, 1770–2. He also became Frau Haydn's lover; he was sent by the Prince on a trip to Italy, whence he did not return to Eszterháza. He became a member of the Academy at Florence in 1782 (on which occasion this self-portrait was painted); when Haydn arrived in London in 1791, he found Guttenbrunn already established there.

V Joseph Weigl, Haydn's principal 'cellist at Eszterháza until 1769, and afterwards a member of the Court Orchestra in Vienna; trompe-l'œil collage, signed (Quodlibet) gedenke öfters an deinen / Freind [*sic*] wan es dir wohl / gehet gars [Gars im Kamptal?] / den 4 Julÿ / 772 / J: M: R: [Johann M. Richter?]'. Weigl, a fine musician, was engaged in 1761 and became a great friend of Haydn's; the composer wrote a number of difficult 'cello solos and the 'Cello Concerto (VIIb:1) of *c.* 1765 especially for him.

A word must be added here about my indications of watermarks in the papers of Haydn and his copyists: they were given principally when (a) the MS. was or is in private possession and possibly difficult of access; (b) if the work has problems of dating; (c) in other cases where it was thought that the information could prove useful. As far as authenticity is concerned, it has been my policy to discuss only works by Haydn for which there is no reasonable doubt as to their genuineness; naturally this does not apply to spurious or doubtful works deliberately analyzed. In this volume, the only principal works discussed about which Haydn's authorship is in any slight doubt are some of the minor church works and *Die Feuersbrunst* (*Das abgebrannte Haus*) which, however, I believe to be a genuine Opera that has come down to us with some of the details (timpani) bowdlerized and some of the music by Pleyel (Overture) and some perhaps by other pupils: I believe that many of the marionette operas, especially those lost, may have been pasticcios of this kind, with Haydn acting as compiler as well as composer.

Eszterháza's opera house disappeared in the nineteenth century, but the great music hall (*Festsaal*) on the first floor (American: second floor) has survived and is now magnificently restored. For those to whom Eszterháza may be too distant geographically, we may recommend a recent recording, made in the music hall, of Haydn's *L'infedeltà delusa*, where the wonderful acoustics may be profitably studied.[1]

ACKNOWLEDGMENTS

My friends at the Országos Széchényi Könyvtár in Budapest were, as always, unsparing of their time and patience; they supplied countless documents in microfilm and xerox copies and answered my many queries with their usual cordiality and efficiency. Many of the documents and all the music, both Haydn's and the operas by other composers, were examined in the course of five trips to Hungary, the last in 1960. Dr Janos Harich, formerly the Archivist of the present Prince Paul Esterházy, has done more than any other single scholar to publish the documents on which the present biography is based, and he also answered my many questions either verbally or by letter. I examined the Archives at Eisenstadt (which includes all the church music, apart from documents) repeatedly in the 1950s and 1960s. My debt to the Esterházy Archives, collectively, is of course enormous.

The following persons and institutions were kind enough to be my hosts on numerous occasions and/or answered questions and supplied photographs of sources: AUSTRIA: Haus-, Hof- und Staatsarchiv, Vienna (Dr Clemens Höslinger); the Gesellschaft der Musikfreunde, Vienna (Frau Dr Mitringer and Dr Otto Biba); the Österreichische Nationalbibliothek, Vienna (Dr Franz Grasberger of the Musikabteilung); the Musikwissenschaftliches Seminar der Universität Graz; the Stadtbibliothek, Vienna; the Benedictine Monastery of Göttweig (Lower Austria); the Benedictine Monastery of Melk (Lower Austria); the Benedictine Monastery of Kremsmünster (Upper Austria, and especially to my old and dear friend, P. Dr Altman Kellner); the Premonstratensian Monastery of Schlägl (Upper Austria); the Archives of the Stadtpfarrkirche (now Cathedral), Eisenstadt; the Burgenländisches Landesmuseum, Eisenstadt (Hofrat Dr Ohrenberger); Archives of the Basilica Maria

---

1 Conducted by Frigyes Sándor, and recorded in 1976 at Eszterháza with a band of 2 oboes, bassoon, 2 horns, timpani and strings (5–4–3–3–1). Hungaraton SLPX 11832/4.

Treu (Piaristenkirche, Vienna; then Dr Otto Biba); Augustinian Monastery of St Florian (Upper Austria); Herr Harald Egger for his kindness in organizing xerox copies of rare periodicals from Graz, the place of his birth; Mr Paul Cobbs for valuable assistance in various Viennese libraries; Count and Countess Gotthard Pilati, Schloß Riegersburg (Lower Austria); Countess Gabriele Mensdorff-Pouilly, Fürstenfeld (Styria) for kind permission to use the Stadion Dépôt in the Haus-, Hof- und Staatsarchiv; the late Count Niklas Salm-Reifferscheidt, Schloß Steyregg (Upper Austria), and his son, the present Altgraf Salm; and Dr Eva Badura-Skoda, Vienna, for sending me a tape of the newly discovered Opera attributed to Haydn, *Die reisende Ceres*, and for copies of her various articles on the subject.

CZECHOSLOVAKIA: Národni Museum, Prague; Former Archives of the Counts Czernin, Jindřichův Hradec (Neuhaus); Schwarzenberg Central Archives, Český Krumlov; the Museum (containing the Archives of the Prince-Archbishops of Olmütz) at Kroměříž (Kremsier); Slovakian Academy of Sciences, Bratislava (Pressburg); National Janáček Museum, Brno (Brünn).

FRANCE: Bibliothèque Nationale, Paris (now incorporating Bibliothèque du Conservatoire de Musique), and M. François Lesure; M. Marc Vignal, Paris, for help in photographing Framery's *Notice*.

GERMANY: the Fürstlich Oettingen-Wallersteinsches Schloßarchiv, Harburg (Bavaria); the Fürstliches Thurn-und-Taxisches Hofarchiv, Regensburg (Bavaria); the Preußische Staatsbibliothek, Berlin (which was partly housed, when I studied the MSS., in Tübingen and Marburg/Lahn); Fürstlich Fürstenbergsches Hofarchiv, Donaueschingen (Baden).

GREAT BRITAIN: British Museum (British Library); Royal College of Music, London; Mr Albi Rosenthal, London and Oxford, for embarrassingly many favours, not least for the document concerning Symphony No. 47 and Canon Holland; Mrs Rosemary Smith *née* Hughes, then London, for having copied out a Burney letter for me in 1953; Mr Roger Hellyer, Oxford; and Mr Christopher Raeburn, who was of great help to me at Donaueschingen Castle in 1957.

HUNGARY: Apart from the Budapest libraries, also the Archives of St Michael's Church, Sopron (Oedenburg).

ITALY: Biblioteca del Conservatorio di Musica 'S. Cecilia', Rome (Signora Emilia Zanetti); Biblioteca del Conservatorio di Musica, Lucca; Biblioteca del Conservatorio di Musica 'Giuseppe Verdi', Milan; Biblioteca Estense, Modena; Count Aurelio Baldeschi-Baleani, Jesi, for allowing me to study his archives; Countess Elisabeth Enzenberg-Esterházy, Terlan presso Merano (Meran), for presenting us with the beautiful illustration of Princess Esterházy, *née* Marchesa Lunati-Visconti; Mr and Mrs F. Gordon Morrill, Florence, who kindly read the galley proofs and made their usual valuable suggestions.

ROUMANIA: Biblioteca Centrală de Stat, Bucharest.

SWEDEN: the late Count C.-G. Stellan Mörner, Stockholm.

U.S.A.: Pierpont Morgan Library, New York, for many and repeated kindnesses; the Library of Congress, Washington, D.C. (especially the late Dr Harold Spivacke and recently Mr Donald L. Leavitt); Mr Rudolf F. Kallir, New York, for making photographs of his Haydn letters; Professor A. Peter Brown, Bloomington, Indiana, for presenting me with xerox copies of Ordoñez's *Alceste* (original in Budapest); and to Mr Edward O. D. Downes, for having read, in 1976, several chapters of the book and for his valuable suggestions, all gratefully incorporated.

U.S.S.R.: Archives of the Council of Ministers of the Soviet Union, Moscow.

I also owe a special debt of thanks to the many persons and institutions responsible for supplying the illustrations, the details of which may be seen on pp. 9, 10. If I have mentioned one or two above, it was because they had to go to immense pains to organize a photographer to come, often to a remote town, to make the necessary photographs.

Vienna, St Cecilia's Day, 1977. H.C.R.L.

AUTHOR'S NOTE

Haydn's music
Vocal music is identified by title and, on the occasion of the first or major reference, by its number in Hoboken's *Haydn Verzeichnis* (vol. II, Vocal Works), Mainz, 1971.

Instrumental music is identified as follows.

Symphonies are referred to by their number in Mandyczewski's list for the publishers Breitkopf & Härtel, which numbering was taken over by Hoboken in his *Haydn Verzeichnis* (vol. I), Mainz, 1955. Symphony No. 95, for example, is I:95 in Hoboken's list.

String Quartets are identified by their opus number and, like all instrumental pieces, by the Hoboken number at the first and/or major reference.

Piano Sonatas are listed by their chronological numbering in the *Wiener Urtext Ausgabe*, edited by C. Landon.

Piano Trios are identified by the new chronological numbering in the *Complete Edition of Haydn's Piano Trios*, edited by H. C. Robbins Landon and published by Verlag Doblinger.

Other instrumental works are identified by their customary title (e.g. 'London Trios' and 'Overture to an English Opera') and by their Hoboken number.

The system of pitch notation used is based on middle C being represented by the symbol *c'*.

Instruments (in order of their customary appearance in the orchestral score) are abbreviated thus: Fl. – flute; Ob. – oboe; Cor ang. – cor anglais; Clar. – clarinet; Bsn. (Fag.) – bassoon; Hn. (Cor.) – horn; Trbe. (Trpt) – trumpet; Trbn. – trombone; Timp. – timpani (kettledrums); V. – violin; Va. viola; Vc. – violoncello; Cb. (B.) – contrabasso (double bass); Cemb. – cembalo (harpsichord); Bar. – baryton.

Documents
In all documents cited in the text the original orthography – whether in English, German, French or Italian – has been retained. Thus, accents have not been inserted where they were omitted in the original document, notably in passages from the Zinzendorf Diaries. The language of the original document is indicated only in those cases which require clarification. Bibliographical references will be found in an abbreviated form in the text, at the end of quotations and in the footnotes; the full titles of works cited are given on pp. 20–22.

The abbreviations 'k.k.' and 'I.R.' (meaning *'kaiserlich-königlich'*/'Imperial Royal') are used interchangeably. Austrian money is abbreviated thus: Gulden (gulden) = 'f.' or 'fl.' (or 'F.', 'Fl.'); Kreuzer = 'k.' or 'kr.' or 'xr.' ('K.', 'Kr.', 'Xr.').

ABBREVIATIONS OF
BIBLIOGRAPHICAL SOURCES

A.M. — Acta Musicalia (from the Esterházy Archives; now Országos Széchényi Könyvtár, Budapest).

AMZ — *Allgemeine Musikalische Zeitung*, Leipzig, 1798 *et seq.*

A.T. — Acta Theatralia (from the Esterházy Archives, now Országos Széchényi Könyvtár, Budapest).

Bartha — *Joseph Haydn, Gesammelte Briefe und Aufzeichnungen*, herausgegeben und erläutert von Dénes Bartha, Budapest-Kassel, 1965.

Bartha-Somfai — Dénes Bartha and László Somfai, *Haydn als Opernkapellmeister*, Budapest, 1960.

Brand *Messen* — Carl Maria Brand, *Die Messen von Joseph Haydn*, Würzburg, 1941 (since reprinted).

Carpani — Giuseppe Carpani, *Le Haydine,* Milan, 1812.

CCLN — *Collected Correspondence and London Notebooks of Joseph Haydn*, translated and edited by H. C. Robbins Landon, London, 1959.

Copyists — In references to MS. copies of scores, individual hands are identified by name (if known) or 'Anon.' with numbers/letters (see Landon, *SYM*, 611, and Bartha-Somfai, 404ff.).

Deutsch *Mozart, Dokumente* — Otto Erich Deutsch, *W. A. Mozart – Die Dokumente seines Lebens*, Kassel-Basel, 1961.

Dies — A. C. Dies, *Biographische Nachrichten von Joseph Haydn*, Vienna, 1810; new ed. Horst Seeger, Berlin, n.d. [1959].

ECP — *Eisenstädter Comissions Prothocoll . . . 1777 bis 1790* (in EH, Budapest).

EH — Esterházy Archives (now Budapest, Forchtenstein or Eisenstadt).

EK — *Entwurf-Katalog* (Haydn's draft catalogue of his compositions, *c.* 1765 *et seq.*; Staatsbibliothek, Berlin).

Enciclopedia dello spettacolo — *Enciclopedia dello spettacolo* (11 vols.), Rome, 1954 *et seq.*

Fitzpatrick — Horace Fitzpatrick, *The Horn and Horn-playing, and the Austro-Bohemian Tradition 1680–1830*, London and New York, 1970.

GdM — Gesellschaft der Musikfreunde, Vienna.

Geiringer 1932, 1947, 1959 and 1963 — Karl Geiringer, *Joseph Haydn*: Potsdam, 1932; New York, 1947; Mainz, 1959; Garden City, N.Y., 1963.

Gerber *NTL*	Ludwig Gerber, *Neues historisch-biographisches Lexikon der Tönkünstler*, 4 vols, 1812–14; new edition by Othmar Wessely, Graz, 1966.
Griesinger	G. A. Griesinger, *Biographische Notizen über Joseph Haydn*, Leipzig, 1810; new ed. Franz Grasberger, Vienna, 1954.
Grove, I, II, III, IV, V	Grove's *Dictionary of Music and Musicians*, first, second, third, fourth and fifth editions.
Harich *Musikgeschichte*	Janos Harich, 'Esterházy-Musikgeschichte im Spiegel der zeitgenössischen Textbücher', in (special number of) Burgenländische Forschungen, Heft 39, Eisenstadt, 1959.
Hase	H. von Hase, *Joseph Haydn und Breitkopf & Härtel*, Leipzig, 1909.
HJB	*Haydn Jahrbuch/Haydn Yearbook*, 1962 *et seq.*
Horányi	Mátyás Horányi, *Das Esterházysche Feenreich*, Budapest, 1959; English edition, *The Magnificence of Esterháza*, London, 1962.
HV	Thematic catalogue ('Haydn Verzeichnis') of Haydn's œuvre (compiled 1805); see Larsen, *HUB*, 53–119; also the final volume of this biography, *Haydn: the Late Years 1801–1809*, 294f.
Index	*Index deren von Sr. hochfürstl. durchlaucht bewilligten Pensionen[,] Conventions, Vermehrungen und neuen Anstellungen von Monath Junio 1788 bis Ende 1790* (EH, Budapest).
Jancik	Hans Jancik, *Michael Haydn, ein vergessener Meister*, Vienna, 1952
Khevenhüller	*Aus der Zeit Maria Theresias. Tagebuch des Fürsten Johann Josef Khevenhüller-Metsch, kaiserlichen Oberhofmeisters. 1742–1776*, 10 vols., ed. Rudolph, Count Khevenhüller-Metsch and Hanns Schlitter (later, ed. Hans Wagner), Leipzig (later Vienna), 1905 *et seq.*
Landon *Beethoven*	H. C. Robbins Landon, *Beethoven: a documentary study*, London and New York, 1970.
Landon *Essays*	H. C. Robbins Landon, *Essays on the Viennese Classical Style*, London, 1970.
Landon *Supplement*	H. C. Robbins Landon, *Supplement to 'The Symphonies of Joseph Haydn'*, London, 1961.
Landon *SYM*	H. C. Robbins Landon, *The Symphonies of Joseph Haydn*, London, 1955.
Larsen *HÜB*	J. P. Larsen, *Die Haydn-Überlieferung*, Copenhagen, 1939.
MGG	*Musik in Geschichte und Gegenwart* (Allgemeine Enzyklopädie der Musik), ed. F. Blume, Kassel, 1947 *et seq.*
Mozart, *Briefe*	*Mozart Briefe und Aufzeichnungen* (ed. Bauer, Deutsch and Eibl), 6 vols., Kassel, 1962 *et seq.*
NA	*Nützliches Auskunftsbuch oder Kommerzialschema für Handelsleute, Fabrikanten, Künstler, Professionisten und die Jenigen, welche in der k. k. Haupt- und Residenz-stadt Wien Handlungsgeschäfte oder andere Verrichtungen zu schlichten haben*, Vienna, 1797.

Neukomm	Sigismund (von) Neukomm, *Bemerkungen zu den biogr. Nachrichten von Dies* (MS. in Pohl's hand, owned by Friedrich Matzenauer, Vienna; published 1959).
NOHM VII	*The New Oxford History of Music*, vol. VII: *The Age of Enlightenment*, ed. Egon Wellesz and Frederick Sternfeld, London and New York, 1973.
Olleson	E. Olleson, 'Haydn in the Diaries of Count Karl von Zinzendorf', in *Haydn Yearbook* II (1963–4).
Olleson *Griesinger*	E. Olleson, 'Georg August Griesinger's Correspondence with Breitkopf & Härtel' in *Haydn Yearbook* III (1965).
PCDI	*Prothocoll über verschiedene hochfürstl. Commissiones, Decretationes, Intimata und andere Buchhaltereys Verordnungen de Anno 1734 [et seq.]*, (EH, Budapest).
Plank	Plank's MS. Diary (Archives of Kremsmünster Abbey), printed in P. Altmann Kellner, *Musikgeschichte des Stiftes Kremsmünster*, Kassel, 1957.
Pohl *Denkschrift*	C. F. Pohl, *Denkschrift aus Anlass des 100-Jährigen Bestehens der Tonkünstler-Societät*, Vienna, 1871.
Pohl I, II, III	C. F. Pohl, *Joseph Haydn* (3 vols.): I, Berlin, 1875; II, Berlin, 1882; III (completed by Hugo Botstiber), Leipzig, 1927. All three vols. since reprinted.
Probst	Franz Probst, 'Daten zur Geschichte des Hochfürstlich Esterházyschen Hoftheaters', in *Burgenländische Heimatblätter* XIV/1 (1952).
PZ	*Preßburger Zeitung.*
Radant *Rosenbaum*	'The Diaries of Joseph Carl Rosenbaum 1770–1829' edited by Else Radant, *Haydn Yearbook* V (1968); also as separate publications in the original German.
Rosenbaum	'The Diaries of Joseph Carl Rosenbaum 1770–1829' (MS. in Osterreichische Nationalbibliothek, Vienna); see Radant above.
Schmid 'Eisenstadt'	E. F. Schmid, 'Joseph Haydn in Eisenstadt', in *Burgenländische Heimatblätter* I/1 (1932).
Somfai	László Somfai, *Joseph Haydn. Sein Leben in zeitgenössischen Bildern*, Budapest and Kassel, 1966; also published in English, London, 1967.
SzM	*Studien zur Musikwissenschaft*, Vienna, 1913 *et seq.*
Valkó I, II	Arisztid Valkó, 'Haydn magyarországi müködése a levéltári akták tükrében', in *Zenetudományi Tanulmányok* VI (1957) = 'I', and VIII (1960) = 'II'.
Wirth I	Helmut Wirth, *Joseph Haydn als Dramatiker*, Wolfenbüttel-Berlin, 1941; Kieler Beiträge zur Musikwissenschaft (ed. Friedrich Blume), vol. 7.
Wirth II	Helmut Wirth, 'The Operas of Joseph Haydn before "Orfeo"', in *Joseph Haydn 'Orfeo ed Euridice'*, Haydn Society, Boston, Mass., 1951.
WZ	*Wiener Zeitung.*
Zinzendorf	MS. Diaries of Count Carl von Zinzendorf, in the Haus-, Hof- und Staatsarchiv, Vienna.

CHAPTER ONE

The Organization of Eszterháza

I. The Castle at Eszterháza (1766–1790)

IT WAS NATURAL for an Austrian aristrocrat, about to build a new castle or *palazzo* in the 1760s, to turn to France and Italy for inspiration and even for the actual workmen – architects and artists in particular. Salzburg, in the middle of the Austrian Alps, was a model of an Austrian town constructed along Italian architectural principles by Italian architects. But the Austrians always managed to give their great Baroque buildings some indefinably Austrian quality, even though they might have been, and often were, constructed by Italians: the great monasteries of Melk, St Florian, Kremsmünster or Altenburg fused local traditions with Italian artists; ceiling frescos by artists south of the Alps looked down on magnificent *Prunksäle* with tall windows opening on to the rolling Austrian countryside; even the famous *Treppenhäuser*, although clearly derived from Baldassare Longhena's stair-hall in S. Giorgio, took the Palladian tradition and transformed it to Austrian requirements.[1]

When Nicolaus Esterházy decided to transform a modest hunting lodge situated on the south side of the Neusiedlersee into a magnificent castle, he did not choose an Italian model; one of the wealthiest Hungarian noblemen of the period, Prince Nicolaus thought in the largest of terms; and the largest of terms, architecturally, meant nothing less than the Palace of Versailles. The first time Esterházy saw Versailles was not, as hitherto believed, in connection with a visit in 1764 to the coronation ceremonies of Joseph II at Frankfurt – which the Prince attended in an official capacity; for it was not until three years later, in the late autumn of 1767, that he first beheld Versailles. That visit was made at a time when Eszterháza Castle was already in an advanced state of completion, so that if one wishes to attach any significance to this visit as far as the formation of Eszterháza is concerned, it can only have concerned details. The marionette theatre, with its lateral niches in the form of *rocailles*, may have been inspired by the cave of Tethys at Versailles, which is also ornamented with *rocailles*; the theatre was first opened in 1773. The visitor to Eszterháza is reminded of Versailles perhaps more by the general layout of the Hungarian castle – the huge *allées* behind the building, the tall trimmed hedges, the arrangement of the castle courtyard, the neat symmetry of the whole plan. In the *Excursion à Esterhaz en Hongrie* of 1784, which is quoted below *in extenso*, we find the rather apt description, 'le petit Versailles de l'Hongrie'.[2]

---

1 P. L. Lauriteen 'The Architectural History of San Giorgio', in *Apollo*, July 1975, p. 11.
2 *Excursion*, 4; Horányi, 46, 54.

In the larger sense, Eszterháza Castle is much more a part of European civilization than its past (and, for other reasons, present) isolation would seem to indicate. Putting it into European perspective for a moment, we may borrow the wise words of Boris Lossky:

A character of great unity may rightly be attributed to the culture of the eighteenth century, but in that case it must also be recognized as having a strong element of complexity.

The 18th century lends itself well to the title of 'Elegant Century' or 'Century of Enlightenment', one of epicurean behaviour and rationalist philosophy. It is also known as the 'French Century', although it should be emphasized that this title is not of French invention but comes from across the mountains and the Rhine.

Historically, the century begins and ends with two events which, although emanating from France, are of European importance: the hegemony of Louis XIV and the imperialism of Napoleon. In the years between, although they are studded with political or economic defeats and setbacks, France maintains her place at the head of a Europe which spontaneously accepts the pre-eminence of her language, her literature and her art and adopts the etiquette of her court for its social usages.

It is taken for granted that foreign sovereigns go to the studios of French artists for their portraits, or to buy paintings to adorn the walls of distant palaces. In the same way French artists, or those trained in France, make triumphant journeys throughout Europe, staying to carry out highly-paid commissions.... 'But was that the whole of European art? Did the powerful wave of French art submerge all national specialities and traditions?' We pose the question as did Louis Réau, principal architect of the 'defence and illustration' of a French Europe, and we accept his answer: 'Art as elaborated at Versailles and in Paris had an all powerful influence on court and society art, which is international, but had no effect on religious and popular art.' It must also be remembered that reservations about French expansion are manifest across the Channel and the Alps: in England because of a fierce Franco–British national rivalry and in Italy from 'the proud consciousness of 18th-century Italians of a national school whose glory stems not only from its past but from the living and is made illustrious with great names'....

The situation is different in Germany and Austria, recovering after the Thirty Years War and the Turkish invasion. Churches and monasteries are rebuilt in thanksgiving. Vast abbeys, libraries, refectories, bishops' palaces and 'imperial apartments' offer a rich field to the Italian fresco painters who before long are joined by native artists trained in the academies of Augsburg or Vienna.[1]

When Prince Nicolaus was in Versailles for the first time, in 1767, he had the French architect Mourette draw up plans for a château; but by this time the hunting lodge in the swamps at Süttör (which was also the name of the castle at first) was already transformed into a kind of *Jagdschloß* or 'hunting castle'. The architect of this first Schloß Süttör was Anton Erhard Martinelli, and there are bills from the year 1721 that show that work on the building was already in progress at that date. Martinelli, at that time only a Viennese master mason, later became court architect to Prince Schwarzenberg and in 1723, after the death of Martinelli's master, the great Joseph Fischer von Erlach, the designer of Süttör Castle assumed the proud title of 'Princely Architect' (*fürstlicher Baumeister*) to the Schwarzenberg family. In 1729, Martinelli received the order from the Austrian War Council to build the *Invalidenpalais* in Pest (now Budapest).

1 Boris Lossky, Introduction to *18th Century Art*, Geneva 1968 (2nd ed., London and New York, 1974); no pagination.

When the Hungarian authorities began to restore Eszterháza (renamed Fertöd) in 1958, small parts of the original Martinelli building were uncovered; it was seen that the proportions derived on the one hand from French models and in some details from the Vienna Court Library (*Hofbibliothek*) which was the work of Martinelli's two masters, Johann Bernhard Fischer von Erlach and his son, Joseph Emanuel.

Fortunately, a general plan in the form of a bird's-eye drawing of Eszterháza has survived (cf. pl. 2); it is thought to have been executed in the mid-1760s, and it did serve, with the usual alterations to be expected from such a complicated plan, as the basis of the present building.

The next name in connection with Eszterháza Castle is Johann Ferdinand Mödlhammer, a mediocre architect who was used in the rebuilding of the Esterházy Viennese winter palace in the Wallnerstraße as well as having been the designer of plans to rebuild the pretty Esterházy Castle at Kittsee opposite Pressburg. Apparently Prince Nicolaus did not consider Mödlhammer, who worked for the family in the 1750s, sufficiently gifted or expert to continue the construction of more than details of Eszterháza; and a new *Baumeister*, Melchior Hefeles, a member of the I. R. Academy in Vienna, was entrusted with the completion of 'le petit Versailles de l'Hongrie'. Unfortunately, nothing has survived of Hefeles' plans and models of 1765, for which bills in the Esterházy Archives bear eloquent witness, except the afore-mentioned, excellently drawn plan, which the Hungarian expert Pál Voit, from whose beautifully illustrated book *Der Barock in Ungarn*[1] we have gladly taken these notes, believes to be the work of Hefeles. The new architect rebuilt the old Martinelli façade and added its present neo-classical elegance; from the former mansard Hefeles constructed a first floor,[2] giving us *inter alia* the famous salon and music room, both of which were an important part of the new design. (Thus we can see the influence that Nicolaus exercized in the physical shape of Eszterháza, where music would play a predominant role.) The beautiful outside double stairway in stone that leads to the first floor, and is in the middle of the castle's façade, is also an addition of the new architect's, as is the stupendous castle gate – in recent years it has become the symbol of Eszterháza itself – which was executed (cast) by Johann Carl Frank, who learned his trade in the factory of J. G. Oeggs in Würzburg.

Extant bills in the Esterházy Archives show that in June 1765, Melchior Hefeles was himself present to supervise construction; a month later we encounter a new name in the history of the castle, Master Mason of the Esterházy Domains (*Domänenmaurermeister*), *Ingenieur* Nicolaus Jacoby, who was ordered to proceed from Eisenstadt to Eszterháza to help with the work. Later, in 1784, he designed some of the plans which were reproduced through engravings in the German-language *Beschreibung des Hochfürstlichen Schlosses Esterháß*. The afore-mentioned plan was apparently the sketch for the (lost) '. . . large plan, drawn in perspective and coloured' which served the master masons and the other workers and for which, in 1765, Hefeles received the large sum of 200 gulden (that sum forming part of a larger bill for all expenses during the year: 348 gulden). It is thought that Jacoby and Mödlhammer executed Hefeles' plans and made some changes which were not always fortunate; but Eszterháza, as we know it, is nonetheless the first great work that Hefeles accomplished. Later he redesigned the Archbishop's Palace in Pressburg and, between 1779 and 1789, created the great Palace at Szombathely for Bishop János Szily; at Szombathely the frescos and murals were painted by no less an artist than Franz Anton

---

1 Budapest 1971, pp. 90 ff.; the plan is reproduced on p. 91; nevertheless its damaged state allows its artistic excellence clearly to be seen.
2 In the United States = second floor.

Maulbertsch. Melchior Hefeles came from the Baroque world of Würzburg, and it is only in his late works – such as the façade of the opera house at Eszterháza – that we find classical elements as well.[1]

The Castle was obviously in a sufficiently completed state by 1766 for Prince Nicolaus Esterházy in that year to sign letters from 'Schloß Eszterház' and for Haydn, in a bill (which we will quote *in extenso* below) dated 11 September 1766, to write of 'strings for the *clavier* in Eisenstadt and [later addition "nach", i.e. taken to] Estorhaz' – Haydn usually wrote 'Estoras' in his letters, which was one of the many spellings used: 'Esterház, Eszterház, Estoraz, Estoras'. This shows that by 1766, music was being played, presumably by Haydn and the orchestra, perhaps even with some singers, at the Hungarian Castle. Until about 1768, however, when the musicians' quarters were completed (the so-called 'music house'), the orchestra, the singers and the strolling players had to be put up elsewhere, in the castle inn or in some of the many guest rooms or servants' quarters.

Actually, Eszterháza Castle was not completed until 1784, at which date the large cascade in front of the main building was put into operation; it had been put into plan as late as 1782. The completion date of 1784 undoubtedly explains the simultaneous publication in that year of the two descriptions, one in German and one in French, which have been listed above, and which were probably given to visitors by the Prince, the Princess or Esterházy officials.

The building contained, when it was completed, one hundred and twenty-six rooms. The huge expense of creating Eszterháza – 13,000,000 gulden – was largely the result of its geographical position. It is perhaps a typical eighteenth-century concept to choose a desolate, fever-ridden swamp as the place in which to construct a fairy-tale castle with an opera house, a coffee house and a Chinese pavilion, and with Joseph Haydn as *Capellmeister*. It is, as it were, a gigantic Baroque conceit; the will of one man is forced upon, and tames, rebellious nature; he creates this fairy-tale castle and six years after its completion – in 1790 – its creator dies and the castle becomes a haunted place, gradually deteriorating until it is almost destroyed by German and Russian troops in 1945. Eszterháza was exactly the opposite of a normal town or village which owes its importance to its geographical position.[2] Eszterháza owes its existence to Nicolaus Esterházy and its fame to Joseph Haydn. Apart from its physical charms – mostly disappeared except for the actual castle building – it lives almost exclusively today for its historical importance.

The huge park, which hardly exists today, once included temples dedicated to the Sun, Diana, Fortune, Venus; a Heremitage and a Chinese pavilion or 'bagatelle' where Nicolaus had his musicians, and Haydn, dress in Chinese costumes and perform for Empress Maria Theresa (September 1773). In front of the Castle was a French garden, and the central courtyard, about which the horseshoe-shaped building stretched gracefully, included a fountain surrounded by fine statues. The front of the building faced north; on the south side was the 'Zier Garten', the *allées* stretching away into the misty distance, while on the right side was the opera house (1768; rebuilt 1781) and facing it on the other side the marionette theatre (1773). The opera house, which no longer exists, was decorated in gold, red and green. There was, of course, a magnificent princely box; there was a room in which the guests might play billiards

---

1 The opera house was destroyed by fire in 1779 and reopened in 1781; we do not know how much of the façade was left standing after the fire, but probably most of it. Voit, 94f., 114. On Maulbertsch, see the standard catalogue, ed. Robert Waissenberger, which in turn grew out of the great Maulbertsch exhibition held in Austria (in several places) in 1974: *Ausstellung anläßlich seines 250. Geburtstages*, Vienna-Munich 1974.

2 Fernand Braudel, *The Mediterranean and the Mediterranean World in the Age of Philip II*, London 1972, Vol. I, p. 317.

between the acts. The auditorium could seat some four hundred people and had eleven rows of seats divided in the middle by a broad aisle. The stage measured some eighty square yards and was sixty feet deep.[1]

The *Beschreibung* of 1784 includes the following section devoted to the two theatres:

> Right at the entrance into it [the opera house] there leads a fine main stairway with double stairs and delicate iron railings to the two entrances into the princely main box and also to the gallery. Next to the entrance, on either side, are chambers, with rest rooms [*Ritiraden*] in each.
>
> This MAIN BOX is supported by red marble Roman pillars which are ornamented to a third of their height by gold ribs, and of which the shaft and capitals are entirely gilt.
>
> The CEILING is very nicely painted, and the GALLERY has polished stone tiles [*Fußtafeln*] and is enhanced by ROMAN PILASTERS, the position of which forms three small closets on each side, between which there are two large *trumeaux*. The tables at the bottom of the pillars are of marble and have on them valuable clocks and vases of Indian porcelain, and are lighted by magnificent gold branched candlesticks.
>
> The GALLERY is supported by delicate arches which rise in half circles from the floor. – The ballustrate is entirely gilt and contains inlaid *cremois* leather, and all the ornaments are gilt.
>
> In the front of the auditorium there are two more boxes facing each other, behind which there are very charmingly decorated cabinets with fireplaces, couches, mirrors, clocks and other necessary objects, the whole beautifully furnished. These boxes also have entrances from the outside.
>
> There are three entrances, one after another, to the PARTERRE, and four hundred persons easily have room there.
>
> The theatre can be heated by FOUR white stoves situated round the sides. The principal colour of the house is marbled red, green and gold; the excellent lighting comes from wall brackets with mirrors.
>
> The outer FAÇADE is decorated by Roman pilasters and five round vaulted windows, three of which have sills [*Risalit*]. It contains a balcony resting all the way across on twelve plain Ionic columns; there is access to the balcony from the rear cabinets inside. The TOP SECTION is ornamented with a group of genii who play the kettledrums and sound the trumpets, and there are also vases and garlands.
>
> The stage itself has an unusually large width and depth. Behind it there are two dressing rooms for the actors, and attached is a wardrobe for the many magnificent costumes.
>
> Every day there is, alternatively, *opera seria* or *buffa*, or German plays, which the Prince always attends and which usually begin at six o'clock in the evening. It is indescribable how eye and ear are entranced. The soul is melted by the music when the whole ORCHESTRA sounds, sometimes by its touching delicacy and sometimes by the most violent power – for the great composer, Her HAIDEN [*sic*], who is *Kapellmeister* in the service of the Prince, conducts it: but also by the excellent lighting, by the lifelike decorations, when clouds with gods are slowly lowered, or are raised from below and disappear in an instant, or when everything is transformed into a lovely garden, a magic wood, a magnificent hall. – Next to this opera house is a well appointed coffee house.
>
> THE MARIONETTE THEATRE. It is situated opposite the opera house, is rather roomy but without boxes or gallery. The whole pit is like a grotto in that all the walls, niches and openings are inlaid with various pieces of metal [*Stuffen*], stones,

---

1 Horányi, 52 *passim*.

conchs and snails, and when illuminated it has a very curious and striking appearance.

The STAGE is rather roomy, the decorations are all delightful and the puppets very well made and magnificently clothed. – Not only farces and comedies but also *opera seria* are given here, and the late MARIA THERESIA graciously deigned to applaud the opera *Alceste*, and the sudden and imperceptible changes of scenery. Here also the siege of Gibraltar was staged with much cunning and military array.[1] – A theatre which is perhaps unique of its kind.

The performances in this theatre as well as in the opera house are free to everybody.

The orchestra was placed below the stage and between the two stage boxes. The well-known picture (it is now in the Theatermuseum in Munich) supposedly showing Haydn conducting a performance of *L'incontro improvviso* at Eszterháza Castle is an attractive eighteenth-century piece; but it cannot depict *L'incontro improvviso* because (1) the musicians are in red uniform, and it happens that Prince Esterházy did not usually (*vide infra*, p. 87) have red uniforms for his orchestra until 1776 (*Incontro* was composed in 1775); (2) because we have recently discovered the detailed list of costumes for the opera in the Esterházy Archives and they are entirely different from those detailed in this picture; (3) in the picture there are no less than six singers on the left side and a group of three, in 'Turkish' costumes, on the right; it must therefore represent a big ensemble scene or finale, and we search in vain for a scene with nine such particular figures in Haydn's *L'incontro improvviso*; and (4) the orchestra shown does not remotely equal the lavish score of Haydn's opera; missing in the picture are Haydn's horns, trumpets, flute, extra percussion and second bassoon (though it may have been playing out of sight to the far left, where the corner of one of the timpani may just be seen). Possibly the Munich *gouache* may have some relation to the interesting engraving by Bellotto of *Le turc généreux*, a ballet given at the Vienna Court Opera on 26 April 1758 (the engraving signed 'par Ber: Belotto, dit Canaletto ... 1759').[2]

The musicians played on two benches running lengthwise, as in the picture, but (see the note) they read their music on a *flat* stand between them. A wall separated them from the first rows of the pit. The music used by the musicians was kept in specially constructed cabinets which were near the small box; this explains how the music could perish so easily and completely in the great fire of December 1779.

The later opera theatre, which is well known to us from many contemporary engravings (though at least one has not survived),[3] was a building on its own; originally, the 1768 theatre, of which no contemporary view of any kind has survived, was attached to a large ball-room known as the 'Chinese dancing room', presumably

1 *Alceste* by Carlos d'Ordoñez was given in August 1775 for the Duke Albert of Sachsen-Teschen and his Consort, Archduchess Marie Christine. Maria Theresa actually saw Haydn's *Philemon und Baucis* in the marionette theatre (1773). *L'assedio di Gibilterra* (composer not known) was staged for the first time in May 1783; see Landon in HJB I, 192.

2 The 'Haydn' picture is reproduced in colour in R. Haas, *Aufführungspraxis der Musik*, Potsdam 1931; in Horányi; and also in Landon, *Das kleine Haydnbuch*, Salzburg 1967. Our attention was drawn to the Bellotto print in the magnificent 'Rococo' exhibition held at Munich in 1958. It is published in R. Haas, *Gluck und Durazzo im Burgtheater*, Potsdam 1925 and also in Horace Fitzpatrick's recent book, *The horn and horn-playing and the Austro-Bohemian tradition from 1680 to 1830*, London 1970. The actual picture is painted in *gouache*, the musicians' heads in ivory. There is no indication anywhere on the back or front of the picture that it represents a Haydn opera, or Eszterháza. Somfai (plate 104) also points out that the stage size of the picture does not correspond with that of Eszterháza. And the musicians in Eszterháza, while they played lengthwise on long benches facing each other, had 'a music stand on which the music *lies*' (our italics) (J. Harich in *HJB* II, 12). We wonder if the attractive picture does not represent one of the 'Turkish' operas by Gluck given at Vienna, such as *Le Cadi dupré* (1761) or *La rencontre imprévue* (1764).

3 Ferdinand Landerer, Professor of the *Ingenieur-Akademie* in Pressburg, sent a bill in July 1780 for an engraved plan of the opera house (which was not yet finished!), some copies of which were prepared for being illuminated from behind. Landerer also helped in the engravings for the 1784 *Beschreibung*. J. Harich in *HJB* II, 14 and *HJB* III, 131 (the actual bill *verbatim*).

because of its decorations: it was in this ball-room that the stove burst, causing the famous holocaust.

The stage itself was, as we have seen, famous for its lightning-quick transformations and the efficiency of its various mechanisms. Fortunately there are two famous eighteenth-century theatres in which we may study the original machinery: the one at Drottningholm (Sweden) and the other the former princely Schwarzenberg theatre in Böhmisch Krumau (Čseský Krumlov), the latter of which we had the good fortune to study in detail in 1959. From various documents, we can see that there were double or even quadruple frames ready to be 'slotted' into place when the scenery changed at the Eszterháza theatre. These frames were of diminishing size, as can be seen clearly on one of the 1784 *Beschreibung* engravings, where eight such frames are shown. They were mounted on castors and could be moved rapidly. At the end of these diminishing frames an 'exchangeable back-cloth closed the upstage, or opened up a further perspective with its painted scenery . . . Judging from the evidence of the Krumlov theatre, [the lifting and sinking machinery] was probably made by means of armchairs suspended from a device rolling along a longitudinal bar. The floor of the auditorium being level and the front of the stage fairly high, the stage was "raked" so as to give the audience a better view. Mirrored sconces provided light for the auditorium, while spirit lamps between the wings served to illuminate the stage. Beams of light coming from the wings can be clearly seen in the print by J. de Fernstein [in the 1784 *Beschreibung*]'.[1]

To the right (if we stand to the rear of the Castle) and behind the opera house were the musicians' quarters, in a spacious building erected in 1768; it contained two storeys and three courtyards. There were a total of seventy rooms, twenty-six on the ground floor and forty-four on the floor above. When the house was completed, the strolling players had at first seven, later nine, rooms at their disposal, as well as three kitchens. Unmarried players and musicians roomed alone, or for short periods two in a room; married couples were given two, sometimes three, rooms. Haydn, as an exception, had a four-room flat. All the flats were provided with simple furniture, towels and linen; heating and light were free, and the rooms were cleaned by two cleaning women; married couples could have their own servant, if they wanted one, at the Prince's expense. In the winter, a princely stoker took care of all the stoves.[2]

Opposite the music house was a large inn, 'in which there are more than twenty rooms for travellers'.[3] Originally the present music house had started life in 1768 as inn-cum-music-house; but with the influx of all the strolling players (*Wandertruppen*), who sometimes stayed for many months at a time, it was obvious that a new inn had to be constructed. The old *Gasthaus* was turned into flats, and a rehearsal room for the orchestra was made out of the former principal hall. The music house was referred to as the 'old inn', and at the beginning not only Dr Wecker but also the apothecary and the new librarian lived there.

In the description by Vályi of 1796, we move into the main building by the 'porcelain house', containing fourteen cupboards and tables with all sorts of Chinese and Japanese figurines; then to the library and the picture gallery. In the east wing

---

1 Horányi, 52ff. The 1784 engravings are reproduced in this book in their entirety.
2 Horányi, 54; J. Harich in *HJB* II, 26, 43 (our translation and summary which we have used here and elsewhere *verbatim*); J. Harich in *HJB* III, 137, 139 (useful documents, corrected from Bartha-Somfai 123). An interesting ground plan of the music house, from the Acta Musicalia of the Esterházy Archives, reproduced in facsimile in Horányi, 77. It will be noted that the physician, Dr Joseph Wecker, had a four-room flat in the musicians' quarters.
3 An entertaining description of the Castle, from which this extract is taken, is found in András Vályi's Hungarian book 'A Description of Hungary' (1796), translated in Voit, op. cit., 88f. J. Harich in *HJB* II, 26, 43 on the inn.

Vályi noted 'the small library of the Prince, which contains entertaining works of foreign – English, French and celebrated German [i.e. non-Hungarian] – authors... Above the bookshelves are two different engravings and three pictures [*Brustbilder*], two [sepia] drawings made from crushed snail shells and very dear, one portraying an Italian fisher and the other a fisher-woman... Hard by is the castle chapel... Next to it a chamber with Indian walls, and adjoining it the Prince's bedroom. Here begins the castle proper [the middle section], on the first floor of which are the living rooms... in the middle the dining room and towards the garden the princely concert-room [or *Prachtsaal*] in white marble with rich gold ornamentation... Underneath this room is the so-called *sala terrena* from the remains of the old hunting castle... The inlay of the white walls is green. The painted ceiling shows various allegorical scenes... the fountains have dragons, snails, a swan and a stork spewing water, the contemplation of which affords the visitor considerable amusement...'. Like the 1784 *Beschreibung*, the 1796 'Baedeker' is tiresomely verbose. Pages are given up to description of vases, clocks, ornaments, 'conceits', and so forth. The concert room, which thanks to the Hungarian authorities still exists in its acoustical and visual magnificence, was begun in 1768. The frescos in the *sala terrena* and in the castle chapel are probably by Joseph Ignaz Mildorfer, while there are other frescos by the regular Esterházy painter, Johann Basilius Grundmann (who is said to have painted the lost portrait of Haydn in uniform, *c.* 1761). Another local painter, Ludwig Guttenbrunn, worked at Eszterháza during the years 1770–72, at which period he accomplished various tasks: (1) he painted Haydn's portrait, of which two versions survive, one now in the Burgenländisches Landesmuseum (*ex coll.* Karajan) and one owned by Mrs Eva Alberman in London (pl. III); it was later engraved in London by Schiavonetti; (2) he painted Prince Nicolaus Esterházy in 1770, and the portrait was magnificently engraved by Charles Pechwill (reproduced in Somfai, No. 92); (3) he was Frau Haydn's lover.[1]

Magnificent as were these rooms, it is easy to see in them a typical Austrian compromise along the lines discussed at the beginning of this chapter: instead of hiring a Maulbertsch or a Paul Troger (to name two good Austrian artists) – not to speak of a great French or Italian master – Esterházy was quite content to use the very mediocre artists Mildorfer, Grundmann and the young Guttenbrunn – whom the Prince sent to Italy on a 'Studienreise' from which, in the event, Guttenbrunn did not return – to decorate his fabulously expensive castle. In fact, expensive though Eszterháza was, the Prince spent the money on things he considered important; and once again we must return to the central theme of this volume, which is, of course, Haydn and the musicians. Other magnates would have sent for a great Continental artist to decorate the *sala terrena*, the upstairs salon and the concert-room (*Prunksaal*); and would have been content with the usual *Tafelmusik* consisting of oboes, horns and bassoons (and, later, clarinets). Esterházy was content with modest decorators and spent a vast sum on Haydn, the opera house, the marionette theatre, and the singers and instrumentalists necessary for their operation.

Before the great concert-room was completed, orchestral concerts were probably held in the *sala terrena*, and possibly operas without costumes (such as *La canterina*) as well. In the complete list of works performed at Eszterháza during the year 1778 (*vide*

---

1 The Haydn portrait is reproduced here from the Alberman version, for the first time in colour; the other version was first reproduced in colour in Landon *Essays* (1970). See also Landon; *Haydn: the Years of 'The Creation'*, p. 497. Guttenbrunn's self-portrait is reproduced in pl. IV.

infra, p. 94), we find 'Academia musica nell'Appartamento', which seems to refer to the Prince's quarters. No doubt, in the years when the Castle was still under major construction, several of the rooms served as temporary concert-halls or even as simple stages.

We have begun our description of Eszterháza with the physical shape of its domains, in the description of which we have been obliged to be briefer than most contemporary documents. Those readers who wish to learn more of things hardly mentioned or omitted – the weapons' collection; the contents of the picture gallery (which was, of course, the basis of the great Hungarian collection now in Budapest); the champs élysées; the 'Dutch pavilion'; the *Wildpark* for deer, pheasants and wild boar; the labyrinth; the stables (new ones were erected in 1769) with their fabulous carriages – these and the other physical aspects of 'le petit Versailles de l'Hongrie' may be examined in the many contemporary sources such as the 1784 *Beschreibung* and the 1796 Hungarian description. We must now turn from 'things' to people, and first to the fantastically complex organization of the Esterházy estates, of which Eszterháza Castle became, for a short period, the centre.[1]

II. The Esterházy family 'Fideikommiß'

THE 'FIDEIKOMMIß', which might be translated as 'Trust Fund', was a law of German origin whereby the family fortune (usually the actual land) could be passed on to one member of the family only, by which the family preserved its power and money intact. In Austria, it was introduced by the Emperor Leopold I in 1687, who made the introduction of such a trust fund a royal privilege and subject to a large tax. The *primo genitur* 'Fideikommiß' for the Esterházy family was established in 1696 by the Palatine Paul Esterházy, mainly from the fortune of his father and from the dowry of his two wives (his niece Ursula and Eva Thököly, daughter of Count Imre Thököly). The huge fortune which Esterházy thus founded was in those days comparable only with the estates of Thököly and Rákóczi, but whereas the two latter fortunes dwindled even in the eighteenth century, that of Prince Esterházy lasted until the present day: in 1938, the law was abolished in Austria, and in 1946 Hungary confiscated the Hungarian estates of Esterházy and incorporated them into the State.

The Esterházy trust fund under its founder Paul contained about 700,000 *Joch* of land (1 *Joch* = 57.546 *ar* in Austria, 43 *ar* in Hungary; 1 *ar* = 100 square metres), divided into thirty-seven estates. Before the First World War the Esterházy estates contained *c.* 400,000 *Joch*; the other aristocratic estates which approached this figure were those of: Count Schönborn with *c.* 230,000 Joch; Archduke Friedrich with 145,000; the Duke of Sachsen-Koburg-Gotha with 141,000; and Prince Festetics with 115,000. The other estates were well under 100,000 Joch.

Haydn's second Prince, Nicolaus 'The Magnificent' (as he was called by his contemporaries), reigned in his estates as if they were a state within a state; he had all the rights of a sovereign. He could mint coins, had his own soldiers (later 'grenadiers'), and had a penal court of justice with an executioner from Oedenburg (Sopron) who was paid separately for executions. His vast administrative staff ran a register of landed property for citizens, issued birth and death certificates, collected levies from the tenant farmers, and also fines. Thus the officials were theoretically open to bribery, and

---

1 J. Harich in *HJB* IV, 5ff., 28ff. (our summary and translation, again used here *verbatim*).

Prince Nicolaus felt impelled to issue a letter on the subject (25 August 1766),[1] wherein he warns them to behave properly towards people in lower positions and in no case to require anything from them except that which was their duty. The princely disbursar acted like a present-day bank, and lent money at a percentage as well as acting like a savings institution (Haydn invested money there, as we shall see, when he sold his little house in Eisenstadt in 1778). In 1776, the trust fund contained numerous estates, each with a director, who in turn was responsible to five inspectors-of-estates.[2] The whole was under the supervision of the *Güterregent* (Estates Director), who was assisted by four secretaries.

The administrative centre was in Eisenstadt Castle: the book-keepers, the general disbursar and the archives. A second section contained the economic or business division: apart from the five inspectors there was a large number of other officials connected with the various estates; wine production, forestry (108 men in the field), garden directors, an iron-foundry, a paper-mill (in Lockenhaus, which produced the famous 'Hirsch' [stag] paper also for Haydn and the musicians) – all contributed to the vast estate. There were the so-called 'house officers' (Haydn was one) in the actual court itself, together with *livrée* servants and lower servants (kitchen, etc.). The Prince had five male *Kammerdiener* (personal servants-in-waiting), four of the 'lower' classes of servants, two runners, two pages (one a Negro) and a bodyguard. The Princess had four ladies-in-waiting, two 'court' servants and a page (who was a dwarf), three personal servants and two runners. Engineer Nicolaus Jacoby, who was (as we have seen) intimately connected with the construction of Eszterháza Castle, and the Prince's favourite violinist, *Konzertmeister* Luigi Tomasini, both began their careers as *Kammerdiener*; but most of that class were barbers by profession.

Twenty-one persons worked in the princely kitchens in Eisenstadt, Eszterháza and Vienna, among them a *chef* ('the taster', from the old tradition when princes were poisoned), five cooks (mostly French), four persons in the 'sweet' (as opposed to the normal) bakery and the court sculptor, who cut the elaborate forms for baking. The wardrobe and laundry were run by three women, the silver pantry by two, and a 'candle-sentry' saw to the lighting. The other household duties devolved upon the twenty-four persons of the *livrée* servants, among whom was for a time Joseph Elssler, later Haydn's (and the princely) copyist.

A physician-in-ordinary saw to the well-being of the Prince and his immediate family. Three other doctors and a surgeon administered to the officials and servants, also to the poor (especially in the hospital at Eszterháza). The costs for medicine and for the hospital (at Eisenstadt the Barmherzige Brüder – Brothers of Mercy – a princely foundation) were undertaken by the princely disbursar.

The princely bodyguard watched over the three most important castles: Eisenstadt, Eszterháza and Forchtenstein. The bodyguard, under a captain, consisted of some 150 picked soldiers who were all about two metres tall (they could not be less than 'six feet', or about 190 cm.), while the drummer was only *c.* 150 cm. There were also seven pyrotechnics experts who shot off fireworks at festive occasions (at Eisenstadt from the Gloriette). The change-of-guard at Eisenstadt Castle was observed with great pomp when the Prince was in residence, and a group of wind instruments ('Harmonie') from the princely orchestra assisted, for which they received an extra fee.

---

1 For the original text, see J. Harich in *HJB* IV, 24, n. 4.
2 I. Eisenstadt, Forchtenstein, Pöttsching, Süttör, Kapuvár, Frauenkirchen, Kittsee. II. Schwarzenbach, Kobersdorf, Landsee and Lackenbach, Deutschkreutz, Lockenhaus, Köszeg, Alsólendva, Nempti (Lenti). III. Csobánc, Kaposvár, Szentlörinc, Dombóvár, Ozora, Ipolypásztó, Buják. IV. Szádvár, Végles, Léva, Biccse. V. Derecske (am Theißbrücken in Hungary).

The court stables (Eisenstadt and Vienna), under the master of the horse, had sixty employees and a further fourteen for the stud-farms (in Göbös near Eszterháza and in Ozara). The beautiful carriages (now at Forchtenstein) were kept at Eisenstadt.

The princely castles, palaces and houses, each with their own concierges, locksmiths, etc., were subordinate to the Castle Inspector, a post held for some time by Michael Kleinrath, a decorator by profession and at first a *Kammerdiener* of the Prince. There was also a princely librarian, a post which later became intimately connected with the marionette theatre (the librarian P. G. Bader was actually Director of the Theatre). The princely musicians (for the chamber and for the choir at Eisenstadt) belonged to the actual court and were 'house officers'.

We shall now examine briefly the salaries[1] of these employees; their income was partly in cash and partly in kind (in the economic section, the salary would mostly be in kind). The best-paid was of course the Estates Director (*Güterregent*) – in Haydn's time Ludwig Peter von Rahier and after his death Stephan von Nagy: his salary was 2,200 gulden, a small fortune, and more than 400 gulden in produce. The physician-in-ordinary came next: Dr Molitor, who also received 2,200 gulden but no produce. The other doctors, Dr Wecker and Dr Genzinger (whose wife would become one of Haydn's intimate friends), received much less, 600 and 300 gulden respectively. The chief judge earned 800 gulden with 40 gulden in goods; the fee for a lawyer on one of the estates was somewhat over 200 gulden. The Castle Inspector received 825 gulden, the Master of the Forests 900. The court painter had 620 gulden, the librarian about 420; an inspector of the estates received 900, an estate director upwards of 700 gulden. The lower strata of the economic section – steward, overseer, etc. – earned in cash between 150 and 200 gulden, plus payment in kind.

All these expenditures had to be balanced against the income. In 1780 the general disbursar's office took in 714,016 gulden, including the income from the various estates (over 500,000); the remainder came from the princely banking activities (lending money, etc.). Prince Nicolaus was a canny man with finances, and at the end of the fiscal year the income from the estate ranged from about 200,000 to 400,000 gulden, rising at the end of the century to over one million (against which, however, greatly increased expenses had to be set). From this income, the major domo's office received *c.* 80,000 gulden p.a. with which to run the palaces and castles; the Princess received 8,000 gulden in two instalments, for her birthday and name-day and as an allowance. The appanages cost a yearly 35,000 gulden, support of relatives and others some 20,000 gulden. We are fortunately in possession of a complete list of the expenditures for the theatrical and musical personnel in the year 1782 (table overleaf); to the total of 27,392 gulden must be added a further 700 gulden for the maintenance of the church choir in Eisenstadt, which included vocal soloists and string players. What could the money purchase? The list overleaf gives the prices of some everyday items.

A *Speckschwein* (a fat, i.e. grown, pig) cost 10 to 12 gulden, a small pig ('Schweindl') 6, a *Frischling* (young wild boar, or 'black pig') 4 gulden. An ox cost 10 or 11 gulden, a milk cow 8, an ordinary cow 6 or 7 gulden. A fathom cord of wood cost 3 to 4 gulden. A merchant from Oedenburg (Sopron) reckoned a pound of American cocoa at 1 fl.[2] [abbreviation for gulden, used throughout this book] 36 kr., chocolate $1\frac{1}{2}$ to 2 gulden, Dutch cheese 20 kr., rice 10 kr., sugar (there were eleven varieties) from 10 kr. to $1\frac{1}{2}$ fl. 100 lemons cost $4\frac{1}{2}$ fl.

---

1 At the beginning of the 1780s; for money and abbreviations used, see note on p. 19.
2 Albert Riedl, 'Halbvergessenes Eisenstadt' in *Eisenstadt. 300 Jahre Freistadt*, Eisenstadt 1948, p. 64, provided the information in the final paragraph. Otherwise Harich in *HJB* IV, 9f. (our summary and trans. 29f.).

SALARIES OF ESTERHÁZY PERSONNEL IN 1782

24 Music Individuals' salaries	9,711 Gulden 14 Kr.	
Their clothing	2,135 Gulden	
Their payment in kind..	932 Gulden 46 Kr.	
	Total	12,779 Gulden
11 Members of the Opera Troupe's salaries	6,879 Gulden	
Their payment in kind..	223 Gulden	
	Total	7,120 Gulden
14 Actors' salaries	4,200 Gulden	
Their payment in kind..	310 Gulden	
	Total	4,510 Gulden
1 Theatrical painter		555 Gulden
1 Machinist..		543 Gulden
1 Garderobier salary 150, in kind 13		163 Gulden
2 Copyist and prompter		340 Gulden
16 Theatrical personnel		1,382 Gulden
	Total	27,392 Gulden

[J. Harich in HJB IV, 9]

PRICES OF EVERYDAY REQUIREMENTS

One *Metze* [3.44 litre, miller's dry measure] of wheat	1 Gulden	30 Kr.
One *Metze* of rye	1 Gulden	
One *Metze* of *Grieß* [semolina or grits; gruel, oatmeal]		
One *Metze Gerste und Hirsebrei* [barley and millet-pap]........................	—	45 Kr.
One pound of bread (*c*. 56 dekagrammes)	—	1 Kr.
One pound of beef [beef, fats, wax prices were county-regulated and the prices announced in the public newspapers]	—	4–5 Kr.
One pound of salt	—	4–5 Kr.
One pound of lard	—	15–16 Kr.
One pound of wax candles	—	10–12 Kr.

[N.B. one pound = 56 dekagrammes]
[N.B. There were various kinds of *Eimer*. In Eisenstadt they usually reckoned according to the Pressburg measure. There was a special measure called the Eisenstadt 'Hamb': 6¾ 'Hamb' = 9 *Eimer* Pressburg measure.]

One *Eimer* of beer	1 Gulden	30 Kr.
One *Eimer Kraut und Rüben* [cabbage (Sauerkraut) and turnip (in U.S. parsnip; beet; here used as a generic name for such root vegetables)]	2–2½ Gulden	

As to clothing, a tailor in Vienna, whose shop was called 'The Frenchman à la mode' (on the Graben) announced in the *Wiener Zeitung* (No. 64, 1782) that he could 'deliver a suit in the latest fashion within seven hours'. A whole suit from the finest material, lined with silk, cost 46 fl. 48 kr. The cheapest suit cost 7 fl. Coat and waistcoat cost 16 fl., coat and trousers 15 fl.; a coat alone cost between 14 and 26 gulden.

At Eisenstadt in the year 1783, the local wine (*Heurige*) cost 1½ to 3 kr. pro half-litre; one *Trunk* [*c*. 1 litre] of beer 2 kr.; one pound of beef 5½ kr.; a sucking pig 21–24 kr.; 1 goose 18 kr.; 4 eggs 1 kr. Masons (*Maurer*) and carpenters (*Zimmerer*) received 27 kr. daily wages. A 'day worker' (*Taglöhner*) received 15 kr., a stone-cutter (*Hauer*) 17 kr. A mason, if he took his salary in goods, could have four chickens, or one sucking pig and one chicken, or 108 eggs.

The provision of care of the sick and pensions for old employees shows Prince Nicolaus to have been ahead of his time in such matters. Those employees who could no longer work, or who were old or infirm, received a pension, and their widows and orphans financial assistance. The amount of the pensions was regulated according to the position of the person concerned. Further pensions could be established through a testamentary clause in the will of a prince or princess: Nicolaus left pensions to Haydn,

Tomasini and Specht. The musicians generally stayed on for as long as they could play, or else voluntarily left the princely service; so that on the whole they did not receive pensions. An exception was the bassoonist Johann Hinterberger, who after seventeen years of service had to leave because of growing deafness; he was given a pension of 250 gulden and six cords of wood and lived comfortably on this pension till his death in 1801; his widow received 150 gulden and four cords of wood. When the tenor Dichtler lost his wife, who dropped dead on the stage at Eszterháza in 1776, Nicolaus gave him in kind an amount equivalent in value to the salary which his wife had received, to help educate his small children. The widow of the bookkeeper Liehtscheidl, who bought Haydn's house, received a pension of 180 gulden annually; the children of the *Cancellista* Johann Novotni received annually thirty gulden and goods worth 124 gulden, while the widow received seventy-five gulden plus goods worth 169 gulden. Nicolaus showed similar *largesse* with his contractor Nicolaus Jacobi, who had been in service since 1746 and worked on Eszterháza Castle; after twenty-nine years of service, he was pensioned off, on 1 January 1775, with a yearly income of 300 gulden, which was to pass undiminished to his widow and children, so long as any of them lived. *In toto*, the estate paid out some 10,000 gulden each year in pensions.

A similarly broad-minded and generous social attitude can be seen in the provisions for the sick. The very first Prince Esterházy established a hospital for the poor in Eisenstadt, and set up a druggist (apothecary) next to the hospital: this was in 1679. In Haydn's time, three doctors, as we have seen, ministered to the sick at princely expense; the necessary medicines were also provided free. Just before Haydn appeared on the scene, Prince Paul Anton founded, in 1760, the hospital of the Barmherzigen Brüder (Brothers of Mercy) in Eisenstadt, thus enlarging the trust set up by the Palatine Paul. A room was set aside for the princely house officers, and the fratres received thirty (later thirty-two) kreuzer per patient per day; for the princely servants there was a dormitory. The oboist Zacharias Pohl died in that hospital in June 1781. Occasionally the doctor considered it necessary for the patient to go for a cure elsewhere, and the Prince paid for this, too. When his contractor Nicolaus Jacoby had to take the cure in Baden, the Prince not only paid for all his medical care but also stood him to free theatre tickets in the Baden theatre. At Eszterháza, the sick were also treated free: Haydn's coachman and his chambermaid were treated there, as were the Jermoli couple, both engaged as singers in the Esterházy troupe. The members of the visiting theatrical companies were also treated *gratis* at the Eszterháza hospital, e.g. 'Acteur Dáhmen' of the Diwald Troupe in September and October 1784. The children of those servants, etc. in straitened circumstances were also treated free in the hospital: we know of one orphan, whose father had been a stoker of the princely furnaces, his mother a servant in the theatre, who was taken to the hospital and cured; afterwards he was given to the theatrical seamstress as an apprentice, at princely expense, because he could do no more heavy work on account of the condition of his feet and 'had not learned anything else': he signed himself 'Lorenz Heim, poor waif from Schrollen' (1785–6).[1]

We may now proceed to fill in the names of the various positions listed above, to clothe, as it were, the skeletons with flesh and blood.

The character of Prince Nicolaus himself will emerge with no little clarity from the many documents we shall quote, so that only a few words need be said here. The

1 J. Harich in *HJB* IV, 21ff., with many more documents; our summary and translation, used here *verbatim* with some small additions, on pp. 34f.

principal characteristic that strikes one if we examine Nicolaus's relationship with Haydn and the musicians is, on the one hand, a severe and pedantic sense of discipline which the Prince sought, successfully, to impose through the means of his equally despotic right-arm, Herr von Rahier; while on the other a real sense of appreciation and a rather benevolent, patriarchal attitude towards his 'musical children'. On the one hand, Prince Nicolaus docks their salary for minor infringements, on the other he showers them with gold ducats if they played and sang beautifully, which they often seemed to have done if we are to judge from the extra rewards they received. No doubt Haydn was a master diplomat, and as we had occasion to observe many years ago (1959),[1] the mild, benevolent Prince Esterházy of the late 1780s is – at least as far as the musicians are concerned – partly the creation of his clever and tactful *Capellmeister*. The Prince was genuinely fond of his consort, Maria Elisabeth, *née* Countess von Weissenwolf; he surprised her with marionette operas for her birthday (March 1775, *vide infra*) and was prostrate with grief when she died in February 1790; but she remains a rather shadowy figure among all the glamour and pomp of Eszterháza where Prince Nicolaus openly kept a mistress. On 26 October 1785, General Miranda, who was visiting Eszterháza, writes: '. . . in the evening went to the opera, saw the Prince, his niece, and his mistress, vulgar woman . . .'. Haydn, writing to his publishers on 27 May 1781, notes that 'Between ourselves, this *Mademoiselle* [Clair] is the darling of my Prince . . .'.[2] Naturally, the official records at Eszterháza hardly refer to the Prince's mistress, so that we are uncertain of her identity.

Of the many relatives of Prince Nicolaus and Princess Maria Elisabeth, we might single out the following names which figure prominently in connection with Haydn.

Prince Nicolaus's eldest son, Anton (who later succeeded his father and was head of the family from 1790 to 1794), had married Maria Theresia, Countess von Erdödy in January 1763; for the festivities at Eisenstadt, starting on 10 January, Haydn had composed his first Italian opera, *Acide*, and conducted an unspecified comic opera. With the Erdödy family, Haydn remained on the best of terms, furnishing operas for the Erdödy Theatre in Pressburg (*vide infra*, pp. 262, 671) and later writing his great quartet series, Op. 76, for another member of the Erdödy family (see *Haydn: the Years of 'The Creation'*, pp. 284ff.), Count Joseph. Haydn's pupil Ignaz Pleyel was a protégé of the Erdödy family. Three years after Countess Maria Theresia died (1782), Count Anton Esterházy married (1785) another Maria Theresia (Marie Therese), Countess Hohenfeld, to whom Haydn later (1794) dedicated his great piano Trios, Op. 70 (XV:18–20).

Prince Nicolaus's second son, Nicolaus Count Esterházy, followed in his father's footsteps and married into the Weissenwolf (Weißenwolf in some documents) family; his bride was Maria Anna Franziska, and they were married in the court chapel at Eszterháza on 3 August 1777. It was for the ensuing celebrations that Haydn composed *Il mondo della luna* and conducted, in the marionette theatre, a repeat performance of one of Eszterháza's most expensive and lavish puppet operas, *Genovefens Vierter Theil*, performed in German.

Maria Anna, Prince Nicolaus's daughter (b. 27 February 1739), married Anton, Prince von Grassalkovics (Grassalkovicz, Grassalkovitch, etc.) on 21 May 1758. The princely Grassalkovics family had grown rich in army commissions during the Silesian (Seven Years') War of 1756–63; they had a magnificent palace in Pressburg, where we find Haydn conducting dance music in November 1772 (*vide infra*, p. 180). On another occasion, for the marriage of Ottilia, Countess von Grassalkovics, with Count

1 CCLN, p. xix.   2 Landon, *SYM* 113; CCLN 28.

Forgács, which took place at Eszterháza on 21 November 1779, Prince Nicolaus offered his guests a wedding present in the form of Felici's *L'amore soldato*,[1] conducted of course by Haydn. Prince Nicolaus's niece, Marianne, Countess Grassalkovics, married Count Viczay (German spelling: Witzay) and lived, during the mid-1780s on her husband's estate Nagylózs (German: Groß-Losing) near Eszterháza. Haydn dedicated to her three piano Trios, Op. 40, published by Artaria in April 1786 (Nos. 19–21, XV:6–8).[2] After Prince Nicolaus died, Prince Grassalkovics attempted to win Haydn as *Capellmeister*, but considering the two other offers (King Ferdinand IV of Naples and the Two Sicilies, and Salomon of London), the idea of spending his declining years in Pressburg was obviously not Haydn's idea of a worthy successor to Eszterháza Castle.

We shall see that the Grassalkovics family plays a not inconsiderable role in Haydn's life at this period. There must have been musical archives (not to speak of family archives) of considerable importance at Pressburg, but all attempts – including a search in 1959 by the present writer – to locate them have thus far proved vain. (Similarly, what must have been another great archive, those of the Cardinal Batthyáni at Pressburg, where Anton Zimmermann was *Capellmeister*, have never been located.)

The Dowager Princess Maria Anna (in some sources: Marie Louise), *née* Marchesa Lunati Visconti, the widow of Paul Anton (who had died in 1762), was a guest at Eszterháza for the celebration of her name-day in July 1773; for that occasion – on 26 July – Haydn composed one of his finest works of this period, the *burletta* entitled *L'infedeltà delusa* (*vide infra*: her portrait in pl. 6, Chronicle pp. 186 ff.).

Prince Nicolaus's grandson, Anton's eldest son Nicolaus (later Prince Nicolaus II), was born on 12 December 1765 and married the beautiful Maria Josepha Hermenegild, Princess Liechtenstein (b. 13 April 1768), on 15 September 1783. The young man was to be the fourth Prince Esterházy under whom Haydn would serve (following his return from England in 1795), and he was particularly attached to Nicolaus's vivacious wife, variously known (in Haydn's correspondence) as the 'Princess Marie' and later as 'Princess Marie Hermenegild' or 'Princess Hermenegild' (see *Haydn: the Years of 'The Creation' 1796–1800* and *Haydn: the Late Years 1801–1809*, *passim*).

In the diary notice of General Miranda quoted above, we read 'the Prince, his niece . . .'. Probably the lady in question is 'ma chère Niece, la Comtesse Poggi':[3] she was born Countess von Lamberg and married Count von Poggi (*recte*: Pocci) in the court chapel at Eszterháza on 16 September 1770. On that occasion Haydn conducted the première of his new opera, *Le pescatrici*.

---

1 The extant score and parts in the Esterházy Archives give Felici as the composer, but the printed libretto for the occasion lists Sacchini as the composer. *Vide infra*, p. 416.
2 Hoboken Vol. I, p. 687; CCLN 50f.; Bartha 147; Horányi 117; Harich, *HJB* VII, 25.
3 From an autograph letter of Prince Nicolaus to M. le Marquis de Frosini, Biblioteca Estense, Modena, Autografoteca Campori, which reads as follows:

Monsieur!

Je vous suis obligé de la peine, que vous vous êtés donné en m'addressait la lettre de Mr le comte de Marchisio, e[t] de la part, que vous prennés à la Situation de ma chere Niece la Comtesse Poggi; et comme je marque mes sentimens sur ce sujet à Mr. le Comte dans la ci jointe, je prens la liberté de vous prier de lui faire tenir cette reponse. du reste mon absence de Vienne m'ayant privé du plaisir de votre entretien personnel, je me reserve cet honneur à mon arrivé a Vienne pour vous prouver, que je suis avec l'estime le plus parfait

Monsieur

votre très humble Serviteur
Nicolas Prince D'Esterhazy

Esterház ce 12 avril 7̄80

The house officers included, among the doctors, Frater Leo of the Barmherzige Brüder in Eisenstadt. Of the 'Sekretariat' (clerk's office) there was Haydn's friend Jacob Kaufmann, who forwarded so many appeals from Haydn to the Prince, and (from 1781) Johann von Szentgály, who later rose to be *Domänendirektor*, Director of the Princely Estates, and who was also to become Haydn's friend.

The blackamoor Frederich de August, the Prince's page, is an interesting figure; referred to in some of the sources as 'English', he lived for a time in the musicians' quarters and was reported on good authority – the princely employee Joseph Carl Rosenbaum – to be the father of the extraordinary violin virtuoso, George Polgreen Bridgetower. The young Bridgetower played in the Haydn-Salomon concerts of 1791 and later (in 1803) Beethoven composed the A major Sonata Op. 47 for him which was later dedicated to Rodolphe Kreutzer. Haydn is supposed to have been Bridgetower's teacher.[1]

The Princess's page was a dwarf, Johann Siedler, usually referred to as 'Monsieur Jean'; Haydn's brother Johann, who was engaged at the Esterházy court as a tenor (*vide infra*, p. 59), taught him music.

Among the interesting men at Eszterháza was the upholsterer, Michael Kleinrath, who later became Castles Director (*Schlösserinspektor*) and sometimes became involved in the theatrical life of the court. On one occasion, Prince Nicolaus ordered the Chief Cashier Züsser to transfer 'to our Inspector Kleinrath immediately the sum of two-hundred Gulden for the purchase of eight operas...' (Esterház, 13 September 1781), to which Kleinrath added the following note, which will have delighted Nicolaus, 'Since of these eight operas three are incomplete, those three have been returned and for the other five only one-hundred-twenty-five gulden (125 fl.) were paid! / Michael Kleinrath mpria / Inspector'.[2] Here we have another case of a self-made man, rising to one of the highest positions within the Esterházy orbit; for Kleinrath was in charge of all the castles and palaces.

The librarian was Philipp Georg Bader, who also occupied himself with the marionette theatre even before the original director, Karl Michael von Pauersbach (*vide* p. 66), left for Russia. Bader wrote the libretti to Haydn's *Dido* in 1776, when Pauersbach was still at Eszterháza (he left at the end of 1778); in 1779, Bader wrote the libretto to another marionette opera by Haydn, *Die bestrafte Rachbegierde*. In February 1778, Bader was made responsible for the total direction of the princely theatres at Eszterháza, the result of which was, *inter alia*, a complete record for the 1778 season which has fortunately been preserved intact (*infra*, pp. 93ff.). As one might expect from a librarian, Bader's libretti show that he was a highly educated man with a dry sense of humour. Bader died in 1779, and was succeeded by Johann Peter Noethen (from 1 January 1780), who had no relation to the theatre.

The princely infantry regiment was a springboard to greater things for at least two men of ambition: L. P. Rahier, the *Regent*, was a captain of the regiment in early life, which may explain the 'military' attitude he tended to show towards his subordinates, Haydn not excluded. Another retired captain, J. A. von Klein, became *Rechnungsführer und Personalchef* (chief clerk and head of personnel); Klein's and Rahier's portraits hang in the princely castle of Forchtenstein.

Apart from Basilius Grundmann, 'Chamber Painter to His Highness', whom we have mentioned above, and the talented young Guttenbrunn, there were other

---

1 J. Harich in *HJB* II, 40ff. (for this whole section); see also *Haydn in England 1791–1795* pp. 65ff; Else Radant in *HJB* V, 110; Landon *Beethoven*, 148ff. Frederich de August apparently came from the British West Indies.
2 Acta Musicalia 17/1114; Bartha-Somfai, 96.

painters in the princely service: Friedrich Rohde (Rodhe), 'cabinet painter', often referred to only by his Christian name; the theatrical painters Alessio Cantini, Pietro Travaglia, etc. will be discussed in the section dealing with the opera troupe, *infra* (pp. 65, 67). On occasion Grundmann had other assistants to help him, for instance in the rebuilding (in Grundmann's case, redecorating) the theatre after the fire. These two other painters from outside were, of course, temporary appointments.

III. Haydn and the Musicians

NO ONE EXCEPT PERHAPS PRINCE NICOLAUS realized what a profound change would be wrought as a result of Eszterháza Castle; possibly not even the Prince could have foreseen how radically the whole court's life would be altered. Originally, when Eszterháza was being built, Haydn lived most of the year at Eisenstadt, making excursions to Vienna in the winter, to the Esterházy castle at Kittsee, and to Pressburg, 'whenever their lordships [*Herrschaft*] so wished'. The Prince gave his *Capellmeister* and musicians a winter vacation when he went to Vienna to pay his respects at court (on New Year's); Haydn usually went to Vienna too, where he could see his publishers and his friends, visit instrument makers, search for new music, and so on. Opera, in the middle 1760s, was an exotic plant in the Esterházy establishment: *La canterina* (1766) was the first attempt, after *Acide* (1763), to introduce Italian opera by Haydn, and it was a modest beginning, suited to the available singers. By 1768, there was a regular opera house at Eszterháza, but until 1776 it was used mainly for the occasional work, usually in conjunction with one of Prince Nicolaus's famous *feste*. All during these years, the Prince cultivated assiduously his rather *outré* string instrument, the baryton, for which not only Haydn but Tomasini, Purksteiner and non-Esterházy composers such as Wenzel Pichl composed chamber music and concertos. The year 1776 seems to mark a certain diminution of interest in the baryton and coincidentally a sudden change in the operatic life of Eszterháza Castle. Whereas opera previously had been a rather sporadic affair, it now developed into a regular season: as long as the operas had been occasional pieces, Haydn composed them – such an exception as Carlos d'Ordoñez's *Alceste* is the typical 'exception that proves the rule' – but when Esterházy wanted a regular season, such as was produced in any European town or city, Haydn could no longer cope alone. At first he turned to the works of his old friend Ditters(dorf) to fill the vacancy, and then gradually to works by other, and primarily Italian *buffo*, composers such as Anfossi, Paisiello or Cimarosa.

From 1776 to 1790, the pattern became more or less set. Haydn composed less and less orchestral and chamber music for his Prince, and became more and more an operatic *Capellmeister*, managing long seasons of mostly 'foreign' operas – Haydn's own production dwindles markedly and comes to a stop in 1784 with *Armida* – which he not only conducted but of course rehearsed and 'edited'. The climax of this operatic activity came in the year 1786, when Haydn conducted 125 performances of eight 'new' operas and nine works already in the Eszterháza repertoire; this scarcely believable feat was repeated in 1788, when seventeen operas (seven 'new' works and ten repetitions) were also staged. It is difficult to understand how Haydn could organize this vast amount of opera as well as compose, in 1786, five concertos for the King of Naples, Symphonies Nos. 82, 84 and 86 (of the 'Paris' series), and several 'insertion' arias for works by other composers being performed at Eszterháza.

Haydn's work in preparing these operas by other composers for the Eszterháza stage did not consist in mere cuts and transpositions, such as every operatic *Capellmeister* made when fitting an eighteenth-century opera to his own local requirements. It is quite clear, now that we are in the fortunate position (which scholars were not, until the 1950s) of being able to study all the extant opera scores and parts in the Esterházy Archives, that Haydn gradually became very cynical in his attitude towards his Italian colleagues. In 1776, we find him making only small alterations to the scores by his friend Ditters(dorf), whereas by 1789 he was capable of transforming a pasticcio such as *La Circe* almost beyond recognition, not only cutting (slashing would be the better word) and changing but adding huge sections of his own composition – an aria, one scene and a brilliant *terzetto*. A recent book by Dénes Bartha and László Somfai, *Haydn als Opernkapellmeister* (Budapest, 1960), sums up Haydn's often flagrant violations of the Italian operas he was obliged to conduct. Apart from writing new numbers – many for his mistress, Luigia Polzelli – Haydn also reorchestrated many arias, adding for example wind instruments where the Italian original contained only strings; and in one particularly crass case speeding up the tempo of an aria in Salieri's *La fiera di Venezia* from Andante Maestoso to Allegro Vivace, a procedure that hardly places Haydn among the ranks of the world's great musicologists. There is no question that this enormous amount of editorial work on the Italian operas of the period gradually prejudiced Haydn violently against opera itself. It cannot be an accident that from 1784 to 1790 he composed no more operas at Eszterháza, particularly in view of the lavish attention he had devoted to his operatic scores from the very beginning. Now that we of the second half of the twentieth century are in a position to study and easily to hear most of Haydn's mature operas, it is ever more clear that such a work as *La fedeltà premiata* (1780) occupies a central position in Haydn's *œuvre* of this period, as indeed does *La vera costanza*, which has survived only in its second (1785) version for Eszterháza. Yet by 1790, when Eszterháza Castle closed its doors, Haydn not only fled precipitately from the geographical area to Vienna (leaving behind valuable music, as he later confessed), he was also escaping from an activity which was basically a total waste of his valuable time, talents and energy. It is, as we have observed, a miracle that he managed to compose as much as he did during the years 1776–90, including many fascinating if problematical operas of his own; but without the crushing amount of work involved in being Prince Esterházy's operatic *Capellmeister*, we might have been the richer for even more great masterpieces like the 'Oxford' Symphony, which must have been squeezed into the operatic duties of the season 1789. Haydn had to turn off his outer ear to the pleasant but basically conventional sounds of Anfossi, Cimarosa, Guglielmi, Paisiello and Martin y Soler (to name but some of the composers represented in the 1789 season) if he were to produce the brilliantly original, nostalgic 'Oxford' Symphony; that he managed to do so remains one of its composer's greatest feats.

The Prince became more and more attached to Eszterháza. The story of the 'Farewell' Symphony of 1772 is, of course, the musical proof of these long seasons, which gradually became intolerable to the musicians. The annual vacations, when the Prince went to Vienna before Christmas and returned in the new year, became shorter and shorter; Haydn was often required to break off his Viennese holiday in the middle and return at once to Hungary to prepare the operas for the coming season. And not only the operas: we must not forget that Haydn also prepared, and in some cases actually wrote, the incidental music for the plays given by the *Wandertruppen* which were engaged every year for the season at Eszterháza. In the lists for the Gotha

Theater-Kalender of the 1770s, these strolling players some of them famous companies, are printed with the significant concluding line 'Musikdirektor H. Hayden fürstl. Esterhazyscher Kapellmeister' (see the Chronicle for a number of such entries).

It may be useful to provide a brief summary of Haydn's financial situation prior to his succession to the title of *Capellmeister* in 1766. Prince Paul Anton had engaged him in May 1761 at 400 Rheinische gulden, plus free food at the officers' table or half a gulden *per diem* instead. When Prince Nicolaus became head of the family after Paul Anton's death on 18 March 1762, one of his first acts (25 June 1762) was to raise Haydn's salary by 200 gulden, and half-a-year later Nicolaus set Haydn's expenses at the officers' table (wine and food) at 182 gulden 30 kr. annually, which sum Haydn could have in cash (decree 1 May 1763). Thus Haydn's annual income was now 782 gulden 30 kr., about double that of two years earlier. On 1 December 1771, Haydn received an additional increase by means of 'a measure (*Maß*) of officer's wine daily' and six fathom cords of wood each year (*vide infra*, 1 December 1771). Apart from this fixed salary, Prince Nicolaus used to give Haydn and the musicians munificent gifts in the form of gold ducats after a particularly satisfactory operatic performance or concert: the details will be found in the Chronicle, *infra*. Haydn's astute biographer, Georg August Griesinger, has an interesting point to make in connection with these gifts of gold ducats. Haydn, writes Griesinger, 'had no idea how famous he was abroad, and he learned of it only casually through travelling foreigners who came and saw him. Many of them, also [Christoph Willibald von] Gluck, advised him to travel to Italy and France, but his diffidence [*Furchtsamkeit*] and his restricted [financial] position prevented him from doing so, and when he dropped a remark on the subject to his Prince, the latter pressed a dozen ducats into his hand, and [Haydn] allowed all such projects again to be dropped' (Griesinger, 16). In ten years the Prince gave Haydn no less than 260 ducats, or some 1,126 gulden.

When the Esterházy chapel organist at Eisenstadt, Franz Novotni (who was a good composer, particularly of church music, one of his Masses being wrongly attributed to Mozart, no less!) died on 25 August 1773, the Prince ordered Estates Director Rahier to find another organist, using Haydn's assistance. The upshot was that the various contestants all proved unsatisfactory, and a compromise was reached whereby Haydn himself was asked to play the organ in the winters at Eisenstadt (when the whole band was in residence there); otherwise the post was to be managed by the Castle Schoolmaster and tenor Joseph Dietzl. The salary was to be so divided that Haydn was paid in kind and Dietzl the 100 gulden in cash. The payment in kind consisted of four dry measures (one *Metze* = 3.44 litres) of wheat, twelve dry measures of rye, and a quarter of a dry measure each of lentils, barley and millet-pap, 300 lb. beef, 50 lb. salt, 30 lb. fats, 36 wax candles, nine liquid-measure kegs of wine, one of cabbage and one of turnips (beets, parsnips, etc.), plus six fathom cords of wood: in cash this would be 179 gulden, 15 kr., which meant that Haydn's salary was now 961 gulden 45 kr. He was now the third highest-paid employee of the entire Esterházy court, after the Estates Director and the physician in ordinary: no doubt this circumstance made the refusal of offers from abroad easier.

On 15 November 1777, the schoolmaster Joseph Dietzl died: Johann Georg Fuchs was given the post of schoolmaster (he was also a tenor), and a year later he got the job of organist which, however, he divided with the church violinist Michael Ernst. The Prince confirmed Haydn's goods for the organist's post in a new contract of 1 January 1779; but Haydn had to pay for a substitute out of his own pocket if he was hindered from playing in the winter (as, no doubt, he frequently was).

The new contract of 1779 replaces the old contract of 1 May 1761, which has been the subject of investigation and comment for some time. In particular, not only the rather offensive wording of the 1761 contract but some of the provisions are now omitted, e.g. '...he shall ...take the more care to conduct himself in an exemplary manner, abstaining from undue familiarity and from vulgarity in eating, drinking and conversations...remembering how displeasing the consequence of any discord or dispute would be to his Serene Highness...' (from clause 3). And the whole of the old clause 4 is omitted entirely: '4. The said Vice-Capellmeister shall be under obligation to compose such music as His Serene Highness may command, and neither to communicate such compositions to any other person, nor to allow them to be copied, but he shall retain them for the absolute use of His Highness, and not compose for any other person without the knowledge and permission of His Highness.' The issue raised here had long been a dead letter anyway.

Other clauses in the old contract were likewise modified: (No. 5) 'The said Joseph Heyden shall appear daily in the antechamber before and after midday, and inquire whether His Highness is pleased to order a performance of the orchestra...'. Or that His Highness 'may not be incommoded with trifling disputes' (clause 6), and similarly clause 8, concerning the instruction of female singers, '...in order that they may not forget in the country that which they have been taught with much effort and expense in Vienna...' and Haydn... 'shall take care to practise on all [the various instruments] with which he is acquainted...'. The new contract is very modern in its terse essentiality.

> This day, according to the day, month and year hereto appended, is ratified between H. Highness, Prince of the Holy Roman Empire, Lord and Master Nicolai Eszterházy v. Gallantha, Hereditary Count of Forchtenstein, Knight of the Golden Fleece, Comendeur [*sic*] of the Military Maria Theresia Order, Chamberlain and Acting Privy Councillor of Her Imp. Royal and Apostolic Maj., General Field Marshal, Colonel and owner of a Hung: Infantry Regiment, Captain of the Noble Hungarian Body-Guard, and likewise Acting Hereditary *Ober-Gespanns* of the *Oedenburg Gespanschafft*; and *Capelmeister* [*sic*] Herr Joseph Haydn, to be considered an Officer, the following contract agreed between them.
>
> *Primo*: Herr Haydn is to conduct himself in a manner which is edifying, Christian and God-fearing.
>
> *Secundo*: *Herr Capell-Meister* is to treat his subordinates at all times with great goodness and forbearance.
>
> *Tertio*: The party of the second part agrees to perform any music of one kind or another in all the places, and at all the times, to which and when H. Highness is pleased to command.
>
> *Quarto*: The party of the second part should not, without special permission, absent himself from his duties, nor from the place to which H. Highness has ordered the musicians.
>
> *Quinto*: Both contractual parties reserve the right to cancel the agreement.
>
> *Sexto*: *Herr Capell-Meister* will receive every two years one winter and one summer uniform, alternately, according to H. Highness's discretion; and he will receive the following (but apart from these items he will receive nothing further either in money or in kind), to wit:

As *Capellmeister*

In cash	782	f 30 Xr
Officer's wine in Eszterház..........................	9	*Eimer* [kegs]
Good genuine firewood in Eszterház	6	*Klafter* [fathom cords]

As Organist

Waitz [wheat]	4	*Metzen* [3.44 litre, miller's dry measure]
Kohrn [rye]	12	
Greißl [i.e. 'Grieß' = semolina or grits]	3/4	
Rindtfleisch [beef].....................................	300	
Saltz	50	*Pfundt* [pound = 56 dkg.]
Schmaltz [lard].......................... alles in......	30	
Kertzen [candles] .... Eszterház......	36	
Weinn [wine]	9	*Eimer*
Krauth und Rueben zusamen [cabbage & beets together]	1	
Schwein [pig]	1	*Stuck* [one whole pig]
Good firewood	6	*Klafter*

Then the necessary forage for 2 horses. Finally two identical copies of this contract are to be prepared and exchanged one with the other, and all previous *Resolutions, Conventiones* and Contracte are declared null and void. Schloß Eszterház the 1st of January 779.

[signed:] Josephus Haydn mpria

Concerning the above payment in kind and the 100 fl. (which latter are not listed in the above contract) which are to be paid in Eisenstadt, there is the following condition that, when I am not able to play the organ myself in Eisenstadt, I herewith agree myself to provide, to install and to recompense an organist.

[signed:] Josephus Haydn mpria

[*Personalakten, Schloß Forchtenstein*][1]

There is, however, another way in which we may observe a graphic illustration of that which occurred in Haydn's inner life between the years 1766 and 1790, to which we might without undue exaggeration apply the same words as Giuseppe Verdi when speaking of his 'middle years', *viz.*, 'gli anni di galera' (the years of the galley): and that concerns the handwriting, the *ductus*, as seen on Haydn's musical autographs. Prior to 'gli anni di galera', Haydn's autographs were on the whole not only well organized, neat, almost scholarly, but they reflected a certain inner stability, a sense of order which, in fact, we know to have been the essential part of Haydn's spiritual life. Let us then begin to examine the autographs written under the extreme pressure of operatic life at Eszterháza Castle. First, we may note that when instruments rest for many bars, they are simply left blank: the copyist was usually provided with the necessary hints in this respect, e.g. when an instrument stopped playing at the beginning of a bar, the rests for *that particular bar* are filled in (but not invariably), and the ensuing total bars are simply left blank. Other, more drastic, abbreviations follow, in particular the 'come Sopra' (as before) which we find when the recapitulation has the same notes as the exposition. Here, Haydn usually leaves one instrument throughout, such as the first violin, as 'orientation' for the long-suffering copyist. But apart from time-saving devices such as that, the autographs themselves begin more and more to show traces of that frantic haste which gradually became the principal underlying fact of

1 J. Harich in *HJB* IV, 10ff., 16 (our summary and translation 30f., 32f.); Novotni's Mass attributed to Mozart: see Landon in *Mozart-Jahrbuch* 1957, pp. 85ff; Bartha-Somfai, 55–9 and *passim*; Haydn's contract of 1761 in facsimile in Valkó I (after 632), and in print *inter alia* Bartha, 41–4; Haydn's contract of 1779 in facsimile in *Joseph Haydn und seine Zeit: Austellung Schloss Petronell Niederösterreich 1959*, after p. 56, and in print (with minor errors) in Harich, *HJB* IV, 76–8.

Capellmeister Haydn's musical, and even personal, existence. The opera productions, their rehearsals, the preparation of the scores soon dominated everything. Haydn's handwriting becomes less accurately formed, more hasty; it is surely more *flüchtig* – a word often used by German scholars which is difficult to translate, but of which the nearest equivalent in English is 'flighty' – and at times reveals a certain pressure that we hardly find in Haydn's earlier autographs. When he was first *Capellmeister* at Eisenstadt, Haydn was certainly a very hard-working man, and in 1762, when writing a Concerto for horn and orchestra (VIId: 3), he mixed up the staves of the oboes and violins when he arrived at the final pages. He had to place new 'headings' for the instruments at the beginning of the page to warn the copyist and, in self-defence, he wrote at the top of the page 'NB' (at the left) and 'im schlaff geschrieben' (written while asleep). But if we examine the page in question (facsimile in Geiringer 1932, p. 92), the neatness and clarity of the notes remain unchanged despite the 'schlaff' that overcame its composer.

The hasty outward appearance of the autographs of the 1780s is also matched by another curious phenomenon: a certain inaccuracy of notation. There are hardly ever mistakes in the actual notes, but the phrasing is now subjected to a kind of shorthand which occasionally borders on the chaotic. How was the copyist, not to speak of the player, supposed to interpret the second violin part, reproduced here, from the *Missa Cellensis* ('Mariazellermesse') of 1782, in the Benedictus? We believe that Haydn meant a rocking motion (2 + 2 slurs, i.e. a slur over every two notes), but the notation is highly ambiguous and is a typical manifestation of the constant pressure under which Haydn was now living. This kind of written *Schlamperei* (an Austrian word for extreme disorganization) now becomes an integral part of Haydn's autographs. There are, it is true, certain signs of this *Schlamperei* in his autographs of the 1760s and early 1770s; his placement of slurs and staccato marks was never as precise as Mozart's, for example, and for a very obvious reason: whereas Haydn wrote for more-or-less the same musicians in the years 1761–90, Mozart wrote (except for those works for Salzburg) for musicians he scarcely knew in his travels to England, France, Italy and Germany; and even when he arrived in Vienna and began to give regular concerts, he probably never knew until the last minute exactly which musicians would play in his Mehlgrube 'academies'. There were exceptions, such as the Stadler brothers, on whom Mozart relied, but the large *gros* of string players in Vienna no doubt came and went at Mozart's subscription concerts with some rapidity; and thus Mozart was obliged to be accurate, in order to avoid wasting expensive rehearsal time. His autographs are far more accurate than Haydn's as far as the placement of phrasing and dynamic marks is concerned, whereas Haydn was undoubtedly used to dictating oral instructions to his players. It was not until Haydn went to London that his autographs gradually become more detailed and more explicit; but the careless phrasing was something that remained with him for the rest of his life – the surely unconscious but nonetheless poignant reminder of the 'anni di galera'.[1]

(a) *The Agents abroad: procuring the Music*
The principal source for the repertoire at Eszterháza was, of course, the Court Opera at Vienna, where not only 'imported' Italian operas were regularly performed (and their scores thus available for ready piracy by the local copyists), but local composers were regularly engaged, and guest composers asked to come, for a season or two, to produce

1 For some *schlampig* phrasing even in *The Creation*, see *Haydn: the Years of 'The Creation' 1796–1800*, pp. 393ff.

A page from the autograph of the *Missa Cellensis*, showing the passage in the Benedictus which Haydn borrowed from an aria in his earlier Opera, *Il mondo della luna* (1777). The instruments (from top to bottom, ignoring blank staves) are: oboes I and II; V. I; V. II; Va.; four vocal parts; organ, Vc.-B.

new operas for the Burgtheater and Kärntnerthortheater. Among the local composers, Gluck's pupil and the arch-intriguer Salieri soon came to hold an enviable position as 'court composer'; of the older men, Florian Leopold Gassmann was much admired at Eszterháza and many of his works performed, even as late as 1790 when Gassmann was long dead. (Gassmann had studied in Italy and had produced his first works at Venice; the Overture to *L'Issipile* of 1758 seems to have had a certain stylistic influence on Haydn's Symphony No. 1 of 1759.)[1] Of the 'foreign' composers asked to come to Vienna to produce new operas, we might mention Pasquale Anfossi (who produced *La vera costanza* in 1776), Giovanni Paisiello (whose arrival in Vienna was fêted by Mozart and, more important, by Joseph II in May 1784 – *vide infra* p. 490 and, after Eszterháza was only a memory, Domenico Cimarosa (who produced, in 1792, his greatest success, *Il matrimonio segreto*).[2] Naturally not only Haydn but the Prince were able to hear (or hear of) the new operas produced in Vienna, and to procure scores for Eszterháza.

Now that we have touched on the actual music, if briefly, it is perhaps the place to establish the Prince's taste. As we can see from many contemporary reports, and from the list of music played at his castles, Prince Nicolaus preferred comic to serious opera. That is not to say that there was no *opera seria* at Eszterháza; we find Bertoni's *Orfeo ed*

1 Gassmann's *sinfonia* (Overture) is published in the *Diletto Musicale* series of Doblinger, edited by the present writer.
2 See *Haydn in England 1791–1795*, p. 126.

Euridice, for example (performed 1788–9) and Traetta's *Ifigenia in Tauride* (performed 1786); but these were definitely the exceptions. Most of the operas conducted by Haydn at Eszterháza were *opere buffe*, and many were taken from the Viennese repertoire. Just as Eszterháza depended on Vienna, we have an interesting case of another opera house in the neighbourhood of Eszterháza that in some respects depended upon it for its basic repertoire, and especially for the new Haydn operas (e.g. *La fedeltà premiata, Orlando Paladino* and *Armida*) : the Erdödy Theatre at Pressburg; we shall have the opportunity of examining the productions of this (in some respects) *dépendance* of Eszterháza later in these pages (p.671).

Haydn and Prince Nicolaus needed agents further afield, however, and the Prince managed to organize two classes of such agents: (1) men that were already engaged as princely agents for other matters, and (2) new men specially recruited, or who offered themselves, for the transmission of the latest operatic scores to Hungary. One of these princely correspondents was the *Consigliere* Leopoldo Mazzini in Rome, who from 1775 received a yearly salary from Esterházy to provide him with all the latest theatrical, operatic, literary and artistic news from Rome (the new princely picture gallery and library were under construction at that time). In Milan it was Venzeslaus (Wenzel) Pichl, musical director and chamber musician to the Archduke Ferdinand; Pichl also received a yearly salary and sent his own and other works to Eszterháza (*vide infra*, p.435, for a *pro memoria* by Haydn, dated 23 December 1780, which concerned *inter alia* the copying of Pichl Quartets); the Bohemian composer also delivered books. In Bologna, the poet P. G. Martelli recruited singers for Eszterháza.[1] But the most important 'informant' was Count Jacob Durazzo, at this time Austrian Ambassador to the Serenissima[2] in Venice, and who was well known in theatrical and artistic circles, not only for having managed the court theatres in Vienna during the 1750s but for having encouraged Gluck and his reform works (*Don Juan, Orfeo*). Durazzo's wife was related to Nicolaus's wife, both having been born Countesses Weissenwolf; Durazzo was often a guest at Eszterháza when Prince Nicolaus was enlarging it in the early 1760s. When Durazzo went to Venice, the friendship with Esterházy continued, and the latter sent wine from the princely estates to Venice. Count Lamberg, also related to the Esterházys through marriage, was at the time in Naples; he, too, must have sent theatrical gossip and news to Hungary, for which he, like Durazzo, received Esterházy wines. As for individual offers, we have examined briefly one which involved Inspector Kleinrath (*supra*, p. 38). The famous composer Friedrich Benda also offered his works to Prince Esterházy, beginning his letter with the flattering words, '. . . Your Serene Princely Highness is accustomed to hear only masterpieces of music from your everywhere famous *Kappellmeister* [*sic*] Haydn . . .', and sending the famous melodrama *Medea*.[3] Sometimes the singers themselves brought or sent for new scores, as when Domenico Negri organized the score and parts to Cimarosa's *L'italiana in Londra* in 1783. Carl ditters(dorf) sold many operas to Prince Nicolaus – *vide infra*, p. 400.

(b) *The Opera Troupe at Eisenstadt and Eszterháza (1766–90)*
There follows a list of the singers who were engaged at any time during this period, with notes on their roles, as far as we know them, and other information that might be considered useful.

1 J. Harich in *HJB* VII, 13.
2 The 'most serene' Republic of Venice.
3 On 10 November 1787. Bartha-Somfai, 143; about Negri, 109; otherwise, J. Harich in *HJB* II, 9ff. 37f. (our summary and translation).

SINGERS (FEMALE)

Benvenuti, Barbara: soprano. Engaged 11 July 1788 – September 1790. Performed in Cimarosa's *Il marito disperato* ('Gismonda') (1788), Martin's *L'arbore di Diana* ('Britomarte') (1789), Paisiello's *Il barbiere di Siviglia* ('Rosina') (1790), Cimarosa's *L'impresario in angustie* ('Doralba') (1790) and *Giannina e Bernardone* ('Aurora') (1790), and in other operas that cannot now be identified. On one receipt she signs herself 'Benvenutte' (Somfai, plate 199). In some sources she is given a different Christian name, Teresa. Bartha-Somfai, 148, 152, 168, 336, 354, 356, 358. She earned 832 gulden *per annum* (*HJB* VII, 108) and was engaged as a substitute for Margherita Delicati.

Bologna, Maria: soprano (younger sister of Matilde). Engaged 17 May 1781 for two years (renewed) – died 16 May 1784, aged 30. Performed in Paisiello's *L'avaro deluso* ('Rosina') (1781), Righini's *Il convitato di pietra* ('Elisa') (1781), Salieri's *La fiera di Venezia* ('Cristallina') (1782), Traetta's *Il cavaliere errante* ('Dorina') (1782), Anfossi's *Il curioso indiscreto* ('Serpina') (1782), Guglielmi's *Il ratto della sposa* ('Dorina') (1783) and Cimarosa's *Il falegname* ('Grazina') (1783). *Eisenstädter Commissions Prothocol anfangend von fasciculo No. 1100 – bis 1753 und zwar von Jahr 1777 bis 1790* (hereinafter abbreviated ECP 2489), Esterházy Archives, Budapest fasc. 2489, items 1332, 1447, 1448. Bartha-Somfai 91, 93, 99ff., 107, 168. Harich in *HJB* I, 43. Haydn referred to her familiarly as 'Mariuccia': see his proposal for *Il ratto della sposa, infra*, p. 68; also for *Il curioso indiscreto, infra*, p. 460. The two sisters were first paid 300 'Cremnitzer Duggatten' together (*HJB* VII, 106).

Bologna, Matilde (Mathilde, Metilde): soprano. Engaged 17 May 1781 for two years (renewed) – September 1790. Performed in Paisiello's *L'avaro deluso* ('Corilla') (1781), Righini's *Il convitato di pietra* ('Donn' Anna') (1781), Grétry's *Zemira ed Azor* (in Italian; 'Zemira') (1782), Traetta's *Il cavaliere errante* ('Arsinda') (1782), Haydn's *La fedeltà premiata* ('Fillide' or 'Celia' in the revised version of 1782), Haydn's *Orlando Paladino* ('Angelica') (1782), Righini's *La vedova scaltra* ('Rosaura') (1783), Sarti's *Giulio Sabino* ('Epponia') (1783), Cimarosa's *Il falegname* ('Elena') (1783), Haydn's *Armida* ('Armida') (1784), Anfossi's *I viaggiatori felici* ('Lauretta') (1784), Sarti's *La Didone abbandonata* ('Didone') (1784), Bologna's *L'isola di Calipso abbandonata* ('Calipso') (1784), Sarti's *I contratempi* ('Carlotta') (1785), Zingarelli's *Montezuma* ('Quagozinga') (1785), Zingarelli's *Alsinda* ('Alsinda') (1786), Traetta's *Ifigenia in Tauride* ('Ifigenia') (1786), Righini's *L'incontro inaspettato* ('Aurora') (1786), Sarti's *Idalide* ('Idalide') (1786), Bianchi's *Il disertore* ('Adelina') (1787), Bianchi's *Alessandro nell'Indie* ('Cleofide') (1787), Cimarosa's *Giunio Bruto* ('Tullia') (1788), Martin's *L'arbore di Diana* ('Diana') (1789), and in other operas that cannot now be identified. ECP

2489, item 1332. Harich in *HJB* I, 50, 61. Bartha-Somfai 90f., 93, 99–102, 108f., 112, 115f., 118, 121, 123, 125, 128–35, 137, 139, 144, 152, 159, 168, 300, 324, 329. Haydn referred to her familiarly as 'Metilde': see his proposal for *La vedova scaltra*, *infra*, p. 68. Matilde Bologna was referred to in the printed libretti as 'Mad.', her younger sister Maria as 'Mlle.'; the elder sister was married to Nunziato Porta, 'Directeur' and chief Wardrobe-Master. Matilde and Teresa Melo received the highest salaries of all the musicians including Haydn: 1,000 gulden *per annum*; at least in 1790 which means that Matilde's salary was considerably raised (facsimile of their final salaries: Somfai, plate 199). Matilde must have been a very remarkable singer; Haydn entrusted her with various taxing rôles in his own operas, such as the dramatic part of Celia in *La fedeltà premiata* and the part of Armida in *Armida*. We have a precious commentary from Count Zinzendorf, who went to hear her when she sang as part of some kind of guest appearance of the Esterházy singers at the Burgtheater on 15 December 1777: '...au Spectacle, La Locanda, la musique est de [left blank – probably Gazzaniga, whose opera was played in 1772 in Vienna and 1778 at Eszterháza]. La Ripamonte jolie actrice sans voix, le Bologna laide avec de la voix...'. A few years later, there seems to have been almost a *Gesamtgastspiel* of the Esterházy troupe at the Vienna court theatre. On 22 February 1783, Zinzendorf reports, '...puis a l'opera Calypso abandonata, ou Mc Bologna et Melle Valdisturla chanterent au Theatre de la porte de Carinthie, musique de Heyden...'. Possibly Haydn did conduct, giving Zinzendorf the impression that Haydn, rather than Luigi Bologna, was the composer. J. Harich in *HJB* 56f., Landon in *HJB* 57n., E. Olleson in *HJB* II, 48, Pohl II, 126. (In point of fact the first performance at Eszterháza in 1783 did not take place till March: J. Harich in *HJB* I, 48.) The two Bologna sisters arrived together with Nunziato Porta (*vide infra*, p. 67) from Venice. Matilde specialized in serious roles ('...Resta fuori in tutte le opere buffe...', Bartha-Somfai, 130).

Bon, Anna and Rosa (range?) – *vide* pp. 64f.

Cellini, Gertrude (Gertruda): mezzo-soprano. Engaged by contract dated Eszterház, 8 August 1769 (J. Harich, *HJB* VII, 61); in the *Prothocoll über verschiedene hochfürstl. Commissiones, Decretationes, Intima und andere Buchhaltereys Verordnungen de Anno 1734* (hereinafter abbreviated PCDI), Esterházy Archives, Budapest fasc. 2488, item 659, dated Esterhaz 13 August 1769 informs of the 'neu aufgenohmene' singer. She received 412 gulden 30 kr., free lodging or in lieu of that 30 gulden, the usual goods and a dress per annum. She left Eszterháza at the end of April 1773. She sang the important part of Eurilda in Haydn's *Le pescatrici*, which shows that she had a mezzo-soprano voice of considerable range; Haydn probably used her as an alto as well. Horányi, 242.

Delicati (Delicatti), Margherita (Margarete): dramatic soprano. Engaged by contract on 1 April 1785 – end June 1787. Performed in: Bologna's *L'isola di Calipso* ('Telemaco') from 17 April 1785, Zingarelli's *Montezuma* ('Leisinga') (1785), Anfossi's *Il matrimonio per inganno* ('Giulietta') (1785), Stabinger's *Le astuzie di Bettina* ('Rosetta') (1785), Cimarosa's *La ballerina amante* ('Ortensia') (1786), Cimarosa's *Chi dell'altrui si veste, presto si spoglia* ('Baronessa Stellidaura') (1786), Traetta's *Ifigenia in Tauride* ('Pilade') (1786), Cimarosa's *I due baroni di Rocca azzurra* ('Sandrina')[1] (1786), Gazzaniga's *L'isola d'Alcina* ('Clizia') (1786), Anfossi's *Il sordo e l'avaro* (? role) (1787), Bianchi's *Il disertore* ('Belinda') (1787), Bianchi's *Alessandro nell'Indie* ('Gandarte') (1787). Bartha-Somfai 124–7, 129–33, 135, 137–9, 143, 168, 277, 316, 342. J. Harich 1959, p. 59; *HJB* I, 61.

Dichtler, *née* Fuchs (Fux), Barbara: soprano. Engaged 1 July 1757 as an apprentice at 20 gulden; raised 10 gulden on 13 August 1758; married the tenor Leopold Dichtler on 28 November 1764 (Haydn as 'best man' for the bride); at this period she earned 100 gulden; as of 1 August 1769 her salary raised 50 gulden, and raised another 50 gulden on 15 September 1772; her goods the usual for the period; as of 28 August 1774, she was to receive an annual 'Kleÿd' (dress). On 19 September 1776, while singing Belinda in Sacchini's *L'isola d'amore*; she dropped dead on the stage; *vide infra*, p. 404. Prince Nicolaus, in a resolution dated 28 October 1776, gave the widower the *Naturalien* (goods) that his wife would have received, to help with raising the four children (Prince and Princess Esterházy were the godparents for the fourth child, Haydn and his wife were godparents of two others). Performed in Haydn's *Acide* ('Glance') (1763), Haydn's *La canterina* ('Don Ettore' [*sic*]) (1766–7), Haydn's *Lo speziale* ('Volpino') (1768), Haydn's *Le pescatrici* ('Nerina') (1770), Haydn's *L'infedeltà delusa* ('Sandrina') (1773), Haydn's *L'incontro improvviso* ('Balkis') (1775), Sacchini's *L'isola d'amore* ('Belinda') (1776), and in other operas and church music that cannot now be identified. Obviously Haydn appreciated Barbara Dichtler's vocal accomplishments; she must have had a light, flexible soprano voice with a fine sense of coloratura (see the beautiful writing for 'Sandrina', especially the E flat Aria in Act II, 'E la pompa un grand'imbroglio', from *L'infedeltà delusa*, which has a nobility and a depth of feeling that tell us something of the person for whom it was so lovingly composed). Bartha-Somfai 63, 66, 168, 379, 385, 389; *HJB* VII, 20, 50f., 77f., 89. PCDI 2488, items 824 (Esterhaz, 15 September 1772: increase in salary), 1096 (*re* death).

Friberth, *née* Spangler, Magdalena (Maddelena): soprano. Engaged as from 1 September 1768 in an 'Intimation' dated Eszterház, 18 September 1768 at 500 gulden *per annum*, plus

free lodging or 20 fl., the usual goods and a new dress each year. She was the daughter (b. 1750) of the tenor, Johann Michael Spangler, who had greatly helped Haydn when he, Haydn, was a starving young man in Vienna. In 1769 she married the tenor Carl Friberth and both left the princely service on 22 May 1776. Performed in Haydn's *Lo speziale* (her début at Eszterháza, as 'Grilletta') (1768), Haydn's *Le pescatrici* ('Lesbina') (1770), Haydn's *L'infedeltà delusa* ('Vespina') (1773), Haydn's *L'incontro improvviso* ('Rezia') (1775) and in other operas of the 1776 season, and in church music, which can no longer be identified. Magdalena Friberth must have been a great actress as well as having been an accomplished singer. Each of the three parts Haydn wrote for her required great 'character', but of course *L'infedeltà delusa* is 'her' opera; Vespina is a great star part and a magnificent tribute to this talented and obviously witty singer. PCDI, item 762 (Eisenstadt 18 October and Esterhaz 27 October 1768); *HJB* VII, 62, 78, 89f.

Griessler (Grießler), Elisabeth: contralto. Engaged as second alto-singer in a 'Comission' dated Eszterház, 28 August 1771. The daughter of the bass singer, Melchior Griessler, she was engaged as an apprentice at 25 gulden in the Eisenstadt church choir, having sung in it *gratis* for two years previously. From 1 November 1775 ('Resolution' of 15 November) her salary was raised to 50 gulden, 'since she sings diligently in the Eysenstädter chorus winter and summer'. In 1782 she married Lukas Wutkowatz (later, in the Hummel era, to direct the princely boys' choir at Eisenstadt) and left the princely service. In her place her younger sister Josepha was engaged. *HJB* VII, 63, 78f. J. Harich in *HJB* VIII, 40f. Pohl II, 375. PCDI 2488, items 1038, 1058.

Griessler (Grießler), Josepha: contralto. Engaged as 'Supernumerar Altistin', as apprentice, on 5 March 1782 (princely 'Resolution') at a salary of 25 gulden *per annum*. Like her sister, Josepha was engaged for the Eisenstadt church choir, and had nothing to do with the life at Eszterháza. *HJB* VII, 120. J. Harich in *HJB* VIII, 40. ECP item 1358 (Esterhaz 5 March 1782: her engagement).

Houdière, Auguste: 'Singerin' in 1766. Nothing is known of her. Pohl II, 261.

Jäger, Eleonora: contralto (with a range including soprano). Engaged on 15 November 1753 at the age of thirty-two as 'chorus singer' at a salary of 150 gulden, 12 fl. lodging money and the usual goods. Since she also sang in operatic performances, from the year 1767 her salary was raised by 23 fl. 30 kr. She also received a new dress every year. In 1773, as a result of a rather complicated situation which shall be examined *infra* (p. 200), she was called to Eszterháza but was not used; she used this pretext to ask for an increase, which was then given her (40 gulden *per annum*). Performed in Haydn's *Acide e Galatea* ('Tetide') (1763) and in

1 'Sandra' in the score used at Eszterháza.

other works that cannot now be identified. A personal friend of Haydn's – he sent her his famous 'autobiographical sketch' of 6 July 1776 to be forwarded to the princely official Zoller – she took a responsible position in keeping the weak Eisenstadt church choir from collapsing entirely. As a member of the princely choir, she was one of the few musicians retained after Prince Nicolaus died in 1790. She herself died, unmarried (Bartha 81, in error), at Eisenstadt on 19 May 1793. She must have been one of those capable, if not brilliant, singers who are the core of any fine ensemble. Her niece, Barbara Pilhofer, sang in the Eisenstadt choir (see *infra* and *Haydn: The Years of 'The Creation' 1796–1800*, p. 51). J. Harich in *HJB* VIII, 39f. *HJB* VII, 50, 62f., 78, 120. PCDI 2488, items 572 (Esterhaz, 22 March 1767: increase in salary), 1059 (Vienna, 3 Dec. 1775: new dress 'like the other singers').

Jermoli, Maria: mezzo-soprano. Engaged, with her husband Guglielmo, on 1 March 1777, for a period of eight months, but they had for some unknown reason to leave by the end of July. They were than re-engaged on 1 October 1779 for one year at a joint salary of 1,200 gulden, 200 more than they had received during their 1777 sojourn. Altogether the Jermolis must have been given preferential treatment, for in 1777, although 'they left the service at the end of Julÿ, they were paid till end 8ber [Oct.]'. They were given a servant at the Prince's expense. Their second engagement seems to have been arranged with some speed – they are not listed on the salary books, officially, until 1 April 1780 – because Barbara Ripamonti was already in an advanced state of pregnancy by the autumn of 1779 and had to be replaced. There was no room for the Jermolis in the music house, and they had to be put up at the princely *Gasthaus* (for which the inn-keeper sent a bill of 15 kr. *per diem* to the Prince) until the end of 1779; the same applied to the famous oboist Colombazzo (*vide infra*). On 31 March 1781, their engagement terminated, and shortly thereafter this excellent 'singer-pair' left Eszterháza for ever. Performed in Gassmann's *L'amore artigiano* ('Angiolina') (1777), Paisiello's *La Frascatana* ('Violante') (1777), Haydn's *Il mondo della luna* ('Lisetta') (1777), Felici's[1] *L'amore soldato* ('Ottavina') (1779), Anfossi's *La forza delle donne* ('Barbarina') (1780), Gazzaniga's *La vendemmia* ('Agatina') (1780),[2] Salieri's *La scuola de' gelosi* ('Contessa') (1780), Sarti's *Le gelosie villane* ('Giannina') (1780), Haydn's *La fedeltà premiata* ('Fillide' [Celia]) (1781). Both Jermolis had the star parts of Haydn's *La fedeltà premiata* (Celia and Fileno), and both roles inspired Haydn to some of his very greatest vocal writing; they must have had not only flexibility but sweeping dramatic power. When the Jermolis left – probably after the April 1781 'farewell' performance of the opera – Haydn had to postpone the next performance of the work

until September; he later rewrote the part of Celia for a soprano, transposing most of the arias a note or two up the scale. The Jermolis went from Hungary to Russia (see Jermoli, Guglielmo). J. Harich in *HJB* VII, 7f. *HJB* VII, 101, 104. ECP item 1270 (Esterhaz, 27 April 1780: Jermoli couple engaged for one year; terms listed). The Jermolis did not actually sing their roles in Haydn's *Il mondo della luna* (1777): *vide infra*, p. 402.

Melo, Teresa (Theresia, Therese): soprano. Engaged 1 July 1790–September 1790. She received the very high salary of 1,000 gulden *per annum*, which suggests that she must have been a very capable artist. We do not know in which operas of the 1790 season she appeared. *HJB* VII, 109. CCLN 108f. Bartha-Somfai 165.

Pilhofer, Barbara: soprano. Engaged by princely 'Resolution' dated 1 January 1788 as an apprentice at 25 gulden *per annum* to sing in the Eisenstadt church choir. Continued in that position after September 1790. *Vide supra*, Jäger.

Polzelli (Polcelli), Luigia: soprano. Engaged together with her husband, the violinist Antonio, by a princely 'Commission' on 15 March[1] 1779 at a joint salary of 110 ducats (or 465 fl. 40 kr.) – the lowest salary of the whole troupe at Eszterháza. Upon their arrival they immediately had to ask for (and received) a monthly advance in salary. Prince Nicolaus, apparently informed of their distressed economic situation, shortly thereafter cancelled the debt of their advance ('Anticipation in Gnaden relaxiret') and paid their monthly salary over again. On Christmas Day 1780, the Polzellis and the trumpeters Markl and Peschko were dismissed before their respective contracts had expired, with 'severance pay' (as we would say today) of two months' salary. It is assumed that Haydn managed to persuade the Prince to rescind the order concerning the Polzellis, and 'biß weitere Hochfürstl. Verordnung' they were allowed to remain in the princely service until the troupe was disbanded in 1790. Performed in:[2] Astaritta's *I visionarij* ('Rosina') (1779), Anfossi's *La Metilde ritrovata*★ ('Nanina') (1779), Gazzaniga's *L'isola d'Alcina* ('Lesbia') (1779), Anfossi's *Il geloso in cimento* ('Modesta') (1778, repeated with Polzelli in 1779), Sarti's *Le gelosie villane* ('Sandrina') (1779–80, 1784), Naumann's *La villanella incostante* ('Lisetta') (1779 as *Le nozze disturbate*, an alternative title), Paisiello's *La Frascatana*★ ('Donna Stella') (1777, repeated with Polzelli in 1779), Haydn's *L'isola disabitata* ('Silvia') (1779), Anfossi's *La forza delle donne* ('Egle') (1780), Gazzaniga's *La vendem-*

---

1 Sacchini? *Vide supra*, p. 37 and *infra*, p. 416.
2 Haydn composed the whole second part of an aria for her; *infra*, p. 423.

1 In another document: 1 March.
2 Haydn wrote many 'insertion' arias for her for inclusion in operas by other composers – all performed at Eszterháza; those works marked with an asterisk are known to contain authentic 'insertion' arias by Haydn, but the list – owing to a confusion of the source at Budapest, occasioned by Haydn's having removed most of those arias after September 1790 – is not complete. Haydn had obviously coached Polzelli lovingly, and did all he could for her mediocre talents.

mia ('Artemisia') (1780), Salieri's *La scuola de'gelosi*★ ('Carlotta') (1780), Anfossi's *La finta giardiniera* ('Arminda') (1780), Anfossi's *Isabella e Rodrigo* ('D. Eleonora') (1781), Righini's *Il convitato di pietra*★ ('Lisetta' and 'Donn' Isabella') (1781), Grétry's *Zemira ed Azor* ('Fatima') (1782), Traetta's *Il cavaliere errante*★ ('Melissa') (1782), Anfossi's *Il curioso indiscreto* ('Emilia') (1782), Sarti's *Fra i due litiganti il terzo gode* ('Contessa') (1783), Cimarosa's *Il falegname* ('Pellonia' [Bellonia]) (1783), Anfossi's *I viaggiatori felici* ('Isabella') (1784), Bianchi's *La villanella rapita* ('Ninetta') (1784), Sarti's *I contratempi* ('Bettina') (1785), Anfossi's *Il matrimonio per inganno*★ ('Rosina') (1785), Stabinger's *Le astuzie di Bettina* ('La Contessa di Belfiore') (1785), Haydn's *La vera costanza* (1779; new version 1785; she sang 'Lisetta'), Cimarosa's *La ballerina amante* ('Betta') (1786), Cimarosa's *Chi dell'altrui si veste presto si spoglia* ('Mirandolina') (1786), Gazzaniga's *L'isola d'Alcina* ('Lesbia') (first performed 1779, repeated with some new additions by Haydn, and new orch. mat. prepared), Caruso's *L'albergatrice vivace* ('Marinetta') (1786), Righini's *L'incontro inaspettato* ('Rosina') (1786), Anfossi's *Il sordo e l'avaro* (? role) (1787), Guglielmi's *La quaquera spiritosa* ('Robinetta') (1787), Bianchi's *Alessandro nell'Indie*★ ('Errisena') (1787), Martin's *L'arbore di Diana* ('Clizia') (1789), Cimarosa's *L'impresario in angustie*★ ('Merlina') (1790); she also sang, no doubt, in other operas of 1788–90, but precise information is now lacking. Luigia Polzelli (born Moreschi in Naples, 1750) was, as is well known, Haydn's mistress; it was certainly the result of his intervention that Antonio Polzelli, obviously a second-rate violinist, and Luigia, a soubrette of no great talents, were retained at Eszterháza all these years. Before they arrived in Hungary, it is thought that they were engaged in Bologna, where Luigia gave birth to her eldest son, Pietro, who became a great favourite of Haydn's (see *Haydn in England 1791–1795*, pp. 59, 115 and *passim*); he became violinist in the Schikaneder's Theater auf der Wieden in Vienna and died in 1796 at the age of nineteen. The second son, Alois Anton Nikolaus (known as Antonio) was born in 1783 and was regarded in the family as being Haydn's son; he too became a violinist and was engaged in the Theater auf der Wieden, later (1803) in the princely orchestra at Eisenstadt. He also composed an operette and several pieces of church music. Of Luigia's sisters, one was in London when Haydn arrived in 1791, and he kindly engaged her to sing in the Salomon concerts (Therese [Teresa] Negri, see *Haydn in England 1791–1795*, pp. 64f.) After Eszterháza was musically dissolved, the Polzellis went to live in Vienna, where Antonio shortly thereafter died. Luigia then went to Italy, sang at the theatres in Piacenza and Cremona, and married the singer Luigi Franchi. Later she returned to Hungary and from 1820 lived in Kassau (Kosice, CSSR), where she died in 1832 at the age of eighty-two (see the following volumes of this biography). The only letter in her handwriting, written after Haydn's death, is now in the Burgenländisches

Landesmuseum. The large literature about Polzelli is mostly based on Pohl II (89 *passim*) who, however, had access to more sources than we do, including at least one lost letter by Haydn of 1793 (Eisenstadt) and Luigia's passport, in which her oval-shaped face and olive-coloured skin are described: no portrait of her has survived. Of the newer literature, the most important is J. Harich in *HJB* VII, 12–19. See also Bartha-Somfai *passim*. *HJB* III, 132. *HJB* VII, 103, 108, 131f. (first contract), also 34, n. 60. ECP item 1236 (first contract, as 'Hochfl. Intimat,' 26 March 1779, also advance on salary 'von 55 Fl. 2 Xr.... welch aber ihme mit Anfang April [1779] monathlich per 2 Ducaten bis zur gänzlichen dilgung des Vorschusses abzuziehen ist'); 1240 (Esterhaz, 9 April 1779: Polzelli's advance 'in gnad geschänket').

Poschva (Boschwa, Poschwa), Catharina (Katharina): soprano. Engaged on 1 January 1776 with her husband, Anton Poschva, oboist. She received 400 gulden *per annum* and a new dress each year; he received 300 fl. and 35 fl. for lodgings, goods and a new summer or winter uniform each year. A 'Hochfürstl. Intimat' of 25 June 1778 indicates that from 5 December 1777 Catharina is to receive 100 fl. cash in lieu of the new dress each year and this sum is to be paid out in monthly instalments; from 1 July 1777 their joint salary is to be raised to 900 fl. On 27 August 1779, both Poschvas were dismissed. Performed in Gluck's *Orfeo* ('Euridice') (1776), Dittersdorf's *Il finto pazzo per amore* ('Eurilla, pastorella...la Sig. Boschwang') (1776), Piccinni's *La buona figliuola* (? role) (1776), Dittersdorf's *Il barone di Rocca antica* ('Beatrice') (1776), Gassmann's *L'amore artigano* ('Rosina') (1777), Haydn's *Il mondo della luna* ('Clarice') (1777), Dittersdorf's *Arcifanfano, re de' matti* ('Garbata') (1777), Guglielmi's *La sposa fedele* ('Camilla') (1778), Piccinni's *L'astratto* ('Clarice') (1778), Paisiello's *Le due contesse* ('Contessina di Belcolora') (1779), Haydn's *La vera costanza* ('La Baronessa Irene') (1779), Anfossi's *La Metilde ritrovata* ('Clarice') (1779). The most important of these roles for us are, of course, 'Clarice' and 'La Baronessa Irene' in Haydn's own operas *Il mondo della luna* and *La vera costanza*, which reveal Madame Poschva as having had a light, flexible, lyric-soprano voice, capable of coloratura but with small sustaining power. Her voice must have had a limited dynamic range, though she could easily sing up to *b''*. (All this supposes, of course, that the part of La Baronessa was not rewritten when Haydn recomposed the work for the 1785 revival at Eszterháza, when, in any case, the part follows the 1779 libretto.) The 'Baronessa Irene, Zia del Conte' is a small part, confined with one major exception (Aria 'Non s'innalsa, non stride sdegnosa') to recitatives and the (many) ensembles. There are charming Arias for 'Clarice'; however, she cannot be counted among the major vocal talents at Eszterháza Castle. Bartha-Somfai 65–7, 69–72, 75, 77, 79, 168, ECP item 1197 (25 June 1778, concerning 'Singerin Poschva' and her husband, lodging money). *HJB* VII, 96. For a theatre scandal involving Poschva, *vide infra*, p. 55.

Prandtner, Maria Elisabeth (Elisabetta): soprano. Engaged as apprentice in the Eisenstadt chorus on 1 August 1774 at a salary of 1 ducat, 12 kr. daily for her upkeep and 'with gracious allowance' (because not strictly required) a dress per year or 100 fl. instead, or (without the dress) 123 fl. 48 kr. *per annum*. She was given to the *routiné* tenor, Leopold Dichtler, to be taught 'Singkunst', for which Dichtler received one ducat per month. Prandtner made sufficient progress that she should sing in opera performances, so that in November 1776 (PCDI 2488, item 1095, Esterhaz, 28 Oct. 1776) she was given an increase of 5 fl. per month. After the death of the soprano Maria Anna Puttler (1778), Prandtner took over Puttler's roles (ECP item 1213, 10 Oct. 1778) and received her salary of 300 fl., 30 fl. lodging, 24 lb. of candles, three fathom cords of wood and the dress. She made her début as 'Dardana' in Haydn's *L'incontro improvviso* (August 1775), and appeared in: Sacchini's *L'isola d'amore* ('Marina') (1776), Piccinni's *La buona figliuola* ('Marchesa Lucinda') (1776), Dittersdorf's *Il barone di Rocca antica* ('Lenina') (1776), Paisiello's *La Frascatana* ('Lisetta') (1777), Piccinni's *L'astratto* ('Angelica') (1778), Anfossi's *Il geloso in cimento* ('Vittorina') (1778), Anfossi's *La Metilde retrovata* (*L'incognita perseguitata*) ('Clarice') (1779), Felici's *L'amore soldato* ('Semplicina') (1779), Gazzaniga's *La vendemmia* ('Lauretta') (1780), Gassmann's *L'amore artigano* ('Costanza') (1777, repeated 1780 with new singers including Prandtner), Sarti's *Le gelosie villane* (1779, repeated in 1780 with Prandtner). In the summer of 1780 she became ill; on 31 August the princely hospital sent in a bill for eighty-seven days' sick-bed expenses for Maria Elisabeth, and on 25 October 1780 she died. Haydn signed for her last monthly salary and seems to have been responsible for her *Verlassenschaft* (death duties). J. Harich in *HJB* 11f. Acta Musicalia (Esterházy Archives, Budapest) 70, 1018. *HJB* VII, 96, 130f. (Dichtler's instruction), 131 (Nicolaus's order that Haydn should receive her final salary, Esterház 2 Nov. 1780). Bartha-Somfai 65–7, 69, 82, 84, 86, 168, 203. PCDI, items 1003 (contract), 1095 (salary increase).

Purghardt (Burghardt), Klara: contralto. Engaged for the princely choir at Eisenstadt on 5 March 1782 (ECP item 1358 dated Esterhaz, 5 March 1782). There is no known termination date for her contract. She was part of the attempt to increase the size of the meagre princely choir.

Puttler (Buttler), Marianna (Maria Anna): soprano. Engaged on 1 January 1776 at a salary of 300 fl., 30 fl. lodging money, 24 lb. of candles, three fathom cords of wood, a dress each year – end of 1778 (but on 10 Oct. it was decided to replace her with Maria Elisabeth Prandtner, q.v.). Performed in Gluck's *Orfeo* ('Amore') (1776), Dittersdorf's *Il finto pazzo per amore* ('Biondina') (1776), Haydn's *Il mondo della luna* ('Flamminia') (1777) and

Guglielmi's *La sposa fedele* ('Lauretta') (1778), as well as other works which cannot now be identified. From the fact that Haydn gave her the role of 'Flamminia' in his new opera, we can judge her voice: a brilliant coloratura soprano with a flawless technique. Bartha-Somfai 65f., 71, 74f., 168. *HJB* VII, 98. Cast misprinted for Haydn's *Il mondo della luna* (p. 71).

Raimondi, Anna: soprano. Engaged from April 1781–July 1782. According to 'Hochfürstlichen Resolution' dated 5 April 1781 she received, from 1 April, a yearly salary of 600 gulden. Performed in Salieri's *La fiera di Venezia* ('Calloandra') (1782) and in other works which can no longer be identified. Bartha-Somfai 90, 98f., 168. ECP item 1327 (Esterhaz, 5 April 1781, about engagement of Anna 'Rajmondi'), *HJB* VII, 106 (terms of contract). 'Calloandra' in Salieri's Opera (autograph: Österreichische Nationalbibliothek, Musiksammlung codex 16.185) is for a virtuoso coloratura soprano with a range to *d'''*.

Ripamonti (Rippamonti), Barbara: soprano. Engaged with her husband, the violinist Francesco, on 21 April 1778 for three years, according to 'Hochf. Resolution', dated 26 April, at a joint salary of 1,100 gulden – dismissed on 10 April 1780. Barbara, without her husband, re-engaged on 15 June 1784 at a salary of 200 ducats – June 1786. Performed in: Guglielmi's *La sposa fedele* ('Rosinella') (1778), Paisiello's *La Frascatana* ('Violante') (1777, repeated in 1778 with Ripamonti), Piccinni's *L'astratto* ('Laurina') (1778), Anfossi's *Il geloso in cimento* ('Flavia') (1778), Gazzaniga's *La locanda* ('Guerrina') (1778), Anfossi's *La Metilde ritrovata* ('Gianetta') (1779), Gazzaniga's *L'isola d'Alcina* ('Alcina') (1779), Sarti's *Le gelosie villane* ('Giannina') (1779–80, 1784), Naumann's *La villanella incostante* ('Ninetta') (1779), Haydn's *La vera costanza* ('Rosina') (1779, also in the 1785 revival), Haydn's *L'isola disabitata* ('Costanza') (1779), Bianchi's *La villanella rapita* ('Mandina') (1784), Gazzaniga's *L'isola d'Alcina* ('Alcina') (Ripamonti also sang the revival of 1786, for which Haydn composed the beautiful 'insertion' Aria 'Sono Alcina', possibly as a farewell gift to this fine singer; *vide infra*, p. 678); it was proposed in the 'Piano Dimostrativo' that Ripamonti sing in Cimarosa's *I due baroni di Rocca azzurra*, but in the event the work was first performed on 6 December, after she had already left Eszterháza. Ripamonti must have been one of the finest singers at the court, with a strong, dramatic soprano voice capable of great flexibility as well (see 'Rosina' in *La vera costanza*). In *L'isola disabitata*, Haydn created one of his most atypical and curious roles for Barbara Ripamonti. J. Harich in *HJB* VII, 5–7 (and esp. 32, n. 11). ECP item 1188. *HJB* VII, 102. Bartha-Somfai 75f., 79, 83, 118f., 124, 129f., 132, 135, 168, 218, 289f., 316, 395. Barbara Ripamonti was at the Teatro S. Moisè in Venice in the year 1768, and again in 1775 in Venice (S. Moisè) as 'prima buffa'. From Venice she and her husband went to Milan, where they were forced to pawn their silver (worth 3,000 gulden). In 1777, Zinzendorf heard her at the Vienna court opera. When they were engaged at Eszterháza, Prince Nicolaus advanced them the money to redeem their pawned silver in Milan. Her first performance at Eszterháza was in Guglielmi's *La sposa fedele* (on 3 May 1778). On 12 January 1780 she was delivered of twins, both of which died shortly thereafter. She was without doubt a singer of exceptional ability.

Sassi, Barbara: soprano. Engaged by 'Hoch Fürstlichen Resolution' on 19 May, to be effective retroactively from 12 May, 1786, at a salary of 800 gulden, six fathom cords of wood and 24 lb. of candles. Remained until September 1790. Performed in Caruso's *L'albergatrice vivace* ('Barberina') (1786), Cimarosa's *I due baroni di Rocca azzurra* ('Madama') (1786), Guglielmi's *La quaquera spiritosa* ('Cardellina') (1787, for the performance of which Haydn wrote his witty 'insertion' aria, 'Vada adagio, Signorina', the first known 'insertion' aria for Barbara Sassi), Paisiello's *Le gare generose* ('Miss Meri') (1787), Cimarosa's *Giunio Bruto* ('Marzia') (1788), Sarti's *I finti eredi* ('Dorina') (1788), Cimarosa's *L'italiana in Londra* ('Livia' in the 1788 revival), and in many other operas, particularly of the season 1789–90, which can no longer be identified. By means of the 'insertion' aria that Haydn composed for her, we can judge Barbara Sassi's voice: a light, flexible soprano voice with a fine top *b* flat''; as an actress she must have had a certain coquettish grace which Haydn takes into good account in 'Vada adagio, Signorina', the only source of which, incidentally, was discovered by the present writer in the Fürstenberg Archives at Donaueschingen Castle in 1957,[1] Bartha-Somfai 22, 53, 124, 129, 133, 137, 140, 144, 148, 152, 159, 168, 274, 311, 316, 321, 323, 325, 328f., 331, 334, 337, 396. *HJB* VII, 108 (contract). ECP item 1560 (her engagement, Esterhaz 19 May 1786).

Sassi (marr. Nencini), Palmira: soprano. Engaged together with her husband Santi Nencini, a bass singer, according to a 'Fürstlicher Resolution' dated 30 August 1785, to be effective retroactively from 15 August, at a joint salary of 1,310 gulden, 40 lb. of candles and 12 fathom cords of wood. Left at the end of July 1790. Performed in Bianchi's *La villanella rapita* ('Mandina') (1784, repeated in 1785 with Palmira Sassi and her husband),[2] Stabinger's *Le astuzie de Bettina* ('Bettina') (1785), Zingarelli's *Alsinda* ('Zelmira') (1786), Cimarosa's *La ballerina amante* ('Rubiconda') (1786), Cimarosa's *Chi dell'altrui si veste, presto si spoglie* ('Ninetta') (1786), Righini's *L'incontro inaspettato* ('Irene') (1786), Anfossi's *Il sordo e l'avaro* (? role) (1787), Guglielmi's *La quaquera spiritosa* ('Vertunna') (1787), Sarti's *I finti eredi* ('D. Isabella') (1788), Cimarosa's *Il marito*

disperato ('Eugenie') (1788), Cimarosa's *L' italiana in Londra* ('Madama' in the 1788 revival), and in many other operas, particularly of the 1789–90 season, which can no longer be identified. A capable soprano voice which, it was (in 1786) considered, would be better suited to serious roles: 'Resta fuori in tutte le opere buffe' (Bartha-Somfai 131). *HJB* VII, 109. ECP item 1525 (Esterhaz, 30 Aug. 1785 re-engagement Sassi & husband). J. Harich in *HJB* I, 62. Bartha-Somfai 22, 53, 124, 129f., 133, 137, 148, 151f., 168, 274, 396.

Spangler, Magdalena: *vide* Friberth, Magdalena.

Specioli, Maria Antonia: soprano. Engaged, with her husband, Antonio Specioli, tenor, on 25 August 1782, for a period of three years – end of August 1785. Nicolaus Esterházy's son, Count (later Prince) Anton Esterházy advanced the Speciolis 231 fl. 54 kr. travel costs which were refunded by Prince Nicolaus on 17 October 1782. They left at the end of August 1785. Their first joint appearance was in Haydn's *La fedeltà premiata* (revival 1782, first performance Sept.), wherin they sang the parts of Amaranta and Fileno, respectively. She also performed in Haydn's *Orlando Paladino* ('Eurilla') (1782), Guglielmi's *Il ratto della sposa* ('Aurora') (1783), Cimarosa's *L' italiana in Londra* ('Madama') (1783), Sarti's *Fra i due litiganti il terzo gode* ('Dorina') (1783), Anfossi's *I viaggiatori felici* ('Bettina') (1784), Cimarosa's *L' amor costante* ('Nespolina') (1784), Bianchi's *La villanella rapita* ('Giannina') (1784), Sarti's *I contratempi* ('Carlotta') (1785), and in Anfossi's *Il matrimonio per inganno* ('Giannina') (1785), the last opera in which, as it happened, both singers appeared together at Eszterháza. Maria Antonio had a fine low soprano voice (almost a mezzo), as we can see from the revised version of the role of Amaranta in Haydn's *La fedeltà premiata*; but she also must have possessed flexibility and vocal agility. Bartha-Somfai 98, 101f., 106, 108, 111, 116f., 119, 124, 126, 168, 274, 278, 296. Harich in *HJB* I, 46f. ECP item 1371 (Esterhaz, 31 Aug. 1782, engagement of the Speciolis for a period of three years).

Tauber, Maria Anna: soprano. Engaged by 'Hoch Fürstl. Intimat' dated Vienna, 30 Dec. 1776 to be effective 1 Jan. 1777, at a salary of 500 fl., 35 fl. lodging money, 24 lb. of candles and six fathom cords of wood, as well as an annual dress. By means of a 'Hochf. Intimat' of 10 January 1778 she was dismissed, effective retroactively from 1 Jan., 'and her salary to cease on that day'. Performed in Gassmann's *L'amore artigiano* ('Madama Costanza') (1777), Dittersdorf's *Arcifanfano, re de' matti* ('Gloriosa') (1777) and in other operas which cannot now be identified. She married the princely marionette director Pauersbach and went with him to Russia at the end of 1778. Pohl II, 374. *HJB* VII, 100 fl. (her contract). ECP item 1174 (Wienn, 10 Jan. 1778: the singer 'Marianna' Tauber dismissed as of 1 Jan.). Bartha-Somfai 69–71, 75, 77, 168. Landon in *HJB* I, 121. *Vide infra*, p. 66.

---

1 Published by the Haydn-Mozart Presse (score, parts, vocal score), edited by the present writer.
2 This was their première at Eszterháza.

Tavecchia (Taveggia), Teresa Amalia: mezzo-soprano. Engaged by 'Hochfürstl. Intimat' dated Eszterhaz, 25 August 1780, effective retroactively from 1 Aug., at a salary of '200 Stück Kremnizer Ducaten, id est...... [original] 860f. dan freyes Quartier, Holtz und Liecht.' Performed in Anfossi's *La finta giardiniera* ('La Marchesa Violante' = 'Sandrina') (1780), Haydn's *La fedeltà premiata* ('Amaranta') (1781), Anfossi's *Isabella e Rodrigo* ('D. Isabella') (1781) and Salieri's *La scuola de' gelosi* (first performed 1780 with Maria Jermoli as 'Contessa'; when revived in April – June 1781, Teresa Tavecchia as 'Contessa'). This excellent singer, for whom Haydn created the taxing role of 'Amaranta' (*La fedeltà premiata*), was married to the highly-paid horn player Anton Eckhardt, who followed her to Eszterháza, was engaged in October 1780, and was given a brilliant solo in *La fedeltà premiata* (Act I, Celia's Aria 'Deh' soccorri infelice'). In one Eszterháza textbook she is listed as 'Taveggia (Eccard)'. This fine singer must have had a low soprano voice, with almost a contralto character, enormous flexibility and some ability as an actress to project Haydn's concept (Amaranta) of '[una] donna vana e boriosa'. Both she and her husband left Eszterháza at the end of July 1781, and on 30 July Prince Nicolaus gave the 'Sängerin Tavechia' an advance of forty-two Kremnitzer ducats for her travelling expenses. *HJB* VII, 98 (contract), 131 (travel expenses). Harich in *HJB* VII, 12. Bartha-Somfai 84, 87, 90, 92, 168. Landon, 'Haydns Oper "La fedeltà premiata": eine neue authentische Quelle', in *Grasberger-Festschrift,* Tutzing 1975, pp. 213–32.

Trever (Dravers), Maria Elisabeth: (? voice) Engaged by 'Hoch Fürstl. Intimat' dated Vienna, 30 Dec. 1776, effective 1 Jan. 1777, for a period of two years at a salary of 300 fl., 30 fl. lodging money, 24 lb. of candles and three fathom cords of wood, as well as a dress each year. Dismissed at the end of December 1778 by two 'Hochfürstl. Schreiben' of 18 and 27 Nov. No record of the operas in which she appeared. *HJB* VII, 101 (contract). Bartha-Somfai 65n., 69, 74f., 168.

Ullmann, Francisca: contralto. Engaged by 'Hochfürstl. Intimation' dated Eszterház, 18 September 1768, effective 1 October, at a salary of 300 fl., 20 fl. lodging money, 20 lb. of candles, three fathom cords of wood and a dress *per annum*. The document adds, laconically: 'mit halben Junii 769. weggegangen' (left in the middle of June 1769). No record of the operas (or church music?) in which she appeared. *HJB* VII, 63 (contract).

Valdesturla (Waldesturla), Costanza (Constantia): soprano. Engaged by 'Hoch Fürstlicher Resolution' dated 11 August 1779, effective retroactively from 20 July, at a salary of 120 ducats or, reckoned at 4 fl. 14 kr., 508 gulden. Ten ducats were advanced to her (for travel expenses, probably) and were to be taken in monthly instalments from her salary. She had free lodgings, wood and light, and was engaged for

two years. According to a 'Hochfürstlichem Intimat' of 5 April 1781, she was to receive a new contract and, effective 20 July 1781, an increase of 100 gulden *per annum*. Performed in Sarti's *Le gelosie villane* (Livietta) (1779–80, 1784), Felici's *L'amore soldato* ('Lisandrina') (1779), Anfossi's *La forza delle donne* ('Clizia') (1780), Salieri's *La scuola de' gelosi* ('Ernestina') (1780), Anfossi's *La finta giardiniera* ('Serpetta') (1780), Haydn's *La fedeltà premiata* ('Nerina') (1781), Anfossi's *Isabella e Rodrigo* ('Ramira') (1781), Grétry's *Zemira ed Azor* ('Lesbia')(1782), Salieri's *La fiera di Venezia* ('Falsirena') (1782), Anfossi's *Il curioso indiscreto* ('Clorinda') (1782), Haydn's *Orlando Paladino* ('Alcina') (1782), Guglielmi's *Il ratto della sposa* ('Donna Ortenza') (1783), Righini's *La vedova scaltra* ('Marionetta') (1783), Cimarosa's *L'italiana in Londra* ('Livia') (1783), Sarti's *Giulio Sabino* ('Voadice') (1783), Sarti's *Fra i due litiganti il terzo gode* ('Livietta') (1783), Cimarosa's *Il falegname* ('Anagilda') (1783), Haydn's *Armida* ('Zelmira') (1784), Cimarosa's *L'amor costante* ('Laura') (1784), Sarti's *La Didone abbandonata* ('Selene') (1784), Bologna's *L'isola di Calipso abbandonata* ('Telemaco') (1784), Sarti's *I contratempi* ('Lucinda') (1785) and in other works which cannot now be identified. She left the princely service on 20 July 1785, when her contract expired. Born in Pisa as Costanza Alessandra Ottavia, this famous singer reached Eszterháza through the services of Pietro Giacomo Martelli in Bologna. The Prince refunded her travel money from Italy when she arrived in Vienna (2 August 1779), at which time she asked for, and received, ten ducats advance (*vide supra*) in her salary. On 22 February 1783 Zinzendorf heard her at the Kärntnerthortheater in *L'isola di Calipso abbandonata* (*vide supra* and *infra*, pp. 47, 473). After she left Eszterháza, she intended at first to sing at the court theatre in Vienna, to which end she procured a fine letter (15 July 1785) of recommendation from Prince Nicolaus. In the event she changed her plans and went to Leipzig, where she was engaged by the Gewandhaus concerts; she married the organist and Music Director Johann Gotlieb Schicht, who had brought her to Leipzig (July 1786). Later Schicht, writing in Gerber's *Neues Lexikon*, recalled that she had sung in Pisa, Florence, Bologna, Prato, Siena, Faenza and Esterházy [*sc.* Eszterháza], and 'there are witnesses still living who recall what she was able to do to the hearts of her listeners with her beautiful, sonorous voice and her expressive singing'. As she grew older, her salary at the Gewandhaus concerts – where she sang for nineteen years – grew steadily smaller (650, then 550, then 400, then 250 and finally a pension of 200 thaler), but her dramatic range increased as her voice lost its initial youth and freshness. In Eszterháza, she began as a light, almost soubrette, voice ('Nerina' in Haydn's *La fedeltà premiata*); by 1799 she was a dramatic soprano, singing Beethoven's 'Ah! Perfido' at a Gewandhaus concert in 1799. Obviously, Valdesturla's was one of the very finest and most 'useful' voices of the Eszterháza fairy-tale. *HJB*

VII, 103f. (contract), 128f. (documents), 130 (her last receipted salary). Gerber *NTL*, IV 58f. Prot. missilium XVII, 472 (Esterházy Archives, State Archives Budapest): Prince Nicolaus's letter of recommendation. ECP item 1246 (11 1779: her contract), item 1327 (Esterhaz, 5 April 1781: new contract). A. Dörffel, *Geschichte der Gewandhauskonzerte zu Leipzig*, Leipzig 1884, pp. 129ff. J. Harich in *HJB* VII, 9–11.

Weigl (*née* Scheffstoss [Scheffstoß]), Anna Maria: soprano. Engaged on 1 January 1760 at a salary of 100 gulden. In 1764 she married the 'cellist Joseph Weigl of the princely *Capelle*, and 'lauth Hochfürstl. Intimat' of 17 June 1764, she was to receive instead of her previous free meals at the officers' table a cash substitute of 180 gulden (obviously more useful for a young married matron). Performed in Haydn's *Acide e Galatea* ('Galatea') (1763), Haydn's *La canterina* ('Gasparina') (1766, 1767) and Haydn's *Stabat Mater* (reprise in Vienna, end of March 1768). When her husband left for Vienna, at the end of May, 1769, she followed him. Haydn was attached to both and was godfather (and Frau Haydn godmother) to their son, Joseph Jr., destined to become a famous composer, at his baptism in Eisenstadt: *vide infra*, 28 March 1766, p. 120. The Haydns were also godparents to a second son, born on 15 July 1768. Anna Maria was obviously a very capable singer if she was especially chosen by Haydn not only for two attractive roles in his operas but above all for the taxing soprano part in the *Stabat Mater*; hers must have been a light, flexible voice with considerable sustaining power as well. *HJB* VII, 51 (contract), 61 (further

contractual information). CCLN 8, 143f. Pohl I, 265.

Zannini, Anna (Marianna): soprano. Engaged 'Laut Hoch Fürstlicher Intimat' dated 'Wienn den 21ten Jan. 1779', effective retroactively from 12 Dec. 1778, for one year at 450 gulden and the usual lodging money, and quantity of wood and candles. She received twenty ducats for travel expenses, but also an advance of 189 fl. 12 kr. which was to be repaid over a period of one year, so that she was to receive only 260 fl. 48 kr., 'or monthly to be paid 21 fl. 44 kr.'. Performed in Paisiello's *Le due contesse* ('Livietta') (1779). Haydn's *La vera costanza* ('Lisetta') (1779) and in other operas which can no longer be determined. Left Eszterháza at the end of August 1779. Probably Valdesturla was engaged to take Zannini's place. Zannini, for whom Haydn created the attractive role of the 'cameriera' Lisetta in *La vera costanza*, must have had a light soubrette voice similar, but perhaps better, than that of *la* Polzelli. Her Aria in Act I, 'Io son poverina, ne ricca, ne bella' is very characteristic of the light soprano voice for which Haydn wrote so much, and so well. *HJB* VII, 102 (contract), 166 (travel expenses). ECP item 1229 (Vienna, 21 Jan. 1779: contract). Bartha-Somfai 77, 79, 168.

Zecchielli, Maria: soprano. Engaged 'laut Löbl. Co[missi]ons Intimat' dated 20 April 1789, effective retroactively from 24 March at an annual salary of 170 imperial ducats or 765 gulden – end of September 1790. Performed in Cimarosa's *L'impresario in angustie* ('Fiordispina') (1790) and in other operas of the 1789–90 season which cannot be identified. *HJB* VII, 108 (contract). Bartha-Somfai 151f., 159, 168, 358.

SINGERS (MALE)

Amici, Giuseppe: baritone. Engaged 'laut l[öbl.] Co[missi]ons Intimat' from 6 March 1790 at a salary of '142 k.k. Duggaten' or 639 gulden – end of September 1790. Performed in Paisiello's *Il barbiere di Siviglia* ('Figaro') (1790) and Cimarosa's *Giannina e Bernardone* ('D. Orlando'), as well as in other operas which cannot now be identified. Obviously a fine baritone voice, capable of taking the lead in Paisiello's great opera. *HJB* VII, 110 (contract). Bartha-Somfai 159, 170, 356, 363.

Bianchi, Benedetto: tenor (baritone). Engaged 'vermög Intimat dd° Eszterhaz den 18ten Apr. 776' for two years retroactively from 1 April at a salary

of 600 gulden, 35 fl. lodging money, 24 lb. of candles, six fathom cords of wood and a new winter or summer uniform each year. At the end of the period, the Prince renewed Bianchi's contract (princely 'order' [*Befehl*] of 12 April 1778 retroactive from 1 April) for three years and raised his salary to 800 gulden. In the winter months, Bianchi either went to Vienna or back to Italy for guest appearances, and often took two months' salary in advance (e.g. on 1 Jan. 1779 he received his salary for January and February in advance) for this purpose. He stayed in Eszterháza until the expiration of his contract at the end of April 1781. At first he intended to enter the service of Prince

Auersperg and provided himself with a good letter of recommendation from Prince Nicolaus.[1] For some reason, the planned engagement with Auersperg fell through, and Bianchi went instead at the end of April to Venice; he sang there at the Teatro S. Samuele, singing *inter alia* 'Bernadone' in Cimarosa's *Giannine e Bernadone*, 'Flautino' in Anfossi's *Gli amanti* and, in the carnival season of 1782, 'Massimo' in Cimarosa's *Il convito* and 'Formicone' in Anfossi's *'Azione drammatica per musica'*. On 6 July 1784 we find him back at Eszterháza, re-engaged by Prince Nicolaus on that date 'Laut Hoch Fürstlicher Intimat', effective retroactively from 1 June, for two years at his old salary. This time he stayed for nearly six years, leaving the princely service at the end of July 1790. Performed in more than forty-two operas while at Eszterháza, including Dittersdorf's *Il finto pazzo per amore* ('Il capitano D. Ercole') (1776), Sacchini's *L'isola d'amore* ('Nardo') (1776), Piccinni's *La buona figliuola* (? role) (1776), Joseph Haydn's *Il mondo della luna* ('Buonafede') (1777), Dittersdorf's *Arcifanfano, re de' matti* ('Arcifanfano') (1777), Guglielmi's *La sposa fedele* ('Pasqualino') (1778), Paisiello's *Le due contesse* ('Leandro') (1779), Haydn's *La vera costanza* ('Villotto') (1779, Gazzaniga's *L'isola d'Alcina* ('Barone inglese') (1779) Sarti's *Le gelosie villane* (?role) (1779), Felici's *L'amore soldato* ('Don Anselmo') (1779),

Haydn's *L'isola disabitata* ('Enrico') (1779), Anfossi's *La forza delle donne* ('Marone') (1780), Gazzaniga's *La vendemmia* ('Conte Zeffiro') (1780), Anfossi's *La finta giardiniera* ('D. Anchise Podestà') (1780), Gassmann's *L'amore artigiano* (1777, revived in 1780 with Bianchi in the role of 'Bernardo'; he also may be presumed to have sung it as well in the 1790 revival), Haydn's *La fedeltà premiata* ('Conte Perruchetto') (1781), Anfossi's *Isabella e Rodrigo* ('Il Commendatore d'Yllesca') (1781), Sarti's *La Didone abbandonata* ('Jarba') (1784), Bianchi's *La villanella rapita* ('Blagio') (1784), Bologna's *L'isola di Calipso abbandonata* ('Mentone') (1784), Zingarelli's *Montezuma* ('Teutile') (1785), Anfossi's *Il matrimonio per inganno* ('Don Volpone') (1785), Stabinger's *Le astuzie di Bettina* ('Il Barone di Lagodoro') (1785), Haydn's *La vera costanza* (revival of 1785: 'Villotto' as before), Cimarosa's *La ballerina amante* ('Don Totomaglio') (1786), Cimarosa's *Chi dell'altrui so veste, presto si spoglia* ('Martuffo') (1786), Caruso's *L'albergatrice vivace* ('Bartolo') (1786), Righini's *L'incontro inaspettato* ('Barone') (1786, Sarti's *Idalide* ('Ataliba') (1786), Cimarosa's *I due baroni di Rocca azzurra* ('Demofonte') (1786), Gazzaniga's *L'isola d'Alcina* (1779, revived with Bianchi again as the 'Barone inglese' in 1786), Anfossi's *Il sordo e l'avaro* (? role) (1787), Bianchi's *Il disertore* ('Corradino'; Haydn wrote the lovely Aria 'Un cor si tenero' as an 'insertion' for Benedetto Bianchi in Scene 4 of Act II)[1] (1787), Guglielmi's *La quaquera spiritosa* ('Kolibacco') (1787), Cimarosa's *Giunio Bruto* ('Procolo') (1788), Sarti's *I finti eredi* ('D. Grifagno') (1788), Cimarosa's *Il marito disperato* ('Marchese') (1788), Cimarosa's *L'italiana in Londra* ('Milord' in the 1788 revival), and in other operas of the 1789-90 season which cannot now be identified. Bianchi's voice was at first a mixture between tenor and bass (low tenor or 'baritone'); typical of this early style is the role of 'Buonafede' in Haydn's *Il mondo della luna,* which is written in the autograph in the bass clef but is in many respects a low tenor part. 'Conte Perruchetto' in Haydn's *La fedeltà premiata* is also written in the bass clef (later, after Bianchi had left, there was a real 'tenor' version). Yet Bianchi sang tenor parts. As his career progressed, his voice must have grown lower in range but did not lose its shining upper register: the 'insertion' Aria 'Un cor si tenero', with its baritone *tessitura* and bass range, shows this late aspect of Bianchi's vocal range. He must have been one of the very greatest and most universal singers of the Eszterháza troupe. Bianchi was married when he came to Hungary, but his wife was sickly and was sent to the cure in St Margarethen near Eszterháza; she was under Dr Genzinger's care when this cure was ordered (December 1776 – Jan. 1777). When Bianchi returned to Hungary he was a widower. In 1787, during his second stay in Eszterháza, he married Josepha Rossi; at that time he was forty. The witnesses were Alois Delicatti and the princely

---

1 'Raccomandazione per il cantore Bianchi. / Il Signore Benedetto Bianchi in qualità di virtuoso di Musica essendo stato cinque anni cio è sin alla fine di questo mese in nostro Servizio e avendo sempre con ogni premura, ed attenzione fato il suo dovere. Noi testimoniamo con nostro piacere le Sue buone qualità, ed anzi Noi racomandiamo a qualunquedegna persona il Sopra nominato Soggetto. In fede di questo lo muniamo di nostra Sottoscrizione e di nostro sigillo.

Esterház ai 30 aprile 781. Nicolo Principe Esterházy

The interesting fact of this warm-hearted letter is that it totally ignores a really scandalous affair in Bianchi's career at Eszterháza. It happened as follows. During a performance of Dittersdorf's *Il finto pazzo per amore* on 24 October 1776, the soprano Catharina Poschva was singing an aria 'wobey Sie sich närrisch zu stellen hatte' (wherein she had to act in a mad fashion). Benedetto Bianchi, who was with her on the stage at the same time, bent down to the floor and using his stick he raised her skirt twice. Madame Poschva did not notice anything until Bianchi was raising her skirt for the third time – probably made aware of what was happening by the uproar in the audience. (Her husband was oboist in the orchestra, moreover.) The following day Anton Poschva and his wife addressed a petition to Prince Nicolaus, asking for satisfaction. The Prince, who had been perhaps absent from the theatre when all this happened, sentenced Bianchi 'to two weeks' imprisonment, a public whipping of fifty strokes and forced him to apologize in front of the audience when he next appeared, which was on 27 October. The apology, in Italian, has been preserved: he apologized first for his lack of respect towards the Prince – how characteristic of life at Eszterháza! –, then for his offensive behaviour to the public and thirdly for his misdeed against Madame Poschva. Acta Musicalia 1366 (Budapest). Horányi: German version (*Das Esterházysche Feenreich*), p. 106; English version, p. 105. Once Bianchi had been punished, all was forgiven and the Prince, as it were, 'wiped the slate': hence the generous letter of recommendation. References for the letter are *inter alia* as follows: Acta musicalia, Esterházy Archives Budapest, No. 1097. Prot. missilium XV (1781), p. 188, Esterházy Archives Budapest. *HJB* VII, 164f.

1 Published in score, parts and vocal score in the Haydn-Mozart Presse, edited by the present writer.

'cellist Valentin Bertoja. At some point, Prince Nicolaus had reason to impose fines on the violinist Antonio Rosetti and Bianchi, but he relented and ordered the princely Chief Cashier Züsser to pay them their full salaries (Eszterháza, 8 February 1778). *HJB* 99 (contract), 109 (second contract), 164f. (documents). PCDI, items 1185 (first contract), 1444 (second contract). Bartha-Somfai 65f., 67–70, 75, 79f., 82f., 85–7, 92, 114, 118f., 121, 125–7, 129–39, 144, 148, 152, 158, 170, 221, 263, 274, 287–9, 316, 318, 321, 329, 331, 337, 354, 396, J. Harich in *HJB* VII, 23f. Landon 'Haydns Oper' (op. cit., p. 216.).

Braghetti, Prospero: tenor. Engaged 'laut Hoch Fürstlicher Resolution' on 19 July 1781, effective retroactively from 1 July, for a period of two years at 200 Kremnitzer ducats or 860 gulden, 24 lb. of candles and three fathom cords of wood. According to a 'hochfürstl. Resolution' of 20 February 1786, his salary is to be reckoned ducats = zecchini, which raised it to 873 fl. 20 kr. He remained until the end of Sepember 1790. Performed in Grétry's *Zemira ed Azor* ('Azor') (1782), Salieri's *La fiera di Venezia* ('Ostrogoto') (1782), Haydn's *Orlando Paladino* ('Medoro') (1782), Righini's *La vedova scaltra* ('Monsieur Le Blan') (1783), Cimarosa's *L'italiana in Londra* ('Sumers') (1783), Sarti's *Giulio Sabino* ('Giulio Sabino') (1783), Sarti's *Fra i due litiganti il terzo gode* ('Masotto') (1783), Cimarosa's *Il falegname* ('Dalmiro' ['Don Dolmiro']) (1783), Haydn's *Armida* ('Rinaldo') (1784), Sarti's *La Didone abbandonata* ('Enea Troiano') (1784), Zingarelli's *Montezuma* ('Montezuma') (1785), Anfossi's *Il matrimonio per inganno* ('Florindo') (1785)¸ Stabinger's *Le astuzie di Bettina* (1785), Haydn's *La vera costanza* (new version of 1785: Conte Errico?), Zingarelli's *Alsinda* ('Parmene')(1786), Cimarosa's *La ballerina amante* ('Bireno') (1786), Cimarosa's *Chi dell'altrui si veste, presto si spoglia* ('Putifare') (1786), Traetta's *Ifigenia in Tauride* ('Oreste'; in Act I, Scene 1, Haydn wrote a great 'insertion' Aria 'Ah, tu non senti, amico'¹ for Braghetti) (1786), Caruso's *L'albergatrice vivace* ('Le Blanc') (1786), Righini's *L'incontro inaspettato* ('Lindoro') (1786), Sarti's *Idalide* ('Enrico') (1786), Sarti's *Giulio Sabino* ('Sabino' in the 1786 revival), Bianchi's *Il disertore* ('Gualtieri') (1787), Bianchi's *Alessandro nell'Indie* ('Poro') (1787), Cimarosa's *Giunio Bruto* ('Tito') (1788), Cimarosa's *L'italiana in Londra* ('Sumers' in the 1788 revival), Martin's *L'arbore di Diana* ('Silvio') (1789), Cimarosa's *L'impresario in angustie* ('Gelindo') (1790), and in other operas which cannot be identified. Braghetti obviously had a strong, dramatic tenor voice; at its finest, it must have been very impressive, with both a good low as well as top range. Haydn's 'insertion' Aria 'Ah, tu non senti, amico' shows Braghetti's voice at its most splendid, as does the great solo part in *Armida*. It is possible that Braghetti later found his way to London, for

Haydn mentions a singer of this name in his London Notebooks and refers to him familiarly as 'the good old Braghetti' (CCLN 293, 301: see also *Haydn in England 1791–1795*, p. 281). It is even possible that Haydn helped him find the job in London. *HJB* VII, 108f. (contract). ECP item 1340 (contract). Bartha-Somfai 90f., 99, 102, 108f., 111f., 115, 118, 123, 125–7, 130f., 133–5, 137, 139, 144, 152, 159, 170, 265, 274, 277, 289, 292, 324, 327, 329, 355, 358, 371f., 395.

Brizzi, Ludwig: *vide* Prizzi.

Crizzani (Crinazzi) N.: (? range). Engaged from 25 June – September 1781. None of his roles is known. Bartha-Somfai 90, 170f. Landon 'Haydns Oper' (op. cit., 216). *N. B.* In ECP item 1333, we read that 'Esterhaz, 28 June 1781, the singer Crinazzi [*sic*] is engaged for four months starting 23 June.' So he was *a priori* intended as a sort of stopgap for the summer season. He signed himself 'Crizzani'.

Di Giovanni, Pasquale: *vide* Giovanni.

Dichtler, Leopold: tenor. Engaged on 1 March 1763 at 150 gulden *per annum*. On 28 November 1764 he married Barbara Fuchs, princely singer (q.v.). Following the death of his first wife, Dichtler married Christine Scheffschick, a widow twenty years older than he. At the marriage, in the Stadtpfarrkirche, Eisenstadt on 28 January 1777, Haydn was a witness. After the death of his second wife, Dichtler married a third time: Anna Maria Krinesz, Church of the Barmherzige Brüder, Eisenstadt, 17 July 1788; he was 49, she 47. Dichtler was frequently slightly ill, and since his salary was not large, Prince Nicolaus often paid his medicine bills. To help out his financial situation, Dichtler often copied music, *inter alia* the huge task of all the orchestral parts for Haydn's *Il mondo della luna* (508 Bögen, more than 2,000 pages). After serving for a quarter of a century in princely *Dienst*, Dichtler resigned on 25 August 1788, 'not' (as he later wrote) 'because of his Prince's dissatisfaction but because of his own with regards his weakened condition in face of the demanding opera studio.' Dichtler was rewarded with a pension for life when Prince Nicolaus died in 1790. In 1792, Prince Anton engaged Dichtler as a double-bass player in the Eisenstadt princely church choir – one more piece of evidence how astonishingly versatile singers were in those days. He died at Eisenstadt on 15 May 1799: a moving letter, written literally on his death bed (2 May 1799), has survived, asking Prince Nicolaus II to help his family (*HJB* VII, 163f.). Performed in about sixty operas, including Haydn's *La canterina* ('Apollonia' [*sic*]) (1766–7), Haydn's *Lo speziale* ('Mengone') (1768), Haydn's *Le pescatrici* ('Burlotto') (1770), Haydn's *L'infedeltà delusa* ('Nencio') (1773), Haydn's *L'incontro improvviso* ('Osmin') (1775). Dittersdorf's *Il finto pazzo per amore* ('Silvio') (1776), Sacchini's *L'isola d'amore* ('Giocondo') (1776), Piccinni's *La buona figliuola* (? role) (1776), Dittersdorf's *Il barone di Rocca antica*

---

1 Published in score, parts and vocal score by the Haydn-Mozart Presse, edited by the present writer.

('Barone Arsura') (1776), Gassmann's *L'amore artigiano* ('Titta') (1777, presumably also in the revival of 1780), Haydn's *Il mondo della luna* ('Cecco') (1777), Dittersdorf's *Arcifanfano, re de' matti* ('Sordidone') (1777), Guglielmi's *La sposa fedele* ('Il conte Lelio') (1778), Paisiello's *Le due contesse* ('Prospero') (1779), Haydn's *La vera costanza* ('Masino') (1779), Anfossi's *La Metilde ritrovata* ('Fabricio') (1779), Gazzaniga's *L'isola d'Alcina* ('Brunoro') (1779, revived 1786), Sarti's *Le gelosie villane* (? role) (1779), Felici's *L'amore soldato* ('Pasquino') (1779), Anfossi's *La forza delle donne* ('Tiziano') (1780), Gazzaniga's *La vendemmia* ('Don Faustino') (1780), Salieri's *La scuola de' gelosi* ('Il tenente') (1780), Anfossi's *La finta giardiniera* ('Il cavalier Ramiro') (1780), Haydn's *La fedeltà premiata* ('Lindoro') (1781), Anfossi's *Isabella e Rodrigo* ('Pasquale') (1781), Paisiello's *L'avaro deluso* ('Don Anselmo') (1781), Righini's *Il convitato di pietra* ('Don Alfonso') (1781), Salieri's *La fiera di Venezia* ('Cecchino') (1782), Traetta's *Il cavaliere errante* ('Stordillano') (1782), Anfossi's *Il curioso indiscreto* ('Aurelio') (1782), Haydn's *Orlando Paladino* ('Caronte') (1782), Guglielmi's *Il ratto della sposa* ('Biondino') (1783), Righini's *La vedova scaltra* ('Runebif') (1783), Sarti's *Giulio Sabino* ('Annio') (1783), Sarti's *Fra i due litiganti il terzo gode* ('Titta') (1783), Haydn's *Armida* ('Clotario') (1784), Anfossi's *I viaggiatori felici* ('Pasquino') (1784), Sarti's *La Didone abbandonata* ('Osmida') (1784), Bianchi's *La villanella rapita* ('Cavallier') (1784), Sarti's *I contratempi* ('Gianastasio') (1785), Zingarelli's *Montezuma* ('Pilpatol') (1785), Stabinger's *Le astuzie di Bettina* ('D. Martino') (1785), Zingarelli's *Alsinda* ('Livango') (1786), Cimarosa's *La ballerina amante* ('Franchiglione') (1786), Cimarosa's *Chi dell'altrui si veste, presto si spoglia* ('Gabbamondo') (1786), Righini's *L'incontro inaspettato* ('Pirolino') (1786), Sarti's *Idalide* ('Ismaro') (1786), Cimarosa's *I due baroni di Rocca azzurra* ('Franchetto') (1786), Bianchi's *Il disertore* ('Berardo') (1787), Guglielmi's *La quaquera spiritosa* ('D. Matusio') (1787), Bianchi's *Alessandro nell' Indie* ('Timagene') (1787), Cimarosa's *Giunio Bruto* ('Aronte') (1788), Sarti's *I finti eredi* ('Cavaliere'; in Act I, Scene 3 Haydn wrote a fine 'insertion' Aria, 'Se tu mi sprezzi, ingrata', for Dichtler, possibly as a kind of farewell present: this oldest working member of the troupe left in August)[1] (1788); and in other works which cannot now be identified. Dichtler, at his prime, must have had a phenomenal voice. The role of 'Nencio' in Haydn's *burletta, L'infedeltà delusa* includes an exposed *b* flat below middle *c'* and runs up twice to high *c'''* in the Aria 'Chi s'impaccia di moglie cittadina' (Act I). Later, as Dichtler lost this brilliant top, Haydn entrusted him with the secondary tenor parts – the typical servants, etc., such as the relatively simple role of 'Cecco' in *Il mondo della luna*. Dichtler obviously had a vast operatic experience and probably sang many of the tenor parts in Haydn's church music of

1 Issued in score, parts and vocal score by the Haydn-Mozart Presse, edited by the present writer.

the 1760s and 1770s. At its best, his voice must have had not only a big range but displayed great musicality, as the subtleties of Haydn's operatic roles for Dichtler in the 1760s and 1770s show time and time again. *HJB* VII, 63f., 80, 157–64 (documents). PCM item 1001 (Esterhaz, 28 Aug. 1774: increase in D's salary of 25 fl. lodging money, 9 *Eimer* of wine and one uniform *per annum*). Bartha-Somfai 53, 63, 66–71, 79f., 82, 85–9, 92f., 99–102, 107–9, 111, 115–19, 123, 125, 127, 130–32, 134f., 137, 139, 144, 159, 165, 170, 234, 262, 302, 316, 321, 324, 329, 331f., 379, 385, 396, 418, 420f. Harich in *HJB* VII, 19–23.

Dietzl, Joseph: tenor. Engaged 1753 as Eisenstadt Castle Schoolmaster, tenor and organist at 62 fl. 30 kr. and *Naturalien*. The *Naturalien* were sufficiently large – Dietzl had a numerous family – that his total salary, with the goods reckoned in cash, amounted to 158 fl., 15 kr. He remained in the princely service until his death in 1777, fulfilling an important place in the Eisenstadt church choir; he remained, of course, in Eisenstadt and had nothing to do with Eszterháza. *HJB* VII, 51, 64, 80f. (documents). ECP item 1157 (Esterhaz, 17 Nov. 1777 *re* Dietzl's death). Valkó I, 641. Harich in *HJB* VIII, 34. See his sons, Johann and Joseph Jr. under orchestral musicians, *infra*.

Ernst, Michael: also boy-singer, later violinist in the princely Eisenstadt church choir. Engaged for the marionette theatre in Eszterháza unofficially in 1773, at the age of eleven; then from 4 September 1774 'lauth obcitirten Hochfürstl. Intimat', effective retroactively from 1 August at one ducat per month, as well as 12 kr. *per diem* food and lodging and a suit of clothes *per annum*. In a letter, dated Eisenstadt 3 August 1805, Ernst makes application for an increase in salary and mentions that he served in the Eszterháza marionette theatre, 1773–76. In another document he is referred to as 'Scholar Michael Ernst', and by now he receives 128 fl. 48 kr. and a suit. There follows the notes: 'According to Hochf. Intimat d° Wienn den 10ten January 1778, he is dismissed from service effective the end of Dec. 777 and this contract is null and void as of 1ª January 778.' We then find that he has been reinstated – another example of Haydn's intervention? – in the Eisenstadt princely church choir as violinist, at the very low salary of 50 gulden *per annum*, in December 1778; and in this capacity he survived the September 1790 *Putsch* and remained part of the band all through the second great period of the late 1790s and early 1800s. He composed church music, mostly for Prince Nicolaus II, including a Mass, a Graduale, three Offertories, eleven German Advent Arias, two Salve Regina, three Ave Regina and two Alma Redemptoris. Harich quotes several letters by Ernst in which it is made clear that he suffered some kind of a stroke at the end of 1777, was incapable of work, and therefore dismissed. He retired with a pension in 1813 and died at Eisenstadt in 1818. The most interesting and important aspect of his career is that it throws some welcome light on the dark period of the marionette theatre and the people who sang behind the scenes. See also Koschwitz, Joseph *infra*. J. Harich in *HJB* VIII, 42f. Horányi 89, 104. Ernst's compositions: Harich in *HJB* IV, 18 (33). Documents: *HJB* VII, 79, 97, 122; VIII, 158–62. PCDI item 1003 (contract). ECP item 1237 (Esterhaz, 5 Dec. 1778; engagement as violinist).

Friberth (Fribert, Frieberth, etc.), Carl: tenor. Engaged on 1 January 1759 at a salary of 300 gulden and a daily allowance for food of 30 Kreuzer, or a cash allowance of 182 fl. 30 kr. *per annum*. According to a 'Hoch Fürstlicher Resolution' dated Eszterház, 23 Oct. 1774, he was to receive, effective 1 Nov., nine *Eimer* of wine each year. Friberth and his wife Magdalena (*née* Spangler), princely soprano,[1] left the princely service on 22 May 1776. Performed in Haydn's *Acide* ('Acide') (1763), Haydn's *La canterina* ('Don Pelagio') (1766–7), Haydn's *Lo speziale* ('Sempronio') (1768), Haydn's *Le pescatrici* ('Frisellino') (1770), Haydn's *L' infedeltà delusa* ('Filippo') (1773), Haydn's *L'incontro improvviso* ('Ali') (1775), and probably in some of the operas of 1776. Friberth must have had a brilliantly flexible tenor voice, and he must have been a clever actor: all his finest qualities are summed up in such an Aria as 'Tu, sposarti' from Act II of *L'infedeltà delusa*, which is musically so intelligent and so moving. He had a range which extended up to high *c'''* (as in Frisellino's first Aria, 'Fra cetre e cembali' in *Le pescatrici*) – though of course we must not forget, in all these high notes for tenors, that in the eighteenth century it was customary for tenors to sing much of their highest range in falsetto. Haydn comments on this quite matter-of-factly when in London.[2] Friberth was a kind of all-round genius. He was capable of writing a good Italian libretto, as he did for Haydn in *L'incontro improvviso*; and he was a composer as well. One is his 'Advent Arias', in a copy by the princely copyist Joseph Elssler Senior on 'stag' (i.e., official Esterházy) paper, in the Archives of St Michael's Church in Oedenburg (Sopron). Friberth also sang in the 1768 Vienna performance of Haydn's *Stabat Mater*, and both Friberths (Carl and Magdalena) were soloists, together with the Esterházy bass singer Specht, in the first performance of Haydn's Oratorio, *Il ritorno di Tobia* (Vienna: 2 and 4 April 1775).[3] *HJB* VII, 63, 79 (documents). ECP item 366 (contract 1759). Pohl I, 270. *MGG* IV, Spalte 944.

In the *Jahrbuch der Tonkunst von Wien und Prag* of 1796, we read (p. 17):

Fribert, Karl Kapellmeister bei der obern und untern Jesuitenkirche, and also at the so-called Italian Chapel. His compositions, which consist mostly of church music and some arias, are distinguished by their clarity, severe correctness and are very pleasant for ear and heart, and without being overladen are brilliantly written. In them he follows a deeply felt aesthetic sense. His voice is supple, flowing and never empty, but has darkened by his having used it in too instrumental a fashion [*noch zu sehr von Instrumentierung verdunkelt*]. In teaching for the voice he tries at all costs to protect it.'

There is also praise for his daughter, Mademoiselle Antoinette. Friberth's *Lieder*, together with those of Leopold Hofmann (*Domkapellmeister* at St Stephan's in Vienna), were published by Kurzböck (Kurzbeck) in Vienna in the 1780s (Pohl I, 270f.).

Fuchs, Johann Georg: tenor in Eisenstadt (princely church choir) 1777, later organist. *Vide* 'Orchestra' (*infra*, p. 71).

Gherardi (Gerardi), Pietro: 'Discantista' (*alto castrato*). Engaged by 'Hoch Fürstlichen Intimat' dated Vienna, 7 February 1776, for a period of two years, effective retroactively 1 Feb., at a salary of 500 gulden *per annum* with the usual free lodging, wood and candles ('Licht') and a winter or summer uniform; after the conclusion of the two years travel money of 100 fl. Performed in Gluck's *Orfeo* ('Orfeo') (1776), Gassmann's *L'amore artigiano* ('Giro') (1777), Haydn's *Il mondo della luna* ('Ernesto') (1777) and Dittersdorf's *Arcifanfano, re de' matti* ('Malgoverno'). He left the Esterházy service at the end of January 1778. He obviously helped in the mad atmosphere of the Dittersdorf farce, successfully revived in our day. But Haydn, in writing 'Ernesto' for Signor Gherardi, gave us one of the most colourless personalities of all his stage works. Like Mozart, when faced with such a problem (Don Ottavio), Haydn pours out stupendously beautiful music for 'Ernesto', but the part remains cold and featureless. *HJB* VII, 99 (contract and departure). Bartha-Somfai 65, 69–71, 74, 170, 189f., 197.

Giovanni, Pasquale di: tenor. Engaged on 1 May 1781 for one year, 'laut Hochfürstl. Resolution', at a salary of 500 gulden *per annum* with the usual free lodging, wood and candles. Left Eszterháza at the end of September 1781. Performed *inter alia* in Righini's *Il convitato di pietra* ('Commendatore Mons. de Giovanni') (1781). *HJB* VII, 106 (contract). ECP item 1332 (Esterhaz, 17 May 1781: contracts for the Bologna sisters, Vincenzo Moratti and Pasquale di Giovanni). Bartha-Somfai 90, 93, 170. Landon 'Haydns Oper' (op. cit., p. 216).

Griessler (Grießler), Melchior: bass. Engaged at Vienna on 1 June 1761, aged thirty-four, as bass singer and violinist. His salary was 200 gulden, a suit or 60 fl., and a large *Deputat*: 4 *Metzen* (3.44 litre, miller's dry measure) of wheat, 12 *Metzen* of rye, one-quarter *Metze* each of lentils, barley and millet-pap, 300 lb. of beef, 50 lb. of salt, 30 lb. of lard, 30 lb. of candles, 9 *Eimer* (Eisenstädter 'Hämb') of wine (Conv. 1769; later only 'wine ... 9 Eimer' without details), ½ *Eimer* of cabbage &

---

1 Born 4 September 1750; *vide* p. 48.
2 See *Haydn in England 1791–1795*, p. 114.
3 Haydn also took with him Tomasini and the 'cellist Marteau. *Vide infra*, p. 214.

58

beets, 1 *Stück* (piece) of pork and six fathom cords of wood. He received an increase 'Laut Intimat der Hoch Fürstlichen Commission' on 17 February 1788, effective 14 February, in kind, *viz.* 2 *Metzen* of wheat, 4 *Metzen* of rye and one-half *Metze* of barley *per annum*. Performed in Haydn's *L'incontro improvviso* ('Il Sultan d'Egitto') (1775) and in numerous church works. He remained in Eisenstadt and was the bass in the princely church choir. He was married when he entered the princely service, and died on 13 January 1792 at the age of sixty-five; his widow received a pension. *HJB* VII, 51f., 81f., 121 (documents). J. Harich in *HJB* VIII, 41f.

Haydn, Johann: tenor. Haydn's youngest brother came to Eisenstadt as a guest of Joseph in 1765; the 22-year-old boy sang, at first without pay, in the church choir. On 28 August 1771 he was officially engaged at a salary of 25 gulden. According to a letter from P. L. Rahier to Prince Nicolaus on 9 September 1775, Johann Haydn was dismissed 'yesterday', but again Joseph intervened with his Prince and we find, 'Laut Hoch Fürstlichen Resolution dd° Eszterhaz den 23ten Novembris 1775' Johann reinstated from 1 October 1775 'für versehung der Chor Dienste' at a raised salary of 50 gulden. According to another Resolution dated 19 Dec. 1782, Johann was to receive, effective 1 January 1783, the same goods (*Deputat*) as received by Eleonora Jäger, to wit 4 *Metzen* of wheat, 8 *Metzen* of rye, ¾ *Metze* of barley, 300 lb. of beef, 30 lb. of salt, 24 lb. of lard, 24 lb. of candles, 9 *Eimer* of officers' wine, ½ *Eimer* of cabbage & beets, 6 fathom cords of wood. In the reminder of Haydn's salary we find 'Für das Gefliegel 2 f. 30 Xr. [*Kreuzer*]', which means 'for the harpsichord'. Johann was often employed as a piano (harpsichord) teacher by the princely court. 'Hansl' Haydn, as he was called, taught the Princess's dwarf page, Johannes Siedler ('Monsieur Jean'), piano in the years 1779–80, for which 'Hansl' Haydn received 4 fl. 14 kr. per month from 'dem Herrn Haus-Hofmeister Vaudrin'. Naturally Johann Haydn could nor possibly live on his fifty gulden and the *Deputat*, and was regularly supported by his brother. He died, aged 60, on 10 May 1805. Joseph Carl Rosenbaum, later a princely employee, reports that 'Hansl' Haydn 'sang through the nose', which is the only contemporary, and hardly flattering, description of his vocal abilities. Like Johann Michael and Joseph, 'Hansl' had been through the Reutter St Stephen's Cathedral Choir School. Dies 28 (denied by other authorities, however: see Pohl I, 71n.). *HJB* VII, 81, 120f.; VIII, 154–6; PCDI item 1038 (documents). J. Harich in *HJB* IV, 14 (Joseph Haydn's financial help to Johann) & VII, 41. Landon, *Haydn: the Years of 'The Creation' 1796–1800*, pp. 51, 327.

Jermoli, Guglielmo: tenor. Husband of Maria Jermoli (q.v.). Engaged on 1 March 1777 – final sojourn ended officially on 31 March 1781. Performed in Gassmann's *L'amore artigiano* ('Giannino') (1777), Paisiello's *La Frascatana* ('Nardone') (1777). Haydn's *Il mondo della luna* ('Ecclitico') (1777), Felici's *L'amore soldato* ('Don Faustino') (1779), Anfossi's *La forza della donne* ('Ogus') (1780), Gazzaniga's *La vendemmia* ('Don Achille') (1780) and Haydn's *La fedeltà premiata* ('Fileno') (1781). Interesting though the part of 'Ecclitico' is, with its enormous tenor range, the splendid role of 'Fileno' in Haydn's *La fedeltà premiata* – perhaps the greatest tenor role the composer ever gave us – shows what a great singer Jermoli must have been: with expressive power, dramatic talents and, as we have said, an astonishing range. When he left Eszterháza, he went to Russia with his wife to enter the service of Catherine the Great, in which capacity he performed *inter alia* as Figaro in the *première* of Paisiello's comic masterpiece, *Il barbiere di Siviglia* (St Petersburg, 1782). Literature: see Jermoli, Maria *supra*. Also: J. Harich in *HJB* VII, 25. Claudio Sartori, *Giovanni Paisiello: Il barbiere di Siviglia*, Milan (Ricordi) 1960. Bartha-Somfai 53, 69–71, 82, 85–7, 90, 168, 170, 192, 197, 215, 222.

Koschwitz (Koschvits), Joseph: choirboy (soprano?). Engaged at the age of twelve, 'laut Hoch Fürstlichen Resolution dd° 12ten Nov. $\overline{774}$ a 1^a Octobris anni praecitati' at a monthly salary of one ducat, twelve Kreuzer *per diem* for food and one suit *per annum* 'by high grace'. A friend of Michael Ernst, Koschwitz was also dismissed from service 'According to Hochf. Intimat dd° Wienn den 10ten January $\overline{778}$ ... effective the end of Dec. $\overline{777}$ and this contract is null and void as of 1st January $\overline{778}$'. Presumably Koschwitz was also a singer in the Eszterháza marionette troupe. *HJB* VII, 79, 97 (documents). J. Harich in *HJB* IV, 18 (33).

Lambertini, Giacomo (Jacob): bass. First engaged 'lauth Hochfürstl. Intimat' at Eszterháza on 17 September 1769, effective retroactively 15 Aug. at 300 f., 30 f. or free lodging and the usual goods; then he left the princely service and was later re-engaged 'vermög Hochfürstl. Intimat dd° Eszterház den 23ten Mertzen 1778' for a period of two years beginning 1 March 'annually without other emoluments in cash 600 f.' Dismissed 'A° 1779. Ende Martÿ beede [Lambertini and Pezzani] entlassen worden.' But it was discovered that bass-baritones were lacking in Eszterháza during the summer of 1782, and thus we find that from August 1782 there is to be given 'to the Singer Lambertini, monthly 50 gulden, as long as we keep him here [in Eszterháza]'. He seems to have travelled a great deal, because large sums of money, presumably travel expenses, are often withdrawn from his salary in 1778–9. Performed *inter alia* in Dittersdorf's *Il barone di Rocca antica* ('Giocondo' in the 1778 revival), and in Piccinni's *L'astratto* ('Don Timoteo') (1778). Another stop-gap engagement. *HJB* VII, 61 fl. & 80 (contracts). ECP item 1181 (engagement 1778). Bartha-Somfai 75, 98 (monthly fee in 1782), 170. PCDI item 664 (engagement 1769).

Majeroni, Pietro: bass. Engaged 'laut
...Co[missi]ons Intimat dd° 16ten Märzen $\overline{790}$',
effective retroactively 6 March, at a yearly
salary of 700 gulden – September 1790. Performed
in Cimarosa's *L'impresario in angustie* ('D.
Crisobolo') (1790), Cimarosa's *Giannina e
Bernardone* ('Bernardone') (1790), and in other
operas that cannot now be identified. He was also
to sing in Paisiello's *Il rè Teodoro in Venezia*, which
was in rehearsal in 1790 when the news of the
Prince's death arrived, just as the copyist was
starting 'Corno Secondo' (left unfinished), and in
which Majeroni was to sing the part of 'Taddeo'.
HJB VII, 109 (contract). Bartha-Somfai 159, 170,
358, 363, 365f. In 1793, Majeroni was singing at the
Teatro del Fondo in Naples.

Mandini, Paolo: bass. Engaged by a decree dated
Eszterháza, 18 November 1783, for a period of one
year and left at the end of October 1784 when his
contract expired. Performed in Cimarosa's *Il
falegname* ('Fabio') (1783), Haydn's *Armida*
('Idreno') (1784), Anfossi's *I viaggiatori felici*
('Gianetto') (1784), Cimarosa's *L'amor costante*
('Armidoro') (1784), Bianchi's *La villanella rapita*
('Il conte') (1784), Sarti's *Le gelosie villane*
('Marchese') (1779, revived in 1784 with Mandini),
and possibly in other, unidentified operas. In
Bianchi's *La villanella rapita*, Haydn had to
transpose what was originally a tenor part down as
much as a minor third to fit Mandini's voice.
Judging from Haydn's writing for Mandini in
Armida, the singer had a baritone range, consider-
able flexibility and an expressive voice. ECP 1419
(engagement). Bartha-Somfai 112, 114–9, 170, 289
(transposition).

Martinelli, Filippo (Philippo): bass. The singer
to be engaged at Eszterháza. The document reads:
'Is substituted for the singer Nencini who left, and
is to remain for the length of the latter's contract,
beginning on 1ª Aug $\overline{790}$, annually 450 f.' One of
the roles he sang was undoubtedly in Mozart's *Le
nozze di Figaro*, which requires four bass (baritone)
parts. *HJB* VII 108 (contract). Bartha-Somfai 159,
170.

Moratti (Muratti), Vincenzo: tenor (baritone).
Engaged 'laut Hochfürstl. Resolution' of 17 May
1781 for two years, beginning on May, at a yearly
salary of 550 gulden. He left Eszterháza at the end
of April 1785, and 'Laut Hochfürstl. Intimat dd° 4
Martÿ $\overline{787}$' he was re-engaged, effective retroactively from 15 February, at 600 gulden, six
fathom cords of wood and forty-eight lb. of
candles. From the size of the 'Deputat', we can see
he was married. 'Left 1ª Jun. $\overline{789}$' concludes the
document laconically. Performed in Paisiello's
L'avaro deluso ('Dottore') (1781), Righini's *Il
convitato di pietra* ('Arlechino') (1781), Grétry's
Zemira ed Azor ('Ali') (1782), Salieri's *La fiera di
Venezia* ('Rasoio') (1782), Traetta's *Il cavaliere
errante* ('Calotta') (1782), Anfossi's *Il curioso
indiscreto* ('Marchese') (1782), Haydn's *Orlando
Paladino* ('Pasquale') (1782), Haydn's *La fedeltà*

premiata ('Conte Perruchetto') (for the 1782
revival), Guglielmi's *Il ratto della sposa*
('Gaudenzio') (1783), Righini's *La vedova scaltra*
('Pasquino') (1783), Cimarosa's *L'italiana in Londra*
('Polidoro') (1783), Sarti's *Fra i due litiganti il terzo
gode* ('Mignone') (1783), Cimarosa's *Il
falegname* ('Sozio') (1783), Anfossi's *I viaggiatori
felici* ('Pancrazio') (1784), Bianchi's *La villanella
rapita* ('Pipo') (1784),[1] Sarti's *I
contratempi* ('Pulcherio' = 'Filiberto' on the actual
parts for Eszterháza) (1785), Anfossi's *Il matrimonio
per inganno* ('Don Fabrizio') (1785), Guglielmi's *La
quaquera spiritosa* ('Conte') (1787), Cimarosa's *Il
marito disperato* ('Conte') (1788), Cimarosa's
L'italiana in Londra ('Polidoro' in the 1788 revival),
and in other operas which cannot now be
identified. The key to Moratti's voice is, of course,
the brilliant parody that Haydn wrote in the role of
'Pasquale' in *Orlando Paladino*, wherein the singer
displays his flexibility, even to trills, his top range,
and above all his abilities as an actor. The fragments
of the tenor transposition for 'Conte Perruchetto'
in the 1782 revival of Haydn's *La fedeltà premiata* –
one whole Aria, 'Salva, salva, ajuto', has survived
in Haydn's autograph – were intended for this
gifted singer. *HJB* VII, 106, 110 (documents). ECP
item 1332 (first engagement), item 1592 (second
engagement). J. Harich in *HJB* I, 41. Bartha-
Somfai 22, 90f., 93, 99–102, 107f. 111f., 116., 119,
125f., 137, 148, 158, 170, 263, 274, 278, 289, 321,
336. Landon, 'Haydns Oper' (op. cit., p. 216).

Morelli, Bartolomeo (Bartholomeo): tenor.
Engaged on 25 April 1785 (princely order of 25
May from Eszterháza) for two years – 'bis inclus:
24. apr.' 1787. His travel money to Eszterháza (bill
of 29 March 1785) was refunded (Acta Musicalia
17/1195, 8 April 1785). The Prince dismissed
Morelli at the end of his contract (ECP item 1592).
Performed in Haydn's *La vera costanza* (? role)
(1785 revival). Stabinger's *Le astuzie di Bettina* ('D.
Pacomio') (1785), Zingarelli's *Alsinda* ('Singeo')
(1786), Cimarosa's *La ballerina amante* ('Petronio')
(1786), Cimarosa's *Chi dell'altrui si veste, presto si
spoglia* ('Gian Fabrizio') (1786), Caruso's
L'albergatrice vivace ('Micheluccio') (1786),
Righini's *L'incontro inaspettato* ('Cardone') (1786,
Cimarosa's *I due baroni di Rocca azzurra* ('Barone')
(1786), Gazzaniga's *L'isola d'Alcina* ('D. Lopez')
(1786 revival), Anfossi's *Il sordo e l'avaro* (? role),
and in other operas which cannot now be
identified. A useful and experienced tenor voice.
ECP items 1478 (engagement) & 1592 (dismissal,
dated Esterhaz 4 March 1787 for 25 April). Bartha-
Somfai 22, 124f., 127, 130–5, 137f., 170, 289, 316.

Negri, Domenico: bass. Engaged on 8
September 1782 for two years – 22 August 1784.
Performed in Haydn's *La fedeltà premiata* (revival

---

[1] The proposal for the costumes names Moratti ['Muratti'] for
'Piaggio' (*recte*: 'Biagio') and Bianchi for 'Pipo', but in the actual
operatic material, Pipo's recitatives have survived in an extra
'Heft' for the singer, and on the cover Haydn himself wrote 'S^r
Moratti', which of course settles the question definitely. Bartha-
Somfai 289.

of 1782: 'Melibeo'), Haydn's *Orlando Paladino* ('Rodomonte') (1782), Guglielmi's *Il ratto della sposa* ('Polidoro') (1783), Righini's *La vedova scaltra* ('Don Alvaro') (1783). Cimarosa's *L'italiana in Londra* ('Milord') (1783), Sarti's *Giulio Sabino* ('Arminio') (1783), Cimarosa's *Il falegname* ('Don Velardo') (1783), Anfossi's *I viaggiatori felici* ('Don Gastone') (1784). Cimarosa's *L'amor costante* ('Marchese') (1784) and Sarti's *Le gelosie villane* (revival of 1784: 'Cecchino'). The rich and amusing part of 'Rodomonte' in Haydn's *Orlando Paladino* shows how gifted this singer must have been. As to his further identity, there are two possibilities that spring to mind: (1) he is merely the 'Signor Negri' who was at Piacenza with Luigia Polzelli in 1792 and to whom Haydn sends greetings (CCLN 127); or (2) he was the husband of Polzelli's sister, Teresa; in which case they went to England, where Haydn knew them[1]. ECP 1373 (Esterhaz, 10 September 1782 *re* Negri's engagement). Bartha-Somfai 98, 101f., 107–9, 112, 114, 116–8, 156, 170, 265, 271, 274, 282f.

Nencini, Santi: bass. Engaged together with his wife, Palmira Sassi, 'Lauth Hoch Fürstlicher Resolution dd° 30ᵗᵉⁿ Aug: 785', effective retroactively from 15 August, at a joint salary of 1,310 gulden, 40 lb. of candles and 12 fathom cords of wood. They left at the end of July 1790. Performed in Stabinger's *Le astuzie di Bettina* ('Giannino') (1785), Zingarelli's *Alsinda* ('Scilace') (1786), Cimarosa's *La ballerina amante* ('Mazzacogna') (1786), Traetta's *Ifigenia in Tauride* ('Toante') (1786), Caruso's *L'albergatrice vivace* ('Pericco') (1786), Righini's *L'incontro inaspettato* ('Gradasso') (1786), Sarti's *Idalide* ('Palmoro') (1786), Sarti's *Giulio Sabino* ('Tito' in the 1786 revival), Gazzaniga's *L'isola d'Alcina* ('Mr. La Rose') (1786 revival), Anfossi's *Il sordo e l'avaro* (? role) (1787), Bianchi's *Il disertore* ('Ormondo') (1787), Guglielmi's *La quaquera spiritosa* ('Togmino') (1787), Bianchi's *Alessandro nell'Indie* ('Alessandro') (1787), Cimarosa's *Giunio Bruto* ('Giunio Bruto') (1788), Cimarosa's *Il marito disperato* ('Corbellone') (1788), Cimarosa's *L'italiana in Londra* ('Milord' in the 1788 revival), Martin's *L'arbore di Diana* ('Doristo') (1789), and in other operas which cannot now be identified. *HJB* VII, 109 (engagement), ECP item 1525 (Esterhaz, 30 Aug. 1785: engagement). Bartha-Somfai 114, 127, 129–35, 137–9, 144, 148, 158, 170, 274, 277, 296, 300, 302, 304, 319–21, 324, 329, 336, 355, 396.

Paoli, Gaetano de: bass. Engaged for two years 'Laut Intimat Sʳ Durchl. dd° 7ᵗᵉⁿ Juny 788', effective retroactively from 1 June, at a salary of 950 gulden, six fathom cords of wood and 48 lb. of candles. From the size of the 'Deputat', we can see he was married. He stayed until the end of September 1790. Performed in Cimarosa's *Il marito disperato* ('Conte') (1788), Cimarosa's *L'impresario in angustie* ('Campanello') (1790) and Mozart's *Le nozze di Figaro* ('Il conte') (1790), as well as other

[1] See *Haydn in England 1791–1795*, pp. 122f.

unidentified operas. *HJB* VII, 110 (contract). Bartha-Somfai 144, 148, 152, 159, 170, 336, 358, 368.

Pesci (Peschi), Antonio (Anton): bass. Engaged 'vermög Hochfürstl. Intimat dd° Esterhaz den 22ᵗᵉⁿ Martÿ 1779 for two years, effective retroactively from 1 March, at a salary of 'Ein hundert ordinaire Ducaten'·or yearly 423 fl. 20 kr. 'Laut Hoch Fürstl. Intimat dd° 5ᵗᵉⁿ April 781 ist mit ihme ein Neuer Contract auf noch 2 Jahre verrichtet worden, und hat a 1ᵃ Martÿ 781 aljährlich zu empfangen . . . . . 500 f.' He left Eszterháza at the end of July 1782. It appears that Pesci travelled from Bologna to Eszterháza; at any rate he was involved in transmitting operas that Pietro Giacomo Martelli, the princely agent in Bologna, purchased for Prince Esterházy; Pesci took with him the vocal parts of two operas, *La giardiniera brillante* and [Anfossi's] *Isabella e Rodrigo*, which cost seven and one-half ducats, and delivered them to Haydn. When Pesci arrived, in 1779, his twenty ducats' travel expenses were recorded. When he finally left, Prince Nicolaus gave him a farewell present of fifty 'ordinari Ducaten' which Pesci went to Eisenstadt, *en route* to Vienna, to collect (he signed the receipt 'Eisenstod 16 Agosto 1782 / Antonio Pesci'). Performed in eighteen operas, of which the following may be identified: Anfossi's *La Metilde ritrovata* ('Fabricio') (1779), Anfossi's *La forza delle donne* ('Timur') (1780), Gazzaniga's *La vendemmia* ('Cardone') (1780), Salieri's *La scuola de' gelosi* ('Basio') (1780), Gassmann's *L'amore artigiano* ('Titta') (1780 revival), Haydn's *La fedeltà premiata* ('Melibeo') (1781), Anfossi's *Isabella e Rodrigo* ('D. Sancio') (1781), Paisiello's *L'avaro deluso* ('Raggiro') (1781), Righini's *Il convitato di pietra* ('Ombriño') (1781), Grétry's *Zemire ed Azor* ('Sandro') (1782), Salieri's *La fiera di Venezia* ('Belfusto') (1782), Traetta's *Il cavaliere errante* ('Ismeno' [= 'Ruffino']) (1782), Piccinni's *L'astratto* ('Leandro') (1778) and in other, unidentified operas. Haydn's writing in the part of 'Melibeo' (*La fedeltà premiata*) shows that Pesci must have had a rich and sonorous bass voice, but it is not known if he had particular abilities as an actor: 'Melibeo' does not require a great 'character actor'. *HJB* VII, 102f., 166f. (documents). ECP item 1235 (Esterhaz, aa March 1789, *re* engagement of Luigi Rossi and 'Anton' Pesci, with salaries listed). Bartha-Somfai 77, 79f., 85–7, 92f., 98–100, 105, 170. J. Harich in *HJB* VII, 29f. (45f.). For Pesci's concert in Prague, see *Miscellanea Musicologia*, VI, Svazek, Prague 1958, p. 45.

Pezzani, Giovanni (Johan, Johann): tenor. Engaged 'vermög Hochfürstl. Intimat dd° Eszterhaz den 23ᵗᵉⁿ Mertzen 1778' for one year, effective retroactively from 1 March, and with no other emoluments apart from his yearly salary of 600 gulden. The document ends: 'A° 1779. End of March both [Lambertini & Pezzani] dismissed. Performed in operas of the 1778–79 season which cannot now be determined. ECP item 1181 (Esterház, 23 March 1778: engagement of

Lambertini, Pezzani). *HJB* VII, 80 (contract). Bartha-Somfai 22, 75, 170.

Prizzi (Brizzi), Aloisio (Ludwig): tenor. Engaged 'Laut Intimat Sr Durchl. dd° 4ten Maÿ 1788. hat selber von 25ten April a: ej:' – *i.e.* retroactively effective 25 April, at a salary of 700 gulden, 24 lb. of candles and three fathom cords of wood. He left Eszterháza at the end of September 1790. Performed in Martin's *L'arbore di Diana* ('Endimione') (1789), Paisiello's *Il re Teodoro in Venezia* ('Sandrino') (1790) and in other operas that cannot be determined. *HJB* VII, 110 (contract), ECP 1648 (engagement). Bartha-Somfai 144, 152, 159, 170, 354, 366.

Rossi, Luigi (Luiggi): bass. Engaged 'vermög Hochfürstl. Intimat dd° Eszterhaz den 22ten Martÿ 1779' for two years, effective retroactively from 1 March, at a salary of 600 gulden. 'At the end of Feb. 781 he left service', concludes the document. Like Antonio Pesci and Anna Zannini, he received twenty ducats in advance for travel expenses (these were recorded in a document). Performed in Anfossi's *La Metilde ritrovata* ('Barone di Trapano') (1779), Gazzaniga's *L'isola d'Alcina* ('La Rose') (1779), Naumann's *La villanella incostante* (= *Le nozze disturbate*) ('Crisante') (1779), Sarti's *Le gelosie villane* ('Mengone') (1779), Salieri's *La scuola de' gelosi* ('Lumaca') (1780) – in this opera Haydn composed a famous 'insertion' Aria, 'Dice benissimo che si marito'[1] in Act II, Scene 2, for Luigi Rossi – and Anfossi's *La finta giardiniera* ('Roberto') (1780). The witty and vocally rewarding Aria that Haydn wrote for Rossi shows that his talents, also as an actor, must have been impressive. An educated man, he published a poem in Oedenburg, composed in Italian and translated into German, entitled 'Al merito incomparabile di Sua Altezza il Principe Nicolo Esterhazi di Galanta' (copy in National Library, Budapest) – which also reveals its author to be a clever courtier as well. He also directed the choreography in the ballets of Haydn's *La fedeltà premiata* (textbook) at its première. A gifted man, then, who was certainly one of the better bass singers of the Eszterháza troupe. *HJB* VII, 102, 130. Bartha-Somfai 53, 77, 79f., 86f., 90, 170, 384. J. Harich in *HJB* VII, 27f. (45). The poem is signed 'In segno di profondissimo rispetto e particolare venerazione, Luigi Rossi.' Budapest (cat. no.) Aprónyomtatvány Tár 1779/81. Horányi 142, 239. ECP *vide* 'Pesci'.

Specht, Christian: bass. Engaged 'lauth Hochfürstl. Intimation dd° Eszterház den 18^t 7[Septem]bris 768', effective retroactively from 1 September, at a salary of 400 gulden, free lodgings of 20 gulden, 20 lb. of candles and three cords of wood. He soon married and received the larger 'Deputat' given to married men (lodging: 35 gulden, 24 lb. of candles and six cords of wood. Performed in Sacchini's(?) *La contadina in corte*

('Berto'?), Haydn's *Le pescatrici* ('Lindoro') (1770), Haydn's *L'infedeltà delusa* ('Nanni') (1773), Haydn's *L'incontro improvviso* ('Calandro') (1775), Piccinni's *La buona figliuola* ('Tagliaferro') (1776), Dittersdorf's *Il barone di Rocca antica* ('Giocondo') (1776) and Paisiello's *La Frascatana* ('Pagnotta'?) (1777). Possessed of a voice with a phenomenal range (F at the bottom of the bass clef to *a'*), Haydn writes for Specht with the affection that characterizes all the bass parts of Haydn's career. At this point an extraordinary thing happens: it appears that Christian Specht lost his voice, and instead of singing took up the viola. In 1778, the Gotha *Theater-Kalender* – *vide infra*, p. 92 – lists him in 1777 as viola player in the Esterházy orchestra; perhaps Prince Nicolaus and Haydn were allowing Specht a trial period as viola player, during which the Prince was generous enough to continue his full salary as a singer. Singers were, of course, paid much more than viola players, and when Prince Nicolaus, on 1 January 1781, wrote out a new contract with Specht as a viola player, his salary was lowered to 300 gulden, which made it the equal of Vito Ungricht, another former singer (q.v.) and later viola player. In the new contract, Specht agrees 'to undertake to play well, particularly in the operas'. In a princely 'Resolution' dated Eszterháza, 5 May 1781, Specht is given five *Eimer* of wine, twelve *Metzen* of rye and six of wheat. 'For his part he agrees to keep in good order, to string, to quill and to tune all the clavier in Eszterház, also those clavier belonging to the singers, and under which it is understood are included the musical clocks in Eszterház and Mon Biyoux [Monbijous, a hunting castle nearby], to which end he is to procure at his expense 'the strings and raven's quills . . .'. The musical clocks were primarily the work of Pater Primitivus Niemecz, princely librarian at Eszterháza[1]. On 31 October 1789, 'in consideration of the fact that in order to tune the clavier and clockworks he has to procure the necessary strings', Specht received one pig *per annum*. After September 1790, Specht had the good fortune to be given a position in Eisenstadt 'in the choir and in other musical functions', and he saw the resuscitation of the princely 'Musique' under Haydn in the 1790s and 1800s; Specht died at Eisenstadt on 21 February 1809, shortly before Haydn's death (May). *HJB* VII, 65, 111 (documents), 167f. (contract as viola player). PCDI item 762 (engagement). ECP, items 1329 (Esterhaz, 5 May 1781 *re* tuning pianos, etc.) & 1669 (Vienna 10 Jan. 1789: pork). J. Harich in *HJB* VII, 30f. (46). Bartha-Somfai 48, 63, 66f., 69, 123, 159, 167, 170, 174, 259, 383.

Specioli, Antonio: tenor. Husband of the soprano Maria Antonia Specioli (q.v.). Performed in Haydn's *La fedeltà premiata* ('Fileno') (1782 revival), Haydn's *Orlando Paladino* ('Orlando') (1782), Guglielmi's *Il ratto della sposa* ('Gentilino') (1783), Righini's *La vedova scaltra* ('Monsieur Le

---

1 Score, parts and vocal score published by the Haydn-Mozart Presse, edited by the present writer.

1 See *Haydn in England 1791–1795*, pp. 201f.

Blan') (1783), Sarti's *Giulio Sabino* ('Tito') (1783), Sarti's *Fra i due litiganti il terzo gode* ('Conte') (1783), Haydn's *Armida* ('Ubaldo') (1784), Cimarosa's *L'amor costante* ('Cavaliere') (1784), Sarti's *La Didone abbandonata* ('Jarba') (1784, Zingarelli's *Montezuma* ('Fernando') (1785), Anfossi's *Il matrimonio per inganno* ('Valerio') (1785), and in other operas that cannot now be identified. Haydn's *Heldentenor,* to whom the great dramatic roles were assigned. Literature: see Specioli, Maria Antonia. Also Bartha-Somfai 98, 101f., 106–9, 111, 115f., 118, 123–6, 170.

Totti, Andrea (Andreas: tenor. Engaged 'lauth Hochfürstl. Resolution dd° Eszterház den 9ᵗᵉⁿ Junÿ 778' for one year, effective retroactively from 1 June, at a salary of 500 gulden 'without any Emoluments'. At the expiration of his contract he was re-engaged for another year with a raise of 100 gulden. He remained until the end of May 1782. Performed *inter alia* in Piccinni's *L'astratto* ('Il Capitan Faccenda') (1778), Paisiello's *Le due contesse* ('Il Cavalier della Piuma Vedova') (1779), Haydn's *La vera costanza* ('Conte Errico') (1779), Anfossi's *La Metilde ritrovata* ('Il conte Asdrubale') (1779), Sarti's *La gelosie villane* ('Marchese') (1779–80). Haydn's *L'isola disabitata* ('Gernando') (1779), Salieri's *La scuola de' gelosi* ('Il conte di Bandiera') (1780), Anfossi's *La finta giardiniera* ('Il contino Belfiore') (1780), Gassmann's *L'amore artigiano* ('Giannino') (revival of 1780), Anfossi's *Isabella e Rodrigo* ('D. Rodrigo') (1781), Paisiello's *L'avaro deluso* ('Conte de Belprata') (1781), Righini's *Il convitato di pietra* ('Don Giovanni') (1781), Salieri's *La fiera di Venezia* ('Grifagno') (1782), Traetta's *Il cavaliere errante* ('Guido') (1782) and in other operas that cannot now be identified. Another *Heldentenor,* to whom Haydn entrusted two brilliant parts. The dramatic Aria 'A trionfar' from Act I of *La vera costanza* shows the exceptional dramatic and vocal powers of this first-rate singer. The following brief biographical details are taken from Harich, 'Musikgeschichte'. Before coming to Eszterháza, Totti sang at the Teatro S. Moisè in Venice (where Barbara Sassi was also a member of the company). When he arrived in Hungary he was twenty-eight. A year later he married a singer (unidentified) at Eszterháza; at the ceremony Francesco Ripamonti (violin) and Luigi Rossi were witnesses; their child, born at Eszterháza, enjoyed no less a person than Countess Viczay (*vide supra,* p. 37) as a godmother. After he left Eszterháza, Signor Totti wished to return and addressed himself to Prince

Nicolaus, who in a charming letter refused:

Al Sigr. Totti.
Signore
Ho capitato la vostra lettere di 26. Marzo passato dalla quale intesi che bramate di tornare un'altra volta nel mio Servizio con Vostra Consorte; ma essendo presentemente proveduto di tre Tenori mi dispiace che per adesso non posso far uso della vostra offerta. Questo non ostante mi facciate di tempo in tempo sapere, dove vi trovate, afin che in caso di qualche mutatione di soggetti ve lo possa avisare. Del resto sono
il vostro ben affezionato
N[icolo] P[rincipe] E[sterházy]
Esterház li 23. avrile 1783.
Prot. missilium XV.5.883 [*HJB* VII, 165]

HJB VII, 102 (contract, 165 (Nicolaus's letter). ECP, items 1193 (contract), 1242 (Esterhaz, 14 June 1779: contract renewed). Bartha-Somfai 75, 79f., 83, 86f., 92f., 98f., 100, 170f., 235. J. Harich in *HJB* VII, 25f. (44f.).

Ungricht, Vito (Vitus): tenor. Engaged 'vermög Intimat dd° Eszterház den 22ᵗᵉⁿ Junÿ 776' for two years, effective retroactively from 10 June, at a salary of 300 gulden, 30 fl. lodging money, 24 lb. of candles, three fathom cords of wood and a uniform each year. Remained in service until the end of September 1790. Performed in Dittersdorf's *Lo sposo burlato* ('Florindo') (1776), Dittersdorf's *Arcifanfano* ('Furibondo') (1777), Piccinni's *L'astratto* ('Giocondo') (1778) and Haydn's *La vera costanza* ('Il marchese Ernesto').A modest singer by the time he reached Eszterháza. Ungricht had been engaged at Prague by Dittersdorf in 1764 for the *Capelle* of the Bishop of Großwardein (now Oradea Mare in Roumania), Baron Adam Patachich. There, he sang bass parts of operas and oratorios, mostly in Latin, and when the *Capelle* was disbanded in 1769, he seems to have followed Dittersdorf to Johannisberg, from which place he then went to Eszterháza. His voice having, it is presumed, failed, he turned to the violin (viola) and became a regular member of the orchestra. Probably he was not a real tenor by the time he came to serve under Haydn, but a kind of baritone (although the part of 'Ernesto' was written in the tenor clef). *HJB* VII, 100 (contract), 110 (repetition of contract). Bartha-Somfai 48, 65, 68f., 71, 79, 123, 151, 159, 167, 170, 174. J. Harich in *HJB* VII, 26f. (45).

THEATRICAL PERSONNEL (ADMINISTRATION, ETC.)

Bader, Philipp Georg: poet (playwright), librarian and, 1778–79, Director of the Theatres at Eszterháza. Died 1779. *Vide supra,* p. 38. Assisted in the organization of the Marionette Theatre 1776–78 (Gotha *Theater-Kalender*), and read roles behind the stage. When he was promoted to be

Director, Prince Nicolaus issued the following document, first published by Horányi:

Instruction
Having entrusted our librarian Bader with the direction of our theatre, we deem it

necessary to issue the following points of instruction, to which he as well as the other theatrical personnel must adhere precisely:

1mo. As to that which concerns the music and actors [singers], and the prompter (to which post the music copyist [Schellinger] has been assigned), our Capellmeister Hayden [*sic*] is to have charge and to maintain the proper order.

2do. Bader will be the full director, and all the persons belonging to the theatre such as carpenters, the wardrobe attendant, servants, guardsmen and others, will be subordinate to him but in such a fashion that he should not without our previous knowledge effect changes, make reductions or enlargements.

3^{tio.} Since Bader has maintained that the painter Travaglio [*sic*] is the most skilful and most able of those capable of lending a helping hand in the direction of the theatre, said Travaglio (being versed in painting, and knowing how to shift and store the scenery) will, in the procuring of the scenery and its disposition, be attached to Bader and will supervise the theatrical personnel, reporting to Bader in each and every matter concerning infractions of discipline without, however, exercising independent authority in that he will continue to be subordinate to our Cabinet Painter [Basilius Grundmann].

4to. He, Bader, is to keep an exact account of expenses, of goods received and all changes (so that everything can be located surely and promptly); he will keep an exact protocol, and therefore anyone having traffick with him shall, if he require it, provide information and detail so that for his part he may render quarterly accounts.

5to. In order that the accounts may in future be precise and available, the wig-maker is to receive 1 fl., the tailor 30 xr. and Frau Handl likewise 30 xr.

6to. In the theatre all the work is to be executed by the following individuals: the 5 carpenters who are already in theatrical service, *viz.* Corbinian, Philipp, Stephan, Johann and the apprentice; also Weber the carpenter and the grenadiers Zimmermann and Andre; each of whom are to receive 7 xr. for each rehearsal and performance.

7mo. If required, the tailor has to provide two journeymen as *gratis* supers, and the decorator [*Tapezier*] and house-carpenter also have to act as supers, *gratis*.

8vo. In order to avoid fire hazards, the chimney-sweep has to stand by during the performance.

9no. One hour after each opera, play or concert [*Akademie*], the corporal on duty together with Grenadier Zimmermann and a guardsman will inspect the theatre-premises, with a view to preventing all possible dangers. Our Sub-Lieutenant will receive the appropriate instructions.

10mo. No guard is to leave the theatre during performances without the knowledge and

permission of Bader, nor must any guard make frivolous requests of any kind. Should such a thing occur, he, Bader, is to report it, so that the culprit may be punished according to the circumstances of the misdeed.

11mo. Frau Handl and all the theatrical personnel are obliged to execute instructions without contradiction and to avoid disorders of any kind, failing which the culprits are to be reported, punished and, should the circumstances warrant, dismissed.

12mo. Except for those persons whose presence is deemed necessary by Bader, no one (no matter what his rank be) shall, under any pretext whatever, dare to enter the theatre's stage during rehearsals and performances.

13^{tio.} Finally, these instructions are to be made known to all the theatrical personnel, and their contents are to be studied, and no one is to contravene them under threat of sure punishment or dismissal. Eszterház, the 14th of February 1778.

Nicolaus Fürst Esterhazy [mpria]

Pursuant to these instructions, it is forbidden without our previous knowledge and permission, to change, increase or reduce any stage property, to which end all orders signed by us are to be registered in our secretariat. Any expenses not so authorized will be charged to the person upon whose instruction they were made.

Eszterház, the 26th of July 1779.

Nicolaus Fürst Esterházy [mpria]
[Horányi: German – *Esterházysche Feenreich* pp. 119–22; English – pp. 118f.]

It was as a result of these precise instructions that Bader drew up the invaluable day-by-day plan of all theatrical activity in Eszterháza Castle for the year 1778, which has by some miracle survived and is presented *in extenso* below (pp. 94ff.).

Bienfait, Albert: 'Maschinist' at the Marionette Theatre. We have records of him for 1775–7, but he may have been engaged as early as October 1774. In 1778 we find him as 'Pantomimenmeister' (Master of Pantomimes) with his own players in Eszterháza. Before coming to Hungary, Bienfait was a member of the French opéra comique in Vienna, where he was an actor. R. Haas, *Gluck und Durazzo im Burgtheater*, Vienna 1925, 17. Horányi 98, 110, 116. Landon in *HJB* I, 118.

Bon, Girolamo (Bonn, Bonno, Le Bon, ['Monsieur Bunon'?], Hieronymus, Hieronymi): impresario and scenic designer. Engaged sporadically at Eisenstadt from 1759; together with his family (wife and daughter, Rosa and Anna, both singers) he helped in the various little Italian comedies at Eisenstadt of 1762, at the conclusion of which he, his wife and his daughter were engaged at a joint salary of 400 gulden on 1 July 1762 (Acta Musicalia 253, Esterházy Archives, Budapest). ECP item 535 (15 April 1765) mentions that 'Le Bon's' contract was renewed, and in another document we read that 'Monsieur Bunon' has a yearly salary of 100 ordinary ducats, 'id est 412 f. 30 xr.' and, underneath, the note 'Vermög Hochfürstl.er Co]mmissi]on dd° 1a 8[October]bris 1772, hat von diesen dato an bis weiteres Hochfürstles beliben Jährle Zulag [addition] 100 stukh ordinaire Ducaten.' Another piece of evidence showing that Bon was still with the troupe in the years 1766 *et seq.* comes from a rather surprising source: the bills submitted by the tailors for the princely uniforms. We find almost all the names misspelled on these documents; usually the tailors were illiterate, and their assistants who wrote the bills managed to misspell almost every musician's name – they were obviously spelled as heard by the tailor's assistant (e.g. 'Capel Meister Heiden. Luitschi [= Luigi Tomasini]. Garnie [= Garnier]' and finally 'Bonno, who is patently 'Bon'; bill of August 1764; *HJB* IV, 80). We find Bon, spelled in various interesting ways, on the following documents of our period: 1766, new summer uniforms; 'Bonn' (*HJB* IV, 81); 1768, new summer and winter uniforms; 'Bono' (*HJB* IV, 81). But, if there is any significance in the omission, he is not listed among the musicians receiving new summer uniforms for the year 1772 (*HJB* IV, 82). By 1 December 1773 he was dead (*vide infra*, p. 201). Bon spent a major part of his career in Russia (from 1735), together with his wife Rosa (*née* Ruvinetti). Their daughter Anna seems to have been born at St Petersburg *c.* 1735. Bon was a Venetian and known in Venetian dialect as 'Momolo'; he also composed, and published (at Nuremberg in 1752) *Sei facili Sonate di violino con il basso*; a few years thereafter (1756) Anna also published some music at Nuremberg. After leaving Russia in February 1746, the Bon family went to Frederick II in Potsdam, then to the Court of Prince Thurn und Taxis in Regensburg. In 1752 this talented man wrote the libretto to *La citella* [*zitella*] *ingannata* given at Antwerp with music by J. F. Agricola. In 1754 he organized the first German performance of Pergolesi's *La serva padrona* at Frankfurt-am-Main, and thereafter we find him at Bayreuth. R.-Aloys Mooser, *Annales de la Musique et des Musiciens en Russie au XVIIIme Siècle*, vol. I (1700–1762), Geneva 1948, pp. 155f. We suggest that this was still Girolamo Bon, whose exquisite scenic designs – Horányi identified them – dated 1762 (from the Esterházy Gallery) show his great talents, and who continued to be the principal stage painter for Prince Nicolaus in this 'interim' period; that is, for the operas *La canterina*, *Lo speziale*, *Le pescatrici* that Haydn wrote for various occasions. *HJB* VII 70 ('Der Mahler Gierolomo Bon')[1] 56, 72 (documents as 'Monsieur Bunon'). ECP item 535, also item 471 (1 July 1762: 'Mahler Le Bon, Weib und Tochter als Singerinnen' engaged). Horanyi 30, 32, 34, 243 and two scenes reproduced in colour: 35, 37.

1 15 April 1765: Bon and his daughter are to earn until further notice 400 gulden and the following *Deputat*: 30f. lodging money, 7 *Eimer* of wine, 7 cords of wood. 'NB left princely service' (no date listed). Perhaps 'Monsieur Bunon' was really someone else.

Cantini, Alessio: scenic designer, known to have designed two operas – Ordoñez's *Alceste* (1775) and *Genovevens Vierter Theil* (1777) – for the Marionette Theatre at Eszterháza, but there is no evidence that he was regularly engaged. On a bill for the decorations to *Alceste*, he is listed as 'architetto e pittore teatrale di S. M. Imperiale'. Landon in *HJB* I, 118, 183, 189.

Elssler, (Elsler), Joseph: princely copyist and theatrical copyist until his death in 1782. Later the principal copyist was Johann Schellinger (q.v.). Elssler Senior was also Haydn's private copyist, but he was not, as Bartha-Somfai appear to suggest, in any private capacity at court. He is listed with the other musicians (*HJB* VII, 118f. for such documents). Joseph Elssler had two sons, both copyists: Joseph Jr. and Johann; the latter became Haydn's copyist and factotum from January 1794 to 1809. Joseph Elssler's (Sen.) handwriting was first identified by J. P. Larsen on a copy of Haydn's *Salve Regina* in G minor (1771) in the Gesellschaft der Musikfreunde. Larsen *HUB* 63. *MGG* ('Elssler': Landon).

Federico, Monsieur: listed on the libretto of the marionette opera (pasticcio?) *L'assedio di Gibilterra* (1783) as 'Pittore di Camera di S. A.', which means 'Cabinet Mahler' in the service of Prince Nicolaus. He probably did other stage sets as well. Landon in *HJB* I, 119, 192. Horányi, 147.

Förster ('Fester', 'Ferster'), Herr: Designed the stage sets for Pleyel's *Die Fee Urgele* (1776) and probably for others, too. Landon in *HJB* I, 119, 191.

Goussard, Pierre: 'Maschinist' at the Marionette Theatre and the Opera House. Born in Paris, Goussard was engaged in 1771 and stayed until 1780. The Gotha *Theater-Kalender* of 1777, reporting for 1776, names 'H. Conßar' as one of the two 'Maschinisten'; in its 1778 issue the name is spelled 'Coußa', which is Gotha's phonetic spelling of Monsieur Goussard. Both times he is placed under 'Marionetten-Oper'. J. Harich in *HJB* II, 23. Landon in *HJB* I, 118, 120.

Grenadiers: the children and wives of the princely grenadiers stationed at Eszterháza were expected to assist behind the stage at the Opera and Marionette Theatres. Sometimes a great many were needed for a single performance, such as the complicated *L'assedio di Gibilterra* (1783) or Haydn's *Dido* (1777) at the Marionette Theatre; for the latter they needed ten rehearsals with ten supers for one performance in September 1778. In two real operas of the 1790 season, probably Mozart's *Le nozze di Figaro* and Salieri's *Axur*, eighteen and thirteen (resp.) grenadier 'supers' were necessary, but of course in costumes and on the stage. Grenadier wives also assisted Frau Handl in the complicated and numerous marionette costumes. J. Harich in *HJB* I, 91f.; II, 23 (42). Landon in *HJB* I, 119. Probably they made up the chorus, since with one exception ('*L'assedio di Gibilterra*'), and the occasional Italian opera transferred from the Opera House to the Marionette Theatre (Traetta's *Il cavaliere errante*, Zingarelli's *Alsinda*; Harich in *HJB* I, 193), all the operas in the Marionette Theatre were done in the German language. If necessary, sixty performers could be organized (as for Sarti's *Didone abbandonata* in 1784: Esterházy Archives 799/46,138; Horányi 150).

Grundmann, Johann Basilius (usually referred to as 'Basil Grundmann' or 'Basilius Grundmann'): princely 'Cabinet Mahler' (*vide supra*, p. 30). He also did operatic scenery, as may be established by various bills in the Esterházy Archives (Horányi 122).

Handl ('Handlin', the suffix 'in' denoting feminine gender), Barbara, wife of the grenadier corporal Johann Handl: 'Garderobière' (Mistress of the Wardrobe), seamstress, also costume-maker for the Marionette Theatre. She was occasionally paid half-a-gulden for such activities. J. Harich in *HJB* II, 24 (43).

Hoffmann, Herr: reader of roles in the Marionette Theatre 1776–78 (Gotha *Theater-Kalender*). Landon in *HJB* I, 120.

Langenfeld, Dr Johann Nepomuk: playwright, princely librarian and Regisseur at the Marionette Theatre in the 1780s. J. Harich in *HJB* II, 22f. (42).

Leeb, Paul: 'Maschinist' at the Opera and Marionette Theatres. First attached to Goussard as an assistant in 1778, from 1780 Leeb was Goussard's successor. J. Harich in *HJB* II, 23 (42).

Mauer, Mademoiselle: reader of roles in the Marionette Theatre 1776–8 (Gotha *Theater-Kalender*). Landon in *HJB* I, 120.

Mayr, Johann: master-tailor at Eszterháza in the 1770s and 1780s. In one of his bills he notes that he is to appear with his apprentices in the theatre before the performances, so that 'the costumes can be organized during the performances, to distribute the costumes previously to the singers, to fit them, and the day afterwards to put them in order'. For this service he received half-a-gulden, but was required to appear when necessary with his two apprentices. J. Harich in *HJB* II, 24 (43).

Noethen, Johann Peter: librarian (from 1780) and assistant at the Marionette Theatre. J. Harich in *HJB* II, 22 (42).

Ochs. Charlotte: reader of roles in the Marionette Theatre 1776–8 (Gotha *Theater-Kalender*). Landon in *HJB* I, 120.

Pauersbach, Karl Michael von: Director of the Marionette Theatre and playwright, 1773–78. Pauersbach was a rather successful author for the

stage in Vienna prior to coming to Hungary. We know of *Die indianische Witwe* (1772), *Die zwo Königinnen* (1773) – played at Eszterháza on 31 August 1773 –, *Schach Hussein* (1773) and *Der redliche Bauer und großmüthige Jude* (1774). Pauersbach was an official (Secretary) at the Lower Austrian *Landrecht* in Vienna, and thus a colleague of the composer Carlos d'Ordoñez, who suceeded Pauersbach as 'Secretary'. On 23 July 1772, Pauersbach sold Prince Nicolaus a 'Marionetten-Theater'[1] for 300 ducats (1,270 gulden), and in 1773 more-or-less regular performances of that theatre began at Eszterháza. In 1773–4, Pauersbach was only part-time in Hungary, for when his and Ordoñez's opera *Alceste* was given at the princely Marionette Theatre in August 1775, the libretto still lists him as 'Kais.-Kön. Nieder Oesterr.. Land-Rechts-Titular-Secretario'. He seems to have began running the Marionette Theatre as a full-time operation in 1776. In 1777, the Marionette Theatre gave guest appearances at Schönbrunn. That year, Pauersbach met Maria Anna Tauber (q.v.), who was singing at Eszterháza, and the two fell in love and married the next year. In March of 1778 Fräulein Tauber appeared as soprano soloist in Joseph Starzer's Oratorio, *La Passione del Redentore* (libretto: Metastasio), performed on the 23 March and 27 March at the Tonkünstler-Societät in the Burgtheater; there she was heard by Emperor Joseph II, who suggested that she be given a trial part in the opera *Lucile* by Grétry. 'I have heard a certain Tauber from Eszterház sing', he said to his Regisseur Müller; 'she has a good voice and something can come of her. Here's a little opera for you; have her study it at once and give Tauber the role of Lucile.' On 29 June, Maria Anna sang the part but was not a success; it was taken away from her and given to Marianne Lange, the first wife of the actor Joseph Lange who later (1780) married Aloysia Weber, Mozart's first love.

Meanwhile Pauersbach was producing his last works for Eszterháza, concluding on 15 September with a revival of Haydn's *Dido*; after that nothing was given at the Marionette Theatre during the rest of the year. Horányi thinks that his wife's failure at the Vienna opera contributed to his decision to leave Eszterháza and go to Russia at the end of the current year (1778). He kept in touch with Prince Esterházy, writing him congratulatory letters on his name-day, or New Year's greetings; after 1784 he was at Regensburg, before that his letters are from Nuremberg, whence he had gone two years earlier. In a letter of 8 October 1784, he offers the Prince a new German translation of *Orpheus*. In his last letter, of 27 February 1789, he mentions that he is again plagued by the illness he had contracted at Eszterháza sixteen years earlier (1773) – probably rheumatism –, and under his doctor's orders he asks Prince Nicolaus to send him some 'guten alten Ungarwein'. In all these letters, we sense a certain nostalgia for the years Pauersbach spent at Eszterháza. Pohl II, 9, 19. Acta Teatralica 4, 10 (Esterházy Archives, Budapest).

1 I.e. the stage, puppets, some costumes, scenery, etc.

Horányi III, 114. Gotha *Theater-Kalender* 1777–8 (details of Pauersbach's activities at Eszterháza, including his reading the roles in the Marionette Theatre). Landon in *HJB* I, 118–22. Klaus M. Pollheimer, 'Karl Michael (Joseph) von Pauersbach (1737–1802). Das Leben und Werk des Begründers und Direktors des Marionettentheaters in Eszterháza', *Beiträge zur Theatergeschichte des 18. Jahrhunderts*, Eisenstadt 1973, pp. 34–78.

Porta (Portha), Nunziato (Nunciato): 'Directeur deren Opern zugleich Aufseher üher die Theater Garderobe'. Engaged on 17 July 1781 (beginning 16 July) at 150 gulden, 24 lb. of candles and three fathom cords of wood. This was an extremely modest salary for a position of such responsibility, and it is no wonder that Porta supplemented his meagre fee by a large amount of music copying. His musical handwriting has been identified by Bartha-Somfai. He also fashioned a number of libretti, including Haydn's *Orlando Paladino* – certainly the most successful Haydn opera during its composer's lifetime. Porta remained with the company until its dissolution at the end of September 1790. *HJB* VII, 119 (contract). Horányi 140. Bartha-Somfai *passim*. ECP item 1338 (engagement).

Rauffer, Franz: director of the Marionette Theatre, October 1774–8 (?). Exactly how the division of labour between 'Director' Pauersbach and 'Director' Rauffer was effected is not made clear by the documents; probably Pauersbach had the overall artistic direction and Rauffer actually ran some of the productions, especially when Pauersbach was absent (as seems to have been the case, for example, for large parts of 1774 and the first part of 1775). Landon in *HJB* II, 116. Pollheimer, 39f.

Rhode (Rodhe, Rohde), Friedrich: Chamber Painter and assistant to Grundmann. Rhode assisted in the scenery of both theatres, when required. J. Harich in *HJB* II, 15 (40).

Schellinger, Johann: Prompter and Theatrical Copyist. Engaged 'vermög Hoch Fürstl[er] Resolution dd° 5ten 8[bris] [Octobris] 780' at 300 gulden, 24 lb. of candles, three fathom cords of wood and free lodgings at Eszterháza. Later, no doubt because of the fact that all his copying was paid separately, a princely resolution decided that 'he must be paid according to the old fashion, that is at 10 fl. monthly', which meant 120 gulden *per annum*. On 9 February 1790 (effective 1 Feb.) he was given an increase of two gulden per month. Schellinger's gigantic copying activity was first revealed to the scholarly world in Bartha-Somfai. In 1786, Schellinger copied 1,749 *Bögen* (one *Bogen* = four pages) of vocal parts at seven Kreuzer per *Bogen* and 1,817 *Bögen* of instrumental parts at five Kreuzer per *Bogen*: a staggering total of 14,264 pages. Haydn countersigned this incredible bill on 29 December 1786. Schellinger

stayed until the end of September 1790. Afterwards we find him in Vienna, copying for Haydn (see *Haydn in England 1791–1795*, p. 487). *HJB* VII, 105, 119 (documents). Bartha-Somfai 136f. and *passim*.

Sicca (Sicka), Herr: 'Figurendirector' (means in charge of the puppets) in the Marionette Theatre 1776–8. Also read roles there. Gotha *Theater-Kalender* 1777–78. Landon in *HJB* I, 119f.

Travaglia, Pietro: Chief Designer for costumes and Scenery at the Opera. Also designed for the Marionette Theatre. Engaged on 1 August 1777 and pensioned in 1798. A pupil of the brothers Bernadino and Fabrizio Galliari in Milan, Travaglia was a gifted stage and costume designer. After the Second World War, his sketch-books, including some signed costumes and sets for Haydn operas, were discovered in Budapest and first published, many in colour, by Horányi – to the astonishment and delight of the theatrical world (see pls. 21–23). Being trained to economise by Prince Nicolaus (who saved in small things that which he spent on the large), Travaglia often used a piece of scenery, or a costume, more than once. With certain modifications, the scenery of Sarti's *Didone abbandonata* (1784) was to be used, together with that for Zingarelli's *Montezuma* (1785), for Zingarelli's *Alsinda* (1786): 'Servirà la decorazione fatta per la Didone però con ricangiamento' (Acta Musicalia 3997). No doubt this made it occasionally difficult when an opera was to be revived; perhaps the scenery had already been transmuted out of existence. Travaglia was also responsible for the lighting. From Horányi we learn that lead-lined alcohol lamps were used for stage illumination (Travaglia sent in bills for 'Spiritus'), and that flash-powder ('Plitz Pulver') was used for lightning and fire (the 'Plitz Pulver' was ordered from the princely pharmacy at Eszterháza). Such effects as the destruction of Carthage and the siege of Gibraltar required vast amounts of 'Plitz Pulver' and 'Schieß Pulver' (gunpowder). Travaglia also supervised the illumination of Eszterháza Castle and the garden. This was accomplished by thousands of jars filled with tallow. For one such illumination, on 12 September 1784 (q.v.), 4,268 tallow lamps were required, of which 2,600 had to be refilled, which latter operation required seven hundred-weight of black tallow. Some idea of the splendour of such tallow-lamp illumination is provided, in our sober age, by the illuminations of the city of Florence and in particular the Cathedral, which is illuminated to the top of its dome with tallow lamps of this kind.

After Eszterháza had, to all intents and purposes, closed down, Travaglia received one position of great honour. He was chosen, with one other designer (who did the fourth), to fashion three sets[1] of Mozart's *La clemenza di Tito* for the coronation ceremonies of Leopold II at Prague in 1791. It was a

---

1 'Le tre prime Decorazioni sono d'invenzione del Sig. Pietro Travaglia, all'attual servizio di S. A. il Principe Esterhazi.'

67

fitting end to a great deal of work quietly and (as we can now see from the rediscovered sketchbooks) excellently accomplished at Eszterháza Castle. J. Harich in *HJB* II, 23. Landon in *HJB* I, 119. Horányi 147–52 and reproductions of Travaglia's sketches *passim*. O. E. Deutsch, *Mozart und seine Welt in zeitgenössischen Bildern*, Kassel 1961, p. 246. Bartha-Somfai 15, 21, 78, 92, 101f., 109f., 115, 117f., 120–2, 126, 131, 133, 136, 144, 147, 157f.

SOME THEATRICAL PROCEDURES

Once it was decided to procure an opera for performance at Eszterháza, there arose the question of casting it with the available forces. We shall see that Haydn sometimes had to omit whole groups of instruments, e.g. the clarinet and trumpet parts, for which he had only occasionally (*vide infra*) the necessary players. The same kind of thing also happened with roles in the operas. When Traetta's *Ifigenia in Tauride* was procured – it was performed in the busy 1786 season – someone made the following note on the score: 'Questa opera così accorciata si può fare con una donna e tre omini, ed anche levando quello che è coperto si può fare con due donne e tre omini.' In fact the original role of 'Dori', as sung in the première of that opera in Vienna (1763), was simply omitted at Eszterháza, where in 1786 Haydn had only six male and five female singers at his disposal. There was also no Italian chorus, and such parts had to be divided among the soloists. There were enough singers to form a German-speaking chorus from among the local personnel, and this explains why it was possible for Haydn to write so many German choruses in his marionette operas.

In the usual bureaucratic fashion of the Esterházy establishment, a plan now had to be submitted for the detailed casting of each opera, and in many cases this so-called 'Piano dimostrativo' was prepared by Haydn himself and survives in the massive material of the Esterházy Archives (either Budapest, Eisenstadt or Forchtenstein). A sample specimen for two operas of the 1783 season may suffice.

Il Ratto della Sposa   di Guglielmi

Aurora. Sorella di Gaudenzio, e cameriera. — 1ma parte		Specioli.
Donna Ortenza. gentildonna ricca — — — 2da parte		Valdesturla.
Dorina. ostessa di compagna — — — — 3^{za} parte		Mariuccia.
Gentilino. giovane affettato — 1mo mezzo carattera		Specioli.
Gaudenzio. Maggiordomo — — — 1mo Basso[1]		Moratti.
Polidoro. Vecchio avaro — — — — — —		Negri.
Biondino. Giovane prodigo — — — — — — —		Dichtler.

La Vedova Scaltra

Rosaura. Vedova. 1ma parte — — — — — — —		Metilde.
Marionetta 2da parte — — — — — —		Valdesturla.
Monsieur le Blan ⎱ Specioli. Braghetti Il Conte Italiano ⎰		
Don Alvaro. Spagnuolo — — — — — — —		Negri.
Pasquino. — — — — — — — — —		Moratti.
Runebif. — — — — — — — — —		Dichtler.

Le gelosie villane[2]

Giulio Sabino Opera Seria[3]

1 Moratti was more a tenor than a bass; Haydn wrote for him in the tenor clef. We see here how Haydn was forced to apportion the roles as best he could.

2 Sarti's opera, revived at Eszterháza in 1784.   3 Sarti's opera, performed at Eszterháza in 1783.

A similar plan for the costumes was drawn up, usually by Nunziato Porta, and astonishing as it appears, it was in the last analysis the Prince himself who made the ultimate decisions: less, perhaps, about the actual costumes – this was a more purely theatrical operation – but certainly with regard to the singers. The question of adapting the operas musically to the exigencies of Eszterháza remained Haydn's province, and all the drastic cuts, elimination of repeated sections and coloratura, tempo changes and, above all, the many additions (Haydn's 'insertion' arias and those by other composers), belonged to the exclusive duties of the *Capellmeister*. It is doubtful if Esterházy was informed about the 'insertion' arias in every case, and certainly not for all those lovingly written for Haydn's mistress Polzelli. Prince Nicolaus certainly approved of Haydn's taste, and the adaptation of these Italian operas 'nell gusto d'Eszterháza' (which meant, *au fond*, 'nell gusto del Signor Haydn'), must have met with the Prince's tacit approval. It is in fact astonishing how little Haydn and the Prince allowed themselves to be influenced by 'outside' sources. Dr Harich makes the good point, in connection with Benedetto Bianchi's repertoire at the Teatro S. Samuele in Venice in 1781–2, that none of these operas was performed when Bianchi returned to Eszterháza in 1784: 'proof how little Prince Nicolaus and Haydn, too, allowed themselves to be influenced by the singers, who of course preferred to sing roles they had studied.'[1]

Another interesting point is the effect of the dreadful, foggy climate on the Italian voices. It will have been observed that many of these singers did not serve at Eszterháza in one uninterrupted sojourn but returned to Italy for a longer or shorter interval, e.g. Bianchi, the Jermolis, Moratti and Ripamonti. Haydn later observed, obviously with some astonishment, that exhausting though the Hungarian climate proved to be for those singers, when they returned from Italy again, their voices had recovered their freshness and bloom.[2]

It is perhaps rather surprising to us to see the large amount of music that these singers had to learn by heart each year – many more roles than they are expected to master in today's repertoire (which is largely static, i.e. historical). Part of this ability to learn so many new parts each season derived from the 'buona scuola italiana', which gave them solid grounding in harmony, counterpoint and technique. Part was the quiet isolation of Eszterháza, where there were hardly any distractions and where the evenings' entertainments were self-provided (unless the singers were given a day off, in which case they could hear German-speaking prose theatre, something which hardly appealed to them). As it happens, we have some documentary evidence that tells us how long a singer needed – on average, of course – to learn a given role. In 1784, Haydn assigned to his singers a new opera, Cimarosa's *L'amor costante*. On the manuscript folder of the recitatives for the role of the 'Marchese', Haydn wrote the name of the singer, 'Sig^r Negri' (Domenico Negri) who, in turn, added the note 'Ricevuta il giorno cinque Aprile 1784'. This meant that Negri had exactly three weeks in which to commit to memory the part of 'Il Marchese di Fiumesecco, uomo ambizioso, e ridicolo' before the première, on 27 April, at Eszterháza. No doubt some

1 Bartha-Somfai 49, 106–8, 308. Harich 1959, p. 35 (Haydn's 'Piano dimostrativo' – not in this particular case his title – in autograph [Esterházy Archives, Eisenstadt] reproduced in facsimile). Harich in *HJB* VII, 24.
2 Griesinger 61. See also *Haydn in England 1791–1795*, p. 334; these singers often let Haydn know that they were doing him a special favour by singing so accurately all his complicated enharmonic modulations, which they had hardly encountered in the, harmonically, rather primitive music of their countrymen.

roles were prepared more quickly, some more slowly, but three weeks was no doubt considered a normal span of time to learn a part by heart.[1]

(c) The Orchestra at Eisenstadt and Eszterháza (1766–90)
There follows a list of the orchestral players who were engaged at any time during this period, with notes on their salaries, their compositions (listed only in general) if they were also composers, and other information that might be considered useful.

Bertoja, Valentino (Valentin): violoncellist. Engaged 18 November 1780. Salary: 100 ducats (430 gulden). *Deputat (Naturalien)*: 24 lb. candles, 3 fathom cords of wood, uniform each year. Contract: two years. At end of period, increase of 50 gulden. Left at end of January 1788. Later, appears to have been in Venice about the year 1800, where he and his brother (also 'cellist) were highly regarded. J. Harich in *HJB* VIII, 24 (with documents), (62). ECP 1305, 1368.

Blaschek (Blascheck; Plaschek), Joseph violinist. Engaged 1 September 1770. Salary: 300 gulden. *Deputat (Naturalien)*: 24 lb. of candles, 3 fathom cords of wood, uniform each year. Contract: two years. Left at end of August 1772. *HJB* VII, 66. ECP 708.

Burgsteiner – *vide* Purksteiner.

Chiesa, Natale: horn player. Engaged 1 August 1782. Salary: 350 gulden. *Deputat (Naturalien)*: 24 lb. of candles, 3 fathom cords of wood, uniform each year. Contract: two years. Left at end of February 1787. *HJB* VII, 117. ECP 1372 (horn players Chiesa and Hörmann engaged). Bartha-Somfai 173.

Chorus, Carl (Carolus, Karl, Clarus): oboist (first). Engaged 15 July 1771. Salary: 240 gulden. 'Free lodging with his family in the Old Apothecary or 30 fl. instead'. Winter: wood and light as provided for the unmarried musicians. Contract: two years. Later his salary was raised to include 343 fl. 20 kr. and the usual uniform. Left 5 May 1776. Chorus was ill in 1774, and Prince Esterházy paid for his cure in Baden. *HJB* IV, 97; VII, 68, 93. PCDI 747, 1036.

Colombazzo (Columbazzo), Vittorino (Victorinus, Victorino; also, very strangely, listed in another later document as 'Franz'; can there have been two Colombazzo oboe players, perhaps brothers?). Engaged 1 September 1768. Salary: 400 gulden. *Deputat (Naturalien)*: 20 fl. lodging money, 20 lb. of candles, 3 fathom cords of wood. Contract: ? Left at end of December 1768. *HJB* 69. PCDI 762. J. Harich in *HJB* VIII, 27f. As *Franz* Columbazzo, oboist. Engaged 12 October 1779.

Salary: 343 f. 25 kr., 24 lb. of candles, 3 fathom cords of wood and a uniform. Contract: one year(?). On 15 March 1780 he was dismissed and given half-a-year's salary; in the dismissal document (*HJB* VII, 133) he is spelled once again 'Colombazzo'. Vittorino, at any rate, was oboist in the service of the Duke of Württemberg in 1767, before he came to Eisenstadt. Afterwards, he appeared many times in Vienna as a soloist, also together with his (previous or later) colleagues Franz Stamitz (horn) and Guglielmo Jermoli. And if Franz is really a misspelling for Vittorino, he was (after he left Eszterháza the second time) in the service of Prince Thurn und Taxis in Regensburg. *HJB* VII, 93 ('Franz Columbazzo'), ECP 1248 ('Franz Columbazzo'). *HJB* VII, 28. Pohl II, 120, 135, 143. J. Harich in *HJB* VIII, 27f. (63).

Czervenka (Cervenka, Cservenkà, Czerwenka), Franz: bassoon and 'orchestral violinist' ('Orgester Geiger'). Engaged 1 April 1783. Salary: 500 gulden. *Deputat (Naturalien)*: 24 lb. of candles, 6 fathom cords of wood. Contract: ? Left at end of September 1790. *HJB* VII, 116. ECP 1395.

Czervenka (Cervenka, Cservenkà, etc.), Joseph: oboist. N.B. In the final pay form for the musicians at Eszterháza (1790), the signature is [copyist: Hautboista Fr. Cservenka] [autograph signature:] Fr. Cervenka. Perhaps these were brothers or cousins, and their identity confused on the Conventionale 1789, Prot.-Nr. 4709, 4710 (*HJB* VII, 107–25 *in extenso*), which is, however, the more odd since they were engaged at separate times. *HJB* 115f., ECP 1431 both list 'Joseph Cservenka', oboist. Engaged on 22 March 1784 retroactively from 1 Jan. (unusual for an orchestral player, not so unusual for a singer, as we have seen). Salary: 500 gulden. *Deputat (Naturalien)*: 24 lb. of candles, 3 fathom cords of wood and a uniform each year. Contract: ?. Left at end of September 1790. See also Somfai, plate 199 (facsimile of pay form, 1790).

Dietzl, Johann: double-bass player and violinist. Engaged 15 March 1775 for Eisenstadt princely church choir, to perform his duties 'when the Chamber Music is away for the summer' and to receive 30 gulden *per annum*. Engaged as part of the

---

1 Bartha-Somfai 283. On the other hand, there is the following note on the score of Cimarosa's *La ballerina amante*:'aus getheilt . . . 16 10bris [December] 785'. The operas was performed at Eszterháza on 2 April 1786, which meant that the singers and copyists had three-and-a-half months in which to prepare it. Perhaps the extremely busy season of 1786 was made more tolerable by distributing the parts well in advance; at least that is what happened in the case of *La ballerina amante*.

main body of musicians: 1 September 1775. Salary: 200 gulden, *Deputat* (*Naturalien*): free lodging in the Old Apothecary, 24 lb. of candles, 6 fathom cords of wood. Contract: ? Increase of 80 gulden *per annum* effective 1 January 1779; another of 25 gulden *per annum* effective 1 Nov. 1789. Remained in princely service, with an interval in the 1790s, until his death (Eisenstadt, 1806). Haydn thought very highly of Dietzl's abilities. *HJB* 85, 95, 114 & PCDI 1038 & ECP 1227 (documents). J. Harich in *HJB* VIII, 25f. (62). CCLN 224 (*Haydn: the Late Years 1801–1809*, pp. 262, 273).

Dietzl, Joseph Wolfgang Jr.: horn player (and later violinist). Engaged 15 May 1765. Salary: 15 gulden per month (as an apprentice) and 17 Kreuzer daily when he played with the 'Banda' at the change of guards. After various increases he was officially engaged on 19 July 1772 at 240 gulden *per annum*. Increases: 1769 (total: 300 gulden counting lodging money), 1773 (343 fl. 25 kr., 35 gulden lodging money). *Deputat* (*Naturalien*): 24 lb. of candles, 6 fathom cords of wood. Contract (see above). Left at end of September 1790 but was retained in Eisenstadt, as a violinist, in the princely church choir. In 1779, because of a complicated reorganization of the many horn players in the Esterházy *Capelle*, Dietzl's salary was reduced to 300 gulden *per annum* (the other 'top' horn players received 462 fl. 30 kr.), and his many appeals to the Prince for an increase fell on deaf ears.[1] *HJB* 70, 87, 117 (documents). ECP 1234 (Rahier on 19 March 1779, 'Musico' Joseph Diezl is given 35 f. 'wegen Quartier' as an increase in his annual salary). J. Harich in *HJB* VIII, 34f. (65f.). Dietzl was also a modest composer: one Symphony in F is in the Esterházy Archives, Budapest. *HJB* IV, 19 (33).

Drobn(e)y (Drobnay), Ignatz (Ignatius): bassoon player. Engaged 1 January 1776. Salary: 500 gulden (ECP: 41 fl. 40 kr. monthly). *Deputat* (*Naturalien*): 35 gulden lodging money, 24 lb. candles, 6 fathom cords of wood, one annual uniform. Contract: ? Dismissed 15 April 1778. *HJB* VII, 97. PCDI 1094 (Vienna 29 Dec. 1775 re 'Drobnay' and the two clarinet players Griesbacher). The 1789 *Schematismus* lists him as a member of the *Hofkapelle* in Vienna, living 'in der Josephstadt 3' (p. 400).

Eckardt (Ekhart), Anton (Antonius): horn player. Engaged 1 October 1780. Salary: 300 gulden. *Deputat* (*Naturalien*): free lodging in

musicians' quarters in Eszterháza, 24 lb. of candles, 3 fathom cords of wood and one uniform each year. Contract: ? Left, with his wife (Teresa Tavecchia, q.v.), at the end of July 1781. *HJB* VII, 104. J. Harich in *HJB* VIII, 33f. (65). Landon 'Haydns Oper' (op. cit., p. 215).

Ernst, Michael: violinist. *Vide* 'Singers, Male' (*supra*, p. 57).

Franz (Frantz), Carl (Carolus): horn player, violinist and baryton player. Engaged 9 April 1763. Salary: 300 gulden. *Deputat* (*Naturalien*): lodging money 30 fl., 30 lb. of candles, 6 fathom cords of wood. Contracts: ? Left at the end of November 1776. Franz went to the *Capelle* of Cardinal Batthyány in Pressburg, leaving there in 1784 and making concert tours. In 1787, he settled in Munich, where he died in 1802. Haydn composed for him the Cantata 'Deutschlands Klage auf den Tod Friedrich des Großen' which Franz performed at Nuremberg in 1788, singing and accompanying himself on the baryton. *Vide infra*, p. 645. Franz must have been a brilliant horn player. We read, in a contemporary criticism, that 'as concerns the execution of chromatic scales by means of [stopping with] the hand, as well as facility in the high and low ranges ... and purity of intonation, scarcely any artist was found in those days who would have come close to him' (Gerber *Lexicon*, p. 439; Paul Bryan in *HJB* IX, 218 and *Haydn-Studien* III/1 [1973], pp. 52f.) Franz was ill for a long period in 1774 and was sent for a lengthy cure at the Prince's expense. *HJB* IV, 98 (cure). *HJB* VII, 69, 86 (salary). Franz appears to have resigned in November 1769 (*vide infra*, p. 160), but it seems that, as usual, the tactful Haydn persuaded him to remain.

Fuchs (Fux), Johann: violinist. Engaged 1 August 1788. Salary: 300 gulden. *Deputat* (*Naturalien*): 24 lb. of candles, 3 fathom cords of wood and a uniform each year. Contract: ? Left at end of September 1790. *HJB* VII, 113. *Index*, item 2 (engagement).

Fuchs, Johann Georg: schoolmaster and organist as well as tenor. Engaged: 17 November 1777. Salary: 62 gulden. *Deputat* (*Naturalien*): Tuning instruments ('Für das Geflügl') 2 fl. 30 kr., 4 *Metzen* of wheat, 8 of rye, $\frac{1}{4}$ each of lentils, barley and millet-pap, 300 lb. of beef, 24 lb. of lard, 24 lb. of candles, 9 *Eimer* of wine, $\frac{1}{2}$ *Eimer* of cabbage and turnips and 6 fathom cords of wood. Contract: from 5 December 1778, when he became organist at Eisenstadt, he earned another annual 50 gulden. Remained in this triple capacity until his death in 1810. Before coming to Eisenstadt, Fuchs had been organist and schoolmaster at the Servite Monastery in Forchtenau near Forchtenstein. *HJB* VII, 81, 119 (contracts). ECP 1157 (Esterhaz, 17 Nov. 1777: engagement), 1237 (organist engagement: Dec. 1778). *HJB* IV, 17 (33) *re* Fuchs' attempt to secure the organist's position in 1773 (refused). In 1777 he was engaged as tenor, but

---

1 'Most Well Born/Highly Respected Herr v. Rahier! As to the supplication of the musician Dieczl [*sic*] in Eisenstadt which has reached me, and in which he asks for a *Deputat* and lodging money, you may intimate to him that if he is not satisfied with his present salary, he may seek his fortune elsewhere. About his place of lodging, however, if he decides to continue in our service, you can give it to him somehow *in natura*. I remain &c. ... /Eszterhaz, 8 March 1779./Your willing/Nicolaus Fürst Esterhazy.' Acta Musicalia No. 4358 (Esterházy Archives, Budapest). *HJB* VII, 144.

after 1780 his principal occupation was that of Eisenstadt Castle Organist. J. Harich in *HJB* VII, 44 (69).

Fux (Fuchs), Peter: violinist. Engaged 1 January 1781. Salary: 400 gulden. *Deputat (Naturalien)*: one uniform each year. Contract: ? Left at end of November 1782. *HJB* VII, 106 (contract). ECP 1314. Born 22 January 1753. (1789 *Schematismus*) he lived in Vienna in the Naglergaße 185 and was in the *Hofkapelle*, listed as a second violinist; in 1797 he lived 'am Stock im Eisen 663'. *NA*. The *Jahrbuch* of 1796 (p. 17) calls him 'an excellent concert violinist. His bowing is strong and pleasant... He has had fine pupils...'.

Garnier (Guarnier), Franz (Franciscus: Frantz): violinist. Engaged May 1761. Salary: 240 gulden. *Deputat (Naturalien)*: ? Contract: ? Dismissed February 1766. Afterwards he was located, in 1778, as 'Musicien de la Comédie de la Ville de Lion [Lyon]'. Valkó I, 634, 641 (documents). Valkó II, 541 (dismissal). *HJB* IV, 15 (32), 42 (documents). See also *infra*, p. 118.

Griessbacher (Griesbacher, Griesbach), Anton: clarinet player. *Deputat (Naturalien)*: 30 fl. lodging money, 24 lb. of candles, 3 fathom cords of wood and a yearly uniform. Dismissed at end of February 1778. *HJB* VII, 98 (contract). PCDI 1094 (Vienna 29 Dec. 1775 *re* 'Drobnay', bassoon player, and the two 'Griesbach's', 'Clarinetisten', who each earned 25 fl. monthly). Later he was second clarinet in the Schikaneder Theatre in Vienna (*Jahrbuch*... 1796, p. 96). He also gave at least one concert in Prague (*Miscellanea Musicologica* VI, Svazek, Prague 1958, p. 45).

Griessbacher (Griesbacher, Griesbach), Raymund (Raymond): clarinet player. Engaged 1 January 1776. Salary: 300 gulden. *Deputat (Naturalien)*: 30 fl. lodging money, 24 lb. of candles, 3 fathom cords of wood and a yearly uniform. The following clause added to each of the Griessbacher's contracts: 'Or, according to high option, free lodging, wood and light'. Contract: two years. Dismissed at end of February 1778. *HJB* VIII, 97 (contract). PCDI 1094 (*vide supra*). Raymund was later a woodwind instrument-maker in Vienna and (*Jahrbuch*... 1796, p. 19) 'Direktor bei der Fürst. Graßalkowitzischen Harmonie, an excellent concert player who performs on the clarinet with the greatest delicacy and purity.' He died on 21 February 1818. Helga Haupt, 'Wiener Instrumentenbauer von 1791–1815' in *Studien zur Musikwissenschaft*, Band 24, Graz 1960, p. 140.

Grisi (Prisi), Attilio (Attilo): violinist. Engaged: 1 September 1786. Salary: 400 gulden *Deputat (Naturalien)*: 24 lb. of candles, 3 fathom cords of wood and a uniform each year. Contract: ? Left at end of September 1790. *HJB* VII, 112 (contract). ECP 1565 (Esterhaz, 10 Sept. 1786, 'Attilo Prisi' engaged).

Heger, Johann Georg: violinist. Engaged May 1761. Salary: 12 fl. 30 kr. monthly but later (decree of 5 July 1762) raised to 200 fl. *per annum*. Contract: ? Left at end of 1766. *HJB* IV, 42, 81. Valkó I, 634, 641.

Hinterberger, Johann (Johannes, Johan): bassoon player. Engaged May 1761. Salary: 240 gulden. *Deputat (Naturalien)*: (last state) 35 fl. lodging money, 24 lb. of candles, 6 fathom cords of wood and a uniform each year. Contract: ? Left: pensioned 1 January 1779. *HJB* IV, 42, 96 (doc.); ECP 1225 (pension); *HJB* VII, 69, 85, 93f. (doc.). J. Harich in *HJB* IV, 22 (35). Hinterberger received an increase of 50 fl. just before he was pensioned, so that his full salary reached 343 fl. 25 kr. and enabled him to have a pension of 250 gulden which was granted him by a special act of dispensation on the part of Nicolaus; Hinterberger was growing deaf. (In Bartha-Somfai 'Hirtenberger', probably a misprint: p. 172.)

Hirsch, Leopold: violinist. Engaged 16 January 1786. Salary: 150 gulden (increased from 1 June 1788 by 50 gulden). *Deputat (Naturalien)*: 24 lb. of candles, 3 fathom cords of wood, a uniform each year. Contract: ? Left at end of September 1790. *HJB* VII, 112f. (contract). ECP 1549 (his engagement). Hirsch was the son of Zacharias (q.v.) and later (1797) lived in Vienna, as a first violinist, 'in der Josephstadt 21' (*NA*), and in 1796 was a member of the German Orchestra (*Jahrbuch*... 1796, p. 92) in the Opera.

Hirsch (Hiersch), Zacharias: flautist, violinist and apparently also oboist. Engaged 1 April 1776. Salary: 400 gulden. *Deputat (Naturalien)*: 35 fl. lodging money (later a free flat at Eszterháza), 24 lb. of candles, 6 fathom cords of wood and a uniform each year. Contract: ? Left at end of September 1790. Hirsch's principal instrument was the flute, but he is also listed on the pay sheets as oboist, and so frequently that an error seems unlikely. In one list of *c.* 1778–9 he is listed as 'Flautroversist / Hirsch zugleich auch Geiger' (*HJB* VIII, 120), and in the Forkel list (*HJB* IV, 26; also *infra*, p. 452) he appears as a violinist. The apparent mystery of one part in the Esterházy Archives' material of Anfossi's *La finta giardiniera* (1780), wherein the flute part is actually (physically) written in the first violin's part for the Aria (Sandrina) 'Geme la Tortorella Lungi' (Act II, Scene 10; Bartha-Somfai 232) is now easily explained: Hirsch started with the violin, switched to the flute ('Subito Flauto') for the Aria in question, and then moved back to the violin. Prince Nicolaus was godfather to one of the Hirsch children. *HJB* VII, 99 (contract). PCDI 1081 (engagement). J. Harich in *HJB* VIII, 27 (63) with documents. In 1797 (*NA*) Hirsch is listed at the same Viennese address as that of his son.

Hoffmann (Hofmann, Hoffman, etc.), Joseph: violinist. Engaged 1 September 1775. Salary 200 gulden (raised on 1 Jan. 1788 by 80 gulden).

Deputat (Naturalien): 24 lb. of candles, 3 fathom cords of wood and a uniform each year. Contract: ? Left at end of April 1787 to become a clerk on the accounts department of the Esterházy administration at Eisenstadt. After 1790 he also played part-time in the Eisenstadt princely church choir. *HJB* 84, 95f. PCDI 1052 (engagement). J. Harich in *HJB* VIII, 21 (60f.).

Hollerieder (Hollerrieder), Johann (Joannes): horn player (also violin and viola). Engaged 1 February 1776. Salary: 250 gulden. *Deputat (Naturalien)*: 30 fl. lodging money, 24 lb. of candles, 3 fathom cords of wood and a yearly uniform. Contract: ? Left at end of September 1780. In 1778, his salary was raised to 300 gulden, and Hollerieder asked permission to marry; this was refused and Hollerieder threatened with dismissal. He now asked permission to remain, which was granted 'only, however, as the Resolution of 22 December 1778 provides, if he does not marry and remains single, particularly since there are no quarters available for married couples'. In 1779, his salary was reduced to its original status of 250 gulden. In 1785, Hollerieder wanted to join the orchestra and mentioned that, apart from the horn, he also played violin and viola. The Prince refused the application, saying that the orchestra was now at full strength (which was true). *HJB* VII, 98 (contract). J. Harich in *HJB* VIII, 33 (65), with documents. Hollerieder was later second horn in the Marinelli Theatre in the Josephstadt (*Jahrbuch . . . 1796*: 'Johann Hollreder', p. 95), Vienna.

Hörmann (Horman, etc.), Johann (Joannes): horn player. Engaged 1 August 1782. Salary: 350 gulden. *Deputat (Naturalien)*: 24 lb. of candles, 3 (later 6) fathom cords of wood and a uniform each year and free lodging in the musicians' quarters. Contract: ? Left at end of June 1786. In a decree dated Esterhaz, 1 October 1782, 'Waldhornist Hörmann' is allowed to take his wife 'zu sich in das Music Gebäu' and to receive quarters and the wood *Deputat* for a married couple. ECP 1372 (contract), 1377 (new arrangements as married man). Bartha-Somfai 172f. Later in the Vienna *Hofkapelle* as second horn: Salieri called him the 'best horn player he had heard in Vienna' (Fitzpatrick, 200).

Kapfer, Johann Georg: oboist. Engaged 1 April 1761. Salary: 240 gulden, later raised to 343 fl. 25 kr. Contract: ? Left at beginning of 1769(?). He was second oboist in the *Capelle*.[1] *HJB* IV, 42. Valko I, 634, 641. Both Kapfers were later oboists in the Parish Church of Mariahilf in Vienna (1783: see O. Biba in *Beiträge zur Musikgeschichte des 18. Jahrhunderts*, Eisenstadt 1971, pp. 35f.). S. Gerlach in *Haydn-Studien* IV, (1976), p. 40.

Kapfer, Johann Michael: oboist. Engaged 1 April 1761. Salary: 240 gulden, later raised to 343 fl. 25 kr. Contract: ? Left at end of 1770(?). In 1773, he was in the service of the Bishop of Wiener Neustadt (*HJB* IV, 15). He was first oboist in the *Capelle. HJB* IV, 42. Valkó I, 634, 641.

Knoblauch, Johann: horn player. See *Haydn: the Early Years 1732–1765*.

Kraft, Anton: violoncellist. Engaged 6 January 1778. Salary: 100 ducats (423 fl. 20 kr.). *Deputat (Naturalien)*: 35 fl. lodging money, 24 lb. of candles, 6 fathom cords of wood and one uniform each year. Contract: ? Left at end of September 1790. Kraft was popular with Prince Nicolaus, who heard him in Vienna and engaged him at once. The Prince was godfather to Kraft's first child, Nicolaus, born in December 1778 and destined to be a great 'cellist himself, and also godfather to a girl born in April 1780; godmother was Prince Nicolaus's daughter, Maria Anna (marr. Grassalkovics). The same godparents appeared for the birth of the third child (May 1781), and Prince Nicolaus was also godfather for the next child (March 1783). For the fifth child (1785), Haydn and Luigi Tomasini's wife, Josepha, were godparents. Kraft, who later went to Vienna and played in the Grassalkovics orchestra, was also a composer; he wrote Trios for two barytons and 'cello, string Quartets and other works. In 1796 he joined the Lobkowitz *Capelle* and in 1802, Anton Kraft and his son Nicolaus intended to join the Esterházy orchestra, but their fees were too high. Prince Nicolaus II nevertheless gave him a yearly present of six *Eimer* 'officers' wine' from the princely cellars. Kraft died in 1820. Haydn wrote for this brilliant virtuoso the famous Concerto in D of 1783 (VIIb:2), which was for a time erroneously attributed to Kraft himself *HJB* VII, 115 (contract and salary increases). ECP 1174 (engagement and contract). In these documents he is referred to as 'Bassetlist' or 'Bassetlista'. J. Harich in *HJB* VIII, 22–4 (61f.), with documents.

Krumpholtz, Johann Baptist: harp player. Engaged 1 August 1773. Salary: 240 gulden (raised 5 fl. per month effective 1 August 1774). *Deputat (Naturalien)*; 30 fl. lodging money, 24 lb. of candles, 3 fathom cords of wood and one uniform each year. Contract: two years. Left at end of February 1776. *HJB* VII, 87 (contract). PCDI 996 (increase, 1774). It is one of the great mysteries of life at Eszterháza that there should be no harp compositions by Haydn for this famous virtuoso, and also none for his wife, with whom Haydn gave concerts for years while in England (see *Haydn in England 1791–1795, passim*). *Vide infra*, p. 188 (reward prior to contract).

Küffel (Khüffel), Ignaz (Ignatius): violoncellist. Engaged 'lauth Hochfürstl. Intimation dd° Eszterház den 18 7bris (Septembris) alljährlich à 1ª 7bris', i.e. effective retroactively from 1 September 1768 (PCDI, item 762, Eisenstadt 27 Oct. and

---

1 For Kapfer's lawsuit over the Will of Prince Paul Anton, *vide infra*, p. 79.

Esterhaz 18 Oct. 1768). Salary: 400 gulden. *Deputat (Naturalien)*: 20 gulden lodging money, 20 lb. of candles, 3 fathom cords of wood and a uniform each year. Left July(?) 1770 (Acta Musicalia 718). *HJB* VII, 67 (contract). Küffel had been in the Salzburg orchestra in 1767 and 1768 (*Mozart Briefe*; Kommentar I/II, p. 160).

Kühnel, Anton (Antonius): clerk in the Works Department (*Bauschreiber*) and double-bass player (*Violonist*) in the princely church choir at Eisenstadt. Engaged as *Bauschreiber* on 22 August 1758, served as musician part-time. Salary: 50 gulden as *Bauschreiber* and 50 gulden as 'violonist'. The various complicated situations, also regarding his double *Deputat*, which arose from his fulfilling two positions, may be seen in *HJB* VII, 53f., 72–5. Later (1771) he received 200 gulden and the *Deputat* only from the Works Department, *viz.*: 12 fl. lodging money 'Waitz 8, Korn 18, Linse, Gerst und Hirbrein [*sic*] jedes 3/8 Metzen, Fleisch 400, Salz 75, Schmalz 50, Kerzen 45 pf. Wein 12, Kraut u. Rüben jedes 1 Eimer, 1 Schwein, Brennholz 6 Klafter'. PCDI 436 (21 May 1761). By a princely 'Intimat' of 14 December 1768, Kühnel was relieved of his duties, and his salary, as a member of the 'Chor Music' (but his missing fee added to his other salary in the Works Department). Like his colleagues Nigst and Johann Haydn, he may have continued voluntarily as double-bass player.

Lendvay (Lendway), Gabriel: horn player. Engaged 1 March 1787 (in a 'Hoch Fürstlicher Intimat' of 17 Nov. 1787, one of the longest of the retroactive contracts; perhaps he was engaged 'on probation'). Salary: 350 gulden. *Deputat (Naturalien)*: 24 lb. of candles, 3 fathom cords of wood and a uniform each year. Contract: ? Left at the beginning of September 1790. *HJB* VII, 118 (contract). ECP 1629 (engagement). In 1800, Lendvay again joined the Esterházy orchestra at Eisenstadt (CCLN 178, see also *Haydn: the Years of 'The Creation' 1796–1800*, p. 567).

Lidl, Andreas: baryton player. Engaged 1 August 1769; new contract 17 January 1771. Salary: (1771) 300 gulden. *Deputat (Naturalien)*: 30 fl. lodging money or free flat, 6 fathom cords of wood and 'money for food *per diem* 30 Xr. Facit 182 f. 30 Xr.' *per annum*. Contract:? Left 15 May 1774. *HJB* VII, 67, 84 (contract). PCDI 660 (*in re* engagement of J. Oliva, F. Pauer, A. Lidl and Z. Pohl), 720 (new contract, with increase in salary). Schubart heard Lidl's 'sweet' baryton playing at Augsburg in 1776. In 1778, Lidl appeared in London, where he later died. He improved the baryton technically, increasing the number of strings below the bridge to 27, including half-notes (*Leben und Gesinnungen . . . Stuttgart* 1793, pp. 29, 122). Junker (*Musikalischer Almanach auf das Jahr 1782*, p. 30) describes Lidl's playing as 'Süsse Anmuth, mit deutscher Kraft verbunden, durch überraschende Bindungen mit der harmonie-vollsten Melodie'. Pohl II, 15ff.

Lindt, Carl: See *Haydn: the Early Years, 1732–1765*.

Makovecz (Makovec), Johann: horn player. Engaged 1 September 1781. Salary: 300 gulden. *Deputat (Naturalien)*: 24 lb. of candles, 3 fathom cords of wood and a yearly uniform. Contract:? Left at end of July 1782. ECP 1349 (Esterhaz, 7 Sept. 1781: engagement). Bartha-Somfai 172f.

Markl, Lorenz (Lorentz): trumpet player. Engaged with the other trumpet player Johann Peschko (q.v.) on 15 March 1780 'Laut Hoch Fürstl. Resolution dd° 16ᵗᵉⁿ Martÿ 780', effective 15 March. Salary: 343 gulden, 25 Kr. *Deputat (Naturalien)*: 24 lb. of candles, 3 fathom cords of wood and a uniform each year. Contract: one year. Dismissed at the end of December 1780 but their salary paid until 17 April 1781 in a lump sum. Two special trumpets were ordered for Markl and Peschko from Nuremberg and arrived on 12 June 1780, costing considerable sums of money in customs duties (both Austrian and Viennese). After leaving Eszterháza, these players went to Russia; 'they play double concertos and in every key' (Forkel, *Musikalischer Almanach* 1782, p. 110). *HJB* VII, 104 (contract). ECP 1264 (engagement). J. Harich in *HJB* VIII, 36f. (66), 145 (document about receipt of Nuremberg trumpets).

Marteau (Martau, Marton; *recte* Hammer), Xavier (Xaverius): violoncellist. Engaged March 1771. Salary 412 gulden, 30 kr.; increases by 50 fl. effective 1 Oct. 1772, and again by 50 fl., effective 1 March 1776. *Deputat (Naturalien)*: 30 gulden lodging money, 30 lb. of candles and 6 fathom cords of wood; later increased to 35 fl. lodging money, and with yearly uniform. Contract: 'at least one year'. Left at end of February 1778. *HJB* VII, 67, 84, 92; Valkó II, 552 (contracts, salary increases), PCDI 776 ('Wienn' 14 Jan. 1772), PCDI 784 (Vienna, 4 March 1772), PCDI 788 (Vienna, 1 March 1772: 'die Versprochene 50 Fl. Zulage Ihme abgesprochen', i.e. his salary increase cancelled), PCDI 817 (21 August 1772: letter from Prince Nicolaus confirming the 50 fl. increase after all), PCDI 1036 (Vienna, 19 March 1775, mentioning the wives of various musicians, including Marteau, and a 50 fl. allowance for separate households when the musicians were in Eszterháza), PCDI 1079 (Esterhaz, 12 March 1776: salary increase). Marteau went from Eszterháza to Pressburg, and we also hear of him in Prague, where he wanted to give a concert with his thirteen-year-old daughter. 'In October 1785 the 'cellist Hammer and his daughter were heard with delight in the Thun's residence' (*Miscellanea Musicologia* VI. Svazek, Prague 1958, p. 51). The very large salary which Marteau (Hammer) enjoyed under Prince Nicolaus suggests that he must have had exceptional abilities, while the raises show that he was appreciated at Eszterháza. Marteau also composed (*Preßburger Zeitung*, 24 Nov. 1779; *HJB* VIII, 179) and was much praised for his performance of his own 'cello concerto at Pressburg on 22 Nov. 1779.

May. Johann (Joannes): horn player. Engaged 1 March 1767. Salary: 300 gulden (27 fl. 30 kr. monthly). *Deputat* (*Naturalien*): as from 1 November 1772 he received 30 lb. of candles, 6 fathom cords of wood and (though it is not specifically mentioned) presumably a yearly uniform. Contract: ? Left at end of July 1774. *HJB* VII, 86 (contract). PCDI 573 (Esterhaz, 7 May 1767 concerning Franz 'Sigl', Johann May and Carl Schiringer, 'neuen aufgenohmene Musicorum', although this does not apply to Siegl, who had been engaged in 1761). PCDI 841 (Esterhaz, 1 Nov. 1772; May's wood and candles). It is interesting to see that it was not until 1772 that May's *Deputat* was considered; we cannot explain this curious fact, nor the absence of his uniform (which would seem to be an oversight in the documents).

Mayer (Mayr) Anton: oboist. Engaged 1 January 1781. Salary: 500 gulden. *Deputat* (*Naturalien*): one yearly uniform. Contract: ? Left at end of September 1790. *HJB* VII, 105 (contract). ECP 1314 ('Wienn', 6 Jan. 1781: engagement). Bartha-Somfai 174f.

Mentzl (Menzl). Franz (Frantz): violinist. Engaged 1 January 1781. Salary: 400 gulden. *Deputat* (*Naturalien*): one yearly uniform. Contract: ? Left at end of November 1782. *HJB* VII, 105 (contract). ECP 1314 ('Wienn', 6 Jan. 1781: engagement). Bartha-Somfai 174f.

Mestrino, Niccolò (Nicolò, known as 'Nicoletti', also in official documents): violinist. Engaged 18 November 1780. Salary: 100 ducats (430 gulden), raised by 50 gulden in November 1782 (three ducats per month withdrawn from salary and sent to Mestrino's wife in Venice). *Deputat* (*Naturalien*): one yearly uniform. Contract: two years. Left at end of January 1784. Born in Milan (1748), this talented violinist went from Eszterháza first to Pressburg, in the service of Count Ladislaus Erdödy, and then to Paris, where his eight violin concertos were published by Sieber and where he died in 1789. *HJB* VII, 105 (contract). ECP 1305 (engagement). J. Harich in *HJB* VIII, 21f. (61), with list of violin concertos on p. 49 (another work in the Burgenländisches Landesmuseum, Eisenstadt, a 'Duo facile et curieux pour deux Violons', is a musical puzzle; reproduced in *Burgenländische Heimatblätter* I/1 (1932), p. v.

Mraf (Mras, Mraw), Franz: violinist. Engaged 16 March 1784. Salary: ? *Deputat* (*Naturalien*): ? Contract: ? Died on 6 June 1786; his last salary was taken and signed by someone else. ECP 1430 (Esterhaz, 20 March 1784: engagement). Bartha-Somfai 174–6. Pohl (II, 18) states that Mraf was engaged by Count Kolowrat in Prague before he joined Haydn's band, and that – by implication – he did not die at Eszterháza but went on to the Batthyány *Capelle* in Pressburg and was, in 1792, with Prince Grassalkovics. Bartha-Somfai quote a

document in the Esterházy Archives in which it is clearly stated 'bis zum Tode dem 6. Junÿ' (176). We cannot explain this discrepancy, but suggest that there was another violinist of the same, or similar, name.

Nickl, Mathias: horn player. Engaged 1 July 1786. Salary: 400 gulden. *Deputat* (*Naturalien*): 24 lb. of candles, 3 fathom cords of wood (raised on 31 Oct. 1789 to 6 fathom cords) and a uniform each year. Contract: ? Left at end of September 1790. *HJB* VII, 118f. (contract). Index, 28 (additional wood). He was later in Vienna, playing the horn part of Beethoven's Quintet Op. 16 in the Tonkünstler-Societät concert of 2 April 1798: see *Haydn: the Years of 'The Creation' 1796–1800*, pp. 100, 316, 545.

Nigst, Franz (Franziscus): violinist. Engaged 1 June 1760. Salary: 50 gulden. This was a part time position; we read: 'The present Master of Rents, so that he will often frequent the princely choir and also make himself useful at the Tafel-Musique [and for the copying of music], receives annually …'. The bracketed portion appears in the *Conventionale* 1760, but is missing in the *Conventionale* 1769; in the latter we read: 'NB. Acc. to Hochfürstl. Intimat dd° Wienn den 10ten Xbris [Decembris] 768 he is removed [*abgethan*]'. Underneath: 'Has acc. to Hochfürstl. Com[missi]on dd° 28t Aug. 1771 annually 25 f.' As *Rentmeister* he received 200 gulden (raised on 1 January 1771 by 20 fl.) and a very large *Deputat* (details: *HJB* VII, 74). *HJB* VII, 51, 66 (contracts). After his 'removal' from the princely choir, he continued to perform there as a first violinist without fee. In August 1771, he was reinstated in the Castle Church Choir at 25 fl. annually (*vide infra*, pp. 83f.); he died at Eisenstadt on 29 October 1773 (*HJB* VII, 83).

Novotni (Novotny), Franz (Franciscus): *Accestista* and Organist. Engaged as *Accestista* 1 January 1763. Salary: 50 gulden. *Deputat* (*Naturalien*): for the details of the large *Deputat*, see *HJB* VII, 58f. Engaged as organist: 30 August 1765. As organist, Novotni received 100 gulden and a second *Deputat* (HJB VII, 65). Like all the positions in the princely Church Choir in Eisenstadt, Novotni's was regarded as a part-time affair, which accounts for his double salary and double employment (*Accestista* is a kind of bookkeeper or clerk). Contract: ? Died 25 August 1773; his position was then filled by Haydn in the winters and by the Castle Schoolmaster Joseph Dietzl in the summers; and later it was given to J. G. Fuchs (q.v.). *HJB* VII, 58, 65, 73, 82 (documents). PCDI 531 (Rahier's letter of 30 Aug. 1765 that Novotni is to receive his father's position as organist with the same salary; Novotni's father, Johann, died in 1765; see also *HJB* VII, 75). Of Novotni's many compositions for the church, one was later attributed to Mozart; see Landon: 'Mozart fälschlich zugeschriebene Messen', in *Mozart-Jahrbuch* 1957, pp. 90f.

Novotni (Novotny), Johann: *Cancellista* and organist. See *Haydn: The Early Years 1732–1765*.

Oliva (Olivo), Joseph (Josephus): horn player, also violinist. Engaged 1 June 1769. Salary: 100 ordinary ducats (417 fl. 30 kr.). *Deputat (Naturalien)*: free lodging or 30 fl. Contract: ? Left: after the *Capelle*'s dissolution in September 1790, Oliva and his companion Franz Pauer (q.v.) applied, in 1793, for positions in the Esterházy establishment. Oliva noted that 'he had served the high princely house as musician for 22 years, diligently and faithfully, but now, alas, he has been a full 3 years without bread and a position and must live in a most wretched fashion, although he is still a man in the prime of life who is capable of work.' The Prince hired both musicians as violinists in the Eisenstadt Church Choir; Oliva was pensioned on 1 May 1794 and died at Eisenstadt in 1806. As the Prince had done in similar cases, he purchased both the instruments (horns) of Oliva and Pauer for 24 ducats in November 1769 to help them financially. On 1 January 1773 Oliva and Pauer each received an increase of 50 gulden *per annum*. On 4 October 1773, a princely decree, 'from special grace (although they, Oliva and Pauer, receive firewood when they are in Vienna) for the previous period as well as the future 3 fathom cords of wood'. Later each received 35 fl. lodging money. The question of flats, with the musicians often living separated from their wives, also arose in Vienna (most of the wives lived at Eisenstadt); and Prince Nicolaus, to have the horn players at his disposal near his winter palace in the Wallnerstraße, obtained a flat for them in the nearby Naglergaße owned by one Juliana Nassatin (= Nassat or Nassati?) during the years 1770 and 1771. As will have been noticed, horn players received more money than violinists, which explains the large number of horn players on the Esterházy pay rolls; but Oliva and Pauer actually played violin in the opera orchestra and are listed on one such document of *c.* 1778–9 under the 'Waldhornisten' but with the proviso 'zugleich auch Geiger' (*HJB* VIII, 120). Forkel's list of 1783 lists both as violinists (*vide infra*, p. 452). Oliva was married and had numerous children, who served as 'supers' and dancers with the opera troupe, e.g. in Haydn's *La fedeltà premiata*. Prince Nicolaus was godfather at the baptism of one of them. In 1774, Oliva gave some 'illegal' concerts – breaking his contract of exclusivity with the Esterházy *Capelle* – and in a letter asked Prince Nicolaus to forgive him; it occurred 'only from bitter and sad necessity, to help my poor wife, who has been so long prostrated by sickness, and her poor five children ...'. He also requested permission to take his wife to Eszterháza, 'so that we could live better by having only one household' and failing that he asked for some kind of help in the situation. The letter is marked '1774. 6ª Aprilis rejecta' – which refers, no doubt, to the proposal to allow Frau Oliva to come to Eszterháza with all her children; this would have created a precedent that the Prince obviously wished to avoid. But the Prince gave Oliva 150 gulden for his sick wife. On 17

November 1777, Oliva was given a supplement of 30 *Metzen* of rye and 6¾ *Eimer* (Eisenstädter *Ham*; or nine *Eimer* 'Preßburger Maaß') of wine, 'in consideration of his many children and until his two sons may be able to earn their own bread, this without further precedence and from an especial act of princely grace ...'. Oliva and Pauer formed a horn team similar to the well-known pair of basset-horn players, David and Springer, who toured the Continent in the 1780s, played with Mozart in the *Masonic Funeral Music* (K. 477) of 1785 and in 1791 at Haydn's benefit concert in London. Oliva and Pauer had been engaged in Prague by Dittersdorf in 1764 for the orchestra in Großwardein (Oradea Mare). *HJB* VII, 70f., 86, 95, 117 and *HJB* VIII 138–41 (documents). PCDI 660 (Esterhaz, 3 Aug. 1769: engagement), 867 (Vienna, 27 Jan. 1773: increase), 1036 (Vienna, 19 March 1775: money for various wives of musicians, incl. Oliva). ECP 1155 (Esterhaz, 17 Nov. 1777: goods 'in consideration of *Waldhornisten* Oliva's two sons ...' etc.). In 1797, after Oliva had been pensioned, we find him listed in *NA* (1797) under the second violins, living in Vienna 'in der Josephstadt 38.'; in the *Jahrbuch* of 1796 (p. 94) he is listed among the second violins of the Orchestra in the German Theatre of the Court Opera. J. Harich in *HJB* VIII, 31f. (64f.) with documents. Oliva's son, Wenzel (Venzl; q.v.), was engaged by Prince Nicolaus.

Oliva, Wenzel (Venzl): violinist. Engaged 1 April 1789. Salary: 150 gulden. *Deputat (Naturalien)*: 24 lb. of candles, 3 fathom cords of wood and a yearly uniform. Contract: ? Left at end of September 1790. On 27 December 1780, Prince Nicolaus gave permission for Oliva and his two sons to undertake a concert tour. *HJB* VII, 113 (contract). J. Harich in *HJB* VIII, 32 (esp. notes 185/6 on p. 51). In the list of final payment for the musicians (Somfai, plate 199), September 1790, he signs himself 'Venzl Oliva'.

Pauer (Paur, Bauer), Franz: horn player, also violinist. Engaged 1 June 1769. Salary: 100 ordinary ducats (417 fl. 30 kr.). *Deputat (Naturalien)*: free lodging or 30 fl. Contract: ? Left: see Oliva, Joseph, *supra* (same situation). Salary increased 1 January 1773 by 50 gulden. Pauer remained in the Esterházy *Capelle* until his death in 1805 and was thus a witness of the last period under Haydn's leadership, with the six final Masses (1796–1802). *HJB* VII 71, 86f., 95, 116 (documents). PCDI 660 (see Oliva, also for PCDI 867).

Peschko, Johann (Johannes): trumpet player. Engaged 15 March 1780 with the other trumpet player Lorenz Markl (q.v.). Salary: 343 gulden, 25 kr. *Deputat (Naturalien)*: 24 lb. of candles, 3 fathom cords of wood and a uniform each year. Contract: one year. Dismissed at the end of December 1780 but their salary paid until 17 April 1781 in a lump sum. *HJB* VII, 104 (contract). ECP 1264 (engagement). J. Harich in *HJB* VIII, 36f. (66), 145 (document about trumpets; *vide* Markl).

Peczival (Pezivall, Petzywal, etc.), Caspar (Kaspar): bassoon, viola and kettledrum player. Engaged (as bassoonist) 1 September 1771. Salary: 15 gulden per month. Increases: (1) 12 Aug. 1772, 2 fl. per month; (2) 18 July (eff. 1 Aug.) 1774, 3 fl. per month, making a total of 240 gulden; (3) 1 Feb. 1777, 5 fl. per month; (4) 1 July 1782, 50 fl. *per annum*; (5) 1 July 1785, 50 fl. *per annum*, making a total of 400 gulden *p.a. Deputat (Naturalien)*: lodging in the 'Old Apothecary' at Eisenstadt, 24 lb. of candles, 3 fathom cords of wood and a yearly uniform. Contract: ? Left at end of September 1790, but was later engaged for the princely Church Choir in Eisenstadt as bassoon player. He died unexpectedly ('Noctu suffocatus improvise obiit') on 1 April 1802 at the age of fifty-four. After the death of Adam Sturm in 1771, Peczival was the only trained timpani player that Haydn had at his disposal until the band's dissolution in 1790. *HJB* VII, 69, 85f., 116 (documents). PCDI 995 (salary increase of 1774), 1366 (increase of 1782), 1501 (increase of 1785). J. Harich in *HJB* VIII, 30 (64).

Pohl, Zacharias: oboe player. Engaged 1 June 1769. Salary: 240 gulden. *Deputat (Naturalien)*: (1769) money for food 17 kr. daily; as with the other musicians, this was changed to 50 fl. *per annum*; 'free lodging, wood and light in the Old Apothecary' when his salary was raised in 1772 to 343 fl. 25 kr. Contract: ? Died at the Hospital of the Barmherzige Brüder in Eisenstadt on 29 June 1781. In 1771, he lost his eye in a scandalous brawl with the 'cellist Marteau (*vide infra*, pp. 172 and 173). *HJB* IV, 96 (death document). *HJB* VII, 68, 92 (documents). PCDI 660 (Esterhaz, 3 Aug. 1769 about four new members, incl. 'Zacharia Pohl'). J. Harich in *HJB* VIII, 28 (63).

Polzelli (Polcelli), Antonio: violinist. Engaged 15 March 1779.[1] Salary: with his wife, Luigia (q.v.), 110 ducats (465 gulden, 40 kr.). No *Deputat*. Contract: two years. Left at end of September 1790. See Polzelli, Luigia for the details, also references: *supra*, pp. 49f.

Poschva (Boschwa, Poschwa), Anton: oboe player. Engaged with his wife, Catharina (q.v.) 1 January 1776. Salary, *Deputat (Naturalien)*, dismissal (27 August 1779) and sources, *vide supra*, p. 50.

Prandtner, Caspar(us): organist. He is listed in an 'Extract was denen Eisenstädter Chor Musicis jährl. sowohl in .Baaren, als Naturalien bezahlet wird betreffend' (1778: Acta Musicalia 70, Esterházy Archives, Budapest) as organist of the princely Church Choir in Eisenstadt, a position which he filled temporarily between *qua organista* Haydn/Dietzl and J. G. Fuchs. Nothing more is known of him. J. Harich in *HJB* VIII, 38. He must have been superseded by 5 Dec. 1778, when Fuchs (q.v.) was given the appointment.

---

[1] In another document: 1 March.

Prisi (Brisi) – *vide* Grisi.

Purksteiner (Burgsteiner, Purcksteiner), Joseph: violinist, viola player. Engaged 15 February 1766. Salary: 16 gulden per month. *Deputat (Naturalien)*: 24 lb. of candles, 6 fathom cords of wood, a yearly uniform and free lodging in Eisenstadt, where he was a member of the princely Church Choir. Contract: ? Left after September 1790; he remained as violinist with the Church Choir until he was pensioned off in Schloß Deutschkreuz, where he died in 1797; his widow Cecilia received a pension. When the Eszterháza opera broadened its scope, Purgsteiner was also used as a viola player, in which capacity he appears in one list of 1778–9 and in Forkel's *Almanach* of 1783. He received salary increases, one of 4 gulden per month (from 1 October 1774) and another of 60 gulden *per annum* (from 1 June 1776), which latter gave him 300 gulden *p.a.* Purksteiner, who may have been a composition pupil of Haydn's, composed the marionette opera, *Das ländliche Hochzeitsfest* (1778), for Eszterháza. One of his works, a Cassatio in F for horns and strings, was circulated in manuscript as by Haydn (Hob. II:F3) but is attributed to Purksteiner as early as 1763 in a manuscript in Göttweig Abbey (copied by Pater Leander). Another Cassatio in G for the same combination was also attributed to Haydn (II:G2) but survives in two sources (Monasteries of Göttweig [Pater Leander] and Seitenstetten ['Purckstainer']) as Purksteiner. In 1763, Purksteiner was about twenty-seven years of age; but since he did not join the Eisenstadt *Capelle* until 1766, one wonders when (or indeed if) Haydn really taught him; certainly the two Cassatios are in the Haydn manner, to such an extent that one would give him the Berensonian description of 'seguace di Haydn'. *HJB* VII, 84, 91f., 112 (documents). PCDI 557 (engagement), 1005 (increase of 1774, where he is listed as 'Secund Violinisten Burksteiner'). ECP 1666 (22 Nov. 1788; a yearly pig), 1752 (P's request of 17 Dec. 1790 to be allowed to perform the *Stadtthurnermeister*'s function, in the princely Church Choir at Eisenstadt, with the latter's salary). J. Harich in *HJB* VIII, 20f. (60), with documents, including complete contract (118) (Acta Musicalia 6).

Reiner, Franz: horn player. See *Haydn: the Early Years 1732–1765*.

Ripamonti, Francesco: violinist. Engaged, with his wife Barbara (q.v.), 21 April 1778. Salary, dismissal (10 April 1780) and sources, *vide supra*, p. 51f.

Ros(s)etti, Antonio Francesco (Anton): violinist. Engaged 1 April 1776. Salary: 400 gulden. *Deputat (Naturalien)*: 30 fl. lodging money, 24 lb. of candles, 3 fathom cords of wood and a yearly uniform. Contract: two years, renewed for three years on 25 December 1777. Left at end of March 1781. Rosetti, usually leader of the second violin section at Eszterháza (in his part for Haydn's Symphony No. 63 we find 'Illustrissimo Signore Rosetti'), was a brilliant and famous composer, whose quartets, symphonies and other works were the delight of *settecento* Europe. While he was in Prince Nicolaus's service, he repeatedly gave concerts during his vacation without permission, for which he was fined (on one occasion, in February 1778, Esterházy writes 'Since I have decided not to enforce the monetary fines imposed on the singer Bianki [*sic*] and on Rosetti, in both cases the subtracted sum is to be added to their salary the next month ...'). It appears, from a document in which Rosetti protests that he was merely earning a pittance on such an occasion and was only improving his work in the Art, etc., that the Prince lost his patience and dismissed Rosetti suddenly. After he left Eszterháza, Rosetti went to the court of the Prince of Oettingen-Wallerstein, where he rose to be *Capellmeister*. He died at Ludwigslust in 1792. *HJB* VII, 100 (contract). PCDI 1082 (engagement). *HJB* VII, 165 (fines, Feb. 1778, cancelled for Bianchi and Rosetti). J. Harich in *HJB* VIII, 19 (59f.), with documents, including complete contract (116f.) and the letter of apology that Rosetti sent, apparently in vain (Acta Musicalia 31; p. 117). Landon *SYM*, 710f.

Rupp, Martin: horn player. Engaged 1 February 1777. Salary: 300 gulden. *Deputat* (*Naturalien*): 30 fl. lodging money, 24 lb. of candles, 3 fathom cords of wood and a yearly uniform. Contract: ? Left at end of September 1781. He earned less than Oliva and Pauer, and tried to improve his salary; and he mentions other 'slights and annoyances' which force him 'reluctantly' to cancel his contract. He would stay if his salary were raised; but since the Prince would not do this, Rupp left Eszterháza and joined the *Hofmusikkapelle* in Vienna at a salary of 400 gulden (in the 1796 *Jahrbuch*, we find him as 'Hr. Rub'); in 1797, *NA* lists him as 'Hr. Martin Rupp, in der Josephstadt 21'. Rupp's son Jacob later became, at Haydn's instigation, a member of the choir in Eisenstadt (see *Haydn: the Late Years 1801–1809*, pp. 345f.). *HJB* VII, 101 (contract). J. Harich in *HJB* VIII, 32f. (65).

Schaudig, Albrecht: oboist, also flautist. Engaged 1 April 1776. Salary: 400 gulden. *Deputat* (*Naturalien*): 35 fl. lodging money, 24 lb. of candles, 3 fathom cords of wood and a yearly uniform. Contract: '... but in such a fashion that he binds himself to remain at least 2 years in princely service'. Dismissed at the end of February 1781. The pay lists in the Esterházy Archives list Schaudig (not 'Schandig') as flute player to the end of June 1776, from July 1776 as oboist, trading places with Hirsch (q.v.), who also played both flute and oboe. *HJB* VII, 100 (contract). *HJB* VII, 105 (in which Schaudig is given an increase of 100 fl., beginning on 1 January 1781; giving him a total of 500 gulden, the same fee as Anton Mayer received; q.v.). PCDI 1081 (engagement), 1314 (salary raised). Bartha-Somfai 174f.

Schiringer (Schieringer, Schöringer), Carl (Karl): bassoon, *violone* (double-bass) and apparently also flute player. Engaged (as double-bass player on 1 March 1767. Salary: 240 gulden. *Deputat* (*Naturalien*): as bassoon player in the 'Harmonie' (wind band), he received 17 kr. daily 'Kostgeld'; also 20 lb. of candles, 3 fathom cords of wood, free lodging in the 'Old Apothecary', a yearly uniform and, from 1 January 1772, 20 fl. lodging money. Instead of the *per diem* of 17 kr., a yearly sum of 50 fl. was then paid. In the pay lists etc., he is always listed either as double-bass or bassoon player until 1788, when he is suddenly described as a flautist (possible, but perhaps also a clerical error). The lodging money of 1772 was paid because Schiringer had married. When in 1775 the whole court was transferred fom Eisenstadt to Eszterháza, and the musicians could not take their wives because of housing shortage, they each received a cash substitute of 50 fl. p.a. Contract: no time specified (obviously the contracts were often vague and did not specify 'one year', 'two years', etc.). Left at end of September 1790. As his family grew, his salary was duly increased: to 343 fl. 25 kr. in 1777; to 400 fl. in 1778 (eff. 1 Jan.), with a corresponding increase in kind – wine, wheat and rye (8 *Eimer*, 6 *Metzen*, 16 *Metzen*) and six fathom cords of wood; and by a final 50 fl. (not 30 fl. as in *HJB* VII, 114), effective 1 November 1789 (confirmed in Index, 29). Schiringer's contract was signed in Pressburg (1 March 1767), where the Prince was on an extended visit with his whole *Capelle*, and where Haydn's *La canterina* was given its first public performance. Schiringer was in the service of Count Csáky in Pressburg, where he was dissatisfied with his salary of 20 fl. per month. Haydn promised him 28 fl. 30 kr. in Eisenstadt, but in the event he only received 20 fl., the same salary as his colleagues. He thereupon wrote to the Prince as follows:

Serene Highness and Noble Prince of the Holy Roman Empire, Gracious and dread Lord![1]

Your Serene Highness will know that two years ago I left without regrets the service of Count v. Csáky in Presbourg, in order to enter Your Highness's service, and for the reason that through the person of Your *Capellmeister* Haÿdn I was assured of a monthly salary of 28 f. 30 xr., since I was earning only 20 f. monthly with the Count v. Csáky; but I as well as the other musicians in the service of the Count could, with his permission, earn quite a respectable side income by playing for the high nobility in Presbourg, in such a way that I certainly earned more than 28 f. 30 xr. If it had not been for the honour of serving such a great Prince, and secondly to earn a more certain income, I surely would not have left the service of the Count to have to suffer a loss of 8 f. 30 xr. monthly. And so I entertain the hope, and entreat

1 The German formula reads: 'Durchleuchtig Hochgebohrner Reichsfürst./Gnädigst Hochgebiettender Herr Herr!'

Your Serene Highness to consider my submissive request to grant to me that monthly salary of 28 f. 30 xr. promised through your *Capell Meister* and graciously to order its implementation through your officials. I am, with most submissive respect,

Your Serene Highness's
most obedient
Carl Schiringer Violonista.

[indorsata: 'rejecta est']
[*c.* 1769]　[Acta Musicalia 74; *HJB* VIII, 136]

As we have seen, when Schiringer married, his salary began to rise with such rapidity that by 1789 he was earning 450 fl. and a large *Deputat*. Another reason for this increase may have been that he soon began to compose good church music, and at least two symphonies, for the *Capelle*. A Mass, a Te Deum, a Regina Coeli, a Salve Regina, two Advent arias, five Ave Reginas and a church sonata have survived in copies in the Eisenstadt Archives (Esterházy Castle; Cathedral), and show that Schiringer was a competent, well-trained composer. His works are rather in the style of Werner and of Haydn's early Te Deum, and in them we find the typical C *alto* horn writing of the Esterházy *Capelle*. *HJB* VII, 69, 85, 94, 113f. (documents). PCDI 573 (engagement). ECP 1154 (increase of 57 f., Esterhaz, 16 Nov. 1777). Index 29 (salary increase of 1789). J. Harich in *HJB* VIII, 29f. (63f.), with documents. James Dack; 'The Church Music of Karl Schiringer, Double-Bass Player in the Esterházy "Kapelle" 1767–1790', in *HJB* IX, 329ff.

Schwenda, Johann Georg: bassoon and violone (double-bass) player – see *Haydn: the Early Years 1732–1765*.

Scolari, Domenico: oboist. Engaged 10 April 1783 (according to Bartha-Somfai 175f., n. 16) or 15 May 1783 (according to ECP 1400). We have no details as to his salary. Left at end of December 1783.

Siegl (Sigl, Sigel, Sügl), Franz (Franciscus, Frantz, Francesco): flautist. Engaged 1 February 1761. Salary: 240 gulden. *Deputat* (*Naturalien*): free lodging, heating and light, and a yearly uniform. Contract: ? Dismissed September 1765, re-engaged 1 February 1767, left again in 1771. A.M. 266, 4159, 175, 49, 67. *HJB* VII, 68 (contract). PCDI 573 (Esterhaz, 7 May 1767 concerning 'Franz Sigl', Johann May and Carl Schiringer). *HJB* IV, 42f., 69f. (documents). J. Harich in *HJB* IV, 15 (32) relates that, concerning the will of Prince Paul Anton (in which the 'house officers' were left one year's salary), 'two of the musicians, the oboist J. G. Kapfer and the flautist Franz Siegl, were not recognized as "house officers" and so received only half the yearly salary; they sued the Prince for the other half through the Lower-Austrian courts, won their case, and were paid.' This occurred in 1773 (*vide infra*, p. 171). S. Gerlach in *Haydn-Studien* IV/1 (1976), p. 40.

Specht, Christian: viola player – see 'Specht' under male singers, *supra*, p. 62.

Stamitz (Stainitz), Franz (Franciscus): horn player. Engaged 25 April 1765(?) or before. Salary: 343 gulden 25 kr. (including *Deputat*). *Deputat* (*Naturalien*): free lodging, heating and light, and a yearly uniform. Contract: ? No known departure date, but presumably left sometime in April 1766. Valkó I, 642. In the Dittersdorf autobiography (ed. Norbert Miller, Munich 1967, p. 60), we read that Stamitz and Leutgeb were horn soloists in the winter season 1751–2 in Vienna. Fitzpatrick gives documentary evidence of a Franz Stainmetz (with various alternative spellings) who played in Paris in the 1750s: in April 1754 he and his first-horn partner – one Syryyneck – played a 'Concerto de Cors de Chasse' at a Concert Spirituel. Later, he is found in Vienna (1773–5). Fitzpatrick 118f., 198.

Steiner, Joseph: bassoon player. Engaged 1 January 1781. Salary: 300 gulden. *Deputat* (*Naturalien*): 24 lb. of candles, 3 fathom cords of wood and a yearly uniform. Contract: ? Left at end of September 1790. *HJB* VII, 116 (contract). ECP 1314 (engagement).

Steinmüller (Steinmiller), Thaddäus (Thadteus, Thadeo, Thadeus): horn player. Engaged 1 June 1761. Salary: 240 gulden. *Deputat* (*Naturalien*): 17 kr. *per diem* 'Kostgeld', later turned into 50 fl. *per annum*, free lodging, firewood, light and a yearly uniform. His salary was, by April 1765, 343 fl. 25 kr. *p.a.* (including *Deputat*). Contract: ? Left April 1772. It was previously thought that Haydn composed his Horn Concerto of 1762 (VIId:3) and the *Divertimento à tre* (IV:5) for Steinmüller, but Bryan rightly points out that Steinmüller was a second horn player and the works in question are clearly for first horn. *HJB* VII, 70 (contract). Valkó I, 634, 642. *HJB* IV, 42f. (documents). P. Bryan in *Haydn-Studien* III/1 (1973), pp. 52f. Fitzpatrick 116f. and *passim* (with much mis-information based on the erroneous fact that Steinmüller was a first horn player; also wrong dates for engagement at Eisenstadt, etc.). Steinmüller had three sons, who were themselves brilliant horn players: Johann, Wilhelm and Joseph (we use the order in which they appear in Cramer's *Magazin*). In the records of the Stadtpfarrkirche in Eisenstadt we know that on 23 September 1763 Haydn was godfather to Joseph Karl Anton; in April 1767 he was godfather to another; and in 1765 the 'cellist Weigl was godfather to another, un-named child (A. Csatkai, 'Die Beziehungen Gregor Josef Werners, Joseph Haydns und der fürstlichen Musiker zur Eisenstädter Pfarrkirche', in *Burgenländische Heimatblätter* I/1 (1932), pp. 13ff.). We have a report on a concert given by the three brothers in Hamburg; it comes from Cramer's *Magazin* (1784, Hamburg, 9 July; pp. 1f.):

On 24 January the Brothers **Johann**, **Wilhelm** and **Joseph Steinmüller** from the

Esterhasi Capelle gave a public concert here in the Schauspielhaus. One was already prejudiced in these virtuosi's favour, since they have a **Haydn** for a Capellmeister, and one was not disappointed; they turned out to be truly virtuosi, genuine connoisseurs of music and its melody and of their instrument. It is rare, very rare, that one can hear three such clever men on this instrument at one time, men who know each other so well and acquired such routine. Their own father is their master. They played a Double Concerto by Rosetti, and one for 3 horns by Hoffmeister: afterwards, various select and tasteful duets and terzettes, played with great correctness and perfection. Their adagios have something very fine and attractive about them, to which the penetrating depth, clarity and power of the 2nd and 3rd horn contribute greatly. On 28 February the three brothers ... gave their last concert ...

Of course the three brothers were not, strictly speaking, members of the Esterházy *Capelle*; but we may presume that their godfather (in two cases, at any rate) gave them the benefit of his musical education. Dlabacž's *Künstler-Lexicon* of 1815 (III, 205) informs us that Thaddäus and his three sons were members of Count Nostitz's band in 1775 (Fitzpatrick, 117, questions the date and suggests 1785). Steinmüller appears in the Esterházy *Conventionale 1769* as 'Dritter Waldhornist', but in the *Conventionals Auszug* of 25 April 1765, and in earlier documents of 1761 and 1762 as 'Anderter [i.e. Second] Waldhornist'. If the Concerto in D for 'second principal horn' (VIId:4) is actually by Haydn, it could have been for Steinmüller (for doubts on the work's authenticity, see Landon in *HJB* IV, 201).

Sturm, Johann Adam (Adamus): violinist and timpani player. Engaged 1737. In the *Conventionale 1760* his salary was 50 gulden. *Deputat (Naturalien)*: 12 fl. lodging money, 4 *Metzen* of wheat, 12 of rye, $\frac{1}{4}$ each of lentils, barley and millet-pap, 300 lb. of beef, 40 lb. of salt, 30 lb. of lard, 30 lb. of candles, 9 *Eimer* of wine (Eisenstädter 'Hämb') $\frac{1}{2}$ *Eimer* each of cabbage and beets, one pig and 6 fathom cords of wood. Contract: ? Died 10 July 1771. *HJB* VII, 53, 66f. (terms). A member of the Eisenstadt princely Church Choir, Sturm did not go to Eszterháza with the other musicians but remained in Eisenstadt. In 1765 (Valkó I, 641) his total salary (including the Deputat transferred into cash) was 169 fl. 57 kr., among the lowest at that time (equalled by Anton Kühnel and Eleonora Jäger: only the young Joseph Dietzl earned less, 158 fl. 15 kr.).

Süssig, Christoph: violoncellist (also violinist, according to Pohl II, 372f.; in our records only 'cellist). Engaged 1 October 1770. Salary: 300 gulden. *Deputat (Naturalien)*: 20 fl. lodging money, 20 lb. of candles, 3 fathom cords of wood and a yearly uniform. Contract: ? Died 8 November

1770. *HJB* VII, 68 (contract). PCDI 705 (Esterhaz, 18 Oct. 1770: engagement).

Tauber, Clemens: 'Bassetlista' (i.e. violoncellist). Engaged 1 February 1788. Salary: 400 gulden. *Deputat (Naturalien)*: 24 lb. of candles, 3 fathom cords of wood and a yearly uniform. Contract: ? Left at end of September 1790. *HJB* VII, 115 (contract). ECP 1643 (Esterhaz, 3 April 1788, effective retroactively from 1 Feb., so perhaps he was first given a trial position). In the pay list for September 1790, he is listed as the second violoncellist (Somfai, plate 199).

Thonner, Johann Georg: 'Cancellista' and member of princely Church Choir in Eisenstadt – see *Haydn: the Early Years 1732–1765*.

Tomasini (Tommasini), Luigi (Aloysius): violinist and leader of the *Capelle*. Engaged as valet-de-chambre and musician. Salary: in May 1761 he received only 12 fl. 30 kr. per month (as did violinist Heger) but from 1765 his salary was raised at regular intervals: 1765 (50 gulden *p.a.* and instead of *per diem* food 182 fl. 30 kr.); 1769 (6 *Eimer* of wine, 6 fathom cords of wood; another increase of 50 fl., wine allowance 9 *Eimer* and additional 30 fl. lodging money); 1777 (100 gulden); 1 Jan. 1779 (total salary: 582 fl., 30 kr., free lodging, 24 lb. candles, 9 *Eimer* of wine, 6 fathom cords of wood); 1787 (100 gulden). In September 1790, therefore, he was earning 682 fl., 30 kr. Contract: ? At the death of Prince Nicolaus, Tomasini received a pension of 400 gulden *p.a.* In 1792, he was re-engaged as *Concertmeister* and remained in that position till his death in April 1808; he lies buried in the Bergkirche, Eisenstadt. The biographical details of his life to the end of 1765 will be found in *Haydn: the Early Years 1732–1765*. About 1766 – the exact date cannot be ascertained – Luigi married Josepha Vogl, apparently an Eisenstadt girl. Haydn was godfather to the first two children and Prince Esterházy himself and his daughter to the third (*vide infra*, pp. 137, 156). Tomasini's children (with dates where known) were:

Joseph: b. 24 April 1767, d. 23 October 1779.
Joseph Franz: b. 19 March 1769.
Theresia Anna Christina: b. 25 July 1770.
Alois Joseph: b. 18 March 1772, d. 18 May 1772.
Maria Anna Theresia Josepha: b. 27 August 1773, d. 2 September 1846; singer in the Esterházy *Capelle*.
Anton Edmund: b. 17 February 1775, d. 12 June 1824; violinist and viola player in the Esterházy *Capelle*. See *Haydn: the Years of 'The Creation' 1796–1800*, pp. 95, 490, and *Haydn: the Late Years 1801–1809*, p. 65.
Theresia Josepha: b. 23 November 1776, d. 15 March 1777.
Franz Basil Nikolaus: b. 14 June 1778, d. 4 July 1778.
Alois Basil Nikolaus: b. 10 July 1779; violinist in the Esterházy *Capelle*. See *Haydn: the Late Years 1801–1809*, pp. 63, 65.

Elisabeth Aloisia: b. 31 July 1780, d. 22 June 1782.

Franz Basil Nikolaus: b. 17 April 1784.

Elisabeth Anna: b. 8 July 1788, d. 2 September 1824; singer in the Esterházy Capelle. See Haydn: the Years of 'The Creation, 1976–1800, p. 46.

Josepha Tomasini died at the age of forty-eight in 1793. On 24 April 1799, Tomasini married again: a cook from Pressburg, Barbara Feichtinger. Of the three children from this second marriage, Haydn was godfather to one, Aloisia (b. 21 May 1804).

HJB VII, 65, 83, 111f. (documents). PCDI 648 (1769), 653 (1769), ECP 1129 (1777), 1628 (1787), 1739 (1790: pension) – documents. J. Harich in HJB VIII, 7ff. (53ff.), also with documents (contract: pp. 78f.) and about the musical careers of the children. Tomasini was a composer. A selection of his interesting works has been published in the DTÖ (edited by Erich Schenk, Vol. 124, Graz-Vienna 1972). St Florian Abbey owns a string Trio copied by Joseph Elssler Sen. and the Gesellschaft der Musikfreunde Tomasini's baryton Trios, also in copies by Joseph Elssler Sen. In the DTÖ there is a catalogue of his works. In the winter of 1783/4, Tomasini gave concerts at Prague (Miscellanea Musicologia VI. Svazek, Prague 1958, pp. 48f.) during the Christmas holidays, when he was on leave from the Prince.

Tost, Johann: violinist. Engaged 1 March 1783. Salary: 400 gulden. Deputat (Naturalien): 24 lb. of candles, 3 fathom cords of wood and a yearly uniform. Contract: ? Left at end of March 1788. Tost was the leader of the second violin section at Eszterháza. In view of his complicated relationship with Haydn, he has become rather a cause célèbre. In 1788 he went to France, taking with him various works by Haydn (vide infra, pp. 709, 724), who dedicated to Tost two of his finest sets of string Quartets, Opp. 54/55 and 64. Tost later returned to Austria, married Maria Anna von Gerlischek (the 'Anna de Jerlischek' to whom Haydn dedicated piano Sonata No. 59, 1790), who seems to have been Prince Esterházy's housekeeper and owned property in Baumgarten. Tost became known as a 'Grosshandlungs-Gremialist' with a cloth factory in Znaim (Znojmo, ČSSR). He seems to have settled in Vienna in 1799. Spohr, in his autobiography, tells of his extraordinary relations with Tost:

Word had hardly gone round Vienna that I was to settle there when, one morning, a distinguished visitor presented himself: a Herr von Tost, manufacturer and passionate music lover, excusing the importunity of his visit by explaining that he had a proposition. After he had taken a seat and I had seated myself expectantly opposite him, he began a hymn of praise about my talent as a composer, and expressed the wish that, for a suitable emolument, everything that I should write in Vienna be reckoned as his property for a period of three

years. I was to give him the original manuscripts and make no copies. At the end of three years the manuscripts would be returned to me, and I would be free to publish them or dispose of them in any other way that I saw fit. After considering this curious proposal for a minute, I asked if this meant that the works were to remain unperformed during the period of his ownership. Tost replied: 'Oh, no! They may be performed as often as possible, but the score must be borrowed from me for each occasion and performed only in my presence.' Nor did he wish to prescribe the form of the composition, although he would prefer works suitable for performances in private circles, such as quartets and quintets for stringed instruments. . . . [Tost later explained:] 'I have two objectives. First, I want to be invited to the musicales where your pieces will be played, and therefore I must have them in my possession. Secondly, I hope that on my business trips the possession of such treasures will bring me the acquaintanceship of music lovers who, in turn, may be useful to me in my business.'

While all of this did not make much sense to me, I had to admit that it indicated a high estimate of the value of my compositions. I found this most pleasantly flattering, and I had no further reservations. Tost accepted the fees that I had set, and further agreed to pay upon delivery. . . .

[The musical journeys of Louis Spohr, translated and edited by Henry Pleasants, Norman (Oklahoma) 1961, pp. 88–91.]

The following document shows that Johann Tost really was an extraordinary character. As will be seen in the course of this volume, Haydn developed what might be called a panic aversion to unscrupulous copyists, who made illegal 'double copies' and sold them abroad, or to publishers. It is scarcely believable, but Johann Tost proposed to establish a gigantic illegal copying 'firm' right at Eszterháza, marketing stolen copies of all the latest operas and other works that flowed into Prince Nicolaus's domains. How he proposed to operate this 'firm' under the watchful eye of Capellmeister Haydn is a problem almost too fantastic to contemplate.

[Johann Tost to the Music Master of the Elector of Trier]
Well born,
Most highly respected Sir!

One would certainly take it amiss that as a stranger I bother Your High Person with this letter, although in defence of myself I must confess that I cultivate only the acquaintance of men of great talent, men whose support is at the same time evidence of their magnanimous activity. Dare I hope to ask for such support? I am in a position where there is a confluence of all the best, carefully selected pieces of music; now I have a copyists' room [Schreibstube] just for the preparation of new music, and I have to serve many and great courts in this manner, so that I take the liberty of asking Your High Person to recommend me to your court as well; my publishing [*sic: verlaag*] work consists mostly of operas, symphonies, concertos and arias, and all at a cheap price. Should I, therefore, be fortunate enough to receive a favourable answer to my proposition, I would offer my services in all sorts of ways (apart from a small reward), and I would miss no opportunity, whenever it arises, of being able to show my unlimited respect, and to assure that I am,

Your well born Sir's

most humble servant

Johann Tost Second directeur

Esterhâaz, 1st May 1787
the address is to me
Jean Tost Musicien
de son Altesse Monseigneur le Prince Regnant
d'Esterhaazy
Esterhâaz.

[Staatsarchiv Koblenz 1 C fol. 252/252. Gustav Bereths; *Die Musikpflege am kurtrierischen Hofe zu Koblenz-Ehrenbreitstein*, Mainz, 1964, 272f.]

The Gotha *Theater-Kalender . . . 1787* (p. 203) lists Tost as Music Director of the Seipp Troupe, Pressburg. Tost seems to have maintained contact with other musicians from the Esterházy *Capelle*, for in 1803 we find Luigi Tomasini, the leader, dedicating to 'Jean Tost' *Trois Duos concertants pour deux Violons*, Oeuvre 11 (Weigl, Vienna, pl. no. 445).

HJB VII, 112 (contract, with note 'Cessat'). Bartha-Somfai 174f. Larsen *HÜB* 114f., where the two Tosts (Johann the Esterházy violinist and Johann the *Grosshandlungs-Gremialist*) are for the first time merged into one. Although the evidence is not conclusive, it seems almost certain that we are in fact dealing with one and the same person. See also Hoboken I, 420, 775 (incorporating valuable research by Victor Luithlen).

Ungricht, Vito: violinist (viola player) – *vide supra*, p. 63. Later Ungricht settled in Vienna, where in 1796 the *Jahrbuch* lists him among the violinists of the National Theatre; in 1797 *NA* lists him under 'Violino secundo' as 'Hr. Vitus Ungericht, in Dorotheerhof auf der 2ten Stiege.'

Weber (Wöber), Fridolin (Fritz): violinist. Engaged 1 April 1788. Salary: 280 gulden. *Deputat* (*Naturalien*): 24 lb. of candles, 3 fathom cords of wood and a yearly uniform. Contract: ? Left at end of September 1788. Fridolin Weber, half-brother of Carl Maria von Weber, was brought, together with his brother Edmund, by their father Franz Anton to study with Haydn in Vienna in 1784. It was obviously Haydn who organized Fridolin's temporary position with the Esterházy *Capelle*. For Carl Maria and the Haydn brothers (Johann Michael and Joseph) sce *Haydn: the Late Years 1801–1809*, p. 279. *HJB* VII, 113 (contract). ECP 1647 (Esterhaz, 24 April 1788: engagement, 'with the salary of the departed Musicus Hoffman' as of 1 April). Pohl II, 372f.

Weigl, Joseph (Josephus): violoncellist. Engaged in May 1761. Salary: 240 gulden. *Deputat* (*Naturalien*): free lodging, firewood and light. Contract: ? Left at end of May 1769. Haydn was a great friend of this fine musician, for whom the beautiful and taxing 'cello solos of Symphonies Nos. 6–8 ('Le Matin', 'Le Midi' and 'Le Soir') were written. In 1764 he married Anna Maria Scheffstoss, the singer. Haydn and his wife were godparents to Joseph, the eldest son, and later to Anton Aloysius (see notes under Weigl *supra*, p. 54). Weigl went to Vienna and joined the Court Orchestra, remaining in that position all his professional life. *NA* (1797) lists him under 'Violoncello' as 'Hr. Joseph Weigel, in der Himmelpfortgasse 1007.' *HJB* VII, 67 (terms). *HJB* IV, 42f. (first salary received). Pohl I, 372.

THE EISENSTADT CASTLE CHURCH CHOIR AND ORCHESTRA

The Castle at Eisenstadt included a chapel with a choir-loft and an attractive Baroque organ; in the loft there was sufficient space for a small choir and chamber orchestra (with trumpets and kettledrums) to perform Masses on Sundays and other church music of a *figuraliter* kind (i.e., with instruments). The ensemble had been created by the Palatine Paul Esterházy (1635–1713), and before Haydn's arrival the group had been directed by *Capellmeister* Gregor Werner. When Haydn was engaged in May 1761, the musical establishment at Eisenstadt was divided into two sections, the church music (castle choir, *Schloßchor*) and the 'Cammer Musique'; Werner was in charge of the former and Haydn directed the latter as *Vice Capellmeister*, but members of the 'Cammer Musique' were expected to perform in church ceremonies as well as at 'Tafel Musique' and at 'Academien' (concerts). The 'Cammer Musique' came to spend more and more time at Eszterháza, leaving only a skeleton group in Eisenstadt to perform church music on Sundays and Holidays, as well as the occasional Requiem or Evening Service. At the beginning of the Eszterháza period, the musicians were, in theory, supposed to spend the winters in Eisenstadt and swell the meagre forces there for church music; but in practice, the Prince came to use Eisenstadt only as a stopping place between Eszterháza and Vienna, and the musicians, following the Prince, were only in Eisenstadt for a brief period in the winter. The Estates Director Rahier often complained to the Prince of the unhappy situation of the Castle Choir after Werner's death in 1766; it consisted of an organist, a soprano, a bass and a violinist, and Rahier suggested hiring an alto, a tenor and another violinist. The Prince agreed, for the church music 'cannot, after all, be neglected.'

[Prince Nicolaus Esterházy to P. L. Rahier]
 Nobly born,
 Highly respected Herr von Rahier! I have received your reports of 28th June, 3rd, 6th and 10th Julÿ. . . .
 N°· 5 it is clear that the Eisenstadt Castle Choir Musique is not sufficient to perform Divine Services, which cannot, after all, be neglected; there is no point in counting the late Adam Sturm this time, because I kept him only as a rentier; consider, therefore, which instruments could be played by which people and for which salary, and let me know your further opinion. . . .
 Eszterhaz, 14th July 1771.

Your willing
Nicolaus Prince Esterhazy.

 [Acta Musicalia 4343, Esterházy Archives, Budapest; *HJB* VIII, 146]

[P. L. Rahier to Prince Nicolaus Esterházy]
SERENE HIGHNESS AND NOBLE PRINCE OF THE HOLY ROMAN EMPIRE, GRACIOUS AND DREAD LORD
 Since our Choir here only consists of
 an Organist
 a Discantist
 a Bassist and
 a violinist
in the absence of the rest of the court musicians, it would be necessary to add
 an Altist
 a Tenorist and
 a violinist,
in my opinion one could engage the daughter of the bass singer Grießler, who for some time has been singing alto without pay, and give her yearly 50 f.; Johann Haiden [*sic*], who has been singing tenor hitherto without pay . . . and the Rent Master Frantz Nigst, who despite the fact that his previous pay of 50 f. and the musician's uniform have been taken from him, continued to play first violin without neglecting in any way his other duties, and ought in grace to have 50 f. annually given to him; according to the old situation as observed in the Conventionale from the year 1723, there were, apart from the above musicians, also a violonist[1] [double-bass player] and a bassoon player, but since all the other musicians are mostly here the whole winter period, perhaps these two could be omitted . . .
 Eisenstadt, 24th Julÿ 1771.

P. L. Rahier.

 [Acta Musicalia 200(199). Esterházy Archives, Budapest; *HJB* VIII, 146]

---

1 'Violinist', probably a misprint for 'Violonist' (double-bass), which instrument was always part of the Eisenstadt church choir.

[Report from P. L. Rahier to Prince Nicolaus Esterházy]
... 7 & 8 About the Eisenstadt Choir Musique, during the summers an altist,
a tenorist and a violinist are absolutely necessary, of which those suggested under
date 24th Julÿ are: <u>Rent Master Nigst</u> will be satisfied with the 25 f. graciously
offered, but Johann Haiden [*sic*] and Grießler on behalf of his daughter (see the
enclosed petitions) hope to receive more, which in my opinion they deserve; but if
Your Highness does not decide to give them more, and turn down their petitions,
I think they would be content to accept 25 f. ...
  Eisenstadt, 21st August 1771.

P. L. Rahier

[Acta Musicalia 199, Esterházy Archives, Budapest; *HJB* VIII, 147]

At this point Eleonora Jäger, who seems to have been quite a character, took it
upon herself to write directly to the Prince about the sad affairs of the church music in
Eisenstadt Castle. 'Your Highness knows', she wrote sternly, 'what a chorus ought to
have, and

> that the choir, as it is normally constituted, has to have at least 4 vocal parts, 2
> violins and the organ in order to perform the usual kind of music; and this is also a
> Parish Church with its unavoidable ceremonies, and we are just 4 persons here,
> and the other 2 have helped out just the last 2 summers because we asked them, and
> all this is something that a great Prince and Lord doesn't have to put up with, so if
> Your Highness would turn his attention to the glory of God, it would be to get
> Grissler's [*sic*] girl who (because I'm singing discant) sings alto, the young Haÿden
> (because the Schoolmaster [Joseph Dietzl, Sen.] plays second fiddle) who has to
> sing tenor, Nigst who plays first fiddle because Sturm is dead and that Nigst
> always helped us out, anyway Your Highness could distribute the jobs to these 3
> persons from your highest grace, so that our music could be supported a little, and
> Your Highness has much too much respect for the glory of God to be ungracious
> with us, and I ask Your Highness this in the greatest submission and in the absence
> of Haÿdn I throw myself at your feet and may it please Your Highness,

I am, Your Highness's
most obedient
Eleonora Jaeger
Singer.

[Acta Musicalia 61, Esterházy Archives, Budapest; *HJB* VIII, 150f.]

 The outcome of all these negotiations was that Nigst was hired as violinist at 25 fl.,
Elisabeth ('Josepha') Griessler at 25 fl. and Johann Haydn at 50 fl. This meant that at the
beginning of our period, the Eisenstadt Church Choir consisted of:

Eleonora Jäger, soprano;
[Elisabeth (Josepha) Griessler, alto;]
[Johann Haydn, tenor;] replacing Joseph Dietzl, Sen.
Melchior Griessler, bass;
Franz Nigst, first violin;
[Joseph Dietzl Jr., second violin;] replacing Joseph Dietzl, Sen., who left the tenor
to Haydn and played violin.
Franz Novotni, organist.

When Novotni died in 1773, Haydn and Schoolmaster Joseph Dietzl, Sen. divided the
organist's post between them; it was later given to Caspar Prandtner, then to J. G.
Fuchs. The tenor part was also filled by J. G. Fuchs before he became the official
organist in December 1778. Michael Ernst, formerly a singer in the Marionette

Theatre, became one of the violinists (December 1778). Nigst died in 1773, and once again the whole problem of the Eisenstadt Castle Choir and Orchestra became acute. This time, the violinists were recruited *ad hoc* until a wholly new solution presented itself; this was in the form of:

THE EISENSTADT 'THURNERMEISTER'

whose name was Anton Höld, Sen. No doubt Höld had sometimes lent the 'Thurnermeister und seine Gesellen' (the Tower Master and his apprentices) for the trumpets and kettledrums which such scores as the church music of Carl Schiringer often require, but which were missing not only in the summer but even in the winter (except for 1780–1, when Haydn had trumpets in his orchestra). There was also the nearby Stadtpfarrkirche (parish church; St Martin's) which had, until 1783 (when Joseph II forbade *figuraliter* church music all over the Monarchy), its own choir and orchestra, whose members certainly can and will have helped out the skeleton forces at the Castle Chapel. So in a sense, the tiny group of four voices (S-A-T-B), two violins and organ was only the basis for the regular church music at Eisenstadt Castle. With that group, many short Masses (the *missa brevis* form) could be performed, for most were written for just that combination; and the missing double-bass player was probably supplied in the person of Anton Kühnel, whose official salary as 'violonist' was cancelled in 1768 but who may have played without fee, like his colleagues.

Anton Höld, Sen., was the town 'Thurnermeister', who fulfilled the dual function of providing the town's music at balls, and so on, and also organizing the music in St Martin's (the rector of which, Carl Kraus, was himself an avid musician),[1] for which latter purpose Anna Barbara Kroyer had in 1753 left the income from a capital sum of 6,000 gulden. Höld is found in Eisenstadt records of 1758 as 'Regiae Civitatis Kismartoniensis[2] Thurnerus'. He died in 1774 and was succeeded by his son, Anton Jr., who 'Laut Hoch Fürstlicher Resolution dd° Wienn den 15ten Marty $\overline{775}$' is to be paid 30 f. for services rendered to the Castle Choir in the period in summer when the *Kammer Music* is absent'. Höld Jr. is listed on this document as violinist, but in general the 'Thurnermeister' and his apprentices consisted of trumpets and kettledrums; and according to another 'Hochfürstlicher Resolution dd° 9ten Apr: $\overline{781}$' Höld Jr. is given 10 *Metzen* of rye and 3 *Eimer* wine 'because he now and in future, with his apprentices, assists in the Castle Choir services'. This suggests that such a work as the *Missa San Antonii de Padua* by Schiringer, composed in 1787 and performed, presumably, on 13 June (St Anthony of Padua's Day) when the main body of the Esterházy orchestra was away from Eisenstadt, will have been possible only with the assistance of the 'Thurnermeister' Höld and his apprentices, and for the simple reason that the work requires two trumpets and timpani *ad libitum*; if we imagine that he wrote the work for performance in the Castle Chapel, not only the trumpets and drums – the *ad libitum* remark does not mean that Schiringer did not have trumpets and timpani available on 13 June 1787, but only that he imagined (quite rightly, as we have seen) that there might arise a circumstance in which the Mass might have to be performed without them – but also most of the choir will have been recruited by Anton Höld, Jr.[3]

1 Haydn arranged to have Prince Nicolaus II Esterházy purchase the music which Kraus left when he died in 1802. See *Haydn: the Late Years*, p. 219.
2 Eisenstadt in Latin (and Hungarian) = Kismarton.
3 J. Harich in *HJB* VIII, 37–44 (66–9). Documents: *HJB* VII, 119–25. *Die Stadtpfarrkirche in Eisenstadt. Sonderheft der 'Mitteilungen' des burgenländischen Heimat- und Naturschutzvereines*, Eisenstadt 1930. J. Dack in *HJB* IX, 329ff. The autograph score and authentic parts (with the trumpets and timpani) are in the Esterházy Archives, Eisenstadt. Another set of parts, without the trumpets and timpani, are in the Archives of the Stadtpfarrkirche (now Cathedral), Eisenstadt, which suggests that the *ad libitum* remark may have been designed, indeed, for a possible performance *outside* the Esterházy chapel.

THE GRENADIERS' *Banda*

Apart from, and occasionally overlapping with, the princely *Capelle* was a wind-band (*Harmonie*) ensemble attached to the princely grenadiers and consisting of two oboes, two bassoons and two horns. At first, from 1766 on, the wind instruments were recruited from the normal ranks of the *Capelle*. They were used for marches, and other pieces suitable for the elaborate ceremony that accompanied the changing of the guard at Eszterháza and Eisenstadt. It will be noted that a description of such a ceremony is given in the *Excursion* of 1784 – *vide infra*, p. 113 – and that 'la Marche musicale est exactement cadencée, fort harmonieuse & de la composition de Hayden: c'est tout dire.' Haydn undoubtedly wrote a great deal of such wind-band music for the grenadiers. Since all the wind-band music of the pre-1790 period has survived only in non-Esterházy sources, we can conjure up the 'fort harmonieuse' style of March only if we look at the pretty and (to twentieth-century ears most unmilitary) 'Marche Regimento De Marshall' which the present writer discovered in the Clam-Gallas Collection, Prague, in a manuscript of the year 1772.[1] There is another attractive March for wind band from Haydn's *Armida* which is undoubtedly the kind of music that our listener heard at the changing of the guard at Eszterháza in 1784 (which, as it happens, is the year *Armida* was first performed).

The princely grenadiers were famous for their great height. The *Beschreibung* of 1784 (p. 40) tells us that 'Their uniform is a dark-blue jacket with red facings and cuffs, and white loops [*Schleifen*], also white vests and knee-breeches; black fur caps with yellow metal badges.' The report continues with a piece of information that explains how it happened that the grenadiers had to form their own 'Banda'. 'A part of the military,' the report continues, 'is in Eisenstadt, to serve the Princess, who resides there.' This was the same situation as that in which the Church Choir and the other musicians found themselves. When the court came to reside at Eszterháza, the Princess remained at Eisenstadt, where the changing of the guard, etc., was accompanied with the same pomp and musical efforts as at Eszterháza; therefore a separate grenadiers' *Banda* had to be organized.

The first reference that we have been able to find, in the records of the Esterházy Archives, is in ECP, item 1466: Esterhaz, 23 July 1779. Here we read that Knopf and Schizenhofer are engaged as horn players with the grenadiers, and one Lattensperger as bassoon with the 'Banda'. These are names that have never appeared on the other musical lists. Their appearance also suggests that after the court moved to Eszterháza in 1776, the situation (like that of the princely Church Choir in Eisenstadt) became acute. In the *Conventionale* of 1789 (*HJB* VII, 123), we find a separate entry, which reads as follows:

Music Banda
Laut Hoch Fürstlichlichen Intimat dd° 3ten May $\overline{783}$, His Highness has granted full powers to Herr Grenadier *Unter Lieutenant* Pavlovsky to re-establish the former Music Banda, and to engage personnel for this purpose according to his wishes, for which purpose H. H. has allotted 260 gulden additionally to the sum hitherto allowed for the former Banda.

Item Laut Hochfürstlicher Resolution dd° 21ten Aug: 1783, to wit beginning on the first of that month and year, the Banda is to receive an additional sum of 3 f. monthly.

---

1 Published with other marches by Haydn, in *Sieben Märsche* (Doblinger, 'Diletto Musicale' No. 34).

We can see, then, that the *Banda* had its ups and downs, and for a time went out of existence. We see shadowy hints of their existence as early as Haydn's first year with the Esterházy court, in 1761:

> Two Bassoons with the Grenadiers' Company.
> Each has annually 50 f., together .... 100 f. and to be paid quarterly at 12 f. 30 xr. They are, for their part, obliged at the high appearance of His Highness to parade and to appear diligently with the Tafel Musique.
> They have been dismissed 1 July 1761.

[HJB VII, 56]

The final document which we could locate is once again in ECP, item 1470: Esterhaz, 30 April 1784. One Aisenreiter, bassoon 'bey der Banda' is to receive Corporal's pay.

THE PRINCELY UNIFORMS

It was customary for the house officers and servants employed by great noble families to wear an official uniform or *livrée*, which was specially in evidence at festive occasions. In Haydn's contract of 1761, this point is particularly mentioned (he is to appear 'at all times, neat and clean, in uniform', also the other members of the band, and 'in white stockings, white linen' powdered, either with pigtail or hair-bag ...'. Every member of the princely band received once a year, at the court's expense, either a summer or winter uniform, which consisted of a coat (jacket), waistcoat (vest), trousers (knee-breeches) and a hat. Curiously, the Italian singers do not seem to have worn the uniforms; of two, Giacomo Lambertini and Benedetto Bianchi, we see that they received suits, but obviously not uniforms; of the female singers, too, not everyone received a dress or cash substitute (only Eleonora Jäger received her cash substitute regularly); after 1773, we cannot trace any documents for female dresses (nor cash substitutes; Miss Jäger excepted). A dress was valued at 100 gulden and the cash substitute paid in this amount. Haydn received his first uniform in Vienna, just after he had been engaged in 1761: his uniform was of far better material, and more elaborately designed, than those of his subordinates: this can be seen by the extant bills from the Viennese tailor. A 'normal' uniform cost something more than ten gulden, while Haydn's cost three times as much. The cloth-maker used expensive Dutch material, in light blue, for Haydn's uniform;[1] for the others a cheaper English material; Haydn's uniform had gold braid and gold buttons, while the rest of the band had silver trimmings. These uniforms seem to have been those for gala occasions, the costs of which, for the whole band, ran to some 1,200 gulden. The summer uniforms, also light blue, were all trimmed with silver.

On 10 January 1763, a great festival was organized at Eisenstadt to honour the marriage of Prince Nicolaus's son Anton to Countess Maria Theresia Erdödy. One of the highlights was Haydn's new opera *Acide* – for the verbatim quotation see *Haydn: the Early Years 1732–1765* – in which the members of the band appeared in dark-red uniforms with gold trimmings.

---

1 Two points concerning 'light blue'. (1) The famous portrait of Haydn in Esterházy uniform, painted by Basilius Grundmann, which was destroyed by the Russians at Eszterháza in 1945, was actually seen, shortly before the end of the Second World War, by Dr Janos Harich, who told us that Haydn was in *blue* uniform (the only photograph of this picture, in black and white, is reproduced in *Haydn: the Early Years 1732–1765*, also frequently elsewhere, e.g. Somfai). Therefore the picture can only have been painted between May 1761 and *c.* 1764, when the musicians received grey (*hechtgrau*) coats. (2) Griesinger (16) tells us that Haydn's father Mathias ('Meister Matthias') 'had the pleasure of seeing his son in the blue house uniform, trimmed with gold ...'. Another authentic description of the first uniform Haydn wore; we suggest that the picture was painted either (a) when Haydn was engaged in May 1761 or (b) upon Prince Nicolaus's accession in 1762. In 1763, as we shall see, the musicians wore a *red* uniform.

It is not clear exactly when Prince Nicolaus again changed the colour of his musicians' uniforms. Harich says at the Prince's accession (1762), but we have seen that in January 1763, the musicians wore red. By November 1764, however, we know from a tailor's bill (*HJB* IV, 80f.) that the winter uniforms were in grey (and presumably the summer uniforms, too); all the winter uniforms were trimmed with gold and the summer uniforms with silver. Haydn makes special mention of 'new uniforms' worn at High Mass on the Prince's Name Day (6 December) 1766; perhaps Haydn was referring to the new grey uniforms.

In 1776, the uniforms were again changed: breeches and jacket were in red, the waistcoat in apple-green cloth. From a bill (*HJB* IV, 84–91, the complete bill with all details of the material used) we can see that Haydn's uniform was the most expensive, while those of the Eisenstadt Church Choir were the cheapest – another instance of the second-rate category into which these musical orphans of the Esterházy establishment were thrust. Those musicians who took care of their uniform received a cash substitute each year in lieu of a new uniform: in Haydn's case this meant 170 or 178 gulden, for the other musicians 75 gulden, from which we can see that Haydn received, in this matter as in others, preferential treatment. Haydn did not take advantage of this extra source of income until relatively late: for the first time he took the cash substitute for a summer uniform in 1784, and one year later for a winter uniform (*HJB* IV, 91f., the documents *in extenso*); in the following year he also drew 340 gulden. In 1784, the Prince allowed his entire band to collect the cash substitute, and the musicians (not Haydn, as we have seen) collected 150 gulden each (document: *HJB* IV, 94). In 1788, Haydn collected another 178 gulden instead of a winter uniform (document: *HJB* IV, 95). It was expected that the musicians apply in writing for such cash substitutes: the disbursar allowed the money to be paid at once (document: *HJB* IV, 95). The last such cash substitute occurred in July 1790, when Haydn received 170 gulden (document: *HJB* IV, 95). All this was a pleasant extra source of income.[1]

THE PRINCELY MUSICAL INSTRUMENTS

Unfortunately, no one in the Esterházy administration ever thought to make an inventory of more than a part of the instruments which remained at Eszterháza Castle; in particular, there seems never to have been a proper list of the enormous number of keyboard instruments. In 1936, when the string, woodwind and brass instruments were recorded in an inventory, *fortepiani* and harpsichords, unless beautifully painted – which is the reason so many, relatively speaking, survived in Italy – were considered more-or-less worthless relics of faint historical interest.

What were the instruments that Haydn and his *Capelle* used? Let us start with the keyboard instruments, about which we have a certain amount of information from the repairers' bills. Horst Walter has compiled a useful survey[2] of the keyboard instruments at the Esterházy court. From the documents we can see that until 1781, only harpsichords (spinets) and a clavichord are mentioned. The harpsichords are called, in horrible local dialect, 'Flüg', 'Flig', 'Flich' (= 'Flügel'), but also 'das Instrument oder cembalum' in Kittsee Castle (1764). In 1764 we also read of 'fürstlichen Klavikordi'. In 1768 there were two harpsichords at Eszterháza (December 1768, receipt by Franz Novotni). After the fire at Eszterháza in November 1779, the *Preßburger Zeitung* reports that 'der schöne Flieg des berühmten

1 J. Harich in *HJB* IV, 19–21; we have used our adaptation and translation *verbatim*, with a few modifications based on other sources, as in *HJB* IV, 34.
2 'Haydns Klaviere', in *Haydn-Studien* II/4 (1970), pp. 257ff.

Kapellmeisters Haiden und die Konzertvioline des Virtuosen Lotschi', by which Luigi Tomasini is meant, were both destroyed in the fire (*vide infra*, p. 420). Naturally, we do not know which 'schöne Flieg' was destroyed, but probably a large harpsichord used for *continuo* work in the opera house. The bills of the Esterházy Archives repeatedly refer to a 'green harpsichord' which belonged to Eisenstadt Castle. In 1767, when Haydn's *La canterina* was performed at Pressburg, two 'Sbinnetr' (spinets) were 'carried up to the princely garden, repaired, quilled and tuned ...' (Valkó II, 541). Since there are bills that refer to keyboard instruments kept by the singers, we may presume that there were a great many large and small harpsichords, spinets and clavichords at Eisenstadt and Eszterháza, and probably also at Kittsee and Monbijou.

In 1781, we find that the famous Viennese piano manufacturer Anton Walter spent twelve days at Eszterháza 'repairing the *Clavier und Flügel Instrumenten*' (bill of 3 March 1781; Valkó II, 590), and countersigned by Haydn himself 'Diese Clavier und Flügel sind von mir genau untersuchet und für Richtig Erfunden worden'. This bill clearly makes a precise difference between pianos (*Clavier*) and harpsichords (*Flügel*). In 1796, Anton Walter came to Eisenstadt to tune two 'fürstliche Pianofortes'. In 1800, Haydn was at Eszterháza and the *Preßburger Zeitung* reports that he played on the 'Fortepiano' – quoted *verbatim* in *Haydn: the Years of 'The Creation' 1796–1800*, p. 565. Probably the only Esterházy keyboard instrument to survive the various vicissitudes to which Eisenstadt and Eszterháza were subjected is the Walter piano now in the Haydnhaus at Eisenstadt.[1]

Apart from the Walter piano, which is not in good condition and is in any case inferior to the two beautiful instruments by that maker in the Kunsthistorisches Museum, Vienna, we have only one record of a piano which used to be situated in the 'Oratorium' at Eisenstadt, *viz.* the rehearsal room next to the great hall (now known as the 'Haydn-Saal'). It appears in a good photograph in the very scarce album of the Männergesangsverein, Eisenstadt, 1909.[2] When the piano disappeared cannot now be established, but Dr Janos Harich believes that it was taken to Eszterháza where, of course, it perished in 1945.

It is possible – indeed, probable – that the two French horns and three string instruments owned by the Burgenländisches Landesmuseum come from the Esterházy orchestra. They are:

1) Violin, 1777, by Antonius Thir, Lauten- und Geigenmacher in Preßburg (signed), black varnish.

2) Violin, 1786, by Johann Radeck, Geigen- und Lautenmacher in Wien (signed), red-brown varnish.

3) Master viola, 1790, by Sebastian Wurzelhofer, Brünn (signed), black (sub-varnish: cherry-red) varnish.

4) Pair of horns, Austrian *c.* 1730, by Johann Hoyer (signed); three windings; brass.[3]

The authentic organs at Eisenstadt (Esterházy Castle; Bergkirche; Chapel of the Barmherzige Brüder; Stadtpfarrkirche [Cathedral]; Franziskanerkirche), although all *settecento* instruments, they were in most cases rebuilt at a later period. They are examined in detail in *Haydn: the Early Years 1732–1765*. The two most important organs in Eisenstadt are without question the magnificent instruments – both by the

1 Victor Luithlen, 'Der Eisenstädter Walterflügel', in *Mozart-Jahrbuch* 1954, Salzburg 1955, pp. 206ff.
2 Through the kindness of Komm.-Rat. Wolf of Doblinger Verlag, Vienna, we were recently given a beautiful example of this extremely interesting album, which includes *inter alia* the first photograph of the Grundmann Haydn portrait and various other photographs, many of which grace the pages of this biography.
3 Preparation for the Haydn Exhibition; list by A. Hahn of the Burgenländisches Landesmuseum, Eisenstadt, 6 June 1975.

same maker, Georg Malleck (1776 and 1797, respectively) and both today in complete playing order – in the Stadtpfarrkirche (Cathedral) and Bergkirche; in particular, that of the former, which has been twice restored by Schuke, Potsdam (1942 and 1975), is a revelation.

In 1936, the following inventory of musical instruments at Eszterháza was made; we give the old inventory number, although it is unlikely that (apart from one baryton) any of them survived the holocaust at the Castle in 1945.

4502	violin	Jacob Steiner [Stainer?] in Absam 1650.
4503	viola	Nicolaus Amatus Cremonen. Hieronimi fil ac Antony Nepos, 1697.
4504	violin	Alexander Nazadure in Ferrara 1769.
4505	violin	Joannes Georgius Leeb fecit Posonii 1797.
4506	violin	Andreas Carolus Leeb, 1802.
4507	violin	Joannes Florenus Quidentus fecit Bonomiae Anno 1743.
4508	violin	Sebastian Dallinger in Wien, 1795.
4509	violin	David Nisle.
4510	violin	Joannes Janek, 1740.
4511	violin	unknown master; repaired: Joannes Havelka Lincii, 1761.
4512	violin	Joh. Bapt. Rogerius Bon in Brixen, Schüler von Nicolai Amati di Cremona, 1697.
4513	violin	unknown master; repaired: J. Nisle, 1811.
4514	violin	Petro Anselmo, Velence, 1753.
4515	baryton	Jacobus Stainer, 1660.
4516	violin	formerly used by Haydn.
4517	double bass	Ignatius Stadlmann, 1776.
4518	baryton	Josephi Stadlmann, Wien, 1750. [This instrument, by a happy accident, has survived and is now in the musical instruments' collection of the National Museum, Budapest. Photograph in Somfai (No. 36). There is also a recording of it, produced by the Burgenländisches Landesmuseum, Eisenstadt ('Aus dem Haydnhaus', TST77938).]
4517 [bis]	violin	Stradivari 1690.
4519	violoncello	Giovanni Grancino in Contrada Cargha di Milano al Seguo della Corona, 1795.
4520	violoncello	Joannes Georgius Leeb fecit Posonii, 1797.
4521	violoncello	Nicolaus Amatius Cremonien. hieronimi filii Antoni Nepos fecit ad 1670.
4522	violin case	for two violins, covered in red leather.
4523	bassoon	
4524	violin bows	eighteen in number.
4525	instruments necessary for playing the 'Toy' Symphony. 3 triangles with sticks to play them. 3 instruments to imitate a cuckoo. 2 small trumpets. 1 wooden whistle. 2 rattles. 3 instruments imitating birds' call, of ivory.	
[4526	plaster-of-Paris impressions of 5 medals commemorating Haydn, including both sides of each].	
4527	kettledrums (a pair).	
4528	trumpet	Joseph Huschauer, 1811.
4529	trumpet	Wilhelm Haas, Nürnberg.
4530	horn	Anton Kerner, Wien 1822.
4531	flute	in a black leather case.
4532	canons in Haydn's handwriting, German, Latin and Italian – 38 pieces framed under glass. . . .	
4533	plan of Eszterháza opera house mounted on white linen and framed.	
4534	spinet, the case of cherry-wood, formerly Haydn's.	
4535	pastel portrait of Haydn [not further identified]. . . .	

[Esterházy Family Archives Fasc. 2229 (4502–35), Országos Levéltár, Budapest. Valkó II, 652f.]

The fate of the musical instruments' collection at Eszterháza – and of all the furniture – will be described *infra*, pp. 749f. Like the theatre and the marionette opera house, the instruments themselves no longer exist.

SOME CONCLUSIONS

If we examine at random some of the musicians' salary lists for our period, we would get a very warped idea of the actual playing disposition of the orchestra. Let us take a typical list from the month of January 1772.

1772. Specification deren fürstl Hoff und Camer Musicis, wie solche vor das Monath februarij aus der General Cassa zu Eisenstadt sind bezahlet worden,

N:º	Nomina	Officia	f	Xr
1	Giuseppe Haydn mpria	Kapell-Meister	47	50
2	Barbara Dichtler	Discantista	12	30
3	Maddalena Friberth mpria	Discantista	41	40
4	Geltrude [*sic*] Cellini	Discantista	34	22½
5	Carlo Friberth mpria	Tenorista	25	—
6	Leopoldo Dichtler	Tenorista	27	—
7	Christian Specht	Bassista........................	33	20
8	Luigi Tomasini	1:ª Violinista....................	40	12½
9	Josephus Blaschek	2:ª Violinista...................	25	—
10	Josephus Purcksteiner	3:ª Violinista...................	16	—
11	Xavier Marteau	Bassetelista	34	22½
12	Andreas Lidl mpria	Paritonista	39	30
13	Carl Franz	1:ª Waldhornist.................	27	30
14	May	2:te Waldhornist...............	27	30
15	Oliva	3:ª Waldhornist................	34	22½
16	Paur	4:te Waldhornist...............	34	22½
17	Hinterberger	1:te Fagotist	28	13
18	Johan Hinterger [*sic*] Caspar Petzyval NB Schiring?	2:te Fagotist	28	13
19	Carlo Schiringer NB Petzival	3:te Fagotist....................	15	—
20	Carolus Chorus	1:te Hautboist..................	28	13
21		2:te Hautboist..................	28	13
22	Thadteus Steinmüller	5:te Waldhornist	28	13
23	Joseph Dietzl	6:te Waldhornist	25	43
	In una Summa		682	20½

[Fascimile: Somfai, plate 93; Esterházy Archives, Budapest]

At No. 18, there is a confusion in that Hinterberger's name appears twice; all the names are autograph in that column, but there are different handwritings for 'Hinterberger' and 'Johan Hinterger'. Also, the different hand which wrote 'NB Schiring[er]?' also wrote 'NB Petzival', indicating that the second bassoon player was actually Schiringer and the third Peczival (*recte*?). Pohl, the second oboist who had lost his eye in 1771, was taking the cure at this point and was absent.

Obviously Haydn had no need of six horns and three bassoons. As we have said, horn players received more pay than many other players, and when making the crucially important initial contract, a player would sign himself as a horn player even if it were clear that he would be frequently playing some other instrument. For one thing, Peczival was a trained timpani and viola player, and he was clearly more useful in his other two functions than as a third bassoon player. Oliva also played violin, and so did Dietzl, while Carl Franz, although a virtuoso horn player, could also play the baryton and thus, if necessary, the 'cello as well. Purksteiner could, and did, play the viola. Thus, if we reshift the orchestra slightly, we find that we have many more strings than is at first apparent, for Schiringer was also a double bass player and, of course, Haydn also played the violin with the orchestra when he was not conducting operas from the harpsichord. The same applied to Lidl, who must have played 'cello or double bass, rather than baryton, in the orchestra. Haydn's pupil, Ignaz Pleyel, who came to study composition in 1772, probably lived with Haydn and no doubt helped with the string section. This meant that the *Capelle* in 1772 could have:

Violins (Violas): Haydn, Tomasini, Blaschek, Purksteiner, Oliva, Dietzl, Peczival (and Pleyel). Violoncellos: Marteau, Lidl, Franz. Double-Bass: Schiringer. To the list of string players, one might add Christian Specht, who became a professional viola player when his voice failed; and the same later applies to Vito Ungricht, who took up the violin (he was not engaged until 1776, and so does not, of course, count in our roll-call for 1772). For the period 1766–76, Haydn's orchestra consisted, as far as the strings are concerned, of about four violins, one or occasionally two violas, one 'cello, one double bass and the wind instruments and timpani as required. After 1776, the size grew to a total of about twenty-four musicians at Eszterháza, consisting, with some fluctuations, of about eight or nine violins, one or two violas, two violoncellos, one double bass, one (later two) flutes, two oboes, two bassoons, and two horns. As we have seen Haydn had clarinets and trumpets for a brief period each, and his timpani were played by Caspar Peczival (engaged 1771, but there are hardly any known, authentic timpani parts in the music Haydn wrote for Prince Esterházy before that date). There is a useful breakdown in Bartha-Somfai of Haydn's orchestra by sections, for the period 1776–90 (p. 49), while Sonja Gerlach has written about the period up to 1776.[1]

Pohl (II, 15) compared the salaries of Haydn's singers and instrumentalists with those earned by members of the *Hofcapelle* in Vienna, for which we have reasonably complete records; and he discovered that on the whole Prince Nicolaus paid rather higher salaries and, of course, provided free lodging, light and heat as well as a yearly uniform. If we examine the lists of the Esterházy musicians, we can see a perfectly average fluctuation such as one would see in any European city or court of the period; but the atmosphere must have been attractive enough, despite the vile climate and the rather pedantic sense of discipline that was maintained by Prince Nicolaus and Rahier (his Estates Director), to entice men and women of European fame to come and, often enough, to stay there for long periods.

The following contract, made between some Prague musicians and the *Primas* of Poland, Archbishop Prince Podoský, in 1767, will provide an interesting parallel to the contracts made at Eisenstadt and Eszterháza. The contract was drawn up in Warsaw on 10 September 1767, and is signed by 'Gabriel Joh. J. Podoský, Archiepsus gen. Primas Regni Pol. et M. P. Lith. primus Princep. Plaschka'.[2] According to its terms, the higher grade of musicians (the violinist and the two horn players) are to

1 *Haydn-Studien*, Band IV, Heft 1 (1976), pp. 35ff.
2 Primas of the Kingdom of Poland and the Grand Duchy of Lithuania. *Miscellanea Musicologia* VI. Svazek, Prague 1958, pp. 99f. The contract is in German.

receive four Spec. ducats (something less than seventeen gulden) per month, the other, lower grade musicians fourteen Bohemian (normal Austrian) guldens per month. Thus the violin and horn players earned for their Polish sojourn slightly over 200 gulden *per annum*, the lesser players 168. (The standard salary for Haydn's musicians in 1761 was 240 gulden *p.a.* In 1769, the top horn players were earning 300 gulden plus emoluments and in one case – that of Joseph Oliva – 100 ducats or 417 fl. 30 kr.) The Prague musicians received a free trip to Warsaw and back. The other terms of this contract read:

> I^{mo} They are to comport themselves at all times in a proper, sober and willing manner.
> 2do Apart from their music, they are without fail to perform other duties appropriate to princely livrée, when the circumstances require it.
> 3 They are not to enter into any other service here in this country, and whenever the one or the other leaves the princely service, he is to return to Prague.
> 4 And in case one decides at the expiration of this contract not to remain any longer, such a decision must be communicated half-a-year before the expiration.
> The present contract shall be valid for two consecutive years, beginning on the 10th of September 1767 and ending on the same date in 1769.
> [Duplicate contracts shall be exchanged, etc.]

Esterházy's terms were better, not only financially but also in the performing of other, non-musical, services 'appropriate to livrée'. At the Esterházy court, the musicians only had to play music and were not required to perform the duties of the other liveried servants. The French Revolution was still a generation away, but there were surely many proud young musicians who preferred to play music for Esterházy rather than to double as musicians and *valets-de-chambre* for a Polish Prince-Archbishop in far-away Warsaw.

Not least, it is quite clear that Haydn was a master diplomat not only with his Prince but also with the musicians. This Chronicle will show that he had a warm, personal relationship with most of them, lifting their babies from the baptismal font, witnessing their marriage, helping with their petitions, and not least, writing such a supreme masterpiece as the 'Farewell' Symphony to help them out of a *cul-de-sac*. Part of the attraction of playing at Eisenstadt and Esterháza was, of course, playing Haydn's beautiful music, but an equally important part must have been to serve under Haydn, *fürstlicher Capellmeister*.

IV. Some characteristic Documents on Eszterháza

The purpose of this section is to provide at the beginning of this volume four characteristic documents describing life at Eszterháza from various standpoints. The first is a vital document from the Esterházy Archives.

(a) The Spielplan *of the Year 1778*
Presumably such a day-by-day plan of all the musical and theatrical activities at Eszterháza was supposed to have been prepared for each year, starting with 1776; if others were made, they have not survived.

LIST*

of operas, academies, puppet shows and plays which were performed from the 23rd of January till December 1778 at the princely theatre of Esterház.

[Esterházy Archives, Budapest. *Fasc. 2461 1–7. l.*]

January

23. *Die Grenadiere*, a comedy. Polyphemus.
27. Mr. Bienfait and Herr Christl. *Arlequin der Hausdieb*, a pantomime.
28. *Arlequin als Todtengerippe*, a pantomime by the same.
30. *Academie*, *Sinfonia*, Aria by Me. Poschwa, Concerto by M. Hirsch, Aria by M. Dichtler, Sonata by Mr. Luigi, Symphonia by Vanhall, Aria by M. Prandtner, the same by M. Bianchi, Synf.

February

1. *Il finto pazzo*.
3. *Academia musica*.
5. *Il finto pazzo*.
10. *Die Grenadier*, a comedy. Bellandra.
11. *Academie*, *Sinfonia*, Aria by M. Bianchi, Concerto by M. Rosetti, Divert. by M. Pichl; Aria by M. Dichtler, Concertino by Pichl, Aria by M. Bianchi, Synf. by Mr. Haydn.
22. *Academia musica nell'Appartamento*.
24. The same.
26. The same.

March

10. The Pauli company began with *Die falschen Vertraulichkeiten* in 3 acts.
11. *Arnaud*, a drama in 2 acts, and *Der Graf Althaus*, a comedy in 3 acts with Mr. Ulrich, and Bachmeyer in the cast.
12. *Il Barone di Rocca antica*.
13. *Trau, schau, wem*. Played by the Schwarzwald family.
14. *William Buttler*, in 5 acts.
16. *Die verstellte Kranke*.
17. *Emilia Galotti*, in 5 acts.
18. *Der Edelknabe* and *Jenny, oder die Uneigennützigkeit*.
21. On the return of H. Highness: *Henriette, oder Sie ist schon verheirathet*.
22. *Il Barone di Rocca antica*.
23. *Der Gläubiger*, a touching comedy in 3 acts.
24. *Die Haushaltung nach der Mode*, farce in 5 acts.
25. *Der Postzug* in 2 acts and *Wilhelmine*.
27. and 28. (Nothing on account of the wind).
29. *La buona figliuola*. With M. Lamberti[ni] in the cast.
30. *Die Schule der Freigeister* und *Die doppelte Hinderniss*.
31. *Die Subordination*.

April

1. *Die 3 Zwillingsbrüder*.
2. *Das Soldatenglück*.
3. *Der Jurist und der Bauer; der Nachtwächter*.
4. *Die Feuersbrunst*.
5. *Il Finto Pazzo*.
6. *Das Duell* and *Die Windmühle*.
7. *Der zu gefällige Ehemann*.
8. *Der Kühehirte* and *Der dankbare Sohn*.
9. *Arcifanfano*. With Mr. Pezzani in the cast.
10. *Miss Fanny* in 5 acts.
11. *Der Schneider und sein Sohn*.
12. *Die Mütter*.
    No performances during Passion Week and the Holy Easter Day.
20. *Montrose und Surrey*, in 5 acts with Herr Meyer in the cast.
21. *Der Schubkarren des Essighändlers*.
22. *Elfriede*. With Herr Meyer's sister in the cast, the later Dittelmeyerin.
23. *Arcifanfano*.
24. *Der Todte ein Bräutigam* und *Der Bettelstudent*.

---

* Foreign names and titles are given in the orthography of the original sources.

25. *Miss Jenny Warton.*
26. *Der Tambour zahlt alles* and *Erispius (?) Liebesstreiche.*
27. *Sophie, oder der gerechte Fürst* with Mad. Mayer in the cast.
28. *Der Zerstreute.*
29. *Der Graf von Sonnenthal* and *Der Bettler.*
30. *Arcifanfano.*

May

1. *Burlie, Diener, Vater und Schwiegervater.*
2. *Die Zwillingsbrüder.*
3. *La sposa fedele.* With Mad. Ripamonti in the cast.
4. *Der Deserteur* and a burlesque, *Der Kapaun.*
5. *Clementine,* in 5 acts.
6. *Die unähnlichen Brüder.*
7. *La buona figliuola.*
8. *Emilie Waldegrau.*
9. *Die neue Weiberschule.*
10. *La buona figliuola.*
11. *Die Gunst des Fürsten,* in 5 acts.
12. *Nicht alles ist Gold was glänzt.*
13. *Der Stolze, oder der Majoratsherr.*
14. *La buona figliuola.*
15. *Der Hausvater,* in 5 acts.
16. Puppet-show *das ländliche Hochzeitsfest.*
17. *Der Teufel steckt in ihm* and *Herkules in der Hölle.*
18. *La sposa fedele.* With M. Totti in the cast.
19. *Das ländliche Hochzeitsfest.* Puppet-show.
20. *die 3 Zwillinge.*
21. *La sposa fedele.*
22. *Der Westindier.*
23. *Gabriele von Monte Vecchio.*
24. *Arcifanfano.*
25. *Der Spleen* in 5 acts.
26. *Emilie, oder die Treue,* and *Lipperl der Weiberfeind.*
27. *Pamela,* Part I.
28. *La sposa fedele.*
29. *Der Deserteur aus Kindesliebe.*
30. *Stella* in 5 acts, by Goethe.
31. *La Frascatana.*

June

1. *Minna von Barnhelm* in 5 acts.
2. Puppet show: *das ländliche Hochzeitsfest.*
3. *Der Furchtsame.*
4. *Arcifanfano.*
5. *Die 3 Zwillingsbrüder.*
6. *Fayel* in 5 acts.
7. *La sposa fedele.*
8. *Der verlorene Sohn.*
9. *Dürumel, oder der Deserteur.*
10. *Der Ungar in Wien.*
12. *La Frascatana.*
12. *Darf man seine Frau lieben.*
13. *Tankred und Sigismunda.*
14. *Arcifanfano.*
15. *Der Bediente, Nebenbuhler seines Herrn,* and *Sind Mann. od. Weibsp. standhafter in der Liebe.*
16. *Henriette, oder sie ist schon verheiratet.*
17. *Der Minister.*
18. *La sposa fedele.*
19. *Der Zerstreute.*
20. *Die seltsame Eifersucht.*
21. *La sposa fedele.*
22. *Medon, oder die Rache des Weisen.*
23. *Der Edelknabe* and *Jenny.*
24. *Die Stimme der Natur* and *der Herr Vetter.*
25. *La Frascatana.*

26. *Der Galeren Sklave.*
27. *Julie und Romeo.*
28. *Die unsichtbare Dame,* and *ein Nachspiel* [after-piece?].
29. *Der Schuster und sein Freund.*
30. *Die verliebten Zänker.*

July

1. *Der englische Waise* and *Die Batterie.*
2. *Arcifanfano.*
3. *Pamela,* Part II.
4. *Adelson und Salvini.*
5. *La sposa fedele.*
6. *Der unvermuthete Zufall.*
7. *Die dankbare Tochter* and *Die Parodie.*
8. *Der Graf von Hohenwald.*
9. *La sposa fedele.*
10. *Der zu gefällige Ehemann.*
11. *Der Bürger,* a tragedy.
12. *L'astratto.*
13. *Die Wahl,* and *Die Nacht.*
14. Puppet show: *Das ländliche Hochzeitsfest.*
15. *Sidney und Sylly.*
16. [*Sophie, oder*] *Der gerechte Fürst.*
17. *Der Krieg, oder die Soldatenliebe.*

August

On the return of H. Highness.
26. *Maria Wallburg.*
27. *La sposa fedele.*
28. *Der Barbier von Sevilien.*
29. *Geschwinde, ehe man es erfährt.*
30. *L'astratto.*
31. *Pamela,* Part III.

September

On the return of H. Highness from Vienna.
8. *Die Wohltaten unter Anverwandten.*
9. *Wie man die Hand umkehrt.*
10. *Il geloso in cimento.*
11. *Arist, od. der ehrliche Mann.*
12. *Der Graf von Olsbach.*
13. *Il Geloso in cimento.*
14. *Der Schneider und sein Sohn,* and *ein Nachspiel* [after-piece?].
15. Puppet-show: *Dido.*
16. *Die falschen Vertraulichkeiten.*
17. *L'astratto.*
18. *Die Poeten nach der Mode.*
19. *Der Hochzeits Tag,* a tragedy.
20. *La sposa fedele.*
21. *Die Wirtschafterin,* and *Der Kühehirt.*
22. *Die verliebten Zänker.*
23. *Der Bettler,* and *Der Bettelstudent* (or: *Das Donnerwetter,* comedy in 2 acts).
24. *La Frascatana.*
25. *Verwirrung über Verwirrung.*
26. *Stella,* by Goethe.
27. *La Frascatana.*
28. *Die Grafen von Sonnenfels,* and *Der Herr Gevatter.*
29. *Minna von Barnhelm.*
30. *Wie man eine Hand umkehrt.*

October

1. *La buona figliuola.*
2. *Miss Burton, oder das Landmädchen.*
3. *Fanny, oder der Schiffbruch.*
4. *Der Gläubiger.*
5. *Die ungleichen Mütter.*

6. *Der Diener Nebenbuhler* and *Der ungegründete Verdacht.*
7. *Der gute Ehemann.*
8. *La Frascatana.*
9. *Die Unbekannte.*
10. *Adelson und Salvini.*
11. *La Frascatana.*
12. *Trau, schau, wem.*
13. *Der Ungar in Wien.*
14. *Der Postzug,* and *der Selbstmord.*
15. *Der Schubkarren des Essighändlers.*
16. *Die seltsame Probe* and *die Feldmühle.*
17. *Derby,* a tragedy.
18. *Il Geloso in cimento.*
19. *Nicht alles ist Gold was glänzt.*
20. *Clementine.*
21. *Der verlorene Sohn.*
22. *La buona figliuola.*
23. *Der Todte ein Bräutigam, der Herr Gevatter.*
24. *Emilie Waldegrau.*
25. *La sposa fedele.*
26. *Das Findelkind.*
27. *Der Schuster und sein Freund,* and *Die Stimme d. Natur.*
28. The troupe of Pauli and Mayer ended their performances at Esterház with *Das gerettete Venedig.*
29. *L'astratto.*
30. The Diwald troupe began with *Amalie oder die Leidenschaften.* With Mlle. Knapp and Messrs. Bartl, Schilling, Dunst and Weiss in the cast.
31. *Die Wildpretschützen* and *Der Tempel der Venus.* With H. Menninger, Mad. Soliman and Mlle. Diwald in the cast.

November

1. *Der Hausregent.*
2. *D'Arnaud* und *Pygmalion.*
3. *Der Schwätzer.*
4. *Die schöne Wienerin.*
5. *La Frascatana.*
6. *Eugenie.*
7. *Die Bekanntschaft im Bade.*
8. *Der Deserteur aus Kindesliebe.*
9. *So muss man mir nicht kommen.*
10. *Der Entsatz von Wienn.*
11. *Der Geschmack der Nation.*
12. *L'astratto.*
13. *Die schöne Wienerin.*
14. *Die Kindesmörderin.*
15. *L'astratto.*
16. *Der Westindier.*
17. *Die Frau als Courier* and *Das Gespenst auf dem Lande.*
18. *Die Bekanntschaft auf der Redoute,* and *Der unbekannte Wohltätige.*
19. *Die Verstellte Kranke.*
20. *Montrose und Surrey.* With M. Morocz in the cast.
21. *Die Batterie* and *Der Gewürzkrämer.*
22. *La Locanda.*
23. *Der Geburtstag.*
24. *La Locanda.*
25. *Emilia Galotti.*
26. *La Locanda.*
27. *Der Graf Waltron.*
28. *Der betrogene Vormund.*
29. *Amalie, oder die Leidenschaften.*
30. *Richard der dritte.*

December

1. *La Locanda.*
2. *Der Kobold* and *Der Soldat.*
3. *Der Schwätzer.*
4. *Der Geschmack der Nation.*

    5. *Louise, oder der Sieg der Unschuld.*
    6. *Il Geloso in cimento.*
    7. *Alle irren sich.*
    8. *Il Geloso in cimento.*
    9. *Alle haben recht.*
  10. *Nancy, oder die Schule der Eheleute.*
  11. *Die Gunst der Fürsten.*
  12. *Die reisende Comödianten* and *Odoardo.*
  13. *Der Bettelstudent* and *der todte Herr Bruder.*
  14. *Der Graf von Olsbach.*
  15. *Der Teufel an allen Ecken.*
  16. *Die reiche Frau.*
  17. *Es ist nicht alles Gold was glänzt.*
  18. *Der Gefühlvolle.*
  19. *Der Schein betrügt, oder der gute Mann.*
  20. *Die Wildpretschützen.*
  21. *Der Jurist und der Bauer* and *Der Einsiedler.*
  22. *Olivie,* a tragedy.

The full commentary on the operas and marionette operas performed during the 1778 season must be reserved for the Chronicle, but a few brief words of explanation and commentary are obviously required.

    Jan. 30: 'Academie' (concert), held in the great hall, one presumes. 'Mr. Luigi' = Luigi Tomasini.
    Feb. 1: Opera by Dittersdorf.
    Feb. 22: concert in the Prince's apartments (chamber music?).
    March 12: Opera by Dittersdorf.
    March 29: Opera by Piccinni.
    April 4: Probably the play by Großmann, not the marionette opera by Haydn.
    April 9: Opera by Dittersdorf.
    April 28: presumably with Haydn's incidental music (Symphony No. 60).
    May 3: Opera by Guglielmi.
    May 16: Marionette Opera by Joseph Purksteiner.
    May 31: Opera by Paisiello.
    July 12: Opera by Piccinni.
    August 28: The Beaumarchais play in German translation.
    Sept. 10: Opera by Anfossi.
    Sept. 15: Marionette Opera by Haydn.
    Nov. 22: Opera by Gazzaniga.

The list shows that, when the Prince was present, there was a play, an Italian opera or a German marionette opera every night. The concerts all seem to have taken place at the beginning of the season; but incidental chamber music was probably not registered (it might have taken place in the morning, or afternoon). It is curious to observe that for the one evening's revival of Haydn's *Dido*, the Prince had the libretto reprinted; and Haydn had a number of rehearsals (see Chronicle). The list gives a vivid picture, in skeleton form, of the variety of theatrical and operatic life at Eszterháza; and we must imagine a similar pattern occurring in the other years between 1776 and 1790.

(b) The Description of Baron Riesbeck (in the Adaptation of Professor Cramer, 1784)

As we have seen, Eszterháza Castle was considered as completed by its creator in 1784, a year which saw a number of descriptions of the Castle. Some of these, like the 'Excursion' and the 'Beschreibung', and perhaps also the long description of the Empress Maria Theresa's visit in 1773, were printed at the instigation of the Prince; others, such as Friedel's report and the present description, simply happened to be printed in that year. We have translated the version of Professor Cramer (a) because it will have had wide circulation among the musical community of German-speaking

Europe, and will have been read by Haydn as well, and (b) because it is considerably longer than the 'official' English translation.[1]

Ditto Esterhazy. Not long after my arrival here [in Vienna] I made a pleasure trip to the residential castle of Prince Esterhazy, which is about a day's journey from Presburg [*sic*]. You certainly know the place from Moore's description in his travel diaries. With the exception of Versailles, there is perhaps in the whole of France no place to compare with it for magnificence. The castle is very large and filled to bursting with luxurious things. The garden contains everything that human fantasy can conceive to improve or, if you will, undo the work of nature. Pavilions of all kinds stand like the dwellings of voluptuous fairies, and everything is so far removed from the usual human operations that one looks at it as if in the middle of a marvellous dream. I will not enter into a description of all this magnificence, but I must say that, at least in the eyes of one non-connoisseur, I found some of it very offensive because too much art prevails. I remember the walls of the sala terrena, which has painted figures that are at least twelve feet [*12 Schuhe*] high, and since the sala is not big enough for a human eye to take them in, an earthbound figure such as myself felt acutely dwarfed. I know that you are for the grand style, and when viewing these monster figures I remembered everything you told my profane ears about the theory of the Roman school, their large designs, etc., but I am sure that had you seen these fantastical figures you would have readily admitted that the grand style was misplaced here.

What increases the magnificence of the place is the contrast with the surrounding countryside. Anything more dull or depressing can hardly be imagined. The Neusiedler See, from which the castle is not far removed, makes miles of swamp and threatens in time to swallow up all the land right up to the Prince's dwelling, just as it has already swallowed up huge fields containing the most fertile land which had been laid out. The inhabitants of this country look for the most part like ghosts, and in Spring they almost always get cold fever. One has figured out that with half the money the Prince spent on his garden, he could not only have dried out the swamp but regained as much land again from the lake. Since the water flowing into the lake is always more than that which flows out, the danger with which these low-lying lands are threatened is really very acute. What would be necessary would be to construct a canal which would take the superfluous water and pour it into the Danube, an operation which would not strain the Prince's capabilities and would in the eyes of certain persons make him more honourable than by the presence of his magnificent garden. On the other side of the castle one doesn't need to make a day's journey to see Tartars, Hottentots, Iroquois and people from Tierra del Fuego living together and going about their various businesses.

Unhealthy as is the country, especially in Spring and Autumn, and although the Prince himself is attacked by cold fever, he is firmly persuaded that in the whole wide world there is no more healthy and pleasant place. His castle is quite isolated, and he has no one about him except his servants and the strangers who come to admire his beautiful things. He keeps a marionette theatre which is certainly unique of its kind. The biggest operas are given in it. One doesn't know whether to laugh or cry when one sees *Alceste*, *Alcide al Bivio*, etc., given by marionettes all finely costumed. His orchestra is one of the best I ever heard, and the great **Haydn** is his court and theatre composer. For his curious theatre he keeps a poet whose ability to fit large subjects into the theatre, and whose parodies of

---

1 *Travels through Germany, in a series of letters; written in German By the Baron Riesbeck, and translated by The Rev. Mr. Maty, late secretary to the Royal Society, and underlibrarian to the British Museum.* 2 vols., London 1787, p. 68.

serious pieces, are often very successful. His theatrical painter and decorator is an excellent artist, although he can display his talents only on a small scale. In short the operation is small, but the outward trappings are on a very large scale. He often engages a troupe of players for several months at a time, and apart from some servants he is the whole audience. They have his permission to appear uncombed, drunk, and dishevelled. The Prince is not one for the tragic and serious, and he likes it when the characters, like Sancho Panza, lay on the humour with a trowel. Apart from a huge group of servants, he also keeps a bodyguard which consists of handsome people.

I was very sorry not to be able to talk to the famous Haydn. He had gone to Vienna to conduct a grand concert. They say the Prince has given him permission to visit England, France and Spain, where he will be received by his admirers with the proper respect, and his purse richly filled. He has a brother [Johann Michael] who is Kapellmeister in Salzburg [Cramer's footnote: 'Seems to be a mistake for **L. Mozard.** C. F. C.'] and not behind him in the art; but he lacks the diligence to reach his brother's fame.   [Cramer's *Magazin der Musik*, 1784, pp. 112ff.]

It is extraordinary that Europe, in 1784, should still be the victim of geographical differences and imprecise history such as we find in the statement about Haydn's brother. In the 'official' English translation of 1787, we find that Johann Michael has been merged with Ignaz Pleyel: 'He has a brother, who is *Maestro di Capella* at Strasbourg . . .'.

Two items require some comments in more detail. The one concerns the players, their appearance, and the statement that they 'lay on the humour with a trowel'. We may perhaps doubt that they appeared 'uncombed, drunk', etc., but there is a wisp of truth perhaps lurking behind the fog of exaggeration. If we examine Ordoñez's *Alceste*, which the Baron perhaps saw, we will note that the actual score of the marionette opera contains at least one set of highly improper words which were changed in the official version which the Archduchess Marie Christine and her consort heard in August 1775. The Chorus in Act I that originally sang 'Ganz gehorsamer Diener, mein Arsch ist kein Wiener' ('Your obedient servant, my arse is no Viennese') transformed its words to 'Ganz gehorsamer Diener, wir seÿnd keine Wiener' ('Your obedient servant, we aren't Viennese') for the Archduchess. Prince Nicolaus was something of a rake in his younger years, and we may imagine that the German comedies, and particularly the Hanswurstiada, were couched in anything but delicate language.

The other matter concerns the unflattering remarks on the peasants who lived in the surrounding villages. Naturally, most of our descriptions are concerned with the Castle, its treasures, its opera house and the people who lived there or visited, either as guests of the Prince or in the more modest 'Wihrtshaus' with its 'more than twenty guest rooms' (*Beschreibung* 1784). No one paid much attention to the peasants, who were colourful additions to the exotic *feste*, dressed in their national costumes and cheering the Prince in their half-drunken state (we read of copious draughts of wine with which they were provided, no doubt to encourage their princely adulation). But here we read that they looked like ghosts and that their outward appearance, at least to the Baron, was very wild indeed. However, as our chief concern is Haydn, we cannot allow ourselves more than a fleeting glance at those extraordinary Croatian, Hungarian, German and Gypsy peasants; but we must have that glance if only because Haydn often had recourse, in his 'exotic excursions' (Bence Szabolcsi), to their folk music and was therefore by no means unaware of their existence.

There is a distinct lack of literature on this aspect of landed society in Hungary and indeed in Austria, but we may be sure that Eastern European peasants were, on the whole, in a medieval state during the eighteenth century. To quote the late Paul Murray Kendall,[1]

> This society was supported by a faceless mass of serfs and peasants, who counted for nothing except to supply their masters with the surplus of agricultural products and with the furnishings which made possible the splendid picturesqueness. If the reader finds little about the rural worker and the city labourer in this biography, the reason is that almost nothing is recorded about them: their lot was monotonous; their existence simple and narrow; the interest they aroused in the chroniclers, nil. They toiled from sunup till sundown, lived on a level, most of them, of mere subsistence, and remained almost invisible upon the social landscape.

We know more of this faceless society in eighteenth-century France because French historians have devoted more attention to pre-1789 civilization than have their Austro-Hungarian colleagues. We believe that the situation of the French peasant was certainly not worse than his Hungarian counterpart, and that the following description from the hand of the great French historian, Pierre Goubert,[2] may be applied to the Hungarian peasantry: those

> two or three million heads of family who make up the majority of the population: small proprietors or non-proprietors, small farmers or *métayers*, stock-breeders without real herds, craftsmen with a handful of tools. Their dwellings were thatch, their crockery wood or earthen, and their clothing and furniture worth not more than a few *livres*. Their aim was quite simply to see the year out. They practically never participated in the parish assemblies (except as silent witnesses, if that); they were never churchwardens, never members of the 'body politic', nor of course syndics or consuls (two rough equivalents of the present-day rural 'mayor'). Except in a few [instances], they never learned to read or write, and received their spiritual food from the Sunday sermon, the cult of local saints and relics, and folk tales retold around the evening hearth. They preserved all the fears, panics, brutality and submission in a kind of obscure mental recess. And they gave their wives as many children as it pleased Heaven to bestow – children half of whom never reached adulthood, while those who did survive had no practical prospects of rising in the world. Their economic, social, political and cultural dependence was total, and as a rule they could hope for no improvement.
>
> In the absence of physical, sometimes of mental resources, and no matter how brave they might be, these dependent peasants were continually threatened. Threatened by epidemics and their own low resistance to infection; by epizootic diseases which bring instant ruin (they could not afford to buy more livestock); and by acute variations in harvests and above all in employment, since they relied on the work they did for other people to buy the bread which they themselves could produce. In cases of economic/demographic crisis ... they lapsed into beggary, vagrancy or death. In this class, it was more usual to sink than to rise.

---

1 *Louis XI*, London 1974, p. 19.
2 *The Ancien Régime: French Society, 1600–1750*, London 1974, pp. 108f.

(c) The Description of Johann Friedel (1784)[1]

Esterhaß is in the county [*Gespannschaft*] of Oedenburg, a few hundred paces from the Neusiedler See. The creator of this delightful and marvellous castle, Prince Esterhaßy, had a dam erected across this lake a few years ago which is easily half-an-hour long if you walk it and shortens the way to Preßburg by five or six hours. This dam is very massive and is planted with trees on both sides. The whole surrounding countryside is a flat field, and rich pasture-land alternates with fruitful arable country. Only at the edge of the lake, bountiful Ceres has yielded a piece of land to Bacchus, and quite a good wine grows there. Now, as I said, a few hundred paces on the other side of the dam rises the majestic Esterhaß, unique of its kind and surely the most magnificent castle in the I. R. crown lands. In front of the main building on each side are the principal sentries of the princely grenadiers, in blue and red uniforms, who are all fine-looking lads over six feet tall. The courtyard boasts a large fountain which is opposite the main double staircase. The building is very extensive and is ornamented with all the rules and delights of architecture. The three storeys contain over 500 [*sic*] rooms, all of them magnificently furnished. Behind the main building, towards the great garden, and on the same line as the neighbouring large courtyards, are the other seigneurial buildings, that is for the house officers, the stables for 100 horses together with a summer and winter riding school, the great theatre, the picture gallery, the quarters for the princely *Kapelle*, opera singers and actors, the barracks for the militia and the commodious inn. At the end of these buildings there are, between alleys [of trees], various houses of all sorts of craftsmen, and these alleys lead on one side to the nearby village of Seplak, and on the other to the village of Schüttin [Süttör] so that when your back is to the alleys you can see in front of you the churches of these villages.

The great garden is an hour's walk in circumference, with broad alleys cut between trees that are hundreds of years old and with many side lanes that lead into thick and cooling bushes and that enliven the eye, tired by all the regularities, with their natural wildness. Everywhere one sees delightful fountains, fine statues, arbours and benches on which to rest. – In this garden there is also a Sun Temple, and Temples to Diana, to Fortune and to Love, all of them wonderfully ornamented and furnished. On the so-called oval place one is just now at work on a Chinese Pleasure House, known as the 'Bagatelle', which has three storeys, a gallery under the eaves and is charmingly situated.

The Orangery is very fine and bountiful; and the Pheasant Reserve quite incomparable. In this garden there is also a marionette theatre, which on account of its splendour and the artfully fashioned puppets as well as their very costly dresses, is quite unique of its kind. At the end of this expansive garden, which is enclosed all round with an iron fence, there is a great thick wood, in which stag and wild boar are kept, but are quite tame and come and nudge the walkers all the time.

The furnishing of the rooms is of a magnificence that almost defies description. The excess can be viewed in the so-called store-rooms, where all these valuables are stored for which there was no room in chambers; and there are so many that one could furnish a whole castle with them. But one must differentiate between these store-rooms and the princely jewel-room, which is not at Esterhaß but at the Fortress of Forchtenstein.

The great theatre exceeds in magnificence and beauty anything of its kind ever viewed. Gold, mirrors and costly marbles adorn it in profusion, but the theatre as such shows the Prince's own excellent taste. Every day there are German

---

1 *Briefe aus Wien von Johann Friedel an einem Freund in Berlin*, Leipzig and Berlin 1784.

plays alternating with Italian *opera buffa*. The music is played by large forces and is as excellent as it would have to be under the direction of such a great composer as *Herr Kapellmeister* Haiden [*sic*]. – In short, everything here is on such a scale and so imposing that even the most unfeeling and casual onlooker must be greatly impressed.[1]

(d) The 'Excursion à Esterhaz en Hongrie' (1784)

Most of us learned of this extraordinary document from its enthusiastic reception in Sacheverell Sitwell's book on Baroque art, which was such an unconventional book in its day.[2] It is certainly one of the most vivid and, to use Sitwell's phrase, 'entertaining' descriptions of court life at Eszterháza, and it gives us particular pleasure to reproduce it here and thus bring its contents to a wider public than it ever enjoyed in its obviously very brief existence as a pamphlet (see pp. 104–16).[3] An explanatory note is given below.

Notes on 'Excursion à Esterhaz en Hongrie':
Friedel: the editions we consulted are all dated 1784, not 1783; the same mistake is made with the *Beschreibung* (last paragraph of pamphlet), which was published in 1784, though the writer of 'Excursion' may have seen a copy at Eszterháza by May 1784. The village 'Schitter' is Süttör. Monbijou, the little *Lustschloß*, is described (*Beschreibung* 1784) as being 'eine kleine Stunde' on foot from the main castle. The Librarian who is the Court Chaplain was in 1784 Pater Primitivus Niemecz (Niemetz). 'Le Sieur *Auguste*' who was 'anglois' = Bridgetower Sen. (*vide supra*, p. 38). Among the people whom our writer met at Eszterháza, the members of the aristocracy are easily recognized. General Jerningham was Charles Jerningham, then British Ambassador to the Court of Vienna and the go-between in Haydn's negotiations with Forster of London: *vide infra*, p. 449. Lieut.-Col. Baron Rosetzki is mentioned twice; he and Stephan von Nagy belonged to the Esterházy *Hof*, Nagy as Superintendent-General.

---

1 Haydn probably saw this report when it was reprinted *in extenso* in the *Preßburger Zeitung*, 10 March 1784.
2 *The Baroque South*, London 1930 (reprinted 1951).
3 The author of the pamphlet is, according to A. Peter Brown and James T. Berkenstock (*Haydn-Studien* III, 3/4, 1974, p. 327), Alphons Heinrich Traunpaur chevalier d'Orphanie.

EXCURSION

À

ESTERHAZ

EN HONGRIE

EN MAI 1784.

Le Maître, le Palais, le Théâtre, & le Bois,
Tout plaît en cés beaux Lieux, tout instruit à la fois.

VIENNE

chez Jean Ferdinand Noble de Schönfeld.

C'est au Chevalier d'A— Gentilhomme provençal aussi aimable qu'instruit, & actuellement Lieutenant au regiment d'Infanterie hongroise qui porte le nom du Prince regnant, que je suis redévable des prémieres notions qu'il me donna a *Gorice* en 1780 du Palais & des Jardins d'Esterhaz qu'il venoit d'admirer & dont il parloit avec cet enthousiasme inné aux vrais Connoisseurs du grand & du beau. Si l'Aürostatie avoit eté déja connue alors, je me ferois d'abord déterminé à me laisser transporter vers l'endroit, dont on me donnoit une idée aussi ravissante que parfaitement exacte. Je brûlois d'un Désir continuel de le voir, mais d'autant plus infructueusement, qu'eloigné à 40 postes de là, je me trouvois trop peu favorisé de dons de Plutus, pour oser songer à entreprendre un voiage pareil.

A 2   Retiré

3

Retiré de l'actualité du ſervice en 1782, je n'eus rien plus à cœur que de réaliſer mes ſouhaits, d'autant plus que j'avois choiſi par preference la Capitale de la Monarchie autrichienne pour ma retraite. Je fus agréablement fortifié dans mon intention après avoir fait la lecture réiterée des *lettres de Friedel à un de ſes amis à Berlin*, ouvrage qui parut en 1783, & ou l'utilité eſt intimement réunie à l'agrement. J'y trouvai avec la plus vive ſatisfaction, dans la derniere de ces lettres, un paſſage ou ce judicieux ecrivain fait mention d'Eſterhaz: cependant ce n'eſt qu'une eſquiſſe en mignature & j'eſperois rencontrer une deſcription étendue, circonſtanciée & digne en un mot de l'objet. Ces conſiderations me firent faiſir avec avidité le deſſein irrevocable de me rendre ſur les Lieux & je l'executai au mois de Mai récemment ecoulé. Je m'y arretai aſſés long tems pour voir, admirer & décrire tout à loiſir. Je ne puis qu'être charmé des heureux ſuccès de mon entreprise, & j'oſe me flatter que tous ceux qui auront la même curioſité feront de mon ſentiment.

Il eſt inconteſtablement décidé, que chaque païs reçu plus ou moins de mains bienfaiſantes de la Nature des marques diſtinctives, telles que la bonté particuliere du climat, la fertilité du ſol, la Réunion des Phénomenes phyſiques, l'aſſemblage des productions innées au don naturel, ou introduites par le ſecours ingenieux de l'art créateur, enfin? un enchainement continu & viſible de ces objets dignes de l'obſervation la plus réflechie,

Les anciens exaltoient avec juſtice leurs ſept merveilles: les habitans modernes du Dauphiné, qui fixent au même nombre celles de leur province, n'ont peut-être également pas tort de les montrer aux etrangers, & de vanter l'exiſtence de leur Montagne renverſée, de leur puits de feu &c. &c. ainſi ſucceſſivement il n'y a guere de contrée ſur nôtre Planete ſublunaire, qui ne ſoit à même d'offrir, dans un dégré plus ou moins eminent, des particularités ſuſceptibles de remarques du philoſophe & de l'examen d'un naturaliſte conſommé.

Ceci poſé pour fondement, il eſt hors de doute, que l'Hongrie ne ſoit une des portions de l'Europe le mieux favoriſées par la nature. Entrecoupée de fertiles campagnes, de rivieres fourmillantes de poiſſons les plus favoureux, abondamment pourvûë tant de metaux précieux, que de tous les mineraux imaginables, elle procure aux commodités de la vie & à la ſanté les préſens variés de Céres & de Pomone, les nectars les plus moëlleux de Bachus, des chevaux vigoureux & infatigables, une quantité de beſtiaux ſi prodigieuſe, qu'on en exporte par milliers chez l'etranger, & tous les avantages combinés de l'induſtrie & du commerce. La nature paroit ſ'être epuiſée pour enrichir l'etendue conſiderable de ce royaume, qui en outre poſſede, auſſi bien qu'Athenes & Rome autrefois, ſes Areopages & ſes Tuſculanes, ſes Epaminondas & ſes Cicerons, ſes Cytheres & ſes Tiburs.

La nation même mérite à tous egards d'être examinée de près: elle n'a aucunement dégénéré de ces Heros celebres,

Les

bres, auxquels elle doit fa courageufe origine. Les Hongrois naiffent tous guerriers & l'impartialité ne peut leur refufer cette qualité généralement réconue. L'utilité de fervices importans qu'ils rendirent dans des tems très modernes, les coups eclatans & décififs qu'ils porterent aux ennemis de leur Rois dans les conjonctures les plus epineufes, font gravés en caracteres ineffacables dans les archives de la fidelité des peuples & de la réconnaiffance réciproque des Princes.

J'efpere de n'encourir aucun réproche de préfomption, en ofant me flatter de rendre un fervice agréable à l'homme de goût & de génie, à l'artifte, au litterateur, au connoiffeur epuré, en un mot, à tous ces individus affts rares, qui compofent la claffe rétrecie, conprife fous le titre de gens du monde, en expofant à leurs regards, l'analyfe exacte d'un fejour de l'Hongrie, le plus délicieux fans contredit des etats hereditaires de l'augufte Monarchia autrichienne: d'un fejour, ou la nature fecondée par l'art étale les richeffes du goût, de l'aifance & de la fomptuofité.

Les perfonnes facrées de Marie Therefe & de François I. d'immortelle memoire, entourées de leur belle & nombreufe famille, daignerent honorer en diverfes occafions ces lieux charmans, de leur préfence chérie & y agréer des fêtes que le patriotifme du Prince tacha de rendre dignes d'elles. Les Miniftres etrangers & regnicoles, les Ambaffadeurs des têtes couronnés, les favans de la prémiere claffe, les artiftes rénommés, ne négligent jamais pendant leur

leur fejour à Vienne ou à leur paffage, d'avoir la fatisfaction d'aller contribuer perfonellement aux eloges autentiques qu'on eft forcé de rendre à cette feconde Ile de Calypfo. Quoique fituée à peu de diftance de la Metropole, très peu d'habitans de cette ville eurent l'occafion de s'y rendre & moins encore de l'admirer. Ce font eux en confequence, ce font les etrangers de diftinction, les Cofmopolites inftruits & les voiageurs des plus fins, qui me fauront gré de les convaincre de particularités d'un Bijou fi à portée d'être vû & qui mérite d'être appreeié.

Le nom de Bijou que je place icy, ne court certainement aucun rifque de pafter pour une expreffion hyperbolique & les fens tomberont aifement d'accord, qu'il ne pouvoit être mieux employé pour donner une idée cathegorique d'un palais, ou les efforts du genie fe font réunis au point, que le premier coup d'œil qu'on jette fur l'exterieur prévient le plus avantageufement en fa faveur, avant qu'on ait eu le tems d'en confiderer les beautés intrinfeques.

Perfuadé d'avance de la réalité de tout ce que mon ami le Chevalier d'A— m'en avoit dit pendant fon fejour à Gorice, je partis de Vienne le 25. du mois de Mai recemment ecoulé & je fus rendu aprés un trajet commode de 12 heures à Efterhaz.

Cet endroit, le petit Verfailles de l'Hongrie, eft fitué dans la partie baffe de ce Royaume, au Cercle, ou Comitat d'Oedenbourg, à 5 1/2 poftes de la Refidence impe-

imperiale & à quelques centaines de pas du fameux Lac de *Neufedel*.

Son Alteffe le Prince regnant NICOLAS ESTER-HAZY DE GALANTHA , & du faint Empire romain, Comte de Frakno, Chevalier de la Toifon d'or, Grand-Bailli du Comitat d'Oedenbourg, Chambellan, Confeiller intime & actuel d'Etat, Marechal des armées de S. M. I. & R. apoftolique, Colonel proprietaire d'un Regiment d'Infanterie hongroife de fon nom, & Capitaine de la Garde-noble hongroife, eft depuis environ vingt ans, le créateur du fuperbe Palais qui y porte fon nom : il fit conftruire en 1780. fur un des marais du Lac une Digue d'une demie-heure de trajet, Cette Levée de plus folides, bordée d'arbres de chaque coté, racourcit de 5 à 6 heures le chemin qu'il falloit faire cy devant pour y arriver de Presbourg.

La campagne des environs eft un Terrain uni & entouré de Prairies & de Champs, dont la fertilité réjouit l'humanité: ce n'eft que fur les bords du Lac que la bienfaifante Cérès abandonna géneroufement au Dieu de la Vigne un petit terrain, qui ne laiffe pas que de produire des vins affés bons.

C'eft à peu de diftance de ces Vignobles que s'éleve majeftueufement le magnifique Palais, l'unique en ce genre de vaftes Provinces de la domination autrichienne.

En face de l'edifice principal font de deux cotés les corps de Garde des Grenadiers du Prince, Cette Troupe eft

eft compofée d'hommes choifs, faits au tour, d'une taille au dela de 5 pieds 8 pouces, & portant l'uniforme bleu avec des paremens rouges, & brandebourgs blancs. La Cour eft ornée d'un beau Baffin en Face de deux Efcaliers qui conduifent au grand Sallon. Le Batiment eft trés fpacieux & richement pourvu des regles attraiantes de l'architecture la mieux compaffée. Trois étages contiennent au dela de 126 appartenens, dont l'aneublement eft d'un goût exquis.

Derriere le corps du logis & vers le Jardin , on trouve en ligne droite les batimens détachés du Palais, avec les cours commodes & fpacieufes de leur dependance. Deux de ces batimens font occupés par la fuite nombreufe des Officiers de l'hotel : les autres font, la belle Ecurie pour 100 chevaux, les manegés d'eté & d'hyver, le Théâtre, la Gallerie des peintures , la demeure des Muficiens, Operiftes & Comediens du Prince, l'Orangerie , le Théâtre des Marionettes , le Caffé, l'Auberge feigneuriale , qui a peu de fes egales, même dans les Capitales.

Au bout de ces batimens on trouve entre des allées les maifons ou logent divers artifans néceffaires dans un endroit auffi peuplé. Ces allées conduifent d'un coté au village voifin de *Séblak* & de l'autre à celui de *Schitter* : de forte qu'en s'y promenant on a en avant & en arriere la perfpective artiftement menagée de l'eglife de l'un ou de l'autre de ces villages.

B

La

6

La Peripherie du Jardin & du bois contigu, nommé en hongrois *Lescb*, est considerable : il est agreablement entrecoupé par des larges allées, que bordent des arbres feculaires & entrelacé de chemins de traverse, qui conduisent à des taillis rafraichissans, ou l'œil fatigué d'un aspect régulier, se trouve ranimé par les Sits que la nature sauvage y présente. Les perspectives les plus pittoresques, Cascades, Berceaux, Cabinets de Verdure, Grottes, Vafes, Statues, Charmilles, Ruines, Boulingrins, Volieres, Colonades, Treillis, Niches, Hermitage, Labyrinthe, Pavillions, Dorures, enfin! tout ce qui peut concourir à l'amenité naturelle & artificielle d'un Jardin des Fées, plonge l'ame dans des sensations d'autant plus piquantes, qu'à chaque pas elle eprouve un nouveau charme, qui par fa combinaison change les heures en minutes.

Sur la place dite ovale on voit un Pavillon chinois nommé *Bagatelle* : il est de deux etages entourés d'une Gallerie & le local est mignon.

Quatre temples consacrés dans le bois au Soleil, à Diane, à la Fortune, & à l'Amour, sont superieurement ornés & l'ameublement en est du dernier goût.

L'Orangerie est de toute beauté & les arbres qu'on y trouve font en grand nombre : la Faisanderie est incomparable. On trouve en outre dans ce Jardin delicieux un Théatre de Marionettes, qui par l'art qui y domine & l'habillement precieux des Poupées, n'a rien d'egal en ce genre de divertissement: on l'evalue à 30000 florins.

A l'extremité du Jardin, se présente un Parc etendu & rempli de Cerfs & de Sangliers assés apprivoisés, pour passer sans occasionner le moindre danger, à coté des personnes qui vont s'y promener. Les ornemens intrinseques du Palais font d'une magnificence dont la description détaillée paroitroit presqu'incroiable: on peut juger de l'abondance qui y regne en tous genres en voiant la Garderobe de l'hotel, ou se conserve un amas des curiosités precieuses qui n'ont pu trouver place dans les apartemens & dont le nombre est si considerable, qu'on en decoreroit commodement un second chateau: on ne doit d'ailleurs pas confondre ce depositoire local avec le Tresor particulier du Prince, qu'on garde dans la Forterelle de *Forchenstein*, en hongrois *Frakno*, située sur une haute Montagne à quelques lieues d'Oedenbourg. La salle de l'Opera surpasse en beauté & en somptuosité tout ce qu'on peut se figurer en ce genre. L'or, les glaces, les dorures, les pendules, les magots & divers autres ornemens de prix y font repandus avec choix sur la Gallerie & dans les Loges. Quand au local, il constate par sa construction l'excellence du goût dès longtems décidé du Prince : on y a tous les jours alternativement Opera italien ou Comedie allemande, ou chacun à l'entrée libre & gratuite. L'Orchestre est nombreux & aussi parfait qu'il ne peut manquer de l'être sous la direction d'un Musicien aussi theoretique que le célèbre *Hayden*, Maître de la Chapelle du Prince, la même dont les brillantes compositions font les delices des Concerts anglois & françois. Enfin, je ne puis mieux conclure qu'en assurant que les objets choisis qu'on rencontre dans Esterhaz font si frappans & si multipliés, qu'ils ne peuvent manquer de faire l'im-

B 2

7

La Levée ſur la digue, dont j'ai parlé d'abord au commencement de cette deſcription, eſt d'une utilité ſi généralement reconnue par les nationaux & par les étrangers, qu'elle ſeule ſuffiroit pour rendre la mémoire du Prince immortelle, ſi elle ne l'étoit déjà dès longtems par les Services importans que lui & tous ceux de cette illuſtre maiſon ont rendus en diverſes occaſions à la Monarchie, à l'etat, à l'humanité en général, & à leurs ſujets en particulier. Cette Levée, auſſi commode que ſolide, porte ſur 12 pieds de profondeur au travers des marais, & couta des ſommes proportionnées à la grandeur de l'entrepriſe. Elle ſera entretenue à perpetuité par la famille, qui a obtenu de la Cour un octroy pour y placer un péage; une Piramide placée à l'endroit ou l'on en jetta les fondemens, indiquera par une inſcription en latin, allemand & hongrois, le nom du Philantrope qui en conçut l'idée & l'époque de ſa Création, qui eſt l'année 1780 : elle eſt aſſés large pour que deux voitures puiſſent y paſſer.

Les deux étages & le Rez de chauſſée du palais contiennent, indépendamment des ſalles & du Belvedere, 126 appartemens. Les batimens ſeparés & de la dependance du Palais ont, m'a-t-on dit, 774 chambres, parmi les quelles celles qui ſont deſtinées aux Cavaliers étrangers ſont d'un ameublement exquis & dans l'enceinte de la grande cour.

On donna le 26 Mai dans la ſalle des ſpectacles, le ſuperbe opera *d'Armide*, nouvellement mis en muſique par le ſieur Joſeph Hayden, qui comme je l'ai déjà dit, eſt le maître de la Chapelle du Prince. La beauté de la compoſition

l'impreſſion la plus vive ſur le ſpectateur le plus inſenſible.

Après avoir couché par écrit les obſervations détaillées ſuivantes, je quittai ce riant ſéjour au bout d'une ſemaine, ravi de remarques que j'avois eu l'occaſion dy faire : ceux qu'une noble curioſité y conduira, feront pénétrés de la réalité de mêmes ſentimens & ſouſcriront avec plaiſir à l'epigraphe que j'ai placée impartialement au frontiſpice de l'excurſion le plus agréable que j'ai faite en ma vie.

La compagnie des Grenadiers du Prince eſt de 146 hommes dont 40 ont au delà de 6 pieds & les plus petits la taille de 5 pieds & 9 pouces.

La *Prairie* eſt un endroit du boſquet au bout d'une allée collaterale du *Temple du Soleil*. On voit au milieu de cette charmante prairie & ſur un Piédeſtal de rocaille une très belle Statue de *Latone*, la *Déeſſe de la Terre*. L'affect & le draperie ſont d'autant plus dignes de l'attention d'un connoiſſeur, que l'ouvrage eſt de l'habile ciſeau d'un ſculpteur ſujet du Prince & habitant du village voiſin de *Szeplak*.

En entrant ſur cette prairie à la droite & en face de cette ſtatue, on decouvre un hermitage factice & conſtruit ſelon toutes les regles adaptées à ces ſortes des batimens. L'œil y eſt agreablement ſurpris par les attraits les plus ſinguliers de l'illuſion: ce morceau merite une attention particuliere.

La

8

position egaloit la pompe de la représentation. Les habillemens heroiques & les decorations ne laissoient rien à desirer. Madame Methilde Bologna jouoit le role d'Armide : le Sieur Prosper Braghetti celui de Renaud : le Sieur Antoine Specioli celui d'Ubalde : le Sieur Paul Mandini celui d'Idrene : Madame Constance Valdesturla celui de Zelmire , & le Sieur Leopold Dichtler celui de Clotarque. Les autres qui ne jouoient pas ce soir, sont Madame Specioli, Mad. Polcell, les Sieurs Morati & Negri. Tous ces sujets sont choisis ainsi que ceux de la Troupe des Comediens allemans.

On voit dans la chambre des Porcelaines un elite des porcelaines de la Chine, du Japon, de Dresde & de Vienne. Ce sont des grouppes, des figures, plats, assietes, tasses, jattes, pots, vases &c. parmi une quantité considerable des pieces dignes de remarque, on admire entre autres un crucifix très artistement travaillé de porcelaine blanche, & les bustes de Joseph II. & de Marie Thérèse de porcelaine de bisuit.

La *Bibliotheque* contient près de 8000 volumes en ouvrages choisis qu'on augmente journellement, divers manuscripts interessans & relatifs à l'histoire d'Hongrie, tels qu'un *recueil de decrets & patentes emanées depuis 1594. jusqu'en 1687. un faveur d'un François Esterhaz de Galantha & ses descendans.* Toutes ces pièces authentiques sont figurées de la main propre des Empereurs Rodolphe II., Matthias, Ferdinand I., Ferdinand II., & Leopold. C'est sous le Regne de ce dernier Monarque que les Comtes Ester-

Esterhazy furent faits Princes du St. Empire romain avec le privilege de placer la lettre L. dans l'ecusson de leurs armoiries. On trouve en autre dans cette bibliotheque une quantité d'excellentes estampes de meilleurs maitres, beaucoup de cartes, des desseins, une pendule artificielle, des globes, &c. une autre bibliotheque privée du Prince occupe deux chambres dans neuf armoires de bois de noyer très artistement construites avec des ornemens dorés : elles renferment les œuvres modernes des ecrivains les plus goûtés de l'allemagne, de l'angleterre, & de la france.

La *Chapelle* est d'une noble simplicité, marbrée en gris avec des dorures, & pourvue de quatre oratoires : l'autel offre un tableau bien desiné & representant St. Antoine de Padoue.

On travaille actuellement à deux magnifiques Cascades colossales, vis à vis de la façade du Palais vers les Jardins & aux cotés de l'allée capitale, dont la perspective à perte de vue donne sur le village de St. Nicolas.

Les contours du pavillon chinois feront embellis par huit grandes statues chinoises, & quatre grottes dans le même goût.

Non seulement il y a de distance en distance des piquets de Grenadiers, mais l'attention du Prince va jusqu'à ordonner un poste de nuit à l'entrée de l'auberge pour la sûreté des effets appartenans aux etrangers,

Le

Le Lieutenant Colonel Baron Rofetzki, Cavalier de la Cour du Prince & le Sieur de Nagy, gentilhomme hongrois & Surintendant général des biens & Seigneuries, accueillent avec bonté & diftinction les perfonnes qui s'adreffent a eux. Une politeffe marquée anime generalement tous les individus attachés au fervice du Prince.

La falle de l'Opera avec les loges, la gallerie & le parterre, peut contenir commodement 500 perfonnes.

On trouve dans le Palais un Cabinet conftruit de toutes les efpèces de bois etrangers des Indes & de l'Amerique: on eft embaumé en y entrant. Ce Cabinet eft evalué à 80000 florins.

Le celebre compofiteur Hayden eft natif de *Bruck fur la Leytha*: fon affabilité eft auffi admirable que fon art.

Efterhaz fourmille d'etrangers pendant tout l'eté, & les fuperbes appartemens du Prince font journellement vifibles, d'autant plus qu'il porte la generofité jufqu'à fe gêner en paffant d'une pièce à l'autre, jufqu'à ce que la curiofité des connoiffeurs foit pleinement fatisfaite.

Le *Jardin d'hyver*, à l'aile gauche du Palais vers les jardins, eft garni de perroquets, volieres, rocailles, ponts chinois, petits ruiffeaux & ce morceau eft d'une elegance achevée.

A la droite de la falle d'Opera eft un *Caffé* avec deux Billiards, d'ou l'on peut être fervi pendant les fpectacles avec diverfes fortes de rafraichiffemens. La jeune & jolie maitreffe du logis joue adroitement au Billiard.

Une chambre de l'auberge feigneuriale eft habitée par un jeune Lettré plein de talens, qui y tient une ecole normale pour une quarantaine d'enfans des perfonnes attachées à la Cour.

La moitié de la compagnie des grenadiers eft avec le Capitaine à *Eifenftadt*, autre magnifique chateau de la famille d'Efterhazy & ou refide actuellement la Princeffe regnante, née Conteffe de Weiffenwolf, Ce palais meriteroit une defcription feparée.

L'uniforme complet du Prince & l'equipage de fon cheval, lorfqu'il fe pofte dans des grandes folemnités à la Téte de la belle Garde dont il eft le Capitaine, eft brodé en perles orientales de plus fines: on l'evalue à 100000 florins.

La *chambre d'armes* contient une quantité de fufils, carabines, arquebufes, piftolets, fabres, & autres armes d'un goût varié. Plufieurs de ces pièces font garnies en or & en argent, & montés en porphire, ivoire &c.

La *gallerie des peintures* occupe l'aile droite du rez de chauffée. On y trouve pas feulement beaucoup d'excellens originaux des ecoles italienne & flamande, mais aussi

C

aussi plusieurs morceaux choisis du pinceau du Sieur Grundemann, très habile peintre du Cabinet de Son Altesse, & qui s'apprete à regaler le public d'une description raisonnée de cette gallerie.

Un grand batiment à la gauche du palais a des logemens commodes pour 250 personnes. Le medecin du corps y loge ainsi que la chapelle du Prince, les Operistes & les Comediens allemans. On y trouve aussi *une Apoticairerie* très bien conditionnée.

Le *Theâtre des Marionettes* est en face de la salle de l'Opera. Le local en est assez grand, mais sans loge ni gallerie. Le parterre a la forme d'une grotte garnie de rocailles & coquillages, qui forment lorsqu'elle est eclairée un coup d'œil etonnant.

Le *Jardin des roses* est un enclos en forme de labyrinthe dans une de grandes allées laterales du bois. Un melange de fleurs de toutes espéces, principalement de celles qui lui donnent leur nom, parfume cet agréable local & procure quelque relache à l'œil fatigué d'avoir admiré tant d'autres objets plus elevés.

Monbijou à une petite lieue en ligne droite du Palais & derriere le village de St. Nicolas qui fait face à l'allée capitale, est à l'extremité du parc. Cette elegante maison de chasse sous la forme d'un charmant pavillon, est appuiée à un parc de chiens, qui sert d'asile à une quantité de Daims. Elle est construite au centre d'un parterre

de

112

de plus rians. Le Prince y va quelquefois jouir du divertissement de la petite chasse pendant le printems. L'architecture de l'edifice est mignonne, avec un toit à la françoise decoré d'une horloge & d'un Belvedere en gallerie, d'où l'on decouvre un terrain varié & etendu jusqu'auprés d'Oedenbourg, qui en est à trois heures de distance : les appartemens ont exactement le même goût & la même magnificence qui regne abondamment dans ceux du Palais d'Esterhaz. Le parterre qui cercle ce lieu de delices, est entrelacé de cabinets, de berceaux, niches, statues &c. & de deux grottes très artistement arrangées, dont l'une sert de Chapelle.

J'eus l'occasion d'admirer dans l'attelier du sculpteur du Prince, derriere la caserne des Grenadiers, les deux superbes Grouppes de grandeur colossale & destinés à l'embellissement des Cascades dont j'ai parlé ci dessus. Ils paroissent à vûe de pays exceder chacun le poids de 25 quintaux. Le premier de ces Grouppes represente la credule *Leda* assise & caressant la tête du Cigne seducteur. On voit de coté Cupidon riant sous cape de la nouvelle reussite du pere des dieux. L'autre Grouppe offre *Andromede* enchainée à un rocher, prête à être engloutie par un monstre marin, & delivrée par *Thesée*. Ces six figures grouppées sont superieurement executées & indiquent aux connoisseurs de la fable, *que les stratagêmes amoureux n'ont pas toujours un succés egal.* Deux petits grouppes de Genies d'une fine allegorie seront postés aux cotés de ces deux pieces remarquables. Le Colonel du corps des Ingenieurs, Baron de Brequin, si celebre par ses vastes connoissances dans la partie

de

10

de l'Hydraulique, trouva les moiens par une machine artificielle dirigée par quatre chevaux, de fournir aux Cafcades & Baffins du jardin le Volume d'eau dont elles ont befoin, & que la nature a refufé au bois.

Cet habile Phyficien eut l'adreffe de decouvrir une veine capitale qui en reçoit quelques autres, & au moien de laquelle l'abondance de l'eau dans le puits eft toujours telle, qu'au bout d'un travail de quatre heures elle n'avoit diminué que de deux pouces.

Le *Pavillon hollandois* fitué dans un des agréables bosquets dont ce bois eft rempli, eft un cabinet à treillage, dont les murs font couverts de carreaux bleuatres de terre cuite à la flamande, & qui reprefentent des figures, des payfages, animaux &c.

Les *champs elyfées* forment un terrain ou l'on trouve de jeux de bague, des chaifes artificielles, des efcarpolettes, & autres amufemens *champetres*.

Une quantité de faifans parcourt paifiblement les allées & les fentiers du bois. Cet agrément joint à la melodie des Roffignols domiciliés dans cette contrée, en rend la promenade incomparable. Un des charmes dont on jouit à Efterhaz eft de n'y être aucunement gené. Defire t'on d'être prefenté au Prince & de lui faire la Cour, on eft affuré d'en être reçu avec l'affabilité qui caracterife les vrais Grands; veut on garder l'incognito, foit parce qu'on n'a pas avec foi des habillemens convenables, ou par d'autres

tres

tres motifs quelconques, on peut egalement compter fur une liberté la plus parfaite. A fix heures chacun fe rend à la falle des fpectacles, & on y prend place au parterre fans le moindre compliment; à l'inftant que le Prince paroit dans fa loge, le coup d'archet fe donne & après une Simphonie dans le dernier goût, on eft enchanté par le fpectacle.

Le fervice & la parade militaire, accompagnée d'une bande de Hautboiftes, s'y fait avec toute la regularité & la precifion imaginable. La Garde monte à onze heures, fait quelques mouvemens, défile en très bon ordre devant les fenêtres du Prince & va occuper les poftes. La Marche muficale eft exactement cadencée, fort harmonieufe & de la compofition de Hayden: c'eft tout dire.

Le Bibliothecaire, qui eft en même tems Chapelain de la Cour, eft un ecclefiaftique inftruit, laborieux & en etat de repondre pertinemment aux queftions fcientifiques qu'on lui adreffe.

La fymmetrie, l'ordre & la propreté qui regnent dans les offices de l'hôtel, correfpondent admirablement avec le refte.

On voit un air de contentement fur tous les vifages & il éclate dans les difcours. Chacun ne peut affés louer les bontés du maître. Tous font des vœux finceres pour fa confervation: la veuve, l'orphelin & l'indigent ont raifon d'y joindre les leurs.

Tout

Tout est payé regulierement à la fin de chaque mois, & souvent il n'est pas encore expiré, que le Caissier arrive déja d'Eisenstadt.

Quand le Prince donne des fêtes, elles font toujours alliées à une somptuosité & un eclat hors du commun. On en vit de superbes en 1773. lorsque l'Imperatrice Reine-Douairiere d'immortelle memoire s'y trouva avec l'Archiduc Maximilien, & les Archiduchesses Marianne & Elisabeth. L'Archiduc Ferdinand, le Duc Albert de Saxe-Teschen, avec leurs Epouses, le Prince de Rohan, Ambassadeur de la Cour de France, & quelques autres Grands de la premiere distinction, honorerent successivement Esterhaz de leur presence. Bals, Concerts, Opera, Feux d'artifice, Illuminations, fêtes champetres, & divers autres divertissemens epuquerent le sejour de ces Hôtes illustres par un enchainement de plaisirs marqués au coin de la splendeur & de la joye la plus epurée.

La belle chaussée de la capitale à Esterhaz passe par *Jebau*, poste: *Minkendorf*, ou campent dans l'automne les regimens de la haute & basse autriche; *Eigesdorf*, ou il y a une fabrique octroyée de Cotton, *Wimpassing*, poste, terre du Prince Esterhazy & frontiere de l'hongrie, que la petite riviere *Leytha* y separe de l'autriche. *Groß-Höflein*; entre ce village & la ville d'Oedenbourg, on decouvre à gauche & à une demie lieue de la chaussée, le magnifique château *d'Eisenstadt*, appartenant egalement au Prince: *Oedenbourg*, ville roiale, poste & capitale du comitat ou cercle de ce nom. *Kolmhof, Heiligenstein & Szeplak.* Entre

tre Oedenbourg & Kolmhof on a à la belle vue d'une allée & d'un château appartenant à la famille des Comtes *Seczény.* Entre Heiligenstein & Szeplak on a le coup d'œil vraiment pittoresque du Lac de *Neusfedel*, qui a 20 Lieues de france de circuit sur 8 de longueur & 4 de largeur,

Le Prince a trois attelages de relais &, un houzard d'ordonnance dans 4 stations sur la route : ces stations sont Oedenbourg, Groß-Höflein, Wimpassing, & Achau, Quoiqu'il y ait un trajet de 22 fortes Lieues de france à franchir depuis Esterhaz jusqu'à Vienne, il n'y emploie communement pas plus que six heures: les heuzards sont en tout au nombre de 12; heur habilement est riche & plein de goût.

Les *Remises* sont remplies d'une quantité de voitures de toute espece, parmi lesquelles on en remarque une qui etoit tirée par des hommes, lorsqu'il plut à l'Imperatrice-Reine de se promener dans le bois. Une autre faite en forme de barque, contient commodement 10 personnes assises en cercle, & est assés legere pour être conduite par quatre chevaux.

Le Sieur *Auguste*, Negre & Page de la chambre du Prince, est anglois. C'est un jeune homme bien bati, fort façoné, extremement attaché à son illustre maitre, & qui se fait le plaisir le plus sensible d'accompagner les etrangers, en leur facilitant les moiens d'admirer les objets remarquables dont ce sejour fourmille.

Le

Le *Belvedere* eft conftruit au deffus de la belle Baluftrade de la façade du palais. Il eft entouré de genies fymboliques, de vafes, & de fujets de la fable.

Les deux entrées principales du jardin font ornées de grilles dorées avec les armoiries du Prince & fon chifre *N. E.* en confiderant ce chifre je me difois à moi même:

N'aiant jamais befoin du moindre eclat factice,
Efterhaz eft connu par maint illuftre trait;
Noble en fes procedés & grand dans ce qu'il fait,
Etrangers ou fujets, chacun lui rend juftice;
Neceffaire à l'etat, utile, & fatisfait,
Entre beaucoup des Grands il brille dans la lice.

Parmi les peintures d'eclat qui brillent à Monbijou, l'amateur examine avec attention le portrait du Prince en chaffeur, au deffus d'une cheminée au premier etage: deux fêtes felon le coftume efpagnol, un chaffeur affis prés du Gibier qu'il a abattu, une petite Sufanne furprife dans le bain par les deux vieillards, une Sinagogue, une Tempéte, & une Cleopatre qui fe laiffe piquer le fein par l'afpic.

L'ecuier du Prince, eft un jeune Suiffe du Canton de *Berne*, rempli d'intelligence dans fon art, de vivacité, & de complaifance envers tous ceux qu'il a l'occafion de pouvoir obliger.

En recapitulant les objets les plus dignes d'être appreçiés, on trouve: le grand fallon, la chambre à coucher du Prince, la façade du Palais, les appartemens en ge-neral,

neral, la Chapelle, la Bibliotheque, la Garderobe, la Gallerie de peintures, la Bibliotheque à la main, la Chambre d'armes, le Belvedere, le Jardin d'hyver, les Ecuries & Menages, la Chambre des porcelaines, la Salle d'opera, l'Orangerie, le Caffé, le Théâtre des Marionettes, les deux Cafcades: les temples du Soleil, de Venus, de Diane & de la Fortune, la ftatue de Latone, l'Hermitage, la Bagatelle, les Champs elyfées, le Pavillon hollandois, le parc des Daims, les Faifans couleur d'or, le parc des Sangliers, Monbijou.

Les perfonnes de diftinction qui etoient à Efterhaz pendant mon fejour, font la Princeffe *Efterhazy*, née Princeffe de *Lichtenftein*, jeune Dame auffi recommandable par les charmes de l'exterieur que par l'excellence de fon caractere: elle a pour epoux le petit fils du Prince actuellement occupé à fon Cours des voiages. La Comteffe douairiere de *Weiffenwolf*, née Baronne de *Salza* de la Boheme, avec l'aimable Comteffe fa fille. Cette Dame eft proche parente du Prince, du coté de feu le General fon epoux, qui etoit frere de la Princeffe Regnante. Les Princes Antoine & Nicolas Efterhazy, fils du *Prince regnant.* Le Lieutenant-General de Cavallerie Comte *Emeric Efterhazy :* le Comte *Jerningham,* General-Major, Cavalier anglois fort inftruit : le Comte *Stahremberg* Colonel & ci devant Commandant de la ville & fortereffe de *Raab,* Le Baron de *Rofersky,* Lieutenant Colonel.

D

On

14

merite d'être fort exacte dans les termes techniques de l'architecture, & d'être la premiere qui ait parue d'un sejour
auffi digne d'être celebré. Il n'est pas moins vrai que les
embellissemens s'y succedent avec rapidité & que le goût
du Prince ne cesse de s'y manifester, au point qu'en com-
binant mes remarques j'ose esperer qu'on ne le trouvera
point deplacées.

On trouve dans Esterhaz tous les arts, professions,
& metiers les plus usités. Il y a jusqu'à un maître de langue, jeune Alsatien de Colmar, qui possede parfaitement
les langues allemande & françoise.

Que de plaisirs frappans, quel comble de splendeur
Quand l'art & la nature allient leurs richesses!
L'agréable Contour d'un bosquet enchanteur
Etale leurs trefors au sein des allegresses.
Euterpe & Melpomene ont un temple sacré,
Ou l'on trouve à la fois le goût & le genie :
Frappé par le local, ravi par l'harmonie,
Le Connoisseur en sort surpris, extasié.
A chaque pas qu'on fait quelque beauté nouvelle;
Cascades, boulingrins mille ornemens mignons,
Du Costume chinois la noble *Bagatelle*, —
Du Seigneur de ces lieux tout annonce les dons.
L'amour accompagné du Cortege des Graces,
Embellit ce sejour par ses appas puissans:
Tout invite à marcher sur ses riantes traces,
On est embarassé du choix des agrèmens.

Il existe déja à la verité une description en allemand
du Palais & des curiosités d'Esterhaz avec huit planches
exactement gravées, imprimée à Presbourg chez Löwe en
1783, & redigée, quant aux plans, par le Sieur de Jacoby, Alsatien & Ingenieur de S. A. le Prince regnant.
On la trouve pour trois florins chez le maître d'hôtel qui
s'est chargé du debit. Mais outre que plusieurs etrangers,
qu'une juste curiosité y attire, ne possedent point la langue
allemande, beaucoup d'observations avoient echappées à
l'auteur de cette description, qui d'ailleurs a le double
merite

V. Summing-up: Haydn at Eszterháza

The reader who has followed thus far the almost incredible operatic activity at Eszterháza may wonder about Haydn; not only how he found time to compose at all, but what he did in the little spare time he had at his disposal. Here, we may use the words of G. A. Griesinger, Haydn's most reliable biographer.

Hunting and fishing were Haydn's favourite pastimes during his sojourn in Hungary, and he could never forget that once he brought down with a single shot three hazel-hens, which arrived on the table of the Empress Maria Theresa. Another time he aimed at a hare but only shot off its tail, but the same shot killed a pheasant that happened to be nearby; while his dog, chasing the hare, strangled itself in a snare. In riding Haydn never developed any skill, because ever since he had fallen from a horse on the Morzin estates [at Lukavec in Bohemia], he never trusted himself to mount a horse again; Mozart too, who liked horseback riding for exercise, was always terrified when doing so. [19]

Prince Nikolaus Esterhazy was an educated connoisseur and passionate lover of music, and also a good violin player. He had his own opera, spoken theatre, marionette theatre, church music and chamber music. Haydn had his hands full; he composed, he had to conduct all the music, help with the rehearsals, give lessons and even tune his own piano [*Klavier*] in the orchestra. He often wondered how it had been possible for him to compose as much as he did when he was forced to lose so many hours in purely mechanical tasks. ...

Although it must be said that Haydn's outward circumstance was anything but brilliant, it nevertheless provided him with the best opportunity for the development of his many-sided talents. 'My Prince was satisfied with all my works; I received approval; as head of an orchestra, I could undertake experiments, could observe that which enhanced an effect and that which weakened it, thus improving, adding to it, taking away from it, taking risks. I was cut off from the world; there was no one in my vicinity to make me unsure of myself or to persecute me; and so I had to become original.' [17]

This volume studies in large measure the story of that brilliant originality.

CHAPTER TWO

Chronicle 1766–1775

AT THE END OF 1765, Haydn faced the first, and worst, crisis of his existence as *Vice Capellmeister* to Prince Esterházy. Haydn's superior, *Capellmeister* Gregor Werner, an old, sick and embittered man who was (as might be expected in the circumstances) insanely jealous of Haydn, had written an appalling letter to the Prince, accusing Haydn of what amounted to criminal negligence in the management of the Castle Choir, its music library and its instruments. There were three results of this accusation: (1) the so-called 'Regulatio Chori KissMartoniensis', a harsh document drawn up, in all probability, by *Güterregent* (Estates Director) Peter Ludwig Rahier, instructing Haydn in his duties and ordering him to draw up a detailed cataloge of the Esterházy music archives and instruments; (2) Haydn's so-called *Entwurf-Katalog*, an immensely valuable thematic catalogue drawn up about 1765 by Haydn and the princely copyist Joseph Elssler, which the composer kept *au courant* until after the London visits; (3) a set of new baryton pieces. The Prince (through Rahier) had recommended Haydn to compose more diligently than heretofore – hence the *Entwurf-Katalog*, to show graphically how many works Haydn had composed up to 1765 – 'and especially such pieces as may be played on the gamba [i.e. baryton], of which we have seen very few hitherto'. There was nothing Haydn could do about the other vicious accusations that Werner had made; no doubt the *Entwurf-Katalog* and the new baryton pieces[1] were responsible for the happy fact that the whole affair was soon forgotten. Our Chronicle opens, then, with the following pleasant conclusion to this unsavoury affair.

[Prince Nicolaus Esterházy to his Estates Director, P. L. Rahier]

[Eszterháza, 4 January 1766.]
... This very moment I received 3 pieces from Hayden [*sic*], and I am very satisfied with them. You will therefore see that he gets 12 ducats from the cashier's office in my name; tell him at the same time to write 6 more pieces similar to those he sent me, and also 2 Solo[2] pieces, and to see that they are sent here at once ...'.
[CCLN 6; Pohl I, 248f.; Bartha 54]

The next month we find Rahier writing to the Prince that '*Kapellmeister* Haydn has been informed about the dismissal of Garnier and Attesti which is to be given to him ...' (Valkó II, 541). The 'dismissal' (*Entlassung*) of Franz Garnier[3] brings up the

---

1 They cannot be identified; no complete autographs of the early baryton Trios have survived; the first complete (and therefore dated) baryton Trio is No. 24 (autograph: Stanford Memorial Library, California, dated 1766); presumably the three pieces were three baryton Trios, perhaps including the lost Trios Nos. 23 (or 18).

2 Haydn probably wrote the 'Solo pieces', which were not, strictly speaking real 'Soli', i.e. for one baryton, but works such as those entered on page eight of *EK* (abbreviation used hereinafter for *Entwurf-Katalog*) 'Divertimento 1mo [and 2–4, with themes] per il Pariton Solo' (Hoboken XII, 20–23), which are lost. Haydn was paid his 12 ducats on 8 January: see the documents in *HJB* IV, 44.

3 The documents that we have been able to see (e.g. Valkó I, 641; Pohl II, 372) list him as 'Franciscus Guarnier'; in two autograph signatures 'Garnier' (*HJB* IV, 38, 42) without Christian name; J. Harich (*HJB* IV, 15 [32]) lists him as 'Lucas Garnier'. We cannot explain this discrepancy. On the important document concerning the re-organization of the *Capelle* after the accession of Prince Nicolaus to the title, Eisenstadt, 5 July 1762 (Valkó I, 634f.), we find 'Anderten [other] Violinisten Frantz Guarnier ... 240 fl.'. We have therefore preferred to retain 'Franz' as his Christian name.

whole question of what we like to call, in military language today, the 'chain of command'. Who dismissed the musicians? From the evidence at our disposal, we believe that most of the dismissals were the direct result of commands from 'on high', i.e., from Prince Nicolaus himself; and usually the dismissals were as a result of some disciplinary infraction (which was, however, hardly ever recorded; the dismissal itself was sufficient). In most cases, the musician who was thus expelled was provided with an 'Attesti', a letter of recommendation to further his career. We have cited one such letter in connection with the singer Benedetto Bianchi (*supra*, p. 55). It is clear that Garnier was given such a letter. Was Haydn consulted? We would like to believe so. Certainly he intervened in cases such as the Polzellis, whose expulsion was rescinded and who stayed on a whole decade, until the *Capelle* was disbanded in 1790. Probably such intervention was managed *sotto quattro occhi*: if Haydn felt strongly, he could probably organize a stay of execution; if he did not feel strongly, the musician in question was allowed to go.

Anno 1766. In the princely choir the following was organized by the Castle Schoolm[aster] for the stringing of instruments.

First for the new violon [double bass] 3 pie[ces] ditto A á

[*sic*] 7 xr:	—	21 xr.
Item 3 pieces ditto f sharp á 8 xr.	—	24 xr.
Item 4 pieces Bas[ett]l ['cello] D á 5 xr.	—	25 xr.
12 pieces covered violin G á 5 xr. makes	1 fl.	—
Item 8 violin pegs á 2 xr.	—	16 xr.
For the good princely Baridon 3 covered Bas[ett]l ['cello] G á 17 xr. makes	—	51 xr.
2 colofoni [resins] bought at	2 fl.	—
Summa	3 fl.	19 xr.

The 5th of Feb. 1766 this sum was paid to me, and I provide this receipt Dat. ut. Supra. Joseph Dietzl Schulmeister.

[Countersigned:] mit accord Joseph Haydn mpria.

[Acta Musicalia VII, 447; Valko I, 646]

Note: There are two interesting facts about this document. The one is the entry about the 'good princely Baridon' (baryton), which refers to the baryton now in the Országos Széchényi Könyvtár, Budapest, and presupposes that the Prince had a second, less 'good' instrument to avoid moving the good one from Eszterháza to Eisenstadt (and to Vienna and Pressburg, too). The second, astonishing fact is that the bill is a mathematical disaster. Mistakes: (1) entry three, five times four makes twenty Kreuzer; (2) the addition, even with the wrong sum of 25 kr. is totally wrong, and to the loss of Herr Dietzl. Properly, the sum (with 20 kr. instead of 25 kr.) should add up to 132 kr., which means 2 fl. 12 kr., and that sum, added to 3 fl., makes 5 fl. 12 kr. With the wrong sum of 25 kr., the total should be 5 fl. 17 kr. All this is scarcely believable, since the bill passed though not only Dietzl's and Haydn's hands but also the princely cashier.

On 3 March 1766, Werner died. Haydn's contract of 1761 had stipulated that '14. His Serene Highness undertakes to keep Joseph Heyden [*sic*] in his service during this time [three years], and should he be satisfied with him, he may look forward to being appointed *Capellmeister*. This, however, must not be understood to deprive his Serene Highness of right to dismiss the said Joseph Heyden at the expiration of the term, should he see fit to do so.' The contract had been written in the days of Prince Paul Anton, of course, but Prince Nicolaus – despite the flurry of events in the autumn of 1765 – was certainly satisfied with Haydn and his promotion to Full Chapel Master took place, in a sense, so automatically that there is no known written record of it in the Esterházy Archives.

Receipt. That I fashioned for the princely Musico Johann Michael Kapfer 12 pieces Hautbois reeds and have been paid correctly by him the sum of 2 fl.
Vienna, 20th March 1766.

Mathias Rockobauer.

[countersigned:] Joseph Haydn mpria.

[Acta Musicalia VII, 448; Valkó I, 646]

Note: Mathias Rockobauer – the clerks who usually wrote out his bills spelled his name in a variety of exotic ways – was an oboe (wind instrument) maker in Vienna. A beautiful cor anglais of his manufacture was on exposition in the so-called *Tanzmeistersaal*, Leopold Mozart's quarters, in Salzburg; the instrument was stolen some years ago and has never been recovered. Kremsmünster Abbey owns an oboe signed 'Rocco Baur'.

On 28 March, Haydn and his wife became godparents to Joseph Weigl's son:

28. huius Baptizatus est Josephus, Legitimus filius Josephi Weigl musici Arcensis, ac coniugis eius Annae Mariae. Levavit Dominus Josephus Haiden [*sic*] Chori Arcensis Regens, cum coniuge sua Anna Maria.

[*Matricula Baptizatorum*, Bergkirche, Eisenstadt; E. F. Schmid; 'Joseph Haydn in Eisenstadt', in *Burgenländische Heimatblätter* I/1 (1932), p. 4 (hereinafter abbreviated 'Schmid "Eisenstadt"'). We have listed the Weigl family *supra*.]

Work delivered for lute-maker items and strings.
First, a Pasetl ['cello] repaired, newly strung, the neck repaired, the bas-bar reinforced:

First, a Pasetl ['cello] repaired, newly strung, the neck repaired, the bas-bar reinforced:	2 fl.	
Strings, a whole set added to it	1 fl.	8 xr.
Two bundles E, 15 batches [*Büschl*] A	5 fl.	24 xr.
4 batches D, 12 sets [*Zug*] G	1 fl.	24 xr.
2 violon [double bass] A	1 fl.	12 xr.
6 sets viola G, 3 of C	1 fl.	3 xr.
Summa	11 fl.	47 xr.

On account of the violloncello [*sic*] 35 xr. taken off, ch[anged end sum to] 11 fl. 12 xr.

Vienna, 4th April 1766.

[countersigned:] Joseph Haydn mpria.

I sign in receipt that these eleven gulden 12 xr. have been paid to me by the Eisenstadt Rent Office,

Johann Joseph Stadlmann, Imp. Roy. Lute Maker.

[A.M. VII, 449; Valkó I, 645]

Note: J. J. Stadlmann was a member of a famous family of string instrument makers in Vienna. Many of his instruments have survived, including the baryton owned by Prince Nicolaus Esterházy, which Stadlmann made in 1750. Barytons by Daniel A. Stadlmann were in the Heyer Collection in Cologne (1715), in the Royal Collection at Berlin (1736), and a baryton by J. J. Stadlmann is in the Metropolitan Museum, New York (1779). Béla Csuka: 'Haydn és a Baryton' in: *Zenetudományi Tanulmányok* (Kodál Zoltán 75. Születésnapjára), Budapest 1957, pp. 682f.

Shortly after Haydn became full *Capellmeister*, he came to two decisions of major importance. The first one was to write a great 'cantata' Mass in honour of the Blessed Virgin Mary, for Whom Haydn had a special sense of veneration – he also dedicated to Her another Mass of this period, the *Missa in honorem B. V. M.* The term 'cantata' Mass means that the work was organized like a cantata, with many individual movements, and that it was on a very large scale, lasting nearly two hours. This great Mass, the beginning of the autograph of which was recently discovered in Roumania,[1] is entitled '*Missa Cellensis | In honorem Beatissimae Virginis Mariae |* dal giuseppe Haydn mpria | 766'. The word 'Cellensis' means that it was intended for the great Baroque pilgrimage church of Mariazell in the Austrian province of Styria. The derivation of the word 'Cellensis' in this connection is 'Celle' = 'Zell'. Many years later, in 1782, Haydn was to write another famous Mass ('*Missa Cellensis*', known in German as the 'Mariazellermesse') for Mariazell. It was also a church with which the Esterházy family had long preserved intimate connections, and the Palatine Paul Esterházy had dedicated a side-chapel there which is to this day reverently preserved. In his youthful years, Haydn himself, a hungry and penniless lad, had made the pilgrimage to Styria and had been well received by the friendly monks at Mariazell.[2] This Mass, then, fulfilled some kind of a private vow concerning the Virgin, Mariazell and its composer becoming full *Capellmeister* to His Serene Highness, Prince Nicolaus Esterházy (who, in turn, will have encouraged Haydn along these ends, not only for the principle of the thing but also because of his family's traditional attachment to the Church there).

The Mass is also a highly important marker along its composer's path to greatness, for it is the biggest work of the period 1750–66 to survive (*Acide* of 1762 exists only in fragments, and *Der krumme Teufel* not at all). All his life, Haydn's dream was to write works on a large scale. During his years with the Esterházy family he was, until 1790, only able to satisfy this side of his career by the large operas that he was, from time to time, called upon to compose; and by the Oratorio for Vienna, *Il ritorno di Tobia*. After he returned from London, most of his efforts were devoted towards large vocal works – the six last Masses, the Oratorios – which he could only write hitherto *en passant*. Now that Haydn also took over Werner's position as Choir Master and director of church music at Eisenstadt, we shall see a sudden and dramatic increase in Haydn's church music. The *Missa Cellensis* is followed in rapid succession by the *Stabat Mater*, perhaps the first work to establish its composer's reputation on a European scale; and by several other Masses as well as numerous pieces of smaller church music which shall be examined in detail in the next Chapter. In every sense, then, Werner's death marked a major turning-point in Haydn's life. We can see it not only in the very fact of the Mass's existence but in its orchestration, with the two high trumpets which Haydn obviously loved but which he did not have at his disposal except in winters at Eisenstadt (by borrowing from the *Thurnermeister*) or Vienna (if the princely forces were there, as sometimes happened).

The second decision at which Haydn arrived was to purchase a house in Eisenstadt. The late Ernst Fritz Schmid,[3] from whose wonderfully detailed article the following information is gratefully taken, thought that a certain re-grouping of the musicians had occurred following Werner's death. Previously, they (and the Haydns) had lived in the house of the former Apothecary on the Oberberg (the part of Eisenstadt above the Castle; the Bergkirche was also there, as was the Hospital and Chapel of the Barmherzige Brüder). Schmid also considered that now that Haydn was *Capellmeister*, he sought to keep a certain distance from the musicians, as indeed his contract of 1761 had clearly specified: '... abstaining from undue familiarity ...'. But Haydn was in

---

1 Landon, 'The newly discovered Autograph to Haydn's Missa Cellensis of 1766', in *Haydn Yearbook* IX (1975), pp. 306ff. With facsimile.

2 Haydn told the story in detail to his biographers Griesinger and Dies. See *Haydn: the Early Years 1732–1765*.

3 'Joseph Haydn in Eisenstadt', in *Burgenländische Heimatblätter* I/1 (1932), pp. 5ff. See also J. Harich in *HJB* IV, 13ff. (31f.) with details of Haydn's various dealings with the Prince about this house. Many of the documents were exhibited in the great *Haydn-Austellung*, Vienna 1932 (p. 8 of the 'Katalog').

fact intimate with many of the musicians, as we have seen, witnessing their marriages and being a godparent to their children; and perhaps a more simple explanation is that, as full *Capellmeister*, he believed that he now enjoyed enough material security to risk buying (if not paying for completely) a little house, which is now the Haydn Museum, No. 82 of the Klostergasse (now Joseph Haydngasse). He purchased it on 2 May 1766 from the widowed owner of the Gasthaus 'Adler' (Eagle), whose husband, Jakob Schleicher, had been a member of the Town Council (*Bürger des äußeren Raths*). Euphrosina Schleicherin, as the documents call her (adding that curious suffix '-in' to denote her sex), reserved the right to occupy the ground-floor quarters during her lifetime. Haydn was unable to pay the full price all at once, but the house belonged to him nonetheless; a year later, he had to borrow money to pay off the rest, for the old lady had died and the remaining sum came due. Fortunately, we have a rather accurate description of the house in the *Grundbuch* (Registry of Property) of 1758, now in the Town Archives of Eisenstadt:

Nr. 78 [former number]; 9th class 5 fl 40 x [tax rate *p.a.*] Owned by *Herr Obrist* [Colonel] Johann von Liptay.
1 Object [*Hofstatt*]
<u>on the first floor</u>
2 fine large stuccoed [*stockendorte*] rooms overlooking the street
1 large kitchen
1 room, not vaulted and 1 wooden hut [*Verschlag*] in the courtyard
1 entry room, small
<u>on the ground floor</u>
One room overlooking the street, not vaulted
One room on the courtyard with kitchen
One large vaulted chamber at the rear
One small cellar with a bigger one attached
One stable for four horses
One vaulted entry with wooden floorboards to the threshing place
<u>Property belonging to house</u>
3 M [*Pfund*, measuring system for vineyards, *c.* 80–100 square *Klafter*] small pasturage
1 *Joch* [1,200 square *Klafter*] arable land [*Haid Acker*]
1 *Joch* [land at] stone grindery [*Steinmühl*]
½ *Joch* in ½ *Jochen* [*vide infra*; in *Grundbuch* of 1771 'in Halb Jochen', 'Halb' referring to a place, not a half measure]
4 plots of woody terrain
1 kitchen garden at the hospital
<u>Cattle</u>
1 cow and
1 calf
<u>Tenants</u>
Simon Großmann, winegrower, has M [*vide supra* for meaning] old vineyard.

E. F. Schmid found that, in 1932, the land attached to the house was still, with the exception of the stone 'grindery' (which was the Eisenstadt town quarry by then), more-or-less that which Haydn himself owned. The '1 *Joch* arable land' is now 1,800 *Klafter* in the flatland below Eisenstadt north of the Wulka Brook. The '3 M small pasturage' are 300 *Klafter* above Eisenstadt, towards the Leitha Mountains. The quarry is south of the Wulka Brook. The '½ *Joch*' (900 *Klafter*) is situated in the flatland north of the Wulka Brook. The four 'plots of woody terrain' are in the so-called 'Hotter', at the level of the Leitha Mountain and are called 'Altlust' (1,839 *Klafter*), 'Burgstall' (900 *Klafter*), 'Rohrgraben' (1,200 *Klafter*) and 'Tränk' (1,000 *Klafter*). One *Klafter* (fathom) meant, roughly, a six-foot measurement. The kitchen garden contained a kind of hut in which, it was reputed, Haydn sometimes composed. This was quite an imposing piece of property, and Haydn was only able to make the final payment at the end of April 1767 (*vide*, pp. 132, 133). Athough many documents have survived concerning Haydn and the house, we are not sure how much it cost him. The remaining 700 gulden were paid on 30 April 1767, but it is nowhere stated what the original sum was: perhaps 1,500 gulden (Haydn resold it later for 2,000 gulden).

On 6 June, the Emperor Franz Stephan, the Duke Albert of Sachsen-Teschen and their followers dined at the princely Castle in Eisenstadt. It is supposed that the *Tafelmusik* for the occasion was provided by Haydn and the *Capelle*, which consisted, as far as the orchestra was concerned, of four violins and viola (not counting Haydn), one 'cello, one double bass, one flute, two oboes, one bassoon and four horns. Haydn played either the harpsichord or the violin, whatever was required. Naturally, we have no idea of what kind of music was offered at such occasions, since no records of that kind have survived, or probably were ever made. Negatively, we may doubt that the operation of 6 June was a very large-scale affair, with singers, for the simple reason that no shower of gold followed the performance, as it would later in the year, probably for *La canterina* (27 July), and certainly for *La canterina* at Pressburg in February 1767 as well as in 1777, after the marionette troupe's *Gastspiel* at Schönbrunn Castle.[1] Apart from *Tafelmusik*, which might have been wind-band music, the orchestra may have given one of their formal concerts, such as were offered in the great hall of Eisenstadt Castle twice a week.

Although the first 'public', i.e. official, performance of Haydn's comic opera, *La canterina*, took place at Pressburg in 1767, we believe that we have discovered what may have been the occasion for the first performance at Eisenstadt. From the important document that Haydn drew up on 11 September (see overleaf), we see that the opera had been given in costume, certainly in Eisenstadt and possibly also at Eszterháza (to which Castle the harpsichord had been transported, but it was reported on this same bill and seems to be a part of the whole operations).

On 27 July, we find Prince Esterházy ordering his Chief Cashier, Johann Zoller, to pay the four vocal soloists who later figure on the title page of the opera's libretto for Pressburg:

Commission

According to which our Chief Cashier Johann Zoller is to pay to the *Capellmeister* Joseph Haÿden [*sic*] 12 ordinary ducats, Annae Weiglin, Barbarae Tichtlerin, Carlo Fribert and Leopold Tichtler each 6, that is together 36 ordinary ducats, and to enter the same in the necessary books. Eisenstad [*sic*], 27th Julÿ 1766.

Nicolaus Fürst Esterhazy

[receipts, signed by:]
Josephus Haydn mpria correctly received
Leopoldo Dichtler Barbara Dichtlerin correctly received
Carlo Friberth correctly received
Maria Anna Weigl correctly received

[Generalcassa 1766, EH, Eisenstadt, Rubr. VIII. Nr. 17; *HJB* IV, 44]

The occasion for this first 'shower of gold' was the name-day of the Prince's eldest son, Anton, later to be the second Prince Esterházy under whom Haydn would serve.

1 J. Harich *Musikgeschichte*, p. 30.

Where did the performance actually take place in Eisenstadt Castle? There are no documents on that subject, but presumably on a temporary stage either in the garden (as sometimes happened) or in the great hall. A similarly improvised stage can have served at Eszterháza, where the theatre was not yet completed.

La canterina is a modest, 'intermezzo'-like Italian *opera buffa*. We shall examine it in detail in the forthcoming chapter, but here a few words about its position in Haydn's *œuvre* may not be amiss. It revealed a new side to Haydn's musical personality: his ability to write genuinely witty Italian opera. It was to be an increasingly important part of Haydn's life in the next quarter of a century, and if posterity has not confirmed this aspect of Haydn as a major part of his creative life, the composer himself undoubtedly did so, and so did Prince Nicolaus. The gold ducats rained on Haydn and the singers for opera, and only for opera; not for symphonies, string quartets or baryton trios – all of which were being composed, and produced, in lavish profusion during these years. It is clear that Prince Nicolaus encouraged Haydn to continue with what had been, with *La canterina*, a kind of experiment. Perhaps, indeed, the great success of the work was indirectly responsible for the building of the opera house at Eszterháza and the gradual shifting of Prince Nicolaus's taste to opera, and in particular *opera buffa*, as the major musical pastime of his life.

The crucial bill for *La canterina*, entirely written in Haydn's hand, reads as follows:

Specification

What I have advanced for some necessities in the Theatre
For the Opera <u>la Canterina</u>

	f —	Xr —
A pair of men's shoes for Madam Dichtler — —	1 —	9 —
For a large fan [*Wäderl*] — — — — — — — = —		20 —
For enlarging a wig — — — — — — — —	1 —	8 —
Hair-ribbons — — — — — — — — — = —		40 —
Red shoelaces — — — — — — — — — = —		8 —
4 grains [*gran*] of rouge — — — — — — = —		16 —
For three boys at 12 Xr each — — — — — = —		36 —
Four pairs of gloves — — — — — — —	2 —	= —

Suma 6 f 17 Xr ide 6f. 17x

What has been delivered in strings	f	Xr
One bundle E. 15 batches A — — — — —	3 —	—
More I bundle E 15 batches A. 6 batches D, 6 sets G	4	6
Item 6 mutes — — — — — — — — —	—	42
Bassetl ['cello] C: and G: 2 batches D: 2 batches A: new hairs on the bow — — — — — — —	1 —	33
Strings for the *Clavier* in Eisenstadt and [added later: 'to'] Estorhaz — — — — — — — — —	2 —	16
24 *Bögen* thick heavy paper — — — — —	1 —	12

Suma 12 f 49 ide 12f 49x

For His Highness
6 books Italian music paper, the book à 24 Xr— — — 2 f 24 ide 2f 24x

Suma 21f 30x

[another hand:] The sum of 21f 30 xr due to me has been paid by the Rental Office, receipted Eisenstadt, 11th Sept. 1766.

[signed:]Joseph Haydn mpria.
[A. M. 451, EH, Budapest; facsimile Horányi 40f.; Valkó I, 646]

Note: the 'ide 6f. 17x' which appears several times at the right of Haydn's sums, the total 'Suma 21f 30x' at the bottom, and the formula for the receipt are all in the same hand, presumably the cashier who also inspected the document and added little checks next to the original sums. The 'heavy thick paper' (*dickes Töckl Papier*) is the characteristic heavy paper from the Esterházy paper mill at Lockenhaus with the stag watermark; it was cheaper, and of inferior quality. The more expensive Italian paper was used, one presumes, for the copying of baryton trios for the Prince; and in fact the Országos Széchenyi Könyvtár, Budapest, still owns, from the Esterházy Archives (Ms. mus. I. 110), a beautifully bound set of baryton Trios (XI:73–96) written on expensive Italian paper. It was a characteristic of the Lockenhaus paper that it was manufactured for Haydn's *Capelle* in tall folio (4°) format, whereas the Italian paper was in oblong format. A reproduction of the cover of the 'pariton' part of Ms. mus. I. 110 in *Haydn Compositions in the Music Collection of the National Széchényi Library*, Budapest, 1960, p. 32.

On 20 September, Haydn was witness on behalf of the bride in a marriage ceremony at the Stadtpfarrkirche:

20 Sept. 1766. Philippus Rolleder caelebs et famulus cum V: Mariana Kammerschmitin. Testes ex parte sponsi D: Johannes Michael Stofinger E: Notarius, ex parte sponsae Josephus Hayden Capelle [*sic*] Magister principis.[1]

On 7 October 1766, Haydn was a witness at the marriage ceremony, in the Bergkirche at Eisenstadt, of his faithful copyist Joseph Elssler to Eva Maria Köstler.

7. huius copulatus est honestus Juvenis, et musicus Arcensis Josephus Elsler, Kieslingensis Sileslita, cum virgine Eva Maria Köstlerin, Sebastiani Köstler fabri ferrarij, et horologiarij montani, ac Catharinae uxoris eius legitima filia. Testes utriusque fuere Dominus Josephus Hayden Capellae Dominalis Magister, et Dominus Petrus Void Cancellista.

[*Matricula Copulatorum*, Bergkirche, Eisenstadt; E. F. Schmid 'Eisenstadt', p. 4]

Prince Nicolaus was at Eszterháza on his name-day, the festival of St Nicholas,[2] but he used the occasion to send, first, the theatre decorator Bon, who had presumably designed the sets and costumes for *La canterina*, a handsome gift of six ducats.

Commission
According to which our Chief Cashier Johann Zoller is to give to the *Operisten* in our service Bonne [*sic*] a present of six ordinary ducats against a receipt and to be entered on the books. Eszterhaz, 4 Dec. 1766.

Nicolaus Fürst Esterhazy

I have received, and hereby give receipt for, the above present which has been correctly paid to me by *Herr* Chief Cashier Joann [*sic*] Zoller, Eisenstadt Castle, 9 Dec. 766:

Idest 24 f 45 Xr: Hieronÿmus Bon

[Generalcassa 1766, Esterházy Archives, Eisenstadt; Rubr. VIII. Nr. 35; *HJB* IV, 45]

Meanwhile, the princely *Capelle*, in their new uniforms, celebrated the Prince's name-day at Eisenstadt, and Haydn took the occasion to write the following letter:

---

1 Harich in *HJB* II, 18 and 32, correcting a wrong transcription of this document, with a wrong date (20 May), in André Csatkai, 'Die Beziehungen Gregor Josef Werners, Joseph Haydns und der fürstlichen Musiker zur Eisenstädter Pfarrkirche', *Burgenländische Heimatblätter* I/1 (1932), p. 15, where we read that on 20 May Haydn led to the altar the widow Christine Scheffschik, about whom *vide infra*, p. 404.

2 'Nahmens Fest' or 'Namenstag' (the modern and more usual form): Festival of the anniversary of one's saint. St Nicholas' Day falls on December 6th.

[To Prince Nicolaus Esterházy. *German*]
MOST SERENE HIGHNESS AND NOBLE PRINCE OF THE HOLY ROMAN EMPIRE
GRACIOUS AND DREAD LORD!

The most joyous occasion of your name-day (may YOUR HIGHNESS celebrate it in divine Grace and enjoy it in complete well-being and felicity!) obliges me not only to deliver to you in profound submission 6 new Divertimenti,[1] but also to say that we were delighted to receive, a few days ago, our new Winter clothes – and submissively to kiss the hem of your robe for this especial act of grace: adding that, despite YOUR HIGHNESS' much regretted absence, we shall nevertheless venture to wear these new clothes for the first time during the celebration of High Mass on YOUR HIGHNESS' name-day. I have received YOUR HIGHNESS' order to have the Divertimenti I wrote (twelve pieces in all) bound. But since YOUR HIGHNESS has returned some of them to me to be altered, and I have not noted the changes in my score, I would respectfully ask you to let me have the first twelve you have at hand for three days, and then the others one after the other, so that apart from the required changes, they may be all neatly and correctly copied and bound: in this connection I would like to ask respectfully in which way YOUR HIGHNESS would like to have them bound?

Incidentally, the two oboe players report (and I myself must agree with them) that their oboes are so old that they are collapsing, and no longer keep the proper pitch [*Tonum*]; for this reason I would humbly point out to YOUR HIGHNESS that there is a master Rockobauer in Vienna, who in my opinion is the most skilful for this sort of work. But because this master is continually busy with work of this kind, and since it requies an exceptionally long time to complete a pair of good and durable oboes with an extra length of reed pipe (as a result of which, however, all the necessary notes can be produced) – for these reasons the cheapest price is 8 ducats. I therefore await YOUR HIGHNESS' gracious consent whether the above-mentioned and most urgently needed two oboes may be constructed for the price indicated.[2] I hope for your favour and grace,

YOUR SERENE AND GRACIOUS HIGHNESS'
most humble
Joseph Haydn.

[5th December 1766][3]   [CCLN, 6f.]

The result of this letter was perhaps not that which its writer expected; instead of the cor anglais, Haydn was, a few days later, given the following Christmas present by Obereinnehmer Zoller:

Commission

According to which our Chief Cashier Johann Zoller is to pay our *Capeln Meister* Joseph Haidn [*sic*] twelve ordinary ducats as a present, against a receipt and to be entered on the books. Eszterház, 7 Dec. 1766.

Nicolaus Fürst Esterhazy

Correctly received the above 12 pieces of ducats the 20th Dec. 766
Josephus Haydn mpria
[Generalcassa 1766, EH, Eisenstadt, Rubr. VIII. Nr. 38; *HJB* IV, 44]

---

1 Divertimenti for baryton, viola and 'cello. We cannot determine exactly which words are described, but they may have been among *HV* 21–31, of which *HV* 24 is dated 1766 (see Larsen, pp. 227ff.).

2 Mathias Rockobauer seems not to have delivered the oboes; at least the Esterházy Archives show no record of his having made them. One receipt, dated 30 December 1766 and countersigned by Haydn, lists only woodwind mouthpieces. Another, of 20 June 1767 (countersigned by Haydn a week later), also lists only mouthpieces for oboes and English horns; while a third, of 25 September 1767, concerns the repair of an English horn. The first document is from a transcript made by Dr Eugen Marton, whose collection is now in the V.Nat. The other two in Valkó I, 649.

3 The date recorded on the letter by the Esterházy administration: the letter was probably delivered by a courier to Eszterháza, where it presumably arrived later on the 6th or on the 7th.

All this was still a reward for *La cantẽrina*, of course, although no specific reason for the gift was mentioned; but the proximity of Haydn's gift to that of Bon suggests the opera as the source of these rewards.

The nine gulden, also for this year, has been correctly paid to the whole *Chor Music* for the annual rorate by the present Rental Office, receipted.
Eisen Statt Castle, 23 Dec. 1766.

[autograph receipt:] correctly received Josephus Haydn mpria.
[Acta Musicalia VIII, 453, Esterházy Archives, Budapest; Valkó I, 647; *HJB* IV, 71]

This operation, which required the services of Haydn and the musicians, was known as the 'Rorate soup'. *Rorate* is the period of Advent in Roman Catholic countries, and Haydn's first Mass is entitled *Missa brevis alla cappella* 'Rorate coeli desuper' ('Drop down, ye dew, from Heaven'). During Advent the early morning Masses were celebrated with *figuraliter* music and the musicians received breakfast at the princely inn, 'Zum goldenen Greifen' ('At Ye golden Griffin'), which breakfast seems to have been some kind of soup, since the bills always call it 'Rorate-Suppe'. Later the church musicians took a total of nine gulden instead of the soup. Haydn had received his Rorate soup for the first time in 1765, which shows that he had already begun to run the church music (Werner, being old and sick, had gradually retired from active service). Up to 1766 Haydn collected the nine gulden for the whole band, and distributed it, but after this date he gave the whole sum to the musicians, without taking any of it for himself. Without specifically mentioning it, therefore, the reader must assume that this little ceremony took place in 1767 (23 Dec.), 1768 (23 Dec.), 1769 (21 Dec.), 1773 (31 Dec.), 1774 (31 Dec.), 1775 (31 Dec.) and 1776 (31 Dec,).[1]

Specification

What I organized during the past year 1766 for the princely choir in Eisenstadt in the way of strings and, with permission, for other things, to wit:

first 12 covered violin strings G. á 5 xr.:	1 f.	
2 detto Bassl ['cello] G á 17 xr.:		34 xr.
2 bundles violin E á 1 f 30 xr.	3 f.	
Item 1 bridge and pegs pr.		5 xr.
One bundle E pr.	·1 f.	30 xr.
Summa	6 f.	9 xr.

Eisenstadt, 27th Dec. 1766.

[countersigned:] Josephus Haydn mpria.
[Acta Musicalia VIII, 454, Esterházy Archives, Budapest; Valkó I, 647. A similar bill for woodwind mouthpieces, 30 December 1766, was mentioned above.]

List

What I accomplished in the way of locksmith work at the instigation of Herrn Heiden *Hochfürstlicher Kapellmeister*, to wit:
First to string a harpsichord [*Eine flich Beschlagen*], and made for it a pair of straight strips [*Bänder*], and nails with clinch attached [*Nögel mit Nied nögl*]: 24 xr.
More, 2 pairs of strips filed down: 24 xr.

---

1 Receipts gathered together in *HJB* IV, 71f. Above text from J. Harich in *HJB* IV, 15f., in our English translation and adaptation p. 32, which we have used here *verbatim*. Probably Haydn and the *Capelle* also performed the service in 1770–72, although no receipts have been found. After 1776, someone else from the Eisenstadt princely Church Choir took over the function. This change again coincides with the court's total transference to Eszterháza.

More, a propping arm with heavy base [to keep the lid open] and a padlock for the case: 21 xr.

More, two wooden screws: 6 xr.
_____

Suma 1 f. 15 xr.

This sum has been paid to me.   Georg Kahrer, Locksmith Master.

[countersigned:] Joseph Haydn mpria.

[1766 bill for end of year: Acta Musicalia, VIII, 456, Esterházy Archives, Budapest; Valkó II, 541]

In this year, the *Wiener Diarium* published, as part of its supplementary series entitled 'Gelehrter Nachrichten' (News of Learned Matters), 26th number, Saturday, 18th Vintage Month (October), an article entitled 'On the Viennese Taste in Music'. As a conclusion to our Chronicle of 1766, we append this article, in which Haydn is given a place of honour. It was one of the first times that an official Austrian newspaper took serious notice of the young composer.

One cannot ever gainsay a nation of taste, as soon as it is capable of having understanding, experience and a susceptible heart: three elements which are important ingredients of it and, after it has been formed, change into its components. Before **Batteux** one did not know how to give it a proper name: one considered it a gift of nature, the lack of which **Aristotle** and **Bossa** could not replace. It is true that most of it is born in us, and like genius it is a force of the soul, of which each one of us receives his due; nevertheless, it would never arrive at its true purpose (which is **perception**) unless **understanding** differentiates the true from the false, and **experience** lights the path like a torch. Therefore taste is a **perception**, which differentiates with certainty between the good, the mediocre and the bad.

This **perception** in music is based, as in all other disciplines, on nature. A people whose taste is sure will never admire effects of art which would displease them in nature; and would never forbid its artists things in which it is mirrored. But never is the **new** and **unexpected** more in demand than in music: however, it must not be quixotic [*abentheurerlich*] if it is to succeed and not to awake displeasure. To this end, then, must be its **purpose**: to **please**, to **move**, to **touch**, and to give **delight**. That which we call **charm** and **grace** in the fine arts is the real pleasure that we receive from them.* A common history affects us only incompletely, through everyday examples, and allows the soul to sigh in a kind of slavery; poetry leads her further on, shows her enchanted places, the most marvellous silhouettes, and our fantasy really and with delight finds them so fashioned; music, to a certain extent, is the first to distribute this delight in full measure: the senses are overcome with joy, pleasures succumb to innocence, a whole heaven of happiness, as it were, surrounds the heart, and we are in Elysium. **Batteux** questions: 'Could a condition be more delightful than that of a person who all at once feels the liveliest impressions of painting, music, the dance and poetry which have all combined to give him pleasure?' But this condition would occupy all the senses and forces of the soul, and would therefore soon become unpleasant. 'For the amount of the parts tire us, if they are not connected one to another in harmony and are not so constituted that they have one common denominator.'

In certain cases the spiritual peculiarities of the listener must be attuned in consonance to those of the composer, if he is to perceive that which is expected of

_____

* Rammler [original footnote].

him. This applies in a contrary sense to the musician as soon as he allies himself with the poet. If the poem as set to music does not produce double the emotion that one had when just reading the poem, or unless it even says something else than that intended by the poet, then the composer has failed his purpose and deserves to be ignored. . . .

One assumes that every nation, every province has its own dialect and taste, which are formed by the governing principle of its leaders. Two or three good writers can transform the literary taste of an entire nation; and as many good composers can do the same for music. The fact that the French are still locked in the dullness of their **Lully**, and the Italians more and more tend to the **bizarre**, while the Germans erect a musical empire – they have no one but their composers to thank for that; and they are the ones about which we would inform our readers, how much and in which *genres* they have done to shape our taste. If we do not list them in the order of their merit, it occurs simply because we put them down as they occur to us. The first is

Herr Georg von Reuttern, Royal Imperial Chapel Master, who is unquestionably the strongest composer to sing the praise of God, and is the model for all the men in this sphere. For who knows better than he how to express the magnificent, the joyous, the trumphant, when the text requires it, without falling into the profane or theatrical? Who is more pathetic, more rich in harmonies than he, when the text demands sadness, a prayer, or pain? His Masses always gather a crowd of people about them, and every man leaves them edified, convinced and wiser than before.

Herr Leopold Hoffmann, his path soars ever upwards. The **serious** with the **pleasant**, **melody** with **correctness**, characterize his pieces above all others. He is the only one to approach the church style of **Hrn von Reuttern**. His Masses are full of majestic and grand thoughts, which elevate and inflame the praise of God and the prayer in the temple. His **musical Oratorio**, which was performed last year by the Carmelites in the Leopoldstadt and was composed in honour of Saint John Nepomuk, shows us a genius who was born for lyrical poetry. Who does not feel everything that one can feel about a bloodthirsty tyrant, when the horrid words of the Hoffmann movement sound: 'ut irrita consilia in vanum abeant &c.'? The menacing pride which lurks in these words flashes from every note, every bar awakes terror in the breast, as the listener hears of the innocent's death. But serious though this style is, as pleasant and attractive is he in his symphonies, concertos, quartets and trios; one may say that **Hoffmann**, after **Stamitz**, is the only one to give to the transverse flute the proper lightness and melody.

Herr Christoph Wagenseil, who is as excellent in composing as in harpsichord playing, has written sundry operas, serenades which have been performed here and elsewhere with the greatest success. All his symphonies are original, solid and professionally composed. His way of playing the harpsichord, and the **soli** in his concertos for that instrument, have something overpowering and captivating about them which will ensure his fame for many years to come. This instrument is little suited to singing melody, for it seems to be made only for accompaniment, and concertos for it are so meagre that one cannot long support them; but the art to give the harpsichord, with the help of the accompanying violins, a kind of melody was primarily reserved for Wagenseil. His delicacy, his clean passages, his strange but not unnatural modulations, with which he modulates in a way peculiar to his art through all the keys, show the discernment of a great master; and he is known for it in many great courts, as well as here.

Wagenseil's most worthy follower is his pupil **Herr Joseph Steffan**. One cannot possibly deny him the novelty of creating beautiful and artless modulations in which art and nature seem to be joined, even if he copies his master. His concertos, divertimentos, galanteries, variations and preludes for the harpsichord will always be applauded by connoisseurs. Although this great harpsichord player has been touched with the illness of scholarship, his smaller pieces nevertheless reflect a spirit which reaches the delightful when he wants to. His allegros are mostly lusty, delightful, full of caprice and learned tricks, melancholy as the preceding adagio might have been as it sighed its course to end.

Herr Joseph Hayden, the darling of our nation, whose gentle character impresses itself on each of his pieces. His movements have beauty, order, clarity, a fine and noble expression which will be felt sooner than the listener is prepared for it. In his cassatios, quartets and trios he is a pure and clean water, over which a southerly wind occasionally ripples, and sometimes rises to waves without, however, losing its bed and course. The art of writing the outer parts in parallel octaves is his invention, and one cannot deny that this is attractive, even if it appears rarely and in a Haydenisch fashion. In symphonies he is as masculinely strong as he is inventive. In cantatas charming, fetching, flattering; and in minuets natural, playful, alluring. In short, **Hayden** is that in the music which **Gellert** is in poetry.

Herr Carl Ditters, his passages are mostly fiery, violent, daring, but they always have a dominating melody that pleasantly and attractively connects them. Whenever he appears, he is new; and one notices that there is a genius in him that seeks to rise up and to reach the highest degree of perfection. Even there when he does not wish to, he pleases, because he understands how the national taste can be linked pleasantly with the art. Up to now a **Ditters** has understood best how to honour the nation, in that he is a good composer as well as a great violinist. His last works, especially the Masses, contain fugues which will stand up to the most severe criticism. In his concertos a brilliant melody usually predominates, which appears to be placed with such order and choice that the work reaches all the perfection of which this instrument is capable. Should not, or can not, time give us a **Bach** [C. P. E. Bach?] in him?

Herr Chevalier Gluck, a man who is really made for the orchestra. A man, who through his **Orpheus**, *Rencontre imprevû, Don Jean* [sic] and **Alexander** has already been made immortal, even if he had written nothing else. A man who animates the works of a **Metastasio**, whom the English like, who delights the French, and us – his notes speak their own thoughts. He has passages wherein the little genius that one has disappears. One dislikes oneself.★ Courage does not come again until the impression he has made upon us gradually disappears. When he describes passion with strong strokes, he dictates the movements of the heart at his will. Always successful, always the leader of our hearts. Every modulation, every movement and fall speak surely to our soul. It is impossible to feel him completely unless one is oneself a poet and composer. So much one can say, however, that he has brought comic opera to perfection, because his genius was the right source to water and to make fruitful the dry French lands. Pity that we have no **Rammler** here; how many **Grauns** we could have to give us honour!

We must still mention **Hrn. Zechner**, secular priest, whose *alla Capella* [sic] style [is noted]: **Hrn. von Ordoniz**, Hrn. **Starzer** and Hrn. **Gaßmann**, of which the first (in symphonies, cassations, quartets) and the latter (in theatre music) have contributed some beautiful pieces. Our composers *à la mode* [*Modecomponisten*], who now and then among their ill-constructed patchwork also produce a novelty, we dare not mention here. Now we are at the point where we can speak a few words to our rivals.

★ Only the *Herren Musiker* will understand us here. [Original footnote].

Recently there have arisen in Germany people who with their prejudiced criticism have taken a strong stand against things that are obviously beautiful; people like the inventors of **Diderot**['s *Encyclopedia*], who live in a valley surrounded on all sides by hills. If such a man stood on one leg and looked over his narrow horizon, he would call out: **I know everything**; **I have seen everything**. When he once climbed his hill in order to examine certain objects more closely, he saw with astonishment what immeasurable spaces unfolded before his eyes. And now he called: **I know nothing; I have seen nothing**. One said to one of our composers that he had been praised by these art critics. 'Oh', he answered, 'they will have set someone else next to me so as to praise him, and by comparison they will disgrace me more than they can ever praise.' This answer turned out to be correct. These art critics – we wish to name them – are the **editors of the Allgemeine deutsche Bibliothek**; they dare to write censorious opinions about our first composers, of which they understand not one single note; and despite this they live in the complete conviction that they have a monoply on good taste. But their 1. St[ück], 2. B[and] Nro. XXV shows the contrary. Their principles are attempts that do not go above sketches or outlines [&c.] .... How very different from these gentlemen is the **editor of Briefe die neueste Litteratur** [*sic*] **betreffend**, how very different! The spirit of the language, the thoroughness of view, the free and unprejudiced but correct judgements, which give these letters their value, are sought in vain in the *Allgemeine deutsche Bibliothek*. In a dozen reviews there is hardly a one which is worth keeping. ...

The editor of the Hamburgischen Unterhaltungen 1. St[ück], who was annoyed about the octave doublings of our composers, must know that most of the Symphonies by **Graun** contain *Andanti* in which the bassoon moves in octaves with the transverse flute; and it occurred to no one to say: **it is as if father and son were begging alms in one tone**. One must have blunted feelings not to appreciate the gentle persuasion of the octave doublings when they cut through a full harmonic background. But what use is there in wasting time over a pride whose dull wit can offend no one. One could not abuse him more than in scorn and silence.

We are now in the middle of what would become a curious kind of Press battle between north and south, or between the better educated, more literary north Germans and the south Germans (and especially the 'new' Mannheim school) with, of course, the Austrians. The Austrians, as this biography will have shown in profuse detail, were not primarily a literary people. Their strength was music, and also theatre, particularly improvised spoken theatre, with its rough charm and excruciating dialect (fully the equal, if that is the right word, of the strongest cockney). They were distinctly at a loss when beginning a battle of words with the verbose intricacies and devious constructions pouring out of Leipzig, Hamburg and Berlin. But more was at stake than a battle of words. The north Germans really had little understanding of the southern art, of that curious mixture of the vulgar and the divine which flourish side by side in the art of Haydn and his contemporaries. They had as little understanding, probably, of the Baroque exuberance that marked the great Austrian and southern German monasteries. Since almost all the German-language criticism was, however, centred in north Germany, it was they who blanketed the critical world with their endless carpings. As time went on, and as Haydn gradually became the leader of his school – in 1766, he was generally regarded as *primus inter pares* – the north Germans began to single him out for attacks of an increasingly vicious nature. Even after Haydn had gone to England, the attacks did not cease, and one of the most virulent is quoted, in all its nauseating verbosity, in *Haydn in England 1791–1795* (pp. 189ff.).

The immediate reason for the long article in the *Wiener Diarium* was *inter alia* the following extract from the *Hamburger Unterhaltungen*, Band 1 (1766):

> A **Hayden** [*sic*] is pleasant, witty and full of inventiveness in his quartets; his symphonies and trios are of the same mettle. Whether, however, his minuets in octaves are to everyman's taste is something I will leave undecided. They are good for amusement; but one easily gets the idea that one is hearing father and son begging by singing octaves: and that is a bad object for musical imitation.[1]

In the course of the Chronicle to the present volume, the reader will be able to follow this series of attacks on Haydn, which would be of little more than academic interest were it not for the fact, as we firmly believe, that they provoked the extraordinary reaction to Haydn's Quartets, Op. 20. Naturally *The Creation* cannot be ascribed to a negative remark in the *Jahrbuch der Tonkunst von Wien und Prag* (1796),[2] and the Op. 20 Quartets are of such decisive importance in the history of music that to ascribe their existence to a German Press war would be impudent. But nevertheless, we know that Haydn smarted under these attacks, and he explicitly mentions the barbs of the north German critics in his autobiographical sketch of 1776 (*vide infra*, p. 399). To a certain, if small, extent, therefore, Op. 20 and the many other serious works of this period are perhaps a refutation of such criticisms as well as a brilliant self-justification.[3]

Chronicle 1767

IN JANUARY 1767, Euphrosina Schleicher died and the whole house at Klostergasse No. 82, Eisenstadt, came into the Haydns' physical possession. Her death forced Haydn to pay off the remaining money for the house sooner than anticipated. Her effects and furniture were auctioned on 16–18 March, and we find Frau Haydn purchasing two items:[4]

> *Fr. Capelmrin* [*Capellmeisterin*]. A box with dried marigold petals [*Land Saffran*, out of which an *Ersatz* saffron is made for colouring food], cinnamon and cloves .... 2 fl. 6 x.
> Fr. Capelmr. 8 ells of the finest linen a 30 x .... 5 fl. 20 x.
> [She also purchased a box with needles and thread and some lengths of linen fabric.]

In order to complete the purchase of their house, Haydn and his wife borrowed 500 gulden from her father – the loan, in the form of a promissory note, was for a year at five per cent – and supplemented the loan with 200 gulden of Haydn's own savings. As noted in the receipt quoted below, the payment of 700 gulden with interest was paid to Frau Schleicher's estate on 30 April:

> Hr. Joseph Haiden [*sic*] *Hochfürstl. Esterházyscher Capelmeister*, because of the Contract *de dato Ratificationis* 2 May 1766 in which he purchased from Euphrosina Schleicher the house in the monastery precincts. Remaining instalment
> Interest on that sum *de dato 1 Novembris* 1766 to the end of April 1767, one $\frac{1}{2}$ year and 5 *per Cento* .... 17 fl. 30 x.

---

1 See H. Unverricht, *Geschichte des Streichtrios*, Tutzing 1969, p. 156.
2 See *Haydn: the Years of 'The Creation' 1796–1800*, p. 13.
3 The present writer gave a B.B.C. lecture on this subject, 'Haydn and the north German critics', some years ago.
4 Schmid, *Eisenstadt*, p. 7.

The capital and the interest were paid, according to a receipt produced by the *Hrn Capelmeister* [*sic*] and signed by the *Tit. Hrn Testaments Executori* [who was Abbot Leopold Hörger, parish priest of St Martin's; the receipt read: 'The 30th of April paid by Hrn Joseph Hayden [*sic*] *Fürstl. Capellmeister* the remaining instalment on the house purchased from the *Fr: Testatricin* ... 700 fl.' 'Half-year 5 *pcento* interest on that sum *de dato 1. 9bris* 1766 to end of April 1767 ... 17 fl. 30 x.'].

We now come to the first public performance, outside Eisenstadt and Eszterháza, of Haydn's *La canterina*. The event took place in the old coronation town of Pressburg (now Bratislava, ČSSR). Fortunately we have an eye-witness account of those days at Pressburg, written by the Imperial Major-Domo, Prince Johann Joseph Khevenhüller-Metsch, who went with the Archduchess Marie Christine and her consort, the Duke Albert of Sachsen-Teschen, when they left Vienna to spend carnival time in the coronation town on the Danube.

[11 February 1767] In the evening the court went to the Primate's garden to see a little Italian comedy, which the *Judex curiae* had arranged to be performed in a theatre that had been erected in a purposely large hall there, and which was performed for [the court's] amusement by his son, his three spinster daughters and niece (daughter of Count Leopold Palffi [*sic*]) and some other cavaliers, also his house officers; all the *caractères* were *en masque* as Arlequin, Pantalon, etc. and distinguished themselves astonishingly well.

On the 12th we dined with their highnesses *en grande compagnie* at Count Christoph Erdödy's and in the evening we accompanied them to a ball and *soupé* at Prince Esterhasy's [*sic*], who for love and respect for their highnesses has established himself at Presburg [*sic*] for the whole of carnival time. ...

The 15th being Sunday, the court went as usual, according to our Viennese ceremony and custom, which obtain here *pro norma* in everything, with open *cortège* to the chapel for sermon and high Mass. At lunch they ate at Count Balessa's and after a *partie de jeu* they went to Prince Esterhasy's, where the Archduchess made up a *partie d'ombre* again, during which the Duke made music with the host, the former on the violin and the latter on a special instrument called the baryton. After the concert they supped and thereupon the whole *compagnie*, and we always with them, went to the Redoute, which was also organized in the Viennese fashion, and at which their highnesses amused themselves with a little card-play until 1 in the morning.

The 16th there was again an invitation *diné* at court and in the evening they went once more to the Primate's garden, where in the theatre appertaining to the *Judex curiae* an *opera buffa* by the famous *compositore* and *Capelmaistern* [*sic*] of Prince Esterhasy, Herrn Handl [*sic*] was produced by his musicians, *virtuose e virtuose* [*sic*], which cost him – supposedly – upwards of 20,000 gulden annually.

The 17th was a small *diné familiare* at the Castle and in the evening the Tuesday ball.

The 18th ... we went at noon to Prince Esterhasy and supped thereafter with their highnesses at the *Judex curiae*, who gave a children's ball and *soupé* for them, and after that the rest of the party danced and was served a *soupé* at separate tables; we had the honour of being asked to join *avec les plus distingués de la compagnie* their highnesses' table.

The 19th there was an invitation lunch at court and in the evening a ball and *soupé* at Prince Esterhasy's. ...   [Khevenhüller VI, 224ff.]

Possibly Prince Nicolaus had heard that Haydn was in grave financial difficulties over the sudden debt that had matured as a result of Euphrosina Schleicher's death.

And perhaps Haydn had composed a new symphony or a set of baryton trios that particularly pleased the Prince. At any event, while Haydn was in Pressburg, and before the new Opera had been produced, he suddenly found himself richer by 99 gulden:

Commission

According to which our Chief Cashier Johann Zoller is to pay our *Capell-Meister* Joseph Haÿdn four and twenty ordinary ducats against receipt and to enter the same in the books. Prespurg, 3rd Feb. 1767.

Nicolaus Fürst Esterhazy

I attest, and herewith provide receipt, that the four and twenty ordinary ducats given by an act of grace were paid as 99 f. by the high princely General Cassa from the hand of Chief Cashier Hn. Joann Zoller in cash. Prespurg, 26th Feb. 767:

Joseph Haÿdn

Idest 99 f   Cappellmeister [*sic*]

[Generalcassa 1767, Esterházy Archives, Eisenstadt, Rubr. VIII. Fasc. 12, No. 7; *HJB* IV, 45]

The performance of *La canterina* 'per divertimento di loro altezze reali' was probably not the only one to take place in Pressburg that Carnival. It is also likely that there were concerts and that the orchestra provided the dance music for the ball which Prince Nicolaus gave on the evening of 19 February. Prince Nicolaus was thoroughly pleased with this first public appearance of his whole *Capelle*, and rewarded them as follows:

Comission

According to which our Chief Cashier Johann Zoller is to give to our Chamber Musig [*sic*], to wit: CapelMeister Haiden [*sic*] 6 ducats; to Luitschi [Luigi Tomasini], Fribert, Dichter [*sic*], Nigst, Grißler, Burgsteiner, Weigl, Hinterberger, 2 Kapfers, 3 horn players, Bon, 4 female singers each 3 ducats. Suma sixty ordinary ducats: as a gift of grace to be paid to them and entered in his books as a real expenditure. Prespurg, 2nd March 1767.

idest 60: ord. ducats.   Nicolaus Fürst Esterhazy

I attest that these sixty ordinary ducats for distribution to the Chamber Music have been paid correctly in cash to me by *Herrn* Chief Cashier Johan Zoller: Eisenstadt, 6th March 1767.

Josephus Haydn mpria

[Generalcassa 1767, Esterházy Archives, Eisenstadt, Rubr. VIII. Fasc. 12, No. 8; *HJB* IV, 45]

This document is of great interest to us because it lists all the musicians taken to Pressburg. Apart from the singers, who must be considered separately, the orchestra consisted of:

Haydn: harpsichord *continuo* (for the opera).
Tomasini, first violin.
Nigst, first or second violin.
Grießler, first or second violin.
Purksteiner, viola.
Weigl, violoncello.
Hinterberger, bassoon.
Two Kapfers, oboists.

Horn players: Joseph Dietzl (also violinist, in which capacity he probably played most of the time in Pressburg); Carl Franz (also violinist); Thaddäus Steinmüller.

Since *La canterina* requires only two horn parts, Joseph Dietzl probably played violin, which meant that there were four violins, one viola, one violoncello (and one bassoon *col basso*), two oboes, two horns and harpsichord (see the Pressburg harpsichord maker's bill of 3 March, *infra*). It is interesting to note that no double-bass player was taken from Eisenstadt; perhaps one was engaged locally, in Pressburg.[1] As for the singers, four (two male, two female) were needed for *La canterina* (*vide infra*), but of the four female singers, two were not needed for the Opera. Perhaps these were Eleonora Jäger and the mysterious Auguste Houdière; but what did they sing? Bon was the theatre decorator and perhaps he brought his daughter, Rosa, or his wife, Anna, so that a female Bon, or two, may have been the two additional female singers rather than Jäger and/or Houdière.

Naturally a specially printed libretto for *La canterina* was organized by Haydn: the printer was Johann Michael Landerer in Pressburg, and 200 copies were ordered in a much larger 4° format than was usual with libretti. From the bookbinder Jakob Georg Finsterbusch, two copies (for Duke Albert and Archduchess Christine) were bound 'with stiff cardboard covered with velvet à 30 xr', the others 'simply covered in various papers à 3 xr'. The libretto reads:

La / Canterina / Opera Buffa / representata / nel tempo di carnovale / per divertimento di loro / altezze reali / [design] /——/ Presburgo, / nella stamperia di giov. michele landerer./1767.

[The Cast:]
Don Pelagio, Maestro di Capella, CARLO FRIBERTH.
Gasperina, Canterina, Maria Anna Weigl.
Appolonia. Finta Madre di Gasperina, Leopoldo
DICHTLER.
Don Ettore. Figlio d'un Mercante, Barbara
DICHTLER.
Tutti in attual servizio di S. A. il Prencipe Esterházy.
La Musica è di GIUSEPPE HAYDN, Maestro di Capella di S. A. il Principe Esterházy.

The music of *La canterina* will be examined in the forthcoming chapter; but we must draw attention to a detail that has caused much confusion, and that is the fact that Leopold Dichtler sang a *female* part (falsetto?), while his wife, Barbara, sang a *Hosenrolle* – therefore the 'men's shoes' for her in the Haydn bill quoted above. This reversal of the roles no doubt added to the hilariously successful first public performance.[1]

Two Pressburg instrument makers hastened to submit their bills on 3 March, as long as the Esterházy court was still in residence there:

Catalogue [of] what I did to the princely instrument during the entertainments
First, newly quilled throughout and with yellow
strings in the 1½ octave at the discant, makes............ 4 sibtzen [17 kr.]
Once again tuned and quilled, makes .... 2 sibtzen
Again teto [*sic*] .... 2 sibtzen

1 *Aus der Zeit Maria Theresias. Tagebuch des Fürsten Johann Josef* [sic] *Khevenhüller-Metsch, Kaiserlichen Obersthofmeisters 1742–1776*, hg. von Rudolf Graf Khevenhüller-Metsch und Dr. Hanns Schlitter. Vol. 7 (1764–1767), Vienna 1917, pp. 224ff. Hereinafter 'Khevenhüller'. J. Harich *Musikgeschichte*, p. 31. Libretto itself: University Library, Budapest, cat. 1007 (consulted 1958). Horányi 41f.

For taking 2 Sbinnetr [spinets] up to the Prince's garden, repairing, quilling and tuning of each Sbinned makes therefore .... 10 sibtzen
[....]

Again the Sbinneder were needed for the musig [*sic*] and for one 2, that makes therefore.................. 4 sibtzen

Again the harpsichord [*Flich*] in the princely court quilled and tuned up again .... 2 sibtzen

For having to carry the Sbinneder back I had to pay the porter .... 2 sibtzen

Again in the princely court, tuned and quilled ... 2 sibtzen

For the wrest-plank [*Stim(m) Kastel*] and for repairing it .... 2 fl.

Summa makes .... 11 fl. 4 xr.

[remark of cashier: 'is to be paid by the Eisenstadt Rent Office with 11 F. Züsser mpr.']

Carolus Joannes Schetz
Organ Maker in Prössburg [*sic*]

Was paid and sincere thanks 11 Fl. in words eleven Gulden the 3rd of Martij 1767.

Carolus Joannes Schetz
Organ Maker in Prössburg

[countersigned:] Josephus Haydn mpria.

[Acta Musicalia VIII, 460, Esterházy Archives, Budapest; Valkó II, 541f.]

Catalogue. What I made for the *Herrn Capellmeister* at His princely Highness Esterházy's.

First 5 violins cleaned and put in order	:	2 gulden	
3 new bows	:	1 ,,	12 xr.
2 violas put in order	:	1 ,,	
1 Bassl ['cello] put in order, with a new bow	:	1 ,,	42 xr.
1 Bassl bow hair replaced with white hair	:	— —	24 xr.
1 Violon [double bass] put in order	:	— —	15 xr.
Bassl strings 12 batches à 3 xr.	:	— —	36 xr.
Summa		7 gulden	9 xr.

Antoni Thir violin maker ...
[Press]burg, the 3rd of March 1767.

[countersigned:] Josephus Haydn mpria.

[Acta Musicalia VII, 461, Esterházy Archives, Budapest; Valkó I, 648]

The interesting fact of this bill is that it shows us all the string instruments – or at least all that needed repairs – of the Esterházy orchestra. Apparently Haydn used the opportunity to have all his string instruments repaired at Pressburg, and he took the double bass (*violone*) with him. The number of instruments almost fits the number of musicians, if we allow that Haydn took with him 'his' violin and viola (we know that he played both), and remembering that there was at the moment no double-bass player in the 'Cammer Music'. The other bill shows that Herr Schetz makes a clear difference between spinets and harpsichords. In the princely palace at Pressburg there were, then, at least two spinets and one, presumably large 'wing-form' harpsichord. In the future, bills of this kind are listed here *in extenso* only if it was thought they contained some piece of valuable information; otherwise they have been summarized.

In the middle of March, Prince Nicolaus went to Eszterháza. He had stayed two full months at Pressburg, and had displayed his orchestra for the first time to the *haute noblesse*. Naturally, we still do not have all the bills for this Pressburg period, for we know[1] that the small orchestra, 'particularly thin in the violin section, was increased by the addition of outside forces, which also played for the dance music at the balls.' Thus Haydn's own group only formed the nucleus of the band that was displayed at Pressburg, but it was probably not larger, in the string section, than 4–3–2–1–1.

Another bill, Eisenstadt, 8 April 1767 is for carpentry work done at the order of the 'Herrn Herrn Kobel Meister': a cabinet of oak 'with 5 feet, all of oak', a new violon case (i.e. for double bass), 'more, the old one for the big [instrument]' was repaired, and 'the apprentice worked three hours at 12 xr. repairing the shelves for the music' – all for a total of 4 fl. 25 kr., which was countersigned as usual by Haydn. The item of interest here is the note of the 'big' double bass. There were, of course, several sizes of 'violoni' and Haydn probably had a large one for orchestral and church music and a small one for chamber music.[2]

A few days later an organ builder from Wiener Neustadt submitted his bill:

> Because of repairing and tuning the princely organ *Positiv* in the choir-loft, and harpsichords [*Fligeln*], on the order of *Titl. Herrn Regentens* v. Rahier, the Neustädter organ builder Joseph Zierengast was paid for 8 days of food and work in Concreto 16 Fl. by the Eisenstädter Rent Office, is hereby attested. [Countersigned:] With my agreement Josephus Haydn mpria.
>
> Eisenstadt, 14th April 1767.
>
> Joseph Zierengast Orgl macher von der Neistat.
>
> [Acta Musicalia, VII, 463, Esterházy Archives, Budapest; Valkó I, 648]

This 'fürstl. Chor Orgl Positiv' has, fortunately, survived; it is usually kept in the rehearsal room next to the great hall in Eisenstadt.

On 24 April, Haydn and his wife were godparents to the eldest child of the Tomasinis; the ceremony took place at the Parish Church of St Martin's at Eisenstadt:

> 24. Aprilis 1767.
> Nomen baptizati: Josephus
> Nomen et Cognomen Parentum: Aloisius Louitschi Inc[ola] et Virtuosis Musicus
>   sub Principe, Uxor Josepha
> Nomen et Cognomen Patrinorum: Josephus Haÿden Capellae Magister sub
>   Principe cum sua Conthorali Anna Maria.

In Vienna, Joseph II's wife, Josepha, died of smallpox on 28 May. In the epidemic that followed, the young Wolfgang Mozart and his sister caught the disease, and so did the Empress Maria Theresa. Leopold Mozart fled to Olmütz and reported, first 'Te Deum Laudamus! Wolfgangerl got over the pox successfully' (10 November) and shortly thereafter (29 November), 'Te Deum Laudamus! My daughter has got over the pox successfully'.[3] When Maria Theresa recovered, the Te Deum that Leopold Mozart had invoked became a reality in Vienna. Khevenhüller reports:

> [On 14 June a Te Deum was ordered to be given at St Stephen's cathedral] in the most magnificent fashion and with various choirs, trumpets and kettledrums at 10

1 J. Harich *Musikgeschichte*, p. 31.   2 A.M. VII, 462. Valkó I, 648.
3 *Mozart: Briefe und Aufzeichnungen: Gesamtausgabe* (ed. Bauer and Deutsch), vol. I, Kassel 1962, pp. 244, 248.

o'clock, and also the same at court in the small chapel at the particular order of the Emperor, who attended together with all the highest family and also the most distinguished families at the court. It was repeated by the court chaplain after 11 o'clock also with trumpet and drum flourishes. This *bruyante Musique* was at the instigation of the late Cardinal Trautsohn *edictaliter* forbidden some years ago; but the present, so joyous occasion suggested to those in high station, and the idea was approved by the court, that during the Te Deum and similar solemn occasions – otherwise not – the trumpets and kettledrums would be allowed to be heard again; which order was received by the people, who always like to see such demonstrations, with the greatest enthusiasm.   [Khevenhüller VI, 246]

It is hard to know how earnestly this 'Verbot' of trumpets and drums was taken in places like Eisenstadt. Obviously Haydn thought his new *Missa Cellensis in honorem Beatissimae Virginis Mariae* a 'solemn occasion', for he used trumpets and drums; which meant, moreover, that he expected it to be played at Mariazell with those instruments. We shall see in 1768 (*infra*, p. 149) that Haydn ordered trumpets and drums from the Oedenburger *Thurnermeister*, but it is not known if they were to be used for a religious ceremony.

On 11 June at Eisenstadt, 'Johann Joseph Stadlmann, k. k. hof Lautenmacher' submitted a bill for 18 fl. 58 kr. for various strings, pegs, etc., partly dating back to 9 January, concluding with the item '3 Violon [double bass] pegs'. When countersigning the document, Haydn wrote 'These strings were required in Prespurg [*sic*] Joseph Haydn mpria', which seems to confirm that not only was the double bass taken to Pressburg but Haydn fully expected to have it played there.[2]

Mathias Rockobauer, the woodwind maker from Vienna, sent in a bill for a dozen oboe reeds (at 10 kr.) and two cor anglais reeds (at 7 kr.), or a total of 2 fl., 14 kr., dated Vienna, 20 June 1767; it was paid, says the document, by Haydn, who in turn collected the money from the Rental Office at Eisenstadt on the 27th.[1]

Our next record of Haydn is again a gift from Prince Nicolaus. He was in Eszterháza, and the Princess, who was in Eisenstadt, arranged to have not only Haydn but also the physician-in-residence, Dr Molitor von Mühfeld, given the money:

Comission
According to which, upon order of the Prince dd° Eszterhaz, 5th July a. c. Chief Cashier Zoller is to give H. Doctor v. Molitor fifty, and the *Kapellmeister* Haiden [*sic*] twelve imperial ducats against receipt and to be paid from, and entered into the books of, the Gral [General] Cassa. Eisenstadt, 6th Julÿ 767.

Elisabeth Fürstin Esterhasÿ gebohrne Gräfin von Weissenwolf

The 9th Julÿ A: C: the above listed 208 f. 20 Xr. in 50 pieces of Imp. Duc. were correctly paid to me from the Gral Cassa Josef Dr. Molitor Edler v Mühlfeld	The 9th Julÿ also received the above listed 50 f. in twelve imperial ducats

Josephus Haydn mpria.
[Generalcassa 1767. Rubr. VIII. Fasc. 12, Nr. 29. Esterházy Archives, Eisenstadt.
HJB IV, 46]

This time we cannot imagine what prompted this gift. We know that a very important work of Haydn's was written in 1767, the *Stabat Mater*, but we have no

---

1 A. M. VIII, 464; Valkó I, 649.   2 A. M. VIII, 465; Valkó I, 649.

record of its performance. Its small orchestral forces (oboes or cors anglais, strings and organ) suggest that it could easily have been performed at Eisenstadt. (It would hardly have been suitable for carnival celebrations in Pressburg.) Perhaps the 50 fl. are a reward for this important work; perhaps for the completion of the new *Missa*; perhaps for yet another performance of *La canterina*. We shall probably never know.

Haydn was godfather to the first child of his copyist Elssler and his wife: Joseph, baptized on 7 August 1767 at the Parish Church of St Martin in Eisenstadt. Joseph was to follow his father's profession and was also to become an oboe player in the princely *Harmonie*.[1]

From Prince Khevenhüller's Diary, we learn of a new opera by the world-famous team of Pietro Metastasio and J. A. Hasse:

> 9 Sept. In the evening at the Theatre next to the Castle [Burgtheater] there was a new opera called *Parténope* by *Abbate* Metastasio for which the music was composed by the famous old Saxonian *Capellmeister* Sr. Hasse; it was given before the whole court except the Empress, who had decided, *pour obliger le public*, to attend the public dining table but no theatrical *Spectacles*. . . . On the 10th [Vestris, the famous ballet dancer, appeared.] As far as both yesterday's and today's *Spectacles* are concerned, they had, apart from the ballet, little success, for the German *Comédie* was a very badly written and stupidly produced extract from the English novel *Tom Jon[es]* and the Opera, as well as for its libretto as for its music was likewise a very weak and *froide* composition, and not like either Metastasio (who recently, for his work *per la riconvalescenza dell'augustissima* entitled 'felicità publicca', was given a *Tabatière garnie de brillans avec le portrait de l'impératrice*) or Signor Hasse; the latter repeated ideas from his *Alcide* [*al bivio*], and the former did not develop the theme and filled it up with tasteless and rather insipid love scenes; to justify himself he professed that he was given strict instructions and was thus inhibited, which in the present well-known circumstances [death of Joseph's wife] is very probable. [Khevenhüller, pp. 263f.]

It is difficult for us to understand the years of triumphal success, in Italy and abroad, which greeted opera after opera by Hasse, usually on texts by Metastasio. What was the fascination of this team for *settecento* audiences? Perhaps the music was the least important part of the operation, and the eye was dazzled by fabulous sets and costumes and the ear delighted by the ravishing singing of Faustina Hasse, the composer's celebrated wife. The actual musical content of those endless Hasse operas appears so thin by any contemporary standards – Handel, Gluck, not to speak of the coming generation of Haydn and Mozart (whose new opera for Milan, *Ascanio in Alba* [1771], would coincide with Hasse's last work for the same occasion, *Ruggiero*)[2] – that one is astonished that his popularity had been so profound and so lasting. If we examine the productions of Hasse in the 1760s, the works that strike us as most likely to have influenced Haydn, who was an admirer of the older composer, are the cantatas, whose suave orchestration and mellifluous vocal line makes us wonder at the emptiness of many of the operas that surround them.[3] But a new wind was blowing, in Vienna, in Venice, everywhere; and the public that had applauded Metastasio and Hasse to the skies ten years ago now found the same face thin and 'froide'. Hasse was, however, the

---

1 Csatkai, op. cit., p. 15f.
2 Also a failure. Leopold Mozart (*Briefe* I, 444: Milan, 19 Oct. 1771) 'In short! *I am sorry* that the Serenate of Wolfg: has so prostrated the opera by Haße that I can't describe it.' Hasse himself, in a letter to Abbate Ortes of 30 Oct. 1771, confirms the failure. Perhaps this second failure, coming after the Viennese *débâcle* of 1767, was instrumental in persuading this charming, cultivated man to retire.
3 See the interesting collection prepared by Sven Hansell and published in the series 'Le Pupitre' by Heugel, Paris, in 1968.

father-figure *par excellence* for young composers: the success story of all time, and even more a Saxonian (the Italians called him 'Il Sassone') who had made a career in chauvinistic Italy with Italian operas. Haydn sent his *Stabat Mater* to Hasse, who thought it an excellent work and said so in public, apparently also to the Empress; Haydn thereupon arranged a performance for the old gentleman.[1]

Before we return to Eisenstadt, another entry from Prince Khevenhüller's Diary commands our attention. On 5 October, a new opera, *Psyche* (libretto by Marco Coltellini, later to serve Haydn with *L'infedeltà delusa*), with music by Florian Leopold Gassmann – soon to be a great favourite at Eszterháza – was given at the Burgtheater in Vienna:

> The music of today's piece found more approbation than that of the first opera [by Hasse]; but the subject and then the *Histoire lugubre d'Orphée et Eurydice*, which was portrayed in the otherwise very well produced ballet, seemed to everybody too sad for the present epoch; and when one thought of the dangerous illness of the bride [of Joseph II], the strange choice of two such sad fables seemed almost like a bad omen when one remembered the curious fact that during the time when the Infanta, first wife of the Emperor [Princess Isabella of Bourbon-Parma], caught smallpox and in her young and so valuable life succumbed to it, they had chosen the same unfortunate *Soggietto d'Orphée et Eurydice per una festa theatrale* [by Gluck] and had performed it several times.   [Khevenhüller, p. 270]

Coltellini and Gassmann were, in fact, much closer to the cultivated amateur of 1767 than Metastasio and Hasse, and closer to Haydn's (and Prince Esterházy's) tastes. In the above report, it is instructive to see how closely music (opera) and everyday life coexisted, and that people automatically thought of the deaths of both Joseph II's wives through smallpox in connection with Gluck's *Orfeo*, Gassmann's *Psyche* and the (anonymous) ballet on the subject of the former.

Haydn's activities are documented for us by the ubiquitous bills in the Esterházy Archives from some of which scraps of information may be gleaned:

> Eisenstadt, 19 August 1767: bill, countersigned by Haydn, from one Balthasar Schlecht, Paroquier 'here' for a wig for the princely opera, presumably *La canterina*. Five Gulden.

> Vienna, 25 September 1767: bill, countersigned by Haydn, from Mathias Rockobauer, saying that 'Herrn Herrn Joseph Heiten' had paid him 40 'kreizer' for repairing an English horn. It is significant that Haydn's new *Stabat Mater*, and *La canterina*, both require cors anglais.

> Eisenstadt, 11 October 1767: bill, countersigned by Haydn and by Rahier, from Jacob Wan Week, princely court bookbinder, for 25 fl. 15 xr.: 'for his most serene Highness ...
> 1) Divert by Hayden with 3 parts, binding and slip-cover: 8 f.
>   Divert. by Neymann [Neumann] with 3 parts, ditto
>   for each 8 Gulden: 16 f.
> For a new slip-cover, makes: 1 f. 15 xr.
> _____
> Summa: 25 f. 15 xr.

---

1 *Vide infra*, p. 144. For an interesting verbal account of Hasse's reaction, given by Haydn to his Moravian friend Latrobe in London in 1791, see *Haydn in England 1791–1795*, p. 58. Gordon and Elizabeth Morrill feel that our views concerning the music of Hasse, as expressed above, do not correctly reflect the essential point being made in the context, viz. that the works of Hasse were taken only as an example (among those of the composer's contemporaries) of the fact that by the period under consideration both the style of composition and public taste had advanced to a new phase, thus rendering 'old-fashioned' the works of the older composers.

This bill was paid to me [etc.] and also H: *Capellmeister* Heyden for four books of Italian music paper: 3 Guld. 6 xr . . .'.

[A.M. VIII., 466, 467, 468; Valkó I, 649f.]

The latter bill is for baryton Trios by Haydn and Neumann; Haydn's dated autographs of the period (Nos. 41, 42, 53) give us the approximate numbers which the Haydn volume contained, but the copy has not survived.

In a bill of Joseph Dietzl (Eisenstadt, 18 November 1767; A.M. VIII, 469; Valkó I, 650f.), listing numerous amounts of new strings and repairs, we learn 'For strings, 7 bundles of small violin E, of which 2 ditto went to Esterhas for the *Cammer Music*'; which tells us that the musicians, and probably Haydn, were in Eszterháza during at least part of the Summer of 1767 (Haydn's presence at Eisenstadt is known to us on 30 April, but afterwards not until 11 June, for example).

Prince Nicolaus decided, in the late Autumn of 1767, to go to Paris. The trip began from Vienna, and at the last minute it was decided that Luigi Tomasini should be part of the entourage. Tomasini had been about to move in with his wife's parents, for economic reasons, when he was hastily summoned to the capital. Instead of travelling with the so-called 'Robotwagen', a conveyance which the princely subjects were supposed to furnish at their own expense, Luigi was given a hackney-carriage with a coachman for which Prince Nicolaus paid. On 19 October, Tomasini was given 100 gulden travelling expenses and left Eisenstadt for Vienna. In the princely entourage were his personal secretary, his *Haushofmeister*, his architect, his 'Travelling Commissioner' (*Reisekommisär*), five *valets-de-chambre* (among them a barber and a blackamoor named Zibas), his gun-master, a page and two runners.

The Prince stayed in Paris a week, but probably the principal reason for the French sojourn was to study the Palace of Versailles, which explains the presence of the architect among the group. The party travelled to Paris via Strasbourg and returned that way; Prince Nicolaus left Paris on 14 November, but Tomasini stayed there to study the musical life of the French capital, for which purpose he was given 125 livres: 'Io [ho] ricevuto a Parigi dal Sig. Magiordomo 50: Fiorini a Chonto [*sic*] che in livre Cento venticinque in Parigi li *14*: novembre 1767 / Luigi Tomassini [*sic*].'

Paris was then unquestionably the musical centre of the world. Haydn must have known that his works were extremely popular in France, for they had been printing his music there since January 1764. Haydn, of course, never had any royalties or any other financial gain from these pirated publications, some of which he probably never even saw; but now, in the person of his friend Tomasini, he had an opportunity to hear about the situation at first hand. It is entirely possible that Tomasini was given Haydn's latest compositions to market in the French capital, and that the Italian established connections, during his further stay in Paris, with one of the principal music publishers, Jean-Georges Sieber, a German émigré who was to publish dozens of Haydn's symphonies, some (e.g. No. 48) in textually so accurate versions that one suspects that the composer himself furnished the engraver's copy. Haydn was actually in correspondence with Sieber at least by April 1789, and that particular letter does not sound like the first of a series but rather as if both men had been in correspondence before. Haydn's principal publisher in Paris was M. de la Chevardière, who had brought out Haydn's early string Quartets and Trios, and many of his early Symphonies. Is it a coincidence that Chevardière issued, in April 1768 (announcement in the *Mercure de France*) another set of 'Six Symphonies ou Quatuor [*sic*] Dialogués' – the title he had used for the early Quartets – which was entitled *Oeuvre IV* and included

Symphony No. 33, a Divertimento in G (II:9), and Symphonies 32, 15, 'B' (I:108) and 25 – all with the wind parts omitted but in textually rather accurate copies? Another house in Paris of importance to Haydn is Venier, which had issued the first symphony by the then unknown Austrian ('les noms inconnus, bon à connaître' was the slogan applied to the new Austro-German symphonic school), also in 1764. Apart from Sieber, Chevardière and Venier, many other Parisian publishers were actively issuing music by Haydn in the 1760s and early 1770s. There were Bailleux ('Rue St Honoré, à la Regle d'Or'); Madame Bérault ('à côté de la Comédie Françoise'); Huberty ('Maître de la viol d'amour, rue des deux écus au pigeon blanc'), who had a daughter who was a fine engraver of music (the family later went to Vienna); Mademoiselle de Silly (Rue du Temple); Simon & Fils ('Imprimeur-libraires de S. A. S. Monseigneur le prince du Condé, rue des mathurins'); 'Le Sr Borelly, rue St Victor vis-à-vis le ferme maison d'un sellier'; the Bureau d'abonnement musical on the Rue du hazard Richelieu (they were to issue the first edition of the 'Farewell' Symphony in 1775); Mademoiselle Girard ('Rue du roule, à la Nouveauté'); and others.

Luigi Tomasini may have found this music too expensive to purchase for his friend Haydn, but he will have looked at it with a professional eye, remembered their contents, talked to the various publishers, and returned to Eisenstadt full of tall tales and, perhaps, a commission or two for future works.[1]

While the Prince was away, Haydn completed Symphony No. 35, the autograph of which is dated 1 December. Perhaps it was intended to greet Esterházy when he returned from his trip (which would have been about the first week of December).

The Prince had not yet taken to engaging strolling players for the whole season at Eszterháza, probably because (a) there was no regular theatre and (b) there were no proper quarters for the musicians and a numerous band of actors and actresses. But Eisenstadt was in 1767 host to such a group of players, the Johann Eder marionette troupe.[2] We may be sure that Haydn looked at the puppets with interest; we know that he was greatly interested in the whole concept of a marionette theatre and would, in a few years, form one of his own.

The great theatrical event of the year was the première of Gluck's *Alceste* at the Burgtheater on 26 December 1767, with Antonia Bernasconi in the title role, Tibaldi as Admète and Salieri at the harpsichord. Prince Khevenhüller was there and reports in his Diary (VII, 280): '... for which Sr. Calsabigi made the libretto, and it was once again to the highest degree *pathétique* and *lugubre*; *par bonheur* there was at the end a ballet by Mr. de Noverre *dans le goût grotesque*, which was highly applauded.' Calzabigi (*recte*) later reports that in the following fifty performances one could hardly hear a sound except for a sigh.[3] We do not know if Haydn was in the audience: it was the Christmas vacation and, theoretically, he could have been. But he certainly saw the handsome score which was printed shortly thereafter, and which included the critically important letter to Grand Duke Leopold of Tuscany that Gluck wrote about the work:[4]

> Royal Highness!
> When I began to write the music for *Alceste*, I resolved to free it from all the abuses which have crept in either through ill-advised vanity on the part of singers

1 J. Harich in *HJB* VIII, 8 (54) and 252 (document from *Haushofmeister* books, Esterházy Archives, Forchtenstein Castle). Landon in Decca notes for Haydn Symphonies, London 1972, 1973, vols. HDNH 7–12, 35–40 for Haydn's publishers in Paris.
2 Probst, pp. 28f.
3 R. Gerber: *Christoph Willibald Ritter von Gluck*, Potsdam 1941, p. 67.
4 *Gluck: Collected Letters*, ed. Hedwig & E. H. Müller von Asow, London 1962, pp. 22f.

or through excessive complaisance on the part of composers, with the result that for some time Italian opera has been disfigured and from being the most splendid and most beautiful of all stage performances has been made the most ridiculous and the most wearisome. I sought to restrict the music to its true purpose of serving to give expression to the poetry and to strengthen the dramatic situations, without interrupting the action or hampering it with unnecessary and superfluous ornamentations. I believed that it should achieve the same effect as lively contours and a well-balanced contrast of light and shade on a very correct and well-disposed painting, so animating the figures without altering their contours. So I have tried to avoid interrupting an actor in the warmth of dialogue with a boring intermezzo or stopping him in the midst of his discource, merely so that the flexibility of his voice might show to advantage in a long passage, or that the orchestra might give him time to collect his breath for a cadenza. I did not think I should hurry quickly through the second part of an air, which is perhaps the most passionate and most important, in order to have room to repeat the words of the first part regularly four times or to end the aria quite regardless of its meaning, in order to give the singer an opportunity of showing how he can render a passage with so-and-so many variations at will; in short, I have sought to eliminate all these abuses, against which common sense and reason have so long protested in vain.

I imagined that the overture should prepare the spectators for the action, which is to be presented, and give an indication of its subject; that the instrumental music should vary according to the interest and passion aroused, and that between the aria and the recitative there should not be too great a disparity, lest the flow of the period be spoiled and rendered meaningless, the movement be interrupted inopportunely, or the warmth of the action be dissipated. I believed further that I should devote my greatest effort to seeking to achieve a noble simplicity; and I have avoided parading difficulties at the expense of clarity. I have not placed any value on novelty, if it did not emerge naturally from the situation and the expression; and there is no rule I would not have felt in duty bound to break in order to achieve the desired effect.

These are my principles. Happily all my intentions fitted admirably with the libretto, in which the famous author, having devised a new plan for the lyrical drama, had replaced florid descriptions, superfluous comparisons, sententious and frigid moralisation with the language of the heart, with strong passion, interesting situations and an ever-varied spectacle. My maxims have been vindicated by success, and the universal approval expressed in such an enlightened city [Vienna] has convinced me that simplicity, truth and lack of affectation are the sole principles of beauty in all artistic creations. . . .

Chronicle 1768

ONE WEEK AFTER NEW YEAR'S DAY, Haydn was best man at the marriage of Joseph Wolfgang Dietzl from the *Capelle*:

[7 January 1768] 7. huius copulatus est iuvenis Josephus Wolffgangus Dietzl, Musicus Dominalis, et Josephi Dietzl ludi Magistri Arcensis, ac uxorius eius Catharinae legitimus filius, cum Virtuosa virgine Elisabetha Weinhofferin, Domini Josephi Weinhoffer, ac pie defunctae Evae consortis eius legitima filia. Testes ex parte Sponsi Dominus Josephus Hayden [*sic*] Chori Magister Arcensis, cum Domino Josepho Weigl musico Dominali Teste ex parte sponsae.
[*Matricula Copulatorum*, Bergkirche, Eisenstadt; Schmid, op. cit., p. 4]

On 20 March, Haydn addressed the following letter to Prince Nicolaus, by way of Anton Scheffstoss:

[To Anton Scheffstoss, 'Secrétaire' and Chief Bookkeeper of the Esterházy Administration. *German*]

†

Eisenstadt, 20th March 1768.

Nobly born,
Highly respected Sir![1]
You will recall that last year I set to music with all my power the highly esteemed hymn, called Stabat Mater, and that I sent it to the great and world-celebrated Hasse[2] with no other intention than that in case, here and there, I had not expressed adequately words of such great importance, this lack could be rectified by a master so successful in all forms of music. But contrary to my merits, this unique artist honoured the work by inexpressible praise, and wished nothing more than to hear it performed with the good players it requires. Since, however, there is a great want of singers *utriusque generis* in Vienna, I would therefore humbly and obediently ask His Serene and Gracious Highness through you, Sir, to allow me, Weigl and his wife,[3] and Friberth[4] to go to Vienna next Thursday, there on Friday afternoon at the FFr.:Miseric:[5] to further the honour of our gracious prince by the performance of his servant; we would return to Eisenstadt on Saturday evening.
If His Highness so wishes, someone other than Friberth could easily be sent up. Dearest Mons. Scheffstoss, please expedite my request; I remain, with the most profound veneration,

Your nobly born Sir's
most devoted
Josephus Haydn, [m.] pria.

P.S. My compliments to all the gentlemen. The promised Divertimenti[6] will surely be delivered to His Highness one of these next weeks.

[CCLN, 8]

If the second known performance of the *Stabat Mater* took place at the Viennese Convent of the Brothers of Mercy, perhaps that institution – or its Eisenstadt branch – had something to do with the first performance in 1767.

In March, Johann May's horn needed to be repaired, and the work was done by the well-known Viennese brass manufacturer, Anton Kerner[7] – his bill was for 3 fl. 30 kr. – which was advanced by May and then refunded to him at Eisenstadt on 31 March 1768 (countersigned by Haydn: A. M. XIII, 771; Valkó II, 542).

---

1 'Wohl Edl Gebohrn/In Sonders Hochge Ehrtester Herr!' Concerning Scheffstoss, see also n.3 *infra*.
2 J. A. Hasse (1699–1783); *vide supra*.
3 Joseph Weigl, the 'cellist, who had joined the band in June, 1761. In 1764 he married Anna Maria Josepha, the daughter of Anton Scheffstoss, who had been engaged as soprano in the church choir in 1760. Haydn was devoted to the family and was godparent to their first child, Joseph (born 1766). See letter of 11 January 1794, *Haydn in England 1791–1795*, p. 230.
4 *Vide supra*, p. 58.
5 The Order of the Brothers of Mercy (Ger.: Barmherzige Brüder), whose Viennese convent in the Leopoldstadt (now 2nd district) is still extant.
6 Baryton Trios. We cannot identify exactly which ones are referred to.
7 Horace Fitzpatrick, op. cit., p. 132 says: 'To judge from surviving examples of his work, Kerner's importance lies in the fact that he was the first to modify the crooked horn of the Baroque so that it conformed to the demands of hand [stopping] technique whilst keeping its basic form intact. Whereas other makers indulged in various experiments with tuba-like bell throats and tightly coiled bodies, it was Kerner's model, with its twice-wound corpus and gracefully flaring bell, which became the standard concert instrument of the Austrian school until the advent of the valve.' It is typical of Haydn to have been so interested in the mechanical aspects of musical instruments, and to have engaged the best Viennese and Pressburgian makers not only for new instruments but also repairs, such as Stadlmann, Rockobauer, Kerner and Walter.

On 11 April at Eisenstadt, one 'Thomas Druckherl Wittib' (widow) supplied Haydn with 85 'Spinderl' (spinet) strings of brass, which suggests that the wear-and-tear on the keyboard instruments must have been particularly acute this past year, perhaps also because of the Pressburg trip: were those instruments taken to the princely palace from Eisenstadt, or were there harpsichords and spinets in all the major Esterházy residences, i.e. Vienna, Kittsee, Pressburg, Eisenstadt, Eszterháza, etc?[1]

The next important composition that must engage our attention is the large Cantata *Applausus*, written for the fiftieth 'Profess' anniversary of the Abbot of Zwettl Abbey, Rayner I. Kollmann (1747–76 Abbot): 'Profess' = taking the vows. Until Leopold Nowak in 1951 suggested that the work had been composed for Zwettl, it was not known for sure for which Austrian monastery it had actually been written. As a very old man, Haydn added this comment to the thematic *incipit* of the work in the *Entwurf-Katalog*, 'in lateinischer Sprache / bey Gelegenheit einer Praelats Wahl zu Crems Münster', i.e. for the choice of a Prelate at Kremsmünster (modern spelling) Abbey in Upper Austria. When this was discovered to be wrong, an alternative possibility was Göttweig Abbey in Lower Austria, where on 7 August 1768 Abbot Magnus Klein was installed; this idea seemed the more plausible in view of Haydn's immense popularity at Göttweig, the Archives of which contained many of the earliest known MS copies of Haydn's works, including the lost violin Concerto in D (VIIa:2). Now, the Joseph Haydn Institut of Cologne has assembled all the documents in connection with the work's publication in the Collected Edition (*Joseph Haydn Werke*), from which source the following information is gratefully taken.

On 29 November 1767, the Prior Placidus of Zwettl Abbey writes to a fellow monk that the Abbey intends to celebrate 'sub rosa' the fiftieth 'Profess' of their Abbot. Although Abbot Kollmann did not wish this celebration to be a grand affair, nevertheless the monks decided to give him a set of porcelain and to organize a new piece of music; for which operation they set aside no less than 600 gulden. On 4 April 1768, the *Haushofmeister* of the Zwettler Hof in Vienna – the great monasteries such as Melk, Göttweig and Zwettl all had 'dependances' in Vienna – sends a complete list of the presents. The beautiful 'Desserte' porcelain from the Imperial Viennese Porcelain Manufacturing Company – it was for thirty couverts in white porcelain – has by some miracle come down to us and may be observed in all its splendour on permanent exhibition in the Österreichisches Museum für Angewandte Kunst, Vienna. This service cost 488 fl. 20 kr. There was a picture, presumably a portrait of the Abbot, which cost 23 fl. 5 kr. together with expenses. 'For the music together with the express letters 104 [fl.]; porter's tip, tip for the messenger from Eißenstatt, cost of packing 1 [fl.] 51 [kr.]' – which means that Haydn received the handsome fee of 100 gulden for the new *Applausus*. The autograph manuscript, which has survived (Gesellschaft der Musikfreunde, Vienna), is signed with the following chronogram by Haydn: 'hVnC appLaVsVM feCIt ioseph haIDn', which will have pleased the learned monks when it arrived in the Monastery. Several beautifully made MS. copies of the libretto were prepared, one in 'yellow Atlas' for the Abbot which reads as follows:

JUBILAEUM / VIRTUTIS / PALATIUM / In quo / Prudentia, Justitia, Fortitudo, / & Temperantia / Columnarum vices sustint, / Accentu Musico adumbrantum / In / Reverendissimo, Perillustri, ac Amplissimo / Domino Domino / RAYNERO / Sac. & Exempt. Ord. Cisterc. Celeberrimi / & Antiquissimi Monasterij B. M. V. de Clara /

---

1 Countersigned by Haydn, the bill of 11 April is in A.M. XIII, 780; Valkó II, 542. Another bill of the date was from Johann Joseph Stadlmann: A.M. XIII, 781; Valkó II, 543. The other bill, for 5 fl. 25 kr., countersigned by Haydn, was for repairs to string instruments.

Valle Austriae / Abbate Vigilantissimo / Ejusdémque Ordinis per utrámque Au- / striam & Styriam [page two:] Visitatore, ac Vicario Generali, / Sac. Caesar. Reg. & Apostol. Majest. / Consiliario / Inclyt. Stat. Provinc. Infer. Aust. à Selectio- / ribus Consiliis / Deputato Perpetuo; / Dum / Jubilaeam sacrae Professionis seriem / Gloriosissimo Annorum Ornatu & Numero / coronavit / DoMInICa, / QVae / speCtata boniPastorIs InsIgnIa / eVangeLIzat. / xv. Kalend. Maji.

In the lengthy Latin dedication, we find still another member of the 'cast', entitled in the libretto 'Sapientia' but in Haydn's autograph 'Theologia'. Presumably the latter was the original wording, but after the text had been sent to Haydn, the Zwettl monks thought to combine the four cardinal virtues with 'Theologia', symbolizing Christian belief.

Before the text begins, in the libretto, we find 'Ad numeros musicos posuit / Nobilis [on one copy, the following words crossed out 'ac Eruditus'] Dominus Josephus Haidn [*sic*] in Aula Celsis- / simi Principis de Esterhazi Musices Director.' Without wishing to be frivolous, we suggest that the cancellation of the words 'ac Eruditus' may have been the reaction to Haydn's letter in which he admitted not knowing how to pronounce 'metamorphosis'. The actual performance took place on Sunday, 15 May, four weeks after the 'Profess' was celebrated (17 April). No one knows who was responsible for Haydn's commission, but the Haydn Institut believes that it might have been *Capellmeister* Werner's son, Pater Johann Nepomuk Paul Werner, a monk at Zwettl who was, until 4 February 1766, *Regens chori figuralis* at the Cistercian Abbey.

Since Haydn knew that he could not be present at the ceremony, he wrote a famous letter (see pl. 15) which he probably enclosed with the autograph when it was sent by messenger from Eisenstadt to the Viennese house of Zwettl Abbey at the end of March 1768.[1] It reads as follows:

[Letter to The Cistercian Monastery of Zwettl in Lower Austria – accompanying the score of the *Applausus* Cantata (1768). *German*]

[Undated: but written *c.* March 1768]

Since I cannot be present myself at this *Applaus* [*sc.*: *Applausus*], I have found it necessary to provide one or two explanations concerning its execution, *viz.*:

First, I would ask you to observe strictly the tempi of all the arias and recitatives, and since the whole text applauds, I would rather have the allegros taken a bit more quickly than usual, especially in the very first ritornello and in one or two of the recitatives; but no less in the two bass arias.

Secondly: for the overture all you need to play is an allegro and an andante, for the opening ritornello takes the place of the final allegro. If I knew the day of the performance, I might perhaps send you a new overture by that time.

Thirdly: in the accompanied recitatives, you must observe that the accompaniment should not enter until the singer has quite finished his text, even though the score often shows the contrary. For instance, at the beginning where the word "metamorphosis" is repeated, and the orchestra comes in at "-phosis", you must nevertheless wait until the last syllable is finished and then enter quickly; for it would be ridiculous if you would fiddle away the word from the singer's mouth, and understand only the words "quae metamo . . .". But I leave this to the harpsichord player, and all the others must follow him. N.B.: our scholars in Eisenstadt – and there are very few – disputed a great deal over the word "metamorphosis"; one wanted the penultimate syllable short, the other long; and

---

1 Sources for above material: (1) *Joseph Haydn Werke*, Reihe XXVII, Band 2 (*Applausus*), ed. Heinrich Wiens [and] Irmgard Becker-Glauch, 1969 – foreword; Kritischer Bericht, 1971.

despite the fact that in Italian one says "metamōrfosi", I have always heard it pronounced "metamorphōsis" in Latin; should I have made a mistake, the error can be easily corrected.

Fourthly: that the fortes and pianos are written correctly throughout, and should be observed exactly; for there is a very great difference between *piano* and *pianissimo*, *forte* and *fortiss*[*imo*], between *crescendo* and *forzando*, and so forth. It should be noted, too, when in the score the one or the other *forte* or *piano* is not marked throughout all the parts, that the copyist should rectify this when preparing the performance material.

Fifthly: I have often been annoyed at certain violinists in various concerts, who absolutely ruined the so-called ties – which are among the most beautiful things in music – in that they bounced the bows off the tied note, which should have been joined to the preceding note. And so I would point out to the first violinist that it would be silly to play the following (as found in bar 47)

– in which the first two notes are to be taken on one bow – in such a disagreeable and mistaken way as

all staccato, and as if there were no ties present.

Sixthly: I would ask you to use two players on the viola part throughout, for the inner parts sometimes need to be heard more than the upper parts, and you will find in all my compositions that the viola rarely doubles the bass.

Seventhly: if you have to copy two sets of violin parts, the copyist should see that they do not turn their pages at the same time, because this takes away a great deal of strength from an orchestra with only a few musicians. The copyist should also see that the *da capo* signs ss are written in one of the violin parts as in the score, but in the other he can put the *da capo* a couple of bars after the sign ss, and then write the sign in its proper place.

Eighthly: I suggest that the two boys [soloists] in particular have a clear pronunciation, singing slowly in recitatives so that one can understand every syllable; and likewise they should follow the method of singing the recitation whereby, for example

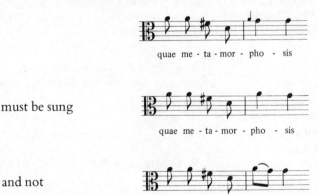

quae me - ta - mor - pho - sis

must be sung

quae me - ta - mor - pho - sis

and not

quae me - ta - mor - pho - sis

The penultimate note 'g' drops out entirely, and this applies to all similar cases. I rely on the skill of the tenor, who will explain such things to the boys.

Ninthly: I hope for at least three or four rehearsals for the entire work.

Tenthly: in the soprano aria the bassoon can be omitted if absolutely necessary, but I would rather have it present, at least when the bass is *obbligato* throughout. And I prefer a band with 3 bass instruments – 'cello, bassoon and double bass – to one with 6 double basses and 3 'celli, because certain passages stand out better that way.

Finally I ask everyone, and especially the musicians, for the sake of my reputation as well as their own, to be as diligent as possible: if I have perhaps not guessed the taste of these gentlemen, I am not to be blamed for it, for I know neither the persons nor the place, and that fact that they were concealed from me really made my work very difficult. For the rest, I hope that this *Applausus* will please the poet,[1] the worthy musicians, and the honourable reverend *Auditorio*, all of whom I greet with profound respect, and for whom I remain

Your most obedient servant,
Giuseppe Haydn.
Maestro di Cap: di Sua Alt:
Sere: Prencipe d'Estorhazy.

[CCLN, 9–11]

Haydn kept a copy of *Applausus* in Eisenstadt: he must have thought it a waste to send such a large work to a remote monastery and, after a single performance, for it to disappear for ever. He therefore turned most of the work into smaller pieces of church music, which shall be examined in the ensuing chapter.

The composer had many friends among the princely personnel, not only among the musicians but, for example, among the grenadiers. On 7 May 1768 we read:

> 7. huius Baptizata est Anna Maria Josepha, Legitima filia Stephani Sekier Granaderij ac uxoris eius Annae Mariae. Levavit Dominus Arcis Capellae Magister Josephus Hejden [*sic*], cum virgine Eleonora Jagerin [Jäger].
> [*Matricula Baptizatorum*, Bergkirche, Eisenstadt; Schmid, op cit., p. 5]

Two years later, on 5 August 1770, Haydn was at Eszterháza, and Sekier's new daughter Clara Elisabeth had Eleonora Jäger and Johann Haydn as godparents (Schmid, 5).

Of the various bills of this Summer, one deserves mention: the bookbinder Jacob Wanweg (a new spelling), who submitted a bill for:

2 Pieces of music bound in red with fine gold 3 parts in a slip-cover, the
slip-cover with French gold à 8 f .... 16 —
1 Piece of music bound in red & gilt paper .... — 34

Suma 16 34

Jacob Wanweg
Hochfürstl: Hoff Buch Binder

[Addition in Haydn's hand:]
These piece of music were Haydn and
Purksteiner Trios which were sent to
His Princely Highness.

With agreement Josephus Haydn mpria.

---

1 The author of the libretto preferred to remain anonymous; probably it was one of the Cistercian monks at Zwettl or a sister monastery.

I herewith give receipt that I have been paid 16 f 32 xr from the Rental Office. Eisenstadt, 7th July 768:

Jacob Wanweg
Hochfürstl: Hoff Buch Binder
[Eisenstädter Rentamt 1768, Nr. 121. Lit. L. *HJB* IV, 78]

Purksteiner was, as we know, a member of the *Capelle*. The bound baryton trios – for that is what both works were – have not survived; Haydn's must have been in the neighbourhood of No. 57 (autograph dated 1768).

On 15 July, the Haydns were godparents to another son born to Joseph and Anna Maria Weigl (the child died a fortnight later):

> 15. huius Baptizatus est Antonius Aloysius Legitimus filius Josephi Weigl musici, ac uxoris eius Annae Mariae, patini fuere Dominus Josephus Heyden [*sic*] Magister Capellae, cum coniuge sua Anna Maria.
>
> [*Matricula Baptizatorum*, Bergkirche, Eisenstadt; Schmid, op. cit., p. 4]

On 17 July we have a letter about engaging trumpets and kettledrums from the Oedenburger *Thurnermeister*:

> [To an Unknown Official of the Esterházy Administration. *German*]
> Nobly born
> Highly respected Sir!
> According to a commission regarding the choir of trumpets and kettledrums, I arranged with the *Herrn Thurn[er] Meister* of [O]Edenburg together with his four apprentices for a fee of 3 species ducats, as follows: he would have performed this service for 2 ducats if he did not have an afternoon service at the Nunnery on that very day; in his absence, he must pay for someone else. For the trip here with the 'Wurst'[1] I have arranged everything with the princely house for the 26th of this month at one o'clock in the afternoon: I hope therefore to have performed my commission satisfactorily. With all veneration, and my profound respects to the two *Herrn* Secretaries and all the other *Herrn* officers, I remain
>
> Your nobly born Sir's
most devoted servant
Josephus Haydn mpria.
>
> Eisenstadt, 17th July 1768.
> [*Haus Hof meister Ambts Rechnung Pro Juli anni 768*, supporting documents, Esterházy Archives, Forchtenstein Castle. G. Feder in *Haydn-Studien* IV/1 (1976), p. 49; not in CCLN]

Haydn probably ordered the four trumpeters and one kettledrummer (if our supposition is correct) from Oedenburg, rather than engaging them from the Eisenstadt *Thurnermeister* either because the Oedenburg players were technically better or because the Eisenstadt group may have been needed for other local services that day. July 26 was St Anne's day, and the name-day of Prince Nicolaus's sister-in-law. For that occasion in 1773, Haydn's *L'infedeltà delusa* was first given. It is idle to speculate for what purpose this large amount of trumpets and drums were required: fanfares, *intrade* in the church, symphonic music, or possibly a solemn performance of

---

1 'Wurst', local name for a princely conveyance which was so ordered that the five musicians – four trumpeters and two timpani players? – arrive at one o'clock.

Haydn's new *Missa Cellensis in honorem Beatissimae Virginis Mariae*, which (because of the presence of difficult *clarino* parts) might not yet have been performed in Eisenstadt? That which makes the document significant is its existence. It explains the 'supplementary' trumpet and timpani parts in such a work as the *Missa in honorem B. V. M.* ('Große Orgelmesse') in E flat, and in Symphonies 38 and 41; in all three cases authentic sources for the supplementary parts exist, but the works were, it would seem,[1] first composed without them. How often did this kind of operation with the Oedenburg *Thurnermeister* occur?

We have seen that trumpets and timpani were usually forbidden in Vienna for church services. The extant parts of the Parish Church St Martin, and the Esterházy Archives, in Eisenstadt suggest that this 'Verbot' was not taken very seriously, for there are a number of works performed all during this period in which the scoring includes trumpets and drums (though the existence of the parts is not, of course, absolute proof that they were in fact used).

On 2 August 1768, a great fire destroyed most of the lower part of Eisenstadt. The Klostergasse, where Haydn lived, was particularly devastated, and the Franciscan Monastery as well as the Nunnery (both on that street) were burned out. Apart from the Parish Church, only nineteen houses in the lower part of town survived. The Castle, being set in its own grounds, escaped serious damage. Apart from his furniture and household goods, many of Haydn's scores disappeared in the flames: apparently there was not enough time to rescue them. Griesinger discusses both the Eisenstadt fires – the next one was in 1776 – and (p. 17) tells us that 'some of Haydn's operas and other compositions were lost in the flames, and it is hardly likely that another copy exists.' One such work that, according to its entry in the *Entwurf-Katalog*, must have been composed about 1768 is the *Missa* 'Sunt bona mixta malis', of which Haydn retained only the Kyrie and part of the Gloria.[1] Considering the great popularity of Haydn's Masses, its disappearance in the 1768 fire would seem to be the only explanation for the fact that no other copy exists. The same applies to a group of several lost piano sonatas.

The town of Eisenstadt drew up a list of the damage to each house. Haydn's was listed as follows:

Numerus urarialis 82 Hr. Joseph Haiden [*sic*] *Fürstl. Capellmeister*

For carpentry repairs and for materials................................	500 fl.
For mason's repairs and materials	160 fl.
For joiner's work [window frames etc.] and glass-maker	100 fl.
Lost of burned and ruined crops, hay, straw and furnishings	388 fl. 27 x.
	Summa: 1148 fl. 27 x.

[*Specification deren Abbrändlern, und des sub dato 2. August 1768 durch die erschröckliche Feuersbrunst so wohl an Häusern, als verbrunnenen Naturalien und Mobilien erlittenen Schadens,* Stadtarchiv Eisenstadt; Schmid, op. cit., p. 8]

At this juncture, Haydn was practically a ruined man. 'But', as the princely Archivist J. Harich phrases it, 'the Prince was not one to fail at such a moment, and rebuilt Haydn's house at his (the Prince's) expense: Haydn had to pay only 50 gulden

---

1 Autograph of the Mass without trumpets and drums, Joseph Elssler copies of the Symphonies (in Pressburg and Prague, resp.), also without trumpets and drums.
2 Discussed in detail in the next chapter.

for rebuilding of the annex.'[1] In the detailed bill for repairs, it will be seen that many days were needed to repair the house, but the final bill was 378 gulden and $67\frac{11}{12}$ Kreuzer. It concludes 'Pro notitia: for this expense *Hr. Capellmeister* was required to pay 50 fl. on account of a newly built room. . . . Frantz Nigst/Rentmaster.' The Haydns had taken the opportunity of enlarging the house and it was thought right that they should pay for that part of the operation. There is a document explaining the operation with the 50 fl. written by P. L. Rahier on 6 April 1769:

> Bonification of Hr. Capellmeister Haydn on account of the newly constructed room in his house.
> His Highness graciously resolved to rebuild the house of the *Capellmeister* Haydn which burned on 2 Aug. $\overline{7}$68 at the expense of the princely estate; but since he built a new room and obliged the estate to pay fifty Gulden for it, the Eisenstädter Rentmaster should collect said 50 fl. from him, *Capellmeister*, and enter the procedure on the books. Eisenstadt, 6th April 1769: / P. L. Rahier
> [Eisenstadt Rentamt 1769, Esterházy Archives, Eisenstadt, No. 76; *HJB* IV, 50]

Haydn also received some financial help from the town, which organized a large-scale charity action: 'Repartitio sacrae Eleemosynae', 12 January 1770 26 fl. $37\frac{4}{16}$ xr., while on 23 February and 14 September 1769 he received 23 fl. 44 kr. 1 Pfennig. (Stadtarchiv Eisenstadt; Schmid, 8.) But his main assistance had come from a really magnanimous gesture on the part of Prince Esterházy, one of the many unexpected acts of kindness that gradually bound Haydn to his Prince with 'hoops of steel'.

On 5 August 1768, the name-day of Princess Maria Elisabeth was celebrated at Eszterháza Castle with balls, illumination, fireworks and with German plays given by a *Wandertruppe*, probably that of *Prinzipal* (Director) Lorenz Riersch, who was engaged to come to Eszterháza for a month. Now that there were quarters for musicians and actors, even if restricted as to space, the Prince could engage larger groups of strolling players, and 1768 was the first season in which this occurred.[2]

The grand official opening of the new theatre was, of course, left to Haydn, who with *Lo speziale* (libretto: Carlo Goldoni) inaugurated the new theatre and began, in the words of Janos Harich, a quarter of a century of theatrical history.[2] Although the handsome printed libretto of the opera specifies only 'nell' autunno dell'anno 1768' as the date of this historic occasion, we believe that the following bill from the Esterházy Archives enables us to date the Opera's première more precisely:

Commission

According to which our Chief Cashier is to pay to

Capell: Meister Haÿden[*sic*]	24 ducats
the female singer Magdalena Spängler	6
Fribert	6
Dichtler and her [Madame Dichtler]	12
and Hanß Georg Ulram ['super'; silent role?]	1

together nine-and-forty ducats against receipt, from the G[ene]ral Cassa, and to be entered in the books. Schloß Eszterhaz, 29th Sept. 768.

Nicolaus Fürst Esterhazy

Correctly received 24 ducats Josephus Haydn mpria 7th Octob[ris] $\overline{7}$68.

Correctly received 12 ducats Leopoldo Dichtler Barbara Dichtler 4th Octob. $\overline{7}$68.

---

1 *HJB* IV, 13f. (31); documents: 49f. 2 Harich in *HJB* II, 24. 3 *Musikgeschichte*, p. 32.

> Correctly received 6 ducats Magdalena Spangler.
> Carlo Friberth per 6 ducats.
> I attest that I have received Hans Georg Ulram's ducat in his absence.

Eisenstadt, 7th Oct. $\overline{768}$:   Frantz Nigst Rentmaster.
[Generalcassa 1768, Rubr. VIII. Nr. 26. Esterházy Archives, Eisenstadt. *HJB*
IV, 46f.]

As we have seen, Prince Nicolaus usually rewarded his musicians the day after an opera performance, and we may thus assume that *Lo speziale* was first given on 28 September. The libretto was printed by Johann Joseph Siess in Oedenberg; it consists of 5 'Bögen' (40 pages) in small quarto format. Three hundred copies were printed at a cost of 5 gulden 30 kreuzer per 'Bogen', and the copies were bound by Anna Maria Heinbeck of Oedenburg. Four copies – two for Prince Nicolaus and his wife, two for the honoured guests of the occasion, Duke Albert von Sachsen-Teschen and his consort, Archduchess Marie Christine – were bound in rose-coloured taffeta, the rest in gold or so-called 'Turkish' paper (the latter meaning paper with various designs: two sorts are printed in facsimile on p. 37 of Harich's *Musikgeschichte*). The title page reads:

> Lo speziale / dramma giocoso / da rappresentarsi / a Esterhaz / nel teatro di S.
> A. il prencipe / Esterhazy / de Galantha &c. &c. / nell'autunno dell'anno 1768.
> Sempronio, Speziale   Carlo Friberth.
> Mengone, Uomo di Spezieria   Leopoldo Dichtler.
> Grilletta, Pupilla sotto tutela di Sempronio   Maddalena Spangler.
> Volpino,   Barbara Dichtler.
> La Musica è di Giuseppe Haydn Maestro di Capella. . . .[1]

The 'gold shower' from Prince Nicolaus shows that once again, Haydn scored a real success with his new Opera. As in *La canterina*, Barbara Dichtler sang a *Hosenrolle*, and Haydn was able, on a larger scale than in the Opera of 1766, to display his genuine talents for *opera buffa*. With all its delicate orchestral effects and its brilliant Overture, *Lo speziale* is a genuinely witty piece of music. Of the special effects, the one calculated even now to delight and astonish is the 'Turkish' scene in Act III. The work will be discussed in the forthcoming chapter.

One of the festivities that took place at Eszterháza in September was a masquerade, in which the 'Hof-Musici', and Haydn himself, participated. The details of this intriguing-sounding *Masquera* are not given in the source – a 'Specification' in the Esterházy Archives.[2]

The bill submitted by Joann (Johann) Joseph Stadlmann for 'lute-maker work', dated Eisenstadt, 14 December 1768, includes work on a 'Passetl' and 'on the Pariton [*sic*] 3 Pass [bass] strings and two Passetl G, 2 D 1 f. 41 xr.' (bill countersigned by Haydn).[3]

---

1 Copy in the Gesellschaft der Musikfreunde, Vienna.
2 On exposition at the Haydn Exhibition, Schloß Petronell (Lower Austria), 1959: Catalogue, p. 49.
3 A. M. XIII, 738; Valkó II, 543.

A few days before Christmas, Haydn had occasion to address an official petition to Prince Nicolaus:

[To Anton Scheffstoss, 'Secretaire' and Chief Bookkeeper of the Esterházy administration. *German*]

✝

Nobly born,
Highly respected Sir!
    I sent you herewith my petition to His Highness, reading as follows:
Your Serene Highness, etc.
    Your Illustrious and Serene Highness graciously gave me to understand, not long hence, that not only was the Rent Collector Frantz Nigst[1] found superfluous as a violinist, but also Joseph Diezl[2] as a member of the band; and moreover I was ordered to demand the 2 uniforms from the former. Concerning the former, i.e., Franz Nigst, I must respectfully persuade Your Highness, and admit myself candidly, that the second violin section in all the operas hitherto produced was, with him, in the best possible hands, because he is the only one capable of leading the seconds: therefore if he were dismissed, one would fear for the future on account of the mistakes which would creep in – that is, unless Your Highness were minded graciously to engage another permanent second violinist, or to have one come from Vienna when we produce operas. Because there are no other players for the seconds except the horn players Frantz[3] and May,[4] with whom one is really not properly equipped. It is true that if the whole band goes to Esterház next year, he could not be in Esterház permanently on account of the rent office, but nevertheless it is my humble opinion that he should be brought to Esterház when the Imperial and Royal Court, or other high dignitaries, are present there. I humbly ask Your Highness, moreover, graciously to allow him the yearly 50 gulden, and also the Winter and Summer clothes (in which he has already seen service in Esterház). Joseph Diezl [*sic*] is in my opinion especially necessary in the choir-loft if the whole band goes off to Esterház, so that the customary church services can be held by him, his *praeceptor* and the boy choristers who are in his apprenticeship. I hear from many people that he cannot possibly support himself with his position as schoolmaster. I ask you humbly to grant him in your graciousness enough so that he can live.

    In case you find anything imprudent in the above, please kindly let me know of it at once. I flatter myself that through my petition and through your confirmation if it, something may have an effect on His Highness.
    Apart from wishing you best greetings for the coming Holidays, and a happy farewell to the old and welcome to the new year, I am,

Highly respected Sir,
Your obedient servant,
Joseph Haydn [m.] pria.

Eisenstadt, 22nd December 1768.

---

1 Violinist in the band from 1760 to 1772.
2 See p. 70. In the copy to Prince Esterházy, Haydn writes 'Dietzl'.
3 Karl Franz, a member of the band from 1763 to 1776.
4 Johann May, a member of the band from 1765 to 1772.

[A second copy, to the prince, has instead of the last two paragraphs addressed to Scheffstoss, the following addressed to the Prince:]

In the next few days I will respectfully send YOUR ILLUSTRIOUS AND SERENE HIGHNESS some new trios,[1] and I most humbly commend myself to your high favour and grace,

> YOUR ILLUSTRIOUS AND SERENE HIGHNESS'
> most humble
> Joseph Haydn.

Eisenstadt, 22nd December 1768.   [CCLN, 11–13]

[Another hand has noted, on the cover of the file, the letter's date and a short summary of its contents in Latin.]

Haydn's petition was successful (for the details of the persons concerned, the previous list of the musicians may be consulted).

Joseph Dietzl, the schoolmaster and violinist, must have sent in his yearly bill – 'Account. What was needed for strings from the 1st of January till the end of December 1768 for the princely Choir in Eisenstadt and also for Esterhass, as agreed'[2] – with a special sense of gratitude to Joseph Haydn.

Haydn's name was beginning to appear with increasing frequency in the German periodicals, and not only Haydn but his Viennese colleagues were regarded with considerable suspicion for their mixture of the serious and comic. In Johann Adam Hiller's *Wöchentliche Nachrichten und Anmerkungen, die Musik betreffend* for 26 September and 3 October 1768, music by the Viennese school is discussed:

> Herr **Ditters'** ... taste is very much for the comic, or rather it is a constant mixture of comic and serious elements that often do not seem to coalesce properly. The [violin] concertos of Herr **Hofmann** in Vienna are better put together, are well conceived and with pleasant melodies; also his harmonic structure is better than with many other newer composers. The same applies to his trios and quartets, that is, if one can accept the planning and style with which these gentlemen fashion their quartets. Herr **Hayden** has composed many quartets, quintets and concertini along these lines. ... In recent times there have been many pieces which because of their new clothing and different style, often lapsing into the comic and trifling, have threatened almost to wipe out [the earlier school of symphonic writers]. One perhaps guesses that we speak of the symphonies by Herren **Hofmann**, **Hayden**, **Ditters**, **Fils** [Filtz], etc. It is true that one does find well written, magnificent and affecting movements in them; the wind instruments are set in such a way that they greatly help to clarify the harmony ... but is not that curious mixture of the noble and the common, the serious and the comic, which so often occurs in one and the same movement, sometimes of a bad effect? Not to speak of those repellent octaves in the second violin or another lower part together with the first violin. [Hofmann's symphonies are criticized as being too long.] **Hayde** [*sic*] knows how to express himself more succinctly, and everything with him has such a pleasing exterior, that he will always have the majority of the amateurs on his side, though the former [Hofmann] enjoys the approbation of most of the connoisseurs. Herr **Ditters** and **Fils** have many fine and beautiful things; they also make far more use of the mixed style than the others. Of the latter we would not even say that a musical library would have to have all his symphonies. Herr **Toeschi** in Manheim

---

1 Baryton trios. We cannot identify exactly which ones are referred to.
2 A.M. XIII, 738; Valkó II, 543.

[*sic*] and also Herr **Canabich** [*sic*] have also written many symphonies . . . ; because of the many good things in them we always wished that their style was more even and sometimes the rhythmic and harmonic modulations better. . . .

[Pp. 99, 107. For a further extract from this article, *vide infra*, p. 174n.]

Chronicle 1769

OUR CHRONICLE FOR THE YEAR opens prosaically with two bills (both countersigned by Haydn) from lute makers, one (Eisenstadt, 1 January 1769) from Johann Sigl, and the other (Vienna, 12 January 1769) from Johann Joseph Stadlmann. The latter delivered a 'Passetl' bow and repaired a double bass (*Violon*), with a note on 'extra strings for them' (double bass A, 'cello A), 27 fl. 51 kr.[1]

Members of the *Capelle*, like all Esterházy officials, were not allowed to marry without princely permission; this ruling gave rise to many dramatic situations, one of which, concerning Joseph Carl Rosenbaum, will be noted in connection with *Haydn: the Years of 'The Creation' 1796–1800*, p. 313f. *Regent* Rahier wrote to the Prince as follows:

> . . . This very moment I was informed that the musician Carl Fribert [*sic*] has yesterday for the second time published marriage banns in the town parish church with the new singer Magdalen Spanglerin, and the banns will be published tomorrow for the third time, and that tomorrow, as *Capellmeister* Haiden [*sic*], whom I asked at once about it, tells me, they will be married at Weigelstorf [*sic*] with the written permission of the parish priest here. Haiden tells me he only heard about it yesterday, and the girl's parents didn't even know. I have learned that Your Highness turned down the request that Fribert submitted in this matter, saying that if they married without Your Highness's permission they would be at once dismissed from the princely service. The princely Castle Chaplain tells me that he entered a protest with the parish priest, and that this afternoon Fribert went to him and asked for the protest to be withdrawn since he anyway intends to leave the princely service with that singer, and so I had Haiden called and ordered him to withdraw the clothes [uniform for Friberth, dress for Spangler] from both of them, and if they had anything else that was princely property they were to return it this very day . . .
>
> Eisenstadt, 24th Jan. 1769.
>
> [Esterházy Archives, Budapest, Fasc. 1526 Fol. 191; Valkó II, 544]

Here we have almost the classic clandestine love affair that is supposed to be the property of novelists: the martinet Rahier – surely he is the man about whom Haydn said, writing from England in 1791, 'Oh my dear gracious lady! how sweet this bit of freedom really is! I had a kind Prince, but sometimes I was forced to be dependant on base souls'[2] – and the stern chaplain; the parish priest obviously in league with the lovers; the remote village where they would marry hastily and in secret; the good Prince who, obviously at Haydn's oral instigation, forgave this breach of discipline and kept his two fine artists – it is all on the order of Romeo and Juliet, except that our Juliet was slightly older (nineteen) and the whole affair had a delightfully happy ending.

---

1 A.M. XIII, 747; XIII, 772; Valkó II, 546, 544, resp.
2 CCLN 118; *Haydn in England 1791–1795*, p. 97.

February is documented for us only in three bills from the Esterházy Archives: (1) 19 oboe and cor anglais reeds, 2 February, 3 fl.; (2) '... from 11 Sept. 1768 to 14 Feb. 1769 Herr Joseph Haydn *Capellmeister* was kind enough to receive 52 spinet strings in agreement, 1 fl. 44 xr. Druckherl's widow ...', to which Haydn added: 'these clavier strings were used at Eisenstadt and also at Estoras'; (3) Rockobauer's bill for six bassoon reeds; all three bills countersigned by Haydn.[1]

On 19 March, the Haydns were godparents to the Tomasinis' second son:

Martius 19ª
Nomen Baptizati: Josephus Franciscus
Nomen Parentum: Aloysius Thomasini Virtuosus Musicus Principis, Uxor Josepha,
Nomen et Cognomen Patrinorum: D[ominus]: Josephus Haÿden Capellae Magister Principis cum sua D[omina]: Conthorali Anna Maria.

[*Stadtpfarre*, Eisenstadt; *HJB* VIII, 9]

Between Haydn's little house, Klostergasse 82, and that of his neighbour, Klostergasse 81, owned by Magdalena Frumwald, a pious (she had the Chapel of Magdalen in Eisenstadt built at her expense) widow, a wall had been put up – at Haydn's (or rather princely) expense after the great fire – which divided the two properties and also served as a prop for Haydn's roof. On 29 April 1769, at 4.30 a.m., Magdalena Frumwald had destroyed the part of the roof that extended over this wall into her property. Haydn promptly went that same day and protested at the town council. Frau Frumwald, when summoned by the council, said that the wall was on her property and that when it had been built she had protested. *Deliberatum est*: the following persons were delegated to examine the situation at first hand: 'Hr. Bernard Müller, Hr. Ludwig Räittner, Hr. Matthias Paur, the town notary and Hr. Anton Heim'. After a report had been made, the worthy town council made the following resolution with regard to the two disputing parties, *viz.*

(1) the wall dividing the houses, which Hr. *Capel Meister* built at his expense *anno* 1768 to replace the old wooden fence [*Laaden Wand = Lattenwand*] is to become property common to both houses for all time; but (2) the fire wall (which Frau Magdalena Frumwald erected at the back between the cellar abutting on the town wall, which cellar was made by her predecessor Hr. Michael Pichler, and the newly built stable of *Herr Capell Meister*, with its wall which was a temporary expedient) is also declared to be property common to both houses, but without Hr. *Capell Meister* having to pay anything towards the expenses of that fire wall; whereas Hr. *Capellmeister* [*sic*] must promise, concerning the new protest that Frau Frumwald has entered (that *Herr Capellmeister* is not to build anything against that wall) that if in time he constructs anything, it must not be to her disadvantage, but also that Frau Frumwald is not to build anything against that wall either. Moreover, Frau Frumwald is guilty of destroying the roof and is to replace the same. *Actum Kis-Martonij in Senatu Anno et Die permiss. Extradat. per me Joannem Adamum Pogacz iuratum Notarium.*[2]

This sensible decision on the part of the town council did not prevent Frau Frumwald from breaking her part of the 'pact': *vide infra*, 15 April 1773. For another lawsuit concerning Haydn's house, *vide* 17 August 1776.

---

1 A.M. XIII, 735; A. M. XIII, 734; A. M. XIII, 746; Valkó II, 545f.
2 Town Archives (*Stadtarchiv*), Eisenstadt; Schmid, op. cit., p. 11.

In April we have two bills in the Esterházy Archives written entirely by Haydn:

Specification

	f.	xr.
3 bundles of Italian strings, 1 fl. 15 xr. the bundle, makes	3	45
4 raven's quills for use in the claviern	1	36
	5	21

Josephus Haydn mpria.

Eisenstadt, 28th April 1769

Specification

What I advanced for Italian music paper for His Highness. 6 books, 24 xr. each, makes: 2 fl. 24 xr.

Eisenstadt, 30th April 1769   Josephus Haydn mpria.

[A.M. XIII, 736 and 737, Esterházy Archives, Budapest; Valkó II, 545]

With the Summer of 1769, another new era begins for Eszterháza Castle: the regular presence of strolling players who were engaged for the whole summer season to stay at the Castle and give performances. As we have seen, there were strolling players in residence for the name-day of Princess Maria Elisabeth in 1768, but we have no documents to inform us which troupe it was and how long they stayed. With 1769 we begin to have records. Acta Theatralia 1 is a letter from an actress named Catharina Rössl (she signs her name 'Rößlin' but we presume the '-in' suffix merely denotes feminine gender[2] as usual), asking the Prince on 19 January 1770 to re-engage her for the 'Hochfürstliches Theater' in the forthcoming season. She and her husband had now left the 'Hellmann-Koberweinische Compagnie' and were now working for a new troupe managed by Franz Passer. Of the members of the Hellmann-Koberwein Troupe, we know that Joseph Hellmann, before he joined forces with Friedrich Koberwein, had been a member of the Menninger Troupe which had 'played' Eisenstadt in 1765. The interesting aspect of the Troupe was that they were attempting to reduce the Hanswurstiada, or buffoonery, in their repertoire and to give serious plays, of course in *hochdeutsch* (whereas the Hanswurst plays were mostly all in dialect). From their winter activities at Pressburg in 1768 and 1769, we know some of their repertoire: Schlegel's *Kanut*, Lessing's *Miss Sara Sampson* and *Minna von Barnhelm*, Voltaire's *Die Schottländerin* (a German translation of *L'écossaise*, 1760, a personal attack on Elie Cathérine Fréron), Lillo's *Barnwell*, Gellert's *Die Betschwester*; Weiß's *Die Haushälterin* and *Die Freundschaft auf Probe*, Molière's *Der eingebildete Kranke* (a German translation of *Le malade imaginaire*, 1673); and comedies by Heufeld and Hafner. The Troupe had been guests of the Empress at Schönbrunn and Laxenburg in 1771. After their first performances at Eszterháza, the Prince signed a contract with them for three years (Acta Theatralia, hereinafter abbreviated 'A.T.', 11); the contract is dated 31 July 1769. In it, the Troupe is, from 1 May 1770, to 'perform, with at least fourteen appropriate and experienced persons, a play every day at any place and hour to be determined by him [Prince Nicolaus], and to take charge of the necessary dresses and plays.' The Prince was to pay them 100 gulden a week and would put at the Troupe's disposal seven rooms with the usual free heating (wood) and lighting (candles). It is interesting to note that the Prince obligated himself to provide the music (i.e., Haydn and the *Capelle*) and illumination, as well as any necessary trips to Vienna or Pressburg. The season was understood to begin on 1 May and continue

---

1 Her husband's name actually was 'Rößl'; Horányi 62.

through 15 October. Mátyás Horányi, from whose immensely valuable book, *The Magnificence of Esterháza* (pp. 57ff.), this information is gratefully taken, explains the probable reason why the contract was termined in October 1769. First, there was disagreement between the two theatrical directors and Michael Kleinrath, Castle Inspector, concerning the distribution of a bonus of 200 gulden which the Prince had given the players at the end of the season. The managers regarded the sum as insufficient. Secondly, there was a disagreement between Catharina Rössl and the managers. Meanwhile, Catharina had become *Schloßinspektor*'s Kleinrath's mistress (A.T. 12), and managed, after resigning from the Troupe, to put Hellmann and Koberwein in such a bad light that Kleinrath declared them to be impostors and had the contract dissolved.[1]

And so it happened that for the season of 1770, the bewitching Catharina Rössl, now with her husband part of the Passer Troupe, came again to Eszterháza Castle, there to delight the Prince with their plays and Castle Inspector Kleinrath with her favours.

Of the bills from the Esterházy Archives for May, one from 'Rockenbauer' (*sc.* Rockobauer) for three dozen bassoon reeds (two gulden) of 14 May 1769[2] is of little interest, whereas the next tells us of a trip that Haydn made to Pressburg to recruit new female singers. The bill is in Haydn's own hand:

Specification

What I advanced for a trip to Presburg made at the order of His Serene Highness to engage new female singers.

The trip from Presburg which took 3 days because of bad weather, arranged at	7 Fl.
The trip from Eisenstadt to Estoras	4 Fl.
Living expenses for 5 days	5 Fl. 30 xr.

Eisenstadt, 16th May 1769   Summa   16 Fl. 30 xr.

Josephus Haydn mpria.

I have correctly received these 16 Fl. 30 xr. from the *Herrn RentMeister* Nigst.

[A. M. XIII, 740; Valkó II, 546; Bartha 64]

Possibly some of these singers were engaged on a temporary basis, but one, Gertrude Cellini (mezzo-soprano) was hired by contract on 8 August; she may have been one of the singers that Haydn found in Pressburg. She was required for the mounting of what is probably the first non-Haydn opera to be given in the new theatre at Eszterháza: *La contadina in corte* (alternate title on the relevant documents: *La contadina ingentilita*), probably the popular work of that name by Antonio Sacchini: a textbook was not, apparently, printed, and the music has not survived, so that we cannot determine the composer.[3]

Rockobauer delivered another dozen bassoon reeds at ten kreuzer each (bill from Vienna, 18 June 1769, signed 'Rockenbauer', countersigned by Haydn), which documents the extraordinary number of reeds that were consumed by the band.

It must have been about this time that Haydn engaged in a new sort of activity. We have parallel reports on the subject from his biographers Griesinger and Dies:

The baryton was ... the favourite instrument of Prince Nikolaus Esterhazy. Haydn, wanting to give his Prince a pleasant surprise, practised on the baryton

1 A.T. 13, 14; Horányi 58.
2 A.M. XIII, 741, written in Vienna (countersigned by Haydn); Valkó II, 546.
3 J. Harich in *HJB* I, 17, 37f.
4 A.M. XIII, 744; Valkó II, 546.

without anyone noticing it, and one evening he quite unexpectedly gave a concert on it. The Prince was rather offended, saying that Haydn wanted to usurp his position with regard to that instrument, and from that hour Haydn never touched the baryton again. [Griesinger writes 'bariton' throughout; p. 19.]

The Prince loved music and he himself played the baryton, which in his opinion should be limited to one key only. Haydn could not be certain of that because he had only a very superficial knowledge of the instrument. Nevertheless, he thought it must be playable in several keys. Unknown to the Prince, Haydn conducted an investigation into the instrument's capabilities, and he acquired a liking for it; he practised it late at night because he had no other time, with a view to becoming a good player. He was, of course, often interrupted in his nocturnal studies by the scolding and quarrelling of his wife, but he did not lose his patience and in six months he had attained his goal.

The Prince still knew nothing. Haydn could not resist a touch of vanity any longer. He played in public before the Prince in a number of keys, expecting to reap enthusiastic applause. But the Prince was not in the least surprised and took the whole thing in his stride; he merely remarked: 'You are supposed to know about such things, Haydn!'

'I quite understood the Prince,' said Haydn to me, 'and though I was at first hurt by his indifference, nevertheless I owe to his curt rejoinder the fact that I gave up my intention of becoming a good baryton player. I remembered that I had already gained some reputation as a *Kapellmeister* and not as a practising virtuoso. I reproached myself for half a year's neglect of composition, and I returned to it with renewed vigour. [Dies, 58]

The excursion was introduced at this juncture because on 1 August, the Prince engaged a professional baryton player, Andreas Lidl, of whose abilities we have spoken briefly above (p. 92). Burney, after Lidl's death, wrote that indeed he

played with exquisite taste and expression upon this ungrateful instrument, with the additional embarrassment of base [*sic*] strings at the back of the neck, with which he accompanied himself, an admirable expedient in a desert, or even in a house, where there is but one musician; but to be at the trouble of accompanying yourself in a great concert, surrounded by idle performers who could take the trouble off your hands, and leave them more at liberty to execute, express, and embellish the principal melody, seemed at best a work of supererogation. The tone of the instrument will do nothing for itself, and it seems with Music as with agriculture, the more barren and ungrateful the soil, the more art is necessary in its cultivation.... [*A General History of Music ...*, vol. IV, p. 1020]

When Lidl played in Paris, the *Almanach musical* wrote the following article entitled 'BARITON inventé par M. LIDLE':

Cet instrument entendu pour la premiere fois à Paris, en 1775, ches M. le Baron de Bagge & dans quelques autres concerts particuliers, a été inventé il y a environ cinquans par M. Lidle, musicien allemand, attaché en Prince Esterhazy & l'un des éleves du célebre Hayden. La forme de l'instrument rassemble à celle du violoncelle; il a sept cordes auxquelles l'inventeur a ajouté, sous le manche, douze autres cordes accordées, de demi-ton en demi-ton, dans les tons graves. Ces douze cordes sont destinées à faire la basse & on les pince avec le pouce, tandis qu'on joue sur les premieres avec les autres doigts & l'archet. Cette découverte ingénieuse a été fort applaudie & méritoit de l'être. M. Lidle est retourné en Allemagne, mais l'on assure qu'il reviendra à Paris, [et] nous souhaitons qu'il y fasse un assez long séjour pour y former des éleves, & pour jouir dans cette capitale des arts de toute la considération que méritent ses talens.

x) Cet instrument est nouveau, mais son nom ne l'est pas [ce qu'on] connoissoit depuis long-terms en Hongrie & à Pétersbourg sous le nom de Baryton, un instrument appellé aussi Viola di gamba, qui n'a rien de ce qui caractérise le Baryton que nous annonçons.

[Hubert Unverricht, *Geschichte des Streichtrios*, Tutzing 1969, p. 160]

It can be seen that Lidl, even if Burney disliked the instrument, enjoyed a considerable reputation throughout Europe. It seems odd that Prince Nicolaus should want to engage a skilled professional, with whom he could play baryton duos, when he could have Haydn at no extra cost. Perhaps the Prince thought it would not be fitting for his *Capellmeister* to play second baryton and even less fitting, no doubt, if he played first. Probably the various works for two barytons, such as the 'Duetto 2do in G per il Pariton Primo, Pariton Secondo' which exists in a copy by Joseph Elssler Sen. in the Esterházy Archives in Budapest (MS. mus. I. 122), and the 'Dodeci Divertimento [*sic*] per il Pariton Primo e Secondo' (ibid. MS. mus. I. 122; Hoboken XII:4, 19), also copied by the elder Elssler, were composed for Prince Nicolaus and Lidl. When one considers that Lidl stayed until May 1774, one wonders what he can have played all those years: perhaps also violoncello in the orchestra, because it is slightly difficult to imagine him systematically playing through, for the Prince's edification, the Haydn *divertimenti* composed for Prince Nicolaus. Here we have a psychological mystery which cannot be explained.

Carl Franz, horn player and baryton performer, resigned in November. Can Andreas Lidl's presence have offended him? It is clear that Franz intended to leave in 1769. *Regent* Rahier reports to the Prince that

I have intimated to the Chief Cashier Zoller to pay the retiring horn player Carl Frantz[1] his salary up to the 15th inst., and I informed the *Capellmeister* in front of the retiring [player] that he [Haydn] is to take into his possession everything that does not belong to him [Franz]. . . .

Eisenstadt, 8th Nov. 1769.

[Esterházy Archives, Budapest, Fasc. 1527, item 341: Valkó II, 544]

Two bills, one by Stadlmann for the repair of string instruments (Vienna, 26 November) and one by Joseph Dietzl (Eisenstadt, 26 November) for strings are revealing for one small fact. We have seen that there was no 'official' violoncello player in the Eisenstadt princely Church Choir as such; yet Dietzl lists, among other items, 'Basl G' and 'Bassl A', which suggests that after all a 'Bassetl' was regularly used at Eisenstadt.[2]

On 9 December, Georg Korer, locksmith at Eisenstadt, submitted a bill which included 'two strips [*Benter* = *Bänder*] for the harpsichord [Flighl]' and a new key for a violin case. And to close our list of documents for the year, Joseph Haydn, as in the past, collected the 'Rorate' money for his musicians on 21 December; while Carolus Flach collected 7 fl. 12 kr., in an undated bill of 1769, for a 'large case [*Verschlag*] for the instrument [harpsichord] 8 feet long, 3 feet wide and 3 feet deep 2 F. 45 xr. More: 6 *Sordino* [mutes] . . .'. Haydn also removed, for reasons unknown, 1 fl. 5 kr. from the *Sordino* part of the bill.[3] It is interesting that in Symphony No. 41 (the Joseph Elssler Sen. manuscript of which in Prague shows watermarks that suggest 1769 as the composition date) mutes are required for both violin parts in the slow movement.[4]

1 Franz was in the end persuaded – probably by Haydn – to remain, which he did until 1776.
2 A.M. XIII, 745, 750; Valkó II, 547. Haydn, who as usual countersigned both bills, removed 15 Kreuzer from Stadlmann's bill.
3 Korer: A.M. XIII, 749; Valkó II, 548. Flach: A. M. XIII, 722; Valkó II, 545. Rorate: A. M. XIII, 748; Valkó II, 547.
4 G. Feder in *HJB* IV, 116, superseding previous information on the subject.

1 Joseph Haydn, engraving by Johann Ernst Mansfeld, published by Artaria & Co., Vienna, 1781; this was the first printed portrait of the composer. The Latin quotation below the portrait is from an ode by Horace; the context in which the words occur reads: 'Tibi, qui possis / Blandus auritas fidibus canoris / Ducere quercus / In amicitiae tesseram.'

2, 3 Eszterháza Castle. *Above*: bird's-eye view of the castle and park by an anonymous eighteenth-century artist; pen and ink and watercolour. *Below*: view from the garden side, showing the opera house to the left of the castle, oil painting (lost), *c.* 1784(?); from an old photograph.

Above
4 Eszterháza Castle seen from the air, showing the entrance court and double staircase.

5 Eszterháza Castle: the great music room (since restoration following damage caused during the Second World War); cf. pp. 749f.

6 The Dowager Princess Maria Anna (*née* Marchesa Lunati Visconti), widow of Prince Paul Anton Esterházy (d. 1762); miniature on ivory. For the Princess's name-day, in July 1773, Haydn composed *L'infedeltà delusa*, which became one of his most successful Operas.

7, 8 Nicolaus, Count Esterházy (the second son of Prince Nicolaus I), and his wife Maria Anna Franziska, Countess Esterházy (*née* Countess von Weissenwolf); both portraits, painted in 1783, were badly damaged in the Second World War. For their wedding ceremonies at Eszterháza in August 1777 Haydn composed his Opera, *Il mondo della luna.*

9 The installation of Prince Anton Esterházy as Governor of the County of Oedenburg on 3 August 1791; parade in the entrance court of Eszterháza with (right foreground) a group of Gypsy musicians (cf. pl. 11). Coloured engraving by János Berkeny.

Below, left
10 Eszterháza: entrance façade of the former Opera House, drawn and engraved by Joseph von Fernstein; published in *Beschreibung des hochfürstlichen Schlosses Esterháß* . . ., 1784 (cf. pp. 25ff.).

Below, right
11 Detail of pl. 9 showing the group of Gypsy musicians in the right foreground: two violinists, a 'cellist and a cimballom player.

14 Archduchess Maria Antonia of Austria (later Marie Antoinette, Queen of France), seated at a spinet; portrait in oils by Franz Xaver Wagenschön. Marie Antoinette's name was associated with Haydn's Symphony No. 85 ('La Reine') when it was first played in Paris in the 1787–8 season; this work was reported to be her favourite of the six 'Paris' Symphonies, and it bore her name in the first French edition, January 1788. Cf. p. 592.

Opposite, top
12 The widowed Empress Maria Theresa, with Emperor Joseph II and members of the Imperial Royal family, by Friedrich Heinrich Füger, 1776. On the right, behind the seated Empress, is her elder son, the Emperor Joseph II; standing, from the left, are Archduchess Marie Christine (holding a box); her husband, Duke Albert von Sachsen-Teschen (handing a picture to the Empress); and the Archduchesses Maria Elisabeth and Maria Anna. (Duke Albert and his wife had just returned from a visit to Italy; the Archduchess Maria Antonia – cf. pl. 14 – had already left Vienna to become Dauphine of France.)

Opposite, below
13 View of Pressburg (now Bratislava, Czechoslovakia), the imperial coronation town on the Danube; coloured engraving by Joseph and Peter Schaffer published by Artaria & Co., Vienna, 1787. Here Haydn gave the first public performance of his Opera, *La canterina*, in 1767 (cf. pp. 133ff.); he visited Pressburg frequently from Eszterháza in the 1770s and 1780s.

15 The first page of an autograph letter from Haydn to the Cistercian monastery of Zwettl in Lower Austria; written in 1768, the letter accompanied Haydn's *Applausus* Cantata and gives guidance as to the correct performance of the work (for translation see pp. 146f.).

16, 17 Autograph pages from Haydn's Quartets Op. 20, Nos. 2 and 5: last page of No. 2 with the note 'Sic fugit amicus amicum', and (below) first page of the Finale of No. 5, with the 'Fuga a 2 Soggetti' marked 'Sempre sotto voce'.

18 Haydn: *La vera costanza*, 1779. A page of the autograph showing part of the Finale of Act I, one of the dramatic highpoints of the opera: (top to bottom) horns; oboes I and II; bassoons I and II; V.I; V.II; Va.; five vocal parts; Vc.-B. Cf. pls. 21, 22.

19, 20 Costume designs by Pietro Travaglia for Haydn's Opera, *Armida*, 1784.

21, 22 Pages from the original libretto of Haydn's Opera, *La vera costanza*, 1779: title page and cast (displayed in the typical diagrammatic fashion of an Eszterháza production). Cf. pl. 18.

Below

23 Design for a stage set for Haydn's Opera, *Orlando Paladino* (first performed at Eszterháza in 1782), by Pietro Travaglia; from Travaglia's sketch-book. Below the design are inscribed the words 'Montuosa ripiena di Nevi per L'opera L'Orlando Paladino' ('mountains covered with snow', etc.).

LA VERA

COSTANZA

DRAMMA GIOCOSO PER MUSICA

DA RAPPRESENTARSI

AL TEATRO D'ESTERHAZ

LA PRIMAVERA

1 7 7 9.

VIENNA

Preſſo Giuſeppe Nobile de Kurzböck.

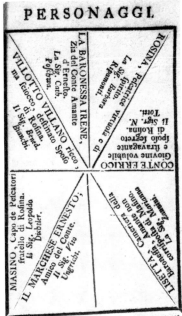

Tutti nel attual Servizio di S. A il Prencipe Nicolo Eſterhazy di Galantha.

24 Haydn: Piano Sonata No. 44 in F (XVI:29). The first page of the autograph, 1774, inscribed 'Divertimento da Clavicembalo' and 'di me Giuseppe Haydn mpria 774'; this was one of works that Haydn sold in MS. copies (see p. 337).

26 Title page of Haydn's *Raccolta de Menuetti Ballabili*, in the authentic Artaria edition of 1784; this set of fourteen minuets for orchestra was sold in parts by Artaria & Co., Vienna (cf. p. 486).

Opposite, below

25 Haydn: Concerto for Violoncello and Orchestra in D major (VIIb:2), 1783. The first page of music from the autograph; the work was composed for the 'cellist Anton Kraft, to whom it was formerly wrongly attributed.

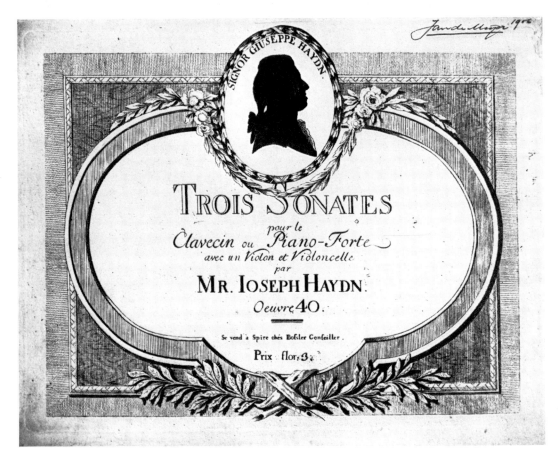

TROIS SONATES
pour le
Clavecin ou Piano-Forte
avec un Violon et Violoncelle
par
MR. IOSEPH HAYDN.
Oeuvre 40.

Se vend à Spire chés Boßler Conseiller.

Prix flor: 3

27 Title page, with silhouette of Haydn, of three Piano Trios (one by Haydn [No. 18; XV:5] and two by his pupil Ignaz Pleyel [XV:3 and 4]), Op. 40, published by Boßler of Speyer (announced 21 January 1786). Haydn sold this same set of Trios to the London publisher, William Forster.

28, 29 Carl Wahr, the famous actor and theatrical director, and Sophie Körner, the leading actress in the Wahr Troupe (cf. pp. 216f.). Haydn was musical director to the Troupe when it played at Eszterháza, and in 1774 he wrote for Wahr the incidental music to Regnard's *Le distrait*.

30 Joseph Martin Kraus, Symphony in C minor: first page of the autograph. This work was composed in Vienna in 1783 for Haydn's orchestra. The bottom stave, for a second pair of horns ('Corni in Ut'), was added later, possibly when Kraus discovered that four horn players were available at Eszterháza: Chiesa, Hörmann, Oliva, Pauer and possibly also Joseph Dietzl. Cf. pl. 32 and p. 478.

31, 32 Wolfgang Amadeus Mozart, plaster cast from a lost relief by Leonhard Posch, Vienna, *c.* 1788–9; and (*right*) Joseph Martin Kraus, portrait in oils by Antonio Pomarolli, 1783.

33, 34 Two of the Italian composers whose operas were much appreciated at Eszterháza: (*left*) Domenico Cimarosa (1749–1801), portrait in oils by Alessandro Longhi; and (*right*) Giovanni Paisiello (1740–1816), engraving by Vincenzo Alloja after a painting by Elisabeth Vigée-Lebrun.

35 A fortepiano built and signed by Anton Walter, the Viennese piano-builder who also serviced the keyboard instruments at Eszterháza; probably from the large Esterházy collection, this fortepiano was formerly at the birthplace of Franz Liszt (Raiding in Burgenland, Austria). Liszt's father had been in Esterházy service and may have given this by then 'old' instrument to the young Franz for practising.

Haydn, in the opinion of a critic in the Hamburg *Unterhaltungen* who was in turn reviewing Hiller's 'Sketch for a Musical Library', 'should have been omitted [from such a library]; *only* in his symphonies he has some excellent ideas, but he certainly cannot be endured on account of his taste and solidity. Keyboard works or worse trios and quartets by him – that is really bad music.'[1] This note appeared *anno* 1769, the year in which J. J. Hummel of Berlin and Amsterdam issued the first edition of Haydn's string Quartets Op. 9, of which Op. 9, No. 4 in D minor is an undoubted masterpiece that – one would have thought – might have found some favour with the Hamburg *Unterhaltungen*.

Chronicle 1770

PRINCE ESTERHÁZY DECIDED that it was time for him to display Haydn and his *Capelle* in Vienna, to which end he secured the loan of Baron von Sumerau's palace in the suburb of Mariahilf. Apparently Prince Nicolaus did not have quarters in his own palace large enough to mount a whole opera, in this case Haydn's *Lo speziale*. The *Wiener Diarium* reports:

> Vienna, 24 March 1770. Yesterday at about noon her I. R. Majest. our most gracious Empress arrived back from Preßburg safely.
>
> As an especially pleasant piece of news which we did not wish to overlook, we would report that last Wednesday the 21st inst. in the quarters of Herr Baron von Sumerau near Maria Hilf an opera entitled The Apothecary by the Princely Esterhasi [*sic*] Kapellmeister, Herr Joseph Hayden [*sic*] was performed by the assembled Chamber Virtuosi of Prince Esterhasi on that day, and upon the request of high personages it was repeated with quite exceptional applause upon the following Thursday in the form of a musical academy and in the presence of many high persons; a fact that reflects exceptional honour on the aforesaid Herr Kapellmeister Hayden, whose great talents are sufficiently known to all lovers of music, and no less upon the aforesaid assembled virtuosi.
>
> [*Wiener Diarium* 24, Saturday, 24 March 1770]

Possibly the lovely second version of Grilletta's 'Caro Volpino amabile' was composed for the Viennese revival of *Lo speziale*.

Among the bills of this period, there is not much of interest: (1) Stadlmann for repair work on string instruments; Vienna, 28 March 1770; A.M. XIII, 731; Valkó II, 549. (2) Two dozen bassoon reeds; Eisenstadt, 1 May 1770; note by Haydn: 'Item repair Herr May [the horn player Johann May?] for 1 dozen oboe reeds 2 Fl …'; A.M. XIII, 720; Valkó II, 548. (3) Bill by Thomas Druckherl's widow for 'yellow strings', 'brass strings' for the harpsichord; A.M. XIII, 721; Valkó II, 548. All three bills countersigned by Haydn.

---

1 Unverricht, op. cit., p. 86.

We have mentioned that in 1770 the Passer Troupe was engaged through the services of Catharina Rössl. In the letter of 19 January 1770, she informs the Prince that the Passer Troupe was to be stationed at Graz for the Winter and could go to Eszterháza any time after Easter. After 'placing herself, her husband and her manager at the Prince's feet', she compares the Passer Troupe to her former group, that of Hellmann and Koberwein ('eben so stark'), and says the new group could offer regular dramas and comedies, plays, operettas, burlesques, pantomimes and spectacular 'interludes'. Passer himself was soon drawn into the affair, submitted the official petition to the Prince (A.T. 24) and a contract (A.T. 22) was concluded on 5 March.

In his petition, Passer stresses that his troupe's behaviour will be better than that of Hellmann-Koberwein. Instead of the latter's fee of 100 gulden per week, he only expected eighty for a company of twelve members. His wardrobe, he said, would be richer than that of his predecessors. In the contract, Passer undertook to give daily performances wherever desired. The season went on longer: from 1 May to 15 October. When they left, they were given a gift of eighty ducats (A.T. 16), which was distributed as follows: the following members of the Troupe received five ducats each – Frau Passer, Herr Rössl, Frau Rössl, Herr Pärtl, Frau Pärtl, Frau Scheibl, Frau Waner, Herr Diwald (later to return as the 'principal' of his own Troupe), Herr Tamaso and Herr Heigl. Passer himself received thirty. These, then, were the players who shared the theatre with Haydn and his Capelle. The fact that they could perform operettas shows that many of them could sing; they can have been put to good use in the new opera, *Le pescatrici*, which contains many choruses.

We may pass over another Rockobauer bill for a dozen bassoon reeds[1] and concentrate on a more interesting bill:

On the orders of His Serene Highness were purchased:
Music paper ten-stave books 6 which *Herrn Capellmeister* Haydn received.
Books with eight staves: 4 Fl. —
10 Books
the book 24 xr. makes 4 Fl. [Haydn adds:] The above 6 books of music paper were properly delivered to me. Joseph Haydn mpria.
The paper with eight staves was for Herr Liedl [*sic*] to write Paridon [baryton] pieces for His Highness. Andreas Lidl Baritonist.
Eisenstadt, 23rd July 1770.
[A. M. XIII, 723, Esterházy Archives, Budapest; Valkó II, 548]

One of the rather mysterious activities of Lidl was, as we see, to copy (compose?) baryton music for Prince Nicolaus.

Two days later, on 25 July, there was an elaborate *Fest* at Kittsee Castle, at which the *Capelle* (and with them Haydn) participated. It was the eve of St Anne's day, and the celebration was in honour of Prince Nicolaus's sister-in-law; there is a bill in the Esterházy Archives, from which we know that the new summer uniforms were worn for the first time on that day:

Spezifica[ti]on
List of the princely Esterhazi [*sic*] Chamber *Musicien* A°. 770. Newly made summer uniforms which they wore for the court *Fest* at Kidsee [*sic*] on 25th July the first time. Nomina Capel Meister Haiden [*sic*] Luitschi Tomasini, Fribert, Dichtler, Specht, Grießler, Oliva, Pauer horn players, Franz, May horn players, Diezl, Steinmiller horn players, Burgsteiner, Bohl [Purksteiner, Pohl], Kapfer,

---

1 A.M. XIII, 725, dated Vienna, 10 June 1770 (countersigned by Haydn); Valkó II, 549.

Sigl, Schieringer, Hinterberger, a new violinist [Joseph Blaschek?], a new Passetist ['cellist: Christoph Süssig?]. The female singers Dichtler and Leonorl [Jäger]. . . .

[A. M. 602, Esterházy Archives, Budapest; *Haydn-Studien* IV/1 (1976), 38n.]

Fortunately we have a contemporary description of this great *fête* at Kittsee. It is from Johann Bernoulli's *Sammlung kurzer Reisebeschreibungen* . . . Jg. 1783 (IX. Band, pp. 294–8) and is signed 'G. F. von R. [Rotenstein]'. From it we learn that five cuirassier regiments were on manœuvres in or near Kittsee and were to be inspected by Emperor Joseph II and Empress Maria Theresa, who went to Pressburg for a week for that purpose.

> . . . Then I came to Kittsee, a princely Esterhasi [*sic*] *Lustschloß*, two hours' [walk] in circumference including the partridge garden; which castle is surrounded by a moat and four bastions with walls and looks like a fortress. The rooms in the castle are handsome, especially the hall in the middle; there one can see eight large pictures of hunts held by the previous Prince [Paul] Antonius. There are also two life-size portraits: one representing the present Prince Nicolaus Esterhasi in the uniform of a field-marshal with the order of the Golden Fleece, the other the present Princess. Among the rooms I particularly liked one covered with Japanese wall-paper, on which all the figures are life-size. From the castle, which lies on a great plain, there is a wonderful view through a long *allée* of quadruple linden trees – the *allée* is paved almost to the Danube, 1¼ hours away – to the castle at Preßburg.
> Anno 1770, 25th July, both their Imperial Majesties, Joseph II and Maria Theresa, Archdukes Ferdinand and Maximilian, the Duke of Sachsen-Teschen, Prince Charles of Lorraine and Princess Charlotte were guests here of Prince Nicolaus Esterhasi. Towards 5 o'clock in the afternoon the All-Highest *Herrschaften* left Preßburg for Kittsee. At the beginning of the long *allée* which leads to the castle, two great pyramids had been erected which were illuminated in the evening from all sides. In the middle of this *allée* two whole oxen (one on each side) were roasting; they were to be given in the evening, together with many *Eimer* of wine and beer, to the assembled subjects of eight neighbouring princely villages (who entertained the All-Highest *Herrschaften* with country dances the whole length of the *allée*). At the end of the *allée* two more pyramids had been erected; from there to the castle entrance was a parade of the princely guards, in light blue uniforms with yellow facings, waistcoats, breeches and tassels – some 200 men strong, all about six feet [*drei Ellen*] tall – and six hussars, six pages in light blue velvet embroidered with silver, two porters, six runners [*Heiducken*], two gun-loaders [*Büchsenspanner*] and 56 servants in magnificent gala *livrée* stood on either side of the courtyard right up to the stairway; on which the whole princely music corps, 36 in number, were placed; 24 princely house officers in silver-grey [*hechtgrauen*] uniforms with gold borders four fingers' wide lined the walls up to the hall's doorway. Above the great gate in the courtyard, everything was adorned with Indian plants, aloes; and the whole of the great high walls covered with 300 orange trees. Moreover, the fortifications and the four bastions were adorned with obelisks, vases and bouquets of stone flowers together with many statues and niches [*Portalen*]. In one corner was a large tent, from which the All-Highest *Herrschaften* could see the manœuvres and attacks of the cavalry regiments encamped there.
> Meanwhile it was evening, and the little building abutting on one side of the castle, all the walls, the stone flowers, statues, vases and niches, the paths in the woods, the orange vases and the entire side of the castle facing the field were illuminated with many thousand lamps of white and green colour. It was a charming sight, better remembered than described. – After eight o'clock the ball

opened in the hall, decorated with many flowers and brilliantly lighted. Any honest man who could show an entrance ticket was admitted. The company was magnificent and brilliant. After ten o'clock the fanfares of trumpets and kettledrums announced *souper*. Thereupon the All-Highest *Herrschaften* and the other guests – 700 were invited to this *fête* – left the hall and went over a bridge that had been put up over the walls and moat and took you down into the open field which was laid out in a half circle. In the middle was a Chinese bagatelle placed against a forest of palm trees, date trees and banana trees, visible on transparent sheets [like a stage set]. In this field were seven huge green tents, each with seven tables set for dinner and usually for at least thirty persons each. The largest and most magnificent tent was intended for the Imperial family and contained a table with fifty couverts; but that which astonished them was a statue made by the pastry cook and showing Julius Caesar's triumphal entry in Rome after his Egyptian campaign. Four other large tables had been erected in the castle. ... After supper, the ball started again and after 1:30 in the morning the court left for Preßburg. The ball continued under about 4 o'clock a.m. I too arrived at Preßburg half-asleep and exhausted and the regiments then began to disperse. . . .

The salient points for us are: (1) Haydn's band on this occasion was enlarged to thirty-six – with local Pressburg forces? – and included trumpets and drums; (2) Haydn obviously conducted dance music and the presence of the singers in the above-mentioned bill suggests that perhaps an opera, cantata or at least arias were performed; there is no concert specifically mentioned; (3) it is possible that there was *Tafelmusik* for the Empress and that Symphony No. 48, of which an authentic copy dated 1769 by Joseph Elssler exists in a remote Slovakian castle, was played for the Empress at this occasion and not only (or also?) at the 1773 ceremonies for her at Eszterháza. No. 48 – about which *vide infra*, p. 198 – is known as the 'Maria Theresa'; (4) there is no mention that Haydn was introduced either to Joseph II or to the Empress. On the other hand, it is specifically recorded that Haydn *was* introduced to the Empress in 1773. The presence of trumpets and drums also suggests that at least two slightly earlier symphonies, which exist in authentic versions without trumpets and drums, but for which these instruments were apparently added later, may have been enlarged for this occasion, *viz*. Nos. 38 and 41, both in C major.

The event of the year 1770 was the marriage of Prince Nicolaus's 'dear niece', Countess Lamberg, with Count Poggi (*recte*: Pocci). We have identically worded reports in the *Preßburger Zeitung* and *Wiener Diarium*, which suggests that both were given what we would now call a 'Press release' by someone at Eszterháza. They read as follows:

[Extract of a letter from Oedenburg in Hungary, 20th September]
At the moment, everyone is talking only about the magnificent fêtes given by Prince Esterhazy on the 16th, 17th and 18th inst. at his splendid castle, Esterhaz, a few miles distant from this town, on the occasion of the wedding of his niece, Countess von Lamberg, to Count von Poggi. Our readers are therefore due a short account of them.
At 5 o'clock in the afternoon of Sunday the 16th, the bridal couple betook itself to the princely chapel, accompanied by Prince and Princess Esterhazy and a large company of invited cavaliers and ladies, to receive the blessing of the church. Then the whole company repaired to the theatre, where a comic opera in Italian, *le Pescatrici* (or The Fisher-Women), was performed with all possible skill and art by the princely singers and instrumentalists, to universal and well-deserved applause. The princely *Kapellmeister*, Herr Hayden [*sic*], whose many beautiful works have

already spread his fame far and wide, and whose flaming and creative genius was responsible for the music to the *Singspiel*, had the honour to receive the most flattering praise from all the illustrious guests.

After the theatre the princely Grenadier Guards presented a warlike spectacle, quite remarkable in its own way, demonstrating the proficiency of well-trained soldiers, as shown in types of attack and defence; the illumination of the star-shells, the exciting sounds of military music and the noise of cannon added greatly to the sight. This day of rejoicing was brought to a close by a splendid banquet for 30 persons.

On Monday the 17th, following a magnificent luncheon for 30 persons, the whole company again assembled in the theatre at 6 in the evening, where two short German plays with arias were performed to great applause by actors in the princely service [Passer Troupe]. On leaving the theatre the company found a number of carriages waiting, in which they repaired to an open place in the large and delightful castle park. The clearing looks like an immense rotunda; enclosing it are lovely trees and trellises, and the eye is caught by a charming fountain in the centre. It was illuminated with so much art and taste that one could hardly cease looking at it. But soon another spectacle drew the attention of the company: a large crowd of peasants, men and women, appeared quite unexpectedly and contributed no little to the company's diversion by their peasant dances and songs, and by the great joy to be seen in their faces. These rustic festivities lasted until late in the evening, and care was taken to enliven them still more by copious amounts of food and wine. Upon returning to the castle there was a dinner for 40 persons, after which everyone went to make ready for a ball, which began soon after. It is not possible to describe the ball in detail here; suffice it to say that all was of the greatest splendour and liveliness, that nothing was left undone to raise it to the highest level of perfection – the illumination of the ballroom, the orchestra, the diverse and delectable refreshments. Although the number of guests grew to more than 400, the ball proceeded in the best possible order, and the company amused itself until 6 in the morning.

On Tuesday the 18th there was a luncheon for 40 persons, and at 6 in the evening the *opera buffa, le Pescatrici*, was repeated to not less generous applause than at the first performance. After the theatre the whole company watched, from the windows of the castle, the fireworks display created by the Prince's own pyrotechnist. Once more, the union of splendour, art and order could be admired. When the fireworks were over, a dinner for 40 persons brought to an end the magnificent festivities of which this report is but a small sketch. One can easily imagine what a deep impression these truly Princely fêtes made on all those who had the honour to be present.

[*Wiener Diarium* No. 77, Wednesday, 26 Sept. 1770; *PZ* No. 78, 29 Sept.; *HJB*
    VIII, 166f. (our version from the translation by Eugene Hartzell, pp. 268ff.)]

Three theatrical painters and the Court Opera tailor from Vienna were imported for the occasion. One of their bills has survived: Paul Eygner's for the making of eight 'fisher costumes for the new opera', which Haydn paid him (4 fl. 54 xr.) and which was receipted by Eygner on 25 September while he was still at Eszterháza.[1]

Joseph Siess in Oedenburg printed the libretto, which contained $3\frac{1}{4}$ 'Bögen' (51 pages), in 200 copies, which were bound by Anna Maria Heinbeck, both of whom had proved reliable in *Lo speziale*. There were 200 copies printed, four of them in rose-coloured taffeta, the rest in gold or 'Turkish' paper. The title page reads:

---

1 A.M. XIII, 710; Valkó II, 549.

Le / Pescatrici, / Dramma giocoso / per Musica. / da Rappresentarsi / nell'autunno / dell'anno 1770. / Nel Teatro di S. A. S. il Prencipe / Esterhazy / de Galantha &c. &c. / in Esterhaz / á Soprono / Presso Giuseppe Siess.

Parti serie

Eurilla. Creduta figlia di Mastricco .... Gertruda Cellini.
Lindoro. Prencipe di Soriento .... Cristiano Specht.

Parti buffe

Lesbina. Pescatrice, Sorella di Burlotto
    ed Amante di Frisellino .... Maddalena Friberth.
Burlotto. Pescatore, Amante di Nerina .... Leopoldino Dichtler.
Nerina. Pescatrice, Sorella di Frisellino
    ed Amante di Burlotto ....Barbara Dichtler.
Frisellino. Pescatore, Amante di Lesbina .... Carlo Friberth.
Mastricco. Vecchio Pescatore .... Giacomo Lambertini.

. . . La Musica è di Giuseppe Haydn . . .
[Pohl's MS. copy, Gesellschaft der Musikfreunde, Vienna, 10955/Textb.]

In order to mount the complicated work, Haydn had to recruit extra forces from Eisenstadt and Oedenburg.[1] This may explain how it was possible for Haydn to use two flutes simultaneously with two oboes (otherwise he used one flute and two oboes, or two flutes without the oboes).

Prince Esterházy, on the day of the second performance, rewarded Haydn and the whole cast and also Eleonora Jäger, who probably sang in the German operetta:

Comission

According to which our Chief Cashier Zoller is to present our *Capellmeister* Haÿden [*sic*] 30 duc: and the hereinafter named, our Chamber Singers, male and female, *viz*.: Fribert and Mad. Fribert, Dichtler and Mad. Dichtler, Specht, Lambertini, Celini [*sic*] and Leonora Jäger each 12 duc., and this is to be entered as a real expense on the books. Eszterhaz, 18th Sept. 770.

Nicolaus Fürst Esterhazy

We the undersigned each acknowledge the gracious above-listed mark of grace and favour, and have received it correctly and in cash from the G'l Cassa, *viz*.:

Eleonora Jaeger   Leopoldus Dichtler 24.D: Giuseppe Haydn 30 Duc.
Giacomo Lambertini   Carlo Friberth   Maddalena Friberth 24
Christian Specht   Geltrude [*sic*] Cellini 12 D:
[Generalcassa 1770, Rubr. VIII. Fasc. 18 Nr. 34, Esterházy Archives, Eisenstadt.
HJB IV, 47.]

We may pass over a bill from J. J. Stadlmann dealing with '6 violin bows having white hair: 2 Fl. 24 xr' and 'Violoncello bow, with hairs', as well as other small repairs and replacements.[2] Our next important event is the re-engagement of the Passer Company. Negotiations for this new contract took place in October, Prince Nicolaus only stipulating that Passer's terms should be not less satisfactory than those for the 1770 season. In Passer's declaration of 31 October, he mentions that he gave performances also outside the Eszterháza theatre ('außer Theatralischen Auffführung') for the Prince – possibly in the park or 'in camera'. Breaking chronology for a moment, we may, with our guide Mátyás Horányi (69f.), follow the negotiations

---

1 Information kindly supplied by Dr Janos Harich from bills in the Esterházy Archives, Forchtenstein Castle. For details of the libretto's printing and binding, see J. Harich, *Musikgeschichte*, pp. 33f.
2 Vienna, 25 Sept. 1770 (countersigned by Haydn): A.M. XIII, 724; Valkó II, 549.

with Passer as they continue from the latter's winter quarters in Graz. On 28 December (A.T. 20), Passer writes *inter alia* that he would try to raise the standard of his Troupe by engaging new members and enlarging the wardrobe, for which he requests a salary adjustment from eighty to one hundred gulden weekly (the old fee that Hellmann-Koberwein received at Eszterháza). The Prince agreed, and on 26 January 1771 the terms were put down on a new contract (A. T. 23). The details of Passer's Troupe for the 1771 season will be discussed *infra* (p. 171).

The bills for the end of the year contain nothing of interest for us: (1) Another bill from Stadlmann, Vienna, 31 December, for string repairs; A. M. XIII, 728; Valkó II, 549. (2) A bill from Druckherl's widow for '45 yellow spinet strings', Eisenstadt, 31 December; A.M. XIII, 730; Valkó II. (3) Dietzl's annual bill for strings, etc., Eisenstadt, for the year 1770; A.M. XIII, 729; Valkó II, 550. (4) Undated bill of 1770 by Carolus Flach in Eisenstadt for carpentry work, including 'Violon [double bass] repaired'; A.M. XIII, 722; Valkó II, 548.

We have mentioned earlier that in 1770 a young painter named Ludwig Guttenbrunn came to Eszterháza to work, and became Frau Haydn's lover. We have this interesting piece of information from the composer himself, who told it to G. A. Griesinger in November 1799. The Guttenbrunn portrait of Haydn, which Breitkopf & Härtel thought to include with their *Oeuvres Complettes* of Haydn as a frontispiece, was now in possession of Frau Haydn. '... Guttenbrunn was once, said Haydn, her lover' and that was why she clung to the picture,[1] which she took with her to Baden.

The documents on which this Chronicle are based do not give us much insight into the private life of the Haydns. From his two principal biographers we learn a few details:

Haydn attached great importance to *order* and *regularity* in everything he did and in all his surroundings. His rooms were always clean and neat, every object stood in its proper place, and even on his fortepiano the papers and music were not in disorder. He dressed completely as soon as he rose in the morning, and only needed to ask for his hat and cane in order to be able to appear at once anywhere, a habit he had adopted in earlier years when his Prince often called for him unexpectedly. [Griesinger, 58]

He frankly admitted that he had always welcomed the sight of pretty women, but he could not understand how it was possible that he had been loved by so many pretty women in his lifetime. 'My good looks', he concluded, 'cannot have led them to it.' [Dies, 134]

In his younger years, he is said to have been very receptive to love. [Dies, 209]

As a youth and man Haydn loved the rough food [*derbe Speisen*] [which was so characteristic of the pungent Hungarian cuisine]. [Griesinger, 52]

One of Haydn's friends was a lady-in-waiting to Princess Grassalkovics in Pressburg; perhaps the composer met her during the long sojourn in the old coronation town which he, the Prince and the *Capelle*, made in 1767. Her name was 'Mademoiselle Catherine Csech', and we know it only because Haydn left her a vast sum of money (1,000 gulden) in his Will of 1801.[2] Perhaps the 'bad weather' to which

---

1 E. Olleson in *HJB* III, 13. *Haydn: the Years of 'The Creation' 1796–1800*, pp. 473, 478.
2 Will: see *Haydn: the Late Years 1801–1809*, pp. 50ff.

Haydn refers in his bill of 16 May 1769 was not the only reason to extend the trip to Pressburg for three days.[1]

We conclude the Chronicle for 1770 with the following petition addressed by Haydn to his Prince:

[To Prince Nicolaus Esterházy. *German*]

[Autumn, 1770]
SERENE HIGHNESS AND NOBLE PRINCE OF THE HOLY ROMAN EMPIRE, GRACIOUS AND DREAD LORD!

In order to purchase my house, I had to borrow 400 gulden in cash some years ago, and now this capital has been recalled. Since I do not have the sum, I wanted to take out another loan in this amount (on which I would pay interest) to repay the debt. But I could not find any creditors here in Eisenstadt, and inasmuch as I have to repay this loan soon, I would humbly ask Your Highness graciously to allow me to have these 400 gulden, against a receipt from the cashier's office, whereby the 50 gulden I receive quarterly from that source (of which the first payment is due to me by the end of January 1771) would be withheld until such time as the whole debt is repaid. I most humbly commend myself to your favour and grace,

YOUR SERENE HIGHNESS'
most humble
Josephus Haydn.

[CCLN 13]

[Another hand has noted on the cover of the file a short summary of the letter's contents (in German), and a third hand has added the following note: 'Vide resolu[tion]em Parts. Miscit. D. Fol. 5', referring to a parallel file. Haydn's request was granted. For Esterházy's reply, *vide* p. 170.]

Haydn seems to have become seriously ill in 1770. He himself placed this illness in connection with the *Stabat Mater*, written for his recovery; he related this version of the work to his friend Latrobe.[2] But we have seen that the *Stabat Mater* was composed in 1767. That Haydn was ill about 1770 is attested by two sources: (1) his brother, Johann Michael, applied for and was granted leave by the Archbishop of Salzburg 'to visit his sick brother' in 1771; in fact, the leave was not used, so that we may presume Michael Haydn heard of his brother's recovery before he set out on the journey.[3] (2) The following episode in Griesinger's biography:

About the year 1770, Haydn succumbed to a fever [*hitziges Fieber*], and the doctor had strictly forbidden him, during his slow recovery, to occupy himself with music. Soon afterwards, Haydn's wife went to church, and before she left the house she gave strict instructions to the maid not to let her master go near the piano. Haydn was in bed and pretended to have heard nothing of this order, and hardly had his wife left than he sent the maid out of the house on some errand. Then he rushed to his piano. At the first touch the idea for a whole sonata came to him, and the first section was finished while his wife was still in church. When he heard her returning, he hastily retreated to his bed, and there he wrote the rest of the Sonata, which he could not identify for me more precisely than that it had five sharps.

[Griesinger 18]

The Sonata is probably the lost B major piano Sonata No. 23. If Haydn wrote a work to 'celebrate' his recovery, it might have been the gravely beautiful *Salve Regina* in G minor of 1771 (XXIIIb:2), also in the Virgin's honour.

1 *Vide supra*, p. 140.
2 Jancik, p. 222.

In 1770, we have another curious German criticism, from J. A. Hiller's *Wöchentliche Nachrichten und Anmerkungen, die Musik betreffend, auf das Jahr 1770* (fifth 'Stück', p. 37):

[Reviews Bailleux's edition of Haydn's Symphonies 17, a spurious work by Herffert Hob. I: Esl, 29, 28, 9 and 3; gives the *incipits*.] [Objects to printing errors, etc.] . . . Altogether these six Symphonies do not seem to be by one and the same hand. The personal and original manner of Herr **Hayden** [*sic*] is found neither in the second, nor in the third or fourth. The second is mostly a failed and unpleasant copy of the **Fil[t]z** style. The third has quite a pretty *Allegro* movement to start, but in the *Andante* the composer has divided the melody in a ridiculous way between the first and second violins, about as follows [imaginary music example]. At the last movement of this Symphony there stands *Presto Fuga*, and whoever wants to call that thing a fugue is welcome to do so; the last movement of the sixth symphony is more deserving of the title 'fugue'. The fourth Symphony has been put into a bearable form not long ago by one of our [Leipzig] composers and the excrescencies [*Auswüchse*] removed; the last movement in six-eight time has been left out of the print altogether; it would been better to have omitted the silly Trio, together with the Minuet! The first, fifth and sixth symphonies are the best of this collection. In the sixth there is, apart from the fugue at end, also a two part canonic minuet which is nevertheless possessed of a by no means unpleasant melody. . . . The first, fourth and fifth are not new to us here . . . The second one is under the name **Herffert** in Suppl. II p. 5 of [the Breitkopf Catalogue].

Herr **Hayden**, for whose genius we have all the proper respect, may concede whether all these works are actually his own, or if their printing does him a service. We are told that there is more than one composer of this name in Vienna; and if we err not in supposing that these symphonies were composed by more than one hand, perhaps it is correct to print the name **Hayden** on the title page, but then the Christian name should be specially listed in front of each symphony so that one can know to whom to ascribe what is good and what is bad in this collection. . . . [Earlier in the review, it is suggested that Bailleux got hold of bad pirated copies of these works and that they were printed without the composer's assent.]

We observe here the vicious practice of printing from spurious texts, without the composer's knowledge, and from that to the next logical step of pirating works by other composers and selling them as Haydn's. This whole practice was particularly rampant in Paris, and it was very harmful to Haydn's reputation, as the above review shows.

Chronicle 1771

LET US ASSUME that the *Salve Regina* (for four solo voices, string orchestra and *obbligato* organ), rather than the *Stabat Mater*, was written to celebrate Haydn's recovery – as a thank-offering to the Blessed Virgin Mary, to Whom intercessions by Haydn were often addressed. The date (1771) is vouched for by the autograph manuscript and also by a fine copy made by the elder Elssler (Gesellschaft der Musikfreunde, Vienna). The solo organ part of the *Salve Regina* in G minor (XXIIIb:2) was, then, probably written for Haydn himself who, like the *jongleurs* of the Middle Ages, was displaying his manual dexterity for Our Lady. Original parts, written on the Esterházy stag-watermark paper, have survived in the Esterházy Archives in Eisenstadt.[1]

[Prince Nicolaus Esterházy to his Chief Cashier Zoller. *German*]
The *Capeln Meister* Haÿden [*sic*] has asked us to advance him four hundred Gulden, for the repayment of which he will turn over to us his quarterly salary of fifty Gulden (of which the first falls due already at the end of this month), so that the whole debt should be paid in two years; and since we agree to this, he[2] will advance to him the said four hundred Gulden and accordingly enter them on the books.

Vienna, 6th January $\overline{771}$.

Nicolaus Fürst Esterhazy.

For Zoller

Receipt

[agreement as above] ... so that the said 400 f. will be completely paid by 30th October 1772. Schloß Eisenstadt, 31st January 1771:

Josephus Haydn mpria

[Generalcassa 1771. Rubr. V. Nr. 5. Esterházy Archives, Eisenstadt. *HJB* IV, 51.]

In January 1771, one 'Comödiant Prenner', principal of the Wiener Neustadt Troupe, offered his services to Prince Esterházy, apparently for the second time; but since the Passer Troupe had been such a success in 1770 and were in negotiation for the forthcoming season, Prenner stood no chance.[3]

On Good Friday (29 March), Haydn conducted an important performance of his *Stabat Mater* in the Basilica Maria Treu of the Piarists (known as the Piaristenkirche) in the suburb of the Josephstadt in Vienna. It was a church with which he would be associated later in connection with the Viennese first performance, and possibly the real première, of the *Missa in tempore belli*. Now, in 1771, Haydn gathered together no less than sixty musicians for this performance, and the annals record that there was a very large congregation. Haydn liked to perform his choral works with large forces, and this is the first time in his career when we have documentary evidence to that effect. All his other oratorios, from *Il ritorno di Tobia* to *The Seasons*, were performed with enormous forces, as this Chronicle will relate.[4]

Of the bills for this period, most are of little interest: (1) Rockobauer's for two dozen bassoon reeds, 4 f., Vienna, 2 April 1771. A. M. XIII, 715. Valkó II, 551. (2) a bill for the repair ('covering') of a pair of mutes for the horns shows that this extraordinary effect was perhaps used in double horn concertos and the like before it officially entered *Kunstmusik* in Haydn's *La fedeltà premiata* in 1781. The bill, from 'Andani [Antony] Kerner' and signed by Joseph Oliva (and Haydn), is dated Eisenstadt 30 [April?] 1771. A.M. XIII, 714. Valkó II, 550. (3) Carolus Flach's bill of the same date for repairs

1 Examined by the present writer in 1957. There are two sets of parts, of which the covers have been since reversed, causing great confusion (see I. Becker-Glauch in *Haydn-Studien* II, 216). Since the matter is of considerable historical importance we establish here the proper contents before it was photographed for the Haydn-Institut (Cologne) and the wrappers reversed. Copy I: Original parts using 'IGP'-*fleur-de-lys* paper and stag paper with 'IGW'; the cover on 'IanoWitz/IGP' paper with elaborate coat-of-arms. Copy II: Owned by Carl Kraus, with the 'Verzeichniß über den Fleiß der Schüler, welche von [empty] im Monate [empty] 178-[empty] sind unterrichtet worden.' Parts on Italian paper with three crescents 'REAL/A' and 'W'. When these covers were switched, Madame Becker-Glauch fabricated a theory dating the stag paper in the 1780s because of the (by the way printed) schoolchildren's [Schüler] formula which Kraus used as the cover. Another lesson that photographs can be very misleading. See our edition of the work for Doblinger, Diletto Musicale 1961.
2 Servants, including, apparently, men of Zoller's and Haydn's rank, were addressed in the third person: 'he [Zoller] will advance him [Haydn]', etc. Nicolaus II Esterházy tried, after 1795 when Haydn returned from England, to continue the 'Er' address, which Haydn forbade. See *Haydn: the Years of 'The Creation' 1796–1800*, p. 22.
3 A.T. 25; Horányi 72.
4 Piaristen Archives: AMT *Liber Officiorum*, p. 3; *Liber Omnium Fratrum Qui in Domino mortui sunt*, pp. 204f. Dr Otto Biba kindly supplied this information many years ago.

on the 'case ... for the large double bass [Violon]' and for carpentry work on the horn cases &c. A.M. XIII, 713. Valkó II, 550. (4) Rockobauer's bill for another dozen bassoon reeds, Vienna, 9 May 1771. A.M. XIII, 706. Valkó II, 550. (5) Widow Druckherl's bill, Eisenstadt, 10 May 1771, for '59 yellow spinet strings'. A.M. XIII, 712. Valkó II, 550. (6) Four dozen oboe reeds and a dozen cor anglais reeds, undated (1771). A.M. XIII, 719. Valkó II, 551. (7) Anton Schaller's undated bill for locksmith's work on two cabinets where the music was kept (1771). A.M. XIII, 707. Valkó II, 551.

When Prince Paul Anton Esterházy died, his Will ordered a year's salary to be paid to all the 'house officers', including the musicians; its implementation, because of inheritance taxes and so on, was greatly delayed. In order to facilitate the documentation, *Regent* Rahier started to collect the old contracts with the musicians,

> some of whom still have their contracts with Prince Antonio of blessed memory, to wit Sub A. A. A. of the alto singer Eleonora Jäger; Sub. B. of the bassoon player Hinterberger; Sub C. of the bass singer Griesler; Sub. D. of the violinist Sturm; Sub E. of the *Kappelmeister* Hayden [*sic*] pretends[!] that he cannot find the contract of the late Prince, God rest his soul, and that it was perhaps lost in the last fire here, therefore he gave the contract which he had made with Your Highness himself; Sub F. That of Michael Kapfer, who is long since gone, and which the *Kappelmeister* [*sic*] had with him. Sub G is an extract of the fees that the musicians had at that time. The other musicians who still served under the late Prince, God rest his soul, *viz*. Fribert, Sigl, Thomasini and Steinmüller, say that they never received a contract.
>
> Eisenstadt, 12th April 1771.
>
> [EH, Budapest, Fasc. 1529 (456); see also Chronicle 1773, *infra*, pp. 183f.]

On 1 May the Passer Troupe took up residence in Eszterháza, having seven (instead of six) rooms at their disposal. When he had signed the contract in January, Passer had wanted to have it rewritten with a terminal date of 10 rather than 15 October so that he could accept a new post beginning on the 15th. The Prince, not wanting to establish a precedent, refused that but said he would allow the company to leave in good time if Count Castiglione, who was arranging for their winter season at Pressburg, would make the request in writing. It was always, with the Prince, a question of 'channels' and 'form'. In the contract, this time, the Prince not only agrees to provide the lighting on the stage but also the scenery. The scenery was entrusted to Stefan Dorfmeister, a painter from Oedenburg. This was a year when the Prince was mostly not in residence but had to be in Vienna; perhaps that is why the documents are scarcer than usual.

The comedians were awarded a bonus of 80 ♯ [ducats] in the year 1771, *viz.*:

Partl et Partlin	12
Rößlin	12
Simon, Simonin	6
Tomaso	6
Dibald	6
Heigl	6
[left blank:]	2
[blank] and his wife	4
Principal Passer	20
	80

13 [bonuses] distributed by Passer himself.

[A.T. 16 *verso*, Esterházy Archives, Budapest; Horányi 68ff., German ed. has list *verbatim* pp. 69f. Dorfmeister: Harich *Musikgeschichte*, p. 34]

The presenting of such a bonus at the termination of the Troupe's contract seems to have been customary; from the above list naming most of the members we can see that it contains many names known to us from earlier seasons.

Archduchess Marie Christine and her consort, Duke Albert of Sachsen-Teschen, were on very friendly terms with Prince Nicolaus. They had (as we see from the entry in Zinzendorf's Diary of 28 May 1772, *vide infra*) a regular suite of rooms at Eszterháza Castle, and since they now resided at Pressburg, they often appeared at Eszterháza, sometimes unexpectedly. In the Summer of 1771, they also paid a visit to the Castle; in the *Baucassa-Rechnungen* for July 1771 (items 18–19) we read of work 'for the arrival of the Hertzogen Albert'. Perhaps the work was to prepare their regular suite which would always be available to them.[1]

On 24 June there was a dreadful affair in the Eszterháza Castle Tavern, in the course of which the oboist Zacharias Pohl lost his right eye; *vide infra*, 21 December, for the outcome of this incident.

Apart from a Stadlmann bill for lute-maker repairs,[2] the next in the meagre list of documents concerns Haydn's family life. On 9 August, Haydn's father-in-law, Johann Peter Keller, wig-maker in Vienna, died. The *Nachlaßakt* lists, apart from 'Frau Anna Haydin zu Eisenstadt', six other children, last of whom was 'Frau Alloisia Sommerfeld zu Preßburg'; with the latter Haydn was soon (1778) to have serious legal difficulties concerning a substantial sum of money she had lent the Haydns who, in turn, were still in debt over their house and its destruction (even if Esterházy had rebuilt it, furniture had to be acquired all over again).[3]

Since the Prince was in Vienna so much of 1771, it happened that the Haydns were in Eisenstadt to be godparents to the Dichtler's second son:

> 18 huius [August] Baptizatus est Josephus Joannes Joachim filius legitimus Leopoldi Dichtler, Musici Dominalis, et consortis eiusdem Barbarae, levavit Dominus Josephus Hayden [*sic*] Chori Magister cum sua conthorali Maria Anna, vices eorundem supplevare Joannes Hayden et Eleonora Jägerin cantatrix.
> [*Matricula Baptizatorum*, Bergkirche, Eisenstadt; Schmid, op. cit., p. 4; *HJB* VII, 20]

It was during this peaceful year that Haydn was able to compose another set of string Quartets (Op. 17), which followed Op. 9, composed about 1768 and published, as we have seen, the next year by Hummel. Op. 17, the dated autographs of which have survived, were also published a year after their composition by Hummel. Symphony No. 42 was also written in this year (dated autograph), and the extraordinary piano Sonata in C minor (No. 33; XVI:20).

In November, Haydn put in a petition, of which the original document (probably in the Forchtenstein Archives) is at present unavailable, for an increased *Deputat* of wood and wine.

> [Summary:] Since he has been in princely service, he has never bothered the Prince with a 'Supplique' and would not do so now unless necessity had not forced him. 'The present very dear times', in which all the households require double expenses, have already made themselves felt and will surely continue to do so in future, and thus he is obliged humbly to ask His Highness if he would grant him

---

1 See Edward Olleson in *HJB* II, 47 (using archive material supplied by J. Harich).
2 Vienna, 8 July 1771. A.M. XIII, 709. Valkó II, 551.
3 The *Nachlaß* papers (legacy) of Keller are in the Archiv des Obersthofmarschallamtes, Haus-, Hof- und Staatsarchiv, Vienna. Schmid, op. cit., p. 4.

'an *Eimer* of officer's wine and half a cord of wood to improve his monthly income'.

[Princely 'Resolution':] Is approved, and the petitioner is to be given a daily *Maaß* of officer's wine and six cords of wood, and the proper officials advised thereof.

[Pohl II, 48; see also PCDI 772 ('Hochfürstl. Resolution ddo Vienna, 1 Dec. 1771 according to which the *Capellmeister* is to receive ...' &c.) and *HJB* IV, 11 (Konventionsblatt)]

J. J. Stadlmann submitted a bill on 17 November with a large list of repairs for various string instruments, including a baryton and a Cremona violin.[1] In December, Dietzl's annual bill was submitted for strings etc., for the Castle Choir; this year[2] again the bill mentions the repair of a 'Bassl' ('cello) bow, A and E strings for the 'Violon' (note the tuning) and A as well as D strings for the 'Bassl' – which shows that there was a 'cello and double bass regularly in use in the Church Choir.

Following the affray of 24 June, in which the oboist Zacharias Pohl lost his right eye, Haydn managed to keep the culprits of the affair from being dismissed, and his way of settling the matter is recorded (21 December) as follows:

[Contract between Zacharias Pohl[3] and Xavier Marteau[4] in Haydn's presence. *German*]

> *Contractum inter Zachariam Pohl et Xaverium Marteau*
> *Musicos, vi cujus hic ob laesum Musici Pohl oculum ad respondas*
> *in curam habitans expensas semet obligat.*

This day on the date and year recorded below is herewith set down and agreed the following settlement and contract between the Princely Esterházy oboist, Zacharias Pohl, and the Princely Esterházy bass-player, Xavier Marteau, because of the scandalous brawl between them which occurred on the 24th of the previous month of June in the Eszterháza Castle Tavern, whereby Zacharias Pohl lost his right eye; to wit:—

Whereas, according to the statements of both parties and various witnesses, it may be surmised that Xavier Marteau did not purposely intend to inflict this damage with his ring on the eye of Zacharias Pohl, but on the other hand, Zacharias Pohl is not entirely guiltless, both parties have therefore agreed, in the presence of *Herr Kapelmeister* Hayden [*sic*], to the following settlement: that Xavier Marteau shall recompense Zacharias Pohl for the costs of the cure and trip arising from the above-mentioned damage, in the amount of forty-nine gulden 13 kreutzer, within six months, at the rate of 8 gulden 17$\frac{1}{6}$ kr. per month, of which the first 8 fl. 17$\frac{1}{6}$ kr. are to be paid on the first of January 1772; but Zacharias Pohl, because of the indemnification here given him as a result of the damage to his eye, shall not and can not demand anything at any time from Xavier Marteau.

As witness thereto both parties have set their hands and their customary seals. Eisenstadt, the 21st of December 1771.

> L.s. Zacharias Pohl, mp
> *hochfürstlicher Hautboist.*
> L.s. Xavjer Marteau,
> *hochfürstlicher Bassetist.*
> In my presence: Josephus Haydn, mpria
> *Hochfürstlicher Capellmeister* L.s.   [CCLN 14]

1 Vienna, 17 November 1771. A.M. XIII, 705. Valkó II, 551.
2 Eisenstadt, 20 December 1771. A.M. XIII, 703. Valkó II, 552.
3 Pohl was engaged in 1769 and remained in the band until his death, in 1781.
4 Xavier Marteau (*recte*: Hammer) was a 'cellist in the band from 1771 to 1778.

We close the Esterházy Chronicle *anno* 1771 with

Specification
What I advanced for His Highness, *viz.*:
4 books of Italian music paper to write the last 24 Trios.
The book at 21 xr. makes: 1 Fl. 24 xr.
These 1 Fl. 24 xr. have been paid to me correctly by the Rental Office.
22 Dec. 1771   Josephus Haydn mpria.
[Whole bill autograph: A.M. XIII, 702. Valkó II, 551]

It just happens that there exists a bound volume of baryton Trios which were composed between *c.* 1769 and 1771: Nos. 73–96 (Esterházy Archives, Budapest, Ms. mus. I. 110: facsimile in the *Haydn Compositions* . . . Budapest 1960, p. 32; of the spine in Somfai, 38). Of these there is a dated autograph for No. 79 (1769), while Nos. 105 and 106 are both dated 1772 on their respective autographs. It appears, therefore, that the paper really was for the only complete volume 'in Prunkeinband' (noble binding) for the Prince to have survived.

Once more the German critics made themselves heard, and to Haydn's detriment. This time the author is the educator and theologian Johann Christoph Stockhausen (1725–84), writing in *Critischer Entwurf einer auserlesenen Bibliothek für die Liebhaber der Philosophie und schönen Wissenschaften. Zum Gebrauch akademischer Vorlesungen*. Fourth edition with corr. and add. Berlin 1771 (foreword dated: Hanau, 20 September 1770). Therein we read:

> Now the works by Heiden [*sic*], Toeschin [*sic*], Cannabich, Filz, Pugnani, Campioni are getting out of hand . . . The mistakes in composition . . . and for the most part a complete lack of knowledge of counterpoint, without which a good Trio was never made, are found frequently in all these men . . . these fashionable Trios are often real solos or duets . . . The same applies to the Quartets of these gentlemen.[1]

As always with these Austrian works, he objects to 'that curious mixture of the comic and serious, of the trivial and touching'. It was a mixture which the north Germans were totally incapable of understanding.

The following year, 1772, Haydn was to compose his epoch-making string Quartets, Op. 20. The whole of Austrian music was in a great emotional crisis, which will be discussed *infra*, pp. 266ff.; yet one would be hard put to find even a faint echo of this great period in the German periodicals, whose critics continued largely along the lines illustrated above.

Haydn, a major part of whose occupation was acting as a diplomat or, if one wishes, a buffer between the musicians and the 'administration', had an able friend in that same administration, to whom he was devoted and who was of immense help to

---

1 *Joseph Haydn Werke*, Reihe XII, Band 3 (Quartets Op. 20, Op. 33), Foreword. A similar criticism of the period reads: 'Some time ago the Trios of Martini [Sammartini] used to be very popular; perhaps they did not deserve to be as much as that, since they were hardly anything but solos, accompanied by a bass and a middle part that just filled in. Now the Trios of the *Herren* Hofmann, Hayde [*sic*] and Ditters have supplanted them in the affections of the connoisseurs; they have beauties of their own, just as do those of *Herrn* Wagenseil, which are, whatever you can say (and which has been said) against his works, original – that much must be said in his defence.' Hiller's *Wöchentliche Nachrichten und Anmerkungen die Musik betreffend*, Jahrgang 3 (1768), p. 104.

him – Anton Scheffstoss. No doubt he was one of the officials who, on the one hand, could keep the military discipline of *Regent* Rahier within bounds and, on the other, had the Prince's ear more frequently than did Haydn (who would have had to seek an interview for each one of his requests). The very beginning of the New Year will show us that Scheffstoss was indeed close to Haydn's heart.

Chronicle 1772

[To Anton Scheffstoss, 'Secretaire' and Chief Bookkeeper of the Esterházy administration. *German*]

†

Eisenstadt, 9th January 1772.
Nobly born and highly respected *Monsieur* Scheffstoss,
    You have my grateful thanks for all your kind efforts on behalf of my wishes, the fulfilment of which is the result of your intercession for me. I would have thanked you long ago and acknowledged my indebtedness, if I were not, and had not been, prevented by illness. Dearest Monsieur Scheffstoss, please also help Marton [Marteau][1] through your kindness to get the 6 cords of wood, 30 lbs. of candles, and 30 gulden lodging money which should be his, and which His Highness promised me to give him; the mistake in this case lies in his contract, according to which he is to receive the same allowance as Lidl,[2] although even in Lidl's contract there is no mention of the 30 lbs. of candles (which, I assure you on my honour, His Highness agreed to grant him). Apart from this please present my respectful compliments to your wife and the Weigl[3] family (to whom I shall write shortly), and to all other good friends. And I remain, with all respect, noble Sir,
Your obedient servant,
Josephus Haydn.

[On the cover of the file, in another hand: 'circa meliorationem Salarii Musico Marton exoperand'.][4]   [CCLN 15]

The other 'intercessions' were Haydn's own additional wine and wood, and of course the solution of the brawl between Pohl and Marteau; but there were probably many others as well. The next day we find Rahier writing to the Prince as follows:

Most Serene and Noble Prince of the Holy Roman Empire,
Gracious Prince and Lord!
    I have communicated today to all the musicians by word of mouth your high order of the 8th, that none of the wives and children of the musicians except for the wives of Haydn, Fribert, Dichtler, Celini and Tomasini are to be allowed to be seen at Eszterház, and there was no one who did not agree to the terms of that high order. . . . Eisenstadt, 10th January 1772. . . .
[A.M. III, 179, Esterházy Archives, Budapest. Valkó II, 554]

Obviously the main problem at Eszterháza was lack of space. If he were to have a regular season of a dozen actors and actresses, there would hardly be room for all the wives and children of the musicians. But that was not all. A document in the Esterházy

1 See p. 74. Hungarianized to 'Marton'.
2 Andreas Lidl, a baryton player, was a member of the band from 1769 to 1774.
3 See p. 144.
4 In the *Prothocoll über verschiedene hochfürstl. Commissiones, Decretationes, Intimata und andere Buchhaltereys Verordnungen de Anno 1734 [et seq.]* (Esterházy Archives, fasc. 2488, No. 776), we learn that Haydn's request was quickly granted: 'Resolution of His Serene Highness, dated Vienna, 14th January 1772, according to which the bass player Marton [*sic*] is to be granted annually six fathom cords of firewood, 30 lb. of candles and 30 fl. lodging money. . . .'

Archives shows that Prince Nicolaus further intended to reduce the size of his orchestra and to cut the salaries of the remaining musicians.[1] Both these ideas contributed to the 'Farewell' Symphony, which was certainly composed in 1772 (autograph) and probably at the end of the season in Eszterháza. In fact, the orchestra was not reduced nor were the salaries cut, but there was a thorough reorganization of the whole band, which resulted in the final division between the Eisenstadt contingent (the princely Church Choir) and the Eszterháza 'Cammer Musique'.

On 25 January, a contract was made out for a new theatrical group: the famous Carl Wahr Company. The terms were no different from those of his predecessor, but Wahr remained a long-time favourite at the Court: 1772–77, five years that made theatrical history at Eszterháza. We do not know where Prince Nicolaus (or indeed Haydn) heard him, but perhaps at Oedenburg in 1770. Wahr was younger than Haydn (the actor was born at St Petersburg in 1745) and had already made a name for himself as a serious actor, and a reliable head of a troupe, when he came to the Esterházy court. He also inspired Haydn to write at least one famous piece of incidental music (to Regnard's *Le distrait*) in 1774.[2]

On 3 February, we have a bill from Jacob 'Wan Weeg', the princely bookbinder, for '3 musical books in fol: bound in fine red and with good gold lettering, slip-cover for it bound in the French style with gold lettering for the title; as agreed per 5 ducats.' This bill is for the baryton trios in the special binding that were discussed when Haydn sent in the bill for the Italian music paper on 22 December 1771.[3]

Mathias Rockobauer sent in three bills: (1) for eighteen oboe reeds, Vienna, 13 February 1772. A.M. XII, 685. Valkó II, 555. (2) a dozen and one-half bassoon reeds, Vienna, 27 February. A.M. XII, 686. (3) 'That I made 24 reeds for Herr Petywall [bassoon player Peczival]', Vienna, 10 March. A.M. XIII, 687. Haydn himself, as usual, countersigned all these bills. There are further documents: (4) J.J. Stadlmann sent a bill dated Vienna, 15 April 1772, for 'lute-maker work ... on a Paridon [*sic*] ... inlay work with ebony ... the belly varnished ... a violoncello newly strung ... glued ... 1 Fl. 34 xr. a long Indian Gampa [*sic*] bow with white hairs, and a silken and golden case [*Schleich = Schlauch*] for it, made for His Highness the Prince ... 4 Fl. ... Summa 62 Fl. A.M. XII, 689. Valkó II, 556. (5) '... Herr Joseph Haydn, princely *Capellmeister* received at Eszterhaz 68 yellow spinet strings, as agreed' a bill dated Eisenstadt, 28 April from Druckherl's widow. A.M. XII, 690. Valkó II, 556. (6) A bill in Haydn's hand, dated 29 April, 'What I spent for His Highness the Prince in Vienna Ao. 1772. Item 6 newly completed Trios with 36 *Bogen* á 7 xr. to be copied, makes 4 Fl. 12 xr. Correctly paid from the Rental Office ...'. A.M. XII, 688. Valkó II, 688. (7) Carl Flach's carpentry bill, Eisenstadt, 30 April 1772 for repairs to the music cabinet. A.M. XII, 689. Valkó II, 555.

On such items is our history of Eszterháza built! From a curious bill that an Oedenburg merchant sent to Eszterháza, we see that for the forthcoming season, new costumes were being prepared. 'Laus Deo Anno 1772, 10th Juny in Oedenburg. Monsieur Haydn should acknowledge the arrival and accord of ... blue taffeta á 28 xr. ... lace from Lyon á 17 xr. ... Johann Georg Munk at the Roman King' (A.M. XI, 610e. Valkó II, 558). The harpsichord strings on 28 April proved insufficient and on 29 June, Druckherl's widow sent 37 more yellow spinet strings (A.M. XII, 697; Valkó II, 557). Rockobauer sent a dozen bassoon reeds (9 July: A.M. XII, 691. Valkó II, 556).

1 A.M. 4355; J. Harich in *HJB* VIII, 35.
2 Wahr: Horányi 72ff.
3 Binding bill: A.M. XII, 684. Valkó II, 555.

This was all in preparation for a huge *Fest* at Eszterháza in honour of Prince Louis de Rohan, Envoy Extraordinary of Louis XV to the Court of Vienna, later Archbishop of Strasbourg and Cardinal, and a key figure in the affair of Marie Antoinette's necklace. Prince Nicolaus offered his guest spoken theatre, ballet, opera and other delights which will shortly be related.

Before we turn to the *Fest* for Prince Louis de Rohan, we have another account of a visit to Eszterháza, from the pen of Count Zinzendorf (whose Diary is of such importance to later volumes of this biography).

[28 May 1772:] ... A ll$^{h.}\frac{1}{4}$ je fus rendu a Suitor [Süttör], ou le P^{ce} d'Eszterhasy d'apresent a bati le beau chateau nommé Eszteras. Descendu a l'auberge, le Prince m'envoya une voiture le Cte Ottocar Starhemberg me mena par la maison, le Grand Salon, les apartemens de LL.A.R.[1] l'immense quantité de vases du Japon, les beaux bras, les feux, les encoignures de glaces peintes dans l'apartement de Me Marie, tout est d'une magnificence qui Vous étonne. Apartment de M^{e} la C^{esse} Antoine Eszterhasy, meublé papier. Lit bleu. On m'avoit destiné une chambre a coté d'elle avec un lit a la Duchesse. Pendules a carillon en grand nombre. Ouvrages d'Ebenisten parfaits. Apartemens de la P^{esse}. Nous dinames a 6. le P^{ce} le C^{tes} Louis et Ottocar Starhemberg, dónt le dernier criblé de blessures est Vice Commandant de Raab, un Colonel Ziska, et le Lieutenant du Prince. Bon diner, puis Concert, deux chanteuses chanterent fort bien. Hayden joua du violon. Le Cte Ottocar me mena en voiture par le parc au temple de Diane, a celui de la fortune, au rond ou les paysans ont dansé l'année passée quand Me Marie [Christine of Sachsen-Teschen] y étoit. Nous fimes le tour du Parc, beaucoup de Cerfs et de Biches Parc aux sangliers. Le plus beau de ce parc est une patte d'Oye comme a Carls [second half of the name illegible], mais seulement a trois branches, tout du bois de chêne qui forme les plus belles charmilles, nombre de sentiers pratiqués dans ce bois, dont je ne pus pas profité tout étant rempli d'eau. Faisanderie. Le flêche du village de Schieblach [Széplak] forme un des points de vûe de la patte d'Oye. La grande Cour du Chateau forme un rod en Arcades, elle est superbe, mais le corps du logis qui etoit le seul edifice existant avant ce Prince cy est surmonté d'un Belvedere construit par lui qui forme un drôle d'effet. Joué a la Pyramide. Dela au Spectacle[.] La Salle est belle, la Tribune du Prince extrémement vaste, on jouoit le Postzug. A droite du Chateau sur la façade du jardin sont la Salle des Spectacles a laquelle sera jointe la Salle des bals, il y a des Ecuries superbes pour 106. chevaus, et plus loin l'auberge ou j'avois descendu ce matin. A gauche des maisons de domestiques. Le Parterre en demi-Cercle devant la patte d'oye n'est pas mal avec des jets d'eau. Sur le Belvedere on voit dit-on, le Chaû [château?] de Presbourg, lorsqu'il fait beau. On reproche a Eszterhas avec raison d'être situé dans un fond, sans vüe et extrémement humide, il est vrai que le seule patte d'oye lui donne dela vüe. Je partis apres le l^{a} acte du Postzug ... a 7^{h} ...

[Edward Olleson, in *HJB* II, 46f.]

Among the large entourage which Rohan brought was a French nobleman, Zorn de Bulach, attached to the French Embassy in Vienna; his memoirs, which include a detailed description of Rohan's visit, are of great value. Another eye-witness was György Bessenyei, an officer of the Hungarian Bodyguard at the Court of Vienna since 1765, since which date Prince Nicolaus had been a captain in the same organization. Bessenyei published not only a poem, in Hungarian ('Eszterházi

---

1 From the words 'LL.A.R.' (their royal highnesses), we see that Marie Christine and her husband, Duke Albert, had apartments regularly at their disposal at Eszterháza. Zinzendorf's guide was Johann Ottokar Joseph, Count von Starhemberg (1722–89). 'Cte Louis' was Johann Ludwig Adam, Count von Starhemberg (1717–78). *Der Postzug oder die noblen Passionen* was a comedy in two acts by Cornelius Hermann von Ayrenhoff.

vigasságok'), about the visit but another one about Marguerite Delphine, solo ballerina from the Vienna Ballet, who appeared during the festivities and later died as a result (*vide infra*). A third eye-witness was the correspondent of the *Wiener Diarium*.[1]

Prince Louis left Vienna for the 'Hungarian Versailles' on 12 July. As he approached the Castle he was 'lost in wonderment' at the surrounding country in the twilight (Bessenyei), and the building was much admired (Zorn de Bulach). We are then told that 'Prince Rohan is accompanied to a large room in the castle where a temporary stage has been erected [the great room in the first storey?]; the heart is quickened. To amuse Rohan, Henry the Fourth is seen at the hunt' (Bessenyei). This was Charles Collé's *La partie de chasse du roi Henry IV*, given (in German, of course), by the newly engaged Carl Wahr Troupe. This was followed by a ballet, for which Prince Nicolaus had actually imported, as ballet-master, one of the great men in his time, Jean Georges Noverre who, it is reported, had already been a guest at Eszterháza in 1771[2] and had at that time produced the ballet entitled 'The Judgement of Paris' (*Das Urtheil des Paris*), which was now repeated for Rohan. Among the dancers imported from Vienna was Marguerite Delphine, fourteen years old and the darling of Viennese audiences: 'Many beauties came from Diana's clouds, also Venus [who was Delphine] on a golden cloud, all from Vienna for a pastoral play to excite and move a gentle heart' (Bessenyei). We may omit most of the long poem on her talents, and content ourselves with the quotation (Bessenyei) that 'breathless silence in the room' greeted her graceful movements. She caught a cold in the draughty vastness of Eszterháza and died a few days after she had returned to Vienna. Haydn and the *Capelle* provided the music for the ballet, of course.

After the ballet there was a banquet, followed by fireworks in the park. The next day (13 July) began with a shooting party, after which Haydn gave a concert. The programme is not recorded, but the new Haydn works for 1772 season included the Symphonies 46 and 47 (No. 45, the 'Farewell' would not have been suitable) and, of

---

1 Bessenyei's poem about the ballerina: 'Delfén'. Horányi 74ff. (German ed., with lengthy quotations from both of Bessenyei's poems). Zorn de Bulach; *L'ambassade du Prince Louis de Rohan*, Strasbourg 1901. The relevant section in Zorn de Bulach's memoirs read as follows:

[P.69:] Le 12 juillet je suis allé avec le Prince à Esterhazy en Hongrie, à 22 lieues de Vienne, domaine appartenant au Prince d'Esterhazy. Celui-ci fit placer des relais de distance en distance, chercha le Prince à Vienne et le ramena de même. A chaque relai se trouvait un de ses hussards qui courait devant, à notre arrivée, ses grenadiers étaient en haie devant le château. Ils sont de toute beauté. Il en à 150 a solde, cammandés par un capitaine, un lieutenant et un sous-lieutenant. Chaque homme a 7 kreuzer et 2 livres de pain par jour. L'entré du château est superbe; une vaste cour orné avec jet d'eau. Le salon du rez-de-chaussée est voûté. Les piliers et les côtes, ainsi que le plafond, sont richement decorés par des guirlandes, de fleurs peintes en or et en diverses couleurs. Deux grottes, l'une vis-à-vis de l'autre. L'eau qui les arose fait un doux murmure et rafraîchit le salon; on va de plain-pied dans le jardin ainsi que dans la cour. Les appartements à droite et á gauche, dont l'un est occupé par le Prince et l'autre par la Princesse, sont de toute beauté. Les deux pièces ou salons du haut sont de la dernière magnificence, dignes d'un souverain. Il fait venir toutes les raretés de Paris. Les appartements de maître sont également très bien distribués et fort bons. En avant du château le jardin forme un parterre immense, au bout duquel se trouve un bois très étendu, dont une partie est réservée auc faisans. Il est coupé vers le milieu par une clôture de pallissades, une enceinte est pour les sangliers, une pour les cerfs et une pour les daims, Ce bois a des routes, et au plus fort soleil on peut toujours s'y promener a l'ombre. Du château trois allées très longues terminées par des points de vue; au bout de celle du milieu on remarque un grand clocher et un village. A une lieue d'Esterhaz se trouve le grand lac appelé Einsiedel [*sc.* Neusiedel]. Il a 7 lieues de long sur 3 de large. Pendant notre séjour qui dura jusqu'au 17, le Prince donna des fêtes et récréations de toute espèce, bals masqués, feux d'artifice, illumination magnifique, des foires; il fit venir plus de 300 couples de paysans qui marchèrent paire à paire avec leurs drapeaux et leurs musique. Chaque communauté arrivait separément. Il est d'usage en Hongrie que, lorsqu'on sort le drapeau qui se trouve dans chaque village, tout court après. Nous eûmes aussi une chasse au daim et une au cerf. Il a une troupe de comédiens, trent musiciens, cent et tant de chevaux, non compris ceux de son haras, qui lui fournit seulement les remontes de son écurie et ceux qu'il offre en cadeau. Le salon du haut est de la plus grande magnificence. Pour l'éclairer on se sert de pres de 500 bougies. Ce prince a aussi une forteresse, des canons. Son droit d'avoir des troupes est un droit féodal. Il a dans son brevet de prince le titre de Durchlaucht, ce que les autres princes à diplômes n'ont point. Les Esterhazy et les Balfi [Palffy] ont bien secouru l'Imperatrice dans la guerre contre la France.

2 Pohl II, 91.

course, the great string Quartets of Op. 20. A number of 'festive' C major symphonies, perhaps with 'imported' trumpets and kettledrums (the latter could be played by the bassoon player Peczival), could have been presented: No. 38 (trumpets and timpani added later by Haydn), No. 41 (trumpets and timpani also added later by Haydn) and No. 48 (dated Joseph Elssler manuscript in Slovakia: 1769; no authentic trumpet and timpani parts have been located).

The Wahr Troupe then gave a tragedy (title not recorded). Bessenyei suggests that 'the tragedy is intended cleverly to pave the way better for frolics and joys'. After a *souper* there was a garden party. Torches flamed over a part of the park, which had booths with refreshments and amusements. A steeple was suggested by a torch-lit building. In the middle of this was a 'small listening hall' (*Diarium*), where 'sundry female singers' sang only of love; 'From their eyes sad woe, from their singers' tongues lust and melancholy' (Bessenyei).[1] The day ended with a masked ball in the beautiful garden clearing.

On the afternoon of the next day, 'the guests saw German players' – obviously the Wahr players again. In the evening there was another firework display and a masked ball, this time presumably in the ball-room. On 15 July, the players gave a tragedy. After *souper* there was a popular gathering (*Volksfest*) in the park clearing, which was illuminated by exotic fireworks. Two thousand peasants, reported Bessenyei, foregathered to drink, carouse, dance and cheer the Prince. It was a kind of 'foire' and the noise was incredible ('le Prince donna des fêtes et récréations de toute espèce, bals masqués, feux d'artifice, illumination magnifique, des foires ...': Zorn de Bulach). Three hundred joyful peasant couples descended on the French guests, each group arriving from its own village under its own flag and with their own musicians. There was yet another masked ball to conclude the day's festivities (Bessenyei).

The final day, 16 August, opened with a deer hunt in the *Thiergarten*; in the afternoon, they shot wild duck on the Neusiedlersee. There were two performances in the evening, a German comedy by the Wahr players, and after that a children's ensemble – Horányi (81) thinks it might have been the famous 'Berner Children's Troupe' which often appeared at Pressburg in the 1770s – gave a German comedy. One wonders what the French guests could make out of these German plays.

---

1 The following bill (A.M. XII, 692; Valkó II, 556), countersigned as usual by Haydn himself, throws some light on this performance by 'sundry female singers':

Payment for the necessities of the Esterhaser Opera.

List of what, on the orders of *Herrn Herrn Capellmeister*, I paid for, and laboured at, in the way of operatic work for the opera singers of Your Princely Highness, *viz.*:

First for Madam Frybergin [= Friberth] a rosy coloured morning dress [*Commot* = French 'commode', 'robe commode'] and a rosy coloured skirt, trimmed with spangles [*Flinterl* = *Flitter*] and white taffeta. Cost of making: 2 Fl. 15 xr.

Secondly for Madam Frybergerin a court [ball] dress in blue taffeta altered ... the blue taffeta dress altered to the former court dress ... Spanish satin, flesh coloured ... a sleeve for a bodice ... for Madame Tüchtlerin [Dichtler] trousers made from green Spanish material ... lilac coloured waistcoat, richly embroidered ... sleeves made ... for Mamsel Lenore [*Mademoiselle* 'Leonore' Jäger] a dress trimmed [*garnihrt*] ... Summa: 8 Fl. 19 xr. Leopold Wöber, tailor master and town citizen. ...

Then for the hairdresser who came from Oedenburg to dress the hair of those three singers, paid: 2 Fl. Which 10 Fl. 19 xr. have been paid to me by the Rental Office here.

The 18th of Aug. 1772.   Josephus Haydn mpria.

Previously, Bartha and Somfai (388f.) suggested that because Madame Dichtler was dressed in man's clothing, *Lo speziale* or *La canterina* (with *Hosenrollen* for *Frau* Dichtler) must have been given. The sources do not include an opera among the entertainments, and there is no record of all the operatic troupe and *Capelle* having been rewarded (which would surely have been the case). We suggest that the 'sundry female singers' performed extracts from Haydn's operas of 1762, 1763, 1766/7, 1768 or 1771 (i.e. the Italian comedies of 1762, *Acide, La canterina, Lo speziale* and *Le pescatrici* in costume), just as the sources indicate, on a temporary little stage in the garden. These works contain many arias dealing with love, woe, melancholy, etc. Another point: there is no record of opera costumes for the male singers.

History records nothing of Haydn's activities at Eszterháza until October. The first item for that month is a bill from one Joseph Stärzer dated Eisenstadt, 22 October:

> Extract. What I did in the way of work for the hunting horn player ...
> Two crooks for lowering half a note: .... 1 Fl.
> Various crook sockets per.: .... 1 Fl. 30 xr.
> _____
> Summa:...... 2 Fl. 30 xr.

Paul Bryan (*Haydn-Studien* III/1[1973], pp. 52f.) plausibly suggests that in this bill, we have documentary evidence for the strange crooks that Haydn used in Symphonies 45 (F sharp crooks) and 46 (B crooks). By using a G horn crook plus the half-note crook Haydn had a horn in F sharp, and by taking a C *alto* horn and adding the half-note crook he had a horn in B *alto*.

Haydn was at Eisenstadt on 31 October: he signed a receipt for money received from Chief Cashier Züsser out of General Cassa funds (Valkó II, 554: A.M. XI, 609). Next we hear of Haydn in Pressburg: on 16 November he conducted the dance music for a ball held at the palace of Prince Grassalkovics, presumably using the princely *Capelle*.[1] Four days later we find Haydn back at Eszterháza, where he and his wife were godparents to his grand-niece, Anna Maria Wimmer, at the latter's christening in the Parish Church of Fertöszentmiklós near Eszterháza.[2]

The musicians were at Eszterháza without their wives. Apparently they came to Haydn to ask if he could help them, and the result of the composer's help was the famous 'Farewell' Symphony. We must also remember the dire threat of Prince Esterházy dismissing some of his musicians and lowering the salaries of others. Here are some documents by Haydn's biographers:

> Among Prince Esterházy's *Kapelle* there were several vigorous young married men who in summer, when the Prince stayed at Esterhazy [*sic*], were obliged to leave their wives behind in Eisenstadt. Contrary to his custom, the Prince once extended his sojourn in Esterhaz by several weeks: the loving husbands, thoroughly dismayed over this news, went to Haydn and asked for his advice.
>
> Haydn had the inspiration of writing a symphony (which is known under the title of 'Farewell' Symphony), in which one instrument after the other is silent. This Symphony was performed as soon as possible in front of the Prince, and each of the musicians was instructed, as soon as his part was finished, to blow out his candle and to leave with his instrument under his arm. The Prince and the company understood the point of this pantomime at once, and the next day came the order to leave Esterhaz.
>
> This is the way Haydn explained to me the origin of the 'Farewell' Symphony, and the variant, that Haydn thereby dissuaded his Prince from the intention of disbanding his whole *Kapelle* and thus assured so many persons of their livelihood, is prettier from the poetical viewpoint but not historically correct.   [Griesinger, 19; the economic part was also true, however; *vide infra*.]

The version in Dies (47ff.) is substantially the same but, as usual, padded out to great length by asides: 'I was young and lusty in those days, too, and thus no better than they', said Haydn apropos of the love-sick musicians. The story continues with Haydn and Tomasini leaving (substantially correct with mistakes in details).

1 Pohl II, 52.
2 Anna Maria. Parentes Joannes Michaël Vimmer et Maria Anna Vimmerin, Patrini Josephus Franciscus Haiden et Maria Anna Haidin Kismartony'. E. F. Schmid *Vorfahren*, p. 264.

The Prince now rose and said, 'If they all leave, we must leave, too.' The musicians had meanwhile collected in the *antichambre*, where the Prince found them, and smiling said: 'I understand, Haydn; tomorrow the men may all leave', whereupon he gave the necessary order to have the princely horses and carriages made ready for the trip.

Haydn's pupil Sigismund von Neukomm, whose notes on Dies are most valuable, has this to report:

> H. told *me* that the Prince, in the course of economic decisions, decided to dismiss the *useless* [*unnütze*] *Kapelle*: *inde lacrymae* which dried up as a result of H's happy inspiration, and the Prince renounced his economic restrictions, whereupon H. in a small new symphony, had the musicians enter, one after another. In *my* version it was not Tomasini but the double-bass player who was the last to leave.[1]
>
> I ought to remark here that all these communications which I received personally from Haydn (mostly from our tête-à-tête conversations at table) occurred in a period earlier than the visits of my friend Dies, in a period when Haydn was strong enough to create his huge work, *The Seasons*.
>
> [Neukomm, p. 29]

We have a contemporary criticism of the 'Farewell', printed in the *Mercure de France* on Saturday, 24 April 1784, probably a review of the first performance in Paris (the work was printed by Sieber in the same year). The review is, among other things, interesting for its negative reaction to the first part of the finale ('bruyant & sans caractère'). We give the criticism here in its entirety:

> ... Le Concert [Spirituel] s'est donné Mardi dernier dans la Salle ordinaire; on a avoir annoncé une symphonie de M. *Hayden*, analogue à cet événement. Voici en quoi elle consiste. Après un morceau bruyant & sans caractère succède un *Andante* d'un chant triste & lugubre, au milieu dequel les cors, d'abord après un trait seul, soufflent leurs bougies, prennent leurs instruments à leurs bras & s'en vont. Les flûtes [autograph: oboes] en font autant; ensuite les bassons, contre basses, violoncelles, quintes, tous défilent l'un après l'autre, instruments sur les dos. La symphonie va toujours, seulement son effet s'affoiblit insensiblement, & il ne reste plus bientôt que deux violons, un sur chaque partie, qui font la même cérémonie, & le morceau est fini. Le départ, qui est écrit sur les parties, & *obligé* comme un *solo*, produit un effet assex plaisant quand on ne s'y attend pas. On raconte ainsi l'occasion pour laquelle M. *Hayden* fit cette plaisanterie. Le Prince d'*Esterhazy* vouloit, disoit on, renvoyer sa musique & ne garder que quelques violons. On exécuta cette symphonie, qui ne plut pas trop au Prince; il demanda la raison de cette bizarrerie. 'J'ai voulu exprimer, lui dit M. *Hayden*, les regrets que cause aux Musiciens qui vous resteront, la perte de leurs camarades, & vous faire en même temps sentir que deviendra votre musique, quand vous n'aurez plus que quelques violons.' La plaisanterie fut goûtée, & les Musiciens conservés.

The review shows that, even twelve years later, various versions of origin of the symphony had begun to circulate (see also Appendix).

In the Dies report on the Symphony, we learn that the usual time for Eszterháza was six months; this agrees with the period, more or less, for the actors – 1 May to 1

---

1 There is a Symphony by Haydn's pupil Paul Wranizky, in which the reverse of the 'Farewell' Symphony obtains, and it is actually conceivable that it was composed under Haydn's supervision. See Jan La Rue; 'A "Hail and Farewell" Quodlibet Symphony', in *Music & Letters* 37/3 (July 1956). Wranizky became Music Director of Johann Nepomuk Esterházy. The young composer (he was born, like Mozart, in 1756) also studied with the brilliant German, J. M. Kraus, who was in Vienna in 1783 and visited Haydn in Eszterháza (*infra*, pp. 471f.): see M. Poštolka in *MGG* 14, 881ff.

November. 'How could [the Prince] have taken it into his head to lengthen [this period] by two months?' asks Dies. If the Prince's announcement to the musicians was made at the beginning of November, the 'Farewell' Symphony might have been composed towards the end of the month. We may assume that the *Capelle* was in Eisenstadt by 6 December, the Prince's name-day (St Nicholas).

Haydn had won a diplomatic *coup* with his great new Symphony, whose merits apart from its programmatic connotation will have been recognized by the great connoisseur for whom it was composed. As a sort of 'thank-offering' Haydn had the equally charming idea of composing a new Mass, which he entitled on the autograph manuscript 'Missa Sancti Niccolai' and dated 1772 'In Nomine Domini'. When Prince Nicolaus celebrated his name-day at the Castle Chapel on 6 December 1772, the princely Church Choir and the *Capelle* will have perhaps even surprised him entirely with a new Mass by *Capellmeister* Haydn. The original parts in the Esterházy Archives at Eisenstadt show enormous haste: Haydn himself copied some of the pages and wrote the Latin text in others, helping Joseph Elssler Sen., whose knowledge of Latin was probably less profound than Haydn's.[1]

The following bills from the period have been preserved: (1) Rockobauer's for 'the two hautbois players of H. High. Prince Esterhazy', two dozen oboe and 6 cor anglais reeds, each 10 xr. . . . A.M. XII, 695; Valkó II, 557. (2) Dietzl's annual bill for extra strings, etc. A.M. XII, 698; Valkó II, 557f. (3) Undated (1772) bill by J. J. Stadlmann for lute-maker work on the Prince's baryton. A.M. XII, 693; Valkó II, 557. (4) Stadlmann's bill for work done between 21 Aug.–18 Sept., Vienna, 31 Dec. 1772. A.M. XII, 699; Valkó II, 558.

Haydn had now come to the notice of the Empress Maria Theresa. Writing to the Archduchess Maria Beatrix in Milan, the Empress notes that

> Ce 12 [Novembre 1772] / Madame ma chère fille . . . Ce que vous me dites sur le *requiem* de Reutter, m'a touchée. C'est aussi ma piece favorite de toutes ses compositions. Pour l'église il fait plusieurs choses assez bien; il faut se mettre à sa place; il faillat que tout fût très court et exécuté par des ecoliers, des enfants. Il faillait donc suppléer pas les instruments et basses. Pour le théâtre, j'avoue que je prefère le moindre Italien à tous nos compositeurs, et Gaisman [*sc*, Gassmann] et Salieri et Gluck et autres. Ils peuvent faire quelque fois une ou deux bonnes pièces, mais pour le tout ensemble je préfère toujours les Italiens. Pour les instruments il y a un certain Haydn qui a des idées particulières, mais cela ne fait que commencer . . .

> [*Briefe der Kaiserin Maria Theresia an ihre Kinder und Freunde*, herausgegeben von Alfred Ritter von Arneth, Band III, Vienna 1881, pp. 148f.]

Once again, we are astonished how slowly musical news penetrated the august precincts of Schönbrunn Castle. 'But that is just a beginning' – in the year 1772 – is a rather astonishing statement about Haydn, whose works had been circulating in Vienna for twenty years or even slightly longer (if we take 1749 to be the correct year to which Haydn assigned his *Missa brevis a due soprani* in F [XXII:1]). We shall see that both Haydn and Mozart suffered from the curious attitude towards their works which characterized not only Maria Theresa but also Joseph II and Leopold II.

---

1 Facsimiles in our critical edition for Faber Music; in Landon, *Das kleine Haydnbuch*, Salzburg 1967, p. 65. See also *infra*, p. 251.

In 1772, Haydn's most celebrated pupil, Ignaz Pleyel, was entrusted to the master as composition pupil. Pleyel's sponsor was Count Ladislaus Erdödy, a family with which Haydn had many contacts at various levels. Pleyel was to become a very famous composer, earning Mozart's praise – Vienna, 24 April 1784:

> ... Then there are Quartets now published by a certain Pleyel; he is a pupil of Joseph Haydn. If you don't yet know them, try to get them; it is worthwhile. They are very well written and very pleasant; you will at once recognize the master in them. Good – and fortunate for music, if Pleyel will in time be able to replace Haydn for us!...[1]

Pleyel had studied with J. B. Vanhal before he was sent to Haydn. In 1791, the Professional Concert engaged Pleyel in competition with Haydn and Salomon: see *Haydn in England 1791–1795*. He remained with Haydn until 1777, a period of five years.

Chronicle 1773

WE MAY PASS OVER the first series of bills[2] and proceed to the final payment of the year's salary from the Will of the late Prince Paul Anton:[3]

[To Prince Nicolaus Esterházy. *German*. Apparently an archive copy in a copyist's hand]

[March 1773]

Most Serene and Noble Prince of the Holy Roman Empire,
Gracious and dread Lord!
    Your Highness intimated to me, through His Highness' secretary Schefstoss[4] [*sic*.] that you would be minded graciously and generously to provide a year's salary to me and to those chamber musicians who entered the service of Your Serene Highness' brother [Paul Anton] (provided that each of us would submit a petition to that effect to Your Highness).
    May I therefore ask, in profound submissiveness, that Your Highness confirm, in your infinite kindness, your willingness to grant us this exceptionally gracious mark of esteem. For this, I shall offer you at all times my most faithful services, and I recommend myself to your serene favour and grace.

Your Serene Highness'
most humble
Joseph Hayden [*sic*]
Capell-Meister

[Address:] To His Serene and Noble Highness, Prince of the Holy Roman Empire, Lord and Sire, Nicolaum Esterházy von Galantha, Knight of the Golden Fleece, Privy Councillor in actual service of His Imperial and Royal Majesty, General Field Marshal of the Imperial and Royal Aristocratic Guards, Captain etc.,

---

1 *Mozart Briefe* III, 311 (VI, 180).
2 (1) Andreas Rockobauer, Eisenstadt (not Vienna), 15 Mar. 1773: 2½ dozen bassoon reeds. A.M. XII, 664; Valkó II, 561. This Andreas was probably a relative (son?) of Mathias. Andreas signs 'Rockenbaur' (perhaps a clerk?). (2) Mathias Rockenbauer, 27 March: 2 dozen oboe and ½ dozen cor anglais reeds. A.M. XII, 665; Valkó II, 561. (3) Stadlmann, Vienna, 28 Mar.: repairs and strings; 'Italian Violon A', work on 'a Pariton', its 'outer case inlaid in mock-oak, lined with green on the inside ...', 'long Indian Pariton bow with a screw ...'. A.M. XI, 668; Valkó II, 562.
3 He died on 18 March 1762, at the age of fifty.
4 *Recte*: Scheffstoss; see also p. 175.

etc. My gracious Prince and Sire: this humble request is submitted *ut intus* by
CapellMster Haydn.

[On the same sheet containing the above address is the following autograph note by Prince
Esterházy: 'If there is no counter-claim, the suppliant should be paid one year's salary according to
the contract then in force, minus ten percent inheritance tax; this sum is to be paid out by our Chief
Cashier's Office, but the sum for the inheritance tax is to be delivered to Doctor Sonleithner[1] after
securing the necessary receipt. Vienna, 1st April 1773. Nicolaus Fürst Esterhazy m.p."]

[CCLN 15f.]

[Haydn's receipt to the Esterházy Cashier for moneys received as a result of the
above petition. *German*]

†

I, the undersigned, herewith acknowledge to have received correctly and in
cash from Herr Züsser, receiver-general of the Princely Cashier's Office, the sum
of 400 Fl. (in words: Gulden four hundred), which according to a decree issued by
His Serene Highness has been bequeathed to me as *qua* staff officer under the
provisions of the last will and testament of his late lamented Highness Prince
Antony Esterházy; and I acknowledge further that I cannot make any other claim
whatever on the Princely house.
Eisenstadt Castle, the 29th of April 1773.

Josephus Haydn [m.]pria
Capell Meister

[CCLN 16f.]

On 15 April the *Ratsprotokoll* (deliberations of the town council) of the free city of
Eisenstadt noted the following:

Hr. Joseph Hayden [*sic*], princely Esterházy Kapellmeister, as the owner of a
citizen's house in the Klostergasse, requests a statement that his Lady Neighbour,
Magdalena Frummwald, has constructed upon their common wall.

We are back to the dreary Frau Frumwald, who broke the town's deliberation
discussed *supra* (p. 156) and illegally made some use of the wall of which the sordid
details, fortunately, have not been preserved in town files.
We may likewise give but brief reference to a further set of bills[2] and proceed to
what was perhaps Haydn's last official act before leaving Eisenstadt for the Summer at
Eszterháza; he and his wife were godparents at the christening of the Dichtler's third
child, Maria Anna; in the Parish Church of St Martin:

30ª Aprilis.
Nomen Baptizati: Maria Anna.
Nomen Parentum et Cognomen: D[omi]nus Leopoldus Dichtler Musicus
Celsissimi D[omi]ni Principis Nicolai Esterházy, Conthoral[is] Barbara. Nomen
et Cognomen Patrinorum: Perillustris D[omi]nus Josephus Hayden Celsissimi

---

1 Christoph Sonnleithner (1734–86), lawyer and also composer (his symphonies were passed off as Haydn's), who managed the Prince's
legal affairs in Vienna.
2 (1) M. Rockobauer, Vienna, 22 Apr.: 2 dozen bassoon reeds. A.M. XII, 667; Valkó II, 562. (2) Anton Kerner, Vienna, 26 Apr.: 'What
I made, with agreement, for the princely *Music Banda*, viz. . . . a hunting horn . . . with all crooks . . . together. [smaller items excluded
here] five Imp. ducats or 21 Fl. 20 xr.' A.M. XI, 610d.; Valkó II, 560. (3) Johannes Mäyer, saddler, Eisenstadt, 29 Apr.: '. . . a travelling
case . . . for the use of the hunting horn [no doubt the one in item 2] . . . 5 Fl. 9 xr. A.M. XII, 668; Valkó II, 562. (4) Antony Spiller, Court
Master-Locksmith, Eisenstadt, 29 April: '. . . At the request of the *Herrn Kabelmeister* [*sic*] . . . hinges for the hunting horn [case], also
hinges for the large double bass [*grossen Bass Geigen*] [case] . . . . A.M. XII. 669; Valkó II, 562. (5) Carolus Flach, carpenter, Eisenstadt, 30
Apr.: 'chest for the hunting horn . . . lining for the Violon . . . and a case . . .'. A.M. XII, 670; Valkó II, 562. (6) Josepha Druckherl,
Eisenstadt, 29 Apr. 1773: '. . . Herr Joseph Haydn *hochfl. Capellmeister* kindly agrees to acknowledge receipt for the 43 yellow spinet
strings, with agreement, for Eszterház . . .'. A.M. XII, 671; Valkó II, 563. The sudden emergence of this amount of bills at the end of April
is easily explained by the fact that the 'season' now began at Eszterháza 'officially' on 1 May, with the advent of the players, and the
Eisenstadt (and Viennese) artisans wanted to collect their debts before the Court and Haydn disappeared into the country.

D[omi]ni Principis Nicolai Eszterházy [*sic*] Capellae Magister cum sua D[omi]na
Conthorali Anna. [Taufprotokoll, Town of Eisenstadt; *HJB* VII, 20]

On 1 May the theatrical season began at Eszterháza. This year, we have records
from Pressburg that show us which plays were given in that town for the Autumn-
Winter season of 1773–4 and thus presumably in the Summer as well; the Wahr
Troupe wintered at Pressburg.

Die Hausplage [by Pelzel]
Die neueste Frauenschule
Regnard's *Le distrait (Der Zerstreute)*
Semiramis
Die verstorbene Ehefrau
Gebler's *Thamos, König von Egypten*
Thamos Junge Brüder
Der Jurist und der Bauer
Shakespeare's *Hamlet*
Collé's *La partie de chasse du roi Henri IV (Die Jagdlust Heinrich des Vierten)*
Großmann's *Die Feuersbrunst*
Orest und Elektra
Shakespeare's *Macbeth*
Der Jude und der Bauer
Amalie
Medon oder die Rache des Weisen, comedy by Christian August Clodius.

A few words about some of these pieces may be welcome. It is now thought that at the
performance of *Thamos, König von Egypten* in Pressburg which took place on 11
December 1773, attended by Archduchess Marie Christine and Duke Albert of
Sachsen-Teschen, Mozart's great incidental music was performed. In the review of the
evening from the *Preßburger Zeitung*, we read high praises for the sets and costumes and
'die wohl harmonisiernde Musik des mit verschiedenen Instrumenten stark besetzten
Orchesters', and this large orchestra with various instruments played (as it is now, and
with good reason, thought) Mozart's K. 345. It is possible that Haydn, who in 1773
himself wrote German-language choruses in his marionette operas, used Mozart's
incidental music if and when the Wahr Troupe did the work at Eszterháza – it would
have been in the 1774 season.

When *Medon* was given at Pressburg on 1 January 1774, the *Preßburger Zeitung*
singled out Sophie Körner and Carl Wahr: '... Herr Wahr in der Rolle des Medons
[hat sich] diesmal selbst übertroffen ... Auch Madam Körnerin hat uns wiederum, wie
allemal, nach ihrer Art entzücket; beyde aber vielen Zuschauern Thränen entlocket'
(*PZ*, 5 January 1774).

It is thought that Haydn's Symphony No. 59 in A, known in some old sources as
'Feuer Sinfonia', might have been written as incidental music to Großmann's play *Die
Feuersbrunst*; but if Haydn did so, it must have been several seasons earlier, for the work
exists in two dated copies of 1769 in the Austrian Monasteries of Göttweig and
Kremsmünster. On the other hand, he did compose music for Regnard's *Le distrait*, but
apparently not until 1774, when the music was reviewed in the *Preßburger Zeitung*;
that same paper also reports on music Haydn was planning to write for *Hamlet*, one of
Wahr's great roles. Wahr's company was altogether such a success with the public in
Pressburg that the readers of the *PZ* actually wrote in and asked for the continuation of
theatrical reviews, which were a relatively new section of the newspaper.

The usual bonus at the end of the season enables us to list the members of the
company; although Wahr's contract with Prince Nicolaus required him to come with
'wenigstens zwölf convenablen gut agirenden Persohnen', the 'principal' always came
with considerably more.

Specification

According to which the high princely present of 100 ducats is to be distributed to the theatre company [*Comische Gesellschaft*] as follows:

M[onsieu]r. Wahr	20 fl.	20	xr.
Madame Körner	20 „	20	„
Körner	20 „	20	„
Seip[p]	20 „	20	„
Litter	20 „	20	„
Litterin [= Mad. Litter]	20 „	20	„
Lorenzo	20 „	20	„
Schimon	20 „	20	„
Mauerin [= Mad. Mauer]	20 „	20	„
Reiner, daughter	20 „	20	„
Reiner, mother	20 „	20	„
Schultz, father	20 „	20	„
Schultz, mother	20 „	20	„
Schultz, daughter	16 „	$53\frac{1}{3}$ „	
Zappe	25 „	20	„
Kessel	25 „	20	„
Kesselin [= Mad. Kessel]	25 „	20	„

At the order of H. Highness the Prince   Jacob Kaufmann
Eszterhaz 30th Oct. $\overline{773}$ Secretaire

[A.T., Esterházy Archives, Budapest; Horányi Ger. p. 86, Eng. (corr.) p. 86]

It will not have escaped the princely eye that Wahr took no more than everyone's share in this bonus and, indeed, less than three of the members who for some reason received 25 gulden.[1]

Haydn was now working on *L'infedeltà delusa*, Marco Coltellini's delightful *burletta* which became perhaps the most successful opera – from the standpoint of stage popularity – the composer ever wrote. In every respect it marked a milestone in Haydn's operatic career and is unquestionably the greatest stage work of the period 1762–75. Its sparkling wit, its tender humanity and its brilliant vocal and instrumental writing must have astonished the audience at Eszterháza as indeed is the case today. These qualities must have been equally impressive to that astute connoisseur Prince Nicolaus, to whom Haydn was supposed (according to the *Regulatio Chori Kissmartoniensis* [CCLN 5]) 'to send us the first copy, cleanly and carefully written, of each and every new composition' – long a dead letter but perhaps, in this case, the explanation for another shower of gold that descended on Haydn's needy person:

Comission

According to which our Chief Cashier Joseph Züsser is at once to give to our *CapellMeister* Haÿdn, as a present against receipt, twenty-five ducats. Eszterhaz, the 27th of Maÿ 1773.

Nicolaus Fürst Esterhazy

The above twenty-five Imperial ducats have been paid to me correctly and in cash from the high princely *General Cassa* by the hand of *Herrn* Chief Cashier Züsser. Estoras, the 30th of Maÿ 773.

Josephus Haydn mpria.

[A.M. XII, 641, EH, Budapest; Valkó II, 563 and, corrected, *HJB* IV, 47]

1 Sources for Wahr sojourn: *PZ* (*HJB* VIII, 169; Horányi German 84). *Geschichte der Schaubühne zu Preßburg*. Preßburg 1793 (reprinted 1927). Horányi English p. 72 (terms Wahr contract) and pp. 84ff.; Ger. pp. 84ff. Haydn's music to 'Die Feuersbrunst': Landon *SYM*, 704. Mozart's K. 345: *Thamos* in *Neue Mozart Ausgabe* Serie II/6/1 (Heckmann) and Alfred Orel, 'Zu Mozarts Sommerreise nach Wien im Jahre 1773', in *Mozart-Jahrbuch* 1951, pp. 47ff.

We suggest that Haydn, to whom the composition of *L'infedeltà delusa* must have meant something very special – note the extravagant signature at the end, on a separate, otherwise blank, page: 'laus omnipotenti Deo et Beatissimae Virgini Mariae', with its reference to Haydn's Patroness in all things, Our Lady – and that upon its completion he took the autograph (still extant) and presented it to Prince Nicolaus, who could read the score as well as any professional musician. And Prince Nicolaus, who was well aware of Haydn's financial difficulties, did the one thing calculated to please Haydn the most: give him a handsome reward of gold ducats. The official première of the Opera was destined for the name-day celebrations of the Dowager Princess Lunati Visconti in July, but it may have been preceded by a special performance for Prince Nicolaus at the end of May.

A report by *Regent* Rahier on 7 October[1] informs us of the celebrations that took place on 26 and 27 July in honour of the Dowager Princess Maria Anna. The Castle and the park were illuminated after the performance of the Opera on 26 July, of which the libretto[2] reads:

L'INFEDELTÀ DELUSA / BURLETTA / PER MUSICA IN DUE ATTI / DA RAPPRESENTARSI / IN ESTERHÀZ / NELL'OCCASIONE DEL GLORIOSISSIMO / NOME DI S. A. LA PRINCIPESSA / VEDOVA / ESTERHAZY NATA LUNATI VISCONTI. / SUL THEATRO DI S. A. IL PRENCIPE / NICOLO / ESTERHAZY / DE GALANTHA, / AI 26. LUGLIO / DELL'ANNO 1773. / A OEDENBURGO, / NELLA STAMPERIA DI GIUSEPPE SIESS.

Vespina. Giovanne spiritosa, Sorella di Nanni, ed Amante di Nencio	MADDALENA FRIBERTH.
Sandrina. Ragazza Semplice, ed Amante di Nanni	BARBARA DICHTLER.
Filippo. Vecchio Contadino, e Padre di Sandrina	CARLO FRIBERTH.
Nencio. Contadino benestante	LEOPOLDO DICHTLER.
Nanni. Contadino, Amante di Sandrina	CRISTIANO SPECHT.

The libretto, forty-four pages in 8° format, was printed in 200 copies by Johann Joseph Siess of Oedenburg and was delivered by the bookbinder Mathias Fischer of Oedenburg on 23 July. Six copies were bound in taffeta, fifty in gold brocade paper ('Procat Gold Papier') and 146 'all'ordinaire'. Ordinary bindings cost 2 kr., gold brocade paper 7 kr., taffeta 36 kr.[3]

After the performance, the guests went to a masked ball at which Archduchess Marie Christine and Duke Albert of Sachsen-Teschen appeared unexpectedly and incognito. The following day there was another ball and fireworks.

In that same letter of 7 October, Rahier provides us with a very interesting piece of information. 'Georg Habentinger, *Directeur* of the *Commedianten* here [in Eisenstadt]' requests payment for expenses of transport and loss [*Schäden*] in connection with his visit, taking his company of seven persons, to Eszterháza, for the performances of two marionette *Spiele*' (plays? operas?), as a result of which he lost the income for four Eisenstadt performances. During most of 1773, this famous Troupe, specializing in Hanswurstiada, was quartered at Eisenstadt.[1] Obviously the Wahr Troupe did not do Hanswurstiada, and to mount these marionette performances, Haydn had to recruit the Habentinger Troupe. Horányi (92) quite rightly suggests that the Habentinger Troupe did not appear in connection with the visit of Maria Theresa, for otherwise it

---

1 A.M. 196, Esterházy Archives, Budapest; Horányi 86.
2 Copy in the Esterházy Archives, Eisenstadt; another in the Stadtbibliothek, Vienna.
3 A.M. 610/b, 610/c, Esterházy Archives, Budapest. Horányi 90f. Valkó II, 559.

would have been mentioned in the many and detailed sources for that famous occasion. What pieces do we have for supposing that a marionette opera might have been done in this period? The only printed libretto other than *L'infedeltà delusa* and *Philemon und Baucis* is *Hexen-Schabbas*, Haydn's marionette opera. But since the sources all say that the marionette theatre was officially opened on the occasion of the Imperial State Visit at the beginning of September 1773, we presume that *Hexen-Schabbas* was first given sometime in late September or before 7 October. Or the Habentinger Company gave spoken plays in dialect with some arias by Haydn's singers – perhaps even *Die Feuersbrunst*, Haydn's marionette opera partly in dialect. It survives in a version with clarinets, which were only in the orchestra from 1 January 1776 to the end of February 1778 (*vide supra*, p. 72), but may have been composed earlier with a reduced orchestration. There are also two versions of *Philemon und Baucis*.[1]

We have seen that the great harp virtuoso, Johann Baptist Krumpholtz, was engaged by Prince Nicolaus on 1 August 1773. He was before that a guest at Eszterháza, however, and must have made a tremendous impression, for at the end of July, the following receipt has been preserved:

> I, Johann Baptist Krumpholtz, acknowledge having received from *Herrn Capellmeister* Haydn a *Gratification* of four Cremnitzer ducats, in Esterhas, the 29th of Julii 1773.   [A.M. XI, 610; Valkó II, 560]

As we said earlier, it is incomprehensible that this great player should have lived for some years at Eszterháza without having been the recipient of a single note of harp music by Haydn; either that, or these harp works have disappeared.

We now come to the state visit by Empress Maria Theresa. Since we have a number of authentic sources, all describing this visit in some detail, we propose to begin with this material, prefacing it with an interesting description of the Empress herself at this time by William Wraxall:

> Maria Theresa's person now retains no trace of the charms which she once possessed; and it is even difficult to conceive from her present appearance, that she ever was handsome. So total a change ought not however, to surprise, when it is recollected that besides her advanced time of life, and the number of children whom she has brought into the world, the small-pox completed the ruin of her features. She caught the distemper from her daughter-in-law, the present Emperor's second wife, twelve years ago, in 1767; and during her illness, her life was in the most imminent danger. Previous to that period, I am assured that she still might have been termed handsome, though she was become large and heavy. In addition to the ravage made in her face by the small-pox, an accident which happened after her recovery, totally altered her countenance, and obliterated whatever remained of her former self. On a journey from Vienna to Presburg, she was overturned from an open carriage. In the fall she bruised her nose and face so violently, that the swelling and inflammation, occasioned by it, threatened to deprive her of sight. The care and skill of her medical attendants prevented that disaster; but the loose gravel upon which she fell, so disfigured her features, that they are no longer recognizable.
>
> The Empress Queen is now grown corpulent, unwieldy, and infirm. Her face, though lacerated by the marks of the small-pox, and the effects of her fall, retains nevertheless such an expression of goodness and benevolence, that when she smiles, her features for an instant become almost pleasing. She owes no advantages

1 Franz Probst, *Beiträge zur Geschichte des deutschsprachigen Theaterwesen in Eisenstadt*, Eisenstadt 1952, pp. 28–30.
2 Landon in *HJB* I, 174, 178ff., 169ff. and *JHW* XXIV/1 (*Philemon und Baucis*) ed. Jürgen Braun, and Kritischer Bericht, 1971.

to the decoration of the toilet, her hair being combed back very flat under her cap, on the crown of her head; and behind, it is cut short on her neck. In order to conceal its being grey, she always wears powder. Every thing about her person is dark and mournful; nor has she ever, since the death of her husband, the late Emperor, worn any dress except the deepest weeds. A black crape cap, which comes very low over her forehead, so as almost to conceal her hair, is little calculated to adorn, or to set off her face. On no occasion whatever has she put on diamonds, or other female ornaments, since she became a widow. Her legs and feet, like those of her mother, being grown feeble, and almost debilitated, she is no longer capable of taking any considerable exercise on foot; and she usually wears gaiters about her legs, on account of the support which they give her when walking. In the Drawing-room she uses a glass, in order to distinguish persons at a few paces distant from her. She is in fact very shortsighted; or rather perhaps, age and infirmities . . . oblige her to have recourse to artificial assistance.

When young, she was exceedingly fond of dancing, masking, and every public diversion: it is almost unnecessary to say, that she has long renounced all such amusements. I have frequently seen her sit down to cards in her drawing-room, on public days; and at the Court balls she usually remains till about eleven o'clock at night, seated as a spectatress of the dances: but, she always retires before midnight; and in her own apartments she never plays at cards, or at any other game. In commemoration likewise of her widowed state, as a sort of austerity which may mark her grief for the loss of a husband whom she tenderly loved, she has never inhabited since his decease, the principal range of apartments in the palace at Vienna. Those in which she lives, have a southern exposition; but, she is so little susceptible of cold, that in the midst of winter she usually has all the windows open during the day, and often cannot bear a fire in her chamber. The Emperor, on the contrary, is so chilly, that he says he is almost frozen when he goes to visit his mother, and is obliged to put on a fur coat in order to enable himself to support, for any length of time, the air of her apartment. Her residence is on the third floor; and the rooms which she occupies, though commodious and spacious, are nothing less than splendid.

Antiquity does not furnish any model of conjugal affection and fidelity more perfect than the one exhibited by the Empress Queen. Like the elder Agrippina, she presses to her heart the urn that contains the ashes of her husband; and time, which has softened, cannot obliterate her grief. Francis died suddenly on the 18th of August 1765, without previously confessing to a Priest, or receiving absolution. Unless prevented by indisposition, Maria Theresa never fails to repair on the eighteenth day of every month, very early in the morning, to the vault of the convent of the Capucins in Vienna, where his remains are deposited. Even in winter, she is there long before dawn, notwithstanding the rigour of the season, and her many infirmities. The vault is lighted up, while on her knees she pours out supplications for the repose of his soul. The whole month of August she considers as a penitential time, dedicated to his memory; and she generally passes it at the palace of Schonbrun [*sic*], in a sort of gloomy and devout retirement, amidst masses, Requiems, and services for the dead. However tinctured with human weakness and superstition, it is impossible not to respect the source, and to honour the principles, which inspire so exemplary a conduct.

[N. William Wraxall; *Memoirs of the Courts of Berlin, Dresden, Warsaw, and Vienna, in the years 1777, 1778, and 1779,* 2 vols. 2nd ed., London, 1800, II, 305–10]

The visit is described by three contemporary sources: (1) a specially printed brochure in French, which exists apparently in only one copy (National Széchényi Library, Budapest, who very kindly, as usual, sent a xerox copy) and has never been reprinted; it is therefore given here complete for the first time since it left the Ghelen Press in Vienna; (2) the report in the *Preßburger Zeitung*; (3) that in the *Wiener Diarium*.

(1) Title page and text of *Relation des fêtes données . . .*, Vienna 1773:

[*Relation des fêtes données . . ., 1773 – cont.*]

IV

nera à dire, que c'est dans l'emplacement le plus heureux qu'il est situé, au milieu d'une plaine immense, dont rien ne borne la vue qui se perd dans l'immensité de son étendue. Une campagne fertile & bien cultivée qui l'environne ; des bois, des villages suffisamment pour couper la vue de temps en temps, présentent de toute part des paysages très agréables. Un grand nombre de bâtimens, de corps de logis, sans compter l'enceinte principale du château, annoncent à l'étranger plustôt une petite Ville qu'une maison particuliere. Le goût, l'élégance des bâtimens, leur propreté satisfait également l'oeil du curieux & du connoisseur. La distribution intérieure en est si bien menagée qu'il y a dans l'enceinte du château plus de vingt logemens de maitre, mais si considérables & tous si bien appropriés, que chaque étranger y trouve les aisances & les commodités de sa propre maison. La beauté, la richesse des ameublemens, & tous les ornemens intérieurs des grands appartemens respirent la magnificence & le bon goût, la finesse dans le choix & la distribution d'une quantité de petits meubles, de la plus rare beauté, font admirer à chaque pas des chefs d'oeuvre en tous genres. Mais tout cède encore à la beauté des jardins , ce que la nature a de plus simple, ce que l'art a de plus recherché s'y font admirer tour à tour. Tantôt confondus, tantôt l'un par l'autre embéllis ; c'est un charme continuel. Leur étendue est immense. La symétrie. la mieux entendue, des berceaux, des cabinets des verdure, des jets d'eau, des statues en ornent les parterres & les bosquets; Un Parc immense peuplé de Dains & de Cerfs les allonge & les continue par trois allées à perte de vue; dont

V

dont le point de réunion est le milieu du grand salon d'enhaut. D'autres allées qui le traversent dans sa largeur font découvrir une quantité de petits bâtimens du meilleur goût & présentent des points de vue charmans. Une quantité prodigieuse d'autres petites allées, les unes régulieres, les autres absolument champêtres, mais toutes formées en berceau par le touffu des arbres, traversent en tous sens les massifs des charmilles. Des jets d'eau, des statues, des bancs de gazon, qui y sont distribués avec le plus grand art, ménagent à chaque pas le plaisir de la surprise & de la nouvauté. Enfin dans une étendue aussi considérable que celle qu'il contient, c'est à dire dans un terrein près d'une lieue de longueur sur autant de largeur, avec cette variété toujours rénaissante, il n'est rien de négligé; tout est tenu avec l'ordre le plus exact & la propriété la plus scrupuleuse. Qu'on se figure d'après cela l'ensemble merveilleux que cela peut produire. Voilà une légère esquisse des beautés qui sont à admirer à Esterhaz, mais dont chacune mériteroit une description toute entiére, pour mettre celui qui ne l'a pas vu, comme celui qui l'a vu, en état de juger que c'est à la fois le séjour le plus magnifique & le plus délicieux.

Les 31. Aoust, tous les Seigneurs & Dames nommés par S. M. I. au nombre de trente, se sont rendus à Esterhaz, ainsi que S. A. R. Mgr. le Prince Albert & S. A. R. Mme l'Archid. Marie qui sont arrivé au soir. Le lendemain, jour au quel la Majesté l'Impératrice & toute la Famille Impériale devoient honnorer cette Fête de leur présence, S. A. Mgrle Prince d'Esterhazy

A 3

VI

hazy eft allé, à leur rencontre jufqu'à Oedenbourg, a eu l'honneur de les y recevoir & de les accompagner jufqu'à Efterhaz où S. M. I. accompagnée de LL. AA. RR. Mgr l'Archiduce Maximilien, Me l'Archiduceffe Marie Anne, Me l'Archiducheffe Elifabeth eft arrivée à dix heures & demie du matin. S. M. I. a été recue par S. A. R. Mgr le Prince Albert, & S. A. R. Me l'Archiduceffe Marie; & après avoir été complimentée par la Nobleffe qui l'attendoit; elle s'eft retirée dans fon appartement, où elle a diné à fon petit couvert, & LL. AA. Rlt. dans le Salon d'enbas à une table de trente quatre couverts.

A quatre heures S. M. I. toute la Famille Implᵉ fuivis de toute la Nobleffe, font allé fe promener dans les jardins. S. M. I. a bien voulu en parcourir quelques endroits à pied; enfuitte fon caroffe fuivi de quinze voitures du Prince & précédé d'une caleche, que conduifoit S. A. Mgr le Prince, l'a conduit dans plufieures allées des jardins, où S. M. I. a admiré plufieurs des petits bâtimens qui y font diftribués, & furtout un Temple dédié au Soleil, l'autre à Diane, d'une très grande richeffe, & celui appellé l'hermitage qui dans la fimplicité eft un chef d'ouvre de gout & d'imagination. Ce grand nombre de voitures, une quantité d'Ecuiers, d'hommes à cheval qui les accompagnoient, une grande affluance d'étrangers de toute efpéce rendoient ce cortége très brillant. De là, S. M. I. eft defcendue à la Salle de l'Opéra, où les Muficiens du Prince ont eu l'honneur d'exécuter avec beaucoup de fuccès un Opéra Italien de la compofition du Sr Heyden Maitre de chapelle; dont les talens font con-

VII

connus' dans toute l'Europe par la compofition de plufieurs autres morceaux de Mufique, qui lui font autant d'honneur, qu'ils annoncent le bon gout du Prince; fa liberalité & fa générofité fixant près de fa perfonne des gens du premier mérite en tout genre, Pendant la durée de ce fpectacle, S. A. Mgr le Prince, pour donner à S. M. I le plaifir du bal mafqué, en fit illuminer la Salle, & y fit trouver une grande quantité de mafques. Incontinent après l'Opéra, S. A. Mgr le Prince l'y conduifit en lui faifant traverfer plufieurs petits appartemens qui y font attenants d'un gout très analogue & très varié; toute la Famille Impériale ainfi que toute la Nobleffe s'y rendirent auffi.

Rien ne peut égaler la magnificence, le bon gout & la richeffe qu'elle refpire. Perfonne ne peut même réfifter au mouvement de furprife & d'étonnement que caufe ce coup d'oeil éblouïfant, lorfqu'on la voit pour la premiere fois. Sa forme eft un quarré long devingt toife de longueur. Tout l'ornement intérieur eft à la chinoife rendu par les couleurs les plus vives; toutes les peintures ont cette touche enluminée qui fait un éffet, on ne peut plus éclatant à la lumière; onze grands luftres y font ufpendus par des guirlandes de fleurs, une double rangée de lampions regne debas en haut de chaque trumeau, des glaces placées dans le milieu de chacun & fur-tout une placée adroitement vis a vis la porte d'entrée répétent à l'infini l'éffet magique de plus de fix cent bougies qui l'éclairent. S. M. I. s'eft placée dans la tribune du fond élevée de quelques marches vis avis la porte d'entrée, au deffus de la quelle eft celle des Muficiens, tous habillés à la chinoife; en forte qu'elle pouvoit jouir à l'ai-

[*Relation des fêtes données . . ., 1773 – cont.*]

VIII

l'aise du spectacle varié, que présente une affluance de masques de tout espéce, au quel donnoit un nouveau prix une musique excellente. Aussi S M. I. en a-t-elle donné des marques de satisfaction, en honorant cette assemblée de sa présence pendant plus d'une heure & demie. Au sortir de là, elle a été reconduite au château où elle a soupé dans son appartement, au petit couvert; & LL. AA. RR. dans le Salon d'en bas à une table de trente quatre personnes. Après souper LL. AA. RR. masquées font retournées au bal, suivies de toute la Noblesse. Il a duré jusqu'à cinq heures & demie du matin; des rafraichissemens de toute espéce y ont été distribués avec le plus grand soin, & une abondance toujours égale la première comme la derniére heure.

Le lendemain, S. M. I. a dîné publiquement dans le grand salon d'enhaut. La table composée de trente cinq couverts, a été magnifiquement servie. Le fut tout qui régnoit le long étoit du meilleur goût; le delfein de la décoration représentoit trois morceaux de grande architecture très reguliére, & dont chaque piéce en détail étoit finie avec le dernier soin; la balustrade qui régnoit autour étoit surmontée de plusieurs médaillons portans les armes des différentes possessions de sa M.té. Le fruit a été composé de plusieurs morceaux de pastillage très artistement inventés entremélées d'un grand nombre de cristaux très bien ornés. Pendant le diner, plusieurs musiciens du Prince, chacun excellent dans son genre, ont eu l'honneur d'être entendus de S. M. I. & d'en mériter des applaudissemens. Mais ce qui a paru le plus intéressant,

IX

fant, a été cette multitude d'étrangers de tout rang, de toute espéce & de gens de la campagne accourus de toute part pour jouir du bonheur de voir leur Auguste Souveraine & qui n'en négligeoient aucune occasion. S. M. I. pour répondre à cet empressement de leur part, a bien voulu permettre qu'ils traversassent la Salle pednant le diner. Leur empressement, l'avidité de leurs regards à la démêler dans le nombre des convives; le murmure des éloges que chacun lui prodiguoit à la façon; leur façon d'admirer qui paroit si stupide, mais qui est si éloquente peignoit au naturel cette vérité de sentimens dont ils venoient lui offrir le pure hommage.

A Quatre heures S. M. I. toute la Famille Imple & toute la Noblesse font allé à la promenade dans le Parc, dans le même ordre que la veille.

Au retour de la promenade, S, M.I. est descendue à la Salle des Marionnettes. A ce mot de Marionnettes, on n'imagineroit jamais que ce dur être quelque chose digne d'attention & de curiosité; aussi est-on à peine revenu de la surprise qu'a causé généralement cette espéce de spectacle dans le goût qu'il est exécuté à Esterhaz. La Salle pour être assortie à ce genre de nouvauté, est aussi du goût le plus rare & le plus exquis. Tout l'intérieur est garni, de droite & de gauche, de grottes en rocaille & en coquillages, dans le fond de chacune des quelles il y a des paysages à fresque très bien apropriés, & dans d'autres des petits jets d'eau qui font un murmure agréable. Toute cette Rocaille est semée de poudre

B

X

dre brillante, qui fait un effet admirable à la clarté de plusieurs lustres qui l'éclairent. Les Comédiens & les Muficiens du Prince ont exécuté un Opéra allemand, intitulé Philémon & Baucis, également de la compofition du Sr Heyden Maitre de chapelle, dout la belle mufique lui a mérité les applaudiffemens des connoiffeurs. La piéce même faite exprès pour le fujet, y étoit très bien adaptée & a été rendue très naturellement. Mais ce qui paroit plus digne encore d'admiration, c'eft, la beauté, la richeffe & le fini des décorations. Les régles de la proportion & de la perfpective y font fi bien obfervées, qu'elles ne laiffent échaper aucunes des beautés de l'enfemble. A l'ouverture du rideau, elles repréfentérent l'Olympe & les Dieux qui y étoient affemblés, & fucceffivement une-nuit, un orage, une forêt, une campagne, un Temple, l'intérieur du Palais le mieux orné ; & enfin une vue des jardins & du Parc d'Efterhaz, mais dans le point de vue le plus riche & le plus naturel : tous ces changemens exécutés avec tant d'exactitude, de juftelfe, de précifion, & de célérité, que la furprife, l'étonnement des fpectateurs & leurs nouvaux applaudiffemens marquoient feuls qu'on s'en étoit apperçu. Une des circonftances de ce fpectacle qu'il ne faut pas ométtre ; eft que lorfque la décoration repréfentoit un Temple ; il parut dans la nuée un trophé environné de plufieurs rayons de gloire, fur les quels étoient foutenues par la Juftice, la Prudence & la douceur, les armes de la maifon d'Autriche, couronnées par la Renommée. A cet afpect toutes les figures de Marionnettes habillées à la hongroife le proiffé-nérent & changérent en choeur les louanges de leurs Au-

XI

Auguftes Souverains, S. M. I. a daigné donner des applaudiffemens à ce fpectacle, elle a paru en être extrêmement fatisfaite, & partager la furprife générale qu'il avoit caufé. Au fortir de là, S. M. I. a foupé publiquement dans le Sallon d'enbas avec toute la Cour. Après fouper, elle a été conduite à une des enceintes du Parc, où fe devoit tirer un feu d'artifice de la compofition du Sr Rabel artificier du Prince. Une double rangée de lenternes conduifoit jufqu'à une tribune placée vis à vis la décoration principale. S. M. I. & toute la Cour placée dans cette tribune, S. A. Mgr le Prince eut l'honneur de lui préfenter l'étoupille. S. M. I. mit le feu à un cordon, qui parvenu très rapidement à l'artifice en fit partir un bouquet de trois cent fufées, & de là, fe communiqua à une piéce de très bon goût, illuminée en feu bleu de ciel, repréfentant à l'artifice les armes de Hongrie acolées de deux aigles éployées, & furmontées de ces trois lettres. V. M. T. Pendant qu'on admiroit cette piéce qui a duré allés long tems, une quantité prodigieufe de fufées tirées de derriére l'artifice, les unes garnies de ferpentaux, les autres d'étoiles, venoient retomber en martinet de chaque côté de cette piéce; d'autres fufées tirées auffi de derriére l'artifice, mais d'une compofition abfolument nouvelle, & montantes prodigieufement haut, venoient retomber jufque fur elles mêmes en pluie d'or en très grand volume, & fe perdant derriére les branches d'arbre, à travers les quelles on les appercevoit encore, faifoient un effet & une nuance difficile à décrire. On mit enfuite le feu à plufieurs autres piéces avancés toutes d'une très belle compofition ; une entre autres a été remarquable

B 2

194

XII

ble par l'activité de son feu & les changemens confi-dérables qu'elle a fournis. Enfin est venu l'illumina-tion de toute la décoration, qui représentoit la façade d'un Palais ornée de trois portiques surmontée d'une tour dans le milieu & de plusieurs autres ornemens d'architecture : une gerbe de feu sous chacun des Portiques représentoient une très belle cascade. Pen-dant la durée de cette illumination, un feu de rem-part de droite & de gauche très bien servi, une quan-tité étonnante de bombes, de pots à feu, de bou-quets de fusées, de mortiers fourérains, & d'autres piéces à grand bruit de guerre ont terminé ce spe-ctacle à l'applaudissement de S. M. I. & de tous les Spe-ctateurs : emportant chacun le regret de n'avoir point eu le tems d'admirer chaque piéce en particulier, tant elles étoient dignes de l'être, par leur exactitu-de & leurs précision. De là, S. M. I. a été conduite à l'Illumination que S. A. Mgr le Prince avoit fait préparer dans une autre enceinte du Parc. La forme de cette enceinte est un oval, mais d'une très gran-de étendue, qui représente très bien celle d'un cir-que, des portiques en treillage surmontés de leurs chapitaux & accompagnés de leurs entablemens fer-ment cette enceinte, au milieu de la quelle est une tribune elevée en colonade orné de guirlandes de fleurs & destinée à voir dans son vrai point l'effet de l'illu-mination. Il seroit difficile de décrire le coup d'oeil éblouissant qu'elle présente. Une double rangée de lampions suivoit l'ordre du dessein & de l'architectu-re avec la plus grande exactitude; tous les portiques étoient surmontés de morceaux de peinture représen-tans des Gloires, des Renommées & d'autres trophés re-

XIII

relatifs, tous aperçus au travers d'une grande quan-tité de lampions qui les environnoient ; d'autres ta-bleaux enluminés & peints d'après des sujets de Van-deik placés dans les encadremens & illuminés par dér-riere offroient le spectacle d'un genre d'illumination inconnu jusqu'à présent; des guirlandes de fleurs agra-phées au haut de la corniche, retroussées à mie-pente, & soutenues en bas par des petits cupidons, éclai-rées par une double rangée de lampions, en feu verd, faisoient une nuance & une variété ravissante. Enfin quon se figure que dans une enceinte qui peut con-tenir plus de huit mille personnes, les lampions étoient tellement multipliés qu'ils n'étoient pas éloignés les uns des autres d'un demi pied, ensorte que chaque losange de treillage, qui a tout au plus cette mesure en quarré en portoit un à chacun de ses angles, ce qui faisoit monter leur nombre à plus de vingt mille. S. M. I. & toute la Cour placée dans la Tribune, des jeunes Paysans, des jeunes Paysannes des Villages des environs, au nombre de plus de mille, conduits par leurs Drapeaux, & dansans au son de leurs in-strumens, à la mode du pays, débuquerent en même temps de dessous les voutes des Portiques. Leurs cris de joie, leurs acclamations les avoient dévancés; ils les redoublerent en criant mille fois : *Vive Marie Therese, & toute la Famille Imperiale*, & chacun à la place qui lui étoit destinée se mit à danser : ensorte qu'on pouvoit jouir à la fois du spectacle de la Fé-te la plus champêtre, & de celui qu'offre tout ce que l'art a de plus recherché.

Voila sans douté de quoi satisfaire l'oeil du simple spectateur, & du connoisseur ; mais quel tableau in-té-

XV

sa joie & son allegresse en cette occasion. Plusieurs arcs de triomphe ornoient les rues par les quelles S. M.I. devoit passer; des inscriptions, des emblêmes manifestoient par tout la joie publique, & consacroient cette heureuse époque. Le Magistrat eut l'honneur de la recevoir aux portes de la Ville, & de la complimenter, & après lui avoir offert six corbeilles des plus beaux fruits de la saison, la conduisit jusqu'à l'Hôtel du Prince, au travers les cris & les acclamations d'une foule innombrable qui bordoit la haye de droite & de gauche, sur son passage. Après y avoir dîné, & donné à tous ces fidels Cytoiens des témoignages de bonté, elle en est partie à quatre heures & demie pour son château de Schönbrun, où accompagnée de S. A. Mgr le Prince elle est arrivée le même jour.

Il faudroit pour terminer la relation de cette Fête, la plus brillante qu'on puisse voir, pour mettre celui qui ne l'a pas vu en état de juger, & lui en donner une idée complette, entrer dans le mérite d'une quantité de gens du premier talent attachés au Prince par les bienfaits, executans sous les yeux, & par les ordres des chefs d'oevre de gout en tout genre; il faudroit ne pas omettre celui essentiel d'un grand nombre d'officiers, dont l'intelligence & les soins parent d'un nouveau lustre la magnificence & la libéralité du Maître; il faudroit rendre sensible l'effet de tous ces ressorts mis en oeuvre à propos pour opérer en même tems; mais dans quel détail on puisse entrer il fera toujours difficil de rendre les justes sentimens d'admiration de ceux qui en ont été les temoins en cette occasion & en plus d'une autre.

XIV

téressant ne présente pas cette assurance de fidels sujets, sur les quels regne par les bienfaits la première Souveraine du monde, s'empressans sur son passage & témoignans cette vive allegresse qu'enfante la reconnoissance, & qui est l'ouvrage de ce sentiment délicieux que n'oint jamais produit le respect ou la crainte: un Prince le premier Seigneur de son Royaume, un Prince dont une suite d'ancêtres inviolablement attachés à l'Auguste Maison d'Autriche assure la fidélité, offrant à Sa Souveraine pendant les douceurs d'une paix tranquille le tribut des richesses, dont le rang, & la naissance l'ont rendu heritier, & d'éployant toute la magnificence pour rendre d'autant plus éclatant le bonheur de la posséder. De quel prix ne doit pas être pour ce Seigneur cette marque publique de bien veillance aussi bien que les témoignages distingués de satisfaction & de reconnoissance, qu'il a reçu en cette occasion? qu'il est flateur de voir ainsi agréer l'hommage de son amour & de son respect! mais aussi qu'heureux font les Princes qui peuvent compter dans leur Empire autant de sujets empressés à saisir toutes les occasions de donner des preuves d'attachement & de zéle; toujours préts à offrir l'hommage de leur fortune & celui de leur sang pour étendre la glorie d'un regne qui fait l'admiration de toute l'Europe!

S. M.I. après avoir comblé les officiers & toute la maison du Prince de présens, & de bienfaits, en est partie avec toute la Famille Impériale le lendemain à neuf heures & demie du matin; & S. A. Mgr le Prince les a accompagné jusqu'à Oedenbourg. Cette Ville, qui depuis plusieurs siecles n'avoit eu le bonheur de voir ses souverains, s'est éforcée de montrer
la

The *Preßburger Zeitung* (No. 73, 11 September 1773) reports:

On the 31st of last month, Their Royal Highnesses the Archduchess [Maria] Christina and her husband Duke Albert betook themselves to Esterház to be present at the visit of the Imperial and Royal Court. After strolling in the princely gardens, Their Highnesses attended a German comedy [by Pauersbach] entitled *Die Zwo Königinnen*. On Sept. 1st, Her Imperial and Royal Apostolic Majesty arrived at Eszterház after a five-hour journey from Vienna, accompanied by the Archduchesses Marianna and Elisabeth, and by the Archduke Maximilian. His Serene Princely Highness arranged various entertainments for the diversion of his Royal guests. After luncheon, Her Majesty went driving in the gardens, the Archduke and Archduchesses promenading on foot beside the carriage. Then the marionette operetta *Philemon und Baucis* or *Jupiters Reise auf die Erde* was performed in the new theatre. This was followed by a festive masked ball. The forenoon of the 2nd was spent strolling in the castle park, and after lunch the little operetta was presented again. The stage showed a Phrygian village, with Philemon's cottage, and a view of fields, vineyards and a landscape. The curtain rose on a fearful thunderstorm; scattered peasants came from all directions, among them Philemon and Baucis, and they it was who opened the operetta. The peasants and an old couple went off, and Jupiter and Mercury entered. The stage then showed Philemon's cottage with two funeral urns which, at a word from Jupiter, were transformed into rose-arbours, where sat Aretus and Narcissa. With a roll of thunder, Jupiter and Mercury then appeared on a shining cloud. Philemon's cottage turned into a magnificent temple, with a statue of Jupiter in the centre. The clothing of Philemon and Baucis took on the appearance of priests' vestments, and several priests and priestesses entered. Then a chorus of neighbours crowded onto the stage, but shrank back in fear of the thunder. Jupiter's statue disappeared, and in its place stood the coat-of-arms of the House of Habsburg, with Glory, Clemency, Justice and Valour grouped about it. Fame came flying in, and crowned the coat-of-arms with a wreath. Divine Providence protected it with a shield, and Time embraced it. The priests of Jupiter disappeared. The Hungarian Nation approached, accompanied by Love of the Fatherland, by Obedience, Devotion and Fidelity, and fell to its knees in veneration of the Imperial arms. Jupiter's temple disappeared, and the stage showed the central portion of the illuminated gardens at Eszterház. Here the neighbours changed into Hungarians too, joining in the final chorus, during which Happiness clasped the Imperial arms with one hand, and with the other showered Plenty upon the Nation from her cornucopia. After this, the rear of the new theatre began to sink before all eyes, and in its stead the illustrious audience saw the splendid illumination in the princely garden, and the fireworks began.

On the 3rd, Her I. R. Apostolic Majesty and retinue returned via Oedenburg to Vienna, while Their Royal Highnesses the Archduchess and the Duke her husband went on to Schloßhof.

[Translation by Eugene Hartzell in *HJB* VIII, 269f.; German in *HJB* VIII, 167f.]

In the *Wiener Diarium* (No. 71, Saturday, 4 September 1773), we read:

Vienna, 4 September: On Wednesday the 1st inst., Her Majesty our ever gracious Empress, together with the Archduke Maximilian and the Archduchesses Maria Anna and Elisabeth, Royal Highnesses, travelled from Schönbrunn to Esterhaz, there to honour with their all highest and highest presences the festivities arranged by the Prince of Esterhazy. On the same day Their Royal Highness the Archduchess Christina and her husband, the Duke Albert of Sachsenteschen [*sic*] also arrived.

Her I. R. Apostolic Majesty also deigned to stay on the domains together with the highest presences until Thursday, the 2nd inst. On the 3rd, however, they partook of luncheon at the princely house in Oedenburg, and from there returned to Schönbrunn. This newspaper will soon publish an account of the festivities at Esterhaz that occurred during the all highest presence of Her Majesty. [This report never appeared.]

From Griesinger's biography, we learned that on this occasion Haydn shot three hazel-hens which the Empress ate. From Dies we hear of another pleasant story. When Haydn had been a choirboy at St Stephen's Cathedral, the boys went to sing during Whitsuntide at Schönbrunn, then in the process of construction and surrounded by scaffolding. The boys climbed the scaffolding and made a racket. The Empress ordered them off and threatened them with a thrashing [*Schilling*, also a coin] if they were found up there again. The next day Haydn climbed the scaffolding, was caught and thrashed.

When ... the Empress came once to Esterhaz, Haydn presented himself before her and most humbly thanked her for the reward he had received. He had to tell the whole story, which caused much merriment. [Dies, 30]

In the *Relation*, we have seen that Haydn and the musicians, dressed in Chinese costumes, gave 'une musique excellente', and that the Empress stayed there an hour-and-a-half. It was presumably on this occasion that Prince Nicolaus introduced his *Capellmeister* to their sovereign. It was always said that Haydn wrote, and conducted, Symphony No. 48 for this occasion which has come down to us as the 'Maria Theresia'. There is, in fact, an old source in Prague with the name 'Santae Teresiae / In C / Sinfonia',[1] but there is an authentic source by Joseph Elssler, Sen., in Slovakia with the pencilled date 1769 on the cover. Perhaps the Empress heard the work on another occasion:[2]

Once when a *Landtag* was held at Pressburg, Prince Nikolaus took his whole *Kapelle* with him. There were parties with the Empress Maria Theresia present.

At one such gathering Haydn conducted a concert (with the violin, as usual) in which four aristocratic amateurs also played. The Empress jokingly said that it would be amusing to see what would happen to the music if the professionals suddenly left the dilettantes to themselves.

Haydn had a sharp ear, intercepted in mid-air the Empress's words and at once arranged with Tomasini ... that as soon as he saw Haydn leave he should break the E-string of his violin and not worry about the consequences.

The Symphony began. At the point of greatest complexity Haydn, unobserved, broke his own E-string. Unfortunately, however, the amateur playing beside him at once offered his own violin. Haydn found a suitable excuse for not taking the violin: he held a handkerchief to his nose, murmured 'Nosebleed!' and left. Tomasini broke his E-string and played his part to perfection. The Symphony began to tilt, staggered, stumbled and after a few bars collapsed.

Haydn, with his ready wit, thus provided the Empress and the whole company with a good laugh. [Dies, 66]

Perhaps that otherwise unrecorded occasion was the beginning of Symphony No. 48's fame. Perhaps, too, Haydn took the first two movements of the Overture to the Prologue to *Philemon* (the music is, except for one orchestral interlude, otherwise lost),

1 Landon *SYM*, 17. Elssler copy: Philharmonia Complete Haydn Symphonies (vol. IV).
2 See also the *fête* at Kittsee in July 1770, *supra*, p. 164.

added the Minuet and Finale, thus creating Symphony No. 50, and played this really 'new' work at the Chinese Pavilion or 'Bagatelle'.

The libretto of *L'infedeltà delusa*, which was the Italian opera given for the Empress on 31 August – in the *PZ* the information is slightly confused here – was reprinted by Joseph Siess in Oedenburg and bound by Mathias Fischer in the following quantities: four in damask silk, fifty in gold brocade paper and ninety 'à l'ordinaire'. The damask silk copies were for the Empress and the Archduke and -duchesses. The bills read:

List. What the undersigned did in the way of printing work for the princely Castle Eszterház, and which was delivered, *viz.*:

An Opera Libretto in 8^{vo,} 3 *Bögen* in length with 200 copies together with the paper at 6 Rfl. makes 18 Fl.

Item the same Opera Libretto was reprinted in 153 copies, the *Bogen* at 5 Rfl. 30 xr.: 16 Fl. 30 xr.

Summa: 34 Fl. 30 xr.

Oedenburg, 14 Sept. 1773.   Johann Joseph Siess, Printer.

[A.M. XI, 610b, Esterházy Archives, Budapest. Valkó II, 559]

The following was prepared for His Princely Highness:
A^{o,} 1773 the 23rd July in Oedenburg.

	F.	xr.
6 Opera Libretti in taffeta at 36 xr.	3	36
50 dto in gold brocade paper at 7xr.	5	50
146 all. ordinaire at 2 xr.	4	52
The 27th Aug. ditto in taffeta	3	36
4 dto in damask	4	
50 in gold brocade paper	5	50
90 all'ordinaire dto at 2 xr.	3	
Summa.........	30 Fl. 44 xr.	

Oedenburg, 10th Dec. 1773   Mathias Fischer, bookbinder

Has been correctly paid to me ... with seven and twenty Guld. ['30 fl. 44 xr.' removed]

[Address;] A Monsieur Monsieur de Haydn Maitre de Capelle A son Altesse le Prince de Esterház.

[A.M. XI, 610c., Esterházy Archives, Budapest. Valkó II, 559]

The libretto for *Philemon und Baucis* was printed in Vienna by Ghelen, but we have no details as to the number of copies printed, etc.

Philemon und Baucis. / Oder / Jupiters Reise / auf die Erde. / Bey Gelegenheit / der höchsterfreulichen Gegenwart / Allerhöchst / Ihro k. k. apostol. Majestät / und / Allerhöchst dero allerdurchlauchtigsten / Erzhauses. / In einer Marionetten Operette zum erstenmale / zu Esterház / auf der fürstlichen Marionetten Bühne / im Jahre 1773. aufgeführt. / Wien, mit von Ghelenschen Schriften.

[Wiener Stadtbibliothek 668/V; another copy A 13 605; another Österreichische
                              Nationalbibliothek, 435 176 B]

Prince Nicolaus did not forget to reward his *Capelle* for their efforts:

Commission

According to which our Chief Cashier is to pay against receipt, and to enter into the books, those five who were in the last opera each ten, but Capell Meister Haÿdn thirty, and the painter Grundemann also thirty ducats.

Eszterhaz, 22 Sept. 1773.   Nicolaus Fürst Esterhazy.

Receipt

According to which we the undersigned, following the princely Comission's *Discretion* [gift] given to us, have received, each one of us, the sum to which he or she is entitled, and have been paid this sum correctly and in cash by *H*[*errn*] Chief Cashier Züsser, for which we acknowledge due receipt. [There follows the list and signatures. Generalcassa 1773, Rubr. V. Nr. 41. Esterházy Archives, Eisenstadt. *HJB* IV, 48 *in extenso*]

We may pass over another bill from Stadlmann[1] and proceed to a letter from *Regent* Rahier on the subject of Eleonora Jäger. From it we learn the highly interesting fact that, instead of *L'infedeltà delusa*, Haydn at first intended to mount a new version of his 1763 *Acide*, to which purpose he actually began composing some new numbers; these will be discussed in the next chapter.

Report and Opinion on the following Circumstance

The singer Eleonora Jäger reports that she had a verbal order from Your Highness himself and thereafter a written confirmation from *Kapellmeister* Haiden [*sic*] to come to Eszterhaz because of the Opera *Acide* and also for another Opera; that because of the living expenses to and fro and also the necessary clothing [*Aufbutz* = *Aufputz*] she spent three ducats; that the Opera *Acide* was not given but another Opera, for which she was the prompter when it was given on St Anne's Day [26 July] and also when it was given in the all highest presence of Her I.R. Apostol. Majesty, and that prompting is much more difficult than performing. At the marionette piece she had a part to sing. That finally all the performers [*Actores*] were given extra fees by Your Highness, but she, who is of them the poorest and most needy, was forgotten.

Therefore her most humble and obedient request is that she receive the above-listed expenses, which the others also regularly receive, and in the future, considering that the times are dear and in view of her 20 years of service, and that of all of them she has the most disadvantageous contract, she would like an annual increase out of grace and favour. She has a poor old father and a poor sister to whom she, out of her childhood love, is wont to give a little money every year, so that of her quarterly salary of 25 Fl., after subtracting her own living expenses, and the little she gives her father and sister, there hardly remain a few Kreutzer [*sic*]; and from that she is incapable of purchasing even the most urgent necessities. I am of the humble opinion, therefore, that her most obedient request would certainly be worthy of your attention, and that apart from recompensing her expenses, she should in grace receive an annual increase of 40 or 50 Gulden. . . .

Eisenstadt, 7th Oct. 1773.

[A.M. III, 196, Esterházy Archives, Budapest; Valkó II, 566]

Hochfl. Resolution ddo. Eszterház, 9th October 1773, according to which the Choir Singer Eleonora Jäger is this time to be recompensed for the expenses enumerated in her *Supplique* in connection with the Opera and moreover an increase in salary of 40 fl. is to be given to her and registered.

[Hungarian National Archives, Esterházy Archives, Fasc. 2488 Nr. 915; Valkó II, 566]

Haydn himself incurred vast expenses in gathering material and persons for this lavish *Fest*, and on 14 November he submitted his list of expenses (138 fl. 32 kr.) to Rahier, who examined them and forwarded the list to the Prince, perhaps because there was a considerable sum involved. Prince Nicolaus ordered his Chief Cashier to

---

1 Vienna, 30 Sept. for violin mutes, strings and keyboard strings [this is a new side of S's activity]. A.M. XII, 674; Valkó II, 563.

deal with the matter.[1] And still the bills had no end. On 30 November Haydn submitted yet another bill in his own hand:

> What I spent for H. Princely Highness, *viz.*:
> 1. The bass singer from Oedenburg for the marionette opera, for five days, each day 3 Fl. as agreed, makes 15 Fl. r.
> 2. The alto singer Griessler from Eisenstadt for 8 days, each day one Gulden, makes 8 Fl.
> 3. Item for the tenor Johann Haydn for 8 days 8 Fl.
> 4. The Hairdresser for both operas 7 Fl. 40 xr.
> 5. The harp player Krumpholtz *Discretion* [gift] 4 Cremnitz ducats makes 17 Fl. 12 xr. Summa: 55 Rfl. 52 xr.
>
> The above 55 Rfl. 52 xr. have been paid to me correctly and in cash from the Eisenstadt General Cassa by the hand of Chief Cashier Joseph Züsser.
> Eisenstadt, 30th Nov. 1773.   Josephus Haydn mpria.
> [A. M., XI, 610a, Esterházy Archives, Budapest; Valkó II, 559]

Countess von Szluha in Oedenburg offered Prince Nicolaus a part of her household effects, including a library, porcelain service, a collection of weapons, paintings, musical instruments, etc. In a long letter from Rahier to Esterházy of 1 December we learn that 'the late Bunon was able [before his death] to examine the catalogue of the books' but found them of no interest for the princely library. (Was 'Bunon' really the same man as Le Bon or Bon?) Rahier thought Haydn ought to be called in to examine the musical instruments. Haydn did just that and made a detailed list with a proposed value of 164 gulden, and on 11 December Rahier reports that 'KapellMeister Hayden' thought the instruments 'could all be used'. The Countess then tried to raise the price and on 28 January 1774, Prince Nicolaus, in a towering (and justified) rage, wrote to Rahier: 'Tell the *Frauen Gräfin* that I take it as no less than an affront, since I only instituted the purchase to please her, and that I have no need of these things whatever . . . and apart from that you are not to proceed any further in this matter . . .'.[2]

On 25 August, Franz Novotni, princely organist at Eisenstadt, died. On 2 December, Prince Nicolaus wrote to Rahier to find another organist who would not be too expensive. He enclosed two petitions and said that Haydn should be called in to judge the men involved. One was Simon Kölbel from Vienna, the other was the Schoolmaster of Forchtenstein, Johann Georg Fuchs. Haydn found the first not good enough and the second worse yet. Thereupon the question of price arose: Kölbel told Haydn that he (Kölbel) earned forty or more gulden per month in Vienna and Rahier added that 'it will be difficult to get one under 400 to 500 f'. Haydn then made an interesting proposition: he suggested that the Eisenstadt Castle Schoolmaster (also tenor) Joseph Dietzl play organ in the summers and Haydn in the winters, and that they so divide the salary that Haydn got payment in kind (*Naturalien*) and Dietzl the cash. The Prince agreed to this idea, and Haydn now became, apart from Rahier and the physician in ordinary, the highest paid employee of the court.[3]

---

1 Rahier's letter: Eisenstadt 9 Nov.; Esterházy's ratification: Vienna, 14 Nov. Hungarian National Archives, Esterházy Archives, Fasc. 1534, pag. 101. Valkó II, 560.

2 The documents of this amusing affair are in the Hungarian National Archives, Est. Arch. Fasc. 1534, pp. 247f., 239–44, 234, 237, 280, 516. Valkó II, 567–70, including the complete list Haydn drew up.

3 J. Harich in *HJB* 16ff. (32f.), with all the supporting documents (pp. 72ff.) which make very interesting reading but which have been reluctantly omitted for lack of space.

Of the bills in the Esterházy Archives for this period, the contents of most may be summarized briefly.[1]

Chronicle 1774

CARL WAHR WAS RE-ENGAGED for the usual season at Eszterháza, and as before spent the winter in Pressburg. The *Preßburger Zeitung* reports on Wahr's performance of *Hamlet* in its issue of 8 January, and we shall see that in the season of 1774–5 many more Shakespeare plays were taken into Wahr's repertoire.

In the following documents, we can see how the musicians were obliged to apply for permission to absent themselves even for a few days, and also Esterházy's insistence on a 'chain of command' which in its pyramid shape required Haydn and not *Regent* Rahier to be the go-between for the musicians:

[Rahier to Prince Nicolaus Esterházy]
P. S. Fribert [*sic*] and she [Frau F.] most respectfully request permission of Your Highness to go to Vienna for 8 or 10 days, because their apartment has been completely shaken up by the recent earthquake and is sagging; it has to be repaired, and also there are other necessities for them to take care of there. . . . P. L. Rahier.
Eisenstadt, 20th January 1774.
[Esterházy's endorsement:] Permission granted for 10 days and no longer, and they are to be reminded that all such applications are to be forwarded to me by no one except Haydn.
Vienna, 28th January 1774.   Nicolaus Fürst Esterhazy.
[Hungarian National Archives, Esterházy Archives, Fasc. 1534, p. 494]

[Rahier to Prince Nicolaus Esterházy]
. . . The musician Lovigi [Luigi Tomasini] most respectfully requests permission of Your Highness to go to Vienna for three or four days to have his musical instruments repaired there, and to take care of some other necessities. . . . P. L. Rahier.
[Esterházy's endorsement:] Permission granted for 4 days, and he is to be reminded that in the future he is to approach me through Haydn.
Vienna, 28th January 1774.   Nicolaus Fürst Esterhazy.
[Hungarian National Archives, Esterházy Archives, Fasc. 1534, p. 457; both documents Valkó II, 570]

Haydn had composed a series of six piano (harpsichord) Sonatas in the previous year, and now had these works (dedicated to his Prince) printed by Joseph Kurzböck (Kurzbeck) in Vienna; the new edition was announced on 26 February in the *Wiener Diarium*, The title page reads:

Sei / Sonate / da / Clavi-Cembalo / che / a sua altezza serenissima / del / sacro romano impero / principe / Nicolo Esterhazy di Galantha / &c. &c. / D.D.D. /

---

1 (1) Caspar Mayer, hairdresser, undated (1773): 'For M[ad.] Dichtler 8 locks [attached to wig] at 15 xr.: 2 Guld . . . M[ons.] Friberth 6 locks . . . A large *Theatro Peruque*, dressed, 10 xr. A.M. XI, 610; Valkó II, 560. (2) Three bills by Rockobauer of 10, 22 and 31 Dec. for reeds. A.M. XII, 675, 676, 679; Valkó II, 564. (3) Adamus Schwarzinger's bill, Eisenstadt, 17 Dec. Haydn rec'd. for musical covers 3 books of tall folio paper at 57 xr. = 2 Fl. 51 xr.' These 'Decken' (covers) were the outside 'wrappers' for manuscript parts and needed to be of heavy and durable paper. (4) The nine gulden 'Rorate' money that Haydn received on 31 Dec. A.M. XII, 678; Valkó II, 564. (5) Dietzl's annual bill for strings, etc. from 1 Jan. through the end of Dec. A.M. XII, 677; Valkó II, 564. All these bills countersigned by Haydn.

L'autore / Giuseppe Haydn / Maestro di Capella della pref. A. S. Ser. / in Vienna, presso Giuseppe Kurzböck Stampatore Orient. di S. M. Imp. R. A. 1774.[1]

These works are the first by Haydn that were printed in Vienna, and the first known authentic edition of any works by the composer; they are Nos. 36–41 of the *Wiener Urtext-Ausgabe* and XVI:21–26 in Hoboken. They are an important milestone in Haydn's career; works such as the great C minor piano Sonata (No. 33; XVI:20) may have been of considerably more importance, but they were disseminated only in manuscript.

Esterházy had the idea that not all the musicians were actually present at Eisenstadt; he therefore wrote to Rahier as follows:

> Most respected Herr v. Rahier!
> Order the *Capellmeister* to come to you at once, and also all the musicians so that you yourself may see, and at once report to me, which of them is absent from Eisenstadt and for how long. . . .
> Vienna, 15th March 1774.   Nicolaus Fürst Esterhazy.
>   [A.M. XX, 1370, Esterházy Archives, Budapest; Valkó II, 572]

Rahier reported (A.M. XX, 1371; Valkó II, 573) *inter alia* that Haydn had gone to Pressburg on Sunday, and that other musicians were, as the Prince has suspected, absent without leave.

> [Prince Nicolaus Esterházy to *Regent* P. L. Rahier]
> . . . I have received promptly the *specification* of the musicians, from which I see that Cristien Spech[t], Xavier Marteau, Carl Corus and Joseph Oliva are absent. You must see that neither *Capel Meister* Heyden [*sic*] nor any of the others notice anything, and you must act as if nothing had happened. However, you must find out how long each of those four above-mentioned musicians has been absent and add up the days, work that out against their salaries, and tell the Chief Cashier to subtract the necessary amount from their monthly or quarterly salaries.
> To make sure, however, this edict must be published in my name right away, so that they do not take an advance on their salaries. . . .
> Vienna, 16th March 1774.
>   [A.M. XX, 1372, Esterházy Archives, Budapest; Valkó II, 573]

The case of Joseph Oliva seems to have cleared itself up at once, for in the letter that Haydn wrote, his name is not even mentioned:

> [To Prince Nicolaus Esterházy. *German*]
>   [*c.* 18th March 1774]
> MOST SERENE AND NOBLE PRINCE OF THE HOLY ROMAN EMPIRE,
> GRACIOUS PRINCE AND LORD!
> Inasmuch as Your Serene Highness has ordered a month's salary to be docked from the musicians Marteau, Specht, and Chorus, I humbly beg to remind Your Serene Highness graciously to remember how in Vienna recently, I myself asked and kindly received permission of Your Highness for Marteau to absent himself for a few days. The reason why he remained a little longer is that he copied some new concerti there, and also had to have his violoncello repaired. Concerning Chorus, there was not enough time to inform Your Highness in advance of the fact that he had the chance to go there [to Vienna] with Dr Bertrand (who

---

1 The dated autographs of Nos. 36–38 (XVI: 21–23) are in incomplete autograph in the Conservatoire, Paris; but the title page reads 'Sei Sonate per Cembalo In Nomine Domini di me giuseppe Haydn 773'. Copy of the print: Nationalbibliothek, Vienna. Larsen (*HUB* 103) suggests that this is the first edition that was ever made by Haydn himself, in the sense that it is obviously an authentic print of which Haydn supplied the printer's copy and the dedication. He probably sold Kurzböck the rights for a flat fee.

prescribed a change of air for him on account of his constant ill health) for nothing, at no cost; and it fell to me to give him permission to go. As far as Specht goes, it so happened that his mother-in-law suddenly fell ill in Neustat. I allowed him to go there just during the three days when he would not miss any of the church services. For this reason I submit my humble and obedient petition to Your Serene Highness, to refrain from insisting on this financial punishment; we ask for such a mark of graciousness in the most profound submissiveness.

Your Serene Highness'

humble and obedient servant,

Haydn.

[CCLN, 17f.]

We may pass over, with brief reference, the bills of this period in the Esterházy Archives[1] and continue with the theatrical season at Eszterháza. As noted above, Shakespeare's plays assumed an ever more important role in Wahr's plans. Apart from *Hamlet* and *Macbeth*, there was a new translation of *King Lear* by Christoph Seipp, a member of the Troupe. His version was attacked by Christoph Martin Wieland in the *Teutscher Merkur* (3. *Vierteljahr,* 1775) for its liberties *vis-à-vis* the original English text, and Seipp defended himself *inter alia* by saying that his version had been appreciated by Prince Esterházy.[2]

It so happens that we have incidental music to *King Lear* which used to be attributed to Haydn. In a MS. at Schwerin the (probably correct) name of 'G. W. Stegmann' is listed. In another copy, at the Conservatorio in Florence, there is no name listed at all. It is probable that this was the music used by Haydn for the Wahr production at Eszterháza, and there are two sources connecting the work with Haydn: (1) an interesting MS. score by Johann Elssler, without the name of a composer, written on small sized paper known as 'kleines Post-Papier' in the Gesellschaft der Musikfreunde (Vienna); (2) a set of MS. parts, also without composer, in the Esterházy Archives at Budapest. Perhaps Haydn reorchestrated the work, because there are several versions of the score.[3] The music is in part rather dramatic and a useful specimen of the kind of *Bühnenmusik* that Haydn used for the incidental music to Wahr's Shakespeare productions. Wahr gave *Othello* at Pressburg in November 1774 (reviewed in the *PZ* on 19 November) and *Macbeth* a month later, so that we may be sure he gave both of them the previous Summer at Eszterháza. Despite Seipp's 'liberties', the Wahr translations were far more accurate than the usual German Shakespeare productions of the period. In the Schröder translation of *Othello*, Desdemona is not strangled, while in Wahr's she is killed, something that the Pressburg audiences thought very impressive (*PZ*, 23 November 1774); Seipp himself played Iago, with Sophie Körner as Desdemona and Wahr as Othello. Wahr also

---

1 (1) M. Rockobauer's bill (Vienna, 1 Apr.) for three dozen oboe reeds. A.M. XII, 654; Valkó II, 571. (2) Another bill from Rockobauer (Vienna, 24th Apr.) for two dozen bassoon reeds. A.M. XII, 655; Valkó II, 571. (3) Widow Druckherl's bill (Eisenstadt, 29 Apr.) that Haydn had received 64 spinet strings 'at Ezterhaz'. A.M. XII, 658; Valkó II, 572. (4) Carl Flach's carpenter bill (Eisenstadt, 6 May). A.M. XII, 657; Valkó II, 572. (5) Organbuilder Martin's bill (Estoras, 16 May) for 'the repair of a *Positiv* and 2 *Clavier* ... 4 Rfl. 30 xr. ...' This is interesting in that we now know that there was also an organ *Positiv* at Eszterháza, presumably in the Castle Chapel. On the same bill, Haydn writes: 'Item for 6 books of unlined music paper for His Highness 1 Fl. 30 xr.' Usually the paper was pre-lined ('rastrirt') with music staves. A.M. XII, 659; Valkó II, 572.

2 1. Vierteljahr 1775, p. 275: 'A certain Seipp, actor in the Wahr Troupe in Hungary, has written a number of wretched plays, among which I would notice only the exceptional arrogance of a King Lear based on Shakespeare ...'. In the 3. Vierteljahr 1775, pp. 94f., we read: 'Herr Seipp ... protests bitterly about the infamous report ... his King Lear is a good piece and pleased Prince Esterházy, and the worst things he wrote are as good as many a Viennese piece by [Christian Gottlob] Stephanie ...'. Here we also sense the omnipresent frustration of a provincial actor *vis-à-vis* the productions of the capital city (in this case Vienna): Eszterháza, for all its brilliance and *panache*, and with even Herr Haydn and Herr Wahr, remained an isolated castle in the Hungarian wilderness.

3 Landon *SYM* 16. The two principal sources as listed above are not in Hoboken (I, 286).

made use of Wieland's translations and gave *Macbeth* at Pressburg on 9 March 1775 in the complete Wieland text.

Among other plays given by Wahr at this period, we may note Christian Gottlob Stephanie's *Spleen* (*PZ*, 23 November 1774); in the same notice we learn, too, of Tobias P. Gebler's *Adelheid von Siegmar* (Adelheid: Sophie Körner; Siegmar: Wahr). There were also Pelzel's *Die Hausplage* (Pressburg: 14 December) and *Die Liebhaber nach der Mode* (Pressburg: 20 December), as well as Goethe's *Clavigo* (Pressburg: 3 December; Beaumarchais: Wahr), which earned fulsome praise in the *PZ*: 'The interpretation of ... Herr Wahr was unforgettable ... And how beautifully was our Maria [Sophie Körner] represented, the young girl full of love and noble pride who, abandoned and dishonoured, sinks to an early grave.'

From the usual bonus paid to the Wahr Troupe at the end of the season, we learn that it consisted of the following members during 1774: Wahr, Madame Körner, Körner, Christoph Seipp, Friedrich Litter, Elisabetha Pärthl, Josepha Prothke, Johann Prothke, Theres[e] Christl, Franz Christl, Franziska Reiner, Carolina Reiner, Cremeri, Schezer with wife and child, Charlotte de Ochs, Pauer with child, Starke, Spieß.[1]

We do not know the reactions to Haydn's letter of *c.* 18 March, but it is probable that the *Capellmeister* managed to get his men pardoned. In a letter from Prince Nicolaus to Rahier dated 'Eszterhaz', 17 May 1774, we read that the 'enclosed apothecary's bill is ... to be paid ... and Doctor Bertrand ... to be rewarded as you see fit. ...

This one time, by the way, I will annul the penalty for *Bassetlisten* ['cellist] Marteu [*sic*], therefore you will have him paid the 25 f. 36 Xr. which was subtracted from his salary, which fact is to be told to the Chief Cashier. ...

[A.M. 4346, Esterházy Archives, Budapest; *HJB* IV, 97. The reward for Dr Bertrand was for the complicated cure prescribed for the horn player Carl Franz. Bertrand received 50 fl. Generalcassa 1774, Rubr. XII. Fasc. 9. Nr. 20. *HJB* IV, 98]

Our next news comes from the following notice in the *Preßburger Zeitung*:

Esterház, June 30.
Persons of high rank from abroad, the Ambassador of Modena and one of the most distinguished gentlemen of Italy, are expected here today. They will stop in Eszterház for two days, inspecting everything of interest. Although His Princely Highness is away, the most pleasant provision has been made for the entertainment of the illustrious visitors. This evening there will be a German comedy, *Der Triumph der Freundschaft*, followed by a serenade and a dinner. Tomorrow the splendid castle and garden, the grand new ballroom, and the new marionette theatre will be viewed. Tomorrow evening is the Italian opera *L'infedeltà delusa*. The music is by *Herr Kapellmeister* Joseph Hayden [*sic*]. This outstanding musician recently composed, for Herr Wahr's company, original music to the comedy *Der Zerstreute*; connoisseurs consider it a masterpiece. One notices, this time in music intended for a comedy, the same spirit that elevates all of Heyden's [*sic*] work. His masterful variety excites the admiration of experts and is nothing short of delightful for the listener; he falls from the most affected pomposity directly into vulgarity, and H[aydn] and Regnard contend with one another in capricious absent-mindedness. The play takes on a new and manifold worth. From act to act the music realizes the play's intention more closely, namely

1 Horányi 92–5.

that of heightening the actors' absent-mindedness. We look forward to hearing music to Shakespeare's *Hamlet* by this adept composer.

[*PZ* No. 54, 6 July 1774; translation by Eugene Hartzell in *HJB* VIII, 270; Landon *Supplement*, p. 38, translation from an inaccurate transcript of this notice; at the relevant time the original newspaper in Budapest was not yet available.]

The new incidental music was for Jean François Regnard's *Le distrait*, and we find enthusiastic notices of it when it was played in successive years by Wahr or other companies in Vienna (6 January 1776) and Salzburg (Wahr Troupe, 1 January 1776, where Mozart was certainly one of the listeners).[1] Haydn later turned this effective piece of theatrical music into Symphony No. 60 ('Il distratto').

L'infedeltà delusa was still being performed, as we see from the above report. It is not clear when Prince Nicolaus returned, but he was in Vienna on 28 July:

Com̄ission

According to which our Chief Cashier is to pay to our *Capeln-Meister* Heyden [*sic*] five and twenty ducats from the General Cassa and to enter them on the records. Vienna, 28th July 1774.

Nicolaus Fürst Esterhazy.

The above one hundred five Gulden 50 Xr have been paid to me correctly and in cash by *Herrn* Chief Cashier Züsser. Eisenstadt, 13th Augusti

Josephus Haydn mpria.

[Generalcassa 1774. Rubr. XII. Fasc. 9. Nr. 33, *HJB* IV, 48]

Either this is yet another reward for a performance of *L'infedeltà delusa* or Prince Nicolaus was also delighted with the new music to *Le distrait* and showed his appreciation in the usual way. We note that Haydn went to Eisenstadt in August. We suggest that he had obtained a kind of leave in order to compose *Il ritorno di Tobia*, commissioned by the Tonkünstler-Societät in Vienna and, as we shall soon see, performed there in April 1775. Haydn must have worked for many months on this enormous work.

We have a report on theatrical life at Eszterháza from a Viennese journal entitled *Historisch-kritische Theaterchronik von Wien* (1774):

[Erster Band, erster Theil, pp. 74ff.] [Summary: Pressburg Theatre has been rented to two persons, a coffee-seller Krimer and a house officer of Count Balessa, and they are only after money; they pay a small rent and the balls alone bring them six times what they spend. The stage is narrow and small, and the theatre is uncomfortable for players and audience alike. Strolling players are permitted.] In the winter of 1773 the well-known (also successful in Vienna) *Herr* Wahr tried his luck in Pressburg. Our Court condescended to appear seven times and he received the applause of the entire nobility. Before I continue, may I permit myself to say a few words about *Herr* Wahr?

Herr Wahr, a clever actor, started with the Vienna theatre, made his own troupe, and first played in Wiener Neustadt during the first winter-month of 1771; there he was fortunate and successful. In those days his troupe consisted mostly of persons to whom the regular theatre was anathema. He educated them with no little effort, and in a short time he was able to perform the best plays. **Prince Esterhazy**, a quite formidable connoisseur and patron of the arts,

---

1 Landon *SYM*, 349. Mozart *Briefe* ... I, 528; V, 360; and reports in a Salzburg newspaper kindly shown to me by the late O. E. Deutsch; *Theaterwochenblatt für Salzburg*, 21. Stück, pp. 241ff.

engaged them. They have already been for the third summer at his summer castle in Esterhaz, and he showered upon them his continued applause and patronage. . . .

[Pp. 126ff.] . . . The present princely Esterhazi and Pressburg Theatre consists of the following persons:
1. **Herr Wahr**. Since he left Vienna, his talents have shone ever more brightly. He chooses the roles himself, and plays his own mostly very well, especially Odoardo Galotti and Hamlet, Oakly, King Lear, Kassander. In his acting there is much truth, which goes to the heart. The public likes him and through his efforts, he has taught the average audience to appreciate good theatre. . . . He plays **Thamos**, as even the Viennese admit, superbly for a theatre like Pressburg. 2. Madame Körner. Plays leading heroines. Her diligence is indefatigable. Her especially fine roles are: **Elektra**, **Sara**, **Roxelane**, **Juliet** in **Romeo [and Juliet]**, and **Minna**. She plays peasant girls and altogether innocent persons with charming naïveté. She is mistress of the language of the eyes, and memorizes easily. 3. **Herr Körner** plays low comic roles rather nicely. 4. **Madame Manner** [*recte*: Wanner] plays old mothers successfully. She gladly gives roles to newcomers to encourage them [Footnote: Note that, ladies and gentlemen; a good example!] 5. **Herr Litter** plays second lovers. He owes most of his art to Hr. Wahr. His declamation is not yet perfect and he lacks the knowledge to differentiate characters. 6. **Madame Litter** substitutes for Madame Körner. She has much expression, and plays some roles well. She has a heavy tongue, but with effort she can overcome this fault. . . .

[Erster Band, zweyter Theil, pp. 12f.] Esterhaz. My Pressburg correspondent has taken pains to gather news from this princely theatre, and has sent it to me at once. The Chronicle, and its correspondent, think that they serve the Hungarian nation if they bring us news of the *divertissements* of one of its foremost members: even these *divertissements* display the [princely] mentality. No prince chooses with more discretion than the Prince von Esterhazi. He shines without extravagance, is a father to his vassals and a protector of the arts. Proof of the latter are the excellent buildings, paintings and exoticisms here. He loves and supports the fine arts and sciences. All his amusements and *divertissements* employ *l'esprit*. Theatre and music succeed one another in providing the listener with the most delicate amusements, and one thinks oneself in an enchanted castle when one attends one of the *fêtes* at Esterhaz. The musical forces of the *Prince* consist of 24 persons, of which each member is a virtuoso on his instrument. Who would not recognize the excellent Joseph Hayden [*sic*], the famous Luigi [Tomasini] and others? . . .

[Erster Band, erster Theil, p. 156] Pressburg. The following pieces of the princely Esterhazi and Pressburg theatres are the result of Herr Seipp's industry . . .: a) *Der Krug geht so lange zum Wasser, bis er bricht.* A comedy in three acts. b) *Adelson und Salvini*, a tragedy after D. Armand's romance. c) *Lucie und Kläry*, a tragedy in 5 acts after Dusch's *Reine Liebe*. d) *Glük und Unglük*, a comedy . . . e) *Olimpia*, a tragedy after Voltaire in 5 acts. f) *King Lear*, a tragedy by Shakespeare. Herr Seipp, in his stage comportment, is supposed to be very similar to Herr Stephanie Jr. [there continues a description of various actresses and actors: Mlle. Reiner, Herr Brokhe, Herr Schlezer (master of costumes), Herr Bodingbauer, Herr Hoffmann (a 'good stage painter')].

Erster Band, zweyter Theil, pp. 29f.] The following persons have meanwhile joined. 1. **Herr Christel**. He made his début as **Gloucester** in **Lear** and afterwards played various different kinds of roles. Fond fathers are his speciality. He has proper declamation but little stage comportment and usually incorrect, stiff action. .... 2. **Madam Christl** plays rarely. She has little comportment, a not very pleasing figure and little diction. ...

[Pp. 39f.] Hungary. / Esterhaz. / ... 3. **Herr Schwarzwald** appeared as Hirschkopf in **Liebhabern nach der Mode**, and was a success. Pedants and peasants are his roles, and he plays them right well. 4. **Madam Schwarzwald** appeared as **Fr[äulein] v. Rechtlieb** in **Liebhabern nach der Mode** and acted excellently. She has a good pronunciation, decorum, a pretty figure, good declamation, and promises to be a good mother for the company; affected roles are supposed to be her strong suit. 5. Mlle **Josepha Schwarzwald**, her daughter aged nine. This most adorable child would certainly please the public of the first theatre in Germany as much as she does this one. Few children can approach her acting. She appeared as **Karoline** in **Liebhabern nach der Mode** and was a notable success. Afterwards she played the **milkmaid** in an after-piece arranged by Herr Seipp from the operetta of that name by [Michel-Jean] Sedaine. ...

[Pp. 57ff.] Esterhaz. / Italian Opera. / Each week at Esterhaz there is one day of opera. The following singers appear: 1. Herr **Friberth**, has a fine tenor voice, knows the theatre well and writes for it as well. 2. Herr **Dichtler**, a good comic actor. His acting is suitable and natural, so that one understands what he wants to say even if one does not speak the language. 4 [*sc.* 3]. Herr **Specht**, a good bass, has only worked in the theatre for a little while but has made good progress already. 4. Madam **Friberth** has a clear and pleasant voice, a good education and much charm. Her timidity sometimes hampers her acting. 5. Madam **Dichtler** has a bright and full theatrical voice, is very vivacious and possesses an excellent memory. These are the principal singers; we have not mentioned the choral singers. This year two operas have been given here: *L'infedeltà delusa* and **La Contadina in Corte**. The music to the first is by the princely Esterhazi Kappellmeister [*sic*], Herr Joseph Hayden [*sic*]. It was given last year in the presence of the Empress and Queen and was admired by all connoisseurs.

Herr Wahr has received music by Herr Hayden especially for the comedy **Der Zerstreute**, and it is exceptional. Haydn has also composed music especially for **Hamlet** as given by the Wahr Troupe.

Marionette productions / It is a remarkable and entertaining operation. Herr von Pauersbach has been appointed its director. There is one performance per week. Three pieces by Herr von Pauersbach have been played. **Die Probe der Liebe** has delicate humour but is rather dull. Also, the names of the persons are too childish and silly. **Genovefens 1. Theil**. A most popular piece. Wit, humour, caprice, marvellous theatre, beautiful music, changes of scenery such as only eye and ear can admire in such a short period. It was given thrèe times. **Genovefens 2. Theil**. The eye has still more than in the first part. Also the music is more beautiful. **Golo**'s dream is beautiful. But why does the devil command this dream to happen? Cannot Golo dream by himself? The devil contradicts the whole order of the piece. The work is very successful. In the whole piece, the pillars are diligence, attention and patience, and Herr von Pauersbach has these three attributes to a high degree. **Genovefens 3. & 4. Theil** is yet to come and is supposed to surpass the first two.

So much about the marionette theatre at Esterhaz, for only few people can imagine what it is really like, and all the expectations of the visitors are surpassed; the Prince spends a great deal on it, and wishes to have everything executed with a very special taste.

[Pp. 88ff.] Hungary. / Esterhaz. / Here, on Sunday 25th August, following [the piece entitled] *Postzug*, was the first performance of the tragedy in one act, **Donna**

Inez. This little piece turned out very well indeed. The actors gave their very best and were so successful that this tragedy will be one of the best after-pieces. When reading it, there seems to be too much action, but in performance this mistake turns out to be an advantage. There is little conversation, the listener sees everything happening. The many scene changes in darkness keep his attention, and he understands all the action and does not dare to guess what will happen. – The theme of the not novel material, jealousy, could have been omitted by the author. The **unfounded jealousy, Fayel, Serena** have their own plan and **Donna Inez** also has hers. If all plays that have jealousy as their theme were to be confiscated, and if a similar prohibition were made for all pieces with love as a basis, what would actors live from?

As far as I am concerned, the piece ought to play in Germany. The last passage, when Garzias stabs **Inez**, was shockingly acted. Herr Wahr dragged Inez (Madame Körner) to the prostrated Juan, dragged her forward, then back to Juan, threw her over Juan's outstretched legs, stabbed her and slung her away, she turning over and over. When the lights came on, what did that man feel, when he saw Inez's brother? His death was pitiable. – We need more such after-pieces, where there is more action than words. Here and there the language could be more plastic, especially in the first scene. The fourth scene is the best for the actors. Why does Garzias address his secretary in the 'du' form? In the eleventh scene Garzias sees his rival enter Inez's room. He believes that he can enter the room and forth-with take his revenge. Nothing prevents him except that he things his rival would hide as soon as he hears the noise. This must be made clearer, otherwise the 12th scene cannot be sufficiently explained. Garzias must be at the point of entering the room in fury, when he reconsiders. With the permission of the author, right at the beginning Garzias touches his wound and lets Ferdinand bind it. In his fury, however, he re-opens this wound and dies as a result. [Footnote:] This is not the place in which the chronicle can register its opinion about the piece's value, and should it be given in Vienna, it will be fairly and openly judged. But this much we may assure our readers, that **Donna Inez** is by the author of the **Ländliches Hochzeitsfest**. We are assured that he several times offered it to the directors of the Vienna theatre, without fee, and this offer was refused every time. We do know which secret reasons prevented the performance of this piece, since it is sure that in accepting such pieces, which really are not beyond criticism, young beginners are encouraged to better efforts; and since, then, we know not these secret reasons, which may have consisted of private prejudices, we would prefer to say nothing; but it will, it is hoped, be permitted us think what we please about it all.

[P. 107.] Hungary. / Esterhaz. / A few days after *Donna Inez*, there was given in the princely theatre: **Olivie**, a tragedy in five acts by Herr Brandes. This piece turned out to be better in performance than it reads. Without doubt it is the worst of the author's. If he continues like this, he will rightly lose all the fame he has harvested. **Olivie** is a warmed-over *Klementine*, and except for the language, is not as good as *Klementine*. All the motives of *Olivie* are the same as the latter. Laura, Bland, Klementina [*sic*] are the same. Every listener who only looks and doesn't read will say: I've seen that piece, but with common people; **Bardonia** is a few degrees more poisonous. If one introduces poison into the theatre, it must achieve something new, otherwise it is disgusting.

Various news items. / Vienna. / The famous Herr Chevalier Gluck has arrived here from Paris this week. But he is to leave soon, to become royal French Kapellmeister with a large salary. [Footnote:] See how local talents are appreciated also outside Vienna!

[Pp. 141, *recte* 157ff.] Esterhaz. / The following pieces have been given here: **Adelheid von Siegmar**, a tragedy that is much better than *Olivie* except for the language. [Footnote:] We reserve our judgement because the piece is about to be given here in Vienna.

Die Räuber, a comedy in one act by Herr Weidmann. Like torture, we find the roguish tone of this piece very capricious [!]. Both after-pieces incidentally have too much of the adventurous, especially *Die Räuber*. The whole decent family escapes its fate so happily, and the robbers with all their care are so quickly under lock and key, that one really doesn't understand how it all happened. In performance it improves. Herr Wahr plays Löwenzahn and Greifenklau in masterly fashion. Herr Litter, put to the torture, is moving. It is one of his best roles.

Der Gefühlvolle, also by Herr Weidmann (it is known in Vienna). Herr Litter is **Musenschutz**, Hr. Wahr **Gesellschaftsfeind**, Hr. Seipp **Mittelding**, Hr. Prokhe **Eduard**, Mde. Körner **Hannchen**, Mde. Litter Sophie. Mde Parthl must realize that as **Anmuthreich** in this piece she must display herself not only as mother but as the mirror of all actresses, and for that [the actress] Huber is of course needed.

Der Schwätzer by Hr. Weidmann. Hr. Wahr **St. Georg**. Hr. Schwarzwald **Rudolph**. Madame Litter as Elisabeth ought to pronounce better the Latin words. Der Schwätzer is one of Herr Wahr's best roles in the comic vein. The piece was a great success.

The **betrogene Philosoph** from the French. A wretched thing. **Der Spleen** by Stephanie Jr. Hr. Wahr Hekingborn. Hr. Brokhe Fletscher, Herr Litter Beaglestedt, Mde Bartl Lady Dorset, Mde Körner Jenny. The piece was well played.

Othelo [*sic*] or the **Mohr von Venedig** by Shakespear. Herr Wahr has dared to produce it, and with great success. Othello, Herr Wahr; Desdemona, Mde Körner; Aemilia, Mde Schwarzwald; Cassio, Herr Litter; Jago, Herr Seipp; Rodrigio, Herr Brokhe – were particularly fine. It was given with enormous fidelity. On the first of September Herr Apelt made his début here in the role of *Der Zerstreute*, but he was not engaged. He has still too little knowledge of the theatre for such roles.

We ought to add that on 26 August Herr Starke was engaged. He made his début as the Captain in *Postzug*. His all too marked Saxonian dialect does not fall happily on our ears. He has much science and exact theoretical knowledge of the theatre, but requires more practice. Otherwise he is a critical connoisseur. . . .

[Pp. 172f.] Hungary. / Esterhaz. / Concerning the German theatre, the following is to be added, viz.: Madame Manner [Wanner] (now madame Kliemsch) is to leave. Madame Parthl remains.

About the Opera we have the following to report, *viz.*: on 25th September was an opera seria entitled **Acide**. The music was by Hr. Joseph Hayden. On the 26th was a comic opera: **la Canterina**, the music also by Hr. Hayden. This opera was excellently acted and sung, so much so that the whole ending had to be repeated. About the marionettes there is nothing to be added except that instead of the previous **Director of the Marionette Plays**, a certain **Herr Rauffer from Vienna** has arrived. He has not given a performance yet. [Footnote:] The first is supposed to take place on 9th October, but one is not sure and it's idle to speculate! Hum!

[Dritter Band, Dritter Theil, Vienna 1774, pp. 45–8.] Hungary. / Esterhaz. / Saturday the 8th of October there was given here: die **Teutschen**, a comedy in five acts by **Hr. Stephanie Junior** played from manuscript. Sixteen persons are involved. Here is a synopsis which must be interesting for Vienna since the author is one of Vienna's favourite poets. [Synopsis follows.] ... Friday was the Opera *lo speciale* [*Lo speziale*]. / Sunday the 15th **Ines de Castro** by Seipp after **de la Motte**. It was enormously successful. The piece was too flat, the long monologues were tiring for the players and audience alike, the language too stiff. To improve it, Seipp rewrote the whole piece. The Queen was made nobler, Pedro more fiery, and Ines given more chances to act. The final scene, in which Ines presents her children to the King, was far more impressive because the scene was prepared and the children, by their speeches, softened the King's heart. [Italics added]

This report is one of the most interesting documents about theatrical life at Eszterháza; in it we have invaluable criticisms about the famous Wahr troupe and particularly the acting of its principal, whose extremely realistic way of presentation – probably based on the brilliant manner of Garrick – slightly disturbed the critic. We also have useful notes about Pauersbach and also the editor's (Christian Hieronymus Moll) new play, *Donna Inez*, but undoubtedly the most sensational part of the report is the news of no less than three Haydn revivals hitherto unknown to scholars, including *Acide*. That *opera seria*, originally performed at Eisenstadt in 1763, was supposed to have been revived for the birthday celebrations of the Dowager Princess Esterházy in July 1773 (*vide supra*, p. 187); but in the event it was not. The various fragments of this later version that have survived, especially the beautiful bass aria 'Tergi i vezzosi rai', were thought, hitherto, to have been written (as it were) for the desk drawer. But now we learn that the opera was rewritten and performed, at least in 1774, and that this new version has only survived in fragments. It is equally fascinating to see *La canterina* of 1766 being performed with such huge success in 1774, and also *Lo speziale*, the work which had been written to open the new theatre at Eszterháza in the autumn of 1768. It is clear from this report that Haydn's earlier operas, far from being merely one- or two-night affairs at Eszterháza, were retained in the repertoire for many years. This fact also renders more easily explicable the various second versions of arias (*Lo speziale*; *Le pescatrici*), cuts (*L'infedeltà delusa*), and the like, which were all the typical side-effects of operatic revivals. It is greatly to be hoped that more numbers of this fascinating theatrical journal may be located by future scholars: who knows what hitherto unsuspected information about Haydn and Eszterháza may be hidden therein.

Rauffer, whose engagement caused the Viennese editor (responsible for the various footnotes in the report) some qualms, did not in the end displace Pauersbach but was obviously a necessary directorial aid in the greatly increased repertoire now being given at Eszterháza.

We still do not know who wrote the music for the various *Genovefens*: Haydn was responsible for them and obviously compiled the music, perhaps 'von verschiedenen Meistern' as he himself records when cataloguing the libretto to *Genovefens Vierter Theil* – the only one of the tetralogy to have been printed, it would seem.[1] Since none of the four was included in the *Entwurf-Katalog*, it is unlikely that Haydn did more than act as an 'editor' for the music.

Haydn received a new summer uniform this year.[2] Otherwise, we hear nothing of him until the following review of *Le distrait* in Pressburg for St Cecilia's Day (22

1 *Haydn: the Late Years 1801–1809*, p. 325.
2 Bill from master tailor J. Franciscus Sellinger (Vienna, 20 Nov. 1774): nine summer uniforms in cloth for the musicians, four dresses for the four chamber singers (female), Haydn's uniform 'trimmed with gold braid [*Posamentier Arbeith*] ... Summa: 139 Fl. 23 xr.'. A.M. XVI, 1071; Valkó II, 572. For complete bills about Haydn's uniform, see *HJB* IV, 80ff. Haydn also had a new summer uniform in 1772, as did Tomasini, Friberth, Dichtler, Specht, Burgsteiner [*sic*], Lidl, Marton [Marteau], Oliva, Paur [*sic*], Franz, Maÿ, Diezl [*sic*], Chorus, Pohl, Schiringer, Hinterberger, Peziwall [*sic*], Grießler – 19 persons – and dresses for *Frau* Dichtler and 'Lenorl Jäger'. Generalcassa 1772. Rubr. VIII. *HJB* IV, 82. Therefore, not all of these men needed new uniforms two years later.

November), a performance at which it is very unlikely Haydn was present:

> Preßburg: ... On Tuesday, St Cecilia's Day, *Der Zerstreute* was given. *Herr von* Hayden [*sic*] has written singular music for it, about which our readers received a first report in an earlier number, in an article from Eszterház. Suffice it to say that it is excellent, quite excellent; the Finale had to be repeated, for the audience would not stop applauding. In the Finale the allusion to the absent-minded man who, on his wedding day, has to tie a knot in his handkerchief to remind himself that he is the bridegroom, is extremely well done. The musicians begin the piece most pompously, remembering only after a while that their instruments have not been tuned.
>
> [*PZ* No. 94, 23 Nov. 1774; translation by Eugene Hartzell in *HJB* VIII, 270]

The day before St Cecilia's *festa*. Haydn received yet another large sum of money from the Prince.

Comission

According to which our Chief Cashier Züsser is to pay to our *Kapelmeister* [*sic*] *Hayden* [*sic*] one hundred Gulden from our General Cassa and to enter the sum on the books. Eszterház, 16th Nov. 774.

Id est 100 f   Nicolaus Fürst Esterhazy

These above-listed one hundred Gulden correctly received by me from Herr Chief Cashier Züsser.

Eisenstadt, 21st Nov. 774.   Josephus Haydn mpria.

[Generalcassa 1774. Rubr. XII. Fasc. 9. Nr. 52. HJB IV, 49]

We cannot tell why Haydn received this particular reward, but we would draw attention to four new Symphonies composed, as the dated autographs inform us, during this year: Nos. 54, 55, 56, 57. Of these No. 56 is unique in that it is the first recorded work that Haydn wrote for the *Capelle* with *a priori* horns (in C *alto*) and trumpets that do not double the horn parts, as well as kettledrums. The other works with separate horn and trumpet parts, Nos. 20, 32 and 33 were composed earlier for the Morzin *Capelle*, while the trumpet and drum parts to Nos. 38 and 41 were composed later. No. 54 was also composed for a much smaller ensemble (oboes, bassoon, horns, strings), to which Haydn later added, in the following order, a second bassoon part and timpani; then a slow introduction; then flutes, and trumpets. (We can see no evidence that this large version was produced, as Sonja Gerlach maintains, in 1776; we favour a much later date, possibly for the second London sojourn.)[1] The evidence of No. 56 shows that during the year 1774, Haydn expected to have trumpets in his orchestra, possibly from one of the *Thurnermeister* (Oedenburg or Eisenstadt). We will see that in 1775, Haydn also had trumpets in his orchestra for the great August festival at Eszterháza. At any rate, these are four magnificent Symphonies and possibly the reason for the reward; it seems unlikely that it was given for the revivals of all the older operas because otherwise the singers involved would probably have been rewarded too.[3]

---

1 *Haydn-Studien* II/1 (1969), p. 54. *Haydn in England 1791–1795*, p. 188.

2 Bills for the end of the year: (1) Rockobauer (Vienna, 1 Dec.) for three dozen oboe reeds. A.M. XII, 660; Valkó II, 573. (2) 'Rorate' money – nine Gulden – for the musicians, paid to Haydn. Eisenstadt, 31 Dec. A.M. XII, 662; Valkó II, 574. (3) Dietzl's annual bill (Eisenstadt, 31 Dec.) for strings and repairs, including items for violoncello and 'Violon' (double bass) A strings. A.M. XII, 661; Valkó II, 574.

3 In November, bills in the Esterházy Archives [Eisenstadt] show that thirty-one 'supers' were involved in marionette production (for that month?) requiring '40 Bögen' (players' scripts?). *HJB* I, 192.

Chronicle 1775

WE SHALL PASS OVER the ubiquitous Mathias Rockobauer[1] and proceed to a notice in the *Preßburger Zeitung*, according to which there was on 7 March the first of the Lenten concerts in the princely Esterházy palace in Pressburg.

> The orchestra was so well filled with foreign virtuosi and various local musicians that the instrumental and vocal music was received with complete satisfaction. . . .
> [*PZ* 20, 11 March 1775; *HJB* VIII, 171]

We do not know if this series was under Haydn's artistic supervision or whether he even participated, but probably not. In the following letter we have really priceless information about Haydn's own 'private' marionette theatre which he organized during the Carnival season of 1774, and about which this letter is the only known reference. It is perhaps the most tantalizing of all the loose ends with which, alas, Haydn's life is burdened for the scrupulous biographer.

> [Prince Nicolaus Esterházy to *Regent* Rahier]
> . . . I know that the *Kapellmeister* Haydn has a little marionette theatre which he produced with the musicians during the last Carnival season. Now I would like to have such a thing organized for the 20th inst., which is the evening before my wife's birthday, and to have it given before my wife at Eisenstadt Castle.
> So it would be necessary to arrange everything with Haydn at once, but in such a way that the Princess learns nothing of it all.
> I await your answer about this and remain, [etc.]
> Vienna, 13th March 1775.   Nicolaus Fürst Esterhazy.

> Post Scriptum: His Highness orders further that Your Well Born Self will be kind enough in the name of the Prince to present his compliments to the Princess and to assure her that the Dowager Princess goes out every day and is quite well. . . .
> [A.M. XX, 1354, Esterházy Archives, Budapest; Valkó II, 577]

The musicians meanwhile succeeded, probably at Haydn's instigation, in getting a cash assistance for their double households when the *Capelle* was at Eszterháza. On 19 March 1775, Prince Nicolaus wrote that

> because they have to leave their wives behind for the summer, each one is granted 50 fl. annually in grace, but they shall not dare to bother us with requests for increases, nor allow their wives or children to come to Eszterház whether we are there or not, otherwise this act of goodness will cease to occur automatically. . . .
> [*HJB* VII, 30]

This *Verbot* was particularly necessary because both the Wahr Troupe and the *Capelle* contained more members than hitherto and there was no room for all the wives and children; later, when the quarters were enlarged, this *Verbot* was lifted and the musicians were allowed to bring their families to Eszterháza.

We now come to Haydn's first major commission for Vienna since he had composed *Der (neue) krumme Teufel* more than twenty years earlier: the Oratorio *Il ritorno di Tobia*. The organization that sponsored it was the Tonkünstler-Societät, a

---

1 Bills of 1 Jan. (two dozen bassoon reeds, A.M. XVI, 1069), 5 Jan. (two and one-half dozen bassoon reeds), 26 Feb. (three dozen oboe reeds, A.M. XVI, 1070 and 1067 resp.) and 10 March (two dozen bassoon reeds, A.M. XVI, 1068); all Valkó II, 576.

group of musicians founded by Court *Capellmeister* Florian Leopold Gassmann in 1771 to provide pensions for the widows and orphans of their members. Since its foundation it had given two double performances annually, one just before Christmas and one during Lent. Following the old Viennese court tradition, the Societät sponsored oratorios in the Italian language, in the intervals of which a concerto was usually performed; there were also, occasionally, other instrumental insertions. In 1772, Gassmann and *Abbate* Metastasio had joined in *Betulia liberata*: in that same year, Hasse and Metastasio had presented *Santa Elena al Calvario*; in 1773, the latter work had been repeated and the new Oratorio was Dittersdorf's *Ester*; while in 1774 the two new pieces had been Bonno's *Giuseppe riconosciuto* and Hasse's *Cantico de' tre fanciulli* on a libretto by Pallavicino.[1]

One of the specialities of this bi-annual meeting was the enormous size of the group that performed these works: some 180 persons. In the 'Letters of a travelling Frenchman in Germany', there is an interesting comment; we print the version of Baron Riesbeck as adapted for Cramer's *Magazin der Musik* (1784, 112ff.), from which source we have already taken the description of Eszterháza (*supra*, pp. 99f.). Music, in the words of this report.

> is the only thing about which the nobility shows taste. Many houses have their own band of musicians, and all the public concerts bear witness that this aspect of art is in high repute here. One can put together four or five large orchestras, all of which are incomparable. The number of real virtuosi is small; but as far as the orchestral musicians are concerned, one can hardly imagine anything in the world more beautiful. I have heard 30 or 40 instruments playing together, and they all produce one tone so correct, clean and precise that one might think one is hearing one single string instrument. The violins are one stroke of the bow, the wind instruments one breath. An Englishman next to whom I sat thought it miraculous that throughout an entire opera there was – I won't say no mistake, but nothing of all that which generally occurs in large orchestras: a hasty entrance, dragging, or too strong a bowing or attack. He was enchanted by the purity and correctness of the harmony, and he had just come from Italy. There are upwards of 400 musicians here, who are divided into certain societies, and often work together many years. They are used to each other and have in common a severe leadership. Through constant practice, and also through the energy and cold-bloodedness which are peculiar to the Germans, they reach such a state. On a certain day of the year these 400 artists come together and give a concert for the benefit of the widows of musicians. I am assured that all 400 instruments play together just as correctly, clearly and purely as if they were 20 or 30. This concert is surely unique in the world.

It is curious that Haydn did not entirely trust the vocal material at his disposal in Vienna; he had his own school, of course, and preferred to make sure that not only three of the vocal soloists were from the *Capelle* but also the leader, Luigi Tomasini, and the principal 'cellist, Marteau. History does not record what their colleagues in the Tonkünstler orchestra thought of this foreign intrusion. No libretto of the two concerts, 2 and 4 April, has survived; and apparently none was printed. The author of the text was Luigi Boccherini's brother, Giovanni Gastone, who had been imported by Luigi and their father when the two latter had played in the Vienna court orchestra in the 1750s. We do not know if Haydn knew the Boccherinis from that period when he was working with Kurz-Bernadon; Boccherini's sisters and a brother (also 'Luigi')

---

1 Pohl, *Denkschrift*, 57f.; *Enciclopedia dello Spettacolo*, VI, 195.

were also in the Vienna *corps de ballet*.[1] Giovanni Gastone had previously worked with Gassmann (*I rovinati*, 1772) and Antonio Salieri (*La fiera di Venezia*, 1772, later to be mounted at Eszterháza – a coincidence?). In literary circles of the period he was a member of the Italian *Accademia degli Arcadi* under the *nom-de-plume* 'Aegindo Bolimeo' – a continuation of the Roman tradition at the time of Cardinal Ottoboni.[2]

The cast
Sara: Magdalena Friberth (from the *Capelle*)
Tobia: Carl Friberth (from the *Capelle*)
Tobit: Christian Specht (from the *Capelle*)
Anna: Margarethe Spangler (sister of Magdalena Friberth)
Azaria/Raffaelle: Barbara Teyber.

The hand-bill (Gesellschaft der Musikfreunde) informs us that on 2 April, the 'princely Esterházy chamber virtuoso' played his own violin Concerto, while on 4 April Marteau played a concerto for violoncello – on both occasions in the interval.

The event was reported in the *k. k. priviligierte Realzeitung*:

> The famous *Herr Kapellmeister* Hayden [*sic*] achieved a general success with the Oratorio entitled 'The Return of Tobias', performed on the 2nd and 4th, and displayed his well-known adroitness once again at its most advantageous. Expression, nature and art were so finely woven in his work that the listener must perforce love the one and admire the other. Especially his choruses glowed with a fire that was otherwise only in Händel; in short, the whole very numerous public was delighted and Hayden was the great artist once again, whose works are loved in the whole of Europe and in which foreigners find the original genius of a master. . . .
>
> O Künstler, dessen Harmonie die Seelen
> Der Fühlenden zum Himmel hebt,
> Der unsrer Väter Thaten melodisch zu erzählen
> Die heil'ge Asche neu belebt;
> Dein Geist setzt durch des Nachruhms goldne Ehre
> Nächst Händeln Dir ein Monument,
> Und hebt Dich in die hohe Sphäre
> Wo Gluck und Bach die Bahn nur kennt.
>
> [14. Stück of 6 April 1775, p. 219]

The Society took in the huge sum of 1,712 gulden; the artists, of course, gave their services *gratis*. The Oratorio was such a success, in fact, that it was three years before the members could bring themselves to invite the composer to join their ranks.

The work was widely circulated in single arias and other pieces in manuscript; Haydn himself sent copies to foreign destinations. It was performed at Berlin in 1777 and, astonishingly, at Rome in 1783 – where Haydn's music was as good as unknown – and where it was probably given because (we must break chronology for a moment) in 1782, Haydn's *Stabat Mater* 'is causing a great deal of commotion here, too . . .' (Cramer's *Magazin der Musik* 1783, p. 168). It was then given in another unlikely place, Lisbon, where Haydn's music was hardly ever played; Schmid (op. cit., pp. 299f.) explains the details. This was on 19 March 1784, the same year in which, as we shall

---

1 Orchestral lists in the Haus-, Hof und Staatsarchiv, where we find a variety of improbable spellings, e.g. 'Bogerini'. See also R. Haas, *Gluck und Durazzo im Burgtheater*, Vienna 1925, pp. 56, 59, 71. Boccherini had composed his epoch-making first string Trios and Quartets in Vienna: see *Haydn: the Early Years 1732–1765*, G. Zechmeister, *Die Wiener Theater nächst der Burg und nächst dem Kärntnerthor von 1747 bis 1776*, pp. 229, 233, *passim*. G. de Rothschild: *Luigi Boccherini . . . London*, 1967, *passim*.
2 E. F. Schmid; 'Haydns Oratorium "Il ritorno di Tobia", seine Entstehung und sein Schicksale', in *Archiv für Musikwissenschaft* VI/3 (1959), p. 293. For Arcadians, see Lina Montalto; *Un mecenate in Roma barocca*, Florence 1955, pp. 146ff., 152f., 193ff. and *passim*.

soon see, the work was revived and rewritten for the Tonkünstler-Societät in Vienna. It was given in Leipzig in 1787, and in an arrangement by Sigismund von Neukomm, at Vienna in 1808.[1]

Its immediate effect in Vienna was that shortly thereafter – the precise date is now the subject of considerable controversy – the Court Opera commissioned Haydn to compose a new opera for them, *La vera costanza* (commission perhaps end of 1776; composed 1778?), the curious history of which will be described shortly. At any rate, it is clear that *Il ritorno di Tobia* caused much discussion in Vienna and brought Haydn physically to the Imperial capital as a potentially dangerous rival to Messrs. Salieri, Bonno, etc.

———

There were now so many keyboard instruments at Eszterháza that it was found profitable to import a repairer for a few days.[2] The amount of 'spinet' strings sent from Widow Druckherl also increased. At this period, Prince Nicolaus was not in residence but visiting his estates in Poland, as a report in the *Preßburger Zeitung* of 6 May informs us; he was not expected back in Hungary before the first days of July. This same report announced a series of balls, plays, marionette 'Spiele' and operas for the coming season at Eszterháza. The principal Troupe was again that of Carl Wahr. The Gotha *Theater-Kalender* of 1776 (pp. 252f.) lists the Company as follows:

Wahr's Theatre Company
Residence: Esterhaz in Hungary and Pressburg. Principal: H. Wahr. Spoken drama and *Singspiel* [this means that many of the Company could sing as well]. Actresses: Madam Christel: smaller parts. Madam Körner: plays leading love-parts; peasant girls. Madam Litter: plays second love-parts. Madam Mauer: old women. Mamsel Reiner: *soubrette*. Mamsel Schlezer: small children's parts. Madame Schwarzwald: mothers, dignified [*Chargirte*] roles. Mamsell Schwarzwald: leading children's roles. Actors: H. Bodingbauer: prompter and small parts. H. Brokhe: leading lover. H. Christel: tender fathers. H. Litter: second lover parts. H. Schlezer: smallest parts. H. Schwarzwald: pedants and peasants. H. Seipp: fathers, peevish old women[!] and character parts. H. Wahr: leading old parts in tragedies. H. Zappe: servants. Music director: H. Haydn, princely Esterhazi *Kapellmeister*.

The list of the members as seen in the annual bonus at the end of the 1775 season reveals a slightly different constitution: 'Herr Wahr, Mad. Körner, Körner, Cristoph Seipp, Friedrich Litter, Elisabetha Pärthl, Josepha Prothke, Johann Prothke, Theres Christl, Franz Christhl, Franciska Reiner, Carolina Reiner, Cremeri, Schlezer, Frau Schlezer and child, Charlotte de Ochs, Pauer and child, Starke, Spieß' (Horányi, German, 95f.) This list is, of course, a more reliable guide than that in the *Kalender*, which was based on information that was sometimes out of date by the time it was printed.

The *Preßburger Zeitung* is once again our primary source for the repertoire of the Wahr Troupe, in residence at the Coronation town during the winter season of

---

1 Hoboken II, p. 28. 1808: see *Haydn: the Late Years 1801–1809*, pp. 354f., 376f.
2 'Receipt. For 10 Fl. which I the undersigned received from *Herrn Capellmeister* Haydn for the repair of two harpsichords [*Flügel*], as agreed daily fee of 4 Fl. – 2½ days. Correctly and in cash ... Eszterház, 25th April 1775. Johann Roth bürgl. Orgl und Instrument Macher in Oedenburg'. Countersigned by Haydn. A.M. XVI, 1065; Valkó II, 577. Other bills of the period: (1) Josepha Druckherl (Eisenstadt, 28 June) for 104 yellow [brass] spinet strings 'auf das Clavier'. A.M. XVI, 1064; Valkó II, 577. (2) Undated bill of 1775 for repairs on violins by Heinrich Standförst, *bürg. dischler* [*Tischler*]. A.M. XVI, 1066; Valkó II, 577.

1774–5. The new actress, Madame Prothke, made her successful début in Stephanie's
Die seltsame Eifersucht at the Pressburg Theatre on 2 April 1775. In a report on 3 May,
the paper advises her to follow Sophia Körner's manner and then adds:

> Preßburg: On 17 April the Karl Wahr Theatre Company opened the house
> here after Lent and played *Adelheit* [*sc.* Adelheid] *von Ponthieu*[1] after 'St. Marc', by
> Hrn. Seipp, member of the Wahr Troupe. At the end the well-known Turkish
> music by Hrn Glanz. [*PZ* 35, 3 May 1775.] The music by Glanz was referred to in
> an earlier report: 'The new Symphony by *Herrn* Glanz, *Kapellmeister* of the I. R.
> Karol Regiment ... consists of all Turkish instruments, most of them *obbligato*.
> There are no string instruments in it. ...'. [*PZ* 105, 31 December 1774]

The same newspaper, in a report from Eszterháza Castle dated 17 August,
announces an elaborate festival there for the arrival of the Court of Vienna, including a
new opera by Haydn, based on a libretto [by Dancourt] arranged by Friberth. We
read:

> Eszterház: ... The ceremonies have been set for the 28th, 29th and 30th. Herr
> Seibert [*sic*], princely singer, has composed the text, and Herr Joseph Heyden [*sic*],
> princely Kapellmeister, the music, to a new opera which will be performed the
> first evening ...
> On the 13th inst. the famous actor Herr Stephanie the Elder came to Eszterház
> from Vienna, staying until the morning of the 17th. *Der Deserteur aus Kindesliebe*,
> *Die Leiden des Jungen Werthers*, and *Der Zerstreute*, with music by *Kapellmeister*
> Hayden, were given at the theatre.
> [*PZ* 67, 23 Aug. 1775; translation by Eugene Hartzell, *HJB* VIII, 271]

It is not clear if this celebrated actor came with his whole company from Vienna or
was simply a 'star' guest of the Wahr Troupe. Goethe's famous *Werther* book, here
adapted as a play, is a central work in the German literary movement entitled *Sturm
und Drang*, in the musical 'preview' of which (one can no longer speak of 'offspring'
since it is known that the musical *Sturm und Drang* preceded the literary movement by
nearly a decade) Haydn would play such a vital role. Regnard's play was still a best-
seller at Eszterháza.

The new opera was to be *L'incontro improvviso*, a Turkish subject so dear to Austrian
hearts of the period; while *Der Deserteur* ... was by Stephanie himself. We now
approach the last grand *festa*, involving all the theatrical personnel, the grenadiers, the
princely *Feldharmonie* (wind band) and, as a colourful exotic backdrop, the peasants.
This time the *Wiener Diarium* contents itself with the bare facts, reporting

> Vienna, 30 August. ... Monday His Royal Highness the Archduke Ferdinand
> with his consort ... and a numerous retinue, left for the princely Esterhazy
> *Lustschloße Esdras* [*sic*] in Hungary, there to honour *Herrn Fürsten von* Esterhazy
> with Their Presence ...   [No. 69, 30 August]

> Vienna, 30 August . . . Yesterday morning H.R. Highness the Serene
> Archduke Ferdinand and his consort ... arrived at Schönbrunn from the *Esterhazi
> Lustschloße Esdraß* [*sic*] in Hungary ...   [No. 70, 2 September]

---

1 This was a piece written for 'a festive occasion' at Eszterháza. *Ein Bändchen Theaterstücken der Ostermesse 1787*, Pressburg 1787, lists
'Adelheid [*recte*] von Ponthieu, verfertigt 1774 zu einer Feierlichkeit in Esterhaz ... ein Schauspiel in drey Aufzügen nach der Oper des
St March ... Dieses Stück ist schon wider Wissen und Willen des Verfassers gedruckt, aber nicht zur Messe gebracht werden.' We see
that illegal copies of plays were just as prevalent as pirated symphonies in Haydn's world. Prince Nicolaus was something of a
connoisseur of the theatrical world, and despite its geographical isolation, Eszterháza was the scene of many important German plays,
some first performances (or new translations).

Fortunately there is a very detailed report in the *Preßburger Zeitung* to guide us through this most elaborate *scena*, where the number of guests at times exceeded anything ever seen at Eszterháza (see the description of the ball, *infra*). We can at once see the vastness of the whole spectacle in the report's beginning. The *Gästehaus*, or inn, was enlarged by no less than an entire upper storey containing twelve rooms. For the servants of this enormous entourage, more than one hundred rooms were arranged in the nearby villages. From the towns of Oedenburg, Pressburg, Güns (Köszeg) and others came hordes of merchants, coffee-vendors and 'hawkers' to see to the comforts of so many guests.

The Court, led by Archduke Ferdinand and Beatrice d'Este left Vienna on 28 August at 3 p.m., arriving at Eszterháza five hours later. The guests were given refreshments at the Esterházy Palace in Oedenburg and were greeted by the town council and local aristocracy. From Oedenburg to Eszterháza a princely courier rode in front of the guests, whose arrival at the Castle was greeted by a salute of cannon. Along the route between Széplak and the Castle, the guests were greeted by crowds of the princely serfs, carrying banners and cheering, and there were trumpet fanfares.[1] In front of the Castle, raised on a platform garlanded with flowers, were trumpeters and kettledrummers, and on both sides of the main entrance the princely grenadiers and princely servants and house-officers stood at attention: twenty-one lackeys in gala uniform, six runners, six *heyducks*, six tall members of the princely bodyguard, the entire princely *Capelle* with Haydn at their head, the princely huntsmen, the administrative personnel, six Hungarian and six 'German' pages greeted the Archduke, the Archduchess and their retinue. It was a scene of pageantry and splendour that had not been seen since the great *feste* of Lorenzo de' Medici.

After the official reception by Prince Esterházy, there was 'ein kleines deutsches Schauspiel' (a small German play),[2] presumably by the Wahr Troupe, in the theatre, followed by the illumination of the park and castle, and a concluding banquet.

The princely *Feldmusik* (wind band) woke the guests on 29 August, the next day. There was an inspection of the Castle, of the great hall, the *sala terrena*, and the marionette theatre, where (if the grammar of the report can be trusted), the company had a gala luncheon. After that, the company were put into carriages and taken through the main garden, where they viewed the Temples dedicated to Diana, Sun, Love and Fortune, also the newly constructed Heremitage. They ended this tour in the princely opera house, where

> the illustrious company ... saw the Italian Opera composed especially for the occasion; it is called *L'incontro improviso* [*sic*], is in three acts and is taken from the French. The poetry is by Herr Seiberth [*sic*], who is in the princely service; the music is by Herr Joseph Hayden [*sic*], *Kapellmeister* to the Prince. The idea and plot are comic in the extreme, the music, as is customary with Hayden, excellent.
> [Eugene Hartzell's translation of *PZ* 73, 13 September]

---

1 The trumpets and kettledrums were probably recruited from the *Thurnermeister* of Oedenburg, of whose services Haydn had availed himself at least once before, on St Anne's Day, 1768: they would have sent, as before, four trumpeters and one kettledrummer. Haydn also used trumpets and drums in his new Opera, and these instruments are also required in Ordoñez's *Alceste*.

2 On September 5, there was a bill for players in the marionette theatre (possibly of *Hanswurst als Sklave*), Esterházy Archives, Eisenstadt. *HJB* I, 192.

The libretto for this occasion reads:

L'incontro improviso. / dram[m]a giocoso / per musica / tradotto dal francesse / e rappresentato / a Esterhaz / in occasione del felicissimo / arrivo / della a.a.l.l.r.r. / il serenissimo arciduca / d'austria / ferdinando. e / della serenissima arciduchessa / Beatrice / d'este / sul teatro di S. A. il prencipe / nicoló Esterhazy / de Galanta / nel mese d'agosto dell'anno 1775 / a Oedenburgo nella stamperia di Giuseppe Siess.

Ali, principe di Balsora, amante di Rezia	Carlo Friberth
Rezia, principesse di Persia, favorita di Sultano d'Egitto nel serraglio...........................	Maddalena Friberth
Balkis, schiava, confidente di Rezia	Barbara Dichtler
Dardana, schiava, confidente di Rezia	Elisabetta Prandtner
Osmin, schiavo d'Ali	Leopoldo Dichtler
Un calandro, inspettore del caravan magazino	Christiano Specht
Il Sultano d'Egitto	Melchiore Grießler

.... Musica di ... Hayden [*sic*] ... La Poesia ... Carlo Friberth.
[Copy: Gesellschaft der Musikfreunde, Vienna: 9212/Textb.]

The bill for printing this work was recently discovered in the Esterházy Archives at Forchtenstein Castle, together with that of the bookbinder. They are:

Catalogue

Of printing work that I the undersigned have done and delivered to the high princely Castle Eszterház, to wit:

An opera libretto in 8tavo four *Bögen* in length, of which 250 copies were printed on clean printers' paper and 50 on fine writing paper, the *Bögen* together with the paper at 7 fl. 30 xr.

Sum for 4 *Bögen*, then	30 fl.
oedenburg, 20 Sept: 1775 [in an unknown hand:] removed	2 fl.
Remainder	28 fl.

Johann Joseph Sieß mpria
Printer

[Haydn's hand:] This bill is to be paid after subtracting 2 fl.

Josephus Haydn mpria

This bill has been correctly paid to me at 28 fl. ...
[Acta varia, Fasz. 145, Gebäu Esterház, 1775, III. Quartal, No. 78. Esterházy Archives, Forchtenstein Castle. *Haydn-Studien* III/2, 95]

What I did for His Highness the
Prince of Eszterhazy for
the opera libretto on
26 Aug: 1775. At the order of H: Carl Friberth.

2 copies in natural satin with gold lettering a 45x	1	30
30 ditto in rosy coloured taffeta a 36xr	18	—
268 partly in gold paper, partly Turkish paper a 3xr	13	24
Suma	32f	54xr

Id est 32 fl. 54xr.

Mathias Pfundtner
Burg: Buchbinder
mpria.

Oedenburg, 20th Sept. 1775.

[Haydn's hand] This bill is to be paid with the sum of 32fl.

Josephus Haydn mpria

Above bill has been correctly paid with the sum of 32fl. Idem qui

Supra mpria.

[Acta varia, as *supra*, No. 79]

We do not know why Haydn subtracted two gulden from the Siess bill, probably for incomplete, mis-printed or damaged copies. Fortunately we also have the complete costume bills for *L'incontro improvviso* (which, as pointed out above, enable us to disprove the picture hitherto believed to represent a performance of this Opera on the stage at Eszterháza: *vide supra*, p. 28). In it, we have not translated some of the terms, such as 'Eln' (= *Ellen*, Eng. ells)

For
Titl: H. Highness Prince v. Eszterhazy
Various Costumes prepared for the Opera entitled
L'Incontro improviso

N° 1 Friberth, Prince Ali from Balsora

16 eln linen	a 18 xr.	4fl	48 xr
20 eln black *chenille* material	a 5 xr:	1	40.
16 eln embroidery	a 40 xr:	10	40.
85 embroidered roses	a 5 xr:	7	5.
9 eln broad silver *bordures*	a 9 xr:	1	21.
3 white feathers	a 1 fl 25 xr.	4	15[.]
one black tuft of heron's feathers	a	—	51.
Buckram and material for lining		—	54[.]
sewing thread		—	30[.]
costume jewels		2	—
cost of making		12	30[.]

N° 2. Madame Friberth, Princess of Persia

9 eln broad silver *bordures*	a 9 xr.	1	21
18 eln embroidery	a 40 xr.	12	—
90 embroidered roses	a 5	7	30[.]
4 eln silver gauze	a 30 xr.	2	—
20 eln black *chenille* material	a 5 xr:	1	40.
14 eln material for lining	q 18 xr.	4	12[.]
one tuft of heron's feathers	a	—	30.
two white feathers		2	30[.]
one black ditto		1	15[.]

Latus		79 fl	32 xr
Transporto		79 fl	32 xr
Whalebone and sewing thread		—	51.
costume jewels		2	—
laces and bows		—	15[.]
cost of making		12	30.
30 eln narrow silver *bordures*	a 3 xr.	1	30.

N° 3. Madame Dichtler, slave and *confiante*

silver *toque* for ornament		4	—
14 eln broad *bordures*	a 9 xr.	2	6.
60 eln narrow ditto	a 3 xr.	3	—
10 eln silver lace	a 15 xr.	2	30[.]
13 eln material for lining	a 18 xr.	3	54[.]
sewing thread and whalebone		—	51.
two white feathers		2	30[.]
one tuft of heron's feathers		—	30[.]
for using some satin		—	30[.]
cost of making		9	—

N° 4.	For Mlle Prandtner a dress of the same kind, costs as in the case of Mad; Dichtler		28	51.
N° 5.	Dichtler as Osmin, a slave and servant of Alli [*sic*].			

7 eln green fustian [*grien Barcan = grüner Barchent*] ......a 42 xr.	4	54.
8 eln red ditto ....a 42 xr.	5	36.
2 eln flesh-coloured linen ....a 30 xr.	1	—
	1	—
20 eln of lace ....a 15 xr.	5	—
11 eln linen ....a 18 xr.	3	18[.]
bows..	—	30[.]

Latus	174 fl	38 xr
Transporto	174 f.	38 xr
sewing thread and material for lining	—	56.
one tuft of heron's feathers	—	48[.]
cost of making	6	—

N° 6 Specht as Calender [*Calandeur*][1]

12 eln grey fustian ....a	8	24[.]
3 eln flesh-coloured linen ....a 30 xr	1	30.
2 eln material for lining ....a 18 xr.	—	36.
sewing thread and camel hair and buttons	—	30[.]
a grey beard..	1	8[.]
cost of making	3	30.

N° 7 Three Calenders [*Galanteurs*][1] of linen

36 eln grey glazed linen ....a 20 xr.	12	—
6 eln flesh-coloured ditto ....a 20 xr.	2	—
7 eln material for lining ....a 18 xr.	2	6.
Three black beards of horsehair	1	3.
Buttons and bows	—	51.
cost of making for all three	6	30.

N° 8 Grießler as Egyptian Sultan

6 eln of *toque*..a 1 f.	6	—
20 eln of *chenille* material ....a 5 xr.	1	40.
2 eln of silver *toque*	2	—
10 eln of lace ....a 15 xr.	2	30[.]

Latus	234 fl	40 xr
Transporto	234 fl	40 xr
50 eln narrow silver *bordures* ....a 3 xr.	2	30
10 eln broad ditto ....a 9 xr.	1	30
6 eln lace for trousers ....a 15 [xr.]...........	1	30
16 eln material for lining ....a 18 xr.	4	48
sewing thread and buckram	—	40
one tuft of heron's feathers	—	51.
cost of making	12	—

N° 9 Two slaves

8 eln red glazed linen ....a 20 xr:	2	40[.]
9 eln yellow ditto ....a 20 xr.	3	—
11 eln white ditto ....a 20 xr.	3	40.
3 eln blue ditto.......................................a 20..................	1	20.
bordure gr[een?]	2	—
two tufts of heron's feathers	—	30.
spangles [*flinderl = Flitter*] and bows	—	30[.]
cost of making	9	30.

N° 10 Six supers as Janizaries

36 eln of yellow glazed linen ....a 20 xr.	12	—
24 eln red ditto.......................................a 20 xr.	8	—
12 eln flesh-coloured ditto ....a 20..................	4	—

1 Calender, a mendicant dervish (O.E.D.). It has been suggested that the 'Three Calenders' may have been, literally, of linen, i.e. dolls or large-scale marionette-like figures; otherwise why 'of linen'?

12 eln unbleached canvas [*Confas* = Fr. *canevas*] ....a 14 xr...............		2	48[.]
120 pieces [? 'st.' = *Stück?*] silver *bordures*...................a 4 xr.		8	—
6 eln of blue glazed linen ....a 20 xr...............		2	—
cost of making for all six costumes		21.	50.
for linen to make six waistbands		2	—
buckram for sashes and waistbands		1	58.

Latus	344fl	15xr
Transporto	344fl	15xr
For making three knitted skirts [petticoats?], each one at 2 fl 30 xr:	7	30.
Suma:	351fl	45xr

Id est: 351 fl. 45 xr

Regulated at 345 fl because most was
previously arranged.   Johgeorg Speckh:
Kleinrath Inspector   I. R. Theatre garderob:

The above sum – f 345 – has been paid correctly and in cash by His Serene Highness Herrn Herrn
Fürsten v. Esterhazy through H. Kleinrath, Inspector

                                                            Johann georg Spöckh [*sic*]
                                                            I. R. Theatre garderob:
Vienna, 3rd Nov. 775.

[Illiterate tailor, who signed bill with three crosses.]

[Acta varia, Fasz. 145, Gebäu Esterház, 1775, III. Quartal, No. 27. Esterházy Archives, Forchtenstein. *Haydn-Studien* III/2, 96–9]

We may add to this important costume bill the fact that Jens Peter Larsen discovered the whole autograph manuscript of the Opera in Leningrad (minus the Overture, which the present writer identified and published separately), as a result of which the authentic text of the whole work could be established and published (*vide infra*, pp. 262 ff.).

To return to our report in the *Preßburger Zeitung*: following this gala performance of Haydn's new Opera, the company received a *Souper* and then repaired to the great Chinese ball-room for a masked ball. The correspondent counted the astonishing number of guests: 1,380 persons.

The morning of the third day was given to a period of rest. Even the princely cannon, which had thundered out to announce the events of the previous days, were silent. Carriages brought the guests to an afternoon drive in the park, and the Prince guided the company to a part in which a village market had been established. On both sides of the *allée* there were twenty-four stalls covered with leaves from which the guests could purchase not only trinkets but jewellery in gold and precious stones. From here they went to a clearing where even Prince Nicolaus outdid himself.

After the high personages had examined the various merchants' stalls, they came to a great open clearing, which reminded one of the great boulevards in Paris. Here one saw: (1) a *pulcinello* [Punch & Judy] theatre; (2) a hawker's stall; (3) a female singer who sang pictures [usually hideous deeds, held up to the audience in form of a picture, while the singer sang verses describing the event; later known as *Moritat*]; (4) a dentist's stand; (5) a dance platform with peasant [folk] music; (6) two musicians' stands. As soon as you entered this section, you were invited to some special pleasantry. Three characters of well-known farcical roles displayed their art, Harlequin, Pierrot and *Balliazo* [*Pagliaccio*], just as in Paris [*sic: commedia dell'arte!*]. Thereafter a dentist, mounted on a horse, arrived, with his assistants mounted on mechanical horses; then a hawker, seated on a waggon drawn by six oxen; the waggon was accompanied by monkeys, lions and tigers. The hawker had on a large sheet a list of all his cures in pictorial form, which he humorously explained. Then each one took his place and displayed his abilities. Monsieur Bienfait, who is in the actual service of the Prince, showed the artful tricks of his marionettes; the cobbler from Paris played his little farce; the hawker hawked his wares; the dentist showed his abilities strutting on stilts eighteen feet high, and how he drew teeth; the 'picture singer' explained her painted murder scene in a French song.

After this *Théâtre de la foire dans le goût françois*, the company repaired to the marionette theatre, where Carlos d'Ordoñez's *Alceste* (German adaptation of Calzabigi's *Alceste* by Pauersbach) was given. The libretto reads:

Alceste / ein parodirt- / Gesungenes Trauerspiel / in drey Aufzügen. / Bey Gelegenheit / Der höchst-erfreulichen Gegenwart / Ihrer königlichen Hoheiten / des / Durchlautigsten Erzherzogs / FERDINAND, / und Allerhöchst-Dero / Durchlauchtigsten Gemahlinn / **Beatrice, von Este**, / in einer / Marionetten Operette zum erstenmale / zu Esterház / Auf der fürstlichen Marionetten Bühne / im Jahre 1775. aufgeführet. / Oedenburg, gedruckt bei Johann Joseph Sieß.

[Copy: Stadtbibliothek, Vienna, 140046]

The interesting music to this work, from Haydn's own library, is now in the Esterházy Archives, Budapest (Ms. Mus. Opera 714); it is probably Ordoñez's autograph score and is entitled 'Musica / Della Parodia d'Alceste' and signed at the end 'O: A: M: D: D[flourish]: G: E: H: A: [flourish]'.

After the marionette performance there were fireworks, and after *souper* another masked ball.

On the morning of 31 August there was a deer hunt in the morning. In the afternoon the Carl Wahr Troupe gave Regnard's *Le distrait* (in German, as *Der Zerstreute*) with the famous music by Haydn. The cast:

Leander:	H. Wahr
Mad. Crognac:	M. Partlinn[1]
Isabelle, ihre Tochter:	M. Prothke
Clarice, Liebste des Leander:	M. Körner
Der Ritter, ihr Bruder:	H. Litter
Valr, Oheim des Leander:	H. Christl
Karl, Bedienter des Leander:	H. Cremeri
Johann:	H. Schlezer
Lisette:	D[emoiselle] Reinerinn.

After the evening meal, the company, with the princely *Feldharmonie* (wind band) went to the great oval clearing in the park, to see the gala illumination:

The place was magnificently illuminated and for ornaments there were large transparent *Konversationsgemälde* [*galant* scenes in the French manner], flower pots and garlands. In the middle was a gloriette, shining and shimmering, on which the lords and ladies could see the whole of the illuminations at once.

A cannon salute brought a swarm of 2,000 Hungarian and Croatian peasants who filled the clearing in an instant and, swinging banners, danced to their own music and filled the air with shouts of joy. This *Volksfest* went on till the early hours of the morning, and as the day dawned on the exhausted folk dancers and the sleepy guests, who were also participants in a final masked ball, the park was softly illuminated by innumerable green lampions.

---

1 The '-in' suffixes have been retained here, for a change, to show how they appear in the sources. H.C.R.L.

It was the last, and certainly the greatest, of the *feste* at Eszterháza Castle on this kind of scale. From 1776, Prince Nicolaus would institute a regular operatic season with works by many foreign, and most Italian, composers; Haydn continued to write works for the stage, of course, but the whole organization was to change completely.

On 9 September 1775, *Regent* Rahier writes to the Prince that

I have received your high order and forthwith yesterday informed Haydn's brother, and today the *Bassetlist* ['cellist] Marteau, that their respective services are terminated, and I have given the order to the Chief Cashier that no one of the musicians, no matter on what excuse, is to receive any money except on Your Highness's order; I have subtracted 1 fl. from the monthly salary of Friebert [*sic*] and Schiringer, and called in the capital from Frau Fribert's father.

Marteau gave to the Castle Inspector here the coat and the waistcoat from his summer uniform, and will betake himself to Eszterhaz at the first available opportunity, where he has his things and the rest of his uniform. Your Highness could deign to order the *Kapelmeister* [*sic*] to receive these other things from him [Marteau] there. . . . Eisenstadt, 9th Sept. 1775.

[A.M. III, 194, Esterházy Archives, Budapest. Valkó II, 579; *HJB* VIII, 154f. (corrected); Bartha 74f.]

This severe order was probably the result of some disciplinary infraction, but once again Haydn managed to intervene, and neither Johann Haydn nor Marteau were dismissed.[1]

Eight days after this letter, Archbishop Prince Migazzi from Vienna was at Eszterháza; a concert was given in his honour, but there are no details of the programme.[2]

We may notice briefly some bills of the period[3] and then proceed to a list of the *Capelle*:

Specifications Quittung [receipt], according to which the following chamber musicians received their salaries *pro Decembris* 1775 . . . :

	Fl.	Xr.
1. Capellmeister Josephus Haydn mpria	48	50
2. Soprano Barbara Dichtler	16	40
3. ditto Maddalena Friberth	41	40
4. Tenor Carlo Friberth	25	—
5. Leopoldo Dichtler	28	—
6. Bass singer Christian Specht	37	30
7. Violinist Luigi Tomasini	40	12½
8. ditto Joseph Burksteiner [*sic*]	20	—
9. ditto Joseph Hoffmann	16	40
10. ditto Johann Dietzl	16	40
11. Violoncellist Xavier Marteau	42	42½
12. Hunting horn player Joseph Oliva	42	42½
13. ditto Franz Pauer	38	32½
14. ditto Carl Franz	27	30

1 The pardon in question is probably contained in the following note from the Esterházy Archives in Eisenstadt, which Pohl (II, 57f., n.) discovered; the document is dated Eisenstadt, 7 October 1775, and reads: 'Since I have forgiven those musicians and reinstated all of them in service, their salary is to be paid to them as before', signed Prince Nicolaus Esterházy.
2 Information from Dr Janos Harich.
3 (1) Mathias Rockobauer (Eisenstadt, 1 Nov.) three dozen [oboe] reeds. A.M. XVI, 1061; Valkó II, 578. (2) M. Rockobauer (Eisenstadt, 15 Dec.) two dozen bassoon reeds. A.M. XVI, 1060; Valkó II, 578. (3) the usual 'Rorate' money that Haydn collected (Eisenstadt, 31 Dec.). A.M. XVI, 1058; Valkó II, 578. (4) Dietzl's annual bill for strings 'and such things' (from 1 Jan. to end of Dec.). A.M. XVI 1059; Valkó II, 578.

[Fl. Xr.]

15. ditto Joseph Dietzl 32 57
16. Oboist Carl Chorus 32 57
17. ditto Zacharias Pohl 28 47
18. Bassoonist Carl Schiringer 32 57
19. ditto Johan Hinterberger 32 57
20. ditto Caspar Petziwal [*sic*] .... 20 —
21. Harpist J. Krumpholtz .... 25 —
22. Soprano ⎫ Josephus Haydn mpria [who signed for them in their absence; they   10 26
23. Alto   ⎬ were the church singers at Eisenstadt.]   10 26
24. ditto   ⎭   10 26

[There follows some increases applying to Nos. 11, 12, 15, 16, 18, and 19, each of whom received 50 Fl. for their double households; *vide passim*.] [Add: six entries of 10 Fl. 50 xr. each]

25. Bassoonist Ignatz Drobney... 25 40
26. Clarinettist Reimund [*sic*] Griesbacher .... 25 —
27. ditto Anthon Griesbacher.. 25 —

Summa:... 847fl.03 xr.
[A.M. XIII, 800, Esterházy Archives, Budapest. Valkó II, 576]

This was an impressive list of musicians for the period. Naturally we have, on paper, a superfluity of horn and bassoon players, but as we have seen, many of them played other instruments. The two clarinet players, for whom not a single note in any of Haydn's works of this period exists (if we except *Die Feuersbrunst*),[1] were officially engaged on 1 January 1776; but, as we see, they were already with the *Capelle* at least a month earlier (perhaps on trial?). Haydn could now muster an orchestra of two oboes, two clarinets, two bassoons, two (four) horns, timpani (Peczival) and about (counting Haydn) four first violins, three seconds, two violas, one 'cello and one double bass.

Our final document, which we present in abbreviated form, is a lengthy letter from *Regent* Rahier to Prince Nicolaus of 29 December:

[Summary:] In the two duplicate copies of the musicians' contracts, 'Leopoldt Dichtler's nine *Eimer* of wine, Frantz Pauer's 50 Fl. [double household] and Melchior Griesler's ½ *Metzen* of semolina' were left out of their respective contracts, and since in their old contracts they were seen to be house officers, they have asked that this term be used in the new contracts. 'Kapellmeister Hayden [*sic*] was extremely sorry to see that in his contract he alone has been made an exception of, in that he is to lose the little *Naturalien* that an organist receives when he is hired and therefore he most submissively asks – inasmuch as he has always up to now fulfilled with great diligence and efficiency all the high commands he has received, and will continue positively to do the same in the future – that he receive in grace said *Naturalien*, which only constitute 112 Fl. 15 xr., without making that exception as was done in his case, and which in view of his services should be his due. So I rewrote the duplicate contracts', reinstating the missing items in the first cases, and adding 'House Officer', whereas 'in the case of the *Capellmeister* I have left out the "N.B." in the organist's clause.' The rewritten contracts were sent with empty spaces for Secretary Kaufmann's signature. . . . Esterházy did not react to all this until 16 June, but then wrote that he had returned the altered contracts for implementation but that 'the Musique does not belong to the privy section of the house, so instead of "House Officer" only the word "Officer" is to be placed. As far as Haydn is concerned, he is obliged, as long as he receives the organist clause's benefits, to see to it that the Eysenstädter organist post is filled', i.e. even if Haydn is absent. 'Vienna, 16 June 1776.'

---

1 For which no precise date has been established.

This was once again one of Prince Nicolaus's Byzantine operations to do with the proper 'Stand'. That which interests us, however, is the new tone in which martinet Rahier deals with Haydn. For some time now, Rahier faithfully transmits all Haydn's wishes, not only for himself but for his musicians, to the Prince and, as we see, intercedes on their behalf. Among the many remarkable achievements of Haydn at Eszterháza, his diplomatic powers must be reckoned second only after his actual music.

As the first era of Eszterháza comes to an end, with that extraordinary festival for Archduke Ferdinand and his consort, we interrupt the Chronicle and turn to the music that Haydn had composed in the years 1766–75, in which he gradually became a European influence, and in which his own style achieved a great unity, polish and depth.

CHAPTER THREE

Haydn as full *Capellmeister*: his new Role as Composer of Vocal Music

IN A BIOGRAPHY OF THIS LENGTH, some decision had to be made about the analyses of large musical works, of which this volume contains a spectacularly large number – all except one of the major operas, for example. Fascinating though these works are, we have forced ourselves to treat the whole of Haydn's musical life as a *crescendo*, and to expand the detail as we move forward. We felt that *The Creation* and *The Seasons*, the 'Salomon' Symphonies, the late string Quartets (from Op. 71 to Op. 103), piano Sonatas and Trios merited careful and at times minute investigation. Space flatly prohibits such a detailed examination of these richly rewarding operas and the many instrumental works of this period: for the symphonies, there is a detailed study in Landon *SYM*, and for the quarters in Finscher (1974) and Barrett-Ayres (1974). Thus the treatment of Haydn's music in this volume is of necessity a survey rather than a detailed analysis in depth.

The works which we shall consider in this chapter are (in chronological order):
Missa Cellensis in honorem B.V.M. (1766);
La canterina (1766);
Stabat Mater (1767);
Cantata, 'Applausus' (1768) and its subsequent use as smaller pieces of Church music (Offertorium, 'Dictamina mea', etc.);
Lo speziale (1768);
Missa 'Sunt bona mixta malis' (*c.* 1768) and *Missa in honorem B.V.M.* ('Great Organ Mass'; *c.* 1768–9);
some smaller Church music;
Le pescatrici (1769);
Salve Regina a quattro voci (1771);
Missa Sancti Nicolai (1772);
Acide, second version (fragment, 1773);
L'infedeltà delusa (1773);
the Marionette Operas of 1773 (*Philemon und Baucis*; *Hexen-Schabbas*) and some lost *Singspiele*;
Il ritorno di Tobia (1775); and
L'incontro improvviso (1775).

Missa Cellensis in honorem Beatissimae Virginis Mariae
(XXII:5) (1766)

Scoring: S-A-T-B Soli; Choir (S-A-T-B). 2 ob., 2 bsn. (written out in Benedictus only), 2 trpt., timp., str., org. The two horn parts for the Benedictus that are found in some sources (not in the autograph) may have been a later addition of Haydn's.

Principal sources: Autograph fragments: (1) Kyrie (dated 1766) and 'Christe eleison': Biblioteca Centrală de Stat, Bucharest; formerly Artaria (*vide infra*, p. 243); (2) Bars 90–123 of Benedictus and first bar of 'Osanna' with the note, '♯ muß ausgeschrieben werden', together with the whole Agnus. Esterházy Archives, Budapest, Ms. Mus. 1. 21. The watermarks of the second fragment appear otherwise only in works of the period 1769–73 and are known as Larsen 8 (*HÜB* 164f.) or Bartha-Somfai (p. 445) 192, and Larsen 9 or Bartha-Somfai 193. In the latter book they are reproduced in facsimile. Larsen 8: Michael Haydn Aria 'Ex Rebus Leopold Dichtler', Esterházy Archives, Eisenstadt, dated 1771; *Missa S. Nicolai*, authentic parts by Elssler Sen., same archives: V. II, Hn. II, Ob. I & II, Sop. (Dec. 1772); Schiringer *Regina Coeli* (Elssler Sen.), Stadtpfarrkirche Eisenstadt; *Le Pescatrici* (*Bogen* 4/5 of Atto III; 1769–70) (Esterházy Archives, Budapest); *Salve Regina* G minor (Berlin State Library: 1771); *Missa S. Nicolai*, autograph (Berlin State Library: 1772); Symphonies 42 (1771), 47 (1772), 50 (1773) (in Budapest, Budapest and Berlin resp.); *L'infedeltà delusa* (1773). Larsen 9: Michael Haydn Aria 1771 (*supra*); Elssler Sen. copy of *Missa S. Nicolai* (Dec.

1772: 'Violone'; *supra*). In some versions the letters 'IGW' are separate from the stag; this is the case in the latter paper and also in the *Missa Cellensis in honorem* [etc.]. Also the same watermarks in: *Le pescatrici* (*supra*: *Bogen* 3/4 of Atto III); *L'infedeltà delusa* (*supra*); *Salve Regina* (*supra*); Symphonies 42, 47, 50 (*supra*); autograph of *Salve Regina* (*supra*) and *Missa S. Nicolai* (*supra*); Baryton Trio 109 ('Fatto a posta nihil sine causa': Esterházy Archives, Budapest, Ms. mus. I. 48.[b]).

Facsimile: The Roumanian fragment complete in *HJB* IX, 308ff.

Some secondary sources: Esterházy Archives, Eisenstadt; MS. parts by an otherwise unknown copyist, and the source (which has the supplementary horn parts in the Benedictus) did not form part of the original material of the princely Church Choir; possibly it came with the legacy of Carl Kraus (died 1802) from the Stadtpfarrkirche. Janaček Museum, Brno (CSSR) A 5710 from Zdǎř-kur (Alt-Brünn), dated 1779 'Descripsit Jacobus Tomassek', which the present writer found under anonymous works in 1959. Göttweig Abbey, 1782. Reliable old parts also in the Minoritenkloster, Vienna, and the Monastery of Klosterneuburg.

Critical edition: Haydn Society G. A. (Brand), XXIII/1, 1951 without either autograph fragments; requires revision. Piano-vocal score (Landon), U.E. (H.-M.P.) 14/15, 1952.

Literature: Brand, *Die Messen*, 52 *passim*; Larsen, *HÜB* 167. Landon in *HJB* IX, 306f.

Until 1951, no printed score of this Mass in its uncut version had been published. The shortened version, for which Haydn can accept no responsibility, was published in score by Breitkopf & Härtel in 1807; it is reputed to have been shortened by Ignaz v. Seyfried (Hoboken II, 79). The extraordinary length of the work made it unsuitable for normal liturgical purposes.

The discovery of the Kyrie autograph, with its dating of 1766, put the work in a much earlier period than had been hitherto assumed. Only the late Carl Maria Brand was always persuaded that, of the proposed Larsen dates 1769–73 (on the basis of the watermarks of the Budapest fragment), 1769 'or even earlier' would be better suited to the work's style.[1] The fact that the experts, from Pohl (who dated the work 1781) to Larsen, Landon (*SYM* 310) and Feder (who even dates the work 1774; *HJB* IV, 108), should not have been able to date this work even approximately on the basis of its style shows that our knowledge of Haydn is only just now beginning to take anything like a solidly scientific shape; but it also tells us something of the stylistic complexities of this, Haydn's first great vocal work as princely *Capellmeister*. As said above, it used to be

---

[1] At the Second Conference of the Haydn Society, Salzburg, Autumn 1950. Present: Brand, Ernst Hartmann (representing Universal Edition and Haydn-Mozart Presse, Salzburg), Erhard Jaeger (General Manager of Haydn Society), Gertrud Meister (protocol), Landon, Larsen, Schmid. Discussion: publication of Masses and Symphonies. For the record, the First Conference of the Society took place in Kiel in October 1949. Present: Friedrich Blume, Brand, Hartmann, Landon, Larsen. Discussion of whole project of *Gesamtausgabe*. Third Conference: Alt-Aussee, Spring 1951. Present: Thomas Crowder (President of Haydn Society), Alan Forbes (Secretary, Boston Office), Gertrud Meister (protocol), Landon, Larsen, Schmid. Subject: preparation of *divertimenti* (Schmid) for *Gesamtausgabe*. At the Second Conference, Brand proposed 1769 or earlier for the *Missa* and was violently attacked by Larsen for this heretical view which, in the event, proved quite correct.

known as the *Missa Sanctae Caeciliae* on the basis of a late MS. in the Österreichische Nationalbibliothek, Vienna, and while the title is unauthentic the connection with the St Cecilia Brotherhood in Vienna is not as fortuitous as might be thought. To see the connection we must look to the work's origins.

It is a so-called 'Cantata Mass', which means that it is much longer than the usual Mass and is laid out, particularly in the Gloria, in cantata-like movements. Mozart's Mass in C minor (K.427) is another famous example of the Austrian school, and of course Bach's Mass in B minor is the most celebrated example of all. Haydn did, in fact, know the Bach Mass, because there was a copy in the Esterházy Archives at Eisenstadt, but it is probable that this was a relatively late MS. (1790–1800?), purchased from Traeg who advertised the work in his 1804 Catalogue.[1] Haydn's immediate predecessors in the local field were Antonio Caldara, whose *Missa dolorosa* (1735) and the magnificent *Missa in honorem Sanctificationi Joannis Nepomucensis* (1726) are most impressive examples of this cantata treatment. The flourishing high trumpets and timpani are also part of this old tradition. Haydn's own teacher, George Reutter, Jr., composed such a work in 1734, known as the *Missa S. Caroli*, which has, as Erich Schenk[2] pointed out some years ago, several points in common with Haydn's *Missa* of 1766: the drop to *piano* at the word 'mortuorum', the drop of a fourth in the 'Passus' symbol and even a transmission of the old *messa di voce* effect from Italy to Haydn via his erstwhile teacher:

[Reutter: *Missa S. Caroli*: 'Gratias']

[Haydn: *Missa Cellensis* (1766): 'Laudamus te']

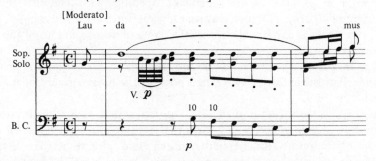

A more immediate source was Florian Leopold Gassmann's *Missa Sanctae Caeciliae*, composed about 1765[3] and probably known to Haydn before he began his own work for Mariazell. The Feast of St Cecilia was celebrated by a Brotherhood (*Brüderschaft*) in

---

1 P. 58, item 151: 'Bach, J. S. Missa a 5 Voci 2 Viol. 2 Fl. 2 Ob. 3 Trombe Tymp. A e B.' Alexander Weinmann: *Johann Traeg, Die Musikalienverzeichnisse von 1799 und 1804*, Band I, Vienna 1973, p. 422.
2 *Anzeiger der phil-hist. Klasse der Österreichischen Akademie der Wissenschaften*, Jahrgang 1953, No. 8, pp. 127f.
3 Franz Kosch in *Studien zur Musikwissenschaft* XIV (1927), p. 235f.

Vienna who gave a Litany on the preceding evening (21 November) and a Mass or concert, usually (if liturgical) in the Cathedral. In 1767, we read in the *Wiener Diarium* (No. 94, Wednesday, 25th Wintermonth [November]) that

> 'the Musical Brotherhood this evening gave the Vespers in honour of the Feast of their patron, which falls on the Sunday. Monday morning this Feast will be celebrated by a solemn High Mass, during which various excellent musicians will be heard in arias and concertos [*sic*].'

Thus it was not so eccentric to connect Haydn's cantata-like *Missa* with the St Cecilia works of his immediate predecessors.

Haydn sets out in many of the movements to be deliberately conservative, just as would Mozart in his Mass in C minor; but both composers have extremely 'modern' and even fashionable movements as well. The jolt between the fabulous eight-part 'Qui tollis' and the saucy, Italian-opera style of the 'Laudamus' in Mozart's K.427 is just as great as the stylistic chasm that positively yawns between the gravely beautiful 'Gratias' in the old fugal style and the 'Quoniam', coloratura-laden and written within a brilliant aria style that also includes trumpets and kettledrums, in Haydn's *Missa*. There are similar stylistic discrepancies throughout this interesting, brilliant, uneven and yet curiously gripping work. The rapt, other-worldly beauty of the slow introduction hardly prepares us for the forthright, almost jaunty style of the Allegro, with its Reutter-like 'dashing violins' and the fanfare-like trumpets and drums. The 'Christe', on the other hand, is not at all conventionally modern but returns to the style of Italian church music of the 1740s (the imitations between the first and second violins at bars 70ff. are typical). The tenor solo is forcefully set off by the various entrances of the chorus, *forte*; and in one beautiful instance, the tenor holds a high *e′* for three bars as the chorus enters with 'Christe eleison' (bars 136–7). The concluding part of this Kyrie section is the first of several fugues which are the glory of the Mass. For years Haydn had obviously longed to get his teeth into church music, and in some respects the inordinate length of the *Missa Cellensis* of 1766 reflects his frustration at the years of forced inactivity in this field.

The Gloria is subdivided into a number of sections:

(1) 'Gloria in excelsis Deo', a brilliant opening with Haydn's 'fingerprint' kettledrum signals (bars 1–2) which reappear several times in the movement, also in the trumpets alone. This is perhaps the most effective and homogeneous of the 'modern' movements up to now.

(2) 'Laudamus te', a very ornate soprano aria, which shows the close proximity of opera to church music in those days. This is possibly the most conventional movement of the work.

(3) 'Gratias', a slow fugue in the 'stilo antico' which shows what contrapuntal power Haydn is able to generate in a form that continued to be ageless for centuries. There are highly individual touches in the sudden *p* and *f* alterations (bars 243ff.) which remind one of similar flashes of inspiration in the 'Qui tollis' of Mozart's K.427.

(4) 'Domine Deus', although using a standard operatic language (three-eight 'slow' Allegro) is so marvellously constructed that it must be reckoned as one of the most original parts of the work. It is in a very broadly conceived form, with huge blocks of music all inter-related in a subtle way. First a long alto solo, then an equally long tenor solo, then a bass solo of great difficulty with enormous leaps ranging from E below the bass clef to *d′*. A moment of curiously gripping unifying power: the series of repeated, Gregorian-chant-like notes at 'Rex coelestis' (alto, bars 379ff.), which is

taken over by the tenor at 'Domine Filius' (bars 435ff.) and finally by the bass at 'Domine Deus' (bars 507ff.), and is always accompanied by a previous modulation: first time after modulation C to G major; then in A minor but moving afterwards to D minor where the repeated notes suddenly solidify into one huge repeated note *d* (bars 446ff.) which goes on for seven bars – a great moment. At bars 524ff., we are in F major and the whole process begins again, but with the various entrances now accelerated: each of the three solo voices (soprano is silent throughout) enter after four bars and form a lovely *terzetto*.

(5) 'Qui tollis', perhaps the most strikingly modern movement of the Gloria. Here again, as in the previous 'Domine Deus', we may observe Haydn's subtle application to large vocal forms of a device which was an integral basis of the Vivaldian *concerto grosso*: the *ritornello* form. Just as in a Vivaldi concerto, the *tutti* returns in various keys (e.g. I–V–II–VI–V–I), the principle was applied by Haydn to such a movement as the 'Domine Deus'. In the 'Qui tollis', which starts in C minor, we may see another application of the *ritornello* principle – here a kind of question and answer: 'Qui tollis' (*forte*, massively chordal) followed by an antiphonal figure (*piano*, only two vocal parts): see bars 579–80 and 581–2. This reappears in the relative major (bars 597ff.), i.e. III, then in VI (bars 619ff.). Parallel to this operation is another one in which there is, literally, a *ritornello* that we first find in E flat (593ff.), then in VI (bars 615ff.) and at the end in the tonic (C minor, bars 631ff.); and in this latter, parallel *ritornello* scheme we find Haydn's language of the period expressed in a whole series of Berensonian 'fingerprints', not least of which are the syncopations so characteristic of this period.[1]

(6) 'Quoniam', a dazzlingly bright aria for solo soprano and full orchestra with trumpets and kettledrums (the ♩♫♩ rhythm of the Gloria is back again, as it almost always is with Haydn's brass and drum parts; after the 'Haydn ornament', the crossed turn, this is the most prominent and typical of the Haydnesque fingerprints). Some of the coloratura is staggeringly difficult (bars 706ff.). Note the old (e.g. literal repetitions of a whole bar as in a Baroque concerto: 709–10) and the new (e.g. the weaving contrapuntal lines of the *p* section with the solo timpani – no trumpets – at 717ff.).

(7) 'In gloria Dei', a magnificent fugue that sweeps along in one huge *forte* outburst: one passage of exhilarating power is a series of syncopations (again) that rise an octave and then fall into the tonic and a fine entrance of the trumpets and drums (bars 776ff.), which have our obligatory rhythm at strategic places throughout.

In the Credo we find the soprano solo entering with the words 'Credo in unum Deum' throughout the whole movement in a kind of super *ritornello* effect: it was a device that Mozart would use with wonderful effect in his 'Credo Mass' (K.257) ten years later. We would draw attention to a last entrance of this 'Credo' at bars 255ff., where Haydn manages to make the *Leitmotiv* audible even though the metre has shifted from four-four to three-four. In the middle section, we have, astonishingly, an accompanied recitative, just as if we are in an *opera seria*; which turns into a beautiful Largo tenor aria. He is joined by the three lower solo voices in the whole Crucifixion scene, which is of hypnotic power (the violins repeating a 'broken' melodic line bar after bar, from 133 to 155). 'But no words' (to quote *SYM*, 311)

can possibly describe the shattering drama of the 'Et vitam venturi' fugue. Here is the culmination of the C major style; trumpets sound forth the gripping theme in

---

1 The 'broken melodic line' on which the bass part is *on* the beat and often marked with a tall *staccato*. Landon *SYM*, 333.

brazen majesty, and the vivid passage work of the violins in constant semiquavers with the bass moving in inflexible quavers (that rock of energy so often found in the previous instrumental works) pass before us like a mighty medieval pageant; at the end, the first trumpet, rising to the highest *clarino* register, flashes like a shining sword across the horizon. It is one of the greatest movements in all Haydn, not equalled until the late masses produced after the second London sojourn.

Of the concluding sections, we would draw particular attention to the individuality of the Benedictus, a stern movement in C minor which is (as *Don Juan* by Gluck would be in instrumental music) the harbinger of the *Sturm und Drang* about to break over Austrian music. It is also the precursor of the great Benedictus in the 'Nelson' Mass. The 'Dona' closing fugue is curiously unsettling and very forward-looking: in it, there is a certain ambivalence (bars 126ff.) that suggests Haydn's growing sense of power and the gradual darkening of his musical horizon.

The first recording of this work was made by the Haydn Society in December 1950.[1]

La Canterina, *Intermezzo in Musica* (XXVIII:2)
Opera in two Acts (1766)

Scoring: Three S (Gasperina, Apollonia, Don Ettore) and Tenor (Don Pelagio), 2 fl., 2 ob., 2 cor. angl., 2 cor., str. (harpsichord [and bassoon] *continuo*).
Principal source: Autograph (missing a small scene in the second Finale: reconstructed on pp. 108f. of *Werke*), Esterházy Archives, Budapest, dated 1766. Ms. mus. I, 1.
Libretto: author unknown. Printed libretto (1767): *vide supra*, p.135.
Critical edition: *Joseph Haydn Werke* XXV/2 (Bartha). Piano-vocal score (Geiringer), Music Press, New York (1947).

Literature: Geiringer 1932, 103f. Wirth II, 15ff. Landon in *NOHM* VII, 184f. Bartha-Somfai 384–6. In this and future listings of this kind, we have attempted to make a sensible selection of the available literature; thus we have selected, of the various Geiringer editions, the one entry which seemed to us the most interesting (in 1932 valuable because of musical examples, missing in 1947); the same applies to Wirth I and II. L. Wendschuh's monograph, *Über Haydns Opern*, Rostock 1895 is so superseded that it was cited only in exceptional cases.

This charming *Intermezzo* is Haydn's modest but effective entry on the *opera buffa* stage. It showed that he could write witty and amusing comic opera that enchanted not only Prince Nicolaus but the whole audience. *La canterina* is the other side of the 1766 coin: having displayed his talents, like a medieval prestidigitator, in all its guises for Our Lady (to Whom the Mass is, of course, dedicated), Haydn now proceeds to show his abilities as a writer of *opera buffa* in the Italian tradition. Barbara Dichtler sang Don Ettore as a *Hosenrolle* and, in the old *commedia dell'arte* tradition, the apparent old mother of the singer (*la canterina*) Gasparina, whose name is Apollonia, was sung in falsetto by Leopold Dichtler. Haydn was quite aware of this tradition, of course, having been intimately connected with the Kurz-Bernadon Company in the early 1750s, whose Hanswurstiada were all based on *commedia dell'arte* figures, often with lewd connotations and interpretations. 'Eh, ruffianaccia cenciosa', says Gasparina to her false mother (Recit., p. 62): in the old Venetian tradition 'Ruffiana' was the name for a procuress (or, if more innocent, a 'match-maker').

1 Rosl Schwaiger (S), Sieglinde Wagner (A), Herbert Handt (T), Walter Berry (B), the Akademie Kammerchor, the Vienna Symphony, Josef Nebois (Baroque *Positiv* of the 17th cent.), conducted by Hans Gillesberger. Recording supervisors: H. C. Robbins Landon, Richard Wadleigh.

Synopsis of the plot: Gasparina and her pretended mother live in the house of, and are supported by, *Maestro di capella* Don Pelagio, who gives Gasparina free music lessons. G. would rather enjoy the favours of the dandy Don Ettore if he would only be more generous. He arrives with a diamond necklace of his mother's and the ensuing scene promises well but is interrupted by the Maestro's arrival. Don E. is passed off as a cloth merchant to the old Don P., who is talked into giving money for a new dress. Don E. is eased out and to cheer him up, a *rendez-vous* is arranged in a coffee house. Don P. sings an aria he has composed and the music lesson begins. A. is sent for some chocolate so that Don P. can propose marriage to G., who avoids answering through A's return. A. so annoys Don P. that he leaves, but in the door he overhears the two women making fun of him and flirting from the window with Don E. Don P. swears revenge. He returns with the police in order to throw the women out of his house. All is lost. A. disappears but G. still persists. Her entreaties are successful, she is forgiven. She faints. Don P., together with A. and Don E., attempt to revive her, which operation is rendered easier by the appearance of a money purse from Don P. and a ring from Don E. 'Viviamo tutti quanti, per poter allegri star ∴'.

A cynical plot which, as Geiringer (1932, 103) rightly remarks, cannot escape the presence of its famous precursor, Pergolesi's enchanting *La serva padrona*, the father of *intermezzi*. But if Gasparina is the modern version of Serpina, Haydn has now increased the number of persons involved from two (the typical number for Italian *intermezzi*) to four; which in turn means that he can provide the little opera with two delightfully light-hearted finales. Here are the first of Haydn's famous ensembles, which will crown *La vera costanza* and *La fedeltà premiata*. Geiringer thinks that the clever way in which Haydn intermixes aria with accompanied recitative shows the influence of Nicola Logroscino: we see this process even in *La canterina*'s opening aria (there was no Overture to the usual *intermezzo*). Parody was always one of Haydn's specialities, and here we find the *opera seria* lampooned mercilessly: huge *ritornelli*, separating tiny fragments of ridiculously pathetic text ('quei dolci lumi? Ite al tiranno!') in No. 2, Don P's recitative and aria that he has newly composed. In the Aria, with the Metastasio-like text 'Io sposar l'empio tiranno', we find a parody of the famous 'obbligato' instruments so beloved in *opera seria* – here two wildly exaggerated horn parts.[1] The most discussed number is Gasparina's C minor Aria 'Non v'è chi mi aiuta', a desperate *Sturm und Drang* outburst with cors anglais, one of the rare times that Haydn ever used these favourite instruments in any key except E flat: as in *Così fan tutte*, part of the whole desperation is parody, but as often with Haydn, he becomes so involved with the girl's pleadings (even if he knows they are all 'stage' pleadings) that he is soon completely identified with them. We shall see this same almost automatic identification with the 'underdog', the downtrodden, the poor, in scenes from *L'infedeltà delusa* and *Die Feuersbrunst*.

In the first Finale, we see clearly that Haydn already possessed a clear concept of how small rhythmic figures must be made to work for the cohesion and unity of such an ensemble. It was a concept inherited from the Italians and may be seen in such a work as Piccinni's famous and epoch-making *La buona figliuola*, which preceded *La canterina* by only a few years, and in other *opere buffe* that followed Piccinni's pioneer efforts, But Haydn's orchestration is more incisive and the rhythm tauter. It is only a step from *La canterina*'s

---

1 Not four as in Landon, *SYM*, 313: the four horns are found on a MS. copy of the score which we studied at Boston in 1946–7, but which are simply a series of doublings etc. to make the two (real) parts easier.

to *La fedeltà premiata*'s

Ques-ti tor - ti, questi af - fron - ti [etc]
[Finale Atto I]

Stabat Mater (XX*bis*) (1767)

Scoring: S-A-T-B Soli; Choir (S-A-T-B). 2 ob., 2 cor angl., str., org. [bsn.].

Principal sources: (1) MS. parts, 4° Italian paper (three crescents of decreasing size, letters 'CS' over 'C'), *c.* 1767–80(?), reliable source that preserves the 'Haydn ornament' (crossed turn), discovered by the present writer in 1959 at St Michael's Church, Oedenburg (Sopron). (2) MS. parts by Johann Elssler of the Neukomm version (newly orchestrated) – see *Haydn: the Late Years 1801–1809*, p. 287 – Esterházy Archives, Budapest, Ms. mus. I. 160. Although this is a very late source, if we ignore the additional orchestration by Neukomm, the source is textually interesting: written in 1803. A parellel source is the (late) MS. score, partly Elssler, in the *Hofburgkapelle*. (3) MS. parts, National Széchényi Library, Budapest, Ms. mus. IV. 67. Last quarter of eighteenth century. (4) MS. score, formerly Göttweig Abbey, signed 'Willibaldus Bürkhofer 1773 19ᶰᵒ 9bris [Nov.]' (complete photocopy: C. M. Brand's Archives; we were shown this in 1952). (5) MS. parts, formerly Göttweig Abbey, 'Comp. P. Marianus 1779 Gottwic.'; both sources 4 and 5 were lost during the Second World War. (6) First edition in score by John Bland, London 1783 (announced in *Morning Herald* of 16–18 Apr. 1783 as being ready in June): 'The celebrated / Stabat-Mater / as performed at the / Nobility's Concert; / Composed by / Giuseppe Haydn ...' (copies: British Museum, Coll. Landon, etc.). (7) Score by Sieber, Paris (announced 17 March 1785 in *Journal de Paris*). Long contemporary review of the work when performed in Paris on 9 April 1781: *Mercure de France* (April 1781, pp. 127ff., with comparison of Pergolesi's work). Sieber title: 'Du Repertoire de M Le Gros Pensionaire du Roy et Directeur du Concert Spirituel – Stabat Mater A Quatre Voix Et Choeurs Dedié Aux Amateurs Composés Par M. Joseph Haydn Maitre de Chappelle de S A S Monseigneur Le Prince Regnant d'Esterhazy. – Executé pour la Premier[e] Fois au Concert Spirituel le 9. avril 1781'. Copy: Bib. Nat., Paris. Review: *Journal de Paris*, 23 April 1786. (8) Score by Breitkopf & Härtel, Leipzig, 1803: 'Stabat Mater a 4 Voci coll'accompagnamento dell'Orchestra composto da G. Haydn. Partitura. [etc. also German]'. Copies: British Museum, etc., etc.

Critical edition: Faber Music (Landon), 1977.

Literature: see *Haydn in England 1791–1795*, p. 58 (documents), *Haydn: the Late Years 1801–1809*, p. 268 (documents). Becker-Glauch in *Haydn-Studien* II (1970), pp. 199ff. Geiringer 1932, 131f. E. Schenk, 'Zur Genese der emphatischen None', in *Grasberger-Festschrift*, Tutzing 1975, 405ff.

Haydn had strong competition from the famous and widely circulated *Stabat Mater* by Pergolesi, which was known in Eisenstadt (copy in the Stadtpfarrkirche, now lost). There are moments of breathless beauty in the Pergolesi setting, not least of which is the wonderful beginning with its Corelli 'perpetual seconds' resolving to thirds over a stalking bass in quavers – a pattern that Haydn had used in the opening movement of his Symphony No. 22 (1764), also (like the present work) using cors anglais. But there are also those sudden lapses into Neapolitan *opera buffa* which upset even Padre Martini, who declared that the whole composition had nothing to distinguish itself from *La serva padrona*.[1] The Aria 'Quae moerebat' with its jaunty syncopations was nearer the stage than the Cross. The great setting by that astonishing composer Franz Beck, written for Paris,[2] was never published; so we have no basis for comparison.

---

1 Alfred Einstein in his interesting foreword to the critical edition of the Eulenburg miniature score (1927).

2 See *MGG*: 'Beck'. The late Dr Sondheimer told us that the autograph score of the Beck *Stabat Mater* is in private possession in France, and that he had once been able to study it for a few hours. He said it was a magnificent and moving work, which we can well believe of one of the most talented of the Mannheim school.

Haydn took immense pains with his setting of the beautiful words by Jacopo de Benedetti (known as Jacopone da Todi, who died in 1306). There are moments when we feel that the composer has completely penetrated the sense of the text. The sorrowful opening, with its interesting melodic leaps and curiously moving harmonies, is certainly as striking in its way as Pergolesi was in his. Haydn's use of the solo voices is now completely assured; he always had a special weakness for the bass, and there are two stirring 'arias', of which the second, a hair-raising setting of 'Flammis orci ne succendar', is one of the great movements. It would also serve, in the coming years, as a model of such writing; we find a similar piece in *Applausus*. As might be expected, Haydn follows a traditional method of dividing the work into various movements, alternating soli with choruses or both. One of the central movements is the large-scale (262 bars) Andante for soli, choir and orchestra with the cors anglais (used in this work only in two E flat sections): 'Virgo virginum praeclara'. Here, Haydn displays his newly found ability to work in a large form (within a large form), and the chorus is handled with consummate mastery, interjecting the word 'fac' into the tapestry of sound woven by the soloists as they sing 'Fac ut portem Christi mortem, passionis fac consortem et plagas recolere. Fac me plagis vulnerari.'

Pergolesi, at the conclusion of this part of the text, sets the words 'Inflammatus et accensus' as a duet between soprano and alto in B flat which is so unchurchly and gay that one wonders if it was this piece that caused Berlioz to speak of the whole work as a musical 'cauchemar' (nightmare). Haydn drops these words entirely and gives us the bass aria 'Flammis orci' mentioned above: we see that he was at considerable pains to circumvent the pitfalls which Pergolesi had failed to avoid. The only conventional sop to the times might be considered the elaborate soprano solo in the middle of the fugal conclusion: here Pohl wishes this solo would disappear (II, 65f.), but its presence is mild compared to some of the coloratura writing in Pergolesi's work.

And yet: despite all its originality and beauty the work appears slightly dated. The reason is possibly its great length and the number of slow movements one after other: there are three in succession at the beginning, and three in the middle as well ('Sancta Maria', 'Fac me vere', 'Virgo virginum'). The same problem will arise in *The Seven Words*, where all Haydn's ingenuity cannot make it easier to listen in concentrated fashion to seven slow movements. The *Stabat Mater* is a flawed masterpiece. If some movements, such as the opening or the 'Virgo virginum', are of limitless beauty, there are also conventional movements that do not rise above the ordinary, e.g. the florid tenor aria 'Fac me cruce'. The work is important in Haydn's development because it gave him the possibility of writing expressive, indeed passionate music in minor keys on a very large scale: no less than seven movements of the *Stabat* are in minor keys, and the music contained therein is usually of a highly charged emotion. The work was also central in establishing its composer as a first-rate writer of vocal music. While Haydn's operas all remained virtually unknown outside the Austro-Hungarian Monarchy – the few exceptions do not change this fact – and all his early Masses never circulated outside Catholic Austria-Bohemia-Bavaria until many years later, the *Stabat Mater* was the first big vocal work by Haydn to appear in print. It was a great success in Paris and London. Haydn himself said to Latrobe that he 'dedicated' the work to the Electress of Saxony, Maria Antonia Walpurgis, widow of Friedrich August II and herself the composer of *Il trionfo della fedeltà*. Haydn did indeed send the work to Dresden, probably in 1772 or 1773,[1] but the dedication was probably in manuscript, as

---

1 Hoboken II, p. 17.

would later be the case in the elaborate MS. dedication (*c.* 1781; MS. score in the Library of Congress) to the Prince of Asturias of *L'isola disabitata* (composed in 1779). The first recording of the *Stabat Mater* was made by Vox in December 1951.[1]

Cantata 'Applausus' (XXIVa:6) (1768)

Scoring: S-A-T-B-B Soli; Choir (S-A-T-B). 2 ob., bsn., 2 cor., 2 trpt., timp., str. with v. solo and harpsichord solo.
Principal sources: Autograph, Gesellschaft der Musikfreunde, Vienna. Original libretto (MS.) Zwettl Abbey.

Critical editions: Joseph Haydn Werke XXVII/2 (Wiens/Becker-Glauch).
Practical edition: Doblinger (Landon), 1969.
Literature: Pohl II, 39ff. Geiringer 1947, 132ff. Nowak 206 (2nd. ed. 184ff.).

The first performance of *Applausus* in modern times (strictly speaking since 1768) took place in connection with a series entitled 'The Unknown Haydn' which this writer gave for the British Broadcasting Corporation in 1958.[2] Later, Erich Leinsdorf conducted the cantata at the Berkshire Festival in Tanglewood (Lenox, Mass.). Although the work was often referred to because of the important letter that Haydn wrote to the monks of Zwettl, it is typical that no one ever bothered to perform it from 1768 to 1958. On the other hand, many parts of the work exist in the form of *contrafacta* (with Latin text) for use as offertories etc., and in this altered guise the music was often played in Austrian and Bohemian churches all through the eighteenth century. Several such arrangements exist in both the Stadtpfarrkirche and the Esterházy Archives at Eisenstadt, where they were entitled, variously, 'Offertorium de Spiritu Sancto', 'Motetto', 'Offertorium de Sancto vel Sancta', and so on; from the watermarks and other factors, many of these arrangements existed by about 1769, and certainly many of them are authentic or had Haydn's blessing. The full list of sources may be seen in the Kritischer Bericht to *JHW*. One of these arrangements starts with 'Dictamina mea' – the 'Applausus' text hardly had to be changed except in details – and ends with the brisk 'Alleluja' (XXIIIc:3) in six-eight time. This *contrafactur* exists in both Eisenstadt Archives. Becker-Glauch (*Haydn-Studien* II/3, 208ff.) is sure that this 'Alleluja' was not written to complete the arrangement, whereas Geiringer (*Musical Quarterly* 1959, 463) says '... it was Haydn himself who was responsible ...' In this arrangement, interestingly, the original *Applausus* trumpets are replaced by C horns (presumably *basso*, since there is no designation). We regard the arrangement as authentic: Haydn would not have tolerated a spurious 'insertion' in his own princely Castle Chapel. The final chorus of *Applausus* exists as a *contrafactur* in an authentic copy at the Castle by the so-called copyist 'Anonymous No. 63' (Bartha-Somfai) – where there are two other copies as well, one with performance dates from 28 January 1787 – with the text 'O Jesu, te invocamus'. For some odd reason, this chorus was also marketed as J. B. Vanhal (*HJB* IX, 364).

The cantata form is not usually a grateful one for musicians in Roman Catholic countries; Protestant composers have always, for a variety of reasons which need not be examined here, fared rather better. Verdi's colleague Boito writes to G. Negri: 'Cantatas are the despair of poets, composers and audience. These hybrid compositions

---

1 Anni Felbermayer (S), Sieglinde Wagner (A), Waldemar Kmentt (T), Otto Wiener (B), the Akademie Kammerchor, Chamber Orchestra of the Vienna Symphony, Joseph Nebois (Baroque *Positiv* of the 17th cent.), conducted by Hans Gillesberger. Recording supervisor: H. C. Robbins Landon.
2 Joan Sutherland (S), Marjorie Thomas (A), Richard Lewis (T), John Cameron (B), the B.B.C. Chorus and the Haydn Orchestra, Charles Spinks (harpsichord), Raymond Cohen (solo violin), conducted by Harry Newstone.

are cold, conventional, rhetorical, and their sole purpose is to fill an hour with boredom.'[1] Like all sweeping statements by brilliant critics – and Boito was surely that – this one contains more than a grain of truth; for it must be candidly admitted that Haydn's *Applausus* is not entirely free of this criticism. There is something slightly mechanical about the C major pomp – Haydn's festival key – of the opening *Recitativo*; but as always, there is great interest in the details. The usual Haydnesque rhythm of the trumpets and kettledrums has this time a motivation in the very theme, wherein ♪♫ ♪♪♪♪ is highly prominent. There is a second section (*p*) – bars 38ff. – which is very characteristic of the period, the whole being welded together by the inexorable quaver basses; and the most interesting thing about this Recitative is the alternation of these two principal thematic blocks. As an intellectual exercise the section is fascinating, but there is a certain impersonal quality in the treatment which we often find in Haydn's C major symphonies of the period. The following 'Virtus inter ardua' with G horns instead of trumpets, is yet another instance of Haydn's many and varied ensemble movements of the 1760s: superbly written with moments of real rapture (the intricate vocal lines at bars 85ff., rising to a genuine *crescendo* and *ff*).

There are two bass arias, both among the finest things in the work: as Haydn's vocal writing continues from 1766, we see more and more clearly his peculiar aptitude for bass arias. We have observed a stormy and dramatic bass aria in the *Stabat Mater*; its parallel here is the D minor Aria 'Si obtrudat', a pure piece of Haydnesque *Sturm und Drang* which is strongly allied to Symphony No. 26 ('Lamentatione'), probably composed in this very year. Once again we note the restless bass line in quavers, becoming ever more a stylistic hallmark of Haydn's style; with it go hand in hand the repeated semiquavers of the violins, which contribute to that nervous energy which is so typical of the Eisenstadt-Eszterháza style in the decade 1765–75. Some of the string treatment depends on the key and metre. In the B flat bass Aria 'Non cymaeras somniatis', which is in B flat and three-four time, the energy is generated by a different kind of semiquavers: as in Symphony No. 35, composed a few weeks before *Applausus* – the Symphony is dated 1 December 1767, and the Cantata was commissioned in the same month – we find broken chordal string writing ♪♪♪ ♪♪♪ ♪♪♪ in more than two dozen bars of the accompaniment (also the viola, which has a highly independent part here). Compare, in the first movement of the Symphony, bars 17ff.

The *Duetto* 'Dictamina mea', which was such a successful *contrafactur*, is another example of C major pomp, with the inescapable Haydnesque rhythm in the trumpets and kettledrums: formally brilliant and slightly cold, with passages of great technical difficulty for the soprano and alto soloists. The middle section of this *da capo* Duet – unlike his operas, where he soon escapes the confines of the *da capo* aria, this Cantata rigidly adheres to the form, perhaps because of its inherent formality – is a curiously archaic piece in C minor which reminds us strongly of Gluck's *Orfeo*.

There are two interesting tenor arias in the middle of *Applausus*, one with a large harpsichord solo part ('O pii Patres Patriae!'), almost on the scale of a concerto: the opening *ritornello* in *Largo* is 28 bars long. The tenor writing is of fabulous difficulty. The other is also a *Largo* with a beautiful violin solo such as we have in the slow movements of Haydn's concertos; the tenor part is, if anything, even more difficult, with runs of inordinate length and fantastic complexity – almost unsingable today (e.g. bars 40–44). The middle section is another extraordinary piece of *Sturm und Drang*

1 *Musicians on Music* (ed. F. Bonavia), London 1956, p. 236.

in D minor where the tenor rises to high *b* flat. In both these huge movements there are double cadenzas in the main sections, one for the singer and one for the solo instrument; in the second Aria ('O beatus incolatus.') there is also a cadenza in the 'B' section. The E flat Aria for soprano, 'Rerum, quas perpendimus', is the one closest to Haydn's operatic style of the period; it is a well-knit and smoothly flowing Andante Moderato, but it is longer than it would be in an opera (because of the *da capo* form).

The long accompanied recitatives are, of course, in the strictest *opera seria* tradition. In fact the whole style of the work is hardly different from an act of a serious opera, and part of the Cantata's stylistic trouble is that it is cast in the form of Haydn's old *Acide* but uses the richer and more involved language of 1768. This is nowhere more apparent than in this beautiful soprano aria, which is simply too long for anything except a Cantata or an *opera seria*. It is even more striking in the recitatives, especially the penultimate number: Haydn keeps our interest from flagging by the interesting *ritornelli*: note typically late 1760-ish syncopations at bars 68ff. and 75ff.

The concluding chorus, also in *da capo* form, returns to the trumpets and drums of C major; in its rather cool brilliance we find real *clarino* writing at the end of the 'A' section, just as we did in the *Missa Cellensis* of 1766. The fact that Haydn expected 'foreign' trumpets – in a remote Styrian pilgrimage church and an even more remote Cistercian abbey in the woods of Lower Austria – to be able to play up to high *c'''* shows that the great *clarino* tradition had not died out (the high *c'''* is only used very sparingly in Haydn's C major symphonies, e.g. No. 20/IV, 243; No. 32/I, 154; high *b''* only No. 33/I, 29, 31).

Applausus cannot be reckoned among the most enduring pieces of the period. Its libretto is too dry, the music too long and the whole subject not exactly calculated to uplift any but the monkish soul of 1768, to whom this combination of Christian virtues and *opera seria* musical language would have been the height of sophistication. A further hindrance for us today is the extreme difficulty of the vocal parts, but in particular the tenor: curiously, the vocal standard of soprano (and to a certain extent alto) coloratura singing is much higher today than that of tenor and bass.

Lo speziale, *dramma giocoso* (XVIII:3),
Opera in two Acts (1768)

Scoring: Two S (Grilletta, Volpino), two T (Sempronio, Mengone), 2 fl., 2 ob., bsn., 2 cor., str. (harpsichord continuo).

Principal source: Autograph (from which are missing: Overture and opening of Act I, Scene 1; Act III, Scenes 1–3, 5, and the beginnings of Scenes 4 and 6), Esterházy Archives, Budapest, Ms. mus. I, 2.[1]

1 Overture – sources as in *L'infedeltà delusa* (*infra*) and also (c) authentic parts by Johann Elssler [copyist 'Anon. 48'], Staatsbibliothek Berlin, cat. 9982/13.

Libretto: Carlo Goldoni, locally adapted (Friberth?). Printed libretto (1768): *vide supra.* p. 152.

Critical editions: *Joseph Haydn Werke* XXV/3 (Wirth). Haydn-Mozart Presse (Landon), in which the missing parts have been reconstructed; in *Werke* only beginning of Scene 1, Act I reconstructed (pp. 19f.).

Literature: Pohl II, 349. Geiringer 1932, 104–6. Wirth I, 13ff. Wirth II, 18–21. Bartha-Somfai 386. Landon in *NOHM* VII, 185f.

This is the first Haydn opera to be revived in modern times. The future editor of the operas in the proposed *Gesamtausgabe* of Breitkopf & Härtel (begun 1907), Robert Hirschfeld, received permission from Prince Esterházy to publish in advance of the Collected Edition an arrangement of *Lo speziale* (1895). With an insertion from *Orlando Paladino* (Duet from Atto II, 'Qual contento') to fill in the missing part of the Third Act, translated into German, with the *secco* recitatives adapted for orchestra, and other liberties, this 'free arrangement' was conducted in 1899 by Gustav Mahler and in 1909 by Felix von Weingartner at the Vienna Hofoper and proved to be extremely popular. It was *inter alia* a regular item in the repertoire of the Vienna Boys' Choir. It is still published by Universal Edition (who acquired the rights from the original publishers, Gutmann).

This is the first of Haydn's three operas based on libretti by Carlo Goldoni, but in each case the composer did not take over the original version of the libretto but a local adaptation. In *Lo speziale*, Goldoni's 1752 version (for the Carnival in Bologna) was more complicated: there are *parti serie* and *parti buffe*. This division was still retained in the 1755 revival (Carnival, Venice) composed by Domenico Fischietti and Vincenzo Pallavicino, but by the time Haydn began to compose it, some local poet had simplified the book, shortening it and eliminating all the *parti serie*. One thinks of Carl Friberth, who made the rather clever adaptation of *L'incontro improvviso* and whose knowledge of Italian was obviously excellent. Since we find such adaptations also in *L'infedeltà delusa* (*vide infra*), the presence of a local poet capable of making these changes seems obvious. We shall probably never learn his name from the documents at our disposal.

Synopsis of the plot: Sempronio, an old apothecary, has a ward, Grilletta, on whom he has matrimonial designs. His other grand passion is travelling, in his imagination, to far places. Grilletta's charms have also awakened two other lovers: Sempronio's assistant, Mengone, who has managed (although not an apothecary at all) to get the job in order to be near his love; and Volpino ('little fox'), a *Hosenrolle* for Barbara Dichtler. Among the fake notary scenes (typical of Italian comic opera) and disguises, the most amusing is Volpino dressed as a Turk in Act III. After various vicissitudes, Mengone is finally united with Grilletta.

One of the peculiarities of much comic opera at this period is the tiny third act which was, at it were, pasted on the more substantial first two acts. This third act is often so much of an afterthought that one wonders why the Italians, Goldoni included, were so attached to the tradition. We find these small third acts in *Lo speziale*, *Le pescatrici*, *Il mondo della luna*, *La vera costanza* and *La fedeltà premiata*. When the Radio-Televisione-Italiana gave the first authentic performance of *Il mondo della luna* (q.v.) in 1954, they had only the first two acts from Brussels and imagined the opera to be complete. These minute third acts constitute something of a problem altogether. Boito, writing to Verdi in 1889,[1] notes, apropos the nature of comedy,

> You have recently read Goldoni and you must remember how in his last scenes, in spite of the marvels of the dialogue and of the character-drawing, the action loses impetus and the interest grows cold. Unfortunately that is the law of the comic theatre. . . . In comedy [at the end of the work] all that happens is that the knot will be untied and the interest wanes as the end is happy. . . . It is impossible to untie a knot without slowing down the pace and when that happens the end becomes a foregone conclusion: the interest is gone before the knot is unravelled. The knot is untied in comedy; it is broken or cut in tragedy.

Realizing, as he apparently did, this insoluble problem, Haydn has recourse to the simplest but most effective trick: he reserves his most interesting music for the flagging third act. In *Il mondo della luna*, the tremendous Duet, the musical and Romantic highpoint of the whole work, is the central piece of *Atto* III. *Lo speziale* is a much more modest work, but even here, Haydn waits for *Atto* III to introduce the most original music of the whole opera: the Turkish scene. (In our reconstruction of the missing scenes, we have attempted to retain some of this tension.)

1 *Musicians on Music* (ed. F. Bonavia), London 1956, p. 190.

Ultimately it is the general public which decides on the success of a resuscitated opera. The public has always been highly amused by *Lo speziale* and the work has never been out of the repertoire in the last three-quarters of a century. (An interesting parallel: the next Haydn Opera to be revived was *L'isola disabitata*, conducted by Weingartner at the Hofoper in 1909; it proved to be a complete fiasco as far as any further operatic life was concerned.) Goldoni's amusing satire was obviously suited to Haydn's temperament. He quickly managed to portray the various characters and scenes. Geiringer (1932, 104) quotes amusing examples of the long-winded phrase that ends the word 'anzianità' and the word-painting of 'L'una prova la lunghezza, l'altra prova la larghezza'. Here we arrive at a central point of Haydn's operatic language. He was later taken to task for his word-painting ('Thonmalerey') in *The Creation*, but if those same critics had known Haydn's operas they would have realized that word-painting was an integral side of his vocal language. All the most beautiful, poignant and often dramatic effects of Haydn's operas are due, in one form or another, to word-painting, or the realization of the word through music. These two examples are the first in a series of such scenes which will culminate in the giant tread of the double bassoon, the worm, the sunrise and the first moonlight in *The Creation*:

[Aria di Sempronio: 'Questa è un altra novità']

Another piece of excellent word-painting is the *Sturm und Drang* Aria of Volpino in G minor, 'Amore nel mio petto', where once again we are not sure how much is a parody of the old Italian 'vengeance aria' and how much is genuine Haydnesque passion of the late 1760s. Certainly its pithiness contrasts violently with the lengthy arias in *Applausus*. The most earthy of these *Thonmahlerey* scenes is the Aria by Mengone, 'Per quel che ha mal di stomaco' which contains several 'NB' signs at the words 'e quel che ha il corpo stitico, le viscere anderà', the 'NB' no doubt being literal manifestations of the apothecary's purges. It is the typical vulgarity of the *commedia dell'arte*.

In the Finales, Haydn has an opportunity to display his love for ensembles, if on a modest scale. The first Finale has a typical forward shift of tempo (bar 72), and the racy three-four Allegro is clearly a preview of the last Finale in *L'infedeltà delusa*. The tempo finally switches to six-eight. Thus the typical conclusions is always marked by a *basic* acceleration of tempo: there may be (as in *La fedeltà premiata*) movements in Adagio within such a frame but the general direction is an increase of speed. In the second Finale, the writing scene, the orchestra plastically describes the notary's busy strokes of the pen: the broken pattern of the strings is an old Italian device. Again, Haydn uses the three-four in his acceleration (Allegro di molto, bar 47) but shifts back and forth from fast to slow.

The key structure is more subtle than in *La canterina* simply because there is more space available. In the earlier Opera, the key structure was progressive: D major to G major.[1] In *Lo speziale*, we have a basic key: G major. The Overture and Act I begin in that key and the Act ends in C; Act II ends in A; Act III back in G. With *Lo speziale* we have perhaps the first of Haydn's interesting experiments in tonal structure on a large scale; it will end with *The Seasons*.[2]

Lo speziale is a light-hearted *opera buffa*. There is no time for real sentiment. And yet, in the second version of 'Caro Volpino', Grilletta succumbs to a real burst of affection for this king of madmen ('siete de' pazzi il re'), and the words 'siete adorabile' are accompanied by a warmth that, we realize, is completely genuine. She feels a gentle admiration for Volpino, 'ma non piacete a me', she simply does not love him, 'Volpino, poverino'. It is music of real charm and psychological insight.

Now that most of Haydn's other operas are available in practical performing editions, we shall see what the reaction to *Lo speziale* will be, and if it will be able, in the future, to hold its own against *L'infedeltà delusa* or the more complicated *La fedeltà premiata* and *La vera costanza*. (One advantage of *Lo speziale* is purely practical: it is an ideal chamber opera, with only four singers and a very small orchestra.)

Missa 'Sunt bona mixta malis' (XXII:2):
lost (c. 1768)

In 1829, Vincent Novello and his wife Mary went from London to Salzburg, where they brought some money to Constanze Mozart-Nissen, and on to Vienna. There, we learn for the first time that sections of this Mass still existed in 1829. 'Artaria has the original MS. of Haydn's Kyrie [of Breitkopf & Härtel's edition of Mass] No. 5, [Simrock's edition] No. 7 in G complete and of the Kyrie and part of the Gloria of a Mass in D minor entitled "Sunt bona mixta malis" which has never been published. These I purchased of him for 6 florins.'[3] Previously it had been supposed that the word 'these' applied to the MSS. of all three works. We have now uncovered evidence that the 'these' were only the fragments of our lost Mass. In the Aloys Fuchs papers preserved in the Benedictine Abbey of Göttweig, we find the following sheet:[4]

---

1 Another reason why the church adaptation of 'Dictamina mea' (*Applausus*) – which begins in C and ends with the G major 'Alleluja' – may be Haydn's after all. We must beware (and German scholars are particularly prone to it) of putting Haydn into a scheme.
2 Orin Moe, Jr. in *HJB* IX, 340ff.
3 *A Mozart Pilgrimage*, London 1955, p. 203. The quotation is from Vincent's diary (Mary also kept a diary).
4 Catalogued 'ad Num XXV'; XXV is a document referring to 'J. Haydens Grabschrift'. In the list, the underlined items have been so marked by Fuchs in red ink.

*Liste des pièces de Musique Autographes de Joseph Haydn,
qui se trouvent chéz Artaria & Co à Vienne.*

		Arg.:ᵗ de Convertl.	
[1]	Symphonie – composée 1765	20	—
[2]	— autre „ 1765	20	—
[3]	— — „ 1773	30	—
[4]	Divertimento à 8 instrumens. 1775.	20	—
[5]	Symphonie composée 1777	12	—
[6]	Divertißment à 8 instrumens. 1778.	25	—
[7]	Menuet, Allegretto et Marche pour l'Orchestre	10	—
[8]	Quatuor p. violon. op. 58. partition	36	—
[9]	6 Quatuor p. violon | : dediés au Cᵐᵗᵉ Appony 1793 :|		—
	Partition [Fuchs: 'Autograph']	200	—
[10]	6 — ditto — ded : à Mr. Zmeskal — dᵉ	150	—
[11]	2 Divertißmens p. le Bariton, Vla et Baße Nᵒ· 39 et 40	12	—
[12]	2 autres — pour les memes instr : Nᵒ : 68 et 69 —	12	—
[13]	3 autres — pour les memes instr : „ 57, 79 et 106	15	—
	de l'an 1768		
[14]	3 Trios p. 2 flutes et Violoncelle	20	—
[15]	2 Marches p. 6 instrumens arrang : p. Clav.	6	—
[16]	Sonate p. le Clavecin. 1793.	10	—
[17]	Marche p. le Clavecin	5	—
[18]	Sonate p. Pfte, Viola [*sic*] et Vcelle. 1785	20	—
[19]	Fragment d'un Trio p. Clavecin, Viol : et Baße	12	—
[20]	6 Sonates p. le Clavecin. 1773, 1774	27	—
[21]	Orlando, opera seria. (3ᵐ Acte.) [() = Fuchs, red ink.]	30	—
[22]	6 pièces de l'op. Il mondo della luna	18	—
[23]	3 pièces de l'opera Alfred	18	—
[24]	Mißa santa [*sic*] Nicolai. 1772 [Fuchs: 'defekt']	40	—
[25]	Kyrie de la meße de Mariazell 1766	27	—
[26]	Die ganz Welt will glücklich seyn —	6	—

[Notes: **1**: No. 28 (now Berlin) or ?. **2**: ? or a misdated No. 9 (now lost). **3**: No. 50. **4**. X:1 or X:3 (both Berlin). **5**: Overture Ia:7 (now Berlin). **6**: probably misdated, and either X:1 or X:3, both of which were in Berlin. **7**: Fragment of a Symphony in C (Hoboken I, p. 87; see first version of Symphony No. 63, last two movements in HCRL's reconstruction, Philharmonia or Haydn-Mozart Presse) and March from *Il mondo della luna* (VIII:5), all MSS. formerly in Berlin. **8**: Quartets, Op. 54, Nos. 1 and 2 (III:58, 59), both fragments (now Berlin). **9**: Quartets, Opp. 71/74 (III:69–74), now Berlin. **10**: Quartets, Op. 20 (III:31–36), now Gesellschaft der Musikfreunde, Vienna. **11**: Trios Nos. 40 and 41 (XI:40, 41), now Berlin. **12**: Trios Nos. 68 and 69 (XI:68, 69), the first in Swedish private possession, the second in the Conservatoire, Paris. **13**: Trios Nos. 57 (XI:57, now Zentralbibliothek, Zürich) – this is the work 'de l'an 1768' – 79 (XI:79, now Conservatoire, Paris) and 106 (XI:106, formerly Mr Walter Johnson, New York). **14**: the 'London' Trios Nos. 1, 2 and 3 (IV:1–3), formerly all in Berlin, No. 3 now unavailable. **15**: Marches Nos. 1 and 2 for the Derbyshire Cavalry Regiment (VIII:1, 2), of which only No. 2 seems to have survived (Berlin). **16**: 'Andante con variazioni' (XVII:6), entitled 'Sonata' on the 1793 autograph (now New York Public Library). **17**: probably the sketch for *March for the Prince of Wales* (VIII:3, wrongly placed, in Hoboken I, p. 543, under VIII:3*bis*), now Berlin. **18**: either (probably) piano Trio No. 20 (XV:7), formerly owned by T. G. Odling, Esq., London, at present (Autumn 1976) in the hands of Sotheby & Co., London, for a future auction; or (possibly) No. 22 (XV:9), now Berlin. **19**: piano Trio No. 18 (XV:5), now Berlin. **20**: Sonatas Nos. 36, 37, 38 (XVI:21–23; now Conservatoire, Paris), 41 (XVI:26; now Berlin) and 44 (XVI:29; now in Swiss private possession). **21**: Act III of *Orlando Paladino* (XXVIII:11; now Berlin). **22**: Six fragments, presumably the so-called 'Berlin autograph' (XXVIII:7; Hob. II, p. 377, Bruchstücke B), which consisted (it is now lost) of five fragments, together with Hob. II, p. 378, Bruchstück D (formerly Robert Haas, now Universitätsbibliothek Tübingen. **23**: XXX:5b–c (Berlin) and XXX:4 (Berlin). **24**: the incomplete autograph, such as Artaria had (Fuchs: 'defective'), of XXII:6 is now in Berlin. **25**: the autograph fragment of XXII:5, now Bucharest. It was sold by Artaria to a 'Russian nobleman' named Balsch. With a miscopied title ('Missa Solemnis [*sic*] ad honorem Beatissimae Virginis Mariae dal Giuseppe Haydn 1766': Pohl I, 260, n. 50; Pohl II, 38) it was thought, wrongly, to have been the autograph of the *Missa in honorem B. V. M.* (Great Organ Mass), and this confusion persisted until the actual autograph was discovered. As a result of this Artaria Catalogue, we may see that Novello bought only the fragments of the *Missa* 'Sunt bona mixta malis' – six gulden would have been far too cheap for the three pieces of church music Artaria owned. Secondly, we may date the Artaria Catalogue precisely as between 1829 and 1835 (when the *Missa* of 1766 was sold). It is possible that the autograph that Novello bought is still among the vast Novello Archives, unknown and uncatalogued. **26**: The *Lied* known as 'Der schlaue Pudel', now Berlin.

Missa in honorem B.V.M. (Great Organ Mass; XXII:4)
(1768–9?)

Scoring: I (original version, 1768–9?): S-A-T-B Soli; Choir (S-A-T-B). 2 cor angl., 2 hr., str., bsn. and organ solo and *continuo*. II (revised version, *c.* 1775?): 2 trpt. and timp. added.

Principal sources (Version I): (1) Autograph, containing the Sanctus, Benedictus and Agnus, Esterházy Archives, Budapest, Ms. Mus. I. 20. Last part of Agnus missing (bars 115ff.). The watermarks, which we traced in 1958, are Larsen 7 (Bartha-Somfai 191), otherwise known to us from the autograph of *Le pescatrici*, Atto I, *Bogen* 2 (1769). In the *Entwurf-Katalog* the entry might be dated 1768–9; the words 'B:V:M:' were added later, and the entry originally read: 'Mißa in E mol / in honorem [blank]'. (2) The parts in the Esterházy Archives, Eisenstadt, are a very late copy by Johann Elssler and others of the re-instrumentation made in the early nineteenth century (by J. N. Fuchs? Hummel?). (3) MS. parts

from Reigern Abbey (Rajhrad), 1774; Janaček Museum, Brno (ČSSR) A. 12.482. There are many other contemporary MSS. (Version II): (1) Authentic MS. by Viennese Professional Copyist No. 2,[1] Augustinian Monastery of St Florian. An important and accurate MS. (2) MS. parts, 'ad Chor gottw[icensis]. Comp: P. Marianus 777', Benedictine Monastery of Göttweig. (3) MS. parts, Benedictine Monastery of Melk. There are many contemporary MSS. with the additional trumpets and drums.

Critical edition: Haydn Society G.A. (Brand), XXIII/1, 1951 without the autograph and without St Florian; requires revision. Practical ed.: Doblinger (Alois Strassl), 1955, with important corr. to G.A.

Literature: Brand, *Die Messen*, 36ff. Geiringer 1932, 124f. Landon in *HJB* IX, 306f.

---

1 For identification, see Landon *SYM*, 45. Haydn's own copy of Piano Trio No. 10 (XV:35), now in the Esterházy Archives, was made by that copyist and another. Thus the anonymous 'No. 2' was a man employed by Haydn himself and therefore to be considered authentic.

The elaborate solo organ part was presumably intended for Haydn himself, yet another offering of his ability to Our Lady. Some nineteenth-century critics were rather scandalized by the triplet figure that the organ plays in the 'Dona nobis pacem', among them even Haydn's biographer Carpani.[1] Nowadays this aspect of *settecento* Austrian church music hardly bothers anyone: it is as much part of the national religious attitude as the exuberant Rococo churches that dot the Austrian countryside, or the whirling *Pestsäulen* (monuments to celebrate the end of the Plague) that stand in the market-places of Austrian towns and villages.

The key of E flat is rather rare for a Mass of this period. It is also rare for Mozart, who began a large-scale and very beautiful Mass for Mannheim in this key (K.322, 1778?), perhaps inspired by our work: both St Peter's Abbey and the Salzburg Cathedral own parts.[2] As we know, Haydn had no trumpets in his band at this period, and the first performance probably took place in the Castle Chapel during the winter (1768?/1769?) without them. When he had trumpets at his disposal, or when requested to add them, perhaps by one of the great monasteries with which he was in contact, he put them into the score (or rather added them on separate sheets). Trumpets in E flat are rather high, and in one stunning passage ('Quoniam', bar 30) the first trumpet rises to high c''' (sounding). The key of E flat is also Haydn's favourite for the cors anglais, as noted above.

The work is something of a stylistic mixture, like all the large-scale vocal works of this period: on the one hand, we have great fugues, of which there are fine examples at the end of the Gloria ('In gloria Dei Patris Amen') and Credo ('Et vitam venturi'). The Kyrie, Sanctus (a monumental opening) and 'Dona' are all 'fugued', if not in the strict sense. The Benedictus establishes that curiously Austrian, pastoral character (with elaborate organ soli) which informs so many of these movements in Haydn, Mozart and their contemporaries: the vocal quartet is used with great effectiveness, and that too is very typical of these movements. In the three-eight 'Gratias', Haydn seems to be following the metre and somewhat the conservatism of his own *Missa Cellensis* of 1766. The 'Et incarnatus' is also very like its older companion: a slow aria-like setting for the solo tenor with 'broken' accompaniment in the strings. The symbolism of 'descendit' (long descending line in the soprano), the sudden *piano* at 'et mortuos', even the melodic lines of the 'Et resurrexit' and 'vivos' are all to be found in the *Missa* of 1766. Many of these are old traditions, found in the works of Haydn's predecessors; most of them will become a standard feature of Haydn's Masses to the end of his life.

The *Missa in honorem B. V. M.* is an uneven work, then, sharing a certain conventionality with bursts of inspiration; in this dualism, it is a typical vocal piece of this period. Haydn, as everybody knows, developed slowly, but he developed surely; and all these works gave him the necessary experience to be able to produce the really great and immortal masterpieces with which this period is crowned, e.g. symphonies such as No. 45 ('Farewell'), quartets such as Op. 20, and vocal works such as *L'infedeltà delusa*. It is not only because the solo organ part in the 'Dona' is frivolous or unchurchly that it disturbs: rather the great fugal line is broken off by a stylistic element that is, to say the least, musically incongruous. Within a few years, Haydn's fugues are to be disturbed by nothing foreign and the style becomes so broad and flexible that there is room for everything in it.

---

1 See *Haydn: the Years of 'The Creation' 1796–1800*, p. 129.
2 Hoboken II, p. 75. Also M. F. Schmid, *Die Musiksammlung der Erzabtei St. Peter in Salzburg*, Katalog Erster Teil (Leopold und Wolfgang Amadeus Mozart, Joseph und Michael Haydn), Salzburg 1970, p. 89. In the later version with trumpets and drums.

Some smaller Church Music
(*Cantilenae pro Adventu*; *Responsoria*; Motetto 'Ens aeternum; Offertorium 'Agite properate')

I. *Cantilenae*

(1) *Ein' Magd, ein' Dienerin* for Sop. Solo, 2 cor., strings and organ (XXIIId:1).
Sources: MS. parts, Esterházy Archives, Budapest, Ms. mus. IV, 75 (later addition: two oboes). *Not* by Joseph Elssler Sen. Copy of *c.* 1774–5. (2) MS. parts, St Michael's Church, Oedenburg (Sopron); with Latin text, 'Atra nocte incubante'; copy owned by 'Novothný Franz'. (3) MS. parts, Stadtpfarrkirche, Eisenstadt. (4) MS. parts, Burgerländisches Landesmuseum, Eisenstadt (also with additional Latin text, 'In turbi da pro cala'): 'Caspar Antoni. / in Wimpassing / 18⅖ 22' but the parts are much older.
Critical edition: Haydn-Mozart Presse, 1957 (Landon).
Literature: Larsen *HÜB* 171. Becker-Glauch (*Haydn-Studien* I, 16).

(2) *Jesu Redemptor* for Sop. Solo, 2 cor., strings and organ (XXIIId:3).
Sources: (1) MS. parts from Gröbming, now Graz, Diözesanmuseum; (2) MS. parts from Kráhiv Druž (now Prague Nat'l Museum); (3) MS. parts from Kuks (also Prague). Discovered by Irmgard Becker-Glauch (*Die Musikforschung* XVII/4, 413; *Haydn-Studien* I, 277; II, 194).

(3) *Mutter Gottes mir erlaube* for Sop. & Alto Soli, strings and organ (XXIIId:2); (no Viola).
Source: MS. parts, Esterházy Archives, Eisenstadt, on stag paper with 'IGW' and a variant of Larsen 11 (Bartha-Somfai 194a): *c.* 1774–5.

II. Four *Responsoria da Venerabili* for Choir (S-A-T-B), 2 cor., str. (no va.), org. (XXIIIc:4 a–d).
Source: MS. parts from Kuks, now Prague (National Museum). Discovered by Irmgard Becker-Glauch (*Musikforschung* XVII/4, 413; *Haydn-Studien* II, 204.
Critical edition: Henle (Becker-Glauch), 1964.

III. *Motetto* 'Ens aeternum' for Choir (S-A-T-B), str., organ (XXIIIa:3). The other instruments (2 ob., sometimes even 2 clar., bsn., 2 trpt., timp.) appear to be a later addition.
Principal Sources: (1) Esterházy Archives, Eisenstadt. There are two covers, one listing only 4 Voci, str. & organ ('Motetta in G'); the other cover ('Coro in G') has the parts (which the first no longer has) which include 2 ob., bsn., 2 trpt., timp., by Viennese Professional Copyist No. 3: a very late copy (watermarks: single crescent; 'w' in frame; 'GA' over 'F', 'EAG', 'GV' over 'A' in curving frame), *c.* 1800–20. (2) MS. parts, Stadtpfarrkirche, Eisenstadt. Original parts ('Motetto de Tempore') on Italian paper ('H' under ornament, 'Real', three crescents, canopy ['Baldachin']), with clarinets, trumpets and timpani added on much later (19th cent.) paper. (3) MS. parts from the Barmherzige Brüder, Graz (now Musikwiss. Institut): 'Offertorium pro Resurrectio Domini S^u P. Joan de Deo Sta Anna ... Sub Regente Chori Fr. Abundio Micksh $\overline{772}$' (with two later horn parts to the original scoring). (4) MS. parts, Göttweig Abbey: 'Chori in G, Tutti, de Tempore ... Comparavit R: P: Marianus' (no wind instr., no timp.). (5) Printed score by Breitkopf & Härtel (1813), with the additional scoring and a supplementary German text 'Walte gnädig'. Copy: H.C.R.L.
Critical edition: Doblinger (Landon).
Literature: Becker-Glauch in *Haydn-Studien* II, 211. Geiringer in *Musical Quarterly* XLV/4, 467f.

IV. *Offertorium* 'Agite properate ad aras' (also with another text: 'Animae Deo gratiae') for Choir (S-A-T-B), 2 ob., 2 trpt., timp., str. (no va.), org. [bsn.] (XXIIIa:2).
Principal sources: (1) MS. parts, Esterházy Archives, Eisenstadt: 'Offertorium' (copy by the young Johann Elssler[?]) on Italian paper (three crescents, canopy ['Baldachin'] with letters 'GF/C', mill of Galvani Fratelli, or 'A / GF / C'). (2) MS. parts, Pilgrimage Church of Mariazell ('Motett Offertorium de Sc^to v: Sc^ta ...'); with text 'Animae Deo gratiae'. (3) MS. parts, Göttweig Abbey: 'Offertorium ... Comparavit R. P. Marianus 1776' with additional va. (4) MS. parts, Conservatorio, Florence (from Pitti Palace): 'Motetto d'ogni tempo' with additional va. and bsn.
Literature: Geiringer in *Musical Quarterly* XLV/4, 467. Becker-Glauch in *Haydn-Studien* II, 211.

This selection of small church music was made on the basis of two factors: authenticity and chronology. A thorough examination of these works from the two standpoints will be found in *Haydn: the Early Years 1732–1765*.

The Advent arias are for local consumption, and the Austro-Bavarian tradition allowed German texts for such works. As with the products of Haydn's predecessors, a simple melodic line and a certain 'folk' quality are the determining characteristics of this *genre*. They were entered on page two of the *Entwurf-Katalog* and were composed at the end of the 1760s or beginning of the 1770s. The beautiful *Responsoria*, all in a slow tempo, are very much in the style of the choruses in the *Stabat Mater*. The second, in D minor, is the first of a series of smaller church works in that key and in the 'severe style', culminating in the late-period *Offertorium* 'Non nobis Domine'. 'Ens aeternum' may have been composed, like the *Missa brevis Sancti Joannis de Deo*, in honour of the founder and patron saint of the Order of the Brothers of Mercy, St John of God; in which case it was written for the tiny chapel in Eisenstadt and was certainly composed with the smaller orchestration (like that of the Mass). The early source from the Graz Mission of this Brotherhood would seem to support this theory. We have no proof if it was Haydn himself who added the wind instruments and timpani, which certainly add weight and colour to this simple piece of *Gebrauchsmusik*. The festive C major *Offertorium* 'Agite properate' (or 'Animae Deo gratae') is in the style of the final chorus in *Applausus*. Neither of these Offertories was entered in the *Entwurf-Katalog* but both are in the Elssler Catalogue of 1805, probably because both were owned by Traeg and in his Catalogue of 1799 (as items 65 and 112).[1] Traeg supplied Haydn with information about, and *incipits* of, several works which the composer no longer owned, such as the Concerto in E flat for two horns and strings (VIId:2).

Le pescatrici, *dramma giocoso per musica* (XXVIII:4) in three acts
(1769, performed 1770)

Scoring: 2 fl., 2 ob., 2 cor angl., 2 bsn., 2 hns., [2 trpt., timp.], str. (harpsichord *continuo*). Vocal parts: 2 S (Lesbina, Nerina), A (Eurilda), 2 T (Burlotto, Frisellino), 2 B (Lindoro, Mastricco), Chorus (S-A-T-B).

Source: Overture (presumably I:106): Library of Congress, Washington (M 1004 A2 H No. 6 P), the only extant source. Opera (in fragmentary state): Esterházy Archives, Budapest, Ms. Mus. I. 3. Written on 4° Esterházy paper from the Lockenhaus mill, with watermarks: (1) Larsen 7 (Bartha-Somfai 191), stag and 'IGW'; (2) the Cavatina of Lesbina, 'Voglio amar', in Act I, and the Coro, 'Soavi zeffiri', in Act III are written on Larsen 8 & 9 (Bartha-Somfai 192, 193), another stag and 'IGW'. Bartha-Somfai (388) have noticed that the Cavatina was on this different paper, but not the Coro. Without burdening the reader with a complete list, we would point out that Larsen 8 (Bartha-Somfai 192) also appears in dated autographs of 1771, 1772 and 1773, while Larsen 9 (B-S 193) also appear in 1771, 1772 and 1773; but both Larsen 8 and 9 appear in the *Missa* of 1766. Therefore there is no evidence that the Cavatina and Coro *must* have been composed later; they *may*

have been later additions, but if so, for which revival? We know of no such revival from any of the Acta Musicalia records.

Libretto: Carlo Goldoni (with extensive revisions; by ? [Carl Friberth?]). Printed libretto: *vide supra*, pp. 165f.

Critical editions: *Joseph Haydn Werke* XXV/4 (Bartha). Reconstruction of entire work: Haydn-Mozart Presse (Landon), using Symphony 57 as Overture (this was before I:106 had been rediscovered).

Literature: Sonja Gerlach in *Haydn-Studien* III, 44ff. Geiringer 1932, 105ff., 108ff. Wirth II, 21ff. Bartha-Somfai 387ff. Landon in NOHM VII, 187.

First performance since 1770: Holland Festival 1965, 1966 (Producer: Werner Düggelin, conducted by Alberto Erede).

Reconstruction: Since the total reconstruction of a Haydn opera of which one third is missing may be considered a rather daring procedure, we reprint here the notes on the subject first published in the 'Guide' to the Holland Festival and in the actual programme notes for the opera as well).

THE RECONSTRUCTION OF 'LE PESCATRICI'

In general it is arrogant to suppose that someone can 'reconstruct' the work of a great genius; if half of a painting by Rembrandt were missing, and there were no sketches extant, it would be a daring man who would presume to complete it. Nor does it occur to anyone to finish the 'Unfinished' Symphony by Schubert; if someone were capable of composing the Finale, that someone would presumably be a genius of Schubert's calibre, and even pre-supposing that such a person might

---

1 Facsimile, edited by Alexander Weinmann (*Wiener Urtext-Ausgabe*): *Johann Traeg, Die Musikalienverzeichnisse von 1799 und 1804*, Band I, Vienna 1973, pp. 225, 226. See also *Haydn: the Years of 'The Creation'*, p. 226 (Concerto for two horns).

exist, it is extremely difficult to project oneself into the past. Composers nowadays do not write symphonies in the style of Schubert or operas in the style of Haydn; if they are geniuses, they write music appropriate to the time in which they live. There has never been, in music, a real neo-classic revival (and we do not forget Stravinsky) as there has been in art, where Poussin, in the early *settecento*, painted imaginary Roman ruins, and where Richter created a *zweites Rokoko* of eighteenth-century ladies and gentlemen drinking tea (a picture which no sensible art dealer, however, would ever confuse with a painting of 1780).

Thus when we decided to 'restore' Haydn's opera, *Le pescatrici*, it was quite obvious that the weight of tradition and the might of common sense were against us. On the other hand, an unfinished opera presents difficulties of a very special kind. Whereas we are quite happy to perform Schubert's 'Unfinished' Symphony as he left it, not even (apart from the recent attempt of Mr Denis Vaughan)[1] bothering to orchestrate the *Scherzo*, for which Schubert left extensive piano sketches, an unfinished opera – or in this case a finished opera of which one-third is irrevocably lost – cannot be performed on the stage. It is one thing if we perform *Moses and Aaron* or *Lulu*: enough is there for the drama to make sense. The gaps in Haydn's *Le pescatrici* are not so well ordered.

What happened in the case of *Le pescatrici* can be reconstructed very simply. Haydn wrote it in 1769 and 1770, and it was first performed at Eszterháza Castle in the latter year. The original parts and the vocal 'short scores' for the singers perished, together with the orchestral and vocal parts of all Haydn's other operas up to that date, in the disastrous fire of December 1779 at Eszterháza. Haydn seems to have had sections of the autograph manuscript in his lodgings in the music house (and also the whole of *L'infedeltà delusa* [1773], most of *Lo speziale* [1768], *Il mondo della luna* [1777], and all of *Philemon und Baucis* [1773], *L'incontro improvviso* [1775], and *La vera costanza* [1778?]). Haydn used music paper which was put out in sheets, or 'gatherings' (*Bögen*), of four pages each; Haydn did not number the pages, but the 'gatherings'. As it happens, there are some gaps in Act I of *Le pescatrici*, a huge gap in the middle of Act II, and no gaps at all in Act III. We also have one(!) copy of the original libretto for Eszterháza, which is doubly important because someone made slight adaptations *vis-à-vis* the original text book of Carlo Goldoni. Otherwise our task would have been quite hopeless.

Thus we were presented with the following aesthetic problem: either leave the two-thirds of *Le pescatrici* as they are, in which case they would have been printed in the *Gesamtausgabe*, would be in all the major libraries, and would continue to be as dead to the musical world as they have been for two hundred years; or we could plunder the music from Haydn's other operas of the period. To the second possibility, there were two immediate and insuperable objections: (1) our publishers, Universal Edition, issue *Lo speziale* and *L'infedeltà delusa* which, respectively, precede and follow *Le pescatrici*, so that one could not, nor did one wish to, serve up *Le pescatrici* mixed up with two other well-known operas. Moreover: (2) it is impossible, unless you are the composer yourself, to plunder earlier works for dramatic music: usually the situations do not match and the new work suffers from music ill suited to the new words; and Haydn's later vocal music is in a different style and not at all suited to the wiry, pithy economy of the period to which *Le pescatrici* belongs.

The publishers and ourselves therefore decided to take a risk – for we were quite clear that it *was* a considerable risk – and to allow the public of the Holland and Edinburgh Festivals to decide if such a reconstruction were possible. It was not our intention, of course, to mystify the critics; no one expects critics to be experts of Haydn's operas from 1762–75 when they can hardly have heard more than one

---

1 Subsequently there has been another attempt, by Professor Gerald Abraham.

or two in their lives. What we wanted to know was if the opera 'worked' on the stage, *malgré* Landon; if one is an honest scholar, the best praise for such additions is that no one notices them in the overall score.

Here then is a detailed list of what was added to the extant score of Haydn's *Le pescatrici* (H.C.R.L., except as noted):

Act I

Overture: we took the first movement of Haydn's Symphony No. 57 in D (1774), which seemed particularly appropriate to the key, D major, and spirit of the opening chorus. [See above for the rediscovered Overture.]

No. 6: Aria of Eurilda in E major ('Voglio goder contenta'): of this only the opening *ritornello* is extant. The following *recitative secco* is also missing, as is what the libretto describes as 'Scena VII. Lindoro con seguito di compani in barca deliziosa s'accosta al lido, e tutti scendono accompagnati da allegro concerto'. For this arrival of Lindoro's boat, we chose a Minuet from an early wind band Divertimento in C by Haydn (No. 7). The following accompanied Recitative is our reconstruction. No. 8, a G major Aria by Mastricco, begins a third of the way in Haydn's autograph (it was cut in the Holland performance), and the last part of Lindoro's D minor Aria (No. 9) is also missing in the manuscript, as is the whole of the ensuing No. 10 (Duetto, at first Lesbina alone); the opening section of the C major Aria that follows is also missing. The rest, from the big E flat major Chorus (No. 11) to the Finale is complete.

Act II

The autograph is complete to No. 19, the Aria of Nerina 'Pescatori, pescatrici', of which only the opening *ritornello* exists; from here to the Finale everything is missing; the opening of the Finale, in G major, can be easily heard: it is the *quartetto* for the four lovers.

Act III

is complete in the autograph. The trumpets and timpani, which would have been on extra sheets (there is no room for them in the MS.), have been reconstructed by the editor; they are present in the overture [Symphony No. 57], however, though a later addition of Haydn's.

Synopsis of the plot: The two fishermen, Burlotto and Frisellino, consider Nerina and Lesbina as their respective brides-to-be. Nerina, Frisellino's sister, is not enchanted by his choice, considering that Lesbina, Burlotto's sister is (a) not hard-working enough and (b) gives herself airs. The two girls are thus at loggerheads. Eurilda, watching such a row, tells her father Mastricco that she despises such 'love' and prefers her freedom. Mastricco, who was given the girl in trust by her nurse, wonders about the girl's past and future. A magnificent ship enters the harbour. Lindoro and his train of followers disembark, and Mastricco is asked to call the inhabitants. Lindoro tells them of a rumour, according to which the daughter and heir of the Duke of Benevento is hidden in this village, and he has come to fetch her. Lesbina and Nerina at once discover royal blood in their veins; Burlotto and Frisellino now address the sisters as princesses in the hope of preserving their affection. Mastricco also offers his own daughter as the candidate to Lindoro who, disgusted at the village's avarice and cunning, decides on a trick to discover the real princess. He piles gold and jewels on a table, among them an old dagger, with which the rightful prince was murdered. The fisher-girls fall over the jewellery, while Eurilda stares at the fateful dagger and, her memories suddenly awaked, faints. The princess is found. The fisher-girls now require urgently the almost lost friendship with their suitors. On the day that the great ship is to leave, their fishermen-lovers dress as cavaliers and in that disguise they offer to marry the girls and take them away on the ship. The girls, *à la Così fan tutte*, fall for the ruse and are furious when they discover the truth. Mastricco, the village elder, brings peace to the discordant quartet and the village gathers to wave the great ship *adieu*, on which are Eurilda and Lindoro, now *promessi sposi*.

This is opera on a much larger scale than *Lo speziale*. It is Haydn's ensemble opera *par excellence*; there are, apart from the finales, 'coro' numbers that open Acts I and III, and two further ensembles in Act I: a sextet ('Bell'ombra gradita') and a magnificent, fast-moving septet ('Fiera strage dell'indegno'), in which the villagers argue with Lindoro. In the Finale there is only one single Aria (Eurilda's 'Questa mano') and four large ensembles. Haydn had seven principals rather than the four of his two previous operas. The interesting sociological structure of the opera – aristocracy and fisher-folk (no middle class) – was obviously one that appealed to Haydn, for we find it, *mutatis mutandis*, also in *Die Feuersbrunst* (where the division can also be made in language, *Hochdeutsch* versus dialect). It is not the lower classes in *Le pescatrici* who have the complicated emotions but the nobility: the *Sturm und Drang* Aria in D minor, 'Varca il mar', one of the great dramatic highpoints, musically, of Act I, is sung by Lindoro; and in the Finale to Act III, we have noble and somehow very poignant 'farewell' music which celebrates the departure of the newly found noble lovers, Lindoro and Eurilda (who, we should add, in truly *noblesse oblige* fashion takes her old foster-father Mastricco with her). The embarking music, in a series of royal fanfares (bars 44ff.) leads to a V cadence, but instead of going back to the tonic, we stay in an endless series of bars all over a dominant pedal point (59ff.), with the harmonies shifting from I_4^6 to V or V^7. By this simple means we have genuine farewell music whch leads to the ship's stately departure and to Haydn's rousing Presto conclusion. The whole opera has a sense of dignity as well as comedy; Haydn's language, even in the one year after *Lo speziale* – he began *Le pescatrici* in 1769 –, has immensely broadened and, in particular, now encompasses a variety of conflicting emotions. *Le pescatrici* is not only larger physically than its predecessor, it is also greater in emotional scope and broader musically, too. Cors anglais appear in E flat (their appearance fast taking on the mark of a Berensonian 'fingerprint'), once in an aria and once in the big sextet of Act I, and lend that curiously melancholic sweetness for which Mozart was to use clarinets. One scene of haunting beauty is the E major Chorus in Act III, 'Soavi Zeffiri, al mar c'invitano'. Haydn always had a special affection for E major and used it with originality all his life, not least to open Part III of *The Creation*. But even more interesting is Haydn's uncanny ability to portray the blue skies of the 'Land, wo die Zitronen blühen'. We shall see again and again how he even conjures up the Neapolitan *canzonetta* (such as in the 'Aria' of the Lira Concerto No. 1's Finale), the lapping of the sea, and here in the last part of *Le pescatrici* we see 'Lindoro's ship illuminated as darkness falls and Eurilda must embark'. And in some miraculous way, Haydn has captured the luminous darkness of a warm Mediterranean night, with 'l'onde placide' breaking in quiet hisses on the beach. All will be well, 'the troubled storms of the sea will disappear when the god of love is the navigator' ('Procelle torbide dal mar spariscono quando si naviga col Dio d'amor'), a wonderfully *settecento* way of thought. *Le pescatrici* is a major achievement and one of those essential works whose beauty, delicacy and strength also fulfil another function: without the experience of such works in the remote swamps of Hungary, we would never have had *The Creation* or *The Seasons* with all their humanity and goodness. The years of experience with Goldoni and Coltellini will one day open to the vastness of 'Chaos' and 'The Heavens are Telling'.

Salve Regina a quattro voci ma Soli (XXIIIb: 2)
(1771)

Scoring: S-A-T-B Soli; strings and organ solo.
Principal sources: (1) Autograph, Staatsbibliothek Berlin, dated '$\overline{771}$' (the last digit is indistinct); Mus. ms. autogr. Jos. Haydn 38. (2) MS. score signed by Joseph Elssler Sen., Gesellschaft der Musikfreunde, Vienna. (3) MS. parts, Esterházy Archives, Eisenstadt, on stag paper. (4) MS. parts from the library of Carl Kraus, now in the

Esterházy Archives, Eisenstadt. For Becker-Glauch's confusion over the covers to these works, *vide supra*, p. 170. (5) Piano score by Tranquillo Mollo, Vienna (1805).
Critical edition: Doblinger (Landon).

Literature: Larsen, *HÜB* 63, 171. Geiringer in *Musical Quarterly* XLV/4, 465f. Becker-Glauch in *Haydn-Studien* II, 215 (misinformation about the Eisenstadt sources).

And yet another work for Our Lady, with a solo organ part for the humble acrobat. Note that the Joseph Elssler MS. is also dated 1771. We believe that it was this work, and not the *Stabat Mater*, that Haydn composed as a thank-offering to the Blessed Virgin for his recovery from the dangerous illness of *c.* 1770 (*vide supra*, p. 168, and *Haydn in England 1791–1795*, p. 58). By now, having studied a series of these large-scale vocal works, we are no longer surprised about the serious tone, the use of G minor (key of the *Stabat Mater*, Symphony No. 39, Quartet Op. 20, No. 3, piano Sonata No. 32 [XVI:44] – Haydn hardly uses the key again except in Symphony No. 83 and Quartet Op. 74, No. 3), the rapt vocal writing, the syncopations ('Salve', bars 7–10, etc.), the involved, often almost tortuous, use of chromatic lines. The work is put into several movements: (1) the opening 'Salve', with extensive organ solo (2) 'Eja ergo', in Haydn's now favourite three-eight metre; C minor *Allegro* (as a contrast to the opening *Adagio*. It appears at first as if the organ is now a *continuo* instrument, but at the end of the E flat cadence it surprisingly appears again as a solo; but only here and at the end of the movement, almost as Haydn were delicately reminding Our Lady of his mortal frailty. (3) Taking a leaf from his Masses, we have a tenor solo ('Et Jesum') with a 'broken' pattern from the string accompaniment. And once again the solo organ appears, this time totally unexpectedly. By this time, however, the astute listener realizes that all these solo entries have a unifying melodic and motivic basis:

a. 'Salve', bars 10f.

b. 'Eja ergo', bars 65f.

c. 'Et Jesum', bars 10f.

and right at the beginning of (4) 'O clemens, o pia':
d. 'O clemens', bars 2–4.

Large works of this kind require some kind of unifying element, and the solo organ accomplishes just that. It would be easy to see in the whole problem a certain symbolic attitude – Haydn *vis-à-vis* Our Lady, to Whom he had a special relationship and particularly in this work, no less a 'Heiliger Dankgesang eines Genesenen an die Gottheit' than Beethoven in his A minor Quartet, Op. 132 (Molto adagio).

The spellbinding, *pianissimo* ending is perhaps the most beautiful thing Haydn has composed up to now – the end of a private (yet public) prayer: 'o dulcis virgo Maria!'

Missa Sancti Nicolai (XXII: 6)
(1772)

Scoring: S-A-T-B Soli; Choir (S-A-T-B). 2 ob., 2 cor., str., org. (bsn. presumably with *continuo*).
Principal sources: (1) Autograph (incomplete), Staatsbibliothek Berlin, Mus. ms. autogr. Jos. Haydn 16; dated 1772 'Missa Sancti Nicolai'. (2) Original performance material (with later title page: 'Missa S. Josephi'), by Joseph Elssler Sen., Esterházy Archives, Eisenstadt. Many additions by Haydn himself, including whole pages of Latin text. (3) MS. parts by Joseph Elssler, St Florian Abbey. (4) Score of the 'Dona' by Johann Elssler, the Latin text by Haydn, Conservatoire, Paris. (5) MS. parts by Joseph Elssler and others (most of the original parts no longer exist), Archives of the Basilica Maria Treu (Piaristenkirche) Vienna; the original material on 4° Italian paper (watermarks: 3 stars and 'FV'); also a later (c. 1800) score with additional *clarini* (trumpets), trombones and timpani. Examined 1959. Facsimile of basso part in Joseph Elssler's hand (beginning) in Otto Biba, *Der Piaristenorden in Österreich*, Eisenstadt 1975, p. 127.
Facsimile: Landon, *Das kleine Haydnbuch*, Faber score (both of perf. material, Eisenstadt with additions by Haydn), *Joseph Haydn und seine Zeit* (Cat., Schloss Petronell, 1959; end of basso [vocal] part in Eisenstadt material).
Critical edition: Haydn Society G. A. (Brand), XXIII/1, 1951, without Eisenstadt or St Florian. Faber Music (miniature score: Eulenburg) (Landon, using the first four sources above).
Literature: Geiringer 1932, 123, 126. Brand *Die Messen* 109ff.

The haste with which this Mass was composed explains some of the shorthand techniques found in it. There was originally no 'Dona nobis pacem' and the choir at Eisenstadt presumably improvised the text for the end of the work: the custom of 'Dona ut Kyrie' was by no means rare in *settecento* Austria. Another confusing piece of shorthand notation is the viola, which was written out only in the 'Et incarnatus' and Benedictus. It is, however, quite obvious that Haydn intended the viola to double the bass part in the rest of the Mass, as will be seen from the fact that in the 'Osanna in excelsis' at end of the Benedictus, the viola doubles the bass line; and therefore it must have been playing in the Sanctus at this point as well. In the viola part of the Faber (Eulenburg) material, our reconstruction of the missing sections may be found. As we have indicated above, Haydn later wrote out the 'Dona' (cf. p. 182).

In Germany and Austria, this work is sometimes referred to as the 'Mass in six-four time', referring to the very unusual metre of the Kyrie. This highly unconventional beginning gives to the work its pastoral character, which is further exploited in many of the other movements, including the equally unconventional Sanctus and the intensely lyrical, rhapsodic Benedictus – the latter another highly developed ensemble piece. This was now a form that so fascinated Haydn that there is hardly a multi-voiced vocal piece of this period in which we cannot find at least one fine example. Another of the characteristic features of the *Missa Sancti Nicolai* is a certain rapturous quality in much of the vocal writing: the Benedictus is perhaps the finest case in point, but also the end of the Credo and even the end of the terse fugue 'Amen' at the Gloria's conclusion. We find the characteristic tenor solo for the 'Et incarnatus', but once again the predilection for the solo voices rather than choir is found in the extraordinary 'Crucifixus', with its composer's newly found delight in complex ensemble writing marvellously and subtly displayed.

This is an optimistic Mass, full of *joie de vivre* and vigorous youthful spirits. It is incredible that it was composed almost immediately after the bleak, tragic 'Farewell' Symphony, Haydn's most intense piece of *Sturm und Drang* writing in the orchestral field. The difference between Mass and Symphony is so breathtaking that one wonders if Haydn's whole attitude to music was not basically and primarily intellectual. Perhaps the 'Farewell' Symphony is a brilliant cerebral exercise in *Sturm und Drang*. Haydn's inner feelings are seldom placed on display, either in his music (at least in this period) or in his letters; one could hardly expect this luxury from a position in which Haydn was accustomed to be fully dressed early in the morning, ready for the Prince's (no doubt sometimes rather eccentric) musical wishes. Haydn was expected to produce vast amounts of intellectually stimulating music of all kinds, and it was not possible to await the muse's kiss. Haydn, if not a 'böhmischer Musikant' was certainly an Austrian 'Musikant', and he had an endless well of pure and not necessarily emotionally involved music awaiting his (or the Prince's) beck and call. It may be that this attitude – if we are correct in our analysis – can explain the astonishing discrepancy in emotional levels between the F sharp minor of Eszterháza's wintry fields and the G major of Eisenstadt's warm winter *Stube* (the well-heated 'good room' in which the composer wrote this thank-offering to St Nicholas and, at the same time, the Prince who bore that name).

Acide, *Festa teatrale* – Second version (XXVIII:1 *bis*)
(1773)

Scoring: 2 ob., 2 cor. angl., 2 bsn., 2 cor., str. Galatea: S. Glauce: S. Nettuno: B.
Sources: Autographs: (1) Fragment of Galatea's Aria 'Troppe felice', probably a supplement to the (lost) version. (2) *Recitativo accompagnato* (Glauce), '[Il] caro tuo tesoro', with str. accompaniment. (3) Aria (Nettuno) 'Tergi i vezzosi rai'. (1) and (3) Esterházy Archives, Budapest, Ms. mus. I. 8 and 16; (2) Staatsbibliothek Berlin (Mus. ms. autogr. Jos. Haydn 55). The paper on which these fragments were written is from the Esterházy mill at Lockenhaus (watermark: Larsen 11, Bartha-Somfai 194a). Bartha-Somfai date their watermark 1762 but this is because they assumed that the fragments belonged to the first version. We now know that they must have belonged to the 1773 setting. The watermark appears in the dated

autographs of Haydn's Symphony No. 54 (1774), in the Divertimento (1775) for baryton, strings and horns (X:5) and in the Eisenstadt parts (Esterházy Archives) of the 'Aria de tempore' *contrafactum* from *Applausus*, 'Dictamina mea' (small differences to Larsen 11 but basically the same paper). In Hoboken (II, p. 348, note 3) it is suggested that the Overture, also written on a (different) Esterházy paper (autograph: Conservatoire, Paris) was composed for the 1773 version. It was not, as the dated set of parts in Göttweig Abbey ('Comparavit R. P. Odo ao. 769') prove.
Libretto: Giovanni Battista Migliavacca (with adaptations for the 1773 version by ? [Carl Friberth?]).
Critical edition: Aria 'Tergi i vezzosi rai', Haydn-Mozart Presse (Landon) – score, parts, vocal score.

The only complete Aria – now available in a modern edition – is an elegant and (as always with Haydn's bass arias) eminently singable piece on a rather extensive scale. No doubt with the successes of *La canterina*, *Lo speziale* and *Le pescatrici* behind him, Haydn felt he had outgrown the *opera seria* conventions of *Acide*. His (otherwise lost) new setting must have contained excellent and stimulating music, as this Aria suggests, but since the first performance was postponed to 1774, we have gained *L'infedeltà delusa*, the greatest opera of the period and certainly (with the Oratorio of 1775) the major vocal achievement of the years 1766–75. The accompanied recitative suggests that Haydn was thinking along the lines of his future (and only other) *opera seria* –

L'isola disabitata – where there are no *secco* recitatives at all, only *accompagnati*. Haydn's minute attention to Italian diction is, as always, omnipresent even in these fragments.[1]

L'infedeltà delusa, *Burletta per musica* in two Acts (XXVIII:5)
(1773)

Scoring: Two S (Vespina, Sandrina), two T (Filippo, Nencio), B (Nanni), 2 ob., 2 bsn., 2 cor., timp., str. (harpsichord *continuo*).
Principal sources: Autograph: (1) Overture, 2nd movt.,[2] Staatsbibliothek Berlin (Mus. ms. autogr. Jos. Haydn 7); (2) Opera itself, Esterházy Archives, Budapest, Ms. Mus. I. 4. Written on 4° Esterházy paper (watermarks: Larsen 8 and 9, Bartha-Somfai 192, 193; stag and 'IGW').

Libretto: Marco Coltellini, with extensive adaptations (Carl Friberth?). Printed libretto: *vide supra*, p. 187.
Critical editions: *Joseph Haydn Werke* XXV/5 (Bartha, Vécsey). Haydn-Mozart Presse and miniature score Philharmonia (Landon).
Literature: Geiringer 1932, 105ff., 108f. Wirth II, 23–5. Bartha-Somfai 389f. Landon in *NOHM* VII, 187ff.

The existence of Marco Coltellini's name in connection with Haydn is known to us only through the following libretto in the Carvalhaes Collection (8272) of the Biblioteca del Conservatorio di S. Cecilia, Rome:

> L'infedeltà delusa, dramma giocoso per musica da rappresentarsi nel teatro degl'arrischiati su la piazza vecchia di S. M. Novella nel carnevale dell'anno 1783. Dedicato al ... Lorenzo Niccolini de' Marchesi di Ponsacco, e Camugliano. In Firenze Nella Stamp. degli Eredi Pecchioni Con Licenza de' Superiori. [Characters: Vespina, Nanni, Sandrina, 'Nardone, Padre di Sandrina', Nencio.] Scena si rappresenta in Campagna vicino a Firenze. Poesia è del Quondam rinomato Sig. Marco Coltellini, Musica è del Celebre Sig. Maestro Michele Neri.

Obviously this 1783 setting must have been preceded by a much earlier one which cannot now be located. Marco Coltellini was an important Italian librettist who was one of those instrumental in effecting the long-needed and in part pre-Gluckian operatic reform: his *Ifigenia in Tauride*, with music by Traetta, was actually conducted by Gluck at Florence in the Winter of 1767. Coltellini was born near Florence on 13 October 1719. In 1758 he arrived at Vienna, where he produced the book for Gluck's *Il Telemaco* (1765) and Mozart's *La finta semplice* (1768). In 1769 he succeeded Metastasio (who thought highly of him) as 'poeta Cesareo', and in 1772 went to St Petersburg, where he died five years later. Even in his *opere buffe*, Coltellini shows strong signs of the reforming tendencies which, of course, he reserved primarily for serious operas; his attitude towards the aristocracy in *L'infedeltà delusa* – the dialogue of which occasionally approaches a Beaumarchaisian stinging wit – and his sympathy with the 'contadini' (peasants) are qualities which, in 1773, must have caused considerable surprise. Lampooning the nobility was by no means as fashionable at that time as it was ten or fifteen years later.

L'infedeltà delusa must have been written while Coltellini was still in Tuscany, for there are numerous local figures of speech. The Florence book's reference to 'in Campagna vicino a Firenze' is, interestingly, dropped in Haydn's version, but not the reference to the 'Marchese di Ripafrata' in Act II. Ripafrata is a picturesque ancient town, situated between Lucca and Pisa, with a gaunt fortress (once owned by a late

---

1 First recordings of Arias in this section: 'Ein' Magd, ein' Dienerin' – Gertrude Hopf, Vienna Symphony Orchestra, conducted by Meinhard von Zallinger (Haydn Society, 1951). 'Tergi i vezzosi rai' – D. Fischer-Dieskau, Vienna Symphony Orchestra, conducted by Reinhard Peters (Decca, 1971).
2 Other principal sources for Overture: (a) Authentic first ed., Artaria (Vienna), 1782; (b) authentic MS. parts, British Museum (London) Add. 32 174, from J. N. Hummel's Library; written by Johann Elssler [copyist 'Anon. 48'].

friend of ours, Cav. N. Nuñes). The libretto was, in any case, completely rewritten for Haydn, and the fact that Coltellini's name is nowhere mentioned in this 1773 version suggests that it was not he who did the revision but probably someone at Eszterháza (Friberth?). Apart from changing 'Nardone' to 'Filippo', there are other and far more sweeping alterations and additions. The opening ensemble – it lays claim to being the greatest single piece of operatic music Haydn ever wrote – with which the Opera begins, 'Bella sera, ed aure grate', is missing from the Florentine and presumably original, although 'revived', setting. In it, the work opens prosaically with a *secco* recitative, 'Ascoltate, caro Padre ...' (Sandrina). Another delightful scene for Eszterháza is that in which Vespina appears as a drunken German servant. Although it might appear that this addition was a brilliant local stroke of genius, designed to amuse Prince Nicolaus and the Dowager Princess Lunati Visconti, in fact the concept is one well known to Italian comic opera of the period. In an interesting collection of Italian MS. operatic music brought back to Ireland by Anna Maria Townley Balfour (later Mrs Anna Maria Dawson) and now in the Trinity College Library, Dublin, we find an anonymous Aria with the text 'Trinche vaine star contente, bone amiche, allegramente', which is astonishingly close to Haydn; though it is unlikely that the librettist or composer of the Dublin Aria – which was copied in Naples (Rome?) in the 1790s – ever heard, or even heard of, Haydn's 1773 setting.[1]

Synopsis of the plot: Vespina and Nanni, her brother, are poor but intend to improve their position: Vespina wants to marry the rich 'contadino' Nencio, and Nanni the only daughter (Sandrina) of another wealthy peasant, Filippo. But the young people have made their plans without Filippo, who persuades Nencio that he should marry Sandrina, a better match. Nanni and Vespina overhear this little intrigue and the clever Vespina decides to take matters into her own hands. She cannot hope for assistance from the terrified Sandrina, so Nanni is made the official accomplice. Filippo encourages Nencio to sing a serenade under the stars in front of Sandrina's window, when two unknown rowdies appear and beat Nencio thoroughly. That being of little more than temporary use, Vespina now begins her enchanting series of masquerades: first as an old hag, she appears in Filippo's house and asks after a certain Nencio, her son-in-law who has left wife and children and disappeared. Nencio then appears and is spurned by the shocked Filippo. Nencio, who is naturally displeased by all this, is now approached by a page (Vespina in disguise) who informs him that the noble Marchese di Ripafrata intends to marry Sandrina. Nencio perceives that Filippo has played totally false with him and when the noble Marchese himself (= Vespina) suggests revenge against Filippo, Nencio is only too willing: the villainous Marchese intends to have a marriage ceremony performed in which Sandrina is given the ring not by the noble Marchese but by a disguised kitchen scullion, and Nencio will be the official witness to this final act of degradation to Sandrina and her scheming father. The ceremony is arranged. Vespina is the notary, Nanni, magnificently attired as the disguised scullion-*cum*-representative of the Marchese di Ripafrata. Filippo, leading his tearful daughter to sign, is mistrustful that the Marchese himself is not present, but is told that the great Lord is away buying clothes and jewellery for Sandrina. The contract is signed; Vespina and Nanni discard their disguises and Filippo sees that he has been betrayed. He is persuaded to make the best of it, and Sandrina is wed to her Nanni and Nencio sheepishly returns to the clever Vespina.

We have seen that Boito's description of the anticlimax in Goldoni's third acts applies in some respects to *Le pescatrici*, where all the action after the discovery of the princess's real identity in Act II is, as it were, rather superimposed. *L'infedeltà delusa* is much more closely knit, with its two acts and swiftly moving plot. Haydn was

1 Cat. (Dublin) D. 5. 41 signed A. M. Dawson, works partly dated 1796, partly (Paisiello *Andromaca*, Teatro S. Carlo Naples) 1797. Watermarks: three crescents, 'BV'. In another volume, D. 5. 37, a print by Luigi Marescalchi (Naples) and the watermarks (animal in a circle) show Naples as the origin of many of the MSS. That volume is signed A. M. Townley Balfour, once 1792 at Nice (did she acquire the MSS. there? or was she actually in Rome or Naples?); there are MS. alterations to the Marescalchi address: originally 'ai Gradoni di Chiaja', changed to 'al Vicolo delle campane nel largo del Castello'. D. 5. 38, still another volume, is also signed 1792 (Nice and, to our astonishment, Paris: what was an Irish girl doing in Paris in 1792? a diplomat's daughter?). One of the works is a piece by Nasolini done at the Teatro Argentina, Rome, in 1792. For information on Coltellini, see the excellent article by Signora Emilia Zanetti in *Enciclopedia dello Spettacolo*. We have used, often *verbatim*, our notes to the Haydn-Mozart Presse/Philharmonia edition.

obviously inspired to write his finest vocal music to date, and with the great experience of his many religious and operatic pieces from the years 1766–73, he was able to give us a masterpiece in every respect. It is significant that *L'infedeltà delusa* has been the most successful of all Haydn's operas on the stage after its revival at the Holland Festival in 1963.[1] It has been performed all over Germany as well as in England, America, Sweden, France (where an entire television film on the work was filmed in Italy in 1973 due to the work's success in Paris and in the provinces, especially Alsace-Lorraine), etc.

Certainly a large part of this extraordinary success, coming as it does nearly two hundred years after the work was first performed, is because of Haydn's brilliant characterization. We single out only a few moments: the serenade that Nencio sings begins like the most Italian of all six-eight *canzonette*; there are even runs for the tenor up to high *c*. But when Haydn sets to music the words 'perchè guai per chi ci casca' (woe to whoever falls into this trap), speaking of the perils of the overpainted city woman as opposed to the innocence of rosy-cheeked country girls, there is suddenly a deathly serious moment: over a pedal point in the horns, there is an astonishingly shocking dissonance which is even visual: the sudden appearance of *c* flat over *b* flat (see *NOHM* VII, 189, for musical example in score; Philharmonia, p. 198). In the preceding 'vengeance' Duetto (which is in D and goes without a break into the E flat serenade, incidentally), Haydn creates a breathtakingly swift and dramatic atmosphere. The words are tossed back and forth in the most realistic fashion; once again Haydn has miraculously caught the swift flow of Tuscan peasants, their *furberia*, and the music almost seems to gesticulate with them. As for atmosphere, the magnificent opening ensemble, to which reference has been made already, again seems to capture with poignant simplicity the day's darkening and the *contadini*, weary from their toil in the fields, pausing to watch the sunset over the blue Tuscan hills. Using a vastly complex kind of *ritornello* form, Haydn binds this enormous, 400-bar 'set piece' into a whole by skilful technical means: it is a great achievement and a milestone in Haydn's artistic development. One final point might be mentioned, and that occurs in Filippo's great Aria in Act II ('Tu, tu, sposarti alla Sandrina?'). Here a short digression must first be made about the key structure of this Opera. It is basically in C major: that is the key of its Overture and Finale to Act II, in which Haydn's festival key is enriched by the now famous high C horns (Corni in C *alto*)[2] and kettledrums. They are used only at the beginning, the end and in Filippo's Aria, the central importance of which is thus underlined by its being linked in key and in orchestration to the pillars of the work. Here we find Haydn being inspired by *Thonmahlerey*, or word-painting. The words 'pien di vizie, e di peccati' (full of vices and sins) are set to extraordinary music with vacillating major and minor harmonies (musical example in score: *NOHM* VII, 189f.; Philharmonia, pp. 300f.), but even more interesting is Haydn's swift and total identification of 'senza amor ne carità', in which the composer sets the *opposite* of that which the text calls for. Instead of describing a man 'without love and charity', the music suddenly enfolds us in a long passage which is not only obviously love and charity but is even marked *dolce* in the score to be sure we do not miss the point.

---

1 It was preceded by the first revival in post-war times (for some earlier and unsuccessful attempts, see Löwenberg's *Annals of Opera*) at the Haydn Festival in Budapest, 1959 (Budapest State Opera). In the Holland Festival performance, the producer was Werner Düggelin and the conductor Alberto Erede (Vespina was Reri Grist). The first recording was produced by the writer of these notes for Chant du Monde, Paris: Emilia Ravaglia (Vespina), Elisabeth Speiser (Sandrina), Giorgio Grimaldi (Filippo), Umberto Grilli (Nencio), Robert El Hage (Nanni). Orchestra of the Haydn Foundation, Rome (Orchestra Sinfonica della R. A. I.). Miles Morgan, harpsichord *continuo*. Antonio de Almeida, conductor. Recorded at Rome in January, 1968.
2 Wrongly C *basso* in *Joseph Haydn Werke*, Overture.

A page from the autograph of *L'infedeltà delusa* showing the great timpani solo in the Finale of Act II; Haydn was the first of the Viennese classical school to realize and exploit the timpani's potentialities. The instruments (from top) are: timpani; horns (C *alto*); oboes I and II; V. I; V. II; Va.; vocal parts; Vc.–B.

Helmut Wirth, writing of this Opera, sums it up in one sentence: 'Although the young Mozart had at this time not entered the circle around Haydn, it may be said that Haydn came very close to his later friend in this work' (Wirth II, 25). *L'infedeltà delusa* is the culmination of Haydn's operatic style beginning with *La canterina* in 1766. With *L'incontro improvviso*, Haydn's writing takes another course, in which the basic element is profusion rather than concentration; and we will note even a gradual renunciation of the ensemble principle that had been one of the chief guiding strategies of his operatic writing during this period.

Philemon und Baucis oder Jupiters Reise auf die Erde (XXIXa:1)
Operette for Marionettes (1773)

I. Prologue *Der Götterrath*: music lost except for one interlude.

II. *Philemon und Baucis*: music later used, except for the end (an apotheosis on Maria Theresa and the Habsburg Family), in the arrangement of the work as a *Singspiel*.

Critical edition: Joseph Haydn Werke XXIV/1 (Braun). Reconstruction, using the *Singspiel* version: Symphony No. 50, first two movements, as Overture to *Der Götterrath*, leaving out the trumpets [*sic*]; in *Philemon*, the flutes omitted [*sic*] because no evidence can be found that Haydn had flutes in his orchestra in September 1773, also the trumpets in the final chorus for the same reason. For a full list, see the above edition and the Kritischer Bericht (1971).

Libretto: C. G. Pfeffel. Printed libretto: *vide supra*, p. 199. The end (not used in the *Singspiel* version) is printed in its entirety in *HJB* I, 170f. The whole libretto in *JHW*.
Literature: Landon, *SYM* 276, 315f.; *Supplement* 37, 60; *HJB* I, 111ff., 168ff. Joseph Müller-Blattau in *Haydn-Studien* II/1 (1969), 67.

Philemon und Baucis, *Ein Original-Singspiel* in One Act
(XXIXb:2) (1773, revised *c.* 1776)

Scoring: 2 S (Baucis, Narcissa), 2 T (Philemon, Aret), 2 speaking roles (Jupiter, Merkur), Chorus (S-A-T-B), 2 fl., 2 ob., 2 bsn., 2 cor., 2 trpt., timp., str.
Principal sources: (1) Autograph, in reduction for voice and keyboard, of the Canzonetta 'Ein Tag der allen Freude bringt', Sibley Library, Rochester, New York. Italian paper (watermarks: three crescents, letters 'REAL' and 'AFC'). Probably not part of the original marionette version. (2) MS. score by Johann Traeg, *c.* 1800, Conservatoire de Musique, Paris. For a complete description see *HJB* I, 172 and Kritischer Bericht, 9ff. (3) MS. parts of the Overture (2 movts.) from Náměšť Castle, Janaček Museum, Brno (ČSSR), without the flute part; A 16.762. (4) MS. parts of the Overture (2 movts.), Stadt- und Universitätsbibliothek, Frankfurt-am-Main, 170/2. Without the flute part.
Libretto: C. G. Pfeffel. Printed libretto: 'Philemon und Baucis. / Ein / Original-Singspiel / in einem Aufzuge'. Page two: 'Die Musik hiezu ist von dem berühmten Hrn. Joseph Haiden, Fürstl. Esterhazischen Kapellmeister'. Copy:

Stadtbibliothek, Vienna, 701/V. No Prologue (*Götterrath*) and a different ending (see *HJB* I, 170f.). One of the Arias, for Merkur (otherwise a speaking role), 'Seelig wer des Tages Stunden', was not included in the Traeg copy; but the other 'new' Aria, 'Dir der Unschuld', is an arrangement of, or the model for, Flaminia's 'Se la mia stella' in Haydn's *Il mondo della luna* (1777). The complete Aria text of 'Seelig' in Kritischer Bericht 18.
Facsimiles: (1) The only extant music from *Der Götterrath* (Prologue), Diana's entrance: *HJB* I, 157f. (2) Autograph reduction of 'Ein Tag': L. Schmidt, *Joseph Haydn*, Berlin 1898, facing p. 72. (3) Extracts from the Traeg copy: *HJB* I, 159.
Critical edition: Bärenreiter-Verlag (Landon).
Arrangement (contrafactum): Baucis's Aria 'Heut fühl ich der Armut Schwere' as: *Aria pro adventu* 'Maria, die reine'. MS. by Carl Kraus on O. W. Wenko and stag paper (Bartha-Somfai 202: 1790), Stadtpfarrkirche Eisenstadt, 67.
Literature: Becker-Glauch in *Haydn-Studien* II/3 (1970), 221f. Landon in *HJB* I, 151.

The Traeg copy includes several instrumental interludes which have turned out to be, in two cases, by Gluck and Carlos d'Ordoñez (from their respective Operas *Orfeo* and *Alceste*) and at the end there is a 'Ballo' which is from Gluck's *Paride ed Elena*: in the

Traeg copy there are parts for flutes and bassoons which the original Gluck score (published by Trattner in Vienna, 1770) does not have. Is this the kind of thing Haydn used for all those ballets at Eszterháza, with the same sort of orchestral retouchings that we find in the operas of his contemporaries? Haydn must have had to use a great deal of music to fill all those evenings of theatrical (incidental) music. Perhaps his pupils helped: certainly Haydn helped himself liberally to Pleyel, who composed the Overture to *Die Feuersbrunst*, the third movement of which Haydn included in his own Overture to *L'infedeltà delusa* (which went from the second movement straight into the first ensemble) when he sold that work to Artaria.

Apart from these versions of *Philemon*, we have a totally lost marionette opera entitled *Hexen-Schabbas* (1773), of which not even the libretto, printed by Trattner in Vienna, has survived. Haydn is also listed as the composer of a lost *Singspiel* entitled *Le Glorieux oder Der Großsprecher* (played by a *Wandertruppe* in Donaueschingen, Winter 1778–9). There is probably more such lost music than we imagine – what, after all, did Haydn play with his marionette troupe in the Carnival season of 1774?[1]

What of the music itself? *Philemon und Baucis*, the first known marionette opera Haydn wrote, is most interesting. Like many of Haydn's large-scale vocal works, it is in progressive tonality (D minor to C major). There are arias, a duet, instrumental interludes (if any are really by Haydn), choruses with soli and a quartet finale which the chorus takes over. The original production must, indeed, have been enchanting. But lacking the atmosphere of Eszterháza, neither the mythological subject nor the fatuous dialogue ('Vergebt des Wurms Verwegenheit ...') is calculated to hold the interest of a modern audience: it is solely Haydn's delightful and, in part, powerful music that retains our fascination. Musicology has no place in judging an opera! One of the most dramatic parts of the work is the Overture, which has some really bleak moments, such as the sinister falling away of the strings in quavers and semiquavers against sustained wind instruments, followed by a fine contrapuntal passage. The opening chorus (Thunderstorm), with Haydn's nervous pattern of repeated semiquavers, is in the best tradition of his symphonic and chamber music, as well as his operas, of the 1760s and 1770s.

Of the arias, one of the best is undoubtedly No. 4, the Canzonetta or Aria of Philemon, 'Ein Tag, der allen Freude bringt', with its finely differentiated dynamic and vocal line: notice the difference between 'O glückliche Zeit' and 'O schreckliche Zeit' and the ending, which dies away 'calando'. The Esterházy copyist Johann Schellinger sent this work (and some dance music)[2] in the arrangement of Haydn's autograph, i.e. for vocal line and keyboard, to Donaueschingen Castle with a fanciful title, 'Freud und Trauerlied'. Schellinger added some curious programmatic descriptions ('thunderclap, which killed them both'). And Donaueschingen even owned a complete piano score of the Opera, which no longer exists (where did they get it? from Haydn, who had dealings with the Fürstenbergs?). Aret's G minor Aria, 'Wenn am weiten Firmamente' (No. 7) is one of the most original parts of the work, with its *obbligato* oboe and *pizzicato* strings, through the dreamy texture of which the second violins, *con sordini*, weave their way in sinuous sextuplets. It will be noted that Aret's high, rather *Heldentenor*-like line contrasts well with Philemon's lyric part, obviously meant to be sung by an older man. Narcissa's meltingly beautiful Aria, 'Dir der Unschuld', can be studied in the *Il mondo della luna* version.

---

1 *HJB* I, 145f., 174f.
2 See *Haydn in England 1791–1795*, p. 487.

Haydn scholars will be struck by the many parallels to *L'infedeltà delusa*. There is a certain stylistic and also textural flavour about Haydn's use of C major in conjunction with high (C *alto*) horns and drums to express emotions of joy, success, triumph, and so on which one does not find in other composers (except in Pleyel's own marionette opera for Eszterháza), nor in Haydn's post-Eszterháza music except as a great exception (end of *The Seasons*). The beginning of the 'Triumph' Chorus (*Philemon*), the Finale of *L'infedeltà delusa* just before the tremendous kettledrum solo ('Quel ch'è fatto, fatto sia'), and the opening of Symphony No. 50 (Overture to *Der Götterrath?*) are all built upon triadic formations rising from '*c*' to '*g*'. The central part of this 'Triumph' chorus is a beautiful quartet which is perhaps the finest single piece in this modest marionette *Spiel*; the technique is now so assured as to be second nature, and the weaving *legato* quavers of the first violin are balanced by a slow vocal line ('Du bleibst in jedem Augenblick der beste Theil, das beste Glück, ein sicherer Trost im Heil und Leide') and the nervous repeated quavers in the accompaniment: these words were of the kind calculated to inspire Haydn's thoughts (almost as if the words were those of our modest prestidigitator addressing himself to Our Lady), and the music transcends the mould.[1] *Auch in der kleinsten Posse erkennt man den Meister ...*

The first complete recording was made at Vienna in 1951.[2]

Il ritorno di Tobia, Oratorio in Two Parts (XXI:1)
(1775)

Scoring: 2 S (Raffaelle, Sara), A (Anna), T (Tobia), B (Tobit), Choir (S-A-T-B), 2 fl., 2 ob., 2 cor angl., 2 bsn., 2 hns., 2 trpt., timp., str.

Principal sources: (1) Autograph of the 'Parte Seconda' from the Library of the Marchioness of Bute, now Gesellschaft der Musikfreunde, Vienna. (2) Autograph[?], in private possession, Paris, of a 'short score' (voice and bass line) of the Aria 'Quando mi dona' and cadenza to the Aria 'Quel felice nocchier'. The photographs that we have seen some years ago suggest that this is *not* an autograph but a contemporary copy. Of the many authentic copies of the score, (3) Library of A. van Hoboken (now Nationalbibliothek, Vienna) and (4) Princes of Oettingen-Wallerstein, Harburg Castle (Bavaria) may be mentioned. For a complete list, see *Joseph Haydn Werke*. (5) The performance material of the former Tonkünstler-Societät was discovered by the author and is now in the Stadtbibliothek, Vienna; it contains a mixture of the various performances – 1775, 1784 and esp. 1808. For princ. sources to Overture, see *L'infedeltà delusa* (*supra*).

REVISION OF THE ORATORIO IN 1784
FOR THE TONKÜNSTLER-SOCIETÄT:

Two new choruses: (1) 'Ah, gran Dio'; (2) 'Svanisce in un momento'. Additional instruments: four (not two as in Hoboken II, 22) horns

and two trombones for (2). Otherwise the 1775 version considerably cut. (2) exists in many sources, also half-a-dozen authentic copies (*inter alia* Eisenstadt, Esterházy Archives) as a Motet 'Insanae et vanae curae' with an authentic timpani part; although the autograph of (2) has none, it may be that the part was added on a separate sheet for the 1784 performance.

Principal sources: Autograph of (2), Esterházy Archives, Budapest, Ms. mus. I. 18.B. dated 1784. Authentic score with corrections and additions in Haydn's hand of the Chorus (with preceding Aria) 'Ah, gran Dio': (a) Burgenländisches Landesmuseum, Eisenstadt (*ex. coll.* Landon); (b) Royal College of Music, London (different ending: *forte*).

Libretto: Giovanni Gastone Boccherini.

Critical edition: *Joseph Haydn Werke* XXVIII/1–2 (Schmid), originally prepared for the Haydn Society. Motet 'Insanae et vanae curae': Breitkopf & Härtel score, 1809, also available in a good modern reprint (B. & H.).

Complete Recording: Veronika Kincses (Sara), Magda Kalmár (Raffaelle), Klára Takács (Anna), Attila Fülöp (Tobia), Zsolt Bende (Tobit), Budapesti Madrigálkórus, Magyar Allami Hangversenyzenekar, conducted by Ferenc Szekeres. Producer: Dóra Antal. Recorded in

---

1 The short analysis from *HJB* I, 156ff., mostly *verbatim*. In view of the well-known legend, a synopsis of the plot was considered superfluous.

2 Vox PL 7660. Soli: Fritz Steinböck (Jupiter), Walter Davy (Merkur), Erich Majkut (Philemon), Susanna Nadic (Baucis), Waldemar Kmentt (Aret), Elisabeth Roon (Narcissa), Chorus of the Vienna State Opera, Vienna Symphony Orchestra, conducted by Meinhard von Zallinger-Thurn. Operatic regie: Walter Davy. Producer: the present writer.

1974. Hungaroton SLPX 11660–62. Motet 'Insanae': see 'Missa in tempore belli' in *Haydn: the Years of 'The Creation' 1796–1800*, pp. 162ff. *Literature*: Pohl *Denkschrift (passim)*; Pohl II, 68ff., 84, 86, 201, 338ff. Geiringer 1932, 134f. E. F. Schmid, 'Haydns Oratorium "Il ritorno di Tobia", seine Entstehung und seine Schicksale', in *Archiv für Musikwissenschaft* VI (1959), 292ff.

When Haydn's Oratorio was revived the third time, in 1808, Rosenbaum went to hear it and wrote in his Diary: 'veraltetes Machwerk, das nicht gefiel' ('an antiquated pot-boiler; it was not well received').[1] Time and Haydn's late Oratorios had relegated *Il ritorno di Tobia* to the category of Interesting Historical Works. Not even the attractive Overture has ever regained its popularity, which is doubly surprising in view of the success of most other Haydn overtures in the last decade or two. The main trouble with the Oratorio is its very Metastasian libretto, a work of the 'Age of Reason'. The Book of Tobias is part of the Apocrypha and was written during the Babylonian Captivity: scholars have found that the battle with the water monster, the use of the monster's liver and heart for miraculous purposes and the evil demon, Asmodi, who murders seven bridegrooms of the young Sara on their wedding nights, are all in the tradition of Babylonian mythology. Instead of using these elements to create a dramatic plot, Boccherini is content to follow the Metastasian idyll, in which moralizing reflections and philosophical ruminations replace any action. The episode with Asmodi is relegated to a recitative (No. 2a): 'Quello spirito immondo sai pur che uccide quanti sposi a Sara ardiscano accostarsi?' Similarly, the battle with the dread water monster is also relegated to a recitative (No. 4a): 'ed ecco un mostro algoso in aspre giuse gli s'avventò ...'. Following an Italian tradition even older than Metastasio, we find what are known as 'Parable Arias', in which events are retold in metaphoric form. Here, Haydn could give full range to his talents for *Thonmahlerey*. To take one obvious example (No. 2b, Aria by Anna): 'Sudò il guerriero, ma gloria ottenne; tremò il nocchiero, ma s'arrichì ... Geme talora l'agricoltore ...; ma lo ristora la messe un dì. Tu passi gl'anni fra pene e pianti, e sono i danni la tue mercè. Chiaro si vede che fra' tuoi vanti un vero merito giammai non c'è ...'. The 'guerriero' is illustrated by the presence of trumpets and martial rhythms, while the 'trembling sea captain' is conjured to metaphorical life by Haydn's 'rolling and foaming billows' (violins). The ploughman ('l'agricoltore') has a Simon-like folk-tune on the oboe. Despite the weight of tradition, however, there are only two real *da capo* Arias, one which (as we have seen in the description of the sources) exists in an elaborated version of the period and is of great interest for that reason (No. 6b, 'Quando mi dona').

Haydn recognized that even in the nine years that separated the work's revival from its première, taste had changed enormously. For the 1784 revival he improved the work greatly by additions and subtractions, the former being the two magnificent choruses and the latter many cuts of all kinds. In its revised form, the work is far tighter musically and constitutes one of the major works of Haydn's Eszterháza years. There are many beauties of all sorts, especially in the rich instrumentation, but contemporary opinion was quite right to single out the choruses in 1775 and even more was that opinion justified in 1784. Thrilling is the switch into minor in the penultimate chorus of Part One, 'Odi le nostre voci', and of rapturous beauty the huge ensemble and fugue with which the work concludes. The key of E flat (Duetto Anna-Tobia, 'Dunque, oh Dio') gives us our cors anglais, but these instruments, usually wedded to E flat, are also used in F major: Sara's extraordinary Aria 'Non parmi esser fra gli'uomini', which uses a vast array of wind instruments in *obbligato* fashion; it is the

---

1 Radant, *Rosenbaum*, German 146, English 145.

largest group of its kind that Haydn had ever employed (flutes, oboes, cors anglais, bassoons, horns), and it is used with consummate delicacy and skill. The work is in the basic key of C major, but Haydn's delight was in the intricate and enharmonic modulations which, many years later, he thought fit to show his English friend, William Shield.[1] The first chorus that Haydn added was of a very special kind. He broke off Anna's Aria, 'Ah, gran Dio' and continued the music with a chorus to which trumpets and kettledrums make a sudden and effective appearance. The contrapuntal splendour of this chorus looks forward to the late Oratorios. The other choral addition of 1784 is the stupendous 'Svanisce in un momento', where for the first time in the revised version, trombones make their belated entry (did they double the choral parts otherwise? did they really make this one solitary *Auftritt*?) and there are four horns, two in the tonic and two in the relative major. This wonderfully powerful D minor piece takes its strength from the text's typical imagery: 'Svanisce in un momento dei malfattor la speme, come il furor del vento, come tempesta in mar ... De' giusti la speranza con cangia mai sembianza, costante ognor si fa ... ed è lo stesso Iddio la lor tranquillità ...'. Here we have another chorus that looks forward: this time to the *Madrigal* 'The Storm', composed in London (1792). Both works alternate between the raging sea (storm) and the 'blessed quiet' ('tranquillità'), the first in quick and the second in slow tempo. The Aria that preceded this chorus is also most unconventional: it is in F minor, with the syncopations typical of Haydn's *Sturm und Drang* style, and it also uses cors anglais to great effect. We are reminded that F minor is fast becoming a favourite: a whole Symphony of 1768 (No. 49, 'La Passione'), an Aria in *L'infedeltà delusa* ('Non v'è rimedio') and now Anna's stormy Aria (No. 13b), with its haunted text ('Come in sogno un stuol m'apparve d'ombre, spettri, mostri e larve ...'). Note that for another text portraying spirits, Haydn would also later choose F minor: the opening Chorus from Act IV of *L'anima del filosofo*. Composers certainly associate keys with ideas, and here is one concrete example. It is curious to note that Haydn seems to have had a fastidious dislike of the clarinet all during these years: although he wrote for it in some early (*c.* 1761–5) divertimentos, he never seems to have used his own players at Eszterháza for the symphonies of this period; or if he did, these versions do not survive. In Vienna he could have had clarinets for *Il ritorno di Tobia*; these instruments were being practised even by the orphans of the *Waisenhaus* (on the Rennweg) in Vienna in 1773.[2] Yet Haydn wrote hardly a note for the clarinet in our period until the *Notturni* for the King of Naples (1790). As we have said before, cors anglais meant to Haydn what clarinets later meant to Mozart.

We cannot enjoy *Il ritorno di Tobia* if we insist on judging it with the aural and spiritual standards of *The Creation*; not even Haydn's contemporaries could do that by 1808. But it would be a pity to miss the many and exceptional beauties with which this score abounds, and if we cannot expect many performances,[3] we are fortunate in living during an age when the whole work, and almost all the other large-scale vocal pieces discussed in this volume, are readily available in score and on records. In some respects, Haydn has come alive as a result of the long-playing record; and if there is such a thing as a Haydn Renaissance, it is in the fact that his *œuvre* is now not only printed but recorded. *Il ritorno di Tobia* is one of the works to benefit most by this

---

1 See *Haydn in England 1791–1795*, pp. 83f.
2 *Wiener Diarium* No. 62, Wed., 4 Aug. 1773: 'a small music concert by the boys of the establishment playing on various instruments, such as oboes, clarinet, violin, organ ...'.
3 One of the first in our times to use the original (i.e. not the Neukomm) orchestration was put on by the Austrian Radio in 1959, conducted by Miltiades Caridis. Another was conducted by Antal Dorati at Washington in 1975.

situation. This is not such a digression from the principle of this biography – 'Scribitur ad narrandum, non ad probandum' – as might at first be thought. . . .

L'incontro improvviso, *dramma giocoso per musica* (XXVIII:6)
in three acts (1775)

Scoring: 3 S (Rezia, Balkis, Dardane), 2 T (Ali, Osmin), B (Calandro), subsidiary roles for further three calandri (Dervishes), an officer (T) and the Sultan (B), 2 ob., 2 cor. angl., 2 bsn., 2 cor., 2 trpt., timp., Turkish instr. (tuned bass drum, cymbals), str. (harpsichord *continuo*).
Principal sources: (1) for the Overture: (a) Fragment of the autograph, Staatsbibliothek, Berlin, Mus. ms. autogr. Jos. Haydn 7, containing bars 1–41; (b) and (c) see *L'infedeltà delusa* Overture sources; the subsidiary MSS. all lack trpt., timp. and percussion. (2) for the Opera itself: (a) Autograph, State Saltykov-Schtschedrin Library, Leningrad, with the closing signature: 'Fine del Drama. Laus Deo et B. V. M. et O. S. [Omni Sancti]', discovered by J. P. Larsen in 1954; lacking the Rezia Aria 'Or vicina' (with surrounding *secco* rec.), which was published by Artaria in score (1783). Haydn obviously tore the original from his

MS. The principal source for 'Or vicina' is, then (b): First edition in score by Artaria, pl. no. 35 (see Hoboken II, p. 367). (c) MS. score of the German translation by F. X. Girzik, with dialogue instead of *secco* recit., Nationalbibliothek, Vienna.
Libretto: Carl Friberth after Dancourt. Printed libretto: *vide supra*, p. 219.
Critical edition: Overture, Doblinger (Landon). *Opera*: *Joseph Haydn Werke* XXV/6 (Wirth). German piano-vocal score: Musik-wissenschaftlicher Verlag (now Bärenreiter) (Helmut Schultz).
Literature: For false portrait of a supposed performance at Eszterháza, *vide supra*, p. 28. Geiringer 1932, 107f. Wirth I, 47ff., Wirth II, 25ff. Landon, *SYM*, 19. G. Feder and S. Gerlach; 'Haydn-Dokumente aus dem Esterházy-Archiv in Forchtenstein', in *Haydn-Studien* III/2 (1974), pp. 96ff. 103f.

Whereas none of the operas hitherto discussed in this Chapter was to our knowledge ever performed outside the Esterházy Court, *L'incontro improvviso* was at least prepared by Girzik for performance at the Erdödy Theatre in Pressburg. Whether the performance took place is doubtful, however; for in the printed libretto of Salieri's *Axur* for the Pressburg Theatre (1788), we find a list[1] of all the singers and orchestral players in the Erdödy Troupe and, even more important, a list of 'Folgende Opern sind seit der Eröffnung des Gräflichen Theaters aufgeführt worden' (The following operas have been performed since the opening of the . . . Theatre). There are no less than four Haydn operas listed: *La fedeltà premiata* (1785), *La vera costanza* (1786), *Orlando Paladino* (1786) and *Armida* (1786); but not this work. Perhaps it was done privately at Pressburg. The other four were all done, it would seem, in German translation, though the source does not quite make this clear.

Synopsis of the plot: Ali, Prince of Balsora, flees from his brother to Persia, where he falls in love with the beautiful Princess Rezia whose father, however, has promised her to another. The two lovers elope but are captured by the Corsairs and separated, Rezia being sold to the Sultan of Cairo, who hopes to win her favours by his gentle behaviour; he allows her considerable freedom. Ali, together with his comic servant Osmin, have many adventures but finally land in Cairo, where he hopes to find Rezia. She spies him from a window and sends a servant to discover his whereabouts.

Osmin, always hungry, finds a group of Whirling Dervishes ('calandri') and attaches himself to them, adopting their mode of dress and

attempting to learn their complex 'begging song'. He tries to persuade Ali to join them too, without success. There appears Balkis, a lady-in-waiting to Rezia, and invites Ali to a mysterious rendezvous in a nearby house, telling him that a lady loves him. Osmin imagines that there may be food and drink involved and since his master hesitates (thinking of his lost love, Rezia), Osmin goes instead and is in fact given delicacies by slaves. Meanwhile Balkis persuades Ali to enter and he, too, is wined and dined by the slaves. Osmin asks Ali to cultivate this new friendship, which annoys the Prince. Another messenger, the lady-in-waiting Dardane appears, and finally Rezia herself, persuaded that Ali loves only her. Rezia plans the escape: as soon as the Sultan goes hunting, they shall flee, and as soon as

1 Copy used: National Széchényi Library, Budapest, Mus. Th. 2874-b.

he leaves Cairo, they start their escape plan. The fugitives now include, apart from the lovers. Osmin, the two lady confidantes of Rezia and a Dervish who is a refugee from Balsora and immediately recognizes Prince Ali. They meet for a final meal and then intend to flee. The Sultan returns unexpectedly. Osmin has another plan: he knows a secret staircase that leads to the carriage-house where the Dervishes have their quarters. There, the group will hide and a caravan-leader will smuggle them out of Cairo. Meanwhile the Sultan has discovered Rezia's and her companions' absence and sets a huge reward on their heads. The fugitive Dervish cannot withstand this temptation and betrays them. Osmin attempts to pass off Ali as a well-known French painter whose eccentricity is legion. That ruse, too, fails, but when Ali receives the Sultan's letter from the officer arresting him, he learns that all is forgiven and, as an example, the faithless Dervish is to be arrested and killed. The group plead for the Dervish's life, and the Sultan pardons him as well, in a magnanimous gesture that must have quickened every Enlightened heartbeat.

The brilliant Overture is now a deservedly popular piece. With its exotic Turkish percussion – including the mystery of *tuned* bass drums in D and A – and racy rhythms, as well as the delicately orchestrated *Andantino* with 'cello solo, it was bound to be an instant success. It was one of the six Overtures that Haydn detached from their respective works and sold to Artaria, who issued them in 1782. The Turkish elements also appear in other numbers of the work, notably in Calandro's first Aria ('Castagno, castagna') and the Duetto on the same theme (No. 8), as well as the *Marcia* in the third Act. In the latter, we note the repeated thirds which was one of the hallmarks of this 'Turkish' music:

The relationship to the Turkish music in Mozart's *Entführung* Overture is clear, though Mozart can have heard only the Artaria version of the Overture to *L'incontro*, i.e. minus the trumpets, timpani and Turkish percussion; it is extremely unlikely that at this stage (1782) Mozart can have seen the score of the Opera itself, though later, after Mozart and Haydn became friends, the latter showed his young friend some of the unpublished Eszterháza operas such as *Armida*.

Friberth wrote a much more balanced third act than is found in the Italian sources that Haydn used otherwise: the over-slight last acts continue in *Il mondo della luna* and even in *La vera costanza* and *La fedeltà premiata*. The whole libretto of *L'incontro* was fashioned to suit Haydn's penchant for witty stage situations. The work is the longest of all the operas considered thus far, and uncut it would last nearly as long as a major Wagner opera. A few of the numbers of special interest may be selected for short analysis. The most beautiful and original is without question the ravishing *Terzetto* in Act I for Rezia and her two confidantes, Balkis and Dardane, 'Mi sembra un sogno che diletta', using cors anglais for the last time in any Haydn opera until *L'anima del filosofo*

(1791). The key is, of course, E flat, which was (by the way) a characteristic key for dream ('sogno') sequences, or as they were then called 'ombra' scenes. It was this extraordinary piece that the first editors of Haydn's *Il mondo della luna*, Mark Lothar and W. M. Treichtlinger, lifted bodily from its rightful place and inserted in their dreadful German adaptation, *Die Welt auf dem Monde* (1932); they rightly recognized its special qualities. The breathtaking chromaticism seems years ahead of its time,

but it only reveals, basically, our total ignorance of Haydn's overall style in this period – one in which vocal music was surely predominant in its composer's mind. Consider that, in the famous autobiographical sketch of 1776 (*vide infra*, pp. 397ff.), not one of Haydn's instrumental pieces is specifically listed.

To return to our *Terzetto*, our astonishment is compounded by the end, where we arrive with formal *settecento* precision at a cadential six-four chord and a triple hold that obviously unleashed a complicated cadenza for the three soloists. Some idea of the Opera's fantastic length may be gathered by timing this *Terzetto*: it lasts about a quarter of an hour!

Haydn, as we have seen in the brief examination of the sources, detached the Aria sung by Rezia in Act II, 'Or vicina a te mio cuore': a brilliant showpiece with flashing coloratura that must have been the success of the evening: Haydn tended to publish his greatest hits, and he preferred issuing them in full score, as would be the case with the great soprano scene from *La fedeltà premiata*, 'Ah come il core' (which for years was judged to be a real solo cantata!). In fact Haydn was beginning to make something of a speciality of these C major soprano 'set pieces': we find an equally arresting one in *Il mondo della luna* (Flaminia's 'Ragion nell'alma siede' in Act I), while the great culmination of this genre is the huge coloratura Aria of the Genio in *L'anima del filosofo* – as much a great summing-up of its kind as is Symphony No. 97 of all the preceding C major works of the festive sort.

Possibly the most subtle of the many interesting numbers is the E major Duet between Rezia and Ali in Act II, 'Son quest'occhi un stral d'amore'. Apart from some brilliantly original harmonic strokes (see bars 28, 51 *et al.*), this lyrical hymn is once again the harbinger of many great love duets in Haydn – perhaps the greatest is that in Act III of *Il mondo della luna*. Helmut Wirth, in speaking of this Duet, says that, in contrast to Gluck's *La rencontre imprévue (Die Pilgrim[m]e von Mekka)*,

> where the aria of Ali is the centre and thus reaches the highest sentiment in the longing of the prince, Haydn already sees the fulfilment of the longing in the classic humanitarian sense.'   [Wirth II, 30f.]

We also have another glimpse into the future: the third-related key structure of this piece in relation to the G major Finale that follows: E major (Duet), modulating to B major (dominant), pivot key (= mediant of) G. This is the sort of complicated key relationship with which the works of the late period abound.

But despite the sonorous orchestration, with its (for Eszterháza) unusual trumpets and extra percussion, despite the funny scenes on the stage, the exotic setting, the brilliant Finales – there was no rain of gold on Haydn and the singers. Harich (*HJB* IV,13 [31]) considers that these gifts had suddenly ceased after 1774 'because meanwhile Haydn's salary had been increased to 1,000 gulden as a result of the new position as *qua organista* of the princely chapel at Eisenstadt'. Yet after the famous *Gesamtgastspiel* of the whole Esterházy Troupe at Schönbrunn Castle in 1777, when Haydn's *Hexen-Schabbas* and Ordoñez's *Alceste* were given, there was another rain of gold for the Marionette Troupe.[1] The gold ducats were particularly profuse in connection with *L'infedeltà delusa* which, the Prince rightly considered, was a turning-point in his *Capellmeister*'s career. *L'incontro improvviso* is not really a first-rate opera: it is too long, too diffuse, and lacks the driving pace of its 1773 predecessor. Curiously, modern audiences feel the same lack of dramatic spirit: despite its much-publicized revival by Helmut Schultz in 1936, and various performances since then (including a complete broadcast by the Vienna Radio in 1959), the work has never been a success. Prince Esterházy, that wise judge of Haydn's talents, did not reward him for this, the most lavish, expensive and expansive Opera so far produced at the Castle; nor do there seem to have been any repetitions after the first performances. Like its 1773 predecessor, this work was also dedicated to the Blessed Virgin (and 'All the Saints' as well): but this time the great *jongleur* was not on his best form.[2]

---

1 A.M. 4361, Esterházy Archives, Budapest: 17 July 1777, receipt signed by Haydn.
2 There is a long review of the Artaria (André's reprint?) edition of the Aria 'Or vicina' by J. F. Reichardt in his *Studien für Tonkünstler und Musikfreunde*, Berlin 1793, pp. 123f. At the end Reichardt writes:
'. . . If this Aria is from an opera, as its appearance clearly indicates, Haydn probably composed the whole opera, and if only I lived nearer to him, I would not cease importuning him to have the score printed. Perhaps not every number therein can, without recourse to the individuality of the character and the situation, be as charming as this Aria; but every one – if we consider this [Aria] from that standpoint – certainly bears the unmistakable stamp of Haydnesque originality'. See Wirth I, 9. For the complete transcript of such a long review of a Haydn aria, we refer the reader to Cramer's analysis of 'Ah come il core' (*infra*, pp. 439ff.). We have had to be slightly selective about these enormous reviews (see our remarks in the Preface, p. 11).

CHAPTER FOUR

Crisis Years: *Sturm und Drang* and the Austrian Musical Crisis

. . . for in the very torrent, tempest, and – as I may say – whirlwind of passion, you must acquire and beget a temperance, that may give it a smoothness.

Hamlet to the players, Act III, scene ii

IN THIS CHAPTER we shall consider the literary and musical scene insofar as Haydn's own compositions are concerned and those of other composers, especially Haydn's pupils and *seguaci*, as follows:

I   Introduction;
II   The German literary movement leading to the *Sturm und Drang*.
III   Haydn's works: (1) Symphonies; (2) String Quartets; (3) Piano Sonatas and Variations; (4) the Piano Concerto in G (XVIII:4) and 'Il maestro e lo scolare' (XVIIa:1); (5) Six Duets for Violin and Viola (VI:1–6); (6) Divertimento a tre (Horn Trio; IV:5); (7) Baryton Trios; (8) various Divertimenti (X:1–12);
IV   Works by other composers and their works: (a) Haydn's pupils (notably Pleyel) and the formation of the 'Second Haydn School'; (b) some *seguaci* of Haydn (J. B. Vanhal; Carlos d'Ordoñez; Mozart, with special reference to the Symphony in G minor, K.183); (c) a literary survey.

I. INTRODUCTION

We now arrive at a curious period in Austrian music. Now that the *oeuvre* of Haydn's predecessors and contemporaries is no longer an unknown continent, traversed only by a few obscure paths beaten by individual scholars into the wilderness of Wagenseil, Holzbauer, Gassmann, Ordoñez, Vanhal and Dittersdorf, we are in a better position to judge the extraordinary series of works, many (but by no means a majority) written in minor keys by Haydn from about 1765 to 1775. When the French scholar Théodore de Wyzewa, in 1909, thought he had discovered a 'romantic crisis' in Haydn's life, and when he tried to ally this crisis to the well-known literary movement usually referred to by the (alternate) title of a play by one of its members, Klinger's *Sturm und Drang* (1776), Wyzewa was unaware of many of the true datings of Haydn's music – not to speak of those of Haydn's contemporaries with whom anyone was then familiar. It was clear to Wyzewa that such works as the 'Trauer' and 'Farewell' Symphonies, or the G minor and F minor Quartets (Nos. 3 and 5 of Opus 20), had some new and special kind of message to impart that was at profound emotional odds with the usual kind of Haydn symphony and quartet produced in the preceding years. The first three volumes of the new Haydn *Gesamtausgabe* had just appeared (1907), including Symphonies Nos. 1 – 40, with a chronological table of what was then thought to be the complete list of 104 Haydn symphonies, prepared by the great Austrian scholar, E. von Mandyczewski. Using this chronological table, Wyzewa could hardly have realized that such a work as Symphony No. 49 in F minor ('La Passione') was not composed only 'vor 1773' but in fact 1768, for the simple reason that the dated autograph was not then known to Mandyczewski.

As for the other Haydn works which might be considered as belonging to the category of *Sturm und Drang*, some (such as Symphony No. 26 ['Lamentatione']) were perhaps dated by Mandyczewski slightly too early ('um 1765'), while other works, such as the *Stabat Mater* were dated too late: the work was then believed to have been composed about 1771, but is now known to date from 1767. Even with the evidence as known in 1909, however, Wyzewa should have seen that a great majority of Haydn's supposed *Sturm und Drang* works had been composed substantially *before* the literary movement of that name began to spread its influence. The key works by Goethe, *Götz von Berlichingen* (1773) and *Die Leiden des jungen Werther* (1774), were published by the time Haydn's 'romantic crisis', or whatever we wish to call it, was virtually finished.

Clearly, the Austrian musical crisis slightly preceded the German literary movement; and it is now plain that the reasons for the Austrian musical crisis, and the spiritual roots from which it took its nourishment, were primarily musical and only secondarily (if at all) literary. Contrary to what has been written, however, both movements were extremely similar in their essential message, in their language and structure, in their relatively short span of life, and not least in the fact that the leading members of both schools later repudiated (either in fact or in word, or both) their *Sturm und Drang* period. We shall therefore try to provide a brief survey of the German literary movement and of the Austrian musical crisis.

II. THE GERMAN LITERARY MOVEMENT LEADING TO THE *'STURM UND DRANG'*

By the time we join the German-language literary school, in the early 1770s, the Age of Enlightenment had shed its warming rays over large parts of the European intellectual scene. Frederick the Great was the first ruler who had tried consciously to apply the theoretical ideas of Rousseau and Voltaire to a political and geographical entity (in that case, Prussia). We know that French influence was paramount, not only in the fact that Frederick (and most of the Austrian aristocracy) preferred to speak and write in French but in the profound influence of French classical drama on German literary circles. The primacy of reason was now incorporated into previous Pietist thought, and in a rational, harmonious and God-defined order, original sin could no longer be considered seriously. Freemasonry, a Brotherhood founded by the British early in the century and which soon spread to France, Germany and Austria, flourished. Maria Theresa's husband, Franz Stephan of Lothringen (Lorraine), was a Mason; and by the 1760s, Lodges had sprung up throughout the Austrian monarchy, bringing to intellectuals the doctrine of Enlightenment, the 'Great Universal Architect's' concept of Divine order and brotherly love. In Freemasonry, which we shall examine in more detail *infra*, there was also a revolutionary seed, a stand against tyranny, bigotism and narrowness of spirit which would lead almost directly to the American Revolution (many of the architects of which, such as Franklin, Jefferson and Washington, were Masons): the Declaration of Independence contains many elements taken from the Charter of the British Grand Lodge. The American Revolution occurred in 1776, the year in which Friedrich Maximilian Klinger (1752–1831) published *Wirrwarr* ('Confusion'), later in the same year renamed *Sturm und Drang*: and it is significant that the action of that play takes place on the American Continent.[1]

The essence of the *Sturm und Drang* movement has been called 'Ich-bezogen', egocentric; but this is only a part of its complex message. *Drang* means not only 'stress' but, since the force comes from within, it might, with Norman Hampson, be called 'the inner voice'. On the one hand, Klinger's play is typical in its confusion, anarchy and breathlessness; but the other elements in the movement as a whole proved to be of more profound and lasting influence. It is wrong to see in the *Sturm und Drang* – the term was in use by 1773,[2] incidentally – only the 'Ich-bezogene', the search for personal happiness or selfish gratification of the senses. Klinger's works have been largely forgotten, but the best spirits of this epoch survived to play a decisive role in the years to come. The diverging interests of the *Sturm und Drang* produced the philosophy of Hamann; the fantasy of Lavater; the logical brilliance of Kant; the charm and *Volksliedverbundene* of Bürger; the great, life-enhancing force of Goethe; and the emergence of Joseph Haydn among the great minds of the epoch.

One of the primary influences was English literature. At the beginning of *Werther*, the heroine (Charlotte) speaks 'mit solcher Wahrheit' of Goldsmith's *The Vicar of Wakefield*.[3] William Heckscher says of these German writers, 'Their catechism was a slender volume which the ageing poet Edward Young had composed in 1759 under the title *Conjectures on Original Composition* ... [It] helped to foster the cult of literary genius as that of an artist unimpeded by the dictates of morals or scholarship. Genius, in the words of Young, "*grows*, is not *made*"'.[4] Another fundamental influence was Thomas Percy's *Reliques of Ancient English Poetry*, a collection of old English ballads (1765), but perhaps one of the most seminal of the English models was James Macpherson's brilliant forgery of poems by an alleged Gaelic bard named Ossian (*Temora*, 1763). And here we arrive at a direct link with Austria, for in 1768–9 – in the very centre of the Austrian musical *Sturm und Drang* – Johann Nepomuk Cosmas Michael Denis (usually only the last of his Christian names is used), S.J.,[5] published with the well-known Viennese house of Trattner 'Die Gedichte Ossians eines alten Celtischen Dichters aus dem Englischen übersetzt'. These Ossian poems had a colossal influence on Austro-German thinking of the period. The 'Ossianic' spirit, with its winter storms, wild ocean cliffs and scudding clouds across a lonely moonlight landscape, was typical of *Sturm und Drang* and is one instance where a single book precedes by some years the actual centre of the movement. The hero, in Goethe's *Werther* (p. 41, l. 11), asks (rhetorically), 'Recently someone asked how I liked Ossian!' and before Werther leaves Charlotte to commit suicide, he reads to her a long passage from Ossian which leaves them both in tears of desperation. The Ossianic cult continued well into the early nineteenth century. Beethoven, in a letter to Breitkopf & Härtel of 8 August 1800, writes: 'These two poets [Goethe and Schiller] are my favourites, as are also Ossian and Homer. . .'.[6] It might be said that Denis's Ossian translations fulfil the same function in the coming literary movement as Gluck's *Don Juan* Finale (1761) was to do for the Austrian musical crisis (*vide infra*).

---

1 Reclam edition (248/48a), Stuttgart 1970 (1974). In this Chapter, abbreviations for titles are used (e.g. 'Heckscher 3n.'); the full titles are listed at the end of Section IV; *vide infra*, p. 393.
2 By Lavater as 'Sturm und Gedrängtheit' (Heckscher, 3n.).
3 Reclam edition 67(2), 1976, p. 24, l. 17f.
4 Heckscher, p. 3.
5 Denis (1729–1800) later became a Freemason.
6 *Selected Letters of Beethoven* (E. Anderson; A. Tyson), London 1967, p. 91.

Part of the *Sturm und Drang* philosophy was, of course, the Rousseauian 'back to nature'. But the Germans, while greatly admiring Rousseau and Voltaire, were also in revolt against the Francophilian invasion of German culture, and some of their 'back to nature' movement derives from an English source – James Thomson's *The Seasons*.[1] To choose but one obvious example, Goethe's *Werther* is built round the changing four seasons: the romance opens with the warmth and hopes of Spring, the tragedy ripens in the Autumn (the American 'Fall' is a better word here) and 'shuts' (as Thomson would have said) with Winter and the hero's suicide.

Not least, it was the giant figure of Shakespeare who became perhaps the greatest single influence on German drama of the period – especially the tragedies, hardly the comedies (a typical comment on the German scene). Goethe's *Götz* stands in the shadow of Shakespearean grandeur, and it was just at this period (1773) that Prince Nicolaus Esterházy commissioned Shakespeare translations from the Wahr Troupe at Eszterháza.

The real beginning of *Sturm und Drang*, apart from the influence of Friedrich Gottlieb Klopstock (1724–1803), is seen in Johann Georg Hamann (1730–88), known as the 'Magus of the North', whose cryptic and paradoxical works suggested that rationalism (*Vernunft*) was not the highest goal but also imagination and spirit (*Geist*): truth was, for Hamann, a matter of subjective belief. His pupil, Johann Gottfried Herder (1744–1803), was inspired by Percy's *Reliques* to produce what he called *Volkslieder* (thus introducing the term into the German language), 'der wahre Ausdruck der Empfindung und der ganzen Seele'. His genius, his great productivity (especially in the field of poetry) and his high humanistic goals soon made him a leading figure. Writing of Herder, Robert Bareikis notes that

> To a large extent, movements in literature arise in reaction to the prevailing trend in contemporary culture, and so it was that the Storm and Stress was engendered in reaction to social, philosophical, and literary aspects of the Enlightenment. It is appropriate that Herder, the founding father of the Storm und Stress, inaugurated his career as critic with his *Fragmente über die neuere deutsche Literatur* (1768), offered as a 'supplement' to a key work of the Enlightenment, Lessing's *Literatur-Briefe* (1759–65).... Already here one can discern Herder's trend-setting approach to esthetics, which would abandon the traditional focus upon the effect of the work of art in favour of a concentration upon the process of creation, the person of the artist, and the work of art *per se*.   [Bareikis, p. 21]

Johann Caspar Lavater (1741–1801), a Swiss theologian and the inventor of 'physiognomy', continued the pattern established by Hamann of a 'positive belief'. Lavater believed in the relationship between the internal spirit and the external view of the individual. Haydn was in correspondence with this young firebrand of the *Sturm und Drang*, who numbered Goethe among his fervent admirers.[2] His best-known work was *Physiognomische Fragmente, zur Beförderung der Menschenkenntiß und Menschenliebe* (1775–8, with numerous plates, many by Daniel Chodowiecki). 'Pseudo-

---

1 See *Haydn: the Late Years 1801–1809*, pp. 93ff.

2 Goethe even managed to introduce Lavater's name into *Werther*. For Haydn's correspondence with Lavater, *vide infra*, p. 454. Lavater seems to have owned a silhouette of Haydn, perhaps indeed the one Boßler published in the 1780s. Griesinger (52) tells us that 'Lavater, who characterized every silhouette in his collection with a verse, wrote under Haydn's portrait:

'Etwas mehr als Gemeines erblick' ich im Aug' und der Nase;
Auch die Stirn ist gut; im Munde was vom Philister.'

('Something more than common I perceive in eye and nose;
The forehead, too, is good, the mouth's a touch of Philistine.')
[Griesinger adds, laconically:] 'The strong, heavy lower lip may have given rise to this opinion.'

science, pietism, and sentimentality are all combined in this, the main work of Lavater, who was a forerunner of the Storm and Stress movement and a prominent exponent of Klopstockian irrationality', writes Bareikis (p. 27).

One of the characteristics of the literary *Sturm und Drang* was that many of its authors failed to live up to the great expectations engendered by their first fruits; this was also to be typical of the later Romantic period itself, to which the *Sturm und Drang* often poignantly looked forward. Johann Anton Leisewitz' (1752–1806) *Julius von Tarent* (1776) is typical of a group of playwrights and authors – mostly of simple background – centred round the so-called *Hain* or *Bund* in Göttingen; the work's rich promise (conflict, in a man, between the state and the heart) was not fulfilled. Similarly, Klinger later successfully pursued a military career and did not live up to the expectations of the plays he wrote in the mid 1770s. Perhaps the most tragic case of non-fulfilment was that of J. M. R. Lenz (1751–92), for apart from 'the impression he made on some fellow writers, he earned little in life but misery, insanity, and finally death abroad [in Russia] in poverty' (Bareikis, p. 26): his *Der Hofmeister* was published in 1774, and, except for it, his most successful work was *Die Soldaten* (1776). 'Tragedy', for Lenz, 'was drama intended for the serious segment of the population, comedy for the people.'

One of the most sensitive and attractive poets of the school was Gottfried August Bürger (1748–94), whose popular, folk-oriented poetry (*Balladen*) was written with great strength of language. Haydn preserved a special affection for Bürger and often set his texts to music.

Sturm und Drang was a movement for young men: many of those under discussion (Leisewitz, Klinger, Lenz, Goethe) were in their twenties in the early and mid-1770s: Goethe was twenty-four when he published *Götz von Berlichingen* (1773) and twenty-five when he issued *Die Leiden des jungen Werthers* (1774), which made him a celebrity overnight and created a whole 'Werther' school.[1] Based on episodes from his personal life, Goethe's *Roman* incorporates Rousseauian principles, shows English influence and is a drama of inflamed passions; but it extols, above all, love between human beings (and not only Werther's love for Charlotte: the hero's warm friendship with Wilhelm, the recipient of the whole correspondence, is equally important). Its humanistic spirit of Enlightenment, its personal warmth but above all the force of expression and exquisite beauty of language were sufficient to place its author among the great minds of European thought. (We have deliberately omitted Schiller from this brief survey, for his principal entry into the field, *Die Räuber*, did not occur until 1781, by which time Austrian music had moved into quite another sphere and Mozart was on the scene.)

'Most of the participants of the *Sturm und Drang* movement outgrew its peculiarities', writes William S. Heckscher in a brilliant survey,

> and turned their backs on the ideals which previously they had defended with so much zest. Much of what in after years has been written on *Sturm und Drang* as a

[1] It also created a new style of clothing. The 'mode à l'anglaise' was the fashionable style in the 1770s and 1780s, but in Germany it was called the 'Werthertracht'. This 'Werther' mode also became the rage in France: blue frock, yellow waistcoat, boots. Simplicity and a certain nonchalance in appearance became the expression of 'progressively minded' people. After Louis XVI's execution, the radicals also dictated masculine mode: powder was synonymous with Royalist, male clothing became simpler than ever: the men renounced 'beautiful' clothing and looked for the 'practical'. It is interesting to observe that Beethoven was completely under the sway of this 'Werther' mode: in the Horneman miniature of 1803 (Landon, *Beethoven*, dust jacket and pl. 103), we see the composer in the obligatory blue frock-coat with yellow buttons; in the Waldmüller portrait of 1823, the composer is wearing the yellow waistcoat (Landon pl. 224), which we may also see Prince Lichnowsky wearing (Landon pl. 41). Beethoven's nonchalant way of dressing ('the other side of the Rhine' mode) was, then, simply the progressive expression. Haydn appeared stiff in his old-fashioned dress, with powdered wig and knee-breeches with stockings (not white, however: Haydn had his principles, too, and white stockings meant *Capellmeister-Dienst* and a servant's status...). L. Kybalová, *Das große Bilderlexikon der Mode*, Prague 1966, p. 223.

literary event, has been written with the disapproving hindsight in mind that was voiced by its ageing proponents. [Heckscher, 1]

With hindsight, however, historians take the *Sturm und Drang* rather more seriously than did some of its proponents in their later years. *Sturm und Drang* meant, in many cases, confusion (*Wirrwarr*), oversized passions, Shakespearean drama translated into Goethian thought (*Götz*, a single man, pitted against fate/society), a certain disorganization of plot and content, a concentration of passion to the near exclusion of order. 'I am torn by passions', wrote Klinger; 'any other man would be destroyed by them ... any moment I would like to see mankind and everything devoured by chaos and then throw myself into it' (Rudolf, 2). Later, settled in St Petersburg and pursuing his military career, Klinger reflected that 'Now I can laugh off my earlier works ...; every young persons looks at the world more or less as a poet and dreamer. One regards everything as being higher, nobler, more perfect – although wilder, more muddled, and exaggerated.' We shall see that many of these characteristics will apply, *mutatis mutandis*, to the music produced in Austria during this period.

III. THE AUSTRIAN MUSICAL CRISIS: HAYDN

Scholars examining the *Sturm und Drang* in Austrian music must have noted, with a certain bewilderment, that Haydn's stormy works in the minor key seemed to coexist peacefully with serene works in major keys. As it happens, this is also typical of the literary *Sturm und Drang*: 'Noteworthy', writes Rudolf (3), 'is a tongue-in-cheek attitude which existed side by side with bombastic words, tragic gestures, and the sensitivity of 'beautiful souls'. Goethe himself, while working on the first version of *Werther*, made fun of the back-to-nature cult in a bold little drama, *Satyros*.'

Just as the literary *Sturm und Drang* movement had a variety of precursors, ranging from Klopstock to Denis's Ossian translations, so the Austrian musical crisis had its predecessors abroad and in the monarchy. The essence of the style was not new: we find it in the north German school, and particularly in the wilful and eccentrically brilliant compositions of C. P. E. Bach, whose music is known to have had a profound effect on both Haydn and Mozart.[1] Such a work as the Concerto in D minor for harpsichord and orchestra (Wotquenne 23) by C. P. E. Bach, written in 1748 (i.e. when his father was still alive), is a clear model for the Viennese masters twenty years later; and it, too, may be said to proceed directly from J. S. Bach's severe and dramatic Concerto in D minor (*BWV* 1052), which has come down to us only as a harpsichord concerto. But in the case of the Austrians, we have a model much closer to home: the extraordinary Finale to Gluck's *Don Juan*, a ballet first produced at Vienna in 1761. This (for its time incredible) music was later used by its composer, minus the introduction, as the Furies' music in the French setting of *Orphée*. Its original score describes Don Juan's descent into Hell, and its D minor ferocity was to prove perhaps the most important single beginning of the whole Austrian musical *Sturm und Drang*. Boccherini modelled a fine D minor Symphony from it, which he entitled 'La casa del diavolo'.[2]

1 Haydn: 'nur den Emanuel Bach erkennt er als sein Vorbild' (Griesinger, 12). Mozart is reported to have said, 'Bach [C.P.E.] is the father, we the children.'
2 First published by Franco Gallini, and now (in a critical edition) in the Collected Boccherini Symphonies, edited by Antonio de Almeida and to be issued by Doblinger (in preparation as of present writing: Summer 1977). M. de Almeida kindly showed us his new edition, and the various sources on which it was based, some years ago.

Before we proceed, we must explain, if very briefly, the transformation that the minor key had undergone in the past two decades. This transformation applies largely to instrumental music of the Italian and Austrian (south German) schools, not (a) to the north Germans and (b) to opera, where (especially in *opera seria*), the minor key was almost always used to express passions, even in this relatively 'dark period'. Even the Italians, such as the 'reform' composer Tommaso Traetta, were, all during the early 1760s, using minor keys as vehicles for expression.[1] (We remember a fascinating revival of Traetta's *Ifigenia in Tauride* (1763) at the Florence Maggio Musicale some years ago, and also the Italian Radio and Television (RAI) revival of *Sofonisba* (1762), which works were certainly of decisive influence on Haydn. In Traetta's *Le serve rivali*, composed for San Moisè in Venice in 1766 and revived by RAI on 16 November 1972, we find at least two passages which Haydn took over almost *verbatim* in his *Le pescatrici*, and *La fedeltà premiata*.)[2] There is, however, a vast difference between Haydn's (extremely rare) use of minor keys prior to 1760, e.g. in the early piano Trios in F minor and G minor (Nos. 5 and 14 [XV:1, f 1]), both preserved in what are probably authentic MSS. in the Archives at Kroměříž (Kremsier). In those works, the use of the minor is in no particular way connected with *Sturm und Drang* emotions but is rather based on the pre-classical, Vivaldian use of minor keys. A Swiss scholar sums up the new use of minor keys as follows:

A symphony in the minor means something out of the ordinary for a symphonist of the eighteenth century. The minor, as the tonality of the outer

1 Rudolf, pp. 14ff.
2 The two Traetta passages and their parallels in Haydn are:

Traetta (*Le serve rivali*)
Atto IIdo
Aria

Haydn (*La fedeltà premiata*)
Atto Imo
Aria 'Già mi sembra'

Traetta

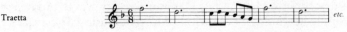

Haydn (*Le pescatrici*)
Finale Atto IIdo (conclusion)

[The Traetta themes were taken down by dictation from the broadcast.]

272

movements, is the vehicle for the expression of passion or grief. This is in contradistinction to a large number of thoroughly festive, joyous concertos of the Baroque era (cf. Vivaldi: Concerti Grossi [Op. 3, Nos. 6 and 11] in A minor, D minor). Philipp Emanuel Bach, on the other hand, uses minor tonality wholly to serve the expression of passion, perhaps most persuasively in the clavier concertos, for example the Clavier (Harpsichord) Concerto in D minor.

[Bernard Rywosch: *Beiträge zur Entwicklung in Joseph Haydns Symphonik* (Dissertation), Turbenthal 1934, p. 65]

Apart from the use of minor keys, the Haydn *Sturm und Drang* style uses a number of technical devices which become typical for these years. A few may be cited here:[1]

(1) The final use of the old *sonata da chiesa* (Italian church sonata) form, i.e. with an entire opening slow movement. There are several Haydn symphonies using this form which were composed prior to our period (Nos. 5, 11, 18, 21, 22, 34), but certainly the form's culmination is the sombre *Sinfonia* 'La Passione' (No. 49 of 1768: misplaced in the chronological list).

(2) An increased awareness of contrapuntal forms. This is a vital part of the new *Sturm und Drang* language, and may be seen most graphically in Haydn's Symphony No. 44 (second movement, Menuetto 'Canone in Diapason'), No. 47 ('Menuet al Roverso'), and the Quartets of Op. 20, three of which (Nos. 2, 5, 6) end with complex double and triple fugues.[2] Other fugal Quartets, also in minor keys, by Ordoñez (Op. 1), Gassmann (*c.* 1767, 1773 and others), and of course the famous contrapuntal master Albrechtsberger, will be discussed in Section IV, *infra*.

(3) Haydn's use of Gregorian plainchant, especially in the *Sinfonia Lamentatione* (No. 26) in D minor, and also (significantly) in the Trio of the 'Farewell' Symphony (No. 45).

(4) An increased use of dynamic marks, especially *crescendo* (which Haydn always uses fastidiously and generally in slow movements: he was not much attracted to the Mannheim school's exaggerated dynamic marks), but also similar dynamic gradations such as 'poco forte', 'calando', as well as sudden *ff* and *pp*. Particularly striking examples of sudden *pp* markings are in the first movement of Symphony No. 44 in E minor ('Trauer') – bar 11 and (even more impressively) at 114.

(5) The use of unison *forte* opening subjects combined with sharp dynamic contrasts within the main subject, as in Symphonies Nos. 44 in E minor, 46 in B major, or 52 in C minor (also, with slight differences, in No. 51 in B flat).

(6) A new sense of long harmonic line, particularly noticeable in the construction of the slow movements, where one sometimes has the impression that time seems to stand still. There are two especially striking examples, one in the 'Farewell' Symphony, the slow movement of which contains this extraordinary modulation, the whole moving at a deliberately stately pace:

No. 45/II (Adagio)

_____
1 In more detail in Landon, *SYM*, pp. 271–341.
2 See Warren Kirkendale's vitally important *Fuge und Fugato in der Kammermusik des Rokoko und der Klassik*, Tutzing 1966.

Another is the slow movement of Symphony No. 54 (1774), one of the longest, most involved and most exaggerated of all slow movements in the present period. In a fast tempo, this new sense of time[1] – which is a new and revolutionary concept in Austrian music of this epoch – may be observed in such a passage as Symphony No. 52/I:

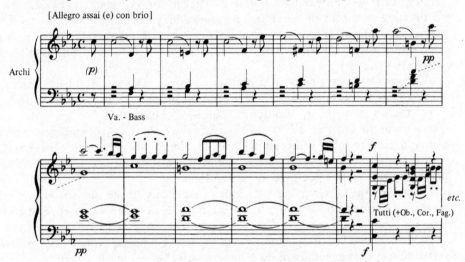

(7) The use of syncopated patterns. Throughout this whole period, we find two basic types of syncopation, of which the first is the typical kind used primarily for accompaniments (and also for the main subject in Symphony No. 26): ♪♩ ♩ ♩ ♪|♪♩ ♩ ♩ ♪|♪ etc., and which will assume gigantic proportions in Mozart (D minor of Haydn Symphony No. 26 = D minor of Mozart, K.466). Among the many Haydn *Sturm und Drang* passages to use this kind of syncopation, we might draw attention to Symphony No. 45's opening movement. The second use of syncopation might be best described as a 'broken melodic line', e.g.:

1 See the fascinating chapter, 'Time as a New Dimension', in Norman Hampson's *The Enlightenment*, pp. 218ff.; also pp. 90f.

Very often the bass part is additionally 'strengthened' by tall staccato points to emphasize the strong beat (as against the off-beat melodic line). This peculiar type of syncopation is often used in slow movements *together* with the first type, e.g. in the *Stabat Mater* (Stabat, bars 25ff.; Sancta Mater, bars 9ff., etc.), i.e. with the bass line stalking on the main beats and the upper line in syncopations of the first kind, or variations of the second kind.

(8) Wide 'leaps' in the thematic material, longer note values. The wide 'leaps' may be seen in Haydn's No. 34/II, 39/IV or 49/II, also in the works of Haydn *seguaci*, such as the Vanhal Symphony in G minor (*vide infra*, p. 382). The leaps are sometimes emphasized by longer note-values and a concentration of the motion in the accompanying parts, *viz.*:

A new momentousness and weight are imparted to the music in this fashion (the musical example is from Symphony No. 52/I).

(9) Orchestration. Naturally, Haydn's basic language has not changed. We find, as we did through the early 1760s, the panache and brilliance that characterize the orchestral and vocal-instrumental scores. The dashing repeated semiquavers (or in quicker time quavers) over a constantly moving bass, which made such a movement as the 'Et resurrexit' from the Mass of 1766 so exhilarating, prevail in many sections of the symphonies; but everything is now intensified. Such a work as No. 56/I seems to provide a climax to the festive C major key, of which there are noteworthy examples (such as Nos. 41 and 48, both *c.* 1769). No. 56 is the first such C major work in which we know that Haydn intended from the beginning C *alto* horns *and* trumpets as well as kettledrums. There is an urgency that underlines this C major brilliance, and the reversible top and bottom line (in double counterpoint at the octave) seems, when the passage comes in minor, to have the same hectic and slightly hysterical sense that we find in another great C major Symphony – Mozart's K.338 (1780) – which perhaps

275

uses Haydn's No. 56 as its model.[1] One other fact that we must consider is that Haydn is always ready for an 'exotic excursion', and in this period one of the most interesting is Symphony No. 51, with its elaborate horn solos, ranging from sounding *ab''* on the top (or *bb''* in the Trio) – (see example below: a and c) – to a whole series of stopped and overblown notes at the bottom of the horn's range (example b):

(Haydn had an interesting predecessor, the composer Christoph Mann, or Monn [*not* the elder Georg Matthias Monn, 1717–50], who wrote a similarly eccentric Symphony in E flat[2] with solo horn parts ranging up to written *ab''*.) The basic orchestra remains two oboes, two horns and strings, to which a bassoon, trumpets, timpani and occasionally a flute were added. In Symphony No. 22 (1764) we had a unique case of cors anglais instead of oboes, but otherwise these instruments are limited to Haydn's vocal music (up to and including 1775). The list of technical characteristics that form the language of this period could be continued at will, but rather than burden the reader with long technical descriptions (which maybe found not only in Landon, *SYM*, but also in both Finscher and Barrett-Ayres)[3] we shall proceed to other ramifications of the *Sturm und Drang* and Haydn.

Professor Wilfrid Mellers singles out an important point:[4]

> The tempestuous features in these works strike one's attention immediately; one should not overlook the fact that they also represent a significant development in Haydn's humour. The funny elements in his earlier work were in the main a

---

1 Haydn's No. 56 appeared in Paris and Lyon in three editions in 1777 and 1778, and Mozart could easily have heard it while still in Paris. The passage in double counterpoint: first movement, bars 29ff., 68ff., 134ff. (E minor), 143ff. (A minor), 199ff. (particularly splendid, ending on a huge pedal point on I_4^6 of C minor).
2 The *Denkmäler der Tonkurst in Österreich (DTÖ)* XXXI (XV/2) 1909 and XXXIX (XXX/2) 1912, attributes it to G. M. Monn, whose D major Symphony of 1740 includes a Minuet and has thus become celebrated with musicologists. It is probably by Christoph Mann and was composed in the 1760s.
3 *Studien zur Geschichte des Streichquartetts: Die Entstehung des klassischen Streichquartetts. Von den Vorfahren zur Grundlegung durch Joseph Haydn*, Kassel 1974. *Haydn and the String Quartet*, London 1974.
4 *The Sonata Principle*, London 1957, p. 22.

simple *buffo* frivolity. Such comic movements as occur in the *Sturm und Drang* works tend – in an abrupt contrast of key, a melodic ellipsis, a sudden pause on concentration of rhythm – to startle as much as to amuse. Procedures that may in some contexts be drama are in other contexts wit: an intense levity that entails a recognition of 'other modes of experience that are possible', and therefore an awareness of instability. Consider the approach to the coda of the presto in Symphony No. 52 in C minor:

All through Haydn's mature music – and in a more poignant way in Mozart's also – one finds this precariousness: the sudden defeat of expectation, the interruption of a norm of behaviour, whether of tonality or of melodic, harmonic, or rhythmic formula. One does not usually find this quality in composers who lived before the Age of Reason, in an age of Faith, whether in God or the State. Bach and Handel are sometimes comic, seldom if ever witty.

The precariousness is another way of saying, perhaps, irrational; and with that word we are back to the German literary movement. The eccentric, the irrational, in such works as Klinger or Lenz have their direct counterpart in Haydn (and his *seguaci*) of this epoch. In the Finale of Symphony No. 46, the previous Minuet is suddenly reintroduced: it is an effect so bizarre as to be almost unsettling. Playing a minuet (and trio) first forwards, then backwards (as in Symphony No. 47) is also highly eccentric, as is the clever introduction of four-four time into three-four (as we find in Symphony No. 65/III):

The irrational is present in many and often very subtle ways. Consider the 'Farewell' Symphony, which is perhaps the greatest single symphonic work of this period:[1] first the key, F sharp minor, which is almost unique in the whole of the symphonic repertoire, and for which (as we have seen in the Chronicle), Haydn's horn players had to have new half-tone crooks forged. In the first movement, the secondary theme does not appear in the exposition at all, but in the middle of the development. Its D major lyricism and poignancy are at sharp, even violent, odds with the fatalistic, striding-down-the-chord first subject, whose accompanying syncopations become an all-pervading element of the whole movement. And that beautiful second subject never again appears. This is irrationality at its most subtle but also its most upsetting. The programmatic Finale may explain why the instruments leave one after the other, but it does not explain the enormous arch of structure and tonality which bring us from F sharp minor (the swift section) to A major (the opening of the final slow section) to F sharp major, the conclusion of the work and certainly the loneliest sound in all of Haydn, and perhaps in the whole of music. Those two solo violins, muted – Haydn and Tomasini – playing in the nearly darkened great hall of Eszterháza completed one of the great intellectual break-throughs of its composer's career, and one that Prince Esterházy immediately understood: Dies (60) says explicitly, 'The so-called "Farewell" Symphony had increased Prince Nicolaus's affection for Haydn.'

Before this whole period was termed 'Sturm und Drang' it used to be referred to as the 'Geniezeit' (the time of genius), which is in some ways a more accurate description of its total effect; for *Sturm und Drang* must be understood in a very wide context if we are not to do injustice to the many works which (in the case of Haydn) are not in the minor key and not 'stormy' in the conventional sense. *Sturm und Drang* was for Haydn *inter alia* an exotic excursion on a vast scale. Certainly he repudiated its message almost completely in the 1780s, reserving a key such as D minor for the literal depiction of tempests at sea (one vital aspect of both the literary and musical movements altogether), as in *Le pescatrici* (composed in 1769), *Il ritorno di Tobia* ('Svanisce in un momento', added in 1784; later 'Insanae et vanae curae'), and the Madrigal 'The Storm' (London, 1792), not to mention 'Rolling in foaming billows' from *The Creation*, all of which are in D minor. The withdrawal from *Sturm und Drang* in Haydn is fully as dramatic and unexpected as its arrival: to paraphrase Erasmus, 'Nihil enim surdius aut impotentius mari commoto, & tamen ad Domini jussum repente versum

---

1 For a sensitive appreciation of this visionary work, see László Somfai's introduction to the beautiful facsimile edition, Budapest 1959.

est in summum tranquillitatem'.[1] And so we dare not forget, side by side with Haydn's fascinating excursion into the world of the passions, the equally important and in Haydn's ultimate career more forward-looking and thus more typical works such as the witty Symphony No. 42 in D (1771). Here, in the first movement, we suddenly (and irrationally) find ourselves in B major (see bars 26ff.) on the way from D major to the dominant; but in the second movement Haydn chastises himself for attempting too eccentric a modulation. After bar 45 of that movement, he had originally sketched a continuation of the first violin part which read:

He had so engrossed himself in new harmonic vistas (*b* sharp) that he had to discipline himself with the stern words, 'Dieses war vor gar zu gelehrte Ohren' ('That was for much too learned ears'). And as if to reassure himself on this point, the Finale turns out to be perhaps the first popular rondo in the typically Haydnesque manner, including delightful wind-band soli and a catchy tune: the D minor section is a tongue-in-cheek *Sturm und Drang* on the level of Goethe's *Satyros*. The key of raging seas turns into D major: 'Est enim tranquillitas quies maris'.

The sea at rest is equally astonishing if we examine the great series of six Quartets, Op. 20 (1772). The bleak drama of the F minor Quartet (No. 5) or the dramatic tension of the G minor Quartet (No. 3) are released in an almost miraculous way in what Somfai[2] believes to have been the final work of the set: the serene (but not undramatic) No. 4 in D, where the irrationality consists primarily in one of the first of Haydn's rather frequent exotic excursions into the world of Gypsy (or if one will, Hungarian) folklore. But if we examine the totality of Haydn's string quartets, it is clear that the drama (and the contrapuntal grandeur) of much of Op. 20 is a grand *cul-de-sac*, just as, *mutatis mutandis*, Symphony No. 45 ('Farewell') or No. 49 ('La Passione') do not lead anywhere. The opening slow movement (*sonata da chiesa*) of No. 49 is the *last* of its kind; and No. 45 is altogether a work *sui generis*. The path to the future is shown in such works as No. 42 (1771) or 55 ('Schoolmaster'; 1774).

The obvious link between Haydn and the literary *Sturm und Drang* is, of course, the theatre, with which the composer was so intimately connected in these years. He is always listed in the Gotha *Theater-Kalender* as a kind of 'house composer' for the Carl Wahr Troupe, and it performed several plays for which Haydn wrote special incidental music. That to Shakespeare's *Hamlet* has, alas, disappeared, as has the music to Goethe's *Götz*[3] – or else Haydn later turned these works into symphonies which we cannot identify (Nos. 44? 52?). Haydn's music for Regnard's *Le distrait* has survived as Symphony No. 60. There is certainly the whiff of the stage in such works as Symphony No. 59 ('Fire'), supposedly composed as incidental music for Grossmann's

1 'For surely, nothing is more obdurate and more passionate than the raging sea; and yet, it was suddenly turned into absolute tranquility at the command of the Lord' (ed. *Opera*, Leyden, VII, 1706, col. 51; English translation from William Heckscher, p. 5, to whose spellbinding analysis of 'Sturm und Drang' the reader is urgently recommended).
2 See his brilliant lecture given at Duke University in April 1969, also his article 'Vom Barock zur Klassik' in *Joseph Haydn und seine Zeit*, Eisenstadt 1972, pp. 64ff., 160ff.
3 See Chronicle, *supra*, p. 208, and *infra*, p. 402.

Die Feuersbrunst.[1] Whether or not it was composed for the Grossmann play (not to be confused with Haydn's marionette *Singspiel* of that name), an old set of parts in the Gesellschaft der Musikfreunde (*SYM*, source 5 on p. 704) is entitled 'Feuer/Sinfonia', and the slow movement is quite typical of Haydn's known theatrical music. A similar piece of almost lunatic irrationality is the slow movement of No. 65, with its curious repeated notes and theatrical fanfares. Here the *Sturm und Drang* would seem to be theatrical in origin, or at least in inspiration.

In a paper read at the Sorbonne in the Autumn of 1956, the present author attempted to show, with many musical illustrations, that the musical *Sturm und Drang* in Austria was not limited to Haydn alone but gripped many other composers, foremost among them Florian Leopold Gassmann, Carlos d'Ordoñez, Carl Dittersdorf and Johann Baptist Vanhal.[2] We shall examine these composers and some others in Section IV (*infra*, pp. 360ff.), but here we would only remind the reader that Haydn was not alone (even if we might consider him, at least in retrospect, as *primus inter pares*) in this whole movement. In Section IV, we shall also examine some chronological problems. Apart from Gluck's *Don Juan* of 1761 and *Orfeo* of 1762, there was a gap in Gluck's real reform (and *Sturm und Drang*) tendencies until *Alceste* of 1767 (published 1768). Was Haydn the first of the Austrian *Sturm und Drang* instrumental composers on a large scale? Whence did the movement come, and why did a whole generation of Austrian musicians consider it necessary?

The Austrians borrowed from their own great contrapuntal tradition; they resuscitated canon and fugue, but more especially contrapuntal development linked with *motivische Arbeit* (working with motifs); they borrowed the severe style of a C. P. E. Bach; they plundered *opera seria* – not only Gluck's but the 'reform' Italians such as Traetta and Jommelli; they turned minor keys into something different from that which they had meant when Vivaldi had died in Vienna in 1740; they, and especially Haydn, turned to folksong (and a step further with Gregorian chant, also a kind of 'peoples' song'), by which they directly allied themselves with similar tendencies on the part of the German writers with their return to *Volkslied* or popular ballad. Haydn, in particular, turned to the rich folklore of the Balkans.

The melody

follows Haydn in divertimento (II:17/VIII, quoted above; II:21, Trio of second Minuet), symphony (No. 60/IV), baryton trio (No. 35, Trio of Minuet), baryton duo (XII:19, opening of second movement), piano sonata (No. 49 [XVI:36] Minuet) and strict canon (*Wunsch* [XXVIIb:43]). It has been traced by Geoffrey Chew[3] to two basic folk-sources: (1) Christmas pastorellas; (2) A Night Watchman's Song (see also Landon, *Supplement*: illustration facing p. 32 and pp. 46f., where an anonymous version of the melody from Metten Monastery in Bavaria is reproduced in facsimile).

1 A MS. of this Symphony in the Mecklenburg Library at Schwerin is subtitled: '1774 für die Wahr'schen Truppe in Esterhaz an dem Stücke: "Die Feuersbrunst" als Zwischenactsmusik geschrieben', but there are two MSS. (see *SYM* 704), from the Monasteries of Göttweig and Kremsmünster, dated 1769. Probably Haydn composed the work about 1766 or 1767 and later (1774) used it, if he had not done so earlier, as incidental music for the Grossmann play.
2 *La Crise Romantique dans la Musique Autrichienne vers 1770. Quelques Précurseurs inconnus de la Symphonie en sol mineur (KV 183) de Mozart,* published in *influences étrangères dans l'oeuvre de W. A. Mozart,* Paris [1958], pp. 27ff.
3 *Haydn-Studien* III/2 (April 1974), pp. 106ff.

This, and some of the Gypsy melodies used by Haydn in the Piano Concerto in D (XVIII:11) and the Trio in G 'with the Gypsy Rondo' (No. 39 [XV:25]), are among the few folk-tunes that can be identified in sources older than Haydn's use of them. Clearly, Haydn had some motive in introducing folk-melodies into his art-forms. In this connection, Carpani (as plagiarized by Stendhal and translated by William Gardiner,[1] Haydn's and Beethoven's admirer, in the year 1817, p. 94) states:

> Some years after Haydn's establishment at Eisenstadt, when he had formed his style, he sought food for his imagination, by diligently collecting those ancient, and original airs, which are to be found among the peoples of every country. The Ukraine, Hungary, Scotland, Germany, Sicily, Spain, Russia were laid under contribution by him.

Naturally, Carpani (Stendhal) has fused into one statement Haydn's real use of Balkan (and other) folk-tunes with his arrangements for Thomson and other British publishers of Scottish, Irish and Welsh airs; but we suspect that a kernel of truth nevertheless remains. Haydn was genuinely interested in folk-song, especially the exotic 'highly spiced' Hungarian-Gypsy lore – he loved their cooking, too (*vide supra*, p. 167). The German poets and playwrights, on the other hand, found their inspiration in English ballads, Haydn in Gypsy melodies, Geoffrey Chew has quoted numerous sources for the 'Nachtwächter' melody and has shown that even in the 'Pastorella' settings, the idea of the Night Watchman (Advent = Dawn) is perhaps closer than expected. In another sacred setting of the Song, 'Nichts Irdisch ewig gewehrt [*sic*]' from the year 1686, we find the melody with the following text:

Nichts Ir-disch e-wig ge-wehrt wie ein Wet-ter-hahn sich ver-kehrt

'Such Hungarian or Slavonic melodies', writes the late Dr Paul Nettl,[2] are to be found extremely rarely at such an early period and perhaps our *Liedbuch* [Vienna, 1686) contains the first monument to a written Hungarian or Slovakian folk-music.' The words here mean 'Nothing earthly remains forever / As a weathercock turns...'.

Curiously, Haydn's German critics did not appreciate this kind of a quotation of folk material: curious, because in Germany at this period, the use of popular ballads on the English model was already very wide-spread.[3] In fact part of the north German resistance to Haydn was just *because* of this new introduction of folk (popular) elements into art-forms such as the symphony and quartet. Geoffery Chew, comparing Leopold Mozart (e.g. *Bauernhochzeit* and *Musikalische Schlittenfahrt*) and Wolfgang Mozart with Haydn, says:

> Leopold is satisfied with the folk tradition for its own sake; Wolfgang needs to escape from the limitations which a sensitive eighteenth-century musician would have felt in it. If Haydn is drawn into this comparison, it will be seen that he occupies a middle and somewhat equivocal place: he tolerates the folk allusion much more than Mozart does, and is prepared to use the very melodies used in the pastorella tradition [quotes Baryton Trio No. 35 as being *in toto*, a pastorella]... To summarise: this example seems to show Haydn permitting

1 See *Haydn: the Late Years 1801–1809*, pp 291, 401f.
2 *Das Wiener Lied im Zeitalter des Barock*, Vienna/Leipzig 1934, p. 42.
3 See J. A. Hiller's bitter criticism of Haydn's very Balkan Minuet & Trio in Symphony No. 28, quoted *supra*, p. 169.

himself to use folk motifs, in the folk way, and perhaps with the folk meaning, more than Wolfgang [Mozart] would have done, but reserving to himself the right to arrange and present the material in a way demanded from a purely musical point of view more than Leopold [Mozart] would have done ... The tastes of their [respective] patrons and audiences must have had something to do with the matter. We know, for example, of the Esterházys' tolerance of the folk idiom [quotes the passage about peasants dancing at the castle festivities in September 1770; *vide supra*, p. 165], without which it would have been impossible for Haydn to have written quite as he did.   [op. cit., p. 121f.]

The geographical position of Eszterháza, being in Hungary, was of great significance for Haydn's adoption of Gypsy (Hungarian) folk elements into his music. Not for nothing do we see, in an elaborate ceremony taking place in the Castle courtyard (see pls. 9, 11),[1] a group of Gypsy musicians playing in a corner. From a Gypsy band at Eszterháza to Gypsy music in Haydn's scores was obviously not a difficult transition, and one appreciated by the Esterházys. Despite adverse German criticism, moreover, Haydn rightly considered that foreigners would find this introduction of Gypsy music original and delightful: Op. 20 (No. 4 with the 'Menuetto alla Zingarese' and other quotations in the Finale), the D major Piano Concerto (XVIII:11) and the 'Gypsy Rondo' Trio (No. 39) all proved to be particularly successful abroad and were reprinted many times in France and England, even in Germany.

The Austrians were clearly dissatisfied with the tone of their earlier instrumental music, which had been delightful, entertaining (also as *Tafelmusik*), witty, clever and not without a certain permanent superficiality. It (and especially Haydn's early quartets) had conquered even the bastions of northern Germany, not without shrill protests from its critical brotherhood; and its very contrast with C. P. E. Bach (not to mention Johann Sebastian) also made it entrancing for the younger generation. We would hesitate to ascribe to this criticism Haydn's renewed attention to counterpoint and the serious tone altogether of the Quartets, Op. 20, and the *Sturm und Drang* symphonies; but certainly there was in Op. 20 a desire to 'wipe the slate clean', to make of the string quartet form something more than a 'divertimento' (though Haydn continued to use that generic term for almost any instrumental music that was not a concerto or a symphony); just as the sudden fugal interest of Ordoñez and Gassmann cannot be ascribed only to Haydn's Op. 20 (some of Gassmann's fugal works may be precisely dated *before* 1773; *vide infra*, p.456), but also to a desire to 'reform' Austrian music altogether. Gassmann's Symphony in B minor, and Vanhal's in G minor or D minor, are fully as revolutionary in their respective *oeuvres* as were Haydn's Symphonies No. 49 or 52 in his.

As for the rest of *Sturm und Drang* and its spiritual influence on Haydn, we might mention one facet of his works, namely his attachment to nature. Haydn and Mozart are often compared, and the former described as a country lad, the latter as a drawing-room hothouse plant; like many comparisons, the superficiality does not exclude an element of truth. Haydn *was* a genuine lover of nature. He had no need of a Rousseauian 'back-to-nature' reminder for the simple reason that, from the moment he left Vienna for Weinzierl to write the early quartets, he lived in the country – and

---

1 Installation of Prince Anton as Governor of the County, 3 August 1791. Also reproduced in colour in Horányi, p. 157; with the Gypsies in detail in Somfai, p. 61.

Weinzierl was followed in rapid succession by Lukavec (Count Morzin), Eisenstadt and Eszterháza. He had no need to escape from the urbanized chaos of Paris or London; and the affectionate descriptions, in Goethe's *Werther*, of the buzz of insects, of the quiet hills and green forests, of the village pump, applies equally to Haydn's everyday environment.

As to infusing music with a deeper message, it is clear that Austria's *Sturm und Drang* was essential to its composers' development. Whether the total progress of music in Europe would have been materially altered if the Austrian 'romantic crisis' had never occurred, is at best an unanswerable question; but we wonder, for example, how much it affected a composer like Luigi Boccherini in far-away Spain (if we except the above-mentioned *Sinfonia* 'La casa del Diavolo' based on Gluck's *Don Juan*). Boccherini's Op. 1, composed in Vienna[1] in 1760, had already pursued a compositional road totally at variance with that chosen by Haydn in his early string trios and quartets. Nearly at the end of his life, we find Boccherini writing to M. J. Chénier (Madrid, 8 July 1799):

> ... so bene che la musica è fatta per parlare al cuore dell'huomo ... la musica senza affetti, e Passioni, è insignificante; da qui nasce, che nulla ottiene il Compositore senza gl'esecutori; questi è necessario che siano ben affetti all'autore, poi devono sentire nel cuore tutto cio che questi á notato; unirsi, provare, indagare, studiar finalmente la mente dell'autore, poi eseguire le opere. Allora vi che arrivano quasi a toglier l'applauso al Compositore, o almeno a partir la gloria con lui, mentre che se è pregio sentir dire, *che bell'opera è questa*, parmi che sia più sentire aggiungere, *oh che angelicamente l'anno eseguita!* ...
> [Autograph, Pierpont Morgan Library, Mary Flagler Cary Music Collection][2]

This is the kind of manifesto which Haydn or indeed Mozart might have written: we may divide it into two parts, the first concerning 'music made to speak to the heart of man ... music without *affetti* and passions is insignificant', the second concerning the important role of the performer (something Haydn also stressed: see his letter on the subject to Prince Nicolaus II Esterházy of 14 June 1802).[3] The essence of *Sturm und Drang*, whether in a Haydn symphony or in *Götz*, was precisely that: music (art) is made to speak to the heart of man; music without feeling (one translation for *affetti*) and passion is insignificant. Yet the words come from Boccherini, a man with whom we do not, on the whole, associate the word 'passion'. No clear case could, perhaps, be put forward for a word meaning different things to different people. Passion for us means, in Haydn, Symphony No. 52; in Mozart, K.466 or 550 (we shall return to that problem in a later chapter); in Boccherini, what? We doubt whether Boccherini's *œuvre*, in its totality, would have been materially changed if he had never heard a *Sturm und Drang* composition (or even Mozart's later transformation of the style in his 'demonic' works). On the other hand, neither Haydn nor Goethe could have become what they did without passing through the eye of the storm (or, indeed, without having created that very eye in large part themselves). Goethe always used to say that he pitied anyone who had never been through a *Werther* period; and the same certainly applies to Haydn, whose great 'Salomon' Symphonies, late Masses and

---

1 See *Haydn: the Early Years 1732–1765* for the documentation regarding Boccherini's early years in the Austrian capital.
2 Our thanks once again to our many friends at the Pierpont Morgan Library, who have kindly allowed us the freedom of its shelves on many occasions.
3 CCLN 205; *Haydn: the Late Years 1801–1809*, p. 227.

Oratorios could hardly have existed (and we do not mean only the D minor of the Kyrie in the 'Nelson' Mass) without the *Sturm und Drang* of *c.* 1766–75.[1]

Haydn's Instrumental Music (*c.* 1766–75)

Haydn's instrumental music of this period falls into several clear groups: (1) Symphonies; (2) String Quartets; (3) Piano Sonatas and Variations; (4) Piano Concerto in G (XVIII:4); (5) Six Duets for Violin and Viola (VI:1–6); (6) Divertimento a tre (Horn Trio; IV:5); (7) Baryton Trios; (8) Divertimenti for one or two barytons (X:1–12), later in part issued by Haydn for flute, horns and strings as 'Opus 31'.

(I) THE SYMPHONIES

In view of the confusing chronology of Haydn's symphonies composed during this period, we have provided a list of the order in which they were presumably composed, set forth in the following manner: (a) year, followed by works known (from dated autographs or other authentic information) to have been written in that year; (b) works believed, from various kinds of evidence, to have been written about the year(s) in question.

Nos. 66–69 are genuine border-line cases which were written, one imagines, partly in 1775 and partly in 1776. The division 1776 in this book was made purely for external, though convincing, reasons: the change in the Esterházy establishment from sporadic operas given at *feste*, and a regular operatic season each year, in the course of which Haydn's duties changed considerably. Naturally, the effects of this change were not immediately discernible in his compositions, but Nos. 66, 68 and 69 are certainly in a very different style from that of the works composed even as late as 1774, as the reader (listener) will soon perceive; whereas No. 67 belongs more to the group at present under discussion. In the forthcoming very brief descriptive analysis of these instrumental works, it will be noted that, contrary to our practice with the vocal works, we do not in general list detailed sources. This is because all the symphonies and their principal sources are readily available,[2] as are the quartets, the baryton works and the piano sonatas and smaller piano pieces (variations, etc.).

1 Literature. I. The German Literary Movement. A large selection of *Sturm und Drang* literature has now been reprinted in fine, inexpensive editions by Reclam (Stuttgart), including: G. A. Bürger *Gedichte* (227); H. W. von Gerstenberg *Ugolino* (141, 141a); Goethe *Clavigo* (96); *Gedichte* (Stefan Zweig; 6782–4) *Götz von Berlichingen* (71); *Die Leiden des jungen Werthers* (67/67a); *Satiren, Farcen und Hanswurstiaden* (8565–7); *Stella* (104); *Der Urfaust* (5273); *Der Göttingen Hain* (authors: Boie, Gotter, Hahn, Hölty, J. M. Miller, G. D. Miller, Stolberg, Voss; 8789–93); J. G. Hamann *Sokratische Denkwürdigkeiten, Aesthetica in nuce* (926/926a); W. Heinse *Aus Briefen, Werken, Tagebüchern* (8201–03); J. G. Herder *Abhandlung über den Ursprung der Sprache* (8729/30); Herder *Von der Urpoesie der Völker* (Shakespeare. Über Ossian und die Lieder alter Völker. Über Volkslieder. Über das Buch [Job] (7794); *Herder, Goethe, Frisi, Möser: Von deutscher Art und Kunst* (H. D. Irmscher; 7497/98); J. H. Jung-Stillings *Heinrich Stillings Jugend, Jünglingsjahre, Wanderschaft und häusliches Leben* (662–666); F. M. Klinger *Sturm und Drang* (248/248a); Klinger *Die Zwillinge* (438); J. A. Leisewitz *Julius von Tarent* (111/2); J. M. R. Lenz *Gedichte* (8582); *Der Hofmeister oder Vorteile der Privaterziehung* (1376); *Die Soldaten* (5899); Schiller *Kabale und Liebe* (33); *Die Räuber* (15); *Die Verschwörung des Fiesko zu Genua* (51); A. Stricher *Schillers Flucht von Stuttgart und Aufenthalt in Mannheim von 1782–1785* (Raabe; 4652–54); J. H. Voss *Idyllen und Gedichte* (2332); H. L. Wagner *Die Kindermörderin* (5698/98a).

II. Bibliography on the Movement itself. H. B. Garland, *Storm and Stress*, London 1952. Ray Pascal, *The German Sturm und Drang*, New York 1953. William S. Heckscher, 'Sturm und Drang: Conjectures on the Origin of a Phrase' in *Simiolus* Jg. 1 (1966–7)/2, pp. 1ff. Norman Hampson, *The Enlightenment*, London 1968. Max Rudolf, 'Storm and Stress in Music', in *Bach* (Quarterly Journal of the Riemenschneider Bach Institute, III/2–4 [1972], pp. 1ff.). Robert P. Bareikis, *The Transition to Modern Germany: The Eighteenth Century* (Exhibition, The Lilly Library, Bloomington, Ind., 1975). Roswitha Strommer, 'Die Rezeption der englischen Literatur im Lebensumkreis und zur Zeit Joseph Haydns', in *Joseph Haydn und die Literatur seiner Zeit*, Eisenstadt 1976.

III. The Austrian Crisis. Théodore de Wyzewa, 'A propos du Centenaire de le mort de Joseph Haydn', in *Revue des Deux Mondes* vol. 51 (1909), pp. 935ff. Landon, Sorbonne 1956 (op. cit.). Barry S. Brook, 'Sturm und Drang and the Romantic Period in Music', in *Studies in Romanticism* IX/4 (1970).

2 Symphonies: Landon, *SYM*, and Philharmonia 589–600 (just now [Summer 1977] in the course of being reprinted; some are also available in *Joseph Haydn Werke* (Henle). Quartets: *Joseph Haydn Werke* (Henle) and also the new critical edition by Barrett-Ayres and Landon (Doblinger). Baryton works: *Joseph Haydn Werke*. Piano works: Sonatas ed. C. Landon (*Wiener Urtext-Ausgabe*), and by G. Feder (*Joseph Haydn Werke*, also reprinted as a practical edition by Henle); Piano music edited by F. Eibner (*Wiener Urtext-Ausgabe*), which is more complete and more intelligently edited than in *Joseph Haydn Werke* and the practical reprint by Henle (ed. S. Gerlach). For the Piano Concerto we shall provide the principal source, since there is no real critical edition as yet.

Symphony No.	Date	Comment
39	c. 1766–7	Entered in *EK* p. 2 at top in pencil; earliest known reference: Göttweig Monastery 1770. Performance probably after 1 March 1767, when the fourth horn player (Johann May) was engaged. Paul Bryan in *Haydn-Studien* III (1973), p. 53.
35	1767	Autograph dated 1 December 1767; entered in *EK* p. 2 after Symphonies Nos. 29, 31 and 28 (all dated 1765 on their respective autographs).
59	c. 1767	The next entry in *EK*; Göttweig and Kremsmünster Monasteries 1769.
38		The next entry in *EK*; Göttweig and Breitkopf Catalogue 1769.
49	1768	Autograph dated 1768; next entry in *EK*.
58	c. 1768	The next entry in *EK*. Minuet & Trio used in Baryton Trio No. 52 (c. 1767)
Overture *Lo speziale*	1768	The next entry in *EK* (top of p. 2); opera performed in the autumn of 1768 at Eszterháza (see Chronicle, *supra*).
26	c. 1768–9	The next entry in *EK*; Göttweig and Herzogenburg Monasteries 1772, but Osek Abbey 1770.
41		The next entry in *EK*; watermarks of authentic MS. parts by Joseph Elssler (Prague) suggest that the copy was made 1769. Göttweig 1771, Osek 1771.
48		Part of a new series of symphonic entries on the left-hand side of page one in *EK*; dated MS. by Joseph Elssler (Slovakia) 1769: see facsimile, p. 297. Breitkopf Catalogue 1773.
44	c. 1770–1	*EK* p. 2; Breitkopf Catalogue 1772.
52		*EK* p. 2 (next entry after 44); Breitkopf Catalogue 1774.
43		*EK* p. 2 (next entry after 52); Breitkopf Catalogue 1772.
42	1771	Autograph dated 1771; next entry in *EK* after 43 but in a different ink (bottom of p. 1, left); Breitkopf Catalogue 1773.
51	c. 1771–3	Breitkopf Catalogue 1774.
45	1772	Autograph dated 1772; top entry in *EK* p. 1, left side; Göttweig 1774.
46		Autograph dated 1772; next entry in *EK* after 45 (also entered once again, three themes below, and later crossed out); Göttweig 1774.
47		Autograph dated 1772; in *EK* four entries below 46 (the entries are: 65 [q.v.], 48, 46 [cancelled]); Göttweig 1774.
65	c. 1772–3	*EK* p. 1 together with works of 1772 (*vide supra*, 47); Breitkopf Catalogue 1778.
[A lost symphony in C (No.63, first version, III/IV)]		Watermarks of MS. (partly autograph): c. 1769–73 (*vide infra*, p. 306).
50	1773	Autograph dated 1773.
64	c. 1773	Authentic MS. by an Eszterháza copyist (Frankfurt/Main) with watermarks: Bartha-Somfai p. 445, group 192; Larsen No. 8. This watermark is found in dated Haydn autographs of 1769 and 1773. Breitkopf Catalogue 1778.
54–57	1774	Autographs dated 1774.
60		Incidental music to *Der Zerstreute* (Regnard's *Le distrait*, performed at Eszterháza and Pressburg in 1774: see Chronicle).

Symphony No.	Date	Comment
68	c. 1774–5	In Keeß Catalogue the work is in chronological proximity of the 1774 symphonies (the Keeß Catalogue is vaguely, not quite strictly, chronological). See S. Gerlach in *Haydn-Studien* II/1 (1969), p. 40. Beginning of a new series of symphonies in *EK*, entered by Johann Schellinger on pp. 25f. Printed with Nos. 66 and 67 by Hummel in 1779.
66	c. 1775–6	Entered in *EK* (p. 25) after 61 (1776); Hummel 1779; Göttweig 1779.
69		Entered in *EK* (p. 25) after 66; Göttweig 1779.
67		Entered in *EK* (p. 25) after 69; Hummel 1779.

Notes on the Symphonies

Symphony No. 39 in G minor

Scoring: 2 oboes, 4 horns, strings and continuo [bassoon, harpsichord].

Haydn's G minor Symphony is original in many ways, not only for the harshness of its language, especially of the first movement and Finale, but for its orchestration. Here Haydn uses four horns, two in B flat *alto* and two in G. This means, firstly, that he can create sumptuous horn chords, and secondly, that he has a pair of horns at his disposal when he modulates to the relative major. Haydn's work had far-reaching consequences. J. B. Vanhal modelled at least one of his two G minor Symphonies on it, even to the four horns, and so, almost immediately, did J. C. Bach[1] and, in 1773, W. A. Mozart (in K.183, also with the four horns). It is also worth recalling that when Mozart started to compose the great G minor Symphony K.550, he first used four horns, two in B flat *alto* and two in G, later reducing them to two.[2]

The first movement of No. 39 is curiously unsettling. The main theme is announced and continued *piano*, and the tension inherent in its thematic layout is heightened by the extraordinary use of silence between the various sections. (This use of rests to increase the dramatic effect becomes a very important detail in Haydn's mature style, of which we are now on the threshold; no one knew better than he how to employ the art of silence, and many of his finest effects are derived by the simple expedient of inserting a pause in the right place.) To give the second part of the melody a still more individual twist, Haydn stretches the last phrase with its characteristic octave skip, so that the theme simply dies away to nothing. The structure of the three component parts (4+6+4) is also cleverly

veiled by the insertion of rests. Having achieved such a restless, almost frustrated atmosphere, Haydn creates a still more unified tension by employing this one theme throughout the movement. Indeed, Haydn cannot escape the hypnotic effect of his principal subject: he modulates from the tonic to the relative major: and the first subject appears, extending itself contrapuntally (see *b* of example). In the development he reaches a superb, five-part tutti (see *d* of example) in which the violins, in imitation sweep through a fine sequence; and again, we see that the oboe part is based upon a tiny fragment of the main theme (see bracketed portion of *a* in example), the string parts being derived from a figure found at the end of the exposition (see *c* of example) which, in turn, developed out of the principal theme. The whole movement is held together by a device which we have come to know well in the previous period: a bass line constantly moving in quavers.

After the force of the first movement, the quiet little Andante, for strings only in E flat is a throwback to an earlier style: Haydn has not yet learned the secret of maintaining tension throughout a whole work. The Minuet is a serious piece worthy of the outer movements, while the Trio, in B flat (the relative major), is again rather jovial. It is only the Finale which really reaches the inspiration of the first movement. Here we have, in a symphony in a minor key, the same highly advanced type of movement which will be discussed in connection with No. 38. If the two middle movements of No. 39 were on the same high artistic level of the outer allegros, we would have had one of Haydn's finest *Sturm und Drang* symphonies; as it is, this flawed masterpiece is one of the most interesting of this strange interim period. What makes this Finale successful is not only the energetic drive and the nervous semiquavers which carry on the restless spirit of the opening movement, but the care with which Haydn has provided a number of dynamic contrasts; thus, the violins rush down the scale into a *subito piano* (bars 14ff.), while after the double bar, the first and second violins have a long passage by themselves, *piano*; and the rest of the development is characterized by continual alterations of *f* and *p*.

1 In his 'Six Simphonies...Oeuvre VI', No. 6 (Terry pp. 264f.), issued in 1770 by Hummel in Amsterdam (pl. no. 113). See Cari Johannson, *J. J. & B. Hummel Music-Publishing and Thematic Catalogues*, Stockholm 1972, vol. I, p. 27. J. C. Bach uses only two horns, but there is an original touch in that the slow movement is in C minor.

2 See *Neue Mozart Ausgabe*, Sinfonien Band 9 (Landon, 1957).

[Symphony No. 39/I]

Symphony No. 35 in B flat

Scoring: 2 oboes, 2 horns in B flat (*alto*), strings and continuo [bassoon, harpsichord].

A felicitous alternation of light and shade deepens and enriches this Symphony, which was completed on the first day of December 1767. It reveals to us a Haydn momentarily captivated by the sunny, melodious sounds of Italy, but who at the same time cast a thoughtful and critical eye on the possibilities of rich orchestral effects. In the first movement, the theme, which seemed to be so friendly in the exposition, suddenly develops a towering contrapuntal anger in the development, while the phrase ♩ ♪♪♪ (originally the basis of a transitional passage) becomes increasingly important and is the basis of a turbulently polyphonic section. The whole development becomes increasingly dark-hued and the keys tend more and more to be minor.

There is a robust little horn figure which accompanies the first *forte* of the recapitulation; it was obviously in B flat *alto* because in some early printed sources it was simply removed as being too difficult (it goes up to sounding *g''*).

The Andante, without wind instruments, is a gentle and warm piece in a light two–four metre with one passage (bars 10ff.) which will remind Anglo-Saxon listeners of *Adeste fideles*. There are some very original syncopations in this movement, reminding us that all syncopations are now important to Haydn's new style.

The Menuet 'Un poco allegretto' is characterized by a triplet upbeat, which gives a certain *insouciance* to the movement; the triplet motion is then continued and broadened in the Trio, alternating between first and second violins. The Finale has something of the swashbuckling adventurousness of the first movement, though without its darker overtones. It is a delightful conclusion to one of Haydn's most winning transitional works. In the Chronicle (*supra*, p. 142) we suggested that No. 35 might have been written to celebrate Prince Esterházy's return from Paris;

if true, that possibility might explain the work's predominantly cheerful character: one would hardly greet the Prince's return with a work like the *Sinfonia* 'La Passione' ....

Symphony No. 59 in A ('Fire')

Scoring: 2 oboes, 2 horns, strings and continuo [bassoon, harpsichord]

We have mentioned the ramifications of the Schwerin MS. (*supra*, pp. 279f.). Whatever its precise origin, it is a highly original and theatrical piece. The acceleration, in the first movement (Presto), from quavers to semiquavers in the main theme (the violins hammering out the note 'A' repeatedly); the sudden shifts from *piano* to *forte*; the tremendous rhythmic intensity – it all seems to suggest music for the stage. The second movement is equally original. It begins for strings alone, in A minor, and is marked by Haydn's characteristic tempo, Andante o più tosto allegretto. It is a spiky, asymmetrical theme which suddenly swerves into C major (the relative major) and a lovely, singing melody almost an aria from an Italian opera. In the second part we modulate slowly back to a long pedal point on the dominant (E) – and the music abruptly switches to A major and the beautiful *cantabile* theme we noticed before when it was in C major. Up to now it has seemed that this will be another of Haydn's slow movements for strings alone; but with the advent of A major, the wind instruments join us. It is a lovely effect. But what are we to make of that shattering *ff* horn call that interrupts the main theme (bars 115f.)? It would be pleasant to imagine that it is related to the military atmosphere of Grossmann's *Die Feuersbrunst* (1773), but we must remind ourselves that there are at least two known manuscript sources of the Symphony dated 1769!

The main theme of the Menuetto is very strongly related to the principal theme of the slow movement, another instance of Haydn's constant attempt to weld the symphonic form into a

288

cohesive whole. The Finale (Allegro assai), with its rousing horn and oboe fanfares, and its racing strings, was bound to be a success. It is one of those Haydnesque movements that contemporary British critics used to call 'phrenzied'; and it is also a very theatrical movement.

Symphony No. 38 in C major

Scoring: 2 oboes, 2 horns in C (probably *alto*), 2 trumpets, timpani, strings and continuo [bassoon, harpsichord].

The sources for this Symphony suggest that Haydn revised it at least twice. There are four passages in the first movement where there were originally rests for the wind instruments: a whole group of early MSS. shows this reading (see Philharmonia 561 for details). The second principal revision is the addition of trumpets and timpani: many of the oldest sources do not contain them. As we know, there were at this period no regular trumpeters or kettledrummers (until the arrival of Caspar Peczival on 1 September 1771 who was a bassoonist but also a kettledrum player). Later Haydn got round this problem by having C *alto* horn parts and kettledrums in his C major works. We have no evidence when he added the trumpets and timpani to No. 38, but they are found in good sources of the year 1769 (Göttweig Abbey and the Breitkopf Catalogue), which suggests another explanation; Haydn actually wrote the Symphony *with* the trumpets and timpani (for example for the great *Fest* in July 1770 at Kittsee Castle) and later sold authentic copies without them, for bands (such as his own) that did not have these instruments available. Perhaps that is why Joseph Elssler's manuscript parts, which Professor J. P. Larsen and the present writer found at the Academy Library in Pressburg (Bratislava) in September 1959, lack the trumpets and drums. The source was owned by the Servite Monastery in Pest (today's Budapest) and is dated 1777 by *them* (not by Elssler, who may have written it many years before that date).

Here we have, in No. 38, one of the first Esterházy symphonies in Haydn's festival key, and with the festival C horns (here also with trumpets) and timpani. These C major works run like a silver thread all through Haydn's long career: from his first works for Count Morzin (which included several festival symphonies: Nos. 32 and 33 in any case, perhaps also No. 20, which is a difficult work to date), to this No. 38, and then to Nos. 41, 48, 50, 56 and 60 (of our present period), to the once-famous 'Laudon' Symphony No. 69 (on the borderline between the end of this period and the beginning of the next), reaching a culmination in the magnificent 'L'ours' (No. 82) which, like No. 90, was written for Paris; and ending with the greatest of them all: Symphony No. 97 (London, 1792).

Although a festival Symphony, we feel the increased poise, compared to earlier specimens of the type, also the sophisticated compositional techniques which we may see, for example, at the beginning of the development, where the theme is broken up and its first six notes ♩♩♪♪ | ♩ used to urge the music into G minor and then D minor and A minor, before we subside into the sub-dominant, F major. This is music very much of the period.

The second movement is still rooted in the Baroque tradition. Here we have an 'echo' movement, so beloved by Baroque composers, even to J. S. Bach in the *Christmas Oratorio* (which it is unlikely Haydn knew). Haydn devises the echo as follows: violin I is without mutes (*senza sordino*), violin II with mutes (*con sordino*). They echo each other in an entrancing way in this delicate and poised Andante molto, made doubly delicate by dropping all the wind instruments and of course the kettledrums; and also by having the entire movement played *piano*. It is a pretty effect.

Many of Haydn's early minuets are (to borrow a term from the pictorial arts) in what might be called 'international preclassical' style, but there were minuet movements which were typically Austrian (such as those in Symphonies Nos. 5 and 9, the one for Morzin and the other for Esterházy). Despite its French spelling, this Menuet is purely Austrian. We are surprised to find the Trio given over entirely to an elaborate oboe solo. But it is only in the Finale that we see Haydn's secret plan. In No. 38's conclusion we find: (1) the most highly-developed example of sonata form found in any Haydn finale to date; (2) interesting use of motifs derived from the main subject; (3) Haydn's first full-scale use of contrapuntal devices in a symphonic finale written in sonata form (as opposed to strict fugues such as the Finale to No. 40); (4) the use of a solo instrument (the oboe) in a concerto-like manner as in the slow movements of Nos. 31, 36 or 72 (misplaced chronologically). What raises this Finale over earlier specimens is the judicious combination of symphonic, polyphonic and *concertante* elements, all of which are neatly fitted into a sonata form mould.

The oboe solo is actually so unexpected, coming at the end of a learned contrapuntal section, that one is tempted to look for an outside explanation. We believe there is one; and we put it forward as a possible reason for this sudden fascination with the first oboe part. On 1 September 1768, Haydn engaged a famous oboe player, Vittorino Colombazzo, who received the very high salary of 400 gulden (and emoluments) a year; he was twice in Prince Esterházy's service, this time only from 1 September to 19 December. Is it not possible that Haydn was perhaps in the middle of Symphony No. 38 when the famous oboe player was engaged, and always ready to display a new performer's talents, the composer wrote the Trio and the Finale to introduce Vittorino Colombazzo to His Serene Highness? There are reasons for supposing that the four horn parts of Symphonies Nos. 13 (1763) and 72 (1763?) were designed to introduce the new sound of four horns to the Prince. Perhaps Symphony No. 38 is a similar tribute to a great oboe player.

Symphony No. 49 in F minor ('La Passione')

Scoring: 2 oboes, 2 horns, strings and continuo [bassoon, harpsichord].

This dark-hued, sombre – even tragic – Symphony, in the unusual key of F minor,[1] stands in the centre of the *Sturm und Drang* movement. It is also Haydn's last symphony in the *sonata da chiesa* form, and unquestionably the greatest. With this work, he obviously thought he had exhausted the *sonata da chiesa* as a symphonic operation (though we must not forget that much later, he wrote a Quartet [Op. 55, No. 2] in F minor with an opening slow movement – coincidence?). There is no doubt that the form of the *sonata da chiesa* suggested to Haydn a serious project: all the earlier works, especially Nos. 21 and 22, have weighty opening slow movements. In the Adagio of No. 49, we seem to sense the winding line of penitents before the Cross. As in all the orchestral works of this period, Haydn takes great pains to lift the music out of its blackness by means of contrasting dynamic marks (see bars 65–7): but in 'La Passione' the questioning spirit prevails almost throughout the four movements.

The wide leaps in the opening theme of the Allegro di molto are fiercely typical of Haydn in these years, as are the lean two-part writing and the syncopations that follow. One notes how carefully Haydn contrasts this heroic opening with the gliding quavers he introduces as soon as the music reaches the relative major (A flat). Yet it is just with this flowing music that Haydn provides his most brilliant touch – the transformation of this relatively serene music in the development back to the original key, in the process of which the sinuous quavers acquire an ominous, almost sinister colour.

The Minuet & Trio are a kind of oasis between the quick movements, and the Trio, with the gunmetal gleam of its high horn notes, is a peaceful and brief interlude before the monothematic concentration of the final Presto. It will be noticed that Haydn has welded this Symphony together not only by its single emotional character but by less apparent means: the opening notes of the Symphony, its basic line (*c – d flat – b flat – c*), serve for the thematic material of all its four movements. In the Allegro di molto, the top notes of the violin, i.e. those at the beginning of each bar, are *c – d flat – b flat*; and the second subject (bars 37ff.) is also related to the basic progression – perhaps more clearly felt when it returns in the tonic minor at bars 126ff. The Menuet's beginning is again the *c – d flat – b flat* line, while the Trio has more or less the same thing in major; and in the Finale the *Urlinie* has a different rhythm and the

intervals are juggled slightly differently. It is an astonishing *tour-de-force* of thematic, or perhaps better, motivic unity in a symphony of this date. The abbots and princes with whom this work was so popular in Central Europe – dozens of old copies have survived – may not have analyzed why they thought this a great work, but that, after all, would not have been Haydn's intention; the technical means which unify any work of art – Giotto fresco or Haydn symphony – need not be known to the layman.

Symphony No. 58 in F major

Scoring: 2 oboes, 2 horns, strings and continuo [bassoon, harpsichord].

This is a typically Austrian chamber symphony, whose delicate string writing and sophisticated (but sparing) use of the wind instruments are reflected in many products by Austrian composers of the period, such as Leopold Hofmann (Cathedral Chapel Master of St Stephen's Cathedral in Vienna), Carl Ditters von Dittersdorf or Carlos d'Ordoñez (an official in the Lower Austrian Law Courts) – all three composers who were well known to Haydn. The comparison also suggests that, at least in its first two movements, this Symphony is hardly different from the products of his contemporaries. As in the Quartets, Op. 9, this period shows Haydn's art in a state of flux: bursts of inspiration side by side with more ordinary, even uninspired, products.

In the second movement, Haydn reverts to earlier practice and omits the wind parts entirely, thus accentuating the chamber musical atmosphere: the writing itself is also rather baroque, very often in just two parts, the harpsichord player being expected to fill in the missing harmonies.[1]

The third movement is a most original *Menuet alla zoppa e trio* (Un poco allegretto) – literally 'limping', which Haydn accomplishes with a dotted rhythm that is deliberately pushed into all sorts of asymmetrical patterns. The Trio is a curious contrast, rather as if a group of slightly sinister Gypsies had suddenly entered the feast: in a moment we are moved far into the world of the Balkans.

---

1 Haydn was much attached to the key, using it in one of the Op. 20 Quartets (No. 5), in a trancendentally great piece for keyboard (the *Andante con variazioni*), in *L'infedeltà delusa* and elsewhere. Although rather rare at this period, the key was sometimes used by Baroque composers, e.g. by Pietro Locatelli. The earliest reference to 'La Passione' is in a MS. copied by a student of law and music at Leipzig, now in the Schwerin Archives.

1 No harpsichord part is ever mentioned on the scores or authentic parts (such as have survived); but in the autograph of Symphony No. 7 we read 'Basso/Continuo' and 'Violoncello con Basso continuo'. See the illustration facing p. 241 in Landon, *SYM*. And C. P. E. Bach (in his *Versuch über die wahre Art das Clavier zu spielen*, says specifically that a keyboard instrument is to be used even if the composer does not specify it. See his Chapter 35 'Von der Nothwendigkeit der Bezifferung' of the 1753 edition (facsimile reprint, Breitkopf & Härtel, Leipzig 1957, ed. Lothar Hoffmann-Erbrecht, pp. 298ff.) Although Bach assumes that the continuo must participate even if the bass is not figured, he says, 'As a result one may see how ridiculous it is to ask a player to accompany unfigured basses' (p. 298). The necessity of a keyboard instrument in Haydn's symphonies ceases after about 1770: such a heavily orchestrated work as No. 41 hardly requires a harpsichord continuo.

In the fast-moving Finale (Presto), we would point out one passage of great harmonic daring which occurs twice, once at bars 47ff. and again at bars 138ff., where Haydn leaps into a bold unison which is violently out of key: it is the same effect that one finds at the beginning of the development in the Finale of Mozart's Symphony in G minor, K.550.

Symphony No. 26 in D minor ('Lamentatione')

Scoring; 2 oboes, 2 horns, strings and continuo [bassoon, harpsichord].

It is natural that our interest in this new period should be concentrated primarily upon symphonies in minor keys, for these not only represent the fulfilment of the new artistic principles gradually being evolved by the composer but are also the finest symphonic works being produced during the years under consideration. Of these transitional symphonies, none is more telling in its expression. The work consists of three movements, of which the last is a minuet. Various writers[1] have suggested that the real last movement may be lacking. This erroneous view was based on a second, false title by which the work seems to have been known: the 'Christmas Symphony'. The idea that 'perhaps a real Pastorale, which should have completed the Symphony, is lost' (Geiringer) derives from this spurious 'Christmas' title. Investigation of all the earliest MSS. shows, first, that only three movements were intended, and secondly, that the work was composed for Easter week and not for the Nativity. The title of the oldest MS., from Herzogenburg Abbey, is 'Passio et Lamentatio', and it was from the remarks penned over the second violin part (see *c* in music example) that the present writer came to the conclusion that the first and second movements illustrate some drama played during the Holy Week. Happily, it has been possible to discover the origin of the entire Symphony through several rare prints, copies of which have been found in various monasteries and churches in Austria.

The model which Haydn took, almost without change, for the first movement of the Symphony is an old drama of the Passion, apparently evolved late in the middle ages[2] and repeatedly printed during the sixteenth to eighteenth centuries. We were able to locate *inter alia* an edition of 1763[1] in the Monastery of St Florian, entitled (in red and black print):

> Cantus Ecclesiasticus / Sacrae Historiae / Passionis / Domini Nostri / Jesu Christi, / Secundum / Quatuor Evangelistas. / Itemque / Lamentationum, / et / Lectionum / pro Tribus Matutinis. / tenebrarum. / Juxta exemplar / Romae editum emendatius. [Etc.] Ex Ducali Campidonensi Typographeo, / Per Andream Stadler, / Anno Domini MDCCLXIII.

The music of all four Passions is of great simplicity, dignity and beauty. Of particular interest is the fact that all four utilize identical motifs; thus, the rising and falling cadence from *fa* to *si♭* given to Christ when He speaks always remains the same; the passage allotted to the chorus is also practically identical throughout, as is the figure 'dixit eis' ('said unto them'), and so forth. The 'Christus' motif is in turn based on the ancient Lamentation chant (see *a* of example, p. 293). The endless repetitions of the original Passions produce a medieval pattern akin to the remote mysticism of the early Christian mosaics at Ravenna. These Passions were well known to Haydn's audience, and the purpose of the Symphony must have been immediately apparent to everyone.[2]

The first subject of the opening movement consists of three parts: (1) a lashing series of syncopations, supported by a stable bass line (*a* of music example) leading to (2) four (2 × 2) leaden *piano* bars and then to (3) a varied repetition of the syncopated idea, still *piano*. This three-part theme is the prelude to the Passion Drama, which is in the key of F major (the relative major of D minor), the modern tonal equivalent of the Gregorian original. Haydn does not modulate to the relative major; he jumps into it at the end of bar 16. The Passion music occurs as the second subject, the old melody being characteristically concealed (as in the 'Alleluja' of No. 30/I or the *Te Deum for the Empress*)[3] in that it is assigned to second violin and first oboe, the first violin covering the whole with a series of constantly moving quavers (the following example shows the original Passion[s], or rather the extracts used by Haydn, and the form

---

1 H. Kretzschmar, 'Die Jugendsinfonien Josef Haydns', in *Peters Jahrbuch* 1908, p. 87; Geiringer 1932, p. 73; etc.

2 Speaking of the origin of the 'Tonus Passionis', U. L. Kirnberger, *Lehr- und Ubungsbuch des Gregorianischen Choralgesanges*, 3rd. ed., Freising 1888, pp. 102f., says: 'The Passion of our Lord is sung after the Gospel according to Matthew on Palm Sunday, on Tuesday in Holy Week after Mark, on Ash Wednesday after Luke, and – especially solemnly – on Good Friday after John. The practice of performing the Passion in an epic-dramatic fashion before the Christian congregation is supposed to go back to the 12th century. In the Papal Choir, the Passion Melody was in use as early as the middle of the 13th century. Baini (*Memorie*, vol. II, p. 112, n. 537) thinks it must have been composed by a Papal singer.'

1 An older copy (second half of the seventeenth century) in the Pfarrkirche at Eferding (Upper Austria) was compared to the edition of 1763. Three further copies of various dates were found in the Monastery of Göttweig, and three more in the Monastery of Herzogenburg. The musical text of the four Passions as well as the Lamentations underwent very few changes in the various editions. As that in St Florian is chronologically the nearest to the Symphony, its text has been used in the musical examples here quoted. The music of the 'Passion according to St Matthew' is also printed in the *Compendiosa ad Cantum Gregorianum . . . Brixinae* Typis Joseph Weger, 1806, pp. 67ff. A further copy, closely related to the edition of 1763, was printed in Vienna in 1761 'ex officina Krausiana' (see Robert Haas, *Wolfgang Amadeus Mozart*, Potsdam 1933, p. 38).

2 Ernst Eberlin (died 1762 at Salzburg) also used this Passion melody in *Der Blutschwitzende Jesus*; Robert Hass (*Mozart*, p. 38) has quoted the Viennese edition of 1761 and Eberlin's interesting transformation of it.

3 See *Haydn: the Years of 'The Creation' 1796–1800*, p. 607.

of the melody in No. 26/I with the remarks of the Herzogenburg MS. attached). The 'Christus' figure as well as the crowd *Tutti* (notice the 'Jud[en]' in Herzogenburg) are quoted in characteristic examples from the original Passions. The end of the 'Jud[en]' passage coincides with a new pattern in the first violins, which abandon their quaver figurations and rush up the B flat scale ('Crucify Him, crucify Him'). The exposition ends with a tense, hammering figure in octave unison.

The development turns back to the syncopated opening subject; the leaden *piano* bars are now given an expressive appoggiatura and used to modulate from F to G minor. The syncopation whips this aside and continues to the dominant of

A minor, where a fragment of the 'Christus' theme enters. The hammering figure pulls the music round to the recapitulation, which is regular until the third part of the main subject, at which point the violins drop to low 'A' and continue their syncopations quietly, the oboe twice climbing up a I_4^6 arpeggio. Then the whole music shifts into D major for the second subject (Passion); instead of the triumphant effect that one might expect, the result is quite the contrary, and the wild, bitter mood only becomes more intensified. The first horn now bites into the orchestral texture, doubling the melody with oboe and second violin. The movements ends with a fanatic concentration on the hammering figure, wrenching the music to

a close like, for example, the *turbae* of a Bach or Schütz Passion.

The wilderness of the first movement is completely altered in the ensuing Adagio. Haydn uses as his principal subject one of the 'Alphabet Lamentations' found in the Passion Print – a typical example is quoted *infra* (*a* of example). The ornaments found in Haydn's adaptation (see *b* of example) are considered to be valuable examples of the traditional embellishments which the singers added *ad libitum* to the melody in the eighteenth century. As we have seen, the 'Christus' melody in No. 26/I was based upon a variant of this Lamentation chant; and thus the two movements are linked together conceptually as well as thematically. In No. 26/II the melody is also hidden in the first oboe and second violin, the first violin having a series of independent figurations which act as a counter-subject. The form of the movement parallels very closely the free adaptation of the chorale prelude used in No. 22/I. (This idea, incidentally, seems to be entirely original with Haydn, for the form is not like the north or south German chorale prelude.) In No. 26/II, each thematic entrance is separated by a series of figurations, during which the second violin and oboe are always silent. Haydn has saved his orchestral colour for the end, where the music is transformed by a radiant modulation to the mediant major (see *c* of example), i.e. a Phrygian half-cadence.

The rather whimsical Minuet & Trio are something of an anticlimax.[1] Judged on its own merits, however, there are some matters of interest. The opening bars (D minor) are questioning, almost tragic; while the last eight bars (F major) are Schubertian, with pert appoggiature. The mood shifts within the time interval of one bar. In the second section there is a fine imitation between violins and lower strings which was possibly the inspiration for the stretto at the end of

---

1 One scribe, in Melk Monastery, omitted it from the Symphony, but wishing to save some attractive music, included it in another collection of Haydn pieces.

Mozart's great *Adagio and Fugue*, K.546 (see example below).

With this Symphony we reach the culmination of Haydn's use of church melodies in the symphonic *genre*. At the same time we have the most striking example of the new symphonic art form, in which we see the composer attempting to infuse his music with a unifying spiritual message.

His efforts towards this goal led him to choose the Easter drama of Christian antiquity which had fascinated artists for centuries, and which had in music perhaps its finest and most noble expression in the Protestant north German school, especially through the Passions of Schütz and J. S. Bach. Haydn's desire to remove his symphonies from the realms of *Tafelmusik* led him to the sterner, more

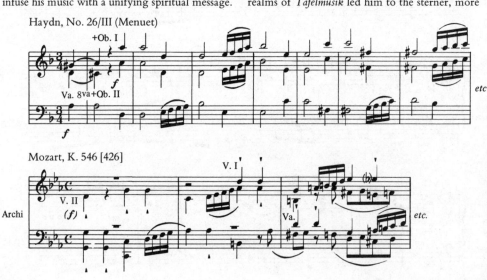

severe art forms of the medieval and Gothic eras; and in taking as his model the old *Volkspassion* he approaches the stirring effects produced by the Reformation upon art in northern Germany. Thus it was that the Catholic Haydn, living amidst an already soft and decaying Baroque grandeur, could through his own experiments raise the art of the symphony far beyond anything known to the preclassical composers of Vienna or Mannheim or Paris (we must make an important exception with the astonishing symphonies of Franz Beck),[1] much less to the composers of the Italian *sinfonia*. The *Sinfonia Lamentatione*[2] breathes the atmosphere of a Riemenschneider, Grünewald or Adam Krafft.

Symphony No. 41 in C major

Scoring: (a) I, III and IV: 2 oboes, 2 horns in C *alto*, 2 trumpets, timpani, strings; (b) II: 1 flute, 2 oboes, 2 horns in C *basso*, strings [bassoon continuo].

No. 41 may have been written originally without the trumpets and timpani, which were lacking in Haydn's band at this period. At least the only authentic manuscript, by Joseph Elssler, which we discovered many years ago at Prague (from the Archives of Kačina Castle), is scored for C *alto* (and *basso* in II) horns but without trumpets and timpani. The watermarks of this Joseph Elssler source (see Philharmonia 592, p. xxx) suggest that it was made in 1769. By 1771, the trumpet and timpani parts had reached Göttweig Abbey[3] and they are clearly a later but authentic addition, also known to us from many other old sources, including the entry in the Keeß Catalogue. Again we think of the great *Fest* at Kittsee in July 1770, where trumpets and drums are specifically mentioned in the Chronicle (*supra*, p. 164): perhaps Haydn did *several* C major symphonies in the

course of the festivities (Nos. 38, 41, 48, all provided with new trumpet and timpani parts).

Haydn's festival key, C major, has a historical explanation. By the time Haydn was a choir-boy in St Stephen's Cathedral in Vienna, the average festival Mass in which he will have participated was in C major, and this would be the key indelibly fixed on his mind as the 'Missa Solemnis' tonality. If we examine fifty such Masses in, say, the old monastery library at Göttweig (with which institution Haydn had at least indirect contact by 1762 and his younger brother Johann Michael as early as 1759), over half will be in C major. Vocally this is a convenient range, because bottom G in the bass clef is about the lowest note most average basses can sing openly, while top G for tenor and (one octave higher) for soprano is also as high as either group can manage without considerable vocal strain: and these G's would also be the dominant of the principal key of C. Trumpets and drums also sound martial in that key. The timbre of these biting C *alto*, or high C horns, together with the trumpets and timpani, is intoxicating; it is a very Haydnish sound, which, moreover, never appears in Mozart's or Beethoven's symphonies (though Mozart occasionally used C *alto* horns). In the orchestral layout of such a work as No. 41, it is fascinating to see how Haydn 'saves' his horn players: the top range with *g″* and very occasionally *a″* (as in the Trio of No. 41), is very difficult to sustain for any length of time, and one notes that it is always used for a special effect. In No. 41, for example, the first trumpet has the top *g*'s in the Allegro con spirito, bars 16/18, as it does in the flaming orchestral passage at bars 165 *et seq.* The very strain of producing the long top *g* in No. 56/I, at bars 212ff., and the barbaric grandeur of the brass at bars 263–6, add great tension to a music already packed with nervous excitement.

We may wonder for what purposes these festive symphonies were written. In a series like the 'Paris' or 'Salomon' works, it is clear that as a 'diversion' it was a good idea to have one of the set in C. In the 1760s, Haydn may have written one or the other of these pieces for performance at an Austrian monastery (he was on friendly terms with several); some were undoubtedly composed for festive occasions at Eisenstadt or Eszterháza, such as No. 50, written (it would seem) to celebrate the arrival of the Empress at the Hungarian Castle on the Neusiedlersee. Is it an accident that both the operas composed or played in her honour in September 1773, *Philemon und Baucis* and *L'infedeltà delusa*, end with C major tuttis and flourishes of the C *alto* horns? It was not until September 1771 that Haydn had a regular timpani player at Eszterháza (*vide supra*, p. 92); from that moment, he could, without recruiting any extra players, write festive C major symphonies with high horns and kettledrums. But every few years he had trumpets and timpani from the Thurnermeister in Eisenstadt or Oedenburg (e.g. for 26 July 1768 at Eisenstadt, for 25 July 1770 at Kittsee, for September 1773 at Eszterháza – see the Chronicle – and in August 1775 at Eszterháza).

---

1 Symphony in D minor, edited from the authentic first edition (by the present writer): Nagels Musikarchiv. Naturally, C. P. E. Bach must also be excepted.

2 As is well known, Haydn used the Lamentation melody in No. 45/III and in a Divertimento for wind band (II:23). It is possible that he received an additional impetus to treat the 'Lamentatio' from his predecessor, Gregor Werner, for there is a number of smaller church works by that composer utilizing the 'Tonus Lamentatio', several of which are preserved in the Burgenländisches Landesmuseum, Eisenstadt. Mozart used a variation of the 'Lamentatio' as the chorale theme in his *Maurerische Trauermusik*, K.477, composed in July 1785: Mozart's treatment of the melody is strikingly similar to Haydn's: the Gregorian chant is assigned to the oboes and clarinets in unison, the first violin overlaying it with figurations and the remaining strings accompanying. The first five bars of the chorale in Mozart's version (bars 25–29) are almost identical with example *a* (*supra*) if the opening 'alphabet' portion is removed. See the new critical edition (Landon) for the *Neue Mozart Ausgabe*, Bärenreiter 4709 (1956), also pocket score. The connection between the Gregorian melody and the *Maurerische Trauermusik* is doubly symbolic: uniting the Church with the Brotherhood, and the 'Lamentatio' of the mourners for the deceased.

3 'Parthia in C. / à / Violini 2/ Oboe 2./ Corni 2 / Clarini 2 / Flautto Traverso / Viola / Tympano / Con / Basso / Del Sigr Giuseppe Hayden. / Comparavit R: P: Odo 1771'.

The first movement of No. 41 is in three-four time, the same metre used in the first movements of three other C major 'festival' symphonies (Nos. 50, 56, 60; not counting the slow introductions). Students of Haydn will notice the clearly defined second subject (something of a rarity), also the new orchestral layout of the strings wherein the violas double the first violins at the octave in those so characteristic 'rushing' passages in repeated semi-quavers (e.g. bars 29ff.). Still another important orchestral device – it can be melodic, too, as we have seen elsewhere – is the use of wide skips as at bars 44ff. Finally, we would point to a famous device of Haydn's during the early 1770s, namely the *fausse reprise* or sham recapitulation, which occurs during the development and leads the unwary listener to believe he is back at the repetition of the initial, expository material. This almost classic 'false recapitulation' occurs here at bar 97, after which we are whirled away into G minor and a long sequence in A minor: the real reprise begins at bar 133.

The second movement has Haydn's favourite sound of muted violins, but the orchestra has changed: the horns are in C *basso* and a flute has joined the woodwind. What a rich tapestry of sound Haydn weaves, the flute in arabesques over a broad oboe cantilena and held horns! The strings tap out a discreet reminder of the 2/4 beat as we are borne aloft in this extraordinarily beautiful and 'rafinée' ensemble. Notice the 'broken' melodic pattern of bars 24ff.: this kind of syncopation, as we have observed, is a frequent occurrence.

The Menuet is more French than anything else, with its pompous trills and triplets; and to offset it Haydn writes a heavenly Trio which is captivatingly Austrian – like the faint echo of some long-forgotten Tyrolean song. The Finale is a *moto perpetuo* in which the pulse of the music is whipped along in quaver triplets (for some reason this sounds quicker if written in two-four with triplets than it had been written in the more conventional six-eight). At the end the brass instruments hammer the repeated chords to a rousing close. No. 41 is the most successful of Haydn's festive C major symphonies up to now.

Symphony No. 48 in C ('Maria Theresa')

Scoring: 2 oboes, 2 horns in C *alto* and F, (timpani?), strings [bassoon continuo].

It was supposed that this brilliant, nervous Symphony had been composed and performed to honour Empress Maria Theresa in Eszterháza, and it was always presumed that it was the one the Empress heard in the Chinese pavilion. Now that we have discovered an authentic manuscript by Joseph Elssler with the pencilled dated 1769 on the cover, we know that No. 48 was certainly not composed especially for the 1773 visit. Perhaps it was the *pièce de resistance* of the great festivity, at which Maria Theresa was present, on 25 July 1770 at Kittsee (*vide* Chronicle). The Elssler copy has no timpani part. Of the ten versions of trumpets and timpani found in other MSS., all are dubious. We

may hope to discover the authentic timpani part, for it is likely that Haydn added one later (even if he may have composed the work without one). In our score (Doblinger and Philharmonia 592), we have added the one from the parts in the Esterházy Archives.[1]

Leaving all these philological questions, it is interesting to observe that, with its new dating of 1769, No. 48 is almost exactly parallel with the Op. 9 Quartets. Haydn's music at this period is still uneven: in Op. 9 there is only one masterpiece, the D minor, while in the Symphonies of 1768 and 1769 there are the outstanding Nos. 26, 41, 48 and the great *Sinfonia* 'La Passione' (No. 49). People may have mistaken the name of No. 48 but the message is right: it is a Symphony for Queens and Emperors, with a brilliance, panache and nervous drive that have not lost their force even after the interval of more than two hundred years. From the tense excitement of the opening (with those reeling horn parts, which have to be heard to be believed); to the ferocious crescendo(s)[2] of the development section; to the quiet intensity of its slow movement (also with difficult and exposed horn solos [bars 50ff.]); to the stamping, driving force of its Menuet (with magnificent fanfares; and what a strange, sombre Trio, with those ominous low C's in the double bass and 'cello parts); to the breathless pace of the Finale, this Symphony seems to have been composed in one great inspirational sweep. There are, throughout, curiously dark-hued shadows which sometimes cloud the music for bars on end. In the first movement, the tense section in *piano* between the two statements of the principal subject; this passage (bars 7ff.) ends in the dominant of C minor. We have spoken of the Trio above. In the Finale, the long, pre-Mozartian

1 Before the discovery of the Elssler copy of No. 48, our knowledge of the Symphony, textually, had been based primarily on these parts in the Esterházy Archives. It now transpires that these parts are absolutely not authentic. Considering that the Esterházy Archives are the sanctuary for much of Haydn's music before 1790, that statement requires some explanation. Six years after the Empress and her entourage left Eszterháza, there was a dreadful fire at the Castle (1779 – see Chronicle, p. 420). All the priceless instruments and the music – except for some autographs that Haydn happened to have in his quarters (which did not catch fire) – including all the orchestral materials of his symphonies composed up to 1779 (some seventy works) were destroyed. Later, Haydn very sensibly went to Vienna and visited some professional copyists who had been pirating his music for twenty years with great financial gain to themselves and none to Haydn. The composer bought a big collection of his earlier symphonies so that he could have the music at Eszterháza and Eisenstadt; and what he bought was parts, much more useful to him than scores. Among his acquisitions was the copy of Symphony No. 48, with two trumpets doubling the horns in the fast movements and a kettledrum part which appears in no other source. It is patently not a Haydnesque addition but it is the only one which (we might say) has a certain authority from having been, as it were, sanctioned by Haydn, at least indirectly: he could, after all, have thrown away the timpani part if he had thoroughly disapproved of it. Nevertheless, we hope that the genuine kettledrum part will one day appear.

2 The first one (bars 95ff.) is in the Elssler MS., the second one (bars 99ff.) was added on that basis by the editor (Landon).

The first page of the difficult first horn (C *alto*) part from Symphony No. 48, from the MS. parts copied by Joseph Elssler Sen.

chromatic inner lines are in striking contrast to the whirling pace of the rest (bars 36ff., 124ff.), and this dichotomy is most dramatically (and in an astonishingly Mozartian way) presented at the beginning of development section – the nervous quavers of the first violin chattering over the long, sinuous and off-beat (beginning on the second beat in many cases, especially at bars 73ff.) lines of the other voices: we are reminded of the introduction to the 'Linz' Symphony (K.425), which is, of course (since Mozart, like Haydn, had perfect pitch), in C major. 'Maria Theresa' is a great and indeed germinal work: its immediate success may be documented in the many contemporary MSS. which circulated throughout the Monarchy and Germany. Of the various editions, the one by Sieber and Imbault in Paris (Imbault also issued the authentic texts of the 'Paris' Symphonies) was published in 1784 (announced in the *Affiches* on 1 April) and seems to have used an authentic text; at any rate textually his edition is remarkably close to the Joseph Elssler MS. (see details in Philharmonia 592, XLVIIff.). Haydn may have sent an authentic copy for publication to either Sieber or Imbault (he

was in touch with Sieber in the 1780s). It is one of the very few Haydn symphonies of this period that survived all through the nineteenth century in various editions, some with elegant, spurious trumpet and timpani parts composed in the Mozartian manner.[1]

Symphony No. 44 in E minor
('Trauer'/'Mourning')

Scoring: 2 oboes, 2 horns (E and G), strings [bassoon continuo].

The name is said to come from Haydn, who expressed a desire to have the slow movement played at his funeral; perhaps the story is apocryphal, but the title, for once, is apt. It is one of the greatest of Haydn's *Sturm und Drang* productions; a new kind of symphony which is neither a chamber work nor a grand one with trumpets and timpani. Here Haydn finally achieved the

1 These spurious, if very competent, trumpet and drum parts, clearly *post*-1800 and with the knowledge of late Mozart within them, may be seen in the Eulenburg score (No. 517); they were first printed by Simrock. See also Landon, *SYM*, p. 690.

form he had sought so long, for the emotional world of the *sonata da chiesa* was successfully transferred to the normal symphonic structure. Not quite normal, though, because Haydn shifts the weight, after the enormously powerful opening movement, to the slow movement but allows a breathing space by inserting the minuet in between. In overall balance, this Symphony is a miracle of judgement.

The first movement has the (for Haydn) unusual marking 'Allegro con brio'; one is reminded of the great C minor Symphony No. 52/I, marked 'Allegro ·assai [e] con brio'. Both have another feature in common: the unison opening, which creates a sense of power and urgency. In No. 44, Haydn divides the first subject into two statements, which might be described: a–b; a–c. This double announcement of the principal theme is something we have heard in No. 39/I and No. 48/I. It gives us a chance to become familiar with the first four notes (in the case of No. 44/I), which play a vital role throughout the movement. We hear them as the bass line of the transition to the dominant and suddenly they emerge in the violins simply as intervals of the fifth. They form the basis of what passes for the second subject and have a decisive part in the development section. It is interesting to see how Haydn increases the tension of this middle part. He uses a motif from the bridge-passage, with the characteristic rhythm ♪♪♪ ♪ ♪ ♪♪♪; and now this fragment 'takes over' the development, growing more and more urgent, until it is compressed to ♪♪♪ ♪ ♪♪♪ ♪, backed by a series of syncopations. The syncopations shift to semi-quavers, and just when we think the music cannot stand any more tension, Haydn pushes the music into *fortissimo* (bar 98) and precipitates us – that is the only word – into the recapitulation, which here assumes an entirely new function: that of being an emotional necessity, a release from the tension of the development section. Instead of the previous double announcement of the main subject, Haydn compresses them into one and adds a passage of great effectiveness just after the *subito pp* (bar 114): the lower strings break from the semibreve into quavers, and though *pp*, what arresting quavers they are! And what a marvellously gaunt sound the oboes have when they enter in this *pp* context: the whole passage has something vaguely Gluckian about it, a classical repose which is doubly effective flanked, as it is, by the most turbulent music Haydn has written hitherto. There is a coda, introduced by a *fermata*: Haydn has reserved his final contrapuntal effect with the main theme, using it canonically with itself.

In a way, that canonic passage is a hint of things to come: for the *Menuetto* is a fantastic piece of contrapuntal prestidigitation: a strict 'Canone in Diapason' (Haydn's marking) between the top and bottom line at the interval of one bar. Nothing could more effectively follow the tension of the first movement. The Minuet releases the tension but is so interesting that the mood is not broken; it is a *tour-de-force* not only contrapuntally but in

overall timing. Often in Haydn's earlier symphonies in minor keys, such as Nos. 26 or 39, the Trio was an anticlimax. Not so in No. 44. Having lowered the tension, Haydn has another and equally effective device for this Trio: extreme lyricism. He has set the stage well: the strings are marked *pp*, and as students of Haydn know, every exaggerated dynamic mark (*pp* or *ff*) in his scores has some structural or emotional function: here it draws discreet attention to the sudden shift into E major, which is a heavenly release after the sombre E minor up to now, and it also focuses our ear on the beautiful *legato* lines of the strings. But great is our astonishment to find the first horn (in E; the second is in G) joining the first violins with the melody and ascending to sounding *e''*, the top of its *tessitura*. The second part of the Trio starts with off-beat *forzati* and suddenly breaks into *ff*. The violent dynamic contrasts of this Trio are typical of *Sturm und Drang*: the older 'terraced' dynamics of the Baroque period[1] will not do for the vastly increased emotions of the new era. This is especially true of the lovely Adagio, like the Trio, in E major, and with the muted violins that we have gradually come to expect and which, from now, become a regular feature of these slow movements. As in the other Adagios, the wind instruments are very sparingly used; but when they do enter at bar 16, it is with a crescendo that surges up to a *forte* only to repeat the effect immediately afterwards. We have noted that Haydn likes to give us hints of things to come. The Trio in E major foretold that key for the slow movement. And now, in the recapitulation of the Adagio, what do we find but the horn once again soaring to top *e''*.

The Finale carries things further than even the first movement would lead us to expect. The unison opening is tensely rhythmic, with those inserted silences that increase the power so effectively. Just as in the first movement, the first (seven) notes of the Finale prove to be essential, and so does another phrase from the first subject

This is essentially a monothematic movement pitched at an emotional level higher than anything since the Finale of Symphony No. 29 (but the quality was different then). It is in abbreviated sonata form, and the development rises to a fine pitch of excitement through a long, slowly rising sequence built upon the first seven notes of the main theme, this being repeated constantly until the tension is relieved by the music hurling itself into a series of semiquavers. The Symphony as a whole was undoubtedly Haydn's greatest achievement in the *genre* hitherto, and is only equalled by

1 By terraced dynamics is meant the straight alternation of *f* and *p*, often to underline a repeated section: the repeats coincide with the phrase even if this starts before or after the first beat

♪ | ♪♪♪ ♪ | ♪♪♪ ♪ | – as opposed to crescendos, off-
   f   *p*   *f*

beat *fz*, and so on.

the 'Farewell' Symphony, a similarly potent and lasting influence. Together with Piano Sonata No. 33 in C minor (XVI:20) and the Op. 20 Quartets, they revolutionized the history of music. The great period of the Viennese classical style has begun, and it is no exaggeration to say that their music was never the same again.

Symphony No. 52 in C minor

Scoring: 2 oboes, bassoon,[1] 2 horns (C *alto*, E flat or C *basso*), strings.

This is another central work in the *Sturm und Drang* movement, big in its scope and emotional range. Like so many of these works (Nos. 44, 46, 51, 56), it begins with a unison passage – always a symbol of strength in Austrian music of this period. The first movement has one most unusual feature: the second subject, seemingly in complete contrast to the first (the dotted rhythm, the *p* marking), comes in twice, the second time with a mournful little extension, *pp*. We say seemingly, because Haydn as usual has taken great pains to weld the movement into a unity by connecting motivic links. Thus the figure of the first subject

(bars 4ff.) has a clear intervallic relationship to this in the second:

while the little tail of the second subject, when it appears the first time –

– is obviously a derivative of the figure

and especially

of the bridge passage. Also, the rhythmic interconnection of all these examples is clear: thus ♩ ♩ 𝅘𝅥𝅮|♩ becomes ♩. 𝅘𝅥𝅮♩, and in the passage between the two entries of the second subject, this same rhythmic figure remains prominent.

The massively powerful development section, in which the double counterpoint is so masterly, goes to work on another section of the bridge passage to the second subject: where the violins have semibreves and the bass line is in crotchets (bars 20ff.). Now, this broadly moving texture is placed against the context of the second subject (a

part of the passage has been quoted *supra*, p. 275). In the recapitulation there are once more the two entries of the second subject, but the second time it is spun out in a *pianissimo* kind of codetta which is most affecting (also quoted *supra*, p. 274). Notice the lean texture of the orchestration, in which the high C horn, hitherto reserved for queenly banquets and princely diversion, fulfils another function. The sound created here is unique in the history of Viennese classical orchestration hitherto.

The second movement is the necessary foil to all this drama. With low C horns, it is almost like a stately Spanish dance: cat-like, reserved, with the sweetly nasal muted violins that Haydn liked so much. The wind instruments are used sparingly, like a delicate watercolour; only once does the texture violently change. At the beginning of the second section, Haydn modulates into D minor and then A minor, with nervous strings and a wash of colour in the winds.

The Menuetto is in a leaden atmosphere, also in contrast with the first movement and often in rather severe two-part texture; but the horns still remain in C *basso*. There are off-beat *forzati* in the second part of the minuet proper which will constitute a major feature of the C major Trio.

With the Finale (Presto, *alla breve*), we are back to the original orchestration with the high C horn. This final movement is a grim *tour-de-force*: it is either loud or soft; only in one section (bars 93ff. of the development) do we have juxtaposed *f* and *p*. Otherwise this is a relentlessly forward-driving movement, perhaps the farthest Haydn ever went in his *Sturm und Drang* style (or at least, it is the equal of that other extraordinary Finale, No. 44's). It carries to a logical conclusion the pattern established in No. 49's Finale. The end is particularly effective: after five massive chords (bars 175ff., *vide supra*, p. 277) we move swiftly to the *dénouement*. It is the severely logical ending of a movement whose total effect was conceived with mathematical precision. This is the grandfather of Beethoven's Fifth Symphony, also created with mathematical and economic precision (especially the first movement).

Symphony No. 43 in E flat ('Mercury'/Merkur')

Scoring: 2 oboes, 2 horns, strings [bassoon continuo]. It is not known why this work was called 'Mercury' in the nineteenth century.

It might be said that Austrian composers *de anno* 1770 wrote two kinds of symphonies. First, there were those 'grand' ones with trumpets and timpani. Often one finds such works specifically listed in contemporary programmes, e.g. 'Grosse Symphonie, mit Trompeten und Paucken'. In Haydn's case, this means C major and *alto* horns with drums, sometimes with trumpets. But the Austrians also cultivated another kind of work, a chamber symphony, with singing allegros. J. B. Vanhal was a specialist in this sort of symphony which often began (unlike most of Haydn's) with a *cantabile* theme, *piano*, on the upbeat. This is not to say that chamber symphonies did not include

---

1 Apparently a later addition: see Philharmonia 593, pp. xxif.

stirring tuttis and many loud passages; but the listener will hear the difference at once between Mozart's chamber Symphony in A, K.201 (or in B flat, K.319), and the 'Grosse Symphonie mit Trompeten und Paucken' which is the 'Haffner' Symphony (K. 385). There is a similar difference between the 'Mercury' Symphony, which is definitely of chamber proportions and sound, and the much more extrovert and louder No. 41 (or 38). Actually, during the period under discussion, Haydn begins to merge the two kinds: not so much with trumpets and timpani (though we soon begin to encounter those instruments in keys other than C, e.g. No. 54) but in overall style. One would hardly call No. 44 a chamber symphony: its scope, its language, its message are all too large in scale for that description.

On the other hand, No. 43 is the Austrian chamber symphony *par excellence*. The *genre* was highly successful, and not only with Austrian monks and German princes. No. 43 figured in the 'Musique du Roy 1782' at the Court of Louis XVI. (No doubt it was Marie Antoinette who specially appreciated hearing something which reminded her of a happier and less troubled childhood...). The whole first theme is intensely lyrical, in fact one of the longest of its kind that Haydn ever wrote; he almost loses himself in the slow-moving crotchets. To balance this *embarras de richesse*, we have a long passage with the usual marching quavers in the bass line and violins in semiquavers; and yet the astute listener will note that this is not a *heavy* tutti. The orchestra is transparent, with the horns providing a 'cutting edge' to the texture. There is a great deal of material to balance the opening subject, but instead of a second subject there is simply a reworking of the principal theme. In the *fausse reprise*, we have one of those theatrical poses that seem to be derived from the *opera buffa* – the careful cultivation of the unexpected. When the recapitulation finally appears, Haydn loses himself in a bemused contemplation of the first subject's lyrical extension.

This is altogether a Symphony in which Haydn frequently allows himself the unusual luxury of dwelling on a subject longer, perhaps, than the material would lead us to expect. In the rhapsodic slow movement, the wind instruments are used very sparingly. The violins are muted, and as in almost all these slow movements, there is a strong sense of nostalgia. Here Haydn is monumentally sidetracked by a little phrase

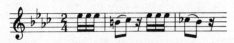

A large part of the development section is concerned with an extension of this phrase, which Haydn pushes to the point of obsession.

The Menuetto is marvellously kinetic and very Austrian. It could hardly have been written by an Italian or an Englishman. Many years later, Haydn was talking to a Swedish colleague after the first public performance of *The Creation*. The conversation fell on Haydn's minuets, and the composer related how he had been given credit for inventing this kind of symphonic minuet; he warned the Swedish colleague not to take them too quickly; the Swede hummed a minuet, and Haydn said, 'That's much too quick' and explained that the bass line would not be clear at that tempo.[1] Of course we know that Haydn's minuets speeded up, reaching allegro in many of the Salomon Symphonies and presto, one-in-the-bar, in some of the late quartets. But in No. 43, we have a superb example of this sturdy, not-too-fast and not-too-slow minuet. The Trio is graceful, starting in C minor but moving to B flat; the ambiguous feeling remains in the second part, too, which again begins in C minor but ends in E flat, the home key (of the Trio, too). The wind instruments are used with the same delicacy as in the slow movement, adding a touch of nasal colour (in the oboes) and an organlike pedal point in the horns. Sparingly though these instruments are used, every student of composition can learn from this Trio how to achieve a perfect balance, in *piano* context, between strings and wind instruments.

Haydn is not letting us forget that this is a chamber symphony, whose strength is in its grace: in the Finale, there is another long, legato subject, just as in the first movement. Haydn is now building symphonies round a central idea, and we shall observe several such central ideas in other works of this period. And just as the long singing theme of the first movement was balanced by a sturdy tutti, the same contrast obtains in the Finale. There is a long coda to this movement, and once again, Haydn dwells long and lovingly on one of his lyrical passages. Time seems to stop, the note values get slower and slower, and finally everything dies away except for the first violin, which goes up to an enigmatic *g* flat. There follows one of Haydn's magnificent silences, and then the music plunges into a last tutti and this elegant chamber symphony is at an end.

Symphony No. 42 in D major

Scoring: 2 oboes, 2 bassoons,[2] 2 horns, strings.

No. 42 is a witty Symphony in the traditional key of D major, the most popular of all keys in eighteenth-century symphonies. Everything

---

1 See *Haydn: the Years of 'The Creation' 1796–1800*, p. 456.
2 We have often mentioned that a bassoon was added 'as a matter of course' to the basso continuo. In several of the works now under examination, we may find concrete proof of the bassoons' role. Haydn's autograph of No. 42 specifies no bassoons at the beginning of the Symphony; but in the middle of the Finale, there is a whole little section of wind band, and the bass line suddenly directs: '2 Fagotti' (to which Haydn later added 'o Violoncelli' in case a band might not have two bassoons). Now obviously the bassoons did not sit through three movements and then play sixteen bars, only to stop playing afterwards. They played with the bass line before. Perhaps they even played in the slow movements of these symphonies, because there is a note at the beginning of No. 47's slow movement, 'Fagotto sempre col Basso', and no bassoon is mentioned before or afterwards in Haydn's autograph of that work. Similar 'sudden' mentions of the bassoon(s) may be found in Nos. 45 (Finale) and 55 (also Finale).

sounds alive in D major, but especially the strings; and Haydn exploits this joyously throughout the work. The first movement starts out like an operatic aria, with 'joking' acciaccature in the violins, followed by a singing melody; and this joke is magnified when the theme is repeated shortly afterwards, by piling up the acciaccature and introducing triplets. This is undoubtedly the first Haydn symphony which shows pervasively the influence of Italian comic opera. (Haydn himself had just completed *Le pescatrici* the year before [1770], his finest stage work to date.) Here is an instrumental piece which could be the *sinfonia* to some *opera buffa*: it is now the unexpected modulation, the quacking bassoon, the strutting horn that inform this music: the *sala terrena* at Eszterháza has become a stage. Previously one sensed, now and then, a certain stiffness in Haydn's music, a certain scholarly bent (much more pronounced in his brother Michael); now, with one sweep of the *buffa* broom, the music is completely relaxed. The two main characteristics of the first movement are brilliance and humour, though both are relieved – as in all great comedians – by a tender side. (Like Watteau, Haydn was 'tendre et peut-être un peu berger...').

The beautiful Andantino e cantabile retains the wind instruments; but they are employed almost colouristically. The melody sounds like an old song, a church tune perhaps; Haydn has learned the trick of writing music so close to folk-songs as to be almost identical with the real thing. It was a conscious effort, too: we have quoted a cancelled passage 'for too learned ears' (*supra*, p. 279). More and more, Haydn felt that *Vox populi* was *Vox Dei...*

The Menuet, so infectious and gay, leads to an enchanting Trio, where the *piano* violins imitate far-away D trumpets, even to their typical trills. In the Finale Haydn also creates a new and revolutionary form: the characteristic Haydnesque rondo. Perhaps this is the first time it appears, at least in a symphony (a similar 'hit tune' Finale, with a different structure, is in the Quartet, Op. 17, No. 3, of 1771). The tune that we seem to know the minute we have heard it; the delightful wind-band sextet that follows the 'B' section, right out of a wind-band divertimento (of which Haydn wrote many); even the *fermata* preceded by a little sentimental journey; the brave end, with the violins in their energetic semiquavers – all these are stylistic details dear to Haydn's famous rondos which conquered Europe in the next decade.

Symphony No. 51 in B flat

Scoring: 2 oboes, 2 horns (B flat *alto*, E flat), strings [bassoon continuo].

This is the kind of symphony that, in the years 1771–4, made Haydn's reputation as a revolu-

tionary thinker. On the exterior, we have a minuet with two trios,[1] a second movement which could be from a horn concerto, and a variety of dynamic markings that must have startled many remote monasteries and castles unused to seeing words like 'calando' (meaning rallentando and decrescendo) and the wild profusion of *f*, *ff*, *p* and *pp*, often in immediate proximity. It was a time for exaggeration: in the first movement, we slide in the exposition from B flat into G minor, and from *pp* to *ff*. Soft string passages with gliding crotchets lead to passages of real contrapuntal ferocity (see the development section, after the *fausse reprise* in E flat, bars 116ff.). Two-part exchanges between the violins seem to come from a string quartet; but rarely does Haydn use his little orchestra with such violence.

The solo horn writing of the slow movement exploits the very top and bottom of the instrument's range (see the musical example, *supra*, p. 276). In the middle section there is a beautiful interlude for strings alone – the violins, as usual, muted – in which Haydn continues the triplets initiated towards the end of the first section. The music dwindles away to the first violins all by themselves. This is real music for a chamber orchestra, for the solitude of Eszterháza and a small audience of genuine connoisseurs.

The MS. parts for the Minuet of this Symphony, now in the Esterházy Archives, have the following 'spiral'. The bass part is only written out once and alternately played in several clefs (see example): this is a joke only for the benefit of the players (it cannot be heard by the audience at all).

The first Trio is for strings alone, with a Lombard (as it is called) snap in the melody; some manuscripts omit this first Trio, which was possibly an afterthought (the chromatic curve into the second part reminds one of the same effect in Mozart's 'Haffner' Symphony, composed a decade later). The second Trio is another page from a double horn concerto (Haydn actually wrote one: it is lost). Here the first horn twice reaches high *bb''*, the highest note ever written for horn: Haydn writes it once more, for an E flat horn, in the Terzetto 'Pietà di me'. And again, the second horn plunges down to the lowest register (see the musical example *supra*, p. 276). It suggests Michael Kelly's words that Haydn's orchestra was indeed a 'band of professors'.

The Finale is one of the earliest of Haydn's famous rondos (that is, always returning to the 'A' section in the tonic; though here Haydn takes care to vary the theme, the orchestration and the dynamic marks when the 'A' returns). For contrast there is a lilting oboe solo in E flat and a ferocious *ff* section in G minor with the wide leaps in the violin

1 Trio I seems to have been a later addition; see Philharmonia 593, p. xxi.

[Symphony No. 51: Minuet]

8 Tact   8 Tact

part that Haydn likes to write at this period. But above all this movement has the high spirits and sense of impish fun (bars 86–88) that have endeared these rondos to everyone for two hundred years.

Symphony No. 45 in F sharp minor ('Farewell'/'Abschied')

Scoring: 2 oboes, bassoon, 2 horns (A, E, F sharp), strings (four violins in the last part of the Finale).

Chronologically, this is probably the last Symphony in a minor key that Haydn was to write for many years (though, as we have seen above, No. 52 just might have been written afterwards). In fact it was to be a full decade before he turned to the minor in a symphony (No. 78, 1782), and by then Haydn's values, and his attitude towards the minor, had changed radically.

Apart from the obvious programmatic connotations, No. 45 is a fascinating and highly original piece of music. With this Symphony he established a tonal precedent to which he would later revert when composing symphonies in the minor: the dispersal of the tonic minor by the relative major and the tonic major:

First movement: F sharp minor
Second movement: A major
Third movement: F sharp major
Finale: F sharp minor (Presto)
    A major (Adagio, part one)
    F sharp major (Adagio, part two, from bar 68).

Here we see Haydn consciously trying to avoid the tonal concentration of such works as No. 49 (all except the Trio being in F minor) and 44 (which employs only E minor and E major).

Formally, the first movement is startlingly original, possibly the most 'far-out' sonata form movement of Haydn's whole career. The horns are crooked in A and E, and by manipulating these two instruments, Haydn can achieve F sharp minor chords (e.g. *f sharp – a*; or *g sharp – b*) in pure intonation. The first subject strides down the F sharp minor triad and is provided with a strangely unsettling accompaniment in syncopated notes (second violin) whenever it appears, in whatever key and at whatever dynamic level. Occasionally the syncopations are taken out of context, as shortly before each double bar (56ff. and 195ff.) when they are given to the first violins: this ominous passage, where the second oboe and lower strings move in legato crotchets, is almost a call to the barricades. What can Prince Esterházy have thought of this dangerously violent music? And why did Haydn never touch the minor key in a symphony for the next ten years?

Prince Esterházy was a trained and performing musician: he will have heard the very odd sound of this movement; and he will have noted that the subsidiary subject appears only once, in D major, in the development section. Afterwards, what seems to be the recapitulation sets in; but it is in its a new kind of *fausse reprise*, in that it starts out like any *fausse reprise* but then turns out to be the real, though false, recapitulation: false because Haydn simply goes on developing the music. This is complete freedom of form, and freedom of musical language, too, on an unprecedented scale. Nothing like it occurs in the Viennese classical school before Beethoven. But though all the rules of this potent Allegro assai are broken, it has a unity (also motivically) and power undreamt of by listeners to Haydn's music even a few years before.

The languid, hauntingly beautiful Adagio is in the relative major, with muted violins. As usual, the wind instruments are employed with monkish fastidiousness: in the first section, up to the double bar, the oboes play only in eleven of the seventy-six bars, the horns not at all. As the Symphony progresses, we shall take note of Haydn's endeavour to make the keys more ambivalent, particularly with regard to major and minor. When the music reaches the dominant, E major, the theme (a derivation of the main subject, with its grace notes) immediately repeats itself, and continues in, E minor; and the same procedure obtains in the recapitulation, of course in A major and minor; whereas in the middle of the development this same section turns up in C sharp minor and *remains* in C sharp minor (bars 110ff.). The lead-back to the recapitulation is with the first violins all by themselves, a forlorn little cadence; and it is not until the recapitulation itself, at bar 127, that the horns enter for the first time in this Adagio, marked *pp* (a difficult entry, 'cold', as they say in horn language, meaning with no preparation whatever). Towards the end of the recapitulation, Haydn develops a passage previously heard in the exposition at bars 58ff. In the second of its statements, he extends the music, modulating in slow motion to what would be, strictly speaking, B sharp minor, the complicated notation of which Haydn avoids by spelling the chord partly in its enharmonic equivalent, C minor (quoted *supra*, pp. 273f.): the violins have, correctly, *d sharp* and *b sharp* respectively, but the violas and bass line have *g natural* (= the notation in C minor) rather than the correct *f double sharp*. It is an extraordinary modulation, so unusual that in the autograph Haydn places a line over the second violin when it plays first *b sharp* and then immediately afterwards *c natural* (the same note).[1] This is not the only time that Haydn writes little notes to himself (or the copyist?) in the autograph: in the first movement, there is another very unexpected and rather *outré* modulation, in the middle of which (bar 150) Haydn writes 'Sapienti pauca', a cryptic remark that he many years later repeated after what appears to have been a meagre dinner with the Storace family in London. In No. 45, 'Sapienti pauca' can also be a warning to the copyist to watch the number of bars (since the pattern of syncopated notes repeats itself here for sixteen bars) – a charming thought that Haydn could correspond with his copyist, Joseph Elssler, in Latin...

1 Philharmonia 592, p. 154 (see also footnote). 'Sapienti pauca' on p. 145.

The Menuet is in F sharp major, but by bar three the basses have a *d natural* which makes the ensuing half close on C sharp sound as if we were going into F sharp minor. The same unsettling syncopations that we noted in the first movement also appear in the Minuet, which ends, in each section, with a curious phrase, just for the violins, marked *pp*. The Trio is based upon a variant of an old Gregorian melody, the 'Incipit lamentatio' discussed in connection with No. 26 *supra*.

The Finale, a Presto *alla breve*, begins in the lean texture and nervous manner of a typical Haydnesque *Sturm und Drang* conclusion. It must have sounded forbidding to many people; the *Mercure de France*, reviewing it on 24 April 1784, thought it 'un morceau bruyant & sans caractère'. There are some interesting details. Just before the end of the first double bar, the first violins have a passage in which they switch back and forth between open a-string and fingered e-string, and this is very odd-sounding. (Many years later Haydn was to create another strange sound, when the violins play half the slow movement of Symphony No. 97 near the bridge [*sul ponticello*].) When we reach the point where the movement ought to conclude, Haydn starts to modulate, following yet another of those queer syncopated sections (bars 127ff.). The music suddenly ends on a half-close (unison C sharp). There is a pause, and to our astonishment an Adagio begins. The bassoon, which was not mentioned in the autograph before, is given its own line, and there are four violin parts. We, of course, know what is going to happen, and so we may study Haydn's preparation with care. The slow movement has the same richly *cantabile* lines that we have come to expect of Haydn *de anno* 1772, and for a while everything proceeds normally. When the dominant (E major) appears, we note that the oboes and the *second* horn have an elaborate solo section, at the end of which oboe I and horn II blow out their candles, take their instruments and leave. (We must remember that in those days, the orchestras played standing.) There then occurs a kind of middle section and a return to the tonic and the main subject. The bassoon emerges from its previous position as part of the basso continuo, has a little solo, and leaves. The wind-band solo that announced the departure of oboe I and horn II is now repeated, in the tonic, for oboe II and horn I (in A; horn II was in E; even such details are meticulously worked out to serve the structure), after which they leave. Each departing player displays his wares, so to speak, before departing. Up to this point, we have had a regular tripartite slow movement, at least formally. But now a gradual shift begins. It is announced by a long and elaborate solo for the stepchild of the orchestra, the *Violone* (as it was then called) or *Contrabasso* (as we call it now). Haydn always had a weak spot for this unwieldy 'great viola' (the literal translation of 'violone'), and even composed a concerto for it, alas lost, as well as some difficult solo sections in earlier symphonies. We are so engrossed by this huge solo in triplets – technically difficult to keep in tune,

even today with our refined 'Koussevitsky' method – that we scarcely realize that the whole tonal basis of the movement has pivoted from the relative major (A) to the tonic major (F sharp), the arrival of which is marked by the contrabasso's departure. Now there are just the four violins, violas and 'cellos left, and they start playing the music of the Adagio all over again, in F sharp. A great stillness seems to settle on this lonely and beautiful music: the 'cello leaves, then the tutti violins, then the viola. Almost imperceptibly, the orchestra has dwindled away to *Capellmeister* Haydn and *Conzertmeister* Tomasini; finally they, too, have their last, forlorn little solo, ending *pianissimo* and *staccato*, blow out their candles and leave.

Felix Mendelssohn conducted this Symphony at one of his 'historical' Gewandhaus concerts in Leipzig, on 22 February 1838. People had almost forgotten this great *Symphonie in Fis-moll*, with which the concert ended; and Mendelssohn had the musicians blow out their candles and leave, just as at that first occasion on the icy marshes of Eszterháza. The public at the Gewandhaus, wrote Mendelssohn to his sister shortly afterwards, was 'jubilant'. Then he added, obviously profoundly moved by the work, 'it is a curiously melancholy little piece' ('Es ist ein curios melancholisches Stückchen').[1]

Symphony No. 46 in B major

Scoring: 2 oboes, 2 horns, strings [bassoon continuo].

In the eighteenth century, symphonies in F sharp minor were as good as non-existent, apart from Haydn's No. 45; B major symphonies were rare, too, because of intonation problems, but they did exist. Haydn may have heard G. M. Monn's B major Symphony, which was played in Vienna when Haydn was a choir-boy at the Cathedral. Our No. 46 is the composer's only Symphony in this remote key, though he wrote a piano sonata in B which is lost.

By this time, we know at once that the four-note unison opening is destined for contrapuntal development. Haydn is very clever in showing us the theme's possibilities. He takes the first three notes and combines them with a kind of Fuxian countersubject: this takes place before the bridge passage. Then, at the beginning of the development, the four notes are combined with themselves canonically, as was done with the similar subject in No. 44. The *fausse reprise* is here on a large scale. At the real recapitulation, Haydn finally presents us with the theme in full contrapuntal dress: used with itself canonically and with the Fuxian countersubject noted earlier. It is a very terse movement and rather dark-hued.

The Poco Adagio is a kind of sophisticated siciliano, which Haydn had used so effectively in an

1 Susanne Grossmann-Vendrey, *Felix Mendelssohn Bartholdy und die Musik der Vergangenheit*, Regensburg 1969, p. 161.

aria from *Le pescatrici* two years earlier. Here, the music is in the tonic minor, and graced with string passages marked *staccato assai*. It has a definite air of Italy, something which we shall often encounter in Haydn's music: astonishing that he could so closely capture the air of a country he had never seen. But though the gently sad atmosphere is south-of-the-Alps, the refined orchestration is Eszterháza. Haydn puts his horns in D, and when he arrives at the relative major, he can support the melody with the horns and bass line (just before the first double bar), a delightful orchestral innovation more often found in the symphonies by Haydn's brother in Salzburg, Johann Michael.

The Menuet, a slowish and graceful movement, is marked by 'sighing' sequences, an old Baroque device of proceeding upwards or (usually) downwards in a pattern such as the passage illustrated.

which he planned to give in his Mehlgrube concerts, on a little slip of paper which is now owned by the Historical Society of Philadelphia. Apart from the palindromic Minuet & Trio, that which Mozart probably found irresistible is the beginning of the Symphony, with its marching horns. This marching rhythm is an all-pervading rhythmic feature of mature Mozart and he no doubt was automatically attracted to a Haydn movement in which the march was so prevalent (it is a very rare rhythm for Haydn, incidentally). This marching phrase grows instrument by instrument, layer by layer. The second subject introduces the greatest possible contrast, a stalking bass in crotchets, chattering triplets in the violins and a lean oboe line on top. All this is unlike the usual Haydn symphony of this period. The development section grows out of the march

[Symphony No. 46: Menuet]

The Trio is quite unprecedented, being *durchkomponiert* (though with double bars) and of a strangely Balkan flavour. The second part ends in B minor, with rather ominous harmonic and dynamic contrasts.

The Finale, marked 'Presto e scherzando', opens in two-part texture, with just the violins. It is a witty, 'joking' (as the title implies) movement, with a flair for the grotesque. The use of silence is remarkable here, adding a whole series of surprising twists to the music. But nothing prepares us for the bizarre, but also touching, effect in the second half. The music comes to a stop on a half-close in the dominant, followed by a fermata, and then the Menuet (characteristically; from bar 15) begins again, and Haydn lets the whole dance movement (without repeats) unfold before returning to the Finale's main subject. This, too, trails off in the first violins, and the music comes to a stop with two whole bars of rests. Then, with a very comical effect, the horns sound a low pedal point and the theme returns in farewell. It is almost a scene out of the *commedia dell'arte*, with Columbine and Harlequin enacting some kind of pantomime in front of us: basically very amusing but with queer overtones.

Symphony No. 47 in G major

Scoring: 2 oboes, bassoon (only mentioned specifically in the slow movement), 2 horns, strings.

We have noted a serious, even scholarly side to Haydn, which manifests itself particularly in the Op. 20 'Sun' Quartets of 1772. Even the little third movement of this work is a palindromic 'Menuet al Roverso' and 'Trio al Roverso'. Perhaps this Minuet was one reason that Mozart admired the work. He jotted down its theme, together with those of two other Haydn symphonies (Nos. 75 and 62)[1] and another, hitherto unidentified piece,

1 Köchel-Einstein, 3rd. edition (1947), pp. 510 and 1009.

theme and becomes gradually more serious, even ominous. The climax of this move from light to dark is the recapitulation itself, where the entire theme is put into the tonic minor. The build-up of the march now sounds menacing and sinister; but the block of oboes and horns, massing itself over the strings, lingers on a moment; suddenly the second subject comes in, and the sun is out from behind the clouds.

The second movement was an old favourite of Dr Burney, who called the theme 'an old organ point',[2] and Haydn stresses the point by requiring a bassoon to double the bass line throughout. Connoisseurs will have relished that in this delicate variation movement (Un poco adagio, cantabile) the theme is constructed in double counterpoint at the octave so that the bottom and top lines can be reversed.

The Minuet and Trio are also constructed with great skill. The players read their music twice for

2 Burney's letter is to the Rev. Thomas Twining; it is incomplete, beginning on the second sheet of paper and was written (as the last paragraph suggests) about 1782. British Museum, Add. 39932, f. 165. Rosemary Hughes (now Mrs Smith) kindly copied the whole letter for us in 1953. '... There have been 6 or 7 of Haydn's Symphonies tolerably cooked for the Harpd. or P.forte – but whole movements being omitted, in 3 of them, for the sake of my scholars, I have adapted and given them to print, and will let you know when they are ready. The 1st Symph. you know. It begins thus, in D [*incipit* of No. 53 Finale, Version 'B' or Overture II:7] &c but the 1st movemt. is omitted, of wch the Base begins thus [*incipit* of No. 53/I after slow introduction, vc.-basso part]. Giordani and Carter have both adapted this symph. entirely, but *secondo di me*, very ill – both having taken unwarrantable liberties with the Author. 2 of the 3 charming Symps. wch you purchased in parts have been likewise printed for the p. forte, but without adagio to either. These you will soon have, entire. There is a delicious Symph. in E♭ – adapted by Giordani [*incipit* of No. 74/I]&c. – get it. Another of the 3 in parts set by Dr Hayes – 'tis in F [*incipit* of No. 67/I]. He has made it

ten bars, up to the double bar, and then they read it twice backwards, arriving at the beginning. The same applies to the Trio. Haydn has taken great pains so that the orchestration and placement of dynamic marks help one to hear the music when it is played in reverse.

The theme of the Finale starts out on a chord without the tonic root, and this scheme gives a strongly anacrustic push to the *piano* section which is not resolved until the *forte*. Another quality of this Finale which appears when he arrives at the dominant is its Balkan snap. (A section of this music, with some sharp dissonances, is quoted in a later volume of this biography.)[1]

These dashing grace notes and syncopated inner parts are Romany legacies, and very much a part of the great heritage of what would later (long after Haydn's death) be called the Austro-Hungarian Monarchy.

Symphony No. 65 in A major

Scoring: 2 oboes, 2 horns, strings [bassoon continuo].

As we have observed earlier, this Symphony may have been conceived as incidental music for some play given at Eszterháza in the early 1770s. Its unusual features in the Andante have been mentioned in part previously (*vide* p. 280). A few brief notes on the Trio and Finale. In the Trio we once again have Gypsy influences (those curious grace notes and that same slightly unsettling quality that we always find whenever Haydn turns to the language of the Balkans).

The Finale is a hunting piece, in 12/8 time, with difficult parts for the horns which, we must not forget, were called 'cors de chasse' (or the local linguistic equivalent thereof) throughout Europe. It is evocative music, as characteristic as Lancret's painting 'A picnic after the hunt'. Nowadays it is difficult for most of us to realize the vital part hunting played in eighteenth-century aristocratic life; but there are many hunting pieces among

Haydn's works, perhaps the most famous being the Overture to *La fedeltà premiata* (later the 'La Chasse' Finale to Symphony No. 73). It was an essential part of life on the great Austrian and Hungarian estates, as reflected in these 'chasse' pieces.

Symphony No. 50 in C major

Scoring: 2 oboes, 2 horns in C *alto*, 2 trumpets, timpani, strings [bassoon continuo].

It is now believed that Symphony No. 50 was put together from the otherwise lost music to *Der Götterrath* (Prologue to *Philemon und Baucis*), which was performed in the marionette theatre at Eszterháza for the Empress Maria Theresa in September 1773. The first two movements of the Symphony were the Overture to *Der Götterrath*, according to this plausible theory (the MS. also included an orchestral piece from *Der Götterrath*, published in *HJB* I, pp. 157f. in facsimile);[1] the last two movements were added later to complete the work. Perhaps this is the Symphony which was, according to tradition, played in the Chinese pavilion for the Empress; Haydn and the musicians were dressed up in Chinese costumes.

No. 50 opens with a stately introduction, something of a rarity in Haydn's works of this period; Baroque specialists will notice that the shortened upbeats and up-dottings are actually written out – 𝄾♪♪♪ and 𝄾♪♪.♪ – a precise form of notation almost never found in a Handelian score, for example, but immensely valuable as a hint as to how these Baroque clichés were performed (Handel had only been dead fourteen years when this Symphony was written). The Allegro di molto is typical vintage Haydn of the period – the strings in semiquavers, the bass in quavers, punctuated by brass and percussion and held together with long phrases (or notes) in the oboes. It is extremely concise music.

Were the Empress's well-known conservative views on music known to Haydn? It is hard to think they were not. Maria Theresa had been taught by Hasse, and to Hasse she remained faithful her life long. It had been Hasse who, in 1767, persuaded the Empress that Haydn's *Stabat Mater* was a great work – something for which Haydn remained grateful his whole life.[2] She also adored Reutter and especially the *Requiem* (*vide supra*, p.

[footnote 2 – *cont.*]

very hard and awkward; but you can simplify – 'tis delightful. There are two printed by Bland for the Harpd. one in G which is begun by the Fr. Horn. I forget how, but something like this [accurate *incipit* of No. 47/I]. 'Seek and ye shall find'. The slow movemt. on an old org. point is admirable for that Instrumt. In this last only mind in the last Allegro or Rondeau how he returns to the subject. There is another in B♭ wch begins with a short Ada° of only 2 or 3 bars [No. 71] that I do not like so well – however among old and common things there is much good and new. . . . What disputes and squabbles about opera Management! If Gallini's [Sir John Gallini] claims to the Theatre are valid, we shall have the dear Pacchierotti another year. . . . – I have stimulated a wish to get Haydn over as opera composer – but mum mum – yet – a correspondence is open, and there is a great likelihood of it, if these cabals, and litigations ruin not the opera entirely . . . The Girls are luckily all out of Town – but wherever they are you are sure of their love – and so take my benediction, though you can *give* a better yourself. vive felice.

1 See *Haydn in England 1791–1795*, p. 580.

1 See Reihe XXIV, Band I (*Philemon und Baucis*) of *Joseph Haydn Werke*, and the Kritischer Bericht, edited by Jürgen Braun.

2 There are various versions of this particular episode, and the sources confusingly say 'Mass' instead of *Stabat Mater*, but in view of Hasse's well-known positive views about the latter work, it seems certain that it was the work which the old Italian master recommended to the Empress. In *A Mozart Pilgrimage* (London 1955, p. 196), we read one version of the encounter as told to Vincent Novello by J. A. Streicher, the piano builder and Beethoven's friend, in 1829:

Streicher also told us that the first Mass which Haydn produced in Public, the Empress Maria Theresa was present –

182). In any event, this Andante moderato is deliberately conservative: it returns to the orchestral layout of Symphony No. 16, with its violoncello obbligato doubling the melody at the octave, which had been composed about a dozen years earlier; and it again turns to the regal French dotted rhythm: deliberate flattery? The scoring is distinctly Haydn's all the same: those octave doublings in his early quartets had created a real *furore*, and a critical scandal, in their time; people had loved or hated them at the first encounter. There is another distinctive feature, too: throughout the first part the oboes are silent; it is not till the second part that they suddenly enter, with the recapitulation. A properly conservative slow movement had no wind parts; this one had almost no wind parts. . . .

The sturdy Menuet uses the chordal skeleton of the introduction to the first movement; there is a sudden shift to the tonic minor in the middle, and the texture and mood become heavier, with the lower parts taking over the semiquavers that have appeared off and on during the first eleven bars. The Trio – Haydn writes on the autograph, 'the rests in the trio must be written out because there are no repeats in the trio' – is also unconventional: it begins just like the Minuet proper and then

swerves into F major and a lyrical oboe solo; and at the end it lingers on the dominant of A, into which key Haydn never takes us, because at that point the Menuet is repeated.

The monothematic Finale (marked Presto) has separate parts for the high horns and trumpets (hitherto *unisoni*): notice, at the end of the first part (bars 60ff.) how Haydn saves the horns' lips by allotting the high *g*'s (and *f sharps*) to the trumpet. The movement develops considerable force as it progresses, particularly that syncopated section that first appears at bars 98ff. and looks swiftly forward to the language of Beethoven: the next time it appears there is even a Beethovenian dissonance: D sharp clashing with E at the same octave (bar 124). The end of the movement contains a wonderfully original modulation through the dominant of D minor into F, but instead of proceeding to F Haydn drops into a deceptive cadence and returns to the tonic – which he now re-establishes in a triple series of fanfares, with high horns, trumpets and kettledrums (reinforcing, originally enough, oboes, violas and 'cello-basses).

It is rather incredible to record that Symphony No. 50 was first published by the Haydn Society in 1951.

[footnote 2 *continued*]

Hasse stood by her and she asked his opinion of the young composer.

Hasse told the Empress that Haydn possessed all the qualities that are required to form the highest style of writing viz. beautiful and expressive melody, sound harmony, original invention, variety of effect, symmetrical design, knowledge of the powers of the different instruments, correct counterpoint, scientific modulation and refined taste. Hasse also predicted that Haydn would become one of the greatest Composers of the Age. This liberal opinion so encouraged Haydn that from that time he exerted himself to the utmost to fulfil the flattering prediction, and he at the same time resolved never to give a harsh or severe opinion himself upon the production of any young Composer but always to do his utmost to encourage their first attempts, and to persevere in their studies with energy and enthusiasm.

Haydn always acted up to this resolution during all his life – and no one was ever more liberal and just to the merit of the productions of others than was this great Master of the Art.

Concerning the performance of this Symphony in the Chinese Pavilion, one notes that while *L'infedeltà delusa* has no parts for trumpets – *Philemon und Baucis* has come down to us only in the *Singspiel* version – Symphony No. 50 does; but they do not start to play their own parts (i.e. seperate from the horns) until the end of the work. We suggest that Haydn did not know until the last minute whether he would have trumpets or not. In G. F. von R. '[Rotenstein]'s report in Johann Bernouilli's *Sammlung kurzer Reisebeschreibungen*, Jg. 1783, IX. Band, p. 282 – Rotenstein was an eye-witness of the Imperial visit – we read that 'trumpets and drums were heard' in fanfares for the Empress, presumably. The trumpets and drums are *not* mentioned in the three other contemporary reports (*supra*, pp. 189ff.) nor the concert using the 'piano-forte' (*infra*, p. 343). In his report of the Imperial visit, Rotenstein also informs us that on the evening of the third day, when the oval courtyard with the iron gates was lighted with 24,000 white and green lamps, a temple had been put up in the middle, 'where the fountain usually is', under which the wind band of the princely musicians gave a concert lasting half-an-hour.

Minuet/Trio and Finale (Prestissimo) of a Symphony in C

Scoring: 2 oboes, 2 horns [presumably in C *alto*], 2 trumpets, timpani, strings [bassoon continuo].

These two movements, preserved in the Preussische Staatsbibliothek, Berlin (Mus. ms. autogr. Jos. Haydn 12), are in score, partly by a copyist and partly by Haydn himself. They have caused much puzzlement among scholars. The last movement, minus the trumpets and drums, was used by Haydn as the Finale of the first version of Symphony No. 63.[1] The watermarks of the paper suggest the period 1769–73. Obviously the Finale's use in No. 63 was Haydn's attempt to salvage some of this fine music, but we can only hazard a guess as to the two movements' original function. Were they part of an otherwise lost Haydn symphony? Or can it be that these two movements were written to complete the Overture to *Der Götterrath* and later discarded? This was soon a period of many similar substitutions (see Symphonies Nos. 53 and 62). The fact that the scoring includes *a priori* trumpets suggests No. 50; of the C major works at this juncture, only No. 56 was written for horns *and* trumpets *a priori*.

These movements were not printed until 1964, when the present writer used them in a reconstruction of Symphony No. 63's first version (q.v.). The Minuet has trumpet parts that rise to *c'''* and is a brilliant and festive piece. The Trio has unconventional modulations, of which the last, *pianissimo*, into C minor is the oddest. The Finale, also a movement with great panache, contains many passage for just the violins, which form a

1 See Philharmonia 594, pp. LXIXf. For No. 63, *vide infra*, p. 561.

striking contrast to the heavy orchestration of the tuttis. As a final possibility, the theatrical gestures of these movements suggest that they may have been intended originally as the end-pieces of incidental music for the Carl Wahr Troupe. That would also explain why the movements remained (except for the Finale's use and then cancellation in No. 63) isolated.

Symphony No. 64 in A major
('Tempora mutantur')

Scoring: 2 oboes, 2 horns, strings.

Recently (*HJB* IX, 328), Jonathan Foster has suggested an ingenious explanation for the Latin title which is found on the authentic MS. parts of the work in the University Library of Frankfurt-am-Main (where the title reads 'tempora mutantur etc.'). Foster writes:

> Probably the most famous epigram by the Welshman John Owen, known as "the British Martial", who lived from *c.* 1565 till 1622, is this, which he entitled *O Tempora*:
>
> Tempora mutantur, nos et mutamur in illis quomode? fit semper tempore peior homo.
>
> In the translation of Thomas Harvey, published in 1677, this runs:
>
> The Times are Chang'd, and in them Chang'd are we:
> How? Man, as Times grow worse, grows worse, we see.
>
> Most Europeans of literary culture in the seventeenth and eighteenth centuries were acquainted with the works of Owen, ten books of epigrams which commanded extraordinary influence, particularly in German literature. The above couplet, and especially the first line, became world-famous. To this day the first line can be seen on clocks and sundials.

Foster then proceeds to fit the first line to the main theme of the Finale.

In this very original Symphony, the central part is the densely written Largo, with its curious form (no double bars at all, and *durchkomponiert*) and its wide range of dynamics. The work occupies an isolated position among all these *Sturm und Drang* symphonies, and looks forward to the equally enigmatic *Capriccio* of Symphony No. 86 for Paris. This Largo's ending, *pianissimo*, is particularly novel, with the second horn at the bottom of its range and the first horn (with viola) suddenly taking the melody away from the violins (see example below).

Something of the other-worldliness of this Largo is, at least formally, found in the Finale, whose asymmetry and enigmatic construction make it one of the most atypical rondos of the period.

Symphony No. 54 in G major

Scoring (final version): 2 flutes, 2 oboes, 2 bassoons, 2 horns, 2 trumpets, timpani, strings. Originally scored for 2 oboes, 1 bassoon, 2 horns and strings. Haydn then added timpani (known in 1776 from MSS. in Göttweig and Laibach [Ljubljana]), then the flutes (at first one flute, then '2 Flauti') and trumpets, possibly for London. See *Haydn in England 1791–1795*, p. 188. The slow introduction was also added later, apparently when the timpani were included. The second bassoon was put into the score immediately afterwards, because there are no known MS. parts with one bassoon. For a contrary view by Sonja Gerlach, that the completed final version (with flutes and trumpets) was made in 1776, see *Haydn-Studien* II/1 (1969), p. 55; we can see no evidence for this assertion.

The introduction is so integral a part of the Symphony that it is almost impossible for us to imagine the work beginning with the Presto. This Adagio maestoso is majestic and stately, with the dotted French rhythm which Haydn so much liked in works of pomp and circumstance. The Presto is

[Symphony No. 64/II]

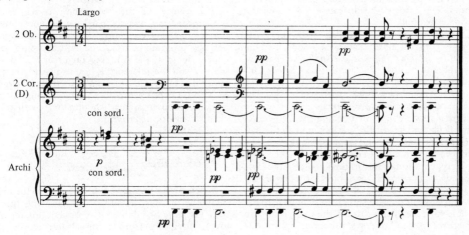

307

[Symphony No. 54/II]

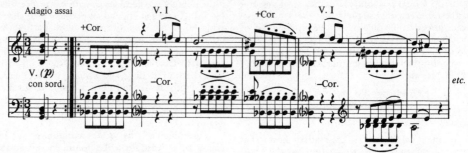

droll, a figure in an *opera buffa*; the tapping rhythm of the strings' accompaniment ♩ ♫♩♩|♩ gradually assumes a leading role. In the development we suddenly find ourselves in E major and the main theme (bars 91ff.): it is one of the first times when a third-related (in this case submediant) key assumes a central place in Haydn's tonal proceedings.

The beautiful slow movement – the longest Haydn ever wrote – is marked Adagio assai. Once again there are muted violins, which lend their peculiar colour to the orchestral palette. Altogether this finely wrought movement sums up all that was admirable in the Eszterháza years. At the end of the first part Haydn moves mysteriously from G to B flat unison, the horns employing their rare seventh harmonic (which Beethoven put to such good use in the Eighth Symphony) – see musical example above; the half cadence contained a striking effective viola part. Towards the end of the second part, there is a crescendo and a full stop on a six-four chord; whereupon, to our astonishment, there is a full-fledged cadenza for the two violins. (Were they soli, perhaps, in Eszterháza? Haydn and the leader Luigi Tomasini? We recall Count Zinzendorf's note of 1772, 'Bon diner, puis concert, deux chanteuses chanterent fort bien. Hayden [*sic*] joua du violon . . .'.)

With the Menuetto we are back again in an *opera buffa*, the appoggiature sounding like Leporello's antics. The Trio, with solo bassoon, is a graceful (also legato) foil.

Haydn is still experimenting with the finale form. We will note that he actually used an opening *sinfonia* of 1777 to *end* the first version of Symphony No. 53; he used that *sinfonia*, incidentally, once again as an opening movement: to No. 62. The present Finale, with its broad sonata form, its powerful development and extended recapitulation (where the opening theme swerves into B flat and gradually works round to the half cadence and the second subject) could well be an opening rather than a closing movement.

Excellent though the original orchestration was (the droll horns and bassoon that opened the Symphony are typical), the added flutes, trumpets, second bassoon and timpani give a rich finish to the whole score; in its full scoring, the work is the size of a first (1791–2) London symphony.

Symphony No. 55 in E flat
('Schoolmaster'/'Schulmeister')

Scoring: 2 oboes, 2 bassoons (only written out in the Finale), 2 horns, strings.

The autograph manuscript of this work is signed and dated but contains no reference to the 'Schoolmaster'; the title was known to Gerber, the great German lexicographer (*Neues historisch-biographisches Lexicon der Tonkünstler*, Leipzig 1812–14). It seems to refer to the second movement (*vide infra*). The first edition was brought out by an interesting publisher in Lyon named Guera, who may have had some connection with Haydn: first, because one of the musicians in the Esterházy band, Franz Garnier, ended up in the 1770s as 'Musicien de la Comédie de la Ville de Lion' (he was later the owner of a music shop there and undertook some publishing on his own); and secondly, because Guera issued the first edition, in rather reliable texts, of several Haydn symphonies: Nos. 55, 56 (*vide infra*), Nos. 57 and 44 together, Nos. 60 and 66 together, and Nos. 80 and 81 together. No. 55 he issued along with a symphony by Vanhal and another by Lochon about 1778.

The first movement is concise even by Haydn's rigorous standards. There is a great deal of contrast, within and between the two subjects; there is also a classical example of a *fausse reprise*. The entire movement is marked by a certain cool objectivity which is at considerable variance with the moods of its numerically flanking partners.

The centre of the Symphony is its slow movement, and was so 'particularly' composed that it must have contained some special message, perhaps programmatical. The dotted figure, of course, suggests the wagging finger of a schoolmaster; and the reference is not all that unlikely, either, for in his *Entwurf-Katalog* there is an *incipit* of a lost Divertimento in D 'Der Schulmeister genannt' (known as the Schoolmaster) with this characteristic dotted rhythm:

When Elssler transferred this theme into the big catalogue of 1805, he added the following title: 'Der verliebte Schulmeister' (the schoolmaster in love), obviously from a verbal instruction of

Haydn's. We suggest that something of this nature obtains in this movement, marked 'Adagio, ma semplicemente'. As usual, the violins are muted. The two characteristic features are, on the one hand, the 'semplice' sections (probably meaning no vibrato for the violins), and on the other, the 'dolce' sections (probably with vibrato), the first emphasising the strict, pedantic teacher, and the other the same teacher shattered by love. Whatever the programme of these variations was, the result was bewitching: particularly the section at bars 81ff. is incredibly moving: as in Haydn's operas, he gets carried away with the subject.

The wrily humorous *Menuetto*, with its *pianissimo* ending, is matched by a Trio which, for once, is exactly what it says: a piece for three instruments – a solo violoncello and two violins (perhaps they were solo, too, in Eszterháza?). Many years later, when in London the first time in 1791, Haydn was to remember this rather wistful Trio and to compose a similar one, with an extensive 'cello solo, in Symphony No. 95.

The Finale is a nimble rondo with yet another irresistible tune. There follows, after the 'A' section (which in turn is subdivided a–b–a), a solo for wind band, right out of one of Haydn's early wind band divertimenti for Count Morzin. Later the music finds itself in a large-scale *cul-de-sac* and slows to a dead stop (and pause), *sempre più piano*. At the end we have one of those typically Haydnesque exchanges: solo oboes – the two violins alone (*pp*) – horns solo – final cadence; but *anno* 1774 this was brand new. It was always one of Haydn's most popular works, and one of the very few 'middle-period' symphonies to enjoy, in the old days, the honour of an Eulenburg miniature score.

Symphony No. 56 in C major

Scoring: 2 oboes, 1 bassoon, 2 horns in C *alto* and F, 2 trumpets, timpani, strings.

In the middle 1770s Haydn's symphonies started to arrive in large quantity in Paris. So avid were the French to hear these new works that they pirated works by almost *any* Austrian or German composer and issued them under Haydn's name. Opus IX meant, in Paris, one of two things: either the string quartets still known under that opus number or 'Six Simphonies a grande Orchestre par Mr Haydn Maître de Musique de Chapelle a Vienne' issued by Madame Berault and containing, in that order, a pirated symphony by Franz Dussek (an old friend of Haydn's); a spurious work for which the real author has never been found; Michael Haydn's music to *Die Hochzeit auf der Alm* (completed at Salzburg on 6 May 1768); Michael Haydn's E major Symphony (Perger No. 5) composed in January 1764; another anonymous spurious work and, for a wonder, Haydn's Symphony No. 30 ('Alleluja'). We must remember that Parisians soon had a very warped idea of what was Haydn....

Still, they had a pretty shrewd idea of what was great Haydn; within a year of Symphony No. 56's arrival in the French capital, sometime in 1777,

three French editions existed: Mademoiselle de Silly, Sieber, and Guera of Lyon (together with a Parisian affiliate). Silly did not bother to engrave the trumpet and timpani parts (Guera, as always, did so), and Sieber noted 'avec timballes et trompettes qui se vendent séparément'; Sieber also noted, in his edition, which included a symphony by J. C. Bach and one by Gossec, 'Ces Simphonies ont été joué au Concert Spirituel et au Concert des Amateurs'.

The French were right. There are five known symphonies of this vintage year 1774: Nos. 54, 55, 56, 57 and 60 – each a masterpiece and each one printed by Guera in Lyon (accident?)[1] But No. 56 shines with exceptional brilliance, due to its scoring: the usual C *alto* horns (which the French, not knowing from the prints that they were *alto*, and probably not knowing C *alto* horns at all, will have played an octave lower), trumpets and kettledrums must inevitably dominate a score which, otherwise, consists of oboes, strings and a bassoon which is part of the continuo except in the slow movement.

The first movement is again based on one of those tension-*cum*-release structures of which we have spoken earlier. The opening theme is typical in this respect: the downward progression in unison resolving in soft string writing; another chordal unison with a strong dotted twist leads back to the opening material. It is beautifully symmetrical; it is also a series of abrupt contrasts, or tension and release. Now one of the hallmarks of this great period in Haydn's symphonies is the contrapuntal texture to which he has frequent recourse. In the richly scored transition we have noted earlier that bars 29ff. are laid out in neat double counterpoint, the first trumpet contributing a strident extra voice, and the oboes following their own course, sometimes doubling the violins or the viola at the octave. After the second subject, the concluding material of the exposition again utilizes the transitional passage by placing the violins' part in the bass, in quavers, each alternate quaver being given a marcato –

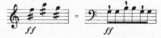

– and thus crotchet stress (violin I bar 29 – bass bar 68); the two variants are eventually placed side by side in the development. Notice the means he uses to communicate this double counterpoint to the audience: the violins are marked *ff* against the *f* of the other instruments at bar 29, while at 68 this *ff* is transferred to the bass along with the accented staccato. Speaking of such delicate details of shading, one notes the timpani's dynamic marks at 206 and 212, the fierce *ff* of the trumpets at 244. Haydn's language has become infinitely more

1 We remind readers that our presumed go-between, Franz Garnier, was finally traced to Lyon by the Esterházy administration so that he could receive the legacy from Prince Paul Anton Esterházy; Haydn's legacy was paid in 1773, Garnier's presumably somewhat later. See Chronicle, p. 118.

(Symphony No. 56/II)

subtle, more complex. The mysterious *pianissimo* drum roll at bar 222 is, it seems, the first time a drum roll appears in the Austrian school.

In the slow movement, we would draw attention to the witty entrance of the bassoon. A passage of dark-hued intensity reminds one almost of Bruckner (37ff.), while the sweeping crescendo (see example) – a dynamic mark that Haydn always uses sparingly and with telling effect – at 68ff. ennobles the middle section of this great *Adagio* (notice the exquisite oboe line which twines round the strings and then flows above them into the upper octave).

Haydn prepares us, in bars 31ff. of the Minuet, for the important triplets of the Finale (bars 82ff.). And what a conclusion it is: stunning trumpet fanfares, whirling triplets, dancing, tongue-in-cheek second subject (note the orchestration, with the held oboe and viola notes – and technically how the oboes take over from each other so that the players will never be too tired); here is all Haydn's knowledge, artfully concealed.

Symphony No. 57 in D major

Scoring: 2 oboes, 2 horns, strings [bassoon continuo]. When the work was announced in the Breitkopf Catalogue of 1774, its scoring also included two trumpets and kettledrums, instruments which Haydn may have added later. A timpani part from the Parish Church of Eibiswald (Styria) has survived in dated MS. parts of 1779 and appers to be authentic. Literature on this subject: Landon, *SYM*, 701f. Also *Joseph Haydn Werke* Reihe I, Band 7 (Wolfgang Stockmeier) with Kritischer Bericht, 1967: timpani part dismissed as spurious and trumpet parts mentioned by Landon also dismissed as fantasy [*sic*]; see Breitkopf Cat.

Landon in *HJB* VI, 210f. The Symphony has been recorded once with the timpani part (Goberman, Library of Recorded Masterpieces), once without it (Dorati in the complete Haydn Symphonies, Decca).

The slow introduction (Adagio) with which the work begins was by no means standard practice in 1774; in those days, only the occasional Haydn symphony included one. Even as late as the 'Paris' Symphonies (1785–6), Haydn was not sure whether the slow introduction should become a regular feature: three of the 'Paris' set (Nos. 84, 85, 86) open with one, Nos. 82, 83, and 87 do not. Subsequently, however, the slow introduction was adopted in all except two (Nos. 89, 95) of the remaining symphonies Haydn composed. The same vacillation is to be found in Mozart's late symphonies, some ('Linz' [K.425]; 'Prague' [K.504], E flat [K.543]) having introductory adagios, and some (G minor [K.550], 'Jupiter' [K.551]) not. Beethoven's First, Second and Fourth and Seventh Symphonies begin with such an introduction.

It would seem, in this brief Adagio, that the world of opera is not far from us – and comic opera, too. The little grace notes seem to be like a figure from the *commedia dell'arte* plucking our sleeves; and at bars 20ff. the short thrusts (*forte-piano*) of the strings with massed wind-band accompaniment are close to the language of *opera buffa*. The main section – no marking in the autograph, but allegro is obviously meant – is sturdy with the bass line progressing in 'walking' octave quavers. In the second subject group, the accompanying bass line at bars 99ff. (with a beautiful, slow-moving second violin line) turns up in the recapitulation in the first horn as well

(which, because of the limitations of its technique, could not have played the notes in A major).

The slow movement (Adagio) is a set of variations on a theme wherein pizzicato chords alternate with ethereal bowed phrases. The whole movement is of an extraordinary purity and 'classical' beauty. It is innocent in a very moving way.

The Menuet (Allegretto) seems to be on the threshold of the waltz: the second violin actually has a Straussian accompaniment. The end of the Minuet proper is a series of staccato crotchets which finally create the D major triad. This triad proves, very cleverly, to be the link to the Trio, in the third-related key of B flat (very unusual for this period).

The Finale (Prestissimo) is an extremely difficult *perpetuum mobile* built upon a traditional theme – it can be traced as far back as the *Canzon vnd Capriccio vber dass Henner vnd Hannergeschrey* (Canzona and Capriccio on the Racket of Hen and Rooster) by Alessandro Poglietti (d. 1683) – see example above. In Haydn's racy transcription there is a new dynamic mark: *mancando* (we would now call it *decrescendo*), which 'falls' into *pp*.[1]

Symphony No. 60 in C ('Il distratto')

Scoring: 2 oboes, 2 horns in C *alto*, 2 trumpets, kettledrums, strings (partly with two viola parts) [bassoon continuo].

We first noted this incidental music to a play by Jean François Regnard (1655–1709) entitled *Le Distrait* (German *Der Zerstreute*: Italian *Il distratto*) in newspaper articles in the *Preßburger Zeitung* and the *Historisch-kritische Theaterchronik* of 1774 (*vide supra*, pp. 205ff.).[1]

Scored for Haydn's customary C major orchestra, with high horns, trumpets (perhaps a later addition; they only double the horns) and kettledrums, *Il distratto* has two more movements than the average symphony of the time. Possibly as a new kind of experiment, Haydn turns to his beloved melodic source, the folk-song: this Symphony contains more traditional tunes than any other of his symphonic works. His idea of a 'distraught' symphony was to pile folk-tunes one on top of another without any apparent connection, and in view of the play for which the music was composed, he takes special pains to create an uproariously mad tonal picture. The first movement, with a majestic slow introduction (Adagio) very similar in character to that of Symphony No. 50 (1773), is perfectly serious, and was undoubtedly intended as the overture to the evening's entertainment. In the midst of the exposition, however, occurs a remarkable dynamic effect, showing us that we expect all sorts of surprises later in the evening: the score is marked 'perdendosi' (literally: dying away), and the strings sink to near-inaudibility, followed by a sudden *forte*; in the recapitulation, the thunder of the kettledrums adds to the surprise.

The second movement is already saturated with the spirit of the evening.[1] According to Robert A. Green, the graceful opening theme suggests the young lady Isabelle, while the rude fanfares (oboes, horns and, for the first time in a Haydn symphony, divided violas) are supposed to portray the Chevalier. The closing material of the exposition suggests Mme. Grognac (bars 43ff.). The middle section brings us a new melody, with *forzato* trills, which in old French editions of this Symphony is described as 'Ancient chant françois'. Green believes this to be a satirical reference to the 'French' mood of the evening. In Fux's *Concentus musico-instrumentalis* of 1701, we 'find a trio sonata in which the upper instrument plays an *Aria Italiana* in a lilting six-eight while the second instrument plays an *Aire française* alla breve' (below).

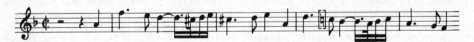

---

1 A report on this work in the *Salzburger Theaterwochenblatt*, on the occasion of Wahr's guest appearance with the play at Salzburg on 16 January 1776, seems to be based on information from Wahr himself. 'Herr Haydn liked the play and it seemed to him that his wit (*Laune*) would find a suitable stimulation in it; he had promised before to give Wahr a keepsake, and so he composed the music for the entr'actes and gave it Herr Wahr exclusively for his own use.' (Wirth I, 61).

The Trio of the ensuing Minuet turns to the Balkans for its melodic inspirations, with Hungarian alternations of tonic and dominant

1 Our edition of *Le distrait* from *Les Oeuvres de M*. *Regnard. Nouvelle Édition, Tome Premier*, La Haye 1729. Robert A. Green, 'Haydn's and Regnard's *Il distratto*: A Re-examination', in *Haydn Yearbook* XI (forthcoming).

minor. Green believes that the exotic Trio is devoted to Léandre (a French adaptation of Leandro from the *commedia dell'arte*). But the next movement is startling indeed. This Presto, in C minor, seems at first to be constructed along the lines of the nervous, tense and headlong finales of Symphonies Nos. 49, 52 or\59; a highly rhythmic first subject leads, upon its entry into the relative major, to repeated semiquavers in the violins with a marching bass line in quavers. In the second part, Haydn begins to hurl Balkan melodies at us (the Chevalier's attempt to dance with Mme. Grognac?); in the middle of one of these, the music jumps from F minor to E flat major, making simultaneous parallel fifths and octaves, and the stamping peasant dance is continued without interruption in the new key. Instead of a re-capitulation, Haydn turns to the tonic major, and the brass and drums enter, supporting a new Slavonic melody. This is perhaps the most characteristic Balkan tune of all (bars 127ff.), and with it Haydn rushes to a close, giving us a musical précis of the intrigues of Act III.

The F major Adagio bears the subtitle 'di Lamentatione' in old manuscript parts in the Benedictine Monastery of Melk. It has not been possible, however, to identify the Gregorian(?) melody which Haydn used as the basis for this movement, 'but' – says Green – 'it calls to mind Léandre wringing his hands over the situation'. Oboe and violin intone the melody, but the horns, trumpets and drums (previously silent in this movement) break into the calm with a war-like fanfare, dragging the rest of the orchestra with them. Some experts think that this represents the entrance of the fake courier in the last scene of the play. (The way Haydn reduces the fanfare's effect by silly, deadpan pizzicati would seem to support this theory, but Green thinks Haydn may be describing the fortunes of the Chevalier.) At the end of the movement, Haydn takes a small motif and repeats it eight times, placing the word 'Allegro' after the fourth entry, so that there is no doubt that we are witnessing the first attempts to write an 'accelerando'. The effect is delightfully bizarre, but the Finale has new and startling tricks in store for us. Starting out like the *moto perpetuo* of Symphony No. 41's or 56's Finale – Prestissimo, with triplet quavers in two-four time – the music barely gets under way before everything stops dead in order that the violinists may tune their instruments, their G-strings have been found to be F-strings! The music proceeds[1] and then again breaks off, this time to introduce the favourite Slavonic melody (quoted *supra*, p. 280) – a strange, secret tune ('The Night-Watchman')

which is slightly frightening; here it 'refers to the lateness of the hour' (Green). But here, we have no time for shadows, and the music proceeds to its breathtaking conclusion. 'Suppose', postulates Peter J. Pirie (*HJB* III, 176), 'we were to describe a symphony in six movements, in a style best described as expressionist, that ran the gamut of irony, savagery, melancholy, and wild humour, with many daring experiments in orchestration? Gustav Mahler? No, Haydn's 60th Symphony. The forward look to Mahler is uncanny in the case of "Il distratto"; yet the environment is much the same, and the line of development direct.'

Symphony No. 68 in B flat

Scoring: 2 oboes, 2 bassoons, 2 horns, strings.

This work has enjoyed a strange, not to say inexplicable, history. It was not widely circulated in manuscript, and when it was printed by Hummel (together with Nos. 66 and 67), huge cuts were made in the slow movement, and the Minuets of all three Symphonies in the set omitted (also the bassoon parts were scrapped and the solo sections worked into other parts). But even some of the extant MSS., such as the one partly by Johann Radnitzky in Milan, omit the bassoons, omit the Minuet and make large cuts, different from those of Hummel, in the slow movement. The Menuetto comes second, as it did in some earlier symphonies (Nos. 32, 44, for example) and many quartets (Op. 17); it is the last time this ever happens in a Haydn symphony, but here this is an important structural reason for reversing the usual order. The prodigious length of the slow move-ment – in which both the first and second parts are repeated – suggested that it be preceded by both Allegro and Minuet and followed only by the vivacious Finale.

In the last four Symphonies here under exam-ination, we can see how the *Sturm und Drang* evaporates: only in No. 67 do we sense its former power. It is as if Haydn had drawn a curtain over the passionate daring of the past decade.

The glittering first movement (Vivace) has a witty second subject with staccato middle strings, rather like an accompaniment to an *opera buffa*; to the charm of which the crossed turns of the first violins and the gliding oboes' notes contribute. The repeated semiquavers, *fortissimo*, of the violins with the same line being shaped *legato* by the oboes (bars 50ff., 142ff.) are very characteristic of Haydn – more of that 'phrenzied' music. But there is now, in Haydn's symphonies, a curiously detached attitude, almost a calculating use of 'phrenzied' *ff* and the other devices of *Sturm und Drang*. There is always wit, but in the Minuet & Trio there is an objective, rather de-personalized atmosphere of considerable variance with the passionate, forward-driving energy of the Minuet in No. 48.

The Adagio cantabile is built round the starkest contrasts: *f* with *p*, legato and staccato, two violins alone with all the rest of the band, and so forth. The accompaniment at the beginning, the staccato skips of a third, move through large parts of the

---

1 The *Preßburger Zeitung* (*vide supra*, p. 212) has described how the absent-minded bridegroom had to tie a knot in his handkerchief to remind himself of his marriage. The last lines of the play read:

Carlin

Ah ciel! un jour de nôce oublier une femme!
Cette erreur me paroît un peu digne de blâme:
Pour le lendemain passe, & j'en vois aujourd'hui
Qui voudroient bien pouvoir l'oublier comme lui.

movement. Georg Feder has drawn attention[1] to the close (bars 123–5) which was to be the basis of the 'forest music' in *Armida* (Act III). 'The soft stationary sound suggests the quiet forest, the firmly rooted trees; the slowly ascending and descending motion the glance of the spectator; the ruffled figure the light motion of the leaves.' There is, incidentally, a strong feeling of the concerto about this slow movement, particularly in the way Haydn reaches a cadence and a six-four chord (ending in bars 31 and 108) in both sections.

After the Adagio's tension and concentration, the final Presto is a calculated relief. It is one of those popular rondos, where we have, to contrast with the main section, the Great Bassoon Joke (bars 31ff.); a miniature oboe concerto (bars 85ff.); the Angry G minor Interlude (bars 167ff.); the Baroque Echo Trick (bars 237ff.); and of course the concluding coda with Haydn's 'phrenzied' violins in semiquavers – altogether a most entertaining and vivacious movement.

Symphony No. 66 in B flat

Scoring: 2 oboes, 2 bassoons, 2 horns, strings.

Haydn's symphonies are now becoming very sophisticated and occasionally rather cool. Here, we have an interesting example, in the first movement, of Haydn's using his own earlier thematic material; for the opening subject – see example – is remarkably close (a) to the first theme of the Overture in D (Ia:7) of 1777 which was later used as the Finale of Symphony No. 53, and (b) to yet a third version, as the opening movement of Symphony No. 62 (c. 1780). It is difficult for us to understand the composer's fixation with this theme and its derivatives; yet there even exists a second authentic version of the Overture in D (printed as an Appendix to Philharmonia 593, pp. 159f.) with different orchestration, so that one can say that Haydn used it no less than five times in about three years, twice as an Overture, twice as a first movement of a symphony and once as the finale to a symphony. Both the accompaniment to

1 'Similarities in the Works of Haydn', in *Studies in Eighteenth-Century Music* (Geiringer *Festschrift*), London 1970, pp. 192f.

the first subject in No. 66 (repeated quavers, B flat) and the elegant second subject – much more prominent than is usual in Haydn – which is marked *dolce e piano*, have something of Johann Christian Bach's suavity and elegance. The wordly, fastidious line of this second theme is a new and slightly unusual side of Haydn's complicated personality: Haydn the epicure, the *grand seigneur* of the musical *settecento*. The continuation, with the second violin in the usual nervous semiquavers (bars 51ff.) and the first violin in syncopated crotchets, is more like the Haydn we know. Of the many felicitous details in this movement, we would like to mention the end of the development: a close in the dominant of D minor, with soft oboes and violins, where suddenly the note *a* becomes the pivotal leading note to the tonic (B flat) and the recapitulation – see bars 102f.

The Adagio continues with the new Haydn as eighteenth-century gentleman: beautifully tailored but definitely reserved. There is a fine crescendo leading to the closing material of the first section: Haydn breaks into sextuplets, and the whole sounds rather like a cadenza, which impression is enhanced by a six-four chord and violin trill. This influence of the concerto in the slow movement of Haydn's symphonies was perhaps initiated (in a different way) by the 'cadenza' in No. 54/II, and is clearly felt in Nos. 66, 67, 68 and most dramatically in No. 71/II (q.v.)

The Menuetto must have been an immediate success: its catchy tune, its poised orchestration (notice how the wind band is suddenly on its own at bars 16ff.), and the humorous lead-back to the main tune in the second part were destined for immediate popularity. The Trio has the scoring of a divertimento: one oboe, one bassoon and no viola in the strings.

The Finale is another rondo of the kind that made Haydn celebrated throughout Europe and even in North and South America (where eighteenth-century MS. parts of Haydn symphonies have been discovered in recent years). It is marked 'Scherzando e presto', and has one particularly ingenious twist to it: namely, the construction of the theme itself in two five-bar phrases. It adds a distinctly piquant touch to the

formal structure of an otherwise typical movement).

the piano, which had to be omitted from the piano reduction.

Symphony No. 69 in C major ('Laudon')

Scoring: 2 oboes, 2 bassoons, 2 horns, 2 trumpets, timpani, strings.

Haydn himself was responsible for the title of this work: it was dedicated to General Laudon, the celebrated Austrian Field-Marshal who defeated the Turks and whose name was in fact Ernst Gideon Freiherr von Loudon (*recte*), 1716–90. Haydn made a piano arrangement and sold it, with a violin part (which, he wrote on 18 June 1783, 'is not at all necessary and may be therefore omitted entirely') to his publishers Artaria; see the Chronicle (8 April 1783), where we read, 'the word "Laudon" will contribute more to the sale than any ten finales' (which Haydn was forced, for technical reasons, to omit from the piano arrangement).

The first movement (Vivace) has an opening theme slightly similar to the famous beginning of the 'Maria Theresa' Symphony No. 48; but in No. 69 we are in a more decorous age, where elegance and poise have supplanted nervous brilliance. The horns are also no longer in the exciting pitch of C *alto*, as they were in No. 48, but have dropped down to C *basso*. By now, Haydn writes more and more extended second subjects, and this one is surprisingly regular (two four-bar phrases), almost a text-book second subject. It almost appears as if Haydn thought that this conformity would appeal to Laudon, who was probably as conservative as most generals are today. The comparison with No. 48 is a striking example of what has happened to Haydn's *Sturm und Drang*. Something has fled from Haydn's personality, and no amount of superb craftsmanship can make up for the loss.

The slow movement, marked 'Un poco adagio più tosto andante', has some original harmonic touches and an unusual approach to dynamic marks, e.g. at the end of each section there is a big crescendo followed by 'perdendosi' (dying away) to *p* and then *pp*. But somehow all these trappings seem to mask an emotional vacuum. The Menuetto is rather pompous and the Trio conventional. One cannot avoid the impression that Haydn did not entertain much sympathy for General Laudon – certainly he did not excite in the composer the flash of inspiration that we find in No. 48 (whether it was written for Empress Maria Theresa or not).

The best movement of No. 69 is certainly the dexterous Finale, another whirlwind Presto with some abrupt dynamic changes (e.g. 45–8) and a really ferocious section in C minor, where the strings are marked *ff*. The lead-back, with a long and delicate solo passage for the first violins (*pp*), is most effective, and so is the end, *fortissimo*, with Haydn's characteristic repeated semiquavers in the violins (which also infect even the lower strings in the final cadence). It is rather ironic that it was this excellent movement, not being 'practicable' for

Symphony No. 67 in F major

Scoring: 2 oboes, 2 bassoons, 2 horns, strings (with two solo violins and solo violoncello).

Without any question, this is one of the most boldly original symphonies of this period: it is also the only one that ever achieved anything like popularity in modern times; for, edited by the great scholar Alfred Einstein, it was played, together with another dozen unknown Haydn symphonies (including Nos. 51, 56, 71, 77, 80, 82, 87, etc.) in the great 1939/40 season of the New Friends of Music in New York, immaculately conducted by the late Fritz Stiedry. That famous season in New York, which was also broadcast (and in the cases of Nos. 67 and 80 recorded by RCA Victor) might, indeed, be said to have initiated the present Haydn Renaissance.

The first movement is in the (for a first movement) unusual metre of six-eight and marked Presto: later, Haydn was to make a six-eight beginning immortal in the 'Clock' Symphony. Textually, our Symphony is based upon a manuscript copied by Joseph Elssler and Johann Schellinger (the Esterházy theatrical copyist), which Haydn sent to the great Benedictine Monastery of Kremsmünster in Upper Austria. Many felicitous details – the odd *mezzo forte* in a viola part to bring into relief an inner voice (bar 147) or the characteristic crossed turn over a note (debased into a trill in the secondary MSS. and prints: Finale, bars 33, 35) – are known to us only through this authentic manuscript, the autograph (like most of this period) having long since disappeared. The second subject still whirls away in a steady quaver flow, though slurred rather than staccato (as the first subject is marked). The development is very long (bars 89–161) and generates enormous strength, using the first theme contrapuntally. It looks forward to the development of No. 101/I.

The Adagio, constructed upon a theme of chamber musical delicacy with muted violins, is of great beauty and strength. After the beginning of the second section (bars 56ff.) a fascinating canon between first and second violins unrolls before us – bar after bar of Bachian complexity, with the two muted violin sections spinning out their delicate threads. At the end of this ingenious movement, when the theme is announced for the last time, the entire string section is directed to play 'col legno dell'arco' ('with the (wooden) back of the bow'). Perhaps Mozart had this great Symphony in mind when he wrote the 'col legno' section in the March in D, K. 335, No. 1 (K.320a, No. 1) in August 1779: Haydn's Symphony will have just reached Salzburg (it was printed that year in Holland and Germany).

After the sturdy Menuetto, the Trio – as so often in Haydn's symphonies of the 1770s – comes as a great shock: almost like the wandering Gypsies in

Háry János. There are two solo violins: the first is to play everything on the *e*-string, *con sordino*, while the second solo violin, also *con sordino*, is to tune its *g*-string to *f*; this second violin part is used like a drone bass. The delicate crossed-turn ornaments in the second part come, once again, only from the authentic Kremsmünster manuscript (in the secondary sources they are, stupidly, trills). It is a breathtakingly original little movement.

The Finale (Allegro di molto) starts normally, with a rhythmically memorable second subject; the closing material in the dominant is what we would expect – but thereafter Prince Nicolaus had the second biggest surprise of his musical life (the first having been the last movement of the 'Farewell' Symphony in the late autumn of 1772). The music stops dead and a brand new movement is inserted, marked Adagio e cantabile, for solo string trio (two violins and violoncello), who are told to play 'piano e dolce'. Time has suddenly stopped moving (not the first occasion on which this has happened in a Haydn slow movement). After an exquisitely beautiful first section, the main body of the orchestra joins in during the second section. We then have a wind-band solo, with strings at the end. After considerable elaboration, the first *Allegro di molto* comes back, to which Haydn adds a bizarre and amusing coda, the violins playing a huge, written-out trill across eight bars, the rest of the instruments mincing their way in chords down the score. The whole symphony has that brilliant eccentricity which was always one of *Sturm und Drang*'s more endearing after-effects; can this have been stage music for some unidenti-fied play at Eszterháza? Or do we have, in its originality, merely Haydn's grand farewell to the 'crisis period'?

Summing up this period, Charles Rosen writes:[1]

> The development of Haydn as a symphonist raises one of the great pseudo-problems of history: the question of progress in the arts. The achievements of 1768 to 1772 are very great ones in a style that Haydn almost at once abandoned. In these years he wrote a series of impressive symphonies in minor keys – dramatic, highly personal, and mannered.... To these symphonies ... must be joined the great Piano Sonata in C minor [No. 33]. The Quartets opp. 17 and 20, written in 1771 and 1772, are all – major or minor – on a level that no other composer of Haydn's time could equal or even approach, and in assessing the level he had reached, one must also add the beautiful slow movement of the Piano Sonata in A flat [No. 31]. None of these works gives a clear indication of the direction Haydn was to take, and one might imagine the history of music to be very different if only he had explored the paths suggested in some of them. They seem to presage not the sociable and lyrical wit of his later work (and of Mozart's), but a style harshly dramatic and fiercely emotional without a trace of sentimentality....

1 *The Classical Style*, London and New York 1971, p. 146; reprinted by permission of Faber and Faber Ltd and The Viking Press, Inc.

(2) STRING QUARTETS

Opus Nine: Six Quartets composed *c.* 1768–70. Entered in *EK* at the bottom of page two in the following, quite different order: Nos. 4, 1, 3, 2, 5, 6; can this order represent the original order of composition? The order as in Hoboken III: 19–24 is from the printed editions. Authentic sources of Nos. 1 and 4 in Gesellschaft der Musikfreunde IX 24982, 24973.

Opus Seventeen: Six Quartets composed 1771. Entered in *EK* in the order Nos. 2, 1, 4, 6, 3, 5. Autographs of all six works, in the order of *EK*, dated 1771 and partly numbered consecutively (1–28, leaving only the last one un-numbered but establishing the authentic order): Gesellschaft der Musikfreunde, Vienna. Thus the different order (in *EK*) of Opus Nine is probably authentic. The order as in Hoboken III: 25–30 is from the printed editions.

Opus Twenty: Six Quartets composed 1772. Entered in *EK* in the order Nos. 5, 6, 2, 3, 4, 1. Autographs of all six works, in six separate fascicles (not consecutively numbered): Gesellschaft der Musikfreunde, Vienna; each work is dated 1772. The order as in Hoboken III: 31–36 is from the Hummel print (1779); other prints (e.g. Chevardière 1774) have a different order, which is discussed below.

Haydn tended to compose string quartets in groups, or blocks, with sometimes many years between such groups. The early quartets (known under Op. 1 and Op. 2) were probably written at the end of the 1750s. There was then a pause until Op. 9, and very likely a pause of a decade (the Op. 3 Quartets are by Pater Roman Hoffstetter [1742–1815] and slipped into the canon of genuine quartets by a clerical error). There follows the intense activity of Opp. 9, 17 and 20, all composed within three or four years of each other. Afterwards there is another long pause until about 1781 (Opus 33), and after that another pause – with the exception of a curious (single?) Quartet (Op. 42) of 1785 – until 1787 (Op. 50).

The first question is: why the long pause after the early quartet-divertimenti? To answer the question we must return for a brief survey of those works. Haydn wrote, to the best of our knowledge, ten (the others in the so-called Opp. 'o', 1 and 2 are either a symphony [Op. 1/5] or sextets with horns [Opp. 2/3 and 5]). As said, they are in five movements, like many of the wind-band divertimenti and cassations for various wind and string groups by Haydn and his contemporaries. Haydn's early biographers stress that the quartet – as opposed to the popular string trio with two violins and 'cello – came into being by accident at Baron von Fürnberg's country estate, Weinzierl Castle, because there happened to be four rather than three string players, i.e. an extra viola player was present. As will be found in *Haydn: the Early Years 1732–1765*, it is difficult to establish the ten works' dates of composition;[1] we would only say here that it now appears that they were composed in the *second* half of the 1750s; that they really did cause an enormous sensation throughout Austria and Germany; but that they were not popular with many north German critics and also not with Emperor Joseph II. Haydn smarted under these critical remarks. Having himself achieved a remarkable success with these early works, through them he founded the first Haydn school, which avidly copied these works and their peculiar formal and musical construction (examples: Albrechtsberger, Franz Dussek and even the earliest quartets by Vanhal, published in 1769 in Paris after, presumably, Haydn had already moved on to the new style of Op. 9). These early quartets all begin with a rather short opening movement in quick metre such as 2/4, 3/8 or 6/8 (exceptions: Opus 1/3 with an opening Adagio and Op. 2/6 with an opening Adagio and variations). The most extended part of the work is usually in the middle, the slow movement, which is often in the style of an Italian serenade such as we also find in the slow movement of the Violin Concerto in C (VIIa:1). The quick movements apart from the minuets are also mostly in quick metres. The charm and facility of these quartet-divertimenti were soon legendary, but Haydn obviously felt no necessity for composing more than ten. The works' structural balance, with the two exceptions noted above, placed their centre of gravity in the middle. The same centre is found in other divertimento (cassatio) works with five movements, but with certain differences (e.g. in the wind-band works, the slow movements are usually more compact because of the requirements of the instruments involved). This peculiar kind of balance is entirely different from many of the three-movement symphonies and concertos, where most of the weight is at the beginning and gradually lessens as the work progresses. The first movement of such symphonies (naturally *sonata da chiesa* works must be excepted, also experimental pieces such as Symphony No. 15 in D) is the longest and formally most involved, with motivic work or, in the earlier works, what is called 'Fortspinnung', the 'spinning out' of motifs, often sequentially; it is usually in some kind of ternary form with the basic harmonic progression (in major) I–V–I (in minor, modulation to the relative major). The second movement, usually a light andante in quick metre on the Italian pattern is followed by a fast finale, also in quick metres, and in a very compressed three-part form (I–V–I); though there are other possibilities (minuet, tempo di minuetto, even a rondo as in Symphony No. 2/III). In the first few years of his symphonic career, Haydn subjected the form to numerous experiments, adding and then subsequently withdrawing a minuet (second place? third place?) and a slow introduction (Symphonies Nos. 6, 7, 15, 25). The details

---

1 Albrechtsberger's brother has meanwhile been located: he actually existed and his name is known to us *inter alia* from a contemporary printed libretto.

belong to the previous volume of this biography, *Haydn: the Early Years 1732–1765*. When he decided to return to the quartet, towards the end of the 1760s, Haydn's style had moved far away from the quartet-divertimento and equally far from the early symphony. It was clear that a strict division between music for the chamber (private music-making) and music for the great hall of castle, monastery or Rathaus (public music-making) had to be effected; thus the innovations, devices (Gregorian chant, *sonata da chiesa* sequence) and experiments made in the transitional symphonies were only partially applicable to the quartet. But we shall see that Haydn had one endless chamber-musical field in which to experiment between 1765 and 1769: the baryton trio.

Op. 9 was constructed in an entirely new manner. There were four movements with the minuet second: the reason for the minuet's position depends on the extraordinary construction of the first movements which, with two exceptions (Op. 9/5 with opening Poco Adagio & variations; Op. 9/6 in the older six-eight metre), are all in eight-eight (slow C) moderato tempo, and are all so long that it would exhaust the listener to follow such an intricate movement with a full-scale adagio – therefore the minuet second. The same procedure also applies to Op. 17 (all moderato except No. 3 [Andante grazioso with variations] and No. 6 [in six-eight]). This new kind of movement tilts the weight enormously towards the beginning of each quartet, even with the six-eight movements which, in view of their light metre and fast speed, are greatly increased in size (Op. 9/6/I: 133 bars; Opus 17/6/I: 200 bars). Finscher, in his valuable monograph (*infra*, p. 393n.), tends to consider this kind of moderato movement a derivative of the baryton trio 'but especially developing from the stimulation of Carl Philipp Emanuel Bach' (p. 192); at other times he notes in these moderato movements 'Mannheimer Tonfall' (p. 198). On the other hand, Isidor Saslav[1] describes these moderati as Italianate: 'As regards tempo and its notation there could indeed be no greater contrast between the original [early quartets] and the following.... The sprightly Viennese allegri molti and presti are replaced by the leisurely Italianate moderato which casts its influence over all the first movements up to and including Op. 50 ...'. If we examine Austrian catalogues of the period (e.g. Lambach of 1768 *et seq.*, Göttweig retrospectively but listing the early dates as they were found on the title pages), there are Italian masters listed but they are usually of a slightly earlier period, such as Vivaldi. Haydn may have heard some of Boccherini's early trios and quartets that he composed while resident in Vienna in the late 'fifties and early 'sixties, but apart from these works, it is questionable how many of Boccherini's early Paris publications (let us say, until the middle of the 1770s) Haydn knew. Of course, Boccherini uses a 'leisurely Italian moderato' – his music is full of them – but Haydn can just as well have adopted the ideas from the countless concerto beginnings of the period (e.g. his brother Michael Haydn's Violin Concerto in B flat of 1760, his Flute Concertos of the 1760s, Anton Filtz's beautiful Flute Concerto in D, Joseph Haydn's own 'Cello Concerto in C); or equally from many German composers, and not only from C. P. E. Bach but also the Mannheim school such as Franz Xaver Richter.[2]

1 *Tempos in the String Quartets of Joseph Haydn* (Dissertation, Indiana University, 1969), p.69.
2 Nowadays, the influence of the Mannheim school is quite rightly considered to be far less widespread, particularly in Austria, than was previously thought. But it was by no means non-existent. Even in remote monasteries such as the Styrian Abbey of Admont, we find MS. copies of Carl Stamitz's Trios (2 violins, basso) known as Op. 14; Carl Stamitz was in his early twenties when Haydn began to compose Op. 9, but the principle is worth noting. We studied the Stamitz MSS. when the Admont collection was still in the Parish Church of Bad Aussee (1951).

Although such ideas as the actual use of the moderato opening may have come from without, it seems clear that the actual initiative to begin quartets after at least a decade was motivated by purely private, musical reasons. Why, after all these years, would Prince Nicolaus suddenly want Haydn to compose quartets rather than the symphonies, operas, baryton trios and other pieces (also, since 1766, church music) in regular demand at Eisenstadt and Eszterháza? By 1768, Haydn was sufficiently popular with the Prince to dare to strike off on his own, as long as such new compositions did not actively conflict with the princely musical and theatrical life; and moreover, these quartets·could be played at once ('nell' apartamento'). Certainly, the presence of Luigi Tomasini may have been an incentive: Haydn is reported to have said, 'no one plays my quartets like Luigi' (who, we must recall, was himself a successful composer, like many others in Haydn's orchestra).

In the quartets, there are several new and interesting factors that place them in a world apart from the symphonies and baryton trios, but also far away from the earlier quartet-divertimenti.

(1) The quartets were composed as a series of six. This was definitely not the case with the earlier works: the traditional Opera 1 & 2 are the selections of a Parisian publisher, M. de la Chevardière, followed by J. J. Hummel of Berlin and Amsterdam. The use of a series does not occur, moreover, in string trios, symphonies or baryton trios (though the latter were often bound in batches of twenty-four for convenience).

(2) These Opera (we include, from this point, Opp. 17 and 20) were thus designed from the outset as sets, each work being in a different key: this differentation did not necessarily occur in the opera by other composers. In Opp. 9 and 17, one of each is in a minor key; in Op. 20, two. When we are able to follow Haydn's manipulations of his own opus sets, as with the Paris Symphonies, for example, we may note that he did not necessarily publish the works in the order in which they were composed; and that, when selling the works to more than one source (and especially to different publishers), Haydn changed the order so that, from catalogue listings ('Six Symphonies en La, Ut, Sol . . .') the works would not be immediately recognizable: that is, in the case of the Paris Symphonies, Artaria, Forster and Imbault might not at once realize that they were in fact publishing the same works simultaneously. This fact may explain why the order of a given set differs between (a) that of Haydn's autographs and/or *EK*, and (b) those of various publishers. In the case of Op. 20, there are no less than four such orders (*vide infra*).

(3) Having displaced the balance of the quartet towards the first movement, Haydn must now increase the weight of the finale to offset this 'nose-heavy' overall structure. In four of the six works in Op. 9 he does so, in two he rather surprisingly does not: the 57-bar Finale of No. 2 is short for the lengthy opening Moderato (109 bars), and the 53-bar Finale of No. 6 is hardly a match, even at presto tempo, for the opening. But otherwise, the new quartet form is established with Op. 9. It will undergo widespread polishing, refinement; and some of its values will be slightly altered (e.g. in the construction of the finales); but such a work as No. 4 in D minor – the first, in all probability to have been composed – is already on the level of great Haydn. It cannot, however, be denied that Op. 9 is still uneven. It was a sophisticated exercise and one that Haydn needed to write, but it is more important historically than it is winning musically. Perhaps the most difficult movements for us nowadays are the moderatos, with their broad tapestry of small interlocking fragments. They are sometimes (No. 3) held together with those ubiquitous repeated quavers; but at other times the quavers do not appear until well after the movement has started (No. 2), and

in some cases the mortar is quite different (No. 1, where the rhythmic variety and complexity are endless).

The minuets require special praise. If there is any single genre in which Haydn was now a supreme master, it is here. He manages to retain the rhythmic vitality of his best symphonic minuets (No. 31), coupled with a fine sense of chamber-musical fitness (the sturdy, octave-led beat of No. 1's Minuet is not necessarily symphonic). Perhaps the most beautiful is the ethereal No. 2's, whose twenty bars are of a purity and subtlety which do not transfer well to the keyboard: Haydn wrote a series of variations on this 'Arietta' (XVII:3) which circulated in MS. as early as 1774 and was printed by Artaria in the 1780s. It shows, for a sensitive ear, how impure is the piano's (harpsichord's) intonation compared to that of four string instruments.

Another speciality is the singing quality of the slow movements. Critics have generally seen, in these richly ornamented violin solos, a tribute to Tomasini. Yet one more feature that occurs in all three opera is the transfer of recitative-like and aria-like (*arioso*) sections (Opp. 9/2, 17/5, 20/2) from the world of *opera seria* (accompanied recitative). In some cases we have the violin imitating a dramatic soprano (Op. 17/5), even to the written-out appoggiature – are there still unconverted on this subject? – but in others, especially in the movement from Opus 20, we have a string quartet assimilating and transferring into a different medium the world of the opera. It is, as Tovey repeatedly stressed, the rhetorical world of opera plus C. P. E. Bach, whose eccentric and brilliantly mannered digressions would not have matched Haydn's earlier style. We shall see other aspects of C. P. E. Bach's influence in the piano sonatas of this period. The influence of the concerto in the slow movements also accounts for the elaborate and difficult violin solos, for instance No. 6's Adagio. The conventional cadences with trill at the end of both parts are a heritage of the concerto, as are the fermate, six-four chords and invitation to a cadenza (which Tomasini, being a composer, will have accomplished with relish and taste) that we find not only in No. 6 (bar 54) but in many other places in the sets.

The D minor (No. 4) was perhaps the most influential. Its serious, dedicated atmosphere, its superbly integrated use of motivic work in the first movement and the deft alliance of counterpoint to the classical style in the fourth movement, were carefully studied by Haydn's contemporaries: we find traces of its compositional technique in Vanhal's String Trio in F minor[1] and String Quartet in C minor, Op. 1, No. 4.[2] Other Vanhal Quartets also show the influence of Opus 9, e.g. the discursive opening movement ('Moderato' in Melk V, 907; 'Allegro moderato' in other sources) of the Quartet in C major.[3] There are many other examples in Vanhal which space prohibits our analyzing, even superficially. But perhaps the most interesting influence of Op. 9, No. 4, is on Mozart, in K.173 (1773). 'The minuet...derives thematically, tonally and formally from the minuet of Haydn's Op. 9, No. 4', writes Hans Keller.[4] There is another detail of even more crucial importance on Mozart's later

---

1 Sieber, Op. 11, No. 3 (announced in *L'avant-coureur*, 16 Nov. 1772; *Mercure de France*, Dec. 1772); MS. parts in the Monastery of Schlägl (Upper Austria) which we studied twenty-five years ago.

2 'Six Quatuors Concertantes... OEUVRE Iᵉ', Huberty pl. 131 (announced in *L'avant-coureur*, 20 Nov. 1769). The copy we used is in the Library of Congress. There are also traces of Haydn's quartet-divertiment in other movements of the series. Three of the Quartets (Nos. 3, 5, 6) are also ascribed to Lolli in the Dunwalt Catalogue, but not No. 4 in C minor which is only known under Vanhal's name, also in the Quartbuch.

3 Breitkopf Catalogue 1773; MSS. in Osek (45A, 56A), Kremsmünster (G 64, 263) and Melk (V, 907); Quartbuch; we used No. 1 of 'Two Quartets... London Printed for BABBS Musical Circulating Library Nᵒ 132 in Oxford Street facing Hanover Square. Where may be had all the above Authors works.' Library of Congress g. 429.f.

4 *The Mozart Companion* (ed. Landon/Mitchell), p. 101.

development, and that is a central phrase in the first subject of Op. 9's Allegro moderato:

The bracketed portion is surely the grandfather of the famous

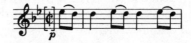

– particularly in view of Mozart's later use at the end of the development

(cf. Haydn's use in G minor, bars 36ff.). The model (Haydn, that is) also has a feature typical of this period, in that the theme appears in the development only in minor keys – first in G minor (in itself an innovation as the starting key of a D minor development section), then A minor: all of which also shows the seriousness of intent.

It cannot be said that the immense success of Op. 9 in Haydn's lifetime – MSS. throughout the Austrian monasteries, Bohemian aristocratic collections, German princely archives (Oettingen-Wallerstein, Thurn und Taxis); printed editions in the early 1770s in Amsterdam/Berlin, Paris and London – has lasted. Whereas the transitional symphonies (Nos. 26, 39, 44, 52, etc.) have made something of a comeback, Op. 9 on the whole has not; and neither has Op. 17. There are perhaps two reasons for this: (a) that the contemporary Haydn symphonies are more interesting and numerous; (b) that the Quartets of Op. 20, which are very popular and respected, have tended to overshadow their immediate precedessors, but not – and this is a curious fact – the much earlier quartet-divertimenti that occupy a position of affection in the public's mind similar to Mozart's so-called Salzburg Symphonies (the Italianate Divertimenti, K.136–8, 1772), which not even the towering musical and intellectual achievements of the later quartets (especially K.387 *et seq.*) have ever displaced from their popularity – once, that is, they were printed in the old Mozart *Gesamtausgabe* (their first[!] edition). Haydn's early quartet-divertimenti – whatever their structural faults and musical weakness (and both are principally viewed in the light of that which their composer later accomplished in the genre) – are winning music, and that could not be said for much of Op. 9, nor on the whole of Op. 17.

Op. 17, too, was more necessary to Haydn's development than to our delectation. Like Op. 9, it was widely circulated in MSS. and printed within one year of its composition by Hummel of Amsterdam/Berlin and Gardom of London, within two years by Sieber of Paris, and reprinted by Welcker of London shortly thereafter; and like Op. 9, Op. 17 has never recaptured the popularity it once so thoroughly enjoyed. The reasons are similar to the eclipse of Op. 9: most of the symphonies composed about 1771 (e.g. No. 44 in E minor) are more interesting to the public, and this is certainly not only because the twentieth-century (if by no means the eighteenth-century) public is more attracted to symphonic (orchestral) works than to chamber music. Symphony No. 44 is better organized and more dramatically expressed than most of Op. 17. Within a year Haydn had caught up and, it must be candidly stated, surpassed with his Op. 20 all his own previous and contemporary symphonies except perhaps No. 45, which is the greatest single work of its genre written before the Paris Symphonies (though some experts on the subject might also wish to include on that narrow platform of greatness Nos. 67 and 77). Op. 17 has become an object for scholarly study for the connoisseur's admiration,[1] but it is more analyzed and discussed than performed. Its merits for Haydn's inner development are obvious but need, perhaps, to be summarized in brief. The often seemingly endless motivic work of Opus 9's moderato movements is tightened, and as a result made more interesting: this does not mean that Op. 17's opening movements are shorter; on the contrary, most are slightly longer:

MODERATO MOVEMENTS IN OPP. 9 AND 17

Op. 9	No. of bars	Op. 17	No. of bars
No. 1	72	No. 1	110
2	109	2	100
3	81	4	130
4	75	5	89

Op. 17, No. 6, is a work closely related to the last of the preceding set: both have 'chasse'-like, that is six-eight, openings; but the whole of Op. 17's contribution to the genre is better balanced:

Op. 9, No. 6	*Op. 17, No. 6*
I. Presto (133 bars); II. Minuet & Trio (34 + 34); III. Adagio (34); IV. Allegro 2/4 (53).	I. Presto (200 bars); II. Minuet & Trio (22 + 20); III. Largo (43); IV. Allegro 2/4 (151).

Everyone has always agreed that the end of Op. 9/6 is unworthy of the work and the set. The argument that Haydn was weary from the strain of composing a whole sextet of works and, as it were, gave up, seems to us unworthy of serious discussion. The fundamental problem with Haydn and in other composers of this period is *the overall balance of all the movements of a given work* and *the internal balance within the individual movements*. Until these two elements are brought into harmony with themselves and with each other, no masterpiece and no perfect series can be evolved. Haydn's problems in creating the classical string quartet were many and profound, and being (as he himself said on many occasions) a slow worker – 'ich war nie ein Geschwindschreiber, und komponirte immer mit Bedächtlichkeit und Fleiß...' (Griesinger, 61) – he had to resort to empirical methods to achieve his goal. Opp. 9 and 17 are precisely part of the famous Eszterháza dictum: 'I was forced to become original', which meant in our case that which even the great and mercurial Mozart called, in his quartets dedicated to Haydn, 'il frutto di una lunga, e laboriosa fatica'. Quartets are in many respects far more difficult to compose than symphonies or even large vocal works; the medium is primarily for the player, and therefore the public values are of far less consequence than private concentration; the listener, as Hans Keller has frequently said, 'is an interloper': 'You can come to understand a symphony by listening to it, but you cannot understand a string quartet without playing it. The string quartet is the esoteric symphony, and the more esoteric a truth, the more absolute the need for its immediate experience.[2]

---

1 Perhaps the future fate for the whole of Haydn? See *Haydn: the Late Years 1801–1809*: 'Haydn and Posterity'.
2 *The Mozart Companion* (ed. Landon/Mitchell), p. 90.

Therefore the problem of the balance remained paramount in Haydn's Opp. 9 and 17, and in the Finale of Op. 17/6 he solved it differently and in a more expanded fashion than in Op. 9/6. Haydn's first, instinctive method was towards pithiness; the discursive, 'mosaic' style was not natural to him and had, as it were, to be conquered. Even as late as the Gloria in the *Missa Sancti Bernardi de Offida* (1796), Haydn's first concept was brevity; he later expanded the movement by 'inserts'.[1] Thus the 53-bar Allegro for Op. 9/6's Finale is Haydn's first instinctive reaction to the problem of closing a work that began with a 'finale' metre (six-eight): he composed a very tightly knit, short movement. The material would not stand for longer treatment and as a conclusion it is much better than its reputation (both repeats must, of course, be taken: that is why they were written). Op. 17/6's Finale uses different material which was designed from the outset for greater expansion and also for interludes such as the switching back and forth from open to fingered string (45ff., 128ff.). It also ends *piano* and that, in itself, requires in a movement of this kind that the material preceding the *piano* is lengthy enough for the *p* to make its structural point; it also presupposes that (given the way the exposition ends) Haydn must add a little tailpiece which puts the final *p* ending into proper perspective (bars 141ff.). This *piano* ending is a surprise (not the dynamic level: we might have expected that from hearing the exposition's *p* ending), and once Haydn has organized the material sufficiently he can indulge in such a luxury. Until he had, with Op. 9, ironed out the structural and technical problems, we could hardly expect ambiguities – Op. 9 is in itself something of an ambiguity, but not self-willed – on a more complex and individual level. The one work of Opus 17 which is in a minor key opens with an ambiguity (and one to which Haydn will return in two other minor-key Quartets, Op. 33/1 and Op. 64/2): the first two notes lead us

to expect E flat: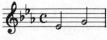

and it is not until the next bar

that C minor bursts upon us. And not only that: the Finale is also tonally ambiguous; its C minor beginning immediately shifts to F minor, to B flat, to E flat and then to the dominant of C minor – all before the principal key has had time to establish itself:

1 *Haydn: the Years of 'The Creation' 1796–1800*, p. 141.

The Minuet is in C major, with that octave skip in the 'cello which one has admired in Op. 9/1 and which is so vital and life-enhancing: therefore our surprise in hearing the Trio's beginning is equal to that of hearing an E flat Quartet become a C minor Quartet in the space of two bars:

Yet another tonal ambiguity. It must be obvious by now that Haydn is consciously trying to establish an overall mood to this work, a device that will permeate at least three of its movements (all the quick ones) in a fashion sufficiently striking to place it apart from its fellows in the set as a distinctive unity. Another such device unites Op. 17, No. 3: *viz.*:

The 'fifthy' character of the theme also extends to the (unquoted) Trio. In the first and last movements, the progression from *b flat* to *e flat* and back again is identical, while in the Minuet the motion is in retrograde; in the Adagio it is (in a different key) also from V to V and back to V with a 'fifthy' progression in the last two quavers of bar 1 as well. The Finale of this work is perhaps the most fetching conclusion in Opp. 9 and 17. With its characteristic use of silence, its memorable (indeed haunting) tune, its brilliant contrapuntal elaborations (bars 10ff., and all except the last $2\frac{1}{2}$ bars in the development) and its wonderfully concise formal efficiency, it shows what technical (and with Haydn this almost always goes hand in hand with spiritual) advances the quartet finale has now reached. It was one way of ending a work, especially one with a long opening slow movement; here (and in Op. 9, No. 5) we have Haydn's quartet transformation of the *sonata da chiesa* form: the opening slow movement – which was often in free, or at least unconventional, form in a symphony of that type (Nos. 21, 22) – has now become a slow theme and variations. It was a type that attracted Haydn throughout his chamber-musical life, and it last specimen is Op. 76, No. 5. An opening slow movement was one further excuse to preserve the placement of the minuet second, thus showing the difference between an orchestral *sonata da chiesa* work and one designed for solo strings. In the symphony the scheme had been:

> Slow (usually adagio) – fast (usually *alla breve*) – Minuet & Trio – fast (quick metre).

There were other designs as well (No. 18) but the quick movement always came second. In the quartet variant of this scheme, we always now find:

Slow movement (theme & variations) – Minuet & Trio – slow movement – fast finale.

The very fact that there are two slow movements shows the difference between the quartet and the public symphony, where the average audience could not be expected to digest two rather long and intricate slow movements within the confines of a single piece. It also meant that the finale needed to fulfil the function of the otherwise missing quick movement: in the case of Op. 9, No. 5, this resulted in a particularly extended *Presto* with 218 bars and both sections repeated, and in Op. 17, No. 3, the construction of a particularly attractive *Allegro di molto*.

Op. 17 is full of rewarding works and delightful individual movements. If it has succumbed to the inexorable laws of survival, it is partly, as Charles Rosen has said, because we insist on judging these works almost exclusively from their position in the totality of Haydn's *oeuvre* rather than on their own very considerable merits:

> Taken on their own terms the works of the late 60s and early 70s inspire admiration: they are defective only when measured by the standards of Haydn's later works. Why then do we impose these standards? Why do we refuse the same tolerance to the early work of an artist that we grant – indeed, insist upon granting – to an earlier style? No one, for example, would reproach Chaucer with a failure to shape his verse in the dramatic speech rhythms of the Elizabethans, Masaccio with a lack of the atmospheric integration of High Renaissance painting, or Bach with a refusal to seek the rhythmic variety of the classical style.
>
> The analogies are, however, less pertinent than we who love so many of the early works of Haydn would like them to be. A style is a way of exploiting and controlling the resources of a language. J. S. Bach's mastery of the contemporary language of tonality was as complete as could be imagined, but in the twenty years between his death and the *Sturm und Drang* symphonies that Haydn wrote in the early 70s, this language had changed significantly: the syntax was less fluid, the relation between tonic and dominant more highly polarized. Haydn's style of 1770, while it had taken account of the development, was not yet able to embrace its full implications. The higher degree of articulation of phrase and polarity of harmony raised problems for continuity that were difficult to solve: the shapes and rhythms move without transition from the squarely regular to the unsystematic, relying in the latter case almost entirely upon repetition or upon Baroque sequences to justify the sense of motion.[1]

It is clear that the Viennese classical style arrived at its full maturity *not* with the Quartets, Op. 33 (Sandberger, Blume, Finscher, Barrett-Ayres), and certainly not as late as Op. 50 (Moe), but with Op. 20. Apart from ourself, and sometimes Professor J. P. Larsen,[2] it would seem that only Professor Kirkendale (pp. 183f.) and Professor László Somfai (*passim*) incline to this view of Op. 20 as the central group of quartets in this period, and as a point of pivotal importance in the works of Haydn and the Viennese classical period altogether. Sir Donald Tovey, of course, at once realized the vital importance of Op. 20, and although his summary has been frequently quoted, it is repeated here because its message could hardly be put more felicitously:

---

1 *The Classical Style*, London and New York 1971, pp. 146f.; reprinted by permission of Faber and Faber Ltd and The Viking Press, Inc.
2 Where there is considerable vacillation about the *Sturm und Drang*: it is played down for Mozart's K.183 in *The Mozart Companion*, p. 173, and in general in 'Der Stilwandel in der österreichischen Musik zwischen Barock und Klassik' (*Der Junge Haydn, Kongressbericht Graz 1970* [1972]; also in 'Zur Enstehung der österreichischen Symphonietradition (ca. 1750–1775)', in *Haydn Yearbook* X (in preparation). In other articles, such as in 'Some Observations on the Development and Characteristics of Vienn[ese] Classical Instrumental Music' (*Studio musicologia* IX [1967], pp. 115ff.), Professor Larsen seems to consider the early 1770s as marking the arrival of the classical style.

With op. 20 the historical development of Haydn's quartets reaches its goal; and further progress is not progress in any historical sense, but simply the difference between one masterpiece and the next. Not all the later works are equally valuable; inequalities of value are relatively more rather than less noticeable, and no later set of six quartets, not even op. 76, is, on its own plane, so uniformly weighty and so varied in substance as op. 20. If Haydn's career had ended there, nobody could have guessed which of some half-dozen different lines he would have followed up: the line of Beethovenish tragedy foreshadowed in the F minor quartet; the Wilhelm Rust line suggested by the fantasia in the C major; a return to fugal polyphony as the main interest; the further development of the comic vein of the D major; the higher and non-farcical comedy of the A major; and the development of (or subsidence into) luxury scoring.

[Tovey, 'Haydn' article in *Cobbett*, pp. 537f.]

The autographs (1772) of Op. 20 do not reveal the order in which the Quartets were composed. Here, in tabular form, is the order as found in *EK*, in the first edition by M. de la Chevardière (Paris), in the Hummel edition and in the late but authentic edition by Artaria:[1]

	QUARTET NO.					
	1	2	3	4	5	6
Entwurf-Katalog, as compiled by Haydn, *c.* 1772, beginning with the Quartets with fugue finale: 'Fuga a 2 soggetti', '…a 3', '…a 4'.	F minor	A	C	G minor	D	E♭
As printed by Chevardière, Paris, in parts with opus number 'XX', *c.* 1774.	E♭	F minor	C	A	G minor	D
As printed by Hummel, *c.* 1779, with the 'Sun' title page; reprinted in Pleyel's complete edition and taken over into the *Haydn Verzeichnis* by Elssler.	E♭	C	G minor	D	F minor	A
		Volume I			Volume II	
As printed by Artaria, Vienna, in parts, *c.* 1800–1; revised by Haydn.	E♭	A	F minor	D	C	G minor

If we examine the autographs, some peculiar characteristics reveal themselves: although written with (even for Haydn) exceptional care and neatness, they nevertheless reveal a barely suppressed state of excitement. There are hardly any other autographs apart from some of the Paris, the 'Oxford' and some of the Salomon Symphonies which reveal this state of constant inner exaltation; but in the cases of the later works, the actual pressure of time was responsible for a certain scribal haste. This does not obtain in Op. 20, but if we study the final 'signatures', this state of inner excitement at once manifests itself:

No. 1: 'Soli Deo et Cuique Suum'.
No. 2: 'Laus omnip: Deo. / Sic fugit amicus amicum.'
No. 3: 'Laus Deo et B: V: M: cum S° [Sancto] S^to' [Spirito; *sc* Spiritu].
No. 4: 'Gloria in Excelsis Deo'.
No. 5: 'Fine Laus Deo'.
No. 6: 'Laus Deo et Beatissimae Virgini Mariae'.

---

1 About the Artaria edition, see *Haydn: the Years of 'The Creation' 1796–1800*, pp. 549f.

Professor Somfai (Lecture: Durham 1969) proposed a new chronological order. This order was based, among other things, on the description in the autograph of the 'cello part. Now there has always been some discussion as to which instrument Haydn actually intended as the lowest part of his early quartets.[1] The contemporary sources for the quartet-divertimenti, including the authentic Fürnberg MSS., all specify 'Basso'[2] but nevertheless it is probable that a violoncello and not a *violone* (double bass) was intended. In the contemporary MSS. of Op. 9, we usually find 'Basso'. On the title page of Op. 17's autograph we find 'Divertimento a quatro [*sic*] p. 2 Violini, Viola, e Basso ...' but the actual instrument reads 'Basso / Violoncello'. (The instruments only occur on page one of the series.) In Op. 20's autographs we find 'Basso' for No. 3, 'Basso' corrected to 'Violoncello' in Nos. 1 and 5, 'Violoncello' in Nos. 2 and 6 and nothing in No. 4. Dr Somfai obviously presumes that some sort of morphological development from 'Basso' to 'Violoncello' may be seen if we re-group the series as follows:

PROBABLE SEQUENCE OF COMPOSITION, ACCORDING TO SOMFAI

	Key	Name of bass instrument in Haydn's MS.	Placing of Minuet movement		Fugue Finale	Haydn's Latin remarks at the end of each MS. fascicle
1	G minor	'Basso'	II		no	'Laus Deo et B: V: M: cum S° Sᵗᵒ'
2	E♭ major	'Basso', corrected to 'Violoncello'	II	old type	no	'Soli Deo et Cuique Suum'
3	F minor	'Basso', corrected to 'Violoncello'	II		yes	'Fine Laus Deo'
4	C major	'Violoncello'	III		yes	'Laus omnip: Deo' 'Sic fugit amicus amicum'
5	A major	'Violoncello'	III	new type	yes	'Laus Deo et Beatissimae Virgini Mariae'
6	D major	none	III		no	'Gloria in excelsis Deo'

In Opp. 9 and 17, the minuet came second; in the later quartets of Haydn's career it came third. Again believing in a morphological development, Professor Somfai has placed the three 'old types' at the beginning and the three 'new types' at the end.

In view of the widely differing sequences, we can only offer some suggestions. Obviously there were contemporary and authentic sources, mostly in parts, which no longer survive. Whence did Chevardière and Hummel receive their sources? Is it possible that Haydn sent them? We consider it very unlikely (there are very bad errors in the Chevardière print), but we consider it entirely possible that there were authentic MSS. in circulation in Vienna, one of which was sent to the offices of Chevardière. Then how to account for the difference in sequence between the Paris and Amsterdam prints? Since one (Paris) came out *c.* 1774 and the other five years later, it is possible that the later sequence (Hummel) also derives from a revised order of Haydn's as found in another no longer extant Viennese copy. That Haydn varied the

---

1 Somfai in *HJB* III (1965), p. 159. Finscher 106ff., 181ff. The problem is linked with the wrong use of the six-four chord, i.e. one that presupposes that (in order to avoid that six-four chord) the lowest note would have been played by a 16-foot instrument. Tovey also mentions this problem (I, 518). See also *Haydn in England 1791–1795*, p. 470.
2 The authentic parts for III: 6, 2, 4, 1, 7, 12 read 'VI. / Notturni. / per due Violini Violae e Basso ...'. National Széchényi Library (Budapest) κ. 44.

order of his works is well known (Paris Symphonies); and in Op. 20 we also have the authentic sequence of Artaria's print which agrees neither with any of those in the earlier prints nor with that in *EK*. We propose, in view of this conflicting evidence, to adopt the sequence of Op. 20 as found in *EK*: it is the only authentic evidence apart from Artaria's, and textual examination of the Artaria print has shown that, by 1800, Haydn was pursuing quite different aesthetic principles. The late sequence is also logical: it ends each volume from a position of strength, i.e. each ends with one of the quartets in minor. Volume II ends with perhaps the most *outré* and 'dangerous' of the six works. Is it possible that in 1800 Haydn was arranging these old pieces so that they would better be able to match Beethoven's Op. 18, of which Haydn must have heard several performances from the MSS.? And so that the player would, in each volume, end with the most dramatic of the three works it contained? We would recall that the revised Op. 20 was dedicated to Nicolaus Zmeskall von Domanowecz, Beethoven's 'Musikgraf'. In *EK*, Op. 9's entry began with the most difficult and uncompromising work: the D minor. Why should not Op. 20 have, as *EK* suggests, begun with the F minor, one of the greatest and perhaps the most pessimistic of the series? This was, after all, the work that Haydn chose to play to Gluck when the latter returned from his Parisian failures (ending with *Alceste*) in 1776.[1]

In his attempt to find a perfect solution of the larger balance for the string quartet form, Haydn in Op. 20 turned to several new methods. The first problem which he attacked head-on was that of the finale and its relation to the earlier movements; it was obviously a question of balance, and by turning to complicated fugal patterns Haydn completely reversed the balance that had obtained in Opp. 9 and 17. The very complexity of the fugues, their density of thought, suddenly shifted the weight, not away from the first and slow movements, but *also* to the finale. A typical work in Op. 9 might be:

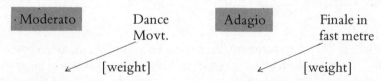

In Op. 20, the weight is distributed in two new patterns: (a) towards the three fugal finales; (b) towards a redistribution of the inner movements. If the minuet comes second, the key of the slow movement (third in position) is either the submediant or, in minor, the relative major, and the metre 3/4, 3/8 or 6/8. If the minuet comes third, the key of the preceding slow movement is the dominant and the metre barred C, four-four or two-four.[2] Thus we have the 'weight' distributions as shown overleaf. Examined in this light, it is clear that Op. 20, No. 4, is the work of the future, with its piquant minuet and light but highly intellectual finale. Judged according to this kind of weight distribution, moreover, Op. 33 is still an experimental set (as far as the distribution of the inner parts are concerned), and we can see why Professor Moe could maintain that the quartet's classical mastery began with Op. 50, in which all these problems are more or less permanently solved.

1 *Vide infra*, p. 395.
2 Somfai 'Vom Barock zur Klassik', p. 69.

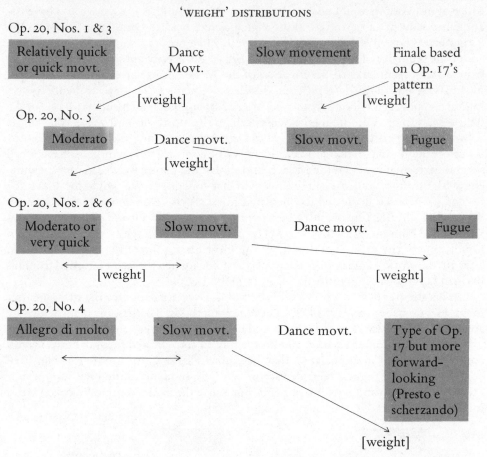

'WEIGHT' DISTRIBUTIONS

Op. 20, Nos. 1 & 3

Relatively quick or quick movt.   Dance Movt.   Slow movement   Finale based on Op. 17's pattern

[weight]   [weight]

Op. 20, No. 5

Moderato   Dance movt.   Slow movt.   Fugue

[weight]

Op. 20, Nos. 2 & 6

Moderato or very quick   Slow movt.   Dance movt.   Fugue

[weight]   [weight]

Op. 20, No. 4

Allegro di molto   Slow movt.   Dance movt.   Type of Op. 17 but more forward-looking (Presto e scherzando)

[weight]

Moving from the large to the small, or from Haydn's balance in 'large dimension' to problems of 'small dimensions', we shall follow the fascinating analysis of one particular problem as it was presented in that memorable Durham Lecture (1969) by Professor Somfai. He called it 'balance in small dimension: the permutation of three elements', and it concerns the beginning of Op. 20, No. 2. With this problem, we are in the midst of Op. 20's intellectual attainments which are here revealed in a formidable way. Music and mathematics are more closely allied than is generally realized by the 'outsider', and here we find Haydn seeking hitherto unknown horizons, exploring problems that are possibly even dangerous for his own sanity (and the sanity of the Viennese classical style as well). By the time we have concluded our cruelly brief discussion of Op. 20, it will be seen that this set really posed problems of a dimension which were explored in quite another way by Mozart in his 'Haydn' quartets but not faced squarely again until Beethoven.

The theme of Op. 20, No. 2, consists of three separate elements:

Schematically the progress of this 'block' may be illustrated as follows:

bar	1	7	15	61	62	63	81
V. I		C	B	A	B	C	
V.II	A	A	C	B	C	A	A
Va.	B	B	A	C	A		B
Vc.	C					B	C
tonality	C	G	C	D	F	A	C

If we analyze this chart from the standpoint of the 'infinite string' we see the following pattern, where the 'A', 'B' and 'C' elements may be continued slantwise *ad infinitum* (or rather as far as the composer chooses to compose):

Infinite String:

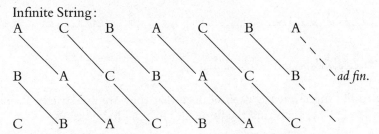

whereas 'Haydn's choice', presented like a cluster of swarming bees, is as follows:

Haydn's Choice:

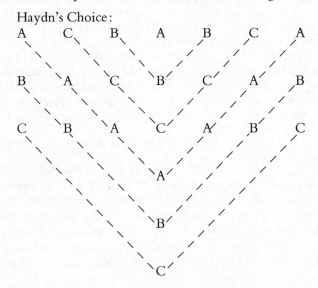

The collision between stylistic elements of the older Baroque and those of the newer classical language are graphically seen in this same section (where, in the following chart, 'CR' = chordal rhythm and 'CH' = chordal harmony). Now if we examine the differences between the autograph's phrasing of 1772 and Haydn's of 1800, we notice a curious thing. By 1800, Haydn realized the disproportionate element in the viola's staccati of bar 1: they were at direct variance with the crotchet rhythm of the harmony. By rephrasing the viola and also the 'cello of bar 2, Haydn turns the phrasing rhythm into minims (Somfai's chart, 1969):

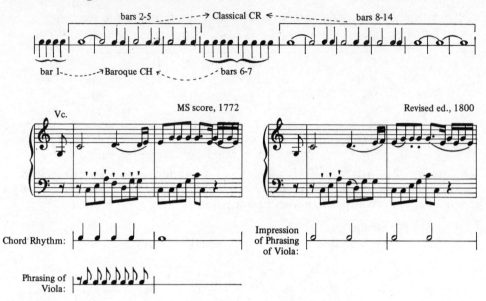

Turning to the fugues, it has been noticed that they are not strictly Baroque in construction. Jan LaRue, analyzing the fugue of Op. 20, No. 2, writes:

> Genuinely contrapuntal styles give an impression of smooth continuity because one part bridges over the articulations in other parts. In a Palestrina cadence, for example, one or two voices may already have begun the points of imitation of the following phrase. [In such works as the fugue in Haydn's Op. 20, No. 2] the coordination of articulations approximately every two or four bars undermines the contrapuntal effect; we may find considerable melodic and rhythmic individuality in the lines, yet if they phrase and cadence together, they obviously lose much or both their independence and total continuity. Similarly, the most striking reason that fugal finales in the Classic period usually do not sound like Baroque fugues may be traced to the overly frequent use of coordinated rather than overlapping articulations.

[*Guidelines for Style Analysis*, New York 1970, p. 47]

Part of this disproportion is a direct result of Haydn's extraordinary dynamic marks (which are seldom observed in performance because they are so violently mannerist and often appear to jaded string players to be moving contrary to the basic spirit of the music, which indeed on the surface they are). The one that springs to the eye in all the fugal finales is the marking 'sempre sotto voce'. If it is true that Haydn wrote that in F minor as the first of the sextet, then the violently disruptive force of the dynamic marks in the context of the fugal form may be explained as a bold experiment:

[minor]		bar 92		bar 145		bar 184
			al rovescio		*in canone*	
Exposition	modul.			F minor		
sempre sotto voce			<	*m. v.*	*ff*	*p* / *f*
[no. of bars] 109			2	33	16	18 / 6

In the A major's fugue, the dynamic level is smoother and only rises to a *forte* at the very end; and the difference may be explained by the entirely different spirit which prevails in this work (*vide infra*):

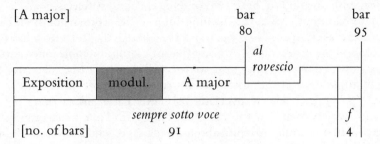

	bar 80		bar 95
		al rovescio	
Exposition	modul.	A major	
[no. of bars]	*sempre sotto voce* 91		*f* 4

LaRue's curious analysis of the C major fugue suggests that he, like most nineteenth-century and even twentieth-century critics, views these fugues with sceptical disapproval. Nowadays, we regard them not as intrusive foreign bodies, but, to quote the American musicologist Warren Kirkendale, 'they belong to the most successful final movements, and the most valuable fugues, that we have. The fact that Haydn later followed other paths does not detract from their value' (Kirkendale, 183). He draws special attention to the bold modulatory pattern (circle of fifths) that takes place in the middle of the F minor fugue, 'looking forward to Beethoven'. 'We have not found such a remote key as A flat minor proceeding from F minor in any other fugue of the eighteenth century' says Professor Kirkendale (186). The subject of the F minor fugue is a well-known Baroque theme (Handel: 'And with His stripes' from *Messiah*; Bach's *Well-Tempered Clavier*, Book II, Fugue in A minor); Haydn may have known it from Antonio Caldara's *Sonata da chiesa*, Op. 1, No. 9, and/or from W. R. Birck's Quartet in G minor (quoted by Kirkendale, p. 137):

It was noted that the last Quartet of Opp. 9 and 17 began with a 'chasse'-like six-eight movement. It is interesting that the last work in Hummel's order of Op. 20 is that in A major which begins with a six-eight Allegro di molto e scherzando. Now it is usually imagined that the fugures of Op. 20 are deadly serious pieces of contrapuntal desperation, and that of No. 5 certainly may be viewed in that light; but the A major fugue, with its dancing patterns and sophisticated cross-rhythms, and despite the fact that G. von Noé considers it the most carefully executed of all Haydn's fugues,[1] is a genuinely lighthearted and humorous piece. It is 'con 3 Soggetti', that in F minor with two and that in C a 'Fuga a 4^tro Soggetti'. On this subject, the theorists rose up in anger. Kirkendale quotes H. F. M. Langlé's *Traité de la Fugue* (1805, p. 4), wherein we may read:

> J'entends toujours parler de Fugues à 2, à 3, et à 4 sujets . . . il n'y a que des ignorants ou des charlatans qui puissent se servir d'une pareille expression; dans une Fugue, il n'y a et ne peut y avoir qu'un sujet, les autres ne sont que Contre-Sujets subordonnés . . . ne lui servent que d'accompagnement.

1 *Die Fuge bei Joseph Haydn* (dissertation), Vienna 1954.

Actually Cherubini's repetition of the last part of this dictum (in his *Cours de Contrepoint et de Fugue*, 1835, p. 105) is much better known and is discussed by Tovey (p. 536; in other connections, p. 535). Strictly speaking, Haydn's fugal finales are *double fugues* with one (in No. 6) or two (in No. 2) countersubjects.

In the quotation of Op. 20/2's opening subject, the astute reader will have noted the new texture, as compared to Opp. 9 and 17, wherein the 'cello now has an entirely different place in the proceedings. Among the almost innumerable innovations of Op. 20, this is an essential one, and we must not forget Tovey's words, 'There is perhaps no single or sextuple opus in the history of instrumental music which has achieved so much …' (p. 533). There is even the obscure Latin instruction 'per figuram retardationis' which occurs in Op. 20/5/III, bars 53ff. Tovey charmingly describes himself as a small boy asking Joachim about this passage, who answered: 'It means that the figures of the violin are always a step behind the chords; it must be played dreamily and tenderly, not stiffly and coldly' – a genuine rubato written expressly into the score, and a hint for all the other slow movements in Haydn's works with this kind of 'dreamy' figurations.

The Gypsy elements in Op. 20/4/III have been mentioned before. They are one more facet of this bewilderingly complex, bold and multi-faceted group of works. Space prevents the detailed analysis that these extraordinary works deserve, and we would close with a warning – Haydn's warning

> Wenn falscher Wahn euch nicht verführt
> Noch mehr zu wünschen, als ihr habt,
> Und mehr zu wissen, als ihr sollt.

The tension of the G minor Quartet's first movement is well known. It is established at once by the division of the main theme into *seven*-bar phrases. At the end of it, we find the curious and slightly sinister tail-piece (Watteau's 'Gilles'? The Gypsies in the merry *Fest*?) –

– which gradually begins to take on a position of increasing significance. The development is so placed that it starts *again* in G minor (another innovation), as if Haydn himself were also starting the 'argument' again. The tension increases to the following passage in B flat, where the initially intrusive figure does, indeed, lead us to the brink of utter catastrophe: that fragmented extract at bars 151f. is profoundly upsetting. We show the passage with the curious differences in dynamic marks between the autograph of 1772 and Artaria's version of 1800 (by courtesy of Professor Somfai's graph, Durham 1969) – see the musical example opposite, above. If there is a single passage in the whole of Haydn that should tell us that he was Beethoven's teacher, this one must be one of the first candidates. (Beethoven made a copy of Op. 20, No. 1: it is now in the Bodmer Collection in the Beethoven-Haus, Bonn.)

Despite the neat, almost scholarly appearance of the autographs, Op. 20 was in fact composed with the aid of complicated sketches, of which only one has survived (for the slow movement of No. 3). It is interesting in that it shows that unlike the later Haydn (cf. Symphony No. 99's sketch), Op. 20 was, like Mozart's own 'Haydn'

(G minor Quartet, 1st Movement, B. 141ff)

quartets, 'il frutto di una lunga, e laboriosa fatica'. Professor Somfai, who published the sketch for the first time,[1] writes: 'The best example'

of the deliberate smoothing-over of the boldness found in the first version may be observed without doubt in the principal theme. The fashion in which Haydn wrote down the sketch of the first bars ... is in fact most interesting: the four instruments are pressed together to a single fifth-tessitura, the melody is given to the 'cello, the sound really vibrates. A magnificent idea (born 'in the fire of inspiration') ... but will it be possible to increase further the beauty, the originality of the sound? Even bars 5–8 of the sketch, it seems, did not continue the lay-out of that first inspiration. ... How much more simple is the solution [shown overleaf] of the final autograph score:

1 'Ich war nie ein Geschwindschreiber...': Joseph Haydns Skizzen zum langsamen Satz des Streichquartetts Hoboken III:33 (Op. 20 No. 3), in *Festkrift Jens Peter Larsen*, Copenhagen 1972, pp. 275ff. The sketches were written on the empty sheets of the early (1760) autograph of the Divertimento II: 16. National Library, Budapest, Ms. mus. I. 47.

Poco Adagio

(3) PIANO SONATAS AND VARIATIONS

Altezza Serenissima! Fra le rare insigni, ed assai note qualità, che adorn[an]o l'Altezza Vostra Serenissima, si contano anche il possesso intiero della Musica tutta, non già del Violino, e dal Baritono, che suona squisitamente ed al pari d'ogni Professore più esperto: Questa cognizione dunque, e la bontà, con laquale l'Altezza Vostra Serenissima hà saputo fin ora riguardare i miei fedeli servigi, a compartire ancora le miei composizioni, mi fanno ardito di dedicare al sovragrande suo merito questo picciol parto del mio talento. . . .

[Haydn's dedication to Prince Nicolaus Esterházy of the Piano Sonatas Nos. 36–41 (XVI:21–26) in the authentic edition by Joseph Kurzbeck, 1774]

Although the chronology of the piano sonatas composed in this period is the subject of considerable speculation, a rough table may be presented – see opposite.

Stylistically, the great, indeed unique, No. 33 continues to cause confusion among scholars who insist on a composer's 'progress'. Pohl (II, 311) remarks on its seriousness and 'solid workmanship, which one hardly wants to attribute to this early period.' The latest writer on Haydn's sonatas, who has devoted a whole book to the early works,[1] resisted to the end the idea that this Sonata could have been written in 1771 and, not believing photographs, actually sent someone to Paris to investigate the date on the autograph itself.

This arises from the totally erroneous belief that Haydn's mind worked like that of a German musicologist, with a proper morphological sense of progress. It is inconceivable, also, to Ms. Wackernagel, that the Sonatas of 1773, dedicated to Prince Nicolaus, could follow hard on the C minor work. Part of this general confusion is

---

1 Bettina Wackernagel, *Joseph Haydns Frühe Klaviersonaten*, Tutzing 1975, pp. 9n., 174ff., 183, 183n.

CHRONOLOGY OF THE PIANO SONATAS

Wiener Urtext-Ausgabe	Hoboken XVI	Date	Remarks
20	18	c. 1766–7 (or later?)	Fragmentary autograph (Paris) suggests period c. 1766–7 or possibly later.
21–27	2a–g	c. 1765–6?	Lost Sonatas (see *Wiener Urtext-Ausgabe* I, pp. 132f. for complete incipits which are given only in fragmentary form in Hoboken). Entry in *EK* c. 1767 (or slightly later?). For a possible later date (1771?), *vide infra*.
28	XIV:5	c. 1765–6(?)	*EK* c. 1767. Fragmentary autograph (Berlin) also confirms this approximate dating.
29	45	1766	Dated autograph (British Museum)
30	19	1767	Dated autograph (Basel)
31	46	c. 1767–8 (or slightly later)	*EK* c. 1767–8 or slightly later.
32	44	c. 1768–70 (or slightly later)	Nos. 32, 29 and 31 issued by Artaria in 1788; No. 32 not in *EK* but presumably belongs to this period & not 1788.
33	20	1771	Dated autograph (Paris); not in *EK*.
34	33	c. 1771–3 (or later?)	Earliest dated reference: print (with Nos. 35 & 53) by Beardmore & Birchall, London 1783.
35	43	c. 1771–3 (or later?)	See No. 34.
36–41	21–26	1773	Dated autographs (Paris) of Nos. 36–38: 'Sei Sonate per Cembalo...di me giuseppe Haydn 773'. Printed 1774. *EK*: '6 gedruckte Sonaten A[nno] 774'.
42–47	27–32	1774–6	Dated autograph of No. 44 (Basel) 1774. Dated authentic copies of set, 1776. *EK*: '6 Sonaten von Anno 1776'.

---

because Ms. Wackernagel seems not to have examined the symphonies and string quartets of the late 'sixties and early 'seventies; otherwise she would have observed precisely the same vacillation between ruggedly individual minor-key works and relatively lightweight, uncomplicated works in the major. There is the same difference between Symphonies Nos. 52 in C minor and 69 ('Laudon') as there is between Sonatas Nos. 33 in C minor and 42 in G. It could hardly be believed that these stormy creations were by the same composer as the *galant* superficialities of a few years later.[1] Part of the confusion with the piano sonatas, at least in the past, was the incorrect chronology of many works. Now that they have been back-dated (perhaps in some cases a little too enthusiastically?),[2] the presence of the C minor Sonata is not all that unique. Alas, some of its immediate predecessors, in D minor and E minor, have been irretrievably lost, but even judging from the *incipits* (especially of that in E minor) we can imagine that they must have been similar in mood, if perhaps not in perfection of language, to No. 33. And with the mention of these lost sonatas we may, for a

---

1 Johannes Ebert (Joseph Haydn; *Der Mann und das Werk*, Mainz 1939, p. 74) writes: 'In all the works of this period, one has the feeling that one has not heard properly and asks – is this still Haydn. Or better: is this *already* Haydn?'
2 Rosen, op. cit., p. 146n. has some perhaps pertinent reflections that No. 32 is now being back-dated too far.

moment, touch on the *raison d'être* of these works altogether. For whom were they written? What accounts for their survival or non-survival?

Considering Haydn's European popularity by the beginning of the 1770s, it is strange that seven piano sonatas of the middle 1760s have totally disappeared. An eighth, No. 28 (XIV:5), was discovered in a private collection and was sold at auction in 1961; it is now owned by the Preussische Staatsbibliothek.[1] Haydn seems to have composed most of these sonatas for pupils. It was not until 1773 that he wrote piano sonatas in series: that set was dedicated to Prince Nicolaus when it appeared in print one year later. Perhaps Haydn was induced to compose a suite of six sonatas by his own example of the Opp. 9, 17 and 20 Quartets or the six Duets for violin and viola. But what persuaded him to withhold the C minor Sonata for nine years? Perhaps Haydn considered that it was a 'private' work, not suited for general distribution.

We have mentioned that the chronology of these works is often open to considerable debate. We shall take as an example the series of lost sonatas, which Haydn seems to have entered in *EK* about 1767 or slightly later. For the cogent reasons why it is considered that Haydn entered the works in *EK* at this date, we may refer to Larsen (*HÜB*, 218f.). When Haydn was seriously ill in 1771 (*vide supra*, p. 168), he had (as he later recalled) composed a piano sonata with five sharps in the signature (*EK*'s entry of the Sonata has only four sharps but it is clearly in B major: see *Wiener Urtext-Ausgabe*, vol. I, p. 132). This would place the lost work more-or-less squarely in the years 1770 or 1771, and also presumably the other lost sonatas as well. But we have to deal with a whole series of imponderables: (a) When was Haydn ill? (The problem has been discussed *supra*). (b) When did he enter the lost sonatas in *EK*? Larsen writes: 'Wir werden also wieder auf die Zeit gegen 1770, oder vielleicht noch um 1767 geführt.' (c) Can Haydn have confused the lost piano sonata in B with the extant Symphony No. 46 in B (autograph: 1772)?

The autograph of the recovered 'lost' Sonata No. 28 lacks the opening pages which would have given us the work's date, and the calligraphy allows of a period *c.* 1765–71.[2] The fact that No. 28 has survived only in one fragmentary, though authentic, source shows how fragile the life-expectancy of many Haydn compositions remained, even at this period: another case is the 'Cello Concerto in C (VIIb:1), which was rediscovered in Prague about the same time as Sonata No. 28. No doubt the fires at Eisenstadt in 1768 and Eszterháza in 1779 were responsible for much destruction; otherwise how can we account for the disappearance of the *Missa 'Sunt bona mixta malis'*, considering that all the other Masses of this period were distributed in MS. copies all over Austria, Bohemia and Moravia? Like our Sonata No. 28, the Mass survived (until 1829) in an autograph fragment. Perhaps Haydn managed to flee with them from the flames at Eisenstadt in 1768 (in which case, however, we are again confronted with the Sonata's chronology; if composed about 1765, why were there no MS. copies in circulation?).

The non-proliferation of these sonatas is the more curious if we consider that Breitkopf apparently did a flourishing business in MS. copies of them: in 1763, they offered a 'Divertimento di Gius. Hayden, per il Cemb. Solo' (Sonata No. 8[5]); three years later (1766), they advertised 'V. Soli del Sigr. Hayden, a Cemb. solo' (Nos. 13, 1,

---

1 The first modern performance of part of this Sonata was given by Charles Spinks as part of a broadcast on Haydn piano sonatas given by the present writer for the B.B.C. in 1961. The lecture is printed in Landon, *Essays*.
2 Reproduction of the first extant page as the frontispiece to Vol. I of the *Wiener Urtext-Ausgabe*, where there is also the much earlier (but undated) autograph to Sonata No. 13 (*c.* 1755?). Another page (the first) of No. 13's autograph in Landon, *Das kleine Haydnbuch*, p. 14.

2, 3 [6, 8, 7, 9] and XVII:7); in 1767, Breitkopf announced yet another set, 'V. Sonate per il Cemb. Solo di Hayden' (Nos. 6[10] and 5, 12, 15, 16 [11–14]). Perhaps news of such ventures suggested to Haydn that he himself begin the sale of his sonatas – thus the printed Sonatas for Prince Nicolaus and the works of 1776 which he sold in MS. copies. Despite the sale of MSS. by Breitkopf (and no doubt Viennese copyists as well), the broad public seemed to know relatively little about Haydn as a keyboard composer. In Hiller's *Wöchentliche Nachrichten* of 1768 (p. 84) we read of Wagenseil and 'Steffani' (Steffan), of whom the writer speaks warmly.

> Herr **Hayden** [continues the report], a famous and worthy composer in another genre, has also written various items for the clavier, but this instrument does not seem to suit him as well as the other [instruments] which he uses in the most fiery and *galant* symphonies.

Until recently, these sonatas were seen to be the dividing point in style between Haydn's earlier keyboard works (including concertos) – based on the characteristic manner of Georg Christoph Wagenseil and his followers (Steffan) – and those which were believed to be under the influence of C. P. E. Bach. Since the entire question of the 'Hamburg' Bach's influence upon Haydn has been placed in serious doubt,[1] we would do well briefly to re-examine the documents and the music in question.

> Griesinger (12): [Griesinger had heard that Giovanni Battista Sammartini was being considered 'the forerunner of Haydn'.] ... So I enquired of Haydn if he had known Sammartini's works in his youth and what he thought of the composer. Haydn told me that he had in fact heard Sammartini's music but had never valued it, 'for Sammartini was a scribbler [*Schmierer*]' ... He recognized only Emanuel Bach as his prototype. ...[2]

> Griesinger (56): No one, moreover, was more inclined to justice on the merits of others than Haydn. He freely acknowledged that most of what he knew he had learned from Emanuel Bach.

> Dies (42f.): Haydn ventured to walk into a bookshop [when he was a young student] and ask for a good theoretical textbook. The bookseller named the writings of Carl Philipp Emanuel Bach as the newest and best. Haydn wanted to see it, to persuade himself; he began to read, understood, found that for which he had sought, paid for the book and took it away with great delight.
> That Haydn sought to make Bach's principles his own, that he studied them untiringly, can be seen even in his youthful works of that period. Haydn wrote in his nineteenth year quartets that made him known to music lovers as a genius with knowledge of composition. Haydn had understood that quickly. As time went on, he procured Bach's later writings. In his opinion Bach's writings are the best, most thorough and useful textbook ever published.
> As soon as Haydn's musical products became known in print, Bach noted with pleasure that he could number Haydn among his pupils; afterwards he paid the latter the flattering compliment that he was the only one completely to understand his writings and to know how to put them to use.

We have, then, authentic evidence that Haydn knew and studied the theoretical and practical (musical) works of C. P. E. Bach, i.e. the famous *Versuch über die wahre Art das Clavier zu spielen* as well as many editions of his piano works, symphonies, and

---

1 By Bettina Wackernagel, op. cit., esp. pp. 63ff.
2 There have been some recent attempts to disprove this theory, i.e. to suggest that Sammartini was a stronger influence on Haydn than the latter cared to admit. The evidence is examined in *Haydn: the Early Years 1732–1765*.

so on. In the recent work on Haydn's early sonatas, Bettina Wackernagel doubts this influence. Most of Ms. Wackernagel's work is here based on negative criticism, and we find Abert, Schmid, Geiringer, Steglich, Lowinsky and other authorities who have tried to draw parallels between C. P. E. Bach and Haydn, doubted in detail and almost *in toto*. We agree that the influence of 'foreign' composers on Haydn is a difficult and delicate problem; we can see that (to quote more of Ms. Wackernagel's negative criticism) Einstein was perhaps wrong when he tended to see Haydn's influence on Mozart's Sonatas K.279–84;[1] we can agree with her that the examples chosen by these authorities were perhaps not always ideal; but we cannot agree with her final summing-up (p. 101): 'One cannot provide precise evidence concerning the influence of Bach on Haydn to the extent that has prevailed hitherto . . . Haydn's acknowledgement of Bach (as reflected in Griesinger and Dies) can be interpreted as meaning that Haydn took from Bach's teachings some quite general advantages . . .'. Yet if we examine Griesinger, we will find a passage not hitherto quoted which reads:

> . . . About this time [when he had been expelled from St Stephen's Cathedral] Haydn came upon the first six sonatas of Emanuel Bach. 'I did not leave my clavier until I had played through them, and whoever knows me thoroughly must discover that I owe a great deal to Emanuel Bach, that I understood him and have studied him with diligence. Emanuel Bach once paid me a compliment on that score himself.' [Griesinger, 11]

Here we have Haydn's very words, and they apply, not to the *Wahre Art* . . ., but to specific *musical* compositions by C. P. E. Bach. And even if the statement is fallacious, we must remember that Haydn's contemporaries thought that he had gone so far as to parody C. P. E. Bach in the Sonatas of 1773 and 1776: '. . . the style of Bach is closely copied, without the passages being stolen'.[2] It is clear that Haydn followed the spirit more than the letter of his great contemporary, but we submit that there are stylistic parallels, and in precisely those works selected by Abert[3] and disputed by Ms. Wackernagel. It is impossible to hear the slow movement of Haydn's Sonata No. 30 (19) without thinking of the 'Hamburg' Bach: the extreme low and high range of the piano does not, in our opinion, derive from Haydn's experience with symphonies but stems from C. P. E. Bach. And as for the first movement, we offer the comparison shown opposite and overleaf.[4]

To conclude our brief excursion on this subject, we must use the words of Sir Donald Tovey:

> What, then, is Haydn's real debt to C. P. E. Bach? It is a pity that the word 'rhetoric' has been degraded to a term of abuse, for it means art the perfection of which is as noble as the noblest cause in which it can be used. Rhetoric is what Haydn learnt from C. P. E. Bach: a singularly beautiful but pure rhetoric, tender, romantic, anything but severe, yet never inflated. This great and comprehensive gift is independent of all reform or progress. The example of Bach's chaotically wild rondos and fantasias may have been necessary in order to stimulate Haydn's far more realistic sense of adventure. But of art forms, the only thing that Haydn adopted from C. P. E. Bach was this device of *Veränderte Reprise*. Its original motive arose from the fact that in any movement, sections marked to be repeated were in fact often varied by the performer on repetition, the repeats being, indeed,

1 Op. cit., pp. 185ff.
2 *Vide infra*, p. 486.
3 'Joseph Haydns Klavierwerke', in *Zeitschrift für Musikwissenschaft* II (1919–20), p. 570; Wackernagel, pp. 90f.
4 We made this point in the B.B.C. lecture (1961): see Landon, *Essays*, pp. 53–5.

C.P.E. Bach: Op. 2 No. 3
(Allegro)

Haydn Sonata No. 30 (XVI : 19)

supposed to be prescribed for that purpose. . . . Now, how does Haydn treat Bach's reprise-device? Besides restricting its use to lyric slow movements, he shows none of the patience which enabled C. P. E. Bach to write out an ornamental repeat of both parts. In the final recapitulatory stage of his movement the ornaments will combine both versions of the exposition or will otherwise throw appropriate light on it. The reprise-movements in Haydn's quartets are the slow movements of op. 9, no. 2; op. 9, no. 4; op. 20, no. 6; and op. 33, no. 3; with which the history of this art-form closes, to be reopened only once, many years later, in the most original and exquisite masterpiece of orchestration Haydn achieved, the slow movement of [Symphony No. 102 in B flat: see *Haydn in England 1791–1795*, pp. 586–90]. [Tovey, op. cit., p. 528]

The Sonatas of 1773 come as a profound stylistic shock after the brooding introspection and, in the Finale, the nearly hysterical force of bars 105ff. – for a quotation, see Landon, *Essays*, pp. 59f. – of the Sonata in C minor; or after the distilled radiance of Sonata No. 31's slow movement. With the Sonata in C minor we have

Haydn's single but monumental contribution to the *Sturm und Drang* in the field of the piano sonata. It was composed in 1771: in that year and the following we have the climax of the *Sturm und Drang*: Symphonies Nos. 44, 45, 52 and the Op. 20 Quartets. Whereupon in 1773 Haydn abandons the style for the formally clear, musically fresh and uncomplicated Piano Sonatas dedicated to Prince Nicolaus. Here the end of the *Sturm und Drang* is announced with a vengeance. If, with the 'Farewell' Symphony (November 1772), the *Sturm und Drang* reached its apogee, there must be a profound significance that the two works written almost immediately afterwards for Esterházy are in such a radically different style: the *Missa Sancti Nicolai* (first performed on 6 December 177[2?]) and the Piano Sonatas of 1773. It would seem that Prince Nicolaus may have been responsible for the collapse of Haydn's dream, and for his 'return to earth' or to normal music-making. Perhaps Haydn was persuaded, too, that such a work as Sonata No. 33 in C minor would hardly entertain the average concert-goer or pianist in London or Paris. At any rate, when he finally published it with Artaria in 1780 (together with some of the most Rococo and empty music he ever wrote: Sonatas 48–52 [35–39]), it was not appreciated: for it can only be to this work that the *Almanach musical* refers when discussing the Artaria set: 'Ces Sonates présentent des traits neufs, des tornûres pleines de hardiesse. Il seroit à souhaiter qu'on fît disparoître de cet oeuvre les morceaux qui ne respondent point à la célébrité de cet Auteur & qui tiennent à l'incorrection [*sic*] & à la dureté du style' (1781, p. 202). The critic may have included in this condemnation the C sharp minor Sonata No. 49 (36). And to these hard words one may compare the glowing words that greeted the Sonatas of 1773 when they were (in 1774) published and reviewed in the influential *Allgemeine Deutsche Bibliothek* (which we may omit since it is merely another of those endless laudatory criticisms which soon covered the pages of the journals).

The readjustment of Haydn's psyche from F sharp minor (as it were) to C major must have been a difficult process, and the 1773 Sonatas lack the stylistic interest of the 1776 Sonatas which were, at least in part, composed in 1774. Once Haydn had overcome the *Sturm und Drang* and began to write in that fatally popular style which was to reach alarming excesses with his pupils and *seguaci*, there always remained a part of his private soul which he reserved for less popular thoughts. And it seems that these flights of originality were not only tolerated but encouraged by Prince Nicolaus (who, after all, must have likewise tolerated and perhaps even encouraged up to a point the *Sturm und Drang* outpourings of the late 1760s and 1770s). Thus we find the marvellously original Symphony No. 67, discussed briefly above, in the midst of a period that did not bring forth the best in Haydn's symphonies; and there are similar works in the 1776 Sonatas, e.g. the first movement of Sonata No. 44 (29) of 1774, wherein the following passage must, to contemporaries such as the writer of the *European Magazine*, have seemed 'even bordering upon madness'. (We quote the second of three such passages; here it leads to the recapitulation.)

* Haydn has these markings in parallel passages.

Another work of genius is the Sonata No. 47 (32) in B minor, in which the Finale in particular looks backwards to the period of 1772. It is also instructive as to Prince Esterházy's tastes that in the six works dedicated to him there is one strict canon (Finale of Sonata No. 40) and also a transcription of the 'Menuet al Roverso' from Symphony No. 47 (now called 'al Rovescio') which seems to have been a favourite of the Prince's: in the baryton trios, we will note a number of movements transcribed from other 'favourite' works (operas, symphonies, etc.). And although the 1773 Sonatas might be termed elegant exercises in Rococo, let there be no mistaking the genius and Scarlattian brilliance of the passagework in No. 38's opening movement (bars 68ff.) and the equally Scarlattian trill in the left hand that extends across several bars later in the same movement (bars 105ff.). Haydn never *progresses* anywhere, and for every piece of stiff formality – the crisp dotted rhythms of the first 1773 Sonata recall Symphony No. 50's introduction, also a formal work played (at least as the Overture to *Der Götterrath*) for Empress Maria Theresa – we find, shortly before or thereafter a movement or a work that denies the style of those surrounding it: we have mentioned Symphony No. 67 and various sonatas, and the same will always apply even in the years when Haydn seems to be pandering to the Philistines of European musical life.

Arietta con 12 Variazioni (XVII:3)
Of the piano pieces listed in Hoboken's Category XVII, No. 2 (Theme and Variations in G, later rewritten in A) belongs to the period *c*. 1765 (and is discussed in *Haydn: the Early Years 1732–1765*), as does No. 1, the *Capriccio* in G (autograph 1765). The Fantasia (XVII:4) and another set of variations (XVII:5) will be discussed in a later chapter (*vide infra*, pp. 644f.). The present *Arietta* comes from a string quartet and was, in its original form, perhaps the most beautiful minuet of the period (*vide supra*, p. 319). The variations are artful, intelligent and have always been popular; and we cannot blame Haydn if, for all their dexterity, they never regain the lambent purity of the theme itself. The melody has been thought to sound Mozartian, and there were indeed MS. copies circulating in Salzburg a few years after the work had been announced in the Breitkopf Catalogue of 1774: one such MS. is now in the Städtisches Museum, Salzburg, and is signed 'Ex rebus Mathiae Essinger 1779' (Hoboken I, p. 786). What is even more Mozartian than the tune are the sophisticated harmonic changes in the accompaniment (bars 5/6, 7, repeated in the second part). One particular point deserves mention: the artistic manner in which Haydn uses the top note of his instrument (f''') in such a way that one never misses the lack of any higher notes and never, indeed, has the impression that a more extended treble range would be necessary or desirable. This well-chosen use of f''' occurs even in Variation I, where the sequence *e flat '''* to f''' (fifth to third-last bar) is treated in a masterly fashion, placing the whole melodic stress of this second part on that f'''.

342

It is known that Sonata No. 33 (1771) contains dynamic marks which are not suitable for a harpsichord,[1] e.g.

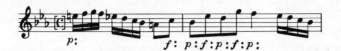

This kind of dynamic change indicates either a clavichord or a fortepiano. We cannot believe that even Haydn's *Capriccio* of 1765 was intended for a harpsichord; it is definitely piano music. Since our records of the instruments at Eszterháza are still deplorably fragmentary, we cannot know if and when Haydn or the Prince acquired a fortepiano, but the most likely candidate would be an English fortepiano in spinet form, of which there were copies all over the Continent by the early 1770s.[2] The well-known portrait of Haydn by Guttenbrunn (see plate III), of which the first version must be dated *c.*1770, shows the composer sitting at an instrument which closely resembles one of these British fortepiani in spinet form. These pianos had a range from F' to f''', whereas Haydn's earlier harpsichords seem at times to have had an upper range of d'''. Perhaps the Sonata in C minor is Haydn's first attempt to write down music especially for this new instrument. The autograph is also entitled 'Sonata', while all the preceding works were called 'Divertimento': thus the C minor Sonata is an exception even to its very title.

We cannot therefore agree with Horst Walter who writes[3] that 'it seems rather unlikely that Haydn in the early 1770s seriously investigated [*auseinandergesetzt*] the pianoforte.' The music under discussion here is not marked by consistently typical writing for the fortepiano, but there is enough of such writing, and sufficient evidence on the autographs (see the musical example just quoted) for us to believe that Haydn or Prince Nicolaus owned, by 1771, a fortepiano of some kind, and probably a British instrument in spinet form. We are persuaded that more evidence will come to light (a) about instruments in Eszterháza and (b) about the importation of British instruments into Austria.[4] It is significant that 'G. F. von R.' [Rotenstein], writing in Johann Bernouilli's *Sammlung kurzer Reisebeschreibungen* (Jg. 1783, IX, Band, p. 282), informs us that he was at Eszterháza for the visit of the Empress Maria Theresa in 1773, and on the second day 'there was *grand table* and a musical concert, auch ließ sich ein Musikus auf einem *Piano – forte* hören'. So it is clear that by 1773 some kind of a piano (square, probably, and English) was heard at a public concert given by Haydn (whose name is, by the way, nowhere mentioned in the whole long report).

There is not enough evidence to show that Messrs. Shudi & Broadwood actually sent Haydn one of their magnificent instruments. In 1773, their books reveal that on 20 August 'Sent the Empress' Harpsichord on board ship', i.e. for Maria Theresa; and it is reported that 'two years later, and probably as a result of this order, another harpsichord was sent to Vienna for Joseph Haydn, which is numbered 762, and is still preserved in that city as a valued relic of the great musician to whom it belonged'.[5] It is

---

1 It is, of course, possible that these dynamic marks were added in the autograph when the Sonata was revised for the printers in 1780.
2 One, dated 1768, was sold at Milan a few years ago; it had been in Europe all its life. Another, from the same collection, is a Franciscus Beck ('Londini fecit 1773') which went to France and from there to Italy; it is now owned by the present writer.
3 Haydn-Studien II/4 (1970), p. 261.
4 Eva Badura-Skoda has uncovered evidence that a fortepiano was used in a Viennese concert in the 1760s. Mrs Badura-Skoda kindly informed us of this important fact; she will publish the evidence in a forthcoming article.
5 William Dale: *Tschudi the Harpsichord Maker*, London 1914, pp. 66f. The instrument in question is now in the Kunsthistorisches Museum, Vienna. See also Grove I ('Tschudi').

dated 1775. The Broadwood records in London contains *no* notice on the subject of Harpsichord No. 762 nor of its having been ordered by, or consigned to, Haydn.[1] There is also no particular reason why in 1775 Haydn would have ordered a large and very expensive harpsichord of this kind unless it was destined for Prince Esterházy's operatic establishment as a large continuo instrument. We lack the evidence to pronounce further on this great harpsichord, but we may add the cautious theory that the only works that might conceivably have been intended for a double-manual harpsichord with Venetian swells (a crescendo device which No. 762 contains) are the Concertos in G and, especially, in D. The keyboard sonatas of this period incline more to the technique of the clavichord or fortepiano, as we have said.

(4) PIANO CONCERTO IN G (XVIII:4);
'IL MAESTRO E LO SCOLARE' (XVIIa:1)

After completing a series of concertos written partly before Haydn entered the services of the Esterházys – these are mostly for harpsichord or organ (with one Double Concerto in F, for violin, harpsichord and orchestra) – and partly during the early years at Eisenstadt – for harpsichord, violin, flute (lost), double bass (lost), horn, 'cello, and so on – Haydn seems to have lost interest in the form. The Piano Concerto in G was entered twice in *EK* (one of the entries was later cancelled) about or perhaps slightly before 1770.[2] It was followed, after about a decade, by the famous Piano Concerto in D (XVIII:11), discussed *infra* (p. 571). The only other concertos of the Eszterháza period known to have survived are (a) the celebrated Violoncello Concerto in D (VIIb:2, 1783) and (b) the five Concertos for the King of Naples (VIIh:1–5), all of which belong in a later chapter.

When the Piano Concertos in G and D first appeared, they were greeted with some scepticism by Cramer's *Magazin der Musik*:

> *Concerts pour le Clavecin ou Forte Piano avec l'accompagnement des plusieurs Instruments Composé par I. Haydn, à Amsterdam, chés J. Schmitt, Nro. 1 & 2.* One is now a little sceptical if everything that appears in his name is really Haydn's. In these two Concertos some traces of Haydn shine forth, but we do not dare to assert that the whole is his work. We do not wish in suggesting this to say that these Concertos are bad; they are very well composed, appear to be brand new but seem to have been composed for some particular connoisseurs. M.
>
> [1785, pp. 882f.]

Too many works 'by Haydn' were appearing, and it was known that many spurious works were being marketed under his name. In fact the concertos reviewed were those for piano in G and D, both of which are indubitably genuine. The reviewer may have a point when he mentions their being composed to order, at least in the case of that in G. In the *Journal de Paris* for 26–28 April 1784 we read an announcement of a forthcoming *Concert Spirituel*: 'Mlle. Paradis exécutera un nouvelle Concerto de Clavecin de M. Haydn'. Some months later, the same Journal could announce Boyer's edition of the work (3 September), the title page of which includes the remark, 'Exécuté au Concert Spirituel par Mademoiselle Paradis'. Maria Theresia Paradis was the blind Austrian pianist for whom Mozart wrote his Concerto in B flat (K.456).[3] It is quite possible that

1 Walter, op cit., p. 285n.
2 Larsen, *HÜB*, 233.
3 She also took that Concerto to Paris. Hermann Ullrich; 'Maria Theresia Paradis und Mozart', in *Österreichische Musikzeitschrift* 1949, pp. 316ff.

Haydn composed this rather superficial G major Concerto for Mademoiselle Paradis, who also acquired the 'rights' to it. This supposition would explain the curious lack of contemporary MS. copies (a state of affairs also, strangely enough, reflected in the D major Piano Concerto). Textually the Boyer edition, engraved (and signed) by Ribière on the title page, seems to have been prepared from a rather inaccurate copy, certainly not from Haydn's manuscript. But it is even more peculiar to find that the oboe and horn parts of the later Hummel edition are different from those of the Boyer, and that the number of bars in the Finale does not correspond in the two editions.[1]

The extraordinary difference between this Concerto and the other instrumental music of the period *c.* 1770 shows that Haydn, even at this relatively early juncture, made a sharp difference between 'public' and 'private' music. We need only to place this work beside the intimate *Divertimenti a otto voci* of 1775 (*vide infra*, p. 356) to see this difference at its most graphic. If, as we assume, this Concerto was intended for Paradis's concert tour (or rather for *a* concert tour, for there is a time lag between *c.* 1770, when Haydn apparently wrote the work, and 1784, when she took it to Paris), the music would have been designed *a priori* for what Haydn imagined the public would like. This is, perhaps, the beginning of the 'popular style' that prevails in most of the works intended for abroad (e.g. piano trios for Forster, the symphonies of the early 1780s [Nos. 76–78, 79–81]). It is particularly evident in the Finale which is dominated by what might be termed Haydn's public wit. It was not for some years that Haydn was able to reconcile his private musical thoughts with works for the broad public. In this respect the D major Piano Concerto is far more successful.

'Il maestro e lo scolare' (XVIIa:1)

In *EK* this work is entered as 'Divertimento per un Cembalo Solo a quatro [*sic*] mani' about the same time as the lost piano sonatas and other works of this category, about 1766–8. There were various editions in Haydn's lifetime, one by T. Skillern in London dated 1780. This pretty and unexceptional Divertimento is in two movements, an Andante with seven variations followed by a Tempo di Menuetto. The pupil copies the master's phrase and then both play together.[2] Apart from this authentic version for one harpsichord/four hands, the present writer owns an Italian MS. score from the Library of the Counts Papafava in Padua which is considerably different.[3] Here the work is scored for two harpsichords and strings, and begins with a hitherto unrecorded opening movement in C and closes with a short quick movement (also in C): the 'maestro e scolare' movement is the centre of the work (in F) and the Tempo di Menuetto movement is omitted in the Papafava version. The MS. would seem to be Venetian in origin (watermarks from a paper-mill in the Veneto) and to have been copied about 1780 or slightly earlier. The string writing in the Andante is ingenious, but it is difficult to say if this version is by Haydn or was put together locally (by some clever Venetian *maestro di musica*?).

Confirmation of the Divertimento's date comes from its use as the first movement of Baryton Trio No. 38.[4] (Trio No. 40 exists in Haydn's autograph, dated 1767, and we presume that this was about the year in which the Divertimento was composed.)

A review of the Hummel edition of *Il maestro e lo scolare* appeared in Cramer's *Magazin der Musik* (1783, p. 73, signed 'W'):

1 The only modern editions, by Karl Schubert (Nagel) and B. Hinze-Reinhold (Peters), are based only on the Boyer print.
2 A good critical edition (*Wiener Urtext-Ausgabe*) by Franz Eibner, 1975.
3 It is discussed briefly in the Eibner edition.
4 The numbering of the baryton trios is Haydn's own and was adopted by Hoboken. Therefore Trio No. 38 = XI:38.

> *Il Maestro e Scolare; o Sonata con Variazioni, a quadri [sic] Mani per un Cembalo, composta da G. Haydn. Amsterdam.*
>
> Since among present-day fashionable pieces of music belong also those for 2 persons at a piano, and there have been composed such pieces by many more and less famous and well-known masters, this publication will be welcome since it is pleasant and diverting for two friends to be able to play at one time on one instrument. The Sonata contains an Andante with 8 variations, which occupies both players pleasingly and by turns. At the end there is a Tempo di Menuetto.

Another German writer, von Eschstruth, in his publication entitled *Musikalische Bibliothek* (II. Stück, p. 195) of 1785, fnds that there is nothing to praise in Haydn's work, for

> if one has continually to hear a melodic chain of the choicest passages, of which each link is presented twice, once in the lower and once in the higher register, the result can only be as disgusting as hearing a collection of witty sayings first sung by the maestro in the bass and then repeated by the pupil in the treble ... [etc., etc.].
>
> [A. Sandberger, 'Zur Einbürgerung der Kunst Josef Haydns in Deutschland', in *Neues Beethoven-Jahrbuch* VI (1936), p. 22]

(5) SIX DUETS FOR VIOLIN AND VIOLA (VI:1–6)

No. 1 in F; No. 2 in A; No. 3 in B flat; No. 4 in D; No. 5 in E flat; No. 6 in C.

In *EK* these six Duets were entered on page 13, first with the title 'Solo per il Violino', later with another, more recent title, '6 Violin Solo mit Begleitung einer Viola'. Larsen (*HÜB*, 226) says: 'Die Handschrift Haydns weist auf die (mittleren?) 70er Jahre ...', but in fact the entry might also be some years earlier. The Bibliothèque de l'Opéra (Paris) owns the violin part of the first two works in autograph (entitled '1mo e 2da'), which are not dated. They are probably the fragments wrongly entered in Haydn's own music catalogue as '2 Sonaten fürs Pianoforte mit Begleitung einer Viola' to which was added the further information, 'blos [sic] Violinstimme; also unbrauchbar'.[1] Johann Elssler, who kept a private collection of Haydn autographs, seems to have given this fragment to Baptiste Petit.[2] The autograph's handwriting admits of a date between c. 1765 and c. 1775. Our first known evidence of the works' date comes from Gerber's *NTL* (II, 580). Referring, apparently, to the Breitkopf Catalogue of 1776–7 (where the Duets Nos. 1 in F and 6 in C are listed thematically), Gerber notes: 'No. 1 aus F und No. 2 aus C kenne ich schon seit 1769 ...'. The first edition of the Duets appeared in Paris in 1775,[3] published by Bailleux: 'Six Sonates à Violon seul avec le Basse, Oeuvre 23'. This arrangement was reprinted by William Campbell in London in 1782. In 1790, André of Offenbach brought out an edition for two violins, many times reprinted (including, oddly, Bailleux). It was not until 1799 that André finally issued the works in their original form; this edition, too, was reprinted several times, also by Artaria in Vienna. The great number of editions (see Hoboken I, pp. 512–4) attests to these works' immense popularity all over Europe; there was even an Italian edition (by Marescalchi in Naples, who printed several works by Haydn in the 1780s and 1790s, a rather bold procedure in a country where that kind of music was only dimly understood).

---

1 See *Haydn: the Late Years 1801–1809*, p. 317, item 132.

2 The autograph has the following note (in German): 'This piece was given by Johann Elssler to Herr Baptiste Petit, and it is the actual handwriting of Herr Kapellmeister Joseph Haydn, which Johann Elssler can vouch for, since he served Herr Kapellmeister as copyist for 22 years'. This would mean, incidentally, that Elssler entered Haydn's service officially in the year 1787.

3 Announced in the *Almanach musical*, 1776; in Bailleux's Catalogue of 1775. Cari Johansson; *French Music Publishers' Catalogues of the Second Half of the Eighteenth Century*, Stockholm 1955, facsimile 5.

It will be seen, in the course of this volume, that there soon arose a considerable difference between what we might term Haydn's 'private' music and his 'public' face – the one he turned to publishers abroad, the 'popular' Haydn, the epicurean man-of-the-world whose music had the easy appeal of Johann Christian Bach. The private Haydn, the one that critics sometimes considered as approaching madness, was the world (to continue the comparison with the Bach family) of the angular, difficult style cultivated by C. P. E. Bach – music for the fastidious connoisseur. One of Haydn's fundamental problems was to effect a working marriage between these two styles. The further the popular style grew away from the private works intended for a limited audience at Eszterháza, the more difficult (or even unlikely) this marriage appeared. The bewilderment of Haydn's critics, then and now, is partially a result of this curious dichotomy; and it was not until he wrote such works as the 'Paris' Symphonies, and Nos. 88 in G and No. 92 ('Oxford'), as well as the Quartets Opp. 54, 55 and 64, that Haydn solved the problem of making his public works private (or vice versa, depending on one's attitude) – a great achievement on which he would be able mightily to capitalize when he went to England. By then his language was (as he said to Mozart) 'spoken all over the world'.

The world of these extraordinary Duets was light years away from that of the sophisticated music that Haydn would write in London. If there is any music of this period that might be chosen as the most uncompromising, intellectually tough and 'unpopular' (in the sense of the 1773 Piano Sonatas), these Duets would well qualify. And yet, the astonishing thing is that they did become popular, and on a European scale (just as did the equally uncompromising Quartets, Opp. 9, 17 and 20); doubtless the Duets' success was also due to their potential didactic use. Whatever the reason, however, these Duets must command our attention not only because they (like the baryton trios) served Haydn well in the grand preparation necessary for the Quartets, but also because they are musically so rewarding. Their principal difficulty is that which we shall also encounter with the baryton trios; of all Haydn's music composed in Eszterháza, these Duets are the least intended for the listener. They are, first and foremost, music for the players.

To arrange the works for violin and 'basso' (by which 'cello is meant) was not difficult. Because of the nature of the viola part, which acts like the (rather high) bass line of an old Baroque violin sonata – sometimes one almost thinks a harpsichord would help, particularly if one had encountered the works for the first time in the 1775 Bailleux edition for violin and basso – the works are really what Haydn first called them in *EK*, 'Solo per il Violino'. The viola is the accompaniment, and we must not expect the independent viola writing of Mozart's famous Duets (in the existence of which, as is well known, Haydn's brother Michael played an important role). It is generally thought that Haydn wrote these works for Luigi Tomasini, who would have appreciated their subtle musical quality and the singing tone which all their slow movements require. Haydn (who was a viola player) may have played the second part. When were they composed? We suggest, using all the evidence at our disposal, *c.* 1766–8 – part of the studies for the quartets. As in the baryton trios, these Duets are a kind of microcosm of Haydn's intimate, chamber-musical style of the late 1760s. We have the allegro moderato or moderato opening movements (Nos. 1, 2, 4, 5) in slow four-four time, which we know so well from the quartets: the combination of the old Baroque 'spinning-out' process with the newer working from motifs; the subtle construction of such a movement by means of rhythmic, metrical and motivic means; and the often mosaic-like appearance of the finished product – all these are the mortar from which Haydn constructed many first movements in Opp. 9, 17 and 20. There is one captivating opening movement in two-four, the Andante of No. 3, where the characteristic element is the repetition of, and concentration on, the note *b* flat:

This is one of these Haydnesque devices that Berenson would call a 'finger-print'; cf., in Haydn's music, Baryton Trio 61/I (which carried this fetching notion to Venetian music lovers, via the rare Zatta print discussed *infra*, p. 353n.), a similar treatment in the famous Lied, 'Eine sehr gewöhnliche Geschichte' (Artaria, 1781)

and the most celebrated example of all, 'Ein Mädchen, das auf Ehre hielt' (quoted in *Haydn: the Late Years 1801–1809*, p. 125). To match this device, which is the nearest Haydn comes to writing a *sonata da chiesa* movement in these Duets (the rest of the work includes an Adagio and a Minuet), we have four melancholy, pensive slow movements in the minor (Nos. 1, 2, 4, 6) which are the glories of this set. It is perhaps counter-productive to single out one of the four, but we cannot refrain from giving the palm to the divinely beautiful Adagio (D minor, *alla breve*) in No. 4, one of those movements so well known to us from Mozart, where the dense emotion is too fragile to be placed in any obvious category, but which at once enfolds the player (and the listener) in its fastidious embrace. And while on the subject of Mozart, the final Tempo di Menuetto for Duet No. 2 –

– has something very Mozartian about it, possibly the combination of the dotted upbeat and trill, as well as the feminine ending of the phrases at bars 2 and 4 (cf. the Finale to Mozart's Violin Concerto in A, K.219, for an analogy).

(6) DIVERTIMENTO A TRE (HORN TRIO, IV:5)

By some miracle, this work has survived in autograph (the only known source), dated 1767 and now in British private possession.[1] Its two movements are, of course, intended primarily as a virtuoso vehicle for the horn player, and the roles of the violinist and 'cellist are secondary. It is now thought that the cruelly difficult horn part – ascending to sounding *a flat''* in the first movement – was written for Carl Franz,

1 First edition, based on the autograph, by the present writer (Diletto Musicale 1, Verlag Doblinger). A photograph of the autograph is in the Toscanini Archives of the New York Public Library.

who was the principal first horn in the band from 9 April 1763 to November 1776. This theory, advanced by Paul Bryan,[1] gains plausibility if we examine Franz's own copy of the Quintet (X:10) which is discussed *infra* (p. 355), and where the technical demands on the player are equally formidable and very much of the same kind. On the whole, Haydn in this Trio utilizes the bright side of the horn's multi-faceted nature, though there are also pedal notes (in the bass clef) which require a rapid shifting of the embrochure.

(7) BARYTON TRIOS[2]

Almost all the baryton trios – Haydn composed 126 (and possibly one or two more) – were produced in the ten years here under investigation. Professor Larsen has provided us with a valuable indication of the works' chronology in *HÜB* (214f., 216). The baryton trios filled many pages of *EK* and because of lack of space spilled on to pages reserved for other categories of works. Professor Larsen writes:

> There can be only *one* explanation of this curious grouping of the baryton trios: the great majority of these works had not yet been composed when the catalogue's [*EK*] first version was prepared. Such an accretion of this kind of works was not planned. For the rapidly growing number of these favourite works of Prince Nicolaus there could be found a place only wherever there was room on the empty staves of the right side and in the broad margins of the left side of the pages, and finally instead of the planned incipits of the vocal works (the titles of which remained standing next to the places for which they were intended). ... It may be safely supposed that only the first twelve Trios belonged to the early plan [of *EK*]; because right after these works there follow (on page 8) baryton works of other kinds and a vocal work, and it is not until the next page (15) that the continuation, Trios 13–22, follows. All this leads us to the years 1765–6, for in 1765 Prince Nicolaus objected to 'the still very few' baryton pieces that Haydn had delivered.

We may therefore assume that Trios 13–126 were composed between 1766 and about 1774. Here are the dated autographs: No. 24 (1766), No. 42 (1767), No. 43 (1767), No. 57 (1768), No. 79 (1769), No. 106 (1772). It is quite clear that after 1774 receipt written by Haydn and signed by Esterházy on 8 November 1778 (*infra*, pp. 404f.) refers to books of music paper with eight staves for 'His Highness for the Bariton, so that this winter the fifth volume of my Trios can be copied'.[3] The season of 1773 was already filled with opera productions, Haydn's own *L'infedeltà delusa*, *Philemon und Baucis* (with *Der Götterrath*) and *Hexen-Schabbas*. In 1774, Haydn revived *La canterina*, *Acide*, *Lo speziale* and *L'infedeltà delusa*; and he had to compose and prepare *Il ritorno di Tobia*. In 1775, there were the great celebrations in August, for which Haydn composed *L'incontro improvviso* and conducted Ordoñez's *Alceste*; and in 1776, the great opera season began. The interest in baryton trios, quite clearly, waned as the fascination with opera – Haydn's and the Prince's – waxed. In 1775, we shall see the great series of 'farewell' Octets (Divertimenti) with baryton that Haydn lovingly composed for Prince Nicolaus (*infra*, p. 356).

The physical characteristics and historical background of the baryton are discussed in the previous volume of this biography, *Haydn: the Early Years 1732–1765*. Obviously

---

1 *Haydn-Studien* III/1 (1973), p. 57.

2 Now all are published in *Joseph Haydn Werke* (five volumes, Ser. XIV, 1–5), mostly edited by Hubert Unverricht.

3 *Haydn-Studien* III/2 (1974), p. 99. The fifth volume was probably Nos. 97–125 (126). This document does not, therefore, 'open the possibility that some of the trios were composed as late as 1778' (p. 104).

space does not permit us more than a cursory examination of these baryton compositions. Although they are, of course, true *pièces d'occasion* and, moreover, composed for an obscure instrument (which has had something of a revival in modern times) that made the trios' composition something of an ensemble problem, the standard Haydn was able to maintain is almost unbelievably high. We must consider that he had to write large operas and oratorios, as well as eighteen quartets, as many piano sonatas, thirty symphonies and a legion of other works all during a period when he was expected regularly to deliver a contrast stream of new baryton trios – and if possible in series of six as well. If, as Hans Keller has said, string quartets are primarily intended for the players rather than the listeners, this could be said with even more justification about the baryton trios. Of all Haydn's chamber music, none was designed more exclusively to give pleasure (only) to the player. He turned the instrument's peculiarly restricted sound into a distinct advantage, experimenting ceaselessly with ensemble works wherein this darkish, alto-tenor-bass texture was cultivated. That is why Haydn apparently considered this special tonal combination eminently successful in slow movements; and these adagios are the pride of the baryton trios. There are perhaps three features of these works that may be singled out. The first is connected with their being specially written for Prince Nicolaus. Because, as we have seen in the Chronicle, the Prince thought that the baryton could be played only in a limited number of keys, the restrictions of the keys used in these trios are considerable: most are in F, C, G, D and A. Secondly, many of the individual movements are arrangements of other works, Haydn's mainly, but also (for instance) Gluck's; these borrowings must reflect Prince Nicolaus's desire to play, in his own chambers and in the form of his special chamber music, pieces of which he was particularly fond – rather like the later arrangements of Haydn's *The Creation* for piano quintet or two flutes for the amateur in the country. Some of these arrangements are as follows:

Trio	Source
2/I	Haydn: also used in a well-known version for harpsichord (reprinted in *Wöchentliche Nachrichten*) written *c.* 1765(?). See XVII:8.
5/I	Gluck's 'Che farò senza Euridice' from *Orfeo* (1762).
29/I	Haydn 'Che visino delicato' from *La canterina*, Act II (1766).
35/III	The famous 'Night Watchman' melody discussed *supra*, p. 280, which also appears in the Baryton *Cassationsstück* (XII: 19, No. 2) and in numerous other Haydn works.
37/I	Haydn Piano Sonata No. 14 (3)/I.
38/I	Haydn Divertimento for Harpsichord 4-hands 'Il maestro e lo scolare' XVIIa:1 (*vide supra*, p. 345).
52/III	Haydn Symphony No. 58/III, 'Menuet alla zoppa'.
64/I	Uses Gregorian 'Alleluja' melody also found in Haydn's Symphony No. 30/I (1765).
76/III	Piece for musical clock XIX:6.
82/III	Minuet also appears as piece for musical clock XIX:5 (the clock wrongly dated 1772 in Hoboken: *vide infra*, pp. 651f.).
97/I, VI, VII	Later used in a Trio for William Forster (IV:9), 1784.
103/I, II	Also used by Haydn in a lost version (*EK*) for harpsichord, baryton and two violins; and again in Piano Trio No. 17 (XV:2).
110/I, II (Trio)	Also used by Haydn in a Divertimento for harpsichord, two violins and 'cello (XIV:8).

It is not always possible to say whether the Trio arrangement is the later one, but in some cases that is obvious.

The third principal feature is Haydn's own attitude towards these little trios. He obviously regarded them as ideal proving grounds for the more important (and also slightly more public) string quartet. The fugal finales in the Op. 20 Quartets have their many parallels in the trios, where they are also found only as finales: Nos. 33, 40, 53, 56, 67, 71, 75, 81 (double fugato) and fully-fledged fugues in Nos. 97, 101 (with the proud title 'Fuga a 3 soggetti in contrapunto doppio') and 114, such as we know from Op. 20. The use of the fugue or fugato as a final movement was known to Haydn not only from Werner but also from the great Gassmann quartets – *inter alia* those of 1773 (op. posth., Bureau des Arts et d'Industrie, 1804) which had two fugues, one at the beginning and one as finale. This procedure, in turn, may also be found in the magnificent *Sinfonia con fuga* in G minor by F. X. Richter (MS. Thurn und Taxis Archives, Regensburg).[1] We find not only fugues but also minuets in the form of a canon ('Canone in Diapente' of Trio 94): we have noted Esterházy's obvious fondness for canonic devices in the Piano Sonatas of 1773. Altogether, apart from using the trios as a kind of grand proving ground, Haydn also allowed them, in reverse action, to reflect all the compositional problems of the larger works. For example, we find in the trios the same Balkan excursions, especially the weirdly haunting Trio No. 109 (trio of minuet):

There are genuine 'siciliano' movements (Nos. 51/I, 77/I, 109/I), into which category the wistful Adagio of No. 36, entitled 'Pastorello' might be placed: the 'pastorello' tradition meant Christmas, which in Italy was also the gently rocking triple rhythm used for the 'siciliano' (e.g. the conclusion of Corelli's 'Christmas' Concerto). There are 'scherzo' movements, anticipating in name the minuets of the Op. 33 Quartets (Trios Nos. 43/III, 76/III) but actually reflecting an earlier kind of scherzo such as was found in the wind-band divertimenti for Count Morzin (also there in 2/4): see Divertimento in D (II:D18)/II.[2] There are 8/8 moderato movements which served as the models for the Op. 9 Quartets, and significantly just in or about the year 1767: Nos. 53/I, 54/I, 55/I, 58/I. There is an astonishing Trio (No. 52) which begins with a kind of accompanied recitative in D minor (with no less than five written-out appoggiature) and proceeds to an arioso, still in the same adagio tempo. At the end there is a place for a cadenza: all this is close to the Op. 9 Quartets. The next movement in the Trio is an Allegro in cut time wherein the plucked strings at the back of the instrument are used with great effect; the work concludes with the 'Menuet alla zoppa' which we know from Symphony No. 58. But here the Trio is, interesting, entitled 'Trio al contrario', which explains the smoothly flowing line in quavers with an occasional semiquaver link but does not explain the queer and faintly sinister quality of

1 On this subject, see the indispensable Kirkendale, op. cit., p. 182.
2 Critical score: Diletto Musicale 33 or Stp (study score) 80, Verlag Doblinger, edited by the present writer.

the piece. We see in such a work as Trio No. 52 one of the many adaptations that Haydn made, in these baryton works, of the *sonata da chiesa*. Another speciality of these trios are the variation movements, often on popular (though original, i.e. not 'foreign') tunes such as the well-known one which was also turned into harpsichord variations (Trio No. 2/I) and is rather similar in character to the finales (also variations) of Symphonies Nos. 31 and 72. For two more movements in the baryton trios, see Nos. 78/I and 81/I.

One of the more intriguing aspects of these works is that in them Haydn perhaps even consciously preserves the great tradition of the Baroque trio sonata. There are more *sonata da chiesa* structures in these trios than in all other categories of Haydn's *œuvre* combined, and occasionally we feel that Haydn is being deliberately old-fashioned. In Symphony No. 6 (1761) the Adagio movement was a gracious tribute to the old Corelli style. In Trio No. 85/I (Adagio) we have another such movement, recalling with almost poignant beauty the glories of the old trio sonata:

One of the first scholars in modern times to devote his attention to these works was Karl Geiringer, whose astute comments (1932, 62ff.) drew many German-speaking musicians' attention to this 'Fülle von feingeschliffenen kleinen Kostbarkeiten'. Among other things, Professor Geiringer drew attention to the following trio of the minuet, entitled on some old manuscripts 'das alte Weib', from No. 82; here the 'old woman' is caricatured with the whining repetitions which in the middle change pitch but in the end return to the original key – just like a senile village conversation:

As Geiringer was publishing his epochal biography – the first full-length monograph to use modern scholarly principles – another scholar drew even more detailed attention to the baryton: Professor W. Oliver Strunk.[1] The interested reader is referred to this definitive study, as well as to Hubert Unverricht's recent study on the string trio as a form.

Haydn must have grieved to see so much beautiful music disappear for ever into the princely library; and he certainly condoned many arrangements[2] of these baryton trios for other combinations (e.g. as flute trio and especially for violin, viola and 'cello) so that other musicians could enjoy these works as well as the few other baryton players.[3] He also made some of the arrangements himself, e.g. from the longest and in many ways one of the most striking Trios, No. 97, 'Fatto per la felicissima nascita di S: A: S: Prencipe Estorhazi' – the only seven-movement work among the trios. It includes, as a rarity, a 'Polonese' with its characteristic

♫♪♪ | ♫♫♪♫ rhythm. Perhaps the work was written in 1771 (the sources are undated). When Haydn turned to the flute (or violin) trios for Forster, this was one of the obscure sources which he plundered to send his English publisher.

The first page of Trio No. 109's autograph is stained by an ungainly water spot, similar to the disastrous ink spot in the autograph of the *Missa Sancti Nicolai*. At the top of the first page of No. 109, there are two underlined notes in Haydn's hand about this water stain: 'fatto a posta' (done on purpose) and 'nihil sine causa' (nothing without its reason). Of the various comments on these remarks (Haydn's annoyance at having to compose so many baryton trios, etc.), the most recent one has been put forward by an excellent young British baryton player, Riki Gerardy, with whom the writer is in friendly contact. Mr Gerardy suggests[4] that

---

1 *Musical Quarterly*, April 1932. For Unverricht, *vide supra*, p. 132n.

2 A particularly intriguing edition of Trios 57–62 (a real cycle, in other words) is that published by Antonio Zatta in Venice: 'Sei Trio / per violino, viola, e violoncello / del Signor Giuseppe Hajden [*sic*]': we used the copy in the Archives of Count Aurelio Baldeschi-Baleani in Jesi. The Count and Countess Silvia were our thoughtful hosts on a long weekend in 1967, when we examined his interesting music collection and also his beautiful Stradivari violoncello piccolo (with the documents from Stradivari himself when Count Aurelio's ancestor ordered the instrument from Cremona). Venice was, apart from a few other north Italian cities (Genova, Milan, Florence, Padua), one of the few Italian centres to cultivate Haydn's music in the 1770s and 1780s.

3 It is unexpected to find, as did the present writer, a large collection of non-Haydn baryton music in the Monastery of Schlägl in Upper Austria. The collection, containing works by Giuseppe de Fauner, Joseph Ziegler and Franz Anton Deleschin, is an important contribution to the scanty baryton literature.

4 In notes to an album of eleven baryton trios which Mr Gerardy and his Esterházy Baryton Trio have recorded for HMV, number SLS 5095.

it is more likely that Haydn's wife was responsible, possibly after some domestic quarrel. We know that she had little regard for his work and would sometimes take sheets of manuscript when needing paper for domestic use. The end of the Pickwickian story may be that future generations will regard this manuscript as an important document relating to Haydn's domestic misery.

What can be the future of these beautiful pieces? Obviously they are singularly unfitted for the concert hall except in conjunction with other pieces (and preferably for other combinations of instruments). Happily the twentieth century has one great asset which will probably be the salvation of works such as these – the gramophone record. No composer has benefited more from the advent of the long-playing record, through the medium of which we are now in a position to enjoy many Haydn operas and (in the near future) a large selection even of his baryton trios and all his early string trios.[1]

(8) VARIOUS DIVERTIMENTI FOR ONE OR TWO BARYTONS, SOME WITH TWO HORNS AND STRINGS (X:1–12), LATER IN PART ISSUED BY HAYDN FOR FLUTE, HORNS AND STRINGS AS 'OPUS 31'

Recently the Joseph Haydn Institut published a rewarding volume of Haydn's music for baryton(s) and other instruments.[2] Some of the duets for two barytons have survived only in dubious arrangements (flute, violin, basso), but one, in G (XII:4), has survived in its original form through a copy by Joseph Elssler. The piece requires an interesting *scordatura* for the plucked strings at the back of the instrument: string 1 = *g* (rather than the usual *a*) and string 8 = *c''* (instead of *c#''*), which is different from the usual Esterházy tuning of (sounding) *a–d'–e'–f#'–g'–a'–b'–c#''–d''*. This raises a parallel problem concerning *scordature* in Trio No. 70. Riki Gerardy writes about this Trio:

> ... it would have required a major retuning of the sympathetic strings of the Prince's baryton which had only ten of these, tuned diatonically. In bar 10 of the Andante there is a G and in bar 12 a G sharp. The instrument would have had to be retuned as follows:

10	9	8	7	6	5	4	3	2	1	
E	D	C#	B	A	G	F#	E	D	A	– normal
D	C♮	B	A	G#	G♭	F#	E	D	A	– retuning

On Haydn's baryton the passage would not have presented a problem:

	9	8	7	6	5	4	3	2	1	
		C♮	A#	G#		F♭	D#			Total – 14 sympathetic
	D	C#	B	A	G♭	F#	E	D	A	strings.

The numbering 1–9 of sympathetic-string notes in the Trios is derived from the 9 strings common to both instruments. The question is: would Haydn have requested the Prince to retune 6 sympathetic strings to play one note? Had the composer wished to demonstrate the virtues of this retuning, surely he would have used the notes concerned more than once in the work. This Trio may well have been written for Karl Franz to play in one of the Court concerts – Haydn's ... biographer Pohl stated that the Prince liked listening to as well as playing the baryton.

---

1 The complete string trios are being recorded by French Decca with the fine violinist Jacques-Francis Manzone, using the new texts prepared for Doblinger by the present writer.
2 *Joseph Haydn Werke*, Reihe XIII (edited by Sonja Gerlach), 1969.

And here we arrive at the question: for whom were these attractive duets composed? The Prince and Carl Franz (or Andreas Lidl)? The Prince and Haydn? Another set of winning pieces is the series of 'Twelve Cassationsstücke' (XII:19) for two barytons and basso (= 'cello), miniature movements written so compactly that they might have been conceived for wind band (the adagio numbers for which are notoriously short because their players are 'short winded'). As it happens, one's suspicions are aroused because there is no use of the baryton's plucked strings and no double stops. Perhaps these were once wind-band pieces for the Princely Grenadiers, or rather a Suite in A major (for that is what the work really is): we shall see that there is a known case in which Haydn reworked a wind-band piece for the princely baryton ensemble. In No. 9 there is an amusing section in imitation of the bagpipes: and to continue our point about the wind band, the double stops in the 'cello – thirteen bars of repeated notes

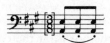

(drone bass) and a closing chord (same notes) – could be played by two bassoons. And this leads us to a proposal. There are many baryton works which do not transcribe well, or at all, such as the pretty Duet in G discussed above; but these *Cassationsstücke* can, without altering a note, be played by two violins and 'cello (also as a small orchestral piece with double bass); or by two oboes (or flutes or clarinets) and two bassoons. Among the many unusual effects we might mention a Polonese (No. 8).

Another unusual piece is a *Divertimento* or *Quintetto* (both titles are authentic) for two horns, baryton, viola and basso ('cello), in D major (X:10). Originally the work was a wind-band Divertimento in D which is lost and known to us only from its entry on page two of *EK*.[1] At least one assumes that the original version was for wind band, but the reverse may also obtain, since the Baryton Quintet was entered in *EK* as early as 1767–8.[2] This is another case where this beautiful music can be presented to a wider public simply by substituting violin(s) for the baryton: the one unmanageable chord (Trio, bar 33) can be adjusted easily. Here is perhaps the first known, or at least earliest written, instruction in Haydn's music for the horn to employ mutes for the work's entire duration. The viola is also muted (and if violin[s] are used instead of the baryton, it [they] should also be muted). The piece is in *sonata da chiesa* form, with extravagant horn solos that remind one of the Cassatio in D for four horns and strings (Hoboken *deest*) and also of Symphony No. 72. (The technique in No. 31 is slightly different.) This particular use of the horns brings us to the threshold of Symphony No. 51 and the *Divertimenti a otto* of 1775. If Carl Franz owned this fabulously difficult Quintet – and his copy, now in the Mecklenburg Library in Schwerin – it is fair to assume that it was written for him; and that he was therefore the man responsible for all those famous C *alto* horn parts, for Symphonies Nos. 31 ('Hornsignal') and 72 with their solo horn quartet, for the Cassatio in D (also with four horns) and for that astonishing collection of Symphonies with C *alto* parts (Nos. 41, 48, 50, 56, 60), in fact for all the difficult

1 'Divertimento a Sei [changed to 'cinq(ue)' / cioè 2 clarinetti 2 corni ['e fagotto' (or fagotti) assumed]'. The *incipit* is in F major but of course the theme was for A-clarinet and therefore the piece was in D major. Hoboken II:5. The Divertimento was entered in *EK* about 1768 or 1769. It is interesting that Haydn was still experimenting with clarinets (after another, earlier attempt or two in 1761): whose clarinets? There is no record of clarinets in the Esterházy band at this period, but perhaps the Grenadiers' Band had, at least, the instruments, and one of the wind-band players could play them. Here is another mystery that cannot be solved from the information now at our disposal.
2 Larsen, *HÜB*, 233.

horn solos of the period. Here are two of the solo passages in the first movement of the Quintet (both passages are repeated):

There is also a 'stopped' note (written *b* below *c'*, sounding *c♯'*) for the second horn; we do not know who Franz's regular second was.

The second movement is like a symphonic allegro of the period and does not in the least reveal its wind-band origin. In fact it does not, curiously, look (or sound) like real chamber music at all, partly because of the way the music is laid out. The Menuet, with its typical octave leap in the bass line, also sounds more like a symphonic minuet. The Trio has two exposed solos for the horns, at the conclusion of which horn I has to sustain written *c'''* for four bars: it is very much like the writing of Symphony No. 31 at this point. The whole Quintet is definitely a work which must be rescued from its ill-deserved obscurity.

Divertimenti a otto voci

for baryton, 2 horns, 2 violins, viola, 'cello and *violone* (double bass): Nos. 1 in D (X:2), No. 2 in G (X:5), No. 3 in A minor (X:3), No. 4 in G (X:4), No. 5 in D (X:1), No. 6 in A (X:6) and No. 7 in G (X:12). Three have survived in Haydn's autograph (1775) in the original baryton version (Nos. 2, 3, 5), of which No. 5 – hitherto among the Berlin State Library MSS. stored in Poland – has just (Summer 1977) been rediscovered and returned to Berlin; it was not yet available to the editor of the new critical edition. We follow here the order and text of these Divertimenti in *Joseph Haydn Werke*, edited by Sonja Gerlach (Reihe XIII, 1969). Six of them were published by Haydn with flute instead of baryton and appeared with Artaria under the title, 'Six Divertissements a 8 Parties Concertantes ... Ouvr. 31' (announced 7 April 1781 in the *Wiener Zeitung*); reprinted the next year by Longman & Broderip, London. A good practical edition, based on Op. 31, by E. F. Schmid of Nos. 4 and 7 (X:4 and 12), is published by Bärenreiter. The new *Joseph Haydn Werke*, apart from publishing all seven works with the baryton part (either Haydn's or cleverly reconstructed by Ms. Gerlach), also prints the flute version of Artaria's and an interesting oboe version (instead of baryton in both cases) which has come down to us in the form of 'Sinfonien' for incidental music in the Hamburg Theatre (where each movement was played as an overture or entr'acte).

These seven Divertimenti are Haydn's farewell compositions to his Prince in the role of baryton player, for there is no evidence that Haydn wrote any baryton music after 1775. The seven were a noble gesture on Haydn's part, and reveal a quite new intimacy between the two men – master and servant on a social level but connoisseur and artist on another and higher plane: for it is increasingly clear that Prince Nicolaus Esterházy was one of the *settecento*'s great connoisseurs, the worthy inheritor of Renaissance princes such as Lorenzo de' Medici or Pope Paul III.

Haydn had composed a whole series of early divertimenti for sundry combinations of strings and wind instruments. Most of these works date from before Haydn's engagement with the Esterházys in 1761, but at least a few – such as the enterprising Divertimento (Cassatio) in C (II:17) for clarinets, horns and strings – are believed to have been written about 1761.[1] We have seen that Haydn often leaves a

---

1 The one dated autograph of this period in which clarinets are specifically mentioned is the Divertimento in C for 2 clarinets and 2 horns: 1761 (II = 14). See the critical edition, Verlag Doblinger, Diletto Musicale 33 or study score Stp 180. The autograph is in Riga (now Latvian S.S.R.).

form, only to take it up again some years later. This occurred during our period with the Mass but also with the string quartet. Now, Haydn returns to the divertimento form which he had, with the exception of some wind-band works and the occasional baryton ensemble piece, more or less abandoned for the last fifteen years. The *Divertimenti a otto voci* of 1775 are of central importance in Haydn's *œuvre*, not least because in them he renewed and revitalized the divertimento form. We shall trace briefly the many innovations, structural and instrumental, that grace these works; but while so doing we should recall that they start an entirely new school of occasional music which, in this period, leads to the great Concerti (1786) and Notturni (1790) for the King of Naples. They also represent an astonishing advance on the techniques, forms and spiritual level of the early divertimento-cassatio; indeed, there is the same relationship between the *Divertimenti a otto voci* of 1775 and the early works in the form, as between the Quartets of Op. 20 and their precursors in Opp. 1 and 2. And the parallel continues, for these early divertimenti became extremely popular and were circulated all over the Austrian lands and in most cases printed in Paris as well. But Haydn, about 1761, renounced these works, just as he renounced the early quartet-divertimento. When the divertimento form came out of retirement in 1775, the results were as far-reaching in their way as in the Op. 20 Quartets.

The most spectacular feature of these works is their virtuoso use of the horn. We have seen that horn players occupied a special position in the musical hierarchy of the middle *settecento* similar to that formerly held by the trumpeters (*clarino* players). Horn players' salaries were usually higher than the others' so that, in the case of Haydn's band, there were (at least on paper) a preponderance of horn players greatly out of proportion relative to the total number of musicians involved; which, however, may be explained by the fact that musicians playing both the horn and another instrument (the violin was a favourite) naturally signed up as horn players to receive the higher salary even if they expected to devote their energies to another instrument. An indication of the horn players' new status may be seen in that seismographically sensitive Italian caricaturist, Pier Leone Ghezzi's amusing sketch of the two 'horn players in the service of the Venetian Ambassador [to the Holy See]'.[1] (Ghezzi also sketched Handel – 'Il Sassone . . . bravissimo suona[tore] di Cembalo' – and moreover drew the only known authentic likeness of Vivaldi.)

The music that these virtuoso horn players – who usually formed a pair – executed has largely disappeared, not least because much of it was composed by the actual performers for the most ephemeral of occasions. But even W. A. Mozart's early brass music – 'Viele Stücke – für 2 Clarini – für 2 Corni – für 2 Corni di Baßetto' and other horn compositions (K.33h, 41b) as well as an entire trumpet concerto (K.47c) – have disappeared; while of Haydn's horn compositions, the Horn Concerto in D (VIId:1) and the Double Horn Concerto in E flat (VIId:2) are lost, the Horn Trio survives in the autograph, the dubious Concerto for Second Horn (VIId:4) also survives in one old copy (Gymnasialbibliothek, Zittau). Thus Haydn's virtuoso horn parts in the *Divertimenti a otto voci* have the double advantage of being gigantic (but rewarding) challenges to the players but also in showing us (and by the hand of a master) what the virtuosi of this long-forgotten art were capable of. The decline in this kind of horn writing from the musical life at Eszterháza dates from Franz's departure and the

---

1 Vatican Museum *ex coll.* Ottoboni, Cod. Ottobon. lat. 3117, f.64. Reproduced in Lina Montalto's useful book, *Un mecenate in Roma barocca . . .*, Florence 1955, p. 107; there are many other entertaining Ghezzi reproductions in this book.

beginning of the regular opera season, both of these events taking place in the year 1776.[1]

On the subject of the horns in these works, Paul Bryan writes:

> Regarding range, the uppermost requirement occurs in [Divertimento] III, whose first horn (in A) must ascend to c''' (sounding a'') while the second horn simultaneously sinks to GG (sounding E). The lowest tone may be observed in [Divertimento] I (with horns in D) wherein the second horn must attack and sustain the factitious note AA (sounding BB), which serves as the very exposed pedal over which the solo violin follows the contrabass (*violone*) in canonic imitation. [Divertimento] I also presents the most florid writing for both first and second horn; the rapidly moving upper-register scale lines as well as the wide-skip figure (ornamented) in the low horn are reminiscent of the writing in the Cassatio in D and Symphony No. 31 – but more demanding. The low horn is presented with a new challenge whereby the low octave is filled in by factitious notes extending the range down to GG for both Horn in G and Horn in A. The longer crook, and the lower range of the Horn in D seems to call forth a more cautious approach, and the only second-partial factitious note used is the above-mentioned AA. Further, these non-natural notes are freely used – similarly to natural notes, i.e. without stepwise approach to or departure from open notes, and sometimes even after a wide skip. Perhaps the most interesting aspect of the Baryton Octets is the manner in which Haydn has integrated the horns into these pieces of genuine chamber music. All are scored with careful consideration of the capabilities of the individual instruments and of the problems and possibilities of balancing them together.... [*Haydn Yearbook* IX (1975), p. 205]

Haydn had used the horns, up to now, mostly in their highest and middle registers. Now, with the exploration of the lowest register, a whole new world is opened with passages such as the following example from Divertimento No. 4 (X:4), Finale, bars 31ff., where the second horn's stopped-factitious notes are set against mysterious low strings. We quote from the arrangement of Op. 31, where the writing looks forward to the Romantic era, when the horn was synonymous with 'Dieu, que le son du cor, c'est triste au fond du bois' – see example opposite.

The novelty is (a) from the purely textural (sound) viewpoint and (b) in a wider context. Although Haydn's virtuoso high-horn writing gradually faded away, except for occasional reminders (Symphony No. 99's Minuet), the low horn's colour remained with his scores for the rest of his life: Symphony No. 92's Finale, Symphony No. 99's first movement (recapitulation), and Symphony No. 104's Finale (opening) are three examples that spring to mind.

One notices in these works yet another farewell: to the form of the *sonata da chiesa*, in which two (Nos. 2 and 3) of the works are cast. We shall find the occasional exception (Quarter, Op. 55/I will be mentioned *infra*) in later works, but these two Divertimenti are the summing-up of a noble Baroque tradition which Haydn had lovingly cultivated for many years. The special position of the adagio opening of these

---

1 The revival of this horn technique belongs to our age. The first C *alto* horns were constructed for the Haydn Society in 1949 and used for the first time in the Society's recording of Symphony No. 56, with the Vienna State Opera Orchestra conducted by Anton Heiller (1950). The first horn was the legendary Gottfried von Freiberg. These horns were subsequently used for *Philemon und Baucis* (Vox, *vide supra*, p. 259) and for recordings with the late Max Goberman. Otherwise the return of the virtuoso horn has been the exclusive merit of British horn players. Haydn's 'Pietà di me' was first played by the late Dennis Brain (the music rises to written g''' for an E flat horn; it was performed in D on this occasion), with Joan Sutherland (sop.), April Cantelo (sop.), Raymond Nilsson (ten.), the Goldsbrough Orchestra, conducted by Charles Mackerras for a B.B.C. Third Programme concert on 17 December 1956. An equally astonishing performance was that of the anonymous first horn player for Karl Haas when he made his first recordings of some of the *Divertimenti a otto voci* in the Op. 31 version for Parlophone and Westminster. Recently Alan Civil has distinguished himself in the performances of all the Op. 31 Divertimenti on ORYX 1740-1 (April 1969), conducted by Leslie Jones.

[Divertimento No. 4, Finale]

two works is typical for the unusual form of the entire set; for they seem, as we suggested at the beginning of this discussion, to define the special relationship between the baryton-playing Prince, now retiring at the age of sixty-one to the more relaxing (if possibly less rewarding) role of musical spectator, and his complicated, reserved, passionate *Capellmeister*, striving for greatness and walking the delicate tightrope between popularity (public approval) and inner satisfaction (private approval). Prince Esterházy himself might be said to play a dual role in Haydn's career, sometimes acting the part of *Vox Dei*, sometimes that of *Vox populi*, i.e. vacillating between private and public approbation (or criticism). It is in the slow movements to these *Divertimenti a otto voci*[1] that we find a purity, beauty and density of emotion experienced at this profundity perhaps only in the Op. 20 Quartets and in such movements as Symphony No. 45's Finale and No. 54's slow movement. In an Adagio such as the slow movement of No. 4 (X:4) we have a standard of excellence and a level of inspiration characteristic of the best in this new divertimento style, and which we shall see later reflected in another great slow movement from a similar work: Notturno III (II:32) of 1790. We are in another world, that of His Highness's chambers in Eszterháza: never was there music fitted to describe that which Haydn later said: 'I was cut off from the world ... I had to become original.' It was Haydn's (and the Prince's) private world; yet it was to be placed at the public's disposal in 1781, when six of the seven works were published by Artaria. (It is interesting to observe that neither Haydn nor Artaria entertained any reservations about the horns' difficulty.) Prince Esterházy no longer insisted on the terms of the old 1761 contract, which required Haydn not to distribute or publish any of the music he composed for the Prince; and of course he was supposed in the first place to compose only for the family. This was now a dead letter and Esterházy had no objections to Haydn publishing even works which, to an astute listener, must have opened a window on one particularly intimate aspect of musical life at Eszterháza.

Perhaps these *Divertimenti a otto voci* are representative of all that was most dignified, rewarding and beautiful in Haydn's active life at Eszterháza; and Prince Nicolaus must have been proud to have stimulated these rich musical revenues from his splendid Hungarian estate.

1 In *Joseph Haydn Werke*, the original Italian titles have been suppressed and German substitutes printed. Needless to say, this operation is unscholarly and, apart from all else, un-international and therefore contrary to the Haydnesque ideal, for which chauvinism was anathema.

IV. THE AUSTRIAN MUSICAL CRISIS:
OTHER COMPOSERS

(a) *Haydn's Pupils (foremost Ignaz Pleyel) and the Formation of the Second Haydn School*
Schools, in art and music, are formed by pupils and (the Berensonian term) *seguaci*
(followers); being a great and influential artist, Haydn was blessed, and burdened, by
many of both. We shall now analyze the advent of that which we turn the 'Second
Haydn School' and some of the principal men who constituted its members. Before
beginning, we must glance backwards to the emergence of the 'First Haydn School'.
This *scuola* was formed during the first years of the 1760s and used as its models several
groups of Haydn's works: (a) first and foremost the immensely popular quartet-
divertimenti which began to circulate about 1760 (dated copies of several in
Kremsmünster and Göttweig Abbeys; (b) secondly, the symphonies which also began
to circulate immediately (Symphony No. 1 is registered in the Catalogue of Bishop
Leopold Egk from Olmütz on 25 November 1759;[1] (c) thirdly, the divertimenti such
as those for horns and strings (II:21 and 22) later adapted (not by Haydn) for string
quartet and known nowadays as Op. 2, Nos. 3 and 5; or the *Divertimento a Nove
Stromenti* in F (II:20) which was even printed in Paris (by Berault, 1772) but was
known in Göttweig by 1763; or the *Divertimento a Sei* (II:11) registered at Göttweig in
1765 and printed (as a flute quartet) by Huberty in Paris (1773); (d) the keyboard
music, mostly piano (harpsichord, clavichord) sonatas but also piano trios and pieces
for harpsichord and small orchestra, which were widely copied in Bohemia. Other
categories of Haydn were known (e.g. wind-band divertimenti and church music) but
they were not yet as widely distributed or as influential as the works of these four
genres listed above. The music of this first period was bright, concise, gay (almost
amounting to flippancy in some cases) and technically adroit. The scoring was
economical except for the usually extravagant horn solos (as in Symphony No. 5/I)
and the concerto- or concerto-grosso-like sections of Symphonies Nos. 6–8, 13/II (solo
for the violoncello), 24/II (solo for the *flauto traverso*), and so on. There was a strong
Italian influence in the serenade-like slow movements (also deriving from the
concerto), but otherwise these works were firmly rooted in the Austrian tradition of
1750, e.g. Wagenseil, Reutter Jr., Holzbauer, etc. Apart from these well established
composers, however, Haydn made an immediate and lasting impression. His *seguaci* of
this first period are discussed in the previous volume of this biography.[2]

The 'Second Haydn School' began in the late 1760s, when the momentum of the
First School was nearly at its strongest. We do not have a list of all Haydn's pupils, but
some have been traced, among them Robert Kimmerling (Kymmerling), later at
Melk Abbey, and several members of the Esterházy band. 'Although', writes the
former Princely Archivist Janos Harich (*HJB* IV, 33), 'there are no documents to
support the theory ... we assume [Haydn] taught music to ... Michael Ernst ...,
Joseph Purgsteiner (Burgsteiner) ... Anton Kraft ... Carl Schiringer (Schöringer) and
Johann Dietzl ...'.

The most important pupil of this period was Ignaz Pleyel who, as we have seen in
the Chronicle, came to study with Haydn in 1772 and remained for five years. In the
available space we cannot analyze in depth the complicated musical relationship
between master and pupil, but briefly it may be stated that Pleyel's first works were
enormously full of promise. Mozart's words, in a letter to his father of 24 April 1784,

---

1 'Das Musikinventar des Olmützer Bischofs Leopold Egk aus dem Jahre 1760 als Quelle vorklassischer Instrumantalmusik', in *Archiv
für Musikwissenschaft* 19 (1972), p. 300.
2 A short résumé of the four Haydn schools is also found in *Haydn in England 1791–1795*, pp. 506f.

are well known: '... there have appeared quartets by a certain Pleyel; he is a pupil of Joseph Haydn. If you don't know them yet, try to procure them; they are worth doing so. They are very well written and very pleasing; you will also at once perceive their master in them. Good – and fortunate for music, if Pleyel will one day be able to replace Haydn for us ...'.[1] As evidence for the superior quality of Pleyel's earlier compositions, we present the (complete) autograph fragment of a Symphony in C from the Conservatoire de Musique (Paris),[2] dated 1778, i.e. shortly after finishing his studies with Haydn (see pp. 362ff.). Pleyel's model was *inter alia* the Overture to *Il ritorno di Tobia* (C minor slow introduction, C major fast section: in Haydn 'Allegro di molto', in Pleyel 'Allegro molto'). The theme of the fast section is also related to its model; Haydn's begins

The Adagio introduction of the Pleyel bears some relationship to the Aria 'Da ist die Katz' from *Die Feuersbrunst* (1776?).[3] In the quick movement, we can see many of the Haydnesque devices that we have studied in this period: the syncopations, the repeated semiquavers (see the beginning of page five of the facsimile), the use of *ff* to increase the tension, the ♩♫♪♩♩♩♩ rhythm in brass and drums (pp. 9f., the top two lines of the score). This is what we would expect from a Haydn pupil; also the solid craftsmanship which impressed Mozart.

But when Pleyel began to capitalize on his master's 'popular style', imitating to a nauseous degree those catchy rondos, sudden silences, jumps into foreign keys after the double bar, etc., he made himself almost as popular as his master but debased the whole Haydn style. Some idea of this debased pseudo-Haydn may be seen easily in the countless chamber works and symphonies in the libraries of Europe. We add (on p. 374) the beginning of Sonata II from 'Three Sonatas for the Piano-Forte or Harpsichord; with Accompaniments for a Violin and Violoncello' Op. XXIII (Longman & Broderip), i.e. Three Piano Trios.[4] The reader will draw his own conclusions. Dr Charles Burney, in his *General History of Music*,[5] writes:

> There has lately been a rage for the Music of Pleyel, which has diminished the attention of amateurs and the public to all other violin Music. But whether this ingenious and engaging composer does not draw faster from the fountain of his invention than it will long bear, and whether his imitation of Haydn, and too constant use of semitones, and coquetry in *rallentandos* and *pauses* will not be soon construed into affectation, I know not; but it has already been remarked by critical observers, that his fancy, though at first so fertile, is not so inexhaustible, but that he frequently repeats himself, and does not sufficiently disdain the mixture of common passages with his own elegant ideas.

1 *Mozart Briefe und Aufzeichnungen*, Gesamtausgabe (Bauer-Deutsch), Kassel 1963, III, 311.
2 W 6, 92, now Bibliothèque Nationale. The beginning initials stand for 'In Nomine Domini et Nomine Mariae'. Note 'in C Basso / Corni obl:'. As a Haydn pupil, Pleyel was used to C *alto* horns in symphonies of this kind (i.e. with trumpets and drums). He himself used C *alto* horns in *Die Fee Urgele* (autograph in the Österreichische Nationalbibliothek, Musiksammlung). Pleyel also adopted, in many of these early works, the so-called 'Haydn ornament' (crossed turn). The Symphony was later published by Artaria (Sinf. Pér. No. 4, pl. no. 95), Imbault (Sinf. Pér. No. 3, pl. no. 74 or 89) and Schott (Sinf. Pér. No. 4, reprint of Artaria[?]). There are MS. copies in Thurn und Taxis (Regensburg), Estense (Modena), Fürstenberg (Donaueschingen, 1596) Archives.
3 See Vocal Score (Schott), p. 49, bars 4–9.
4 We have the facsimile from Dr Alan Tyson, who also drew attention to the work in question in his article (quoted *infra*).
5 Vol. IV, pp. 915f.

[Pleyel: Fragment of a Symphony in C, 1778]

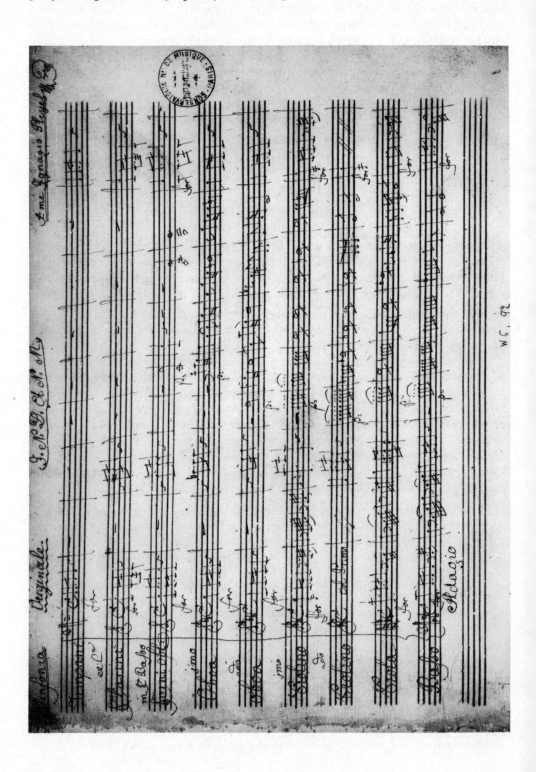

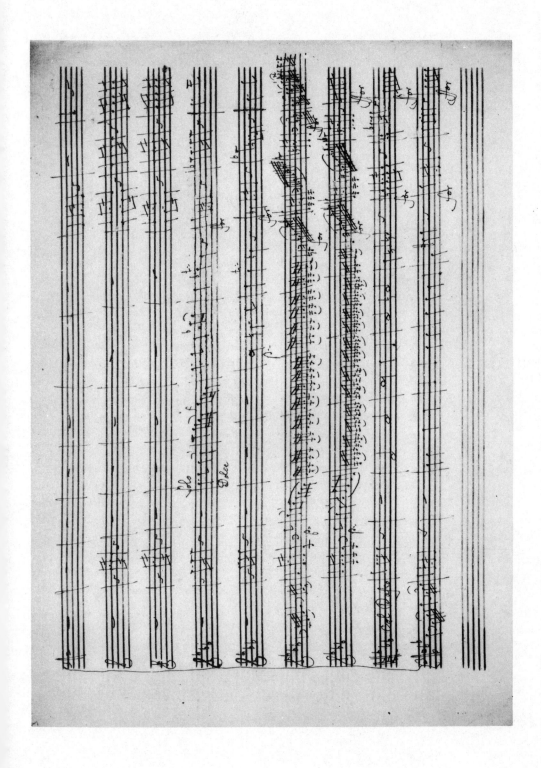

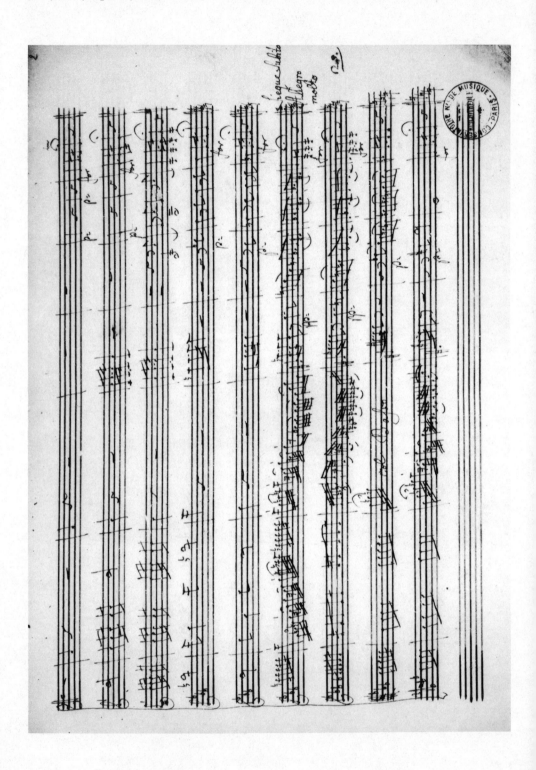

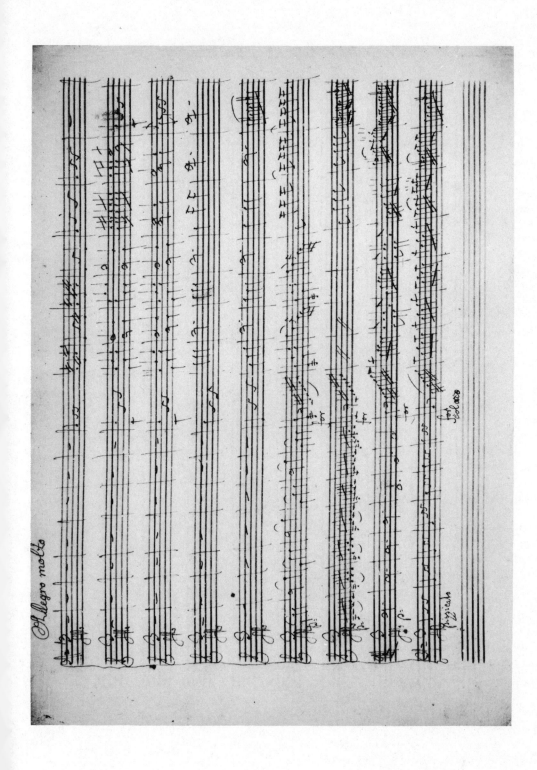

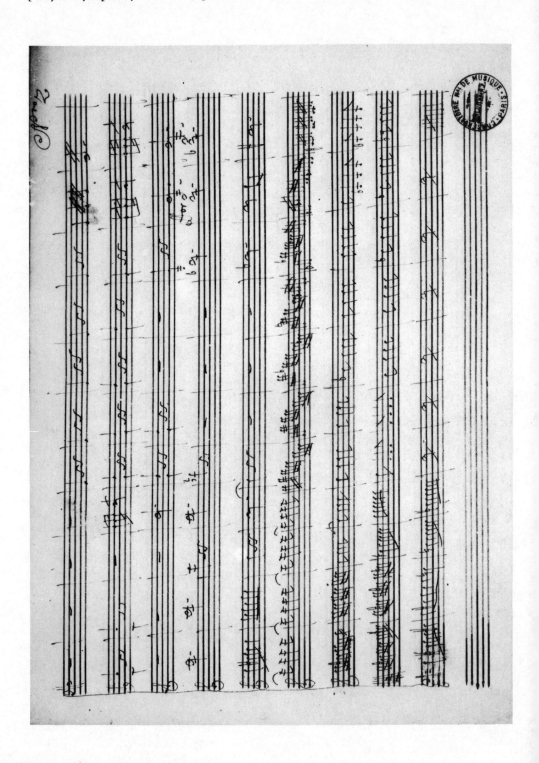

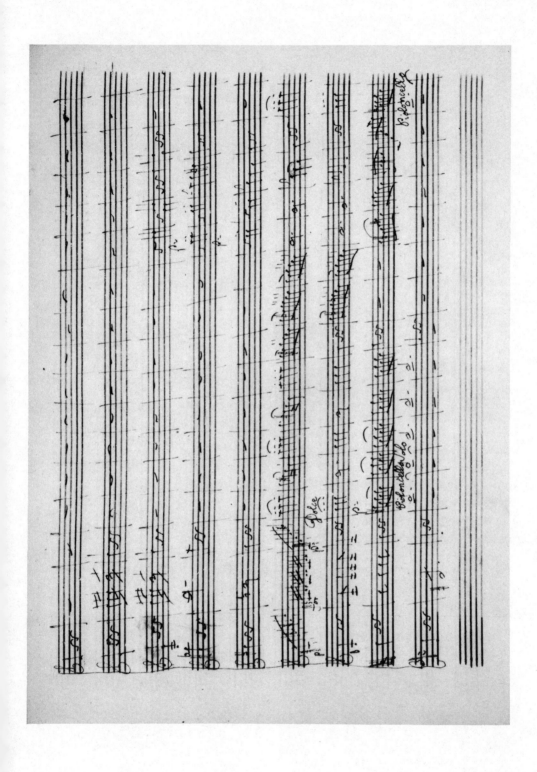

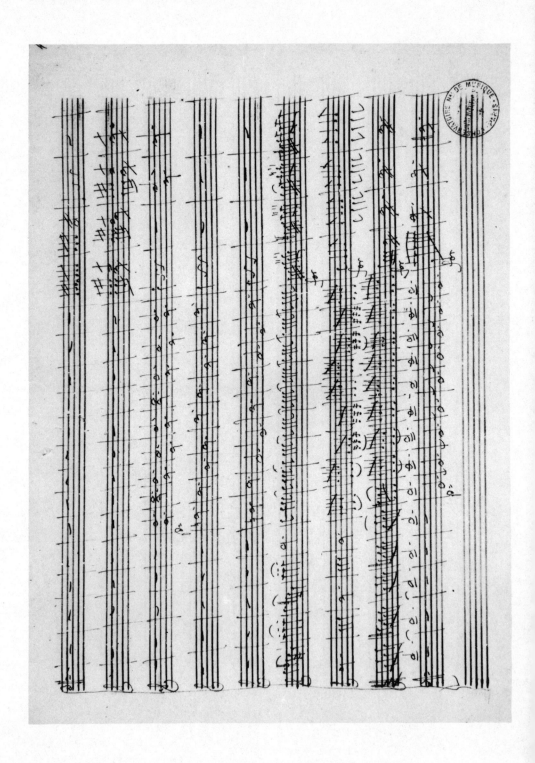

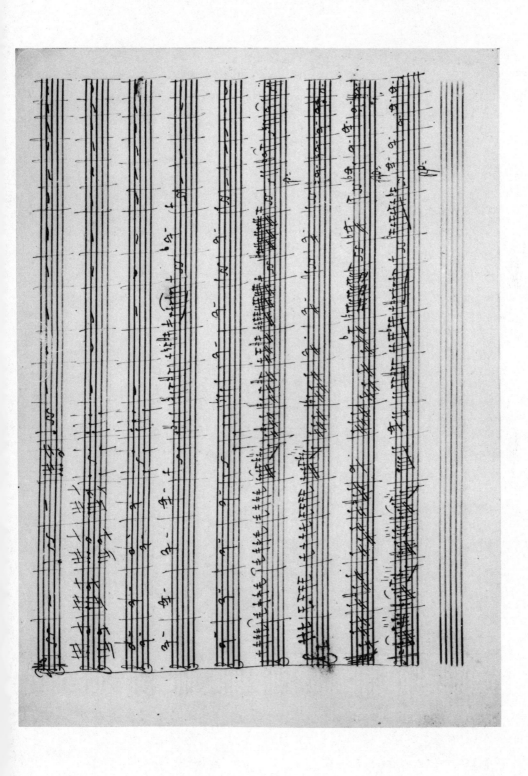

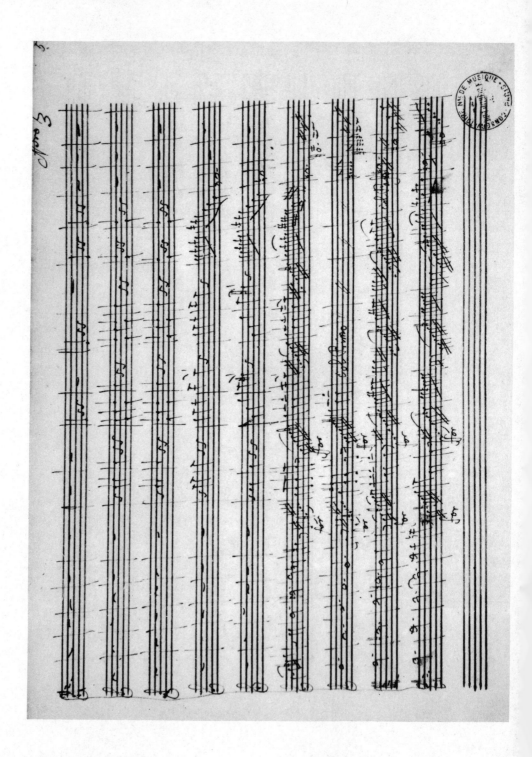

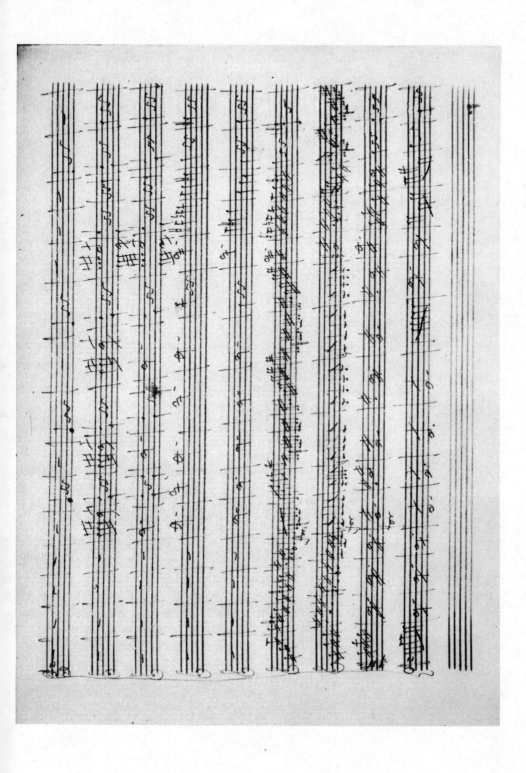

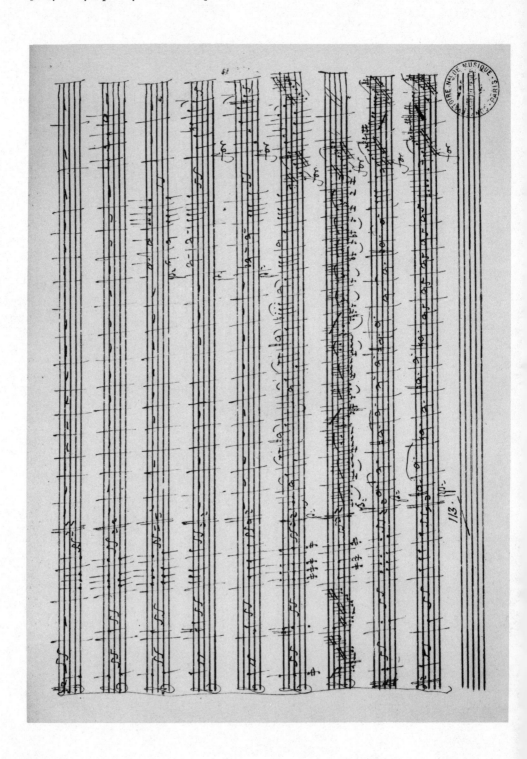

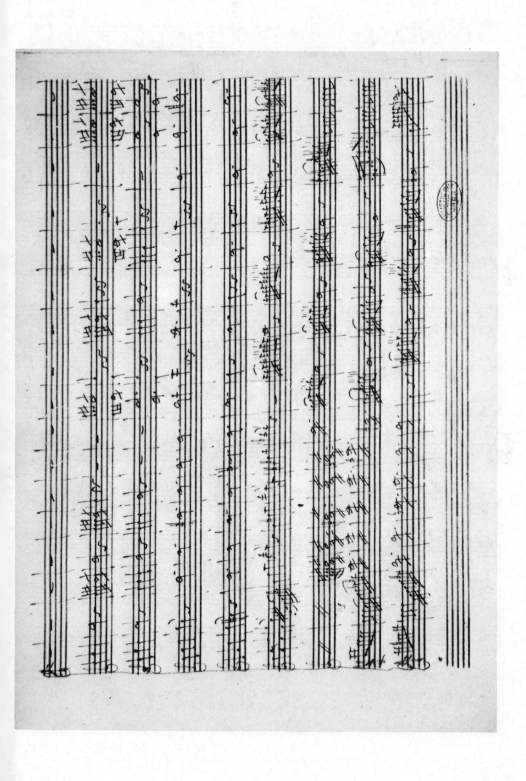

The opening of the piano part of the Sonata (Trio) in C, Op. XXIII, No. 2, by Ignaz Pleyel, in a contemporary edition published by Longman & Broderip, London (cf. p. 361).

We now proceed to a document on Pleyel's life, written (on the occasion of his death on 14 November 1831) from what is clearly first-hand information; it appeared in the *Revue Musicale* and was shortly thereafter translated and reprinted in *The Harmonicon* (1832, pp. 25ff.):

MEMOIR OF IGNATIUS PLEYEL.
(From *La Revue Musicale*.)

IGNATIUS PLEYEL was born in the year 1757; he was the twenty-fourth child of Marten Pleyel, a schoolmaster residing at Ruppersthal, a village within a few leagues of Vienna, by a lady of noble birth, whose family had disowned and disinherited her on account of her unequal marriage. His mother died in childbed of him, and his father, after having fourteen more children by a second wife, died at the patriarchal age of ninety-nine.

Educated as is usual with the youth of Germany, the young Ignatius learned the rudiments of music almost as soon as he learned to speak; the bent of his genius towards the art showed itself early, and so decidedly, that his father sent him to Vienna to study the piano-forte under Vanhall. Until he was fifteen years old he had no other master, but about the year 1772, the Count Erdœdy, a Hungarian noble, took him under his protection, and placed him as a pupil and boarder with Joseph Haydn, paying for his board and instruction a hundred louis per annum, a sum, for that period, by no means inconsiderable. During five years Pleyel continued an inmate of Haydn's house, applying himself with unremitting assiduity to his musical studies under the guidance of that great master.

A circumstance, singular in itself, and the more so, from its having escaped the researches of all the biographers of Haydn, was very near destroying for ever the friendship and good understanding which prevailed between him and his scholar. It was a custom of Haydn as soon as he had finished any new work, to lay it aside for some time before he again looked at it, for the purpose of retouching and correcting. It happened that, under the influence of low spirits and chagrin, this great master had written six quartetts, all in a minor key. According to custom, he left the manuscript on his piano, and, as was also usual with him whenever he had finished a new work, he dismissed from his mind, and forgot entirely the subjects and ideas on which he had been working. Some time afterwards, Haydn felt inclined to revise these quartetts, of which he thought favourably, but he sought for them in vain; they had disappeared, were no where to be found, and all attempts to recover them ended only in disappointment. Pleyel, who alone had access to Haydn's house and apartment, was suspected by him of having stolen the missing quartetts; and notwithstanding all the protestations of his pupil to the contrary, he continued for a long time firm in that opinion. At length, however, the sincere and devoted attachment of his young pupil convinced Haydn that his suspicions must be unfounded: he restored him to his friendship, and thought no more of the circumstance, except occasionally to regret the disappearance of what he considered one of his best productions. The most singular part of the whole affair is, that the thief, whoever he may have been, did not attempt to derive any advantage from his robbery; these stolen quartetts never saw the light.

In 1776, when Pleyel was in his twentieth year, and had nearly completed his studies, Gluck returned to Vienna, after bringing out his opera of *Alceste* in Paris. He had not been many days in the Austrian capital, before he paid a visit to Haydn, who played to him his quartett in F minor then just written. The beauties of so fine a composition could not be lost upon the great restorer of lyric tragedy, who, accordingly, bestowed on the quartett warm and well-merited applause. Haydn then requested his guest to hear a specimen of the composition of his *favourite pupil* Pleyel: this also was praised by Gluck, who said, 'My young friend, you understand very well how to put notes on paper; you have now only to learn how and when to blot them out again.'

In 1777 Pleyel left Haydn, and returned to his patron, Count Erdœdy, who had appointed him his Maestro di Capella. This situation, though in many respects both advantageous and pleasant, did not entirely satisfy the young musician, who nourished an intense desire to visit Italy. The Count at first opposed this fancy, but yielded at length to the repeated solicitations of his protégé, gave him leave of absence, and supplied him with the means of carrying his wishes into execution. Pleyel accordingly set out for Naples. Once arrived in Italy, he soon became acquainted with all the celebrated artists who shed their lustre over that Augustan age of Italian music; Cimarosa, Guglielmi, Paisiello, were numbered among his friends; his taste was formed by hearing such singers as Marchesi at Milan, Guadagni at Padua, the Gabrielli, Pacchierotti, &c. Nardini was then still living, and in full possession of his unrivalled powers on the violin. Pleyel had frequent opportunities of hearing and admiring him. He was also intimate with Pugnani, and, indeed, with the majority of those great artists whose united talents rendered that period perhaps the brightest and most astonishing in the whole history of Italian music. At Naples he was presented to the king, who received him with great kindness, and required him to compose some pieces for a species of lyre or guitar, upon which his majesty sometimes performed, a task which the young German executed with facility, and much to the royal satisfaction.

Although the bent of his genius was towards instrumental writing, Pleyel determined, while at Naples, to try his hand at theatrical composition, and produced an opera on the story of Iphigenia, which was represented with success at the great theatre, and subsequently translated into German. The manuscript German score is preserved by M. André of Offenbach, who has published a pretty recitative and rondeau from it in his collection of airs arranged for the piano-forte.

It was not till 1781 that Pleyel returned to his native country, and then his stay there was but short. The recollection of Italy was uppermost in his mind, the desire to return thither his strongest wish; in the following year he again quitted Germany and proceeded to Rome, where he was present in February, 1783, at the production of Cherubini's comic opera, *Lo Sposo di tre Femmine*. His second visit to Italy, however, was not so long as his first. The advanced age of Francis Xavier Richter, then Master of the Chapel in the Cathedral of Strasburgh, rendered it necessary that he should have some assistant in performing the duties of his office; the appointment of deputy, together with the reversion of the situation expectant on the death of his principal, was offered to Pleyel, who accepted the proposal, and settled in Strasburg[h] before the end of 1783. His new post imposed upon him the necessity of writing for the church, in which species of composition he composed several pieces which were well thought of, but were unfortunately all destroyed, together with the compositions of Richter, in a fire which happened at Strasburgh a few years after. Richter died 12th Sept., 1791, and Pleyel became Chapel Master of Strasburgh Cathedral.

It was during the ten years between 1783 and 1793 that Pleyel produced the greatest part of his works. His violin quartetts and sonatas for the piano-forte acquired the highest popularity; editions upon editions were published at Vienna, Berlin, Leipsic, Offenbach, Paris, London, and even in Holland, while the number of copies sold was almost incredible. No instrumental music of that class was endured but Pleyel's, and his reputation eclipsed that of all his contemporaries. He also wrote some symphonies; and although his style had hardly the grandeur requisite for this species of composition, their easiness of execution, and the elegant melodies which they contained, rendered them pretty popular.

A weekly concert, called 'The Professional,' had existed for some years in

London, under the management of several distinguished artists and amateurs of music. In 1791, Salomon, a violinist of great celebrity, determined to give a series of twelve subscription concerts in the Hanover Square Rooms, and in order to strengthen himself for the approaching struggle with his 'professional' rivals, engaged Haydn to furnish a new grand symphony for each night. Haydn went to London, where his symphonies, the last twelve he wrote, produced an extraordinary sensation, and the success of his enterprize in the first year encouraged Salomon to continue it the following season. The directors of the Professional Concert now felt the necessity of resorting to some new attraction, in order to interest the curiosity of the musical world, and recall the amateurs who were fast deserting them, and gathering round their spirited competitor. They engaged Pleyel, who went to London towards the end of 1791, and wrote for them several symphonies. The first concert under his conductorship was given on the 13th of February, 1792; the success of his music was prodigious; he surpassed himself, and showed that he was worthy to contest the palm even with his illustrious master. He wrote three symphonies, of which one in E♭ was particularly admired as an excellent composition. Unfortunately, the 'Professional Concert' was discontinued a few years after, and by the dispersion of its library Pleyel's symphonies, of which he had not preserved any copies, were lost to the world*.

By his engagement in London, Pleyel had realized about twelve hundred pounds; this, together with some former savings, enabled him to purchase an estate a few miles from Strasburgh, to which he retired when the Revolution, by overturning the Catholic worship, deprived him of his office in the Cathedral. His retirement, however, was far from being unmolested; the situation which he had filled classed him among the *Aristocrats;* seven times during the year 1793 he was denounced, and only preserved his life by a timely flight of concealment. At length he was arrested in the middle of the night, and led prisoner before the municipal authorities of Strasburgh. Interrogated on the subject of his opinions, Pleyel professed civism, in proof of which he was required to compose the music for a kind of drama, which a Septembrizer had written to celebrate the anniversary of the 10th of August. Refusal being out of the question, he undertook the task, only requesting permission to retire to his own house, that he might work more at his ease. This favour was granted him, but under the surveillance of two gend'armes, and, moreover, of the poet whose effusions he had been thus commanded to set to music.

After seven days and nights of almost uninterrupted labour, the task was achieved, and the author returned to Strasburgh to direct the performance. Amongst the instruments in the score, he had written a part for seven church bells, tuned to the notes of the gammut; these bells had been selected from those of several neighbouring churches, and hung up for the occasion in the tower of the cathedral. The first burst of these unusual instruments in a common chord produced so overpowering an effect that the composer fainted. The impression made by this fine composition is not yet forgotten by the inhabitants of Strasburgh; the score is preserved in the author's family.

Disgusted by these events, Pleyel sold his estate at Strasburgh, and in the spring of the year 1795 removed with all his family to Paris. The constantly increasing success of his compositions suggested to him the idea of securing to himself the profit which the music-sellers of the capital had hitherto derived from his labours, by becoming his own editor. This first led him to open a music shop,

---

* [original footnote:] Thus the French biographer. Truth, however, obliges us to remark, that Pleyel did not, in the opinion of his English hearers, approach at all near to Haydn; on the contrary, his inferiority was universally felt and acknowledged, even by those who relied upon the support of his talents. In two seasons more, Salomon, supported by Haydn, drove his rivals entirely out of the field.

to which he subsequently added a piano-forte manufactory; his establishments were successful, but the unremitting attention they demanded, withdrew him gradually from composition, so that long before his death, he had entirely given over writing. In his interims of leisure, nevertheless, he composed twelve quartetts, which remain in manuscript, but which, in point of construction, are much superior to any of his published works, and prove that his self-imposed silence did not result from any failure of his talents. These quartetts have excited the admiration of many distinguished performers, and especially of Messrs. Dussek and Onslow.

After a long career of labour, M. Pleyel withdrew far from the capital to a country estate, where he indulged his partiality for agricultural pursuits, and was living in a happy retirement, when the Revolution of July filled him with alarm on account of his property. His health was already beginning to yield; anxiety of mind increased his illness; and, after three months of almost unremitting pain, he died on the 14th of November, 1831.

Pleyel entered into the married state in 1788, and had eight children. His eldest son, M. Camille Pleyel, has distinguished himself both as a piano-forte player and composer: indeed, the demands which his manufactory of instruments makes upon his time and attention, have alone prevented his attaining a brilliant reputation.

Between the years 1783 and 1797, Pleyel's productions were exceedingly numerous; a correct and complete list of them would be very difficult to obtain, and it would be hardly possible to distinguish, in many instances, his original compositions from arrangements of them by himself. He is known to have published twenty-nine symphonies for a full orchestra, besides several symphonies concertante for violin, tenor, violoncello, and wind instruments; nine sets of violin quartetts, five sets of quintetts, [etc.]. . . .[1]

We must break our chronology for a moment and continue the story of Haydn and Pleyel, which in 1784 took a very surprising turn. The facts are told in Framery's *Notice sur Joseph Haydn* (1810).[2]

When Pleyel had ceased being Haydn's pupil he moved to Strasbourg, where he began to make a name for himself, especially with pianoforte works; and as an act of homage to his old teacher he sent Haydn two sonatas [trios], which were so to speak the first-fruits of his talent. Some time later Haydn received from a London music merchant, 'whose name I think was Forster', a request for three new sonatas of his composition, for which he was offered a good price on condition that they were sent straight away. Haydn was busy with 'un grand ouvrage' [*Armida*], but not wishing to lose the offer, sent Forster, along with one sonata that he had just composed, the two that Pleyel had sent him – not thinking that Pleyel would put them to further use.

About the same time a partner of the firm Longman and Broderip, who was passing through Strasbourg, bought a number of Pleyel's already popular works and overcame Pleyel's reluctance to including the 2 sonatas in the purchase. The Longman and Broderip edition of 'Pleyel' and the Forster edition of 'Haydn'[3]

1 Concerning the Haydn quartets in the minor key, either he actually wrote six in the proximity of Op. 20 and they are irretrievably lost, or the autographs of Op. 20 are meant. Now it is a curious point that Haydn obviously did not have these autographs when making the revised editions for Artaria in 1800, nor do they appear in the catalogue of his music effects (see *Haydn: the Late Years 1801–1809*, pp. 316ff.). But Artaria later owned these autographs and offered them for sale (*vide supra*, p. 242). We can do no more than offer these facts without providing 'connecting information'. The part about Haydn playing Op. 20, No. 5 (F minor), to Gluck shows, however, that the writer made a distinction between Op. 20 (which was clearly never lost) and the lost quartets. In Naples, Pleyel wrote Lira Concertos for the King of Naples. Franz Xaver Richter died in 1789, not in 1791. For Pleyel's activity in England, see *Haydn in England 1791–1795*, pp. 108, 119f., 121f., 127f. and 130 *passim*; see also the later volumes of this biography. MGG X, 1353–9, corrects *Harmonicon*'s data.
2 We follow the summary in the article by Alan Tyson, 'Haydn and two Stolen Trios', in *Music Review* XXII (1961).
3 Op. 40, containing Trio 18 (XV:5) and the two Pleyel works (Hoboken XV:3 and 4).

appeared in London at almost the same time. Forster, astonished to see the works he had bought from Haydn published by a rival firm under Pleyel's name, started a lawsuit against Longman and Broderip – who in their turn were astonished by Forster's edition of works well-known in Strasbourg as being by Pleyel; consequently 'ils répondirent donc à l'assignation par une assignation semblable'.

Haydn had meanwhile got leave and arrived in London; and his embarrassment on being informed of the situation was not decreased by the appearance of Pleyel. Not knowing what to say to 'the judges' they decided to tell – the truth. The judges and publishers recognized their good faith, and instead of a judgement 'on fit un accommodement. Haydn en fit quitte pour le frais', which are enormous in London, and gave three new sonatas of his composition to each of the two publishers.

Alan Tyson, who rediscovered all this important information, also found yet another source: an edition of the three Trios published by Pleyel himself (1799?) – one by Le Duc under Pleyel's name was already listed in Hoboken – which contained the following note inserted on a sheet of paper (watermark date 1822) inserted as a fly-leaf:

> The [two] first of these light pretty Sonatas were composed by Pleyel when a pupil of the celebrated Haydn and [got] accidentally mixed amongst his papers, on looking over the wreck of which after having suffered very severely by a fire which broke out in his House at Vienna, he found these two Sonatas, and not knowing how to account for their being there, he composed and added a third, which is infinitely more scientific – and having corrected improved and prepared them for Publication, he sent them for this purpose to Broderips in London, where they were so favourably received as to produce a very unprecedented Sale.
>
> Pleyel, then at Strasbourg, met a friend recently arrived from London, and enquiring what new musical Compositions were most in Vogue he played him one of his own Sonatas published under Haydn's Name which Pleyel immediately recognizing for his own, a warm discussion arose between him and his late Master, who proposed to him such a Compensation for the mistake as his pecuniary Embarrassments would permit which not being satisfactory, – the Affair terminated in a Law Suit, and Pleyel obtained a Verdict against the unfortunate Haydn for £500 damages.
>
> This unfriendly Act (under the existing Circumstances) has been generally considered by no means in a favourable Light on the part of the Pupil.

Dr Tyson has uncovered further evidence[1] that the lawsuit took place in 1794 and was 'settled out of court'. A final piece of evidence cited in the article is from Dr John Callcott's *A Musical Grammar* (London 1806). Callcott was Haydn's pupil, and this lends weight to the following statement on page 172 of his book: a point of harmony is illustrated by an example taken from 'what are called Haydn's Sonatas, Op. 40' and the phrase is explained by a footnote: 'The first two of these *three* Sonatas were composed by Pleyel, and only the last in G by Haydn.'

We have only one suggestion to make in explanation of this unsavoury episode. We believe that the facts as stated by Framery are essentially correct – we shall examine another salient point from Framery in connection with *La vera costanza* (*infra*, p. 528) – but that the origin of the Pleyel trios may be slightly different. In view of Haydn's

---

1 'There is no record at Stationers' Hall under the year 1785 [when Forster issued the Trios] to indicate that Forster took steps to safeguard his copyright in the trios he had bought by depositing the obligatory copies. But he appears to have done just that nine years later, since on 13 January 1794 he entered at Stationers' Hall 'A Favorite Overture in all its parts Composed by Giuseppe Haydn of Vienna and published by his Authority' and also the Opp. 40 and 42 [Nos. 22, 17 and 23] piano trios, both 'composed by Giuseppe Haydn of Vienna'. The records at Stationers' Hall further state that a certificate of entry for each of these works was given on 2 June 1794.' See also *Haydn in England 1791–1795*, p. 119.

letter to Eybler of 1789, asking for some minuets (*infra*, p. 717), we wonder if Haydn did not, perhaps, *commission* the trios from Pleyel in a similar fashion, with the clear intent to re-sell them (as was patently the idea with the Eybler minuets). It was not the only time that Haydn helped himself to the works of his pupil; we shall see that the Overture to *Die Feuersbrunst* was composed by Pleyel and that Haydn, moreover, used the little Finale to round off the two-movement Overture to *L'infedeltà delusa* when he prepared that work (and some other overtures) for publication at Artaria's (*vide infra*, p. 519).

As for the stylistic similarities between Pleyel and the two Opus 40 Trios, we refer to the musical example (facsimile) reproduced above: the Pleyel Trio shows a distinct relationship to Op. 40/1 (XV:3), which may be consulted in any old edition of the Haydn trios (Peters, for example, vol. I, p. 237). Later, when Breitkopf & Härtel was preparing the *Oeuvres Complettes* of Haydn's (mostly pianoforte) music, the composer assuaged his guilty conscience by suggesting that Opus 40/1 was actually by Michael Haydn.[1]

(b) Some 'Seguaci' of Haydn's

The 'Second Haydn School', which formed its style round the new and powerful works emanating from Eszterháza in the late 1760s and early 1770s, was soon well represented at the copyists' offices in Vienna and also abroad, especially in the Parisian publishing houses. The traffic in spurious compositions 'by Haydn' grew apiece: many of the *seguaci*'s works were sold to Paris in MS. and published as 'Haydn'. Nowadays the most famous case is probably that of P. Roman(us) Hoffstetter, whose quartets were engraved by Bailleux in 1777; before publication, however, Bailleux erased (but not completely, so that the name 'Signor Hoffstetter' can be read underneath the later superimposed name of Haydn) the original name from the plate and substituted Haydn's.[2] We shall examine more situations of this kind *infra*, pp. 661ff.

We are forced to be highly selective in dealing with the myriad number of these *seguaci*, most of whose music has been long (if at times also unjustly) forgotten. We shall therefore select three such *seguaci* for a brief treatment here: Vanhal, Ordoñez and Mozart (with particular reference to his Symphony in G minor, K.183).

The most talented, and one of the most prolific, composers of this 'Second Haydn School' was Johann Baptist Vanhal (Wanhal, etc.). The facts about his life are astonishingly few, and those (as given to us in *MGG*)[3] may be summarized as follows. He was born on 12 May 1739 at Neu Nechanitz (Nové Nechanice) in Bohemia, and died, almost entirely forgotten, in Vienna on 20 August 1813. He studied with Dittersdorf and, like Dittersdorf and Gluck, made an Italian journey in 1769–71. After that, he had a nervous breakdown which was at that time described as an outbreak of religious mania. He was then taken by Count Johann Nepomuk von Erdödy to recover on his estates in Croatia. In 1780, Vanhal settled in Vienna and gradually degenerated into a facile composer of salon music. It was one of the great tragedies of Viennese musical life at that time.

Vanhal began composing in the 1760s, and by 1771 his works were being offered for sale along with the other Austrian masters.[4] The *Wienerisches Diarium* No. 22 of 1771 had an advertisement by Simon Haschke offering 'Eine Quantität Sinfonien, als

1 See *Haydn: The Late Years 1801–1809*, p. 253; also *Haydn in England 1791–1795*, pp. 119f.
2 H. C. Robbins Landon and Alan Tyson, 'Who Composed Haydn's op. 3?', in *Musical Times* 105 (1964), pp. 56f.
3 Vol. 14, Sp. 1255ff., by Milan Poštolka.
4 Hannelore Gericke, *Der Wiener Musikalienhandel von 1700 bis 1778*, Graz & Cologne, 1960, pp. 104f.

von Hern. Ordenitz, Hofmann, Ditters, Haydn, Vanhal [etc]). Göttweig Abbey owned several of Vanhal's symphonies in 1768 and 1769, while Breitkopf was offering his symphonies as early as 1768. We have mentioned some of Vanhal's quartets *supra* (p. 319). He took Haydn as his model not only figuratively but literally. In a Symphony in A major (see example) from Bailleux's Op. 25[1] we note that the model was the second movement of Symphony No. 5 by Haydn (*c.* 1757–60):

[Vanhal: Symphony in A major, opening]

Another Symphony, in G minor with four horns (announced by Breitkopf in 1771), uses Haydn's Symphony No. 39 as its model, and here[2] we may observe the Haydnesque *Sturm und Drang* at its full flowering. We cite the opening of the Finale, a first-rate *seguace*'s adaptation of the bold style in Haydn that we have been examining throughout this chapter. (The second movement contains unusual and beautiful solo parts for violin and viola: Vanhal wrote some beautiful viola concertos, of which we particularly admire one in C major with trumpets and kettledrums.)

1 Copy in the Conservatoire de Musique, Paris.
2 Diletto Musicale No. 38 (Landon), edited from MSS. in Prague (Osek Monastery) and Kremsmünster Abbey.

[Vanhal: Symphony in G minor, Finale]

In these Vanhal pieces of the time, we may trace many Haydnesque details – the wide skips in the melodic material, the repeated quavers in the bass, the syncopations, the repeated semiquavers in the violins, and so forth. Another fine example is the Symphony in D minor, also with four horns[1] (announced by Breitkopf in 1771), of which we cite the beginnings of the first and last movements. The slow movement exists in two versions, one in the very unusual key of G minor (strings alone, rather in the old-fashioned style of Haydn's No. 39/II or 58/II), which meant (like the J. C. Bach Symphony in G minor) that all the movements were in a minor key.

---

1 MSS. in Kremsmünster (H 36, 359), Osek (Prague 179A), Göttweig 1778, Regensburg (Thurn und Taxis), Frýdland (Clam-Gallas Archives, Schloß Friedland, now Prague), etc.

[Vanhal: Symphony in D minor, opening]

[Vanhal: Symphony in D minor, first movement – *cont.*]

[Vanhal: Symphony in D minor, first movement – *cont.*]

Violoncello

[Vanhal: Symphony in D minor, Finale]

[Vanhal: Symphony in D minor, Finale – *cont.*]

Of the 110 Vanhal symphonies in our thematic catalogue,[1] a few appear to be by other composers,[2] but it may be stated with confidence that he composed as many symphonies as did Haydn. If we analyze the number of works in the minor key we arrive at the following results:

C minor: 2 (No. 2, a magnificent work, was known to Mozart through a MS. dated 1771 in the Monastery of St Peter, Salzburg.)

D minor: 3

E minor: 3 (No. 1, with four horns [two in G, two in E], in the Esterházy Archives)

F minor: 1

G minor: 2

A minor: 2

With this total of thirteen works, Vanhal outnumbers Haydn's minor-keyed works by three. It is significant that, like Haydn, most of Vanhal's symphonies in a minor key were composed in the period *c.* 1768–72. We agree with Professor Barrett-Ayres when he writes (op. cit., p. 326):

I feel that these two composers, Ordoñez and Vanhal, represent the two main streams of mid-eighteenth-century Viennese musical thought: Ordoñez, serious, sombre, inclined to look back towards pre-classical and Baroque times, but ready to experiment, and the owner of an original mind....

But we think he has not examined the right works of Vanhal to label him 'an ephemeral, light-hearted composer, writing principally for the day, a musician who found it easy to copy others and whose principal concern was to please ... a music to be enjoyed and perhaps forgotten ... his music lacks imagination and distinction...' (op. cit., pp. 327, 326.) Vanhal certainly became the composer described by Professor Barrett-Ayres, but at the period of which we are speaking he was, in our opinion, the most original and powerful of all the Haydn followers.

The present writer's interest in the music of Carlos d'Ordoñez dates from the Haydn Society Conference at Bad Aussee in 1951, when it was decided (by Landon, Larsen and Schmid) that of all the dubious symphonies attributed to Haydn, only one, in A major (I:A6), might be considered genuine. Subsequently the work turned out to be Ordoñez (most MSS. missing in Hoboken, *inter alia* Donaueschingen 1772, Count Pachta [Prague]) and was discussed as such by the author at a conference in Harvard University, 1957.[3] Later we prepared a complete thematic catalogue of Ordoñez's compositions which, among other things, revealed strikingly how many of his works were once attributed to Haydn: string trios, quartets, symphonies, divertimenti.[4] In recent times, Professor A. Peter Brown has made a thorough investigation of Ordoñez's life and works and is about to publish a complete thematic catalogue which is a model of its kind.[5]

---

1 We have prepared a complete thematic catalogue of the works of J. B. Vanhal (begun 1951).

2 Koželuch (a D major Symphony), Kohl (a B flat Symphony), Dittersdorf or Sandel (Symphony in A); some other works are wrongly attributed to Carl Stamitz, to Novotny (our D minor Symphony, no less) and a great many to Haydn.

3 'Problems of Authenticity in Eighteenth-Century Music', in *Instrumental Music* (ed. D. G. Hughes), Cambridge 1959, p. 35.

4 The catalogue was used *in toto* in a dissertation by Iain Watson (University of Aberdeen). In 1969, A. G. Wilson, as part of a thesis for Aberdeen, made working editions of several Ordoñez quartets and symphonies. The first Ordoñez Symphony published in modern times was that in C for two choirs of trumpets and timpani with orchestra, Universal Edition (Landon); it had previously received its first modern performance in this writer's series on the preclassical symphony for the B.B.C. in 1956. See also *MGG* (Landon), where a brief summary catalogue of Ordoñez's music is listed. In Zinzendorf's Diary for 23 April 1775 (at a concert given by Count Thun), he notes that Ordoñez is a 'fils naturel de Mr. de Buquoy.'

5 See his useful articles, 'The Chamber Music with Strings of Carlos d'Ordoñez: A Bibliographical and Stylistic Study', in *Acta Musicologica* XLVI/2 (1974), pp. 222–72; also 'Structure and Style in the String Quartets of Carlos d'Ordoñez', Copenhagen Congress 1972, vol. I (Copenhagen 1974), pp. 314ff.

Ordoñez's fugal writing has been discussed by Kirkendale and Barrett-Ayres.[2] We shall therefore add a few remarks on the subject of Ordoñez's orchestral music. He wrote about seventy symphonies which are among the most striking and original of the Viennese *seguaci* of Haydn's (though, strictly speaking, Vanhal was much more a real *seguace* than Ordoñez, whose first known Symphony in C was already at Göttweig by 1756, thus antedating Haydn's first work in the genre). Ordoñez's fugues, in the Fuxian manner, are part of a vast contrapuntal (fugal) tradition which the Viennese always cultivated – being by nature slightly old-fashioned and inclined to be conservative in their ideas – and not only in church music. We find fugato finales in his symphonies, e.g. in a Symphony in A (Doksy Archives, Prague) and in an E major Symphony (Doksy, Florence Conservatorio [Pitti Palace]); and as the second movement of an F major Symphony (Doksy).

The serious side to Ordoñez's music has been mentioned by Barrett-Ayres. In the symphonies, we have a number of serious, weighty works in minor keys: one in C minor (Florence Conservatorio, Kroměříž [Kremsier, twice]) with trumpets and kettledrums; three in G minor (one lost; No. 2 in Nationalbibliothek, Vienna; Schwarzenberg Archives, Český Krumlov [Krumau] and Florence Conservatorio; No. 3 only in Biblioteca Estense, Modena); and a most rewarding Symphony for strings in F minor (Rajhrad [Brno], Modena). To illustrate this side of Ordoñez in an orchestral work, we have chosen the opening part of the Overture to *Alceste*, given at Eszterháza in 1775 (pp. 391–2). We have taken our text from the copy of the score that Haydn owned and which is partly in Ordoñez's handwriting. We have seen (*vide supra*, p. 257) that Haydn used part of Ordoñez's *Alceste* in the later version of *Philemon und Baucis*.[2]

Ordoñez died in shameful poverty in Vienna on 6 September 1786: Professor Brown showed us a transcript of the *Verlassenschaft* from the Archiv der Stadt Wien. It is yet another case of a well-known and respected colleague of Haydn's dying in abject poverty – Dittersdorf, Boccherini and Mozart are three other infamous cases. It was one more lesson to Haydn how frail was the economic basis on which an eighteenth-century musician lived, and died.

Admirers of Mozart will perhaps be surprised to find his name listed as a *seguace* of Haydn's, but the description is entirely accurate for the very short period under present discussion. We have mentioned the string quartets that Mozart wrote in the shadow of Op. 20. We will now turn to another interesting case: Mozart's so-called 'little' Symphony in G minor, K.183.

It is clearly another work based on Haydn's Symphony No. 39, and like its model it, too, is scored for four horns, two in G and two in B flat *alto*. Mozart was with his father in Vienna from July to the end of September, when Wolfgang had ample opportunity to hear the latest music by Haydn and his contemporaries. The obvious fruits of this encounter were, firstly, the choruses for *Thamos* (later revised in 1779: K.345), and secondly, the G minor Symphony K.183, probably composed in October 1773.[3] It is a work as unlike its symphonic companions (K.200, 201) as is the

---

1 Kirkendale op. cit., pp. 35f. & *passim*; Barrett-Ayres op. cit., pp. 122, 131f., 319ff. and *passim*.
2 The Ordoñez score, which we studied *in situ* in 1958, is now in the National Széchényi Library, Budapest, Ms. Mus. Opera 714. Professor A. Peter Brown gave us a xerox copy of the whole opera, and we have had many fruitful discussions and exchanges of ideas on Ordoñez, Haydn and many other topics when this writer was a guest lecturer at Indiana University in 1976.
3 See Köchel, 3rd edition (Einstein), p. 248. The dates of these three works were later scratched out, probably when Mozart needed them in Vienna in the 1780s and saw no reason for the copyists to realize that they were 'older' works. Mozart asked his father for several of these 'older' works, including K.183, in a letter from Vienna dated 4 January 1783. Mozart, *Briefe und Aufzeichnungen*, III, 248.

[Ordoñez: Overture *Alceste* (1775)]

[continuation overleaf]

Symphony in G minor, Op. 6, No. 6, in the catalogue of J. C. Bach's orchestral works. Both are 'single shots', never repeated by J. C. Bach and not repeated in this particular fashion by Mozart; but that is another story. We are concerned with this early G minor Symphony. Einstein[1] writes: 'In [K.183] ... the choice of key alone transcends the boundaries of simply "social" music, and even contradicts the nature of such music. What purpose of the day can this document of impetuous expression have served?' Unique though the work is in Mozart's symphonic *œuvre* at this period, however, it is curiously un–Mozartian and reveals a certain lack of balance. Overwhelmed by the impression of the *Sturm und Drang*, Mozart tried his hand at one

1 *Mozart*, p. 223.

391

[Ordoñez: Overture *Alceste* – cont.]

himself, and borrowed the use of the four horns, and other technical devices, from Haydn and/or Vanhal. Wilfrid Mellers writes admirably of the work:[1]

The little G minor Symphony, K.183, is fascinating both for its resemblances to and differences from Haydn's minor moods in his *Sturm und Drang* compositions. It has the same passionate repeated notes and brusque changes of dynamics which we noticed in Haydn's G minor Symphony (No. 39). But whereas Haydn is fierce, Mozart is melancholy; and the difference consists in the sweetly singing quality of

1 Op cit., p. 39.

Mozart's themes as compared with Haydn's explosiveness, and in the persistently sighing appoggiaturas:

This does not mean that Mozart's melancholy is limp. It is acute, because it is already inherently dramatic. It is worth noting that whereas Haydn and C. P. E. Bach and Beethoven – who were not *primarily* lyrical composers – prefer to unify their material as closely as is consistent with their dramatic intentions, Mozart and J. C. Bach, who naturally think lyrically, can afford to introduce more obvious contrasts between their themes. Even Mozart's A major Symphony, K.201, which is a radiant piece, places sinuously chromatic melodies alongside airily dancing *buffo* tunes: and contains the longest and most exciting development that Mozart had yet created.

'Storm and Stress' was, however, an element inherent in Mozart's temperament, rather than absorbed from without.

In 1772, Charles Burney received a letter from Hamburg (probably from his friend Christoph Daniel Ebeling), in which the writer stated about Haydn, 'His mixture of serious and comic is disliked, particularly as there is more of the latter than the former in his work and, as for rules, he knows but little of them.'[1] When this new series of Haydn's quartets, symphonies and other music reached northern Germany, the critics would never be able to state such a postulate quite so boldly (though, as we shall see, Haydn never lacked for enemies and critics his whole life long).

A summary of the musical literature is given below.[2]

1 Percy Scholes, *The Great Dr. Burney* I, 198ff. and Geiringer 1947, p. 66.
2 The literature on the musical topics discussed in this Chapter is very large, and at best we can here provide only a survey. For convenience, we have broken up the references to subjects.

Symphonies: Geiringer 1932, pp. 73ff. (also in the other editions). B. Rywosch, *Beiträge zur Entwicklung in Joseph Haydns Symphonik 1759–1780*, Turbenthal 1934. Landon, *SYM*, pp. 271–357. C. Rosen, *The Classical Style*, London and New York 1971, pp. 146ff.

Quartets: Cecil Gray, *The Haydn String Quartet Society*, vols. 1, 4, 5, 8 (Op. 20, Nos. 1, 2, 4, 5), 1932ff. Geiringer 1932, pp. 45ff. (also in other editions). M. M. Scott, Analytical Notes to Haydn's Opus 17, Haydn Society (Boston), 1951. Geiringer, Analytical Notes to Haydn's Opus 20, Haydn Society (Boston), 1952. R. Sondheimer: *Haydn, A historical and psychological study based on his quartets*, London 1951. L. Somfai (selection), 'Vom Barock zur Klassik. Umgestaltung der Proportionen und des Gleichgewichts in zyklischen Werken Joseph Haydn's, in *Joseph Haydn und seine Zeit*, Eisenstadt 1972, pp. 64ff. W. Kirkendale, *Fuge und Fugato in der Kammermusik des Rokoko und der Klassik*, Tutzing 1966. Rosen, pp. 111ff. R. Barrett-Ayres, *Joseph Haydn and the String Quartet*, London 1974. L. Finscher, *Studien zur Geschichte des Streichquartetts . . .* Kassel 1974. J. Webster, 'The Chronology of Haydn's String Quartets', in *Musical Quarterly* LXI/1 (1975), pp. 17ff.

Sonatas: H. Abert, 'Joseph Haydns Klavierwerke', in *Zeitschrift für Musikwissenschaft* II (1919/20). Geiringer 1932, pp. 94ff. (also in other editions). C. Landon, Forewords to Haydn's Sonatas in *Wiener Urtext-Ausgabe*, 3 vols., Vienna 1963–6. Rosen, pp. 146, 150f., 358f. B. Wackernagel, *Joseph Haydns Frühe Klaviersonaten*, Tutzing 1975.

Mozart, K.183: H. C. Robbins Landon, 'La crise Romantique dans la musique autrichienne vers 1770. Quelques précurseurs inconnus de la Symphonie en sol mineur (KV 183) de Mozart' (lecture at the Sorbonne, October 1956, printed in *Les influences étrangères dans l'oeuvre de W. A. Mozart*, Paris [1958], pp. 27ff. J. P. Larsen in *The Mozart Companion* (ed. Landon & Mitchell), London 1956, pp. 173ff.

Much of the other specialized literature has been quoted in the course of the chapter.

CHAPTER FIVE

Chronicle 1776–1784

WITH THE ADVENT OF A NEW KIND of theatrical and operatic season at Eszterháza – operas were, from 1776 to 1790, staged regularly – it was necessary to adopt a different organization of the material. At the outset of each season, therefore, we shall list (1) the Italian operas, in their order of presentation (as far as this is possible); (2) the German marionette operas, also in chronological order (as far as this is possible); (3) the constitution of the German-speaking players and their repertoire. In listing the libretti of operas not composed by Haydn, we have renounced indications of line divisions.

Christoph Willibald von Gluck: Orfeo, ed Euridice Azione Teatrale per Musica. Da rappresentarsi al theatro d'Esterhaz l'anno 1776. [putto] – In Oedenburgo, Nella Stamperia Di Giuseppe Siess.

Personaggi.

Orfeo, il Sign. Gherardi.
Euridice, la Sign. Boschwang. [Poschwa]
Amore, la Sign. Buttlerin. [Puttler]

Libretto: Stadtbibliothek, Vienna. First performance: February. The alto castrato Pietro Gherardi was obviously engaged especially for the part of Orfeo (7 Feb., retroactive to 1 Feb.) and then kept on and given the occasional part – also in Haydn's *Il mondo della luna*. The harp part was played by J. B. Krumpholtz, who left Eszterháza at the end of February. Therefore *Orfeo* can only have been given during this month (probably several times). The parts were copied by Johann Schellinger (bill in EH, from information sent by Dr Janos Harich on 26 July 1777). What did Haydn do with Gluck's parts for cornetto, three trombones and chalumeaux? The trombones were probably omitted entirely, and the other parts given to oboe and/or cor anglais. Not in Harich, *Musikgeschichte*, or Bartha-Somfai. Harich, *HJB* I, 13; *HJB* IX, 93.

Carl Ditters (von Dittersdorf): Il finto pazzo per amore. Operetta a quattro voci. Da rappresentarsi al Theatro d'Esterhaz l'anno 1776. Oedenburgo, nella stamperia di Giuseppe Siess.

Il capitano D. Ercole, amante di Eurilla	il Sig. Bianchi.
Eurilla, pastorella	la Sig. Boschwang.
Silvio, pastore	il Sig. Dichtler. [Poschwa]
Biondina, vivandiera, amante di D. Ercole	la Sig. Buttlerin. [Puttler]

First performance: April (Harich, *Musikgeschichte*, 38). Libretto: 300 copies printed. Eszterháza performance material: EH, Budapest, Ms. Mus. OE–18 (score and parts), by Johann Schellinger and Anonymous 2, with cuts and minor changes by Haydn, also in the orchestration of 'L'idol mio fu questo un giorno' (Atto II, Scena 3). Bartha-Somfai 66, 179f. Copy of Eszterháza libretto: Országos Széchényi Könyvtár, Budapest, 160937.

Antonio Sacchini: L'Isola D'Amore Operetta Giocosa Per Musica, Da Rappresentarsi Nel Teatro D'Esterhaz L'Estate Dell' Anno 1776. In Oedenburgo Nella Stamperia di Giuseppe Siess.

Belinda, Fanciulla nobile Scozzese amata, ed abbandonata da Giocondo	La Sign. Barbara Dichtler.
Giocondo, Governatore dell'Isola	Il Sign: Leopoldo Dichtler.
Marina, Pescatrice	La Sig: Elisabetta Prandtner.
Nardo, Pescatore	Il Sig: Benedetto Bianchi.

Libretto: EH, Eisenstadt. Eszterháza performance material: EH, Budapest Ms. Mus. OE–103 (parts only) by Anonymous 3 (a Vienna copyist?) and (the duplicate string parts) by Anonymous 4 and Johann Schellinger, with cuts and minor changes by Haydn. Harich, *Musikgeschichte*, 38. Bartha-Somfai, 66, 180.

Nicolà Piccinni: La buona figliuola. Dramma giocoso per musica in tre atti. Da rappresentarsi nel teatro d'Esterhaz. L'autunno dell'anno 1776. In Oedenburgo, Nella Stamperia Di Giuseppe Siess.
[cast included Marianna Puttler, Catharina Poschwa, Maria Elisabeth Prandtner, Benedetto Bianchi, Leopold Dichtler and Christian Specht; the exact cast list cannot be supplied since no copy of the libretto is now known]
Libretto: 300 copies printed. No Eszterháza performance material has survived (burned in 1779 fire?). Harich, *Musikgeschichte*, 38. Bartha-Somfai, 66, 180.

Carl Ditters (von Dittersdorf): Lo sposo burlato. Intermezzo a quatro [*sic*] voci. Da·rappresentarsi nel teatro d'Esterhaz. L'autunno dell'anno 1776. In Oedenburgo, Nella Stamperia di Giuseppe Siess.
[no cast list since no copy of the libretto is now known]
Libretto: 400 copies printed and bound by Oedenburg bookbinder Mathias Pfundtner. Eszterháza performance material: EH, Budapest Ms. Mus. OE–34 (score and parts) by Anonymous 5, 6, 7, 8. Harich, *Musikgeschichte*, 38. Bartha-Somfai, 66f., 181.

Carl Ditters (von Dittersdorf): Il Barone Di Rocca Antica Intermezzo A Quatro [*sic*] Voci Da Rappresentarsi Nel Teatro D'Esterhaz. L'Autunno Dell'Anno 1776. In Oedenburgo Nella Stamperia Di Giuseppe Siess.

Il Barone Arsura. Possessore del feudo di Rocca antica	Il Sign. Leopoldo Dichtler.
Beatrice, Amante del Barone	La Sign.ra Catharina Poschwa.
Gicondo, Fattore del Barone	Il Sign. Giuseppe [*sic*] Specht.
Lenina, Vilanella, ed Amante di Giocondo	La Sign.ra Elisabetta Prandtner.

Libretto: 400 copies printed. Copies: two in EH, Eisenstadt. Eszterháza performance material: EH, Budapest Ms. Mus. OE–63 (score and parts). Autograph score by Dittersdorf. Parts by Anonymous 9. Cuts and small changes by Haydn. Harich, *Musikgeschichte*, 39. Bartha-Somfai, 67, 181f.

GERMAN MARIONETTE OPERAS 1776

In the Gotha *Theater-Kalender* for 1777, which of course reports on events taking place in 1776, we read (p. 253):

Presburg [*sic*], actually Esterhazy [*sic*] The Prince von Esterhazy supports here:
I. Italian Opera ·
Director: H. von Bauersbach [*sic*]. Musical Director: H. von Hayden. Female singers: Mad Böschwang [*sic*], Mamsell Butler [*sic*], Mad. Friebert, Mamsell Prandtner. Death: Mad. Dichtler, a born Viennese, died on 21 September 1776. It occurred on the stage, as she played Belinde in the Opera, l'isola d'Amore; hardly had she spoken the words, 'non posso più sostenermi in piè' when she sank to the stage, dead. [Male singers omitted by mistake?]
II. Marionette Opera
Director: H. von Bauersbach. Machinists: H. H. Conßar [*sic*] and Bienfait. Poets: H. von Bauersbach, H. Bader. The roles read by: Mamsell Ochs, Mamsell Mauer, H. H. Bader, Bauersbach, Hoffmann, Sicca. Note: This theatre must be noted because of its exceptional magnificence. Every new performance costs 600, even 800 gulden. Performed are translations [*Parodien*] of the Operas *Alceste, Dido, Demophon, Genovefens 1. 2. 3. 4. Theil, der Hexensabbath, Philemon und Baucis*, etc.

The following is an attempt to present the marionette season of 1776:

Joseph Haydn; *Dido*. First performance in March with repetitions (10 performances) up to July. The opera required ten 'supers'. Libretto by Philipp Georg Bader, printed by Siess and bound by Fischer in Oedenburg (no copy extant: see 1778 for a reprint, presumably using the same plates). The orchestral and vocal parts were made by Johann Schellinger. The 'supers' were played by the Grenadier's children.

Pauersbach's *Demofoonte* (*Demophon*), with music by ? (not Haydn) was also given in March. Copyists' bill for '52 Bögen' of players' scripts, signed by Bader, indicate that the following three plays were performed before 25 October (the bill's date): *Wilhelmine, Martin Velten, Pigmalion*.

From the Gotha *Kalender* we learn that Ordoñez's *Alceste* was repeated (first performance: 1775); this information is confirmed by other EH sources. The four parts of *Genovefa* were also repeated (see 1774), also *Hexen-Schabbas* (see 1773), and the new version of *Philemon und Baucis* (see 1773 and also pp. 257ff.).

Ignaz Pleyel: Die Fee Urgele. Oder was den Damen gefällt. Eine Marionetten-Operette in vier Aufzügen. Nach dem franzoesischen des Herrn Favart. Zu Esterház, auf der Fürstl. Marionettenbühne. Im Wintermonathe [November] 1776 aufgeführet. Oedenburg, gedruckt bey Johann Joseph Siess.

Libretto: 500 copies printed. Copies: Burgenländisches Landesmuseum, Eisenstadt; EH, Eisenstadt. Autograph score: Österreichische Nationalbibliothek, Musiksammlung, S.m.15560. The Eszterháza performance material has not survived (burned in 1779 fire?).

Uncertain: Joseph Haydn's *Die Feuersbrunst* (*Das abgebrannte Haus*). The presence of clarinets in the score suggests that the work must have been performed between 1 January 1776 and the end of February 1778 (the dates of the clarinet players' engagement at Eszterháza). *Vide supra*, p. 225.

Our archive material shows that *Genovefens Vierter Theil* was not produced until 1777; perhaps this was an earlier version (*vide infra*, pp. 403ff.).[1]

THE GERMAN THEATRICAL TROUPE 1776

[Gotha *Theater-Kalender* of 1777, pp. 239f.:]

Wahr's Theatre Company

Residence: Esterhazy [*sic*] and Salzburg. *Principal*: Herr Wahr. *Actresses*: Mamsell Herdlidschka: soubrettes and love-parts. Madam Klimetsch: comic mothers, procuresses, nagging and delicate roles. Madam Körner: leading love-parts, heroines, peasant women, naïve roles. Mamsell Mautausch: love-parts and young roles. Mamsell Reiner: secondary love-parts, young gentle roles and soubrettes. Madam Riedl: noble, tender mothers. Madam Rößner [*sic*]: beginner's parts. Mamsell Schlötzer: leading children's parts. *Souffleuse* [promptress]: Madam Reiner. *Actors*: H. Bauer: secondary parts; he is the scenery painter. Mamsell Bauer: small children's parts. H. Bulla: petulant, nagging old ladies and other dry roles. H. Haym: officers, crude petit-maîtres and intriguers. H. Klimetsch: small servants and pedants. Herr Körner: comic servants, Jews, caricature parts. H. Litter: lovers, young heroes, knights, sometimes tender fathers. H. Riedl: comic old women, servants, comic roles of the lower type. H. Roßuer [*sic*] [*sc.* Roßner]: gentle old women, soldiers. H. Schienagl: lovers, young parts and cavaliers. H. Schlötzer: old servant-women and peasants. H. Schlötzer Jr.: children's roles. H. Schulz: fathers and servants. H. Spieß: serious and dry parts. H. Wahr: leading lovers, noble fathers, heroes, moving, whimsical roles and parts requiring a noble deportment. H. Zappe: chief servants and bumpkins. *Débuts* for 1776: Mamsell Herdlidschka as Julchen in the *Schwiegermutter*. Madam Hülverding as Louise in the same comedy. Madam Riedl as Frau von Kapellet. H. Bulla as Katesby in *Richard*. H. Hülverding as the younger Count Finsterthal and H. Müller as Karling in *Minister*. H. Riedl as Niklas in *Wölfe unter der Heerde*. H. Roßner [*recte*] as the President in *Wilhelmine von Blondheim*. H. Schulz as Paulo in *der neuen Arria*. H. Thomas as Wilkin in *Albert I*. Left in 1776: H. and Mad. Christel, H. and Mad. Prothke, H. Cremeri, H. Seipp. *Schedule*: Daily at Esterhazy [*sic*]; at Salzburg on Sundays, Mondays, Wednesdays and Fridays. *Note*: the troupe plays tragedies and comedies.

With the engagement of no less than seven new singers[2] and the enlargement of Wahr's troupe to twenty and the orchestra by the addition of clarinets, Esterházy's establishment was now at its largest since the beginning of Eszterháza Castle.

Possibly to celebrate this great leap forward, Prince Nicolaus ordered new winter and summer uniforms for Haydn and the musicians: they were with red coats and waistcoats of 'apple green'; the knee-breeches were also of red.[3] The hats had golden

---

1 Literature: Harich, *Musikgeschichte*, 39 (Pleyel), Bartha-Somfai, 67 (Pleyel). Landon in *HJB* I, 172, 175, 178, 183, 190–3.

2 Benedetto Bianchi, Pietro Gherardi, Catharina Poschwa, Maria Elisabeth Prandtner, Marianna Puttler, Maria Elisabeth Trever and Vitus Ungricht.

3 The exact specifications by Harich in *HJB* IV, 84ff., where it can be seen that Haydn's uniform was made of much more expensive material. Together with the hat, it cost 238 fl. 37½ kr. The tailor made uniforms for twenty-four musicians (apart from Haydn) costing 6,858 fl. 39½ kr. (including Haydn's uniform and three dresses for female singers) for summer and winter uniforms. The three ladies' dresses were made of (1) green and lilac, (2) green and rose-coloured, and (3) of blue and *souris* [mouse-coloured] embroidered taffeta. Included in this large bill were, moreover, the uniforms for three church musicians (presumably the Eisenstadt contingent) and 'two scholars' (Ernst and Koschwitz). We might add that Haydn's coachman also wore livrée, the cost of which was borne by Prince Nicolaus. See *HJB* IV, 78f.: 'As ordered by the Herr hauss hoffmeister for Mosieur Heitten's coachman a set of livrée consisting of a coat, waistcoat, breeches and a great-coat 4 f. . . . Jacob Ent, Master Tailor in Esterhaz' (April 1790, EH Eisenstadt Haushofmeister Nr. 33).

buttons and the uniforms were trimmed with gold. (Yet another nail in the coffin of the supposed pictorial representation of *L'incontro improvviso*: Haydn, conducting from the harpsichord, is wearing quite the wrong-coloured uniform: greyish white with a touch of blue.)

On 6 January, *Der Zerstreute* (*Le distrait*) by Regnard was given at the Kärntnerthor Theatre in Vienna, and the *Priviligierte Realzeitung* (p. 107) reports that

> ... Before the comedy and between each act was performed a new, appropriate symphony, especially written for this piece by the famous Jos. Haiden [*sic*], Kapellmeister in the service of Prince Esterhazy.

Symphony No. 60 (as it turned out to be) was fast becoming one of its composer's most celebrated works.

We may pass over the usual Rockobauer and similar bills[1] and proceed to a set of Six Minuets for small orchestra (IX:5) of which the autograph, in the Berlin State Library, is dated 1776. We suppose they were written for some Carnival celebrations, perhaps for Eszterháza. There is also a set of Twelve Minuets (IX:6) which include the first four of the 1776 series (IX:5) as Nos. 9–12; this new series is for the Eszterháza orchestration of flute, oboes, bassoons, horns (C *alto*) and kettledrums, i.e. without trumpets. Both these attractive series remain at the present writing (1977) unpublished.

The following letter is one of the very few of this period:

[Contents of a letter from Haydn to Prince Nicolaus Esterházy. *German*]

[Estoras], [March] 1776.[1]

> Haydn informs the Prince that Count Erdödy,[2] 'because of his satisfaction with the pupil he entrusted to me', has given him two horses and a carriage. But as he is not capable of supporting the horses, he asks the Prince 'in his serene graciousness to grant him hay and oats'.   [Pohl II, 23]

Certainly the most important document of the year is the following autobiographical sketch:

[Autobiographical sketch; to Mademoiselle Leonore.[4] *German*]

Estoras, 6th July 1776.

Mademoiselle!

> You will not take it amiss if I hand you a hotchpotch of all sorts of things as an answer to your request: to describe such things properly takes time, and that I don't have; for this reason, I do not dare write to Mons. Zoller personally, and therefore ask for forgiveness.
>
> I send you only a rough draft, for neither pride, nor fame, but solely the great kindness and marked satisfaction that so learned a national institution has shown

---

1 Rockobauer: bills for three dozen bassoon reeds, A.M. XVI, 1043, 10 Jan.; three dozen oboe and cor anglais reeds, A.M. XVI, 1046, 12 Feb.; one Jacob Bauer Instrumentenmacher Vienna, 9 Feb. 1776, for two dozen bassoon reeds. The 'Rorate' money signed by Haydn on 31 Dec. in A.M. XVI, 1047. Joseph Dietzl's listing of replaced strings etc. from 1 Jan. to end of Dec. on A.M. XVI, 1048 – all these bills were countersigned 'Josephus Haydn mpria'. A tailor's bill, also countersigned by Haydn, on 6 Nov. (Vienna: Martin Ernst Unger), A.M. XVI, 1075. Valkó II, 580.

2 Pohl does not give the exact date. However, the *Prothocoll ... de Anno 1734* (see *supra*), No. 1091, includes the following note, the contents of which show that the Prince granted Haydn's request, and the date of which indicates that Haydn's letter must have been written sometime during March: 'Resolution of His Serene Highness *d*[*e*] *d*[*ato*] Esterház, 29th March 1776, according to which *Cappelmeister* [*sic*] Haydn is to be issued the necessary fodder for 2 horses.'

3 Here it is undoubtedly Count Ladislaus of Pressburg who is meant, and the pupil is Pleyel, Erdödy's protégé, whom the Count sent to Haydn as a pupil in composition in 1772.

4 Mademoiselle Leonore was later the wife of Prince Esterházy's *Wirthschaftsrath* (economic adviser) and *Güterdirector* (estates' director), Lechner. Haydn was requested to write this sketch for a publication entitled 'Das gelehrte Oesterreich', in which it appeared in volume I, 3rd *Stück*, p. 309 (1776). The editor, Ignaz de Luca, seems to have applied for it in a very roundabout manner to a 'Mons. Zoller' (see beginning of the letter), who was an official in the Prince's service, who in turn asked 'Mademoiselle Leonore'. See Pohl I, 75 and II, 381.

towards my previous compositions, have induced me to comply with their demand.

I was born on the last day of March 1733,[1] in the market town of Rohrau, Lower Austria, near Prugg on the Leythä.[2] My late father was a wheelwright by profession, and served Count Harrach,[3] a great lover of music by nature. He [my father] played the harp without knowing a note of music, and as a boy of 5, I correctly sang all his simple little pieces: this induced my father to entrust me to the care of my relative, the schoolmaster in Haimburg,[4] in order that I might learn the rudiments of music and the other juvenile requirements. Almighty God (to Whom alone I owe the most profound gratitude) endowed me, especially in music, with such proficiency that even in my 6th year I was able to sing some Masses in the choir-loft, and to play a little on the harpsichord and violin.

When I was 7, the late *Capellmeister* von Reutter[5] passed through Haimburg and quite accidentally heard my weak but pleasant voice. He forthwith took me to the choir house [of St Stephen's Cathedral in Vienna] where, apart from my studies, I learnt the art of singing, the harpsichord, and the violin, from very good masters. Until my 18th year I sang soprano with great success, not only at St Stephen's but also at the Court. Finally I lost my voice, and then had to eke out a wretched existence for eight whole years, by teaching young pupils (many geniuses are ruined by their having to earn their daily bread, because they have no time to study): I experienced this, too, and would have never learnt what little I did, had I not, in my zeal for composition, composed well into the night; I wrote diligently, but not quite correctly, until at last I had the good fortune to learn the true fundamentals of composition from the celebrated Herr Porpora[6] (who was at that time in Vienna): finally, by the recommendation of the late Herr von Fürnberg[7] (from whom I received many marks of favour), I was engaged as *Directeur* at Herr Count von Morzin's,[8] and from there as *Capellmeister* of His Highness the Prince [Esterházy], in whose service I wish to live and die.

Inter alia the following compositions of mine have received the most approbation:

The operas	*Le Pescatrici* [1769: perf. 1770] *L'incontro improvizo* [*sic*] [1775] *L'infedeltà delusa*, performed in the presence of Her Imperial and Royal Majesty [Maria Theresa, in 1773].[9]
The oratorio	*Il Ritorno di Tobia*, performed in Vienna [in 1775]
The *Stabat Mater* [1767],	about which I received (through a good friend) a testimonial of our great composer Hasse,[10] containing quite undeserved eulogiums. I shall treasure this testimonial all my life, as if it were gold; not for its contents, but for the sake of so admirable a man.

1 *Recte*: 1732.
2 *Recte* (or rather in modern German orthography): Bruck-an-der-Leitha.
3 The family owned a winter palace in Vienna (still extant – opposite the Schottenkirche) and a castle in Rohrau. Haydn remained devoted to the family throughout his life. In 1793, Harrach erected a monument to Haydn in his castle gardens at Rohrau – a gesture which naturally delighted the composer.
5 *Recte*: Hainburg (on the Danube). The school rector, Johann Mathias Franck (Frankh), who was then still alive, died in 1783, shortly before his 75th birthday. See Pohl I, 23.
5 J. A. Georg von Reutter, Jr. (1708–1772).
6 Nicolo Porpora (1685–1766), an Italian composer whose vocal music, in particular, was much admired at that time.
7 Haydn's first quartets were written about 1757 in Fürnberg's Summer Castle at Weinzierl, near the Monastery of Melk (Lower Austria). See Fritz Dworschak, 'Joseph Haydn und Karl Joseph Weber von Fürnberg' (*Unsere Heimat*, 1932).
8 Haydn was engaged in 1759: Morzin's castle was in Lukavec (Bohemia).
9 This clause ('performed ...') is written in the autograph to the right of *L'incontro improvviso*; we have placed it here in its correct position.
10 See *supra*, p. 144.

In the chamber-musical style I have been fortunate enough to please almost all nations except the Berliners; this is shown by the public newspapers and letters addressed to me. I only wonder that the Berlin gentlemen, who are otherwise so reasonable, preserve no medium in their criticism of my music, for in one weekly paper they praise me to the skies, whilst in another they dash me sixty fathoms deep into the earth, and this without explaining why; I know very well why: because they are incapable of performing some of my works, and are too conceited to take the trouble to understand them properly, and for other reasons which, with God's help, I will answer in good time. *Herr Capellmeister* von Dittersdorf,[1] in Silesia, wrote to me recently and asked me to defend myself against their hard words, but I answered that one swallow doesn't make the Summer; and that perhaps one of these days some unprejudiced person would stop their tongues, as happened to them once before when they accused me of monotony. Despite this, they try very hard to get all my works, as Herr Baron von Sviten,[2] the Imperial and Royal Ambassador at Berlin, told me only last winter, when he was in Vienna: but enough of this.

Dear *Mademoiselle* Leonore: You will be good enough to give this present letter, and my compliments, to Mons. Zoller for his consideration: my highest ambition is only that all the world regard me as the honest man I am.

I offer all my praises to Almighty God, for I owe them to Him alone: my sole wish is to offend neither my neighbour, nor my gracious Prince, nor above all our merciful God.

Meanwhile I remain, *Mademoiselle*, with high esteem,

Your most sincere friend and servant

Josephus Haydn [m.p.] ria

[CCLN 18–21]

Apart from being the most important single document about Haydn's early years, this letter is interesting from several other points of view. We note that Haydn considered his most successful works three operas, an oratorio and the *Stabat Mater* – not a word about his symphonies, sonatas, trios, and only a brief mention of chamber music altogether. We notice, too, that Haydn smarted under the derogatory criticisms of the north German press, some examples of which have been included in the foregoing Chronicle.

On 17 July 1776, another terrible holocaust ravaged Eisenstadt, destroying within two hours the town hall, the Franciscan church and monastery, the brewery and this time the Parish Church; 104 houses were destroyed and sixteen people died. Once again the Prince rebuilt Haydn's house and altogether paid out more than 7,000 gulden to owners of damaged or destroyed property. Haydn's house was more badly damaged in this than in the previous (1768) fire, and it cost Esterházy 450 gulden to repair it. Now that Haydn was living most of the year in Eszterháza, he may have thought it a disadvantage to have almost his entire capital in a house at Eisenstadt that he hardly used, and we shall see that in 1778 he sold it. We do not know if Haydn was in Eisenstadt when the fire happened, but probably he was at Eszterháza. No doubt many autograph scores perished in this conflagration.[3] (See also Appendix, p.760.)

Another reason that surely encouraged Haydn to sell his newly repaired house was that his neighbour Frau Theresia Späch sued Haydn for having repaired his roof in a

---

1 Carl Ditters von Dittersdorf (1739–1799), one of Haydn's oldest friends, was the principal opera composer of the 1776 season at Eszterháza.
2 Gottfried van Swieten. This diplomat and patron of music was to play a decisive role in Haydn's later life, as the translator and arranger of the libretti of *The Seven Words* (choral version), *The Creation* and *The Seasons*. See also *infra*, p.753.
3 Harich in *HJB* IV, 31 (our translation and adaptation, with additions). Document concerning the rebuilding charges: *HJB* IV, 54f.

fashion detrimental to her side of the property.[1] We have seen the lawsuit between Haydn and his other immediate neighbour, Magdalena Frumwald, about an equally trivial matter (p. 156).

It appears that the musicians were required at Eisenstadt for some ceremony in late November:

[Prince Nicolaus Esterházy to *Regent* Rahier]
... Since all the musicians are to go to Eisenstadt this coming Thursday the 28th, it is necessary to obtain 8 entirely covered waggons which are to arrive here on the coming Wednesday evening. ...   [A.M. XX, 1359. Valkó II, 581]

They returned to Eszterháza in November for Pleyel's *Die Fee Urgele*.
On 16 December Carl Ditters von Dittersdorf wrote to Prince Esterházy:

... I understand that Your Highness was gracious enough to applaud my Operette *Il finto pazzo*. From Your Highness's request through Herr v. Pauersbach I had the honour of waiting on Your Highness with yet two others, viz. *Sposo burlato* and *Barone di Rocca Antica*.

Now it happens that our Court here has, on account of my most gracious Prince [Patachich], decided entirely to abolish opera here. Therefore I can submissively offer Your Highness six further Operas, viz.: *Arcifanfano*; *Tutore e la pupilla*; *I visionarj*; *Marescalco* (a French opéra comique entitled *Le maréchal ferrant* translated into an Italian opera); *La contadina fedele* and *La moda o sià gli scompigli domestici*, for all of which I have composed new music. The chamber musician Ungricht,[2] who is in your service, knows all these Operas and can inform Your Highness that they would all fit Your Highness's theatre.

Apart from this I have a proposal to make to Your Highness: I take the liberty of enclosing a libretto put together by a certain Giacomo della Tavola partly from other operettas and partly also in the new kind of poetry.

I intended to write this piece during the coming Lent and then to produce it the following summer. But since opera will no longer be done here, this has been cancelled and it is a pity that the libretto will not be set to music. If Your Highness so commands, I will do the music for Your Highness's theatre and I promise myself a gracious approval. ...
          Johannisberg, 16th Dec. 1776

Your most submissive
Carl Ditters v. Dittersdorf.
[A.M. I, 87; Bartha-Somfai 67f.]

Prince Nicolaus bought all six of the Operas mentioned and performed *Arcifanfano* in 1777 (*vide infra*, p. 403), but for some reason *I visionarj* seems to have been lost and is also missing in most catalogues of Dittersdorf's works. The other five are in EH, Budapest.[3]

In November Haydn began teaching two of the female singers at Eszterháza: Elisabeth Prandtner and Elisabeth Griessler, for which he was paid one ducat per month by Prince Esterházy (see 22 November 1777, *infra*, p. 406). We have the written documents about these two singers, but one imagines that Haydn's teaching activity, all during these years, was probably very extensive – one more part of his heavy duties as Princely *Capellmeister*.

---

1 Ratsprotocoll No. 253, 17 Aug. 1776. Schmid, 'Eisenstadt', p. 12.
2 *Vide supra*, p. 63; Ungricht had been with Dittersdorf in Großwardein and Johannisberg.
3 OE 15 (*La moda*), 59 (*Arcifanfano*), 60 (*La contadina fedele*), 61 (*Il tutore*), 62 (*Il Maniscalco* [*recte*]).

It was seen that Haydn conducted *Orfeo* at Eszterháza; it was certainly a better audience than the fickle ones in Paris who applauded *Iphigénie en Aulide* (1774) but greeted *Alceste* (1775) with cool disapproval. The Paris performances, including that of *Orphée*, may not have been the best. In Swinburne's *Memoirs*[1] we read:

Paris, April 30th, 1774.
Last night we were at the new opera of Orphée, by Gluck. I was vastly disappointed: the best of the music resembles in style and force the common burlettas; but, to do it justice, the performers sang it abominably, not quite in the French–, yet not in the least in the Italian–style. Some of the dances, too, are ridiculously grovelling and vulgar; but this he did in imitation of Boyes, I suppose, to make the rest of the opera show off better. The dancers are very bad, a thing uncommon on the French stage, where at least one sense should have repaid for what the other underwent.

Gluck left Paris in May, arriving in Vienna shortly thereafter. The meeting with Haydn, therefore, must have taken place during the second half of the year.

Haydn's name had circulated all over Europe and had reached America *inter alia* by means of the Moravian Brotherhood: the composer J. F. Peter had taken with him to the United States his copy, made on 12 December 1766, of Haydn's Symphony No. 17.[2] Now, shortly after the historic Fourth of July, 1776, we read[3] of Haydn being performed in Charlestown, South Carolina. Haydn may have been pleased at this piece of information, but nearer to home the appearance of an extraordinary pamphlet will have annoyed him acutely. It is a work by C. L. Junker entitled *Zwanzig Componisten, eine Skizze* (Berne 1776), which was largely reprinted in 1792 under the title *Portfeuille für Musikliebhaber* and has been quoted in another volume of this biography.[4] We will therefore confine ourself to some short extracts:

. . . Viennese music. . . . [since] the dignity it enjoyed under Wagenseil, . . . has [under Haydn] sunk into too much triviality . . . Hayden [*sic*] is eccentric and bizarre; – and projected without control. . . . Hayden's caprice, I said earlier, has apparently had evil effects on music . . . [etc., etc.] But just name me one single, solitary product of Hayden, in which caprice is not at the bottom of it all! You won't find any. . . .

Chronicle 1777

ITALIAN OPERAS 1777

In the Gotha *Theater-Kalender auf das Jahr 1778* (p. 235), we read:

Esterhazy [*sic*]
The Prince von Esterhazy supports
I. Italian Opera
Director: H. von Bauersbach [Pauersbach]. Musical Director: H. von Hayden. Female Singers: Mad. Buschwang [Poschwa], Mamsell Buttler [Puttler], Madam Jermolli, Mamsell Tauber, Mamsell Tepree [Trever], Mamsell Prandtner. Male Singers: H. H. Bianchi, Dichtler, Irrhardi [Gherardi], Jermolli, Specht, Ungrig [Ungricht]. Note. The orchestra consists of 30 persons, mostly virtuosi, so that it may be counted among the finest orchestras.

---

1 Henry Swinburne in *Secret Memoirs of the Courts of Europe*, Philadelphia, n.d., (2 vols.) I, p. 15.
2 See *Critical Edition of the Complete Symphonies* (Landon), vol. III (Philharmonia), p. xxxvii.
3 'Über den Zustand der Musik in America, besonders Charles-Town in South Carolina, in den Jahren 1776 bis 1783' (extracts in von Eschtruths *Musikalische Bibliothek*, Marburg/Gießen 1784, I. Stück).
4 *Haydn in England 1791–1795*, pp. 189ff.

II. Marionette Opera

Director: H. von Bauersbach. Machinists: H. H. Couße [*sic*] and Bienfait. Poets: H. von Bauersbach, H. Bader. The roles read by: Mamsell Ochs, Mamsell Mourrin [*sic*]. H. H. Bader, Bauersbach, Hoffmann, Sicca.[1] Note. During the past year there was a new performance [*Genovefens Vierter Theil*] which cost 6,000 fl. and was so magnificent that the Empress herself demanded to see it. Thereupon a Theatre was built at Schönbrunn, and the marionettes and decorations taken to Vienna.

On pages 101ff. we read of Carl Wahr's Troupe leaving Eszterháza and going to Pressburg in July – much earlier than usual. On pages 114f. we read the usual list of Haydn's works which has remained more or less unaltered since 1776;[1] but in 1778 there is the addition 'und neuerlich zur Göz [*sic*] von Berlichingen'.'

Florian Leopold Gassmann: L'amore artigiano. Dramma giocoso in tre atti. Da rappresentarsi nel teatro d'Esterhaz la primavera dell'anno 1777. – Vienna, presso Giuseppe Nobile de Kurzbek. . . .

Madama Costanza, Cittadina Vedova	La Sigr. Maria Anna Tauber.
Giro, Parruchier Francese	Il Signor Pietro Gherardi.
Bernardo, Vechio Calzolaro ⎫	⎰ Il Sign. Benedetto Bianchi.
Giannino, Legnajuolo ⎬ Parti Uguali:	⎱ Il Signor Guglielmo Jermoli.
Rosina, Figlia di Bernardo ⎭	La Sigra Catharina Poschwa.
Angiolina, Cuffiara	La Sigra Maria Guigl. Jermoli.
Titta, Fabro	Il Signor Leopoldo Dichtler.

Libretto: Országos Széchényi Könyvtár, Budapest, IM. 1258, printed in an edition of 500 copies. Eszterháza performance material: EH, Budapest, Ms. Mus. OE–17 (score, minus the third Act, and incomplete vocal parts; all the orchestral parts). A conglomeration of three different performances at Eszterháza (1777, 1780, 1790) makes it difficult to single out the changes for the 1777 season; in any case, there are large-scale cuts, changes and substitutions in this material. Three new arias by Haydn for the 1790 revival will be discussed *infra* (pp. 647f. and 733f.). At one time or another, six 'insertion' arias were used in this Opera. Copyists: Johann Schellinger, Anonymous 10, 14, 15, 16 and in later parts (1790) Anonymous 12. Harich, *Musikgeschichte*, 39. Bartha-Somfai, 70, 182–8.

Joseph Haydn: Il / Mondo / Della / Luna. / Dramma Giocoso / In Tre Atti. / Rappresentato / Sul Teatro d'Esterhaz, / All'Occasione degli Felici Sponsali / Del / Signore Nicolo, / Conte Esterhazy / Di / Galantha, / Figlio di S. A. S. / E / La Signora Contessa / Maria Anna / Weissenwolf. / L'Estate Del Anno 1777. / In Vienna / Presso Giuseppe Nob. De Kurzbeck, Stampa- / tore Orient. di S. M. Imp. R. A.

Ecclitico. Finto Astrologo.	Il Signor Guglielmo Jermoli
Ernesto. Cavaliere.	Il Signor Pietro Gherardi
Buona Fede.	Il Signor Benedetto Bianchi
Clarice, Figlia di Buona Fede.	La Signora Caterina Poschwa
Flamminia, Altra Figlia di Buona Fede.	La Signora Maria Anna Puttler
Lisetta. Cameriera di Buona Fede	La Signora Maria Jermoli
Cecco. Servitore di Ernesto.	Il Signor Leopoldo Dichtler

Tutti in Attual Servizio di S. A. S. Principe Nicolo Esterhazy di Galantha.

Libretto: 500 copies ordered. Only known copy: EH, Eisenstadt. The Jermoli couple did not sing in the first performance because they had left Eszterháza in July. The Eszterháza performance material no longer exists (destroyed in the 1779 fire?). The sources will be discussed *infra* (pp. 524ff.). Bartha, *Musikgeschichte*, 40. Bartha-Somfai, 71, 188–197. Günter Thomas in *Haydn-Studien* II/2(1969), pp. 122–4.

Giovanni Paisiello: La Frascatana. Dramma giocoso in tre atti. Da rappresentarsi nel Teatro d'Esterhaz. L'estate dell'anno 1777. – In Vienna presso Giuseppe Nob. de Kurzbeck. . . .

Libretto: 500 copies printed (none has survived). The Eszterháza performance material has also not survived. For this Opera, Haydn composed his large-scale 'insertion' Aria di Donna Stella, 'D'una sposa meschinella', with its elaborate solo oboe part.[3] Harich, *Musikgeschichte*, 40. Bartha-Somfai 71, 198.

---

1 Repeated (up to 'Note') in Gotha *Theater-Kalender . . . 1779*, pp. xxxviif.

2 'Hayden, Kapellmeister zu Esterhaz in Ungarn. Eine Oper, l'infidelta [*sic*] delusa und zwey Simphonien zum Zerstreuten und zum Hamlet, für die dasige Truppe &c.' Under Pauersbach we read that he has written *Die Probe der Liebe* and *Genovefens 1. 2. 3 und 4. Theil* (another indication that the latter must have been ready in some form by 1775 or 1776 at the latest).

3 Haydn-Mozart Presse (Universal Edition, ed. Landon 1961), score and parts (also piano score). Autograph in EH, Budapest, Ms. mus. I. 10.

The following Opera was given in the 1777 season but no libretti were (as far as we know) printed: Giovanni Paisiello: *Il marchese villano (La contadina di spirito)*. Eszterháza performance material: score, EH Budapest, Ms. Mus. OE-25, which is not that used for the 1777 première but for the 1788 revival. The original parts of the 1777 première, prepared by Johann Schellinger, have disappeared. This work, first given at Rome in 1767, was entitled *Il marchese Tulipano ossia Il matrimonio inaspettato*; the EH score is listed as *La contadina di spirito o sia Il matrimonio inaspettato*. Harich in *HJB* I, 20, 82f. Bartha-Somfai, 334.

Carl Ditters von Dittersdorf: Arcifanfano Re De' Matti[.] Dramma Giocoso, Satirico / In Tre Atti / Rappresentato Sul Teatro D'Esterhaz. L'autunno dell'Anno 1777. In Vienna Presso Giuseppe Nob. De Kurzbeck. . . .

Arcifanfano Re di Matti	Il Signor Benedetto Bianchi.
Furibondo, Poltrone	Il Signor Vito Ungricht.
Garbata, Donna Allegria[!]	La Sign. Catterina Poschwa.
Sordidone, Uomo Avaro	Il Signor Leopoldo Dichtler.
Semplicina, Donna ritrosa	La Signora Maria Anna Puttler.
Malgoverno, Giovane Prodigo	Il Signor Pietro Gherardi.
Gloriosa, Donna superba	La Signora Maria Anna Tauber.

Libretto: 500 copies ordered. Only known copy: EH, Eisenstadt. Eszterháza performance material: EH, Budapest, Ms. Mus. OE-59 (autograph score and orchestral parts, copied by Joseph Elssler and Johann Schellinger) with some cuts and re-orchestration in one Aria ('Vi miro fiso', Atto I). Harich, *Musikgeschichte*, 40. Bartha-Somfai, 71f., 198f.

From the 1776 season, Dittersdorf's *Il barone di Rocca Antica* and Sacchini's *L'isola d'amore* were repeated. Harich in *HJB* I, 20.

GERMAN MARIONETTE OPERAS 1777
The vast new production for this year was:

[Music by various masters, perhaps also including Joseph Haydn:]
Genovefens / Viertel [*sic*] Theil, / eine Marionetten Operette, / in dreyen Aufzügen. / Auf der fürstlichen Marionetten Bühne zu Esterhaz / im Somer 1777, zum ersten male aufgeführet.
The libretto was printed by Siess of Oedenburg in August 1777 and bound by Pfundtner. Pohl's MS. copy of the libretto (Gesellschaft der Musikfreunde 11.576/Textbuch) is the only known source extant. The printing was in honour of the marriage festivities of Count Nicolaus Esterházy, but the première was in April. Eszterháza performance material, by Johann Schellinger (his bill of November 1777 in EH, Eisenstadt), has disappeared (destroyed in the fire of 1779?). The music is lost.
For the *Gastspiel* at Schönbrunn Castle, Ordoñez's *Alceste* and Haydn's *Hexen-Schabbas* were given: see *infra*, July. Landon in *HJB* I, 183ff., 193. Bartha-Somfai 72f.

THE GERMAN THEATRICAL TROUPE 1777
Carl Wahr's Troupe returned to Eszterháza for the last time this season, but for some reason he left as early as July and went to Pressburg and to Pest (Budapest) in August. Of his repertoire, the only piece of which we have some kind of hint is a German translation of Charles Simon Favart's *Les trois sultanes*, entitled *Soliman II, oder Die drei Sultaninnen*, which Wahr had given at Vienna in 1770. The leading female role, 'La Roxelane', is the title of the slow movement in Haydn's Symphony No. 63, which was obviously put together as incidental music for the play: the opening movement is identical to the Overture to *Il mondo della luna*, but in the latter version the orchestration is bigger (*vide infra*). Landon, *SYM*, 359, n. 16 (for 'Eisenstadt' read 'Pressburg').

THE SCHMALÖGGER BALLET TROUPE 1777
As Carl Wahr's season neared its end, Prince Nicolaus engaged this well-known ballet company. On 12 April they gave the Ballet 'Der junge Werther' (after the Goethe *Roman*) and on 1 June:
Achilles und Daira ein heroisch pantomimischer [*sic*] Ballet in fünf Aufzügen; von Joseph Schmallögger dem Ältern. Zum erstenmal vorgestellt auf dem Hochfürstlichen Theater zu Esterhaz den 1ten Juny 1777. Ödenburg, gedruckt bey Johann Joseph Siess.
The libretto was dedicated to 'Nicolao Esterhazy de Galantha, etc., etc., Meinem gnädigsten Herrn'. The parts were played by Schmalögger himself, Theresia Schmalögger, Martin Borst and Carl Schmalögger. Joseph Schmalögger had been the ballet director for the Carl Wahr Troupe. Probst, p. 35.
And thus we see Haydn in yet another role at Eszterháza – as the conductor of a ballet company. His life certainly did not lack for variety.

We shall pass over a detailed study of the bills for instrument repairs, etc.[1] and merely point out that Haydn seems to have used his brief yearly sojourn in Vienna to arrange for these bills to be submitted so that the instrument makers could receive their money quickly.

Dichtler's wife, Barbara, had collapsed and died on the Eszterháza stage in September 1776. The Prince assisted him in educating the motherless children by continuing the payment in kind (*Naturalien*) which had been part of Barbara's contract. On 28 January 1777, Dichtler married again, with princely permission, the widow Christine Scheffschick, who was almost twenty years older than the bridegroom. The ceremony, at the Stadtpfarrkirche in Eisenstadt, included Haydn and the clerk in the Esterházy Buildings Administration, Kühnel:

> 28 Jan. 1777. Dominus Leopoldus Dichtler C. Principis Musicus cum Honest. vidua Christina Scheffschikin sponsus 39 sponsa 58 ann. Nomen et cognomen Testium: Perill D. Josephus Heiden C. Principis Capellae Magist. Sponsae D. Kühnel, aedificiorum C. Principis Scriptor et Posses. hujas.[2]

We now find Haydn's name in a document where we would hardly expect it, namely in the 'Berechnung / über / Empfang, und Ausgab / Bey denen den Fasching 1777. hindurch / in den kai: könig: Redouten Säälen / abgehaltenen 13. maskirten Bällen' (expenses and income from the thirteen masked balls held at Carnival time in the I. R. Redoutensaal rooms 1777), which occurred in the period 9 January–11 February – see opposite.

It would seem that the operatic season at Eszterháza began in April, when Gassmann's *L'amore artigiano* was first performed in the opera house (it ran until October 1777) and *Genovefens Vierter Theil* was first(?) performed in the marionette theatre (it ran until August 1777).[3] On 1 June Haydn wrote the following letter:

> [To First Lieutenant Seitz, an official in the Esterházy administration. *German.*]
> *Monsieur* Seitz!
> You are herewith requested please to issue to Herr Svoboda[4] on presentation of the enclosed receipt two bundles of E-strings. I remain, *Monsieur,*
> Estoras, 1 June 1777.   Your obedient
>   Josephus Haydn [mp]ria.
>   *Capell Meister*

We now arrive at the *Gastspiel* given by the Esterházy marionette theatre in Schönbrunn Castle, in honour of the Elector of Trèves and his sister, the Duchess Kunigunda of Saxony. The *Wiener Diarium* (No. 62, 12 Heumonat [July]) reports:

> After H. R. H. the Elector of Trèves with his Madame Sister, H.R.H. Duchess Kunigunda of Saxony, accompanied by the highest I. R. gentlemen, had deigned to honour everything here with their high presences, they left Schönbrunn on

---

1 Mathias Rugenbauer (Rockobauer), Vienna 1 Jan. for 3 dozen bassoon reeds, 6 fl., A.M. Fasc. XVI, 1056; Antoni Schintler, Vienna 1 Jan. for 2 dozen bassoon reeds, A.M. Fasc. XVI, 1051; J. Bauer, Vienna 9 Jan. for 2 dozen bassoon reeds, 4 fl., A.M. Fasc. XVI, 1055; M. Pauer Instrument Macher, 14 Feb. 1777, 8 fl. which 'I have received from the Messrs. oboists for oboe and cor anglais [repairs], A.M. Fasc. XVI, 1053; and the usual yearly bill for strings and repairs for the instruments in the Eisenstadt church choir, A.M. Fasc. XVI, 1050 – all these documents in EH, Budapest, and countersigned by Haydn. Valkó II, 584f.
2 Harich in *HJB* II, 32, and VII, 22. The previous assertion by Csatkai ('Die Beziehungen … Werners, … Haydns und der fürstlichen Musiker zur Eisenstädter Pfarrkirche', in *Burgenländische Heimatblätter* I/1 [1932], p. 15) that Haydn gave away Widow Scheffschik at a previous marriage on 20 May is, as we have seen (*supra*, p. 125), wrong.
3 Harich in *HJB* I, 32 and Landon in *HJB* I, 183.
4 Not in the list of musicians; he was probably a valet or servant. His autograph signature on the same document reads 'Joseph Swoboda'. About Seitz see also *Haydn: the Years of 'The Creation' 1796–1800*, p. 261.

Pag: 12

Expenses
For the music in the I. R. Redouten Säälen and expenses incurred

No.		f.	x.
21	For HUBER Pangratz, Music Director, for the musicians, 43 in the large and 27 in the small rooms, together 70 and for the composition of 36 minuets and 12 German Dances with the copying expenses, for 13 balls à 220 f each time, together according to Receipt N° 21	According to the price regulated in the contract A° 773 2860	
22	For HEIDEN Joseph, fürstl. Esterhasischen Kapelmeister for the composition of 12 minuets [later:] against receipt signed by W[ell] B[orn] Franz Bernhard Edler von Keeß ut N° 22	According to order of H[err] B[aron] v: Kirnmaÿr 51	12
23	For BORSARI Joseph for copying the same ut N° 23	*viz.* 6	46
24	For ASPELMAIER Franz for the composition of 18 minuets and 12 German Dances............................... 101.36 For costs of copying.......................... 12.55 Together ut N° 24........................	*viz.* 114 3032	31 29

Summa of the expenses for the music in the I. R. Redouten Säälen and the expenses incurred, three thousand two-and-thirty Gulden 29 X.

Id est 3032 f. 29.X.

[Underlined words not underlined here]

[Haus-, Hof und Staatsarchiv, Hoftheater-Rechnungen S. R. 35, p. 12: photograph kindly provided by Dr Clemens Höslinger of that institution.]

[Notes: Pancrazio (Pankraz) Huber and Franz Aspelmayer were well-known composers. At least one Divertimento IID:20 (identical with II:Es7) attributed to Haydn was actually composed by Pancrazio Huber: Lambach Cat. 1768, see also Breitkopf Catalogue 1772, and one spurious Haydn Symphony (I:Es6) is attributed to Aspelmayer and also to Pierre van Maldere. About Keeß, *vide infra*, p. 663. We cannot identify Haydn's go-between, Kirnmayr. See also Günter Thomas in *Haydn-Studien* III/1(1973), pp. 8f. From all the available evidence, it would seem that the Haydn Minuets must be the Twelve (IX:6) which also used some of the 1776 Minuets (IX:5) discussed *supra*, p. 397. Haydn was not badly paid for his dances. Carlos d'Ordoñez was paid 102 fl. 24 kr. 'für die componierte Music zur deutschen Operette, Diesmal hat der Mann den Willen' and 12 fl. 36 kr. 'item für Copiatur 12 von selben componisten simphonien ...'. 'Fünfte Kais. Königl^er Obersten Theatral Hof Directions Casse Halbjährige Rechnung' 18 April–2 Nov. 1778, S. R. 14. Haus-, Hof- und Staatsarchiv, Vienna. In other words, Haydn received half (exactly!) of Ordoñez's fee for an entire opera.]

Wednesday afternoon for the Belvedere, to see there the magnificent picture gallery, and from there to the Salesian Nunnery in the Rennweg, and in the evening to the Schloß theater at Schönbrunn for the opera, which was given by the Princely Esterhazi [*sic*] Troupe and received the applause of the all-highest guests. [On Thursday evening they went to an Italian opera at the Kärntnerthortheater.]

Friday noon the Princely Esterhazi Capelle, having received the gracious applause of the all-highest and highest persons at the opera on Wednesday, could be heard again at the Emperor's *Tafel* in Schönbrunn ...

And four days later we read:

Vienna, 16 Hay Month [July]. Saturday [at the Burgtheater] ... The joy on the part of the public when glimpsing the all-mildest Mother of the Country immediately turned into a general rejoicing, and delighted pleasure inflamed every heart at this unexpected grace ...

On Sunday ... Mass in the Schloßkapelle at Schönbrunn ... in the afternoon ... to the Augarten, then to the Prater ... [where there were] fireworks ... On Monday [a visit to the] porcelain factory..., lunch at Prince Franz von Lichtenstein's [*sic*] ..., thereafter back to Schönbrunn ... where in the evening there was once again a magnificent Singspiel by the Princely Esterhazi Troupe given to the all-highest applause.

From documents in the Esterházy Archives (Eisenstadt), we learn that the Vienna guest-appearance was directed by Pauersbach (order for the necessary carriages to take the troupe to Vienna, and so on); that the Italian operatic personnel remained in Eszterháza, and probably Haydn too, and gave performances during the marionette troupe's absence; and that 'zwey Operetten' were given at Vienna. On 11 July 1777, a bill was paid to the Oedenburg printer, Siess, for having twelve copies of Ordoñez's *Alceste* (1775) bound 'in roten Atlas'; while on 8 July, the Viennese publisher Trattner was asked to bind up thirty-three copies of Haydn's *Hexen-Schabbas* (in the document: 'Hexen-Sabat') 'in blauen Atlas'. These were the two operas, therefore, that Pauersbach presented at Schönbrunn.[1]

We believe, however, that the operatic 'performances' at Eszterháza were actually rehearsals – perhaps with costumes – for the new Haydn Opera, *Il mondo della luna*. The reason for our assertion is that the whole Esterházy orchestra, with the exception of Joseph Dietzl (who was probably in Eisenstadt – in a document in the Esterházy Archives of the following year he is referred to as the 'violinist Joseph Dietzl in Eisenstatt')[2] and Johann Hinterberger (referred to in that same document as being 'already old and deaf') was sent up to Schönbrunn. In another of those famous 'showers of gold', Prince Nicolaus rewarded all the members of the marionette troupe and the whole orchestra for their participation in the two Operettas, including three female singers, the two 'pupils' (Ernst and Koschwitz), two children, the prompter-*cum*-copyist Johann Schellinger, the singers Dichtler, Specht and 'Ungericht'. This 'Regale' was received and signed for by Haydn on 17 July 1777.[3]

On 3 August, the Prince's second son, Count Nicolaus, married Maria Anna Franziska, Countess von Weissenwolf, at the court chapel at Eszterháza. We can find no records that state on which day Haydn's new Opera, *Il mondo della luna*, nor *Genovefens Vierter Theil* (for which a libretto had been specially printed), were actually performed. The bridal couple were rather older than was usual at that time: she was thirty and he thirty-six. Pietro Travaglia, engaged on 1 August, prepared the scenery 'in great haste' for *Il mondo della luna* and Leopold Dichtler copied the entire vocal and orchestral material for this long work.[4]

We have seen that Dichtler taught singing to Elisabeth Prandtner (*vide supra*, p. 51) after she was first engaged in 1774. For some reason, she was 'transferred' to Haydn, together with Elisabeth Griessler, in November 1776. Now, a year later, we read:

---

1 Landon in *HJB* I, 114f.
2 Letter from Prince Nicolaus to Peter von Rahier of 5 Dec. 1778; A.M. 4359, *HJB* IV, 95f.
3 EH, Budapest, A.M. 4361. S. Gerlach in *Haydn-Studien* II/1 (1969), p. 52.
4 Harich, *Musikgeschichte*, 40. Document: 'Copiatura Dell opera Il Mondo della Luna: / Follia ..... 508 / Summa 42 f: 20 Xr: / Leopoldo Dichtler. / The above two-and-forty Gulden 20 Xr. are to be paid from our General Cassa and booked. Esterház, 25th Aug. 777. / Nicolaus Fürst Esterhazy. / I apologize most submissively that I did not return this order for payment to you, because my children at a moment when I turned my back knocked over a whole inkwell on it; and I think you won't need it; so I'll keep it till I get to Eisenstadt, so I can show you. Meanwhile many thanks for the *Obligation* [payment?] and I remain with respect / Your most obedient Dichtler'. Generalcassa 1777, Rubr. 20. Fasc. 14. Nr. 10. EH, Eisenstadt. *HJB* VII, 159f. Document: 'Receipt P[e]r 42 f: 20 Xr / Which I the undersigned have received in full and in cash from H. Chief Cashier Züsser for the copying of the opera Il mondo della Luna for which I do attest herewith Esterhaz 29th Augusti 777: / Id est 42 f: 20 Xr / Leopoldo Dichtler'. Ditto Nr. 10.

Comission

According to which our Eisenstadt Chief Cashier Züsser is to pay to our Kapellmeister for his instruction of two female singers twenty-four Kremnitz ducats against a receipt. Eszterház 22nd Nov. 777.

Nicolaus Fürst Esterhazy

Receipt

Pr [*per*] four-and-twenty Cremnitz ducats which I the undersigned received through the Chief Cashier Züsser in full and in cash, for which I give this receipt. Estoras 26th Nov. 777.

Josephus Haydn mpria

[Generalcassa.1777. Rubr. XII. Fasc. 9. Nr. 33, EH Eisenstadt. *HJB* VII, 34 & 79]

Our Chronicle for 1777 closes with the appearance of three singers (later to be members of the Eszterháza company) at the Vienna Opera. They were all engaged in the ensuing years: Ripamonti and Totti in 1778, and both the Bologna sisters in 1781. Our source is Count Zinzendorf's Diary:[1]

[15 December 1777] au <u>Spectacle</u>. La <u>Locanda</u>, la musique est de [empty space: probably Gazzaniga, whose setting was given at Vienna in 1772 and at Eszterháza in 1778 – a coincidence?] La Ripamonte [*sic*] jolie actrice sans voix, la Bologna <u>laide</u> avec de la voix. Todi [Totti] a de la voix. . . .

It was probably during his annual stay at Eisenstadt in the winter of 1777–8 that Haydn composed his *Missa brevis Sancti Joannis de Deo*[2] (the so-called 'Kleine Orgelsolomesse') for the chapel of the Brothers of Mercy, the pretty organ (almost exactly the same age as Haydn himself) of which is still extant. The very restricted size of that organ loft seems to have dictated the small forces used in the Mass: two violins, organ and continuo. It is thought that Haydn himself played the solo organ part (and of course the continuo). The Mass was also used by the Esterházy Castle Chapel (MS. parts in EH, Eisenstadt), and was ideal for performance in the period when the main orchestra was at Eszterháza; so perhaps Haydn actually composed it with them in mind as well. (The saint to whom the Mass is dedicated, St John of God, was the founder and Patron Saint of the Order of the Brothers of Mercy.)

Chronicle 1778

ITALIAN OPERAS 1778

[Pietro Guglielmi? Giuseppe Sarti?] La sposa fedele. Dramma serio-giocoso per musica. – Da rappresentarsi nel teatro d'Esterhaz. L'anno 1778. – In Oedenburgo, Nella Stamperia di Giuseppe Siess. [No composer's name listed].

Rosinella	La Sign. Barbara Ripamonti.
Pasqualino	Il Sign. Benedetto Bianchi.
Lauretta, serva	La Sign. Maria Anna Puttler.
Il marchese di Vento Ponente	Il Sign. N. N.
Camilla, nipote del Marchese	La Sign. Catharina Poschwa.
Valerio, magiordomo	Il Sign. Lambertini.
Il conte Lelio, amico del Marchese	Il Sign. Leopoldo Dichtler.

1 Zinzendorf's Diary for this month shows that he was a constant visitor 'chez la P<u>sse</u> Eszterhasy regnante', where he met the Emperor three times; on 20 December '. . . l'Empereur nous parla beaucoup de son voyage en france.' See his entries for 13, 14, 16, 17 and 20 December.

2 The undated autograph (Gesellschaft der Musikfreunde, Vienna) has a watermark consisting of 'GF' (Galvani Fratelli) and an ornament with three stars within it and a half-moon suspended from it; and three crescents. The same watermark occurs in the Overture Ia:7 (dated autograph, Berlin State Library, 1777). The Mass is registered at Göttweig, 1778.

Libretto: Országos Széchényi Könyvtár, Budapest Sign. 206.203, printed in an edition of 500 copies. The Eszterháza performance material no longer exists (destroyed in 1779 fire?). First performance on 3 May, repeated each month until 25 October. Pohl II, 368, and Horányi (English) 202, give Guglielmi, and Harich, *Musikgeschichte*, 41, gives Sarti as the composer. Bartha-Somfai 75 point out that Guglielmi's Opera was the one given at Vienna in 1776.

Nicolà Piccinni: L'astratto, ovvero il giocatore fortunato. Drama [*sic*] giocoso. – Da rappressentarsi [*sic*] nel teatro d'Esterhaz l'estate 1778.

Personagi [sic]
[star form]
Il Capitan Faccenda, fratello di Laurina: il Sig. Andr. Toti. [*sic*]
Laurina, Gardiniera [*sic*] Amante di Leandro[:] la Sig. Barbara Ripamonti.
Leandro, Giovane astratto e Giocatore di Lotto, figlio di D. Timoteo: il Sig. Giov. Pezzani.
Giocondo, Servitore: il Sig. Vito Ungricht.
Clarice, figlia di D. Timoteo[:] la Sig. Cath. Poschwa.
Don Timoteo, uomo stravagante: il Sig. Giacomo Lambertini.
Angelica, figlia di D. Timoteo, la Sig. Elisabetha Prandtner.
[Also a complete German translation by P. G. Bader]

Libretto: Stadtbibliothek, Vienna, A 14835.
The Opera is actually a pasticcio, for there are arias in it by Salieri, Guglielmi and Rutini. Eszterháza performance material: EH, Budapest, Ms. Mus. OE–27: score (not quite complete) by a Viennese(?) copyist and one viola part. In the score there are simplifications, transpositions and cuts in Haydn's hand, also changes in Joseph Elssler's hand. Bartha-Somfai 76, 200–2. First performance: 12 July, repeated until 15 November.

Pasquale Anfossi: Il geloso in cimento. Dramma giocoso per musica. Di Giovanni Bertati. Da rappresentarsi al teatro d'Esterhaz l'estate 1778. Presso Giuseppe nob. de Kurzböck.
Libretto: printed in an edition of 500 copies (none has survived). Of the Eszterháza performance material, this 1778 version has not survived (destroyed in the fire of 1779?): but it was re-copied for the 1785 revival and is discussed *infra*, p. 670. First performance: 10 September, repeated until 8 December. Harich, *Musikgeschichte*, 41. Bartha-Somfai, 76, 202.

Giuseppe Gazzaniga: La locanda. Dramma giocoso per musica. Da rappresentarsi nel teatro d'Esterhaz dell'anno 1778. [Giuseppe Kurzböck, Vienna.] In Haydn's *Opernliste* 1784: Piccin(n)i. *HJB* IX, 92.
Libretto: 300 copies ordered, also a new edition of the title page and one additional aria, also 300 copies (perhaps an 'insertion' aria by Haydn?): none has survived. Eszterháza performance material: score, orchestral parts and some of the vocal parts; the score is probably of Viennese origin, the material was copied by Joseph Elssler and Johann Schellinger. There are two 'insertion' arias, both in Act I, but as usual now incomplete and without the vocal parts necessary for their identification. We know that Elisabeth Prandtner sang in this Opera, because in Act III, Aria del Guaritore 'Chi viene a chiedere del Guaritore', bar 45, Haydn wrote 'NB da Capo / ma solamente in assenza della Prantner'. Haydn also made cuts (e.g. Scene 1 of Act III), transpositions, etc. Harich *Musikgeschichte*, 41. Bartha-Somfai, 76, 202f. First performance: 22 November, the last on 1 December.

Five operas from previous seasons were repeated in 1778: Dittersdorf's *Il finto pazzo, Il barone di Rocca Antica* and *Arcifanfano*; Piccinni's *La buona figliuola* and Paisiello's *La Frascatana*. (We would remind readers that the entire season, operas, marionette theatre and plays, has been preserved: *vide* pp. 93ff.)

GERMAN MARIONETTE OPERAS 1778

Joseph Purksteiner: Das ländliche Hochzeitsfest. Libretto printed by Siess in Oedenburg. Copy formerly in Sándor Wolf Museum, Eisenstadt; sold to Galerie Fischer, Basel; no other copy known. First performance: 16 May, repeated until 14 June. The music is lost. Landon in *HJB* I, 191f. The play, written by Pauersbach,[1] is listed in the Gotha *Theater Kalender* of 1777, p. 197 (*Das ländliche Hochzeitsfeste, ein Faschingsstück*, i.e. a Carnival piece), and was probably the basis for the *Singspiel*.

Joseph Haydn: Dido, / eine parodirte / Marionetten Operette / in drey Aufzügen, / von / Philipp Georg Bader. / ——— / Aufgeführt / auf der / Hochfürstlichen Marionettenbühne / zu / Esterház / im Herbste 1778 / ——— / Die Musik ist von Hrd. Joseph Haiden, / Hochfürstl. Capellmeister / eigen hiezu verfertigt. / ——————— / Oedenburg, / gedruckt bey Johann Joseph Sieß.

---

1 A copy of the libretto, printed in Pressburg and Leipzig in 1773, is in the Stadtbibliothek, Vienna, A14835.

Avertissement
This Operette is a parody . . . [original] and if that is the case, one is not required to follow the truth in matters of chronology. The tragedy is thus turned into comedy, and the poet is permitted to bring into one period Nuremberg, Vienna, Carthage and Hirschau. The same is true of the dialogue! One presents heroes and kings, queens and princes, as partly tragic figures and immediately thereafter has them talking in low and silly tones, just like the most common people. Moreover, such pieces are designed for the eye and the ear . . . [original]. Without that, marionette pieces are impossible! Whereby one should recall that the shorter they are, the better they succeed, and the more variety they have, the better.

Bader

Libretto for this revival (first and only performance was on 15 September): Stadtbibliothek 23520-A (now on exhibition in the Haydn Museum), Vienna. The 'Figurendirector' for the 1778 performance was Sicca (Sicka), and there were fifteen days for the necessary ten rehearsals. Landon in *HJB* I, 175–8 (with the beginnings of the musical numbers as listed in the libretto), 193. This was apparently Pauersbach's farewell to Eszterháza, and it was a typically generous act to print (or rather reprint) Haydn's and Bader's libretto just for this one occasion. After that, there were no more performances at the Eszterháza marionette theatre in the 1778 season. The music, as we have said when first discussing *Dido*, is lost.

THE GERMAN THEATRICAL TROUPES 1778

With a very long season – January to December – Prince Nicolaus had to engage several companies:

(1) Pantomime Troupe of Albert Bienfait, formerly of the Esterházy Marionette Troupe (as 'Maschinist'), and Franz Christl, formerly of the Wahr Troupe. Their contract, dated 23 January 1778 (A.T. 58, EH Budapest), specified that they would give pantomimes with at least five persons between 24 January and 3 March 'as frequently as His Highness sees fit'. Horányi (German), 111; (English), 110.

(2) But who performed the plays *Die Grenadiere*, *Polyphemus* and *Bellandra* which we find in January and February, i.e. before 10 March and the début of the 'Paulische Truppe'? We believe we have found the answer in the 'Fiskalbuch der Freistadt Eisenstadt von 1766–78', where we find the following entry: 'Anno 1778 the 11th of August the actress Theresia König [Königin], who has come here from Esterhaz and for some days gave plays here, paid the tax levied upon her by the Herrn Stadt Richter [Judge of the Town] consisting of four seventeen [Kreuzer pieces].'[1]

(3) The Pauli Troupe, who began their season at Eszterháza on 10 March, with actors Ulrich, Bachmayer, Lamberti and Mayer; and actresses Mayer's sister (later Frau Ditelmeyer), Schwarzwald mother and daughter (formerly with the Wahr Troupe). Johann Mayer, Pauli's co-director, later formed his own company. Horányi, 110f.

(4) On 4 July 1778, a contract was signed with the Diwald Troupe (A.T. 33, EH Budapest), in which Diwald binds himself to give plays with fourteen skilled actors and actresses from 1 November. He assured the Prince that his ensemble is superior to Pauli & Mayer, he also agrees to bring an imposing wardrobe and if he could stay at Eszterháza until the beginning of Lent he would replace any players who might have meanwhile left the company. Franz Joseph Diwald, who had previously played at Pressburg, Baden, Pest and Oedenburg, now became the Prince's main theatrical company, remaining at Eszterháza until 1785. Diwald's tour, in 1778, began on 30 October and ended on 22 December. Horányi, 114–6.

Haydn was presumably in Vienna early in January to settle the usual instrument makers' bills.[2]

The Eisenstadt *Ratsprotokoll* No. 233 of 30 May 1778 announces that Haydn's sister-in-law, Aloysia Sommerfeld, *née* Keller, 'citizen wigmaker in Preßburg', has begun a lawsuit against 'Hrn Joseph Heiden Fürst Esterhazyschen . . . Capellmeister and house owner here' which is to be given a final hearing on 25 August. On 31 May, *Ratsprotokoll* No. 234 of 31 May informs us that if, in the course of the lawsuit against Haydn and his wife, 'Hr. Haiden sells his house here, the proceeds are to be sequestrated

---

1 Franz Probst, *Beiträge zur Geschichte des deutschsprachigen Theaterwesens in Eisenstadt*, Eisenstadt 1952, p. 33.
2 Antonius Schindler, Vienna, 1 Jan., for 1½ dozen bassoon reeds, A.M. Fasc. XVI. 1034; Mathias Pauer Instrument Maker, Vienna 1 Jan., 6 fl. for three dozen bassoon reeds, A.M. XVI. 1054; Jacob Bauer Instrument Maker, Vienna 4 Jan., 'receipt for two dozen bassoon reeds which I gave Schiringer . . . per 4 Fl . . .', A.M. XVI. 1035; later in the year we find another bill from Jacob Pauer [*sic*], Vienna 1 Nov., 'receipt. Four Gulden . . . for two dozen oboe reeds', A.M. XVI. 1039; and the yearly bill for repairs etc. to instruments of the Eisenstadt church choir, Johann Georg Fuchs (Eisenstadt, 29 Dec.), 16 Fl. 33 xr., A.M. XVI. 1038. All these bills are countersigned by Haydn. Valkó II, 585f.

and turned over to the lawcourts'.[1] Haydn's debts were, no doubt, a result of the two fires at Eisenstadt. The other documents, unfortunately, are no longer extant, but since there is no entry in the *Ratsprotokoll* for 25 August, the suit seems to have been settled out of court. Haydn bore his sister-in-law no ill-will and remembered her children in his Will of 1801.[2]

On 12 May 1778, we have a tailor's bill for a new summer uniform for Haydn,[3] of which the coat cost 147 fl. 54½ kr., the waistcoat in apple green material 61 fl. 51 kr., two pairs of breeches 19 fl. 27 kr., and '1 fine hat' with various gold buttons, braid, etc. 11 fl. 40 kr. Prince Nicolaus was quite willing to pay for the most expensive material.

On 27 October 1778, Haydn sold his property in Eisenstadt to the princely book-keeper Anton Liechtscheidl, who paid 2,000 gulden; on that same day, Haydn took 1,000 gulden to the princely disbursar who paid him five per cent p.a., or fifty gulden, which the composer received in semi-annual payments, the last time on 13 December 1808. In the years 1802–4 Haydn transferred the income to his younger brother Johann, who was then living in straitened circumstances at Eisenstadt.[4] The contract reads:

Obligation

Pr. one thousand Gulden, id est 1,000 f Rn which we the undersigned have received from our Capell-Meister Joseph Haÿden against an annual 5 per cent interest to be paid semi-annually: we promise and obligate ourselves not only to pay the interest at semi-annual intervals but to repay the capital itself in good, ready money upon the notice being given a quarter of a year beforehand by either party. Witness thereto is this our autograph and the princely seal. Eszterhaz, 28th Oct. 1778.

[L. S.]Nicolaus Fürst Esterhazy mp.

This was the first capital Haydn ever owned, and he referred to it when he, many years later, told his biographers Dies and Griesinger that he had 'barely 2,000 gulden capital'[5] when he left Austria for England in 1790. He probably repaid his debts, *inter alia* to Frau Sommerfeld, with the remaining 1,000 gulden. The sale of the house is registered in the Eisenstadt *Ratsprotokoll* No. 372 of 29 October 'sub dato 27. Octobris anni cur. . . . erga relationem'.[6]

We now arrive at one of those documents in the Esterházy Archives (Forchtenstein Castle) which is much more revealing than would at first appear:

Specification for Necessary Music Paper

6 Books oblong format with 10 staves, 6 Books quarto format with 10 staves, and 2 Books oblong format with 12 staves, and 3 Books oblong format with 8 staves: the book at 50 Xr. Makes

11 fl 20 Xr.
Josephus Haydn mpria

---

1 Schmid, 'Eisenstadt', p. 10.
2 See *Haydn: the Late Years 1801–1809*, p. 52 (entry 43). Also in the Will of 1809, *ibid.*, p. 380 (item 24), with 200 gulden (Will of 1801: 100 gulden).
3 A.M. Budapest, Fasc. LXVI. 4160. Valkó II, 586f. in extenso.
4 Harich in *HJB* IV, 31f.; we have used, mostly *verbatim*, our summary and translation. The document in *HJB* IV, p. 61.
5 See *Haydn in England 1791–1795*, p. 319.
6 *In extenso* in Schmid, 'Eisenstadt', p. 12.

        For my new opera
First the 6 Books oblong format with ten
lines for the vocal parts. 2ndly the 6 Books
quarto for the orchestral parts, 3rdly the 2
Books with 12 staves for the finale in the opera
and the 3 Books with 8 Lines for His Highness for
the Bariton so that this winter the 5th volume
of my Trios can be copied.
The above specified paper will be purchased by our House Inspector Kleinrath and
sent here as soon as possible. Eszterhaz the 8th Nov. 778.
Nicolaus Fürst Esterhazy.
        [EH Forchtenstein, Acta varia, Fasz. 186; *Haydn–Studien* III/2 (1974), p. 99]

The new Opera was *La vera costanza*, and thereby hangs a curious tale. Here are the
documents from Griesinger and Dies:

> The Emperor [Joseph II] wanted to hear his [Haydn's] opera *La vera costanza*,
> but through intrigues the parts were so badly assigned that Haydn withdrew the
> score.   [Griesinger, 35]

> [Dies gives a list of Haydn's previous operas and concludes with *Il mondo della
> luna*. They were so positively discussed that] the Court at Vienna requested an
> opera by Haydn for the Court Theatre. He accepted the offer with pleasure and set
> *La vera Costanza*, Dramma giocoso.
>   The opera was finished. Naturally Haydn had weighed the capabilities, and
> the vocal range, of every singer and written the parts accordingly to fit their
> needs. How great was his astonishment when he saw his choice of roles overruled
> and was told that he had no right to distribute the parts as he saw fit. They wished
> to force another cast on him. Haydn answered, 'I know what, and for whom, I
> compose'; he refused to be forced and took his case to the Monarch. Emperor
> Joseph agreed with Haydn's rights and sought to mediate but found incredible
> opposition, to the extent that Haydn said he would sooner not have the opera
> produced than to struggle any more against the cabal. . . . 'I did not give the opera.
> I packed my things and went to my Prince and told him the whole story. The
> Prince did not condemn my action but arranged to have the opera given at
> Esterház in 1779. The great Emperor Joseph was in the audience.'   [Dies, 62f.]

Armed with this information, we examined the entire accounts of the *Hoftheater*
(Court Theatre), now in the Haus-, Hof- und Staatsarchiv in Vienna, for the period
1775–79. There is no mention whatever of Haydn or his *La vera costanza*, but in
January 1777, the Court Theatre performed Pasquale Anfossi's work of that name
which had been performed with success in Italy and Spain. We have also examined, in
the same Archives, the *Protocollum separatum aller Hand-Billets vom 3. Nov. 1774 bis 13.
Juli 1778*, and there is no record of Haydn in these important copies of Joseph II's
'Hand-Billets' of the period.[1] It is clear that Haydn has confused the issue, and that if
there were negotiations, they never proceeded beyond the informal stage. Moreover,
it is quite clear that on 8 November 1778 Haydn had not yet composed the finale (to
Act II?); otherwise he would not have requested the paper for it. And finally, there is

---

1 Nor is there any record in the semi-annual bills of the Hoftheater Cassa, in particular the crucial period under investigation: 'Fünfte
Kais. Königl^ER Obersten Theatral Hof Directions Casse Halbjährige Rechnung . . . 18ter April bis inclusive 2ten October 1778.' Hof
Theater S. R. 14, Haus-, Hof- und Staatsarchiv, Vienna. In the Imperial *Handbillets* of 1778 we may ascertain that Joseph II was away on
manœuvres with the army and did not return to Vienna until the middle of November 1778: in these *Handbillets* (vol. II, 1778) there is
no mention of theatrical activities whatever.

evidence, which will be discussed below, that Haydn knew and made use of Anfossi's setting. The whole opera was destroyed in the 1779 fire at Eszterháza and later Haydn wrote most of it down from memory (or composed parts wholly anew) for the 1785 revival.

Haydn's relationship with Joseph II was not a cordial one. We wonder if the whole story is not in reverse, and that Joseph II himself prevented the Viennese production of *La vera costanza*. In the *Oracle* for 27 January 1792, we read:

> HAYDN, though in instrumental composition so *varied* and *original*, has yet but slender merit as a Writer for the *Voice*. He once wrote, however, an *Opera* at Vienna, and the late EMPEROR would not hear of its being performed.

Now it happens that we have documentary reports that Joseph II actually heard two Haydn operas: (1) In December 1784 he went to *La fedeltà premiata* (Kärntnerthortheater, Vienna), and (2) he went to hear *Armida* in Pressburg. The first instance will be discussed *infra*; the second is known to us from the Gotha *Theater-Kalender ... 1787*, where, on p. 203 (in a report about the Pressburg Theatre), we read:

> On 16 Oct. [1786] Armide [*sic*] by Haydn was given, which was attended by H. M. the Emperor. Oral reports of a friend, who attended several performances, appear very favourable but would require too much space ... [but see n. 1, p. 413]

Joseph II was certainly not at the Eszterháza première of *La vera costanza* and his opinion of Haydn was altogether unfavourable, and especially where his operas were concerned. When Dittersdorf had his famous interview with Joseph II, we hear the following exchange:

> *Emperor*: What do you say to Haydn's compositions [for the theatre].
> *I* [*Dittersdorf*]: I've not heard any of his theatrical pieces.
> *Emperor*: You haven't missed anything; for he does just like Mozart [to full accompaniments]. What do you think of his chamber music pieces?
> *I*: That they create a sensation in the whole world, and rightly.
> *Emperor*: Don't you think he trifles [*Tändelt*] at times and altogether too much?
> *I*: He has the gift of trifling without, however, lowering the art.
> *Emperor*: Well, you're right. (After a pause:) Some time ago I drew a parallel between Mozart and Haydn. Make one yourself, too, so that I can see if it agrees with mine. ...
> *I*: What kind of a parallel would Your Majesty draw between Klopstock and Gellert?
> *Emperor*: Hm! – that both are great poets – that one must read Klopstock more than once to understand all his beauties – but that Gellert's beauties lie exposed at first glance.
> *I*: There Your Majesty has my answer.
> *Emperor*: Then Mozart would be compared to Klopstock and Haydn with Gellert?
> *I*: That is my opinion.
> *Emperor*: Charming! Now you've given me a stick to use against [the Court musician and deadly enemy of Haydn and Mozart] Greybig [Franz Kreibich] and to beat him over the nose with it ...
> [Dittersdorf, *Lebensbeschreibung* (ed. Miller), Munich 1967, pp. 228f.]

On another occasion, Joseph II was discussing music with the Berlin composer and writer, J. F. Reichardt, and was no little astonished to hear the Emperor say, apropos of

Haydn, 'I thought you Berlin gentlemen did not like such jokes: I myself don't think much of them either.'[1]

To return to Eszterháza, Haydn also received a new winter uniform this year: Johann Franciscus Sellinger, a Viennese Master Tailor, delivered his bill on 20 November, for Haydn's uniform and for the uniforms of nineteen musicians and 'more for the two Eisenstadt musicians 2 suits with red waistcoats and golden borders'.[2]

Our Chronicle for the year closes with a letter from Prince Nicolaus to Peter von Rahier, from which we give some extracts:

... Since my chamber musicians and the singers, male and female, receive free lodgings here, I wish that their *Deputaten* [goods] will no longer be issued to them

1 Took place in 1783 (Dittersdorf's in 1786): *AMZ* XV, 667. See also O. E. Deutsch, 'Joseph Haydn und Kaiser Joseph II' (1910), reprinted in *Musikalische Kukukseier* (a collection of Deutsch's essays, ed. Hans Weigl), Vienna. Joseph II's supposed presence at *Armida* in Pressburg: in the *Hochgräflich-Erdödischer Theaterallmanach auf das Jahr 1787* (p. 77), the performance of 16 October 1786 was postponed to 3 November because Count Johann Nepomuk Erdödy was ill, but then it was 'performed with great magnificence and universal approbation.' Joseph II's presence would certainly have been mentioned.

In Reichardt's *Vertraute Briefe* (ed. Gugitz), vol. II (1915), p. 110, he writes, referring to his visit to Vienna of 1783, 'I can very well remember that in the time of Emperor Joseph, who himself played a great deal of music and who, in a long discussion that I had with him about the theory and practice of music, revealed much good and profound knowledge about music, Haydn's wonderful symphonies, which delighted half of Europe by that time, were not allowed to be given in the court theatre. The Emperor continued to lump them in one pot – probably through the exertions of those composers who were close to him – with Haydn's earliest cassatios, which appeared to him only as burlesques and unworthy of higher art. But the Emperor loved *opera buffa* very much.' Reichardt amplified his conversation about Haydn in his sketches for an autobiography, published in the *AMZ*, 1813: 'Reichardt was then [Summer, 1783] introduced to Emperor Joseph and had rather a long conversation with him about music in which the Emperor very often expressed himself very forcibly in his naïve[!] Austrian German ... The conversation could agree least about Haydn, whom Reichardt mentioned with respect and regretted missing in Vienna. 'I thought' [etc. as in main text] – and fell over that excellent musician in a pretty formidable way, that musician who had already written the finest of his symphonies and quartets. Reichardt however soon learned that a pleasant but rather limited violinist and instrumental composer, Kreibich [Franz Kreibich, 1728–97], was the chamber music director of the Emperor and played first violin in his small chamber concerts; he was a great antagonist of Haydn's, and had arranged things with the Emperor to the extent that in the Imperial Theatre, only rarely were works by Haydn allowed to be played. The vocal compositions of this fine master were also not allowed to surface in Vienna [*La vera costanza*!], though of course they were almost all written in the usual Italian style. [Reichardt goes to hear a wind band concert by the I. R. band:] ... Some pieces by Mozart were also exquisite. Nothing by Haydn was played.'

We believe the taste of Joseph II to have been of vital importance in Mozart's life, and in the *general* aristocratic attitude towards Haydn; and in both cases, Joseph's negative attitude was of catastrophic effect, particularly in Mozart's case. (Haydn, being employed in a remote Hungarian castle, only felt the overtones of his Monarch's disapproval.) But that Joseph was a genuine connoisseur of Italian *opera buffa* and a generous supporter of their creators, we propose to establish here and in later portions of this volume. We use Joseph's letters to his Ambassador to the Court of St Petersburg, Ludwig Count Cobenzl: *Joseph II and Graf Ludwig Cobenzl. Ihr Briefwechsel* (ed. A. Beer and J. von Fiedler), Vienna 1901. Page numbers simply added in [ ] at the end of each quotation; vol. I (1780–4), II (1785–90), 'Vienne, 12 sept. 1781 [sur le voyage à Vienne de Maria Feodorowna: le clavecin était trop grand pour porter et] 'l'instrument qu'elle aimait le mieux étoit un pianoforte organisé, au défaut de celui-ci, un simple pianoforte, et celui-ci manquant encore un clavecin ordinaire ... ces clavecins organisés qui ne sont pas même connus à Vienne ...' By 'clavecins [pianofortes] organisés' is meant a grand fortepiano with damper mechanism and probably 'Fagottzug' (bassoon stop) and/or other 'Veränderungen', e.g. lute-stops. Interesting that such pianos were still very rare in Vienna in 1781. [I, 225].

Cobenzl sends Joseph II the score of Paisiello's *La serva padrona*. Joseph thanks him for it and (24 Feb. 1783) adds, 'Je compte le faire éxecuter après Pâques par une nouvelle troupe de Bouffons Italienes, que j'ai fait engager et qui doit être bonne. Vous me ferés aussi plaisir de me procurer tous les ouvrages en ce genre et non serieus de la composition de Païsiello à mesure qu'il en paraîtra de nouveaux ...' [I, 370] Cobenzl to Joseph II, St Petersburg, 17 Dec. 1783: 'Paisiello a eu une petite rixe avec le comité qui dirige les spectacles, au sortie de laquelle on l'a mis au arrêts au pain et à l'eau [ces charmants Russes ...] Il a demandé son congé que L'Imp^ce n'a pas voulu lui donner. ... Il se propose de passer et de s'arrêter quelque tems à Vienne ...' [I, 448].

'Vienna ce 9. Juin 1784 ... C'est pour prendre les occasions qui se présentent pour vous souhaiter le bon jour, que je vous écris ces lignes par le Maitre de Chapelle Sarti. C'est un très bon compositeur, dont je crois que vous serés fort content, au moins il a écrit des opera, buffe e serie, qui ont fait les délices de l'Italie et de l'Allemagne. Outre cela c'est un homme qui a vu et avec quel on peut causer. Je ne scais pas s'il plaira autant que Paisiello à l'Impératrice parcequ'il est un peu douceraux ...' [I, 478f.].

Joseph II actually had Paisiello's *La serva padrona* staged. Zinzendorf's Diary for 26 March 1786 relates '... à l'opéra La serva padrona, musique nouvelle de Paisiello au lieu de l'ancienne de Pergolese. Benucci et Storace jouèrent ...'. Zinzendorf preferred Sarti. Diary, 13 Aug. 1783, *re* Paisiello's *Il barbiere di Siviglia*: '... musique de Paisiello charmante, il y a des morceaux admirables ... L'Empereur fit repeter l'air du bachelier ... gioja e pace ... mais l'action de la pièce perd par la musique et l'opera des litiganti [Sarti, *Fra i due litiganti il terzo gode*] me plait toujours infiniment mieux', but Zinzendorf thought it much better when Paisiello himself conducted: 14 May 1784, 'Cet ópera a été beaucoup mieux rendu que l'année passée après remettant le presence de Paisiello y contribue ...'. In the *Berliner Literatur- und Theaterzeitung 1783* (p. 555), we read about Sarti's *Fra i due litiganti*, 'Never was an opera more generally successful, also the music is the finest [*trefflichsten*] that I ever heard.'

For the best side of Joseph II's multi-faceted nature, see his touching farewell to his theatre director Rosenberg written shortly before the Emperor's death (20 Feb. 1790) and quoted *in extenso* in R. P. von Thurn, *Joseph II als Theaterdirektor*, Vienna 1920, pp. 84f.

2 Quoted *in extenso* in *Haydn-Studien* III/2 (1974), pp. 100f.

in Eisenstatt but in Süttör [*sc.* Eszterháza] ... as from 1 January 779 ... and thus they are to receive nothing more in Eisenstatt, either in cash or *in natura*, nor substitute lodging money, but the Choir Musicians in Eisenstatt are to go on receiving their emoluments as found in their contracts. In view of his many years of service, I have decided to grant the already old and deaf Choir Musician Johann Hinterberger a pension for life instead of the previous contract, beginning on 1 January 779 with 250 f. in cash and 6 fathom cords of wood ... and the violinists Joseph Hofmann and Johann Dietzl, who are here, are to be granted an increase of 80 f. beginning on 1 January 779. I have decided to adjust the salaries of the violinist Joseph Dietzl in Eisenstatt and the singer Christian Specht here to be of the same cash value as that of singer Vitus Ungericht and have therefore ordered the Chief Cashier to pay to the first two no more than Ungericht receives, that is 300 f. annually in cash as of 1 January 779.

   ... Eszterház, 5th Dec. 778.

Your Willing
Nicolaus Fürst Esterhazy
[A.M. 4359, EH Budapest; *HJB* IV, 95f.]

Chronicle 1779

ITALIAN OPERAS 1779

Giovanni Paisiello: Le Due Contesse. Intermezzo per Musica. Da rappresentarsi Al Theatro D'Esterhaz La Primavera 1779. Vienna Presso Giuseppe Nob. de Kurzböck.

> La Contessina di Belcolore, la Siga. Catharina Poschwa.
> Il Cavalier della Piuma Vedovo, Viaggiatore ridicolo, il Sig. N. Totti.
> Livietta, Cameriera, che finge Contessina, la Sig. Mariana Zannini.
> Leandro, Gentiluomo, Amante della Contessina, che si vergogna d'esser geloso, il Sig. Bened. Bianchi.
> Prospero, Maestro di Casa della Contessa, Cugino di Livietta, il Sig. Leop. Dichtler.

Libretto: EH, Eisenstadt. Eszterháza performance material: EH, Budapest, Ms. Mus. OE–75 (score of Italian [Roman?] origin; Livietta's vocal part; orchestral parts by Joseph Elssler, Johann Schellinger and Anonymous 12) with transpositions, mostly downwards, to accommodate the local singers. First performance: March. Harich, *Musikgeschichte*, 42. Bartha-Somfai, 78, 204f.

Gennaro Astaritta:[1] I visionarj, dramma giocoso per musica. Da rapprensentarsi ne' teatri privilegiati di Vienna l'anno 1774. Presso Giuseppe Kurzböck, stampatore orient. di S. M. Imp. R. A.

Libretto: EH, Eisenstadt. The Eszterháza performance material is lost. In some cases, such as this one, Prince Nicolaus was able to take over a libretto already printed for an earlier Viennese performance. The princely financial section was always attempting to reduce costs of the operas, and suggested not printing the libretti; we have seen that the costumes and scenery were often used for more than one work. *I visionarj* was first given in March. Harich, *Musikgeschichte*, 42. Bartha-Somfai, 78. Horányi (English), 117.

Joseph Haydn: LA VERA COSTANZA / DRAMMA GIOCOSO PER MUSICA / DA RAPPRESENTARSI / AL TEATRO D'ESTERHAZ / LA PRIMAVERA / 1779. / [ornament] / VIENNA / Presso Giuseppe Nobile de Kurzböck.

Personaggi

LA BARONESSE IRENE, / Zia del Conte Amante d'Ernesto. *La Sig. Cath.* / *Poschwa.*
ROSINA, Pescatrice virtuosa e di spirito. *La Sig. Barbara* / *Ripamonti.*
CONTE ERRICO / Giovine volubile / e stravagante / sposo segreto / di Rosina. / *Il Sigr. No.* / *Totti.*
LISETTA, Cameriera della / Baronessa, Amante non / corrisposta di Masino. / *La Sig. Marianna Zannini.*
IL MARCHESE ERNESTO; / Amico del Conte. / *Il Sig. Vito* / *Ungricht.*
MASINO, Capo de Pescatori / fratello di Rosina. / *Il Sig. Leopoldo* / *Dichtler.*
VILLOTTO VILLANO, ricco / ma sciocco, destinato Sposo / di Rosina. / *Il Sig. Bened.* / *Bianchi.*

[For a facsimile of the original libretto, with its characteristic fan-like division of the 'personaggi', see pl. 22]

---

1 In Haydn's *Opernliste* of 1784: Guglielmi. Harich in *HJB* IX, 91f.

... La Poesia e del Sigr. Francesco Puttini. / La Musica e del Sigr. Giuseppe Hayden Maestro de Capella di S. A. il Prencipe. ... / Inventore, e Pittore delle Scene. / Il Sign. Pietro Travaglia alivo [*sic*] de Sign. Galliari.

Libretto: Gesellschaft der Musikfreunde. Eszterháza performance material: destroyed in the fire of 1779. See revival at Eszterháza, 1785, *infra*, p. 670. First performance (1779): April. Harich, *Musikgeschichte*, 42f. Bartha-Somfai, 79. Landon in *HJB* I, 131f. Horst Walter, Foreword to *La vera costanza, Joseph Haydn Werke* XXV/8 (1976).

Pasquale Anfossi: Metilde ritrovata. Dramma giocoso per musica. Da rappresentarsi nel teatro d'Esterhaz l'anno 1779. Oedenburgo, nella stamperia di Giuseppe Siess.

Il conte Asdrubale	Il Sigm. Andrea Totti.
Gianneta	La Sign. Barbara Ripamonti.
Il barone di Tarpano	Il Sign. Luigi Rossi.
Clarice	La Sign. Cathari. Poschwa.
Il conte Ernesto	Il Sign. Leopoldo Dichtler.
Nanina Cameriera	La Sign. Luigia Polzelli.
Fabricio Fattore	Il Sign. Antonio Pesci.

Libretto: Országos Széchenyi Könyvtár, Budapest Sign. 287725. The first performance of this work, better known as *L'incognita perseguitata*, took place in July and was the Eszterháza première of Luigia Polzelli (engaged in May). Eszterháza performance material: EH, Budapest (score and the orchestral parts, both from abroad, with many local corrections etc. by Haydn, copied by Joseph Elssler, Johann Schellinger and Anonymous 23). Haydn used the introduction, speeded up (*più presto*), as the conclusion to the Opera. Apart from the usual transpositions downwards, and some cuts and tempo accelerations ('Allegretto' to 'Allegro'), Haydn shortened a cadential formula (Atto II°, Sc. 8, Aria d'Ernesto), removed several arias (including one of Nanina's) but composed for the pretty new Italian soubrette a new Aria in Act I, 'Quando la rosa'. Harich, *Musikgeschichte*, 43f. Bartha-Somfai, 79f., 205–9 (facsimile of page one of 'Quando la rosa' as pl. 11; the whole Aria recorded on the accompanying gramophone record by Judith Sándor and the Staatliches Konzertorchester [Budapest], cond. Erwin Lukács, Qualiton LPM 1561). Aria 'Quando la rosa' (XXIVb:3) published by Haydn-Mozart Presse (Landon), score and parts, also piano score, 1961.

Giuseppe Gazzaniga: L'isola d'Alcina. Dramma giocoso per musica. Da rappresentarsi nel teatro d'Esterhaz. L'anno 1779. [Vienna, Kurzbeck.] Possibly Kurzbeck used the same plates as his printing of this libretto for the Vienna Opera in 1774 (copy: Budapest Sign. 207.005). The Eszterháza performance material was destroyed in the fire of November and had to be re-copied for the revival of 1786 (q.v.). Harich, *Musikgeschichte*, 43. Bartha-Somfai, 80, 132, 209.

Giuseppe Sarti: Le gelosie villane. Dramma giocoso per musica. Da rappresentarsi nel teatro d'Esterhaz l'anno 1779. Oedenburgo, nella stamperia di Giuseppe Siess.
Copy of libretto: formerly EH, Eisenstadt (at present mislaid). The following persons sang: Costanza Valdesturla (as Livietta: her first performance; she was engaged in July), Luigia Polzelli (as Sandrina), Barbara Ripamonti (as Giannina), Benedetto Bianchi (as Jaquino or Narduccio), Leopold Dichtler (as Jaquino or Narduccio), Andrea Totti (as Marchese), Antonio Pesci (role?) and Luigi Rossi (role?). The Eszterháza performance material for 1779 was destroyed in the fire and was re-copied for the 1780 revival (q.v.). Harich, *Musikgeschichte*, 43. Bartha-Somfai, 80, 89, 118, 209.

J. G. Naumann: La villanella incostante [Le nozze disturbate]. No textbook is known to have been printed; perhaps one for an earlier (Dresden?) performance was used. Of the cast, it is known that Barbara Ripamonti sang the role of Ninetta. Eszterháza performance material: EH, Budapest, Ms. Mus. OE–16 (only the score survived the fire), Haydn made the usual transpositions downwards, cuts (several arias) and other changes. Bartha-Somfai, 85, 217–9. Harich in *HJB* I, 20, and *HJB* VII, 7.

Franchi: Il finto cavalier Parigino.[1] No textbook is known to have been printed. No details of the cast are known. Eszterháza performance material: EH, Budapest, Ms. Mus. OE–88 (no score, vocal and orchestral parts). Harich in *HJB* I, 20, and *HJB* IX, 94 (item 21). Bartha-Somfai, 377, also 240.

Nicolà Piccinni: L'incognita perseguitata. Haydn's *Opernliste* of 1784 lists two versions of this Opera, one (as *Metilde ritrovata*) by Anfossi and another, under this title, by Piccin(n)i. The texts of both are identical. It is not certain if the Piccinni version, of which EH, Budapest (Ms. Mus. OE–28), owns a score of foreign (Viennese?) origin, was actually performed, since the EH sources confuse this work with

1 The composer is so listed in a princely order of 14 Sept. (*vide infra*, p. 416); in Haydn's *Opernliste* 1784 as Piccin(n)i. In the later Esterházy 'Inventare' as anonymous. In Bartha-Somfai as Monza because their only source (Sonneck) lists Monza as the composer of one such setting.

the one (using the alternative title) by Anfossi. Harich, *Musikgeschichte*, 44. Bartha-Somfai, 378, also 79f. Harich in *HJB* IX, 92, 94 (where the Piccinni version is listed among the works of the 1779 season; but in *HJB* I, 20f., it is not). We doubt if the Piccinni work was ever actually performed; to give two works with identical texts in one season would seem very unlikely.

Alessandro Felici: L'amore soldato. Dramma giocoso per musica. Da rappresentarsi in occasione delle nozze de Signori Conte Forgács, Contes. Ottila Grassalkovich. Nel teatro d'Esterhaz, l'anno 1779. – Oedenburgo, Nella stamperia di Giuseppe Siess.

Don Faustino Uffiziale	Il Sigr. Guglielmo Jermoli.
Ottavina, Figlia di D. Anselmo	La Signora Jermoli.
Don Anselmo, Vecchio Av[a]ro	Il Signore Benedetto Bianchi.
Lisandrina, Ortolana ...	La Signora Costanza Valdesturla
Semplicina, Nipote di D. Anselmo	La Sigra. Elisabetha Prandlerin.
Pasquino, Servitore.	Il Sigr. Leopoldo Dichtler.
... La Musica del celebre Maestro Antonio Sacchini.	

The libretto for this occasion (21 December) was ordered in 200 copies, but since the first performance was much earlier (in October), we wonder if there was not a first edition of the libretto which has not survived; a similar procedure obtained with Haydn's *L'infedeltà delusa* (July and September 1773). Copy: Országos Széchényi Könyvtár Sign. 209062. In Haydn's *Opernliste* 1784 under Piccin(n)i. Eszterháza performance material: 'L'amor soldato. Dramma giocoso ... del Sig. Alessandro Felici', EH, Budapest, Ms. Mus. OE–64. It is unclear why the libretto was printed as Sacchini and why Haydn remembered it as Piccinni. The EH material includes a score and orchestral parts, both from abroad. Haydn made the usual cuts (including whole arias), wrote a new recitative (Atto Iº, Sc. 5)[1] and rewrote other sections. One Aria (possibly an insertion by Haydn) was removed: Atto IIº, Sc. 8, 'Voi che forse in cor provate'. In the next scene, an aria was substituted for another and the second version later cut (but the first remained in the libretto); in Sc. 12, the score's aria is cut and the (different) aria of the textbook has not survived. There are similar discrepancies between score and libretto in the 'Scena ultima'. The curious differences between score and textbook suggest that the textbook may in fact be the Sacchini version and the MS. score the Felici, which differences, suggested Bartha-Somfai (213), 'may have been acknowledged by the Prince with a certain aristocratic nonchalance.' Harich, *Musikgeschichte*, 43f. Bartha-Somfai, 82f., 209–13. Harich in *HJB* I, 30f., and IX, 92.

In September, various operas were ordered for the princely archives, including Felici's *L'amore soldato* (Haydn: 'a 7 persone'), Guglielmi's *L'impresa dell'opera*, Colla's *La pupilla ed il ciarlone*, Michel's *Il rè alla caccia*, Sarti's *La giardiniera brillante*, Franchi's *Il parigino finto* and Piccin(n)i's *L'americano* and *Gli stravaganti*.[2]

Using Haydn's *Opernliste* and the various catalogues, it has been suggested that Michel's *Il rè alla caccia* (no libretto; Eszterháza performance material in EH, Budapest, Ms. Mus. OE–71) and the following work were first given in 1779: Piccinni's *La schiava riconosciuta (Gli stravaganti)*,[3] but at present we can find no concrete evidence for either in that year. We have archive material showing that Piccinni's work was performed there in 1781, and the Piccinni Opera is discussed at that point in this biography (*vide infra*, p. 438). There are no printed libretti for (1) Guglielmi's *L'impresa dell'opera*, but the performance material ordered for Eszterháza has survived: EH, Budapest, Ms. Mus. OE–65 (apparently from Dresden

1 In the EH score, Sc. 5 is Sc. 4 of the libretto. Pasquino's Aria, 'Bella cosa è il comandare', was cut and a new one substituted. The score of it is missing, but the parts show the *incipit*. The tempo Andante was crossed out and 'Allo' (Allegro) added in red crayon:

2 Commissions-Protocoll No. 29, 14 Sept. 1779, and Secretariats-Protocoll, Band 1780, EH Eisenstadt. *HJB* I, 31, and IX, 117n.
3 Harich in *HJB* IX, 90, items 31 and 00, also 94, item 29 (where the Piccinni work is, however, not given. See also Bartha-Somfai, 94, and Harich in *HJB* I, 36f.

and used by the Koberwein Company: Bartha-Somfai, 375);[1] (2) Colla's *La pupilla ed il ciarlone*, where the EH material (also from Dresden?) has survived: Ms. Mus. OE–101. See Bartha-Somfai, 378 (wrong composer), and Harich in *HJB* IX, 91. In Haydn's *Opernliste* 1784 as Astaritta; (3) Sarti's *La giardiniera brillante*, possibly in rehearsal in November 1779, seems to have perished in the fire. It may be also possible that these three operas, as well as Michel's *Il rè alla caccia* and Piccinni's *La schiava riconosciuta* were in an advanced state of rehearsal when they were partially destroyed in the conflagration, and later only partially replaced.

Of works from earlier seasons, Anfossi's *Il geloso in cimento* (première 1778) and Paisiello's *La Frascatana* (premiere 1777) were also performed during the 1779 season.[2]

Presumably the final work of the 1779 was:

Joseph Haydn: L'ISOLA / DISABITATA / azione teatrale / in due parti / per musica / del celebre signor / abbate / pietro metastasio / poeta cesareo / da rappressentarsi [*sic*] in occasione del gloriosissimo nome di S. A. il principe / nicolo Esterhazi / di Galantha / l'anno 1779 / ————— / Oedenburgo, nella stamperia di giussepe [*sic*] Siess.

La Musica è del Sigr. Giuseppe Haydn . . .

PERSONAGGI

COSTANZA, moglie di Gernando	Sigra. *Barbara Ripamonti*.
SILVIA, sua minor sorella	Sigra. *Luigia Polzelli*.
GERNANDO, consorte di Costanza	Sig. *Andrea Totti*.
ENRICO, compagno di Gernando	Sig. *Benedetto Bianchi*.

Copy of libretto: Gesellschaft der Musikfreunde, 7992 Textbuch. First performance: 6 December (there were repetitions in that same month). The Eszterháza performance material of 1779 has disappeared; the final Quartet, 'Sono contento', a score by Anonymous 23, came from Haydn's library

1 We cannot agree with Bartha-Somfai that this Opera was not performed at Eszterháza. Since they have not dealt with the insertions, we propose to do so here, using our notes of December 1958. Atto IIo, Scena VII (No. 3 of the EH score). The Conte's Aria was written once more, using the original words. The orchestral parts are there, too.

With its rapid six-eight conclusion, this Arìa might well be by Haydn. Atto IIo, Sc. IX (No. 4 of the EH score), the Aria di Tortorella is preceded by a new secco using the original libretto's words and a new Aria, over which Haydn wrote, in red crayon, 'Ex G'. The Aria text is *not* in the original score:

Perhaps Tortorella was sung by Polzelli; the style of the new Aria is very like many of the new 'insertion' arias which Haydn composed for her. Atto IIo, No. 6, Aria di Bottacino. Guglielmi's Aria had the text, 'Forte, spirito, del foco'. The new Aria is as follows:

The orchestral parts are still there. The use of *mf* and other stylistic factors make it unlikely that Haydn composed this Aria.

2 Harich in *HJB* I, 20f.

and may have been part of the conductor's score such as we know from other Haydn operas (*La fedeltà premiata*): Anon. 23 made other copies in the year 1779, e.g. Anfossi's *Metilde ritrovata* and Haydn's Symphony No. 75.

Vide infra, p. 534, for the authentic musical sources of *L'isola disabitata*, Harich, *Musikgeschichte*, 45f. Bartha-Somfai, 83, 214.

GERMAN MARIONETTE OPERA 1779

Joseph Haydn: Die / bestrafte Rachbegierde, / ein / Singspiel / in drey Aufzügen / von / P. G. B. [Bader] / ———— / Aufgeführt / zu / Esterhatz [*sic*] / auf der / Hochfürstlichen Marionettenbühne, / im Jahre / 1779.

Libretto: printed by Siess in Oedenburg in August 1779 and bound by the Oedenburger bookbinder Fischer; Siess's bill of 25 August. Copy: Music Library, University of California, Los Angeles. The music was apparently destroyed in the fire. Landon in *HJB* I, 187ff. (with first lines), facsimile of the libretto's title page on p. 143.

THE GERMAN THEATRICAL TROUPE 1779

[Gotha *Theater-Kalender* . . . *1780*, p. 234:]

The Diwald Company

Residence: Esterhazy [*sic*]. Principal, H. Diwald. Actresses: Madam Diwald, leading lady in comedies and tragedies, young and naïve roles. Mams. Knapp, second heroines in comedies and tragedies. Mams. Diwald, secondary roles. Mad. Schwarzwald, tender mothers, highly comical women. Mamsell Schwarzwald, young, gentle and naive roles. Actors: Hr. Diwald, petulant old ladies in tragedies, comic & nagging old ladies in comedies, servants, peasants and low comedy roles. H. Dunst, second gentle lovers and young heroes. H. König Sen., gentle fathers, soldiers. H. König Jr., lesser lovers and servant roles. H. Kirchmeyer, also acts occasionally in secondary roles. H. Morocz, old women and serious roles. H. Münzenberger, prompter, also occasionally plays pedants. H. Partl, leading gentle fathers and serious roles. H. Schilling, leading lovers, young heroes and comic roles. H. Schwarzwald, pedants, old and serious servants. H. H. Suttor, Hipfel, secondary roles. H. Weiß, angry lovers and servants. Music director, Hr. Hayden, fürstl. Esterhazischer Kapellmeister.

Franz Diwald's contract for the 1779 season was signed in November 1778. He agreed to present a play daily but also to supply actors and actresses for reading roles in the marionette theatre, and the period was from Ash Wednesday and 18 October; but in another copy of the contract (A.T. 37) for 1779, the Troupe agreed to remain until 18 December. In the intervening months Diwald and his players went to Oedenburg and Wiener Neustadt.[1] We have no list of the plays given for the 1779 season.

This year the bassoon player and kettledrummer Caspar Peczival was in Vienna on New Year's Day to collect the bassoon reeds for Eszterháza.[2] On that same day, Haydn received his new contract with Prince Esterházy, the details of which have been communicated *supra* (pp. 42f.).

At the beginning of February, Haydn was impelled to write the following letter to the Tonkünstler-Societät:

[To Thaddäus Huber, Secretary of the Tonkünstler-Societät in Vienna. *German*]

Estoras, 4th February 1779.

Nobly born,
Most highly respected Sir!

It was with considerable astonishment that I read through your letter of 18th January 1779,[3] and also the declaration appended to the end thereof (which I am

1 Horányi, 116f.

2 'Receipt. For three dozen bassoon reeds which Herr Caspar Petzyval, bassoon player, paid for in cash per 6 Fl. . . . J. Pauer . . . Vienna, 1 Jan. 1779', countersigned by Haydn. A.M. Fasc. XVI.1040. Valkó II, 587.

3 The circumstances of this letter are briefly explained as follows. In 1775, Haydn had written the oratorio, *Il ritorno di Tobia*, which was performed at one of the benefit concerts of the Tonkünstler-Societät. Most of Vienna's finest musicians belonged to the Society, and Haydn naturally wished to join. In the session of 18 November 1778 Haydn's petition was considered, and in view of his previous services to the Society, 'but mainly because of the services he is to perform in future (he is to submit a declaration to that effect)', his petition was approved. The Society added the clause that 'the demands for services to be rendered as per the enclosed declaration shall never be indiscreet', and this clause with the use of the word 'indiscreet' seems to have infuriated Haydn (with some justification). The real point, however, was that most of Haydn's bitterest enemies were members of the Society – a fact which the 'foreigner' (i.e. non-resident of Vienna) felt very strongly. But because he was a non-resident, he would have been required to pay a reduced entrance fee (see end of the letter). See *Haydn: the Years of 'The Creation' 1796–1800*, p. 246, for the happy end of this episode. See Pohl, I, 84.

supposed to sign and return), in default of which I am threatened with the immediate cancellation of my admission – THOUGH THIS IS ALREADY AN ACCOMPLISHED FACT; for the fact that the worthy Society admits me only under the proviso that I shall compose oratorios, cantatas, choruses, symphonies, etc., as they require, flatly contradicts the circumstances of the session wherein my admission was considered. In the presence of *Herr Kapellmeister* von Bonno,[1] Herr von Starzer,[2] and the other honourable men, I directly protested against such a binding and obligatory declaration, for the following obvious reason: to satisfy a demand of this extraordinary kind would require two or three months every year, and therefore I should be unable to fulfil the duties required by my gracious Prince and Lord. But provided a clause reading 'if time and circumstances permit me' were added, I agreed gladly to sign this declaration with all the demands enumerated above. Whereupon this my proposal was unanimously accepted, and my admission approved. In order to validate my admission, I was ordered to deposit on the spot the sum of 368 fl. 10 kr., in the presence of the assembled company, for it was particularly explained to me that as soon as the money was deposited, my admission would become valid. I deposited the money, and was thereupon admitted WITHOUT any such declaration. – I was congratulated. – I expressed, in all humility, many thanks for my admission. Of course, in matters of this kind, the whole affair should have been entered into the protocol by the duly authorized notary, and a declaration of this admission as an accomplished fact presented to the newly admitted member; but a worthy Society has not yet seen fit to do so in my case. Moreover:—

This clause, with the so-called DISCREET demands, depends in my opinion wholly on the fancy, or the envy, of some of the members; in time it might depend largely on those who have the least possible insight into the art of composition, for they could judge as DISCREET that which is INDISCREET (for instance, a whole oratorio instead of a few symphonies). I should be forced to compose the most DISCREET oratorios *in plurali* as a result of the INDISCRETION which they consider their right; and if not, the majority of the *vota* – purely out of DISCRETION, of course – would demand my suspension *sine jure* (just as is now threatened). Why? Perhaps because I, freely and without any gain to myself, have provided the worthy Society with many good services and useful advantages? Perhaps because I am a 'foreigner'?[3] In my case, the 'foreign' means only that my person is of no use to the aborigines [*Inwärtigen*]: through my works I'm quite aboriginal enough, and if not the composer, oh well, his children are there in almost every concert and provide many nice advantages.

Now, my good friend! I am a man of too much sensitivity to permit me to live constantly in the fear of being quashed: the fine arts, and such a wonderful science as that of composition allow no gyves on their handicraft: the heart and soul must be free if they are to serve the widows[4] and collect profits. One more thing:—

This generous provision of 300 fl. I regard as a well deserved reparation for the 1,000 fl. which the Society made on my *Ritorno di Tobia*, especially written for them free of charge. God the all-wise Provider of us all will also protect me and my wife, through my most gracious Prince and Lord, especially since I am convinced that even the least of persons in the Princely Esterházy house has received an adequate pension. Therefore, on the 15th inst., Herr von Kleinrath,

1 Giuseppe Bonno (1710–88) was Court *Kapellmeister* in Vienna.
2 Joseph Starzer (1726–87) was a well-known composer of the time; his ballets were especially highly thought of. Burney heard him play first violin (together with Carlos d'Ordoñez, Count Brühl and Weigl) in some Haydn quartets, given at the English Ambassador's house in Vienna. See *The Present State of Music in Germany, etc.*, London 1773, I, p. 290.
3 'Auswärtiger', i.e. a non-resident of Vienna.
4 Of the composers – it was for their benefit that the Society existed.

Princely Esterházy Inspector, will appear in my name, and to him the worthy Society will repay my 368 fl. 10 kr. in cash.

For my part, however, despite such a crude and threatening treatment, I shall 'if time and circumstances so permit' compose various new pieces for the widows at no cost. I remain, Sir, with due respect,

> Your obedient servant,
> Josephus Haydn, m.p.
> *Kapell-Meister.*

> [CCLN, 22f.]

In March, the violinist Antonio Polzelli and his nineteen-year-old soprano wife, Luigia, were engaged; she was to become Haydn's mistress and he was probably the father of her son, Alois Anton Nikolaus ('Antonio'). Her presence can hardly have contributed to the stability of Haydn's already shaky marriage.

We have the following contemporary description of the fire at Eszterháza from the *Preßburger Zeitung*:

Wednesday, 24 November 1779.

From Eszterház we receive the unpleasant news that last Thursday the 18th at 3:30 a.m. a dreadful fire broke out in the world-famous Chinese ball-room, which because of its magnificence, taste and comfort was so admired by all visitors. As a result, the adjoining water works with the tower, and the theatre, which was so excellently appointed and which contained not only a grand box for the Prince but also two comfortable side-boxes for the other guests, were entirely destroyed. The fire was dreadful to behold and glowed now and again the next day, because the ball-room was mostly painted with varnish and in the theatre was stored a large quantity of wax lights. The fire must have burned in the roof for some hours, because the whole of the valuable roof was in flames, and also the beautiful walls were almost consumed by the time the fire was discovered. – The origin of this unexpected occurrence was as follows: as is well known, the 21st inst. was the day set for the exalted marriage of Count Forgátsch with the noble Countess Miss Graschalkowitz. For this celebration the stoves in the ball-room were to be previously lit. There were also two Chinese stoves therein which were more for show than for actual use. They were neverthless lit despite all previous warnings. They probably exploded from the heat and thus the fire spread. It would have spread even further if not for the wise order to remove the roofs of the nearby buildings, and for the fact that heavy rains and strong winds lessened the fire's effect and finally extinguished it. The damage, according to several eye-witnesses, is estimated to be more than 100,000 gulden. Two beautiful clocks; the magnificent theatrical costumes; all the music collected at great effort and expense; the musical instruments, including the beautiful harpsichord [*Flieg*] of the famous *Kapellmeister* Haiden [*sic*] and the concert violin of the virtuoso Lotsch [Luigi Tomasini] – all were lost to the flames, which reached their height at 8:00 a.m. His Highness the Prince, despite the inclement weather, was at once present at a time when a speedy rescue seemed distant.

Since various high persons had already arrived for the festivities, a brand new opera [*L'amore soldato*] was given in the marionette theatre on the 21st.

Haydn lost many works in this fire – certainly all the marionette operas except *Philemon und Baucis* and *Die Feuersbrunst*, and all the performance material of the Italian operas up to *L'isola disabitata*: the fragments of the autographs that have survived were probably by pure accident in Haydn's rooms (*Acide, La canterina, Lo speziale, Le pescatrici, L'infedeltà delusa, L'incontro improvviso, Il mondo della luna*). The material for

L'isola disabitata was obviously in Haydn's rooms for revision: otherwise there would have been no première on 6 December. We shall discuss the problem of *La vera costanza* later. It seems, moreover, that the orchestral parts of all Haydn's Esterházy symphonies (1761–November 1779) also perished in the fire.

The opera troupe moved into the marionette theatre and the marionette theatre – its activity was sharply diminished in any case by the absence of Pauersbach – moved into the pavilion in the garden.[1]

The Prince was not a man to allow even a holocaust to interrupt his theatrical activities, and on 18 December – a month after the fire – the ceremony of laying the foundation stone of the new theatre, to be constructed from plans by Michael Stöger, was performed.[2] To celebrate this event, Haydn completed a very original Symphony – No. 70 in D – of which the parts, by Joseph Elssler and other copyists, are entitled '779 die 18te Xbris / Sinfonia'. It contains a sombre and beautiful 'Specie d'un canone in contrapunto doppio' for its second movement and a fantastic triple fugue ('a 3 Soggetti in contrapunto doppio') which is itself a miniature programmatic reference to the fire: it begins in D minor and is a terrifying evocation of the raging flames, but it concludes in D major and obviously refers to the happy event for which it was composed.

On 23 December, Leopold Dichtler submitted his bill for re-copying *L'amore soldato*,[3] which seems to have been partially destroyed in the fire.

We may conclude the year with two interesting references to Haydn, one from England and one from Spain. The English source is a MS. score of Haydn's Symphony No. 47, owned by Mr Albi Rosenthal of London and Oxford, who kindly supplied the following information about it:[4]

Sinfonia

a 8

Par

Giuseppe Haydn

1779

[36 pages of music in folio. On the cover: 'Bought in the sale of the Rev. J. Holland Rector of Stanton St. John, Alfrid[?]. Holland was son of Canon Holland (W.) of Chichester who was a prominent member of Almac[k]'s, where Haydn was entertained & welcomed when he entered London in 1790 [*sic*]. Canon Holland made his acquaintance in Vienna where the MS. was written with another when made Member of a Philharmonic Society & when the King of Spain presented him with a gold snuff box.']

The reference to Spain comes from a poem by the well-known Don Tomas de Yriarte:[5]

---

1 Harich in *HJB* II, 39.

2 A.M. 3983; Horányi, 124.

3 'Copiatur ... for organizing a brand new score and the study[!] parts. [104 *Bögen* score, 141 *Bögen* parts] Suma der Bögen 245. The Bogen at 5 means 20 f. 25 Xr.' Nicolaus himself ordered the bill to be paid by the Süttör Administration, 'Eszterház den 23ten Xbr 779'. Commissions-Protocoll 1779, Nr. 79. EH Eisenstadt, *HJB* VII, 160.

4 Letter of 29 December 1959.

5 *La Musica, poema por D. Thomas de Yriarte, con superior permisso: en Madrid en la Imperenta Real de la Fazete, 1779.* Third edition 1789, translations into: French ('La Musique, poëme, traduit par J. B. C. Grainville, et acc. de notes par Langlé. Paris, an VIII'); English ('Music, a didactic Poem, translated by John Belfour. London 1807'); and Italian ('La Musica, poema, tradotto da Gius. Carlo de Ghisi. Firenze, 1868.'). Pohl II, 179f. The original Spanish print has six engravings and consists of five parts; Haydn occurs in the fifth part, which is in praise of German instrumental music.

Sólo á tu númen, Háyden prodigioso
Las Musas concedieron esta gracia
De ser tan nuevo siempre, y tan copioso,
Que la curiosidad nunca se sacia
De tus obras mil veces repetidas.
Antes séran los hombres insensibles
Del canto á los hechizos apacibles,
Que dexen de aplaudir las escogidas
Cláusulas, la expresion, y la nobleza
De tu modulacion, ó la estra ñeza
De tus doctas y harmónicas salidas.
Y aunque á tu lado en esta edad numeras
Tantos y tan famosos Compatriotas.
Tú solo por la Música pudieras
Dar entre las naciones
Vecinas, ó remotas
Honor á las Germánicas regiones.
Tiempo há que en sus privadas Academias
Madrid á tus escritos se aficiona,
Y tú amor con tu enseñanza premias;
Miéntras él cada dia
Con la immortal encina te corona
Que en sus orillas Manzanáres cria.

Chronicle 1780

ITALIAN OPERAS 1780

Ninety-three performances are known to have been given in this season (Harich, *HJB* I, 33).

Pasquale Anfossi: La forza delle donne. Dram[m]a giocoso per musica. Da Rappresentarsi nell teatro d'Esterhaz nella primavera l'anno 1780. Oedenburgo nella stamperia di Giusep[p]e Siess.

Ogus, Principe	Il Sigr. Jermoli.
Clizia, damigella della Principessa	La Sigra. Valdesturla.
Egle, Principessa di Ginopoli	La Sigra. Luigia Polzelli.
Barbarina, Contadina	La Sigra. Jermolli.
Tiziano, Custode degli amanti	Il Sigr. Leopoldo Dichtler.
Timur, capitano d'Ogus	Il Sigr. Pesci.
[Arabachir, sacerdote indovino]	[Leopoldo Dichtler].
[Ufficiale d'Ogus]	[Guglielmo Jermoli].
Marone, adjutante	Il Sigr. Bianchi.

Libretto: 200 copies printed; copy: EH, Eisenstadt. First performance: 17 February, repeated (31 performances) until October. A large number of 'supers' were required: two decorators, two or three decorators' assistants, sixteen Grenadiers, two boys and three girls. Eszterháza performance material: EH, Budapest, Ms. Mus. OE–100 (incomplete vocal parts, orchestral parts, the former by Joseph Elssler and Johann Schellinger, the latter ordered from Italy). Haydn made transpositions downwards, simplifications (for 'Signora Jermoli', e.g. Atto I°, No. 3) and added one Aria (his own?) in A major (no text available) in Atto I°, radically changed one Aria for Polzelli ('Se provasse un pocolino') at the outset of Atto II° and added a large scene (his own? 'Ma dimmi almen tiranno') in E flat during Atto II°. Since the score is missing, which would have contained Haydn's autograph(s), we cannot determine Haydn's authorship. Concerning the Aria for Polzelli, to which Haydn added flutes, oboes and horns, *vide infra*, pp. 648, 684 for 'Vada adagio' (with similar *incipit*). Harich, *Musikgeschichte*, 46f. Bartha-Şomfai, 84f., 214–7. Harich in *HJB* I, 26f.

Giuseppe Gazzaniga: La vendemmia. Dramma giocoso per musica. Da rappresentarsi nel teatro d'Esterhaz. Nella primavera l'anno 1780. Oedenburgo, nella stamperia di Giuseppe Siess.

Agatina, Pastorella	Mad. Jermoli.
Artemisia	Mad. Polzelli.
Lauretta, cameriera	Mlle. Prantner.
Don Achilles, Marchese	Mons. Jermoli.
Conte Zephyro	Mr. Bianchi.
Cardone	Mr. Peschi.
Don Faustino	Mr. Dichtler.[1]

Libretto: 200 copies printed; copy: EH, Eisenstadt. First performance: 27 April, repeated (9 times) until November and also in 1781. Eszterháza performance material: EH, Budapest, Ms. Mus. OE–20 (score and parts, both of Italian origin). Haydn made the following changes: transpositions downwards (in one case, Atto I°, Sc. 3 from B flat to F, no less), cuts (considerable), adding of numbers (Atto I°, Sc. 12, Aria di Cardone 'Hò tanto, tanto collera', also used in Piccinni's *Enea in Cuma* [Ms. Mus. OE–79] and probably not by Haydn; Atto I°, Sc. 14, Aria in D [no text extant]; Atto II°, Sc. 5, Haydn cut the second part of Gazzaniga's Aria 'Ah crudel' and replaced it with his own *Presto* on a new text, 'agl'a monti, al colle, al prato'; published [Landon] in Haydn-Mozart Presse [XXXIc:5, HMP 112–3, 1961]; the orchestral material for this Aria was written by Haydn himself[!], Joseph Elssler and Johann Schellinger; for the Aria 'Hò tanto, tanto collera' by Anonymous 27 and Schellinger; for that in D by Anonymous 28 and Elssler); and Haydn made other, smaller changes as well. Harich, *Musikgeschichte*, 47. Bartha-Somfai, 85f., 219–23, facsimile of page one of Haydn's completion, 'agl'a monti' as No. 12. Harich in *HJB* I, 27f.

Antonio Salieri: La scuola de' gelosi. Dramma giocoso per musica da rappresentarsi nel teatro d'Esterhaz nell'estate l'anno 1780. Oedenburgo, nella stamperia di Giuseppe Siess.

[Cast from a costume proposal:]

La Contessa, moglie del Conte	Mad. Jermoli
Il Conte di Bandiera, marito moderno sposo della Contessa	Mr. Totti
Ernestina, moglie di Blasio, annojata dalla gelosia del marito	Mlle Valdesturla
Blasio, biandainolo marito geloso di Ernestina	Mr. Peschi
Carlotta, cameriera prima di Ernestina, poi cameriera della Contessa...	Mad. Polzelli
Il Tenente, uomo di spirito, amico del Conte, cugino di Blasio	Mr. Dichtler
Lumaca, servitore di Blasio, amante di Carlotta	Mr. Rossi

Libretto: 200 copies ordered (none has survived). First performance: 27 July, repeated (13 times) until November and also in 1781 (10 times).[2] Eszterháza performance material: EH, Budapest, Ms. Mus. OE–9 (score and parts, both probably from Trieste). Haydn made several important changes and additions. Atto I°, Sc. 1: Aria di Carlotta (= Polzelli); Haydn added oboes and horns and rewrote substantial passages; facsimile of one page as No. 13 in Bartha-Somfai; later he transposed the whole Aria up one note; the parts are by Haydn himself(!) and Joseph Elssler; Haydn rewrote the oboe parts when transposing the work to B flat (see facsimile 14 in Bartha-Somfai). Atto II°, Sc. 1. Haydn composed (adapted?) a new insertion Aria for Polzelli, probably using Salieri's original text 'Il cor nel seno'. The parts are by Joseph Elssler, the score in part by Johann Schellinger. Sc. 2. Haydn composed a new Aria for Lumaca (= Rossi), 'Dice benissimo'. The parts were copied by Joseph Elssler and there is, curiously, also a score by Lorenz Lausch, a Viennese copyist, in EH (Ms. Mus. I. 156) which is from Haydn's library. The piece (XXIVb:5) was published by Johann Traeg in 1802 (piano score) and reprinted by Breitkopf & Härtel in 1806. New edition (Landon), Haydn-Mozart Presse 104–5, 1964. Sc. 3 uses, in EH, a printed score (Antonio Palmini, Venice) of Salieri's Duet 'Quel visino è da ritratto'). There are the usual cuts and transpositions by Haydn. There are some Haydn sketches on spare pages, also for the Lied 'Trauergesang' (printed in 1783): Bartha-Somfai 228f. Harich, *Musikgeschichte*, 47. Bartha-Somfai, 86f., 223–9. Harich in *HJB* I, 28f.

---

1 From the costume proposal of 16 April, A.M. 4025. The actual libretto reads as follows:

Agatina, creduta Pastorella	La Sigra Jermoli
Il Conte Zeffiro, Adulatore, e scroccone	Il Sigr. Bianchi
D. Achille Marchese di Pioggio Antico Amante d'Agatina	Il Sigr. Jermoli
D. Artemisia creduta Dama	La Sigra Polzelli
Cardone Affittuario del Villagio, Amante D. Agatina	Il Sigr. Pesci
Lauretta Cameriera di S. Artamisia [*sic*]	La Sigra Prandner
Pancoto Padre di Agatina [dumb role]	
Agrestone Zio della sudetta [dumb role]	
D. Fausto Amante di D. Artemisia	Il Sigr. Dichtler

2 When Teresa Tavecchia sang La Contessa.

Pasquale Anfossi: La finta giardiniera. Dramma giocoso per musica. Da rappresentarsi nel teatro d'Esterház. L'autunno dell'anno 1780. Oedenburgo, nella stamperia di Giuseppe Siess.

La Marchesa Violante, sotto nome di Sandrina	La Sigra. Teresa Taveggia.
Il Contino Belfiore...	Il Sigr. Totti.
Arminda, Dama Milanese	Sigra. Polzelli.
Il Cavalier Ramiro	Sigr. Dichtler.
Roberto, Servo di Violante sotto nome di Dardo [*sc.* Nardo]	Il Sigr. Rossi.
Serpetta, Cameriera	Sigra. Valdesturla.
D. Anchise Podesta	Il Sigr. Bianchi.[1]

Libretto: 200 copies. Copy: Országos Széchényi Könyvtár. First performance: 29 October, repeated (four times) in October and November, As 'supers' there were two girls, three boys, five Grenadiers and three assistants. Eszterháza performance material: EH, Budapest, Ms. Mus. OE–41 (score and parts, both apparently of Italian origin). Haydn's changes include many changes in Polzelli's role (Arminda). Atto I°, Sc. 4, Haydn added a new Aria, using Anfossi's text, 'Noi donne poverine', for Sandrina: E flat, Largo and Allegro assai. The parts are by Joseph Elssler. The use of *sf* (rather than Haydn's usual *fz*) and the extended divisi violas suggest that Haydn was not the composer. Sc. 7, Haydn transposed Polzelli's Aria, 'Si promette facilmente', from A to G, added oboes and horns and even changed Anfossi's melody, made cuts (127 bars' original, 82 in Haydn's version); the parts were copied by Johann Schellinger. The melodic change is as follows:

Sc. 9. Haydn replaced Serpetta's Aria 'Appena mi vedon' with another, from Naumann's *Le nozze disturbate* (where it was a Cavatina of Ninetta, 'La donna a bella rosa si assomiglia'), transposed from B flat to G. This insertion is not in the Esterházy libretto. Atto II°, Sc. 2, Polzelli's Aria, 'Vorrei punirti' was rewritten by Haydn, the melody changed, many dynamic marks added and also oboes and horns added by Haydn himself in the parts. It would seem quite clear that she was by now Haydn's mistress. Sc. 6, Schellinger added a bassoon part (probably at Haydn's oral instigation. Atto III°, Scena ultima: this final chorus was added (by Haydn?) and the short score is written by Schellinger and signed 'Fine (780)':

Apart from these larger changes, there are also the usual cuts, transpositions, etc. Harich, *Musikgeschichte*, 47f. Bartha-Somfai, 87, 229–33. Harich in *HJB* I, 29f.

Four operas from earlier seasons were repeated:
Felici's *L'amore soldato*: March (two performances), July (one).
Haydn's *L'isola disabitata*: Sunday, 12 March. The disappearance of this new work from the boards is in direct connection with the dismissal of Haydn's *prima donna*, Barbara Ripamonti, on 10 April; she was obviously irreplaceable.

1 Costume proposal of 2 October (A.M. 4005) in Harich *Musikgeschichte*, 48: 'Tavecchia', 'Armina' (not 'Arminda'), 'Ramire' (not 'Ramiro').

Gassmann's *L'amore artigiano*: May (three performances), June (five), July (three), August (two), September (one) and October (one). The Prince was especially attached to this Opera, and after his wife's death in 1790, Haydn repeated it (q.v.).

Sarti's *Le gelosie villane*: June (five), July (two), August (two), September (two), October (three), November (three), also in 1781 and 1784. Harich in *HJB* I, 30ff. Eszterháza performance material was newly copied for the 1780 reprise by Joseph Elssler, Johann Schellinger and Anonymous 23, 30, 31, 32, 33. Apart from the usual cuts and transpositions, Haydn made the following large-scale changes: in Atto II°, Sc. 3, he replaced Sandrina's (Polzelli's) Aria 'Se volessi far l'amore' with a Rondo in A of which only Elssler's bass part has survived; for the 1784 revival yet another Aria was substituted (q.v.); Atto III°, Scena ultima, was revised and greatly shortened. Bartha-Somfai, 234–7.

GERMAN MARIONETTE OPERA 1780
[no records of any performances known]

THE GERMAN THEATRICAL TROUPE 1780
[Gotha *Theater-Kalender* 1781, pp. CLI, CLII:]

Residence: Esterhazy [*sic*]. Principal, H. Diwald. Actresses: Mad. Diwald [etc., as in 1780 Gotha]. Madam Kettner, second heroines in comedies and tragedies. Mams. Diwald [as before]. Mad. Schwarzwald [as before]. Mamsell Schwarzwald [as before]. Actors: Hr. Diwald [as before]. H. Dunst [as before]. H. König Sen. [as before]. H. König Jr. [as before]. H. Kirchmeyer [as before]. H. Morocz [as before]. H. Münzenberger [as before]. H. Partl [as before]. H. Schilling [as before]. H. Schwarzwald [as before]. H. H. Suttor, Hipfel [as before]. H. Weiß [as before]. H. Walter, petulant old ladies, also some serious lovers. Music director, H. Hayden, fürstl. Esterhazischer Kapellmeister. Note: Prince Esterhazy, a protector and friend of the Arts, had the opera house, destroyed by fire, rebuilt in a much finer and more costly fashion, and it was opened on 15 October – the name-day of the Late Empress – with the tragedy, Julius von Tarent [Johann Anton Leisewitz], and a prologue especially written for the occasion, performed by this company.[1]

On 15 March a contract was made with a second theatrical company, Franz Merschy (Mörisch) and his Children's Troupe, according to which Merschy promised to add two new members to his group of seven children and to give comedies, tragedies, *Musikspielen* (whatever they were) and pantomime or ballet. He also agreed to supply the musical accompaniment (which is odd), to provide for pleasing costumes and to write a pantomime. For his services he received twenty-five gulden weekly, [2]up to 31 December.

The intense activity occasioned by the rebuilding of the Eszterháza opera house seems to have required Haydn's presence by the middle of January. Instead of settling the bills in Vienna himself, Haydn wrote the following

Specification

for the necessary strings, *viz.*

4 bundles E	
2 bundles A	for the violin
1 bundle D	
12-G	

For the viola
4-G, and 4-C.

---

1 It will be seen that the Theatre was not ready by 15 October. The report must have been sent off before that date, but it is curious that the Empress is referred to as 'late' (*I. W.* = Ihre Weiland], because she did not die until 29 November 1780: perhaps the 'I.W.' was added by the Gotha editor. The 'Prolog zum Julius von Tarent, im Character des Julius: für ein gesellschaftliches Theater' is contained in the Gotha *Kalender* of 1781 but has been omitted here as being a little too peripheral for this Chronicle. 'Mad. Kettner' was 'Mamsell Knapp' in the 1779 list; she married a Joseph Klettner(!) at Eszterháza in 1780. *HJB* III, 135.

2 Horányi, German, p. 132; English, p. 128. The Children's Troupe cost the Prince nearly 1,000 gulden, Diwald's more than 5,000. Harich in *HJB* II, 25f.

> For the violoncello
> 6-A.
> 4-D.
> 2-C.
> 3-G.

For the violon [double bass]
2-A and a covered A
two ordinary violon bows

6 violon bridges, 6 violin pegs, 2 viola bridges, 2 viola pegs, two ordinary violin bows, 2 boxes of resin, 18 bassoon reeds.

6 books of oblong Italian music paper with 10 staves

> Josephus Haydn mpria Capell Meister.

In the absence of H. Highn. The Prince . . . [another hand:] passed for payment by the General Cassa . . . Stephan Nagy *Regent*.
Esterház, 15th January 1780.
> [A.M. XVII.1132. Valkó II, 598f. (with wrong date: '1783'). *HJB* III, 149.]

The principal activity, then, was the construction of the new theatre. The Prince ordered his building engineer, Michael Stöger, and his architect, Paul Guba, to start on the new opera house, which was to open on 15 October. We can follow the building's progress in the 'Extract über die bey dem neuen Comaedi Haus verrichten Mauer Arbeit 1780'. Although *Ingenieur* Stöger was to submit the new plans, in fact Court Master-Carpenter Augustin Haunold, who had done most of the exquisite interior work in Eszterháza, proved to have the better idea, which the Prince accepted.[1] In the actual construction, a sort of race between Haunold and Stöger developed, each stealing the other's ideas, so that in the end no one knew which ideas were whose. In any event, this dispute slowed up the work. The façade had to be changed (this was Haunold's plan) according to that of the famous Schönbrunn Court Theatre, and most of the doors and windows, which were in the process of construction, had to be altered according to Haunold's ideas.

The stonecutter for the project was the Eisenstadt 'Steinmetzmeister' Balthasar Em(e)rich, who was ordered to complete all his work by the end of April, and in the contract Esterházy was so anxious to speed matters that he inserted a clause reading that Em(e)rich 'would have to have some of his honorarium docked' if he were not to finish in time. Em(e)rich also examined the stones left over from the fire, which was so devastating that only a very few could be used in the new building.[2]

The whole of February and the first half of March were spent in taking down the main walls which had already been erected: the Prince made further changes in Haunold's plans, and the whole building had to be begun again from the very foundations. At the end of April the main walls were up again, according to new plans; the Eszterháza interior decorator, Paul Glück, had forty princely Grenadiers to

---

1 Stöger, in a letter to Prince Nicolaus (A.M. 3983), points out that the foundation stone was laid on 18 December 1779 according to his plans. Haunold's plans were finished on 26 January 1780. In the ensuing battle for architectural supremacy, a third (and presumably unprejudiced) voice was called in: Peter Mollner, 'P. P. Fortifications and burg. Baumeister', wrote a report in which he says that he is not competent to decide whether the two architects had, or had not, borrowed each other's ideas. The contract with Paul Guba, on 28 December 1779, stated that the Prince would pay for the building materials, and everything else was to be Guba's responsibility. Horányi, 124. Otherwise our report is taken, mostly *verbatim*, from our translation and adaptation of Harich in *HJB* II, 38f.
2 In Peter Mollner's report, he objects to the fact that the foundations were not thicker than the walls erected on them. Otherwise, 'in general the whole arrangement is most pleasing and has been made with great artistic skill, with much industry and strict accuracy, a great credit to the designer'. Horányi, 125f.

help him put on the 'French rafters'. The actual roofing was done by the Eisenstadt 'Ziegeldeckermeister' Sebastian Gamsjäger, who had to get his brother Johann from Wiener Neustadt – also a 'roofing master' – to help him finish the job in time. The roofing tiles were delivered from the princely kilns in Széplak, whose chimneys smoked night and day, turning out tiles for the theatre. In August, the new roof was painted, Master Gamsjäger using 'Braunrot' (red earth), linseed oil, ten 'Eimer' of beer and six 'Eimer' of ox-blood. He considered this curious mixture absolutely water-tight; but in that same month a fearful thunderstorm broke over Eszterháza and the rain started to penetrate the building, with ruinous effects. For three days and nights the princely Grenadiers attempted to save the interior; they rushed home and got their own bedspreads with which they covered the furniture (the Prince rewarded them handsomely for that). In the autumn, there was another raging storm, and it was then decided (since by this time the actual stage decorations were in progress) to put in another roof under the riled roof.

The main façade was the joint work of stone-cutter and sculptor. Stone statues of children playing musical instruments, vases, etc., decorated the gables of the entrance roof, the corners, and so forth. Johann Friedrich Schrott[1] executed these figures.

The interior decoration began in July, when the roof was put on. Haunold was responsible for this work. The Prince's director, Stephan von Nagy, as head of a commission set up for the purpose, checked all the advance contracts and tried to keep prices down; he removed 1,500 gulden from the final bill of Haunold. This bill, incidentally, also informs us how the orchestral pit was set up: 'two rows of benches for the musici' accommodated the players, and a long music stand was erected for the players' parts. A wall divided the pit from the parterre. Thirty benches and twenty-four seats were placed in the parterre, the benches being upholstered with cow-hair and covered with red fabric. The benches in the gallery were similarly designed. The principal box and two smaller boxes rested on pillars.

The glass for the building was delivered by the Oedenburg 'Glasermeister' Joseph Gruber, whose estimate of costs in July was the very same day approved by the Prince. Work could not begin till October, however. The inner sides of the panes, i.e. those inside the house, were painted silver; the blinds and the large balcony over the main entrance were green.

The stage decorations were entrusted to Pietro Travaglia. Despite overtime – the workers continued at night, by candlelight – these decorations were not ready till the end of November. The lighting of the house was entrusted to the Oedenburger Master, Franz Leitgeb, who in July delivered fifty lamps for the parterre (set in metal and on strong rods); but the eighty-four lamps for the stage lighting were not ready until November.

Heat for the various rooms was furnished by tiled stoves, which were ordered from Vienna, Oedenburg and Széplak. In the three boxes, stone-mason Balthasar Em(e)rich placed magnificent open fireplaces, executed in marble 'in Neapolitan fashion'. These were delivered in November.

The interior painting and gold decorations for the ceiling, at first entrusted to Court Painter Basilius Grundmann and his apprentices, did not proceed quickly enough, and two other painters from outside had to be engaged. Grundmann hoped that these assistants would finish their work 'in about three weeks'; but although he wrote this at the beginning of October, the assistants were still there in December.

---

1 A.M. 4006, 4027, the latter reproduced in *HJB* II, 31 (n. 20). Schrott (Schroth) made an estimate of 180 f. for his work, but the Prince, who was now in a frenzy of cutting down the vast expenses, made a counter-offer of 150 f., which Schrott accepted on 1 June 1780.

They seem to have been capable workers. One of them was Gaetano Pesci, perhaps a relative of the princely singer Antonio Pesci. Further gold decoration was subcontracted to the Vienna Master, Ludwig Mazzini, who had done such work at the castle before; his first estimate was no less than 5,000 gulden to which – after studying the situation – he added another thousand; the commission, under Nagy, managed to reduce this enormous bill to 4,600 gulden. Master Mazzini, too, was not ready in time, and was still working by February 1781.

The stucco and imitation marble work was done by the Vienna Master, Martin Keller who, together with Mazzini, had worked at Eszterháza from the castle's inception. His first estimate, 4,000 gulden, was of course 'regulated' by the commission, and the Prince made him promise to finish his work by the end of September. But the Court Painter Grundmann did not order the necessary paint for Keller till October, and thus Keller was late, too.

Pietro Travaglia, who was entrusted with the stage decorations, submitted his estimate for an opera with five changes of scenery on 6 April; his detailed estimate, which the Prince at once approved, shows clearly that Haydn's new Opera, *La fedeltà premiata*, is the one described. It was to be, apart from Leisewitz's *Julius von Tarent*, the *pièce de résistance* for the inaugural ceremonies of the new theatre. By the middle of September, Grundmann was busily at work on the actual scenery. Travaglia had a number of local assistants, including a locksmith, a lathe worker and a cabinet maker. The ropes were delivered by 'rope-maker' Matthias Hesz from Szentmiklós. The stairways for the building were made in wrought iron by 'Schlossermeister' (master locksmith) Martin Rieger from raw material produced by the princely iron works in Csobánc (on the northern bank of lake Balaton). The locksmith was the last worker in the new theatre. The planned performance for 15 October was out of the question: the parterre was cluttered with scaffolding, and the various 'Handwerker' were all over the interior.

Ferdinand Landerer of Pressburg prepared an engraving on copper plates of the theatre, before it was quite finished (July 1780); unfortunately, no copy has survived.[1]

The marionette theatre, which now housed the opera company, had a stage too small for its new purpose; it was therefore enlarged and other changes and repairs made.[2] It was in fact February 1781 before Haydn and his musicians could open the new theatre with *La fedeltà premiata*.

Having interrupted the chronological presentation in order to relate the adventures of the new theatre's construction, we may now return to the Chronicle proper. We have a list of the musicians drawn up on 1 January but with comments added in the course of the year (see table opposite).

It is not always known from which sources Haydn replaced the instruments destroyed in the fire, but on 15 January, the great instrument-maker Anton Kerner delivered three new French horns.[3]

---

1 *Vide supra*, p. 28.
2 Pietro Travaglia's bill of 23 January 1780: *HJB* III, 143, where (*passim*) may be found most of the documentation relating to the construction of the new theatre.
3 Generalcassa 1780. Fasc. 12, Rubr. 21. No 1. Vienna, 15 Jan. 1780. The three pairs of horns with all the necessary 'mutation crooks' cost 30 Imperial Species ducats. Order to pay signed by Prince Nicolaus, Vienna, 17 Jan. *HJB* III, 151f.

Chamber Music, Situation and [annual and monthly] Cash Salary, 1 January 1780

1	Capelmeister Haiden	782.30	65.12½	
2	Female Singer Ripamonti & husband	1100.—	91.40	on 10 Apr. she and her husband left the service, up to then their salary set against debt.
3	d° Valdesturla	508.—	42.20	
4	d° Pranterin	300.—	25.—	died Oct., her salary paid till end Oct.
5	d° Polcelj & husband	465.40	28.48	dismissed end Dec. 7̄8̄0, salary paid till end Feb. 7̄8̄1.
6	Singer Dichtler	332.30	27.42½	
7	d° Bianky [*sic*]	800.—	66.40	
8	d° Totti	600.—	50.—	
9	d° Ungricht	300.—	25.—	
10	d° Rossi	600.—	50.—	
11	d° Bescy [Pesci]	423.20	35.16½	
12	d° Specht	300.—	25.—	
13	Violinist Tomasini	582.—	48.32½	
14	d° Rosetti et quart.	450.—	35.50	
15	d° Burgsteiner	300.—	25.—	
16	d° Hofmann	280.—	23.20	
17	d° with N° 2 Rippam.			Apr: 10th: see N° 2.
18	d° with N° 5 Polcelj			see N° 5.
19	Violoncellist Kraft	458.20	38.11½	
20	Violonist Joh. Diezl	280.—	23.20	
21	Hunting horn: Oliva	462.30	38.32½	
22	d°　　　Paur	462.30	38.32½	
23	d°　　　Ruepp	300.—	25.—	
24	d°　　　Hollerieder	250.—	20.50	Left in Sept.; acc. to decision of Secret. Kauffmann, the Sept. salary is to be divided between him & his successor.
25	d°　　　Jos. Diezl	300.—	25.—	
26	Hautboist Columpazo	343.25	28.37	Resigned 15 Mar. and paid half-a-year's salary.
27	d°　　　Pohl	343.25	28.37	
28	Bassoonist Schiringer	400.25	33.22	
29	d°　　　Pezival	300.—	25.—	
30	Flautist Hirsch	400.—	33.22	
31	Copyist Schellinger	120.—	10.—	Has a new salary from 1 Oct., see below.
	Trumpeter Joh: Peschko	Newly engaged		Both dismissed end Dec. but their salary paid till 17 Apr. 7̄8̄1.
		343.25	28.37	
	d°　　　Lor: Merkl	343.25	28.37	
	Jermoli and his wife from 1. Apr.	1200.—	100.—	
	On 1 Aug. [soprano] Tavechia engaged	860.—	71.40	
	On 1 Oct. hunting horn player Ant. Ekhart engaged.	300.—	25.—	
	The prompter Schellinger 1.d° [Oct.]	300.—	25.—	On 6 Oct. sent notice of termination of contract and from 1 Jan. 781 the old salary of 10 f. per month.
	On 18 Nov. Viol: Mescrino [*sic*]	430.—	35.30	
	d° Bassetlist ['cellist] Bertolja	430.—	35.30	

[Generalcassa Handbuch für 1780, EH, Eisenstadt; *HJB* III, 131–3]

Haydn had entered into negotiations with the leading music publisher in Vienna, Artaria & Co., and the correspondence which begins with the following letter is revealing not only to students of Haydn but also as valuable documentation concerning eighteenth-century music publishing in general:

[To Artaria & Co., Vienna. *German*]

Estoras, 31st January 1780.

Nobly born Gentlemen!

I send you herewith the 6th pianoforte Sonata,[1] because it is the longest and most difficult: I will certainly deliver the 5th in the next few days; meanwhile I remain, in the greatest haste, *Messieurs,*

Your most obedient servant,
Josephus Haydn [m.] pria.

[No address. Artaria's clerk notes: 'Esterhase 31 Jan. 1780'.] [CCLN, 24]

Readers will recall that Haydn had composed some minuets for the Redoutensaal balls for the Carnival season of 1777. Apparently the reception of the works was such that a new set was commissioned, and in the 'Ausgab. / Auf die Musico [Musici?] in den k: k: Redouten Saälen u: dießfällige Spesen' (expenses for the music[ians] in the I. R. Redoutensaal rooms 1780), which occurred between 9 January and 8 February, we find Haydn once again represented (see opposite).

The correspondence with Artaria now continues:

[To Artaria & Co., Vienna. *German*]

Estoras, 8th February 1780.

Nobly born Gentlemen!

I send you herewith the 5th and last Sonata, and I would ask you to send me all 6 once more for correction; in any event, I hope to gain some honour by this work, at least with the judicious public; criticism of the works will be levelled only by those who are jealous (and there are many); should they have a good sale, this will encourage me to further efforts in the future, and to serve you diligently at all times in preference to all others. I remain, *Messieurs,*

Your wholly obedient servant,
Josephus Haydn
Capellmeister.

[CCLN, 24f.]

[To Artaria & Co., Vienna. *German*]

Estoras, 25th February 1780.

Most highly respected Gentlemen!

I send you herewith the corrected proofs of all 6 Sonatas, and ask you to study them as carefully as possible: those numbers marked in red are the most urgent of all. The approval of the *Demoiselles* von Auenbrugger is most important to me, for their way of playing and genuine insight into music equal those of the greatest masters. Both deserve to be known throughout Europe through the public newspapers.

Incidentally, I consider it necessary, in order to forestall the criticisms of any witlings, to print on the reverse side of the title page the following sentence, here underlined:

Avertissement

Among these 6 Sonatas there are two single movements in which the same subject occurs through several bars: the author has done this intentionally, to show different methods of treatment.[2]

1 Artaria's first Haydn publication was six pianoforte Sonatas dedicated to the *Demoiselles* Francisca and Marianna von Auenbrugger, op. 30 (Nos. 48–52, 33; XVI: 35–39 and 20). These two talented ladies, both excellent pianists, were the daughters of the well-known physician and scholar, Leopold von Auenbrugger, from Graz. The Sonatas were published on 12 April 1780: announcement in the *Wiener Zeitung*.
2 Artaria did include an 'Avertimento' which reads: 'Tra queste sei Sonate vi si trovano due Pezzi che cominciano con alcune battute dell'istesso sentimento, cioè l'Allegro scherzando della Sonata No. II, e l'Allegro con brio della Sonata No. V. L'Autore previene averlo fatto a bella posta, cangiando però in ogn'una di esse la Continuazione del Sentimento medesimo.'

[Pag:] 8.

Expenses
For the music in the I. R. Redouten Saälen and expenses occurred

NB N°		fl	xr
On 11, 13, 18, 20, 25 Jan. 780 only in large rooms, otherwise in both rooms NB This year 6 German Dances more 22 ·	For HUBER Pankratz Music Director, for the musical personnel comprising the ORCHESTRAS, 43 in the large rooms and 27 in the small, together 70, and for the 36 minuets and 18 German Dances which he composed, together with the costs of copying, as per receipt N° 22	For 8 balls in both rooms à 220 f. each time — 1760 f. For balls only in the large rooms à 139 f. each time — 834 Together according to regulated tariff correct 2594	—
23.	For ASPELMEIER Franz for composing 24 German Dances ut N° 23	Acc. order H. Bar: v. Kirnmaÿer 48	—
24	For UHRL Joseph Copyist, for copying the Aspelmeier German Dances and for the Haiden Minuets ut N° 24 77 Bögen à 7 X	makes 8	59
25.	For HAYDEN Joseph for composing 18. Minuets ut N° 25 according to 2 receipts	makes 50	—
		2700	59
	Summa of the expenses for the music in the I. R. Redouten Saälen and the expenses incurred two thousand seven hundred Gulden 59 Xr. Id est: 2700 f 59 Xr.		

[Haus-, Hof- und Staatsarchiv, Hoftheater-Rechnungen S. R. 37, p. 8: photograph kindly provided by Dr Clemens Höslinger of that institution.]

Notes: For Huber, Aspelmayer and Baron Kirnmay(e)r, *vide supra*, p. 405. We cannot identify the Eighteen Minuets which Haydn delivered and perhaps even conducted, though it was usual for Huber to conduct also the 'foreign' compositions, and Haydn was probably at Eszterháza except for a very brief vacation at New Year's. See also Günter Thomas in *Haydn-Studien* III/1 (1973), pp. 8f.

———

[letter continues:]
For of course I could have chosen a hundred other ideas instead of this one; but so that the whole *opus* will not be exposed to blame on account of this one intentional detail (which the critics and especially my enemies might interpret wrongly), I think that this *avertissement* or something like it must be appended, otherwise the sale might be hindered thereby. I submit the point in question to the judicious decision of the two *Demoiselles* Auenbrugger, whose hands I respectfully kiss. Please send one of the six copies you promised me to Herr Zach von Hartenstein[1]

1 *Das Österreichische Adelslexikon*, Vienna 1822 (edited by F. G. Nägeli von Mühlfeld) lists two Austrian aristocrats under the name of Zach von Hartenstein: Johann Franz (raised to the nobility in 1764) and Joseph (raised to the nobility in 1756). Both are listed as 'Postoffizier', i.e. officials in the Postal Department. The *Hof- und Staats-Schematismus*, Vienna 1785, p. 5, lists only 'Franz Zach von Hartenstein, k.k. Oberst Hof-Postamtsverwalter Adjunkt'.

through the Royal Bavarian post-office, but the other 5 are to be addressed to Estoras.

I hope soon to receive an answer to the above point, and have the honour to be, most respectfully,

Your most obedient servant.
Joseph Haydn

[No address]   [CCLN, 25]

On 15 March, two trumpeters were hired: Johann Peschko and Lorenz Markl. Prince Nicolaus, as we have seen (*supra*, p. 74) ordered two trumpets for the new players which arrived from Nuremberg in the middle of June. Haydn, who hardly seems to have written a single note for his clarinet players except in *Die Feuersbrunst*, immediately included trumpet parts in *La fedeltà premiata*, but he seems to have had an inkling that they would not last long at Eszterháza, for their parts in the Opera are always 'covered' by the horns; in the event they were dismissed at the end of the year. The newly added trumpet parts in Symphony No. 70 (Esterházy Archives, Budapest) were probably added for the new players, and we shall soon see that Haydn set about replacing his destroyed timpani (Symphony No. 70 also has an autograph timpani part which Haydn added later): see letter of 7 November *infra*.

The correspondence with Artaria continues as follows:

[To Artaria & Co., Vienna. *German*]

Estoras, 20th March [1780].

Most highly respected Sir!

Everything that you write to me meets with my entire approval; I only regret one thing, that I cannot have the honour of dedicating these Sonatas to the *Demoiselles* von Auenbrugger myself.[1] I remain, with all due respect, Sir,

Your obedient servant
Josephus Haydn

[Address:] Monsieur
     Monsieur Artaria et Compag
     press: a
                 Vienne.
[Artaria's clerk notes: 'Haydn/ Esterhas 20th March/ 1780'.]

[CCLN, 26]

[To Artaria & Co., Vienna. *German*]

Estoras, 29th March 1780.

Messieurs!

I received in the past day or two a letter from Herr Humel,[2] Royal Prussian Musical and Commercial Advisor, in which among other things I read with astonishment that my Sonatas have been sent to Berlin some time ago. Please therefore don't forget completely about my five copies. I remain, *Messieurs*, very respectfully,

Your most obedient servant,
Joseph Haydn.

We do not know what was behind the princely dismissal of the Ripamonti couple in April. Haydn had created the part of Rosina in *La vera costanza* for her and must have been sorry to see her leave; she had had troubles of her own (her twins, born in

---

1 Many eighteenth-century dedications were made by the publisher rather than the composer.
2 J.J. Hummel, the famous music publisher of Amsterdam and, later, Berlin.

January, had died shortly thereafter). In fact the circumstances of their dismissal are unclear: in one document (quoted at the beginning of this year's Chronicle), it is stated that they 'left the service', i.e. voluntarily; in another (Conventionale 1773, Prot. 4687, *HJB* VII, 102) it says specifically 'were dismissed 10 Apr. 780'. In any event, Prince Nicolaus gladly re-engaged her four years later, without her husband, and she was able once again to (re)create Rosina in *La vera costanza*.

Haydn's fame was spreading, even to Italy (where the musical taste was entirely different). 'The Prince', we read in Dies (75)

> rejoiced with Haydn when the Philharmonic Academy in Modena in 1780 rendered homage to Haydn's merits by granting him membership in their Society and surprising him with its diploma.

Haydn sent *L'isola disabitata* as a gift to the Society, according to Dies: perhaps the authentic Esterházy score, now in Turin, is the one Haydn sent to Modena. From Griesinger (45) we learn that the diploma was dated 14 May 1780.

Several bills from Johann Michael Schadlbauer are of this period. A word should be said about the nomenclature of these 'books' of music paper, which Schadlbauer delivered along with harpsichord quills and strings. We have for 1780 his bill for twenty-four books of Venetian paper and four 'of the German kind'. In those days the paper was sold per 'Ries': one 'Ries' consisted of twenty books, one book of twenty-four *Bögen* (four pages). In 1780 Schadlbauer delivered 576 *Bögen* of Venetian paper to Eszterháza and slightly under 100 *Bögen* of the inferior 'German' paper.[1]

The orchestral musicians earned extra money by copying. We read:

Copiatur Conto
Dell opera
Le Gelosie villane

	Bögen
Dichtler	59
Pezivall	63
Peschko	41
	163

[Haydn's hand:] These 163 Bögen are properly written and checked by me.

Josephus Haydn mpria
Capell Meister

[Countersigned by Prince Nicolaus, 19 June 1780 and used as receipt.]

[A.M. 1097. *HJB* VII, 161]

We find Prince Nicolaus interesting himself in violin strings and writing a little note to Haydn to organize the matter.[2] Shortly afterwards we find him as godfather *in absentia* for the master cook Defarge and 'the musician Pulcelly ... and [Haushofmeister Vautrin] should pay the costs of 29 f 36 X and enter it in the books.

---

1 The bills, not countersigned by Haydn, are of the following dates: Vienna 'At the Golden Lamp' 18 May (8 books Venetian paper at 40 Xr. and 23 yellow spinet strings), Vienna 3 Aug., Vienna 23 Sept. and a composite bill by Prince Nicolaus listing raven quills and harpsichord strings (1 Oct.), as well as music paper, which is interesting in that it shows that the theatrical continuo part was still played on the harpsichord and not on the fortepiano. On 24 Nov. Schadlbauer sent a bill for '4 books of music paper in the German fashion' 2 f. 48 Xr. A.M. 1095, 1091, 1094, 1090 and 1089. *HJB* III, 146f. Another document by Haydn is quoted *supra*, and yet another *infra*, 21 Nov.

2 'Haydn. 4 bundles of e-strings are necessary ...[etc.] Eszterház 19 June 780. N. F. E.' Com.-Prot. 1780. No. 200. *HJB* VII, 150. Thereafter we find a bill from Wenzl Peller for various strings (*HJB* VII, 150), and another of 13 Oct (*HJB* VII, 150f.). Peller was a 'bürgerliche Saitenmacher in Altlerchenfeld zum König David sub N° 84' in Vienna. There are also bills from other makers: J. J. Stadlmann, 30 Nov. 1780 for strings and resin.

Esterhaz, 20th June 1780. Id est 29 f 36 X / Nicolaus Fürst Esterhazy / protocollirt.'[1] Polzelli's daughter died soon thereafter.

The exact description of Haydn's summer uniform and its cost (with two pairs of breeches: 133 f. 59⅜ xr.), as well as the same information for the other musicians (less costly, as usual), is preserved in the Budapest Archives.[2] It contains no information of special importance (colour, etc.).

On 1 August, Teresa Amalia Tavecchia, a fine soprano, was engaged; she was to sing in Haydn's *La fedeltà premiata* (Amaranta), and three months later she persuaded Haydn and the Prince to engage her husband, Anton Eckhardt, a horn player, for whom Haydn presumably wrote the muted solo horn part in that Opera (*vide infra*, p. 539). At the end of October, when Eckhardt had joined the troupe, Maria Elisabeth Prandtner, who had sung so often and so faithfully, died; Haydn signed for her last salary and supervised her last financial affairs.[3]

Haydn, looking forward to *La fedeltà premiata*, the score of which requires timpani at several important points, wrote the following letter to replace the burned instruments at Eszterháza:

[To Stephan von Nagy, Regent of the Esterházy Estates. *German*.]
Nobly born,
Gracious Sir!

On the order of His Serene Highness, Your Grace should instruct the administrator of Forchtenstein Castle[4] or the inspector-general of ordinance there to send at the earliest possible opportunity a pair of good military kettledrums [*Feld Paucken*] (such as are kept in the arsenal there) to Estoras: to this end one should, in my humble opinion, request the Forchtenstein schoolmaster and the *Pater Regens Chori* of the *Serviten* Order to give their expert opinion as to the best and most useful instruments. I remain, most respectfully,

Your Grace's
Obedient servant,
Josephus Haydn
CapellMeister.

Estoras, 7th November 1780   [CCLN 27]

Five days later, a theatrical scandal broke over Eszterháza. On the night of 12 November, Johann Schilling, whose speciality in the Diwald Troupe was playing 'young lovers', tried – with the assistance of the prompter Jacob Münzenberger – to elope with *Prinzipal* Diwald's wife. They were caught and Schilling was imprisoned for a fortnight in Kapuvár on a diet of bread and water every second day and a prohibition to return to Eszterháza as long as the seductive Madame Diwald was in residence there. The accomplice, Münzenberger, spent three days in prison, also on dry bread and water. We have seen in this Chronicle that there was enormous sexual freedom at Eszterháza (Haydn *colla* Polzelli, Frau Haydn *mit dem* Guttenbrunn, Castle Inspector Kleinrath *mit der* Catharina Rössl); but eloping with a married woman and lifting the skirts of a soprano singing on the stage were not found amusing.[5]

1 Com.-Prot. 1780. Nr. 207. Haushofm. 1780. Nr. 415. *HJB* III, 152. Was Haydn already the father of this girl?
2 A.M. Fasc. LXVI.4160. Valkó II, 588f.
3 'Dear Züsser! Although the singer Prantnerin died on the 25th ult., nevertheless he is to pay the entire month's salary to the Kapellmeister. Esterhaz, 2nd November 1780. Nicolaus Fürst Esterhazy'. A.M. XVI.1099. Valkó II, 588.
4 Forchtenstein Castle, an ancient fortress belonging to the Esterházy family, in the province of Burgenland. The castle stood good service in the second Turkish invasion of 1683. A photograph of Forchtenstein may be found on the jacket of Nowak's *Haydn* (Vienna, 1950). The *Serviten* Monastery still owns some contemporary MSS. of Haydn's works (*Missa Sti. Joannis de Deo*, etc.); and some scraps of instrumental music we found there in 1958 – e.g., part of Haydn's Symphony No. 35, the reverse sheet of which was used to copy a piece of church music – suggest that the collection must have been much more extensive at one time.
5 The elopement described in A.T. 40. Horányi, 126.

Another receipt shows that even the vast amount of music paper which had been ordered throughout 1780 was not sufficient:

> Since the music paper recently purchased has been entirely used up, partly for the new opera [*La fedeltà premiata*] and the rest for the Pichl Quartets, and since all the vocal parts to the afore-mentioned opera must still be copied, the following music paper is required, viz.
> 6 books oblong with 10 staves
> 6 books quarto with 10 staves
> 3 books oblong with 12 staves ⸻⸻⸻ the book costs 40 Xr. makes
> 10 f.
> Josephus Haydn mpria
> Capell Meister

[with Prince Nicolaus's order for the purchase:] Esterház 23 Dec. 780.
Nicolaus Fürst Esterhazy.

> [A.M. 1131; facsimile in Bartha-Somfai as No. 3. *HJB* III, 148f.]

A bill for bassoon reeds by Jacob Bauer 'at the sign of the golden bassoon' in the suburb of Vienna may be mentioned briefly.[1]

We shall close our Chronicle with two bills for copying:

Copiatur Conto
Dell Opera La fedeltà premiata
The whole orchestra of the whole 1st act, makes in Bögen 142: the Bogen at 5 Xr. means in cash: 11 f 50:

Leopoldo Dichtler

These 142 Bögen are correctly written and have been checked by me.
Josephus Haydn Capell Meister

[Prince Nicolaus's order to pay the bill signed on 23 December 1780.]
[Leopold Dichtler signs the receipt, Eisenstadt, 9 January 1781.]

> [A.M. 1085. *HJB* VII, 161f.]

Nota
Concerning the music which I the undersigned copied for His Pl. Tit: Hochfürstl: Highness.
First, 6 Trios, which made   22 Bögen
2ndly, 6 ditto, which made   24 Bögen
3rdly, 6 Quartets   43 Bögen

Total   89 Bögen

The Bogen at 5 x comes out to 7 f 25 x

Anton Kraft.

[Prince Nicolaus's order to pay the bill signed at Eszterháza, 29 December 1780; Kraft's receipt on 31 December.]

> [A.M. 1084. *HJB* III, 145f. Note the enormous size of one act of orchestral parts to a Haydn opera, over 500 pages. Kraft was the famous 'cellist for whom Haydn would in 1783 write the D major 'Cello Concerto VIIb:2]

---

1 Vienna 27 Nov. 1780: a dozen bassoon reeds. A.M. 1088. *HJB* III, 152. In another 'Specification' of 21 Nov. 1780, Haydn orders '3 bundles of violin e-strings, 3 g-strings, 2 covered double bass A-strings, 2 g and one C for the viola, a whole set for the violoncello. Two boxes of resin. Music Paper / To copy the new Quartets by Pichl and for the duplicate parts of the new opera. 4 books with 10 staves. 12 bassoon reeds. Esterhaz, 21 Nov. 780. Josephus Haydn / Capell Meister'. With a summary of three bills, one from Stadlmann for strings (10 f. 41 x., mentioned above), one from Schadlbauer for music paper (2 f. 48 x., also mentioned above), and the bill from Bauer. Countersigned by Nicolaus Fürst Esterházy. A.M. 1086. *HJB* III, 148.

Chronicle 1781

ITALIAN OPERAS 1781

Sixty-nine performances are registered. (Harich in *HJB* I, 39).

LA FEDELTA / PREMIATA. / DRAMMA GIOCOSO / PER MUSICA. / DA RAPPRESENTARSI / NELL' / APERTURA DEL NUOVO TEATRO / DI S. A. IL PRINCIPE NICOLO D' / ESTERHAZY DI GALANTHA. / L'AUTUNNO DELL'ANNO / 1780. . . . Le Decorazione, e Machine sono Diverzione [*sic*], ed esecuzione del Sigr Pietro Travaglia Allievo de celebri Frattelli Galeari [*sc.* Galliari], in attual servizio di S. A. il Principe NICOLO ESTERHAZI di Galanta etc.

INTERLOCUTORI

Fillide, sotto il finto nome di Celia, Amante di Fileno.
        La Sigra Jermoli.
Fileno, Amante di Fillide.
        Il Sigr Guglielmo Jermoli.
Amaranta, donna vana, e boriosa.
        La Sigra Teresa Taveggia.
Conte Perrucchetto, uome di umore stravagante.
        Il Sigr Benedetto Bianchi.
Nerina, Ninfa volubile in amore, innamorata di Lindoro.
        La Sigra Valdesturla.
Lindoro, fratello di Amaranta, addetto à servigj del Tempio, innamorata prima di Nerina, e poi di Celia.
        Il Sigr Leop. Dichtler.
Melibeo, Ministro del Tempio di Diana, innamorato di Amaranta.
        Il Sigr Antonio Pesci.
Diana
        l'istessa La Sigra Valdesturla.

Tutti in attual servizio di S. A. il Principe Nicolò Esterhaz [*sic*] di Galantha. . . . La Musica è del Sig. Giuseppe Hayden [*sic*] Maestro di Cappella di S. A. il Principe Nicolò Esterhazi di Galantha, ed Academico Filharmonico di Modena. Inventore, e Direttore de' Balli, e del Battimento Il Sig. Lugi [*sic*] Rossi.

Libretto: An edition of 200 copies, with a complete German translation, was ordered from the printer Joseph Siess in Oedenburg; it was therefore exceptionally large (159 pages). Copy: Stadtbibliothek, Vienna A 108.599. Eszterháza performance material: except for most of the autograph, it has disappeared. See the 1782 revival and also p. 537, where the working score of the 1782 revival is discussed. First performance: 25 February, repeated twice in that month, then in March (eight), April (one) and September (five) and in 1782–4: one of the greatest successes of Haydn's operatic career at Eszterháza. The problem of the singers' departure and the substitution of new ones are discussed *infra*, pp. 460f. Harich, *Musikgeschichte*, 48f. Bartha-Somfai, 87f. Harich in *HJB* I, 33f. Landon, 'A New Authentic Source for "La Fedeltà Premiata",' in *Soundings* II (1971–2), revised in *Beiträge zur Musikdokumentation* (Franz Grasberger *Festschrift*), 1975.

Pasquale Anfossi: Isabella, e Rodrigo o sia La Costanza in amore. Dramma giocoso per musica. Da Rappresentarsi nell' teatro D'Esterhazy Nella primavera del anno 1781. [Oedenburgo, nella stamperia di Giuseppe Siess.]

Il Comendatore d'Yllesca, Padre di D. Isabella	Il Sig. Benedet. Bianchi.
D. Isabella, Amante di D. Rodrigo	La Sigra Teresa Taveggia Eccard.
D. Rodrigo, Amante di D. Isabella	Il Sigr Andrea Totti.
Ramira, Damigella di D. Isabella	La Sigra Costanza Valdesturla.
Pasquale, servo confidente di D. Rodrigo	Il Sigr Leop. Dichtler.
D. Eleonora, Nipote del Commendatore	La Sigra Luigia Polzelli.
D. Sancio, Amico del sudetto ed Amante di Isabella	Il Sigr Antonio Pesci.

Libretto: 200 copies. Copy: EH, Eisenstadt. Performed only five times in April. Eszterháza performance material: EH, Budapest, Ms. Mus. OE–42 (score and parts of Italian origin). Haydn made the following changes, apart from the usual cuts and transpositions. Oboes and horns added (by Haydn) to Aria 'Saper bramante' in Atto I° (copied in the parts by Joseph Elssler). Sc. 12, tempo added by Haydn, also many dynamic marks added throughout the rather bare original score. Atto II° Sc. 9, Aria 'Non ama la vita' a large cut and six bars added in Haydn's autograph (coloratura for the soprano), also bassoon parts; actual parts by Elssler (dup.) and Haydn. Sc. 11, addition of oboe and horn parts in Schellinger's hand (Haydn? Schellinger?).[1] Harich, *Musikgeschichte*, 49. Bartha-Somfai, 91f. (interesting document, showing that Antonio Pesci organized the score and parts from Pietro Martelli in Bologna; Haydn countersigned the order for payment of 8½ ducats on 5 Oct. 1781), 237–9. Harich in *HJB* I, 34f.

Giovanni Paisiello: L'avaro deluso. Dramma giocoso per musica. Da rappresentarsi nel theatro d'Esterhazy l'anno 1781. / Der verspottete Geitzige. Ein lustiges Singspiel, aufgefuehret, auf dem hochfuerstl. Theater zu Esterház. Im Jahr 1781.

Corilla, Orfano proveduta di ricca dote, amante del Conte	Mad. Matilde Bolognia [*sic*].
Conte di Belprata	Mons. Totti.
Rosina, Sorella di Corilla, amante di Don Anselmo	Mselle Bologna.
Il Dottor Medico, Avaro, e fanatico per la lingua francese	Mons. Moratti.
Don Anselmo	Mons. Dichtler.
Raggiro, Servitore in Casa del Dottore	Mons. Pesci.

Libretto: 200 copies for this large (143 pp.) libretto, for which the printer Joseph Siess in Oedenburg also supplied a complete German translation. Copy: Nationalbibliothek, Vienna, Théater-Sammlung 629.418 A. First performance: May (total six perf.), repeated in June (six), July (three), August (one), also in 1782. There are several alternative titles of this work: *La discordia fortunata ossta L'avaro deluso* (EH, Secretariats-Prot.), *La gelosia di se stessa o sia L'avaro deluso* (score, EH, Budapest). Eszterháza performance material: EH, Budapest, Ms. Mus. OE–24 (score of Atto I°, fragmentary orchestral parts and sections of Corilla's part). Haydn made various cuts. Sc. 10, an insertion aria added ('Infelice sventurata, non ha pace questo cor', not identical with Haydn's Aria on a text that begins similarly of 1789). Harich, *Musikgeschichte*, 49. Bartha-Somfai, 92f., 239f. Harich in *HJB* I, 35.

Gennaro Astaritta: Il Francese bizzarro.
Libretto: printed by Joseph Siess in Oedenburg in June: no copy has survived. Cast unknown. First performance: July (four perf.), repeated once in August. Eszterháza performance material: EH, Budapest, Ms. Mus. OE–88/a (Sc. 1–8, Atto I°, score of Italian origin[?]). Haydn made the usual cuts and trnspositions. Atto I°, Sc. 2, Aria 'Se d'una bella Giovane' was replaced by another aria, now missing. Bartha-Somfai, 93, 240f. Harich in *HJB* I, 36.

Vincenzo Righini: Il convitato di pietra o sia Il dissoluto. Dramma tragi-comico per musica. Da rappresentarsi nel' teatro d'Esterház nell'estate l'anno 1781. [Oedenburg, Siess].

Attori

Don Giovanni Tenorio, Cavaliere Napolitano	[Andr. Totti]
Don Alfonso, Ministro del Rè di Castiglia	[Leopold Dichtler]
Il Commendatore di Loioa Castigliano	[Pasq. di Giovanni]
Donn'Anna, Figlia del Commendatore	[Matilde Bologna]
Donn'Isabella, Figlia del Duca d'Altomonte	[Luigia Polzelli]
Elisa, Pescatrice	[Maria Bologna]
Ombrino, Pescatore	[Antonio Pesci]
Corallina, Ostessa	[Maria Bologna]
Tiburzio, Garzone d'Osteria	[Antonio Pesci]
Lisetta, Cameriera di Donn'Anna	[Luigia Polzelli]
Arlechino, Servo di Don Giovanni	[Vincenzo Moratti]
La Poesia e del Signor Nunziato Porta.[2]	

Libretto: 200 copies. Copy: Országos Széchényi Könyvtár. First performance: July (two perf.), repeated in August (one) and September (two). Nunziato Porta, in a document signed Eszterház, 14 Aug.

---

1 Our notes on the EH material (1958) register an 'insertion' aria towards the end of Atto II°. This aria has been removed from the score and all the parts except V. I & II (one part each, in the other it was also removed), and we strongly suggest that this is another lost aria by Haydn. The violin parts, in Joseph Elssler's hand, are written on oblong Italian paper (watermark 'A'), and Elssler has the following title 'Nro [blank] Aria del Atto 2do'. The *incipits* are:

2 Harich in *HJB* I, 36 has combined the characters from a Viennese libretto of 1777 with his reconstruction of the entire cast, which is only partly listed in the Esterházy libretto.

1781 (and countersigned by Haydn), shows that this opera was purchased in Vienna: *vide infra*, p. 449. This was Porta's most important libretto. Eszterháza performance material: EH, Budapest, Ms. Mus. OE–84 (score and orchestral parts), the orchestral material was copied by Schellinger and two Viennese copyists (Schellinger was active as a copyist before he came to Hungary). Haydn, apart from the usual cuts and transpositions, added a chorus (probably not his own), 'Tira, tira' in Atto I°, Sc. 1 between Overture and Introduzione. Sc. 2, an aria by Luigi Bologna, 'Amor tristarello' was substituted for the original one, 'Se voi mio caro'. Sc. 6 the strings marked 'tacent' and only wind band ('Feld Parthia') used – not Haydn's change. Haydn, however, changed the tempo of the Duet 'Per esempio' from Andante to Allegro. Sc. 8, Haydn made a new modulation to the second of two available arias. In Sc. 10 there are also two versions of the Aria 'Dall squarciate vene'). Sc. 11, the original aria cancelled and a new one by Niccolò Jommelli substituted, 'Odio, furor, dispetto'. Atto II°, Sc. 8. Haydn added, it would seem, his own insertion here: a big *scena* for Donna Isabella, Rec. acc. 'Mora l'infido' and Aria 'Mi sento nel seno'. This *scena* was, of course, for Polzelli; alas, it has survived only in fragments. It was copied by Haydn himself, Joseph Elssler and Schellinger (who apart from having copied some of the material while still in Vienna, also made new additions for the Eszterháza performance). *Incipits* in Bartha-Somfai, 244f. Sc. 10: the original text was a 'licenza' addressed to the Viennese nobility. This was changed in Eszterháza to address the local patron ('Di NICCOLÒ ripeta il nome ognora'. Haydn seems to have re-composed this scene, but it has not survived. Harich, *Musikgeschichte*, 49f. Bartha-Somfai, 93f, 241–6 (with facsimile of some sections of the new Polzelli *scena* as No. 19).

Nicolà Piccinni: La schiava riconosciuta (ossia Gli stravaganti). Libretto printed by Joseph Siess (his bill: 20 August, A.M. 4009); no copy has survived. First performance: end of August, repeated in 1782. Eszterháza performance material: EH, Budapest, Ms. Mus. OE–81 (score and orchestral parts of Italian origin). Apart from the usual cuts and transpositions, Haydn made the following changes, Atto I° Sc. 1 ('Introduzione'), Haydn accelerated the tempo from Andante con moto to Allegretto. Arminda's Aria, 'Che tortura', rewritten by Haydn, adding coloratura passages and making Piccinni's form tighter; also enriching the violin writing. The parts were written by Joseph Elssler (score contains Haydn's autograph of 14 pp.). Sc. 2: the original Aria of Lelio, 'Quel lab[b]ro', was replaced by a shorter Aria, 'Quant'è vezzosa' (composer?). Sc. 7: instead of Piccinni's 'Marchia' a new aria was inserted (parts: Schellinger), of which we have the *incipit* but not the text (score wanting, vocal parts missing for whole opera): Bartha-Somfai, 247. The aria is possibly by Haydn. Atto II°, Sc. 2: Arminda's Aria, 'Una semplice agnelletta', was rewritten by Haydn (fourteen bars replaced by a new version in Haydn's autograph) and reduced from 161 to 88 bars. The parts for the changes are by Joseph Elssler. In Sc. 5, Arminda's Cavatina, 'Dove vado, sventurata', was also subjected to small changes and many dynamic marks added, including a sharp crescendo (p — rinf. — crescendo — ff) within two bars. Bartha-Somfai suggest that Polzelli may have sung the role of Arminda. Sc. 6: Lelio's Aria, 'Sentimi o faggio amico', was replaced by another Aria (text?; *incipit* Bartha-Somfai, 249), the composer of which cannot now be established. Parts by Schellinger. Bartha-Somfai, 94, 246–9. Harich in *HJB* I. 36f.

Four operas from earlier seasons were repeated:
Gazzaniga's *La vendemmia*: March (one).
Sarti's *Le gelosie villane*: March (two).
Salieri's *La scuola de' gelosi*: April (one), May (eight), June (one).
Sacchini's(?) *La contadina in corte*. First given in 1769 (*vide supra*, p. 158), this opera perished in the 1779 fire and had to be replaced by new material (see Chronicle, 14 August). In Haydn's *Opernliste* of 1784, the composer is listed as Piccin(n)i; but in 1782 Sacchini's Opera of that title was given in Vienna (Pohl II, 379), and Nunziato Porta organized the new material from Vienna. Since libretto (if one was printed), score and parts have all disappeared, the identity of the composer is problematical. Roles for the 1781 revival: Travaglia's 'Verzeichnis für die neue Oper La contadina ingentilita' (this was the alternative title of the work):

Tanncia	one of the Bologna sisters
Sandrina	one of the Bologna sisters
Ruggiero	Pasquale di Giovanni
Berto	Vincenzo Moratti

[Since a positive identification of the opera is not possible, these roles were not added to the singer's *curriculum vitae*.]

Revived for the first time: June (three perf.), repeated in July (two), August (two) and in 1782. Bartha-Somfai, 94, 105. Harich in *HJB* I, 37f. *HJB* IX, 89, item 29.

GERMAN MARIONETTE OPERA 1781

[no records of any performances known]

THE GERMAN THEATRICAL TROUPE 1781

The Diwald Company, whose constitution has been listed above, continued to be the resident troupe at Eszterháza until the end of the 1785 season. We shall list the Company once again in the Chronicle of 1784. Between its constitution in 1781 and 1784, we must rely on three undated letters from Diwald to the Prince (A.T. 39, 38, 32). In the first, Diwald promises to engage Ditelmeyer for buskin [*Kothurn*] parts and to replace Frau Schwarzwald by another actress for motherly roles. In the second letter Ditelmeyer is included in the list but also Frau Schwarzwald. Ditelmeyer had been, in 1778, a member of the Pauli-Meyer Troupe. In the list of players given in the second letter, eight are known to us from the 1780 Gotha list and the other six are new: Herr and Frau Diwald; Herr, Frau and Fräulein Schwarzwald; Ditelmeyer, König, Schilling, Münzenberg, Olperl; Herr and Frau Heigel; Herr and Frau Riedel. In the third undated letter, Diwald lists his members as: Franciscus Nuth, Carolina Nuth, Theresia Schwarzwald, Joseph Schwarzwald, Anna Alram, Franz Alram, Joseph Alram, Theresia Ulam, Gottlieb Pärtl, Johann König, Jacob Münzenberg, Joseph Sartorius, Emilia Diwald and Franz Diwald. In this third letter, Diwald promises to enlarge the male and female wardrobes.[1]

The opening of the new opera house took place, as we have noted briefly, on 25 February with Haydn's new Opera, *La fedeltà premiata*. Unlike most of Haydn's earlier operas, which never circulated outside Eszterháza, Haydn was now becoming so famous that even his operas, although composed for a remote Hungarian castle, began slowly to circulate on German stages, and usually in German translation. *La vera costanza*, *La fedeltà premiata*, *Orlando Paladino* and *Armida* were all translated into German for the Erdödy Company (*Prinzipal*: Hubert Kumpf) in 1785 and 1786 and in this new guise circulated across Germany in the 1780s and 1790s. Breaking chronology for a moment, we may mention that Haydn, whenever he printed parts of his operas, tried to persuade his publishers to issue the section(s) in full score. Of *La fedeltà premiata* he published the most daring and beautiful *scena* from Act II, 'Ah, come il core', with Artaria in full score in 1783 (omitting the kettledrum part), which was much admired, even in Italy – where Haydn's music, like that of his compatriots, penetrated only very slowly and with considerable difficulty; there the Artaria score was copied and sold in MS. Apart from the few MSS. listed in Hoboken (Vol. II, p. 402), there are Italian copies even in such a remote place as Lucca.[2] The Artaria print of 'Ah, come' was also given a close analytical review in Cramer's *Magazin der Musik* which, as we know (*vide infra*, p. 490), was sent to Artaria by Haydn. The review is signed 'C. F. C.', i.e. Cramer himself, in the form of a letter to Mademoiselle Meta von Wintheim of 10 November 1783:

> [Precis: Discussion of proper vocal style and proper declamation as contributions towards the true art of music: 'to move the heart' and to use the right language to express the thoughts. Author suggests using German instead of Italian, 'unless the singer and listeners speak perfect Italian'. It would be useful to show, by analyzing a single important composition, how important the art of declamation is. Hiller showed us how to ornament six Italian arias by Graun, Hasse, Anfossi etc., and while such ornamentation is, if applied correctly, and sparingly, permissible, it could lead to mis-use, to display rather than to move, as in present-day Italy. As perfect examples of operas which contain 'throughout a sense of true expression': Gluck, Salieri, Benda. There follows side by side Italian text of 'Ah, come il core' and Cramer's line-for-line German translation. Cramer is clever enough to suggest that the work is 'torn out of' an opera, and that Haydn's descriptions therein 'are as varied as the narrow confines of his text allow'. He then continues]

---

1 Horányi (German), p. 132; (English), p. 130.

2 Biblioteca del Conservatorio di Musica, Collezione Marchese Bottini (uncatalogued), MS. score 'Scena è Aria / Del Sig:re Giuseppe Haydan' [*sic*] on small 'post paper' (watermarks: 'GM' in coat-of-arms, 'AL MASSO') with an exquisitely printed frame on the title page, obviously used for the sale of various MSS. of this kind: 'Vendesi due Soldi da Giovanni Chiari Rigatore di Carta da Musica nelle Cond——' [rest torn off]. Haydn's *Arianna a Naxos* was similarly popular in Italy and sold in MS. throughout the country.

After a suitable introduction, or if you will ritornello, of the two violin parts in unisono, playing the most delicate melody in triplets, a simple recitative section gives us the general tone that the Aria will have. We perceive the fear of expectation, 'Ah, come il core mi palpita nel seno!' sings Phillis [footnote: Cramer wonders if Phillis is not a badly chosen name, with its pastoral connotations and its 'fate seen through rose-tinted glasses'. 'It is a small matter, *au fond*; but the piece itself is small, too; the more reason that there should be nothing whatever in it to disturb the truth of the illusion'. Naturally the names involved come from the opera.]. These notes must be sung with a pure voice, without too much expression of fear, since Phillis does not know yet why she should tremble. She will learn that when she has read the letter that brings her the news of her unhappiness.

In the following passage 'Per Phillide [*sic*] infidel morì Fileno', I see a shoal on which even the best singer could founder. If she merely follows the rules of the school, the singing method; if she gives the notes that set the tone (*Phil—del—ni[no]*) a real accent and if she infuses into 'Fileno', the final cadential period of the recitative, a strong, abrupt expression – then she has quite missed the real point.

For correct as this kind of singing would be in a very passionate section, it would be out of place here.

From the following question, 'che lessi?' we gather that these words are not the words of the soprano but are from a letter which she has just received with palpitations of the heart, with tremors of fear; and now she reads therein the news that her lover, her Philene, has died for her, faithless Phillis. The singer has to convey all this by her whole bearing. How would she in fact read such a sad message? I think: with shaking uncertainty, with a voice that tremulously seems to betray, by what her eyes see, that which her heart cannot believe; she will hardly be able to spell out this Job's message. So instead of a strong expression, the most uncertain and shaky of voices. At each rising accent, hardly any raise of volume! And finally the closing cadence almost disappearing! Only then is the whole scheme properly served.

That this is Haydn's intention may be seen unmistakably by the broken line of notes which taken together only make sense as a whole phrase. The rests which he places after the individual notes would be unpardonable if they were not meant for this purpose. Especially the half bar of rest after just the opening: '*per——*'! But if the singer recites fearfully, as if she could hardly express the horrible sense of the words, then how true are these rests; how excellent these apparent mistakes.

The more tremulously uncertain these words are sung, the stronger will be the contrast with the following exclamation: 'omnipotenti Dei! che lessi?' which are marked *f* (not without reason) and presto. This must be sung energetically and quickly.

The rests between the words: 'che lessi? — *Ah mia &c.*', and between the following: '*pietà* – – – *tu per salvarlo &c.*' must obviously not be too short. Although these are words of passion which allow of no dragging melody, the individual sentences are exclamations. These are thoughts which the soul does not suddenly connect, between which she must pause. So that it depends more or less on the smallest bit of rest to show whether the singer has felt, or has felt not enough, the passage. [Footnote with a long quotation from Lessing concerning movement, also in music.]

One cannot stress sufficiently the enormous importance in vocal music, and altogether in declamation, of the length and brevity of rests, how very much their longer or shorter length contributes to give colour to the speech.

At the word '*tu*' Haydn did not put the note in the right place. He placed it on the weak beat, when it ought to be on the strong. It is not '*tu per salvàrlo*' (u – u – u) but '*tù, per salvarlo*' (–, u u – u). One must therefore sing it as if it were written

or even better, one puts a rest after the word '*tu*' and sings the two syllables 'per sal–' in semiquavers, thus:

I admit that I don't understand the following word: '*legge*'. Perhaps because I don't know the plot of the piece well enough. What kind of a law is meant here? The law of blind necessity, perhaps? The way it stands, the expression is faulty. The same applies to '*ingrato*', not the proper word to go with '*forte*' [footnote elucidating this point with a sermon which contains a similar anticlimax of adjectives]. But —— the Italian poets do not take the propriety of their adjectives that seriously.

The singer's wild emotion disappears after the first cry of self-accusation. Now there is a section with an accompaniment in gentle broken chords by the second violins, the first violin having in the middle a fine melody curving downwards whose expression, in order not to be too gentle, is informed by a masterly dissonance to which bassoon and second oboe contribute a contrary effect; this gives the whole a dark colour and of necessity provides an exceptional effect. It leads to a section that once again is capable of the most varied interpretation. Here again are shoals for the singer. The first exclamation '*Ohime!*' is melancholy; it cannot be sung with sufficient pathos. But if the singer continues with the same pathos she is declaiming wrongly. The words '*di fosco velo si copre il giorno*', sung in tempo, during which the broken accompaniment stops for one whole bar; even more the strong '*io gelo*', in a falling diminished fifth (it must be 'pulled' from note to note in the same way the violinists play *sull'istessa corda*), with the beautiful modulation from D major through C natural (chord of 2nd) to B (chord of seventh), accompanied in rocking motion by the first violins – these are not just words of **melancholy**, they are words of **shaking fear**. The voice, which with velvet melancholy calls out '*Ohime*' must suddenly switch to a muted tone, as it were *tremolo con sordini*. At the words '*il piè vacilla*', the first violin takes on increased motion in consequence of the melody being perhaps too charming; but all this is justified and the whole well blended by the new twist given to the harmony [description of bars 40–42] – a really great stroke of genius! The exclamation '*oh Dio!*' must be held by the singer in a doleful but not shrill manner and may perhaps be embellished by a modest ornament, thus:

If one rightly expresses the various nuances of this passage, one has declaimed properly.

The Recitative's accompaniment now admirably blends with the theme of the Aria proper, and the passage is the more remarkable in that the gentleness is in great contrast to the foregoing harshness in the modulation. The horn and flute announce the theme; and it is indescribable what effect is brought forth in the sad loveliness of this movement, with its violin *pizzicati* and the two violas [Artaria's marking]; how wise is this anticipation of the vocal entry, which the listener will now recognize when the principal voice has it. Before this happens, however, there is the *arioso* section '*Ombra del caro bene, fra i mirti*' &c., whose connected intervals in stately procession must be produced gently and quietly, not too quickly. (Here a remark about the pronunciation of the syllable '*mio*' is perhaps advisable [footnote explaining that in Italian certain words admit of two pronunciations, a quick and a slow one – '*Dio*' or '*Di-o*', whereby the 'i' of the quick one must not be pronounced as if it were 'j', i.e. '*Djo*'. Another illustration from the Greek]). Another repetition of the theme by horn and flute! Then, at the words '*teco sarò*' the singer's calm may be raised to an expression of joy.

In a moment the effect passes like water over the dam. The singer thinks she hears her lover calling her from the banks of the Lethe, reproaching her for her complicity in his death. The '*che sento*?' must be sung with a fearful and frightened voice. The next sentence again fearful, but without too rapid an expression. Strong tone at '*funesti*'.

Here I have to complain of a real mistake in expression on the part of the composer: but it is the **only** one. The singer actually addresses her lover and repeats the words which he used: '*fuggi*' &c. But why does Haydn divide the words from the previous ones, '*mi rispondi*'? – If I quote someone else, do I insert a long pause between the words quoted and my own? Nothing further from the truth! I recite them in one breath. I identify myself with the person, take on his personality: if he is violent, I am violent, if gentle I am gentle, etc. I don't stop to think like a bad actor who hasn't learned his role quite by heart. But this is what H. does to his singer, in that he divides the words '*funesti*' and '*fuggi*', not only by a crotchet and two minim rests in the vocal part but also through the *a tempo* two notes of Violins I & II, making it impossible for her to rectify the mistake by quick recitation. He set a full stop where a colon should have been placed. Not to remark that at these words (one sees the fact also by the outburst up the scale that follows) the tempo must be accelerated and the marking *presto* should not have been forgotten. Also the '*Tu m'uccidesti*' must be accentuated; instead of the interval

an appoggiatura must be sung:

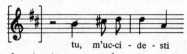

tu, m'uc-ci - de - sti

as is well known from the singing manuals.

And now the Aria, in two parts: a gentle, imploring one and a violent end. The economy therein is admirable. Equally great and appropriate the relationship between the parts. Well prepared by the orchestra the singer's entrance, ranging later from gentleness to cutting and explosive misery over the cruel results of her innocent love. No unnecessary, silly repetitions! No artful contortions of the vocal chords in melismatic sing-song; and also no mere declamatory and unperiodical melody! And the accompaniment! What an accompaniment! One can take this Aria as a model of real description of feeling, and of a judicious musical arrangement.

The theme itself, which remains exclusively in that range which comes from the chest with full strength and unmixed force . . .: can one imagine a theme more satisfying, singable, touching? It is as if it came from Hasse's soul, in the most noble and greatest of taste – Oh how different from the fearfully contrived melodies that characterize a certain school here, and proof that the great well-spring of pure song has not yet dried up for him who has the genius to find it. With what a fulness it starts in the dominant, to come to the tonic via the third, insinuates itself by neighbouring notes up, then down, then up still another note [bar 73] and then in the gentlest fall it slips into silence, disappears, wilts! This theme has such magic for my ear and heart that I could sing it to myself for days on end without getting tired of it.

Also the words are put together according to their sound in such a way that I cannot believe any language could offer syllables which are more beautiful and hardly any which could equal them. The delightful alternation of vowels and consonants! Lots of 'o's, 'a's, a couple of soft 'e's to offset the 'a's and 'o's; and so that the sound is not too feminine through the use of 'l' and 'b' some rolling masculine syllables on 'r'. [There follows a long digression concerning articulation, vowels, etc.]

I wished in fact to say that among all consonants I know, 'r' is the one, properly spoken, [which is of primary importance. Pronunciation of 'r' in two ways, guttural and rolling. Long footnote on French pronunciation of 'r': pp. 1097–1104.]

Returning to our beautiful Aria theme, we should add that it begins with a semibreve [bar 71] which gives the singer the opportunity of introducing a fine, swelling crescendo. In the next bar the note or rather grace note 'a' must be accented. [Long description of accents]

'*Ah, non chiamarmi infida!*' The request is said twice. A less wise composer would perhaps have repeated '*ombra del caro bene*' or the whole sentence. Not nearly so good! Also the declamatory effect is entirely appropriate when the first time the request is in the high register [bars 75f.] and then in a lower [76–8]. That's the way we ask in real life: **first** in a lively way, then with increasing modesty. With an exclamation of approval it's the other way round. **Its** vehemence increases by repetition and requires raising the pitch and increasing the speed.

The singer supports her request by a well grounded reason: 'Such a reproach would be unjust; she loved her Philen most faithfully!' The musical interpretation used between request and reason is well presented. At the word '*ombra*' the vocal line sinks down an octave, as low as possible, and remains there in those dark regions for half a bar, rising by third and fifth. Here [bar 82] the appoggiatura can be of very plastic effect.

Haydn, instead of doing what other composers would have done (*e.g.* **Graun** and **Hasse** who were, I hope, not motivated by their own genius in this respect but influenced by the spirit of their times . . .) – instead, as I say, of Haydn, after announcing the theme, beginning it anew, taking the letter 'a' in '*cara*' and using it for a series of roulades, and putting the theme through its paces in small figures in the manner of sonata form (wrongly taking a leaf from rhetoric, which has to do with clear ideas, and transferring it to the realms of music, which is a dark art) – none of all that! The address '*ombra*' &c. is repeated once and the request '*Ah, non chiamarmi*' &c. twice with, in turn, the most fitting sense of declamation the second time in a lower range. God be praised for this noble, true simplicity.

At the second repetition a fermata is called for [bar 87] . . . [and the singer may add a cadenza]. But not a long, involved one with intricate modulations but simply, as your mother [Madame von Wintheim] with wise precaution did. She did no more than to run up the diatonic scale to the octave and then to jump with great precision down to the lower octave. A desperate, dangerous interval, which must be done perfectly if song is not to turn into howling. One can simplify the intonation and give the melisma still more beauty if in descending one takes in f sharp and the upper d sharp as well.

In Haydn's praise we must remark on the properly unsatisfactory nature of the cadence on the second interval [f sharp: bar 87].

The fermata on '*infida*' is not a formal caesura on which to construct any kind of edifice, and just as feeling dictates, it must not disturb the vocal line's progress. Such fermatas are actually pleonasms in the musical notation and do not mean more than the pauses that are placed over them. The singer's sentence, moreover, is not yet finished at this point; she must once more assure of her unwavering love; this occurs twice, the first time with a pattern on the word '*ombra*' which is like a phrase in the bass line (excellent because of the horrible implication of the word – adjacent intervals would have meant **nothing** here), and the next time even more brilliantly in that Haydn does not, as every ear would expect, go to the dominant of the key in which the piece is based, but to the second. To add another dark nuance he … introduces d sharp [bar 99] to the cadence. How horrifying this ending is, can be heard even by an untrained ear; and it is very original, too; as one cannot in fact count Haydn among the masters *qui semper chorda oberrant eadem* (always harping on one string). The novelty of his transitions is generally known and admired.

For the singer of this Aria I ought to add that since, in the course of her protestations, the melismatic figure

appears four times, she would do well the second time to add the following variant:

The more delicately and gracefully she applies her *calando* here, the stronger will we believe her '*fida*'. It seems to me to be a good idea to apply a fermata here throughout the score where there are two quaver rests [bars 89, 94]: this suspension is entirely appropriate; the singer reflects a moment after '*fida ti amai*' and then continues with greater conviction.

And now all of a sudden the emotions of that miserable woman flame up, brilliantly prepared by the orchestra in a wild lament over the desperation of her love which caused Philen such grief. Bass and viola hasten up the diatonic scale, and the first violins have the same trend but are enlivened by intervals of the third, while the second violins have almost the same effect with their figure [bar 101] – what variety there is in all this liveliness! – and now everyone retires before the singer … The dotted passage in thirds [bar 101] for the vocal part is a powerful wild effect: [*u–n*]*a pietà fe*[*-dele*], which must be sung not in a dead but a strong, lamenting voice. These nuances are not easy to differentiate, but in declamatory passages there is a great difference between the tone of shock and that of grumbling indignation. Excellent, too, the inversion of the words (at '*Tiranna*'), where bitter unwillingness is increased to the highest potential by a chromatic change; until at the words '*infelice amor*' we reach an original modulation, in bitterly protesting tone, that takes us to the dominant of B minor [bars 114f.].

It is reasonable for the singer to remain a bar in these dark-hued thoughts, accompanied by the sad echo of the orchestra [bar 115]. She may express her sorrow as delicately as she can, but not in the form of a cadence; she would be advised to sing as *calando* as possible and then by means of an upbeat continue to address her dead lover. At the words '*caro*' the vocal line sinks to darkness again, rises again dully (do not exaggerate the accents here!) and has a breathtaking leap of a tenth from c sharp [bars 119f.]. The e must sound loud and clear, but not with an *éclat de voix* about which Rousseau complains in his nation's vocal school. Excellent from the declamatory and rhythmic standpoints is Haydn's second repetition of '*ah, non chiamarmi infida*', squeezed into $1\frac{1}{2}$ bars, where originally they required $2\frac{1}{2}$ and had long notes: an effect of acceleration which the violins continue in dashing patterns. And so the restless accompaniment fights, in light and (where the voice dominates) in darkness, with the voice until the final cadence. Before this occurs there is a fermata [bars 135f.] where a small cadenza may be added; there is also a small melisma, but only half-a-bar long and for all its small size requires practice, because of the swift tempo, if one is to leave it cleanly. It ends with a passage which of course one has heard before; but this typical *aria di bravura* conclusion is, like eating bread, something of which one never tires because it has truth and melody. Opera composers who know their business like to end an act with such a cadence, which continues to sound long after in the listeners' ears and assures the departing singers of loud applause. [Comparison with Salieri; reflections on 'borrowings', etc.]

I must almost fear that you will have had enough of my chatter. I have nothing to add; once I decided to analyze this fine Cantata by Haydn, I could not be more brief even at the risk of seeming to be microscopic. . . . C. F. C.

[Magazin der Musik, 1783, pp. 1075–1115]

This Chronicle has shown often enough that apparently unimportant receipts are sometimes of crucial importance in tracing Haydn's life and movements. For example:

Conto. I the undersigned worked 12 days repairing the clavier and harpsichord instruments, per accord two Gulden for each day, makes a total of twenty-four Gulden.

Esterhaz, 3rd March 1781.   Anton Walter, Organ and Instrument Maker.

[Haydn's countersignature:] These clavier and harpsichord [instruments] have been examined closely by me and found in order.

Josephus Haydn mpria
Capell Meister.
[A.M. Fasc. XVII.1128. Valkó II, 590]

Anton Walter, the greatest fortepiano builder of his age, was summoned to Eszterháza in February 1781. We believe there is an obvious explanation for Walter's presence: in the fire of 1779, Haydn's theatre harpsichord was completely burned. In the bill a precise difference is made between pianos (*clavier*) and harpsichords (*Flügel*); why summon Walter unless he had actually delivered at least one grand fortepiano? We suggest that after November 1779 Haydn followed the modern trend and substituted a fortepiano for the old large harpsichord (concert and theatre), but the singers of course probably had numerous spinets, harpsichords; and perhaps, as we have suggested, there were also English square pianos as well. Perhaps the Walter fortepiano now in the Haydn Museum (Eisenstadt) was originally an Eszterháza instrument. Walter was a witness to the première of *La fedeltà premiata*, as the date of his bill indicates (3 March and at the Castle for twelve days).

On 12 April died in Vienna the famous old Italian poet, Pietro Metastasio, whom Haydn had known since he lived in the same house (*c.* 1750: Michaeler-Haus) in Vienna; Haydn had set only one of Metastastio's dramas, *L'isola disabitata*, the old-fashioned style of which was rapidly putting it out of the operatic running. The poet was eighty-three.

On 14 April, Haydn and his wife were godparents at the baptism of Anna Elssler in the Parish Church of Süttör.[1] On 1 May died Maria Theresia, *née* Countess Erdödy, for whose wedding celebrations in 1763 with (Paul) Anton, eldest son of Prince Nicolaus, Haydn had composed his first Italian *opera seria*, *Acide*.

On 27 May we have the following informative letter from Haydn to Artaria:

[To Artaria & Co., Vienna. *German*]

Estoras, 27th May 1781.

Nobly born,
Most highly respected Sir!

I am most obliged to you for the 4 copies, so beautifully engraved.[2] Concerning the *Lieder*,[3] I have completed 14 of the same with all possible diligence, and the number would have been completed long ago if I had had the texts of them; I cannot quite understand why *Herr Hofrath von Greiner*[4] does not return them to me, since at one time they were in my hands. I only wanted his opinion as to the expression contained therein, and sent them to him *via* Herr Walther, the organ-builder; but now I receive no answer from either of them. If you would be good enough to try to press the matter with Herr Walther, I should be most obliged to you, for I assure you that these *Lieder* perhaps surpass all my previous ones in variety, naturalness, and ease of vocal execution. I rather doubt, however, that you will take them, for in the first place I ask 30 ducats, secondly 6 copies, and thirdly the following short dedication, to be placed on the title page:

Collection of German Lieder
for the pianoforte,
dedicated
as a mark of special homage
to
Mademoiselle Clair
by
Mr. Joseph Haydn
Chapel Master to Prince Esterházy.

Between ourselves, this *Mademoiselle* is the darling of my Prince. You will certainly see for yourself what an impression such things make! If you agree to these points, I shall not fail to complete the others one after the other. These *Lieder* however, must appear first on Elizabeth Day, for this is the name-day of the fair lady.

---

1 A. Csatkai, 'Haydnra és zenekarára Vonatkozó a Datok a Süttöri Anayakönyvekböl', in *Zenetudományi Tanulmányok* VIII (1960), p. 670. Pohl II, 192.
2 Of the *Sei Divertimenti* (fl., 2 horns, str.), Op. 31, published in April (pl. no. 7).
3 Artaria accepted the *Lieder*, which they published in two sets: the first in December 1781, the second two years later. Concerning the dedication, see *infra*, p. 586.
4 Franz von Greiner, a well-known music-lover in Vienna. His daughter, Caroline Pichler, wrote memoirs which are a useful source of information about contemporary Vienna. Mozart, Haydn, Salieri, Paisiello and Cimarosa were all friends of the house. See Artaria-Botstiber, p. 12, also *infra*, p. 503.

Now something from Paris. Monsieur Le Gros,[1] *Directeur* of the Concert Spirituel, wrote me the most flattering things about my *Stabat Mater*, which was performed there four times with the greatest applause; the gentlemen asked permission to have it engraved. They made me an offer to engrave all my future works on the most favourable terms for myself, and were most surprised that I was so singularly successful in my vocal compositions; but I wasn't at all surprised, for they have not yet heard anything. If they only could hear my operetta *L'isola disabitata*[2] and my most recent opera, *La fedeltà premiata*,[3] I assure you that no such work has been heard in Paris up to now, nor perhaps in Vienna either; my misfortune is that I live in the country.

I enclose Herr Boccherini's letter:[4] please present my respectful compliments to him. No one here can tell me where this place Arenas is. It cannot be far from Madrid, however; please let me know about this, for I want to write to Herr Boccherini myself.

I remain most respectfully,

Your most obedient servant,
Joseph Haydn.

P.S. Many people are delighted with my portrait.[5] Return the oil-portrait to me in the same case.

[CCLN, 27f.]

On 30 May, during one of the visits of Duke Albert von Sachsen-Teschen and his wife, Archduchess Marie Christine, to Eszterháza, there was an extraordinary concert held in, of all places, the picture gallery; it was directed, of course, by Haydn. Idle though it is to speculate on the programme, we cannot refrain from suggesting that this concert may have seen the first performances of some of Haydn's latest string quartets, namely Opus 33, which he offered for sale in MS. on 3 December (*infra*, pp. 454f.).

In June we have two bills ('Specifications') written by Haydn himself concerning the organization of music paper and strings etc.[6]

Another letter to Artaria is dated 23 June:

[To Artaria & Co., Vienna. *German*]

Estoras, 23rd June 1781.

Nobly born,
Most highly respected Sir!

I received with the greatest pleasure the oil-portrait together with the twelve copies you enclosed of the beautifully engraved portrait. My gracious Prince,

1 Joseph Le Gros (1739–93) was a singer in the Paris Opéra. In 1777, he assumed the directorship of the Concert Spirituel. See Pohl II, 175.
2 Performed at the Esterháza Theatre on the Prince's name-day, 6 December 1779.
3 Performed at the Eszterháza Theatre on 25 February 1781.
4 Boccherini wrote to Artaria from Arenas in February 1781 as follows: '... Spero mi faranno un favore, che io stimerò moltismo ed è che se alcuno di lor Sigri (come è probabile) conoscesse il Sigr. Giuseppe Haidn [*sic*] scrittore, da me, e da tutti aprezzato al Maggior segno, gli offra i miei rispetti, dicendoli che sono uno de i suoi più appassionati stimatori, e ammiratori insieme del suo Genio, e Musicali componimenti dei quali qui si fà tutto quel apprezzo, che in rigor di Giustizia si meritano ...' (Artaria-Botstiber, p. 11; Pohl II, 180, n. 6.)
5 Artaria published a series of portraits (engravings' of well-known persons, musical and otherwise. In June 1781, Haydn's portrait, painted and engraved by J. E. Mansfeld, was announced. Although Haydn was pleased with it (it is the earliest picture of Haydn which we can date with certainty), the engraving is not a good likeness; at best one can describe it as 'flattering'. See pl. 1.
6 'Specification of strings to be ordered, viz: two bundles of Italian fifths (*Quinten*), the bundle à 2 Fl. . . . 4 Fl. / two bundles of the ordinary kind à 1 Fl. 30 xr. . . . 3 Fl. / one bundle of A. . . . 1 Fl. / 10 bunches [*Büschl*] D, the bunch à 6 xr. . . . —[Fl.] 48 xr. / 12 bunches G à 4 xr. . . . —16 xr. / 4 violin pegs à 4 xr. . . . 16 xr. / 2 viola pegs à 4 xr. . . . 8 xr. / four Bassetl ['cello] A à 5 xr. . . . 20 xr. / four Bassetl D à 5 xr. . . . 20 xr. / One Bassetl bridge but somewhat higher than usual. . . . 34 xr. / Josephus Haydn mpria / Capell Meister Summa . . . 12 Fl. 8 xr.' [Countersigned by Prince Nicolaus, Eszterház, 10 June 1781, 'to be purchased in the finest quality ...'. A.M. Fasc. XVII.1121. Valkó II, 591. 'Specification of music paper to be ordered, *viz*. 6 books quarto with 10 staves, the book à 40 xr. . . . 4 Fl. / 6 books oblong with 10 staves dto. . . . 4 Fl. / 2 books oblong with 12 staves dto. . . . 1 Fl. 20 xr. / Summa 9 Fl. 20 xr. / Esterház, 16th June 1781 Josephus Haydn mpria. / Capell Meister.' A.M. Fasc. XVII.1120. Valkó II, 590.

however, was even more delighted, for as soon as his attention was drawn to it, he immediately asked me to give him one. Since these 12 copies are not enough, I would ask you, good Sir, to send me another six at my expense. You can subtract the sum from my fee for the *Lieder*, six of which I shall send you in a few weeks.

Fifteen are now finished, but among them is one[1] which the strict censorship may perhaps not allow; it is one of those which you yourself gave me, and you shall have the words of it in a few days. I should be sorry about this, for I have composed a remarkably good air to it. To this day I have not received the other *Lieder* from Herr von Greiner; they are certainly lost. You would therefore oblige me if you would procure a dozen others from Herr von Greiner, but only good ones and varied, so that I may have a choice: for it often happens that a certain poem has a real antipathy to the composer, or the composer to the poem.

Moreover, I agree to the stipulated price of one ducat a piece, but no one should know anything about this. Also I do not want any money until all the proofs have been passed. I am still in doubt about the dedication: i.e., whether I should dedicate it to her [*Mademoiselle* Clair] or to someone else. But enough – I reserve this right, and 12 free copies.

As soon as I come to Vienna, will you be kind enough, good Sir, to present me to the worthy Herr von Mansfeld?

Meanwhile I thank you for the copies [of the music][2] and the other portraits and remain, Sir, most respectfully,

Your obedient servant,
Joseph Haydn.

[No address: Artaria's clerk notes: 'Haydn/ Esterhaz 13 June 1781/ ans. 5th July'.]

In his MS. autobiography (Gesellschaft der Musikfreunde), Abbé Maximilian Stadler, a friend of Haydn's and Mozart's, tell us that he visited Haydn at Eszterháza in July. Stadler was also at Eszterháza when Haydn had just received the commission to compose *The Seven Words*.[3] On 4 July, Haydn's former patroness, the Dowager Princess Esterházy, *née* Marchesa Lunati Visconti, died at Eisenstadt, aged seventy-one. Count Zinzendorf writes: 'La bonne Princesse d'Esterhazi est morte hier au couvent d'Eisenstadt a 11ᵉ du soir. ... à 70 ans elle avait l'air d'en avoir cinquante.' Haydn had composed *L'infedeltà delusa* in her honour, and it is possible that his gravely beautiful *Libera* was composed for her Requiem at Eisenstadt.[4]

There follows a well-known letter to Artaria, dated 20 July:

[To Artaria & Co., Vienna. *German*]

Estoras, 20th July 1781.

Nobly born,
Most highly respected Sir!

I send you herewith the first 12 *Lieder*, and will endeavour to send you the second dozen, good Sir, as soon as possible: some of them are written twice over, in case my handwriting should not always be entirely legible, but I would prefer that you engrave them from my autograph.

In the third *Lied*, please note that following the completed text, at the bottom, the words 'N.B.' must be engraved in just the same way as I have indicated below the text.

---

1 The twelfth, 'Die zu späte Ankunft der Mutter', in which the daughter cries to the mother: 'It has happened, so you might as well go away again.'
2 Probably either the Sonatas, Op. 30 and/or the Divertimenti, Op. 31: see *supra*.
3 *Vide infra*, p. 616. See also *Haydn in England 1791–1895*, pp. 113f., 415, and *Haydn: the Years of 'The Creation' 1796–1800*, p. 479.
4 The *Libera* was more probably composed for the death of the reigning Princess in 1790, but we cannot be sure. On the *Libera*, see Landon in *HJB* IV, 140ff. Pohl II, 192.

You will find the words of the 4th, 8th and 9th *Lieder* in Friebert's[1] *Lieder*, as published by Herr von Kurzböck,[2] but in case you cannot get them, I shall send them to you. These 3 *Lieder* have been set to music by *Capellmeister* Hofmann,[3] but between ourselves, miserably; and just because this braggart thinks that he alone has ascended the heights of Mount Parnassus, and tries to disgrace me every time with a certain high society, I have composed these very three *Lieder* just to show this would-be high society the difference: *Sed hoc inter nos.*

You will find the texts of the 10th and 12th *Lieder* among those you sent me, and I enclose herewith the texts. Under No. 12 you will find the text of which I recently expressed some doubt as to the censorship.

Those notes which I have marked in red should be engraved in very small type; They appear in only very few of the *Lieder* and are indicated by a 'NB' in front of each line.

Above all I ask you to engrave the musical signs as I have written them: for instance, you will find the following: ∿ ∞ *tr* ∾ and likewise the *da capo* sign *ss* such as appears in every *Lied*. Please return the printed *Lied* which I have attached to No. 7.

I pray you especially, good Sir, not to let anyone copy, sing, or in any way alter these *Lieder* before publication, because when they are ready, I shall sing them myself in the critical houses. By his presence and through the proper execution, the master must maintain his rights: these are only songs, but they are not the street songs of Hofmann, wherein neither ideas, expression nor, much less, melody appear.

You once again make me your debtor for the portraits you sent; but do they sell? I'm curious. In any event the frame-makers and gilders have profited by those you sent to me.

When you have an opportunity, please send back the cardboard cover in which the *Lieder* were packed: such material is not to be had here.

Meanwhile I remain, most respectfully,

Your most obedient servant,
Josephus Haydn mpria.

[No address; Artaria's clerk notes: 'Haydn / Esterhas, 20. lugl. 1781 / risp. – 20. 7ber' and further down the page, 'NB. / Bocherini']

[CCLN, 30f.][4]

On 14 August, Nunziato Porta submitted his bill for two operas in the Eszterháza repertoire, Sacchini's(?) *La contadina in corte* and Righini's *Il convitato di pietra.*[5]

Haydn now entered into profitable negotiations with the British music publisher, William Forster. The go-between was General Charles Jerningham, British Ambassador to the Court of Vienna and a welcome guest at Eszterháza (he is mentioned in the *Excursion* of May 1784, *vide supra*, p. 103). The correspondence with

---

1 Carl Frieberth, the former member of the Esterházy *Capelle.*
2 Joseph von Kurzbeck, who had issued Haydn's Sonatas Nos. 36–41 (XVI:21–26) in 1774.
3 Leopold Hofmann, whose name is well known to readers. He was then *Kapellmeister* at St Peter's Church and later Cathedral Chapel Master at St Stephen's in Vienna.
4 The autograph of this letter was not available when we published CCLN in 1959. We have subsequently been given photographs by the owner, Mr. R. F. Kallir, New York City, to whom we are most grateful.
5 'Conto. La Contadina in Corte portata da Vienna appartenente a me sottoscritto. Partitura, parti cantanti e Orchestra. Importa in tutto Fl. 32. 24 [xr.]. / Il Convitato di Pietra come sopra con tutte le parti dell'orchestra, e delli Cantanti e partitura ed anche con diverse aggiunte fatte al detto spartito, importa in tutto 51 Fl. 36 [xr.]. / Summa: 85 Fl. Nunziato Porta. Eszterház, den 14ten Augusti 1781. [in Haydn's hand. *German*] I have correctly received these 85 Fl. from Chief Cashier Züsser. / Josephus Haydn mpria. / Capell Meister / Estoras, 5 Oct. 1781.' A.M. Fasc. XVII.1117. Valkó II, 592. Bartha-Somfai, 94.

Haydn did not begin for several years and is presented, as usual, chronologically, but we may present the other material here.[1]

William Forster was also a well-known maker of stringed instruments, and in *Haydn in England 1791–1795* (p. 232) we note that he repaired Haydn's viola in 1794.

[1] Our information is taken principally from (*a*) Sandys & Forster, *The History of the Violin*, London 1866 (hereinafter 'Sandys-Forster') and (*b*) file of material, mainly Haydn's autograph letters to the firm, from the publisher, now in the British Museum, MS. Egerton 2380, ff. 1–25; the MSS. that Haydn sent to Forster, with the exception of Symphonies 74 and 70, are in Egerton 2379, ff. 1–386b, and 2334, ff. 1–35.

Warned to expect the first work from Haydn (Symphony No. 74), Forster consulted a solicitor, who on 17 August submitted the following bill:

Attending Mr. Forster in conference on a contract, intended to be entered into by Mr. Forster with Mr. Haydn, for Mr. Forster's purchasing of him and printing his compositions, and advising thereon.

Taking Instructions for drawing Agreem^{ts} between Mr. Haydn and him, and for the sale and purchase of Mr. Haydn's Musical Compositions by Mr. Forster.

Drawing same, fo. 15.

Attending to read over and settle same.

Engrossing same for Execution.

Attending and advising Mr. Forster as to the mode of execution of same by Mr. Haydn, and which he was to communicate to Genl. Jerningham, who had undertaken to get it signed by Mr. Haydn at Vienna. [Sandys-Forster, 301]

Forster immediately brought Sir Charles Jerningham into the affair, who a few days later wrote as follows:

Sir/I received Your favour 21 ins.^t & send here inclosed a letter for Mr Giuseppe Hayden to whom I have written very circumstantially & inclosed to him a procuration which he is to gett drawn up either in French, German, or Latin, & authenticated by two wittnesses & a publick notary, which gives it full force in all Countries; you may depend on it that what I have sent to M^r. Hayden is to the full as strong as the letter of Attorney you sent me in which theres nothing but a repetition of words. If you receive from Hayden a letter for me send it to Lady Jerninghams in Grovener [*sic*] square she will take care I get it[.] when Hayden has sent you his procuration to print his musick lett me know it and am Sir Your most obed^t humble serv^t Charles Jerningham. Cawsey August 24th 1781. [CCLN 70, misdated]

From Sandys-Forster, we learn when Haydn's various MSS. arrived in London, viz:

On the fly-leaf of one of the old account-books for 1786 is written, 'The dates of the years when Haydn's works came', which are as follows:—

Augt. 22, 1781	Haydn's Ov^t. N° 1 [Symphony No. 74]			
June 20, 1782	Do	„ „ 2 [„ No. 70]		
Feby. 14, 1784	Do	Do	„ 4 [„ No. 76]	
„ 24, 1784	Do	Do	„ 5 [„ No. 77]	
May 6, 1784	Do	„ „ 6 [„ No. 78]		
July 6, 1784	Do	Trios, op. 38 [Trios IV:6–11]		
Novr 22, 1784	Do	Ov^t. N° 7 [Symphony No. 81]		
„ 26, 1784	Do	Do „ 8 [Overture to *Armida*]		
Decr. 6, 1784	Do	Do „ 9 [Symphony No. 80]		
Jany. 3, 1785	Do	Sonatas, op. 40 [Piano Trios XV:3/4 (Pleyel) and No. 18 (XV:5)]		
Decr. 26, 1785	Do	„ op. 42 [Piano Trios 22, 17, 23 (XV:9, 2, 10)]		

July 16, 1787. Recd. of Haydn M.S.S. of the Crucifixion published under the title of 'Passione'. Ten guineas was paid for this instrumental piece; and the Postage cost fifteen shillings.

5 Octr. 1787. Received the M.S.S. of Haydn's quartets, op. 44. Twenty guineas was paid for these; and the Postage cost twenty shillings. [*The Seven Words* and Quartets, Opus 50]

Sandys-Forster provide us with an enlightening balance for the costs to an eighteenth-century publisher (*The Seven Words*):

	£	s.	d.
65 Pewter plates, at 1s. 6d. per plate..	4	17	6
Engraving the same, at 4s. 6d. do..	14	12	6
Copper title and engraving..	1	11	6
66 quires of perfect paper for 75 copies, at 1s..	3	6	0
Printing 75 copies, at 1s. 2d.	4	7	6
Cost of the manuscript	28	15	0
	10	10	0
Making in the aggregate	£39	5	0

Fifty copies were first printed and in 1817–8 another twenty-five. The full price of each copy was fifteen shillings, but many were sold to subscribers at 10s. 6d. each, and most of the remaining copies probably went at the trade price of twelve shillings. A total income of forty-five pounds would be expected, but it is known that some of the second printing were disposed of as waste paper. Mr. Forster will have been lucky to have made five pounds on the whole transaction. [p. 312] [Summary HCRL]

Among Haydn's friends for whom Forster made instruments were violas for Dr. Wolcot (*alias* Peter Pindar, whose 'Storm' Haydn set to music) and Gaetano Bartolozzi, a violoncello for Thomas Holcroft (1787), a violin for Miss Abrams (1789) and in 1790 another violin and a viola, a violin (a copy of a Steiner) for Holcroft in 1791 and one of his 'best violoncellos' (No. 20) for our ancestor, the Rev. Mr. Landon (1758–1838), D.D. of Whittington, Provost of Worcester College, Oxford, and in 1802 Vice-Chancellor of the University.[1]

On 24 August, Haydn again ordered more strings.[2]

On 13 September, Prince Nicolaus ordered two hundred gulden to be paid by Chief Cashier Züsser to Inspector Kleinrath 'for eight operas that were purchased'.[3]

We may mention a receipt by Haydn of 15 September[4] and pass on to the following bill by Schellinger:

Conto. / The work I did on operas from 1st April to Sept. 1781 – the Bogen at 5 xr.

	Bögen	
Discordia Fortunata	79	[*ossia L'avaro deluso* by Paisiello]
Sinfonien 12. duplicate parts	86	[Haydn's?]
Francese bizzaro	69	[Astaritta]
Gli stravaganti	81	[*ossia La schiava riconosciuta* by Piccinni]
L'infedelta fedele[5]	82	[the original 'working' title of Haydn's
	397	*La fedeltà premiata*]

Makes 33 Fl. 5 xr.   Giov. Schellinger Souffler mpria.
[Haydn's hand] I have found these 397 Bögen to be correct, reckoned at 5 xr. per Bogen

Josephus Haydn mpria
Capell Meister

[Prince Nicolaus's order for payment, Esterhaz, 18th Sept. 1781. A.M. Fasc. XVII, 1108. Bartha, 102f. Valkó II, 590]

Antonio Pesci helped to organize new operas for the Eszterháza repertoire, and at the end of September we find him writing to the Prince as follows:

---

1 Sandys-Forster 320, 321, 338. Larsen, *HÜB*, 116ff. *Account of the Family of Landon of Mornington and Credenhill Co. Hereford*, London 1912, pp. 4, 14.
2 'Specification of strings to be ordered, viz.: 4 bundles E, the bundle at 2 Fl. . . . . . makes 8 Fl. / 1 bundle A . . . . 1 Fl. 30 xr. / half a bundle D . . . . . 1 Fl. 30 xr. / 6 G . . . . . — 24 xr. / 2 viola G . . . . . . — 10 xr. / 2 violoncello A . . . . — 10 xr. / an ordinary violon [double bass] bow . . . . . 1 Fl. 17 xr. Summa: 13 Fl. 1 xr. / Estoras, 24th August 1781 Josephus Haydn mpria / Capell Meister. / This conto has been correctly paid to me . . . Vienna, 6th Sept. 1781. / Michael Ignatz Stadlmann I. R. Court Lute and Violin maker.' A.M. Fasc. XVII.1115. Valkó II, 592.
3 Michael Kleinrath notes: 'Since of these eight operas, three were incomplete, these latter were returned and, for the other five, only one hundred twenty-five gulden (125 fl.) were paid.' These operas came from the effects of Joseph Bustelli in Prague and the money received by Peter Bianchi 'als Joseph Bustellischer Executor Testamenti', Vienna, 12 Oct. 1781. A.M. XVII, 1114 and 1113. Another letter by Nunziato Porta informs us that two of these operas were Traetta's *Il cavaliere errante* (Eszterháza 1782) and Guglielmi's *Orlando Paladino*, performed at Vienna on 19 June 1777. (The libretto for that occasion, printed by Kurzbeck, of which we own a copy, lists no composer.) The two operas were in score, and Haydn needed the second one as the textual basis for his own forthcoming work on the same subject (1782). Porta informs the Prince that seven months ago [Nov. 1781] he wrote, according to a princely order, to Braunschweig (Brunswick) to organize the two operas. During the negotiations Bustelli died in Vienna and in his effects were *inter alia* these two operas, which could be had at half the price (the rest of the financial details may be omitted). 'I also purchased the Opera *La vedova scaltra* [Righini] in score, in Vienna; 17 Fl.' The other two operas cost 18 Fl. Prince Esterházy passed the letter for payment on 20 June 1782. A.M. 64/4002. Bartha-Somfai, 96f., facsimile of Porta's letter, useful for identifying the handwriting (we find it in the Paris copy of *La vera costanza*, mostly in Haydn's autograph, of 1785), as No. 4.
4 Haydn received from Secretary Jacob Kaufmann the salaries (one month) of Kraft and 'Makovec', 'cellist and horn-player, resp., a total of 68 f. 36½ xr. A.M. XVII, 1116. Valkó II, 592.
5 These 82 *Bögen* represent changes and additions that Haydn was obliged to make as a result of his losing *inter alia* Celia *Vide infra*, p. 540. Cimarosa's Opera, from which Haydn took the libretto, was entitled *L'infedeltà fedele*.

A Monsieur Pietro Martelli in Bologna per Commissione di Musica data da Mons. Pesci

Per le Parti Cantanti delle due Opera Isabella e Rodrigo. Giardiniera brillante [Anfossi & Sarti]¹ Zecchini 7½. Per Saldo delle altre Due Opere che sono state già pagate resta un Zecchino, che sono in Tutto Zecchini 8½.

Antonio Pesci.

[Prince Nicolaus's approval for payment, 27 September 1781; Haydn's countersignture, Estoras, 5 Oct. 1781. A.M. XVII, 1109. Bartha-Somfai 92.]

The opera season at Eszterháza ended much earlier than usual (in September), because the Prince was away from the Castle.

The Prince made a journey to Paris. One document on the subject reads as follows:

[*Musikalischer Almanach für Deutschland auf das Jahr 1783*. Leipzig im Schwickertschen Verlag, pp. 100f.:]

Princely Esterhazische Kapelle at Esterhaz in Hungary. (Since last winter [1781–2] the Prince undertook a journey to Paris, which will last half-a-year if not a whole year, his Kapelle was reduced to only a few members. This list contains, therefore, the Kapelle as it was before said reduction.)

Director and Kapellmeister.

Joseph Hayden [*sic*]. Also plays the first violin.

Violinists.

Luigi Tomasini, Pauer. Nicoletto Mestrino. Ungricht. Hirsek [*sic*]. Fux. Menzl. Hofmann. Oliva. Potzelli.

	Viola-players.
Specht. Burksteiner.	
	Oboists.
Schandick. Mayer.	
	Horn-players.
Rupp, Mackoveicz.	
	Double-Bass-players.
Schringer. Dietzl.	
	Violoncellists.
Kraft. Pertoja.	
	Bassoon-players
Peczivall. Stainer.	

Singers, Male & Female
(actually opera singers)

Madame Bologna.	Demoiselle Bologna.
„ Raymondi.	„ Baldisdurla.
„ Polczelly.	Madame Pragetta. [*sic*]
„ Totti.	„[!] Pesci.
„[!] Dichtler.	„[!] Crinaczi.
„ Jermolj, absent	
„[!] Jermolj, absent	

Although the names are badly misspelled, the list is not uninteresting, and gave many people a first-hand (though Bowdlerized with the usual Austrian confusion over 'd', 't', 'b', 'p', etc.) account of Haydn's *Kapelle*. The Prince left after 27 September, when he signed a document, and was back by February 1782. For his return, tradition

---

1 Since *La giardiniera brillante* has not survived in EH and is not even listed in Haydn's *Opernliste* of 1784, we cannot identify the composer, but it was undoubtedly Giuseppe Sarti's setting of 1768 (Rome).

says that Haydn composed (assembled) his new Symphony No. 73 ('La Chasse'), using the favourite Overture to *La fedeltà premiata* as the Finale (Pohl II, 191).

About this time, the Tonkünstler-Societät in Vienna came with a request to Haydn: for a proposed revival of *Il ritorno di Tobia*, the composer should make changes in the score. The protocol contains Haydn's answer in the third person:

If the Society guarantees benefit tickets or another *bonification* for his efforts and expenses, he will shorten the Overture [*Symphonie*] and choruses and would take over the rehearsals and performances, for he flatters himself that the Society, as a result of his large circle of acquaintances and generally good reputation, would take in 100 ducats more.   [Pohl II, 86]

The Society did not accept Haydn's conditions and gave, instead, Hasse's old Oratorio, *Elena*.

The story of Haydn's relations with Spain must wait for a later chapter, but one part of it must be related here. Haydn sent, some time in the first half of 1781, a score of *L'isola disabitata* to the Prince of Asturias, later Carlos IV.[1] The *Wiener Zeitung* of 6 October reports:

His Catholic Majesty, the King of Spain, unexpectedly rewarded the princely Esterhazi *Herr Kapellmeister* Joseph Hayden [*sic*], long celebrated through his original compositions, for some music sent [to Spain]; the reward was a golden, jewel-studded tabatière and that which must far outweigh gold and jewels in the eye of a great artist, namely the flattering way it was presented. The Secretary of Legation of the Spanish Court, accredited to the I. R. Court, had, upon the explicit order of his monarch, to bring the present personally to Esterhaz and, apart from presenting the gift in person, he was to report to Madrit [*sic*] upon the box's delivery and also to assure [Haydn] of the ever well disposed wishes of his Catholic Majesty.

[*Anhang zur Wiener Zeitung Nr. 80. Sonnabend den 6. Weinmonat 1781*]

On 18 October Haydn writes to Artaria as follows:

[To Artaria & Co., Vienna. *German*]

Estoras, 18th October 1781.

Sir,

In great haste I inform you that next Monday I shall send you the proofs together with 6 new *Lieder*. Some small matters, and the 6 new Quartets[2] which must be ready in 3 weeks, kept me from the *Lieder*; but I shall deliver them in 14 days at the latest. I would like – if it is possible to have them quickly – to receive three new, gentle *Lieder* texts, because almost all the others are of a lusty character. The content of these can be melancholy, too: so that I have shadow and light, just as in the first twelve.

Your most obedient servant,
Joseph Haydn.

Please send me some more of my portraits.

1 The handsome score by a copyist, with corrections by Haydn (e.g. pp. 161, 171, 179, 192, 198, 302), is in the Library of Congress, M1500 H44 16 case, which institution kindly supplied a microfilm (we studied the MS. itself in 1955). The title reads: 'L'isola / disabitata / Azione Teatrale in due Parti / dedicata / a / sua A: R: il serenissimo Principe d' ASTURIAS'. The dedication reads: 'SERENISS:MO PRINCIPE / VOSTRA ALTEZZA REALE, che in mezzo alle sue utili e rispettabile occupazioni, sá mettere a profitto i monumenti destinati al necessario riposo, coltivando le scienze amene, suol adoprare la Musica, come una di quelle più proprie per la recreazione, e talvolto si degna di onorare le miei deboli produzioni, sentendole ed eseguendole ancora. Questa particolare mia felicità, che ignoravo fin ora, e la notoria benignità del' ALTEZZA VOSTRA REALE mi da coraggio per dedicare alla MEDESIMA la Musica dell' Isola disabitata da me composta; e che con la più profonda sommissione pongo a suoi REALI PIEDI. / SERENISS.MO PRINCIPE / DELLA REAL ALTEZZA VOSTRA / Umilissimo Devotissimo / Giuseppe Hayde.' [*sic*]
2 The Quartets are those known as Op. 33 (from Artaria's numbering).

[Address:] Monsieur
    Monsieur Artaria et Compag. press:
    Kupferstecher Comp.
           à
      Vienne.
[Artaria's clerk notes: 'Haydn. 1781 —/Esterhaz 18th Oct./ (rec'd) 22nd ditto / (ans.) 23rd ditto'.]   [CCLN, 32]

Haydn had completed his six new Quartets known to us as Opus 33. Instead of consigning them directly to a publisher, he decided to offer them to several selected patrons by subscription MSS.: no less than three such letters were sent from Vienna on 3 December (and probably many more have not survived):

[To J. C. Lavater, Zürich.[1] *German*. Only the signature autograph]
Zürch [*sic*]
Most learned Sir and
Dearest Friend!
    I love and happily read your works. As one reads, hears and relates, I am not without adroitness myself, since my name (as it were) is known and highly appreciated in every country. Therefore I take the liberty of asking you to do a small favour for me. Since I know that there are in Zürch [*sic*] and Winterthur many gentlemen amateurs and great connoisseurs and patrons of music, I shall not conceal from you the fact that I am issuing, by subscription, for the price of 6 ducats, a work, consisting of 6 Quartets for 2 violins, viola and violoncello *concertante*, correctly copied, and <u>written in in a new and special way (for I haven't composed any for 10 years)</u>. I did not want to fail to offer these to the great patrons of music and the amateur gentlemen. Subscribers who live abroad will receive them before I issue the works here. Please don't take it amiss that I bother you with this request; if I should be fortunate enough to receive an answer containing your approval, I would most appreciate it, and remain,
                     Most learned Sir,
                       Your ever obedient
                       Josephus Haydn m.pr.
                       Fürst Estorhazischer
                       Capell Meister

Vienna, 3rd December 1781.
To be delivered to Prince Esterhazi's house. In Vienna.

                                [CCLN, 32f.]

[To Prince Krafft Ernst Oettingen-Wallerstein,[2] Wallerstein Castle (Bavaria). *German*. Only the end, from 'humble . . .' to '*Capell Meister*' autograph]
Most Serene Highness,
Gracious Prince and Dread Lord!
    As a great patron and connoisseur of music, I take the liberty of humbly offering Your Serene Highness my brand new *à quadro* [Quartets] for 2 violins, viola [and] violoncello *concertante* correctly copied, at a subscription price of 6 ducats. They are written in a new and special way, for I have not composed any for 10 years. The noble subscribers who live abroad will receive their copies before I

---

1 Johann Caspar Lavater (1741–1801), a well-known Swiss writer, was one of the most talented and curious figures of the German-speaking *Sturm und Drang* literary movement. He was also a master of the silhouette and developed the science of physiognomy.
2 Prince Krafft Ernst Oettingen-Wallerstein, one of Southern Germany's most ardent patrons of music, maintained a band of virtuoso musicians, including the composer Rosetti (for some years *Kapellmeister*). In the following years the Prince became more and more enamoured of Haydn's music: see correspondence up to 1789.

issue them here. I beg for your favour, and a gracious acceptance of your offer, and remain ever, in profound respect,

Your Serene Highness'
humble and obedient
Josephus Haydn,
Fürst Estorhazischer Capell Meister.

Vienna, 3rd December [1781][3]
[Address:] To be delivered to Prince Esterhazi's house in Vienna.

[CCLN 33f.]

[To Robert Schlecht, Abbot of Salmannsweiler in *Land* Baden. *German*. Only the signature autograph]
Reverend and Gracious Sir!

As a great patron and connoisseur of music, I take the liberty of humbly offering Your Reverence and Grace my brand new *à quadro* for 2 violins, viola et violoncello *concertante* correctly copied, at a subscription price of 6 ducats. They are written in a new and special way, for I have not composed any for 10 years. My church pieces, symphonies, concertos, operas are also at your gracious disposal. The noble subscribers who live abroad will receive their copies before I issue them here. I beg for your favour, and a gracious acceptance of your offer, and remain ever, in profound respect,

Your Reverend Grace's
humble and obedient
Josephus Haydn mpria
Fürst Estorhazischer Capell Meister.

Vienna, 3rd December [1781].

[Address:] To be delivered to Prince Esterhazi's house in Vienna
       Reverendissimo, Amplissimo ac Doctorissimo
       Domino, Domino Roberto Schlecht, Sacri. R. I. Abbati
       in Salmansweyl Dignissimo patrono meo Grasiosissimo p. p.
          p[er] <u>Ratisbonn</u>
             <u>ulm</u>
          à
          <u>Salmansweyl</u>[2]
[Badisches Generallandesarchiv Karlsruhe Sig. 98/1405. G. Feder in *Haydn-Studien* I/2 (1966), 114–6; not in CCLN]

Of the MS. copies that Haydn presumably sold, only one incomplete set seems to have survived: four Quartets (Op. 33, Nos. 1, 2, 5 and 6) in the Benedictine Monastery of Melk (cat. VI. 736–9), authentic MSS. prepared under Haydn's supervision.[3]

Perhaps the first performance of these Quartets before a larger audience – if we except the afore-mentioned concert given at Eszterháza on 30 May (where the presence of the Quartets is, of course, purely hypothetical) – took place in connection with a visit to Vienna of the Russian Grand Duke Paul (from November 1796 Tsar Paul II) with his consort, Maria Feodorovna (Fiodorowna), *née* Princess of Württemberg, accompanied by Duke Friedrich Eugen von Württemberg and consort, together with Prince Ferdinand and Princess Elisabeth (Maria Feodorovna's sister) of Württemberg. Princess Elisabeth was the fiancée of Archduke Franz (later

---

1 The year is missing, but see St. George's (Privy Councillor and Cashier) answer of 18 February 1782, *infra*.
2 For a copy of Haydn's Symphony No. 24 acquired by Salmannsweiler in 1773, see Landon, *SYM*, 652, source 6.
3 See the new critical edition (Doblinger), ed. Barrett-Ayres and Landon.

Franz I). The Russian grand ducal pair travelled as the Count and Countess von Norden ('of the North'), the Württemberg pair as Count and Countess von Gröningen. Among the many festivities in their honour was a whole series of Gluck operas (*Alceste, Iphigénie en Tauride, Orfeo, Die Pilgrimme von Mekka*) and on 24 December the famous contest between Mozart and Clementi. In the grand ducal suite was none other than Friedrich Maximilian Klinger, which gave the author of *Sturm und Drang* the opportunity to meet the composer of the 'Trauer' and 'Farewell' Symphonies. On Tuesday, Christmas Day, the Countess von Norden, who was taking piano lessons with Haydn, gave a concert in her apartments, at which some (all?) of Op. 33 were introduced to the fashionable world:

Vienna:
... We must add to our report of the concert given in Countess von Norden's rooms on December [25th][1] that the music was by the princely Esterhazy *Kapellmeister*, the famous Herr Hayden [*sic*], and that the quartet played on that occasion was performed by Messrs. Luigi Tomasini, Apfelmayr [Franz Aspelmayr], Weigl and [Thaddäus] Huber. It was received with gracious applause by the illustrious audience, who were pleased to present Herr Haydn, as composer, with a magnificent enamelled golden box set with brilliants, and each of the other four musicians[2] with a golden snuff-box.
[*Preßburger Zeitung* No. 4, 12 January 1782. *HJB* VIII, 182 and 274, the latter in
Eugene Hartzell's translation, here used.]

Joseph II was not amused. He took the Grand Duke Paul on a visit to his music library and there the Emperor showed him the op. posth. string quartets by F. L. Gassmann (1773) with the fugues: 'Those are still the roses growing on my Gassmann's grave'. (When Gassmann had died and his widow had thrown herself at Joseph's feet, the Emperor was also moved to tears and said: 'I have lost not only an excellent artist but also an honest man'). It is to be doubted if any I. R. tears were shed at the first performance of Op. 33 ...

When the Count and Countess of the North went on to Venice, the old Baldassare Galuppi came out of retirement – he is said not to have written any harpsichord music since 1760 – and composed the elegiac and beautiful 'Passa Tempo al Cembalo' in honour of the high guests.[3]

On 29 December, Artaria announced (*Wiener Zeitung*) Haydn's *XII Lieder* (XXVIa:1–12), no doubt to coincide with the various grand ducal festivities. Haydn will surely have given a copy to the Countess of the North, to whom, many years later, he would dedicate the *Mehrstimmige Gesänge*.[4]

Haydn may have thought he was playing a trump against Leopold Hofmann with the new *Lieder*, but the German press did not take kindly to them, mainly because of the texts. (We shall consider the problem of Austrian literary taste later in this volume: see pp. 501 ff.)

634) Lieder für das Clavier, gewidmet aus besonderer Hochachtung und Freundschaft der Fräulein Liebe, Edlen von Kreuznern, von Joseph Haydn, Fürstl. Esterhazischen Capellmeister. Erster Theil. Wien, bey Artaria 1782.

1 In the paper '26th', but there are other wrong dates in *PZ*'s reports on the events in which the Count and Countess von Norden participated. On 5 Jan. the paper says that the group was on the 26th at the Tonkünstler-Societät, whereas their annual performance was on 22 and 23 Dec. The dates corrected from the *Wiener Zeitung*.
2 Tomasini, Aspelmayr and Huber were themselves quartet composers of some distinction.
3 Pohl II, 183–6. Baldassare Galuppi, *Passatempo al cembalo: Sonate* (trascrizione e revisione di Franco Piva), Fondazione Giorgio Cini, Venice 1964. F. M. Klinger, *Sturm und Drang*, ed. Jörg-Ulrich Fechner, Stuttgart 1974, p. 147.
4 See *Haydn: the Late Years 1801–1809*, p. 330.

These *Lieder* are not quite worthy of a Haydn. Presumably however he did not write them in order to increase his fame, but to give pleasure only to connoisseurs, male and female, of a certain kind. No one will therefore doubt that Herr H. could have made these *Lieder* better, if he had wanted to.

Whether he should not have done so in the first place is another question.

[Cramer's *Magazin der Musik* 1783, pp. 456f.]

For a further review, see Forkel's *Musikalischer Almanach für Deutschland*, 1783, p. 17.

Op. 33, on the other hand, was an unqualified success even in north Germany. In Cramer's *Magazin der Musik* (1783, p. 153), with news of concerts in Hamburg, we read that Schick (violin) and Trickler ('cello)

played in the Westphalian House at a private concert two Quartets from Opus 19 [= Op. 33] by Haydn with such an admirable agreeableness and dexterity that there was not one of the many listeners present who was not particularly moved and delighted.

Chronicle 1782

ITALIAN OPERAS 1782

Ninety performances are registered (Harich in *HJB* I, 39).

A. E. M. Grétry: Zemira ed Azor.

Libretto: 400 copies by Kurzbeck in Vienna (no copy survives). Porta undertook the Italian translation and was paid separately for it. First performance: February (two perf.), repeated in March (three) and April (one). As 'supers' there were thirteen Grenadiers and three scenery assistants behind the curtain. The cast can be reconstructed from Travaglia's costume proposals:

Zemira	Mad. Bologna
Fatima	Mad. Polzelli
Lesbia	Mlle Valdesturla
Azor	Mons. Braghetti
Ali	Mons. Moratti
Sandro	Mons. Peschi

Eszterháza performance material: EH, Budapest, Ms. Mus. OE–7. score with the title '... Nell'Italiana favella tradotto / Vienna 15 Giugno 1780', which renders Porta's supposed 'new' translation problematical; there are also orchestral parts and fragmentary vocal parts bearing Haydn's holograph date for the rehearsals (or distribution of the parts) 'a 24^{tro} 9bre $\overline{781}$'. Haydn made only very moderate changes in this work: some cuts, some acceleration of tempi (Atto I°, Sc. 3 'Allegretto' to 'Presto' or 'Allegro'; Atto II°, Sc. 10 'Largo non troppo' to 'Andante'). Atto III°, Sc. 6. Grétry's stage orchestra of clarinets, horns and bassoons could not be mounted at Eszterháza, and Haydn had to rewrite the clarinet parts in V. I, II and Fl. (of the pit orchestra), while bassoons and horns were also given to the pit orchestra. One set of parts is by Haydn, the other by Johann Schellinger. Some other changes were incorporated into the parts by Joseph Elssler. Harich, *Musikgeschichte*, 50f. Bartha–Somfai, 99f., 252–4. Schellinger's bill for copying the vocal parts, 115 *Bögen*, of 20 June 1782 (A.M. XVII.1135) quoted on pp. 99f. Harich in *HJB* I, 40.

Antonio Salieri: La fiera di Venezia. Comedie per musica di Gio. Gastone Bocherini [*sic*] Lucchese. Da rappresentarsi nel' teatro d'Esterhaz l'anno 1782.

Ostrogoto	Mons. Braghetti.
Calloandra	Madama Raimondi.
Grifagno	Mons. Totti.
Cristallina	Madselle Bologna.
Falsirene	Madselle Valdesturla.
Rasoio	Mons. Moratti.
Belfusto	Mons. Pesci.
Cecchino	

[sung by Leopold Dichtler]

Libretto: 200 copies were ordered from Joseph Siess in Oedenburg. Copy: EH, Eisenstadt. First performance: February (two perf.), repeated in March (three), April (four) and July (one). Eszterháza performance material: EH, Budapest, Ms. Mus. OE–10. Johann Schellinger submitted a bill for 118

Bögen (A.M. XVII.1135), mostly vocal parts (all have disappeared). EH has the score and orchestral parts, which came from Vienna. Haydn made the usual cuts and accelerations in tempo (Atto II°, Quintetto 'Chi va di quà', 'Andante con moto' to 'Allegretto', Sc. 6 'Andante maestoso' to 'Allegro vivace'[!]). In Atto I°, Sc. 6, 2nd part of Calloandra's Aria 'Col zeffiro' was rewritten and shortened, and the new version entered in the parts by Anonymous 40. Harich, *Musikgeschichte*, 50. Bartha-Somfai, 99, 250–2. Harich in *HJB* I, 40f.

Tommaso Traetta: Il cavaliere errante nell'isola incantata. Dramma eroicomico per musica. Da rappresentarsi nel teatro d'Esterhasi l'anno 1782.
Libretto: 200 copies were ordered from Joseph Siess in Oedenburg. Porta's proposal (September 1781) gives us the cast:

Arsinta [Arsinda]	Madame Bologna.
Zauberin [Melysa]	Madame Polzelli.
Dorina	Mlle. Bologna.
Guido............................	Mons. Totti.
Collotta [Calotta]	Mons. Moratti.
Stordillano.......................	Mons. Dichtler.
Die Zauber-Rolle [Ruffino] ...	Mons. Peschi.

First performance: March (three perf.), repeated in April (four) and July (one). Some documents: Travaglia's proposal for the costumes and decorations (1781) was, in the Prince's absence – see Chronicle 1781, Autumn –, approved by Regent Stefan Nagy with the note: 'In the absence of H. High. since he demanded to see the above-mentioned Opera, everything must accordingly be prepared' (Secretariats-Protocoll, Jan. 1782). Johann Schellinger's bill for copying 'Il Cavaliere errante 139 Bögen' is included in A.M. XVII.1135. Eszterháza performance material: score of Act I and some fragmentary vocal and string parts of the remainder; Schellinger's bill was apparently only for the (mostly missing) vocal parts. EH, Budapest, Ms. Mus. OE–96. We do not mention changes made before the material arrived from Vienna (e.g. substitution of the Overture by another) or Haydn's usual small changes (cuts). Atto I°, No. 2, a new aria (composer?) for Calotta ('Carlotta') was substituted. Sc. 5, Aria (Melysa = Polzelli) 'Agli amanti' replaced by another, probably Haydn's in B flat, which is very similar to Haydn's insertion Aria 'D'una sposa meschinella' in Paisiello's *La Frascatana* (Eszterháza 1777). Sc. 8. Traetta's Aria (Ruffino) 'Fate a mio modo' was replaced by Luigi Bologna's Aria, 'Amor tristarello', which we know from Righini's *Il convitato di pietra*; the replacement had been made in Vienna. Haydn first tried to fit Traetta's original words to Bologna's Aria, then substituted a third version (text has not survived). Atto II°, No. 4: the acc. rec. 'Misera che farò' was re-composed (apparently by Haydn). No. 8: Traetta's acc. rec. 'E soffirò' led to an Aria already replaced in Vienna by another; Haydn had the whole scene sewed up and replaced both rec. and aria by another (his own?), of which, alas, only fragments survive; *incipits* of all this material in Bartha-Somfai, 256ff. In our notes (December 1958) to the Budapest MS. we have noted other replacements not in Bartha-Somfai, and we add them here. No. 11, Arsinda's Aria 'Una voce lusinghiere dolce' was replaced with another (our notes: 'probably not by Haydn')

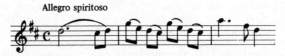

while No. 12 is yet another insertion, this time in score (contrary to Bartha-Somfai) and parts for a character named 'Ismene' (bass clef, 'Veggo già un nembo in sorgere'):

See also Section II (Marionette Theatre). Harich, *Musikgeschichte*, 51. Bartha-Somfai, 100, 254–9. Harich in *HJB* I, 41.

Giovanni Paisiello: L'innocente fortunata.
Libretto: printed by Joseph Siess in Oedenburg (A.M. 64.4007); no copy survives. First performance: April (immediately removed; it was the only Paisiello failure in Eszterháza). Johann Schellinger's bill for the vocal parts of 20 June 1782, 'L'Innocenza fortunata 168 Bögen' is in A.M. 17.1135. The cast cannot be determined. Eszterháza performance material: EH, Budapest, Ms. Mus. OE–76 (score and orchestral parts, probably of Italian origin). Haydn made only small changes (cuts). Atto I°, Sc. 5, a new Aria was substituted before the material arrived with the text, 'Bell'Italia, bel paese':
Tenor (D. Trippone) *Cavatina* (watermarks of score: three crescents in an unusual order ⌒⌒)

Andantino

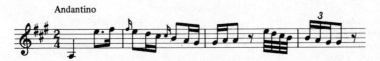

No. 7: a new Aria was substituted ('Si mio ben t'amai fedele'):

Andante con moto

(from our notes, Budapest, December 1958). Bartha-Somfai, 100, 259f. Harich in *HJB* I, 42.

Pasquale Anfossi: Lo sposo disperato.

Libretto: printed by Joseph Siess in Oedenburg (A.M. 64.4001); no copy survives. First performance: August (seven perf.), September (five), October (one) and November (one). Johann Schellinger's bill for some (missing? duplicate?) parts, 'Lo Sposo disperato 41 Bögen', A.M. XVII.1152. The cast cannot be determined. Eszterháza performance material: EH, Budapest, Ms. Mus. OE–99 (most of the vocal parts, except for Atto I°, Nos. 2 and 7, and the orchestral parts). The material was probably Viennese. Apart from the usual cuts, etc., Haydn made the following changes: Atto I°, No. 4. Aria replaced by a *Cavatina*, 'Giusto ciel' (parts by Anonymous 47 and Schellinger), probably not by Haydn. Atto II°, No. 15. Aria replaced another, 'Arrogante chi credi' (parts by Anonymous 10 and Schellinger), probably not by Haydn. Bartha-Somfai, 101, 200f. Harich in *HJB* I, 42.

Pasquale Anfossi: Il curioso indiscreto.

Libretto: Instead of ordering a new one from Siess, Porta, in his first list of proposed costs for the Opera, notes that there are no copies at Eszterháza, but 'I will try to get some from a person in Vienna. . . . I hope to get at least a dozen.' The Prince made some changes on the proposed list of roles and Porta had to make an *addendum* (approved in September 1782), in which we read *inter alia* 'More 5 opera libretti already printed, bought at 17 xr.' Porta bought copies of the Kurzbeck libretto (Vienna 1783) of which the printer had prepared proofs as early as September 1782. First performance: September (seven perf.), repeated in October (two), November (three) and in 1783. Johann Schellinger's bill for some (missing? duplicate?) parts, 'Il curioso indiscreto 50 Bögen', A.M. XVII.1152. Eszterháza performance material: EH, Budapest, Ms. Mus. OE–35: score, fragmentary vocal parts (Serpina's part), orchestral parts – probably ordered from Dresden, but the score (used in Dresden) is of Italian origin. Apart from the usual cuts, Haydn's changes were as follows: Atto I°, Sc. 8. Emilia's Aria, 'Deh' frenate i mesti accenti' was transposed from B flat to A, and Haydn added his own autograph parts for oboes and horns: Emilia was sung by Polzelli. Haydn even rewrote Anfossi's theme:

Anfossi

Allegro

Anfossi:

Haydn

Allegro

Haydn:

The parts were copied by Joseph Elssler. Atto II°, Sc. 5. In Dresden a new Duetto (Serpina, Prospero), 'Guardate che figura' was added, and this time Haydn slowed down the tempo, from 'Allegretto grazioso' to 'Andante'. For Anfossi's Opera, we have Haydn's own proposal for the cast:

459

Il curioso indiscreto.

Clorinda 1ma parte...	Valdisturla [*sic*]
Emilia 2da	Polzelli
Serpina 3za	Mariuccia Bologna
Contino 1mo mezzo Carattere	[empty]
Marchese 1mo Buffo	Morati [*sic*]
Prospero	Pesci
Aurelio...	Dichtler

Bartha-Somfai, 103, 266–8. Harich in *HJB* I, 43.

Giovanni Paisiello: I filosofi immaginari ossia Gli astrologi immaginari.
Libretto: no Eszterháza libretto survives, and no records can be found in which one was ordered. First performance: October (last week), repeated in October (three perf. more), November (three), December (three) and in 1783 and 1784. Johann Schellinger's bill for copying orchestral parts (they were reckoned at 5 xr. per page, vocal parts at 7 xr., because of the additional work in adding a [usually foreign] text), 'Astrologi imaginari 49 Bögen' is in A.M. XVII.1152. The cast cannot be determined. Eszterháza performance material: EH, Budapest, Ms. Mus. OE–11: score by a Viennese copyist (probably Wenzel Sukowaty) and incomplete orchestral parts, also of Viennese origin. Haydn's very few changes (he obviously thought highly of Paisiello's abilities), apart from cuts, consist of putting Paisiello's characteristic clarinet parts into the oboe parts instead, there being no clarinets at Eszterháza in these years, and accelerating the tempo (Atto I°, Sc. 7, 'Andante' to 'Allegretto'). Bartha-Somfai, 103f., 268f. Harich in *HJB* I, 43–5.

Joseph Haydn: ORLANDO / PALADINO / DRAMMA EROICOMICO / IN TRE ATTI. / MUSICA / DEL CELEBRE SIGR. GIUSEPPE HAIDEN. / DA RAPPRESENTARSI / NEL TEATRO D'ESTERHAZI, / L'ANNO 1782.

ATTORI

[arranged from middle clockwise round the star-like disposition:]
ANGELICA, / Regina del Cattai. / *Madama Bologna.*
ORLANDO, Paladino. / *Mons. Specioli.*
PASQUALE, / Scudiero d'/Orlando. / *Monsieur / Moratti.*
MEDORO, amante d'Angel. / *Monsieur Braghetti.*
ALCINA / Maga. *Mlle. Val-* / *desturla.*
LICONE / Pastore. *Mons.* / *Dictler.*
CARONTE [no name listed]
EURILLA, / Pastorella. / *Madama* / *Specioli.*
RODOMONTE, / Re di Barbaria. / *Mons. Negri.*
Tutte nell'attual Servizio di S. A. il SIGR. / PRINCIPE NICOLO ESTERHAZI di / Galanta.
La Musica è del sudetto Sig. Giuseppe Haiden, / Maestro si S. A.
La Poesia è del Sigr Nunziato Porta.
Pastori.   Selvaggi.
Pastorelle.   Saraceni.
Ombre.

[next page:] ... Le Decorazzioni sono del Sig. Pietro Travaglia, Pittore Teatrale di S. A.

Libretto: printed by Joseph von Kurzbeck in Vienna (EH, Budapest, Fasc. 799). Copies: Országos Széchényi Könyvtár, Sign. 160.963; fürstl. Fürstenbergsches Hofarchiv, Donaueschingen. British Museum, London, Add. 32174 (from J. N. Hummel) First performance: 6 December (Prince's name-day), repeated three times, also in 1783 and 1784. Eszterháza performance material: Johann Schellinger's bill for copying the work, 'Orlando Paladino 319 Bögen' (A.M. XVII.1152), on 19 Dec., and the vocal parts have, by some miracle, survived (almost all the performance materials of Haydn's operas composed after 1779 were passed on to other opera houses), and they are not only by Schellinger but also Joseph Elssler, Anonymous 10 and Anonymous 48 (Johann Elssler?). Haydn himself wrote the singers' names on their respective parts, 'Valdesturla', 'Braghetti', 'Negri', etc. EH, Budapest, Ms. Mus. I. 152. Haydn made one important correction to Sc. 3, Aria by Alcina. The text at first read, 'A un mio accento, a un guardo solo'; Haydn changed this to read, 'Ad' un guardo, a un cenno solo', and this later version is the one found in the printed libretto. There are other holograph corrections by Haydn in these authentic and important parts. Harich, *Musikgeschichte*, 52. Bartha-Somfai, 101f., 265f. Harich in *HJB* I, 45.

Four operas from earlier seasons were repeated:
Paisiello's *L'avaro deluso*: March (one), April (two).
Sacchini's(?) *La contadina in corte*: May (one), June (one), July (four), September (two).
Piccinni's *La schiava riconosciuta (Gli stravaganti)*: July (two).
Haydn's *La fedeltà premiata*: September (one), October (four), November (three), December (one), also in 1783 and 1784. Because so many of the original cast had left and were replaced by new singers, it was decided to print a new libretto, only in Italian, and with a new cast:

LA / FEDELTA / PREMIATA. / DRAMMA PASTORALE GIOCOSO. / MUSICA / DEL SIG. GIUSEPPE HAIDEN. / DA REPRESENTARSI [*sic*] / IN / ESZTERHÁZ. / [vase of flowers] / l'anno, 1782.

interlocuturi [*sic*]
[arranged from middle clockwise round the star-like disposition:]
FILENO, *Amante di* / *Fillide* / Mr. Specioli.
AMARANTA, *donna vana,* / *e boriosa.* / Md. Specioli.
CONTE PERRUCCHETTO, / *uomo di umore stravagante.* / Mr. Moratti.
MELIBEO, *Ministro* / *del Tempo di Dia-* / *na, innamorato di* / *Amaranta.* / Il Sigr. / Negri.
DIANA, *l'istessa,* / La Sigra Valdesturla.
LINDORO, *fratello di Amaran-* / *ta, addetto à servizj del Tem-* / *pio, innamorato prima di* / *Nerina, e poi di Celia.* / Il Sigr. Leop. /Dichtler.
NERINA, *Ninfa* / *volubile in amore,* / *innamorata di* / *Lindoro.* / La Sigra Val- / desturla.
FILLIDE, *sotto il finto nome* / *di Celia, Amante di Fileno,* / Md. Bologna.
Tutti in attual servizio di S. A. il Principe Ni- / colò Esterhazy di Galantha.
Coro di Ninfe, e Pastori. Cacciatori, e Caccia- / [t]rici. Seguaci di Diana.
Ballo di Pastori, e Pastorelle.
L'azione si finge nelle Campagne di Cuma.

Joseph von Kurzbeck delivered 400 copies (A.M. 64.4000), of which one is in the Országos Széchényi Könyvtár, Sig. 206.265. Johann Schellinger's bill for copying the changes (principally in Celia's part), 'La fedelta premiata 17 Bögen', is in A.M. XVII.1152. Eszterháza performance material: two volumes of the score by Anonymous 48 (Johann Elssler?), *ex. coll.* Landon (who discovered the source in Milan), Burgenländisches Landesmuseum, Eisenstadt; many additions in Haydn's hand. This Opera's revival marked the début of the couple Specioli (engaged from 25 August). Harich, *Musikgeschichte*, 52. Bartha-Somfai, 101. Harich in *HJB* I, 46f. Landon (see 1781 première).

ITALIAN MARIONETTE OPERA 1782

Traetta's *Il cavaliere errante* was given alternately in the opera house and in the marionette theatre, now restored to its previous function after serving as the opera house until February 1781. Some of the performances listed above were therefore with puppets (a precise division into opera and puppet theatre for these Traetta performances is no longer possible). Harich, *Musikgeschichte*, 51 and *HJB* I, 41.

THE GERMAN THEATRICAL TROUPE 1782

The Diwald Company (see Chronicle 1781, p. 439).

Early in the new year, Haydn wrote to Artaria:

[To Artaria & Co., Vienna. *German*]

Estoras, 4th January 1782.

Monsieur!

To my astonishment I read in the Vienna *Diario* that you intend to publish my Quartets[1] in 4 weeks; I wish you had shown sufficient consideration for me to delay the announcement till I had left Vienna: such a proceeding places me in a most dishonourable position and is very damaging; it is a most usurious step on your part. At least you could have waited with the announcement until the whole *opus* was completed, for I have not yet satisfied all my subscribers: Mons. Hummel[2] also wanted to be a subscriber, but I did not want to behave so shabbily, and I did not want to send them to Berlin wholly out of regard for our friendship and further transactions; and by God! you have damaged me to the extent of more than 50 ducats, since I have not yet satisfied many of the subscribers, and cannot possibly send copies to many of those living abroad: this step must cause the cessation of all further transactions between us.

I would only ask you to send a copy of the *Lieder*, bound in red taffeta, to Herr von Liebe[3] and an ordinary copy to my brother-in-law, Keller,[4] and three

---

1 Op. 33.
2 See p. 432.
3 The songs were dedicated to Francisca, daughter of Anton Liebe von Kreutzner, who was to receive the copy bound in red taffeta. Kreutzner ordered, also in 1782, a new solemn Mass from Haydn for performance in the pilgrimage church at Mariazell (the *Missa Cellensis* in C, called the 'Mariazellermesse').
4 Joseph Keller, whose son later boarded with Haydn's old friend, Anton Stoll, at Baden. See *Haydn: the Years of 'The Creation' 1796–1800*, p. 554.

copies to me. You can substract the sum from the second dozen. Meanwhile I remain, respectfully

> Your obedient servant,
> Joseph Haydn.

[No address; Artaria's clerk notes: 'Haydn/Esterhasj 4th Jan/1782/ans. 14th ditto'.] [CCLN, 34]

The reason for Haydn's wrath is the following announcement inserted by Artaria in the *Wiener Zeitung*:

> [After announcing the new *Lieder*, we read] Also the 6 brand new Quartets . . . composed by this great man are in a forward state of engraving and we hope to issue them in approximately four weeks. [*WZ* 104, 29 Dec. 1781]

This meant that all Haydn's subscribers, many of whom had not yet received their MS. copies, would learn that their quartets were about to be available for mass consumption, and at a price of four gulden instead of six ducats. Artaria was decent enough to postpone their publication until 17 April (*Wiener Zeitung*), but Haydn had difficulties on the subject, *inter alia* with Gottfried van Swieten and Conrad Breunig (*infra*).

[To Artaria & Co., Vienna. *German*]

> Estoras, 20th January 1782.

Nobly born,
Most highly respected Sir!
I must apologize for having written my last letter to you in the heat of anger, and I hope that nevertheless we shall remain good friends. There is no doubt that I gave you the Quartets so that you could engrave them, but it never entered my head that you would put it right into the newspapers.

Well, it happened that way; another time both of us will be more cautious. I shall send you the *Lieder* with the next mail. I thank you for those you sent and remain, most respectfully,

> Your most obedient servant,
> Josephus Haydn mpria.

[Address:] Monsieur
    Monsieur Artaria et Compag
    press:

        à
      Vienne

[Artaria's clerk notes: 'Haydn 1782/Esterhasi 20th Jan./rec'd 23rd ditto/answered: (not filled in)'.] [CCLN, 35]

On 26 January there appeared in Berlin No. IV of the *Literatur und Theater-Zeitung* bearing the *impressum* 'bei Arnold Weber'. In it we have the following report:

> News of the princely castle Esterhaz in Hungary
> . . . The Prince . . . always divides a part of his entertainment with everyone. Whenever friends of some standing come to Esterhaz and take up quarters in the *Gasthaus*, he sends his carriage, has them taken to his castle and invites them to dine with him. Every day there is theatre, three times a week Italian opera and the same for German plays. The entrance is free for everyone. When new pieces are given, he has the libretti printed in Oedenburg and distributed to the audience. His wish that in this magnificent castle there should always reign happiness and politeness, is followed explicitly by his personnel. . . . Most rooms in the castle are designed for great rulers who from time to time come here. The Prince and dowager Princess

live on the rez-de-chaussée.... The Prince has some four hundred clocks, each one of different and beautiful workmanship. Among the most remarkable that I saw was one with a stuffed canary which every hour sings an aria [*sic*] like a real bird, and the beak, breast and the whole body move like a real bird. . . . and [there are] various clocks with all sorts of music. A similar musical plaything is an armchair which, when you sit in it, begins to play various pieces and continues with new ones. . . . From the garden one arrives at the theatre. It burned to the ground some $1\frac{1}{2}$ years ago ... and now it is there again with renewed brilliance. Everything is larger. . . . his chamber musicians wear a uniform (green coats with red and gold), and at their head is Haydn, a man whose music is admired in Italy, England and France. . . .

The following correspondence has to do with the famous Op. 33 and Haydn's MS. subscription copies:

[To Artaria & Co., Vienna. *German*]

Estoras, 15th February 1782.

Nobly born,
Most highly respected Sir!
    Herr Breunig,[1] with whom I am engaged in a most unpleasant correspondence, and to whom I sent a copy of the passage in your last letter concerning the quartets of my composition which he offered you, has sent me the enclosed disgusting letter with the most impertinent threat that I should immediately forward this letter to you for his satisfaction; otherwise Herr Breunig must believe I am a liar. You will therefore have to defend not only me but also yourselves: but the further away from Herr Breunig you can put me, the more satisfactory will be your service to me. I remain, Sir, most respectfully,

Your wholly obedient servant,
Josephus Haydn mpria.

P.S. About the songs, please have a little patience for a short time. I would like to see at least one single copy of my Quartets.
[No address; Artaria's clerk notes: 'Haydn / Esterhazy 15. feb: $\overline{782}$'.]

[CCLN, 35f.]

[To Haydn from St. George, Privy Councillor and Cashier to the Court of Prince Oettingen-Wallerstein. *Draft in German*]
Monsieur,
    Since I received neither an answer to my letter which I sent to you as early as 24th December, nor anything of the music we expected, my gracious Prince has instructed me to ask you for it once again: I do so herewith, and would ask you to be good enough to send whatever you have ready of the new *à quadro*[2] to His Serene Highness, at this address, but to inform me thereof, so that I can see that payment is made to you without delay. In expecting this, I have the honour to be, Sir, with every expression of my esteem ...

S.

Wallerstein, 18th February 1782. [CCLN, 36]

---

1 Conrad Breunig, a composer from Mainz, whose '6 Duetti per due Violini' Artaria had issued in 1776, offered Haydn's Quartets (Op. 33), obviously pirated from one of the advance subscription copies in MS. Artaria very decently refused to accept them.
2 Op. 33: see Haydn's letter to the Prince of 3 December 1781, *supra*.

On 20 June Prince Nicolaus passed for payment two bills, one by Haydn and one by Schellinger, to which we may add another 'Notta' by Haydn of 28 July.[1]

In the middle of July (Artaria's note on his answer and the letter's arrival supply us with the approximate date of the letter's expedition from Eszterháza), Haydn wrote to his publishers in Vienna:

[To Artaria & Co., Vienna. *German*]

[*c.* 22 July 1782]

Nobly born,
Most highly respected Sir!

On the very day that I received your kind letter of the 2nd ult., I had the misfortune to injure my left foot so severely by a fall that I have not been able to leave the house up to now, and have had to live on a strict diet: this explains why my answer to you, which is long overdue, was delayed.

I foresaw the consequences of my bringing Herr Hummel[2] into the business of the ·Quartets just as easily as you will see, in the future, the unfortunate consequences entailed on me; for among many other people, Herr Baron van Sviten[3] gave me distinctly to understand that in future I should dedicate my compositions directly to the public. I hope you will see that this state of affairs is due to your over-hasty announcement, and that this very precipitation obliged me to offer my Quartets all over the place.

I send you herewith the enclosed[4] letter, and only regret that I cannot at present write to Herr Boccherini in my own hand, but when occasion offers, please present my devoted respects to him.

Many thanks for the copies[5] you sent me. As to the pianoforte Sonatas with violin [i.e., trios], you will have to be patient a long time; for I have to compose a new Italian opera, and the Grand Duke and Duchess and perhaps His Majesty the Emperor will be coming here for it.[6]

Your defence against Breunig is excellently done. He received it recently against a signed receipt. Meanwhile I remain, Sir, most respectfully,

Your most obedient servant,
Josephus Haydn, m.pria.

[No address; Artaria's clerk notes: 'Haydn 1782/Esterhaze dto./rec'd. 27th [July]/
11 Agosto] [CCLN, 37f.]

---

1 (*a*) 'Specification for the music paper necessary for the brand new Opera [*Orlando Paladino*], *viz*: 6 books quarto with 10 staves, 10 books oblong with 10 staves and 4 books oblong with 12 staves. Suma: 20 books, the book a 40 xr., makes together 13 Fl. 20 Xr. Josephus Haydn mpria, / Capell Meister'; approval by the Prince 'Esterház, 20th June 1782'. A.M. XVII.1136. Valkó II, 593f. Bartha-Somfai, 102. (*b*) Conto for 1782. What was copied for the 4 operas listed below, the Bogen at 5 xr: *viz*:

For Zemire und Azor	115 Bögen
La fiera di Venezia	118 ,,
Il Cavaliere errante	139 ,,
L'innocenza fortunata	168 ,,

Soma   540 Bögen, makes 45 Fl.
Joan. Schellinger, Prompter & Copyist.

[Haydn's handwriting: The above-listed 540 Bögen have been carefully examined by me and found to be correct. Josephus Haydn mpria, / Capell Meister.] A.M. XVII.1135. Valkó II, 593. Bartha-Somfai, 104. This bill, too, was passed for payment by the Prince on 20 June. (*c*) Haydn's hand: 'Notta. Strings which ought to be ordered, *viz*. for the violin: 4 bundles E, one-and-one-half A. / 12 sets [*Züg*] D, and 12 G for the viola. / 3 complete rows of strings for the violon [double bass]. / 2 A and 2 F♯. / 2 boxes of resin. / 2 ordinary violin bows. / Esterhaz 28 July 1782. Josephus Haydn mpria / Capell Meister.' Valkó II, 594.
2 Haydn had obviously sold the Quartets to Hummel, who announced them in May 1782.
3 *Recte*: Swieten.
4 The original is not clear. Nohl reads 'beide' (both), but Pohl's MS. copy suggests 'beilig[ende]' (enclosed), and Professor Bartha, who examined the autograph for us in Budapest, is inclined to agree with Pohl's reading.
5 Of the Quartets, Op. 33 (see P.S. in letter of 15 February).
6 The opera was to be *Orlando Paladino*. The planned visit of the Russian Grand Duke Paul, with his wife, Maria Feodorovna (*née* Princess of Württemberg), did not materialize.

This was followed, a few weeks later, by another:

[To Artaria & Co., Vienna. *German*]

Estoras, 16th August 1782.

Nobly born,
Most highly respected Sir!
    Many thanks for the Cantata[1] you sent, which is very neatly engraved; as to the Overture of my new opera[2] (which isn't composed yet), I cannot let you have this Overture before the first performance, but if you would like two others from my operas that no one – not a living soul – owns, you can have them at 5 ducats apiece. I promise, by the way, to make up half-a-dozen for you. Next week I shall send you 4 new *Lieder*. Meanwhile I remain, most respectfully,

Your most obedient servant,
Joseph Haydn.

[Address:]   Monsieur
      Monsieur Artaria et Compag
      press:
         à
           Vienne.

[CCLN, 36f.]

On 5 September, Haydn countersigned a bill for strings.[3] And three weeks later we have the following letter to Artaria:

[To Artaria & Co., Vienna. *German*]

Estoras, 29th September 1782.

Nobly born,
Most highly respected Sir!
    At last I can send you the five Symphonies [Overtures] you wanted, neatly and correctly written and also well constructed; I rehearsed them myself with my orchestra; I assure you that you will make a considerable profit by their publication, for their brevity will make the engraving very cheap. I would ask you to put the 25 ducats (N.B.: full weight) into a little box, seal it up, and wrap or sew it in an oil-cloth cover, and write nothing on it except *à Mons. Haydn*; for I don't want anyone in my house here to know of my transactions. You can deliver the box to the Prince's porter,[4] and just tell him that it contains some money, and then I shall get it safely from the porter. In any event, you can get from the porter a receipt which says that he has safely received the box.
    The 5 *Lieder* are also herewith enclosed: you must engrave them in the order in which I have numbered them. I shall try to complete the remainder as soon as possible and remain, meanwhile,

Your wholly obedient servant,
Josephus Haydn.

[No address; Artaria's clerk notes: 'Haydn 1782 / Estoras 29th Sept. / received 3rd Oct.']
                [CCLN, 38f.]

---

1 'Ah, come il core mi palpita', issued in score (pl. No. 29), from *La fedeltà premiata*.
2 *Orlando Paladino*. Artaria accepted the offer, and the set grew from two to five and then six, as the next letters show.
3 'Nota. What I did in the way of lute-maker's work. ... Summa: 7 Fl. 30 xr. [Haydn:] The above-listed strings have been correctly delivered to me ...'. A.M. XVII.1143. Valkó II, 594.
4 Herr Rosenbaum, whose name appears on the envelopes of later letters.

[To Artaria & Co., Vienna. *German*]

Estoras, 20th October 1782.

Nobly born,
Most highly respected Sir!

I cannot understand why you did not receive my last letter fourteen days ago, in which I reported that when I was last in Vienna, I had made an agreement myself with your partner[1] for five ducats for each piece, to which *Mon.* Artaria[2] willingly agreed. I also wrote that instead of *Sinfonie* you were to put *Overture*;[3] so this resolves your doubts. I have been very annoyed at the delay, for I could have had 40 ducats from another publisher for those 5 pieces, and you make such a fuss about something from which (considering how short the pieces are) you will derive a thirty-fold profit. Your partner has long since had the sixth piece. So finish the affair and send me either my music or my money, and with this I remain, most respectfully,

Your most obedient servant,
Joseph Haydn.

[Address:]   Monsieur
         Monsieur Artaria et Com
                à
             VIENNE

[Artaria's clerk notes: 'Haydn 1782 / Estoras 20 October / rec'd 22 ditto / ans.23 ditto'.]   [CCLN, 39]

Some bills at the end of the year may be noted briefly.[4]

A review of an important publication – Hummel's Oeuvre XVIII, Libro III (Symphonies Nos. 75, 63, 70, 71, 62 and 74), Haydn's latest symphonic output – occurred in the *Musikalisches Kunstmagazin*, edited by Johann Friedrich Reichardt (Berlin, 1782, p. 205):

Both these works [the quartets issued by Hummel as Op. 19, i.e. Op. 33] are full of the most original fancies, of the liveliest and most pleasing humour. Probably no composer has combined such originality and versatility with such

---

1 Probably either Tranquillo Mollo or Giovanni Cappi.
2 One of the young Artaria nephews, Carlo or Francesco.
3 Despite Haydn's request, the works appeared as 'Sei Sinfonie a gran orchestra opera XXXXV'; they include overtures from his earlier operas *Lo speziale* (1768), *L'incontro improvviso* (1775), *La vera costanza* (1778?), *L'isola disabitata* (1779), the oratorio *Il ritorno di Tobia* (1774, perf. in 1775) and *L'infedeltà delusa* (1773).
4 (a) 'Receipt. For three imperial ducats which I the undersigned received correctly and in cash for the repair of all the hunting horns and their crooks from Herr Joseph Haydn ... Vienna, 30 January 1782. [Passed for payment by Prince Nicolaus ('... Haydn should pay ...'), Esterhaz, 18 December 1782.' [Countersigned by Haydn, Vienna 1 Jan. 1783.] A.M. XVII.1151. Valkó II, 593. (b) 'Nota ... Italian 'Cello [*Pasetl*] G. C. E. ... bows ... violon [double bass] A ... Summa: 13 Fl.' (countersigned by Haydn), 19 Dec. 1782. A.M. XVII.1154. Valkó II, 595. (c) 'Conto / That which was copied for the hochfürstliche Theat. in the way of operas and symphonies from 1 June to 12 Decemb. 1782 / the Bogen agreed à 5 xr.

For Symphonies by various composers 98 Bögen	
Opera D. Giovanj	19 Bögen
La fedelta premiata	17
La Contadina in corte	19
La Schiava riconosciuta	28
Lo Sposo disperato	41
Il Curioso indiscreto	50
Astrologi imaginarj	49
Orlando Palladino	319
Soma 639	[recte: 640]

[Haydn's hand:] Above-listed 639 Bögen have been precisely examined by me, the undersigned and found to be correct. / Josephus Haydn mpria / Capell Meister.' [Passed for payment, Esterház, 9 December 1782. Haydn's receipt for the money through Joseph Züsser, Vienna, 1 Jan. 1783.] A.M. Fasc. XVII.1152. Valkó II, 595. Bartha-Somfai, 105. Bartha, 121f. (d) Haydn's winter uniform 'Anno 1782' (with many references to gold braid, gold knee ribbons, etc.), cost 137 fl. 27 xr., A.M. XVII.1150. Valkó II, 594f.

466

charm and popularity as has **Haydn**: and few pleasing and agreeable composers have the good technique that **Haydn** has most of the time. It is very interesting to follow **Hayden**'s [*sic*] output from a critical standpoint. Even his first works, which we came to learn some twenty years ago, showed his own good-natured humour; it was then, however, more a youthful petulance, an unrestrained joviality, combined with a superficial harmonic treatment; gradually, the humour became more manly and the whole more thoughtful, until – through higher and more steadfast inspiration, more mature study of the Art, and especially an increased knowledge of how an effect is best made – a mature originality and an assured artist were reflected in all his works. If we had but one **Haydn** and one C. P. E. **Bach**, we Germans could assert with impunity that we have our own style, and that our instrumental music is the most interesting of any land.

This was the year in which Haydn's *Lieder*, dedicated to Francisca Liebe von Kreutzner, were circulated all over German-speaking Europe (they had been announced on 29 December 1781). It was also the year in which Haydn dedicated a great Mass, the *Missa Cellensis*, to Francisca's father, Anton, a retired military man (Haydn's autograph dedication reads 'fatta per il Signor Liebe de Kreutzner, composta di me Giuseppe Haydn 7̄8̄2̄') who had been raised to the nobility on 20 March 1781. Probably the old gentleman swore to dedicate a Mass to Our Lady and to have it performed in the famous pilgrimage church of Mariazell. Haydn had already written one such vow for Our Lady in Mariazell (the *Missa Cellensis in honorem B. V. M.* of 1766) and he, too, had much to be thankful for. His opera librettos at Eszterháza now had his name on the title page, and 'Haydn' was a name known and revered throughout musical Europe. So perhaps Haydn added his own private prayer of thanks to Our Lady when he sent off this life-enhancing Mass to Anton Liebe, Edler von Kreutzner.

Many years later, Haydn thought it was in 1782 that he wrote a little song entitled 'Der schlaue Pudel'. Griesinger tells the story as follows:

About the year 1780, an officer's daughter wrote to Haydn from Coburg that she had gone for a walk with her fiancé (a captain), his dog, and a friend; the captain praised his poodle's talents and wagered that the dog could find a thaler that he would hide under a bush. The wager was accepted. They were home again when the captain called to his poodle, 'Lost! Go and find it!' The dog at once returned to the place where his master had been walking. By chance a journeyman tailor had sat down in the shade of the bush in question. When he was resting, he saw the thaler and put it in his pocket. Soon the poodle arrived. It smelled the thaler and nuzzled the tailor. Overjoyed to have found, within the hour, a thaler and a poodle who paid him attention, he went to an inn in the town. The poodle watched over the tailor's clothes all night; but when the door of the room was opened early in the morning, it stole out with the tailor's trousers and brought them, with the thaler, to his master.

This little adventure was turned into verse with the title 'The Sly and Ever-ready Poodle' (*Der schlaue und dienstfertige Pudel*) and Haydn was supposed to set the poem to music for the officer's daughter. She wrote to him that she was poor, that she had heard of his kind heart, and hoped he would be satisfied with the enclosed ducats. Haydn composed the verses at once. He returned the ducats and wrote to the beautiful lady that as punishment for her poor opinion of him – as if he would not offer his talent *gratis* to a worthy person! – she must knit him a pair of garters. The garters, of red and white silk with a painted garland of forget-me-nots, in fact arrived, and Haydn kept them carefully with his jewellery.[1]

This was also the year when Haydn fully intended to travel to England – the whole episode will be related in another chapter – and for that purpose completed three new Symphonies, among them No. 77 in B flat, one of the greatest works of this period: a felicitous combination of heart and intellect, and the most convincing piece of evidence that Haydn's strivings towards 'the popular style' were not proceeding unrewarded.

Chronicle 1783

ITALIAN OPERAS 1783

A total of 105 performances are registered (Harich in *HJB* I, 52).

Pietro Guglielmi: Il ratto della sposa.
Libretto: none seems to have been printed, or at any rate no printer's bill has been located. The cast has been quoted *supra* (p. 68) in Haydn's suggestion for casting the work. First performance: March, repeated only twice. Eszterháza performance material: Schellinger sent in a bill (with other works: A.M. XVII.1161) for '8 Bögen Singstimmen und 19 Bögen Orchesterstimmen'. The score, orchestral parts and the vocal parts of 'Polidoro' (Haydn added the singer's name, 'Negri'), EH, Budapest, Ms. Mus. OE–66 were purchased abroad (Polidoro was sung by 'Mons. Biondini'; the first violin was played by 'Strobach'; some insertions are signed 'Paolo Bonaga'; all this suggests Prague as the MS.'s place of origin). Apart from cuts, Haydn made almost no changes. Atto I°, Sc. 5. A new Aria for Donna Ortenz(i)a, 'Imparate o zittellucce', by Paolo Bonaga was substituted, who was possibly responsible for Aurora's insertion Aria, 'Non ti muove' in Sc. 6; he also composed Sc. 11, Biondino's Aria 'Se voi sapete'. Atto I°, Sc. 1, secco: Polidoro's words 'proteggo l'onestà' were changed by Haydn to 'proteggo l'innocenza'. Donna Ortenz(i)a's Aria, 'Le donne, Padron mio', was transposed from A to B flat and the bassoon part cancelled; new parts by Schellinger. Sc. 7 Aurora's Aria, 'Basta sol' was replaced by another, possibly Bonaga. Atto III°, the Finale, 'Viva, viva li sposi contenti', is an insertion by Vincenzo Righini. These insertions were all done (in Prague?) before the Opera reached Haydn. Bartha-Somfai, 106f., 269–71. Harich in *HJB* I, 48.

Vincenzo Righini: La vedova scaltra.
Libretto: none seems to have been printed, or at any rate no printer's bill has been located; possibly they used the Vienna textbook of 1778. The cast has been quoted *supra* (p. 68) in Haydn's suggestion for casting the work. First performance: March, repeated in April (three perf.), June (three), July (two), August (three), September (one) and October (one). Eszterháza performance material: Schellinger's bill (A.M. XVII.1161) lists 184 Bögen of vocal parts and 296 Bögen of orchestral parts. The score (of Viennese origin), the orchestral parts and fragmentary vocal parts are in EH, Budapest, Ms. Mus. OE–82. On V. I part 'Sig. Luigi 7̄8̄3̄' at beginning and 'Fine dell'opera 7̄8̄3̄' at the end; on V. II 'Sig. Tost'. Of the vocal parts only those of 'Rosaura' and 'D. Alvaro' (on the cover 'Negri') have survived. Apart from cuts, Haydn made the following changes. Atto I°, Sc. 2, a new Cavatina for Rosaura, 'Tutti schiavi' (composer?) was substituted for the original Aria, 'La sospirata calma'. Since in the score there is only a canto-basso 'short score', with cues for violin I, Bartha-Somfai suggest that Haydn is not the composer (otherwise there would have been a full autograph score, probably torn out later, as usually happened). Copyist: Schellinger (also 'short score'). In Sc. 7 Haydn made a drastic cut: Righini wrote a slow introduction (4 bars), followed by 16 bars of Allegretto, and then the voice enters with the theme of the slow introduction. Haydn simply removed the Allegretto section. Sc. 8. Rosaura's Aria, 'Affettati, spasimati', was replaced by another, possibly Haydn's on the same text (the inserted V. I part, by

---

1 Griesinger, 20f. The date of the song from Griesinger's correspondence with Breitkopf & Härtel: see *Haydn: the Late Years 1801–1809*, p. 343. The autograph of the pretty little song (1½ pages of actual music) is in the Preussische Staatsbibliothek, Berlin, Mus. ms. autogr. Jos. Haydn 32. A similar version in Dies, 124ff. It ends, however, as follows: 'Shortly after, she sent the garters, adding that she was ill, and if Haydn received no further news of her within the fortnight, he might count her among the souls departed this earth. No news came, and probably the young lady, who suffered from consumption, grieved herself to death over the failure of her marriage plans.'

Schellinger, is dated 1783). Sc. 9 (cut), Sc. 10 (mostly cut) leads to a new Aria for 'Monsieur', 'Morirò da voi lontano':

Andante sostenuto

Mo - ri - ò, mo - ri - [rò]

(ob. obbl., orch.); in the score there is only a 'short score' and parts by Anonymous 46 (duplicated parts by Schellinger). The Aria is not by Haydn (he cut bars 1–7). Atto II°, Sc. 5, 'Marionette' sings an aria which seems to have disappeared. In Sc. 9 Rosaura's Aria, 'Il Francese scieglierò' is replaced by another, 'Sventurata in quanti affanni', with ob. obbl. Score has a 'short score' by Schellinger; the parts are by Anonymous 10 (Porta?). The theme and orchestral disposition show an affinity with Haydn's insertion Aria, 'D'una sposa meschinella' (*vide supra*, p.402); the scoring of this insertion for Rosaura is for horns and strings. It is an attractive piece, possibly even by Haydn (an earlier 'insertion' aria?). In Sc. 11, as in Atto I°, Sc. 7, Haydn made a similar cut: Righini prefaced the Allegro section with 36 bars of introductory material – 8 bars' exposition of the *Affetuoso* section followed by 18 bars 'Fortspinnung': Haydn promptly cut those 18 bars. In Sc. 14 Marionette's Aria, 'Marionette non son io' was replaced with another, 'E tanto il furore', not by Haydn ('short score' and it was put into the Opera *a priori* by Schellinger). Bartha-Somfai also list a costume proposal of 16 December 1782, approved by the Prince (A.M. 3990). Bartha-Somfai, 107f., 271–4. Harich in *HJB* I, 49.

Domenico Cimarosa: L'italiana in Londra.
Libretto: none seems to have been printed; they probably used the Viennese libretto (the performance there was also in May). We have a costume proposal (A.M. 3989) of 19 April 1783:

Livia	Mad. Valdesturla.	[1787–8	Sassi
Madama	Mad. Speciolj.	revival:]	Nencini
Sumers	Mons. Braghetti.		Braghetta [*sic*]
Milord	Mons. Negri.		Bianchi and Nencini
Polidoro	Mons. Morati [*sic*].		Moratti

First performance: 4 May, repeated in May (three more perf.), June (one) and in 1788. There were rehearsals on 30 April, 2 and 3 May. Eszterháza performance material: Schellinger's bill (A.M. XVII.1161) lists 193 Bögen of vocal parts and 29 Bögen of orchestral parts. The score and the orchestral parts (which came from Italy), and incomplete vocal parts are in EH, Budapest, Ms. Mus. OE–14. The score notes 'In Parma Nell'Autunno dell'Anno 1780'. The inside of the score lists the cast of the 1787 revival (*vide infra*, p.685). In Eszterháza 'new' parts for bassoons (Schellinger) and 'Basso' (Joseph Elssler, who died in 1782, and Schellinger) were prepared. The two extant vocal parts are Milord ('Sr. Negri / Sr. Bianchi [1788]) and Madame ('Sra. Specioli, Sigra. Nencini [1788]). Haydn made very few changes (mostly cuts) in this witty and beautiful work. Atto I, Sc. 12: Polidoro's Aria, 'Dammi la mano', was replaced by another, 'Che contento, che piacere', of which the composer's name has been erased on the score ('Authore . . . . . gallo'). In Sc. 13, Milord's Aria, 'Sire, io vengo ai vostro piedi', Haydn cut bars 4–22 of the orchestral introduction. Bartha-Somfai (109) tell us of an interesting receipt in connection with *L'italiana in Londra*:

Esterhasi di Settembre 1783.
Ricevo io sotoscritto dal Sig. Maestro Giuseppe Haiden Fiorini 34. xr. 24. dico trentaquatro, e carantani ventiquatro, e questi per un spartito vendutoli intitolato L'italiana in Londra cio è Primo e Secondo Atto con tutti li libri del Orchestra Copiati, di più Fiorini uno e carantani quarantadue. Spesi per francatura alla posta da Bologna sino a Mantova che forma in tutto la Somma di Fiorini Trentasei, e carantani sei; in Fede,
Fiorini 36 × 6   Io Domenico Negri

[Haydn's hand. *German*] Above-listed sum 34 Fl. 24 xr. together with the shipping costs per 1 Fl. 42 xr. together 36 Fl. 6 xr. for the Opera Italiana in Londra, which His Highness the Prince will buy, the score and the orchest. parts, from the singer Negri, I attest to be correct.
Josephus Haydn mpria
Capell Meister

[Passed for payment by Prince Nicolaus, 30 September 1783. Haydn's autograph receipt for the money paid by Chief Cashier Züsser, Estoras, 6 Oct. 1783.]
[A.M. XVII.1165. Valkó II, 597. Bartha-Somfai, 109. Bartha, 131]

This reveals one interesting way in which Prince Nicolaus procured his new scores. Bartha–Somfai 108f., 274–6. Harich in *HJB* I, 49.

Giuseppe Sarti: Giulio Sabino. Dramma per musica. Da rappresentarsi nel teatro di S. A. il Sigr. Principe Esterhazy de Galantha. 1783.

Attori

Epponia	Sigra. Metilde Bologna.
Giulio Sabino	Sigr. Braghetti.
Voadice	Sigra. Valdesturla.
Annio	Sigr. Dichtler.
Arminio	Sigr. Negri.
Tito	Sigr. Specioli.

Libretto: 200 copies ordered from Joseph Siess in Oedenburg. Copy: Országos Széchényi Könyvtár, Sign. 207.006. First performance: 21 May (after eight stage rehearsals), repeated in May (two perf.), June (two), July (three), August (three), September (three), October (three), November (three) and in 1784, 1786 and 1787. On 17 and 18 May there were double rehearsals, starting at 9:00 a.m. and again at 2:00 p.m. (on the 18th there was a performance of Haydn's *Orlando Paladino* in the evening, while on the 17th there were morning and afternoon rehearsals also for the marionette theatre's production of *L'assedio di Gibilterra*). On the day of the première there was yet another rehearsal for the crowd scenes, involving four boys and thirty-three Grenadiers. Eszterháza performance material: Johann Schellinger's bill (A.M. XVII.1161) for the copying lists 180 Bögen vocal parts and 189 Bögen orchestral parts. Because the Opera was so long in the repertoire, various parts were lost and some arias perhaps replaced: Schellinger (A.M. XVIII.1211) wrote a bill in 1786 for 48 Bögen. The score is lost, but the orchestral parts and most of the vocal parts (Epponia, Annio, Arminio, Tito, Sabino) have survived: EH, Budapest, Ms. Mus. OE–32. On the V. I part (first desk), there is the following signature at the end: 'in 12 Stund copirt / gio Schelling [*sic*] / die 1 Mag / $\overline{783}$'. The rest of the parts by Schellinger and Anonymous 14 and 32. As far as can be determined, Haydn made only the usual cuts and transpositions. In one Aria (Atto I°, Sc. 4), he cut a *b flat''* held for four bars (Epponia); in Atto I°, Sc. 6, the vocal cadenza and the lead into it are cut, also Atto II°, Sc. 2. Atto III°, Sc. 3: in Tito's Aria, 'Bella fiamma', Haydn cut three sections of coloratura. Harich, *Musikgeschichte*, 53. Bartha–Somfai, 109f., 276f. Harich in *HJB* I, 49f.

Giuseppe Sarti: *Fra i due litiganti il terzo si gode, ossia I pretendenti delusi*.
Libretto: printed by Joseph Siess in Oedenburg (no copy survives). We have the cast from Porta's costume proposal of 7 July 1783 (A.M. 3988):

Dorina	Mad. Speciolj.
Livietta	Mad. Valdesturla.
Contessa	Mad. Polzelli.
Conte	Mons. Speciolj.
Mignone [*recte* Mingone]	Mons. Morati.
Titta	Mons. Dichtler.
Masotto	Mons. Praghetti [*sic*].

First performance: 10 August, repeated in September (four perf.), October (two), November (three) and in 1784. Eszterháza performance material: Schellinger's bill (A.M. XVII.1161) is for 189 Bögen vocal parts and 297 Bögen orchestral material. The score, orchestral parts and some of the vocal parts are in EH, Budapest, Ms. Mus. OE–4. The score comes from the Viennese copyist Wenzel Sukowaty. The parts, by Schellinger, are signed on the first V. I part: 'die 20 July / 20 Stund. $\overline{783}$ / Joan Schellinger'. Haydn added the names of the singers: 'M. Moratti' (Mingone), 'S^{ra} Specioli' (Dorina). The Sukowaty score includes many insertions, *inter alia* by Anfossi, 'Martini' and Storace. Atto I°, Sc. 2: Aria of the Contessa, 'Vorrei punirti indegno' is in fact Arminda's Aria from Atto II° of Anfossi's *La finta giardiniera*, also sung by Polzelli in 1780 (*vide supra*, p. 424). At that time Haydn had re-orchestrated the Aria; this time the Aria was played without those additions but with a cut (bars 60–65), an old-fashioned modulation to D major in between a cadence in F and the Aria's 'A' section in B flat. Sc. 5, Masotto's Aria 'In amor ci vuol finezza', is by 'Martini' (= Martín y Solar or Soler). Sc. 6, Dorina's Aria, 'Compatite miei Signori', is 'del Sig. Storace'.

In Atto II° we come to one of the most surprising operations in the history of the Eszterháza operatic establishment. Sc. XIII (Dorina) takes places in a 'Folto bosco, con diverse strade formate da varj massi, e da orride spelonche', and Dorina sings a *scena* in E flat (oboes, horns, strings). In the Eszterháza score, this was No. 9, changed locally to 20 (they preferred consecutive numbering for the whole of each work rather than by individual acts). On 9 October 1790, the *Morning Herald* announced this *scena* as 'O ime [*sic*] dove m'asendo [*sic*] by Signor Haydn'. The only recorded copy of this print, by Longman & Broderip is in the Hoboken Collection and is a proof copy with many corrections, including the name of the composer added to the proof as 'Del D^r. Joseph Haydn' (Haydn was not 'Doctor' until July 1791!). There is no doubt that this attractive *scena* was composed by Sarti, although there are numerous variants for the later part. The text as in the Eszterháza score is that found, for example, in a Dresden libretto of 1784 (Library of Congress ML48 s9457), but the Aria there begins 'Cara voce del mio bene'. (The 'Haydn' English print as 'Senza il caro amato'). In the Milan libretto (L. of C. s9454) of 12 September 1795, the recitative is also different after line 2 and the Aria reads 'Meschinella abbandonata'. In the Stuttgart libretto (L. of C. s9458), 1785, we find for the first time three additional lines of recitative not in the Dresden libretto but in the Eszterháza score: 'Perchè non mi ricerca, ma chi sa / Se a me più penserà? Perchè quel core? / Non sente parte almen del mio dolore.' Yet another Aria with the words 'Sola in braccio al mio periglio' is found as the conclusion of this *scena* in the libretto for Barcelona, 1784 (L. of C. ML 50 F18 s3, of 1784), of which the L. of C. also owns the music (M1505 s336), where however also the beginning is different:

L. of C. M1505 s33 is another source of our work: it begins with the accompagnato as we know it and then has the 'Rondo' 'Sola in braccio', of which the *incipit* is:

But despite all this textual chaos, Sarti is the composer. How did Haydn's name become attached? We have seen that many of the vocal parts of the EH materials have disappeared, retained by the singers; perhaps one of them sold this Aria, even thinking it was at least 'arranged' by Haydn. Hoboken (vol. II, p. 202), who assigns the number XXIVa:Es1 to the work, suggests the Allegro part of the Aria, 'Un momento più funeste' also occurs in Cimarosa's *La Circe*, Atto II°, Sc. 8, sung by Ulisse (A major, text at beginning identical, then different). The words do not occur in the pasticcio *La Circe* given at Eszterháza in 1787 (q.v.). We have to thank the Országos Széchényi Könyvtár for sending us photographs of the *scena* from the EH score. The scene also occurs in the Viennese score (Österreichische Nationalbibliothek, Musiksammlung) which was used for the performance on 28 May 1783. This is obviously not the place to discuss in further detail the ramifications of the Haydn version *vis-à-vis* the many Sarti versions. Harich, *Musikgeschichte*, 54. Bartha-Somfai, 111, 277–9.

Domenico Cimarosa: Il falegname. Commedia per musica da rappresentarsi nel teatro di Sua Altezza il Signor Principe di Esterhazi. L'anno 1783. In Vienna presso Giuseppe Nob. de Kurzbeck.

Libretto: no copy survives. It was in Italian and German and required 165 pages. The cast may be seen from a costume proposal (A.M. 3984, 18 November 1783):

Anagilda	Mlle. Valdesturla.
Don Verlardo	Mr. Negri.
Sozio	Mr. Morati [*sic*].
Fabio	Mons. Mandini.
[in another copy, EH, Eisenstadt: 'Don Fabio']	
Dalmiro	Mr. Braghetti.
[in Eisenstadt 'Don Dalmiro']	
Grazina	Mad. Bologna.
[in Eisenstadt 'Mlle. [i.e. Maria] Bologna']	
Pellonia	Mad. Polzelli.
Elena	Mad. Pologna [*sic*].
[in Eisenstadt 'Mad. [Metilde] Bologna']	

First performance: end of November (total: three perf.), repeated in 1784. Eszterháza performance material: Schellinger lists the work in his bill (A.M. XVII.1161) with 196 Bögen vocal parts and 299 Bögen orchestral material. The score, orchestral parts and most of the vocal parts are in EH, Budapest, Ms. Mus. OE–12; the score was apparently ordered from Vienna, where the work was given on 25 July. On the first V. I part we find 'Fine dell'Opera / di 20 7bris / 783 / in 18 ore'. Apart from cuts and transpositions, Haydn made the following changes: in Atto I°, Sc. 11, an insertion aria was added (parts by

Anonymous 58, not part of the Eszterháza copying establishment), of which the short score was by the late Joseph Elssler:

In Atto II°, Sc. 1, Grazina's 'Voi donne poverine' was replaced by Luigi Bologna's 'Damerini, care e belli'. In Sc. 6 Anagilda's Aria seems to be from another Cimarosa work (it has a separate title page) or is a later insertion by the composer: 'Voi notturne aure serene'. In Atto III° the Finale (chorus) seems to have been omitted. Harich, *Musikgeschichte*, 53f. Bartha-Somfai, 111f., 279f. Harich in *HJB* I, 50f.

Four operas from earlier seasons were repeated (Bartha-Somfai, 112. Harich in *HJB* I, 51f.):
Paisiello's *I filosofi immaginari*: March (two), April (three), May (two), June (three), July (two), August (two), September (two), October (two), November (three) and in 1784.
Haydn's *Orlando Paladino*: March (four), April (one), May (three), June (two), July (two), August (two), September (one), October (three), November (one) and in 1784.
Haydn's *La fedeltà premiata*: April (two), May (one), June (one), July (two), August (one), September (one), November (one) and in 1784.
Anfossi's *Il curioso indiscreto*: May (one), July (two), August (one) and October (one).

ITALIAN MARIONETTE OPERA 1783

[Pasticcio:] L'assedio di Gibilterra. Azzione [*sic*] teatrale per musica. – Da rappresentarsi con le marionette nel piccolo teatro di S. A. il signor principe Niccolo Estherhazy [*sic*] de Galanta. 1783. [Le prime cinque decorazioni sono] Del Digr. Pietro Travaglia Pittore Teatrale di S. A. Veduta della Fortezza di Gibilterra al naturale. Mare. Di Monsieur Federico Pittore di Camera di S. A. Campo di San Rocco illuminato vagamente alle Cinese. Di Monsieur Pierre Goussard Macchinista di S. A.
Libretto: 200 copies ordered from Joseph Siess in Oedenburg. Copy: Országos Széchényi Könyvtár, Sign. 1258 (facsimile of first three pages in Horányi, 106–8). No composer is listed and the entire material has disappeared. In Haydn's libretto catalogue (*Haydn: the Late Years 1801–1809*, p. 322) no composer is listed. First performance: 17 May after months of intensive preparation and rehearsals: this was one of the most difficult works ever staged at Eszterháza: there were six further rehearsals in August in preparation for another performance on 20 August (A.M. 3974a). Apart from the general rehearsal in the morning of 17 May, the work was repeated several times that month (a total of thirteen days' service for the marionette theatre in May is registered, without specifying which days were rehearsals and which performances). There is even a bill from the Apothecary (a so-called Chemist's bill) for services needed 'in the marionette theatre for the Opera: L'assedio di Gibilterra', probably gunpowder etc. for the siege. The parts for the Opera were copied by Johann Schellinger (91 Bögen vocal parts and 160 Bögen orchestral material). Harich has located a document in Eisenstadt in which Haydn refers to the composer of *L'assedio* as Pietro Guglielmi. Pohl (II, 9) gives Giuseppe Sarti, without giving a source. Harich, *Musikgeschichte*, 53. Bartha-Somfai, 110. London in *HJB*, 192 (using new archive material from EH, Eisenstadt).

THE GERMAN THEATRICAL TROUPE 1783

The Diwald Troupe was still in residence. See Chronicle 1781, *supra*, p. 439.

On New Year's Day, *anno* 1783, Haydn signed a receipt for payment for music paper.[1] Later in January there follows a letter to Artaria:

1 Haydn's hand: 'Specification / of music paper required for the 2 new Operas Julio Sabino and La Vedova Scaltra / For the vocal parts / 8 books Italian oblong with 10 staves / For the orchestra / 12 books Italian quarto with 10 staves / the book per 40 xr. makes together – – 12 Fl. / Joseph Haydn / Capell Meister'. Passed for payment by Prince Nicolaus, Esterház, 19 Dec. 1782 and Haydn's holograph receipt dated Vienna, 1 Jan. 1783. A.M. XVII. 1153. Valkó II, 596. Bartha 123. We may also add three other bills of the year: (*a*) Haydn's 'Specification of music paper required, viz.: 4 books quarto music paper with 10 staves / 2 books oblong with 12 staves / 4 books oblong with 10 staves / 2 books quarto with 12 staves / the book per 40 xr. makes together 8 Fl. / For various strings: 3 bundles E. — 6 G. — 2 violoncello A . . .'; passed for payment by Prince Nicolaus, Esterház, 15 May 1783. A.M. XVII. 1171. (*b*) Stadlmann's 'Notta. / a 'cello [*Pasetl*] strung with Italian strings, repaired the fingerboard, newly strung a Pariton [*sic*], glued the neck . . . an Indian violoncello bow . . . violin bows . . . Summa: 12 Fl. 22 xr . . .'; Haydn's hand: 'the above-listed repair of the Pariton and violoncello of 25 January, together with the other things listed, is correct and I attest to it . . .'; passed for payment by Prince Nicolaus, Esterhaz, 30 Sept. 1783. A.M. XVII.1163. Valkó II.1163. (*c*) A 'Notta. A violoncello as agreed together with an Indian bow with screw: 27 Fl. 44 xr. / A case with lock and metal hoops [*Pändern*] and lined with green material [*duch*]: 7 Fl. / Summa: 34 Fl. 44 xr.' Haydn's hand: 'Above violoncello together with the case as was ordered by his princely highness was properly received by me . . .'; passed for payment by 'N. F. E.', Esterhaz, 30 Sept. 1783. A.M. XVII.1164. Valkó II, 597.

[To Artaria & Co., Vienna. *German*]

Estoras, 27th January 1783.

Nobly born,
Most respected and honoured Sir!

You will certainly receive the *Lieder* together with the Symphonies[1] by the end of this month, through our palace superintendent [*Haus Hof Meister*] or *via* the Hussars: don't be angry at me, because upon my return home I caught a severe catarrh and had to stay in bed for a fortnight.

I remain, most respectfully,

Your ever obedient servant,
Joseph Haydn.

[Address:]   Monsieur
Monsieur Artaria & Compagn
à
Vienne

[Artaria's clerk notes: 'Haydn 1783/Esterhaz 27th January / rec'd 30th ditto/ ans'd 11th February'.]   [CCLN, 40]

We move for a moment to Vienna, where Count Zinzendorf, on 22 February, writes in his diary: '... puis a l'opera <u>Calypso abandonata</u>, ou Me Bologna et Melle Valdisturla chanterent au Theatre de la porte de Carinthie, musique de Heyden ...' (Olleson, 48). It seems that Haydn conducted a *Gesamtgastspiel* at the Kärntnerthortheater, with Metilde Bologna and Costanza Valdesturla, of Luigi Bologna's Opera, which was performed at Eszterháza in November 1784. We assume that Haydn conducted; the opera season at Eszterháza did not begin till March, with Guglielmi's *Il ratto della sposa*.

In March and April we also have letters to Artaria:

[To Artaria & Co., Vienna. *German*]
Nobly born,
Most highly respected Sir!

Next Monday you will receive the Symphony (full of mistakes)[2] and also some *Lieder*.

I cannot understand what you write me about the trios of Count von Durazzo;[3] it's just the other way round: I never received from him, but the Count did receive from me a thematic list, and only yesterday I sent his nephew a catalogue. Possibly the letter and the catalogues went astray: would you please therefore let me have the exact details on the next post-day, for I value Count Durazzo's house above all others. Meanwhile I remain, Sir, respectfully,

Your most obedient servant,
Joseph Haydn.

Estoras, 20th March 1783.

[Address:]   Monsieur
Monsieur de Artaria et Compagne
à
Vienne.

[CCLN, 40]

1 Previously we thought that the Symphonies must be Nos. 76–78 (see *The Symphonies of Joseph Haydn*, p. 388, n.48); we now consider that Haydn was referring to the proofs of the *Sei Sinfonie* (see letter of 20 October 1782, *supra*).
2 Symphony No. 69 in C, written about 1778. Haydn subsequently dedicated it to the Austrian *Feldmarschall* Laudon (or Loudon). Artaria published only a piano arrangement, which Haydn either made or looked through.
3 Johann Jacob, Count Durazzo, formerly Director of the Vienna Stadttheater nächst dem Kärnthnerthor, was appointed Austrian Ambassador to Venice in 1764.

[To Artaria & Co., Vienna. *German*]

Estoras, 8th April 1783.

Nobly born,
Most highly respected Sir!

I send you herewith the Symphony,[1] Sir, which was so full of mistakes that the fellow who wrote it ought to have his paw [*Bratze*] chopped off. The last or 4th movement is not practicable for the pianoforte, and I don't think it necessary to include it in print: the word 'Laudon' will contribute more to the sale than any ten finales. My continued unhappy condition, that is, the present necessity to remove a polypus on my nose, made it impossible for me to work up to now. You must therefore have patience about the *Lieder* for another week, or at most a fortnight, until my enfeebled head, with God's help, regains its former vigour. Please have the goodness to present my respects to Count Durazzo,[2] and tell him that I cannot remember the themes of the trios nor can I recall having received them. I searched carefully all though my music and papers, and could find no trace of them; if it please the Count, however, I shall send him a catalogue of all my trios. I await the favour of your reply and remain, Sir, most respectfully,

Your wholly obedient servant,
Joseph Haydn.

P.S. Many thanks for the copies
you sent me.[3]

[Address:] Monsieur
Monsieur Artaria et Compag
à
Vienne

[CCLN, 41]

Vienna was host to a young composer, Joseph Martin Kraus, whom we shall soon (October) encounter at Eszterháza. Meanwhile, on 18 April, he went to hear Haydn's *Stabat Mater* at the convent church of the Brothers of Mercy. 'But I had expected much more – much more. The performance was middling.' He taught composition to Paul Wranizky and was much attracted to Fräulein von Born, 'an excellent pianist' and the daughter of Ignaz von Born, Master of the lodge 'Zur wahren Eintracht'. At the end of the Summer he met Joseph II: 'I had the favour of speaking to His Majesty – but I couldn't win a really lasting picture of his feeling for the arts and wouldn't bet on it as being very reliable.'[4]

Two reviews in Cramer's *Magazin der Musik* may be quoted here, the second dated ('letter from Königsberg, April 1783'):

50) *Trois Sinfonies a grand Orchestre composées par Mr. G. Vanhall. Oeuvre 10. chès J. J. Hummel à Berlin & Amsterdam.*

These 3 Symphonies distinguish themselves among others by this so well known and famous man, and they are full of good thoughts and a select accompaniment. They rather approach the newest Hayden [*sic*] symphonies, but are more difficult than easy; and one cannot advise putting out the parts without having played though them at least once. . . . May Herr Vanhall as he grows older not be hindered by waning strength from giving us more such symphonies, which

---

1 See previous letter.
2 See previous letter.
3 Possibly of the *Sei Sinfonie*, which had appeared that winter (letter of 20 October 1782, supra).
4 K. F. Schreiber, *Biographie über den Odenwälder Komponisten Joseph Kraus*, Buchen 1928, pp. 65, 67, 81.

will be so much more welcome, the more spoiled we become by the delightful ones by Hayden [*sic*].

M. N.

[Page 92]

Herr **Joseph Haydn**, who without further ado need merely be mentioned in order that through his name everything, like Montesquieu's tombstone ('Erudiebam reges'), is expressed; he who in his wonderful sonatas provided many a piano player with *antispasmotica* against sorrow and misfortune; could he take it amiss if the so impressive list of languishing violinists hereby request from him in the most friendly and submissive fashion to remember them with the speedy publication of a little opus with violin sonatas for their empty larders? As far as clarity of engraving is concerned, we don't have to recommend Messrs. **Artaria** to him, since they are well enough known to him anyway. As for trouble required of the great man, isn't it payment enough if every violinist offers up his unfeigned thanks? The newspapers report that Hr. **Haydn** has gone to England; his brow crowned with laurels, he will surely return to the fatherland that loves and respects him; and if his talents are properly rewarded, he will return loaded with good guineas. If this sheet should come to his notice, may he fulfil the wishes of the German violin players who respect him.

★★★ki.

[Pp. 582f.]

Haydn was now in contact with another German publisher, Heinrich Philipp Boßler of Speier (Speyer), who issued the following open letter in the German periodicals:

From my friend, the Princely Esterhazi [*sic*] Kapellmeister, Herr **Joseph Haydn**, I have the commission to accept subscriptions at **six gold ducats for three new, very magnificent, beautiful and not all too long Symphonies**, which he intends to deliver by the end of June; I request, therefore, the resp. connoisseurs to send their orders to me post free, with 4 Kreutzer fee for registering them. **From this very same great, very famous composer** I have the pleasure of announcing to friends of music a subscription for **six thoroughly beautiful new Divertimenti** scored for violin, viola and bass. Subscription price **1 Gulden 40 Kreuzer** [*sic*] for the well known excellence of my publishing house's copies on very fine paper with handsome, clear engraving. At the same time will also appear **three very beautiful and not all too difficult new Trios** for 2 flutes and violoncello by the **famous Badian Kapellmeister Herr Schmittbauer.** Subscription prince 1 Gulden Rheinländisch. Afterwards the price will be raised as much again. Speier, 27th May 1783.[1]

Bossler,
Hochfürstl. Brandenb. Onolzb. Rath.
[Pp. 805f.]

---

1 We quote from Cramer's *Magazin der Musik*, 1783. Also in the *Teutscher Merkur*, May 1783, p. LXXIIIf. The Symphonies are the 'English' works that Haydn composed in 1782 for a proposed London concert tour which did not materialize. Boßler was, of course, helping Haydn to market MS. copies – otherwise 6 gold ducats would be far too expensive for a print. The Divertimenti (in other sources 'Divertissements') are probably authentic arrangements of Baryton Trios XI:123, 103, 101, 114, 124 and 108), a category of works that Haydn was trying, not very successfully, to sell in a more easily playable form. Like all Boßler prints, the Divertimenti are rare. Hummel's reprint, as Op. 21, achieved better circulation. Boßler also issued other Haydn Baryton Trios: Nos. 74–76 as 'Trois Trios pour le violin, alte & basse', Op. 32; and separate editions of XI:111 and 112 in the series 'Soirées Amusantes ou Récréations pour les Amateurs de Musique' (1784 and 1785: Op. 32 cannot be dated exactly but was certainly printed by 1788). Copies: Divertimenti – Bruxelles (Conservatoire). XI:74–6 – Westdeutsche Bibliothek, Marburg/Lahn. XI:111 – Benedictine Monastery of Einsiedeln. XI:112 – Landesbibliothek, Stuttgart. H. Unverricht, 'Haydn und Boßler', in *Festskrift Jens Peter Larsen*, Copenhagen 1972, pp. 287–92.

In June, we have a letter to Artaria:

[To Artaria & Co., Vienna. *German*]

Estoras, 18th June 1783.

Nobly born,
Most highly respected Sir!

I send you herewith the Laudon Symphony [No. 69], for which the violin part is not at all necessary and may be therefore omitted entirely. Please send me either the music or the first strophe of each of the 2nd part of the *Lieder*, so that I can complete the missing ones. Many thanks for the pianoforte Sonatas by Clementi,[1] they are very beautiful; if the author is in Vienna, please present my compliments to him when opportunity offers. I remain, Sir, most respectfully,

Your wholly obedient servant,
Joseph Haydn.

P.S. As to the pianoforte Sonatas with violin and bass, you must still be patient, for I am just now composing a new *opera seria*.[2]

[Address:]   Monsieur
         Monsieur Artaria et Compag
                à
              Vienne.

[Artaria's clerk notes: 'Haydn 1783./Esterhaz 18th June/ rec'd 20th and/ans'd 18th July.']   [CCLN, 42]

In Cramer's *Magazin der Musik*, Haydn could read, in a report from Paris in May (pp. 834ff.), that 'The choice of symphonies met with the greatest success, and those of Haydn stood out particularly.' The success of Holzbauer's *Miserere* – the one to which Mozart added choruses (K.297a) which are lost – is noted, also the *Stabat Mater* by the revolutionary *Sturm und Drang* composer, Franz Beck, the most talented of the Mannheim school after Franz Xaver Richter; it 'called forth an astonishing number of people'.

In a report from Vienna in the same magazine, June 1783 (pp. 842ff.) we read:

... The music that we receive here from Berlin, Saxony and the rest of the north has almost always little success here; whereas our music is supposed to please almost always there [in the north]. What can be the reason for that, considering that in the former places there is no lack of great composers? Some think that regularity and too much art are the reason. Our local music is surely singing, laughing, pleasant and expressive [*sprechend*], and if this were so with all the other arts and sciences here, Vienna would be the Athens of Europe. ...

The next letter that concerns us is from Haydn to Boyer in Paris, offering him Symphonies Nos. 76–78:

[To Boyer, music publisher in Paris. *German*]
Nobly born,
Most highly respected Sir!

I did not receive your esteemed favour of 2nd June until my return yesterday, and noted your requests with much pleasure; I doubt, however, whether I can satisfy your wants, for the following reasons. First, I am not allowed, according to the terms of my contract with my Prince, to send any of my own autographs abroad, because he retains these himself. I could of course make two scores of a work, but I don't have the time and don't really see any adequate reason for doing

1 Probably Artaria's edition of Op. 7 and/or Op. 9 (pl. nos. 32 and 36).
2 *Armida*, first performed at the Eszterháza Theatre in February 1784.

so. For if a piece is neatly and correctly copied [in parts], it is able the more quickly to be engraved. Secondly, you must rely on my word of honour, and not believe in a scrap of paper. Last year I composed 3 beautiful, magnificent and by no means over-lengthy Symphonies,[1] scored for 2 violins, viola, basso, 2 horns, 2 oboes, I flute and 1 bassoon[2] – but they are all very easy, and without too much *concertante*[3] – for the English gentlemen, and I intended to bring them over myself and produce them there: but a certain circumstance hindered that plan, and so I am willing to hand over these 3 Symphonies. N.B. No one has them up to now: you will therefore have the kindness to let me know at your earliest convenience what you are capable of paying me for them, that is to say, how much you want to let yourself in for, because my circumstances are such that he who pays the best for my work is the one who receives it. On the other hand, I assure you that these 3 Symphonies will have a huge [*gewaltige(n)*] sale. Awaiting the favour of your early reply, I remain, with the greatest respect,

> Your well born's
> most obedient servant,
> Josephus Haydn mpria.

Estoras, 15th July 1783.
[Address in a copyist's hand:]
> Monsieur
> Monsier Boyer, au Magazin
> de Musique, Rue neuve des petits
> Champs, cideyant Rue du Roulle,
> à la Clef d'or N^{ro} 83

A Paris

[CCLN, 42f.]

The Prince purchased yet another violoncello (he had bought one earlier in the year – *vide supra*, p. 472n.). We read:

I herewith attest to having received 6 Cremnitz ducats from Herr *Capell Meister* Haydn for a Bassi violoncello.

> Mathias Thier bürgerl. lauten und Geigen
> Macher zu Wien.[4]

The composer Joseph Martin Kraus, born the same year as Mozart (and died one year later), arrived at Eszterháza in October. Here are the documents from Kraus's letters and his travel diary:

3 October 1783: [Kraus receives orders to meet King Gustav III] ... Then I will go for a little while to Esterhaz to take leave of my Haydn.... give my dear Hoffstätter [Roman Hoffstetter, the composer of Haydn's 'Op. 3' Quartets] heartfelt greetings. – Vanhall presents his compliments to him, for I told him [Vanhal] that he is just as dear a man [*Herzensmann*] as he [Hoffstetter]. ...

1 Symphonies Nos. 76–78 (E flat, B flat, C minor). Torricella issued them in July 1784: an announcement in the *Wiener Zeitung* specifies that Haydn himself corrected them. He also sold them to Forster in London, where they appeared in 1784. Boyer, too purchased the Symphonies and published them as Op. 37.
2 There are in fact two bassoon parts.
3 In 1959, when CCLN was first published, the end of the letter (from the clause 'for the English gentlemen ...' was known only in summary from a British antiquarian catalogue. Meanwhile the present owner of the letter, Mr R. F. Kallir, New York, thoughtfully provided me with a photograph of the entire letter which is therefore printed here for the first time. Note that the words 'beautiful, magnificent and by no means over-lengthy' ('schöne, prächtige und nicht gar zu lange') is nearly the wording of the above-mentioned announcement by Boßler (original: 'neue, sehr prächtige, schöne und nicht gar zu lange'), which must be a direct quotation from a lost letter from Haydn to Boßler.
4 Haydn's hand: 'I have received in order and already paid for the above-listed violoncello which was ordered by his princely highness ...'. Passed for payment by Prince Nicolaus, Esterhaz, 30 September 1783. Receipt for the money in Haydn's hand, Estoras, 6 Oct. 1783. A.M. XVII.1166. Valkó II, 598.

18 October 1783: Eszterháza. I fulfil my promise to write again from a place where I have thoroughly enjoyed myself . . . The Prince here was most condescending towards me, and from the monetary standpoint something would surely be there for me if I had time and inspiration – and if I could stand the Hungarian way of life better . . . The theatre is built with enormous luxury – but with little taste and still less reflection. The orchestra is what you would expect under the direction of a Haydn – therefore one of the best. It is in fact not larger than 24 men, but makes an outstanding impression. – The first two violinists and the 'cellist are Italians – the rest are almost all Bohemians. In Haydn I got to know a right good soul, except for one point – that's money. He simply couldn't understand why I didn't provide myself with a drawer full of compositions for my trip, so as to be able to plant them whenever necessary. I answered quite drily that I wasn't cut out to be a Jewish salesman. *Satis!* Sterkel wrote him and asked for some arias for his sister and offered as an equivalent several arias from his Neapolitan opera; Haydn shook his head, for that wasn't ringing coin of the realm! It's a curious thing with most artists. The closer one examines them, the more they lose the halo with which the Messrs. Amateurs and critics invest them. My compliments to my dear Hoffstätter. . . .   [Schreiber, op. cit., pp. 68f.]

Haydn later said that Kraus was the first genius he had ever met, which is interesting (a) because it shows that Haydn had scarcely met Mozart by October 1784 and (b) Haydn never thought of himself as a genius 'in that class'. Kraus brought with him the magnificent Symphony in C minor which he had especially composed for the occasion in Vienna (two of the four horns were added later, probably for Eszterháza). This great, humane and profound Symphony[1] obviously impressed Prince Nicolaus, too, with his connoisseur's ear. Haydn's opinion of Kraus has been quoted at length in *Haydn: the Years of 'The Creation' 1796–1800*, pp. 250f., 256f., 268, etc. Haydn said, about Kraus, to Marianne Ehrenström: 'J'y reconnais Kraus. Quelle profondeur de pensées – quel talent classique' (Schreiber, 71). We can only agree: his early death was a tragedy for eighteenth-century music.

The following receipt by Schellinger gives us a useful list of his copying activities:

Conto. The copying work which was done the whole year from 1 January to end of November 1783:

Operas	Vocal parts á 7 xr.	Instr. parts á 5 xr.
Il Ratto della Sposa	8	19
La Vedova scaltra	184	296
Italiana in Londra	193	29
Opera seria Il Giulio Sabino	180	189
L'assedio di gibilterra Marionetti	91	160
Fra i due litiganti	189	297
Il Faglegname	196	299
Sinfonie per Theatro	—	19
Soma: 230 Fl. 27 xr.	1041	1308

Johan Schilling [*sic*] Copyist Souffler mpria

[Haydn's hand:] Above-listed sum for 1,041 Bögen vocal parts (the Bogen as agreed a 7 xr.) and the 1,308 Bögen instrumental parts with the Bogen at 5 xr. have

---

1 A critical edition of J. M. Kraus Symphony in C minor, ed. Richard Engländer, in Vol. 1 of Works by Joseph Martin Kraus, *Monumenta Musicae Svecicae*, Stockholm 1960.

been carefully examined by me, the undersigned, and found to be correct. Estoras, 24th Nov. 1783. Josephus Haydn mpria. / Capell Meister.
[A.M. XVII.1161. Valkó II, 597f. Bartha-Somfai, 113. Bartha, 132.]

Haydn had made a Symphony (No. 73 'La Chasse') round the hunting Overture to *La fedeltà premiata* and had given it to Christoph Torricella, who published it in July 1782 (*Wiener Zeitung*, 24 July). Of the various interesting copies, we would single out one in the British Museum, entitled 'Spectat Illustrissimo DD^{mo} Conti Esterhazi de Gallantha' (*not*, as stated in Landon, *SYM*, 721, and elsewhere, Haydn's holograph addition). Now we find it reviewed in Cramer's *Magazin der Musik* (1783, pp. 491f.):

> This symphony is quite as worthy of its author as the newest Op. 18 ... [Hummel ed.; *vide supra*, p. 466], and in no way needs our praise. In listening to it, the very beginning and the wonderful workmanship of the following parts reveal the hand of the great master, who seems to be inexhaustible in new ideas. It goes without saying, of course, that there are in this, as in all his symphonies, difficulties and unexpected progressions which require trained and correct players, and cannot be entrusted merely to good luck, without the closest study of the key-signatures, and without knowing the work. So let this be a warning to amateurs and hesitant players, who dare not essay this work without knowing it exactly beforehand, else they shame themselves. We hope, indeed, that Heydn [*sic*] will crown this great epoch of the symphony with more such wonderful pieces, and thereby reduce all bad writers of symphonies to silence, or to improving their superficial products, through which none but themselves can derive any pleasure.

We close the Chronicle for 1783 with two further reviews from Cramer's *Magazin der Musik* which will show that (a) Koželuch was regarded as a Haydn *seguace*, a position which neither will have found very amusing and (b) that the degeneracy of Vanhal, that great hope of the late 1760s, was now proceeding apace:

> *Trois Sonates pour le Clavecin ou Forte Piano dont la troisieme est à quatre Mains composés & dediés à son Excellence Madame la Comtesse Hortense D. Hatzfeld née Comtesse Zierotin, par Monsieur Leopold Kozeluch. Oeuvre VIII. à Vienne. chés Christoph Torricella [etc.]*
>
> Three very well composed Sonatas, very brilliant, full of new thoughts and charming melody. There is hardly a composer who so closely approaches the style of Haiden [*sic*] in this field as Herr Kozeluch, without however being just an imitator. New as this author is, he was little known in our part of the world, but he now is very successful and his works are in great demand; and this is still and sure proof of the musical public's approval.   [Pp. 921f.]

[Pp. 925f.] [Vanhal Tre Sonate Op. XXX Artaria. Mainly for amateurs with unskilled fingers] but who love good and sensitive melodies. And in this respect they are admirably composed. Particularly in the slow movements one finds a so simple and touching melody that one is glad to spend the time to play through them. Of course such things have to be regarded as *bonbons* or *bisquit*, which one cannot enjoy too much or too often. Otherwise they don't agree with one. ...

Chronicle 1784

ITALIAN OPERAS 1784

This year 104 performances are registered (Harich in *HJB* I, 59).

Joseph Haydn: ARMIDA / DRAMMA EROICO. / DA RAPPRESENTARSI / NEL TEATRO / DI S. A. / IL SIGR PRINCIPE REGNANTE / NICCOLÒ ESTHERASI [*sic*] / DE GALANTHA. / POSTO IN MUSICA / DAL SIG MAESTRO

HAYDEN. / L'ANNO 1784. / [vignette] / IN OEDENBURGO, / NELLA STAMPERIA DI GIUSSEPE [*sic*] SIESS. . . . *Le Decorazzioni sono del Sigr. Travaglia Pittore Teatrale di S. A.*

ATTORI

ARMIDA.	*La Sigra Metilde Bologna.*
RINALDO.	*Il Sigr Prospero Braghetti.*
UBALDO.	*Il Sigr Antonio Specioli.*ʼ
IDRENO.	*Il Sigr Paolo Mandini.*
ZELMIRA.	*La Sigra Costanza Valdesturla.*
CLOTARCO.	*Il Sigr Leopoldo Dichtler.*

La Musica è del sudetto Sigr Maestro Giuseppe Haiden.

Libretto: 500 copies ordered from Siess, who had 200 bound; the remainder were soon bound and in circulation. Copies: Gesellschaft der Musikfreunde, Vienna, 9210/textb.; Biblioteca del Conservatorio di Musica, Rome, Carvalhaes 1212. First performance: 26 February, following the usual four stage rehearsals and one general rehearsal. The work required a large apparatus of 'supers', including six stage musicians, four girls and 34 Grenadiers dressed in Roman and Turkish costumes. A further eight Grenadiers helped with the scene-shifting. The 'Stabenen-Ausweis' (List of Supers) informs us that the general rehearsal and the previous one as well were given with all the decorations and machines but without costumes. Some of the costumes for *Armida* in Travaglia's sketches have survived (see pls. 21, 22). Travaglia's proposals for the stage sets were submitted on 6 August 1783 and approved by the Prince one day later. The many costumes made this a particularly expensive work to produce; they cost nearly 500 gulden (approval by Prince Nicolaus on 13 October 1783). Repetitions: a total of 54 performances, the most popular opera ever produced at Eszterháza: February (two more perf.), March (three), April (two), May (three), June (one), July (one), August (two), September (four), October (three) and in 1785, 1786, 1787 and 1788. Eszterháza performance material: Schellinger's bill (A.M. XVII.1186) lists 184 Bögen vocal parts and 193 Bögen orchestral material; it is no longer in EH, which owns only two sources from Haydn's legacy: (a) score of Act III by Johann Elssler and (b) Duet with preceding recitative: Scene IX (Finale) of Atto I°, 'Oh amico!', Ms. Mus. I. 153 and I. 157 resp. Both these scores are not part of the original performance material. Some documents: (a) Nunziato Porta's costume proposal = A.M. 3985 (*vide supra*); in that proposal, Valdesturla was supposed to sing not only 'Zelmira' but also appear as a (silent) 'Ninfa' (Atto III°, Sc. 2); (b) Travaglia's proposals for the stage sets, A.M. 3986 (6 Aug. 1783) suggests that one could save money by using decorations from earlier operas, *viz.* Haydn's *La fedeltà premiata*, Haydn's *Orlando Paladino* and Sarti's *Giulio Sabino*; but all three operas were still performed in 1784. Among the eye-witnesses of *Armida*, we have quoted one, *supra*, p. 109. Another is the famous Italian composer, Giuseppe Sarti, three of whose operas were being given at Eszterháza in 1784 (*vide infra*). On a trip from Italy to St Petersburg, Sarti visited Vienna, where he met Mozart, and went on to Eszterháza, where he could hear four of his own works and where he listened to *Armida*, which he found most impressive.[1] Concerning the author of the libretto, *vide infra*, p. 550. Harich, *Musikgeschichte*, 54. Bartha-Somfai, 114f., 281. Harich in *HJB* I, 53f.

Pasquale Anfossi: Die glücklichen Reisenden. Ein Singspiel. Aufgeführt auf dem hochfürstlichen Theater zu Esterhazy. Wien, bei Joseph Edlen von Kurzbeck. 1784. – – I viaggiatori felici. Dramma giocoso per musica, da rappresentarsi ne'teatri di Sua Altezza il Signor Principe d'Esterhasi. L'anno 1784. Presso Giuseppe Nob. de Kurzbeck.

Libretto: in two languages throughout: no copy survives. Cast (from a costume proposal, 16 April 1784, EH, Budapest, Fasc. 799, Nro. I.46; a parallel file in Eisenstadt placed to the right when differing):

Gianetto	Mons. Mandini.
Gaston [Don Gaston]	Mons. Negri.
Pasquino	Mons. Dichtler.
	Mons. Murati. [Moratti]
Pettina [Bettina]	Mad. Specioli.
Isabella	Mad. Polzelli.
Lauretta	Mad. Bologna [Mlle. Bologna][2]

First performance: 21 March (two perf. in all), repeated in April (four), May (two), June (three), July (two), August (one), September (one), October (three) and in 1787 and 1788. Eszterháza performance material: Schellinger's bill (A.M. XVII.1186) lists 288 Bögen vocal parts and 189 Bögen orchestral material. The score (from Vienna), the orchestral material (V. I, first part, Atto II° missing) and Don Gastone's part are in EH, Budapest, Ms. Mus. OE–33. The Viennese performance took place on 29 Dec. 1783. Schellinger dated several of the parts '1784'; on 1st V. I part, 'Sig. Luigi'; Haydn added 'S: Negri' in

---

1 N. E. Framery, *Notice sur Joseph Haydn*, Paris, 1810, pp. 22ff. For Framery's tale of *Armida* and Pleyel, see our reconstruction of the true facts, *infra*, p. 759.

2 Mlle. (Maria) Bologna died on 16 May; theoretically, she can have sung the first performance on 21 March. She may have been ill by that time, however, and replaced by her sister, Metilde.

the part of 'Don Gastone'. Apart from transpositions (downwards) and cuts, the small changes Haydn made are as follows: Atto I°, sinfonia: of the three movements, Haydn cut the last two. Sc. 7. Isabella's (Polzelli's) Aria, 'Dove mai s'e ritrovato', had to be transposed from E flat to D, and then down to C to accommodate Polzelli's limited range, and Haydn rewrote the last cadenza for her, simplifying it. Sc. 12, Terzetto 'Voi pergoletti amori': Haydn for once slowed the tempo from 'Andante espressivo' to 'Adagio'. Harich, *Musikgeschichte*, 55. Bartha-Somfai, 115f., 281–3. Harich in *HJB* I, 54.

Domenico Cimarosa: L'amor costante. Dramma giocoso in due-atti. Da rappresentarsi nel teatro di S. A. il Sigr. Principe Regnante Niccolo Esterhasi de Galantha. L'anno 1784. In Vienna, presso Giuseppe Nob. de Kurzböck.
Libretto: 200 copies ordered. Copy: EH, Eisenstadt. Cast (from a costume proposal by Porta, 17 May 1784, EH, Budapest, Fasc. 799, Nro. I. 46; a parallel file in Eisenstadt placed to the right when differing):

Armidoro	Mons. Mandini.
Marchese	Mons. Negri.
Cavallier [Cavaliere]	Mons. Specioli.
Nespolina	Mad. Specioli.
Laura	Mad. Valdesturla.
....	Mons. Dichtler.

The actual cast, from the libretto itself, shows that Porta must have made widespread changes in the book, which no longer agrees with Giovanni Bertati's original (e.g. Gazzaniga's setting, Venice 1787); this new version is also the one used for the Vienna performance of 1787 (i.e. the names of the roles, not of course the singers):

Il Marchese di Fiumesecco[,] vomo [*sic*] ambizioso, e ridicolo.	Il Sig. Negr. [*sc.* Negri]
Armidoro, ufficiale di spirito amante di Laura.	Signor Mardini [Mandini]
Nespolina, cameriera astuta.	Signora Specioli.
Il Cavalier del verde.	Signor Specioli.
Laura, Figlia del Marchese.	Signora Valdestiula [*sic*]

The role for Dichtler (as proposed in the first casting) had been eliminated. First performance: 27 April, repeated in May (four perf.), June (two), July (two), August (one). Eszterháza performance material: Schellinger's bill (A.M. XVII.1186) lists 289 Bögen vocal parts and 181 Bögen orchestral material. The score (probably from Italy: 'In Roma Alla Valle 1782'), orchestral parts and fragmentary vocal parts are in EH, Budapest, Ms. Mus. O E–53. Schellinger dated V. I first part '1784'; Haydn noted 'Sigr. Negri' on the rec. of the role 'Marchese', next to which is (Negri's?) notice 'Ricevuta il giorno cinque Aprile 1784' which (as we have pointed out before) gave him 22 days to learn the whole Opera. The duplicate V. I parts also by Anonymous 14 and 32. Haydn's minor changes include: Atto I°, Sc. 2, Armidoro's Aria, 'Che piacere, che contento', was subjected to a large cut (bars 80–103); there are other, similar cuts in Sc. 10 (Marchese's 'Mi rallegra') and Sc. 12 (Nespolina's 'Sono schietta'), and in Atto II, Sc. 3, an extraordinary cut (Duetto Armidoro-Marchese, 'Lai, lai lai') at bars 158–79. Harich, *Musikgeschichte*, 55. Bartha-Somfai, 116, 283f. Harich in *HJB* I, 54f.

Giuseppe Sarti: La Didone abbandonata. Dramma per musica. Del celebre Sig. Abbate Pietro Metastasio. – Da rappresentarsi nel'teatro di S. A. il Sig. Principe Regnante Niccolò Estherasi [*sic*] de Galantha. L'anno 1784. – In Oedenburgo, nella stamperia di Giuseppe Siess. . . . Le Decorazzioni sono del Sigr. Pietro Travaglia Pittore Teatrale di S. A.

Personaggi[1]

Didone[,] regina di Cartagine	Mad. Bologna.
Enea Troiano.	Mr. Braghetti.
Jarba, Rè de Mori sotto nome di Arbace	Mr. Bianchi.
Selene, Sorella di Didone . . .	Mad. Valdesturla.
Araspe, confidente di Jarba.	Mr. Specioli.
Osminda, confidente di Didone.	Mr. Dichtler.

La Musica è del celebre sigr. Maestro Giuseppe Sarti all'attual servizio di S. M. I. di tutte le Russie.

Libretto: 200 copies ordered (A.M. 4021 of July 1784). Copy: Országos Széchényi Könyvtár, Sign. 208.421. First performance: 26 July, repeated 29 July and in August (two perf.), September (three), October (two) and in 1785. The battle scenes, requiring 24 Grenadiers (a total of 36 Grenadiers were

---

1 Only the roles, not the singers, are listed. We follow Bartha-Somfai and add the singers' names using (*a*) costume proposal, EH, Budapest, Secr. Prot. III. 132 and (*b*) a parallel file in Eisenstadt; we place the latter's differences (when present) to the right.

required) – 12 as Moors and 12 as Trojan soldiers –, caused much difficulty; the première, set for Sunday 25 July, had to be postponed a day, and between the première and the next performance, the 24 'fighting' Grenadiers had fencing rehearsals for two whole days. Eszterháza performance material: Schellinger's bill lists (A.M. XVII.1186) 198 Bögen vocal parts and 189 Bögen orchestral material. The score (from Vienna?), the orchestral parts and fragmentary vocal parts are in EH, Ms. Mus. OE–90. On the vocal part of Jarba, 'Sig. Bianchi', and on that of Osminda 'Dichtler'. Apart from Schellinger's work, V. I dup. and II dup. were also copied by Anonymous 14 and 30; at end of V. I first part, the date '26 Juny'. Haydn's changes were small and apart from cuts and transpositions downwards, we find: Atto II°, Sc. 3, part of *secco* rewritten. Otherwise, Haydn's changes are so minimal that we might be tempted to seek an explanation why this old Opera – the first performance took place at Copenhagen in 1762 – was so respectfully treated: and we believe that the Opera's performance was a direct result of Sarti's personal presence at Eszterháza, or rather his planned presence. Whether he actually arrived in time for the première is doubtful: he had left Vienna on 9 June (Mozart to his father: 'I will fetch Paisiello with a carriage, so that he can hear my compositions and my female pupil; – if Maestro Sarti did not have to leave today, I would have taken him along too. – Sarti is a good, honest man! – I played a great deal for him ...'. Mozart, *Briefe und Aufzeichnungen*, vol. III, Kassel 1963, p. 318), and presumably arrived at Eszterháza about the evening of the 9th or, more likely the 10th. It is unlikely that he could stay until 26 July, but in June he could have heard his own *Fra i due litiganti* or *Giulio Sabino*. Harich, *Musikgeschichte*, 55f. Bartha-Somfai, 118f., 286–8. See also Gerber *NTL* III, 20 (mentions performance Eszterháza).

Francesco Bianchi: La villanella rapita. Dramma giocoso per musica di Giovanni Bertati. Da rappresentarsi nel teatro di S. A. Principe Regnante Niccolò Esterhasi de Galantha. L'anno 1784. In Oedenburgo, Nella stamperia di Giuseppe Siess.
Libretto: 200 copies ordered and 150 bound by Mathias Pfundtner (Aug., A.M. 4021). No copy survives. Cast (from a costume proposal by Porta, E II, Budapest, Fasc. 799, Secr. Prot. III.131; a parallel file in Eisenstadt placed to the right when differing):

Mandina	Mad. Ripamonti.
Giannina	Mad. Specioli.
Ninetta	Mad. Polzelli.
Piaggio [Biaggio]	Mons. Muratti [Moratti].
Pipo	Mons. Bianchi.
Graf [Il Conte]	Mons. Mandini.
Cavallier [Cavaliere]	Mons. Dichtler.

Further documents: (a) costume proposal by Travaglia for a special decoration of 24 July 1784 (EH, Budapest, Fasc. 799, Secr. Prot. Nr. 4. 158): '... For the Opera La vilanella rapita it is necessary to make a peasant cottage 17 feet [*Schuh*] high, 7 feet wide ... Item a decoration, which is a small *Rompiment* and shows the distance ...'; (b) Haydn's request for music paper (A.M. XVII.1180; Valkó II, 601; Bartha-Somfai, 120): 'Specification / Paper required for the new Opera La Villanella Rapita and for the duplicate parts of the newly purchased Symphonies, *viz.* / 8 books oblong with 10 staves / 12 books quarto with 10 staves / the book at 40 xr. Summa: 13 Fl. 20 xr. Esterhaz, 17 July 1784 ...'. First performance: 29 August after three stage rehearsals and a general reharsal, repeated in September (three perf.), October (one), November (five), December (one) and in 1785, 1786 and 1787. Eszterháza performance material: Schellinger's bill (A.M. XVII.1186) is for 296 Bögen vocal parts and 193 Bögen orchestral material. The score (by the Venetian copyist Giuseppe Baldan), the orchestral parts and the recitatives of Pipo (Haydn: 'Sr Moratti') are in EH, Budapest, Ms. Mus. OE–39. Apart from Schellinger, Anonymous 14 and 32 assisted in duplicate V. parts. Apart from the usual transpositions downwards and cuts, Haydn made the following changes. Atto I°, Sc. 2, Conte's Aria, 'Bel godere al campagna', originally sung by Mandini, was transposed for his benefit from A to G and, when he left at the end of October 1784 put back in the original key for Mandini's substitute; the Aria was later cut entirely. The same applies to Sc. 14, Mandina's Aria, 'Quando che a me', transposed from B flat to G for Ripamonti's benefit and when she left (1787), put back in the original key. In Sc. 15, Ninetta's (Polzelli's) Aria, 'Quando i miei paperi', transposed *up* from F to G to avoid the mezzo range. In both Finales (Atti I° e II°) Haydn later cut the concluding Presto sections either entirely (Atto I°) or in part. Harich, *Musikgeschichte*, 56. Bartha-Somfai, 119f., 288–90. Harich in *HJB* I, 56. See also Gerber, *NTL* III, 391 (mentions perf. Eszterháza).

Luigi Bologna: L'isola di Calipso abbandonata.
Libretto: none seems to have been printed; perhaps the Viennese libretti were used (see Chronicle for 22 Feb. 1783, where Haydn seems to have conducted a performance at Vienna: *supra*, p. 473). First performance: 11 November, repeated 5 December and in 1785, 1786, 1787, 1788, 1789 and 1790 – a total of 41 performances and after Haydn's *Armida* the most popular opera at Eszterháza. Eszterháza performance material: copied by Johann Schellinger (Baucassa-Secretariats-Protocoll, EH, Eisenstadt) 21 vocal parts and 19 orchestral parts (a different kind of reckoning than his usual 'Bogen'). Alas, the entire performance material has disappeared from EH, so that we can say nothing of Haydn's changes. The cast,

however, may be reconstructed from a costume proposal of 10 Nov. 1784 (EH, Budapest, Fasc. 799. Secr. Prot. IV. P.183):

Callipso	Mad. Bologna.
Telemaco	Mad. Valdesturla.
Mentone	Mons. Bianchi.

The proposal for scenery by Travaglia is in the same archives IV.P.180. Gerber, *NTL* I, 462 (where 'a copy of the score ... is wrongly attributed to Haydn' and listing the work, as in all these references, as performed at Eszterháza under Haydn's direction in 1786, which in this case, and also Bianchi's *La villanella rapita*, is true). Bartha-Somfai, 120f., 290. Harich in *HJB* I, 56f.

Seven operas from earlier seasons were repeated:
Sarti's *Fra i due litiganti il terzo gode*: March (one), April (two), May (one), June (one), July (one) and August (one).
Cimarosa's *Il falegname*: 9 March.
Paisiello's *I filosofi immaginari*: March (one), April (one), May (two) and June (one).
Haydn's *Orlando Paladino*: March (one), May (one), June (two), September (one) and October (two). A total of thirty performances and the ninth most popular opera in the repertoire.
Sarti's *Giulio Sabino*: March (one), April (two), June (two), July (one), August (one) and in 1786 and 1787.
Haydn's *La fedeltà premiata*: 29 June. A total of thirty-six performances and the fifth most popular opera.
Sarti's *Le gelosie villane*: July (three) and August (two). For this revival, Haydn seems to have composed a new Aria for Sandrina in Atto II°, Sc. 3 (now sung by Polzelli), scored for oboes, horns and strings: *incipit* Bartha-Somfai 236 (add *ff* to beginning of bar 3). The original text at this point was 'Se volessi far l'amore'. The new parts were copied by Johann Schellinger.
For the reprise of *Orlando Paladino*, some unbound textbooks for the 1782 première were now given to the bindery (EH, Budapest, Fasc. 799, Secr. Prot. I.68. Bartha-Somfai 122). Harich in *HJB* I, 57–9.

MARIONETTE THEATRE 1784
No performances registered for this year.

THE GERMAN THEATRICAL TROUPE 1784
[Gotha *Theater-Kalender auf das Jahr 1785*:]
The Diwald Company
Residence: Esterhazy [*sic*] in Hungary, Principal and Director: Herr Diwald. Actresses: Mad. Diwald, leading lady in comedies and tragedies, young and naive roles. Mad. Kopp: soubrette, some heroines, sings and is the first ballerina. Mad. Klimetsch, formerly Wanner: old, comic women and Jewesses. Mad. Schwarzwald: tender mothers in tragedies, comic women in comedies. Mlle. Schwarzwald: second heroines in comedies and tragedies. Mad. Pfeil: secondary roles. Actors: H. Diwald, petulant old ladies in tragedies, comic and nagging old ladies in comedies, leading servants, peasants and low comedy roles. H. Dahmen, first and second lovers in comedies and tragedies. H. Kopp, serious heroes, gentle old women in tragedies, eccentric old women and serious lovers in comedies, first ballerino. H. König: gentle fathers and soldiers. H. Prandt: first lovers, young heroes in tragedies, also 2nd lovers in comedies; dances. H. Prillmayer: lovers in comedies and tragedies. H. Schwarzwald: pedants, old women and serious servants. H. Schletter (poet of the company): also occasionally plays small roles and is the prompter. H. Weiss: 2nd lovers in comedies and tragedies, Jews. H. Pfeil: secondary roles. Children's roles played by: Nicolaus Diwaldt, Eleonora Pielin [*sic*; Pfeil?], Stephan Kliemetsch. [Premières in 1784:] Schiller's *Fiesco* and *Kabale und Liebe*. [?] *Maria Stuart* [Schiller's play not yet written; Kormat after Vondel?]. [H. Schletter's arrangement of] *Das stumme Mädchen* and Schletter's *Irrtum in allen Ecken*; *Der argwöhnische Liebhaber*; *Liebrecht und Hörwald*; *Hannibal, Gerechtigkeit und Rache*; *Die Neugierigen*; *Das vermeinte Kammermädchen*. [?] *Verbrechen aus Ehrsucht*; [?] *Kommst du mir so, so komm ich dir so*; [?] *Die Weltweise*; [?] *Karl von Freystein*; [?] *Der Besuch nach dem Tode*; [?] *Die reiche Freyerin*.
Horányi (Ger. 133, Eng. 131), examining a document for 'Supers' of November 1785 (A.M. 3968), shows that the Diwald Company also performed Shakespeare's *Macbeth* and *Hamlet*, probably however premières of their forthcoming last season, 1785 (q.v.).

Before we begin the Chronicle proper, we would draw attention to a long list of Eszterháza operas, Haydn's and as many of those by other composers as he could remember, which he appears to have made (for an unknown purpose) in 1784. One work, *I contratempi*, was not performed until 1785, but Siess delivered the libretti in

September 1784 and the work was apparently ready for the stage by 1784; on the other hand, the last two premières of 1784, *La villanella rapita* and *L'isola di Calipso* do not appear in the list; thus, we may date the list in the first half of 1784:

Spezificatione di tutte Le Opere

1	Il Tuttore, e la Pupilla	Ditters +
2	Il Marescalco	Ditters +
3	L'Ucellatrice	Jomelli +
4	Zemir et Azore	Gretry /1782/
5	Arcifanfano	Ditters /1777/
6	Orfeo	Gluck /1776/
7	Finto pazzo	Ditters /1776/
8	Ratto della Sposa	Guglielmi /1783/
9	Visionarj	Guglielmi /1779/
10	Baron di Rocca antica	Ditters /1776/
11	Sposo Burlato	Ditters /1776/
12	La buona Figliuola	Piccini NB 1776/
13	L'amor Soldato	Piccini /1779/
14	Finta giardiniera	Anfossi /1780/
15	Le Nozze disturbate	Anfossi /1779/
16	Abramo un Oratorio	Miszlibeszeck +
17	La forza delle donne	Anfossi /1780/
18	Le vendemie	Gazzaniga /1780/
19	Scola dei gelosi	Salieri /1780/
20	La locanda	Piccini NB /1778/
21	La Metilde ritrovata	Piccini /1779/
22	Il Cavalier Errante	Anfossi /1779/
23	L'amor Artigiano	Gassmann /1779/
24	Enea in Cuma	Piccini +
25	Isabella e Rodrigo	Piccini /1781/
26	Incognita persequitata	Piccini /1779/
27	Innocente fortunata	Paisiello /1782/
28	Il Finto Parigino	Piccini /1779/
29	La Contadina in corte	Piccini /1781/
30	Rè alla Caccia	Michel /1779?/
31	J Stravaganti	Piccini /1779?/
32	J Pescatrici	Gugliemi +
33	Pupilla, e Ciarlone	Astarita +
34	Italiana in Londra	Cimarosa /1783/
35	Idolo Cinese	Rust +
36	Il Francese Bizzaro	Astarita /1781/
37	L'astrato	Piccini NB /1778/
38	L'assidio di Gibilterra	Gugliemi /1783/
39	Il Convitato di Pietra	Righini /1781/
40	Isola d'Amore	Sachini /1776/
41	La Figlia Ubbidiente	Bosi +
42	Lo sposo disperato	Anfossi /1782/
43	Le gelosie villane	Sarti NB /1779/
44	L'amore in Musica	Piccini +
45	La discordia fortunata	Astarita /1781/
46	La Secchia Rapita	Salieri +
47	Ipocondriaco	Nauman +
48	Il Tamburo Notturno	Paisiello + /1788/

49	L'Americano	Piccini +
50	La Fiera di Venezia	Salieri /1782/
51	L'amor Senza Malizia	Ottani +
52	La Donna Colerica	Paisiello +
53	il Curioso Indiscreto	Anfossi /1782/
54	il Falegname	Piccini /1783/
55	Julio Sabino	Sarti /1783/
56	la Vedova Scaltra	Righini /1783/
57	Fra due Litiganti	Sarti /1783/
58	J Filosofi	Paisiello /1782/
59	L'Amor Costante	Cimarosa /1784/
60	Viaggiatori felici	Anfossi /1784/
61	J Contratempi	Sarti /1785/
62	Didone Abbandonata	Sarti /1784/
63	Jl Mondo della Luna	Haydn /1777/
64	Acide	/1763/
65	La Canterina	/1767/
66	Lo Speziale	/1768/
67	L'Jncontro Improviso	/1775/
68	Le Pescatrice	/1770/
69	L'Jnfedelta delusa	/1773/
70	L'Jsola disabitata	/1779/
71	la Fedeltà premiata	/1780/
72	Orlando Paladino	/1782/
73	Armida	/1784/

nebst 5 Marionetten Opern

Besides 5 marionette operas, i.e. Haydn's *viz*: (1) *Philemon und Baucis* with the Prologue, *Der Götterrath*, September 1773; (2) *Hexen-Schabbas* (Autumn 1773?); (3) *Die Feuersbrunst* (*Das abgebrannte Haus*) (1776–7?); (4) *Dido*, March 1776; (5) *Die bestrafte Rachbegierde*, 1779. In itself, this important list of five marionette operas, supplemented by *EK*, which lists *Philemon und Baucis*, *Dido* and the *Opera comique vom abgebrannten Haus*, and the authentic libretto listing Haydn as composer (*Die bestrafte Rachbegierde*), account for four of these puppet works. *Hexen-Schabbas* (is listed by Dies as Haydn (p. 75), and so is *Genovefens Vierter Theil* (p. 75), also in *HV* (p. 64, No. 1) and Griesinger (16). Until we locate a copy of the lost printed EH libretto of *Hexen-Schabbas*, a decision as to its authenticity will be impossible: it is unlikely that the music of either *Hexen-Schabbas* or *Genovefens 1. 2. 3.* or *4. Theil* will ever be discovered. Haydn, in his libretto catalogue, listed the *Vierter Theil* as 'by various masters'.

Notes: We follow the publication by Harich in *HJB* IX, 89f., with his explanations. The dates added, e.g. '/1784/' refer to the first performances at Eszterháza. The little cross means that score and parts were then available but the works never performed; the 'NB' signs cannot now be explained. The works with cross are:

1. Dittersdorf's *Il tutore e la pupilla*.	44. Piccinni's *L'amore in musica* [recte (?): Marcello di
2. Dittersdorf's *Il maniscalco* [recte].	Capua's *L'amore et musica*].
3. Jomelli's *L'uccellatrice*.	46. Salieri's *La secchia rapita*.
16. Mysliveček's Oratorio, *Abramo*.	47. Naumann's *Ipocondriaco*.
24. Piccinni's *Enea in Cuma*.	48. Paisiello's *Il tamburo notturno* (later, 1788, the work was
32. Guglielmi's [recte: Piccinni's ?] *La pescatrice*.	actually performed).
33. Astaritta's (Colla's?) *Pupilla, e Ciarlone*.	49. Piccinni's *L'Americano*.
35. Rust's *Idolo Cinese*.	51. Ottani's *L'amor senza malizia*.
41. Bosi's *La figlia ubbidiente*.	52. Paisiello's *La donna colerica*.

Haydn seems to have prepared this list from memory, as a result of which he wrote the wrong composers for twelve operas:

9. *I visionarj*. Guglielmi instead of Astaritta.	21. *La Metilda ritrovata*. Piccinni instead of Anfossi.
13. *L'amor soldato*. Haydn writes 'Piccini'. The libretto (EH) read, incorrectly, Sacchini; in reality the composer was Felici.	22. *Il cavalier errante*. Anfossi instead of Traetta.
	25. *Isabella e Rodrigo*. Piccinni instead of Anfossi.
15. *Le nozze disturbate*. Anfossi instead of Naumann.	26. *L'incognita persequitata*. Haydn writes 'Piccini'. Both
20. *La locanda*. Piccinni instead of Gazzaniga.	Anfossi and Piccinni set the text of this work, identical with No. 21. In fact, Anfossi is the correct composer.

29. *La contadina in corte.* Probably Sacchini instead of Piccin(n)i.

32. *I pescatrici.* Haydn writes Guglielmi but it is believed he meant Piccinni's *La pescatrice*, which is still in EH (Ms. Mus. OE–26, Budapest).

44. *L'amore in musica.* Haydn writes 'Piccini' but in EH the work is listed as Marcello di Capua's *Amore et musica* or *Amore e Musica* (Budapest, Ms. Mus. OE–70).

45. *La discordia fortunata.* Astaritta instead of Paisiello.

54. *Il falegname.* Piccinni instead of Cimarosa.

Seven operas in this list have totally disappeared from EH (Nos. 1, 4, 9, 20, 32, 33, 34) and three operas are in EH catalogues of 1806 and 1858 which do not figure on Haydn's lists: Paisiello's *Le due contesse,* Haydn's *La vera costanza* and Guglielmi's *L'impresa dell'opera.* Apart from the earlier marionette operas by Haydn and other composers, Paisiello's *La Frascatana,* his *La contadina di spirito,* Guglielmi's *La sposa fedele,* Anfossi's *Il geloso in cimento* and Gazzaniga's *L'isola d'Alcina* are missing in Haydn's list; were all known to have been performed before the fire of November 1779; and therefore must be presumed to have been destroyed in that fire and are therefore missing in Haydn's list. Haydn's *La vera costanza* (Eszterháza, 1779) is also conspicuous by its absence; it, too, no longer existed when the list was prepared.

Before turning to other matters, the receipts for the year may be mentioned briefly.[1]

On 31 January, the *Wiener Zeitung* announced Artaria's publication of Haydn's *Raccolta de Menuetti Ballabili* (IX:7); after giving details of the scoring, the announcements adds: '. . . made for the Art Shop Artaria & Comp., in which they may be had on Tuesday, 3 February, for 1 fl. 30 [xr.]. For 12 years no dance minuets by Herr Haydn have been issued [*herausgegeben*], and these will be surely welcome.' We cannot imagine to which 'issue' (publication?) Artaria refers: one of 1772, but apart from Hummel's early publication of Fourteen Minuets (1766) (IX:4), we know of no such publication.[2] Artaria issued them in good time for Carnival.

Haydn was in close touch with Artaria:

[To Artaria & Co., Vienna. *German*]

Estoras, 3rd February 1784

Nobly born,
Most highly respected Sir!

I shall send you the missing *Lieder* next Friday or Saturday; I would only ask you to let me know the key of the final printed *Lied,* and how its text begins, so that I can decide the keys of the ones to follow. Meanwhile I remain, Sir, most respectfully,

Your wholly obedient servant,
Joseph Haydn.

N.O. Please present my compliments to the Bavarian house[3] and Herr von Hoffmann.

1 (a) Haydn's 'Specification' for 6 books of quarto music paper with 10 staves, 6 books oblong with 10 staves, 4 books oblong with 12 staves at 40 xr. per book, 10 Fl. 40 xr., passed for payment by Prince Nicolaus, Vienna, 23 Jan. 1784; A.M. XVII.1175; Valkó II, 600. (b) 'Specification' for strings signed by Haydn for 4 bundles E 12 Fl., 1 bundle A 2 Fl., 6 C-strings 30 xr., 3 boxes of resin 21 xr., signed by Haydn; passed for payment by Prince Nicolaus, Eszterház, 1 May; EH, Budapest, Secr. Prot. II. No. 83. Fasc. 799; Valkó II, 599. (c) Haydn's 'Specification' for more music paper: 10 books quarto with 10 staves, 10 books oblong with 10 staves, 4 books oblong with 10 staves, the book at 40 xr., total 16 Fl., passed for payment by Prince Nicolaus on 8 May; A.M. XVII.1177; Valkó II, 600. (d) Haydn received money instead of a summer uniform, Fl. 178, 18 xr. Esterházy's order to Michael Kleinrath to find out the sum, Esterház, 10 May; Kleinrath's answer, Vienna, 28 May; Haydn's receipt for the money, Estoras, 28 June. A.M. Fasc. XVII.1190, 1191; Valkó II, 600. (e) Franz Czervenka's bill for 36 bassoon reeds and 2 E-flat keys from Pressburg, Eszterháza 1 Feb. to end of Nov. 1784; Haydn's note that he has given them to Pezival [*sic*] Eszterház, 26 Nov., and passed for payment by Prince Nicolaus; EH, Budapest, Fasc. 799. Secr. Prot. IV.188; Valkó II, 599. (f) Haydn's 'Specification what is required for two new operas for music paper, viz. / 10 books quarto with 10 staves and / 8 books oblong with 10 staves / the book per 40 xr. makes 12 Fl.', passed for payment by Prince Nicolaus, Esterház, 5 Dec. 1784; A.M. XVII.1184; Valkó II, 601f. Other documents are listed in the course of the Chronicle.

2 Hoboken I, p. 554.

3 It is not clear what is meant by the 'Bavarian house'.

N.B. I have mislaid among my papers the print of the *Lieder* you sent me long ago, and cannot find it any more.

[Address:]   Monsieur
        Monsieur
        Artaria et Compag
          à
          Vienne

Herr Rosenbaum[1] is asked to expedite this.
[Artaria's clerk notes: 'Haydn – 1784/ Esterhatz 3 febr[i] / rec'd – 6th/ ans'd 6th.']

[CCLN, 43f.]

Most of the letters to Haydn have disappeared; this one, being from a 'high personage', survived long enough to enter the authentic biographies (Dies):

[To Haydn from Heinrich, Prince of Prussia.[2] *German*]
    I thank you for the Quartets[3] which were sent to me, and which give me much pleasure. Please accept the enclosed trifle[4] as a token of my particular satisfaction. I remain, with sincere esteem,

Your ever well-disposed[5]
Heinrich.

Berlin, 4th February 1784.   [CCLN, 44]

Haydn, full of his *Armida*, writes to Artaria as follows:

[To Artaria & Co., Vienna. *German*]

Estoras, 1st March 1784.
Dearest and best Friend!
    The day after tomorrow, this coming Wednesday, you shall certainly receive the *Lieder*. Yesterday my *Armida*[6] was performed for the 2nd time with general applause. I am told that this is my best work up to now. I ask *Fräulein* Nanet Peyer,[7] whom I embrace a thousand times, to forgive my mistake; she may rest assured that not I, but the press of work, is responsible for it. Meanwhile I remain, most respectfully,

Your wholly obedient servant,
Haydn.

In haste
[Address:]   Monsieur
        Monsieur d'Artaria
          a
          Vienne

Herr Rosenbaum is asked to expedite this at once.

[CCLN, 44]

As it happens, we have a complete table of performances at the opera house in March 1784, given in the list of various theatrical 'supers' from EH, Budapest (Horányi in *Zenetudomány Tanulmányok* VI, 1957, p. 735, corrected by Harich in *HJB* I, 14n.), which the reader will find enlightening (see overleaf).

---

1 Prince Esterházy's porter, and the father of Joseph Carl (see *Haydn: the Years of 'The Creation' 1796–1800, passim*).
2 Heinrich, Prince of Prussia, brother of the King, Friedrich II.
3 Op. 33, to which the Prince probably subscribed directly from Haydn.
4 A gold medal and the Prince's portrait (Dies, p. 70).
5 'Ihr wohlaffectionirter'.
6 Haydn's new opera.
7 Nanette Peyer (see also letter of 5th May 1786) was *Kammermädchen* to Count Apponyi at Pressburg.

[Performances at the Eszterháza opera house, March 1784:]

Comparsen für den Monath Marty 1784.
Opern und Comedien und Bandisten Proben

Martius	[Work]	Bandisten à 10 xr	Mädl à 10 xr	Buben à 3 xr	Stabenen à 5 xr	Gehilfen à 5 xr	fl.	xr.
1	Comedie						5	10
2	Production Armida	6	4		34	8		5
3	Comedie	—				1		30
4	Production Litiganti				6	2		10
5	Comedie							
6	Deto							
7	Production Armida	6	4		34	8	5	10
8	Comedie				24		2	—
9	Production Falegname							
10	Comedie							
11	Production Filosofi	—	—	1	12	2	1	3
12	Comedie	—			12		1	10
13	Prob. Orlando	—						—
14	Production Orlando	—	6	3	15	8	3	4
15	Prob. Viaggiatori felici				12		1	—
16	Production Armida	6	4	—	34	8	5	10
17	Prob. Viaggiatori felici				12		1	—
18	Production Julius Sabin [Giulio Sabino]		—	4	33	6	3	27
19	Prob. Viaggiatori felici				12		1	—
20	Prob. General Deto			—	12		1	—
21	Production Viaggiatori felici	—	—	—	12	—	1	—
30	Production deto	—	—	—	12	—	1	—
	Comedie	—	—	—	12	—	1	—
[Totals:]		18	18	8	276	43	32	59

On 10 March, the *Preßburger Zeitung* reprinted the report on Eszterháza Castle which originally appeared in *Briefe aus Wien von Johann Friedel an einem Freund in Berlin* (1784, *vide supra*, pp. 102f.). On the 17th, the same paper tells us of a concert given by Count Grassalkovics, in which it would seem that Haydn's newest Symphonies Nos. 76–78 were played – they were circulating briskly in authorized and unauthorized MSS.[1]

> . . . All the works performed were exquisite. The symphonies of the immortal Hayden [*sic*] stand out so wondrously, that only a sensitive ear can judge them, and the pen can only feebly describe them. Elevated in expression, inexhaustible in invention, new in every musical thought, unexpected and astounding at every turn, their mild harmoniousness melted the senses of connoisseurs and laymen alike. . . .   [HJB VIII, 274]

On 19 March, Haydn's *Il ritorno di Tobia* was given at the Court in Lisbon in honour of the name-day of the Infante Don Giuseppe, Prince of Brazil.[2] But Haydn was occupied with his work at much closer hand. He had now thoroughly revised it, made extensive cuts, and added two magnificent choruses. The list of performances at Eszterháza contains a gap, from 22 to 29 March, and it was during this period that Haydn went to Vienna to rehearse and prepare the new production of his Oratorio. (Concerning the new additions, *vide supra*, pp. 259ff.) Haydn had a great cast for his Viennese revival; most of the singers are known to us from Mozart, but Carl Friberth had sung in the première nine years before –

Anna Storace	Anna
Catharina Cavalieri	Raffaelle
Theresia Teyber	Sara
Valentin Adamberger/	
Carl Friberth	Tobia [on the 30th Friberth][3]
Steffano Mandini	Tobit

On the first evening, 28 March, Nancy Storace's husband, John Abraham Fisher, a violin virtuoso from Ireland, played his own concerto, and on the second evening, 30 March, Georg Anton Kreusser's Flute Concerto was played by Herr Johann Philipp Freyhold from the Electoral Chapel Orchestra in Mainz.

When he returned to Eszterháza, Haydn had occasion to write two letters to Artaria:

---

1 Two months later, on 15 May, Mozart writes to his father: 'I know for certain that Hofstetter copies Haydn's music twice – I *really* have his newest 3 Symphonies . . .'. Mozart, *Briefe und Aufzeichnungen*, vol. III, Kassel 1963, p. 313.

2 Libretto printed; copy in Biblioteca del Conservatorio di S. Cecilia, Rome, Carvalhaes 13296.

3 Adamberger was ill. The following sheet was distributed to the audience (copy: Gesellschaft der Musikfreunde, Vienna): 'Notice. Herr Adamberger had suddenly to renounce the vocal part of Tobia in Haydn's Oratorio, as a result of which the Musical Society was placed in an embarrassing position; Herr Kapellmeister Karl Friberth, member of said Society, took over the part at our urgent request.' It is not certain whether Friberth performed on both occasions; the programme sheet for the 28th still has Adamberger's name, whereas on the 30th Friberth's name was inserted. Of these singers, Theresia Teyber was Mozart's Blondchen in *Die Entführung*, Cavalieri was of course Constanze, Adamberger was Belmonte, and Mandini was Count Almaviva in *Figaro*. About Teyber, Schmid ('Haydn's Oratorium "Il ritorno di Tobia"', op. cit., p. 302) points out that in the printed announcements she is listed as 'Mlle. Teiber' or 'Signora Teiber', and that possibly Barbara Teyber, who had participated in the 1775 performance as Rafaelle (and Azaria), may have been meant; though Schmid believes that the famous Theresia is the lady in question. Possibly Haydn rewrote the alto part of Anna for Nancy Storace's soprano voice. There is a score, discovered by the late Dr Schmid in the archives at Zittau before World War II, with Anna as a soprano, with many additional coloratura passages. Alas, this score no longer exists. When we discovered the orchestral and vocal material of *Il ritorno di Tobia* in the former Tonkünstler-Societät Archives (now Rathaus, Vienna), the material was mostly for the 1808 revival and we could no longer determine what Nancy Storace actually sang in 1784. Schmid, p. 299, n. 1.

[To Artaria & Co., Vienna. *German*]

Estoras, 5th April 1784.

Nobly born,
Most highly respected Sir!
    Although I have always received more than 100 ducats for my quartets[1] by subscription, and although Herr Willmann[2] also promised to give me this sum, I agree to your offer of 300 fl. with the following stipulations; first that you are patient until July, though all six should be finished by then; secondly, I demand either 12 copies or my choice of the dedication. If this proposal is agreeable to you, I shall await your draft of a contract: those quartets which I am at present working on, and of which half are finished, are very short and consist of three pieces only; they are intended for Spain.[3] On the next post-day I shall send you an article, i.e., an analysis of my Cantata[4] which you engraved, and which has been a great success. Professor Kramer[5] from Kiel sent it to me together with a letter.
    Farewell, meanwhile: I am pressed for time.

Your most obedient servant,
Joseph Haydn.

[Envelope:]   Monsieur
      Monsieur d'Artaria et Comp
      à
         Vienne.   [CCLN, 45]

[To Artaria & Co., Vienna. *German*]

Estoras, 8th April 1784

Nobly born
Most highly respected Sir!
    In my last letter I forgot to ask you to have someone deliver a copy of the new *Lieder* in my name to Fräulein von Liebe.[6] She now lives in the Leopoldstadt.[7] The Prince's porter will be able to tell you where. More on next Wednesday.

Josephus Haydn [m.] pria.

Please could you get for me the German book on composition, in 4to format, by *Capellmeister* Fux, entitled *Gradus ad Parnassum*. I would be much obliged to you. N.B.: Herr von Liebe lives at No. 10.

[Address:]   Monsieur
      Monsieur d'Artaria
      à
        Vienne

[Artaria's clerk notes: 'Haydn 1784/Esterhaz 8. Apr./ rec'd the 10th ditto/ ans'd the 29th ditto'.]   [CCLN, 45f.]

    On 1 May, the famous Italian composer, Giovanni Paisiello, arrived in Vienna. Mozart records the fact in a letter to Salzburg, but we have a recently discovered letter from Paisiello to a member of the Imperial Court in St Petersburg:

---

1 Op. 50 ('Prussian'), which did not, however appear till December 1787 (see *infra*).
2 Probably Maximilian Willmann, 'cellist in the service of Prince Grassalkovics and not, as in Hoboken (p. 408n.), Johann Ignaz, the violinist, who was later leader in the Theater an der Wien under Count Palffy's patronage.
3 It is doubtful if Haydn really completed his set: the single quartet, Op. 42 (autograph: 1785), may belong to it.
4 'Ah, come il core', from *La fedeltà premiata*.
5 *Recte*: C. F. Cramer, who wrote the forty-two page analysis himself. It was published the year before, in Cramer's *Magazin der Musik*. *Vide supra*, pp. 439ff.
6 Francisca Liebe von Kreutzner, to whom both sets of the *Lieder* were dedicated: see *supra*, p. 461.
7 A suburb of Vienna, now the 2nd District.

Eccellenza

Fin dal primo di questo corrente mese che sono arrivato in Vienna, onde von voglio mancare di farne stare inteso l'Eccellenza Vostra e insiemamente fargli sapere che siccome ho avuto l'onore di essere stato presentato a S. M. I. e R. L'Imperatore il quale mi ha ricevuto molto graziosamente, avendo mi fatto l'onore di fare una conversazione di un ora, e più ha voluto ancora ingaggiarmi a comporgli un opera per il di Lui Imperial teatro. Sicchè sono obligato di fermarmi qui almeno due mesi, Le parole del libro le farà l'abbate Casti .... Vienna li 8 Maggio 1784 Umiliss^mo dev^mo: ob^n: serv. / Giovanni Paisiello.

[Autograph in the author's collection]

Joseph II, who talked to Paisiello for one hour, obviously thought him a far more interesting composer than Haydn and/or Mozart. Paisiello's new commission was *Il rè Teodoro in Venezia*, and the first performance took place on 23 August; Mozart was at the first performance and during it was seized by renal failure – the first sign of the uraemia from which he was later to die. Paisiello and Abbate Casti were present, some time in 1784, at a quartet party attended by Michael Kelly, the entertaining Irish singer who formed part of a curious and interesting English colony at Vienna during this period;[1] Kelly writes:

[... Storace gave a 'quartett party' to his friends.] The players were tolerable; not one of them excelled on the instrument he played, but there was a little science among them, which I dare say will be acknowledged when I name them:

The First Violin	HAYDN.
„ Second Violin	BARON DITTERSDORF.
„ Violoncello	VANHALL.
„ Tenor	MOZART.

The poet Casti and Paesiello formed part of the audience. I was there, and a greater treat, or a more remarkable one, cannot be imagined.

On the particular evening to which I am now specially referring, after the musical feast was over, we sat down to an excellent supper, and became joyous and lively in the extreme. ...

In the midst of my devotion to tragedy and comedy, I did not forget what I owed to music; and what more favourable opportunity could offer for evincing my devotion to the science of harmony than that which presented itself, of visiting the immortal Haydn? He was living at Eisenstadt [Eszterháza?], the palace of Prince Esterhazy, in whose service he was, and thither I determined to go and pay my respects to him; accordingly, accompanied by a young friend of mine of the name of Brida, a young Tyrolese merchant, I set off ...

I had the pleasure of spending three days with him, and received from him great hospitality and kindness. The Prince Esterhazy lived in regal splendour. ... his band was formed of great professors; – Haydn was his maître de chapelle. There was at Eisenstadt, merely for the amusement of the Prince, his family, suite, and vassals, an Italian Opera, a German and a French theatre, and the finest Fantoccini in Europe.

At this delightful place Haydn composed the greatest part of his immortal works. I saw and admired the different artists employed by the Prince, who unanimously gave His Highness an enviable character for generosity and exalted goodness. His vassals absolutely adored him.

1 The libretto for the Paisiello is in Italian and German (copy: author's collection). Deutsch, *Dokumente*, 201. *Reminiscences of Michael Kelly* ... 2nd ed., 2 vols., London 1826, I, 237ff. MS. Diary of Lord Barnard (later the Duke of Cleveland), Raby Castle, for 1786. S. M. Ellis: *The Life of Michael Kelly* ... London 1930, pp. 119f.

The country about Eisenstadt is delightfully picturesque, abounding in woods and water, and all kinds of game. The Prince had the goodness to desire Haydn to take one of his carriages, that we might drive about and see all the beauties of this terrestrial paradise, for such I thought it. His Highness was very partial to shooting, hunting, and fishing.

We took our departure on the evening of the third day, delighted and flattered with the gracious kindness we had received, and with light hearts arrived at Vienna. [*Reminiscences*, pp. 218f.]

We cannot, of course, date any of these occurrences, but it seems certain that Haydn met Sarti, Paisiello and Mozart some time in 1784, Mozart very possibly at the Tonkünstler-Societät concert in 1783. Haydn's contact with the intriguing English colony in Vienna was perhaps fleeting, but he certainly knew the Ambassador and the singers/musicians (Nancy Storace and her brother Stephen, and of course Kelly). Nancy Storace welcomed him in England and 'waved to him' from the orchestra when he received his doctor's degree at Oxford (1791); Mozart's first Susanna was herself a great flirt in Vienna; she became Lord Barnard's mistress, and he led a carefree life, as the following entry in his Diary shows:

[July 12:] Je me suis lévé à onze heure, dinai à l'Augarten; Mr. Powlett, Mr. Morgan et Lord Strathaven ont pris du Thé avec moi; allai à l'Opera, soupai au Casino avec Mr. Powlett, Morgan et O'Kelly; allai à minuit chez Milord Crawford et Captain Wale et Prince Ventimiglia, ou J'ai resté jusqu'à six heure du matin.

The difference between Haydn, composing at top speed and organizing a large operatic establishment, and the life led by the elegant few, was indeed astonishing.

On 16 May, Maria Bologna died at Eszterháza. In the *Generalcassa-Handbuch* (EH, Eisenstadt) there is the following entry about the Bologna sisters:

Bologna Sisters. The youngest died on 16 May, but they get their whole salary because another sister is to come here. [Later:] From 1 Sept. the salary of the [dead Maria] Bologna stopped. [Harich in *HJB* I, 43]

The Third Bologna sister could not come. On the day that the popular 'Mariuccia' died, there was opera as usual at Eszterháza Castle . . .

There follows a letter to Artaria:

[To Artaria & Co., Vienna. *German*]

Estoras, 18th May 1784.

Mon tres chere Amy!

As to the Quartets,[1] the agreement remains; as to the extract[2] from my *Armida*, I cannot yet say for certain, because I would like to show it to the world in its entirety. I am grateful to you for Cramer's *Magazin*[3] and am your debtor for it. I would ask you only to send to me at my expense 2 copies of the last *Lieder*, and also of the first.

Meanwhile I remain, as always,

Your wholly obedient servant,
Haydn.

---

1 Op. 50.
2 'Auszug': Haydn may mean here 'Piano-vocal score', in which case 'in Ihrer ganzen gestalt' would mean 'in full score' rather than 'in its entirety.'
3 See also letter of April. Artaria must have sent a new number.

[Address:]   Monsieur
                    Monsieur d'Artaria
                         a   [Artaria's clerk writes: 'Haydn – 1784/
                      Vienne.   Esterhaz 18th May/ rec'd 20th'.]

                                                          [CCLN, 46]

In 1784, the Prince seems to have agreed to a new(?) system, whereby the musicians could take a cash substitute instead of their uniforms. At any rate, 1784 is the first year in which such documents for this substitute survive:

[To Joseph Lex, Esterházy Administration Bookkeeper, Eisenstadt. *German*]
                                              Estoras, 20th May 1784.
Well and nobly born,
Most highly respected Herr Bookkeeper!
    I ask of your noble self what would be the price of my winter uniform[1] with all its appurtenances including hat and tailor's bill, how much it costs His Highn. and would you write me on the first post day, for which courtesy I shall remain indebted to your noble self, and I remain with every respect
                              Your
                                        most obedient servant
                                        Haydn mpria
                                        Capell Meister
[Address:] Dem Hoch, und Wohl gebohrnen Herrn
Lex Fürst-Estorhazischen BuchHaltern
zu zustellen.
               à
            Eisenstadt.
[In an unknown hand: '137 f. 27xr NB 140f.']
[Acta Varia, Fasz. 12, Bündel Nr. 5, Jahr 784, EH, Forchtenstein. *Haydn-Studien* III/2 (1974), pp. 101f., 105. Not in CCLN.]

On 8 June, Travaglia submitted a proposal for the scenery of two operas, *L'incontro improvviso* and *I contratempi* (EH, Budapest, Fasc. 799, Secr. Prot. II.97), the latter of which was for Sarti's work which was performed in 1785. As for the first, either the Prince planned a revival of Haydn's 1775 Opera, which was entirely within the realms of possibility since at that time the whole autograph was still in the Archives (it was later – in the nineteenth century – given to a visiting Russian dignitary); or, as Bartha-Somfai suggest (122), Travaglia actually meant Righini's *L'incontro inaspettato*, which was performed in 1786.
    A few days later, as we have seen, Giuseppe Sarti arrived at the Castle.
    Repairs to the musicians' quarters, where there were various changes – 'Burgsteiner received a kitchen, in which were a small larder [*Handspeis*[2]] and other kitchen utensils belong to the Frau Capellmeister, which were removed and put in the corridor' – are related in a document dated 6 August.
    On 31 August, the Frankfurt *Staats-Ristretto* announced Boßler's authentic edition of three new Piano Sonatas by Haydn: Nos. 54–56 (XVI:40–42) dedicated to Princess Marie Hermenegild Esterházy, *née* Princess Liechtenstein. She had married Prince Nicolaus (grandson of Nicolaus I and himself later Nicolaus II) on 15 September 1783,

---

1 Haydn and the musicians also received cash substitutes for their summer uniforms (Haydn's was valued at 170 fl.). *HJB* IV, 91.
2 Or 'Handspieß', which would mean a hand-roaster for meat or bread. EH, Budapest, Fasc. 799. Secr. Prot. III.129. Valkó I, 656.

and perhaps these attractive and graceful Sonatas were Haydn's wedding present to her.[1] A contemporary review appears in Cramer's *Magazin der Musik* (1785, p. 535):

> *Trois Sonates pour le Pianoforte composées par J. Haydn, Oeuvre 37, a Spire chès Bosler [sic], Conseiller.* These Sonatas are written in a style different from the previous ones of this famous master; but they are not less valuable. The first in G major is in fact only a short, very melodious movement of which each part consists of eight bars. Then is a mineur (G minor). Both are then varied in an excellent fashion. The final Presto in G major is also similarly worked out. In the variations the finest taste predominates. The 2nd Sonata in B flat is a masterpiece of its kind, and also the final *Allegro molto*. The 3rd in D major also has its mineur and is varied perhaps even more excellently than the first. The composer shows himself in these variations, which are so well written for the instrument, much like a clever and tasteful soprano when she repeats her aria. Incidentally, the Sonatas are more difficult in performance than one might at first believe. They require the greatest precision and much delicacy of style.
>
> L.

On 12 September there was a special *Fest* at Eszterháza Castle: it was to honour two things, first the forthcoming eve of Princess Marie Hermenegild's and Count (Prince) Nicolaus's wedding anniversary (15 September), and also because, in the reigning Prince Nicolaus's eyes, Eszterháza Castle was now completed. This was the year for both the German and French descriptions of the Castle and there are various other hints that he now considered his architectural masterpiece to be perfectly accomplished. On that evening, 4,268 tallow lamps were used, and 2,600 refilled, consuming some seven hundred-weight of black tallow.[2]

The following letter concerns Haydn's little vegetable garden at Eszterháza:

[To Prince Nicolaus Esterházy. *German*]

Submissive
pro Memoria

Serene Highness and Noble Prince of the Holy Roman Empire, Gracious and Dread Lord!

Since Your Serene Princely Highness also allowed the bassoon player Drobney,[3] formerly in your service, to have a garden next to the former wooden huts, which I bought, with the express permission of Your Serene Prince Highness, for 25 f. after he had been dismissed from service; and since then, to improve it, I invested 50 f. in it: now, however, Your Serene Prince Highness has decided to take over this garden, but because of the double expenses, to plant the new substitute garden which was graciously intended for me is too inconvenient. Therefore my submissive and respectful request to Your Serene Princely Highness is graciously to allow me at your high discretion some money for the fruit trees and other things growing there, also for the small amount of gardening tools [*gärtner vorrath*].[4] For which high grace I remain, in deepest submission,

Your Serene Princely Highness'
humble and obedient
Haydn. Capell Meister.

1 Copy in the Gesellschaft der Musikfreunde, Vienna. In 1783, Joseph II allowed all the children of princely families to use the title 'Prince' or 'Princess' (previously they were Counts or Countesses).
2 EH, Budapest, Fasc. 799, Proth. 3.156. Horányi 152.
3 Ignaz Drobney, dismissed on 15 April 1778. The Prince obviously needed the space where the garden was for something else and offered Haydn a substitute garden, which the composer thought would be too much trouble. See also the duplicate protocol in Budapest, fasc. 799, Secr. Prot. IV.168. Valkó I, 656.
4 'Gärtner-Vorrath' might also mean seeds, seedlings, etc.

[Clerk's hand:] We herewith order that our Administrator at Süttör shall pay to our Capelmeister [*sic*] Joseph Haydn ten ordinary ducats for his garden (now taken over by us), the fruit trees, other things growing there and gardening tools, and this sum should be taken from our Süttör Building Cassa and should be entered in the books.

Esterház, 5th October 1784.

Nicolaus Fürst Esterhazy.
protocollirt.

[Haydn's hand:] Which above-listed ten ordinary ducats have been paid in cash with 43 f. (forty-three Gulden), and are herewith receipted, from the princely Building Cassa in the person of the Süttör Administrator, H. Johann Vadász.

Süttör Office, 8 October 1784.   Josephus Haydn mpria
                                                        Capell Meister.

[Eszterházer Bau Cassa Rechnungen, 1784, Extra ausgaben No. 60: EH, Forchtenstein Castle. G. Feder in *Haydn-Studien* IV/1 (1976), pp. 49f.]

We now arrive at the first mention of three new Haydn Symphonies, Nos. 79–81:

[To Nadermann, music publisher in Paris.[1] *German*]
Nobly born,
Most highly respected Sir!

   Since you, good Sir, accepted three of my Symphonies last year, once again I offer you three brand new Symphonies,[2] very diligently composed and neatly and correctly copied, for the price of 15 ducats; I would deliver them by the end of November. If, good Sir, you accept this offer, I shall devote my energies to delivering to you at the first opportunity the pianoforte piece which you asked for in your last letter. In the hope of receiving the favour of an early reply I am, with the most sincere esteem, Sir,

                                     Your wholly obedient servant
                                         Josephus Haydn.
Estoras, 25th October 1784.

[CCLN, 47]

Haydn's fame was now so widespread that there was a long report on him in the *European Magazine*, which we reproduce in facsimile overleaf.

---

1 This letter was published for the first time in 1838 (*Neue Zeitschrift für Musik*). The man who discovered it, C. A. Mangold, reports that he found it in a bundle of old music, and that it is addressed to Nadermann, who – as Mangold does not mention – became Boyer's successor a few years later. Mangold does not, however, give the actual address and it is possible that none was included on the letter. Either Nadermann was a partner in Boyer's business earlier than we knew, or else the letter is really addressed to Boyer. Perhaps the bundle of music had belonged formerly to the Nadermann music business, and Mangold was not aware that Nadermann was Boyer's successor (and thus that the letter may have been addressed to Boyer). The connection between this letter and that to Boyer of 15 July 1783 is, however, obvious. In conclusion it should be said that (1) Boyer really bought Symphonies Nos. 76–78 and issued them; (2) that he did not buy Nos. 79–81; (3) Nadermann issued neither.
2 Symphonies Nos. 79–81, which Haydn also sold to Torricella of Vienna (see letter of 20 November, *infra*) and (except No. 79) to Forster.

EUROPEAN MAGAZINE,

AND

LONDON REVIEW;

FOR OCTOBER, 1784.

For the EUROPEAN MAGAZINE.

An ACCOUNT of JOSEPH HAYDN, a CELEBRATED COMPOSER of MUSIC.

[With an excellent Engraved LIKENESS of him.]

GIUSEPPE HAYDN was born at Vienna about the year 1730. At a very early age he discovered a most uncommon taste and propensity to music, which to facilitate, his parents placed him in the Jesuits College, where he was educated, and in which place he had full time and opportunity to improve and indulge himself in his favourite science.

The progress he made while he was in college was so rapid, that before he was acquainted with the rudiments of harmony he composed a great number of symphonies, trios, sonatas, &c. in which the early dawnings of a soaring genius appeared; and although they wanted that regularity and consistency that a grammatical education never fails to bestow, yet in every thing he composed there appeared a wildness of nature and luxuriance of fancy that at once bespoke what he would in after-times produce, when that wildness was somewhat tamed, and that luxuriance pruned by the steady hand of science, and the sober guidance of art.

The fertility of Haydn's genius made such an impression on all his friends, that they earnestly requested him to lay aside his pen for some time, and apply himself solely to the study of counterpoint, without which no author, be his genius ever so exalted, can be correct. He took their advice, and, by close and unremitted application, in a very short time became a perfect master of harmony in a regular and grammatical form.

With these advantages, it is no wonder if we now behold Haydn outstrip all his competitors. And as envy never fails to pursue merit, the masters in Germany were so jealous of his rising fame, that they entered into a combination against him in order to decry his works and ridicule his compositions; nay, they even carried it so far as to write against him; and many pamphlets in the German language appeared in print to depreciate him in the public esteem, alledging his works were too flighty, trifling, and wild, accusing him

at the same time as the inventor of a new musical doctrine, and introducing a species of sounds totally unknown in that country. In the last position they were perfectly right: he had indeed introduced a new species of music: it was his own, totally unlike what they had been used to—*original, masterly*, and *beautiful*.

Amongst the number of professors who wrote against our rising author was Philip-Emanuel Bach of Hamburgh (formerly of Berlin); and the only notice Haydn took of their scurrility and abuse was, to publish lessons written in imitation of the several stiles of his enemies, in which their peculiarities were so closely copied, and their extraneous passages (particularly those of Bach of Hamburgh) so inimitably burlesqued, that they all felt the poignancy of his musical wit, confessed its truth, and were silent.

This anecdote will account for a number of strange passages that are here and there dispersed throughout several of the sonatas that have been reprinted in England from the German copies, of which we shall point out the few following passages by way of illustration. Among others, Six Sonatas for the Piano-Forte or Harpsichord, Opera 13 and 14, are expressly composed in order to ridicule Bach of Hamburgh. No one can peruse the second part of the second sonata in the thirteenth opera, and the whole of the third sonata in the same work, and believe Haydn in earnest, writing from his own natural genius, and committing his chaste and original thoughts upon paper. On the contrary, the stile of Bach is closely copied, without the passages being stolen, in which his capricious manner, odd breaks, whimsical modulations, and very often childish manner, mixed with an affectation of profound science, are finely hit off and burlesqued.

It has often been said, that the compositions of our author are very unequal; that some are replete with elegance and scientific knowledge, whilst others are extravagant in the excess, and even bordering upon madness

To this it must be observed, that many of these pieces that seem to border on the extreme were written at the express command of the Prince of Estoras *, whose ideas of music are truly eccentric, insomuch that he often chuses the plan on which Haydn is to compose particular symphonies that are to be adapted for three or four orchestras, that are situated in different apartments, which are to be heard singly, response to each other, and join together according to the will of the Prince. Under these circumstances it is no wonder if many of his pieces appear wild, extravagant, and even unnatural; but when he is left to follow the natural bent of his own genius, he is always new, elegant, and delightful.

The national music of the Germans is by nature rough, bold, and grand; and although they do not possess the softness of the Italians, yet it must be confessed that in instrumental music, and particularly that for wind instruments, they have excelled all other nations. This in a great measure may be owing to their not cultivating vocal music more than they have done, to which the harshness of their language seems to be an eternal bar; and it is a general observation, that wherever vocal music is in the highest estimation, instrumental is in some degree neglected. Hence it is that the Italian overtures are in general so insipid, and the German symphonies so capital.

Amongst the professors who have distinguished themselves by their compositions in Germany for these last thirty years, Richter and Stamitz the elder seem to be the most conspicuous; their works are truly masterly, notwithstanding which, they are of the old school; and by some they are thought to favour rather too much of the church stile. It seems therefore, that the refinement of music in Germany was reserved for Haydn to accomplish, which he has in a very ample manner established by originality, novelty, and beautiful air, in which it is thought he has excelled his predecessors and competitors.

It must not be understood, that for the sake of pleasant melody, and sweet air, our author has neglected and laid aside that part of music that constitutes the great master, namely *imitation* and *fugue*. With these strokes of art all his capital music abounds. From his hands they neither appear pedantic nor heavy, being continually relieved by pleasant touches of fancy, and luxuriant flights of endless variety.

Hitherto we have only spoken of Haydn as an instrumental composer. We shall now introduce him in an higher stile, and present him like a heaven-born genius soaring to the *highest elevation* of his art, by adding his lays to those of poetry, and giving double force to language by the energy of his music. And here we behold him, not in a servile manner trying his genius on trifling airs, but imposing on himself a task worthy of his great mind. The subject he made choice of was the *Stabat Mater*, in which his talents found ample scope for that dignity and sublimity so essentially necessary in sacred music.

Haydn's *Stabat Mater* was performed at Vienna about 17 or 18 years since, at which all those masters who had written against and criticised on his former productions were present. They heard with attention, though not without prejudice; and, to their honour be it recorded, gave ample testimony of the merit they had so long doubted, and so often ridiculed.

Haydn has composed several operas in the Italian language, which have been performed at Vienna, in Saxony, and Berlin; also others which have been performed at the Theatres of the Prince of Estoras, and the Empress at Vienna.

The pension that Haydn receives annually from the Prince of Estoras renders his situation so easy, and his mind so unembarrassed, that his genius has full liberty to display itself whenever he chuses to take up his pen; to which, from nature and long habit, he has acquired such an aptitude, that what would appear tiresome and fatiguing to other people, becomes ease and relaxation to him. This account for the vast quantity of music of all sorts and denominations that he has composed, which, upon a fair statement of the matter, will appear in quantity to exceed what any other person has composed, Handel only excepted.

The universality of Haydn's genius cannot be more strongly proved than by the vast demand for his works all over Europe. There is not only a fashion, but also a rage for his musick; and he has continual commissions from France, England, Russia, Holland, &c. for his compositions, expressly written for individuals, or for the music-sellers resident in these kingdoms: and it was, perhaps, a circumstance of this nature that first gave rise to the epistolary correspondence and friendship that subsists between our author and the celebrated Boccherini, whose residence is in Spain.

Those who are best acquainted with Haydn's character, all unite in the following opinion:

As a man, he is friendly, artless, and undesigning;

As a husband, affectionate, tender, and exemplary;

As a performer, neat, elegant, and expressive;

As a composer, chaste, masterly, and original.

* Haydn has been in the service of the late and the present Princes of Estoras in Hungary, in all about twenty-eight years.

For

This account is, of course, full of inaccuracies and misstatements. Nevertheless it was very widely read. Opp. 13 and 14 (Hummel's numbering) are Piano Sonatas Nos. 36–41 (XVI:21–26, Hummel's Op. 13) and Nos. 42–47 (XVI:27–32, Hummel's Op. 14). This article was soon published in translation in Cramer's *Magazin der Musik* (1785, pp. 585ff.), where the editor felt obliged to 'disown' the contents with sundry footnotes. Cramer was particularly shocked about the references to C. P. E. Bach, and also about Haydn's various operas performed in Vienna, Saxony and Berlin. 'Lie upon lie', adds Cramer. Of course, the whole affair with C. P. E. is totally unfounded. When this article appeared in German, C. P. E. Bach read it and felt constrained to write an open letter in the Hamburg *Unpartheiische Korrespondent* of September 1785:

> My way of thought and my occupations have never allowed me to write against anyone: the more was I astonished about a passage in a recent article in The European Magazine in England, where I am accused in a mendacious, crude and shameful way of having written against the good Herr Haydn. According to my news from Vienna and even from members of the Esterhazi [*sic*] Kapelle who came to me, I must believe that this worthy man, whose works continue to give me much pleasure, is surely as much my friend as I his. According to my principles, every master has his true and certain value. Praise and criticism cannot change any of that. Only the work itself praises and criticizes the master, and therefore I leave to everyone his own value. Hamburg, 14th September 1785. C. P. E. Bach.

Bach was seventy-one when he wrote this short but effective reply. The following letter from Haydn is to Artaria and the last of the year:

[To Artaria & Co., Vienna. *German*]

Estoras, 20th November 1784.

Dearest Friend!

Don't be angry at me that I cannot fulfil any of your wants just now; the 3rd Symphony[1] is now ready, but you cannot have it before my arrival in Vienna because of some small profit which I shall try to make on all three. The main difficulty in everything is the long sojourn of my Prince in Estoras, even though he doesn't have much to amuse him, since half of the theatre is sick or away. So you can imagine what trouble I constantly have to amuse His Highness.

You will therefore be good enough to be patient until I have the pleasure of seeing you personally. Meanwhile I remain, with profound esteem,

Your most sincere friend and servant,
Joseph Haydn [m.] pria.

My respectful compliments to the Bavarian house.

[Address:]   Monsieur
            Monsieur d'Artaria
                    a
                VIENNE
[Artaria's clerk writes: 'Haydn / Esterhaz 20th Nov./1784'.]

[CCLN, 47f.]

---

1 Nos. 81, 80 and 79 (in that order) were published as Opp. 38, 39 and 40 in March 1785. Haydn sold them to the Viennese publisher Torricella who, after having engraved the first one (No. 81), ceded the rights of all three to Artaria, who then issued them. Torricella was obviously in straitened financial circumstances at this time, and shortly afterwards went bankrupt; Artaria subsequently acquired most of Torricella's plates, which were sold by public auction.

Schellinger's summary bill for the opera season is as follows:

Conto

What was copied for the princely theatre in the way of operas from 1 January 1784 to the end of November, as agreed the vocal part at 7 xr., the instrumental part at 5 xr.:

Operas	Bögen Vocal Parts	Orchestral [Parts]
L'amor costante — — —	289.	181
Armida — — — —	184.	193
Viaggiatori felici — —	288.	189
Gelosie villane — — —	49.	29
Didone — — — —	198.	189
Contratempi — — —	194.	192
La villanella rapita — —	296	193
	1,498.	1,166.

Makes 271 f. 56 xr. [sums heavily corrected]

Joannes Schilling [*sic*]
Theatrical Copyist
3 Oct. 784

1,166

[Haydn's hand:] Above listed 1,498 Bögen have been found to be correct by me the undersigned. Estoras, 3rd December 784.

Josephus Haydn mpria
Capell Meister

[Passed for payment by Prince Nicolaus, Esterház, 4 Dec. 1784 and money collected by Schellinger, Vienna, 3 Jan. 1785. A.M. 1186. Facsimile 5 in Bartha-Somfai. Valkó II, 601, Bartha-Somfai, 123, Bartha, 142.]

Haydn had moved to Vienna for the Christmas season. The most important event of the period was the performance of *La fedeltà premiata* in a German translation by Emanuel Schikaneder and Hubert Kumpf. This troupe gave a whole series of German operas at the Kärntnerthortheater, and for the première of 'Die belohnte Treue', as it was now called, on 18 December; Emperor Joseph II and the whole court were present, as the local newspapers inform us. We may be sure that Mozart was there to hear the work of his new friend. The *Wiener Zeitung* reports that 'the house was so full by 6:00 p.m. that despite the large capacity more than 600 persons had to be turned away' (22 December, p. 2905). On the same day *Das Wiener Blättchen* writes, '... With the excellent music of a Heiden [*sic*] and the right performance of it, the work could not fail to gain general applause'. The *Wienerische Kronik* for 1785 (p. 438) also reported that

> On 18 Dec. [1784] Herr Schikaneder and Kumpf gave an opera, die belohnte Treue by Haydn, this man who is just as unappreciated as Handel whom the English, after his death, gave a place in the royal vaults of Westminster [Abbey] so that, as a wit observed, posterity could know where the kings of England lie.

It was in 1784 that Haydn received the commission to compose six grand symphonies for the Concert de la Loge Olympique in Paris. The details will be discussed *infra*, pp. 606ff.

We will now break off our Chronicle to turn, in the ensuing Chapters, to Haydn's entry into the literary world of the Viennese salons; to his joining the Freemasons; to his friendship with Mozart; to the works of the period 1776–84; to the dissemination of his music all over Europe and the rise of still further *seguaci*; and to the works of the last years at Eszterháza, 1785–90.

CHAPTER SIX

Haydn and Viennese Society:
the Salons; Freemasonry; Mozart

THERE IS NO QUESTION that in Empress Maria Theresa's time, the Austrian literary world lagged far behind that of England and France, even of Germany. This was largely because of the censorship imposed on all foreign books and articles, especially those which the authorities considered in any way dangerous. Dr Burney, entering Vienna in 1772, had his books confiscated and it was a considerable operation to pry them loose from the censor.[1] Robert Pick, in his biography of the Empress, relates the following revealing story:

> Once Gottfried van Swieten proposed that a monthly, published in Bavaria, and 'which ridicules good humouredly ... the dialect and other characteristics of the population' be admitted to her dominions. 'The world is so frivolous nowadays', she replies, 'so little well-meaning and everything is made sport of and looked upon as a *bagatelle*.' No, those 'booklets' must not be imported. Van Swieten was bold enough to disagree: had not 'sarcasm' since time immemorial helped people grow aware of their shortcomings, and had not many religious authors themselves made use of 'irony and fables' to that end? 'I for one have no love for whatever smacks of irony', she declared. 'Rather than improve men, it irritates them. It is inconsistent with the love of one's neighbour. Why should people waste their time writing such stuff, or reading it?' Austrian speech, she went on (involuntarily puncturing the myth of her great familiarity with it), did not lend itself to 'that kind of light joke', and anyway, some scribblers 'might hit on the idea of publishing similar little stories here under cover of a Bavarian imprint, and that I could not possibly tolerate.'

'There is nothing', says Pick, 'to show that Maria Theresa gave [such a book as Montesquieu's *L'esprit des lois*] even a cursory reading. Except for devotional literature and Italian poetry, she never, for all we know, read a book.'

We cannot concern ourselves, in the limits of this biography, with Joseph II's widespread reforms, in both church and state, which had such vast repercussions on Austrian life. At Eszterháza, all these reforms went totally unnoticed. But in Vienna, they were the talk of the town and as far as the literary world went, they had an indirect effect on Haydn. The censorship which had reduced Austria to a literary nursery was lifted and literary salons flourished in Vienna. Haydn, who spent most of the year as princely *Capellmeister* in Hungary, longed for Vienna and its stimulating intellectual atmosphere.

Perhaps the foremost salon in Haydn's world was that of Franz Sales, Hofrat von Greiner (1730–98), a protégé of Maria Theresa. He served as Court War Secretary in the Bohemian-Austrian Court Chancery, was ennobled in 1771 and given the title *wirklicher Hofrat* in 1773. He was of assistance in the problem of importing foodstuffs to

---

1 Scholes I, 217. Robert Pick, *Empress Maria Theresa: The Earlier Years 1717–1757*, New York 1966, pp. 236 and 193n.

Vienna, and as a trained lawyer he was put to work on problems of inflation, the levelling of a tax on alcohol and the abolition of statute-labour in Bohemia. He was a member of the I. R. Study Society (*Studiengesellschaft*) which organized *inter alia* the school system. 'Greiner', says Roswitha Strommer,[1] 'is the prototype of the enlightened, thinking and active civil servant'. A contemporary describes him as 'a smooth, right-thinking, understanding, active man, worthy of respect; protector of the sciences and the enlightenment, enemy of hypocricy and bigotry, and the warm friend of all those who display talents and ability . . .'.[2] His famous daughter, Caroline Pichler, a poet and diarist of local distinction, relates in her memoirs[3] that 'everything in the way of new poetical works that appeared here or abroad was at once known to us, read and discussed.'

Another contemporary, Joseph von Hormayer, writes that

> His house in the Mehlgrube on the Neuer Markt was a temple of music, a collecting place of *le bon ton* and everything that was excellent from local and foreign artists, whether of equal or higher birth. No excellent foreigner was refused the house's noble hospitality, its encouraging and educated circle of friends.
> [*Taschenbuch für die vaterländische Geschichte* 34, 1845, p. 115]

Caroline Pichler recalls that Mozart, after improvising on 'Non più andrai', jumped up from the piano, sprang over chairs and tables and miaowed like a cat. 'Haydn and Mozart', adds Frau Pichler primly,

> whom I knew well, were persons who displayed in their contact with others absolutely no other extraordinary intellectual capacity and almost no kind of intellectual training, of scientific or higher education. Everyday character [*Sinnesart*], silly jokes, and in the case of the former [Mozart] an irresponsible way of life, were all that they displayed to their fellow men, yet what depths, what worlds of fantasy, harmony, melody and feeling lay hidden in that unlikely outer shell. Through what inner revelation came their understanding of how to bring forth such gigantic effects, and to express in notes such feelings, thoughts and passions that every listener is forced to feel with them, that his very soul is so profoundly touched?
> [*Allgemeine Theaterzeitung*, Vienna, 15 July 1843. *Denkwürdigkeiten* I, 293ff.]

Caroline von Greiner (before she married) corresponded with Lavater; it was probably through the Greiner salon that Haydn came to know Lavater. The Hofrat, though a bad amateur poet himself, had good taste, and among those who frequented his hospitable house on the 'New Market' (see colour plate III in *Haydn: the Years of 'The Creation' 1796–1800*) was Lorenz Leopold Haschka, the author of 'Gott erhalte' which would in 1797 make his name immortal, and who was from 1777 secretary to the Hofrat; and 'with him', writes Caroline, 'the Muses entered our house'. It was rumoured by Vienna's evil tongues that Haschka enjoyed more than the literary favours of Frau von Greiner. Poets, playwrights, scientists, scholars and doctors frequented the salon. The Hofrat was an ardent Freemason, and many of his brother Masons were welcome guests: Johann Baptist von Alxinger (the poet), Freiherr von Gebler (of Mozartian fame – he furnished the text for *Thamos, König von Egypten*, K.345), Freiherr von Jacquin (also Mozart's friend), Gottfried van Swieten, and Mozart himself. In the summer, the 'at home' took place in the Greiner's house in the

---

1 'Wiener literarische Salons zur Zeit Joseph Haydn's, in *Joseph Haydn und die Literatur seiner Zeit*, Eisenstadt 1976, p. 98.
2 *Österreichische Biedermanns-Chronik*, Erster Theil, Freiheitsburg [Vienna?] 1784, pp. 66f.
3 *Denkwürdigkeiten aus meinem Leben* (ed. E. K. Blümml), 2 vols., Munich 1914, I, p. 49. On Greiner, see also Alfred Arneth, *Maria Theresia und der Hofrath von Greiner*, Vienna 1859.

nearby countryside (Hernals). Sometimes plays were given in the Mehlgrube salon, such as Lessing's *Minna von Barnhelm*; but also pantomimes, which were a speciality of another great Viennese salon, that of Ignaz von Born, a famous natural historian and Master of the Lodge 'Zur wahren Eintracht' (to which Greiner also belonged). In short, the Greiner salon was a place in which Haydn's budding literary ambitions could be nurtured. Haydn's small but interesting library – its contents are described in detail in *Joseph Haydn und die Literatur seiner Zeit* (Maria Hörwarthner's article, 'Joseph Haydns Bibliothek – Versuch einer literhistorischen Rekonstruktion', pp. 157ff.), from which this material has been gratefully taken – owes its origins to Haydn's contact with the Viennese salons.

Apart from Hofrat Greiner, whose name has figured often in Haydn's letters of the previous Chronicle, the composer was also a welcome guest at Anton Liebe von Kreutzner's and at Hofrat von Keeß's house, where orchestral concerts were given (*vide infra*, p. 663). Later his favourite salon was that of Frau von Genzinger in the Schottenhof (*vide infra*, p. 720).

When Haydn began to write *Lieder* on a large scale, he turned to Greiner for help in choosing the texts, not being himself 'un uomo di lettere'. We have seen that these modest and pretty songs were treated harshly by German critics, whose opinion of their Austrian literary colleagues was still conditioned by their fate under Maria Theresa. Christian Gottfried Körner, discussing the possibility of Haydn as a composer for song texts, writes from Dresden to Schiller on 29 March 1802, 'I rather doubt if he [Haydn] understands a good poem, since he has always lived in very bad society'[1] – an odd remark. The basis of it is the north-German suspicion that Austrians as a nation had no literary taste at all. 'The literary historian', writes Roswitha Strommer (op. cit., p. 119) recently (1976), 'will have to avoid a judgement in value on those terms'. The Weimar school, which had invented literary *Sturm und Drang* and renounced it later, had also lost any appreciation they might once have had for an authentic Rococo poetry. The Austrians, as always basically conservative, were in the 1780s still immersed in the delicate, pastel shades of Rococo literature – Gellert (Haydn's favourite), Klopstock, Weisse, Bürger, Eschenburg, Gotter – all of whom furnished texts for Haydn even as late as the 1790s and 1800s (Gellert's texts for the *Mehrstimmige Gesänge* of 1796, Bürger's 'Spinning Song' in *The Seasons* of 1801). Haydn was swept into the literary life of Vienna. One of his literary contemporaries wrote in 1782:[2]

> Reading has now become a necessity for us; almost everyone with any money at all has a private library, even if it is only to wallpaper a few rooms; whoever can read has at least half-a-dozen books.

Haydn met many distinguished Freemasons at the Greiner salon, and no doubt Ignaz von Born encouraged Haydn to join the lodge 'Zur wahren Eintracht'. Certainly, Haydn's new friendship with Mozart must have involved serious talks on Freemasonry, and it will have impressed Haydn that his young fellow-composer joined the lodge 'Zur Wohlthätigkeit' on 14 December. Leopold Mozart, who visited his son and talked to Haydn in February 1785 (*vide infra*, p. 508), also joined on 1 April 1785.[3] Haydn had for some time been considering joining a society to which many of

---

1 Pohl II, 361. Schiller's *Briefwechsel mit Körner*, p. 277.
2 Aloys Blumauer: *Beobachtungen über Österreichische Aufklärung und Literatur*, Vienna (Kurzbeck), 1782, p. 54.
3 In the announcements of the lodge 'Zur Wohlthätigkeit' on 28 March 1785, we read 'proposed: Chapel Master Mozart [Leopold] and Joseph Brashy; since both will shortly leave, we have requested a dispensum for them'. Both saw the light on 1 April 1785. *Haydn as a Freemason*, 1967, p. 28.

his Viennese friends belonged. At the end of December 1784, he officially applied to join the Masons:

> [To Franz Philipp von Weber, *Hofsecretaire* and Master of Ceremonies at the Masonic Lodge 'Zur wahren Eintracht', Vienna. *German.* Only the signature autograph]
> Nobly born,
> Most highly respected *Herr Hoff Secretaire*,
>   The highly advantageous impression which Freemasonry has made on me has long awakened in my breast the sincerest wish to become a member of the Order, with its humanitarian and wise principles. I turn to you, Sir, with the most urgent request that you have the great kindness to intervene on my behalf with the Lodge of the Order, in order to implement this my petition, as indicated above.
>   I have the honour to remain, with profound esteem,
> Your obedient servant,
Josephus Haydn,
CapellMeister to Prince Esterházy.
>
> Vienna, the 29th of the Christmas Month
> 1784.   [CCLN, 48]

With this letter Haydn placed himself as a candidate for the lodge 'Zur wahren Eintracht'. His sponsors were the Hungarian Chamberlain Anton Georg, Count von Apponyi from Pressburg, who had himself joined the Brotherhood in Mozart's presence shortly before Christmas, 1784; the Court Secretary von Weber, to whom Haydn wrote the letter, and who was Master of Ceremonies at the lodge; and Heinrich Joseph Walter von Aland, 'Privy Councillor to his Highness, the Elector of Trier and ... accredited Resident Minister at the Imperial Court.'

It was in the so-called 'Henikstein House' in the Wollzeile that Haydn saw the light. By 1785 the lodge 'Zur wahren Eintracht' had about 200 members, including Count Saurau and Court Councillor Sonnenfels, both acquaintances of Haydn's. One of Haydn's oldest Viennese friends, Georg Spangler, was also a member; Spangler was a tenor, now *Regens chori* at the Church Am Hof, and later became *Regens chori* at St Michael's Church in Vienna. We can follow Haydn's admission to the lodge 'Zur wahren Eintracht' from the original protocols, which fortunately have survived the anti-Masonic purges and are now in the Haus-, Hof- und Staatsarchiv in Vienna. The following notes have not been previously published in their entirety, though Otto Erich Deutsch (1932) and Carl Maria Brand (1941) have given us substantial extracts:[1]

> Vienna the 10/1 5785 [10 Jan. 1785]. The Lodge Zur Wahren Eintracht was opened and the members listed in the Protocolle Praesentium were present. 1. After the Lodge of the First Grade had been opened, the ballots for the aspirants Pfangler and Anton B[aron] v[on] Tinty were held; both white. After the usual congratulations, their initiation was set for 14/1 [14 Jan.] ... 3. It was decided to circulate among the Lodges the names of the aspirants Joseph Haydn, Princely Esterhazy Chapel Master, and Baron Hallberg von Brussels ...'.

---

1 Deutsch: 'Haydn bleibt Lehrling', originally in the *Neue Freie Presse*, March 1932, reprinted in *Musica* 13. Jahrgang, Heft 5 (1959), pp. 289ff. Brand: *Die Messen von Joseph Haydn*, Würzburg 1941, pp. 197ff., a very interesting and informative chapter on Haydn and the Freemasons, with many quotations from contemporary documents. Our present translation from *Haydn as a Freemason*, 1976, pp. 28ff., using the original documents.

Three days later the protocol tells us:

.... Then Brother Wolfgang Mozard [*sic*], at the request of his Hon. Lodge Zur Wohlthätigkeit, was advanced to the Second Grade with the customary ceremonies.

A few days later, we read:

Vienna the 24/1 5785 the Lodge Zur wahren Eintracht was opened ... 5. The aspirants B[aron] Hallberg and Joseph Haydn were ballotted white and after the usual congratulations their initiation was set for 28/1. Hallberg's protector Br. Knorr Sen., proposed by Master of the Chair Born. Haydn's protector Br. Weber, proposed by Apponyi and Walter. ...

On 28 January everything was prepared for Haydn's initiation, and as the protocol tells us, 'Mozart from the Lodge Wohlthätigkeit' appeared to welcome his friend. But Haydn had to go to Eszterháza and apologized in a letter to his protector Count Apponyi (the autograph was recently discovered in Hungary):

[To Count Anton Georg Apponyi, Vienna. Only signature autograph. *German*]
High and Well born Count,
Gracious Sir!
    ... Just yesterday I received a letter from my future sponsor Herr v. Weber, saying that they had anxiously awaited me last Friday [28th January] for my initiation, to which I am looking forward intensely; but through the inefficiency of our Hussars, the letter of invitation did not arrive punctually and the whole thing has now been postponed till next Friday. Oh if only it were that Friday! So that I could have the enormous good fortune of being among a group of such worthy men. Herr Hoffmann,[1] my pupil, takes the greatest pleasure in being able to provide Mademoiselle Bayer[2] with the three Dietzl Sonatas;[3] but I am even more proud to be instrumental in their expedition for such a great genius as my dearest Nanette; she deserves to sit at the top of Parnassus and to be worshipped by all men of the Muses: most gracious Count, I take the liberty of sending her a thousand kisses.
    As for Your Grace, the Count, I am with the greatest respect and submission, and with my most humble kiss-of-the-hand to the so beautiful and most gracious Countess,

Your most humble servant
Joseph Haydn mpria.

Estoras, 2nd February 1785.

P.S. Herr Hoffmann doesn't have any concerto by Dietzl.
[On reverse side: 'ddto 2ten et accept. 7ª Febr. 785. Joseph Haydn']
[CCLN 49, incomplete; subsequently autograph discovered in the former Apponyi Archives, County Archives Szekszárd, Hungary, and first published complete in Bartha, 144f.]

The protocol for the day originally set for Haydn's initiation reads:

Vienna the 28/1 5785 the Lodge Zur wahren Eintracht was opened ... 2. The foreign aspirant Hallberg was presented for initiation, since the profane [*Profane*] Haydn was hindered from coming; the initiation was done with the usual ceremonies.

---

1 We cannot identify Haydn's pupil, Hoffmann, except that he was a 'Livonian' (Dies, 207).
2 Nanette Peyer or Payer, *vide supra*, p. 487, and *infra*, p. 679.
3 Probably Trio Sonatas by Joseph Dietzl: his Trio Sonatas Op. 1 appeared at Hummel's in Amsterdam.

On Friday, two weeks later, we discover that Master of the Chair, Born, was absent and his place taken by Brother Anselm:

> ... 3. In the same fashion the initiation of the second aspirant took place, i.e. in the year 5785 the 11/2 was presented the foreign aspirant Joseph Haydn, son of Mathias, 51 years old, born 1 May, of Rom. Cath. faith, of bourgeois parentage, born in Rohrau in Austria, at present Princely Esterhazy Chapel Master, hitherto received in no known Order, and out of sincere desire and will ... [here the entry in the MS. breaks off ('ut supra usque ad finem'); the formula then went on, as we can supply it from other entries] to become a member of the Ancient and Honourable Society of Knightly Freemasons, not driven to this by his own curiosity, nor seduced, driven or persuaded to this end by another; wherefore he was elected by ballot according to the statutes of the Hon. Society and accepted into the Lodge of this Order of St John as a Freemason, apprentice and brother.

On this evening in Vienna Mozart gave the first of six Friday concerts in the town Casino 'Zur Mehlgrube' (Flour Market) on the Neuer Markt and was thus prevented from attending Haydn's initiation. Usually the new apprentices were greeted with a speech, and on that Friday Brother Holzmeister made one for Haydn. Joseph von Holzmeister is listed in contemporary records as 'Chief Clerk of the Imperial War Ministry' and later 'Commissary for the Field'; the speech was later printed in the *Journal für Freymaurer*, Zweyter Jahrgang Zweytes Vierteljahr, Vienna 5785 [1785]:

> Sparta stood unopposed against its enemies, and the soul of the country was happy in the times of its Lykurgen, when every citizen was equally strongly united in love for the fatherland, in the firm belief of the goodness of its laws, every citizen equally resolved to become a part of the whole's harmony and to use his strength for the general well-being.
>
> Rome was the Queen of the World and her sceptre, wide in scope, was unbreakable as long as her rulers served wisdom and her states remained united; and the Germans were a free, strong and happy people as long as their princes were unanimous in their desire for the common good, as long as their lands were not divided, as long as the spirit of noble independence and propriety was the spirit of the whole nation.
>
> Do you not think, my Brothers, that these glimpses of history are not too large in scale to serve as a good example for something smaller than whole states? Every society which serves some purpose and has at its disposal the means by which to reach that said purpose, every society which is organized along certain definite lines is of necessity a little state in itself; general concepts, taken from the rules of nature, fit the state and equally well the society. A state whose constitution rests upon the harmony of its rulers, its aristocracy, its citizens, can count upon an outward greatness and fixed line of purpose, can hope for the fulfilment of its wishes and can expect a measure of inner peace; and so every society may with impunity expect that its progress towards the goal it has established will be certain, and that nothing will stand in the way of its prosperity, as long as each member regards the whole in the same light and the harmony of its purpose remains undisturbed by the discords of secondary considerations.
>
> I regard with distaste the thought that in Masonic circles there was once a time when they were disunited in their purpose, when the name of hetherodoxism was bandied about in their temples, where not infrequently brother hated brother, or at least regarded him with contempt; and all this because the creed of one was not the creed of the other. And I bless the epoch when our goal is certain, our strength in unbroken line assured, our progress unbehindered: and the goal the most

beauteous and noble! Worthy of the dignity of the human soul, and in concord with the divine source from which its noble precepts spring.

Do you not agree with me, my Brothers, that in this, the goal of Masonry is precisely defined, and at least in this respect the harmony of the order as a whole defined and its establishment secured? Without the identical desire in every heart success cannot crown our efforts.

The happy purpose of music is emotional and pleasurable. One gathers together all the marvellous instruments of the Art, and one executes the most songful of melodies: and yet, if every instrument, apart from the duties to which it is assigned, does not also heed the effect of the other instruments, at times subduing his own strength to that of the others, the point of the whole will be missed, and instead of moving and delightful music there will be an impossible cacophony of regulated but unpleasant tones.

I know of no more dignified, no more delightful concept, none wherein the upright man can find true happiness and real joy, than a society of noble human beings, each driven by the same thirst to drink from the spring of wisdom; who seek not to be parsimonious with the knowledge that is given them in the Temple of Truth, but on the contrary seek to share it with the others for the common good; a society in which neither the smile of fortune, nor the chance of birth, reign, but in which the wisest and best are given the leadership; a society in which a shining enlightenment does not give rise to jealousy but rather is a source for emenation; where the manly handclasp is the sign of a heart expanded to much greatness, not the mask of a false friendship; where the clear-eyed lead the mistaken to the truth without rancour; where man may open his heart to man without having to fear prejudice, hate or intrigue; a society in which the meetings represent a day of joy for each member, a day to which one looks forward with impatient delight, and which one leaves with the deep pleasure gained from good deeds accomplished and with the joy of an intellect satisfied.

And this dignified and inspiring idea is realized in the Society of Freemasons; it can be, indeed must be, the characteristic of the order as a whole, and of each lodge; it must be the central point, the essential strength, through which Beauty is defined in the whole of Nature; without it Nature itself must fall, and the starry firmament must again sink with the earth into chaos – harmony.

It is this which gives us patience with those weaker than ourselves, gives us forgiveness for those who err, gives us a frank, open appreciation of the merits of each one of our brothers; it is this which supresses in us ignorance and egotism, and which makes love speak in our breasts; it is this which supresses personal satisfaction in preference to the common good; it is this which awakens in us the desire for common points of view, jointly arrived at and jointly maintained; it is this, finally, which lends a supple tolerance to our way of life and in our common friendship renders us pleasant companions.

You, newly elected Brother Apprentice, know especially well the designs of this heavenly gift, harmony; you know its all-embracing power in one of the most beautiful fields of human endeavour; to you this enchanting goddess has granted part of her bewitching power, through which she calms the stormy breast, puts to sleep pain and sorrow, brightens melancholic and cloudy thoughts, and turns the heart of humans to joyful speculation; she not infrequently rises to the heights of passion herself – but to praise all her charms to you would be superfluous. I content myself if in this small and imperfect picture – I would rather describe it as a sketch –, if in this brotherly talk I have awakened in you the desire to remain steadfastly true to your goddess friend also in this circle, new, my brother, to you.

Even more will I think my task accomplished, my desire fulfilled, if I have contributed to persuade my brothers of the utter necessity of this fundamental stone of Masonic architecture; if I have strengthened and encouraged the attention which you have ever lavished on this heavenly goddess.

In the following membership lists of the lodge, 'Haydn Joseph' is listed as 'Auf Reisen' (abroad), i.e. in Eszterháza. Now that we know that Haydn's patron, Count Ladislaus Erdödy, had his own lodge 'Zum goldenen Rad' ('At the golden wheel') in Eberau Castle (now Burgenland, then Hungary), of which Ignaz Pleyel was a member,[1] it seems likely that Eszterháza Castle incorporated a *Winkelloge* in these years which Haydn attended, for his name does not appear in the attendance protocols of the lodge 'Zur wahren Eintracht' after the beginning of 1785. On the other hand, Haydn had contact with the French 'Loge Olympique', which was the host for his 'Paris' Symphonies, composed in 1785 and 1786; and in Haydn's effects were Masonic Songs for the lodge 'Zur wahren Eintracht' which, of course, the censor immediately withdrew ('unbrauchbar', was the comment written on the Elssler Catalogue entry, No. 72; see *Haydn: the Late Years 1801–1809*, p. 306); the Masons were prohibited in Austria from 1795 until 1918.

There was, no doubt, an element of 'la chose à faire' in Masonry at that time. Caroline Pichler (whose father was a Mason) writes:

> A characteristic feature of the reign of the Emperor Joseph II was the movements which flourished openly in the social world through the so-called secret societies. The order of Freemasons carried on its activities with an almost absurd publicity. Freemason songs were printed, composed and sung everywhere. Freemason insignia were worn as pendants on watches; ladies received white gloves from apprentices [they still do]; several articles of fashion, such as white satin muffs with blue-edged seams, representing Mason's aprons, were known as 'à la franc-maçon'. Many men joined out of curiosity . . . Others had different motives. At that time, it was not unadvantageous to belong to this brotherhood, which had members in every circle and had known how to entice leaders, presidents and governors into its bosom. For there, one brother helped the other . . . There were all sorts and varieties of Masons . . . and during the last years of the reign of Joseph II, they caused a great deal of mischief.
>
> [Translation from Landon, *Beethoven*, pp. 54f.]

On 11 February, Leopold Mozart arrived in Vienna to visit his son and daughter-in-law in their large flat (just now [1977] being restored to its Mozartian state) in the Domgasse, in the shadow of the great Gothic Cathedral of St Stephen, so full of memories and sentiment for every Viennese. On the next day, 12 February, Wolfgang gave a quartet party in honour of his new Masonic Brother, Haydn; two of Haydn's lodge Brothers, the Barons Tinti, were also present. The report which Leopold wrote to his daughter is perhaps the most quoted remark that Haydn ever made:

> Saturday Evening Herr Joseph Haydn and the two Barons Tindi [*sic*] were here; the new Quartets were played, the three new ones that he [Wolfgang] wrote to go with the other three which we already own; they are a little easier than the others but composed brilliantly. Herr Haydn said to me: 'I tell you before God, and as an honest man, that your son is the greatest composer I know, either

---

1 Herbert Seifert: 'Die Verbindungen der Familie Erdödy zur Musik' in *Haydn Yearbook* X (1977), esp. n. 6. A printed list of members, 29 July 1785, Haus-, Hof- und Staatsarchiv, Vienna, Vertrauliche Akten der Kabinettskanzlei, Karton 72: 'Those who left the [lodge]: Ignatius Pleil, Compositeur bei Ladisl. Graf von Erdödy, Apprentice.' A charming 'Winkelloge' (i.e. not an official member of the St Johannis group whose head, in Austria, was of course in Vienna) is still preserved in Schloß Rosenau in the Waldviertel (Austria), where there is now (1977) an interesting historical Freemasonry Museum. All the eighteenth-century decorations are still preserved.

personally or by reputation. He has taste and, apart from that, the greatest knowledge of composition [*Compositionswissenschaft*].'

[Mozart *Briefe und Aufzeichnungen*, vol. III, Kassel 1963, p. 373.][1]

Haydn had heard all six Quartets on 14 January, the day on which Mozart completed the final work, K.465, and entered it in his Catalogue. We know of this from a letter of Leopold Mozart to his daughter in St Gilgen of 22 January 1785:

> [P. S.] This moment I have received 10 lines from your brother, in which he writes that his first subscription concert starts on the 11th of Feb ..., that I should come soon, – that last Saturday he had his 6 Quartets, which he has sold to Artaria for 100 ducats, played to his dear friend Haydn and other good friends. At the end it says: 'Now I must sit down again at my concerto I've just begun' [K.466, completed on 10 February (Catalogue)].   [Mozart, *Briefe* ..., vol. III, 368]

When did this great friendship begin? From evidence quoted in the Chronicle (*supra*, pp. 491 and 499), we believe it must have begun in 1784. The succeeding three volumes of this biography are full of authentic accounts of the friendship, and from the biographical standpoint we would like to limit ourselves to a few quotations. We have quoted one characteristic account from Niemetschek's *Leben des K. K. Kapellmeisters Wolfgang Gottlieb Mozart, nach Originalquellen* (see *Haydn: the Years of 'The Creation' 1796–1800*, p. 336). Here are some short but interesting *vignettes* from that same biography, in the English translation by Helen Mautner (foreword by A. Hyatt King, London 1956):

> ... Mozart ... became a most sincere admirer of the great and incomparable Joseph Haydn, who had already become the pride of music, and now, since Mozart's death, remains our favourite and our delight. Mozart often called him his teacher.   [31f.]

> In Vienna, above all, his piano-playing was admired; for although Vienna had many great masters of this instrument, which had since become everyone's favourite, yet nobody could come up to our Mozart! His admirable dexterity, which particularly in the left hand and the bass were considered quite unique, his feeling and delicacy, and beautiful expression, of which only a Mozart was capable, were the attractions of his playing, which together with his abundant ideas and his knowledge of composition must have enthralled every listener and made Mozart the greatest pianist of his time.   [31]

> [*Entführung*] created a great stir; and the cunning Italians soon realised that such a man might be a menace to their childish tinkling. Jealousy now reared its head with typical Italian venom. The monarch, who at heart was charmed by this deeply stirring music, said to Mozart nevertheless: 'Too beautiful for our ears and an extraordinary number of notes, dear Mozart'. 'Just as many, Your Majesty, as are necessary', he replied with that noble dignity and frankness which so often go with great genius. He realised that this was not a personal opinion, but just a repetition of somebody else's words. ...

> I cannot describe the sensation it made in Vienna from my own experience – but I was witness to the enthusiasm which it aroused in Prague among

---

1 Ludwig Finscher, in his Foreword to the new critical edition (*NMA*), Werkgruppe 20, Band 2, Kassel 1962, thinks that the Quartets were played by Leopold and Wolfgang Mozart and the Freiherrn Anton and Bartholomaus Tinti. We beg leave to doubt that. Leopold was an old man and was probably happy to listen rather than to play the difficult new works. We suggest that Haydn was one of the participants (perhaps as viola?).

knowledgeable and ignorant people alike. It was as if what had hitherto been taken for music was nothing of the kind. Everyone was transported – amazed at the novel harmonies and at the original passages for wind instruments.   [32f.]

[Quartets dedicated to Haydn 1785] ... Not only does the homage of an artist like Mozart enhance Haydn's fame, but it is also to Mozart's credit, and makes us realise the tenderness of his feelings, considering that he himself had such wonderful talent.

Certainly Mozart could not have honoured Haydn with a better work than with these quartets, which contain a mine of precious thoughts and which are, indeed, models of composition.

In the eyes of the connoisseur this work is of importance equal to any of his operatic compositions. Everything in it has been carefully thought out and perfected. One can see that he has taken the trouble to deserve Haydn's praise.

[33f.]

[*Le nozze di Figaro*] was performed in Vienna by the Italian Opera Company. If it is really true, as has been definitely asserted – and it is difficult to disbelieve reliable eye-witnesses – that disgruntled singers out of hate, envy and ill-will, tried to spoil the opera by continually making mistakes at the first performance, the reader may gather how much the whole coterie of Italian singers and composers feared the superiority of Mozart's genius and how right I was a short while ago in my remarks about *Die Entführung*. They slandered him and did their best to belittle his art. ... It is said that the singers had peremptorily to be called to their duty by the late monarch, as Mozart in his dismay had come to the royal box during the first act and had drawn attention to what was happening. [At Prague] the enthusiasm shown by the public [for *Figaro*] was without precedent; they could not hear it enough. A piano version was made by one of our best masters, Herr Kucharz; it was arranged for wind band, as a quintet and for German dances ... in addition, there was the incomparable orchestra of our opera, which understood how to execute Mozart's ideas so accurately and diligently ... The well-known Orchestra Director Strobach, since deceased, declared that at each performance he and his colleagues were so excited that they would gladly have started from the beginning again in spite of the hard work it entailed.   [34f.]

[Mozart at Prague in 1787, applause for *Figaro*] In answer to a universal request, he gave a piano recital at a large concert in the Opera House. The theatre had never been so full as on this occasion ... We did not, in fact, know what to admire most, whether the extraordinary compositions or his extraordinary playing: together they made such an overwhelming impression on us that he felt we had been bewitched. ... The symphonies which he composed for this occasion are real masterpieces of instrumental composition, which are played with great élan and fire, so that the very soul is carried to sublime heights. This applies particularly to the Symphony in D major, which is still a favourite in Prague, although it has no doubt been heard a hundred times.   [36f.]

We can judge what fine sensibility he had, and how keen his artistic feeling was, when we hear that he was wont to be moved to tears during the performance of good music; particularly when listening to something composed by the two great Haydns.   [65]

He was always very touched when he spoke of the two Haydns or other great masters. We would not have suspected that we were listening to the almighty Mozart, but rather to one of their enthusiastic pupils.   [68]

He loved her [Constanze] dearly, confided everything to her, even his petty sins – and she forgave him with loving kindness and tenderness. Vienna was witness to this. . . .

His greatest pleasure was music. If his wife wanted to give him a special surprise at a family festivity, she would secretly arrange for a performance of a new church composition by Michael or Joseph Haydn.   [72]

This is obviously not the place to enter into Mozart's financial troubles, but we would point out that the fee Artaria paid him for the 'Haydn' Quartets (K.387, etc.) was considerably higher than the fees Haydn received for similar works, of which our Chronicle contains many details. Similarly, the picture painted in most Mozart biographies is that of a misunderstood genius; but this is not that which emerges from the Niemetschek biography. And what, for example, did Giovanni Paisiello, who visited Vienna and listened to Mozart several times in 1784, think of him? As it happens, we know. The document comes from that little known but extremely valuable book, *Aneddoti piacevoli e interessante, Occorsi nella vita di G. G. Ferrari*, of which extracts may be found in *Haydn in England 1791–1795*, pp. 154f. To redress the picture of the universal misunderstanding of Mozart's music, we present the following extract, again using the pretty translation from *The Harmonicon*:[1]

> Shortly after this, I was so unfortunate as to lose the society of my good friend Attwood, who set out for Vienna, in order to complete his studies under the celebrated Mozart. He arrived in that metropolis at the very moment this great composer published his six Quartets, dedicated to Haydn, and sent me a copy as a present, with a letter, in which he advised me not to form an opinion of them till I had heard them executed several times over. I accordingly tried them with some dilettanti and professors, who were friends of mine, but we could execute only the slow movements, and even those indifferently. I scored several of the parts, and among others the fugue in G, in the first quartet. I showed it to the [celebrated composer Gaetano] Latilla, who, after looking over the first movement, pronounced it to be a masterly piece; but when he had examined the ingenious combinations and modulations of the second part, and came to the bars where the subject is resumed, he laid down the copy upon the table, exclaiming in perfect ectasy, 'This is the most magnificent piece of music I ever saw in my life.' . . . A manager of one of the theatres at Rome, of the name of Gasparoni, paid Paisiello a visit. He came to know whether the composer could recommend him a maestro of abilities, one above the common; for since he was unable to engage either himself, Guglielmi, or Cimarosa, he could not find a composer in Italy who was worth two farthings. Paisiello immediately proposed Mozart, as a young man of transcendent talent. He added, 'that he could not say for certain whether his music would please at first, being somewhat complicated; but that should Mozart once take, it would be all over with several masters in Europe.'

This episode occurred in Italy, where Mozart's and Haydn's music was little known and little appreciated; it also shows that the Italians were not as chauvinistically thick-witted as their biographers north of the Alps often consider them as far as the eighteenth century is concerned.

That Mozart's music was difficult and met with resistance is, of course, all too true. In the article about Mozart in the *AMZ* (I, 854f. of 1799), we learn of further details of

---

1 Ferrari, 2 vols., London 1830. *Harmonicon* 1830, p. 371f.

his life as told by his widow, among other things that the Minuet & Trio of K.421 were written as Constanze was having her first child. The report continues: 'The Quartets' – referring to the set of six dedicated to Haydn –

> occasionally had a curious fate. When the late Artaria sent them to Italy, they were returned 'because there were so many printer's errors'. Gradually they were accepted. But all the same even in Germany these Mozart works did not fare better. The late Prince Grassalkowich for example had these Quartets performed by some of the players in his *Kapelle*. One time after another he cried, 'You're not playing correctly', and when they assured him that they were, he tore up the notes on the spot.

How many works by Mozart did Haydn know from the years 1781–90? It is difficult to establish, but from available evidence we are sure that he heard *Le nozze di Figaro*, *Don Giovanni* and *Così fan tutte* and there were ample opportunities for him to have heard *Die Entführung aus dem Serail*, e.g. in January 1786.[1] Haydn knew, of course, the six Quartets dedicated to him (K.387, etc.), and at Eszterháza he knew, but did not perform, the Arietta 'Un baccio di mano' (K.541, *vide infra*, p. 713). The Esterházy Archives owns copies of the last three Symphonies in MS. (now Budapest, K.543, 550, 551), but it is not known when they were acquired and it is difficult to imagine their performance, prior to 1790, because Haydn's band lacked trumpets and, of course, clarinets (no problem in the first version of K.550). How, in fact, did Haydn intend to cope with this problem in *Figaro*? He was probably witness to some of Mozart's piano concertos, and we know that Haydn played in performances of the late Quintets (K.515, 516, 593, 614).

While there are times in Mozart's Viennese music in which we can clearly trace Haydn's influence – a typical case in point is the Finale of the Piano Concerto in D, K.451 – they are relatively few and far between. In Haydn's case, we believe that prior to the 'Prussian' Quartets, Op. 50 (1787), Mozart's influence is negligible, and we propose to show (*vide infra*, p. 627) that it was largely negative: as would be the case with Beethoven, Haydn either withdrew (no more operas, no more piano concertos, no quintets) or he was at great pains to try to preserve his own personality. The occasional chromatic 'slither' back to the tonic in Haydn's music and other such borrowings do not alter the fact that, however massive Mozart's personality was, its direct influence on Haydn was far less than is usually asserted: most of the critics who have written on the subject knew less than one-tenth of Haydn's music and quite frankly were in no position to write about Haydn at all.

In a biography of Haydn, we must cope with the phenomenon, the miracle, of Mozart in a pitifully limited space. At the risk of superficiality, therefore, we must of necessity be brief. The principal differences between the two composers are almost too well known to require comment, but perhaps a few technical details might be mentioned. The main difference in orchestration between the two is Mozart's *density*, which is of course part of his density of thought. The trumpets are used in a lower tessitura, whereas with Haydn they are still very Baroque, or at best pre-classical, in texture. The cor anglais in Haydn is the clarinet in Mozart, but altogether, it is astonishing what a difference a second flute, two clarinets, two (Haydn often had

---

1 *Wiener Theaterkalender auf das Jahr 1787* [Vorwort: 1 Dec. 1786]. Mozart's Opera was given at the Kärntnerthortheater in January. In February they also gave *Der Schauspieldirektor* and Salieri's *Prima la musica, poi le parole*.

only one) bassoons and two trumpets make in Mozart's scores. Haydn's fastidious, spare orchestration has its own delicate beauty, but inevitably it pales in front of the gorgeous wash of colour displayed in Mozart's scores. Haydn was a master of irony, and Mozart is a master of ambivalence, where the subtlety goes so far (as in *Così fan tutte*, an astonishing masterpiece that has only come into its own in the twentieth century)[1] that, as it were, the emotion sometimes turns totally upside-down. It is a pity that the word 'courtly' has acquired something slightly pejorative which has nothing at all to do with the word's original and true meaning (*OED*: '(of speech, gesture, etc.) such as are heard or seen at Court, easily ceremonious, (of persons) having courtly ways'.) Who does not think of the great scenes in *Don Giovanni* (Atto I°, Sc. XX; Atto II°, Sc. XIII; *NMA* II/5 [1968], 212, 393), as 'easily ceremonious'? At the risk of belabouring a point made frequently in this biography, the all-pervasive rhythm

♩ ♫·♩ ♩ is an integral part not only of the courtliness which is so much a part of Mozart's intricate personality, but also a sign of the tighter, more exciting rhythm that informs his scores. The intellectual fascination of Haydn's scores is matched in those of Mozart, and the latter are clothed in radiantly attractive colours. Another aspect of Mozart's scores which springs to the eye is the accelerated tempo of the allegros, 4/4 instead of 8/8 and barred C instead of 4/4: but not only will this technical aspect occupy us when examining Op. 50 by Haydn (where we see direct results of this particular detail in Mozart's style), but it must be considered in a larger context. Haydn's operas move slowly; everyone at Eszterháza had unlimited time, especially Prince Nicolaus, 'for whom nothing was too long'; Mozart's move quickly, and not only within the allegro. Consider *Le nozze di Figaro*, Atto I°: Sinfonia: Presto, barred C. No. 1 (Duettino) Allegro, 4/4. No. 2 (Duettino) Allegro, 2/4. No. 3 (Cavatina) Allegretto, 3/4. No. 4 (Aria) Allegro, 4/4. No. 5 (Duettino) Allegro, 4/4. No. 6 (Aria) Allegro vivace, barred C. No. 7 (Terzetto) Allegro assai, 4/4. No. 8 (Coro) Allegro, 6/8. No. 9 (Aria) Vivace, 4/4. A slow movement does not occur *at all* until the Countess's Cavatina, 'Porgi amor', at the outset of Atto II°. Let us take Atto I° of Haydn's *La fedeltà premiata*, perhaps his most successful large-scale Opera (by large-scale we mean in length, in number of participants and in overall complexity). Sinfonia: Presto, 6/8. No. 1 (Introduzione) Allegro, 3/4 – Adagio, 4/4 – Adagio, barred C – Allegro, 3/4. No. 2 (Aria) Presto, 6/8. No. 3 (Aria & Recit.) [Poco adagio], 3/4. No. 4 (Aria) Presto, 4/4. No. 5 (Aria) Allegro con brio, 4/4. No. 6 (Aria) Adagio, 3/4. No. 7 (Aria) Poco andante, 2/4. No. 8 (Aria) Adagio, 3/4. No. 9 (Aria) Allegro di molto, barred C – Adagio – Presto – Adagio – Presto. No. 10 (Aria) Allegro assai, barred C. No. 11 (Aria) Andante, 2/4 – Largo, barred C – Allegro, 4/4. No. 12 (Aria) Vivace, 4/4 – Adagio, 3/4 – [Allegro], 4/4 – Presto, 3/4. No. 13 Finale: Vivace assai, 4/4 – Adagio, 3/4 – Presto, 2/4 – Presto, 6/8 – Vivace assai, 4/4 – Adagio, barred C – Presto, 2/4 – Presto, 4/4 – Presto, barred C. It is only in the Finale, incidentally, that we find the same sense of forward-moving time that is so typical of *Figaro*; and although the forward drive of *Figaro*'s Atto I° is (as it happens) connected with an entire series of rapid or relatively rapid tempi, the presence or absence of an adagio or largo has little to do with this overall concept of swift movement. We believe that Mozart's mercurial sense of tempo was the one single aspect of his prismatic style that gripped

---

1 We recall, with equal astonishment, Donald Mitchell's and our defence of this great work against bitter attacks by Colin Mason; we also remember Jens Peter Larsen's dismissal of *Così* at Budapest in 1959, which ruined a pleasant dinner party given in our honour by the late Bence Szabolcsi, good friend and wise counsellor. Old ideas die hard.

Haydn's imagination. If the reader finds difficulty in applying this theoretical concept to the actual scores, let him consider Part I of *Die Schöpfung* (*The Creation*). Here we have that same sense of forward-moving drive which is not in the least retarded either by the vastly slow-moving Largo which is 'Chaos', nor by the other less-than-allegro sections (e.g. 'Nun schwanden', Andante; 'Nun beut die Flur', Andante; the Sunrise, Andante): the whole moves forward as inexorably as Genesis itself. And we must not forget that *Figaro*'s subtitle is 'La folle journée', and that the entire action of the work takes place within twenty-four hours.[1] It is in the work's concept of time that we realize that Mozart was thirty when he composed this epochal masterpiece, from which all modern opera derives.

Concerning the demonic side to Mozart's nature, it, too, has in recent years been subjected to intensive study – we recommend Charles Rosen's penetrating remarks on K.466 in *The Classical Style*, pp. 227ff. And as for the incredible beginning of the G minor Symphony, K.550, we refer readers to Denys Parsons's statistical analysis[2] of 7,387 themes of thirty major classical composers, the G minor's theme was found to belong to the bottom (ninth) choice of patterns. Twenty-six of these composers 'banished [this pattern] to the bottom place.' Thus it can be seen statistically that which we guessed stylistically: that K.550's beginning is one of music's greatest leaps forwards, and that its novelty remains untarnished after nearly two hundred years. As one example of Mozart's genius, we may select an extract from the penultimate of the 'Haydn' Quartets, K.464's slow movement, where towards the end a 'drum' rhythm (in Austria the work is called 'The Drum' by quartet amateurs) suddenly enters quietly – the 'battle afar off'. Here we have the quintessence of Mozart's ambivalence, emotions of fathomless depth clothed in the purest of D major; this Quartet was also one of Beethoven's favourites.[3] 'That is a work! In it Mozart said to the world: "See what I could create if the time had come for you!"'

[*Neue Mozart-Ausgabe*, Werkgruppe 20, Band 2 (Finscher), 1962, pp. 130ff.]

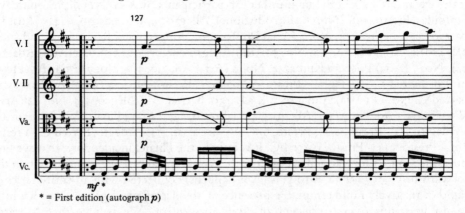

* = First edition (autograph *p*)

1 The first production we have ever seen to take cognizant account of this changing from morning (Act I), high noon (Act II), afternoon (Act III), to evening (Act IV) proceeding, at bars 445/8 of the Finale (Eulenburg pp. 710f.), to the sunrise was Luchino Visconti's magical production at the Rome Opera (conducted by Carlo Maria Giulini).
2 *New Scientist*, 24 March 1977, pp. 688f.
3 Carl Czerny to Otto Jahn. Friedrich Kerst, *Die Erinnerungen an Beethoven*, 2 vols., Stuttgart 1913, I, 51. Landon, *Beethoven*, p. 53.

Haydn repeatedly said that Mozart was the greatest composer he knew, 'either personally or by reputation'. He did not change his opinion even after he had met, taught and listened to Beethoven. A hundred years ago, Haydn's categorical statement on Mozart will have been regarded as an eccentric whim. As the twentieth century progresses, the music of Mozart means increasingly more to music-lovers and musicians. Indeed, it is *essential* to many of us, like life itself. And to many of us, moreover, Mozart still remains the greatest of all composers, all-embracing in his universality, timeless in his appeal, his poignance as real as it was to the few that really understood him during that magnificent decade, from 1781–91.[1]

'And yet ... it was different from the freshness of spring; the image and the gaiety of it were tinged with despair ...'.

1 We would not dare to list even a small Mozart bibliography, but we would draw attention to two great books in German which have never been translated into English: the great biography by Hermann Abert, Berlin 1923/4 (latest edition: Leipzig 1956, three volumes), and Robert Haas's splendid monograph, Potsdam 1933 (2nd edition, 1950). A penetrating article which we recommend strongly is Edward E. Lowinsky's 'On Mozart's Rhythm' in *Musical Quarterly* XLII/2 (1956), pp. 162ff. There are many interesting articles in the *Mozart Jahrbücher* published by the Internationale Stiftung Mozarteum in Salzburg. Quotation: from Isak Dinesen, *Seven Gothic Tales*, New York 1934, p. 120.

CHAPTER SEVEN

Haydn's Works 1776–1784

THE WORKS OF THIS PERIOD, grouped by types for the purpose of discussion, are as
follows:

Operas: *Die Feuersbrunst* (*c.* 1775–8?); *Il mondo della luna* (1777); *La vera costanza*
(1778?); *L'isola disabitata* (1779); *La fedeltà premiata* (1780); *Orlando Paladino* (1782);
Armida (1784); also 'insertion' arias for works by other composers performed at
Eszterháza.

Masses: *Missa brevis Sancti Joannis de Deo* (1777?); *Missa Cellensis*
('Mariazellermesse'; 1782).

Symphonies: single works (Nos. 61, 53, 63, 70, 75, 71, 62, 74, 73); Nos. 76–78
(1782); Nos. 79–81 (1783–4); also Overtures.

Concertos: for Violoncello and orchestra (VIIb:2; 1783); for Harpsichord or
Fortepiano and orchestra (XVIII:11; *c.* 1780–3?).

Dances and Marches.

String Quartets, Op. 33 (1781).

Piano Trios Nos. 17–19 (XV:5, 6, 7).

Piano Sonatas: Six Sonatas (Op. 30, Artaria, 1780; Nos. 48–52 and 33; XVI:35–39
and 20); No. 53 (XVI:34; *c.* 1780?); Three Sonatas (Op. 37, Boßler, 1784; Nos. 54–56;
XVI:40–42), dedicated to Princess Marie Hermenegild Esterházy; the same works for
String Trio (Hoffmeister, 1788);

Flute Trios for Forster, Op. 38 (IV:6–11; 1784).

Lieder.

The Operas

Die Feuersbrunst (Das abgebrannte Haus), Singspiel
(Marionette Opera; XXIXb:A; *c.* 1775–8?)

Scoring: S (Colombina), S T (Steckel, Odoardo,
Leander, Hausknecht [scullery boy] Geist [Ghost]),
Baritone (Hanswurst), 2 fl., 2 ob., 2 clar., 2 bsn., 2
cor., 2 trpt., timp., str.
Principal Source: A copy of the score in MS.
prepared by Johann Traeg *c.* 1800, using Haydn's
autograph (which Traeg owned) as the basis, Yale
University Library. The score was formerly in a
French country estate and sold, together with the
Traeg copy of *Philemon und Baucis* (q.v.) which
is now in the Conservatoire Library, Paris
(Bibliothèque Nationale), by Arthur Rau in 1935.
A single copy of Leander's Aria 'O meiner Augen
Weide', transposed into D and arranged for piano,
is in the Österreichische Nationalbibliothek,

Musiksammlung, as part of a collection of Haydn's
songs. *Libretto:* ? Pleyel Overture: *vide infra.*
Critical edition: Schott, London 10779 (piano-vocal
score; full score and parts of hire) (Landon).
First performance in modern times: A student
performance at Yale University preceded the first
public presentation at the Bregenz Festival, 1963.
The cast: Hanswurst (Oskar Czerwenka),
Colombina (Rosl Schwaiger), Leander (Heinz
Hoppe), Steckel (Kurt Equiluz), Odoardo
(Claudio Nicolai), Geist (Karl Terkal), Wirth
(speaking role: Hugo Gottschlich), Priest (speak-
ing role: Robert Marencke), Chorus and Ballet of
the Vienna State Opera, Vienna Symphony
Orchestra, conducted by Robert Heger. Producer:

Adolf Rott. A performance with marionettes (director: Norman Shetler) was given during the Haydn-Tage, Eisenstadt, 1977, conducted by Bernhard Klebel.
Literature: Landon in *The Times*, 13 and 14 June 1961. Landon in *HJB* I (1962), pp. 111ff. with a complete thematic catalogue (pp. 178–183) of the *incipits*. A. van Hoboken in *Neue Zeitschrift für Musik* 1963, No. 10, pp. 396f. Eugene Hartzell in *HJB* II (1963/4), 102–9. G. Feder in *Haydn-Studien* II/2 (1969), pp. 114–8.

The only score of the work contains all the music but only the 'cue lines' of the dialogue before each musical number. Therefore, our score is a reconstruction of the whole plot. Leaving aside our additions, it is clear that Haydn's opera was written around Hanswurst, a likeable vagabond chimney-sweep who tries, successfully, to win Colombina's heart. Colombina's father is Odoardo, a crotchety old gentleman, and Colombina's first suitor is the dandy, Leander. We combined the two roles of Steckel and the Hausknecht, each of which has only one aria to sing (Hausknecht's Aria, No. 21, is thus assigned to Steckel). The house burns up at the end of Act I, and it was to this dramatic incident that Haydn referred when he listed the opera in *EK* as 'Opera comique Vom abgebrannten Haus'. The score gives us all the typical disguise scenes in which Hanswurst appears during the second act, also the happy end in which Colombina and Hanswurst are united in a duet.

The following factors assist us in dating the work. In *EK* (p. 18), Haydn continued to add opera titles to the earlier Esterházy productions: *Acide*, 'Opera la Cantarina', 'Applauso', 'Opera lo Speziale' and 'Opera le pescatrici', the last four with *incipits*. About 1777, thinks Professor Larsen,[1] the next batch of operas was added, consisting of 'Opera l'incontro improviso', 'Oratorio il Ritorno di Tobia', 'Opera l'infedeltà delusa', 'Opera il mondo della luna' – all without *incipits* – and in the upper right-hand part of the page

Opera comique Philemon und Paucis [*sic*]
Opera comique Didone abbandonata
Opera comique Vom abgebrannten Haus.

The latest of these operas, whether German or Italian, was composed in 1777, which may be assumed to be a *terminus post quem non*. *Die Feuersbrunst* is the only work of the period to include clarinet parts (in two numbers, characteristically, in E flat in Act I, Leander's 'O meiner Augen Weide' and the Ghost's single Aria, 'All Kummer'). Haydn had the clarinet players, Anton and Raymond Griessbacher from December 1775 to 1 March 1778, and thus the opera must have been written within this period. Except for the closing chorus of Act I and the 'Dragon Music' just before the end of the opera, Haydn's two flutes are used instead of oboes. A similar situation exists in the Traeg copy of *Philemon & Baucis*, where there are also two flute parts which the Haydn Institut have, rather high-handedly, simply dismissed from their new scores because Haydn did not have (at least on paper) two flute players during this period (*vide supra*, p. 429); in the *Philemon* edition, the trumpets were omitted by the Haydn Institut for similar reasons. Now it is clear that Haydn was not enamoured of these peculiar restrictions at Eszterháza and entirely possible, even likely, that he enlarged the *instrumentarium* of his scores whenever possible and whenever they were destined for a 'foreign' orchestra. We imagine that the presence of two flutes rather than one, and the two trumpets together with the two horns, are later additions, but we note that *Il mondo della luna* (1777) has two flutes, two horns *and* trumpets. Perhaps Ignaz Pleyel,

1 *HÜB*, 238.

who furnished the Overture,[1] may have helped in such problems: the timpani part of the score which, as it stands, cannot possibly have been composed by Haydn, may have been composed by Pleyel (or indeed someone at Traeg's): although corrupt timpani parts also occur in other Haydn MSS. of the period, e.g. the authentic performance material of Symphony No. 53 in the Esterházy Archives (copied by Joseph Elssler and others), in which the timpani part of the minuet and finale (Version A) cannot be by Haydn.

It seems to us possible that Haydn composed this work for his own marionette theatre, which we know was in existence in the Carnival season of 1774 and was, moreover, used by the Prince in a birthday surprise for the Princess in March 1775. *Die Feuersbrunst*, written partly in Lower Austrian dialect

> Nä, nä, nä, s'Haus gib i net her,
> Er mache was er will: mänt er, es wär zu viel,
> So gib ich's doch nit her.
> Will er an gnädig Herren machä,
> Uns arme Bauern nur auslachä,
> So lachen wir alsdann, wann ihm wird Angst und Bang.

and with social and critical overtones that remind one faintly and sinisterly of the Peasants' Wars' – 'He'd play the gentleman or peer now, at us poor peasants he would sneer now' (from the above quoted Aria) – hardly suggests even the marionette theatre at Eszterháza, where the text of Haydn's other German operas (*Dido* and *Die bestrafte Rachbegierde*) is not in dialect, and not of this particular kind of 'low comedy'.

Like the other figures of this type of Viennese popular 'plays with music', Hanswurst is clearly a derivative of the Venetian *commedia dell'arte*. Haydn's first operatic patron, Felix Joseph von Kurz-Bernadon (for whom Haydn wrote *Der krumme Teufel*), was a great Hanswurst specialist, sometimes acting 'Bernadon' and sometimes Hanswurst, but almost always with the characteristic disguises (*Verkleidungsszenen*). In *Bernadons Reise in die Hölle*,[2] we find Bernadon appearing as 1. Traveller, 2. Cavalier, 3. Hussar, 4. Gypsy Woman, 5. Croatian, 6. Barber, 7. Doctor, 8. Affected lady, 9. Runner, 10. Night Watchman, 11. Man without a head, and 12. Bridegroom fetched by the devil. 'Amusing arias will be sung the whole time.' In Haydn's opera, we find Hanswurst appearing as a soldier, as a gentleman, as a milliner and as a beggarwoman. As for the *commedia dell'arte*, the very names are known to us from countless plays and pictures: Colombina, Leandro (= Leander), Odoardo, and were taken over in the Austrian *Volkskömodie*. In Philip Hafner's (1731–64) *Megära*, we find Hanswurst, Colombine and Leander all together, and in *Die bürgerliche Dame*, which Hafner wrote in 1763, Hanswurst and Colombina appear as 'zween Mustern heutiger Diensboten' (two models for today's servants).[3] The people on stage to a certain extent represented stock figures, or archetypes: Colombina is the typical girl in the comedy, usually (in the Viennese versions) of the lower classes, though in Haydn's work she has been educated for better things, speaks *hochdeutsch*, and is ruined by the fire. Odoardo, in Kurz-Bernadon's plays, is the typical fussy old father, while

1 The Pleyel sources are listed on p. 178 of *HJB* I, 178; to them add: Boßler (Speyer), No. 1 of 'Trois Simphonies' Op. VII (1780s). In the Pleyel sources, a minuet occurs between the slow movement and finale, and this minuet was not, obviously, used in the *Feuersbrunst* score. Haydn also borrowed the finale of the Overture (possibly this section was really Haydn's and used by Pleyel when publishing the symphony?) for use as the concert ending of *L'infedeltà delusa* when he needed a conclusion to that Overture in the first edition of Artaria. The Pleyel Overture to *Die Feuersbrunst* is published (Landon) by Edition Eulenburg. Note that the orchestration of the finale differs in many significant details from that of *L'infedeltà delusa* Overture, finale, in the concert version. For the timpani part of the opera, see also *HJB* I, 153f.
2 Birnbaumer I, 69. The literature is listed *infra*, p. 521 n.
3 Kindermann V, 47.

Hanswurst and Colombina are a typical 'low' pair, the ancestors of Papageno and Papagena. In Kurz-Bernadon's works, Colombina was often Kurz's wife, Antonia ('as Colombine . . . at the end, as a bride in a white dress'). Ghosts and fabulous beasts, the use of hell, are stock figures in the *commedia dell'arte* and also in the Viennese versions thereof. Similarly, Italian sensuality was easily translated into Viennese sexuality; the overtly licentious character of Hanswurstiada did not appeal to Maria Theresa, whose censors actually forbade Haydn's *Der krumme Teufel* and, soon, Bernadon altogether. Although the arias had 'set' words, much of the dialogue was improvised, and in these improvisions, sexual licence and political lampoons combined to outrage the aristocracy. These were the plays of, by and for the people. Both the supernatural and the sensual appear in Haydn's *Die Feuersbrunst* – a 'Dragon's Music' before the end, and such references as the Hausknecht's Aria on the subject of Hanswurst 'as a cavalier': 'Count Hanswurst will soon have her in bed'. Leander is, of course, the typical 'affected cavalier' (mimicked by Hanswurst) but also the typical duped figure of the *commedia dell'arte*.[1] The Italian influence, indeed, even extends to that extraordinary mixture of German and Italian that we find in *Der krumme Teufel*, where a whole Italian *intermezzo* appears within the German *Singspiel*. Or consider 'Hanns-Wurst als Savojard' in *Die lustige Bauern-Hochzeit zwischen Hanßel und Gredel [sic], oder Hanns-Wurst der verliebte Maus-Fallen-Krämer* (The merry peasant marriage between Hanßel & Gretel, or Hanswurst the infatuated purveyor of mouse traps):

> Chi voi Hechel, Mause-Fall,
> Chi vol was comprare?
> In der Kuchel, in der Stall
> Er kann aplicare,
> Ist vielleicht in eurem Haus
> Uno razzo, oder Maus? . . .[2]

Being a German *Singspiel*, we cannot expect the kind of elaborate ensembles that Mozart was to transport into *Die Entführung* from Italian opera: instead, we have concluding choruses for Acts I and II, which Haydn could easily mount, using local forces (whereas he would have had difficulty in finding enough grenadiers, etc., to learn by heart Italian choruses). If our theory is correct, and this was, as it were, an 'off-Eszterháza' production, we may note that there are considerably more numbers in minor than ever appeared in any other Haydn opera: no less than six numbers are in minor (though two end in major). Once again, this sudden flowering of the minor key suggests that Haydn's renunciation of the *Sturm und Drang* was perhaps not entirely, or certainly at the beginning, of his own volition. There are also some curious undertones which show a different kind of originality than that of the Italian operas, e.g. No. 9 (Aria: Hanswurst) –

---

1 Birnbaumer I, 59.
2 Birnbaumer I, 85.

There is a certain menacing quality to that music which we also find in Hanswurst's 'Aria as a milliner' (*Haubenhefterin*), where the text calls forth 'Lauter Höllengeister' (ghosts of hell) which the man, against whom Hanswurst warns, 'vomits from his face'. Haydn's music, strangely unsettling, shows us quite a new side to his operatic personality and reminds us that Haydn composed, or at least had some part in, the marionette opera, *Hexen-Schabbas*, from which this Aria might easily have come.

It is altogether interesting to study the passages in this opera which gripped Haydn's imagination, and they are – apart from the comic scenes which obviously appealed to his sense of humour – in particular two: Colombina's Aria, 'Wie wallet mein Herze', in Act II, the most beautiful piece in the whole opera and the most touching aria on the subject of love that Haydn ever wrote. Its radiant melody is in the key of E major for which Haydn always had a special affection, and which appears in his vocal pieces to the end of his life (Part III of *The Creation*). We are instantly reminded of Filippo's Aria 'Tu, tu, sposarti', from Act II of *L'infedeltà delusa*, where the music is transfigured by a similar wave of affection to match the words 'senza amor ne carità'. The second point in the work which has always caused an intense silence to fall on the opera house in the performances we have witnessed is Hanswurst's falsetto Aria as a beggarwoman (*als Bettelweib*) – Haydn's knowledge of the horrors of poverty was first-hand, and his sympathy flowed out to the broken old woman, reduced to begging for a crust of bread and perhaps a cup of soup. His E minor Aria (Adagio) even has moments of humour – he relishes his ability to show the beggarwoman's shortage of breath, her pounding heart (old and faint, *pp*, as Haydn's score shows us), but it is all done with an unfailing sense of charity and tenderness.[1]

The other German operas, except for *Philemon und Baucis*, have not survived. In the Benedictine Monastery of Seitenstetten, there was discovered the music to a play in

1 Literature on the background of the *commedia dell'arte* and its transformation into Hanswurstiada: Karl von Görner, *Der Hans Wurst-Streit in Wien und Joseph von Sonnenfels*, Vienna 1884, Robert Lach, *Sebastian Sailers 'Schöpfung' in der Musik*, Vienna 1917. Robert Haas, 'Die Musik in der Wiener deutschen Steggreifkomödie', in *Studien zur Musikwissenschaft* 12. Heft, Vienna 1925. *Deutsche Komödienarien 1754–1785 (Denkmäler der Tonkunst in Österreich* XXXIII, Band 64 (Hass), 1926. The second volume of this project, ed. Camillo Schoenbaum and Herbert Zeman, appeared as vol. 121, 1971). E. K. Blümml and Gustav Gugitz, *Alt-Wiener Thespiskarren: Die Frühzeit der Wiener Vorstadtbühnen*, Vienna 1925. Max Pirker, *Teutsche Arien, Welche auf dem Kayserlich-privilegirten Wienerischen Theatro in unterschiedlich producirten Comoedien, deren Titul hier jedesmahl beygerucket, gesungen worden*, Band I (all that appeared), Vienna 1927. Otto Rommel, *Die Alt-Wiener Volkskomödie: Ihre Geschichte vom Barocken Welt-Theater bis zum Tode Nestroys*, Vienna 1952. Heinz Kindermann, *Theatergeschichte Europas*, Band V ('Von der Aufklärung zur Romantik', 2. Teil), Salzburg 1962, pp. 13ff. Ulf Birnbaumer, *Das Werk des Joseph Felix von Kurz-Bernadon: Versuch einer Genealogie und Dramaturgie der Bernadoniade*, 2 vols., Vienna 1971. Herbert Zeman, 'Das Theaterlied zur Zeit Joseph Haydns, seine theatralische Gestaltung und seine gattungsgeschichtliche Entwicklung', in *Joseph Haydn und die Literatur seiner Zeit*, Eisenstadt 1976, pp. 35–60.

Upper Austrian dialect by Maurus Lindemayer entitled *Die reisende Ceres*, attributed to Haydn. The title page reads '[sign of the Cross] Comͣaedie Arien / a / 4 vocibus / 2. violino / Viola / e / Violone / Auth: Giuseppe / Hayden / Ad me / Josephi / Fierlinger mpria'. Pretty though the music is, in its present textual state the score cannot be more than an arrangement of a (lost) Haydn original: the orchestration and the tempo markings are thoroughly corrupted in the Seitenstetten source, in particular the horn parts which are in their present state either spurious or bowdlerized. There is no reason to believe that Haydn set a piece in Upper Austrian dialect, though he had good relations with several Benedictine monasteries (concerning which see *Haydn: the Early Years 1732–1765*), and his music was much admired in the Upper Austrian monasteries of Kremsmünster, Lambach, Schlierbach and Wilhering. The first performance of *Die reisende Ceres*, edited by Eva Badura-Skoda and conducted by Ernst Märzendorfer, was given during the Salzburg Festival 1977 at Hellbrunn Castle.[1]

When Mr Christopher Raeburn and the author were at Donaueschingen Castle in 1957, Mr Raeburn was kind enough to interrupt his own Mozart research and to copy out the following play-bills from the repertoire of the Franz Grimmer Troupe which was 'playing' Donaueschingen in the season 1778–9. The first is *Le Glorieux* (*Der Großsprecher*), translated from the French original (Falbaire), with music by Haydn; and the second is *Der krumme Teufel* (or as it was now called, *Der hinkende Teufel*):

LE GLORIEUX, oder **Der Großsprecher**, Eine komische Oper in zweyen Aufzügen, Von Herrn Fenovillot von Falbaire, aus dem Französischen übersezt. Wird heute **Mit Hochobrigkeitlicher gnädiger Bewilligung** Von der Franz Grimmerschen Suite producirt, und mit möglichster Accuratesse bearbeitet werden.

Personen.

Don Julio, der Großsprecher.

Frau Alberta von Zankersdorf.

Petina,
Charlotte, } ihre Töchter.

Peter, Diener des Julio.

Vorbericht.

Um dieses vortrefliche Singspiel nach seinem Karakter zu beurtheilen, kann man es billig eine Opera Pastice, oder sogenannte Opera mezo Seria, mezo Buffa, nennen. = = Es ist ein Drama, von dergleichen Gattung wir seit unserm Aufenthalte hier noch keines aufgeführt haben. Wir schmeicheln uns folglich auch um so zuversichtlicher, daß wir uns, und dem Verfasser mit der Production desselben Ehre machen, das einsehende Publikum aber durch diese neue Abwechslung theatralischen Zeitvertreibs auf die angenehmste Art unterhalten werden. Der Stof selbst, als auch die von dem berühmten Herrn Joseph Haiden dazu gesezte und an Ausdrücken ungemein reiche Musik werden sich alles Beyfalls würdig finden lassen: = = Neuheit hat in jeder Sache eine besondere Wirkung, noch mehr aber muß eine solche Neuheit reizen, wenn sie von einem Genie herrühret, und dieß können wir von dem heutigen Stück mit Wahrheit sagen. Der Verfasser hat eine ganz neue Bahn betreten, und uns ein karakteristisches Singspiel geliefert, das von denen gewöhnlichen Opern

1 Score to be published by the Universal Edition. See Eva Badura-Skoda, 'An unknown Singspiel by Joseph Haydn?', in *Report of the Eleventh Congress Copenhagen 1972* (International Musicological Society), I, 236ff.; 'The Influence of the Viennese Popular Comedy on Haydn and Mozart', in *Proceedings of the Royal Musical Association*, vol. 100, London 1974,' pp. 185ff.; 'Zur Salzburger Erstaufführung von Joseph Haydns Singspiel "Die reisende Ceres"', in *Osterreichische Musikzeitschrift* Heft 7/8, 1977, pp. 317ff.

Comiquen in Absicht auf das Niedrig = komische gänzlich abweichet, und uns ganz neue und besondere Scenen darstellt; kurz, man muß es sehn, um sich von allen Schönheiten desselben zu überzeugen. Möchte es uns doch gelingen, sie alle so anschaulich zu machen, wie sie der Verfasser geschildert hat, denn dürfen wir an dem vollkommnesten Beyfall nicht zweifeln.

[in handwriting]
zu dem ein lustiger Prolog = zum Schluß ein Ballet.

[Translation]

Le Glorieux, or Der Großsprecher, a comic opera in two acts by M. Fenovillot de Falbaire, translated from the French. Will be produced today, with permission of the highest authorities, by the Franz Grimmer Troupe and played with the greatest possible accuracy.

Cast
[see the German]
Preface

In order to judge the character of this excellent *Singspiel*, one might easily call it an opera pastiche, or a so-called opera *mezzo-seria, mezzo-buffa*. It is drama of a kind not hitherto produced during our sojourn here. We flatter ourselves therefore the more that we shall do honour to us and to the author; and that the perceptive audience will amuse itself to the utmost when hearing this new kind of theatrical pastime [*sic: Zeitvertreibs*]. The play itself, as well as the highly expressive music which the famous Herr Joseph Haiden has composed will surely be worthy of every success. Novelty has its special effect in any work, but how much more effective must novelty be if it comes from a genius; and that we can truthfully say about today's piece. The author has tread an entirely new path and given us a characteristic *Singspiel* entirely different in purpose from the low comedy of the usual opéra comique; he has portrayed new and special scenes; in short, one has to see it to be convinced of all its beauties. If we are successful in portraying everything as graphically as the author has here described it, we cannot fail to win the public's full approbation.
[In handwriting:] A merry prologue to begin; at the end a ballet.

Mit gnädigster Bewilligung. Heute wird von der Franz = Grimmerschen Suite deutscher Operisten und junger Schauspieler vorgestellt werden, Ein mit den artigsten Verwicklungen versehenes, und mit vollkommener Lustbarkeit angefülltes, extra wohl ausgearbeites von Herrn von Kurz verfertigtes

Lust = und Singspiel,
in Versen und drey Aufzügen
genannt:
LE DIABLE BOITEUX,
Oder:
Der hinkende Teufel.

Personen.

Arnoldus, ein Mediciner.	Lepold.
Argande, seine Schwester.	Zwey Notarien.
Fiametta, ein Ziehmädel.	Der hinkende Teufel Asmodeus.
Bernardon, Diener des Doktors.	

Die Musik ist von dem berühmten Herrn Hayden, Kapellmeister, des Durchlauchtigsten Fürsten Esterhazy.

Um von dieser Piece nicht viel Großsprechens und Rodomandaten zu machen, so versichern wir in Kürze nur so viel, daß sie wegen denen vielen vorkommenden Arien und intriguanten Passagen, eine drr [*sic*] lustigsten und kurzweiligsten Piecen des Grimmerschen Theaters seye, bittende, uns mit zahlreichem Zurspruch zu beehren.

Den Beschluß macht ein neues Ballet,
Genannt:
Das Kind in der Wiege.

N.B. Um allen Unordnungen vorzubeugen, und weder Publikum noch Schauspieler zu genieren kann niemand aufs Theater gelassen werden.
N.B. Man bittet, die Comödien = Zedel bis zur Abreise aufzubehalten.

[Donaueschingen Archives]

[Translation]
With most gracious approval. Today the Franz Grimmer Troupe of German operatic singers and young actors and actresses will perform: A comedy and Singspiel in verses and three acts called LE DIABLE BOITEAUX or *Der hinkende Teufel* by Herr von Kurz, a piece with the most delightful intrigues and of the most amusing kind, particularly carefully worked out.

Cast
[see the German]
The Music is by the famous Herr Hayden, Kapellmeister of
His Serene Highness, Prince Esterhazy.

In order not to make too many promises or rodomontades about this piece, we will in short say that because of its many arias and intricate passages, it is one of the most merry and entertaining pieces of the Grimmer repertoire, and we ask you to honour us with a large attendance.
The conclusion will be a new ballet entitled, *Das Kind in der Wiege*.
N.B. To avoid all confusion, and not to upset public or actors, no one is allowed on the stage.
N.B. It is requested that the playbills be retained until the Troupe leaves.

Since not another trace of the intriguing *Le Glorieux* (XXIXb:B) has ever been found, we can add nothing about the work's authenticity or chronological position. *Der krumme Teufel* (XXIXb:1) continued to enjoy a thriving life of its own as late as 1778–9, and it is a real mystery how this *Singspiel*, the most popular opera Haydn ever composed, has not survived except for the libretto (in several versions).

Il mondo della luna, dramma giocoso
(XXVIII:7; 1777)

Scoring: (first version, 1777?): 3 S (Clarice, Flaminia, Lisetta), A Castrato (Ecclitico), 2 T (Ernesto, Cecco), B (Buonafede), 4 choral bass parts ('Scolari', 'Cavalieri'), 2 fl., 2 ob., 2 bsn., 2 cor., 2 trpt., timp., str. (harpsichord *continuo*) (Second version, as first performed in August 1777): Ecclitico – tenor; Ernesto – alto castrato; Lisetta – alto. Note that, as in *Die Feuersbrunst*, Haydn used two flutes, two horns and two trumpets, but no clarinets (which he had in the orchestra in August 1777).
Principal Sources: Four autograph fragments: **A** EH Budapest, Ms. Mus. I.138 and (Overture fragment) Ms. Mus. I. 42. Overture (*Sinfonia*) signed 1777. End of opera signed 'Fine dell'opera / laus Deo et B. V. M. e[t] O: S:'. **B** Preussische Staatsbibliothek, Berlin (Grüssau, Poland), Mus. ms. autogr. Jos. Haydn 27 (photographs owned by the Staatsbibliothek and H.C.R.L.). **C** Bibliothèque de l'Opéra, Paris, Ms. 138. **D** Universitätsbibliothek Tübingen (from the coll. of Robert Haas, Vienna). Johann Traeg owned a complete autograph and made MS. copies for sale, c. 1799–1800, of which two have survived: 1) Österreichische Nationalbibliothek,

Musiksammlung Codex 17 621 (even includes 'In Nomine Domini' at the beginning) and 2) National Janáček Music Library, Brno, ČSSR, from Náměšť (Namest) Castle – does not include 'In Nomine Domini' (which the first copyist may have included without knowing what it really meant); cat. A17023.
Libretto: Carlo Goldoni (Galuppi: Teatro S. Moisè, Venice, 1750) with the revisions used in the setting composed in 1775 by Gennaro Astaritta (c. 1749–1803) for S. Moisè, Venice.
Critical edition: Bärenreiter 3186 (Landon, 1958), at which time **A** and **D** were not yet available.
First performance of the critical edition: Holland Festival 1959. Ecclitico: Michel Hamel; Ernesto: Luigi Alva; Buonafede: Marcello Cortis; Clarice: Mariella Adani; Flaminia: Biancamaria Casoni; Lisetta: Bruna Rizzoli; Cecco: Paulo Pedani. The Netherlands Chamber Orchestra, conducted by Carlo Maria Giulini (who had previously performed Acts I and II in the original version for RAI in Rome). Producer: Maurice Sarrazin.
First recording: Ecclitico: Luigi Alva; Ernesto: Lucia Valentini Terrani; Buonafede: Domenico Trimarchi; Clarice: Edith Mathis; Flaminia:

Arleen Augér; Lisetta: Frederica von Stade; Cecco: Anthony Rolfe Johnson; Orchestre de Chambre de Lausanne; Choeur de la Suisse Romande; conducted by Antal Dorati; recorded in September 1977 (producer: Erik Smith) and released in 1978 – Philips 6769 003.
Literature: Geiringer 1932, 110f. Wirth I, 107 *et passim*. Wirth II, 32f. Bartha-Somfai, 71, 188–97. Günter Thomas in *Haydn-Studien* II/2 (1969), 122–4. Landon in *NOHM* VII (1973), pp. 192ff.
Synopsis of the plot: The old Buonafede is a vigilant father who keeps a firm grip on his two daughters, Clarice and Flaminia, as well as his servant-girl, Lisetta. Ecclitico, posing as an astronomer, is in love with Clarice and his friend, the rather stiff cavalier Ernesto, loves Flaminia, while Ernesto's servant, Cecco, has designs on Lisetta. Ecclitico's name derives from Ecclitica, the sun's orbit, and using his knowledge of astronomy he shows Buonafede life on the moon seen through a telescope: the delightful visions are arranged by Ecclitico's 'scolari'. Seeing the success of this operation, Ecclitico persuades Buonafede to make a trip to the moon, where his scholars and Cecco as the Moon Emperor create an enchanted atmosphere in which Buonafede is induced to arrange the triple marriage (Ecclitico-Clarice, Ernesto-Flaminia, Cecco-Lisetta). At the dénouement (end of Act II), Buonafede is furious at being duped but resigns himself to the inevitable, including Lisetta's marriage; he had designs on the girl himself. In Act III, which is a typical Goldoni 'appendix', the high-point is the great love duet between Ecclitico and Clarice, followed by the 'Coro' with the words, 'Dal mondo della luna a noi ci vien fortuna, ci vien prosperità!'

Haydn expended a great deal of loving attention on this large-scale opera, the biggest since *L'incontro improvviso*. He rewrote almost the whole work, partly (it would seem) from an artistic standpoint, e.g. the tripartite Intermezzo-Recitativo-Aria of Buonafede (Sc. 3, Atto I°), and partly because the Jermoli couple, destined to sing Ecclitico and Lisetta (and even printed in the cast list of the 1777 première) left before the work was performed. Originally Haydn intended to give the alto castrato Pietro Gherardi the role of Ecclitico but than changed his mind and allotted the rather featureless part of Ernesto to the singer. Of this earlier version, we have issued Ernesto's beautiful Aria, 'Begli occhi vezzosi', in the version for tenor in F major;[1] later Haydn rewrote it in E flat and then in D for castrato.

This was the first of our Haydn operas resuscitated at the Holland Festival: it was followed by *L'infedeltà delusa*, *Le pescatrici* and *La fedeltà premiata*. *Il mondo della luna*, which had already been revived in a heavily revised version by Mark Lothar and W. M. Treichtlinger in 1932 (Edition Adler), proved to be a substantial stage success, to which the then current cult of Sputniks and Thors no doubt contributed. It contains many witty and delightful moments. We might single out the richly scored Aria con balletto that Buonafede, enchanted with life on the moon, sings in Atto II°: 'Che mondo amabile', where the singer is instructed to whistle together with the woodwind. Haydn took great care with the secco and accompanied recitatives: there is a wonderful colouristic touch in Scene 10 of Atto I°, just before the Finale (when Buonafede – 'good faith' – is taken on the trip to the moon), when after a long secco, the strings enter at bar 115 on a C major chord and Buonafede sings 'Mondo, mondaccio mio, per sempre t'abbandono'. The keys are used to symbolize earth and moon. The earth presents itself in C major with the Overture and again when Buonafede says he will leave it for ever. The moon is shown as the curtain opens on Atto I° (the stage directions say: 'night with the moon and a star-studded sky', and to the text of 'O Luna lucente' E flat rises softly from the pit. Thus when Ecclitico takes Buonafede on his trip to the moon (Finale Atto I°), the key is also E flat; and while looking at the telescope, Buonafede is accompanied first in D and then in E flat. The climax of Atto II° (Finale) moves into D major, and this is now the key in which the opera also ends at the end of the last act. The large-scale finales have always been admired: that of Atto II° is 437 bars long and is skilfully constructed: as the tension mounts, the tempi increase. Starting with an 8–8 Moderato, we move to 2–4, then

1 Haydn-Mozart Presse, 1964 (score, piano score, parts). HMP 122–3.

3–8, then Presto 2–4 and (the same tempo) barred C. It is a typical piece in which the basic pulse remains the same and is simply divided or the metre halved (e.g. Presto in two-four and then barred C).

Flaminia's music is most interesting. Her big C major Aria, 'Ragion nell'alma siede', has now become a feature and speciality of Haydn's operas – a brilliant coloratura display-piece which, however, is taken far from the realms of empty fioratura by a beautiful middle section in C minor with softly undulating strings in quavers. We will find just this same procedure in the Genio's brilliant Aria in *L'anima del filosofo* (1791).[1] Flaminia's Aria in the next act, 'Se la mia stella' (F major), has felicitous solo wind writing and was also used in the *Singspiel* version of *Philemon und Baucis*.

Haydn hardly attempts any characterization of his stage figures: the plot was not destined for such treatment. Yet even at its face value, such a figure as Ernesto remains rather unreal and un-lifelike, without flesh and blood. Haydn compensates for this by writing exceptionally fine music for him, as Mozart was to do with a similarly stiff figure, Don Ottavio. He does the same thing with the (strictly speaking) unnecessary third act, about which we have spoken before in connection with *Le pescatrici* and *Lo speziale*. Starting with a brusque Intermezzo in G minor (pivot from earthly D major to what follows), Haydn then proceeds to write the greatest single piece in the whole opera: the B flat Duet, 'Un certo ruscelletto', whose magical slow melody and undulating semiquavers in the accompaniment bring us close to the world of Mozart; but even here, Haydn's omnipresent sense of irony leads him to abandon the star-studded heavens of his B flat Largo for a pert little Presto, 'Ah furba, furbetta, da me che pretendi?'

To sum up: vastly more complex in every respect than *Die Feuersbrunst*, much more interesting on the stage than *L'incontro improvviso*, Haydn's *Il mondo della luna* is an important step in his development as an operatic composer. Like almost everything Haydn composed for the stage at this period, it is far too long (uncut, it would run to about three hours and twenty minutes), and of course with our historical hindsight, we miss the guiding hand of a Mozartian character development. This was the third and last of Goldoni's libretti set to music by Haydn, and if we may find some aspects of the book static and, literally, out of this world, Goldoni was infinitely more witty, better organized (even in this Astaritta version, with which Goldoni probably had nothing whatever to do) and with more genuine variety than the book of the next opera that Haydn was unwise enough to set.

The heavily symphonic Overture served Haydn as the beginning of what would become a very popular Symphony (No. 63, 'La Roxelane'); but as we shall see, he had to reduce the large orchestration to more normal Eszterháza proportions and in doing so we of course lost some of the splendid original orchestration: *vide infra*, pp. 561ff.

La vera costanza, dramma giocoso per musica
(XXVIII:8; 1778?)

Scoring (only revised version of 1785 has survived complete): 3 S (Rosina, Baronessa Irene, Lisetta), 3 T (Conte Errico, Marchese Ernesto, Masino), B (Villotto), 1 fl. (in Anfossi's scene, 'Mi quale ascolto', 2 fl.), 2 ob., 2 bsn., 2 cor., timp., str. (harpsichord *continuo*).

Principal sources: (1) The performing score for the 1785 revival at Eszterháza, partly written by Haydn and partly by several Esterházy copyists (including Johann Schellinger, Pietro Travaglia and the young Johann Elssler), Conservatoire de Musique, Paris (now Bibliothèque Nationale, Ms.

---

1 See *Haydn in England 1791–1795*, pp. 349f.

1383/1384); with a list of the original cast ('1ma Signora Ripamonti', 'Bianchi', the others illegible); signed by Haydn at the end 'Fine dell'opera Laus Deo 785'. (2) Score from the Esterházy workshop with many holograph corrections, Conservatoire de Musique, Brussels. (3) Score from the Esterházy workshop, National Janáček Music Library, Brno, ČSSR, from Náměšť (Namest) Castle partly by Johann Schellinger; in the Count's Recit. 'Mira il campo' and Aria 'A trionfar', this source has C *alto* horns, timpani 'e Tamburo' in both Rec. & Aria. (4) Scores, one by Johann Schellinger (signed at the end 'JSch – Esterhaz') and the other also from the Esterházy workshop, Landesbibliothek, Weimar. (5) Of the single sources, we may single out some extracts: Esterházy scores of three numbers, 'Tutta ... 1779', Benedictine Monastery of Göttweig – Finale (Atto II°), Rosina's 'Eccomi' & 'Care spiagge', also a score of Rosina's *Scena* 'Misera' and Aria 'Dove fuggo'. The latter is also found in the Gesellschaft der Musikfreunde, Vienna, where it is marked 'Scrit[t]a p: la Ripamonti l'anno 1779 à Esterhaz', and a set of parts, copied by Joseph Elssler (died 1782) of Rosina's Scene 'Eccomi giunta al colmo' and Aria 'Care spiagge' in the Österreichische Nationalbibliothek, Musiksammlung. Overture; issued by Artaria as No. 4 of 'Sei Sinfonie' 1782 – an authentic concert version.
Libretto: Francesco Puttini, revised by Pietro Travaglia.
Critical editions: Universal Edition (Landon, 1975); *Joseph Haydn Werke* XXV/8 (Walter), 1976. German adaptation by G. Schwalbe and W. Zimmer as 'List und Liebe', Henschelverlag 1959 (distribution in the West: Universal Edition).
First performance in modern times: Deutschlandsender, 1959. Masino: Dietrich Musch; Rosina: Eva-Regina Schulze; Conte Errico ('Erminio'): Martin Titzmann; Baronessa: Hannelore Kuhse; Ernesto: Hans Ziehnert; Villotto: Rainer Süss; Lisetta: Hannelore Diehn. Kammerorchester der Staatskapelle Schwerin, conducted by Kurt Masur. The Henschelverlag German version.
First recording: Rosina: Jessye Norman; Lisetta: Helen Donath; Conte Errico: Claes H. Ahnsjö; Villotto: Wladimiro Ganzarolli; Masino: Domenico Trimarchi; Baronesse Irene: Kari Lövaas; Marchese Ernesto: Anthony Rolfe Johnson. Orchestre de Chambre de Lausanne, conducted by Antan Dorati. Philips 6703 077 (producer: Erik Smith), 1977. Using Universal Edition material.
Literature: Geiringer 1932, 111. Wirth I, 39ff. *et passim.* Wirth II, 33ff. Landon in *HJB* I, 132ff., 215f. Landon in *NOHM*, VII (1973), pp. 191f.
Synopsis of the plot: Baroness Irene cannot succumb to Marquis Ernesto's charms until she is able to break up the relationship of her nephew, Count Errico, to the fisher-girl Rosina, and to find a suitable match for him. To this end she embarks on a ship together with Ernesto, her lady-in-waiting Lisetta and the wealthy and slightly dim-witted Villotto, whom she proposes to marry off to Rosina. She has no idea that Rosina and Errico are secretly married: the Count had to leave her shortly after the marriage, and Rosina has a young child. A violent storm drives the ship to a fishing village on the coast, and Masino, Rosina's brother, helps the ship's passengers to find safety on land; he places them in Rosina's house. The Baroness loses no time in proposing to Rosina a marriage with Villotto: Rosina's confusion is considered maidenly inexperience. Masino tries to help his sister by frightening off Villotto. Suddenly Count Errico appears and threatens Villotto with death if he does not desist from his plans. There now begins a curiously sadistic attempt to test Rosina's fidelity. Errico acts aloof and cool, driving the confused Villotto, who hardly knows how to unite the Baroness's machinations with Errico's threats, into Rosina's arms. In a secret rendez-vous, which is of course overheard by the Baroness and her nephew, Ernesto attempts to persuade Rosina to marry Villotto so that Ernesto will not lose the chance of marrying the wealthy Baroness. The confusion reaches its highpoint when the jealous Count attempts to force Villotto to kill Rosina or be killed himself. Villotto's escape from this displeasing prospect is to request time to make his last will. Lisetta, informed of everything by Rosina, attempts to persuade the Count of Rosina's faithfulness, and the Count, never a very reasonable man, suddenly sees himself as Orpheus seeking his Eurydice. He must find Rosina and make amends for everything. Rosina, in desperation, has taken her child and fled to the mountains, where she finds refuge in a ruined tower, and there Masino, also exhausted, falls asleep after fleeing the village. Villotto pursues and decides that it would be more interesting to kill Masino rather than Rosina, who, he thinks, has certain charms which death would render uninteresting. Lisetta, however, arrives to prevent murder, and hard on her heels arrive the Baroness and the Marquis, also looking for Rosina. At the end, Count Errico arrives; he is greeted by a small boy who directs the Count to the boy's mother, lying unconscious. The Count finds Rosina, and in the midst of their grand reconciliation arrive the Baroness, the Marquis, Lisetta, Villotto and Masino. They accuse Rosina of whorish aspirations, which the Count proudly denies, saying that Rosina is his wife and worthy of respect. After one last intrigue, which we will pass over in silence, the Baroness presses Rosina to her heart and, in turn, gives her hand to the ever-ready Marquis.

The recent attempts of Austrian historians to rehabilitate Haydn's literary taste pale before the inanities of the libretti which he set to music, one after the other, in this period. After (as it were) abandoning Goldoni, we move to Puttini, which was supposed to be the basis of Haydn's entry into the operatic world of Vienna. Bad enough to choose such a fatuous book, worse to choose one already set to music by Pasquale Anfossi for Vienna in 1776. Leaving apart the question of the Vienna commission, we must now proceed to the history of the opera. Apparently it was destroyed in the fire of 1779. There were, however, certain numbers which had been copied beforehand and even circulated by Viennese copying houses, and Haydn himself sold the Overture to Artaria in 1782 (turned into a five-movement 'Symphony' by the addition of a ballet from *Il mondo della luna* and by using the opening scene of the opera for the third and fifth movements). In 1785, the Prince persuaded Haydn to revive *La vera costanza*, and to this end Haydn had to remake the score. He and his team of copyists therefore proceeded as follows: the copyists wrote out the music that had survived complete. This was: (1) Overture, i.e. the first two movements of the Artaria concert version; (2) Aria No. 2 (Baronessa), 'Non s'innalza'; (3) Rec. and Aria No. 12 (Rosina) (Landon 13), 'Misera' and 'Dove fuggo'; (4) an insertion that Haydn bodily lifted from the Anfossi setting, (Haydn's) No. 14 (Landon 15), Rec. and Aria (Conte), 'Mi quale ascolto' and 'Or che torna'; and (5) Rec. and Aria (Rosina), 'Eccomi giunta al colmo' and 'Care spiagge'. Haydn then sat down with the printed libretto and wrote out the rest of the work in his own hand. Did he have any other sources? We have drawn attention to the story, related in Framery's *Notice sur Joseph Haydn*,[1] of Pleyel's having secretly copied *Armida* which is burned up in the fire(!) and then presenting Haydn with his 'lost' work. If, as we assume, Pleyel secretly copied *La vera costanza*, he may have made some kind of 'shorthand' version of it, perhaps a 'short' score. Be that as it may, the autograph of 1785 shows clearly that Haydn actually rewrote many of the recitatives, and the reason we know that is because a series of sketches to the 1778 version, in Haydn's hand, has survived: the sketches are (1) in the Preussische Staatsbibliothek, Berlin[2] and consist of sketches to Scenes 1–3, Aria No. 4 (Rosina) 'Con un tenero sospiro', Aria No. 6 (Lisetta) 'Io son poverina', and (2) in the Conservatoire de Musique (now Bibliothèque Nationale, Paris), which include sketches for Scenes 13–15 of the Finale to Atto I° and, most importantly, to the Rec. and Aria No. 14 (Landon 15). When Haydn prepared the 1785 score, it will be seen that he completely rewrote the recitatives, which are quite different from those of the sketches, but retained the music of the arias – except, that is, for No. 14 (15). In 1778, he had obviously composed this number, but in 1785 he simply had a copyist insert the pretty setting by Anfossi (which had, however, two flutes as against Haydn's one). The Anfossi setting is not only in the Paris 1785 score (i.e. the Eszterháza conducting score for the 1785 revival), but Haydn allowed it to be included in workshop copies for abroad: both the Brno and Weimar MS. scores include the Anfossi setting without noting that Haydn is not the composer, but in the revised Brussels MS. score, it is, significantly, dropped. Otherwise, Haydn used two kinds of ink when writing the 1785 score, and this is particularly clear in the ensemble scenes of the first act: he first penned the vocal parts, and only after they were complete did he add the orchestral sections. This would lead credence to the theory that Pleyel's 'score' was primarily a kind of shorthand vocal score, which Haydn could use, relying on his (obviously exceptional) memory to complete the rest of the score.

---

1 See Appendix, p. 757.
2 The sketches were in depot at Marburg when we studied them: Mus. ms. autogr. Jos. Haydn 29. 4° format, 32,1 × 22,8 cm. with watermarks: horizontal chain-lines, letters GF (Galvani Fratelli) under ornament. Our watermark master-lists give so many varying dates for the GF paper – including one as late as 1787 (Mozart Quintet K.515, autograph, Library of Congress) – that we cannot attempt a dating through the watermarks.

From the 1785 Eszterháza revival, the work made its way to Pressburg, where it was given in German translation by Franz Xaver Giržik for the Erdödy Theatre under the direction of Hubert Kumpf (first performance: 30 January 1786, repeated in 1786 and 1787). In its new guise as 'Der flatterhafte Liebhaber oder Der Sieg der Beständigkeit' (or 'Die wahre Beständigkeit') it was given in Pest in 1789, at the Landstraße Theatre in Vienna in 1790, and at Brünn (Brno) in 1792, but contrary to what Mr Horst Walter says in the Preface to the new edition (*Joseph Haydn Werke*, p. IX), it was certainly not 'ein durchschlagender Erfolg', which are words that should apply to Mozart's *Die Entführung aus dem Serail* or Paisiello's *Il barbiere di Siviglia* and not to an opera which, when played at Brünn in 1792, 'pleased less than the beautiful music deserved.'[1]

What was in Haydn's mind when he opened the libretto of a work like *La vera costanza* and began to compose it? Contrary to the assumption of Helmut Wirth (*Haydn als Dramatiker*, 1941), we do not believe that, like Mozart or Richard Strauss, he demanded changes in his textbooks or that he had a 'shaping hand' in the writing of new libretti,[2] i.e. ones especially designed for Eszterháza, such as *L'incontro improvviso* or (it would seem) *La canterina* and certainly *Die Feuersbrunst* and the other German operas. This is the reason, too, why Haydn was perfectly content to re-compose libretti which were already in circulation by such renowned masters as Anfossi (*La vera costanza*), Cimarosa (*L'infedeltà fedele* = *La fedeltà premiata*) or *L'isola disabitata* which (as we shall see) had been set *inter alia* by Holzbauer, Jommelli, Traetta and Naumann. In fact, with the exception of *Armida* (q.v.) all the Italian operas of this period arrived at Eszterháza shop-worn, some very much so, and even *Armida* was largely plundered from a setting used by Gazzaniga. Part of this curious attitude on Haydn's part was, of course, that he never expected his operas to circulate beyond Eszterháza, and he must have been surprised to see his *La vera costanza* performed (and the full score thereof printed) as 'Laurette' in Paris in 1791.

Although he was always captivated by certain parts of these libretti, Haydn must have regarded large parts of them with a jaundiced eye, and we may note a certain cynical sense of humour with which Haydn approached points in the text which another composer would have regarded as a dramatic highpoint. Haydn treats as a farce the storm at the beginning of *La vera costanza*, with its inviting text, 'Che burrasca, che tempesta, che paura' – inviting because of what an opening operatic storm might be if taken seriously (obviously we think of Verdi's *Otello* and Wagner's *Die Walküre*). Haydn does not take it seriously and treats it with the same Don Alfonso touch as he would in the 'Queste due vittimi' scene (the Finale of Atto II° in *La fedeltà premiata*).

Nevertheless, *La vera costanza*, like all these stage works, served its composer admirably as a proving ground for all those large-scale forms which he could not display in his instrumental works (sonatas, quartets, symphonies). He was also experimenting in the development of the popular style, the ramifications of which pervade almost every work of this period. At the end of the Introduzione to Atto I°, we have an interesting application of this popular style, i.e. the transference of a perky Viennese instrumental tune to a vocal work (of which we have seen many examples in *Die Feuersbrunst*:

---

1 *Haydn in England 1791–1795*, p. 100.
2 See also Georg Feder in *Haydn-Studien* II/2 (1969), pp. 126ff.

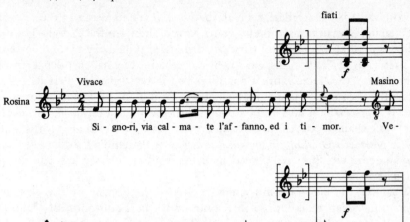

No. 3, Masino's Aria, 'So che una bestia sei', is another example of such a witty and fetching melody. But lest it be thought that Haydn was only concerned with the light, popular style, we may consider No. 7, Conte Errico's Recitative, 'Mira il campo all'intorno', and Aria, 'A trionfar', in which the score includes C *alto* horns and (the only place in the whole opera) timpani (in some sources also 'tamburi', military drums, as well). This Aria is a magnificent gesture and composed in a totally new form. It starts like a typical 'war' aria, of which we shall see other examples (also with high horns and drums) in *Orlando Paladino* and *Armida*. There is then a gentle middle section in G, with an attractive solo oboe part, which is broken off in a kind of fast accompanied recitative and a new swift section, but in C minor – an almost unprecedented step in Haydn's and other composers' operas of the epoch – completes this extraordinary and powerful number. 'Oimè! che smania orribile' is the excuse for sweeping series of syncopations that rage through the orchestra and lash out at the words 'e fuori già dal mondo'. When we are witnesses of such a spectacular moment – and there is another towards the end of *Armida* – we must regret that Haydn's heart and mind were less involved in many stretches of his operas.

The highpoints of the work from the musical standpoint are the ensemble finales, which also occupy positions even longer than those of *Il mondo della luna*. The Finale of *La vera costanza*'s first act contains 633 bars, that to the second act 651 (some comparisons: *Il mondo della luna*, Atto I° Finale – 188 bars, Atto II° Finale – 437 bars; *La fedeltà premiata*, Atto I° Finale – 822 bars, Atto II° Finale – 506 bars; *Orlando Paladino*, Atto I° Finale – 539 bars; Atto II° Finale – 433 bars). There are a thousand felicitous details in these finales: consider the shift from the 'broken' accompaniment to the smooth quaver legati (also marked *pp* as a further way of drawing attention to itself) and the entrance of G minor, 'Oh, che gran giorno è questo' (opposite).

Mozart experts know that he often writes a peculiarly piercing tenor line, lying rather high in the *tessitura* and having a kind of emotional power of its own: it is very hard to describe in words the combination produced on the sensitive listener of an extreme legato line which is not tense in itself combined with a tessitura in which the very character of the voice is rather 'tight' and thus tense. But those familiar with Mozart's operas will remember the music of Don Ottavio: not only the arias (above all

'Dalla sua pace') but also the extraordinarily moving section in the Sextet (No. 20), when he and Donna Anna enter and the music swerves into D major with 'seinen hellen Trompetenklängen' and, as Abert continues, hits us 'fast mit physischer Gewalt'.[1] This 'edle und warme Art der Kantilene' is not only Ottavio's property; it is a whole Mozartian concept that we also find in *Die Zauberflöte* (Tamino) and, of course, in *Così fan tutte* (though not in *Figaro*, there being no real principal tenor part in the opera). We had always imagined – never having heard quite this kind of highly strung legato in Italian opera of the period, not even in Paisiello who, however, often seems to be on the edge of writing such tenor parts – that this must have been Mozart's personal contribution. It was not, as matters turn out, Mozart's but Haydn's. As an example, we cite a few bars from the Finale of Act I:

1   *W. A. Mozart*, 7. Auflage, Leipzig 1956, vol. II, 437.

Apart from the lay-out of the parts (the characteristic crossings of the tenor above the [written] soprano line), listeners will be struck at once by the Mozartian quality of the music altogether: which again shows that we have musical-historical facts all wrong. (Mozart borrowed from *La vera costanza*, incidentally, when composing his Imperial parody, 'Ich möchte wohl der Kayser seyn', K.539, in 1788: cf. 'So che una bestia sei', Masino's Aria in Atto I°).

The Finale of which this extract is part must certainly rank as the greatest part of the opera and one of the finest Haydn ever wrote, surpassed only by those in *La fedeltà premiata*. It is in a number of separate sections; but the whole has a unity and forward-drivingness, a beautifully balanced series of tensions and releases, the subtlety and craftsmanship of which one scarcely believed to have existed before *Figaro*.[1]

In the construction of these finales, Haydn makes use of a rather complicated technical device which was also previously thought to be primarily Mozart's invention. We cite from the most civilized account of the matter known to us:

[George Hogarth, *Musical History, Biography, and Criticism: Being a General Survey of Music from the earliest Period to the Present Time*, London, 1835, pp. 264ff. Hogarth (1783–1870) was Charles Dickens's father-in-law and critic of the *Morning Chronicle*. Referring to Mozart's operatic school, he writes:]

Its chief peculiarity consists in the fullness of the orchestral parts; and hence it has been called, by M. Choron and others, the *dramatic symphony*. In the operas of Mozart, the accompaniments, even of the airs, display a richness of harmony, and a variety on the combinations of the different instruments, previously unexampled; while, during the long finales and other concerted pieces, in which the most animated and busy scenes of the piece are carried on, the music of the orchestra consists of a series of movements which are written and played in the symphony style, and, instead of accompanying, are accompanied by, the performers on the stage, who carry on the dialogue in a succession of vocal phrases written *upon* the instrumental symphony, while their motions are regulated by its time.... This method, accordingly, was so attractive, that its universal adoption has made all the older music of the stage appear meagre and unsatisfactory; and modern audiences will hardly listen with patience even to the masterpieces of Gluck, Piccin(n)i, or Paisiello; an unhappy, but necessary consequence of the ceaseless changes to which every description of music – save the highest of all – is liable ...

1 This section is taken, usually *verbatim*, from our discussion of the opera in *HJB* I, 215–8.

In Scene XV of this Finale, 'Che miro, Rosina?' we find a fine example of this 'fragmented' use of the voice to *supplement* the action in the orchestra, in the manner so well described by Hogarth:

In the Finale to Atto IIº there are equally many memorable pages. The magnificent F sharp minor section, 'Presto si cerchi' includes a breathtaking contrast, *pp*, 'anche sotterra s'ha da trovar' which is yet one more example of the kind of word painting (*Thonmahlerey*) which always moved Haydn to his finest efforts. The ending uses a Viennese popular tune of the kind that grace many a Haydn instrumental finale:

In this section, we suddenly find a totally unprepared third drop to B flat, which serves to illustrate 'Che stupore'; and we are suddenly reminded of a similar drop into B flat during *The Seasons*.[1] This is a typical case in which these operas serve as uniquely valuable training grounds for tonal, formal and orchestral-vocal experiments on the large, indeed panoramic scale. Without these operas we would have never had the effortless mastery so constantly revealed in the late Masses and Oratorios.

The last number of Finale II is constructed with an eye for canonic entries (a speciality in Haydn's operatic finales, as we shall see):

Towards the end, there is a double announcement of a section which includes the following, highly original harmonic twist. (Note, yet again, the lovely tenor 'crossing' above the soprano written line at bars 4ff. of the example overleaf.)

The text tells us: 'I know how it will end', but in comic opera of the kind Haydn was now setting to music, the ending is never *that* certain, and this is what Haydn whispers in our ear with his deceptive cadence – an ambivalent shadow passes over the music and once more we are poignantly reminded of music's greatest master, whose own matchless stage works were soon to persuade the perceptive Haydn to abandon the field in which he was now toiling with such interesting results.

1 *Haydn: the Late Years 1801–1809*, p. 147.

The point about these finales is that, using traditional Italian forms, Haydn has written pieces in the great Viennese classical style: by having recourse to motivic stress, developmental technique and the other tools of the Viennese symphonic and chamber musical forms, Haydn has wedded Italian opera to Viennese intellectuality. Historically, these finales composed from 1777 to 1782 – unless those of *La vera costanza* were entirely rewritten in 1785, which is of course possible – are milestones, in that they carry considerably further a synthesis which one can see as early as *Lo speziale* (1768) but which, until *La vera costanza*, was not developed to such an extent either in scope or in formal intricacy. Musically, too, these finales show that at this period Haydn really was pouring the major part of his creative fantasy into operas and not into symphonies (most of which are mediocre potpourris) or quartets (we must remember that between 1772 and 1781 there are none, and none except Op. 42 [1785] after that till 1787).

L'isola disabitata, azione teatrale
(XXVIII:9; 1779)

Scoring: 2 S (Costanza, Silvia), T (Gernando), B (Enrico [Ernesto]), fl., 2 ob., bsn., 2 hns., timp., str. *Principal sources*: (1) Autograph. (a) Bars 1–57 of the Overture, Preussische Staatsbibliothek, Berlin (during World War II in Grüssau, Poland); photographs: J. P. Larsen. (b) Quartetto (No. 13) in Haydn's shortened and revised version, 1802 (with '2 Clarini o Corni in C. alto'; in earlier sources no provision for trumpets), signed 'Fine G: H mpria'; Dr A. Wilhelm, Basel. (2) Authentic MS. score, 1781, by Anonymous 23, with corrections by Haydn (*vide supra*, p. 453), Library of Congress, Washington, D.C. (3) Authentic MS. score Biblioteca Nazionale, Turin, mostly by

Anonymous 48, i.e. probably the young Johann Elssler. (4) MS. score in German, 'Die wüste Insel', with corrections by Haydn, Preussische Staatsbibliothek, Berlin, cat. 9913/4. (5) Authentic MS. score from the Esterházy work-shop, Landesbibliothek, Weimar. (6) MS. score (possibly from the Esterházy workshop?), Zentralbibliothek, Zürich. (7) Quartetto (No. 13) in authentic MS. score by Anonymous 23, EH Budapest, Ms. Mus. I. 82. Of the Overture's sources, we may mention: (1) Artaria's first edition, as No. 1 of 'Sei Sinfonie' 1782 – an authentic edition. (2) MS. score, probably by a professional Viennese copyist in the 1780s,

Gesellschaft der Musikfreunde, Vienna, XII 7524.
Libretto: Pietro Metastasio, first set by Giuseppe Bonno (Vienna 1752).
Critical edition: Bärenreiter-Verlag, Kassel, 1976 (Landon). Overture: Edition Eulenburg 1124 (Landon, 1958).
First performance in modern times: Vienna Court Opera, 1909 (in connection with the Haydn Centenary), conducted by Felix von Weingartner.

First recording (using new Bärenreiter edition): Silvia: Linda Zoghby; Costanza: Norma Lerer; Gernando: Luigi Alva; Enrico (Ernesto): Renato Brunson; Orchestre de Chambre de Lausanne, conducted by Antal Dorati; recorded in May and June 1977 (producer: Erik Smith) and released in 1978 – Philips 6700 119.
Literature: Wirth I, 142ff., Wirth II, 43–5. Bartha-Somfai, 214.

When Weingartner performed *Die wüste Insel* (in German) in 1909, it proved to be a resounding failure. Alfred Heuss, writes in the *Zeitschrift der Internationalen Musik-Gesellschaft* (1908–9, pp. 311f.) that

> One made . . . a mistake with the performance of Haydn's serious one-act [*sic*] Opera *Die wüste Insel*, a thoroughly unhappy, textually (Metastasio) impossible, embarrassingly dull work. Haydn held it in high esteem, and he certainly laboured hard at it, but the result turned out to be entirely negative. Whoever, in a weak moment, turned to such a text in order to compose it shows a total lack of dramatic instinct.

Part of the trouble, of course, is our attitude to Metastasio, the *opera seria* as such, and the plot, which is as follows:

Synopsis of the plot: Gernando, accompanied by his wife Costanza and her younger sister Silvia, sets sail for the West Indies, where they are to join his father. A storm drives the ship to a deserted island. Pirates kidnap Gernando, leaving the two sisters to fend for themselves as best they can. After three years, Gernando manages to free himself and attempts the almost hopeless task of finding the lonely island and its inhabitants. Gernando is accompanied by his friend Enrico (in many MSS.: 'Ernesto'), with whom Silvia is in love. The final 'Quartetto' unites the two loving pairs in a classical *settecento* happy end.

Although it is, compared with its surrounding companions, a relatively short work, in 1802 Haydn considered it too long:[1] 'I must only change something of the Finale, a Quartet, because it's too long'. As Haydn said in that connection shortly thereafter

> [Griesinger to Breitkopf & Härtel]
> . . . He would like to have the Opera printed with the original text, i.e. the Italian. What he has crossed out should not be included; for his old Prince, for whom he had to compose this Opera, nothing was too long . . . Hn. believes this Opera to be a good example for would-be composers, on account of the recitatives: it's a little work that, in its present form, can be performed in every private theatre.

The severe pruning that Haydn made in the final Quartet made no real difference in the slow pace of the opera as a whole, which moves in a Hassian or Gluckian tempo rather than a Mozartian and is thus almost impossible to stage nowadays. Probably with the sound of Gluck's *Orfeo* still in his ears (Eszterháza, January–February 1776), Haydn abolished entirely the secco recitative in his new Opera and wrote only accompagnati; strictly speaking, a harpsichord is not necessary at all in this work. If it is very doubtful whether *L'isola disabitata* can ever enjoy a stage life any more, we are in a perfect position to relish the music through the medium of the gramophone record, which is ideally suited to works of this kind: the same applies, we believe, to *Armida* (q.v.). If we therefore concentrate on some of the interesting musical aspects of the score, it is because we are convinced that there is no stage future for this original and unconventional music.

1 *Haydn: the Late Years 1801–1809*, p. 218. Length of operas: p. 222.

Although Haydn was not generally interested in character development, the figure of Silvia in this Opera, played by Luigia Polzelli, occupies something of a special position. 'The only person about whom a development can be spoken', writes Wirth (I, 150f.)

> is Silvia who, at the beginning a young girl untouched by problems of any kind, becomes a loving woman in the course of the Opera, something which, however, is made plausible only by the musical treatment.

It is not too far fetched to imagine that Haydn's heart was already lost to Luigia, and that in some respects her 'progress' in this Opera represents a biographical sketch, in the course of which she became, literally, Haydn's loving woman. Knowing all the insertion arias that Haydn touchingly composed for his not terribly talented mistress, it is intriguing to note that even in this Opera, the Aria (Silvia) in the 'Seconda parte', 'Come il vapor', seems to be an Eszterháza addition, for it is not in Metastasio's setting of 1752. (There are also changes in Enrico's Aria in the 'Parte prima', 'Chi nel camin', and in the Finale [Quartet].)

The Overture, in four parts (slow introduction – fast – a slow dance in 3/4 – shortened repetition of fast), is the finest of Haydn's operas to this date. Usually, Haydn was content to preface his scores with a heavily symphonic overture which might have been the first two movements of any Haydn symphony – e.g. *Lo speziale* (with a short third movement, possibly the concert ending?), *L'infedeltà delusa*, *Philemon und Baucis*. The one-movement Overture to *Il mondo della luna* later became the beginning of a symphony. But in *L'isola disabitata*, the Overture is a real introduction to the deserted island; the middle section is perhaps designed to show the constancy of the principal female singer. The fast sections return to the most severe *Sturm und Drang* style of the early 1770s and show us that Haydn has not forgotten how to write in the language of passion.

In view of the lack of 'movement' (ensembles), Haydn has resort to the old Baroque device of solo instruments. In Silvia's Aria, 'Fra un dolce deliro' in Part I, a slow (Andante) piece, Haydn scores for solo flute and bassoon. (We shall see a similar outpouring of soli at the end of the work.) But great is our surprise to see in Silvia's Accompagnato, 'Dov'è Costanza', the same use of the flute and bassoon. This is the kind of device that Haydn uses throughout the Opera to cement the loose structure of the music together. Motives, such as the 'chisel' theme at the beginning of the Opera (Costanza is chiselling a message into a stone), return later. The use of the flute and bassoon in connection with the innocent Silvia also marks the final Quartet. In this same Accompagnato Haydn uses the second horn in the typical 'stopped' note that we found in the Baryton Divertimenti à otto:

and which we shall encounter in Melibeo's Aria, 'Sappi, che la bellezza', in *La fedeltà premiata*. But despite all this loving attention to detail, an Aria such as Silvia's 'Come il vapor' (Part II), especially composed for Polzelli, is not really anything more than a vehicle to display her (mediocre) vocal talents. 'It is', says Wirth (II, 45), 'a typical example of the old *simile* aria belonging more or less to every *opera seria*.' What is much more original occurs shortly thereafter. In a highly expressive Aria, Costanza declares herself tired of life: 'Ah, che in van' (with a remarkable passage each time for the words 'ma si lunga è questa morte'). After a short recitative, Gernando appears and begins to sing the same music (in a different key: C instead of B flat), and shortly after that, the long-separated lovers meet; Haydn has foreseen this in his music. In a succeeding kind of 'scena', we note that Gernando is accompanied by a solo violin (another Baroque excursion), and shortly thereafter a solo violoncello also appears on the scene and the horns (just before) move into C *alto*. The scene is set for a glorious, oratorio-like (even *Fidelio*-like) Quartet Finale, which is like an enormous *symphonie concertante*. It is opened by a huge ritornello for the solo violin, then follows Costanza, then another large ritornello for the solo violoncello. The pairs of lovers are thus given instruments with which to identify them to us: Costanza and Gernando by solo violin and solo 'cello, Silvia by the solo flute, Enrico by the solo bassoon. It is a beautiful tripartite movement (slow middle section) of no less than 365 bars which is a worthy predecessor to Mozart's glorious but operatically problematic 'Martern aller Arten' from *Entführung*.

L'isola disabitata, then, is more an oratorio than an opera; it is a musically rewarding 'Operette' (Haydn's term) but of no consequence in the history of opera; and it is perhaps significant that it did not enjoy more than a few performances at Eszterháza in 1779 and 1780 (see the Chronicle, *supra*).

La fedeltà premiata, dramma giocoso per musica
(XXVII:10; 1780)

Scoring: (Haydn's approved final version) 4 S (Amarante, Nerina, Fillide [Celia], Diana), 2 T (Lindoro, Fileno), 2 B (Peruchetto, Melibeo), fl., 2 ob., 2 bsn., 2 cor., 2 trpt., timp., str. (harpsichord *continuo*).

Principal sources: 2 fragments of the autograph: (1a) EH, Budapest, Ms. mus. I. 6; (1b) Preussische Staatsbibliothek, Mus. ms. autogr. Jos. Haydn 24, (2) Complete authentic MS. score by Anonymous 48 and 30 (lacking Lindoro's Aria in Atto II°, 'Non vi sdegnate', which Haydn cut), Biblioteca Nazionale, Turin, corrected by Haydn. (3) Complete piano score in German ('Die belohnte Treue'), including the only complete text (in reduction) of 'Non vi sdegnate', Fürstlich Fürstenbergisches Hofarchiv, Donaueschingen. (4) Vols. II and IV of what was originally a four-volume authentic score, the conducting score for the 1782 version, by Anonymous 48 (i.e. probably Johann Elssler), with many corrections by Haydn, including changes to Celia's part and dynamic marks not in any other source, discovered by this writer in a Milan bookshop, now Burgenländisches Landesmuseum, Eisenstadt. (5) Authentic printed score of Celia's Scena in Atto° II, 'Ah, come il core' in its original state, D major, but without the timpani part; Artaria (pl. no. 1783), 1783: copy in Melk Monastery. (6) Some single arias, also including Joseph Elssler's copy of 'È amore di natura' as S.m. 3402 and the score of 'Placidi ruscelletti' as S.m. 9843, in the Österreichische Nationalbibliothek, Musiksammlung.

Libretto: G. B. Lorenzi as *L'infedeltà fedele* (Naples, 20 July 1779, with music by Domenico Cimarosa): Haydn owned a three volume MS. score of the Cimarosa opera, now in EH, Budapest, Ms. Mus. OE–10. See Bartha-Somfai, 249f. *Haydn: the Late Years 1801–1809*, p. 314, item 217.

Critical editions: *Joseph Haydn Werke* XXV/10 (2 vols., G. Thomas, 1968); Universal Edition (Landon, using also source 4 which *JHW* could not, since at the relevant time source 4 was not yet available; 1970).

First performance in modern times: Holland Festival 1970 (using Universal Edition's material): Diana: Sophie van Sante; Melibeo: Frangiskos Voutsinos; Celia: Romana Righetti; Fileno: Pietro Bottazzo; Nerina: Helen Mané; Lindoro: Eduardo Giménez; Amaranta: Eugenia Ratti; Perrucchetto: Renato Capecchi. The Netherlands Opera Choir, the Netherlands Chamber Orchestra, conducted by Alberto Erede. Producer, sets and costumes: Jean-Pierre Ponnelle.

First recording: Celia: Lucia Valentini; Fileno: Tonny Landy; Amaranta: Frederica von Stade; Perrucchetto: Alan Titus; Nerina: Ileana Cotrubas; Lindoro: Luigi Alva; Melibeo: Maurizio Mazzieri; Diana: Kari Lövaas. Orchestre de Chambre de Lausanne, conducted by Antal Dorati. Philips 6707 028 (producer: Erik Smith). Grand Prix du Disque, 1976.

Literature: Wirth II, 36f. Bartha-Somfai 87f., 91, 234, 262–5. Landon, 'A new authentic source for "La fedeltà premiata" by Haydn', in *Soundings* 1971–2 (German in Grasberger *Festschrift* 1975, with revisions). Marc Vignal in *HJB* VIII (1971), pp. 295–8.

Synopsis of the plot: In a small village in the neighbourhood of Cumae, the inhabitants must sacrifice each year a faithful loving couple to the sea monster in atonement for having once offended the goddess Diana. It is the duty of the devious priest (Melibeo) to find the pair and to prepare them for the sacrifice: as he assures Amaranta, whom he wishes to marry, he is immune from the goddess's curse. The village inhabitants have gathered by the temple to pray to the goddess for mercy, since the time for the sacrifice is drawing near. Amaranta brings a pair of doves to Diana and listens with pleasure to Melibeo's compliments. The priest can also be of use, for her brother Lindoro (a temple servant) wishes to leave Nerina, a nubile nymph, and to conquer a mysterious and attractive stranger, the beautiful Celia. Melibeo is glad to act as a go-between in this operation but is nonplussed by the sudden arrival of the slightly deranged Count Perrucchetto, fleeing before wild beasts and finding a haven in Amaranta's willing arms. Her beautiful eyes induce him to forget the snarls of the wild animals and in front of the disconcerted priest, the two begin to flirt.

Meanwhile Nerina could find a stranger, Fileno, who is looking for his lost lady-love, to whom she could pour out her wounded heart. He promises to persuade Celia to drop her new lover (Lindoro), but he soon discovers in Celia his lost love, who was then called Fillide. She, considering the fate of lovers in Cumae, swears never to have seen Fileno, and from this moment she attempts to save them from the slavering jaws of the sea-monster, whereas he is filled with thoughts of revenge at what he supposes is her faithlessness. Melibeo, who wishes to please Amaranta, faces her with an ultimatum: either she gives herself to Lindoro or (since he has discovered her secret attachment to Fileno) she must die with her lover. Some satyrs, pursuing nymph Nerina up to the gates of the temple, seize Celia instead, saving her from an unpleasant decision.

Celia frees herself from the lusting satyrs and returns to her fate. Melibeo still insists on the choice and Lindoro is ready to offer his hand, and since he is a temple assistant under Melibeo's protection, they (as a couple) need have no fear of the sea-monster. The flirtation between Amaranta and the mad Count has reached a point where Melibeo fears he has lost the lady. He must therefore remove the Count from circulation, if possible permanently. Fileno, in order to punish the (as he imagines) faithless Celia, flirts with Nerina.

The great feast of Diana begins with a hunt in which the whole village participates. Amaranta is attacked by a wild boar which Fileno kills with a well placed arrow. Count Perrucchetto, who took refuge in a convenient tree when the wild boar rounded the corner, makes sure the animal is dead and gently awakens Amaranta, who has fainted, and persuades her that he has slain the boar (which, to his consternation, shows signs of being still alive).

Fileno has decided to end his life and carves his intention, and his regrets at Celia's faithlessness, on a tree stump. His knife breaks in the attempt and robs him of a proper instrument for suicide, and he runs away. Celia, seeking him, reads his message and thinks him dead. (This is the occasion of the Opera's greatest scene, 'Ah, come il core'.) In desperation, she throws herself into a cave. Melibeo is now able to set his plans for revenge into operation. He tells the Count, who cannot resist feminine charms of any kind, that Celia awaits him in her cave, to which place the Count rapidly betakes himself. To general astonishment, the Count and Celia, adorned in white sacrificial robes, are led to kneel before the sea-monster's arrival ('Queste due vittime'). Amaranta is beside herself; she and Lindoro want to save the two faithless victims, but Melibeo is adamant. Fileno wants to die with his former love, even to die before her; he throws himself into the waves, from which the monster rises, spreading panic among the Cumaean population. His noble sacrifice moves Diana, who now appears in the flesh, to forgive the village its former sins. Fillide (alias Celia) is united with Fileno; Amaranta becomes a Countess; Lindoro has his nubile nymph Nerina. The devious priest is killed by the goddess's bolt of lightning, as the curtain falls on general jubilation and the sound of trumpets and kettledrums. Faithfulness is rewarded: la fedeltà è premiata.

Haydn of course laughed at certain aspects of the libretto, as must we. And the libretto even makes fun of itself in places. The lunatic Count, when he arrives in a fright over the wild beasts, sings an Aria, 'Salva … salva … aiuto', which Haydn places in G minor and is a clear parody of the *Sturm und Drang* which he had just employed with particular force in the Overture to *L'isola disabitata*. No doubt Haydn's attitude was here conditioned by the text itself, for Perrucchetto, fainting in terror, yet manages to stammer his wish for 'un fiaschetto di Bordò' (Bordeaux). And we have mentioned Haydn's tongue-in-cheek treatment of 'Queste due vittimi' (Finale of Atto II°). The whole of Count Perrucchetto's music, indeed, was an open invitation to parody, and in the scene where the wild boar is supposedly killed, only to show that it is still alive, forcing Perruchetto up his tree again, Haydn writes a merry A major Aria ('Di questo audace ferro') which, in Jean-Pierre Ponelle's treatment, brought the house down in Holland (1970). Parody changes to irony, however, when Melibeo sings, in Atto II°,

A page from the autograph of *La fedeltà premiata*, showing part of Celia's Aria in Act I, 'Deh soccorri', in which the original version of the Largo began with a muted horn solo (top line); this solo passage was later changed to bassoon (after the horn player Anton Eckhardt left Eszterháza).

Sappi, che la bellezza
Senza la gentilezza
È un fonte senza l'onde
È un arbor senza fronde . . .

and the second horn has a series of stopped notes to illustrate the thought and to show, as it were, Melibeo's devious character:

But the most original use of the horn occurs in Celia's Aria (Atto I°), 'Deh soccorri un infelice' where, after an opening Andante, the music stops and a Largo in barred C begins. We include the page of the autograph in question: the top stave is that of the horns, and the original version was for 'Solo con sordino'.[1] After Teresa Tavecchia (Haydn's first Amaranta) and her horn-playing husband Anton Eckhardt left

1 In a concert held at Hamburg on 20 December 1783, the Boeck brothers from the princely Batthyani *Capelle* in Pressburg gave a concert which was reviewed in Cramer's *Magazin der Musik* (1784, pp. 1400ff.). The use of mutes (*Sordinen*) was especially commented on, 'an echo is produced that was most striking and surprising'. The reviewer hopes a composer would write specially with that effect in mind (as would the Pressburg-based Anton Zimmermann in his 'Echo' Symphony: see *SYM*, 814, No. 86; the work has two solo and two ripieno horns and mutes are used). One of the Boecks played two notes at once, the main note and the fifth (this was the second horn). Haydn, clearly, was fascinated by all these new effects for the previously limited horn.

Eszterhàza, Haydn apparently had no one to play this taxing horn solo and changed it (also on the autograph) to 'fagotto'. Later Celia's part had to be given to another singer and transposed upwards, and Haydn retained his change to bassoon, thinking, too, that if the opera were played outside Eszterháza – and Haydn obviously knew of the impending performances at Vienna (1784) and, later, at Pressburg – it would be safer to give the passage to the bassoon and not to a muted horn. Here, however, we have reversed our usual procedure, which is always to allow Haydn's last word to be printed, and retained the muted horn part, an innovation of Mahlerian finesse: Haydn only sacrificed the original idea because he was forced to do so, and we see no reason to follow his forced decision. (The *Joseph Haydn Werke*, incredibly and unmusically, does not even *mention* the muted horn part in the actual score.)

Haydn's imagination was fired by his task. Probably he was infected by the excitement of writing a new work for opening the rebuilt Eszterháza opera house; but whatever the reason, *La fedeltà premiata* is surely the most rewarding of all the operas considered in this section. If it lacks the eminently successful stage quality of *L'infedeltà delusa* – the most successful of all Haydn's operas on the stage – it has gained, since 1773, immeasurably in sophistication and depth. Like all these operas, it is too long, especially the first act: if performed complete, the work would run to nearly four hours. But the tension that Haydn manages to create, also on the stage, in the central portion of the second act, is remarkable. This particular section begins (according to the 1782 libretto) with Fileno singing, in an 'orribile grotta', the Rec. 'Bastano i pianti' and the ensuing D minor Aria, 'Recida il ferro' – this is the situation in which the knife breaks and he cannot commit suicide. Haydn's form has become as free and unfettered as his imagination, and the end of the Aria turns into a recitative and then a short concluding ritornello. (The same interruption of an aria with a recitative also occurred in Atto I°, Amaranta's B major Aria, 'Per te m'accesse amore'.) We then have Celia's great *scena*, 'Ah, come il core', with its fine flute solo and its almost unbelievable (even for Haydn) interruption where the whole orchestra engages in three gigantic unison *decrescendi*: here the timpani suddenly enter 'con un continuo bischero, ed in fine perdendosi' while the horns are, apparently, supposed to 'flutter-tongue' the note (it is marked with a whole series of dots and the note 'e sempre tremolante, ma in fine perdendosi'. The huge analysis of this great piece by Cramer has been quoted above (pp. 433ff.).

It seems gratuitous to select points from a series of arias as matchlessly beautiful and ingeniously composed as those of *La fedeltà premiata*, but perhaps a few points may be welcome. In *Haydn in England 1791–1795* (pp. 341ff.) we point to a series of pedal points that appeared several times in *L'anima del filosofo* (1791), all *piano*, and with a certain characteristically sombre undertone. We have a remarkable premonition of this same kind of music in Fileno's first Aria in Atto II°, 'Se da' begli occhi tuoi', where we have the following lead-back to the recapitulation (see the musical example opposite). With this passage of ravishing beauty, we arrive at an interesting point of speculation: how carefully did Mozart study *La fedeltà premiata*? We cannot imagine that he missed the Christmas performance of 1784 when, a few months later, we know that he was Haydn's intimate friend. And the proof of Mozart's study is surely such a passage as the one just quoted, which has the very special 'Mozartian' quality of a lead-back which would in fact become a hallmark of Mozart's own style. Those who know his music well will recognize the point, for his scores are full of these emotionally laden 'retransitions', usually over the dominant pedal point and with the same shifting chromatic lines as in Haydn's example. (A characteristic and particularly beautiful

[Allegro con moto]

Non ti sdeg-nar, ___ ben mio, non ti sdeg-nar, ben

mio s'ar - do per te, ben mio, per te _____

[Tutti]

lead-back of this kind is found in the slow movement of Mozart's Piano Concerto in D, K.451 [1784], which also has the most Haydnesque movement in all Mozart – the Finale

Allegro di molto

where even the *tempo* is Haydnesque – 'di' molto: Mozart otherwise writes 'Allegro molto' or 'Molto allegro'.) And is it coincidence that in this same Aria we have that all-pervading Mozartian march rhythm?

Just as Symphony No. 47, with its march rhythm, fascinated Mozart (*vide supra*, p. 304), his attention will have been swiftly drawn to this Aria, from which, in the event, he drew inspiration from another quarter, as we have just seen. This march rhythm is associated with Fileno in the manner which we have observed in *L'isola disabitata*, for in his Aria, 'Miseri affetti miei' (Atto I°), our attention is riveted on that very rhythm which is introduced in a spectacular manner. The Aria starts (B flat) as if it were a normal ritornello but then stops short in the middle of its Allegro di molto course to introduce

Apart from establishing the dotted rhythm so dramatically, the Aria is another example of the unparalleled freedom with which Haydn now treats the form:

Allegro di molto ritornello (26 bars)	Adagio vocal entry (20 bars)	Presto new material (61 bars)	Adagio return to 2nd pt. (10 bars)	Presto shortened return to 3rd pt. (19 bars)

It is a piece full of the passion that we remember in the works of 1772: the middle part of the 3rd section (bars 69ff.) is one of the great moments of this Opera – and there are many. To an undulating string movement of ⅜ ♩ ♩ ♩ | ⅜ ♩ ♩ ♩ Haydn here re-introduces the text 'Miseri affetti miei', and gradually the *pianissimo* woodwind and later horns creep into the background. The reader will have gathered that *La fedeltà premiata* is an adroit mixture of serious and comic elements (Fileno and Celia being of course the *parti serie*). Next to Fileno's and Celia's music, the most interesting part, from the strictly musical standpoint, is that of Amaranta, who is treated with considerably more sympathy in Haydn's score than the libretto's description, 'donna vana, e boriosa', would warrant. Her first piece of music, embedded in the opening ensemble, is an Adagio of rare beauty and long lines, 'Prendi, o Cintia'. Her Aria later in the same act, 'Vanne...fuggi...traditore!' is in the (for Haydn) rare key of B minor, which is part of Haydn's complex and subtle system of key relationships: Amaranta's second large-scale appearance in Atto Iº is in Scene IV, where she has an Aria in B major ('Per te m'accesse amore) – hence the B minor Aria later in the act, which by the way contains a memorable 'second subject'

Cruel as it is to treat with such brevity a subject which certainly deserves far more ample space, we must pass over the delightful hunting Overture, in honour of Diana, which Haydn later used as a Finale(!) to Symphony No. 73. The glory of *La fedeltà premiata*, and surely its lasting claim to immortality, are the ensemble finales that conclude the first and second acts (the third is, as usual, an 'appendix' consisting, apart from recitatives of the ubiquitous duet between the serious lovers, Diana's literal appearance as the *dea ex machina*, and the final chorus). We have noted above that the Opera is composed in a sophisticated chain of keys: like *Le nozze di Figaro*, it is a D major work, beginning and ending in D. Act I ends with a Finale the basic key of which is B flat (third-related, then, to D), while Act II ends with a Finale in E flat, the Neapolitan sixth, as it were, of the home key. But great is our astonishment to see that *within* the finales, Haydn has recourse to a whole series of third-related keys which, characteristically, progress *downwards* in thirds (i.e. towards the darkness, away from the light – see the same treatment in his dealings with chains of fifths *away* from the tonic, e.g. in Quartet, Op. 71, No. 3: *Haydn in England 1791–1795*, p. 469) to match the catastrophic action in the libretto. In Atto Iº, the Finale's scheme is: B flat – G major – G minor – E flat – C major – A flat – G minor – B flat – G minor – B flat. The end of the A flat section, and the end of the downwards cycle of thirds, is marked by Perrucchetto's words 'E ben, lo dirò io: costei, signore mio, deve costui sposar' ('Well, I'll tell you then: you, sir, have got to get married'), i.e. Lindoro must marry Celia. In Atto IIº, Finale, the scheme is: E flat – G major – C minor – C major – G minor – E flat. The climax is, of course, the C minor section, 'Queste due vittimi', which is quite as cynically treated as Melibeo himself (who speaks the words), but the orchestration, with flute, bassoon and lower strings pizzicato, is breathtakingly original even though we sense the presence of Gluck's *Orfeo* behind the score. Haydn scoffs at the action in his C major section: as Celia moans, 'Ah mio Fileno . . .' the violins show us that it is all, basically, *opera buffa*:

The G minor section has massive orchestration and Hungarian harmonies spiced with off-beat *forzati* to describe the words 'Delira il meschinello, è pazzo in verità': there was something slightly mad about the dark, secret world of gypsies (synonymous, in Haydn's music, with Hungarian). For purposes of comparison, we may list the two comparable finales in *Le nozze di Figaro* (1786). Finale Atto IIº: E flat – B flat – G major (Sc. X, Figaro's entrance) – C major – F major – B flat – E flat. Finale Atto IVº: D – G – E flat – B flat – G – D. It will be seen that Mozart also flirts with *Terzverwandtschaft*, though less ostentatiously than Haydn in *La fedeltà premiata*: but the basic organization, also the application of symphonic devices to large-scale vocal forms, is the same in both works.

As a stage piece, *La fedeltà premiata* cannot take its place in the great operatic tradition which Mozart founded, but in Haydn's *œuvre* it occupies a place of pride. With its open-hearted, witty, profound, meticulously constructed music, it is without question the most important work of its period, dwarfing symphony, sonata and quartet. Haydn was quite right to regard it with special affection.

Orlando Paladino, dramma eroicomico (XXVIII:11; 1782)

Scoring: 3 S (Angelica, Eurilla, Alcina), 4 T (Orlando, Pasquale, Medoro, Licone), 2 B (Rodomonte, Caronte), 1 fl., 2 ob., 2 bsn., 2 cor., in No. 15 (Atto II°, Pasquale's Aria 'Vittoria, vittoria') 2 cor. in C *alto* or trpt., timp., str. (harpsichord continuo).
Principal sources: (1) Autograph (a) British Museum, Add. 32172 (from the legacy of J. N. Hummel) Atti I° & II° (lacking two sections, from bar 57 of Aria No. 15, 'Vittoria', to bar 24 of Aria No. 17, 'Aure chete': two sets of 'Bögen', Nos. 7 and 8 of Haydn's numbering); Atto III°, Preussische Staatsbibliothek, Berlin, Mus. ms. autogr. Jos. Haydn 28, signed at end 'Fine dell' Opera – Laus Deo et B.V.M.' It is presumed that Haydn removed sections 7 and 8 from his autograph, which included the Duet, 'Quel tuo visetto amabile', which was performed, with another text, 'Quel cor umano e tenero', in a *pasticcio* given in London in 1794 and which Haydn performed, with the original text, at his benefit concert, on 4 May 1795 in London: see *Haydn in England 1791–1795*, pp. 254, 306–9. (2) The vocal parts of the first performance at Eszterháza, copied by Joseph Elssler, Johann Schellinger, Anonymous 10 and Anonymous 48 (Johann Elssler?). EH, Budapest, Ms. Mus. I. 152. Facsimiles: Bartha-Somfai, 421, *Werke*, vol. II. Haydn added the names of the various singers to each part: 'Braghetti', 'Valdesturla', etc. In Alcina's Aria No. 6 (Atto I°), Haydn changed the text from 'A un mio accento, a un guardo solo' to 'Ad'un guardo, a un cenno solo', which change is also incorporated in the printed textbook (see *Werke*, pp. 71f.). There are also changes in the text of Eurilla's part. (3) MS. score with German text from the Mannheim performance of 1792, EH, Budapest, Ms. Mus. I. 154. Haydn made corrections in the German text (see Bartha-Somfai, facsimile 21). He owned the score himself (see *Haydn: the Late Years 1801–1809*, p. 314, item 218). (4) Duet No. 16, 'Quel tuo visetto', copied by Johann Radnitzky, Benedictine Monastery of Göttweig (from the coll. of Aloys Fuchs). (5) Print, by Torricella of Vienna, of Duet No. 16, 'Quel tuo visetto' for voice and harpsichord (copy in Library of Congress M. 1552, A.2.H.2.: title in Landon *Supplement*, 42n.). Perhaps this print, which must be prior to 1785, was the reason why this item was removed from the autograph. (6) Authentic copy of No. 1

('Introduzione') by Anonymous 63, Stadtbibliothek Leipzig. On the title is the remark: 'Ho corretto nel Mese d'Aprile 1790', which is similar to another (Viennese?) copy of Angelica's Aria (Atto II°), 'Aure chete' in the Gymnasialbibliothek, Zittau: 'Ho corretto nel Mese di Gennaro 1790'. (7) A MS. score sold by M. Arthur Rau at the same time as the Traeg copies of *Philemon* and *Feuersbrunst* and now in the Conservatoire de Musique (Bibliothèque Nationale, Paris). The various prints by Simrock (pl. no. 73, 1798–9) and Rellstab (1799–1800) have no claim to authenticity and are in German translation.
Libretto: Nunziato Porta, using (a) his own adaption of Carlo Francesco Badini's libretto (London 1771, music by Guglielmi) for Prague, 1775 (music by Guglielmi) and (b) new numbers especially for Eszterháza. The Prague setting was performed at Vienna on 19 June 1777 (textbook owned by the present writer); but neither Porta's name is mentioned, nor is any composer listed (which had been the case in Prague: 'Dramma eroico comico di Nunziato Porta', 'La Musica è del celebre Signor Pietro Guglielmi'; copy of the libretto in the University Library, Prague). Badini's libretto was a straight comedy; the Prague version changed this to a 'heroic comic' drama, as was then the fashion. Many sections of the Guglielmi 1771 setting could be incorporated in the Prague 1775 setting, but the new numbers seem to be by several composers. Thus the Prague setting is really a pasticcio, and this is without question the reason why Guglielmi's name was omitted in the Vienna 1777 setting and the work listed, as it were, under a nameless composer. Literatures: Geiringer and G. Feder in *Werke*, foreword. A. van Hoboken: 'Nunziato Porta und der Text von Joseph Haydns Oper "Orlando Paladino"' in *Symbolae historiae musicae* (Federhofer *Festschrift*), Mainz 1971.
Critical edition: Joseph Haydn Werke XXV/11, 2 vols. (Geiringer).
First recording: Angelica: Arleen Augér; Rodomonte: Benjamin Luxon; Orlando: George Shirley; Medoro: Claes-H. Ahnsjö; Alcina: Gwendolyn Killebrew; Licone: Gabor Carelli; Eurilla: Elly Ameling; Pasquale: Domenico Trimarchi; Caronte: Maurizio Mazzieri. Orchestre de Chambre de Lausanne, conducted by

Antal Dorati; producer: Erik Smith. Philips, 6707 029.
Literature: Geiringer 1932, 113f.; Wirth I, 127ff.; Wirth II, 37ff.; Bartha-Somfai, 101f., 265f.; Geiringer 1968, 80, 264, 332f., 373.
Synopsis of the plot: The errant knight Orlando (Roland) with his comical shield-bearer Pasquale is searching for Angelica, whose favours the knight wishes to enjoy. But she has eyes only for the young Medoro and flees with her lover to a lonely castle. From far-away Algeria arrives Rodomonte, eagerly awaiting single combat with Orlando; Rodomonte too looks for Angelica, to whom he wishes to offer his services. He finds some shepherds who, terrified, tell him that Orlando is not in the neighbourhood but that a loving couple has hidden in the nearby castle (Angelica and Medoro). The shepherdess Eurilla, a kind-hearted child of nature, warns Rodomonte of the dangers involved in challenging Orlando, but he is sure of his prowess and takes with him the shepherd Licone to show the way. Rodomonte promises to protect Licone against Orlando, a promise which Licone is not entirely sure Rodomonte can keep.

Meanwhile Angelica sits in her lonely castle and tells of her love for Medoro and her fear that she will be forced to give him up. She calls the fairy Alcina, who promises assistance. Medoro has seen a knight in armour and learns that he is the shield-bearer of Orlando. The trembling Angelica makes Medoro promise to hide from the raging errant knight.

Pasquale is in fact looking for a place to sleep and eat, when he is challenged to single combat by Rodomonte; but Pasquale will only fight with his fists. Eurilla appears and tells Rodomonte that Orlando is searching for him. Rodomonte immediately conjures up visions of victory, and Pasquale persuades Eurilla to bring him some food.

Orlando, in his turn looking for Rodomonte, stumbles on a pretty fountain on which the names of the two lovers are engraved. In a rage he demolishes the fountain. When Pasquale appears, the knight reproaches him for thinking only of eating and not of combat. He sees Eurilla slinking away and seizes her; in terror she tells all that she knows of the lovers. Orlando rages. Eurilla and Pasquale hasten to Angelica and warn her; while they escape, they meet Rodomonte, still looking for Orlando. Suddenly Orlando appears and everyone is in a state of shock, but Alcina (the sorceress) saves this potentially unpleasant situation by turning the knight into a beetle.

In a forest, Orlando and Rodomonte meet for single combat, but before Rodomonte can cover himself with glory, Eurilla appears with the news that the lovers are in flight. Orlando dashes off. Rodomonte, furious, is not soothed by the attractive attentions of Eurilla and chases her away.

Medoro has rushed to the ocean and wishes for death. Eurilla comes and he gives her his last words for Angelica. As she is about to fulfil this commission, Pasquale appears, and Eurilla, using Alcina's voice, almost robs him of his senses. Pasquale finally discovers the ruse and returns to Angelica, who in her loneliness and desperation is about to hurl herself into the sea. She finds Medoro, but hardly are they reunited when the mad Orlando roars on the scene. Once again Alcina saves the situation. Orlando decides that this new element must be removed from circulation and sends Pasquale, chattering with fear, to the grotto of the sorceress to challenge her. This was a mistake, because she turns Orlando into stone on the spot. Meanwhile, Angelica, Medoro, Eurilla and Rodomonte are also en route to Alcina and discover the trembling Pasquale, who relates his knight's last adventure. No one, in true *settecento* fashion, wishes for revenge and Alcina obligingly turns Orlando back into flesh and blood. She then takes the knight into her cave and the others return to their normal lives.

Alcina has taken Orlando to the river Lethe, where Caronte resides, and requests the latter to bathe Orlando with the water so that his rage will abate. Eurilla and Pasquale, meanwhile, have returned to their castle and are considering marriage, when Orlando appears and asks them to join him. In the forest Angelica and Medoro are attacked by wild men and Medoro is wounded. Rodomonte and Orlando appear and mix into the battle. Angelica is left behind and believes Medoro dead (he reappears later). Alcina, Rodomonte and Orlando return. Orlando has forgotten his mad love for Angelica and offers her his knightly services. At a touch of Alcina's magic wand, the forest is turned into a beautiful garden, and as the curtain falls, all sing of love.

Haydn's Opera enjoyed a real success when it was translated into German as 'Ritter Roland', first at the Erdödy Theatre in Pressburg (1786) and then at Prague, Brünn, Vienna, Pest, Mannheim, Donaueschingen, Frankfurt-am-Main, Cologne, Graz, Nuremberg, Berlin, Hanover, Bremen, Leipzig, Munich, Augsburg, Königsberg, Hamburg, Breslau and St Petersburg. It was also, as we have seen, a great success at Eszterháza. But critical voices, even in 1792, noted that 'excellent though the music is, nevertheless this opera did not entirely please' and it was thought the introduction of Cimarosa's *Maestro di Capella* was 'more to present-day taste.'[1] And in our day, although a perfectly acceptable German piano score was published by Ernst Latzko

---

1 *Haydn in England 1791–1795*, pp. 197f.

(Leipzig, Max Beck Verlag) in 1931, it was not a success and there have been no performances at all in recent years (except for a fine radio performance in Budapest, 1959, which the Hungarian Radio kindly played for us then). Yet all the present-day Haydn experts are persuaded that this is perhaps Haydn's finest opera. Certainly it presented a fine vehicle for Haydn's sardonic wit, and the figures of Rodomonte and Pasquale, in particular, are most amusingly portrayed. '*Orlando Paladino*', writes Helmut Wirth (II, 42),

> terminates Haydn's activity in the sphere of *opera buffa* and simultaneously represents a peak in the history of comic opera. And yet a tragic sentiment is hidden behind the gay mask, which the poet Jean Paul describes in Haydn's case as 'like an expression of disdain for the world'. The eagerness for new ideals can be felt everywhere, and *La fedeltà premiata* and the heroic-comic 'Knight Roland' are, with *La vera costanza*, nothing else but a step towards wholly serious opera.

When, some years ago, we were examining the autograph sections in the British Museum, we wondered how it would be possible, nowadays, to stage a work in which Atto I° consisted of the Overture, an 'Introduzione' (ensemble), and then nine straight arias (some with accompagnati), preceding the magnificent Finale. It is the same in Atto II°: three arias, a duet, an aria, an accompagnato, a duet, an accompagnato, two arias and then another marvellous Finale. Atto III° has only arias, accompagnati and a final 'Coro'. It seems to us that the only Haydn operas that are likely to hold the stage nowadays (even if in limited fashion) are those in which there are at least some ensembles or other diversions apart from the finales; and in Haydn's case, this means largely the earlier works where, conversely, we lack the flowering maturity of *La fedeltà premiata*. Even if the intervention, in *Orlando Paladino*, of supernatural powers is treated as a farce, i.e. the figure of Alcina, it is difficult for a modern audience to take it at all.

The Overture is the first single-movement work in a Haydn opera – racy, light, a prelude more to a farce than a grand 'heroic-comic opera'; but it shows at once what Haydn's intentions are. Space prevents more than a few observations. Wirth (II, 38f.) notes Haydn's interesting use of keys in connection with Orlando, who 'presents himself in two principal keys: E flat major and A major'.

> E flat major is his personal heroic world out of which his craze has sprung. But by adhering to this key Haydn pokes fun at the hero in the second act, as he flees from Alcina's dragon. However, the moment he comes under Alcina's power in the cave (this is of course brought about by witchery) her key, i.e. C minor or C major, sets in, and not before he is again transformed to his normal state does Roland sing in E flat major, whereby he plainly shows that he is not yet cured from his craze. In the A major region he is easier to deal with and more practical, for this key belongs to the circle in which the passionately desired Angelica moves. A major is finally also the key of the last rondo in which the cured Roland is returned to the world.

A similar operation obtains with Rodomonte, a 'sabre-rattling bumpkin squire' (Wirth): his basic key is B flat, and when he appears in the Finale of Atto I° it is in the key of B flat (*Werke*, pp. 170ff.). But at the outset of Atto II° he sings a 'storm' Aria in D minor – a persiflage on Haydn's many D minor arias which were, of course, well known to Prince Nicolaus. Similarly, Pasquale's 'war' Aria in the same act, 'Vittoria', with C *alto* horns or trumpets and kettledrums, is a farcical blueprint of Haydn's own C major Arias of this kind: 'Trombette suonate, le glorie cantate del grande Pasqual'.

We must not fail to mention his delightful 'music' Aria (Atto II°, 'Ecco spiano'), imitating all the devices of an Italian virtuoso, including a run to high *d''*.

The Opera has a curious tonal structure: it begins in B flat and ends in A. Atto I° has a Finale in the new key (A), with subdivisions as follows: A major – D major – B flat – B major – G major – A major. The immediate juxtaposition of B flat with B is immensely effective. In Atto II° we move from D minor to the Finale's key of C major: (Finale:) C major → E flat → A flat → C major – A major → C major – B flat major – F major – C major.

The tonal complexity is matched by music, in these finales, of bewildering panache and audacity. But as we have said, it takes a very long time, and especially on the stage, until we arrive at these two great climaxes. Atto III°, though slightly longer than its Italian prototypes, is nevertheless something of an anticlimax. Haydn used the melodic structures of the final 'Coro' in his last (1791) Opera, *L'anima del filosofo* (Atto II°, Coro 'Finchè circola il vigore') and also in a little *Coro* with different words, 'Su, cantiamo' (see *Haydn in England 1791–1795*, pp. 356f.):

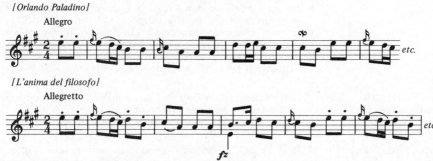

And what are we to do with this interesting, if rather un-stageworthy Opera? The answer, it would seem, must be the gramophone record, where we can enjoy all its beauties without having to worry about its effect on a provincial audience: that same critic, writing about the Mannheim production of 1792, noted that 'many parts of the music were incomprehensible to the amateurs' [*Nichtkenner*] and it is true (as we have often said) that a brawling Neapolitan audience in the eighteenth century would have hardly detected many of the subtleties of an average Haydn opera. And, as that same critic observed, 'the story itself is dreadfully handled by the poet.' Haydn, as Griesinger said many years later, was 'predestined for bad texts',[1] and *Orlando Paladino* is, alas, no exception.

Although, as we regretfully believe, there is hardly a theatrical future for *Orlando Paladino* – unless we follow Walter Legge's intriguing proposal to do it as a glorified marionette play –, it would be grossly unfair to Haydn not to add a few words on certain details of the work. The references are to the new Henle score (Geiringer).

Number and page ref.	*Comment*
	Atto I°
Overture (pp. 3ff.)	Notice the resemblance to Symphony No. 77 in key, atmosphere and also certain technical details.
Introduzione, 'Il lavorar' (pp. 21ff.)	This winning ensemble is typical of the work's central position in Haydn's operas of this period (1780s), looking back on the one hand to certain stylistic attributes of Haydn's own stage works – cf. Rodomonte's 'Zitti tutti' (bars 76ff.), the repeated semiquavers reminding us of *L'infedeltà delusa* (No. 4, Nanni's Aria 'Non v'è rimedio', bars 106ff.; No. 6, Vespina's

1 *Haydn in England 1791–1795*, p. 197. 'Es scheint Haydn sey zu schlechten Texten prädestiniert': Olleson in *HJB* III (1965), p. 30.

	and Nanni's Duet, 'Son disperato, bars 21ff., 31ff., 61ff., Philharmonia pp. 133, 163ff.) – but in an uncanny way presaging Mozart of the *Figaro* years.
Medoro's Aria, 'Parto' (p. 89)	The *pianissimo* passage at bars 35ff., used to describe 'è giunto il tuo penar', is of astonishing modernity. The key is A flat minor (instead of the A flat major we have hardly become exposed to), and the special 'twist' is that appoggiatura in the vocal part at bar 37.
(p. 94)	The unexpected arrival of F minor (characteristically 'underlined' by the simultaneous use of *pp*) in the middle of this section is illustrative of Haydn's subtle sense of tonal architecture. The Aria begins slowly in F minor; the second section is in F major (Allegro). In his usual way, Haydn shuffles the text, here introducing the words of the slow section, 'Parto' (etc.); and to stress this textual aberration, the music *also* returns to the previous key of F minor and even the actual pattern of the slow section, speeded up (cf. bars 97ff. on p. 94 with bars 1ff. on p. 86) here but so composed that the Allegro's basic tempo is retarded. It is one of Haydn's great structural *tours de force* in this Opera.
Pasquale's Cavatina, 'La mia bella' (pp. 100ff.)	Although this enchanting little piece is in the best Italianate serenade tradition (i.e. *siciliano* or *pastorella*), the music recalls Haydn's *Die Feuersbrunst* at two levels: the melody is reminiscent of Colombina's 'Wie wallet mein Herze' in Act II (also in E major), while Pasquale's slither down (instead of up) from *a* sharp to *b* at bars 18f. and 21f. recall Hanswurst's slither up the octave in *Die Feuersbrunst's* No. 6 (Aria 'Was fang i armer Würstel an?', second section). In the case of Pasquale, the description is for 'morirò', in Hanswurst's, 'I must hang myself'. Coincidence is out of the question: we have here two sides of the same coin.
Pasquale's Aria, 'Ho viaggiato in Francia' (p. 116)	The two sections where Pasquale must whistle ('fischiando'), calculated to bring the house down, look back to Buonafede's Aria from Atto II°, 'Che mondo amabile', of *Il mondo della luna*, where there is also a delightful whistling sequence.
Angelica's Aria, 'Non partir' (pp. 122f.)	At bars 25 and 27 we have yet another look towards Mozart in the ambiguous use of *g* and *b* flat in the middle of a dominant seventh progression to D major. This is the Mozart of *Don Giovanni* rather than *Figaro*, moreover. Note also p. 125, bars 45ff. for another *Don Giovanni*-like sequence to D minor (rather than D major), also p. 127, bars 74ff.
Orlando's *Scena*, 'Angelica, mio ben' (pp. 131ff.)	There is a strong stylistic similarity to Haydn's Cantata, 'Miseri noi' (cf. bars 1ff. with bars 8ff. of the *Scena*). Apart from that, bars 55ff. (p. 135), with the remarkable *pianissimo* section to draw attention to the words, 'Oimè, che fiero duolo!', are one of the many brilliant instances of Haydn's allying heightened emotion with exaggerated dynamic marks.
Finale dell'Atto I^{mo} (p. 162, Angelica's scene, 'Sento nel seno')	Note Haydn's curiously fastidious and almost impersonal treatment of 'un tetro orror di morte', precisely as in the Cantata 'Miseri noi', where 'Funesto orror di morte' (bars 77ff.) is composed in tranquil E flat. The beauty and originality are all in the harmonic progressions of Angelica's scene (cf. top of p. 164), but this general treatment, of which Giuseppe Sarti is also accused by his modern critics, is difficult for us to accept, used as we are to the totally involved, emotionally committed music for such occasions composed by Mozart.

Atto II°

P. 173	One of several jarring confrontations of totally opposed keys in this Opera – here from B flat to B with appropriate change of orchestration (first appearance of flute in the Finale). See also pp. 56f., where B flat is followed by A with Haydn's note between, 'S' aspetti un momento', presumably to soften the clash. See also pp. 180f., G to A major within a fast moving context.
P. 175 (bars 262ff.)	This great vocal quartet, with its polyphonic layout, looks forward to Haydn's own late Masses (e.g. *Missa Sancti Bernardi*, Gratias, bars 79ff.) and shows once again the crucial importance of these operas in Haydn's later career.

P. 187 (bars 377ff.)	Notice the witty use of *piano* ('Che terribile sembiante'): if nowhere else, surely this passage shows beyond question that Haydn treated this whole libretto with sophistication, with tenderness (how could he do otherwise?), but above all with delicate irony.
Medoro's Aria, 'Dille che un infelice' (p. 219)	Bar 38: note the tremendous harmonic sequence to illustrate 'del mio duol, de' mali miei...' – *Thonmahlerey* of the kind we find throughout Haydn's vocal music, whether of the 1760s or 1790s. It was in this fashion that Haydn's imagination was caught by his libretti. This Aria is formally speaking one of the most astonishing of the Opera: note on p. 226 how the slow section returns for six bars just before the end of the Vivace: here is a clear anticipation of (1) Kraus's Symphony in C minor, (2) Mozart's Quintet in D, K.593 and (3) Haydn's own 'Drum Roll' Symphony, No. 103, for which *vide infra*, pp. 752f.
Duet, 'Quel tuo visetto' (pp. 237ff.)	This is perhaps *the* popular hit of the Opera, and Haydn was quite right to think that it would stand up well even in the galaxy of his last benefit concert in London (1795) – see *Haydn in England 1791–1795*, pp. 306ff. With its wittiness and its *chic* melody, not to speak of the delightful sense of rapport between the two lovers, Haydn clearly thought it could represent, for the English audience of 1795, what he could write in the way of *opera buffa*. History may have proved him mistaken, but one would be sorry to miss this side of his personality.
Angelica's Aria, 'Aure chete' (pp. 248ff.)	Note the wonderfully original harmonic structure of this Aria's opening section, which moves from D major (tonic) to D minor and then, with a whole change of key signature (like a late piano trio) to F major and then back to D major.
Duet, 'Qual contento' (pp. 270ff.)	This particularly attractive piece was added, it would seem, later, but is so cleverly constructed round motifs known to us from the preceding recitative that no one would ever suspect that it was not part of Haydn's original scheme.
Orlando's Aria, 'Cosa vedo!' (pp. 284ff.)	Another of Haydn's curious treatments of a passionate text by cheerful E flat music (see Orfeo's 'Perduta un'altra volta' from Atto IV° of *L'anima del filosofo* for the classic example: *Haydn in England 1791–1795*, pp. 339f.). In *Orlando's* case, it is yet another example of Haydn's ironic indifference to the libretto's content. Perhaps for this reason we are given a spectacular display of motivic unity: cf. V. II, bars 26ff., 55ff., then wind band (with characteristic stopped horn) in quavers at bars 68ff., V. II, bars 82ff.
Finale dell'atto 2do (p. 334)	The spectacular modulation into C major (from A via A minor) underlines a fundamental change of action. Pasquale is required to explain his presence to Rodomonte ('Parla, perchè qui sei?').

Atto III°

Pp. 350ff.	'Torna la calma' is one of the many magical moments in this great score, the 'calma' being expressed by one of Haydn's famous pedal points, growing over fifteen bars of unchanged repeated *c*'s in the bass line to a *crescendo* of Rossini-like proportions – 'fugge il timore, comincia l'alma a respirar'. It was the *lieta fine* (to a drama in which he obviously did not believe) that attracted Haydn's loving attention.
Caronte's Aria, 'Ombre insepolte' (pp. 360ff.)	Another example of Haydn's magisterial treatment of the bass voice, of which the melody looks forward to Haydn's great *Scena di Berenice* (bars 76ff.).
Orlando's Aria, 'Miei pensieri' (pp. 369ff.)	This extraordinary piece begins like a recitative, and might be out of Bellini, Donizetti or even early Verdi. The actual Aria, one might think, would have begun in the hands of a lesser man at the upbeat to bar 4. But then (bars 15ff.) we see Haydn making this 'introduction' an integral part of the music by reintroducing it in a more elaborate state. This music and that discussed above (relating to p. 94) are possibly the most original and beautiful moments in the Opera.
Angelica's Aria, 'Dell'estreme sue voci' (pp. 385ff.)	On p. 391 we have one last glimpse into late Mozart: the sinister wind echoes (*c* flat – *b* flat) which describe 'Fra tanti tormenti che m'uccide?'. (*N.B.* The singer must perform her appoggiatura at bars 65 and 67 exactly like the wind instruments' – cf. the 'Applausus' letter, *supra*, pp. 146ff.).

Armida, dramma eroico
(XXVIII:12; 1783, perf. 1784)

Scoring: 2 S (Armida, Zelmira) 3 T (Rinaldo, Ubaldo, Cloterco), B (Idreno), 1 fl., 2 ob., 2 bsn., 2 cor. (in Aria No. 1 (Rinaldo's 'Vado a pugnar', Atto I°, and Finale, Atto III°, 2 cor. in C *alto* or trpt., timp.)[1], str. (harpsichord *continuo*). In *Marcia* No. 4 (Atto I°) 2 clar., 2 bsn., 2 cor., perhaps a stage band played by the Princely Grenadiers, who had clarinets in their ensemble: '6 Bandisten' were among the 'supers' required at Eszterháza.

Principal sources: (1) The autograph, which – though complete – is now divided in two sections: (a) The main body, Royal College of Music, London, with the superscription 'Armida Atto Primo di me giuseppe Haydn mpria $\overline{783}$'; at the end of Atto I° 'Fine dell'atto I^{mo} Laus Deo'; of Atto II° 'Fine dell'atto 2do Laus Deo'; of Atto III° 'Laus Deo et B.V.M.'. (b) The section missing in the main body, i.e. Atto II°, the end of Rinaldo's Rec. ('Armida') and the whole of the ensuing Aria, 'Caro e vero', Armida's scene 'Barbaro' and Aria 'Odio, furor' and the beginning of the next secco (Sc. VIII), Houghton Library of Harvard University. In the nineteenth century, (a) was sold by Puttick & Simpson at their auction of 26 May 1853 for five guineas; today, it would fetch £50,000 at a minimum. (2) MS. score, mostly by Johann Schellinger, National Janáček Music Library, Brno, ČSSR, A 17019 (late copy, after Schellinger had left princely service: watermarks: star-fish with six points, single crescent, 'EGA', three crescents, 'BV'; probably *c.* 1800 – these watermarks also in the first performance material of *The Seasons*, Stadtbibliothek Vienna. (3) MS. score from the Esterházy workshop (three copyists), Sächsische Landesbibliothek, Dresden. (4) MS. score by Johann Schellinger (signed 'Sch') with corrections and additions by Haydn, Preussische Staatsbibliothek, Berlin, 9912/1. (5) MS. score from the Esterházy workshop, same library, 9912. (6) MS. score from the Esterházy workshop, Zentralbibliothek, Zürich. (7) MS. score by several authentic copyists which Haydn sent to Dr Burney, Reid Music Library, Edinburgh. With Dr Burney's nameplate. (8) MS. score by an authentic copyist (Johann Elssler?), Burgenländisches Landesmuseum, Eisenstadt. The MS. contains watermarks (three crescents, eagle, 'REAL') which suggest that it was copied before 1791. It consists (Hoboken numbering) of Nos. 7a–b, 9, 11a–b, 12a–b, 14 and Atto III° except for the opening recitative. In the Finale of Atto II° (*Werke*, p. 232), Haydn has added an explanatory note (facsimile: Geiringer 1932, p. 125): 'NB: the composer asks that in this and several similar passages, viz.

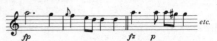

his purpose and true expression be reached, in that in all the parts, the first stroke of the forte be of the shortest duration, in such a fashion that the forte seems to disappear instantly.' This is interesting because in the autograph Haydn wrote the *f* and *p* quite far apart: [symbol] . (9) Artaria issued piano scores of Ubaldo's Rec. ('Valorosi compagni') and Aria ('Dove son') from Atto I° and Rinaldo's Rec. ('Quai prende il bosco') and Aria ('Torna pure') in 1787 (pl. no. 101). In view of the multitude of primary sources, we may omit mention of reliable and in part authentic scores in the Gesellschaft der Musikfreunde (IV 33853), Prague (National Museum, acquired at the present writer's instigation from private possession in 1959), etc.

Libretto: Probably adapted by Nunziato Porta from various sources, including the anonymous settings by Gazzaniga (Rome, 1773) and Naumann (Padua, 1773) (*Werke*, foreword, p. vii).

Critical edition: *Joseph Haydn Werke* XXV/12 (Wilhelm Pfannkuch), 1965.

First performance in modern times: Armida: Gundula Janowitz; Rinaldo: Waldemar Knecht; Idreno: Günter Reich; Ubaldo: Werner Hollweg; Clotarco: Horst Laubenthal; Zelmira: Nancy Burns; Cappella Coloniensis, conducted by Ferdinand Leitner. Radio Cologne (Westdeutscher Rundfunk), 1968.

Literature: Geiringer 1932, 89, 114–6. Wirth I, 151ff. Wirth II, 45ff. Bartha-Somfai, 114f., 281. Landon in *HJB* VI (1969), pp. 213f. Landon in *NOHM* VII (1973), pp. 195f.

Synopsis of the plot: The background: Ismene has enchanted the forests so that the Franks are unable to construct any siege machines and thus free Jerusalem. Furthermore, the sorceress Armida has brought Rinaldo, the best Frankish fighter, into her power and has seduced him, with her manifold charms, away from his duty. Goffredo, King of the Franks, now proceeds to send out Ubaldo and the Knight Clotarco, with soldiers, to free Rinaldo.

Armida, Zelmira and Idreno see the knights approaching and attempt with every means to keep them away from the territory, but this is in vain and soon they are at the foot of the mountain at the top of which Rinaldo is living, in Armida's castle. Idreno tells of the approaching enemy and Rinaldo is ready to fight, but Armida has her doubts and begs her lover to keep himself hidden: Rinaldo promises to do so. From the battlements he sees the magnificent knightly train approaching, and faint memories of his earlier life stir in him. Zelmira is sent out by Idreno to lure the Franks into a trap, but she promptly falls in love with Clotarco and the plan misfired. Ubaldo enters

---

1 Timpani are, inexplicably, missing in the Finale. In Ubaldo's Aria (Atto II°), 'Prence amato', Haydn calls for '2 Trombe o 2 Corni in C alto'. In Idreno's Aria (Atto II°), 'Teco lo guida', C *alto* horns or trumpets are specified.

the castle and finds Rinaldo, who (as happened to crusaders living in the Holy Land) has changed out of all recognition. Ubaldo talks earnestly to Rinaldo, reminds him of his early life, his valiant deeds, and persuades him, despite his love for Armida, to return to the Frankish camp. Armida intervenes and wins back the wavering Rinaldo. As a last resort, Idreno will pretend to sue for peace and again lure the enemy into a trap. As a sign of peace, Ubaldo demands Rinaldo's freedom. Idreno assures him that Rinaldo can stay or leave as he pleases. Yet again Armida intervenes and Rinaldo swears his love for her, but Ubaldo's contempt reminds him of his duties. Armida faints and when she recovers, Rinaldo has gone.

Full of joy, Rinaldo takes up his old life in the camp. Armida appears and wants to remain with him, a procedure which Ubaldo refuses to tolerate. It requires all Ubaldo's powers of persuasion to keep Rinaldo in the camp. Rinaldo's task is to pass the enchanted forest in safety. At first he is surrounded by nymphs, who ask him if he comes as a lover or as a warrior. Rinaldo approaches a great myrtle tree and is about to pierce it with his spear when the tree opens and out steps Armida with her magic wand, mesmerising Rinaldo with her love. But when he rejects her love and is about to split the tree, Armida with a wave of her wand conjures up the Furies, who fall on Rinaldo, who prays to gods for strength to carry on his knightly duties. He rams his spear into the tree and, with a clap of thunder, he finds himself in the middle of the Frankish camp. The magic spell is broken. Rinaldo is proud of his moral victory, but his heart is heavy when Armida, Idreno and Zelmira enter the camp. He swears of his love to Armida and bids her to wait for him, but Armida's love has changed to hate. In the Finale, the cast ponders the lovers' sad fate as, in the background, the Frankish troops march out to battle for Christ and Country.

Like the 'Chanson de Roland', *Armida's* story was an old one, going back to Tasso's *Gerusalemme liberata*, which had also served Monteverdi in his epochal 'Duel between Tancredi and Clorinda'. Lully, Pallavicino, Handel, Gluck, Anfossi, Salieri, Sacchini, Gazzaniga and Righini had all treated the story; as the poem 'moved' into the eighteenth century, a *lieta fine* was introduced: in Gluck's setting of 1755, Rinaldo promises to return after he has completed his military service, and Armida promises to wait for him. In the libretto for Haydn's version, printed by Siess in Oedenburg, we read, after the contents, the note: 'The fable is well known, and if one or the other point has been altered, this was done in order to enhance the other theatrical effects.' The Porta-Haydn arrangement is not without its effective moments, and *Armida*, which was soon translated into German and given by Hubert Kumpf in the Erdödy Theatre at Pressburg (première: 3 November 1786), was a modest success in Haydn's lifetime. It was Prince Nicolaus's favourite opera and received, with its 54 performances, more applause than any other work in the history of the Eszterháza Theatre. No doubt it was primarily the princely approval which moved Haydn to write to Artaria on 1 March 1784, 'I am told that this is my best work up to now' – an opinion which modern Haydn enthusiasts would hardly share, but which shows the central position of Haydn's operas in his mind during the period under discussion. The lavish production at the Esterházy theatre, with its huge supplementary cast of 'supers', stage bands, etc. – more than fifty persons –, no doubt contributed to the general success. *Armida* was given at Pest in 1791 and at the Theater auf der Wieden, as an 'academy' (i.e. in concert version), on 25 March 1797, and in an 'arranged' form at Turin (Imperial Theatre, first performance: 26 December 1804).

The Overture is one of Haydn's very finest: it is what is termed a 'potpourri', that is, it uses literal quotations from the opera itself. We have come a long way from the Overture to *Acide* (January 1763), a three-movement work which so closely resembled the contemporary symphony that it was easily sold as a concert piece (e.g. to Göttweig Abbey in 1769), for it had absolutely nothing to do with the content, the mood or the structure of the opera to which it belonged. *Armida* could be (and was) sold as a concert piece,[1] but it is closely bound up with the drama that follows. In the principal theme, Rinaldo's conflict between duty and passion is made clear, while the march-like

---

1 Supplementing the list of the sources for the Opera proper, we may add: (1) the authentic MS. parts that Haydn sent to Forster on 8 Nov. 1784, now British Museum, Eg. 2379; (2) authentic MS. parts, EH, Budapest, Ms. mus. I. 104.

secondary theme is a reminder of his military duties. The development describes the turbulent scenes of his love for Armida and his guilty conscience. The middle movement, a plaintive allegretto, which is taken from Atto III°, Sc. II ('Orrido bosco'), the enchanted woods through which Rinaldo must pass: the allegretto is used to introduce the seductive nymphs, among them Zelmira (*Werke*: Overture, middle part, pp. 12ff.; Sc. II of Act III, pp. 265ff.). Haydn now introduces a kind of accompanied recitative in which the first violin imitates the soprano (with the appoggiature all *written out*): Armida's pleadings and (implicitly) his refusal. In B flat minor (Vivace) Haydn now introduces the Furies' music (*Werke* 14 and 290), Armida's revenge; but although the sudden *forte* in the Overture is a dramatic moment, Haydn has reserved the really hair-raising version for the Opera itself. The march-like theme returns and we know (because Haydn tells us) that Rinaldo will return to his Christian duty. (We might note that one possible source for the slow movement's foretelling an actual moment in the ensuing Opera is Mozart's *Entführung*, which Haydn might have seen sometime between its première and the winter of 1783/4.)

By way of introduction to the music, we may quote our short description in the *New Oxford History of Music* (VII, 195):

> Of all Haydn's operas for Eszterháza, this one has the fewest ensembles. Except for the final duet there are none in Act I; in the second act there is only the final terzetto, which Helmut Wirth (II, 47) rightly calls 'the peak of the opera' while the third act contains 'a short piece in which everyone appears'. So, in a sense, Haydn has renounced the principles which created the earlier masterpieces, *Le pescatrici* and *L'infedeltà delusa*. The sacrifice has its good and bad points: we miss the rich and varied sound of the large-scale ensembles, as well as the variety that they lend in breaking the chain of arias and recitatives. On the other hand, Haydn was able to achieve an increased concentration on the individual characters. As the plot unfolds, the character of Rinaldo develops, both in musical and in dramatic terms; the violent struggle within himself between his Christian duty and yielding to Armida's charms is admirably set off by the simple, military 'right and wrong'-ness of Ubaldo, who sees through Armida long before Rinaldo does. Incidentally, it has been said, with considerable justification, that the central figure in the operas is not Armida but Armida's *selva incantata*, the enchanted forest which colours the action much as the city of Nuremberg does in *Die Meistersinger*.

A few points must suffice: No. 1 is Rinaldo's 'war' Aria, 'Vado a pugnar', with its obbligato *alto* horns or trumpets, and timpani, which we now remember in several previous operas. We bring this up because in *La vera costanza, Orlando Paladino* and *Armida*, Haydn adopts a very curious attitude towards the drums: they are only used once in the first two of these works and only once in *Armida*. In the three other places where we would expect the drums (i.e. Idreno's Aria 'Teco lo guida' [Atto II°] Ubaldo's 'Prence amato' [Atto II°] and the Finale of Act III, where there are *alto* horns and/or trumpets), they are silent: Ferdinand Leitner adds them, and we believe quite rightly, to the Finale, but it is a curious lapse on Haydn's part, a negligence which we do not find in *L'infedeltà delusa* or, indeed, in *La fedeltà premiata* (or even *Il mondo della luna*). We believe it is symptomatic of the haste with which everything operatic now occurred in Eszterháza.

It is not until the end of Atto II° that we finally have an ensemble, the splendid Terzetto 'Partirò', and if the music seems to have moved very slowly in the preceding part of the Opera, we are rewarded, in Atto III°, with what may be considered the greatest operatic scene Haydn ever wrote. Consulting the plot, it will be seen that Rinaldo enters the 'horrible woods' and meets the nymphs. He looks: 'all round high trees rise into the air and nothing else is to be seen'. Reminding us that this exquisite music, Rinaldo's Rec., 'Questa dunque è la selva?, has striking affinities with the close of Symphony No. 68's slow movement, composed in the 1770s, Georg Feder writes:[1] 'The soft stationary sound suggests the quiet forest, the firmly rooted trees; the slowly ascending and descending motion the glance of the spectator; the ruffled figure the light motion of the leaves'. It is *Thonmahlerey* in the finest Haydnesque tradition. After Zelmira's beautiful Aria, the musical contents of which we first heard in the middle of the Overture, Rinaldo has a short accompanied recitative, the progress of which is broken off by the most beautiful Aria in the Opera, Armida's hauntingly sad 'Ah non ferir'. In a dramatic dialogue between the two star-crossed lovers, Armida sees that this time she will fail. She summons the Furies. The music, which we also heard in the Overture, is perhaps the most thrilling moment in all Haydn's stage music: the gaunt unison and 'open' fifth syncopations in the horns, the swooping scales upwards from instrument to instrument, the racing semiquaver strings. It is truly a great moment: *Werke*, 290ff. Rinaldo's last scene, completely free, arietta alternating with accompanied recitative, shows a man almost demented by his divided emotions. The brisk C major Finale, with its C *alto* horns but, as we have said, no timpani, is a conventional ending; but even in its conventionality, Armida's big 'insertion' after the march of the departing Crusaders, 'Vanne, crudel spietato, va tra le morti e il sangue', 'go to your dead and the blood', is remarkably passionate. The war trumpets – very similar to the trumpet calls in Creonte's 'war' Aria in Atto II° of *L'anima del filosofo*[2] – call Rinaldo and Ubaldo to their soldiers, and in C major splendour we have an incongruous conclusion to the last Haydn Opera composed at Eszterháza.

Insertion Arias

The only complete insertion arias of this period – Haydn's concentration of this form will come between 1785 and 1790, when he composed over a dozen – are:

(1) For Paisiello's La Frascatana – Aria di Donna Stella, 'D'una sposa meschinella' (XXIVb:2), a magnificent C major 'display' piece of 1777, with an important *concertante* oboe part, first published by the present writer in 1961 from the autograph in EH, Budapest, Ms. mus. 10 (Haydn-Mozart Presse 128–9);

(2) For Anfossi's La Metilde ritrovata – Aria di Nannina, 'Quando la rosa non ha più spine' (XXIVb:3), a modest, pretty little G major Andante for *la* Polzelli of 1779, also our edition, 1961, from the autograph in EH, Budapest, Ms. mus. 0 – 38;

(3) For Salieri's La scuola de' gelosi (1780) – Aria di Lumaca, 'Dice benissimo' (XXIVb:5), a witty and charming work which might be from the lips of Don Alfonso. It was first published by Traeg in 1802 and in critical edition by us, using the various autograph fragments (Metropolitan Opera Guild, Conservatoire de Musique Paris [Bibliothèque Nationale], the former Geigy-Hagenbach Collection, Basel), the Joseph Elssler parts of the first performance (EH, Budapest) and the copy of the score by L. Lausch (EH, Budapest) from Haydn's own library: Haydn-Mozart Presse 104–5, 1964.

1 *Studies in Eighteenth-Century Music* (Geiringer Tribute), pp. 192f.
2 Quoted in *Haydn in England 1791–1795*, p. 349.

The Masses

Missa brevis Sancti Joannis de Deo (Small Organ Mass)
(XXII:7; 1777?)

Scoring: S Solo (only Benedictus), Choir (S-A-T-B), 2 v., *basso continuo* (org. solo and *continuo*).
Principal sources: (1) Autograph, Gesellschaft der Musikfreunde, Vienna signed 'laus Deo: B. V. M. et Sⁱ Joanni de Deo'. (2) The parts in the Esterházy Archives, Eisenstadt: 'Missa Sancti Joanes, / de Deo. / a 4ᵀᴿᴵ Vocalibus Solo / 2ᵉ Violinis 2. Clarinettis / 2ᵉ. Fagottis 2. Cornui oder / 2ᵉ Clarinis / et / Violone, Organo Solo. / Auth: / Sig Giuseppe Haydn'. There are two sets of sources: (a) the original, small instrumentation and (b) a later adaptation, with added wind parts and an extended Gloria section; we are concerned only with (a). Watermarks of the 4° paper, 35 × 23 cm., with a stag not hitherto recorded in Larsen or Bartha-Somfai, in which the letters ('IGW' are sometimes superimposed across the body of the stag; the second watermark, also a stag with superimposed 'IGW', is similar to, but not identical with, Larsen 12 (*EK* last two pages, see *HÜB*, 166) and also occurs in the papers found in the Stadtpfarrkirche (now Cathedral) of St Martin, Eisenstadt. Of the many attempts to make the tiny Gloria, with its telescoped texts, longer, we must mention Michael Haydn's, charmingly accomplished, with two trumpets (which he had found in his non-authentic source of the Mass), Salzburg, 16 July 1795 (now Staatsbibliothek, Munich). A new version of the Benedictus, made to replace the ornate Rococo organ solo and solo soprano, was composed by Haydn's old friend, Johann Georg Albrechtsberger. It is included in the material of the Mass in the Imperial Hofburgkapelle: we own a full score, made by the late Dr C. M. Brand in 1946, which he kindly presented to us many years ago. The *incipit* is shown below (scoring as in the original, only 2 v. & b. c.)
Critical edition: *Joseph Haydn Werke* XXIII/2 (Landon, Füssl), 1958. Score reprinted by Bärenreiter (Tp. 95, 1962). Schirmer (Landon).
Literature: Brand, *Die Messen* 131ff. Geiringer 1932, 124f. (with facsimile of first page of autograph, showing how some *continuo* player enlarged his notes for greater legibility).

Poco allegro

This Mass is in the telescoped 'missa brevis' tradition, i.e. the texts of the Gloria and some of the Credo are so composed that the four vocal parts sing different text simultaneously. This means, in the case of the present Gloria, that the soprano sings 'Gratias agimus', the alto 'Domine Fili', the tenor 'Domine Deus' and the bass 'Et in terra pax hominibus'. This pernicious habit, it is thought, arose from the habit of singing these short Masses at Advent-tide when the churches were freezing cold; but it was one of the musical traditions that needed urgent reform. At Salzburg, incidentally, even the *missa brevis* form was composed in such a way that the text was clearly understandable.

Apart from the problem of the telescoped texts, however, this Mass has always been extremely popular in Austria and the surrounding Catholic countries. It has a quiet spirit of devotion, even of mysticism, which is most appealing: the slow and rapturous Kyrie (Adagio); the poignant Crucifixus, part of a beautiful slow-paced (Adagio) insert in the Credo; but especially the Benedictus, which seems to fit perfectly into those delicate, small Rococo chapels that grace the Austrian countryside. It is thought that the small size of the Chapel of the Brothers of Mercy at Eisenstadt dictated the restricted number of instruments, and that Haydn himself played the highly ornate, *verspielte* organ solo on the fine instrument of the early 1730s. Certainly the most magical moment in the work is the transformation from the stern Agnus Dei to the Dona nobis, which enters almost imperceptibly. At the very end of this intimate movement, Haydn instructs everyone 'perdendosi' and 'pianiss.' and the music dies away to three softly repeated notes: it is the 'still small voice' of a very private prayer which we are fortunate enough to overhear.

Missa Cellensis (*Mariazellermesse*)
(XXII:8; 1782)

Scoring: S-A-T-B Soli; Choir (S-A-T-B). 2 ob., 2 bsn., 2 trpt., timp., str., *continuo* (org.; also bsn. when not solo).

Principal sources: (1) Autograph, formerly Benedictine Monastery of Göttweig, sold (through personal intervention of Adolf Hitler) to the Preussische Staatsbibliothek, Berlin, in 1937; signed 'Laus Deo et B: V: Maria' and with the dedication 'Missa Cellensis / Fatta / per il Signor Liebe de Kreutzner / e / composta / di me giuseppe Haydn mpria / 782' (on the title page). (2) The MS. parts in EH Eisenstadt are from the legacy of Carl Kraus, *Regens chori* of the Stadtpfarrkirche St Martin in Eisenstadt, and are not (Hoboken vol. II, 87f.) from Elssler's workshop; the parts were acquired from the Kraus legacy in 1802. All the MS. copies of the work consulted – there are many in Austria, including (2), and also including the (late) first edition in score by Breitkopf & Härtel (pl. no. 3454, issued in 1823 in an edition of 400 copies – the earlier B. & H. editions, twenty years previously, had been printed in editions of 1,000: *sic transit gloria mundi*) – contain certain vocal ornaments and arabesques not found in (1) but perhaps added later by Haydn in the Gratias (see

Bärenreiter score, pp. 18–21); or they represent the kind of ornaments which the singers automatically added, and as such are also valuable for our knowledge of the performance practice of the period.[1]

Critical editions: Joseph Haydn Werke XXIII/2 (Landon, Füssl), 1958. Score reprinted by Bärenreiter (Tp. 96, 1962). Schirmer (Landon).

Literature: Brand, *Die Messen* 143ff. Geiringer 1932, 127. Landon, *SYM*, 395. Landon, *Essays*, 72f.

1 Some first recordings: *Missa in honorem B. V. M.* (Great Organ Mass) – Soli, Akademie Kammerchor, Vienna Symphony, conducted by Ferdinand Grossmann (J. Nebois, organ), Vox 1951. *Missa Sancti Nicolai* – Vienna recording, conducted by George Barati, Lyrichord 1961. *Missa brevis Sancti Joannis de Deo* – Hedda Heusser (S), Akademie Kammerchor, Vienna Symphony, Anton Heiller, org. (on a 17th cent. *Positiv*), conducted by Hans Gillesberger, producer: H.C.R.L. Lyrichord, 1952. *Missa Cellensis* – Soli, Akademie Kammerchor, Vienna Symphony Orchestra, conducted by Hans Gillesberger; Haydn Society, 1949; producer: H.C.R.L.

The insertion aria 'Quando la rosa' is included in Bartha-Somfai; Judith Sándor, Hungarian State Concert Orchestra, conducted by Erwin Lukács; Qualiton LPM 1561. 'Dice benissimo': D. Fischer-Dieskau, Vienna Symphony Orchestra, conducted by Reinhard Peters (Decca, 1971).

If we examine the contemporary MSS. of the *Missa Cellensis*, it soon becomes apparent that they are relatively late: Göttweig Abbey, always one of the first to acquire new works by Haydn, copied the *Missa brevis Sancti Joannis de Deo* in 1778, about a year after it had been written; but the *Missa Cellensis* in 1791. Melk Abbey acquired it in 1792, Seitenstetten Abbey 1793 and in the Archives of the publishers Schott there is a score 'Terminato li 2 di Novembre 1795' (Hoboken vol. II, p. 88).

There are, we believe, two reasons for this curious state of affairs. First, Haydn probably made an arrangement with 'Signor Liebe de Kreutzner' to whom the work was dedicated that Kreutzner have the 'exclusive rights' for the work's performance for a certain period: this was the procedure, at any rate, with Haydn's and Beethoven's works of the 1790s and 1800s (see the later volumes of this biography). But an even more potent reason for the Mass's non-proliferation originated in Schönbrunn Palace: the so-called Josephinian Reforms. Joseph II has been the occasional subject of this volume, particularly concerning his attitude towards music, based on contemporary documents. As we have said before, it cannot be within the scope of this volume to discuss Joseph's reforms, which caused such a profound shock in their day; but his reforms of church music directly concern us.

Joseph sought to curb the Church's powers in the crown lands. The monasteries, in particular, were subjected to his cold scrutiny, and his Enlightened eye did not look kindly on those institutions unless they also fulfilled the function of educating the populace (many Benedictine Monasteries, such as Kremsmünster, organized a school: in Kremsmünster there was a 'Ritter Akademie', an academy for young noblemen): the contemplative orders were in many cases forced to disband, and the rich church furnishings, libraries and furniture were auctioned. Joseph also introduced the vernacular into church services, and insisted in the economy and simplicity of the service. In a letter of 10 September 1782, the Emperor proposed that 'figuraliter' music (i.e. with orchestra) be allowed on Sundays and certain holidays, 'in which way the bothersome expenses for music and the other burdens of the clergy and their assistants might be avoided ...'. All litanies, benedictions and vespers with music were to be discontinued. Naturally, these proposals were not greeted with joy, especially among the many church-music players in Vienna. The Archbishop of Vienna, Cardinal Migazzi (who had been a guest at Eszterháza and loved Haydn's music – for the fifty-year jubilee of his priesthood, he had a Haydn Mass played at St Stephen's Cathedral) asked for some modifications in a letter to the Emperor of 21 January 1783, *inter alia* that the Archbishop continue to celebrate vespers on high holidays 'with the same solemnity' as before; to which Joseph II replied, 'The archbishop may celebrate vespers as he pleases, with all the instrumental music, especially if he defray the musical expenses out of his own pocket.' Despite Migazzi's misgivings, the 'Order of Service for Lower Austria' was published as a court decree on 25 February 1783 and became law on 20 April. Similar restrictions on the use of instrumental music – only Sundays and holidays – were soon promulgated in other parts of the monarchy. In the *regolamento* for Lombardy (under Austrian rule) we read that the instrumental music 'non sia strepitosa, ma decentemente moderata'.

Like most of the Josephinian reforms, his attempt to reduce the amount of instrumental music was successful only for as long as he lived. After his death in 1790, instrumental Masses again flourished; but the disbanded monasteries remained, in almost all cases, disbanded, and the many Viennese church musicians who had been obliged to seek other occupations or, at best, new positions, could not return to their former posts because those posts had been, meanwhile, permanently removed form the ecclesiastical budget. Although we cannot blame the Josephinian reforms entirely, they were certainly part of the reason that Mozart composed no more Masses after that in C minor (K.427), in 1783, and no church music at all (except the *Ave verum*, that miracle of beauty, for the Parish Church at Baden, in 1791) during his residence in Vienna, before the *Requiem*; and that Haydn wrote no more Masses, after the one under discussion, before 1796.[1]

The 'Mariazellermesse' is one of its composer's most popular Masses in Austria and Catholic southern Germany. Its combination of *Volkstümlichkeit* and polyphonic grandeur has always appealed to the Austrian sense of Baroque churchliness, whereas the popular, cheerful music of the Kyrie, with its powerful, massive choral writing, its trenchant trumpets and timpani, its gay and jubilant violin parts might prove puzzling for many Anglo-Saxon ears, attuned as they are to Protestant hymns and – if any *figuraliter* music enters the Sunday services – a Bach fugue or Tallis anthem. But if we adopt Haydn's standards, it is clear that with this *Missa Cellensis* and *La fedeltà premiata* he reached, and reached with astonishing panache and intellectual vigour, the popular style for which he had been so long and so diligently searching in his instrumental music. And there is no doubt that the sense of faint superficiality, even triviality, which we find in piano sonatas such as No. 48 (XVI:35) or No. 53 (XVI:34) or in symphonies such as No. 69 ('Laudon') or No. 66 in B flat, and which was a partial consequence of Haydn's searching for the popular idiom, is in no way reflected in either Mass or opera. In other words, Haydn found his equilibrium first in vocal music and then in instrumental music, for it can be argued that it is with such Symphonies as Nos. 86, 88 and 92 ('Oxford'), with the Quartets,

1 Brand, *Messen* 187ff. R. G. Pauly, 'The Reforms of Church Music under Joseph II', in *Musical Quarterly* XLIII/3 (1957), pp. 372ff., from which useful article we have quoted pp. 377f. For the situation among the Viennese musicians after the 'Verbote', see Otto Biba, 'Die Wiener Kirchenmusic um 1783', in *Beiträge zur Musikgeschichte des 18. Jahrhunderts* I/2, Eisenstadt 1971. Migazzi: *Haydn: the Late Years 1801–1809*, p. 82.

Opp. 54, 55 and 64, and with Piano Sonatas Nos. 58 (XVI:48) and 59 (XVI:49) that Haydn reached the level of his vocal music of the period and achieved in the field of purely instrumental music that perfection of the popular style which he had, in the Masses of 1777(?) and 1782, and in the Opera of 1780/1, found some years before in vocal music.

In its overall form and style, in its orchestration, in its consistent use of the four vocal soloists, the *Missa Cellensis* of 1782 establishes the pattern that was to characterize Austrian church music after 1790, including Haydn's own last six Masses (1796–1802). To this crucially important work of 1782 we must add Mozart's last two completed works in the form – the great Mass in C minor (K.427) was (a) not completed and therefore could not be used in regular Mass services and (b) was not printed until 1840: the 'Coronation' Mass (K.317), of 1779 and the so-called *Missa Solemnis* (K.337) of 1780. Both these works became immensely popular and were circulated all over Austria, Bohemia and southern Germany. Haydn's chapel at Eisenstadt also owned them.[1]

There has been a great change between Haydn's last C major Mass, the 'first' *Missa Cellensis in honorem B. V. M.* (1766), which had been composed in the large 'cantata' mass form, and the 'second' *Missa Cellensis* of 1782. The earlier work followed a long tradition and was written in the prevailing church-music style of the period, whereas the present work is a fusion of the traditional church-music style with the principles of the new symphonic style. Thus, the slow introduction (very impressive in the way it builds up, starting with the bass voices and *continuo*) makes use of a *ff* > which we would never have found in the older *Missa*, with its 'terraced' Baroque dynamics. The symmetrical theme of the ensuing *Vivace* is in the newest popular style: soprano solo, taken over by chorus with the trumpets and timpani entering for the first time. The violins of bars 31ff., in imitation (not strict), could be from a string quartet or symphony, and we find ourselves modulating, as in sonata form, to the dominant; there, Haydn follows his own monothematic sonata form principles, and we have the first subject again, this time for alto solo and with the words 'Christe eleison'. There is even a kind of development section and at bars 100f. a recapitulation in which the original soprano solo is omitted. And to cap this fantastic transcription of sonata form into Kyrie, there is even a coda. The sound of the trumpets and kettledrums, cutting through the texture in a particularly effective way just before the pause that introduces the coda, is, in one of the great Baroque churches of Austria, an experience that simply cannot be duplicated in a concert hall. We also note, when hearing Haydn's Masses in these large churches, how well he has written the scores from an acoustic standpoint.

---

1 Both entitled 'Missa Solemnis' and both acquired, it would seem, before 1790. The trombone parts were omitted, since the Eisenstadt chapel had none at this period. In EH, Eisenstadt (where these two copies are kept), there are also the following other church works by Mozart: Masses, K.194 (186h), 220 (196b), 140 (Anh. 235d, authenticity disputed), K. 257 ('Credo Mass'), K.258, K.275 (272b; with 2 ob., 2 bsn., 2 hns., 2 trpt., timp. and va.) and K.259 (with 2 ob.). One copy of the *Graduale ad Festum Beatae Mariae* (K.273) of 1792 has been discussed in *Haydn in England 1791–1795*, p. 113. There is a second copy at EH, Eisenstadt, 'Auth: Sig^RE Wolfgang Mozart / requiescat in pace / T St: / Xbris 794 Eisenstadt'. *Offertorium de B. V. Maria*, 'Alma Dei creatoris' (K.277 [272a], copied by Anonymous 63 before 1790 (one of Mozart's few Marian compositions, collected by a man who dedicated most of his large-scale works in the 1760s, 70s and 80s, to the Virgin: coincidence?). *Offertorium de tempore* 'Misericordias Domini' (K.222 [205a]) in two copies, one *c.* 1790 and one later in the 19th century. The following interesting arrangements were copied, according to our comparison of the watermarks with comparable material, *c.* 1790–1800, when Haydn was in charge of the church music for Prince Nicolaus II: *Motetto* 'Jesu Rex tremenda' (transcription of *Thamos*, K.345 [336a], 'Gottheit'; *Motetto* 'Splendete te, Deus' (transcription of *Thamos* 'Schon weichet dir, Sonne'); *Motetto* 'Nos pulvis et cinis' (transcription of *Thamos*, 'Ihr Kinder'); all three for the original scoring with choir and large orchestra, including trombones (which were simply not used). Naturally, all these sources are in MS. parts. Early nineteenth-century sources: *Graduale* 'Vias tuas' (transcription of the Terzetto 'Soave sia il vento' from *Così fan tutte*, K.588); *Alma* (transcription of *Die Zauberflöte*, K.620, 'O Isis und Osiris') by *Regens chori* Carl Kraus (d. 1802). Later MSS. (*c.* 1810 and later: *Ave verum* (K.618), *Requiem* (K.626); Breitkopf & Härtel score of 1800 and parts in MS., copied perhaps very shortly thereafter). Sources of *c.* 1830: *Regina coeli* (transcription of K.323, a Kyrie = Anh. 118), Diabelli score (pl. no. 3423) & MS. parts. The *Vesperae de Domenica* (K.321) is a late copy of *c.* 1830–50.

The Gloria is worked out in several sections. The opening is one of Haydn's most joyous and his 'fingerprint' rhythm in the kettledrums  is heard twenty-three times in forty-nine bars. The next section is a lyrical Gratias of great melodic beauty (Allegro, 3/8 time), of which the innocent theme is:

The use of the 3/8 time is a carry-over from the earlier Mass tradition (Gratias of *Missa in honorem B. V. M.*, Domine Deus of the *Missa Cellensis* of 1766) and never appears again in a Haydn mass. Another old-fashioned feature is that 'Fagotti' appear as obbligato instruments only in this movement and simply doubled the bass otherwise; Haydn would, in later years, never return to this shorthand method of notation.

At bar 160, the music suddenly enters F minor, the chorus enters, the oboes and bassoons are marked *ff* (with long-held lines), and the Qui tollis begins, a fine movement in a somewhat old-fashioned 'severe' style which is an admirable contrast to the open, rather folk-song-like quality of the 'Gratias' Aria. The Quoniam (Allegro con brio) re-introduces trumpets and kettledrums and is in that same breathless, forward-driving style as beginning of the Gloria. There is a magnificent fugue 'a due soggetti' (as Haydn would have marked it in a quartet or symphony – fugues being a matter of course in a mass, he did not do so here). The pedal point – first dominant, then tonic – leads into the most brilliantly written bars of the Mass (271ff.), with the inverted pedal point first given to first violins and then another dominant pedal point where the previous semiquaver movement of the violins is transferred to the violas

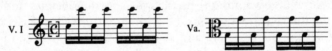

In between there is the following bar (272) which is rivalled in brilliance only by Symphony No. 56/I, bars 263–6:

558

The same orchestral glitter marks the first part of the Credo, where we can see the layout of the late Haydn Masses perfectly anticipated: the oboes filling in the harmony, trumpets and drums punctuating the whole with stabs of rhythmic intensity, the choir singing the words in crotchets and occasionally in quavers (or minims). The lower strings are in quavers throughout and the violins mostly in semiquavers, the repeated notes being calculated for the church with its reverberating acoustics (♪♪♩♩ ♫♫♩: see also E. T. A. Hoffmann's remarks on this particular point and their relation to Haydn's Masses, as quoted in *Haydn: the Years of 'The Creation' 1796–1800*, p. 167).

The Et incarnatus is a tenor 'Aria' which begins in A minor, modulates (as one would expect) to the relative major (C) and then (as one would not expect), the key signature changes to C minor and the procedure is repeated in this new key: i.e. theme in C minor, modulation to relative major. The Crucifixus introduces the choir and free imitation and is another fine example of the 'severe style'. This entire middle section is without brass and drums, which rejoin the group together with a recapitulation of the opening material for the text 'Et resurrexit'; but here again we have a curious throw-back to the 'telescoped' kind of approach used in the *missa brevis* form, in that no less than *four* texts are presented simultaneously, viz. soprano 'Et resurrexit, etc., alto 'Et in Spiritum Sanctum' etc., tenor 'Et iterum venturi' etc., and bass 'Qui cum Patre' etc. This barbaric practice was never repeated by Haydn again, and in the edition by Verlag Böhm of Augsburg (general editor: the late Alfred Schnerich), this problem – insuperable for actual use within the church service – has been cleverly solved by repeating the material and disentangling the texts. (The Böhm solution of the *Missa Brevis Sancti Joannis de Deo* is less successful for the simple reason that the movements concerned, Gloria and the Credo sections flanking the Et incarnatus, which was never 'telescoped', are so short that the many repetitions necessary to disentangle the texts completely destroy Haydn's compact formal scheme.) The Et vitam is another stirring fugue, short, immensely compact and very effective.

The Sanctus starts with an Adagio whose melodic basis is a Marian pilgrimage song of considerable antiquity. There is again, in this Adagio, a sense of rapture and at the same time a wonderfully original use of the trumpets and timpani, both for massive tutti entrances (e.g. bars 15ff.) and for *piano* accompaniment of the opening section when it returns in bars 11–4. Haydn, of course, had no trumpets in his band at Eszterháza except for a brief period in the year 1780; and he now rejoices in these instruments, so closely associated with festive Masses in Austria and so much a part of the great Baroque tradition. The second part of the Sanctus is in Allegro ('Pleni sunt coeli et terra') which turns into a fugato for the words 'Osanna in excelsis'. Haydn's indulgence in the fugue, all during this Mass, almost seems to be compensation for the fact that fugues had less and less place in the 'popular style': and the exceptions are always musically important (e.g. Symphony No. 70, Finale).

Haydn seldom borrowed from himself, and one of the curious exceptions is his Goldoni Opera, *Il mondo della luna* to which, it would seem, he was especially attached: (1) he used the Overture as the basis for Symphony No. 63; (2) he fashioned a substantial part of the Flute Trios, Op. 38, for his British publisher William Forster, from sections of the Opera; (3) he took the entire Benedictus from Ernesto's beautiful Aria from Atto II°, 'Qualche volte non fa male'. It is an interesting comment on the close application of the Haydn's new style to chamber, opera pit and church, that such an operatic aria could fit into the church so easily – indeed, as effortlessly as 'Tönet ihr Pauken, erschallet Trompeten' could become 'Jauchzet, frolocket' (Bach's *Christmas Oratorio* and the secular Cantata which formed its famous opening Chorus). Of course Haydn chose well: the G minor Aria is no piece of Italianate frivolity but a carefully worked-out piece of music that begins archaically with dotted Baroque patterns and trills that sound like a *concerto grosso* composed two generations earlier. Naturally Haydn chose the Aria primarily for its middle section, which is first in the relative, then in the tonic, major, and is one of the many melodic sources for the second part of 'Gott erhalte' (the Aria is quoted in *Haydn: the Years of 'The Creation' 1796–1800*, p. 274): this is one of Haydn's great, indeed immortal melodies, and he was quite right to salvage it from an Opera that had, by 1782, become relegated to the library shelves in Eszterháza.

Yet another example of the 'severe' style confronts us for the Agnus Dei in C minor (no trumpets, no timpani), a worthy introduction to the greatest fugue of them all, the life-enhancing 'Dona nobis', whose brilliantly syncopated theme was given to Beethoven as a subject for study:

Vivace

Do - na no - bis, pa - - - - [cem]

When he was a pupil of Albrechtsberger, Beethoven was given this theme to work on, probably in the year 1794.[1] This final 'Dona' fugue may be considered as one of the finest choral fugues in Haydn's *œuvre*: surely he never surpassed its exaltation or its immaculate construction. It is a short fugue, like all in this Mass, and without any interruptions from the soloists and, incidentally, only one single contrast in *piano* (bars 66–9), ending in a great deceptive cadence that looks forward to a similar one in a similar position in the *Missa Sancti Bernardi de Offida*.

It was Haydn's great farewell to the Mass form, which he was to take up again in 1796, when he returned from England a much changed man. The 'Mariazellermesse' is, indeed, 'The Great Precursor'.

The Symphonies

SINGLE WORKS

Nos. 61, 53 ('L'impériale'), 63 ('La Roxelane'), 70, 75, 71, 62, 74, 73 ('La Chasse')

CHRONOLOGY

No.	Date	Remarks
61	1776	Autograph dated.
53	1777–9(?)	Finale Version 'B' dated (autograph) 1777. Without the slow introduction: Breitkopf Catalogue 1779/80. With introduction and Finale 'B': Seitenstetten Monastery, 1781. Without introduction and with Finale 'B', 'as performed at Messrs Bach and Abel's Concerts' printed by Blundell (London): last Bach-Abel concert on 9 May 1781 (Terry: *John Christian Bach* [Landon edition 1967] 165).
53	revised version *c.* 1781–2(?)	Finale Version 'A': EH, Budapest. Copied after (or during – therefore not yet in library and not destroyed) fire in Nov. 1779. Principal copyist: Joseph Elssler (d. 26 Oct. 1782).
63	1777–80(?)	First movement as Overture to *Il mondo della luna*: 1777. Finale: First version – part of a Minuet & Finale, composed between *c.* 1769–73 (*vide*

---

1 Catalogue by V. A. Heck XXVI (September 1926) with a reproduction of Beethoven's fugue as 'Tafel I'.

supra, p. 306). Finale: Second version – inserted later (by Joseph Elssler) into EH parts, copied after (or during) fire, Nov. 1779. MS. copies in Monasteries of Melk and Göttweig: 1781. Hummel edition: 1781.

70	1779	EH parts dated 18. Dec. 1779.
75	1779	EH parts dated 1779.
71	1779–80(?)	First movement's bassoon part in several versions, 'starting' with one not written out but only marked col basso' (Schwerin). This suggests that the movement may have been composed before the rest of the Symphony, which has a normal bassoon part. MS. parts, Gesellschaft der Musikfreunde (Vienna): 1780 ('Fidelis Candon [Landon?]').
62	1779–81(?)	EH parts, Budapest, copied after (or during) fire of 1779. Hummel edition: 1781.
74	1780–1(?)	Haydn's MS. parts for Forster arrived in London on 22 August 1781; Hummel's edition: 1781.
73	1780–2(?)	Finale's original use, as Overture to *La fedeltà premiata* composed in 1780, first performed 1781. No. 73/II based on Haydn's Song *Gegenliebe* (1781?). First edition of the Symphony: Torricella, Vienna, July 1782.

The effect of the new operatic régime at Eszterháza on Haydn's symphonic production is reflected in three ways: (1) the number of works decreases sharply *vis-à-vis* the previous decade; (2) the style of the *opera buffa*, with all its ironic overtones and its musical message makes itself ever more increasingly felt; (3) the quality of the symphonies declines, partly because most were hastily written and some even potpourris of various earlier works, and partly because Haydn's search for the popular style led him to pander to the lowest common denominator. Haydn's mind was not rapier-quick (as was Mozart's) but, like Beethoven, he worked slowly, and needed not only time (which he now did not have) but many examples on which he could experiment.

Haydn, from his present viewpoint, was quite right in judging the public's reaction, for Symphony No. 53 (a potpourri work) turned out to be one of the most successful of all his symphonies: apart from countless MSS., it was rapidly printed by Blundell (1781?), Preston (1783), Hummel (1783–4) and Sieber, Paris (1785?) and arranged for piano and published in several English editions (Longman & Broderip 1782, Preston 1783, etc.). The famous second movement was even given words and proved to be sensationally popular; it was later one of the themes placed on the Haydn monument in Rohrau (1793). Haydn's speciality was rapidly becoming these catchy 'semi-slow' (i.e. Andante or Allegretto) double variation movements, often with alternating major and minor sections, and always in the new style which carefully eschewed any deeper emotions. His next international success was with another potpourri symphony, No. 63, which was put together from *Il mondo della luna* (first movement), his incidental music for C. S. Favart's *Les trois sultanes* (Wahr Troupe, Esterháza 1777?) and an older finale, which Haydn later replaced with one more in the current popular taste. In the process of fashioning this pastiche, he sacrificed much of the finely symphonic orchestration of the Opera Overture and also the original Finale, discarding the second bassoon part of the Overture and the trumpets and drums of both corner movements.[1] In the process, Haydn got into some trouble with the pitch of his horns (*alto* or *basso*) and other details. Yet the Symphony, with its brilliantly composed *La Roxelane* movement (the heroine of the Favart play and so entitled on the original EH parts), proved to be a resounding success: contemporary editions by Le Duc, Paris (1779), Boyer & Le Menu, Paris (1782), Sieber, Paris (1782), Hummel,

---

1 The original Finale also lacked a flute and bassoon(s).

Berlin & Amsterdam (1781), Bland, London (1784?) and in piano arrangement, 'by Sig^r. Giordani', Preston (London) 1783. Haydn seemed to have his finger on the international pulse.

Even when the symphonies were not potpourris, they were composed hastily and copied in phenomenal haste: if we glance at the EH copy of No. 75, we find the copyists taking over from each other in the middle of a part. It would seem, from the evidence of the MS., that Haydn was composing the Finale when the copyists were completing the parts to the first three movements.

Some curious evidence of Haydn's constantly changing orchestra may be seen in the bassoon parts. For a while, Haydn had only one bassoon, and this meant that when he adapted *Il mondo della luna* Overture, the second bassoon had to be removed. For a time, moreover, there was no flute. Can this be the explanation for the first movement in the EH parts of No. 62? Originally there was no flute part to this Allegro, but Haydn later added one in his handwriting (facsimile of a page in Landon, *SYM*, plate XXVI) and wrote the following little note to his player, Zacharias Hirsch: 'Freund! Suche das erste Allegro'. Altogether, there is something rather mysterious about this Symphony. The first movement uses the frame of the Overture in D (Ia:7) of 1777 (when, however, Haydn had Hirsch in the orchestra!), which has no flute part. Haydn originally used this Overture as the opening to some stage piece, because one of the two autographs (the only complete one: Berlin Staatsbibliothek), at the end of movement, modulates to the dominant of C major; this passage was, of course, omitted when Haydn used the movement for another purpose. The second autograph (Vienna Stadtbibliothek) has a widely differing orchestration and may have been an earlier version because this orchestration has not survived elsewhere. Haydn then used the Overture as the Finale of Symphony No. 53 (to which he also later added the slow introduction). When this happened, the following loose ends remained: (1) Haydn composed a timpani part for the first movement, but apparently none for the rest of the Symphony.[1] When it was played at the Bach–Abel concerts, the timpani simply stopped playing after the first movement, and in this semi timpani-less state it was also printed by Blundell. (2) The same situation obtained with the flute part, except that it played through all three movements, stopping only at the Finale. When J. J. Hummel printed No. 53, he found this situation unsatisfactory and added flute and timpani parts to the Finale.

Haydn then made yet a third version of this Overture (Ia:7) and used it to begin No. 62; as we have seen, it began its life without a flute. Since, however, the music was already very well known in England, when William Forster issued No. 62, he dropped the first movement. Many years later Forster issued No. 53, which was not originally part of his catalogue; his descendant (in Sandys-Forster, p. 313) refers to No. 53 as 'The London, or the celebrated in the Key of D'. But great is our surprise to find the second movement of No. 62 in the tonic, and a very odd piece with vast descrescendo signs that, in this number and extent, are unique in Haydn of this period. Its highly theatrical content make one wonder if this, too, is not an Overture or entr'act for one of the Wahr plays. The wonderfully original off-tonic opening of the Finale is also theatrical. The fact that Haydn could use the Overture Ia:7 interchangeably as a first and final movement shows that he had not yet solved the question of the finale as a genre. Haydn himself was worried about it, and wrote a new, formally interesting

---

1 The timpani part in EH for the Minuet and *Capriccio* Finale ('A') is so amateurish that we must ascribe it to a pupil or one of the musicians (copyists?).

'Capriccio' as a new Finale for No. 53. (In France, Sieber thought the Overture Ia:7 was too well known in its form as No. 62's opening movement, for Le Duc in Paris had issued No. 62, possibly importing Hummel's 1781 edition; when, therefore, Sieber issued No. 53 he removed the Overture Ia:7 and substituted an entirely new Finale, referred to as 'C'; it is doubtful if this 'C' Finale is authentic.)[1] An even more curious situation obtains with No. 73. In what is apparently the earliest MS. copy, part of the collection of Haydn's friend and Viennese patron, Ritter von Keeß, the order of the work is as follows:

> First movement: Overture to *La fedeltà premiata* (with parts for two trumpets and kettledrums, as in Haydn's autograph 1780).
> Second movement: as in other version.
> Third movement: ditto
> Finale: Slow introduction and Allegro, otherwise the *first* movement as the work has otherwise survived.

The trumpets and drums disappear after the 'Chasse' movement, which gave the Symphony its name. When Torricella published the work, the order was the one we know today but the trumpets and timpani of the Finale were omitted. In the joint Parisian edition of Imbault & Sieber of 1784, the trumpet and drum parts of the Finale were retained. In Forster's edition, they were omitted.

Side by side with the new kind of popular, rather quick 'slow' movement, based on a folk-song-like tune, and set out in variations – of which Nos. 53 and 63 contained the most celebrated specimens – there now arises another kind of slow movement: the use of a slower tempo and a sort of 'hymn tune'. The most interesting example in the ten works under discussion is No. 75's Poco Adagio. Although in variation form – Haydn was increasingly fascinated with the intellectual capabilities of this technique – it is based on a much more serious kind of melody, one so serious in fact that in London, Haydn noted in his diary that an English clergyman had listened to this movement and found in it a premonition of his coming death (which in fact occurred shortly thereafter).[2] We may note with interest how, as Haydn's popular style becomes increasingly refined, these two types of slow movements persist in his symphonies (and other works, too, of course) to the end of his career: the catchy, folk-tune melody with variations has its culmination in two marvels of the London period, the slow movements of Nos. 94 ('Surprise') and 103 ('Drum Roll'), while the hymn-tune type of melody will be the basis of No. 88's justly celebrated Largo, of No. 92's Adagio, of the slow movement of No. 98, so close in spirit to 'God save the King', and of course the culmination of this hymn tune in the 'Gott erhalte' variations of Quartet Op. 76, No. 3, where the melody is, literally, a hymn.

The greatest of these ten works is surely No. 70, written to celebrate the laying of the corner-stone of the new theatre at Eszterháza just before Christmas of 1779 (see Chronicle, p. 421). Haydn used the occasion to write his best music, and that meant, in the back of his Fuxian-trained mind and Church-oriented soul, counterpoint. Thus the opening movement acts like a bright Overture to the extraordinary second movement, marked (on Haydn's original MS. parts) 'Specie d'un canone in contrapunto doppio' – a grave, dignified canon in which the top and bottom lines can be, and are, reversed. The movement is cast in double variation form, the canon being

---

1 See our edition: Haydn-Mozart Presse (Philharmonia's complete edition of the Haydn Symphonies, Vol. 5) or Haydn Society *Gesamtausgabe*, Ser. I, vol. 5, pp. 141 ff.
2 *Haydn in England 1791–1795*, p. 152.

in D minor and its 'foil' in D major. There is behind this music, a great sense of nostalgia, as if Haydn were saying to himself: if I were not composing in that fatal popular style, this is what I would be composing. The Minuet acts (as did the first movement in its way) as a foil to the Finale, which is marked Allegro con brio and, like the slow movement, is in D minor. It starts off with a whiff of the theatre (those five repeated *d*'s, Harlequin softly opening the drawn curtain?), but at bar 26 there is a *fermata* and suddenly four of those repeated *d*'s turn into a gigantic triple fugue of incandescent power; Haydn marks this section 'a 3 soggetti in contrapunto doppio', just as he had done with the fugues of Op. 20, of which he had been so justly proud. It is a movement of unparalleled power in Haydn's symphonic *œuvre* hitherto and once again a tribute to the fastidious connoisseur for whom it was written, and for whom it was not necessary to compose symphonies with tap-room melodies and racy rondo finales. When Haydn played the Symphony, he could not use timpani because they had been destroyed in the theatre pit. But later he recruited timpani from Forchtenstein Castle and when they arrived, he added, in his own hand, timpani parts for this work (one page reproduced in Landon, *SYM*, pl. xxvii) and had a copyist prepare trumpet parts doubling the horns (omitting one high note in the first movement). These parts for trumpets and drums were prepared when copies had already been sent from Eszterháza to London, Berlin and elsewhere, and so the parts survive only in the Esterházy MS. and were not known to anyone until we published the Symphony.

THE 'ENGLISH' SYMPHONIES OF 1782: NOS. 76–78

With these three works, Haydn began a new trend in his symphonies: they were, (a) as far as we know, the first such works written as a series and (b) composed for a foreign performance. As matters turned out, this proposed London visit fell through, but we know of no other symphonies, at least since 1761, that Haydn wrote especially for abroad. After the potpourri works just discussed, Nos. 76–78 are more carefully composed and in fact sometimes rise to the level of the *Missa Cellensis* or *La fedeltà premiata*. It is curious to see what Haydn now does with the first symphony composed in a minor key since the *Sturm und Drang* period. Of course, we immediately think of the grand Symphony in C minor No. 52, one of the highpoints of that epoch, which now seems so far away. The first movement of No. 78 contains flashes of the old C minor fire, and the contrapuntal extensions of the unison main theme are ingenious and, in the development, stirring. But the popular style would admit of no continual use of *Sturm und Drang*: the second movement (E flat) is placid and unadventurous; the Minuet is in C major; and the Finale, though it starts in C minor, has a C major partner which is in the usual dance (or folk-song) style. If No. 78 came as a shock to those with the sound of Nos. 44, 45 or 52 ringing in their ears, an even worse shock was awaiting the connoisseurs of Op. 20 Quartets.

'They are all very easy', wrote Haydn about these works to M. Boyer, and the easy is also used in the Boswellian sense ('I was easy'). Thinking of London, Haydn will automatically have thought of the famous Bach-Abel concerts, where his 'Festino' (as it was called) Symphony No. 53 had been such a resounding success. In 1782, Johann Christian Bach, the elegant, successful man-of-the-world was still alive, and his presence is even now startlingly conjured up by that magnificent Gainsborough painting: the faintly smiling mouth, the *air* of success surrounding the man. Is it an accident that the first of the new English set, and especially the first movement, has something Christian Bachian about it? That tonic pedal point, the 'cello in quavers, the violins in patterns of thirds above (bars 2ff.) reminds us of many such passages in the 'London' Bach, e.g. the Overture to *Lucio Silla* (Mannheim, 1776, published as a concert symphony in William Forster's Op. 18, No. 2), where after an opening flourish there is the same drop to *piano*, the repeated quavers in the bass line, the violins in rhythmic figures in thirds. But along with this nod to fashion, there are, as always in Haydn, flashes of originality: the murmuring sound of 'B' section in the slow movement which is in B flat minor, with long lines in the wind instruments and pulsating *pp* strings beneath; the explosion of 'C' section – the movement is in A-B-A'-C-A''- Coda – in G minor, which has the drive of the Overture to *L'isola disabitata*. These are all things that bear the stamp of genius. The Trio of the *Menuet* is in pure

waltz time, even to the ♩ ♩ ♩ of the accompaniment (notice the pizzicato only in V.II and Vc.-B.); it is also immaculately orchestrated, with the horns rising in thirds, only to fade away after they have reached *a* flat–*c* (sounding):

There is also a very Haydnesque sound here, flute – bassoon – violin I with the theme in three octaves simultaneously. The whole little movement is a model for *settecento* Viennese popular style.

It was Karl Geiringer who, with his usual perspicacity, drew attention to Symphony No. 77's outstanding development section in the first movement (see the long musical example in score, Geiringer 1932, p. 76). In those days, the score was hardly known, even to connoisseurs. No. 77, in all its movements, is filled with genius, from the contrapuntal splendours of the first, to the vivid inspiration of the slow movement, the *scherzo*-like verve of the Menuetto (marked Allegro rather then Allegretto), and the scintillating panache of the Finale, the fantastic contrapuntal development of which even outdoes that of the opening Vivace.

THE SYMPHONIES OF 1783–4: NOS. 79–81

Another group of three symphonies – all the rest of Haydn's symphonic *œuvre* (except possibly Nos. 88 and 89) was composed in groups – which proved to be as popular as Nos. 76–78. The 'English' set had appeared, more or less simultaneously, in Vienna (Torricella, dedicated to Prince Nicolaus Esterházy, another of Haydn's thoughtful gestures), Paris (Boyer), London (Forster) and Berlin-Amsterdam (Hummel). Nos. 79–81 came out together in Vienna (Artaria), Berlin-Amsterdam (Hummel), while No. 79 was published in London by Bland, and Nos. 80, 81 and *Armida* Overture by Forster; Guera of Lyon published Nos. 80 and 81 with a symphony by Carlos d'Ordoñez, and Le Duc of Paris were the agents for the Artaria edition. Haydn was now an international best-seller.

There is no outstanding work on the level of No. 77 in this set of 1783–4. Each of the three works has many details to delight the connoisseur. One of the problems that Haydn has now solved to his satisfaction is the character of the finale, which was still not entirely satisfactory in the first ten works examined in this chapter. The Overture Ia:7 does not really sound like a Finale; nor does, for that matter, the last movement of No. 62; No. 70's triple fugue was obviously a *tour-de-force* which could not be repeated. The basic difficulty was to create a movement which was intellectually stimulating and yet sounded like a conclusion and not another first movement. Haydn gradually came more and more to the rondo and a quick metre, but to make it interesting he soon injected elements of the sonata into this rondo, creating the sonata rondo form which was to be such a brilliant success in the 'Paris' (and of course 'Salomon') Symphonies. These finales soon came to be the typical products of Haydn's wit, and one fine example is that of No. 80, with its bizarre syncopations, droll woodwind, false entries, and so on.

Even in a cool work like No. 79 in F, there are touches of beauty in every movement: the passage in the first movement at bars 123ff. is of breathtaking originality. The purity and beauty of the slow movement have a certain innocence which the extreme sophistication of the orchestration (especially the wind parts) belies: at the end Haydn breaks off and gives us 'un poco allegro', a kind of *Kehraus* (or 'go-home' music of an Austrian dance series) that introduces a rather curious atmosphere into this hitherto Rococo exquisiteness: it is as if Haydn were bringing us back to the *Puszta*.

If Talleyrand, talking of life before 1789, had wanted to choose one piece of music to sum up all that was dignified, beautiful and typical of the age, he might have chosen this miracle of a Menuetto in No. 79, whose stately beauty is graced by Haydn's most ingenious orchestration (cf. the oboe line in bars 21ff. or the flute entrance at bars 58 and 60).[1]

Symphony No. 80 is a mock-heroic Symphony. The ferocious beginning cannot possibly prepare us for the waltz-like frivolity of the second subject. The violent contrast is carried a step further in the development, where statements of this waltz are separated by a tense extension of the first subject (bars 93–109). This is the total negation of the *Sturm und Drang*, and it was certainly not to everyone's taste. That there would be another way of treating D minor and C minor would be shown from another part of the Austrian monarchy: from Vienna, in Mozart's K.466 and 491 (1785 and 1786). In No. 80 the tonal scheme is the same, *mutatis mutandis*, as in No. 78: second movement in the relative major (here, B flat); third movement in the tonic minor and major (in No. 78 all in the major); Finale in the tonic major (in No. 78 minor and major). There is not very much minor tonality in No. 80, and it was not the time or the place for it, either. Haydn, at this point in his life, was the Great Entertainer, whether for Prince Esterházy's opera house (and as a conductor of Cimarosa, Paisiello and Sarti) or for the international music market. Great Entertainers do not write *Sturm und Drang* symphonies, and by the time Haydn came back from London to write the 'Nelson' Mass and *The Creation*, Europe was a very changed place and he a very changed man.

No. 80 is altogether not a conventional work, and if its D minor is not the Mozartian D minor of K.466, the Trio of Minuet uses a derivative (almost the reverse) of the old Gregorian *incipit lamentatio* melody that Haydn had used in Symphony No. 26. The colouring of No. 80's Trio, with the oboe and horn doubling the melody, also reminds us of a similar procedure in Nos. 26/II (final announcement of the theme).

1 It is not our practice to draw attention to gramophone records except as a statistical adjunct to the sources, but we cannot refrain from mentioning the exquisite playing of the Parisian Orchestra in the new (issued 1976) Philips recording of this Symphony conducted by M. Antonio de Almeida, previously available on Irmac (France) 6710.

The opening of No. 81, with the F natural that slides quietly into the J. C. Bachian G major opening, is much admired. The whole work has the sleek elegance which now marks Haydn in the role of the Great Entertainer, but the robust Minuet still shows the hand of its clever *jongleur*; and the Trio ends up, wistfully, in the minor: the slight touch of the *Puszta* again.

No. 81 marks the end of Haydn, the Great Entertainer. For in 1784 or 1785 two commissions arrived from far-off places that would much change Haydn the man as well as Haydn the musician, the second obviously acting on the first, as with all artists. The first was a request, from Cádiz in Spain, for an oratorio without words on The Seven Words of the Saviour on the Cross; the other a proposal to write six large symphonies for the Parisian Concert de la Loge Olympique; both of which commissions Haydn accepted and which must have greatly liberated his spirits from the rigorous and time-consuming duties as opera *Capellmeister* at Eszterháza.

OVERTURES

We are concerned, here, only with 'concert' Overtures, or rather works which cannot be identified with Haydn's operas; and the two works concerned are Ia:7 in D, which has been discussed above, and Ia:4. The latter first appeared in an edition by Hoffmeister, Vienna, about 1785 or 1786, and is scored for the usual small orchestra of flute, two oboes, two bassoons, two horns and strings.[1] On the occasion of the Soviet State visit to Vienna in 1960, an exhibition of Soviet-Austrian documents was given in the Haus-, Hof- und Staatsarchiv in Vienna, at which, to our general astonishment, the long lost autograph of Ia:4 was exhibited. It is signed 'Finale' and on the right side 'Jos. Haydn mpria' ('Jos.' added later? in an unknown hand?). At the end 'Fine / laus Deo'. The MS. comes from the collection of Prince Youssoupoff and includes a signed declaration of the MS's authenticity signed by Prince Youssoupoff at St Petersburg on 21 May 1888; it is now in the Archives of the Council of Ministers of the Soviet Union in Moscow. The only use of the work as a Finale which is now known is as the conclusion of Symphony No. 53 in a (Traeg?) MS. owned by the Conservatorio Giuseppe Verdi at Milano (cat. 296A). Perhaps Haydn wrote this third Finale for No. 53. Stylistically Ia:4 is rather closer to Symphony No. 80, and is a cleverly constructed and bright movement which has, in recent years, become rather popular as a concert

1 Edited from the Hoffmeister print by the present writer, Diletto Musicale, Doblinger, 1959 (miniature score; Stp. 177).

overture. Since our edition was published before the autograph was known, a few points may be of interest.[1]

1 We do not agree that the Hoffmeister print, because it differs from the autograph, is not authentic (Sonja Gerlach in *Haydn-Studien* II/1 [1969], p. 59). On the contrary, we consider it astonishing that she can state that the print is 'certainly not authentic'; we believe the changes represent changes that Haydn himself made, and for which the autograph gives us the evidence. 116 and 118: hn. II = hn. I. At 124–40, the violins in the autograph have staccato quavers and not semiquavers, but at 124 V. I has the first four notes as in our score, i.e. semiquavers, with Haydn's note 'NB' to the copyist to continue along those lines. 124ff. represent a dramatic acceleration and are, of course, authentic. The following interesting change was removed by Haydn (by crossing out and changing) at bars 155ff.:

At 175, 177: hn. II = hn. I. 210ff.: V. I slurred ♩ ♩ | ♩ ♩ | ♩ ♩ | ♩ . 214/5: whole orchestra slurred barwise. 216/9: only slur in autograph over vc.-b. 216/7. There are other small differences as well, but we believe that most of Hoffmeister's changes are the result of an authentic, later MS.

Concertos

Concerto for Violoncello & Orchestra in D (VIIb:2; 1783)
(orchestration: 2 oboes, 2 horns, strings)

As this biography has often shown, Haydn's concertos have come down to us in an extreme paucity of sources or not at all. This now famous Concerto appeared in Haydn's lifetime in an authentic edition by Johann André of Offenbach-am-Main 'd'après le manuscrit original de l'auteur'. Recent research indicates that it was issued in 1804 (not 1806) and was thereafter reprinted by Vernay in Paris.[1] No other contemporary sources except the autograph is known. André, thinks the late Wolfgang Matthäus, may have acquired the manuscript from Anton Kraft, the Esterházy 'cellist for whom the work was supposedly composed – 'perhaps on the occasion of a concert that the 'cellist gave in Frankfurt-am-Main. In 1799 André

1 Walter Lebermann in *Musikforschung* XIV/2 (1961), correcting Hoboken's date of 1806 for the André and 1803 for the Vernay prints. Hoboken's proposed dates were based on O. E. Deutsch's plate number catalogue and Hopkinson's *Dictionary of Parisian Music Publishers 1700–1950* (London 1954). Deutsch's *Music Publishers' Numbers . . .* London 1946 has, as far as Haydn and André is concerned, been superseded by the late Wolfgang Matthäus, 'Das Werke Joseph Haydns im Spiegel der Geschichte des Verlages Jean André', in *HJB* III (1965), pp. 54ff. Haydn's Concerto is discussed on p. 84, where the close relationship between Mme. Vernay, *née* Révillon, and André is discussed. Her edition of the Haydn Concerto is a licensed republication of the Offenbach print.

published Three Sonatas for Violoncello by Kraft, and on the title page Kraft is expressly listed as Haydn's pupil.'

The autograph, formerly the property of 'Herr Meinert in Dessau' (Aloys Fuchs' MS. cat.),[1] then Julius Rietz in Dresden, was later owned by Breitkopf & Härtel and is now in the Musiksammlung of the Österreichische Nationalbibliothek.

Critical Editions: (1) Edited by Leopold Nowak from the autograph, published by the Austrian National Library: full score 1963. Unfortunately, there are very bad mistakes (misreading of Haydn's abbreviations:

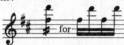

and similar matters): a proposed article on the subject by Karl Trötzmüller for the *HJB* II was withdrawn because Nowak was then director of the music division and Trötzmüller feared the

consequences of his devastating review. (2) Eulenburg 769 (Wilhelm Altmann, 1935), based on André, is a carefully edited score, but without the benefit of the autograph. The present writer has prepared the performance material now available for this Eulenburg score (Praeclassica series), adjusting such Haydn abbreviations as noted above (1st. movt., bar 25 compared to 91 and 186; only bar 25 is written out). (3) Edition Peters (K. Soldan, 1934, based on André print). *Literature*: Leopold Nowak, 'Ein Haydn-Autograph und sein Schicksal: Das 'Cello-Konzert in D-dur, op. 101', in *Biblos*, Jahrgang III (1954).

As a result of an article in Schilling's *Lexicon der Tonkunst* (1837, IV, 207f.), this authentic work was wrongly attributed to Anton Kraft: '... just this very concerto by Kraft is the one which later, after Haydn's death, was published posthumously under his name (André, Offenbach) and up to now considered a genuine work of Haydn's, whereas the writer of these lines has it from the best source that it belongs to our Kraft'. It was, of course, presumed that the source was Kraft's son Nicolaus.

There is no mystification in all this. Nicolaus Kraft undoubtedly heard from his father that Haydn and Anton Kraft had collaborated on the Concerto: the 'cello part was certainly 'tailor-made' for Kraft, and all those brilliant technical effects – indications for flageolet notes (marked 'flautino' in the autograph and André: see I, 175), for various strings ('sul G' at I; 50, 'sul D' at I, 153) are never found in Haydn's earlier C major Violoncello Concerto (VIIb:1) – show that this is a typical eighteenth-century attempt on the part of the composer to display the talents, tone and musicianship of his soloist.

We know that Haydn was desperately busy with the opera house in these years and we wonder how it was possible for him to undertake a large-scale *pièce d'occasion* such as this one. The autograph is clear and neat (for facsimile, see pl. 25) but there are notational problems of which one has been mentioned above. Another is the attractive oboe solo that occurs in I, 24, five bars before the first solo entrance. This pretty little figure

does not appear at the corresponding place at the end of the movement (bar 185): should we presume Haydn forgot it (he always wrote out his recapitulations from memory) and add it, at least in small print? We believe that not all Haydn's differences of this kind should be adjusted, but at least a critical edition must point them out.

Ever since Breitkopf & Härtel issued the dreadful arrangement by G. A. Gevaert in 1890, in which Haydn was reorchestrated and trimmed to Victorian size, this

---

1 *Thematisches Verzeichnis der sämmtlichen Compositionen von Joseph Haydn ... zusammen gestellt von Aloys Fuchs*, Vienna 1840, p. 53, No. 4. Preussische Staatsbibliothek, Berlin, Mus. th. ms. Kat. 606.

Concerto has been the delight of 'cellists the world over – less the delight of audiences, who are obliged to listen to passages of fabulous virtuosity which are the pride of the soloists and anathema to any except the highly trained listener:

The work sounds extremely long: the 8/8 opening Allegro moderato also probably enjoyed a huge cadenza (which will have been more tasteful than the appalling efforts played by most 'cellists – including those by Enrico Mainardi which the new 'critical' edition by Nowak dares to perpetrate), as did the other two movements. There is, moreover, an extraordinary lack of tension in this music, even considering the era in which it was written (the discovery of the 'popular style'), a placidity which is at curious odds with the *Missa Cellensis* of 1782, not to speak of works like the String Quartet, Op. 33, No. 1, or Symphonies Nos. 70 or 77. 'Here we go gathering nuts in May' springs, of course, to the cynical Anglo-Saxon mind when we encounter the pleasant rondo meanderings of the Finale (6/8), which is also full of virtuoso passages fascinating to the soloists and painful to the listener (e.g. bars 119ff., where one always cringes to hear if the octaves will be in tune, which they occasionally are). One remembers with sadness and perplexity that for many years, this Concerto would be the only work by Haydn in the yearly season of the Boston Symphony or the Philadelphia Orchestra. And not only are we used to another concerto language from Mozart, and at this very period too, but in every respect the earlier C major 'Cello Concerto by Haydn is far more interesting for the listener: the Finale generates an electric tension of which the D major work never even has a spark. And our ears are now attuned to the greatest of all Haydn's concertos: that for trumpet and orchestra in E flat (VIIe:1). Against any and all of these sister works, Haydn's famous D major 'Cello Concerto will simply not stand up, except as an exercise for 'cellists. It is curious that no one ever wrote a really great 'cello concerto: not Schumann, not Saint-Saëns, not Vivaldi, certainly not Boccherini (though we must not judge his works by the disgusting arrangement of the B flat Concerto for 'cello), and not even Elgar (the most interesting, in many respects). Perhaps this otherwise noble instrument does not lend itself to virtuoso and musical treatment, *à la même fois*, on a large scale.

Concerto for Harpsichord or Fortepiano and Orchestra in D
(XVIII:11; *c.* 1780–3?)

In this work the orchestra consists of 2 oboes, 2 horns and strings.

Sources: (1) MS. parts, possibly copied from one of the contemporary prints, Preussische Staatsbibliothek, Berlin, 10060. (2) Printed parts by Boyer & Le Menu, Paris, announced in the *Journal de Paris* on 6 July 1784, and on 7 August in the *Mercure de France*. (3) Possibly authentic first edition, in parts, Artaria & Co., Vienna, Op. 37, announced in the *Wiener Zeitung* on 25 July 1784. (4) Printed parts by Longman & Broderip, Op. 37, announced in the *London Recorder* on 26 September 1784. (5) Printed parts by Hummel, Berlin–Amsterdam, 'Concert ... Libro I' issued *c.* 1789(?). (6) Printed parts by Bland, London, 'No. [1 in ink]', 1788. (7) Printed parts by Schmitt, Amsterdam 'Concerto I Op. XXI', 1785. (8) Schott, Mainz, reprinted from Boyer & Le Menu edition, 'Copié après le Journal de Piéces de Clavecin' (= Boyer's sub-title), announced on Christmas Day 1784 in the *Wiener Zeitung*.

Critical editions: Edition Peters (K. Soldan, 1931, based on the contemporary MS. parts in the Berlin Library and the Artaria and Schott prints; reprinted in Edition Eulenburg, No. 791.

Cadenzas: A whole collection of MS. cadenzas, copied together, is from the library of Archduke Rudolph (not a good source for Haydn, textually) and is now in the Gesellschaft der Musikfreunde, Vienna. It is impossible, except for one or two cases, to attach the cadenzas to the right Haydn concertos, because so many are in the same key (F, C, D, G) and the copyist may also have included Haydn's 'concertini' and 'divertimenti' (Hoboken, Gruppe XIV) among the concertos. Two have been selected for the Eulenburg edition discussed above (pp. 43f.), from which the student may gather the general style of these cadenzas, for which there is no evidence of authenticity whatever. N.B. in the 'Cadenza to the 2nd

Movement (p. 27)', stave 1, bar 1, r.h. 10th note is, of course, *f* sharp, not *e*; stave 3, last 2½ bars must be played as arpeggios, as in the ensuing bars. More interesting contemporary cadenzas to Haydn's early concertos and piano trios are discussed in *Haydn : the Early Years 1732–1765*, *inter alia* the interesting Albrechtsberger autograph of his 'Concerto per l'Arpa' (1773), from the Albrechtsberger Archives in EH, Budapest, 'Ms. Mus. 2404 (watermarks: eagle and 'HELLER'), which includes 'zum Concert in F Ferma del Signor Hayden' in Albrechtsberger's autograph.

One inferior MS. and no less than seven contemporary printed editions of this popular Concerto show that printing was gradually usurping completely the previous position of the professional copyist who sold (usually unauthorized) MSS. of such works to the Austrian monasteries, the Bohemian castles and the German princely archives. The point had now been reached when such new music was more often acquired in a printed edition.

We have no authentic MSS. but the Artaria print cannot be – at this stage of Haydn's relationship to them – anything but an authentic print. And we have further evidence of its authenticity in that Haydn offers what can only be this work to Forster on 8 April 1787 (*infra*, p. 691), ignorant of the many British editions that had meanwhile flooded the market. Curiously, this work is listed neither in *EK* nor in *HV* (the 'Cello Concerto in D appears in *HV*, not in *EK*), and the earliest mention of its existence is the publishers' announcements listed above from Hoboken, vol. I, pp. 822f., and the listing in the Breitkopf Catalogue of 1782–4.

Although like its sister concerto of this period (for 'Cello in D), it is in many ways a typical product of its period, another attempt to explore the popular style in every *genre*, nevertheless this Piano Concerto has always won the hearts of audiences, and not because it is (as it were) forced on them by the soloists. They have an enormous repertoire from which to choose, including the eighteenth century, and this Haydn Concerto is popular because the music is popular. It moves much faster than its sister: the opening Vivace is 4/4 and not 8/8, and the increased speed is also internal as well as external. We are back to the pithy, wiry style of the Haydn we know and love, with its chain sequences of syncopations (bars 31ff.) – which become an integral part of the movement's structure, *forzati*, and motivic elaborations. For a pretty example of the latter, the 6th, 7th and 8th notes of the main theme

become the basis for a huge part of the development section (end of first part in dominant, modulation with our *fz* and syncopations, already deftly presented in the earlier sections, to B minor): from 138ff., this three-note fragment is tossed between various members of the orchestra, but always including the piano's left hand. 'Harpsichord or Fortepiano': and of course, Haydn really writes in such a way that either instrument can be used. The repeated quaver groups in the left hand sound better on the harpsichord; a broken pattern (as in Mozart's K.482, piano's first solo, left hand) is better for the fortepiano. In the developmental passage discussed above, the piano's right hand has a long section of broken semiquavers which sound attractive on either the older or newer instruments.

The slow movement, particularly beautiful, and retaining the wind instruments (hitherto a rarity in works of this kind, also in Haydn's), reaches heights of poetry in the sextuplet chain suspensions (bars 21ff., also later) with long-held string accompaniment. The figure ♪♪♪ | ♩ ♪ (at bars 4ff.) will quietly but firmly dominate vast stretches of the middle part (end of the exposition and the whole

The beginning of the Finale of Haydn's Piano Concerto in D (XVIII: 11), from a contemporary (perhaps the first) edition by Boyer of Paris. The movement, Allegro assai, is also marked 'Rondo Hongrois', i.e. making use of Gypsy and/or Hungarian folk-melodies.

middle section which is, surprisingly, in E minor when of course we expect E major – the movement is in A and we are in the dominant). That marvellous passage with the suspensions and lingering string accompaniment greets us in the recapitulation as well (bars 55ff.), and after the cadenza we have a huge pedal point in the horns which, dropping to *piano* brings us to the end of this original and heartfelt movement. The last three notes were a private gesture only for the oboe players: the second oboe takes the top line, the first the bottom (one of those many times when Haydn writes only for the players' benefit: this effect cannot be heard at all).

Haydn had flirted with Gypsy (= Hungarian) music in his great String Quartet in D major from Op. 20, No. 4, but this 'Rondo all'Ungherese' ('Ungarese', etc.) is a *tour-de-force* of breathtaking originality and sweep. We seem to see the dancing figures, whirling before our eyes in front of the campfire on those endless, lonely Hungarian plains, the charm and slightly forbidding aspect of which have captivated any Western visitor of perception and imagination. Haydn displays what must have been his encyclopaedic knowledge of Gypsy folk melodies, with their repeated phrases of hypnotic force, their chain trills (the section in the minor), syncopations, the typical 'biting' grace notes ♩ ♩ , and all the other tricks of the great *primas* – fortunately, a tradition which (although since modified in the course of two hundred years and by the inevitable 'outside' influences that have altered the original style) continues to flourish in Hungary and in Burgenland (the province of which Eisenstadt is the capital) to this very day. Haydn performed a unique service (a) in writing down these fascinating Balkan melodies and (b) introducing them into 'art music' and thus saving them for posterity's delight and emulation. The first page of this celebrated Finale in the Boyer-Le Menu first edition is reproduced here (p. 573) as it must have appeared to the astonished eyes of the Parisian *haut monde* in the Summer of 1784, for many members of which this will have been the first introduction into the magic, secret, exotic world of the Balkans.

Dances and Marches

DANCES

Six Minuets (IX:5; 1776); Twelve Minuets (IX:6; 1776–7?); Fourteen Minuets IX:7; 1783?); Twelve Minuets (IX:8; 1784?); and *Six Allemandes*... (IX:9; 1786 or before).

Six Minuets (IX:5; 1776) for fl., 2 ob., 2 bsn., 2 hn., str.
Source: Autograph, Preussische Staatsbibliothek, Berlin, Mus. ms. autogr. Jos. Haydn 52. Unpublished.

Twelve Minuets (IX:6; 1776–7?) for fl., 2 ob., 2 bsn., 2 hn., timp., str., including, as Nos. 9–12 the same minuets as Nos. 1–4 of IX:5.
Source: MS. parts, Gesellschaft der Musikfreunde, Vienna. Unpublished.

Raccolta de Menuetti Ballabili (Fourteen Minuets [IX:7] 1783? before?) for fl., 2 ob., 2 bsn., 2 hn., timp., str.
Sources: MS., arranged for piano and containing Nos. 1, 14, 4, 8, 10, 6 (with No. 3 as Trio), 7 (with No. 13 as Trio) and 11. Authentic printed edition in parts by Artaria & Co., Vienna, announced on

31 January and 4 February 1784 in the *Wiener Zeitung*. Copy in Országos Széchényi Könyvtár, Budapest, к 1190 (for title page see pl. 27). Based on this authentic edition, Longman & Broderip issued 'Fourteen Favorite Minuets for the Harpsichord with a Violin Accompaniment Composed by Sigr. Haydn'.
Critical editions: Breitkopf & Härtel, Partitur-Bibliothek 3420 (parts Orch.-Bib. 2777), ed. T. W. Weiner, 1932. Verlag Doblinger, Vienna-Munich, Diletto Musicale 301 (Landon, ed. 1967, pub. 1970).

Twelve Minuets for ? (IX:8; 1784? or before?). Only piano arrangement has survived.
Sources: (1) Authentic arrangement (or at least authentic edition) by Artaria & Co., Vienna, announced on 9 April 1785 in the *Wiener Zeitung*. (2) MS. from the legacy of Aloys Fuchs, Göttweig

Abbey, in the order: 4, 5, 6, 7, 12, 8, 9, 1, 2, 10, 11 and 3. (3) Edition, probably based on Artaria, by Bignon, Paris with a different Trio for No. 11; *c.* 1785? (4) Various other reprints by (a) Birchall & Andrews, London, *c.* 1785–90?; (b) Longman & Broderip, London, 1785 (ann. *Public Advertiser* 26 Sept.); (c) Haueisen, 1785.

Modern editions: Various selections edited by Hugo Riemann (Augener, London) and Nana Krieger (Universal Edition, Vienna: 'Kleine Tänze für die Jugend'). No critical edition exists. N.B. The Artaria edition was originally sold by Haydn to Torricella, who announced it in the *Wiener Zeitung* on 12 January 1785; after Torricella's bankruptcy, Artaria purchased the plates of this work and also Haydn's new Symphonies Nos. 79–81. That the Dances were originally scored for orchestra is suggested by Torricella's notice, '12 Menuets,

brand new and very fine, along with various others which were produced at the Casino in the Trattnerhof...'. Hoboken, vol. I, pp. 555f.

Six Allemandes à plusieurs instrumens [*sic*] for fl., 2 ob., bsn., 2 hn., 2 trpt., timp., str. (IX:9) (1786 or before).

Sources: (1) Authentic first edition in parts by Artaria & Co., Vienna, announced on 3 January 1787 in the *Wiener Zeitung*. With the trumpet parts (correct Hoboken, vol. I, p. 557). Copy in British Museum. (2) MS. parts, 'Menuettinj Tedeschi 6. . . . Di Sig. Giuseppe Haydn' (oblong format, 25·5 × 20·2 cm.; watermarks 'FA' in Baroque coat-of-arms). St Peter's Abbey, Salzburg. *Critical edition*: Verlag Doblinger, Vienna-Munich, Diletto Musicale 52 (Landon, 1960).

We have slightly disturbed the chronology by including the one known set of dances composed in the final period treated in this volume (the *Six Allemandes*). If we examine (a) the Chronicle and (b) the music of these robust and infinitely varied dances, we shall see that although it is known Haydn composed such music for the Redoutensaal in Vienna and the Grassalkovics Palace in Pressburg, the actual music is all, without exception, composed with the Esterházy forces in mind. We have C *alto* horns substituting for trumpets and only in IX:9 parts for trumpets (which Haydn sometimes had for special occasions). We even have the single bassoon with which Haydn had to make do from April 1778 to the end of 1780, which is the reason for our dating of IX:9 (which has one bassoon) '1786 or before'. We consider it probable that these 'outside' commissions for dance music were filled simply by supplying Eszterháza (or as the case may be Eisenstadt, Vienna or Kittsee) music which Haydn had already composed for local consumption.

No doubt a great deal of Haydn's dance music is lost, particularly of the very early period but also of the Eszterháza years: dance music of the eighteenth century was particularly perishable because it was usually kept separate from the 'concert' music (as was, too, the music for wind band). None of the Grenadiers' wind-band music, and no dance music, has survived from the Eszterháza Archives unless it was kept, and thus preserved, in Haydn's own library, or in contemporary Viennese copies. The Gesellschaft der Musikfreunde is particularly rich in Haydn dances of the period, mostly in unique copies, and fortunately most of the Redoutensaal music for the I. R. Court Balls has survived and is now in the Musiksammlung of the Österreichische Nationalbibliothek.

What are we to do with this large collection of Haydn dances, minuets and *Deutsche Tänze*? They are hardly suitable for the concert hall unless they are of such astonishing beauty that they can rival the London Symphonies – and this is the case with the Twenty-Four Minuets IX:16, with Mozart's late dances, and some of Beethoven's (the so-called 'Mödling' Dances are particularly appealing, as are the *Contre-Tänze* of *c.* 1802, WoO 14). But these are exceptions; and even Beethoven's beautiful and historically important Redoutensaal Dances of 1795 (WoO 7, 8) are rarely performed today.[1] Again, these are works ideally suited for the gramophone

1 At the *Haydn-Tage* in Eisenstadt in 1976, we devised a concert with the Vienna Philharmonic Orchestra, conducted by Theodor Guschlbauer, in which were given Haydn's Twenty-Four Minuets (IX:16), Mozart's *Deutsche Tänze*, K.605, and Beethoven's Redoutensaal *Deutsche Tänze* of 1795 – all composed within five years of each other. The effect on the public of the Haydn-Saal in the Eszterházy Castle was electric.

record, on which (as we have seen with the sensationally successful series of Mozart's complete dances conducted by Willi Boskovsky and produced by Erik Smith for Decca) such music can be appreciated in an atmosphere perhaps less attractive than in the Redoutensaal of Vienna or the Chinese Ball Room at Eszterháza, but surely more congenial than in the concert hall.

MARCHES

(1) *Marche Regimento de Marshall* (Hoboken *deest*; 1772?) for 2 oboes, 2 bassoons and 2 horns; (2) *[Marcia]* (Hoboken VIII:6; *c.* 1780–90) for 2 clarinets, 2 bassoons and 2 horns.

Sources: (1) MS. parts from the Clam-Gallas Collection of Friedland (Frýdlant) Castle (now National Museum, Prague, cat. 1192, dated 1772; (2) autograph, Bibliothèque du Conservatoire, Paris (Bibliothèque Nationale).

Critical editions: (1) Diletto Musicale No. 34/1 (Landon; (2) Diletto Musicale No. 34/2. Both Verlag Doblinger, Vienna-Munich 1960.

We have again broken our chronological rule and placed together, at this point, the two surviving Marches of the period. The first was discovered in Prague by the present writer. It may have been composed a few years before the MS.'s date of 1772: the music however has a passage (bars 10f., 26f.) which is almost a literal quotation of the ritornello's conclusion in the *Cantilena pro Adventu,* 'Ein' Magd, ein' Dienerin' (*vide supra,* p. 245), of which the EH copy in Budapest has watermarks that suggest a date 1773–5. The second March is probably the only known piece of music that Haydn wrote for the Eszterháza Grenadiers, who employed clarinets in their little band. This was the kind of unmilitary, unmartial music that sounded as the Grenadiers, six feet tall, stood to attention in the great courtyard of the Castle. Haydn also allowed this pretty little March to be used in a musical clock that Pater Niemecz constructed in 1793 (XIX:25; MS. copy of this version in the Gesellschaft der Musikfreunde lists Niemecz as 'Librarian of H. Highness the Reigning Prince Anton Esterházy': see Hoboken, vol. I, p. 834).

String Quartets, Op. 33
('The Russian'; III:37–42; 1781)

Six Quartets composed in 1781; not in *EK*; no autographs extant. Of the many authentic MS. copies that Haydn sold, the only ones to survive are in Melk Abbey: III;37, 38, 41, 42 (Melk VI.736–9), from which the authentic order cannot be deduced.

(1) *Order of the contemporary editions.* The order now followed in Hoboken is that of *HV*, which in turn follows the Pleyel Complete Edition. We show, in tabular form, the differences between it and the three earliest and probably authentic editions (authentic in that the publishers involved were in likelihood subscribers, if not directly then at second hand, of Haydn's MS. copies, to which we have added Schmitt's early (authentic?) edition.

Pleyel's Edition 1802 *et seq.*	Hoboken vol. III	Artaria 1782	Guera 1782–3	Hummel 1782	Schmitt 1783?
No. 1 (B minor)	37	No. 3	No. 2	No. 2	No. 6
No. 2 (E flat)	38	No. 2	No. 3	No. 3	No. 1
No. 3 (C)	39	No. 4	No. 1	No. 4	No. 2
No. 4 (B flat)	40	No. 6	No. 4	No. 5	No. 5
No. 5 (G)	41	No. 1	No. 6	No. 1	No. 4
No. 6 (D)	42	No. 5	No. 5	No. 6	No. 3

[Kerpen 1783 is an unauthorized reprint of Artaria with the title page in mirror, later acquired by Forster as pl. no. 47; Napier is an authorized reprint, with a new title page, of Artaria. There is also an edition by Sieber of Paris, announced on 16 January 1783.] If the order of Pleyel might have been dictated on musical grounds (*viz.* placing the heaviest, most serious work (in the minor) as No. 1 and as the link between the rest of the set and the previous Quartets, Op. 20, then adding the other three works of the 'heavy' scheme – Allegro moderato opening movements and the slow movement third, and ending with the lighter constructions – works beginning Vivace assai and with the slow movements second), the curious divergence of the order in the four early editions can only be explained in two ways: (a) either Haydn deliberately sent copies which he knew would be used for engraving in different orders so that the publishers in question would not immediately discover that they were all simultaneously issuing the same work or (b) the order is the publishers' in each case. But that seems very unlikely, for the only reason to change such an order would be to disguise the fact that, let us say, Hummel simply pirated Artaria's edition and wished to put Artaria off the trail of his piracy. There are textual differences between the prints that suggest that probably most are independent of each other. Schmitt's even put the Scherzo before the Adagio in III:42 (Op. 33/6).

(2) *Critical editions*: Verlag Doblinger, part of the Complete String Quartets: Opp. 9, 17, 20, 33, edited by Reginald Barrett-Ayres (1968 *et seq.*), 1978 *et seq. Joseph Haydn Werke*, XII/2 (Opp. 9, 17) (G. Feder), 1963. Op. 20 and Op. 33 *JHW*, XII/3 (G. Feder). For Opp. 42, 50, 54, 55 and 64, see Op. 64, *infra*, p. 655.

Pleyel was Haydn's pupil and a famous composer in his own right in those days when he began to issue his monumental collected edition of his master's string quartets. Haydn liked the project because, he said, you could trace his progress in the art; but Pleyel went even further than the sources at his disposal. If we follow Somfai's analysis of the set's structure, we may divide the six works into two distinct groups:

(i) Nos. 1, 2, 3, 4 with Allegro moderato opening movements in 4/4; a dance movement called 'Menuetto', 'Scherzando' or 'Scherzo'; the slow movement, usually in slow 3/4 (Adagio; Largo) tempo, once (No. 1) Andante (6/8); Finale in quick metre and fast tempo (Presto 2/4 or 6/8). This gives rise to a scheme that Somfai[1] gives as follows:

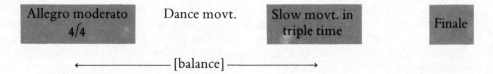

(2) Nos. 5, 6 with a very fast opening movement, marked Vivace assai in quick metre (2/4, 6/8); a slow movement of weighty size and in 4/4 time; Scherzo; Finale: Allegretto, 6/8, 2/4. All four movements in the tonic, I and III–IV major, II minor. Somfai's scheme:

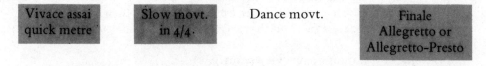

In an extraordinary way, Haydn proceeds with the same problems of overall structure and the distribution of weight with which he had wrestled so manfully in Op. 20 nine years earlier. It is clear that Haydn poured into Op. 33 the whole of his intellectual abilities, to a depth and breadth far beyond the capabilities of his own contemporary

---

1 *Joseph Haydn und seine Zeit*, Eisenstadt 1972, pp. 70, Tafel 5.

piano sonatas, for example, and usually beyond any but a few – exceptional – symphonies of this period. These are works of crucial importance in Haydn's artistic career, and with this statement we arrive at a musicological battle which has raged over these works for over half a century and which shows no signs of abating. Briefly, the origins of this battle – which has the same importance to Haydn scholarship as the argument about the number of angels able to sit upon the head of a pin to theology in the middle ages – are as follows. The German scholar Adolf Sandberger, writing in the *Altbayrische Monatshefte* for 1899,[1] promulgated the theory that with Op. 33 Haydn had arrived at the perfection of the Viennese classical style; that Haydn himself had realized this fact when, in 1781, he offered the works to various potential clients and described his products as 'auf eine gantz neue besonderer Art' ('in a new and special way'); that the essence of this new style, as opposed to the 'crisis' works of Op. 20 with their exaggerated use of minor, fugues, etc., was the development of 'motivische Arbeit'. Sandberger's theory was taken over by Blume in his influential article of 1931, but was sharply attacked by Larsen who maintained that the new 'motivische Arbeit' had been slowly arrived at in the symphonies of the 1770s; that this new technique, although of eminent importance, also for the nineteenth century, was not to be called *the* turning-point in Haydn's style; and that Haydn's use of 'gantz neu' is not a stylistic description but a mercantile slogan. Bartha (1965) followed Larsen and Finscher followed Blume and Sandberger. The latest word to date was spoken by the young American musicologist James Webster who (1976) writes:

> The weakest link in Finscher's argument, however, is his exaggerated claim that Op. 33 'created' Classical quartet style. The 'Op. 33 hypothesis', an invention of Adolf Sandberger about 1900, is neither historically nor stylistically persuasive. Numerous Austrian quartets originated in the 1770s, and several sets of quartets were published by the firm of Artaria before Op. 33. The 'resonance' of Op. 33, of which so much is made [by Finscher], turns out on closer inspection to consist of one Viennese 'command performance', a couple of reviews, and a single quartet-party on tour; in actuality the dissemination of Op. 33 was not significantly greater than that of earlier Haydn quartets.... Thus Op. 33 was merely one prominent event in the rapidly increasing production of string quartets in the 1780s.

'Gantz neue besonderer' may be a mercantile *Werbeslogan* but to anyone with a pair of ears it should be obvious that Op. 33 is certainly written in a new and special way. The musicologists have, as usual, confused historical and musical importance. The argument is not whether the perfection of the Viennese classical style was reached in Op. 33 – why single out this series rather than Op. 20, or the symphonies of *c*. 1772, or even *L'infedeltà delusa* or the *Missa Cellensis* of 1782? – but what makes Op. 33 different from its predecessors. And that there is a gigantic difference *on the whole* is indisputable.

Orin Moe (1975) sums up one viewpoint:

> '...In comparing Opus 33 to the Opus 9, 17 and 20 Quartets, we notice something new. There is a light, popular touch about these quartets, something not heard since Opus 1 and 2. The themes are folk-like, the formal outlines clear.

1 'Zur Geschichte des Haydnschen Streichquartetts', reprinted in his *Gesammelte Aufsätze zur Musikgeschichte*, Munich 1921. Larsen, *HÜB*, 83n., CCLN 32–4 (also *supra*, pp. 453 ff.); Bartha, 108n.; Finscher 1974, pp. 238ff.; James Webster in the *Journal of the American Musicological Society* 1976, pp. 546f. Sondheimer 1951, pp. 94f., 102, 105. Blume, 'Joseph Haydns künstlerische Persönlichkeit in seinen Streichquartetten', in *Jahrbuch der Musikbibliothek Peters* 1931. Orin Moe, 'The Significance of Haydn's Opus 33', *Haydn Conference*, Washington, D.C., 1975.

The outward simplicity, however, frequently conceals an inward complexity. All this might be said about the late symphonies, and indeed there is much in common between them and Opus 33. These Quartets are both the summation of the popularizing tendencies found in many of the symphonies of the preceding decade and the first clear anticipation of a style that will be especially characteristic of the late symphonies, a style which will not make a mature appearance in that genre until 1785. . . .

If one had to concentrate on one particular stylistic element in which Op. 33 differs fundamentally from Op. 20, it must surely be the sense of humour which in some (but not all) of the works of Op. 33 finds a boisterous and even hilarious outlet: the pizzicato effects, the stuttering theme of No. 2 (which used, rather obviously, to be called 'The Joke'), the use even of Gypsy tunes in a semi-humorous fashion (No. 3, Finale) – all these are manifestations of this humour. Sir Donald Tovey in his Haydn article for *Cobbett's Cyclopedic Survey of Chamber Music* (1929), writes

> The 'Russian' Quartets, op. 33, are the lightest of all Haydn's mature comedies. In one place in the old Breitkopf catalogues the opus appears with the alternative [and, *pace* the Melk MSS., authentic] title of Divertimenti. . . . [p. 538]

In a note that Cobbett himself added, the editor wrote: 'The music of this quartet [Op. 33/3] gives the impression that at this period of his life Haydn must have felt exceptionally happy.' Although this biography is not the place for such speculation, perhaps the reader will forgive us if we point out that Op. 33 was composed in the first flush of Haydn's affair with Luigia Polzelli (who had arrived at Eszterháza in 1779 and was certainly Haydn's mistress by 1781). When in London, he wrote to her (14 January 1792, CCLN 126), '. . . perhaps I shall never again regain the good humour that I used to have when I was with you. Oh! my dear Polzelli: you are always in my heart'. She was, quite clearly, always in his music of the 1780s, and especially in Op. 33.

Several 'new' features may be confronted with elements taken over from Op. 20 and from the other music that lay between. The most obvious of the innovations is the use of 'Scherzo' or 'Scherzando' instead of Minuet (except in No. 1, the most conservative of the set and the only one in which the serious style precludes comical touches); but upon examination this turns out to be a novelty in word only: the movements hardly differ from the previous minuet movements. Another innovation of a more profound nature is the character of the slow movements: they often have a rhapsodic, yearning intensity and differ from those of Op. 20 in that Op. 33's are of a much denser texture, substituting massive, concentrated emotion for the earlier *arioso* kind of movement (e.g. Op. 20, Nos. 3, 4 & 5). Haydn may have been able to arrange the more simple Finale of Op. 33, No. 5, for piano (our 'diplomatic' transcription of the composer's autograph is published in 'The Great Composers' series: *Haydn* [Faber, London 1972, pp. 54–6]), but he would have found it uncongenial to do so with the tightly knit instrumental web of the slow movements. Sometimes the music seems to look forward to later Haydn in an uncanny way: the two-part texture of Op. 33, No. 2's Largo sostenuto, starts as if it were transcribed from an earlier baryton trio but then a murmuring 'cello part seems to be from an Op. 76 quartet. Similarly, the recitative-like first violin solo at the end of Op. 33, No. 5 (II, bars 41ff.) is taken up in a similar fashion in *The Seven Words* IV ('Eloi, Eloi, lama sabachthani?', bars 100ff.), even to the

breathless broken-quaver accompaniment $_p$ ♪ ⅄ | ♪ ⅄ ♪ ⅄ ♪ ⅄ | (♩). The ominous figure of bars 8f. (and later) has been singled out by critics, too.

The only work of the set which has achieved real popularity is that in C, known, rather simple-mindedly, as 'The Bird' (No. 3), because of its profuse use of grace notes which apparently reminded nineteenth-century listeners of garden twitterings. The Gypsy Finale, in our opinion, did as much as the first movement's acciaccature to win the public's attention: and not only the 'Kolo'-like first subject but perhaps even more the dark-hued and as usual slightly sinister A minor section (bars 23ff.). Of course, we know these Gypsy effects from Op. 20, No. 4; but in the present work they are expanded (and were expanded even further in the Finale of the D major Piano Concerto previously examined).

Although No. 1 looks back in its general mood to the seriousness of Op. 20, it contains elements that are not only new but astonishing. Perhaps the most original and effective *coup-de-génie* in Op. 33 is the tonally and rhythmically ambiguous opening, which starts out in D major and does not reach B minor (tonic) until half way through bar two:

In this same Quartet, we find another feature which will become an integral part of Haydn's later style. It might be called a 'haunted tune', so impressing itself upon us with its novelty that Haydn can afford to quote it three further times. It first appears with the 'jutting' melody in the lower strings and then reversed. It is a procedure to which Haydn often has recourse, i.e. the introduction of a particularly effective passage not as the first subject but later in the movement and repeating it. The passage in question is:

and Tovey was quite right to single it out (op. cit., p. 538). We find the same pattern in the Andantino grazioso from the Quartet Opus 74, No. I (1793), where the 'hit tune', or rather the 'hit accompaniment' in softly bouncing octaves, appears first at bars 38ff., then at bars 80ff., and at 120ff. Anyone familiar with the later Haydn can find other, similar examples: it is an adjunct of Haydn's surprise technique.

We noted in the earlier quartets of this period a systematic attempt to weld the various, outwardly disparate movements together by the use of similar themes or intervals or whatever. We find a particularly striking example in this present B minor Quartet; but note that it is not with the opening theme of the first movement, but with a later passage, that Haydn begins to establish this inter-movemental relationship (opposite, top). That ever astute critic, Cecil Gray, has pointed out a similar and equally subtle thematic relationship within the first movement of Opus 33, No. 6. 'Very few movements in music', he writes

can show such a logical continuity of thought, one idea leading imperceptibly and without a break into another. Note the way in which even the second subject, presented canonically by all four strings

has already been subtly and unobtrusively anticipated in a passage based upon bar 5 of the first subject:

[*The Haydn String Quartet Society*, London 1933, p. 4]

Perhaps the immediate proximity of the intensely serious and the intensely comic was not to everyone's taste. The single pizzicato unison that ends the slow movement of Op. 33, No. 5 (some aspects of which were mentioned above) verges on comedy, at the end of a most serious, even tragic, movement. The most profound, rapturous slow movement of the set, the Largo from No. 4 – it looks forward in many ways to the great slow movement of Op. 76, No. 4, not only with its soaring violin part (bars 31–4: cf. Op. 76/4/II, bars 48/50) but also the quietly undulating 'cello part at the end (bars 60ff.; cf. Op. 76/4/II, bar 73) – leads, a movement later, to pizzicato slapstick. We presume Joseph II was a witness to the famous grand-ducal performance of these works in Vienna, and we can imagine his total disapproval of such a procedure. When Haydn, in the great series of Quartets Opp. 54, 55, 64 (1787–90), was able to dampen slightly this effusion of high spirits, and yet to retain the rhapsodic quality of his slow movements – we take his great craftsmanship for granted – he attained that perfection of the popular style, and with it the perfection of a new classical style (note that we do not say 'the' classical style, for Haydn had already perfected one by 1772), which Haydn was now seeking, and very near to attaining. In this search, we notice how symphony and quartet vie with each other in achieving the new goal – the great and final series of quartets in this period is preceded and accompanied by the greatest symphonies of Haydn's career up to this juncture.

Robert Sondheimer (1951) summed up the essence of Opus 33 in a series of chapters of which we may cite the following extracts:

> During the period of nearly ten years between Op. 20 and Op. 33 ... great changes had been brought about in the art of music. The almost forgotten older generation of pre-classics, that of Sammartini and Wagenseil, had in the meantime died out, and the revolutionary assault of younger composers, which had still been so powerful at the end of the 60's, had by now lost its force... The Gluck campaign in Paris, which had broken out in the middle of the 70's, had been the last outburst of revolutionary ardour in the pre-classical world of music. It had inflamed the great mass of the general public which habitually only flocks together when the final issue is no longer in doubt, and for whom the easiest way to music leads through the portals of the opera-house....
>
> On the other hand, one may ascribe a general significance to an instruction of Boccherini's Paris publisher given in the middle of the 70's, to write in a light and pleasing manner, and may conjecture that Haydn yielded to it in his Op. 33....
>
> A master of form, aware of his superiority, may easily be induced to strike a witty pose. Hence, the quartets of Op. 33 seem elastic and attractive in comparison with those of Op. 20, which are somewhat ponderous in gait.... During [Op. 33] Haydn, though in his quest for the applause of the multitude he does not stoop to an unscrupulous display of crude effects, yet shows an intellectual naivety such as always crops up somehow in a man who covets power, and which is indispensable to the acquisition of popularity....

Two contemporary criticisms of a 'private concert' in Hamburg were printed in Cramer's *Magazin der Musik* (1783). On 17 November 1782, a violinist named Schick and a 'cellist named 'Tricklir' played 'at a private concert in the Westphalian House two Quartets from Op. 19 [Op. 33] by Haydn with such an admirable charm and dexterity that not one of the many listeners remained unmoved...' (p. 153). Later we read:

> ... These works [Op. 33] are praised and cannot be enough, considering their greatly original humour and the liveliest, most pleasant wit found therin. I know that Bach in Hamburg, who in the normal course of events avoids those loveless, severe and tortuous products of lesser talents than his, and who by nature has a most delicate palate, expressed his complete satisfaction about these works, especially since Schick and Triklir [*sic*] played them so brilliantly....

Piano Trios Nos. 17–19 (XV:2, 5, 6)
(XV:2, *c.* 1772, rewritten *c.* 1784–5; XV:5 and 6, 1784)

Piano (harpsichord) trios had occupied Haydn's mind rather intensely twenty-five years before, during the Morzin period and before, and he had composed over a dozen. His activities at Eisenstadt and Eszterháza seemed not to require works of this kind, and it was not until 1784 that Forster's request for new works in the *genre* awakened in him an interest to continue writing such trios. The earlier trios treated the 'cello as part of the *continuo* but the violin often had quite intricate solo passages; the principal part was, of course, the harpsichord. Taste had now changed slightly, and it was apparently the amateurs who 'accompanied' the keyboard parts; thus the string parts are even simpler than before. Publishers and composers soon realized that it was ideal drawing-room music for the rising bourgeois classes – those talented ladies, for example, who played the fortepiano well and to whom Haydn dedicated some of his trios and piano sonatas, accompanied by two friends who could (as Haydn later said of the Prince of Wales, later George IV) play their instrument 'tolerably well'. From now until 1797, Haydn poured increasingly interesting, original and often very beautiful music into the piano trio form.

The first work that concerns us chronologically started life as a baryton piece, or rather as several baryton pieces. The Trio's first two movements form the Moderato and Menuet (but not the Trio) of Baryton Trio No. 103, composed *c.* 1772 (the autograph of No. 105 is dated 1772). These two sections must have been particularly popular with Prince Nicolaus, for we next find the work listed in *EK* with the music as we know it from the trio version as 'Divertimento per il Cembalo con Pariton e Violini'. The Finale, an Adagio with variations, was also a 'Solo per il Bariton' (*EK* p. 7: Hob. XII: 13) but that version is lost; so is the version with baryton, harpsichord and violins. But in the Esterházy Archives we have a MS., which came from Haydn's collection, entitled 'Divertimento per il Clavicembalo a Due Violini con Violoncello'; there is only one violin part and it is difficult to see what the lost violin part should have played (EH, Budapest, Ms. mus. I. 144). This work is assigned the number XIV:2 in Hoboken. In this trio version, Haydn sent it to Forster, who received it on 28 October 1785. The work shows its age but is so bright and attractive that Haydn considered it could survive the competition of its fellows composed in 1785 (Nos. 22 and 23, issued with No. 17 as 'Three Sonatas . . . Op. 42': *vide infra*, pp. 681f.). Because of the work's original state, there is a more extensive violin part than was usually the case in the 1780s, but the 'cello is mostly there for colouristic reasons.

Trio 18 is the work composed by Haydn to augment the two stolen Pleyel trios into the usual group of three, and begins with an entire slow movement. It is from the outset clear that this is piano and not harpsichord music (for which instrument No. 17 was written). Perhaps fortified with the violin solos of No. 17, Haydn gives the violin an important part in this beautiful, rhapsodic Adagio non tanto. The second movement is as rhythmically taut as the previous Adagio was free, and the Trio closes with a 3/4 movement of the kind often encountered in Haydn's later works in this *genre* (form: A–A'–A'', the latter being closer to the original 'A'). That which astounds is the difference between this work and the pale Pleyel *seguace* style of the other two works; but perhaps it is easier for us to distinguish the difference between master and pupil than for the amateurs (in the best, eighteenth-century meaning) of that time.

Trio 19 (1784, autograph formerly in Eisenstadt; now lost) is the first of three published by Artaria and dedicated to the Countess Marianne von Witzay (Hungarian: Viczay), Prince Nicolaus's niece who lived on an estate near Eszterháza. We shall discuss the set with the others of the period later in this book, and here it is only necessary to point out its interesting two-movement form – typical for the piano trio as opposed to the usual piano sonata – and to say a word of its general style. There is a world of difference between this swiftly moving music, with its rapid runs and the felicitous interchange between violin and piano (the 'cello doubles the bass, as usual), and the rather intricate, involved, heavily ornamented style of Haydn's contemporary piano music. The trios are, at this stage, much more modern and to our ears they wear better than the sonatas. Perhaps this is because Haydn was, in the trios, trying to gauge the temper of his unknown audience (Vienna, London, Paris, Madrid) whereas the sonatas seem, with some notable exceptions, to have been written for pupils and pulled out of the drawer to satisfy the publishers' demands.

Piano Sonatas

(a) Six Sonatas, Op. 30 (Artaria, 1780): Nos. 48–52, and 33; XVI:35–39, and XVI:20, dedicated to Caterina and Marianna von Auenbrugger.
(b) No. 53 (XVI:34; *c.* 1780?)
(c) Three Sonatas Op. 37 (Boßler, 1784): Nos. 54–56; XVI:40–42, dedicated to Princess Marie Hermenegild Esterházy.

These are surely the works of this period that wear the least well nowadays. Their age shows, as we noted above, in the excess of ornamentation (first movement of No. 51), in an over-indulgence of the Alberti bass (first movement of No. 48, where it is also 'inverted', e.g. without pause from bars 72–99) and from a somewhat empty style in the adagios (No. 48). For teaching purposes, these sonatas have always proved to be popular, and perhaps we are all overexposed to their rather fragile charms. It would be wrong to overlook their many beauties, of which we may single out a few. The C sharp minor Sonata (No. 49) is one of two minor-key works in Op. 30 (the other is the great C minor Sonata, No. 33); but compared to No. 33 it lacks the single-mindedness of the earlier work (1771), and the Scherzando movement in the middle (A major) is something of a shock, stylistically, compared to the solid and rather severe opening, and the melancholic Menuet with its wistful C sharp major (7 sharps!) Trio. Altogether we cannot escape the impression that these six works were composed at various times between 1771 and 1780. Sonata No. 50, a very famous work, is in the modern style and has a brilliance and virtuoso panache that the others often lack, and the slow movement is a magnificent recollection of the great Baroque period, with its rolling chords and dotted rhythms; it leads into a 'Presto, ma non troppo' in the latest rondo style. No. 51, on the other hand, sounds like a work of the 1760s, also its rather aria-like slow movement in *siciliano* time. The Finale again suffers from excessive ornamentation (seven crossed turns or 'half trills' in the first eight bars).

The E minor Sonata (No. 53) is also a very popular work, probably because of its original opening movement in the new fast time (Presto, 6/8, as opposed to the 4/4 of, say, No. 51's opening). We know nothing about its origin except that it was first published in London as one of three sonatas (Nos. 35[43], 34[33], 53) by Beardmore & Birchall. They were entered at Stationers' Hall on 26 July, 27 November 1783 and 15 January 1784, respectively. Brilliant though the first movement is, the Adagio is rather empty and the intricate figurations are suitable to the pupil's fingers but hardly calculated to awaken his enthusiasm. It leads (half cadence) to the Vivace molto, where the Alberti bass is rather too all-pervading – ninety-eight out of 136 bars. Haydn now has a new word, 'innocentemente' which he used as a title for this Finale and for that of No. 50. It puzzles slightly, as it did Cecil Gray when discussing the slow movement of Piano Trio No. 45 (1797): 'Personally', wrote Gray, 'I do not find it particularly innocent in character, but rather arch, coy and subtle.'[1] Possibly Haydn meant that which we would, in our modern idiom, call 'deadpan'.

---

1 *A Limited Edition of Haydn Trios*, London 1940, p. 9.

The word is applied, with more obvious justification, to the beautiful opening movement of Sonata No. 54, the first dedicated to Haydn's later Princess, Marie Hermenegild, for whom he always seems to have had an affectionate place in his heart. These are sophisticated and gentle sonatas which really seem to be destined for a lady's hand. (The dynamic marks of all these sonatas show that they were intended for the piano and not the harpsichord, but these three works are particularly crowded with pianistic terms – 'calando' is the newest of these terms.) Students have always relished the variety with which he treated a single theme, and in the works under discussion two entire movements are built on the same material: No. 49's Scherzando (middle movement) and No. 52's opening Allegro con brio; this was the occasion for the foreword which Haydn felt obliged to print (*vide supra*, p. 430). We cannot escape thinking that Haydn is treading a thin line, in most of these works, between connoisseur, pupil (also his own?) and professional. Princess Marie was a connoisseur, of course, and that may explain the particular charm and cultivation of Sonatas 54–56; and who except a connoisseur would know how to appreciate a harmonic twist such as the *g* flat that Haydn introduced in bar 2 of No. 55:

It is not within the scope of this biography to discuss arrangements, but of these three Sonatas there exists an arrangement so interesting that it warrants at least brief mention. About 1788 – the exact date is not certain, but before 5 December 1789, when the edition was advertised in Dresden (Hoboken, vol. I, 508) – Hoffmeister brought out 'Trois Trios pour violin, viole et violoncello' which turn out to be expert and sensitive string trio versions of Sonatas 54–56. Hoffmeister's version proved as popular as the piano sonatas and was soon reprinted all over Europe, first by André (January 1790), and later by Bland. André even made a second edition.[1]

Our problem is whether Haydn himself made this adroit edition. It seems, otherwise, an odd thing for Hoffmeister to do: we will not say it is a unique occurrence but certainly a rare one. String trio is also a most unlikely medium into which to transpose piano sonatas. We cannot determine Haydn's part, if any, in this operation, but we can commend these fine string trio adaptations, which were done by a master (perhaps Hoffmeister himself?).

The Flute Trios for Forster, Op. 38
(1784; IV:6–11)

These attractive works were put together by Haydn for William Forster, and Haydn's engraver's copy has, fortunately, survived (British Museum, Egerton 2379, ff. 125–48), with Haydn's autograph title: 'Sei Divertimenti a tre Violino 1mo o Flauto traverso Violino 2do Violoncello' and signed 'di me giuseppe Haydn mpria $\overline{784}$'. Following

---

1 Hoboken, vol. I, p. 508, and Wolfgang Matthäus in *HJB* III (1965), pp. 64f.

Forster's edition as Op. 38, they were reprinted by various publishers, including Traeg in Vienna, 1802–3, Op. 100, under which alternative number they are also known. There is no critical edition.

Haydn plundered his *Il mondo della luna* to make up many of these movements: add to the list in Hoboken, IV:8 Poco Adagio = Aria No. 25 of Clarice in Atto II°; IV:10 Tempo di Menuetto = No. 23 Balletto, Atto II°. Apart from the Opera, Haydn took IV:9 from his Baryton Trio No. 97, using the first, sixth and seventh movements. Despite the fact that many movements are adaptations, the music is delightful and has often been played (and recorded) in recent times. For colouristic purposes, one naturally prefers the flute version. These are of course *pièces d'occasion* but particularly well done – like the famous 'London' Trios for two flutes and 'cello that Haydn would compose exactly ten years later. Probably the merited success of these 1784 works suggested to Lord Abingdon and his friends that Haydn might be persuaded to compose more music of the same kind.

Lieder

Artaria published the first twenty-four of Haydn's *Lieder* in two parts: Part I, dedicated to Francisca Liebe von Kreutzner, appeared in December 1781 (*Wiener Zeitung*, 29 December), Part II in April 1784 (*WZ*, 24 April). They were a great success in their time, but as we have seen they were very severely criticized for their lack of literary pretensions. They suffer now from the fact that Haydn's own English songs and 'canzonettas' are so much superior. Not only the glories of 'O tuneful voice' or 'The Spirit's Song' but even the touchingly beautiful late work 'Ein kleines Haus' (XXVIa:45), composed on 20 July 1801 (perhaps for a friend in Eisenstadt? – one of the princely singers), rather put into permanent shade the often attractive efforts of this period. To the twenty-four *Lieder* must be added several occasional works, notably 'Der schlaue Pudel' (XXVIa:38), which is charming, and the nostalgic 'Bald wehen uns des Frühlings Lüfte' (XXVIa:47). Their almost total neglect nowadays is unfortunate but, one fears, inescapable. Of course, they are superior to the efforts of Leopold Hofmann and Carl Friberth (both of whom published *Lieder*, some of them charming, in Vienna), but they must compete not only with Haydn's canzonettas, etc., but also the entire wealth of Beethoven, Schubert, Schumann, Brahms and Hugo Wolf: and against this competition these first Haydn *Lieder* simply have no chance. It is sad, but true, that if *Lied* No. 13 had survived in its original form as the Aria of Selene in Haydn's *Dido* (text by Bader: 'Jeder meint, der Gegenstand den er sich erwählet'), we would probably hear its fresh, folk-song like melody more often than we do as a concert song. And we miss a number of beautiful works: the G minor *Lied* No. 5 ('Hör auf mein armes Herz so bang zu schlagen') is a delicately sad piece in Watteau-like pastel colours. Sometimes we have extraordinary overtones: *Lied* No. 7 'An Iris' has a melody very like Haydn's witty Aria di Cardellina 'Vada adagio, Signorina' (Guglielmi's *La Quaquera spiritosa*, Eszterháza 1787), even to the same key (B flat). As always, when Haydn writes a religious song (No. 17, *Geistliches Lied*), we are given something special: in this case a sober, G minor setting that looks forward to the beautiful *Mehrstimmige Gesänge* of 1796 *et seq*. The combination of gay and pensive is very well thought out, both in the first as well as second sets. We expect the witty songs, such as No. 14, 'Lachet nicht, Mädchen', with its gay imitations of B flat *basso* horns, but one is perhaps surprised to see how many quiet, thoughtful and even melancholic texts Haydn chose. As we say, it is a pity for the high quality of the music, and the texts are not nearly as impossible as the north German critics (and their blind followers, even down to C. F. Pohl) have made out. These *Lieder*, in their totality, show a particularly well-balanced Haydn, who, in these works of the smallest scale, wished to show that miniature forms are worthy of special attention. It is a secret that all great composers have known.

CHAPTER EIGHT

The Grand Dissemination:
Haydn's Music Abroad

IN THIS CHAPTER we have selected three countries – Spain, France and England – with which Haydn now began to have increasingly close contacts. The reader will wonder why Germany is omitted from the list: this is because in a sense Germany and Austria may be treated as one, mainly because of the common language. The diffusion of Haydn's works in Austria, Bohemia, Germany (and to a lesser extent Switzerland – Einsiedeln Monastery, for example – and Italy) by means of manuscript copies began much earlier and has therefore been placed in the first volume of this biography. There is another reason why Germany (or Holland, the Scandinavian countries and Switzerland) and Italy do not figure in this chapter and this is because although Haydn was cultivated in these countries to a smaller (Italy) or greater (Germany) extent, this cultivation did not lead to his being asked to write music for them. Spain produced *The Seven Words* and a multitude of other works, some (like the Quartet, Op. 42) extant but most, alas, destroyed in the Spanish Civil War. France was responsible for *all* the symphonies from 1785 to the time Haydn left for England – a huge list – and at least indirectly for the first 'Tost' Quartets (Opp. 54/55). England, of course, would soon occupy a unique position in Haydn's life, and the documents here included show that his visit had been prepared by his music and also because England had expected him in 1782 in person. The Prince of Oettingen-Wallerstein did commission three symphonies from Haydn, but in the event the composer simply sent the Prince his latest works written for the Comte d'Ogny. Therefore, there are special and, we believe, persuasive grounds for concentrating on these three particular European countries.

Finally, we include a section on the problem of pirated copies and spurious works, together with a note concerning the Terzetto, 'Pietà di me'.

SPAIN

Spain was host to a number of distinguished foreign visitors, two of whom, Luigi Boccherini and Gaetano Brunetti (whose interesting works are just now being rediscovered, mainly through the efforts of the American conductor, Newell Jenkins), made the country their second home. Haydn's music was adored in Spain, and we have quoted, in the preceding Chronicle, a laudatory poem by Yriarte and the correspondence concerning *L'isola disabitata* and its friendly reception by the Spanish royal house.

In 1947, Nicolás A. Solar-Quintes[1] surprised the musical world by his revelations from Spanish Archives of Haydn's relations with the Countess-Duchess of Benavente

---

[1] 'Las relaciones de Haydn con la Casa de Benevente', in *Anuario Musical*, Barcelona 1947, pp. 81–88. See also the fine summary by G. Feder in *HJB* IV (1968), pp. 1341.

and Osuna (María Josefa Alonso Pimentel, First Lady at the Court of Madrid), to whom the composer sent his latest works. He was also in close contact with the Duke of Alba (José Álvarez of Toledo, Gonzaga and Caraciolo, Prince of Paterno and Montalbán). Haydn sent to Spain Masses, quartets, duets, operas (specifically mentioned: the libretto of *Orlando Paladino*), a chorus with the preceding *sinfonia* (which Dr Feder thinks, no doubt rightly, must be the Overture and opening Chorus of *Il ritorno di Tobia*), another *sinfonia*, 24 minuets and 24 *Contretänze*. In Dr Feder's summary, we read:

> The works were sent from 1783 to, at least, 1789; the transactions were conducted *via* a Spanish middleman in Vienna, Carlos Alejandro de Lelis, who negotiated with the Spanish poet Tomás de Iriarte (Yriarte), the agent of the Countess. On 20 October 1783, the necessary contract between Haydn and Lelis was drawn up. This follows from a supplement, a 'spiegazione ulteriore', which was added as a result of previous differences of opinion, and signed by both parties on 12 February 1785, in Vienna. This further declaration states that Haydn is obligated to give all his compositions to Mr. de Lelis, excepting those commissioned by other persons for their private use. The number of compositions may vary in accordance with the circumstances, but should not be fewer than twelve each year. These twelve are understood to be only symphonies, quartets, quintets[!], sextets and concertos. Mr. Haydn will endeavour to see that there are always eight symphonies in this number. He obliges himself to deliver six pieces to Mr. de Lelis in the first six months of the year, and the other six in the last six months. If Mr. de Lelis should withdraw from the contract due to negligence on Mr. Haydn's part in fulfilling the contract, Mr. Haydn will return the last half-year's remuneration he had received in advance. If either of the two parties commits a breach of contract, he loses all claims and pays 100 gulden fine.

The duets listed are, as far as we can tell, those for violin and viola (VI:1–6). In a curious apology, Haydn writes, in de Lelis's words, '... porque no gusta trabajar con instrumentos que non son de su facultad, y en cuya especie de composición no sobresale', in other words that he had written them without wind instruments for which he did not write outstandingly – a strange excuse if we consider all the fine wind writing with which the Spanish were as well acquainted as any other peoples. We imagine that the Spanish had wanted Haydn to write some kind of concerto or *sinfonia concertante* with woodwind or brass, and that the composer used the excuse not to have to compose the work(s) especially for Spain when he could, as it were, rifle the archives at Eszterháza for dozens of other works.

According to the documents, a similar problem arose with the composition of quartets. Between 30 June 1784 and 24 March 1785 Haydn sent Yriarte two quartets without wind instruments, although the Countess had asked for works written with the eccentric combination of violin, oboe, tromba (or trompa? horn?) and violoncello. Similarly the Duke of Alba had ordered quartets from Haydn for the past two years. In the Chronicle (*supra*), we read in Haydn's letter to Artaria of 5 April 1784 about quartets which are 'very short and consist of three pieces only; they are intended for Spain'. The only quartet of this period to survive is Op. 42, and thus it seems likely that the others, if written, have disappeared in Spanish archives or, more likely, were destroyed in 1936. With the two completed works (quartets), Haydn served both the Countess-Duchess and the Duke of Alba, who '... y pagado la misma suma por otros dos', noted de Lelis. Whether Haydn delivered the other two for which he had been paid the same sum is not known.

It is unlikely that the '24 minuets' can be the late works which have been discussed in *Haydn: the Years of 'The Creation' 1796–1800* (see especially p. 89), with their typically 'Viennese' clarinet writing in the *chalumeau* register. (See also ibid., p. 91n., for note of the fruitless search in the Archives of the House of Alba.) Some idea of the works which Haydn sent to Madrid can be seen (a) in the large collection of symphonies which Jan LaRue discovered in the Archives of the Palacio Real in Madrid and (b) in another large collection of symphonies and overtures from South America, obviously of Spanish origin, now in the Library of Congress, Washington, D.C., from which derives the only known copy of *Le pescatrici* Overture (*vide supra*, p. 246). Research in Spanish archives has always been hindered by almost insuperable difficulties, as our old friend Frederick Marvin (the editor of Soler's harpsichord sonatas) has often related; and one can only hope that if that unhappy country ever reaches inner political stability, its scholars may one day begin the archive research which is so urgently needed.

FRANCE

In January 1764, the Parisian musical world took note of a new publication: it consisted of four string quartets (Op. 1, Nos. 1–4) by Haydn and two flute quartets by Carlo Giuseppe Toeschi, issued by the well-known house of M. de la Chevardière. Two months later, Parisian journals announced a new entry in a series of symphonies by 'Noms inconnus, bons à connaître': No. 14 'Del Sig^r Heyden' which Venier, another successful music publisher, was in the process of issuing. The work was Haydn's Symphony No. 2. In that same year, Chevardière issued 'Six Sonates en Trio pour deux violins & basse... par Mr Hayden, Maître de Chapelle à Vienne' – the first publication of Haydn's string trios. From that point until Haydn's death in 1809, Parisian publishers made a fortune on his music which, at least until the early 1780s, was mostly published without his approval and with no financial benefit to him whatever. This extraordinary state of affairs, whereby a publisher could simply pirate a composer's works or an author's books, persisted in most of Europe until the nineteenth century.

But if Haydn never saw a penny from all these publications in Paris during the mid-1760s, he must have heard sooner or later that his works were extremely successful in France. Viennese bookshops actually imported some of these French prints: van Ghelen offered for sale in January 1772 three Haydn symphonies printed by Huberty in Paris, and Ghelen or others may have done so before that date. In any case, by the beginning of December 1767, Haydn will have had first-hand information about his popularity in France from Prince Nicolaus, who (as we have seen in the Chronicle) went to Paris, taking Luigi Tomasini with him. It is thought that Haydn's relations with Jean-Georges Sieber, a German émigré who was to publish dozens of Haydn's symphonies, may have had their origins in the Esterházy-Tomasini visit.

It was not only in Paris that Haydn's music flourished. Soon the French provinces found his music not only enjoyable but profitable. In Lyon, the enterprising firm of Guera began to issue Haydn's works about 1777. The Guera copies are textually so reliable that one wonders if Haydn was in correspondence with Lyon. Actually, one of the musicians in the Esterházy orchestra, Franz Garnier, had gone to Lyon to play in the theatre orchestra there (*vide supra*, p. 72), and was located there in 1778 by Esterházy agents, wishing to pay him a legacy which Prince Paul Anton had left all his musicians. Can Garnier have been the go-between?

Haydn's works were by about 1770 so popular in France that the publishers could not get hold of them quickly enough; those unscrupulous ladies and gentlemen therefore procured all sorts of works by Haydn's *seguaci* in Vienna and the Austrian provinces – favourites proved to be Haydn's brother Johann Michael in Salzburg, Dittersdorf, Ordoñez, Leopold Hofmann and Vanhal – and published their works under Haydn's name. Entire *opera* of forged Haydn thus appeared in Paris. The most famous case is that of the so-called 'Opus 3' (Pleyel's numbering in his collected edition) Quartets, which arrived in Paris as the works of one *Pater* Roman(us) Hoffstetter. M. Bailleux simply erased Hoffstetter's name from the already engraved plates and substituted Haydn's (but the original attribution can still be seen). In fact, as many spurious 'Haydns' as real ones appeared in Paris from 1765–75, but from 1775–80 *more* spurious than real Haydn compositions were published in France.

Nevertheless, the really great successes of the period – for the spurious Op. 3 Quartets did not become famous until the nineteenth century (mainly because of the famous 'serenade' movement in Op. 3/5) – were genuine Haydn. Symphony No. 56 (1774) made its Parisian début in the 1776–7 season at the Concert Spirituel and the Concert des Amateurs was engraved three times at the end of 1777 and beginning of 1778: by Guera (who now had a Parisian office on the Place des Terreaux), by Sieber and by Mademoiselle de Silly.

Some inkling of this vast success could be read in the *Mercure de France* which, being the leading French journal of its day, was certainly subscribed to by the librarian of Eszterháza, Herr Bader. In its issue of 15 September 1779, we read:

> Concert Spirituel. Le jour de la Nativité il y eut, selon l'usage, un Concert Spirituel au château des Tuileries. On en fit l'ouverture par une symphonie de Hayden, qui fut très-applaudie, & qui méritoit de l'être: noble & véhément, toujours gracieux, toujours varié, le génie de ce Compositeur semble en effet inépuisable: parmi le grand nombre d'Ouvrages qu'il a publié, aucun ne se ressemble; chacun a son caractère distinctif; & le plus souvent on ne reconnoît Hayden qu'à ses menuets. Il semble même avoir le secret d'animer les Musiciens; l'orchestre paroît se complaire & s'identifier avec lui; jamais il n'est plus attachant que dans l'exécution des ses chef-œuvres.

Shortly thereafter, in its issue of 16 November 1781, we read:

> ... Le Concert [Spirituel] du Vendredi premier Novembre... La Symphonie d'Hayden, par laquelle le Concert a commencé, a été fort bien exécutée, & a plû généralement. Ce charmant Compositeur, par le brillant, la grâce, la nouveauté de ses idées, a trouvé l'art de se couvrir de gloire & de se placer au premier rang dans un genre que les Grand-Maîtres de son pays, les Stamitz, les Toeschi, &c. sembloient avoir épuisé; car il faut convenir que c'est à l'Allemagne qu'on doit les meilleurs Compositeurs Symphonistes. . . .

The next great success was Haydn's *Stabat Mater*, about which we have learned in the foregoing Chronicle (p. 447). After all this French success, it is not surprising that the Parisians soon seized the initiative. In particular, we owe the existence of Haydn's famous 'Paris' Symphonies to a remarkable French aristocrat: Claude-François-Marie Rigoley, Comte d'Ogny (1757–90), one of the backers of the celebrated Parisian concert organization, Le Concert de la Loge Olympique. This group of Freemasons, led by the young d'Ogny, decided to commission six new symphonies from Haydn. Since d'Ogny played such an important role in Haydn's symphonies of this period, a few words about this 'long-distance' patron may not be amiss.

D'Ogny was born at Dijon in September 1757, the second child of Claude-Jean Rigoley, baron d'Ogny, and Elisabeth d'Alencé (the title of count comes from his mother's side of the family). The name was an old and respected one, whose history can be traced back to the fifteenth century. D'Ogny's father was Intendant Général des Postes, a position which his son inherited in 1785; Ogny *père* was also a backer of the Concert des Amateurs, and apparently music played an important part in the family life. The now famous 'Catalogue de la Musique de Monsieur le Comte d'Ogny' (British Museum), discovered by Barry Brook in 1954, shows that the Count owned, in Professor Brook's words, 'une des plus riches collections musicales privées qui aient jamais été rassemblées au XVIIIe siècle'.[1]

D'Ogny was an extremely handsome man – his portrait, engraved by Edmé Quenedey, is reproduced in Somfai, p. 97 – and kept a mistress who was the subject of the following anecdote by Sophie Arnould (who created the part of Iphigénie in Gluck's *Iphigénie en Aulide* in 1774 at the Paris Opéra):

> ... Mlle Beaumenard, mistress of fermier général d'Ogny, who had presented her with a magnificent rivière of diamonds. Some one was praising before Sophie Arnould this splendid necklace, but said that its only fault was that it was much too long and therefore fell too low over the wearer's figure. 'C'est qu'elle retourne vers sa source', said Arnould.[2]

The correspondence between the Concert de la Loge Olympique and Haydn has not, unfortunately, survived; but H. Barbette, writing in *Le Menestral* of 1871, gives us some valuable details as to the negotiations, which seem to have begun in 1784 or early in 1785. It seems that the Comte d'Ogny asked the chef d'orchestre, le Chevalier Joseph-Boulogne de Saint-Georges – a swashbuckling lady-killer who was himself a prolific composer – to write to Haydn and settle the details. The Concert agreed to pay Haydn 25 louis d'or for each of the six symphonies, 'ce qui avait paru à Haydn un prix colossal, car jusqu'alors ses symphonies ne lui avaient rien rapporté', and a further 5 louis d'or for the publication rights.

Haydn wrote two of the symphonies (Nos. 83 and 87, dated autographs in the Bibliothèque Nationale, Paris) and possibly a third (No. 85, the complete autograph has not survived) in 1785, and three (Nos. 82, 84, 86, first and third in dated autographs also Bib. Nat., Paris, the second in private Swiss possession, also dated). The order in which Imbault printed the first edition (*vide infra*) was: 83, 87, 85, 82, 86, 84, which may actually represent the order in which Haydn composed them and sent them to Paris; while Sieber's edition preserves Imbault's order except that No. 85, by then known as 'La Reine de France' and a popular work, was taken out of its third place and put first. We shall see later in the Chronicle that Haydn suggested a new order to Artaria: 87, 85, 83, 84, 86, 82 – which, however, Artaria did not follow (he printed them in the order we know today). At any rate, five of the autographs survive, and they were once a part of the Comte d'Ogny's music library for there is a note, on the title page of the autograph of No. 82, to the effect that the manuscript was sold at 'la vente de feu Cte d'ogny le 10 février 1791', the Count having died on 4 October 1790, leaving 100,000 livres in debts.

1 See Barry Brook, *La Symphonie Française dans la seconde moitié du XVIIIe siècle*, Paris 1962, vol. 1, pp. 340f., 342, *et passim*. It is from Professor Brook's excellent book that we have gratefully taken the information concerning d'Ogny and Saint-Georges.
2 *Sophie Arnould d'après sa correspondence et ses mémoirs inédits*, par Ed. & J. de Goncourt, Paris 1877. The Memoirs of Sophie Arnould...; ed. Robert B. Douglas, Paris 1898, p. 33. We are indebted to Mr Walter Legge for this amusing story of Paris before 1789.

Parisian orchestras of this period were much larger than those of the Austrian and German provincial courts; and much larger, of course, than Haydn's modest band of twenty-four at Eszterháza. The Concert de la Loge Olympique, 'rempli indépendamment des professeurs par les plus habiles amateurs de Paris', boasted some forty violins and ten double-basses. It is said that only Freemasons were permitted to play in the orchestra.[1] The musicians wore splendid 'sky-blue' dress coats with elaborate lace ruffles and played with swords at their sides. A contemporary engraving of the 'Salle de Spectacle de la Société Olympique' shows us that it was a sort of theatre, with boxes in tiers. The concerts were patronized by the nobility, and Marie Antoinette found the B flat Symphony her favourite: when Imbault engraved the authentic first edition in parts, No. 85 bore the proud title, 'La Reine de France'. (Incidentally, Louis XVI was fond of Haydn, too: among the *Musique du Roy 1784* preserved in the Bibliothèque du Conservatoire at Paris is Symphony No. 53.)

The first performances of the 'Paris' Symphonies appear to have taken place in the season of 1787. They were soon given by the Concert Spirituel as well, and reviewing their concert given on Saturday, 5 April 1788, the *Mercure de France* wrote:

> On a exécuté à tous les Concerts [l'année dernière], des Symphonies de M. Haydn. Chaque jour on sent mieux, & par conséquant on admire davantage les productions de ce vaste génie, qui, dans chacun des ses morceaux, fait si bien, d'un sujet unique, tirer les développemens [*sic*] si riches & si variés; bien différent des ces Compositeurs stériles, qui passent continuellement d'une idée à l'autre, faute d'en savoir présenter une sous des formes variées, & entassent mécaniquement des effets sur des effets, sans liaison & sans goût. Les Symphonies de M. Hayden, toujours sûres de leur effet, en produiroient encore davantage, si la salle étoit plus sonore, & si sa forme étroite avoit permis au Directeur de ce Concert d'en disposer l'Orchestre plus avantageusement. On a exécuté aussi quelques Symphonies de M. Guénin,[2] & c'est pour elles un assez bel éloge que de dire qu'elles ont été applaudies à côté de celles de ce grand Maître [Haydn]...

In January 1788, the same *Mercure de France* printed the proud announcement of the Parisian music publisher Imbault, who advertised for sale the six new works:

> Ces Symphonies, du plus beau caractère & d'une facture étonnante, ne peuvent manquer d'être recherchées avec le plus vif empressement par ceux qui ont eu le bonheur de les entendre, & même par ceux qui ne les connoissent pas. Le nom d'Hayn [*sic*] répond de leur mérite extraordinaire.

Imbault went to particular pains to state, on the title page of his edition,[3] 'Gravé d'après les Partitions originales appartenant à la Loge olympique'. One curious remark in this first edition calls for brief comment: in the middle of the famous flute solo in the slow movement of No. 85 (see Philharmonia vol. IX, p. 186, bar 90), we find the words 'Mot de gué': the words mean something like a 'yodel', or expression of joy – a shout or exclamation. Lacking any sort of explanation, one is tempted to think that Imbault included this remark to indicate that the audience began to applaud, or cheer, at this point in the score. But perhaps the remark is Haydn's (the autograph of No. 85 is lost); at any rate, its precise meaning is lost in the mist of time.

---

1 *Österreichische Freimaurerlogen: Humanität und Toleranz im 18. Jahrhundert*, Schloß Rosenau bei Zwettl, 1976, p. 81. Luigi Cherubini composed a Masonic Cantata for the Loge Olympique.

2 Marie Alexandre Guénin (1744–1819), an interesting composer whose symphonies have recently been resuscitated with good effect. One of them was attributed, wrongly, to Haydn: see Landon, *SYM*, p. 902, No. 17.

3 We used the copy in the Burgenländisches Landesmuseum. Another is owned by the British Museum.

We have noted that Sieber reprinted these Symphonies. When he did so, he had to get permission from the Monseigneur le garde des finances – this was standard practice for all publishers in those days – and by some miracle we have the 'expertise' which was furnished by no less a man than the famous French composer Grétry:

> P. G. N°. 49. J'ai vu par ordre de Monseigneur le garde des finances six Symphonies de M. Joseph Haydn, dont une en ut maj., une en mi *b*, une en sol, une en Re, une en ut mineur et une en si *b* [*sic*]. j'ai vu en outre la conception qu'on a fait l'auteur a M. Sieber, et je crois qu'on peut lui de permettre la publication.
>
> Gretry
>
> Paris ce 9 janvier 1788

[autograph owned by the Collection Larousse. *La Musique* (Larousse), Paris 1965, vol. II, p. 69.]

We cannot explain satisfactorily the reference to 'la conception' that Haydn made to Sieber. The first publication rights were obviously Imbault's; possibly Sieber had to secure Haydn's permission to reprint the works.

When Johann Tost went to Paris in 1788 he took with him the manuscripts (parts?) of several new works by Haydn: Symphonies Nos. 88 and 89, and the Quartets Opp. 54/55 (one opus, in reality). Tost had the rights to sell these works in Paris, which he did (to Sieber, who brought them out in 1789). We shall see that Johann Tost also sold as Haydn a new symphony by the young Adalbert Gyrowetz (*vide infra*, pp. 663ff.). So in a sense all these works were composed with an eye to the Parisian public.

The success of the 'Paris' and 'Tost' Symphonies persuaded Monseigneur le Comte d'Ogny to order three new symphonies from Haydn for the Concert de la Loge Olympique. Haydn had meanwhile received an order from his south German patron, Prince Krafft Ernst von Oettingen-Wallerstein (the relevant correspondence is included *infra*, pp. 706, 727), to compose three new symphonies. Being a shrewd businessman, Haydn decided to satisfy both of his 'corresponding patrons' (if we may misuse the French Academy's term, corresponding member). In 1788 he composed two of the works (Nos. 90 and 91). The autographs of both turned up within the last fifty years. Comte d'Ogny owned both works, and No. 91 is dedicated to him in Haydn's hand, 'Pour Mons: le Comte d'Ogny' (autographs: No. 90, Library of Congress; No. 91, Pierpont Morgan Library, New York). In 1956, the autograph of No. 92 was bequeathed to the Bibliothèque Nationale in Paris among a bundle of mostly worthless music; it was first exhibited in the beautiful Mozart Exhibition at Paris in 1956. It too bears an autograph dedication to the Count (first two pages of music reproduced in Landon *Supplement*, facing p. 49): 'Pour S[on] Excellence Monseign[eur] le Comte d'Ogny' (on the otherwise blank title page, which also has Haydn's signature and the date 1789). We shall follow the history of the Symphonies' delivery at Wallerstein Castle in the forthcoming Chronicle.

The French publication rights of Nos. 90–92 had been assigned this time to Le Duc, who engraved the parts 'Du Répertoire de la Loge Olympique' from the autograph manuscripts (Le Duc's name is even found on page three of No. 92's autograph). Le Duc published the three symphonies in 1790, the year that Count d'Ogny died.

There is a curious postscript which concerns Symphony No. 85 ('La Reine de France') and Marie Antoinette. After Louis XVI and his family were imprisoned in the *Temple*, we hear of the following event:

Another of those who came to the Temple was Lepitre, a young professor who became a member of the provincial Commune on December 2nd [1792]. With him on duty one morning was Toulan, a man who did all he could to make life bearable for the royal family. There was a harpsichord by the door of Madame Elisabeth's room, which he tried to play, only to find it was badly out of tune. Marie Antoinette came up to him: 'I should be glad to use that instrument, so I can continue my daughter's lessons, but it is impossible in its present condition, and I have not succeeded in getting it tuned.' Lepitre and Toulan sent out a message, and the harpsichord was tuned the same evening.

'As we were looking through the small collection of music that day upon the instrument we found a piece called *La Reine de France* [Haydn's Symphony No. 85]. "Times have changed", said her Majesty, and we could not restrain our tears.'
[John Hearsey: *Marie Antoinette*, London, 2nd ed. 1974, p. 100.]

ENGLAND

Haydn's success in England received a marked impetus when Symphony No. 53 ('L'impériale) was given at the Bach-Abel concerts in 1781. After J. C. Bach's death, Abel carried on the concerts for a season but they were not successful, despite the fact that a new Haydn Symphony, No. 74, was performed.[1] Haydn's future friend, Willoughby Bertie, Fourth Earl of Abingdon, then took over the concerts and published his plans in the *Public Advertiser* on 13 July 1782: there were to be twelve, given in the Hanover Square Rooms, and the report stated that Haydn and Friedrich Hartmann Graf were already engaged. On 23 November 1782, the *Morning Herald* reports that Graf had arrived and that Haydn, 'the Shakespeare of musical composition is hourly expected' (Roscoe, 204). In fact Graf had not arrived at all. On the 25th we read:

> The *musical world* are rather alarmed, lest the celebrated *Haydn* should decline visiting England. His stay is so much courted by persons of the first fashion and eminence on the continent, so engaged is he in his studious avocations and domestic concerns, that Lord Abingdon, who is at the head of the new *Festino* concert, has yet received no positive assurance that he will come over.
> [*Morning Herald*, 25 November 1782; Roscoe, 204]

On the 27th we read in the *Public Advertiser* that 'Hayden certainly joins his Talents to the Band'. But of course Haydn did not come, and the *Morning Herald* on 6 February 1783 had to report:

> Neither Haydn nor Graaf, the musical composers for the new concert, are yet arrived, though they have been expected for more than a month past: in consequence of this disappointment, we understand that the noble conductors of this fashionable assembly are not a little *disconcerted* themselves! [Roscoe, 204]

Two days before the first concert was supposed to occur, the *Morning Chronicle* on 17 February reported that Graf had arrived. 'But as to Haydn – we have got neither him nor his music – however the music is certainly to come – the musician, most probably, will remain at Vienna' (Roscoe, 204). Meanwhile, news of the concerts was sent to Germany by correspondents of Cramer's *Magazin der Musik*. In the 1783 volume (pp.

---

1 William Forster's advertisement in the *Morning Herald*, 20 February 1782. Our knowledge of this pre-1791 scene in England comes from two excellent articles: (1) Christopher Roscoe, 'Haydn and London in the 1780's' in *Music & Letters* 49 (1968), pp. 207ff; and (2) Cecil B. Oldman, 'Haydn's Quarrel with the "Professionals" in 1788', in *Musik und Verlag*, Kassel 1968, pp. 459ff. Hereinafter abbreviated 'Roscoe' and 'Oldman'.

564ff.) we read of the size of the Nobility's Concert: 16 violins, 7 basses, 3 violas, 2 oboes, 2 flutes, 2 horns, 2 clarinets, 2 bassoons; and a typical programme is reproduced in flawless English on p. 549. In a letter from London of December 1783 (pp. 106ff.), the *Magazin* reports:

> **Hayden's** intention, of which I wrote you recently, to come here has turned out to amount to nothing. He has categorically turned down our offer but promised to compose anything we wish if he receives the sum of £500.

We know that Haydn went so far as to compose three new symphonies for the *Festino* concerts: Nos. 76–78. The question that we cannot answer is: did he send them to the Earl of Abingdon? We believe he did not. In July 1783 he was offering them to Boyer in Paris, but if they had been performed in London in the 1783 season, they would have (by July) become common property. Probably some of the works that Haydn sent to Forster before these particular symphonies, e.g. Symphony No. 70, were the 'new' pieces performed in the 1783 season (Forster's edition of No. 70 appeared in December 1782). In the *Magazin* we read that 'The third concert on 3rd March was distinguished by a new, not yet heard original Symphony by Haydn, which connoisseurs declared to be unique of its kind; and to hear it in another concert, was the general wish, even before it was ended.' The description would fit well the 'new' work with its triple fugue and canon. At the fifth concert, on 17 March, we read (pp. 228ff.) that it 'began with a Symphony by **Haydn**, which was declared to be a masterpiece of its kind ... In the 8th concert on 21 April was a new Symphony by **Haydn**, pronounced by connoisseurs to be very learned and brilliant, and in its good performance none of the beauties were lost which that great master had infused into it ... The 9th concert on 28 April began with a Symphony by Mozart which was very brilliant ...'.

Haydn's presence, it seems, was still expected. The *Morning Post* (19 July 1783) writes:

> The great Hayden, next autumn, comes to London. Phlegm, and, in all pecuniary concerns, extreme caution, are among the leading characteristics of this great composer; insomuch so, that last winter he could not, without uncommon assurances, he prevailed upon to send his new music over to Lord Abingdon's Grand Concert. [Roscoe, 205]

And Haydn was still the biggest drawing card of the new musicians. He even entered the precincts of Vauxhall Gardens, the sanctuary of British music and their composers. In a newspaper clipping (no paper named) of 15 May 1783, we read:

> *Haydn's* Symphonies, which were introduced for the first time at Vauxhall on Tuesday evening last, must cease to have their wonted effect, unless Mt Bartholemon [*sic*] will simplify his manner of playing them, and the performer on the organ will confine his finger [*sic*] to those powerful *fortés*, which only require such assistance.[1]

Abingdon organized a subscription series of twelve concerts for the 1784 season, but for some curious reason they were totally unsuccessful. Thereupon Wilhelm Cramer and Luigi Borghi, two violinists, founded the Professional Concert. Rumours of Haydn and England continued to filter back to the Continent, and in a letter from

---

1 'Maître' ('Mt'?) François Hippolite Barthélémon, later Haydn's warm friend. See *Haydn in England 1791–1795*, pp. 168–70 *et passim*. This clipping is in the Bodleian Library's Vauxhall Collection, and was kindly sent to us by Mr Roger Hellyer.

Vienna of June 1784, the *Magazin der Musik* (p. 194) reports that the English have decided to erect a monument to Haydn in Westminster Abbey, the unveiling of which is to wait until Haydn arrives personally. This may have been idle speculation on the part of some of Haydn admirers, but anything seemed possible in that foggy, mad island. The latest proposal was to kidnap Haydn and bring him to England. The *Gazetteer & New Daily Advertiser* (17 January 1785) reports:

> There is something very distressing to a liberal mind in the history of *Haydn*. This wonderful man, who is the Shakespeare of music, and the triumph of the age in which we live, is doomed to reside in the court of a miserable German Prince, who is at once incapable of rewarding him, and unworthy of the honour. *Haydn*, the simplest as well as the greatest of men, is resigned to his condition, and in devoting his life to the rites and ceremonies of the Roman Catholic Church, which he carries even to superstition, is content to live immured in a place little better than a dungeon, subject to the domineering spirit of a petty Lord, and the clamourous temper of a scolding wife. Would it not be an achievement equal to a pilgrimage, for some aspiring youths to rescue him from his fortune and transplant him to Great Britain, the country for which his music seems to be made?
>
> [Roscoe, 205]

The Professional Concert gave a series of twelve in 1785, on Wednesdays (starting on 2 February and ending on 11 May). There were still hopes of luring Haydn to England: on 16 September 1785, the *Morning Herald* writes:

> The report of the celebrated *Haydn's* intention of visiting this country, is again revived. Those however, who know him best, are of opinion, that he will never honor this land of *heresy* with his presence. This great genius is so great a bigot to the ceremonies of religion, that all his leisure moments are continuously engaged in the celebration of masses, and in the contemplation of purgatory, but what gives a greater gloom to his mind is, the unfortunate temper of his wife – she, good woman, has no relish for the beauties of *harmony*, nor is her voice of the *melodious* sort – hence his domestic comforts are few – and he is glad to seek consolation in the *bosom* of the Church.
>
> [Roscoe, 206]

On 2 November, the *Morning Herald* reports that Haydn has now abandoned his intention of visiting England; it suggested that

> his music he has been told is not in estimation with the King. Mr. Bates, who had the management of the great organ [at the Westminster Abbey Handel Commemoration in 1784], also dislikes his compositions, and as *occasion* offers, speaks his disapprobation – *piano* and *forte*, against him!
>
> [Roscoe, 206]

Joah Bates was later to become Haydn's friend in London. All these were, of course, excuses; Prince Nicolaus would simply not allow Haydn to leave. Since this non-arrival in England is otherwise inexplicable, we might add a few words from Haydn's biographer Dies, who tells us (pp. 73f.):

> Haydn owned a little house in Eisenstadt which twice fell prey to flames. The generous Prince Nicolaus both times hurried there and found Haydn in tears, comforted him, had the house rebuilt, and provided the necessary furnishing. Haydn, much touched by the Prince's generosity, could repay him only with love, attachment, and with the products of his muse. Touched to the heart, he wished to prove his gratitude. He swore to the Prince to serve him till death should bring to a close the life of the one or the other, and never leave him even should he be offered millions.

It was that simple. But of course the English could know nothing of Haydn's simple but earnest vow. The *Public Advertiser* of 8 October 1785 said that 'He certainly undertakes to write for the Hanover-square concert; his genius is yet in its full vigour; and what may we not expect from its exertions, if we may judge from what we have already experienced?' (Roscoe, 206); while on 6 February 1786 the *Morning Herald* reports that 'Haydn wishes it [the Professional Concert] prosperity, and has composed some pieces that will be played there, full of his phrenzy and fire' (Oldman, 460; Roscoe, 206). On 10 October 1786, the *Morning Chronicle* reports that Sir John Gallini was in Vienna 'for the express purpose of engaging the celebrated Haydn as composer to the Opera House for the ensuing season'.

On 23 November the *Morning Post* writes:

Haydn! The musical world will shortly be gratified with the arrival of the celebrated HAYDN in England. This *Shakespeare* of composers has entered into an engagement with the conductors of the Hanover square Concert to visit London in January next. The articles for this purpose were signed in the beginning of this month at Vienna. It is stipulated in the agreement that he is to compose a new *Overture* or *Concerto* for every night's performance; of course we shall have twelve original pieces from that great master. He is to be paid four hundred guineas for this service besides a clear benefit.   [Roscoe, 207]

The next day, the *Morning Post* was forced to modify its enthusiasm:

It is said we shall shortly be gratified with the arrival of Haydn amongst us. We should think from his advanced age that this circumstance is rather to be wished than expected; besides, it is well known, that the Earl of Abingdon offered him 500 guineas and a free benefit some years ago, on conditions similar to the present which were refused. That he may have been engaged to furnish a new Overture, or Concerto for every night's performance, it is probable; but then there is no necessity for his coming hither to compose them.   [Roscoe, 207]

The *Gazetteer*, continuing the discussion, writes on 5 January 1787:

Whatever may be asserted to the contrary by the retailers of musical anecdotes of the day, it is certain that Haydn has offered his services to the Hanover-square Concert, and he has sent them the terms on which he will engage. Mr. Hammersley, the Banker, has now become the negociator, and as his *notes* are in as great estimation as those of Haydn, there is little doubt but that he will prevail on him to visit England.   [Roscoe, 207]

On the 17th the same paper informs us that

The Professors, to whom music is but a *drug*, complain that the *musical* Apothecary in Pall-Mall does not *gild the pill*—though he cannot say with his brother, 'My poverty, but not my will, consents'.   [Roscoe, 207]

The Professors seemed to have entered serious negotiations with Haydn, not only for his music – among the new works he sent over for the 1789 season were the Opus 54/55 Quartets, which were subsequently engraved by Longman & Broderip and issued with the note 'Performed at the Professional Concert Hanover Square 1789': we have examined this print for our edition as part of the Doblinger Complete Quartets and may state here that it is not only clearly authentic but a slightly earlier version than that issued by Sieber in Paris (*vide infra*, pp. 635ff.).

But as for Haydn the man, we read in the *World* on 17 January 1787:

Haydn—of composers by far the most original, and the best, is to remove from Vienna. The professional concert are in treaty with him. An offer of £400 sterling, has been forwarded for his acceptance—£100 to be paid to him in Vienna on his departure—the other three on his arrival in London. All guaranteed by Mr. Hammersley the banker—of course as good as the Bank. [Roscoe 207]

We now have an interesting and authentic account of a visit to Eszterháza by that clever young man Gaetano Bartolozzi, son of the famous engraver, with both of whom Haydn had frequent contact in England from 1791–5; Haydn was a witness at Gaetano's marriage to Therese Jansen on 16 May 1795.[1]

A *musician*, it would seem, has as little honour in his own country as a *prophet*, and of this the celebrated *Haydn* furnishes a remarkable proof. The Prince of Esterhagy [*sic*], to whom this great composer is *Maitre de Chapelle*, though he affects the highest admiration of the works of Haydn, who is constantly employed in his service, yet his only reward is a pittance which the most obscure fidler in London would disdain to accept, together with a miserable apartment in the barracks, in which are his bed and an old spinnet, or clavichord. In this situation, so unworthy of his genius, was Haydn found by Mr. Bartolozzi, who lately went to visit him. He seemed to be highly pleased with Bartolozzi's account of the encouragement given to music in England, and of the high estimation in which his compositions were held. It was upon this occasion that Haydn first expressed a desire to visit London, which was the origin of the negociations now on the tapis between him and the managers of the Hanover-square Concert. [Roscoe, 208]

We shall see that Sir John Gallini again enters the picture (see his correspondence with Haydn, or rather *vice versa*, in the ensuing Chronicle, p. 696). The documents for 1788 are so many and are almost self-explanatory (the few notes will be found at the end, p. 602) that it was thought best to present them *en bloc*:

A. Haydn is certainly a great Composer; but he often copies from himself. – In some pieces lately sent to the Professional Committee, and to Longman and Napier,[1] they were in many passages nearly the same.

The World, 25 Feb. 1788.
[Oldman, 460]

B. HAYDN'S DEFENCE
A CARD[2] OF VINDICATION from Mr. HAYDN, of Vienna, on his Character being unjustly attacked by a certain Musical Committee in London.
1. Mr. Haydn sent three Symphonies to that Committee, but having intrusted a Copy thereof to a Music Seller at Vienna, it was clandestinely transmitted to a Music Shop in London, by which means it was published without the author's consent.
2. As a compensation to the Committee, an Oratorio[3] by Mr. Haydn was presented to them, in lieu of the Symphonies.
3. Mr. Haydn received a few Guineas on Account, for the three Symphonies abovementioned, which he has returned, and never wishes to have any correspondence whatever with persons who have attempted to injure his character without any just cause.
4. The public have been repeatedly deluded by Newspaper paragraphs, into a belief that Mr. Haydn was engaged by the Committee to visit London, and

---

1 *Haydn in England 1791–1795*, p. 309.

assist at a certain Concert;[4] the whole of which was fabricated to answer sinister purposes, and to impose on the credulity of a generous Nation.

5. As Mr. Haydn hopes he has hitherto maintained the character of an honest man through life, he is in justice to himself bound to publish these facts to the English Nation, whose generous approbation of his Music will always merit his warmest and most grateful acknowledgments. Vienna, Feb. 28, 1788.

JOSEPH HAYDN
The World, 29 March 1788.
[Oldman, 461; Roscoe, 209]

C. Haydn, the composer, lately suffered very much in the estimation of musical people, on account of his having sent to the conductors of the Professional Concert, who had transmitted him money for new music to be performed there, some compositions which had been previously published in this country. He has, however, fully vindicated his character, in shewing that the works sent to this country were intended for Spain,[5] by refunding all the money thus transmitted to him, and by making the Professional Concert a present of an Oratorio of his own composing, which though of no use to them, is a tribute of his liberality and good will.

The Morning Post, 21 March 1788.
[Oldman, 461; Roscoe 208]

D. The Committee of the Professional Concert, find themselves under the necessity of intruding a few lines on the public, in order to vindicate themselves from the malevolent and unjust accusations which appeared in an Advertisement entitled "Haydn's Defence", and which was published in this Paper. They beg leave to inform their Subscribers and Patrons, that the original Contract of Sig. Haydn's, together with all his Letters and Answers, are deposited at Messr. Ransom, Morland and Hammersley[6], No. 57, Pall-Mall, for their inspection, to prove the falsity and malice of that Advertisement.

The World, 3 Apr. 1788
[Oldman, 461; Roscoe, 209]

E. An ANSWER to the first part of HAYDN'S DEFENCE.

A Card having appeared in the World and the HERALD, stating first – Mr. Haydn sent three Symphonies to the Musical Committee in London; but having entrusted a copy thereof to a music-seller in Vienna, it was clandestinely transmitted to a music shop in London, by which means it was published without the Author's consent. The above illiberal paragraph having been inserted by one Dittenhoffer,[7] a German Musician, in justice to Mess. Artaria and Company, music-sellers at Vienna, we think it incumbent in us to contradict so false and scandalous a paragraph, the said Symphonies being wrote purposely for Messrs. Artaria and Co. and in order to remove every doubt of this matter, Mr. Haydn's original receipt in full for the copy-right of the said Symphonies, and also Messrs. Artaria's receipt to us for the sole right of printing and publishing the same in London, may be seen at No. 13, in the Haymarket. LONGMAN AND BRODERIP. [8]

The World, 3 Apr. 1788 [printed immediately below D].
[Oldman, 462; Roscoe, 210]

F. HAYDN

The difference between this celebrated Composer and the conductors of the Professional Concert, does not arise from any fault on either part but is the effect of pitiful rancour in an individual; who, from motives of private pique, has contrived to affect this misunderstanding.

HAYDN, besides his great musical genius, possesses the repute of an honest man, and the Managers of the Professional Concert have also separately such characters as give them a claim to respect for their private merits, fully equal to what their public talents deserve.

The malignant individual alluded to, has been induced to work this temporary dissension merely because, being obscure in life, and having no talents that were entitled to distinction, he was refused the freedom of the Professional Concert; in consequence of which he wrote to Haydn, reviling the Committee, and offering himself as a friend to the vilified Composer.

HAYDN, duped by his professions, intreated him to rescue his character, and on this foundation the vindictive gentleman has obtruded his mischievous nonsense on the world.

The Morning Post, 7 Apr. 1788.
[Oldman, 462; Roscoe, 210]

G. There seems to be some inconsistency in the story of *Haydn's Symphonies*, which is not removed by the counter-advertisement. It is very likely that both parties may be in the right, and that the fraud ought to be placed at the door of some *starving copier of Music*, who will frequently play this trick with the works of a *celebrated man*.

The Morning Post, 12 Apr. 1788.
[Oldman, 462; Roscoe, 210]

H. HAYDN'S DEFENCE

1. MR. DIETTENHOFFER'S Name being mentioned, as the inserter of an illiberal paragraph concerning a Musical Committee, renders it necessary to inform the public, that what was inserted, was extracted from a letter of Mr. Haydn's, which some of the Committee have seen in the presence of a certain seller of music.

2. If it may be supposed, that Mr. Diettenhoffer sent the paragraph alluded to, it must have been in consequence of the intimacy and warm friendship for that excellent master, the great Haydn, whose honour he thought injured. Mr. Diettenhoffer was educated at Vienna, and has been in constant correspondence with that Musical Phenomenon; he has likewise received very honourable protection from some of the Nobility and Gentry of this country, and he would be much concerned to engage in anything which might in the least sully his reputation. It must clearly appear, that Mr. Diettenhoffer could only have been considered as agent, not the author of the paragraph, which has occasioned such discord among the Sons of Apollo.

3. The Committee should certainly know, that signing the engagement at Pall-Mall, was not sufficient to induce Haydn to travel to London. The paper should have been signed and approved by a banker at Vienna, and the Four Hundred Guineas,[9] or security agreed on, should have been transmitted to Mr. Haydn, which last circumstance was never performed by the Committee.

4. There is some reason to hope, that Mr. Haydn will visit London, and compose for another Concert,[10] when, without doubt, he will fully defend himself, support the character of an honourable man, as well as the greatest composer in music.

The World, 12 Apr. 1788.
[Oldman, 463; Roscoe, 211]

I. HAYDN'S DEFENCE

BELLA, HORRIDA BELLA!

The Shrill Trumpet has sounded, all the Fiddle Sticks are raised, the bass viols grunt, the flagelet squeaks, nothing but wounds, bloodshed, and slaughter will ensue. The Musical Committee and their magnanimous leader, the Haymarket Apollonean Hero, or seller of sol-fa, have armed themselves, under the pure banners of their own virtue and integrity. HAYDN, the great Vienna HAYDN prepares, not for flight it seems, but to meet his heroic Opponents: England may, dreadful to reflect! London will be the scene of direful action! Hospitals are preparing for the wounded, young Surgeons are gaping for dislocations, fractures, fiddle stick wounds, and operations; new recruits are enlisting to gain immortal honour by discordant deeds. Heaven send, that during the bloody Musical Conflict, the French or Spanish may not invade our British territories, and annihilate English Liberty!

Sancta Cecilia ora pro nobis!

The World, 15 Apr. 1788.
[Oldman, 463; Roscoe, 211]

[Notes:]

1 We cannot identify the pieces in question, but suspect that they concern Symphonies 53 (with Finale 'B') and Symphony No. 62, the first and last movements of which are based on the same music.

2 Card: a term used in the eighteenth century for any personal announcement in the Press.

3 *Il ritorno di Tobia;* autograph formerly owned by the Marchioness of Bute.

4 The Professional Concert.

5 Haydn imagined that there would be no rivalry between his Spanish and his London patrons since it was hardly likely that there was any contact between the two. Is the work *The Seven Words?*

6 The late Dr Oldman established that the banking firm of Ransom, Morland and Hammersley, 'after several earlier amalgamations, was finally absorbed into the firm of Barclay, Bevan, Tritton & Co. in 1888. This latter was the forerunner of the present Barclay's Bank Ltd. I have been assured, however, by Barclay's Archivist that none of the Ransom records before 1796 have survived.' Haydn also used the bank when it was known as Hammersley & Co. See *Haydn: the Late Years 1801–1809*, pp. 288f. Thomas Hammersley subscribed to *The Creation:* see *Haydn: the Years of 'The Creation' 1796–1800*, pp. 626, 632n.

7 Joseph Diettenhofer, a Viennese musician living in England. See *Haydn in England 1791–1795*, pp. 97f.

8 Longman & Broderip were obviously not yet aware that Haydn had composed the 'Paris' Symphonies for the Concert de la Loge Olympique.

9 In Haydn's letter to Gallini of 19 July: £500.

10 The Salomon Concerts.

A few words of explanation may be required. The 'three Symphonies' in Document E are obviously three of the 'Paris' set, which Haydn had sold in MS. copies to various patrons and sold to Artaria, Imbault, Sieber, Forster and the Professional Concert. The Professionals were to start their series of 1788 in February, but in January printed copies of 'their' three 'Paris' Symphonies were on sale in London (Longman & Broderip's importation of Artaria? Forster's?).

The Professionals apparently neglected to send a proper contract to Haydn, but who knows if he would have signed it. In view of all this publicity, it is no wonder that Haydn's arrival in England, on New Year's Day 1791, was the occasion for much speculation and curiosity.

HAYDN'S COPYISTS; PLAGIARISM; TERZETTO, 'PIETÀ DI ME' (XXVb:5)

We have quoted in the Chronicle (p. 489) Mozart's letter in which he writes that a certain Hofstetter 'des Haydn Musique dopelt copirt'. The subject of pirated prints and spurious attributions – quite apart from the problem of the *seguaci* as such – has appeared at intervals throughout this biography. Unscrupulous copyists plagued composers all through the century. On 12 March 1750, Giuseppe Tartini sent a letter to 'Sig Conte mio Padrone, e Signore', with six concertos composed for 'Sua Altezza il Sig:ᵉ Prencipe di Lobcovitz [*sic*]', in which he writes *inter alia*

...La mia delicatezza mi obliga pasind[i] fargli sapere, che hò occasione di dubitare, che il copista mi abbia trafugato con doppia coppia uno di questi sei concerti et è quello in b mì cerfa minore. Non son sicuro, ma molto temo. Mi son oppresso abastanza col medesimo; ma se lo hà trafugato, nulla giovarà perchè l'animo è ostile ...   [Autograph, Pierpont Morgan Library, New York]

Haydn had no doubt had his bitter experiences with copyists who had 'trafugati con doppia coppia', and in a letter of 7 October 1789 he explains how it was done: 'the rascals put a piece of paper *a parte* under the music, and thus by degrees they secretly copy the part they have in front of them'. Of course, the problem is not limited to musicians, and in *Haydn in England 1791–1795* (p. 42), we have shown that Lady Montagu suffered from similar plagiarism in the literary world. It was not exclusively an eighteenth century problem, either. In his fascinating book *Lysias and the Corpus Lysiacum*,[1] Professor Kenneth Dover has shown that Athenian booksellers in the late fourth century B.C. unscrupulously attached the names of famous orators, e.g. Lysias and Demosthenes, to speeches composed by comparatively unknown speech-writers and litigants; hence the great number of spurious or doubtful works listed under the names of the great orators in the first catalogue of the Alexandrian Library compiled by Callimachus in the early third century BC.[2]

If we confine ourselves only to the symphonies – 160 spurious works in this form have thus far been recorded by Larsen, Hoboken and Landon – we find the following composers' names:

C. F. Abel	Klug	Antonio M. G. Sacchini
Casimir Antonio Cartellieri	Franz Körzel (2)	Giuseppe Sarti
Anton (Matthaeus?) Czibulka	Leopold Koželuch (2)	Baron T. von Schacht
Carl Ditters(dorf) (9)	J. M. Kraus	Johann Michael Schmid(t)
Franz Dussek	Laus(en)mayer	Joseph Schmitt (2)
Anton Filtz (3)	Pierre van Maldere (3)	Franz Schneider
F. L. Gassmann	Louis Massoneau	Joseph Schuster
Marie Alexandre Guénin	P. A. Monsigny	J. F. X. Sterkel
Adalbert Gyrowetz (2)	Leopold Mozart	Gottfried van Swieten (3)
Johann Michael Haydn (20)	Sebastiano Nasolini	Christoph Sonnleithner (2)
Herffert	Neubauer	J. B. Vanhal (12)
F. A. Hoffmeister (2)	Carlos d'Ordoñez (3)	J. G. F. Wassmuth
Leopold Hofmann (6)	Wenzel Pichl (4)	Francesco Weigert
Ignaz Holzbauer (2)	Ignaz Pleyel (4)	Winkler
Robert Kimmerling	Gaetano Pugnani	Anton Zimmermann (2)
J. F. Kloeffler	Franz Anton Rosetti (2)	

The list for the spurious Masses would be even longer and the names obscurer. What could Haydn do to protect himself against thefts of his own works (he could hardly prevent misattributions unless, as was the case with his pupil Pleyel, Haydn himself was responsible). He had a number of copyists at Eszterháza, Johann Schellinger and the Elssler family, also the many musicians who earned a few extra gulden by copying music. But after the experience of Johann Tost, who wanted to open up his own music copying establishment at Eszterháza, Haydn may have become suspicious of his group at Eszterháza. There was another reason why Haydn soon began to establish his own copyists' circle not in Hungary but in Vienna, where he spent a month (sometimes

1 Berkeley & Los Angeles, 1968, Chapter II and especially pp. 159–161.
2 We are indebted to Professor Dover, who took the trouble to write this summary himself, which we gratefully include here.

longer) at Christmas time: Haydn's increased contacts with foreign patrons, and a natural desire that this activity take place somewhat in secret and away from the inquisitive eyes and ears of Esterházy officialdom and the other musicians, suggested that he engage non-Esterházy musicians to do the necessary copying. In the 1780s, this Viennese copying grew ever more important. We know some of the names: Johann Radnitzky, who signed his name on several copies that Haydn signed and sent to Forster. There were two Radnitzkys: Peter and Johann, both copyists, but for reasons explained by us in another place (*SYM*, 30n.), Johann, who died a pauper in January 1790, was probably Haydn's copyist, not his brother Peter (who also died a pauper in 1832 – music was a precarious profession at best). Another copyist whom Haydn occasionally used in Vienna was a man named Schmutzer, who also signed many of his copies (he also worked for Ritter von Keeß: see *SYM*, 39), but alas the most important of them all is known to us only as 'Anonymous 63' (Bartha-Somfai's term). Formerly confused with Johann Elssler, it is now clear that Anon. 63 was a most reliable copyist in his own right. It is now believed that Joseph Elssler's son Johann, who later became Haydn's valet-de-chambre and copyist (after 1794, when he went with Haydn to England), began copying music for Haydn in the 1780s, and that his handwriting is identical with one of the Esterházy copyists identified as Anonymous 48.[1] It is certain that Schellinger made some copies of Haydn's music in 1793,[2] but we do not know if Haydn employed him or if he was working on his own. It is important for us to know, because of an interesting *pasticcio* that Schellinger made, entitled 'Alessandro il grande, Opera Seria in 3 atti Dal Sig[r] gius. Haydn' (XXXII:3; MS. in the Gesellschaft der Musikfreunde). Traeg marketed this Opera, for it is included in his Catalogue of 1799. The music includes pieces from Guglielmi's *Debora e Sisara*, Haydn's *La fedeltà premiata* (two numbers), *Orlando Paladino* (one aria), *Armida* (two arias) and a fascinating piece which must now concern us: 'Pietà di me, benigni dei',[3] which we know from England. It is scored for two solo sopranos, tenor solo, with cor anglais, bassoon and horn obbligati, and orchestra (E flat). The MS. in the British Museum by Johann Elssler (Anonymous 63?) on what is known as 'small post paper' (Add. 34073) is accompanied by a piano-vocal score in another hand, on which is the following note: 'This very rare M.S. formerly belonged to my kind friend Mr. Shield, who told me that he rec[d] it from Haydn himself, on purpose to be sung by M[rs.] Billington – at the time Haydn visited England. I have no doubt that this is the identical copy from which Mrs. Billington sang on the occasion. V. Novello.' The *particella* does in fact have Mrs Billington's signature on the right-hand top corner.

We therefore need to know when Schellinger made the copy of *Alessandro*, i.e. during his tenure as Esterházy copyist or later? We can find no evidence that 'Pietà di me' was composed before 1790, and the Gesellschaft der Musikfreunde *Alessandro* copy cannot be dated any more precisely than *c*. 1790. The fact that Traeg advertised the work in 1799 cannot assist us in dating it, but it might indicate that Schellinger was working for Traeg and that his copy is really a commercial Traeg copy of the 1790s, made after Schellinger left Hungary.

And what of the music? The horn part is the most difficult Haydn ever wrote: it often reaches sounding *a* flat″ and even goes up to the incredible note, sounding *b* flat″

---

1 See our article 'A New Authentic Source for "La Fedeltà Premiata" by Haydn', in *Soundings* II (1971–2).
2 See *Haydn in England 1791–1795*, p. 487.
3 Günter Thomas in *Haydn-Studien* II/2 (1969), 122. Landon, *SYM*, 861f. *Haydn in England 1791–1795*, pp. 28, 29n., 311, 377. Critical edition: Verlag Doblinger, Vienna-Munich, edited by the present writer (1978).

– the highest note ever written for the horn.[1] It is the kind of writing that we find Haydn using in works presumably composed for Carl Franz, and no doubt Franz could have played the music. But the crux of the matter lies in the cor anglais part. It was noted that in *L'anima del filosofo* Haydn wrote cor anglais parts going down to *d* and *e* flat in the bass clef, notes that connot be played on a normal cor anglais in F: there seem to have been English horn players in Britain capable of playing these notes (on an instrument with extended compass).[2] We also suggested in that volume that there is a suspicious similarity to 'an additional new Song, composed here for the occasion by BIANCHI, to be sung by Madame BANTI, accompanied by the English Horn, Violoncello, French Horn and Bassoon Obligati, by Messrs. FERLENDIS . . . [&c.]' (June 1795).[3] If we examine the cor anglais part of 'Pietà di me', we note that it too goes below the normal compass of an instrument in F. It appears that for the moment, 'Pietà di me' must be assigned to the English period, but of course the evidence is slight. The music, which apart from the vocal and instrumental fireworks is often of great beauty and even solemnity, might have been composed at any moment between c. 1780 and 1795 (the latest possible date, for obvious reasons). It is one of the most interesting *pièces d'occasion* that we have from Haydn's pen, and highly unconventional, not to say bizarre.

---

1 First performance in mòdern times: B.B.C. Third Programme, 17 December 1956: see *supra*, p. 358n.
2 *Haydn in England 1791–1795*, pp. 311, 330.
3 The *True Briton*, 16 June, 1795.

CHAPTER NINE

The Musical Results of Haydn's Internationalism: Works of 1785–1790

THE WORKS OF THE YEARS 1785–90 which we shall consider here are:
the 'Paris' Symphonies, Nos. 82–87;
The Seven Words for Cádiz;
Concertos for the King of Naples;
Quartets for Spain and for the King of Prussia;
Symphonies Nos. 88 and 89 for Paris (via Tost);
Symphonies for the Comte d'Ogny and for Prince von Oettingen-Wallerstein, Nos. 90–92;
the First Series of Quartets for Johann Tost (Opp. 54, 55);
Piano Trios for Vienna and London;
Piano Sonatas for Vienna and Leipzig, the Fantasia in C and the VI Variations;
vocal works: *Deutschlands Klage*; *Arianna a Naxos*; Cantata, 'Miseri noi';
'insertion' arias;
pieces for musical clock;
Notturni for the King of Naples;
the Second Series of Quartets for Johann Tost (Op. 64);
the Farewell Song, 'Trachten will ich nicht auf Erden'.

THE 'PARIS' SYMPHONIES NOS. 82–87
(1785–1786)

Some kind of stand has to be taken about the diverse chronological possibilities of the Paris Symphonies (we shall now drop the quotation marks), and we shall follow the order in which Haydn (vainly) asked Artaria to engrave the works: 87, 85, 83, 84, 86, 82 which has the merit (a) of not contradicting the five dated autographs and (b) being the composer's preferred sequence.

Symphony No. 87 in A (1785)

Scoring: 1 flute, 2 oboes, 2 bassoons, 2 horns and strings.

This stepchild of the Paris Symphonies seems to have been forgotten quite fortuitously – something that often happens to the *œuvre* of prolific artists. There are always a few masterpieces by the great painters, writers and musicians that never lose their popularity; but among the vast output of a Titian, Haydn, Verdi or Dickens, there are works that come and go in the public's esteem, and to a certain extent even Beethoven is subjected to this treatment. Why should his *Geschöpfe des Prometheus* be hardly known while the First Symphony is world-famous?

The strong opening subject of the first movement, with agile bass (and bassoon) quavers, has the same kind of rhythmic lead as that of the Finale of No. 86:

C ♩ ⅎ♪♫♫♩ | ♪ etc. The first subject stays *forte* until the beginning of the bridge passage to the dominant, where we are introduced to a gliding bass line in minims over repeated semiquavers in the violins: this section plays an important role in the development section. The six-note figure in the same rhythm but with different intervals greets us when we reach the dominant (bar 37) and is also the rhythmic basis of the second subject (bars 48ff.). This internal unity is further strengthened by the fact that all the sections mentioned above have an accompaniment in quavers. This central and unifying organization is present throughout the rest of the movement.

Observers of this period in Haydn's life will have noticed two basic types of slow movements in the symphonies: the one is the variation, or double variations, in rather quick time (usually Allegretto), and in a quick metre (2/4 is a favourite, but also barred C or 6/8); the other is a real slow movement, almost always Adagio, and very often in Haydn's preferred 3/4 metre. To the first category belong the 'slow' movements of Nos. 82 (Allegretto, 2/4), 84 (Andante, 6/8), 85 (Allegretto, barred C), 89 (Andante con moto, 6/8), 90 and 91 (Andante, 2/4); while to the second belong the really slow movements of Nos. 83, 86, 87, 88 and 92, all of which are in 3/4 except for 92 (2/4), and all of which except 83 (Andante) are marked either Adagio or Largo. To this group, as noted, belongs the beautiful and rhapsodic slow movement of No. 87, whose broad, flowing lines and intricate orchestration place it among the finest of the period. Another characteristic of these adagios and largos is the hymn-like quality of their main themes, especially noticeable in Nos. 87 and 88. We also note the increasing freedom with which Haydn uses the wind instruments, and in particular the fine passages for solo woodwind (with or without horns, sometimes with soft string accompaniment). One such remarkable passage will be noted in connection with the slow movement of No. 84; here, in No. 87's Adagio, we find a kind of cadenza for flute and oboes at bars 37 (with upbeat)–42, greatly elaborated at bars 87 (with upbeat)–97, at first with violin I accompaniment and then without, but with the horns and two bassoons added. One more striking and typical feature may be mentioned: the 'apotheosis' with which Haydn, now in his fifties, provides the codas of his real slow movements: a strong sense of autumnal beauty, of slanted rays of the sun, pervade these poignant, lyrical passages. Technically, this sense of 'dying fall' is produced by two main factors: a pedal-point, usually tonic, and the tendency to reach out to the sub-dominant, using the flattened seventh, together with the use of the *minor* subdominant (six-four chord with the sixth flattened). We find this at the end of No. 87 and, with even more sense of finality, at the end of No. 92; later we shall notice particularly beautiful examples in Symphonies Nos. 94, 97, 102 and, perhaps most poignantly of all, in the last of them all: No. 104, 'The 12th which I have composed in England'.

The sturdy Menuet has a catchy little 'whip' flick ♫ ♩. that pushes the music forwards with a slightly Balkan twist. The Trio is a difficult oboe solo, rising in the second part to *e'''*. The Finale (Vivace) is a monothematic movement in which, as the music unfolds, we see that the main theme has been planned so that it can be used contrapuntally. If we may be permitted a final piece of analysis *à la* Berenson, we would note that Haydn in this period often ends his symphonies with three chords, separated from the rest, i.e. in No. 87 ♩ ⅎ − | ♩ ♩ | ♩ − ‖. One also finds this ending in Symphonies Nos. 80, 83, 84, 85, 88, 89, 92 (and later in Nos. 95 and 101 as well). It is never found in a single mature Mozart symphony.

Symphony No. 85 in B flat ('La Reine de France'; 1785?)
Scoring: 1 flute, 2 oboes, 2 bassoons, 2 horns and strings.

'La Reine' has always been a popular work, and no doubt its initial success was materially assisted by Marie Antoinette's approval. Later it was admired for being *the* Haydn Symphony of the late Eszterháza years *par excellence*: for its formal subtlety and, perhaps, for possessing special 'grace and favour' which illuminate each of the four movements with a certain radiance.

The introduction is vaguely French, and not so vaguely as far as its dotted rhythm is concerned, for it smacks of the old French Overture, the rhymic force of which lived on, *mutatis mutandis*, in many late eighteenth-century introductions such as this one. One of Haydn's characteristics is pithiness, and this whole introduction sets the stage in exactly eleven bars. The curtain opens on an extraordinary two-part theme, the bass line of which moves down a ninth in very precise quavers over a long held cantabile upper line. This theme, or derivatives of it, dominate the entire movement. The first subject actually includes not only this theme but a middle section which begins with a semiquaver progression up to B flat, and then goes down the B flat chord in crotchets; this middle section is widely used in the course of the movement (bars 24 *et seq.*); the first subject then continues with a variation of the *a* section. Georg Feder has noted[1] that in the middle of the transition Haydn indulges in a rare luxury: he quotes himself, in this case (bars 62ff.) the beginning of the 'Farewell' Symphony (1772), which is in F sharp minor; the (not very exact) quotation is in F minor. For the second subject, we are given the *a* part of the first subject with the top line for solo oboe. Unless one is prepared to call the closing material of the exposition a 'subject' (which it would be academic to do), there is no real second subject. Possibly for this reason the first subject is tripartite and much longer than usual (bars 12–41).

The themes of Haydn's quicker slow movements often sound like folk-tunes (e.g. Nos. 53, 63). In No. 85 we have a 'Romance' (Haydn's title) which actually *is* an old folk-tune of French origin, 'La gentille et jeune Lisette' (it is quoted in Pohl II, 275). Haydn was paying a pretty compliment to his Parisian public; but apart from that the theme sounds just like Haydn. In this most sophisticated movement (which returns to nature in the same fashion as the Petit Trianon . . .), we note the beautiful section (bars 45ff.) in E flat minor, with its gliding first violin line above the tune, and a fastidiously beautiful flute solo as the next variation. The final variation is still in Watteauian pastels and ends with a tiny coda, *pianissimo*. One of Haydn's most interesting *seguaci*, Baron Theodor von Schacht (1748–1823), used this movement as the basis for his own 'Romanze Variée' in an E flat Symphony which was formerly attributed to Haydn (Landon, *SYM*, Appendix II, 83; Hoboken I:Es 11) but discovered by Jan LaRue to be by Schacht.[2]

The Menuetto is springy and with some comical effects for the horns (bars 34, 36), but the Trio is an exquisitely proportioned movement. Beginning with a bassoon solo (which Haydn arranged for one of the musical clocks), a tutti takes over in the second

1 'Similarities in the Works of Haydn', in *Studies in Eighteenth-Century Music* (Geiringer *Festschrift*), London 1970, p. 191.
2 'A new figure in the Haydn masquerade', *Music & Letters* 40/2 (1959), pp. 1–8 (offprint).

part which breaks up into a huge pedal point (F, horns), over which various wind instruments spin out a derivative of the bassoon theme: time stops dead, the rules are broken and we are in a magic world.

One of the sensationally new effects in the Finale of that great masterpiece, Symphony No. 77, was Haydn's eminently successful attempt to write a sonata movement with a rondo-like theme. In the Finale of No. 85 we have the same process carried a step further: this is a genuine sonata rondo. The theme is a racy Presto and one of those fetching Haydnesque melodies which revolutionized music in the 1780s. The new formal element is that Haydn's tendency towards monothematicism even in sonata form is now, as it were, legalized by assuming rondo guise: this manifests itself *inter alia* in that the main theme comes back at the end of what would be, in straight sonata form, the exposition, but in the *tonic*, not the dominant: then the development section begins (which did not exist in strict rondo). A great *tour-de-force* to end one of the *ancien régime*'s most persuasive and winning products.

Symphony No. 83 in G minor ('La Poule')

Scoring: 1 flute, 2 oboes, 2 bassoons, 2 horns and strings. The sub-title 'La Poule' is supposed to describe the 'clucking' second subject of the first movement and is a nineteenth-century designation.

There was once a time in Haydn's life when G minor was a very serious, even tragic key; not quite with the special overtones that it had for Mozart, but very much out of the ordinary, e.g. *Stabat Mater, Salve Regina*, Symphony No. 39, Quartet, Op. 20, No. 3, where Haydn steered near to the desperate near-lunacy with which Mozart's music sometimes grimly flirts (the twelve-note cataclysm at the beginning of the Finale's development in K.550). But *anno* 1785, Haydn's style, as we have seen, had undergone the transformation from music's most revolutionary thinker to Europe's most popular composer. The beginning of this new G minor Symphony reminds us, briefly, of the old *Barrikadenmensch* (if we may for a moment anticipate the language of socialism) of 1772, with its heavily accented minims and the unusual *c* sharp, as well as the urgent series of dotted figures. But Haydn had no intention of returning to the world of 1772, and smoothly pilots us to the relative major and the famous 'La Poule' theme: the appoggiature in the violins scoff at the earnest G minor opening, and at the entry of the solo oboe in bar 52 tragedy, or if you will deadly seriousness, has been supplanted by doggerel. It was the kind of lightning change for which the nineteenth century never forgave Haydn. Even less comprehensible to them was the alternation of the 'clucking' second subject with the first four notes of the main theme, as Haydn proceeds to do in the development section. The end of the movement abandons the minor altogether and finishes in the tonic major.

Perplexed as the Victorian mind might have been about the tongue-in-cheek first movement (for there can be no doubt that Haydn was being highly ironical), the wholly serious, beautifully sculptured Andante which follows probably left them totally confused. For one thing it is in E flat, a very ambivalent key in that it can be judged as the submediant of G minor, a typically eighteenth-century key for a slow movement of a G minor symphony (e.g. Mozart's K.550) except that Haydn's 'La Poule' ended in G major; which gives a strong third-related feeling to the E flat which is not dispelled, either, because he never returns to G minor as the principal key. There is a dramatic surprise after we reach the dominant: the second violins and viola get softer and softer ('sempre più piano'), to be violently interrupted by a *ff* outburst. This passage was later shortened by Haydn (one of the repeated 'sempre più piano' bars was removed). The loveliest moment of all occurs in a huge pedal point (bars 63ff.), in which Haydn has several lines going at once over a long held B flat in the horns, the flute striking a shaft of sunlight into this very autumnal and almost Mozartian lead-back (but by 1785 it is unlikely that Haydn knew very much of Mozart's music – we will take up this point in connection with the Op. 50 Quartets, *infra*).

With the Menuet we are squarely in G major and a gay, bucolic dance with a strong *two-three* emphasis to the accompaniment in many crucial places. The Trio is a flute solo supported at the lower octave by the first violin. The Finale (Vivace) has something of 'la chasse' about it, probably because it is in the very unusual 12/8 time; it is altogether a very outdoors piece, the kind of music which, arranged for wind band, one might have expected to hear at someone's hunting picnic or garden party. Since a large part of Haydn's make-up was intellectual, we are treated to a stupendous modulation at the beginning of the development section: here, only the violins race ahead in quavers, all the other instruments leaning on heavily accented minims; later Haydn changed this passage, but after he had already sent the autograph to Paris, so that the lower strings also have quavers. The happy end, a real *lieta fine* in the operatic sense, is a long way from the atmosphere of the work's beginning; and more than anything else, it is this deliberate negation of the *Sturm und Drang* which places this symphony in a class totally different from a Kraus or Mozart symphony in the minor and also from Haydn's own world of 1772.

Symphony No. 84 in E flat (1786)
Scoring: 1 flute, 2 oboes, 2 bassoons, 2 horns and strings

Never one of the more popular Paris Symphonies, this elegant and superbly constructed work has much to recommend it to amateur and connoisseur (*Kenner und Liebhaber*) alike. Not the least of its many beauties is the stately and often ethereal Largo introduction: note the magical entrance of the first violin into the wind-band solo at bar 11. The succeeding Allegro, *alla breve*, is a masterpiece of witty and sophisticated thought, very monothematic (is there really any second subject at all?), very carefully paced, and with a latent power kept in leash by the immaculate crotchet pulse which underlies almost the whole movement. In the development, there is a marvellous modulation to F major (bars 132ff.) where this curious feeling of leashed power is strongly felt.

The second movement, too, develops great strength as it progresses. The theme is deceptively simple, at least at first sight and hearing, but the off-beat *forzati* tell us that the rhythmic pattern is by no means conventional. Formally, the movement is organized like a straight set of variations, the principal section being in the usual tripartite subdivision of *a-b-a'*. Variation II (though it is not so marked) is in the tonic minor, and here for the first time the wind instruments enter. Variation III is, like the theme itself, for strings only. Variation IV, a massive tutti with only two bars of *p* in the whole section, turns the rather delicate theme into a marching, surging affirmation: this is the proud music of a man who could write for kings and princes but was not ashamed of being a wheelwright's son, whose language was (in his own words to Mozart in December 1790) 'understood all over the world'. This grand and noble tutti slows for a moment and then, like a concerto, masses itself into a six-four chord with pause: this is now a regular feature in Haydn's slow movements of this period, and a conscious attempt to unite some of the concerto's formal principles with the symphony. The 'cadenza' is an enchanting variation in canonic imitation, based on the main theme, for solo woodwind accompanied by pizzicato strings: of a saturated beauty, with rich inner lines and a fantastic sense of the capacities of every wind instrument: it could be from a text-book on orchestration. And its sense of yearning is magnified by the fact that it ends on another huge pedal point over F, leading to the final, simple statement of the main subject's first part.

With the Menuet we are back in the poised world of the opening movement, where everything is ordered and worked out with the impeccable craftsmanship for which Haydn's music was so famous. The Finale (Vivace) has an agile main theme in the typical style of Haydn's maturity; it is the kind of movement that was born to be a popular success. The racy transitions in repeated semiquavers, with their sense of thrusting energy, and the mysterious standstill at bars 56ff. (but time does not really stand still, for quavers soon break out in the bass to remind us that this is a Vivace in two-four time): all this is characteristic of the best in the Paris Symphonies. It is again a very monothematic movement, which is not to say that Haydn does not develop 'secondary' ideas; for that mysterious standstill becomes enormously magnified in the development section (bars 173ff.) and provides Haydn with an attractive lead-back to the recapitulation.

Symphony No. 86 in D (1786)

Scoring: 1 flute, 2 oboes, 2 bassoons, 2 horns, 2 trumpets, timpani and strings.

Haydn's order may or may not be chronological; it is surely morphological. He starts the set with the lightest of the six and ends with the two heaviest (also the two with trumpets and drums), saving the most popular and at the same time the most weighty Finale to end the whole set.

No. 86 is perhaps the greatest of the Paris Symphonies: certainly the most majestic in its quick movements, the most profound in its slow. The Adagio introduction (the beginning of Haydn's autograph score is reproduced here) is more extended than usual and forms a compact world of its own. In bar three, there is an off-beat *forzato* which plays a role later in the movement (cf. 59, 60), and it will be found that many elements of this Adagio – rhythmic, dynamic, structural – turn up later in the Symphony. The introduction moves in a very suave way right into the ensuing Allegro spiritoso: the half-close of the Adagio slides, with a six-chord, into the supertonic and, rather fantastically, the quick movement starts on the off-tonic. The first subject, or the first part of the first subject, is a little wisp of a theme four bars long. There then ensues a huge tutti which is dominated by the rhythmic fragment ♪ | ♫♫ ♪♫♫ ♪ | ♫♫ or its derivative ♪ | ♫♫♫♫ etc. In the *ff* dominant, which Haydn goes to great pains to establish by hammering out the dominant of the dominant, we are given the little first theme: that is why Haydn was so intent on establishing A major, because the first subject is now, *mutatis mutandis*, off-dominant. In view of the fragmented nature of this first subject, we are treated to an extended and fully developed second subject (65ff. with upbeat), containing a characteristic tail in slithering chromatics; and there is a vigorous concluding section (notice the sudden added dynamic power added to stress the sudden new modulation from A major to C sharp minor in six-four position). In the development section, which is very long (bars 86–150), we see the immense possibilities of the little first subject: it is treated primarily as an ideal vehicle for extended modulations,

The autograph of the opening of the slow introduction of Symphony No. 86; there was no room for the trumpet ('clarini') and timpani parts, which were added on separate sheets at the end of the autograph.

particularly in the lead-back to the recapitulation. Because, however, this is a particularly well balanced movement, we also have a generous treatment of the second subject in this broad development section. The whole movement is a brilliant display of what Haydn can do with seemingly innocent, even undistinguished, thematic material.

The slow movement is marked, in the autograph manuscript, 'Capriccio: Largo'. 'Capriccio' always meant, in Haydn's usage, formal freedom and a kind of rondo treatment in the manner of C. P. E. Bach – which is not the Haydnesque rondo with its A-B-A-C-A division but much more closely related to the Baroque ritornello form. The principal subject, that is, returns throughout the movement: it is taken from the bass part of the Symphony's Adagio introduction, and this subject provides a tonal and spiritual base from which Haydn's spirit may rove. It returns (after being stated) in the tonic, G major, at bars 33ff. and, using itself as a modulation just before, at 54ff. and, with great effect, in the tonic minor at 71ff. As a foil to this main subject, which moves at a stately pace and in slow dynamics (a big 'swell mark', that is crescendo and decrescendo, is placed under the two dotted minims of violin I), we have a partially double dotted and otherwise very intricate melodic line to set off the stateliness of the main subject. The difference between the two principal groups of themes lends a curiously veiled and ambivalent quality to this extraordinary and uncharacteristic movement. Who is to describe its brooding emotional state, interrupted several times by tutti sections of frightening intensity?

The Menuet, like the whole Symphony of generous proportions, shows us what an intricate artistic form this dance movement has become: how symphonic, too, and how serious. It is possible to analyze this Minuet in two ways: in the old, conventional manner of A-B-A, or in a new fashion, whereby Haydn has superimposed on the basically tripartite form a kind of sonata structure with exposition (A, ending at the double bar), development (bars 13ff., the 'B', and notice how the principal theme is used contrapuntally), recapitulation (upbeat to 39–54) and even with a little coda, which we realize after Haydn leads us to a deceptive cadence and pause (fermata) at bar 54. But we have said nothing of the majesty, poise and strength of this beautiful music. The Trio is one of Haydn's winning melodies, orchestrated in a distinctly waltz-like way, and with the trumpets and drums silent.

The Finale (Allegro con spirito) is in sonata form, with two distinct subjects, though the second is clearly an offspring of the first, having the same five-note lead-in. Altogether, the movement is in the iron group of the rhythmic lead, which turns up constantly, even in the timpani part all by itself (bar 125). It is also, *in toto*, a remarkable example of how Haydn's wit and charm are contained in an intellectual framework of great complexity: so that all the gaiety and warmth have substance, as they always must in great art.

Symphony No. 82 in C ('L'ours') (1786)

Scoring: 1 flute, 2 oboes, 2 bassoons, 2 horns in C *alto* or 2 trumpets (first, third and final movements), 2 horns in F (slow movement), timpani and strings. The subtitle 'L'ours' (the bear), a nineteenth-century conceit, is supposed to describe a captive bear dancing to the music of the Finale – an unlikely situation at best.

No. 82 is the latest in the long and distinguished series of festive symphonies in C major with high horns (from 1769), in this case or trumpets, and kettledrums. It is also, in its flanking movements, one of the most aggressive and powerful symphonies Haydn ever wrote. Both these outer movements are, moreover, very highly organized from the standpoint of thematic breakdown. The first subject (*ff*) at the beginning of the first movement is separated into several interconnecting segments: the rising broken chord (*a*), the *piano* contrast (*b*) and the long series of fanfares (*c*) on this characteristically Haydnesque rhythm ♩♪♫ | ♫ ♫♫♪ | etc. The theme uses itself, even while modulating to the dominant. With a derivative of (*a*), the upper woodwind meanwhile have the following 'rhythmic lead' ♩. | ♩. ♫ | ♩. ♫ (*a'*), in which the quavers act not as the second half of the bar in question but as 'lead-ins' to the following bar. Thus a sense of impetus, or forward-going, is established. This kind of technical device, here applied with craftsmanship and *élan*, is 'motivic work' of the finest sort. It is instructive to see how Haydn combines (*a*) with (*c*) and (*a'*), the (*c*) being restricted only to the kettledrums, to produce a dashing transition whose apparently effortless sweep is the result, which we must feel unconsciously even if we are not aware of the formal aspects, of rigorous intellectual self-control. This stunning transition ends with a series of violent discords (bars 51ff.), a sort of Neapolitan sixth (*a* flat–*e* flat–*c*) into which is introduced simultaneously the jarring note *g* at all levels of pitch, i.e. clashing at the interval of a second through three whole octaves. The second subject, very delicately scored (with one bassoon providing the only bass voice), is not only, with its 'closing material', much fuller than is often the case with Haydn, but a real contrast to all the vigour and nervousness of the opening material. The little figure (bars 78/80) with the syncopated minim, is brilliantly extended by contrapuntal devices in the development section (bars 150ff.), itself a model of concise and well-organized thought. At the end of the movement, there is a short coda based on the (*c*) figure of the opening subject which begins *f* and plunges at bar 255 into *ff*, bringing the movement to a swift and very loud conclusion.

We have provided this typical movement with perhaps a more detailed analysis than usual because in its organization and especially its orchestration it is the kind of music that electrified audiences all over Europe in the sunset of the *ancien régime*.

Some of Haydn's double variation movements had already achieved the status of being world-wide celebrities by the time the Paris Symphonies began to circulate all over Europe in 1788. One such success had been the second movement of Symphony No. 53 in D ('L'impériale'), which had even been printed in Philadelphia; another had been 'La Roxelane' movement from Symphony No. 63. Both are in that rather 'unslow' tempo (No. 63 is actually marked 'Allegretto o più tosto Allegro') and alternating major and minor (or minor and major) sections. The Allegretto movement of No. 82 has these characteristics and like its predecessors the main subject sounds like a folk song. The movement is laid out as follows:

> A (major: a–b–a form)
> B (minor: a–b–a')
> A' (major: tripartite but varied)
> B' (minor: tripartite but varied)
> A'' (major: tripartite but varied still further)
> Coda

The contrasting major and minor sections are linked by similar rhythms and *Urlinien*. This is a popular and successful movement, the orchestration of which is lightened by removing the timpani (and of course the trumpets, which in some authentic sources are permitted to double, not to substitute for, the horns in movements I, III and IV).

The Menuet is French not only to the letter (spelling) but in spirit as well: sophisticated, with measured staccato crotchets in the bass line, and pompous quavers at critical points in brass and kettledrums. The Trio, like the previous movement almost a folk-tune, is orchestrated with the utmost *finesse*: there happens to exist a sketch of the Trio (reproduced in Haydn Society's *Complete Works*, Ser. I, vol. 9, p. 308) which shows that all these apparently effortless movements were the result of much thought and even complete drafts in score. We cannot – to return to the music itself of this Minuet & Trio – re-iterate the point often enough: this is the world of Marie Antoinette, the Comtesse de la Tour du Pin, of Catherine the Great, of George the raffish Prince of Wales (later George IV) – not the sombre, doom-ridden, tragic world of Mozart's K.504 (introduction) or K.550 or the Adagio and Fugue K.546. That world was certainly round the corner, but in 1788, when Haydn's Paris Symphonies were simultaneously printed in Vienna, London, Berlin, Amsterdam and Paris, Europe was still basking in sunlight: though it was much later in the day, and the sun much lower, than anyone realized.

In the Finale, we are back to the kind of formal *tour-de-force* that informed the opening movement. The orchestration is most original, with a drone bass (bagpipes, *Dudelsack, cornamusa*: it is an international sound) and, at first, just the first violins, to which the middle voices join in harmonious support only during the last four bars.

Whereupon the solo woodwind and timpani take the music into their hands, to relinquish it to the drone, this time in fifths with the violins settling into g''. With the whirlwind transition (which begins after a pause), we are again in the world of Haydn's contrapuntal grandeur, motifs being played off against motifs but the whole marked by a long arch that is carefully guided by the master-craftsman. Like the first movement we have here a marked contrast in the second subject and closing material (bars 66ff. with upbeat); and like the first movement, we have an enormously organized development section, with vast extension of previous material, in this case the first few bars of the music. Haydn never leaves it for a moment: we are plunged (after the dominant, G) into F major, then into E flat major, G minor, C major, A minor and gradually to the dominant of C, in the course of which tonal journey Haydn builds up an enormous tension that is only resolved by the recapitulation. There is a coda in which the timpani, always very active in this hard-textured Symphony, have a roll in semiquavers over nine bars, marked ff, and pushing home the last entry of the drone bass.

One of *L'ours*'s admirers was Richard Wagner, who (as we have seen in the Appendix of *Haydn: the Late Years 1801–1809*) was a connoisseur of Haydn. On 26 February 1878, we read in Cosima's Diary, 'Then R[ichard] needed some music and played the "Bear" Symphony by Haydn, with much delight over the last movement; then he showed friend Seidl the Andante of the G major Symphony by Haydn and told him that it is among the most beautiful things ever written, and how it sounds!'[1]

With the Paris Symphonies, Haydn had perfected his new popular style. Although he was not the master of minor-key works that he would later become once again, the works in the major key are indeed 'd'une facture étonnante'. In them (and in No. 83's slow movement) he achieved a breathtaking synthesis between energy and grace, between profundity and popularity, between art music and folk-song. He had successfully weathered the crisis of *Sturm und Drang* and the decision to abandon *Sturm und Drang* principles for a new popular style, which (it may be said) Haydn invented and brought to a fine gloss of perfection.

'THE SEVEN WORDS' FOR CÁDIZ
(XX:1) (1786)

Scoring: 2 fl., 2 ob., 2 bsn., 4 hn. (using unusual crooks of B flat *basso* and C *basso*), 2 trpt., timp., str. *Principal sources*: (1) Authentic MS. parts by Anonymous 63 and 30, sent by Haydn to Forster (arrived in July 1787), British Museum, Egerton 2379, fol. 149–90. (2) Authentic first edition in parts, Artaria & Co., Vienna, 'Opera 47', pl. no. 114, announced in the *Wiener Zeitung* on 7 July 1787. (3) Authentic MS. score by a British copyist, London, 1791, with many corrections and additions in Haydn's hand, Pierpont Morgan Library, New York. This score was made in connection with the performance Haydn conducted at the Hanover Square Rooms on 30 May 1791 and repeated on 13 (not 10) June. *Haydn in England 1791–1795*, pp. 82, 85. Haydn had a score made up from Forster's edition. Among the many contemporary sources which have nothing to do, directly, with Haydn, we may mention Johann Michael Haydn's copy in score, Bayerische Staatsbibliothek, Munich, Mus. Mss. 328. Michael made the work from the parts, as a note on the score by Neukomm informs us.

Authentic arrangement for string quartet: Artaria & Co., Vienna, 'Opera 48', pl. no. 113. V. I is the same as in (2) and thus has pl. no. 114. Copies of the orchestral version: Gesellschaft der Musikfreunde, Hoboken Collection, now Österreichische Nationalbibliothek, Musiksammlung; of the string quartet arr.: Hoboken coll., Thurn und Taxis Archives, Regensburg.

Critical edition: *Joseph Haydn Werke*, Reihe IV (1959, Hubert Unverricht), also as miniature score, Bärenreiter-Verlag, Kassel, min. score 92 (1961).

1 Cosima Wagner, *Die Tagebücher*, vol. II (1878–1883), ed. Martin Gregor-Dellin and Dietrich Mack, Munich and Zürich 1977, p. 50.

Literature: Robert Sondheimer, *op. cit.*, pp. 109ff. Dénes Bartha, 'Die Entstehung der "Sieben Worte" im Spiegel des Haydn-Nachlasses in Budapest', in *Zenetudományi Tanulmányok* VIII, Budapest 1960, pp. 146ff. H. Unverricht, Foreword to miniature score (*vide supra*), 1961 and the best available discussion of the work's origin and sources in *JHW*, Kritischer Bericht, 1963. For the vocal version see *Haydn: the Years of 'The Creation' 1796–1800*, pp. 97f. and 180–3. Orin Moe, 'Haydn's *Seven Words*: An Analysis', *Revista Musical Chilena* 1976. *Sketches*: One set in the Hamburg Staats- und Universitäts-Bibliothek was sent to Silesia during the Second World War and has disappeared. Another set from the Breitkopf & Härtel Archives, now in the Hessische Landes- und Hochschulbibliothek, Darmstadt; they have been reproduced in the Kritischer Bericht, pp. 41a–44a (with fold-out). This set of sketches is to *Sitio* and *Terremoto*.

When Haydn sent the score of the vocal version to Breitkopf & Härtel in 1801, he dictated the following foreword to his go-between G. A. Griesinger:

> About fifteen years ago [1786] I was requested by a canon of Cádiz to compose instrumental music on *The Seven Last Words of Our Saviour on the Cross*. It was customary at the Cathedral of Cádiz to produce an oratorio every year during Lent, the effect of the performance being not a little enhanced by the following circumstances. The walls, windows, and pillars of the church were hung with black cloth, and only one large lamp hanging from the centre of the roof broke the solemn darkness. At midday, the doors were closed and the ceremony began. After a short service the bishop ascended the pulpit, pronounced the first of the seven words (or sentences) and delivered a discourse thereon. This ended, he left the pulpit, and prostrated himself before the altar. The interval was filled by music. The bishop then in like manner pronounced the second word, then the third, and so on, the orchestra following on the conclusion of each discourse. My composition was subject to these conditions, and it was no easy task to compose seven adagios lasting ten minutes each, and to succeed one another without fatiguing the listeners; indeed, I found it quite impossible to confine myself to the appointed limits. [Translation: Geiringer 1947, p.77]

Abbé Stadler happened to be with Haydn when he received the commission from Cádiz. In his autobiography, Stadler relates:

> He also asked me what I thought of it all. I answered that it seemed to me advisable that over the words an appropriate melody should be fitted, which afterwards should be performed only by instruments, in which art he was in any case a master. He did so, too, but whether he had intended to do so anyway, I do not know. [Pohl II, 215]

We have confirmation of the Stadler part in the proceedings from the Diaries of Vincent and Mary Novello, who visited Vienna in 1829:

> Stadler was with Haydn when he received the commission to write the seven Adagios – and as he seemed comparatively at a loss to proceed in introducing sufficient variety in writing seven Adagios directly following each other, it was the Abbé Stadler who advised him to take the first words of the text and write a melody to each which should be the leading feature of each movement; he followed the Abbé's advice and with a success that requires no eulogy from me.
>
> A *chanoine* afterwards adapted words, but not in a satisfactory manner, and Baron Swieten engaged Joseph Haydn to adapt some words to the music himself which he accordingly did. Stadler said he preferred these beautiful compositions without the words just as they originally were conceived by their Author.
>
> Mentioned with great praise the Quartetto of Haydn [Op. 20, No. 5] in F minor with the Fugue (which Pinto arranged for the Piano Forte).
>
> Haydn did not play the Organ much but his brother Michael was a good performer.

In Novello's edition (vocal score) of *The Seven Words*, some of the above conversation was incorporated, with the addition that 'L'Abbé Stadler also corroborated the truth of the tradition that Haydn himself considered this "the very finest of all his works". V. Novello. London. Sept. 6th, 1829.'
[*A Mozart Pilgrimage, Being the Travel Diaries of Vincent & Mary Novello in the year 1829. Transcribed and compiled by Nerina Medici di Marignano, edited by Rosemary Hughes*, London 1955, p. 172. Hereafter: 'A Mozart Pilgrimage'.]

When Haydn was in England in 1791 and *The Seven Words* was to be performed, the *Morning Chronicle* published an article dealing with the work's origin which we have placed here rather than in *Haydn in England 1791–1795*. In this article, we learn that Haydn, after receiving the commission, found it most difficult to keep to the exact limit of ten minutes, and wrote to the Bishop of Cádiz, asking if he could here and there exceed the prescribed limit. The Bishop wrote at once, saying that Haydn could lengthen his music if he wished to and that he (the Bishop) would limit his sermons to ten minutes, leaving the rest of the time for Haydn's music.[1]

In Hoboken, vol. I, p. 845, we have an interesting account of how the work came to be commissioned. The church for which it was intended was not the cathedral but the grotto Santa Cueva, built underground as part of the Parish of Rosario in 1756. A well-known priest, José Saluz de Santamaria, Marquès de Valde-Inigo, conceived the idea of asking Haydn to compose music for the religious exercises that were held in the grotto. The Marquès turned to a friend, Don Francisco Micon, Marquès Méritos, who was also in touch with Haydn, and Don Francisco wrote to Austria explaining in detail the religious exercises and the part that the music should have in them. It is thought that Haydn's autograph perished in the Spanish religious wars of 1835 (Unverricht, in Kritischer Bericht, 21).

We know that in 1786, Haydn's activities as opera *Capellmeister* reached their height. It seems almost incredible that in this very year, when he had to conduct 125 opera performances at Eszterháza (see Chronicle *infra*, p. 675), he managed to write three of the 'Paris' Symphonies, probably all the Concertos for the King of Naples, two insertion arias (one of great complexity) and, probably as the last work of the year, began *The Seven Words*, perhaps finishing it in 1787. The sketches show, however, that Haydn was composing in frantic haste, so that the tails of the crotchets almost turn into quavers through rushing from one note to the next; Unverricht (ibid., p. 41a) reports that Haydn wrote so long as the pen contained any ink, and when it went dry he of course dipped it and continued: one can trace this process (which saved time: when writing 'properly' you dip the quill much more often to ensure an even distribution of ink and no lighter patches). 'The exterior picture of these sketches makes an almost Beethovenian impression', concludes Dr Unverricht.

Nevertheless Haydn believed that he had solved the problem well. Griesinger (21) informs us that 'Haydn often said that this work was one of his most successful', and contemporary opinion certainly bore him out. Of the many contemporary criticisms, we may single out one which describes a performance in Bonn in 1787 (which Beethoven, being in Vienna at the time, did not attend):

Letter from Bonn, 8 April 1787. On 30th March there was a performance of great expression here at court under the direction of Herr Concertmeister Reicha of a new composition by Joseph Hayden [*sic*]. It consists of seven adagios on the seven Words of Christ on the Cross and closes with a Presto which describes the

---

1 The summary from our preface to the Eulenburg miniature score 162 (1956).

earthquake at the death of the Saviour. The idea of expressing these thoughts by purely instrumental music is curious and daring and only a genius like Haydn would take such a risk. I won't try to ascertain if a single member of the audience could and would think of the word 'sitio' (thirst) when hearing the fifth Adagio. But every movement, even without the Latin superscriptions, is most interesting and entirely worthy of a Haydn. These seven adagios seem to be intended for Good Friday, on which Day the Catholics visit the graves of the saints, pray there, and make music. . . .   [Cramer's *Magazin der Musik* 1787, p. 1385]

Hubert Unverricht (miniature score's Foreword, 1961) writes of the work's effect, that

besides the 'Paris' Symphonies, it was mainly . . . *The Seven Words* which was the foundation of his fame all over Europe in the seventeen eighties. . . .

Robert Sondheimer's interesting comments on the music will complete our introductory summary:

When a man reaches his fifties, it often happens that he enters a period of earnest introspection. He feels that he must concentrate his powers. Not that his aim in life has become any less problematic, but he clings more tenaciously to essential values because they might easily retreat beyond his grasp by a sudden diminution of his vital energy. As is evident in the quartets of Op. 20 and Op. 33, Haydn had pondered the question of how his aims could attain an ultimate significance, without, however, transgressing the formal sphere of music. Now, from a remote corner of the Continent, he had received a commission which no artist might dare to carry out solely by means of technical dexterity. To depict the 'Grünewald' Crucifixion in pure instrumental music; to breathe life into the profoundly moving subject, and to place the result before a generation of still deeply devout believers, it was necessary for the secret flame of genuine feeling to be revealed, and for man himself to stand beside the artist, as is indicated in the picture by the group of mourners beside the Crucified. It was the preclassical ideal which took command of Haydn. The conviction of having been able to do it justice made him feel proud, for he had been all his life on its track without ever having desired to embrace it. Now at last, the mature man is possessed with the dark, mystic awe which had left the crude peasant youth cold. . . .

The scheme of the work is as follows:

Introduzione, D minor, Maestoso ed Adagio;
Sonata I ('Pater, dimitte illis, quia nesciunt, quid faciunt'), B flat, Largo;
Sonata II ('Hodie mecum eris in Paradiso'), C minor, Grave e cantabile, ending in C major;
Sonata III ('Mulier, ecce filius tuus'), E major, Grave;
Sonata IV ('Deus meus, Deus meus, utquid dereliquisti me?'), F minor, Largo;
Sonata V ('Sitio'), A major, Adagio;
Sonata VI ('Consummatum est'), G minor, Lento, ending in G major;
Sonata VII ('In manus tuas, Domine, commendo spiritum meum'), E flat, Largo;
Il terremoto, C minor, Presto e con tutta la forza.

The Seven Words has always been a connoisseur's work, and its very nature prevented it from becoming the kind of popular success that *The Creation* and *The Seasons* would achieve. It is curious that for many years, it was the string quartet version that was played the most. (Haydn also approved a piano version which Artaria published.) The string quartet adaptation, which Haydn made, was never intended to supplant the original version but to enable the work to be played by amateurs unable to marshal the large orchestra necessary for the full score. 'The Earthquake' sounds especially unfortunate in the string quartet version. As for the orchestral *versus* the later choral version, preference must remain largely a matter of personal inclination; but it would be a pity to miss the extraordinary piece for wind band that Haydn inserted in the 1796 version.

There is a kind of impersonal severity to the introduction, scored only for oboes, bassoons, horns and strings. As the piece progresses, we notice that it is haunted by the dotted figure with which it begins: ♩ ♪..♪ ♩ ♩ becomes ♩ ♪..♪ ♪ and ♪♪ ♪♪

and that Haydn charts its course with a skill which is superb even for music's greatest craftsman. The singleness of purpose which we must feel in looking at the 'Grünewald' picture is reflected in the overall mood, in the motivic concentration, and in the course of the whole from *ff* to *pp*. There are also numerous cross-references to be made between the introduction and the rest of the work, one of the more obvious being the transference of the introduction's dotted patterns to

♪..♪♪ ¿ | ♪.. ♪ ♪♪♪ | ♪.. ♪ ♪ (our musical example shows how Haydn

Pa - ter,   Pa - ter, dimitte   il - lis

'fitted' each of the Words to the first violin part: they are, of course, not to be sung but are simply a kind of mental indication to the players and readers of the music). In Sonata I we note for the first time that Haydn (retaining the small orchestra of the introduction) asks for *low* B flat horns. In Sonata II for the first time he used the four horns: being in C minor, horns I & II are in E flat and III & IV in C *basso*. Here we have sure proof that these high C and B flat horn parts were Esterházy specialities that Haydn never expected 'foreign' orchestras to duplicate.

In Sonata II (C minor), we notice the refined use of the four horns – here, Haydn could put to good use all his experiments in the Divertimenti, Op. 31, and elsewhere: it is, however, interesting that he fully expected Cádiz horn players to be able to play stopped notes (see p. 15 of the miniature score). This rich horn orchestration is matched by a quite unprecedented effect: the use of a muted solo 'cello doubling the melody (first violin). When the second theme appears, the same muted solo 'cello continues to support the first violin. This subject, of great length, has a running semiquaver accompaniment (second violins) and reminds us strongly of the famous subsidiary theme in the Benedictus of the *Missa Cellensis* of 1782 = Ernesto's Aria in *Il mondo della luna*). The rapturous sound of this vision of Paradise is perhaps one of the moments that Wilfrid Mellers had in mind when he wrote (op. cit., p. 30):

> These seven adagios all, like the andante of Symphony No. 104, combine a sublime lyrical serenity with intense tonal drama. The themes are, however, more Italianate than the Masonic hymns of Haydn's last years. Perhaps for this reason the music has a meditative ecstasy which makes it seem more Catholic in spirit than any music Haydn wrote.

At the end of this section, we find the derivative of this tune which looks forward to 'Gott erhalte'

The first 49 bars of this Sonata are to be repeated. The music ends in C major.

Sonata III ('Mother, behold they son') is in Haydn's favourite key of E major and provides an interesting contrast of two elements: the main theme –

♩ ♪♩ | ♩ ♪♩ | ♩ ♫♫ | ♩ ♪ – with its stress of the first beats, and a
Mu-lier,   ec-ce   fi - - lius— tu - us

long series of syncopations, which in the middle section – all these movements can be construed to be in sonata form – is intensified by chain *fz* (score, p. 31). A flute first appears here.

Sonata IV (F minor) again makes interesting use of four horns, two in E flat (used when the music modulates to A flat because in those days it was not customary to use horns in A flat; but with E flat horns Haydn has enough available notes to justify their presence) and two in the home key of F. Haydn has dropped the flute again, nor will he use trumpets and timpani before the Earthquake. The first part of this Sonata is also marked with repeat signs. This sombre music, in Haydn's often cultivated key of F minor, is a reminder of the Symphony 'La Passione' that Haydn wrote in 1768. Haydn creates a vivid picture of loneliness and abandonment: the orchestra, in the first part, drops away, leaving only the first violins to play by themselves (score, p. 37). This idea occurs at several places later in the movement (p. 40, especially at p. 42, then at 43f.). In this fashion Haydn seeks to display musically the Saviour's Words, 'Why hast Thou forsaken me?'

The critic from Bonn in 1787 wondered if the audience identified the music of Sonata V with 'I thirst': yet this movement's originality lies, in our opinion, in Haydn's depiction of exhaustion and thirst. Two flutes make their first appearance. After two *coups d'archet*, we have a series of running pizzicati

♫♫ ♫♫ | ℅ | ℅ which create a curiously hypnotic effect: this is the

exhaustion, one feels, as these pizzicati go on and on for fourteen bars. Over them, in

bars 4f., droops ○ | ♩ and this figure appears in various combinations of wind
Si - tio

instruments and first violin. The quietly plucked strings suddenly (bar 18) turn into raging bowed quavers, perhaps the body racked in pain. It is gruesomely descriptive of physical torment and one of the most moving of all the sonatas.

Sonata VI is another marvellously original interpretation of the words 'Consummatum est' and we believe that Haydn himself considered it the greatest movement: he used to sign it in visitors' common-place books, e.g. in Clement's

(*Haydn in England 1791–1795*, p. 86). The music begins *ff*: ♩ ♩ | ♩ ♩ | 𝄒 |;
Con-sum - ma - tum est.

'And when Jesus had cried with a loud voice, he said, Father, into thy hands I commend my spirit' (Luke xxiii, 46) – and Haydn applies the 'loud voice' to 'Consummatum est'. After this *ff* opening, the four notes are used softly, with entwining subsidiary voices in quavers. Haydn's meditations on these four notes are of the greatest complexity and reveal him once again in his old role of *jongleur* before the Almighty.

Haydn has reserved his most comforting music for Sonata VII, in E flat, a key in which he would write some of his noblest music. How moving the expiring Spirit (score p. 71), with grimly repeated bass quavers and the stuttering breath of life above

in the muted violins ♩ 𝄾♫ 𝄾♫ 𝄾♫♫ | ♩ 𝄾♫ etc., and a moment of

blinding inspiration at the end, when the quavers continue softly and life itself seems
to expire in the gentle thirds of the melody:

Finally, all movement stops and Sonata VII dies away in a long unison with flute and
horns: 'Attaca subito il Terremoto, ma senza sordini' (and the violins have three bars
of rest to remove their mutes). The relevant passage in Matthew xxvii reads:

51 And, behold, the veil of the temple was rent in twain from the top to the
bottom; and the earth did quake, and the rocks rent;
52 And the graves were opened; and many bodies of the saints which slept
arose,
53 And came out of the graves after his resurrection, and went into the holy
city, and appeared unto many.
54 Now when the centurion, and they that were with him, watching Jesus,
saw the earthquake, and those things that were done, they feared greatly, saying,
Truly this was the Son of God.

Haydn's earthquake must have been a piece of awesome power in 1787, but our
ears, used to Berlioz, Wagner and Mahler, tend to find it slightly tame unless it is

performed in a spectacular way. The series of cracks (p. 80: ♪♪. ♪♪. ♪♪.)

require the 'tutta la forza' that Haydn requests; at the end we have, for the first time in
any music known to us from the *settecento*, the marking *fff*.[1]
One of *The Seven Words'* admirers was Richard Wagner. In Cosima's Diary[2] for
Wednesday, 13 March 1878: 'Evening with our friend Count Du Moulin. "One can
write music without melody just as little as one can speak without thinking," said
R[ichard] in the course of the conversation, "the melody is the thought for music."
Many amusing examples from the thin, *pauvre*, schrum–schrum two and two bar
melodies of Meyerbeer. To offset this R. sings the Aria of Don Ottavio and says: "Ah!
That's *melos*, that comes out to meet a person." Also about *The Seven Words* by
Haydn: during these days R. spoke of them with the greatest admiration and said they
are deeply moving.'

1 A recording produced by Abbé Carl de Nys for the series Archives Sonores de la Musique Sacrée was made in the Church of Santa
Cueva with its remarkable reverberation time.
2 Op. cit., 57f., 58n.

CONCERTOS NOS. I–5 FOR THE KING OF NAPLES
(VIIh:1–5; 1786)

No. 1 in C, No. 2 in G, No. 3 in G, No. 4 in F, No. 5 in F.

Scoring: 2 lire organizzate, 2 horns, 2 violins, 2 violas and 'cello.

Principal sources: For each work there is one MS. (score or parts) from Haydn's estate, now EH, Budapest. For the details, see the editions.

Critical editions: *Joseph Haydn Werke*, Reihe VI

(Makoto Ohmiya), 1976. Verlag Doblinger, Diletto Musicale 41–5 (Landon), 1959.

Literature: Harry R. Edwall, 'Ferdinand IV and Haydn's Concertos for the Lira Organizzata', in *Musical Quarterly* XLVIII/2 (1962), pp. 190ff. See the forewords to the critical editions.

In the year 1785 or 1786, Haydn received a commission to write a series of concertos for King Ferdinand IV of Naples. It was a very curious commission, and its execution must have taxed even Haydn's ingenuity; for these concertos were to be written for two strange instruments, the so-called 'lira organizzata' – a kind of hurdy-gurdy into which was built a miniature organ. The instrument has been described in detail by Edwall (pp. 190f.) but since no restored example has survived and there is no one alive who can play the lira organizzata, interest in its probable sound is slightly academic; the more so since the actual notes can be played by a recorder, flute or oboe (and best by a combination). This lira was a favourite instrument of the *lazzaroni* – the people of Naples; the Bourbon King, though often a rough and uncouth monarch – he was married to Maria Carolina, a daughter of Maria Theresa, and his life has been admirably described by Harold Acton[1] – had a genuine affection for his people and for all their peculiar customs. It is therefore quite characteristic that his favourite musical instrument should have been this eccentric hurdy-gurdy. The lira on which the King played, however, was not the simple instrument of the Neapolitan street. The Austrian *Legationssekretär* in Naples, one Norbert Hadrava, perfected this instrument and taught the King to become a virtuoso on it. This Hadrava was the man who asked various foreign composers to write new music for the lira, and Adalbert Gyrowetz, Johann Franz Xaver Sterkel, Ignaz Pleyel and others received well-paid commissions for lira concertos and divertimentos. Hadrava's correspondence with Haydn has not been preserved, but from a letter to another composer, Sterkel,[2] we can imagine the letter Haydn must have received:

Naples, 12 October 1785.
... you should compose three concertos for two organized lyres for His Majesty.... one in the key of C, the second in F, and the third in G. Please take care that the ritornelli are shorter than those of your first concerto; for the rest, you should adjust the melodic line of the lyre to fit that of an oboe, but without too much to the oboe's contemplative nature. ...

1 *The Bourbons of Naples*, London 1956. Mr Acton, who subsequently became a friend when we lived near Florence, was kind enough to search for the lost autographs of the Haydn music for Naples. On subsequent occasions, many friends continued the search, and we ourselves spent weeks in Naples and Caserta, but to date no trace of the original scores has been found. The Mozart Concerto for lira in the Conservatorio di Musica, Naples, is a MS. score of the period but clearly spurious; it will no doubt be found to have been composed by one of the many *Kleinmeister* – Gyrowetz, Sterkel, Pleyel – who also wrote concertos for the King.

2 First published in Augustin Scharnagl's useful monograph, *Johann Franz Xaver Sterkel*, Würzburg 1943. The correspondence in which this letter appears is in a series of letters by Hadrava to Johann Paul Schultesius in Livorno (Leghorn). Hadrava was a composer in his own right, while Schultesius (1748–1816) was a Protestant Pastor who subscribed to *The Creation*: see *Haydn: the Years of 'The Creation' 1796–1800*, p. 630. Hadrava is thought to have been born about 1750. This correspondence is in the Musiksammlung of the Österreichische Nationalbibliothek, S.M. 8979 and is dated from Caserta, Naples and Capri, 1783–1799. Scharnagl, 75, 83f., 104f. Sterkel, in Hadrava's letter from Naples of 27 September 1785, is not painted in glowing terms. 'I could tell you many other pleasant tricks of St., for instance that in one place in Italy he copied Haydn's latest sonatas and put his own [Sterkel's] name on them, for which he was taken to task by a pupil of Haydn's [Pleyel] ...' (Scharnagl, 82). Our translation from our B.B.C. Haydn Series of 1958, the scripts of which were reproduced by mimeograph for the B.B.C. Transcription Service.

In this letter, there are two points which explain much of the peculiar character of Haydn's concertos for the King of Naples. The first is the restricted tonal scope of all the works he wrote for the lira – C, F and G major are the only principal keys allowed. The second is the range of the lira, which, as the report says, is about the same as that of an oboe.

Bearing these limitations in mind, Haydn did not attempt to write complicated double concertos, but rather ensemble music for two liras – the King and Hadrava – with two horns and a string quintet: in other words, enlarged chamber music very much along the lines of the *Divertimenti a otto stromenti* (Op. 31). There is seldom any attempt to write strict concertos but rather Haydn neatly combined the concerto form with the divertimento: there is also no strict division into tutti and solo but a constant intermingling of both. On the other hand, Haydn retained the use of the cadenza and wrote some beautiful examples.

Haydn knew his music was destined for Naples, and it is another tribute to his uncanny instinct that he actually manages to write whole movements that sound like Neapolitan serenades. In the Finale of Concerto I, Haydn breaks off his principal section to introduce a short Adagio which will have made Ferdinand think he was hearing a transcription of an opera aria. The slow movement of No. 2 *is* a transcription: it is the insertion Cavatina 'Sono Alcina' that Haydn composed in 1786 for Gazzaniga's *L'isola d'Alcina* (XXIVb:9). Of course the King had no idea of Haydn's insertion, but the sound of the slowish aria will have had pleasant associations with the opera house.

These works continue the style of the Op. 31 baryton works for Prince Nicolaus. The concertos of 1786 establish a new and eminently successful concerto-divertimento style and Haydn seems to have been intrigued by the commission and anxious to create a new and special language for the works. In this he succeeded beyond all expectations. The sophistication at times recalls J. C. Bach, but with all Haydn's intellectual brilliance and a sense of warmth that pervades every one of the five works. Perhaps the most striking movement is the first of Concerto V, based on the old theme known to us in the Finale of Haydn's Symphony No. 13 and soon to become world-famous as the Finale theme in Mozart's 'Jupiter' Symphony (K.551). The first twelve bars function as a kind of introduction and have nothing to do with the rest of the exposition. 'The function of these bars', writes Jan LaRue (*HJB* I, 210),

> resembles a slow introduction except in tempo. And we fully understand the introductory function only when we reach a parallel passage over a dominant pedal that precedes the recapitulation.

It is characteristic that the entire development section of this movement is in minor key, and as Edwall (202) points out, the three appearances of the opening 'Jupiter' music – at the beginning, in the middle and at the very end (nowhere else) – 'suggest a fresh combination of rondo principles with those of sonata-allegro and concerto forms.'

These graceful, vigorous and inventive works occupy the same position of excellence in Haydn's *œuvre* as 'Eine kleine Nachtmusik' would do in Mozart's. One of the greatest experiences of our life was when, in 1958, we spent several weeks in the Esterházy collection of the friendly National Széchényi Library, Budapest, copying these works and in some cases scoring them from the parts. In the evenings, with the late Professor Bence Szabolcsi, we played them, probably for the first time since 1786, on the piano four-hands and marvelled at their perfection.

Haydn lavished a great deal of care and affection on the five lira concertos which have survived (we presume he wrote the usual set of six). It must have pained him a little to think of all this beautiful music disappearing into the depths of southern Italy; and he retained copies of the works for his own, and Prince Esterházy's use. By assigning lira I to the flute and lira II to the oboe, Haydn could produce at short notice chamber music without changing a single note of the original scores. He thought sufficiently highly of his new concertos to incorporate the second and third movements of the F major Concerto V (of which we have discussed briefly the opening movement) as the slow and final movements of Symphony No. 89. (He could hardly use the first movement which was too 'chamber music' and formally too far removed from the symphony.) But an even more famous case occurs in Concerto III. It opens with a brilliant Allegro con spirito on the broadest scale and is one of the most scintillating movements of the series – also the only one of the five to be published prior to the Doblinger editions of 1959 (Karl Geiringer had edited it for Edition Adler, Berlin, 1932). Our ears are, however, in no way prepared for the second movement which turns out to be the music of the 'Military' movement (Symphony No. 100/II) with which Haydn scored the greatest triumph of his London career after the 'Surprise' Symphony (No. 94). The transformation of the beautiful 'Romance' into the 'Military' movement has been discussed elsewhere.[1] Suffice it to say that, once the later version is in our ears, we tend to miss the linking music between the end of one section and its repetition or continuation, that is to say, the three beats of rest disturb one. Almost uncanny that Haydn would sense that this movement from his Concerto for the King of Naples and the Two Sicilies would prove to be such an instantaneous success in London: the audiences reacted with 'shouts of joy' and even the ladies 'could not forbear'. This was the vindication of Haydn's popular style with a vengeance, and total proof, if any further be required, that by 1786 Haydn had brought this popular style to an apex of perfection which would soon be the admiration of the whole civilized world.

Quartets for Spain (Op. 42, 1785; III:43) and for the King of Prussia (Op. 50, 1787; III:44–49)

OPUS 42, IN D MINOR (1785)

Principal sources: (1) Autograph, Preussische Staatsbibliothek, Berlin, Mus. ms. autogr. Jos. Haydn 34, signed 'giuseppe Haydn mpria 785'; at end 'Fine Laus Deo'. Watermarks: three crescents of decreasing size; 'REAL', 'CS'. Tempo of I at first 'Allegretto ed Innocentemente', the word 'Allegretto' cancelled and 'Andante' substituted.

(2) First, presumably authentic edition, by Hoffmeister, Vienna, pl. no. 32, 1785–6 (in chronological proximity to the Overture Ia:4, Hoffmeister, pl. no. 37).
Critical editions: Complete Quartets, Verlag Doblinger (Barrett-Ayres), in preparation; *Joseph Haydn Werke*, in preparation.

This Quartet has always puzzled critics. Pohl (II, 44) even wrote that 'from its value [*Werth*] it belongs to the first eighteen [Quartets]...', and Geiringer (1932, p. 52) calls it 'a foreign body in the firm suite of Quartets up to now'. It is easy to confuse brevity with superficiality, and it is quite clear that Haydn received a Spanish commission for short quartets (see Chronicle, letter of 5 April 1784, *supra*, p. 490). Tovey (op. cit., p. 540) provided a spirited defence of the work, when he wrote:

---

1 *Haydn in England 1791–1795*, pp. 561f., where the chronological proximity of Haydn's 'Romances' of 1785(?) in Symphony No. 85 and 1786 (present work) with Mozart's K.466 (1785) is also mentioned.

The slow movement is, as Pohl says, *anspruchlos*; and this unpretentious movement will do as well as any other part of the quartet to prove that Haydn could not have written it any earlier ... If he had only had the luck or cunning to call it a cavatina, nobody would have failed to see the point of this melody without development, without a contrasting second theme or middle section, without sign of dramatic action, extending itself before us till we note, first, that it is not going to be a mere theme for variations; secondly, that it is becoming broader than any melody that we have ever heard worked into larger designs with other themes; finally, that it is rounding itself towards a conclusion, and is sufficient in itself, and justified by sheer contrast for its position in a work of dramatic action.

The scheme of this miniature later Quartet is:

    I   Andante ed Innocentemente, D minor, 2/4. A whole opening slow movement;

  `II   Menuet & Trio: Allegretto D major, 3/4;

  III Adagio cantabile, B flat, *alla breve*;

  IV Finale. Presto, D minor, 2/4.

Haydn, as can be seen, makes the little work seem much longer by reintroducing the old *sonata da chiesa* form, but bringing it 'up to date' in its tonal scheme (in 1764, twenty years earlier, Haydn would have written D minor four times or D minor followed by D major three times, as in Symphony No. 34). Two points may be mentioned: the first is that in the Minuet the first violin ascends a scale and reaches d''''. It is interesting in itself that Haydn thought Spanish violinists would have no trouble negotiating this high range; but it is also symptomatic of a new predilection for using his leader in a very high register, and we find it throughout Opp. 50, 54/55 and 64. Can it be that Haydn now had Johann Tost or some Viennese violinist in mind rather than his old friend Luigi Tomasini? (Tost, however, was leader of the *second* violins at Eszterháza; which, of course, does not prevent him from being a specialist in high notes.) The other point of special note is the way in which Haydn has constructed the Finale, using his theme

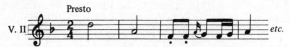

in constant fugato style. One immediately thinks, with Barrett-Ayres (op. cit., p. 186) of the Finale in the first (K.387) of Mozart's 'Haydn' Quartets, finished on New Year's Eve, 1782. But of course Haydn himself has many finales with this kind of fugato technique (as opposed to the straight fugues of Op. 20), not least the celebrated Finale of Symphony No. 77 (beginning of the development).

OPUS 50 (1787)

These six Quartets ('Prussian') are, respectively, in the keys of B flat, C, E flat, F sharp minor, F and D.

Principal sources: (1) MS. parts on 'small post paper' sent to William Forster by Haydn and signed by him; with remarks by the firm, 'sent 20 Sept' 1787'. Sandys-Forster, p. 310: '5 Oct' 1787. Received the M.S.S. of Haydn's quartetts ...'. British Museum, Egerton 2379, fol. 1–54. (2) MS. parts from Haydn's library, which later belonged (except for one) to J. N. Hummel, from whose legacy they were purchased by the British Museum: Nos. 1, 2, 4–6 = British Museum, Add. 32174, ff. 102–146f.; No. 3 = EH, Budapest, Ms. Mus. I. 132. All these MSS. on 'small post paper'. (3) MS. parts, EH, Budapest of Nos. 1, 2, 4–6. Ms. Mus. I. 131, 133, 134, 135, 136. (4) Authentic printed parts by Artaria & Co., Vienna, announced in the *Wiener Zeitung* on 19 December 1787; pl.

no. 109 'composés et dediés a sa Majesté Frederic Guillaume II Roi de Prusse par Ioseph Haydn Oeuvre 50me.'

Critical editions: Complete Quartets, Verlag Doblinger (Landon, 1975), in preparation; *Joseph Haydn Werke*, in preparation.

This crucial series of Quartets begins with a solo passage for the violoncello –

– subtle flattery for his Majesty, a well-known amateur 'cello player. But whereas Mozart's Quartets for Friedrich Wilhelm II contain a great deal of soloistic writing for the King, Haydn, apart from this one pretty compliment, continues in Op. 50 to write in the same structure as before.[1] But something else has happened. If we were to hear the beginning for the first time, with no knowledge of the printed score, we might at first imagine that we are hearing **C** ; but before long, even without a score, it is clear that Haydn has adopted an entirely new system of tempo. At the risk of becoming over technical we must explain the background for this vital innovation; and there is no doubt in our mind that the halving of the old eight-eight pace into barred C was the one direct influence which we may trace to Haydn's study of the Six Quartets (K.387 etc.) that Mozart dedicated to him in 1785. We have spoken above of Mozart's increased pulse, in overall terms (we examined *Figaro*) as well as in this technical aspect: Haydn pondered the inner significance of such a beginning as Mozart's K.428 or Mozart's K.499 (August 1786), an Allegretto which nevertheless has the same halved time: . The problem has been lucidly presented by Isidor Saslav (op. cit., pp. 70ff.):

> ... For the first time in his first movements Haydn employs the unmodified allegro barred C, in Op. 50/1/I. Also for the first time Haydn uses the unmodified word 'allegro' over a movement in four-four, Op. 50/6/I. This is the true classical allegro making its first appearance in the quartets. The influence of Mozart's quartets dedicated to him ... is no doubt of the greatest significance to this development. The appearance of these two tempi for the first time in Op. 50 mark these six works as the beginning of Haydn's last period and these tempi dominate the first movements to the very end as well as making more and more frequent appearances as finales. A last farewell to the previous style is the 2/4 allegro moderato, Op. 50/5/I. [Some musical examples conclude with the 'Cello Concerto VIIb:2, first movement and the Quartet, Op. 64/1/I (barred C).] The above examples strongly indicate that Haydn's barred C does indeed serve the purpose of halving the beat values of [the] previous sort of measure, in this case that of the pre-classical allegro four-four. Henceforth the smallest values found in Haydn's new barred C will be triplet quavers, with occasional semiquavers, where in the pre-classical allegro the smallest values were triplets of semiquavers and demisemiquavers. ...

Why did not Haydn simply label the movement allegro di molto in 4/4? If we compare a typical fast finale in 4/4 from the earlier years such as Op. 9/2/IV or Op. 20/4/IV with the new Op. 50/1/I we see that in the earlier movements an explicit

---

1 For a short reference to Mozart's K.565, 589, 590 and their structural problems as a result of the 'cello's domination, see Hans Keller in *The Mozart Companion* (1956), pp. 131f.

four beats in the bar is manifested in the form of drum-fire quaver pulses whereas in Op. 50 the attempt is made to dissolve the subdivisions into larger units, half-, even whole bars. The smallest unit is the triplet quaver, in the earlier movements, the semiquaver. The earlier genre is largely scherzando, buffo; the new is a combination of the galant, the lyric, and the energetic: in short, the classical allegro as we know it.

Mozart's presence in Haydn's life, apart from the older man's intense pleasure in the younger man's music, must have also been a considerable musical shock, the results of which also had the negative effect that Haydn simply stopped writing operas and piano concertos – fields in which, he believed, he should and could not compete with the 'divine Mozart'. Yet if we examine the Op. 50 Quartets, which are Haydn's first works *known* to have been composed in the string quartet form after Mozart's K.387 etc., we see that Haydn has preserved his own personality remarkably well. He took the one element which, although total and revolutionary, speeded up the basic tempo but did not materially change his *style* as such. He did not follow the example of the tragic D minor Quartet K.421. His own F sharp minor Quartet (Op. 50, No. 4) seems to assert his own style, his own renunciation of *Sturm und Drang*, of the language of tragedy, almost 'mit Nachdruck', or as if he were stressing the point. Nevertheless, as Tovey (op. cit., p. 543) writes, 'The F sharp minor quartet is a great work.'

> It shows for the first time [in the quartets] Haydn's definite renunciation of tragic ends to sonata movements, and his now typical association of the minor mode with a passionate, somewhat blustering temper, ending with a recapitulation (in these circumstances regular) in the tonic major, so that everything turns out well. ... In striking contrast to the happy end of the first movement, the final fugue, quietest and deepest of all the ... instrumental fugues since Bach, strikes a note so tragic that Beethoven's C sharp minor quartet is the first thing that one can connect with it.

If one might think that the meltingly beautiful pedal point ('cello triplet semiquavers) with the weaving quavers of the strings above which constitute the end of Op. 50, No. 3's slow movement, might owe something of its tremulous spirit to the end of Mozart's slow movement in K.464 (quoted *supra*, pp. 514f.), Haydn displays his own special kind of slow movement in 'The Dream' (Op. 50, No. 4's 'Poco Adagio'). Mozart's ambivalence seems to display itself best in andantes; Haydn's greatest slow movements are his sustained adagios, of which this one has the fleeting but haunting power of a dream – intense in a way that we will learn in the slow movements of Op. 76. It is preceded by a movement containing one feature which is positively riveting, and that is the way Haydn develops and modifies the little phrase:

The wit lies in the harmonic sophistication, so that we never know what marvellous harmonic twist Haydn has prepared for us.

The only work of this remarkable set of six that has achieved general popularity is No. 6, which is popular because it embodies the essence of Haydn in its four wonderfully contained movements. Its off-tonic beginning has always excited attention, and when we resolve, in bar 4, the question, the 'cello has a fascinating rhythm rather like that of a child's skipping rope

The sudden shifting into D minor at bar 11 is as effective as totally unprepared. The mournful little *siciliano* tune of the slow movement (Poco Adagio) develops a profusion of intricate arabesques in demisemiquavers, sometimes melodic variants, sometimes throbbing accompaniments, and with all its complicated modulations we hardly notice that we are being carefully guided from D minor to D major. About the Minuet, Cecil Gray[1] writes that it is 'one of the most attractive of Haydn's minuets in his string quartets, and a wonderful example of his genius in achieving originality in a conventional form through the simplest means. Not even Mozart himself excels Haydn in this.'

> [The Finale, continues Gray], one of the most brilliant and original of Haydn's finales, which is saying a lot, is chiefly based on the exploitation of a peculiar technical device known by the French name of *bariolage* (derived from the Latin *variolagium* – alternation), the same note being sounded in alternation upon two adjacent strings. ... Here Haydn chiefly uses it by alternating notes on the open strings with stopped notes. The subtle difference of tone-colour thus obtained is largely responsible for the irresistible fascination of the movement. What is, perhaps, most remarkable about it, however, is the way in which Haydn repeats the effect throughout the movement with such resource that one never wearies of it, as one might easily do if it were done by another hand.

Haydn had flirted with *bariolage* on many occasions, first in a lunatic Minuet of 1765 from his Symphony No. 28, then grimly in the fast section of the 'Farewell' Symphony's Finale, and occasionally in the Quartets prior to Op. 50 (Op. 17, No. 6, Finale). It is a Haydnesque gesture and something that, one feels, would never have occurred to Mozart, at least not on the gigantic scale here displayed.

Another point which critics have always stressed is the monothematicism, about which Robert Sondheimer (op. cit., 141) writes:

> The content of the movement is not to be disjointed by contrasting themes in the exposition. The first subject, therefore, does not immediately make way for the intermediary episodes: it is retained as long as possible by repetitions and expanded with supplementary material. Thus, the roots combine into a strong growth which gives the exposition solidity from the first. Eventually, however, the main stem of the music has to spread out into a number of branches, and thereby ebbs away like a great river in a delta ... The varied activity of the sonata movement is not impeded, but plays round the main train of thought, like widenings in a narrow street. That is why in his quartets, time after time, Haydn tends to form the second subject from ingredients of the first ... The place assigned to the second subject is [in certain quartets] like a blind alley from which it has to run back into the main avenue.

1 *Haydn String Quartet Society*, Vol. 7, p. 12 (1938).

Haydn had managed to assimilate the (for him) most important total aspect of the Mozartian manner without removing the originality, wit, depth and unity of the 'Prussian' Quartets. We shall soon see yet a further intensification of Haydn's preoccupation with Mozart in the first 'Tost' Quartets (Opp. 54/55).[1]

Symphonies No. 88 and 89
for Paris *via* Johann Tost (1787)

SYMPHONY NO. 88 IN G ('Letter V'; 1787?)

Scoring: flute, 2 oboes, 2 bassoons, 2 horns, 2 trumpets, timpani and strings.
Literature: Landon, *SYM*, 412 *passim*. Jan LaRue,

Guidelines, op. cit. 1970, pp. 161ff., with analysis 'which compactly illustrates that composer's ingenuity in conceiving subtle derivations.'

This popular Symphony is a particularly successful blend of gaiety and towering intellectual strength: in that respect it is closely allied to No. 92, which may explain the particular success of both works. Before proceeding to 'Letter V', we would point out a striking innovation, or rather a double innovation: the Symphony begins with Haydn's usual 'light' scoring, i.e. without trumpets and drums. It was in fact not usual to have trumpets and drums in a G major Symphony in those days, and for purely technical reasons: G trumpets (known as 'English trumpets') were too high-pitched: their scale did not begin until g'', whereas the alternative course – using C trumpets – would mean that they were rather limited (again for technical reasons). Haydn's Symphony No. 54, which has trumpets and drums and is in G, was originally composed in 1774 without the trumpets, and it has been suggested[2] that the large orchestration (flutes were also added) was made for England. The timpani part of Mozart's brilliant G major Symphony, K.318, seems also to have been a later addition. Thus, no one in Paris *anno* 1788 would have expected trumpets and kettledrums in a G major symphony, and they will have been very surprised to see them patiently sitting through the first movement. When the second movement, in D, commenced, listeners will have still wondered what those instruments were doing at the back of the stage, because in slow movements of symphonies, trumpets and drums were almost never used; Haydn and Mozart had never done so before 1783. Thus their astonishment at hearing the trumpets and drums enter after forty bars of the slow movement must have been considerable. This is the first Haydn symphony with a slow movement to use them. Mozart's first (and last) was in the 'Linz' Symphony K.425 (1783), but the Parisians had never heard a note of it, and would not for many years; though the Viennese knew it, and possibly Haydn did, too. It is doubtful if anyone outside Salzburg knew Michael Haydn's great Serenade in D of 1785 (*vide infra*, p. 672) which uses trumpets and drums in its extended slow movement. Many years later, in the Leipzig *Allgemeine Musikalische Zeitung*, we read of the tremendous effect that was created with the introduction of these instruments into slow movements by Haydn and Mozart – even in 1798, people still recalled it.[3] This is the kind of thing that we would do well to remember, because our ears, bombarded by the weight of horns, trumpets, trombones, tenor tubas, bass tubas and contrabass tubas of German

1 Literature: Tovey in Cobbett's *Survey* (1929), pp. 540ff. Gray in *Haydn String Quartet Society*, vols. 4 (1935) and 7 (1938). Sondheimer, 1951, op. cit., 141 *passim*. Barrett-Ayres, 1974, op. cit., pp. 183, 202ff. Orin Moe, 'The Significance of Haydn's Opus 33', Haydn Conference, Washington, D.C., 1975.
2 *Haydn in England 1791–1795*, p. 188.
3 Quoted *in extenso* in *Haydn: the Years of 'The Creation' 1786–1800*, pp. 339f.

Romantic music (and two pairs of kettledrums in *Die Walküre*), hardly hear the innovation any longer.

If anyone wanted to know why Haydn wrote slow introductions to most of his late symphonies, he might try playing this first movement without the Adagio. The introduction is particularly necessary in movements where the quick section begins *piano*, and this is the case in Symphonies Nos. 84, 85, 86, 88, 90, 91 and 92. Conversely, the other Symphonies, Nos. 82, 83, 87 and 89 all begin *forte* and have no introduction. The opening theme of the Allegro in No. 88 is too delicate, too 'fragmented', to come in 'out of the cold'. This first movement is undoubtedly an intellectual *tour-de-force* of the first magnitude, the detailed analysis of which would occupy more space than is at our disposal (see literature). Like all Haydn's greatest formal complexities, one can listen to it with much enjoyment even lacking such an analysis; but we would make the point that the Parisian audiences of 1788 were highly educated musically and without doubt understood and appreciated the intellectual side of the Allegro.

The great slow movement, of which Brahms is reported to have said, 'I want my Ninth Symphony to sound like that', is a variation movement built upon one of Haydn's hymn-tunes and marked Largo. Among its many spectacular features is the shining orchestration, that which in German is called 'durchbrochen', 'broken through', the opposite of massive. This finely wrought score gives the theme's announcement to solo oboe supported (an octave below) by solo violoncello, and accompanied by solo bassoon, second horn, viola and bass line. The effect is as original as Wagner's Prelude to *Tristan* if we attune our ears to 1788, which is admittedly difficult nearly two hundred years later. How Haydn gradually enriches the theme as the movement progresses is a wonder to behold.

The Menuetto, in G, with C trumpets and kettledrums in low G and D, is a scene out of Breugel: stamping peasants dancing round kegs of wine and tables groaning with harvest feast. If one seeks the difference in a single minuet between Haydn and Mozart, one may compare this rich, earthy peasant scene with the fantastic sophistication and fastidious elegance of the 'Jupiter' Symphony's Minuet, both composed within a year of each other. In No. 88, there is, to celebrate the timpani's entering the closed world of G major, a neat little solo in two places (bars 11f., 41f.). In the Trio, the banquet is over, and much wine has been consumed: the bagpipes come, droning to the drowsy couples in the afternoon sun. It is another painting in vivid colours, and as earthy as the Minuet itself. Marie Antoinette might have been reminded of Le petit Trianon when she heard it; men from the country will have recognized its authentic accents.

The Finale is one of the most intricately composed, yet brilliant sounding, movements in the *corpus* of Haydn: a sonata rondo which is a perfect tribute to the Viennese predilection for combining intellect and beauty. Notice in the development how – after returning rondo-like to the tonic key – Haydn suddenly launches into a *fortissimo* canon between upper and lower strings which continues, before our fascinated eyes and delighted ears, bar after bar: this is surely one of the great contrapuntal feats of the Viennese classical symphony.

SYMPHONY NO. 89 IN F (1787)

Scoring: 1 flute, 2 oboes, 2 bassoons, 2 horns and strings.

Placed beside the glowing strength of No. 88, No. 89 seems at first a rather pale companion. In fact, the Symphony is reserved, cool and of immaculate formal design, rather like the perfectly fashioned German porcelain figurines of that period. It is often said that Haydn opened the doors of the eighteenth-century salon and let in the fresh air; no doubt this is on the whole true, and we only need to recall the barn-yard richness of No. 88's Minuet; but for No. 89 he momentarily closed the doors again.

As said above, the slow movement and Finale were borrowed from Concerto V for the King of Naples one year earlier than the Symphony (of which, unlike No. 88, we have the dated autograph, 1787, in the Fitzwilliam Museum in Cambridge). The Concerto was composed, as we have seen, for two lire and string quintet. Haydn retained the form of the slow movement more or less unchanged (though of course re-orchestrated), but he enlarged the Finale with the highly symphonic section in F minor, whose rather ferocious off-beat *forzati* add strength and orchestral colour to an otherwise rather Rococo movement. Another interesting addition to the Concerto in this Finale are the indications 'strascinando' ('dragging'), which give a very Viennese lilt to the returns of the main subject.

Perhaps the most original part of the work is the Menuet. It begins with a rustic wind-band solo and the first part ends with a rather coy flute solo. At the beginning of the second section, the bass voice is first the horns and then the bassoons: it all sounds very droll. The end of the Minuet proper is a long tonic pedal point which suddenly bursts into *ff* in a very Beethovenian manner, both as regards the 'layout' of the parts as well as the repeated quavers: here is a foretaste of the Eighth Symphony.

Symphonies for the Comte d'Ogny and the Prince von Oettingen-Wallerstein
Nos. 90–92 (1788–9)

SYMPHONY NO. 90 IN C (1788)

Scoring: 1 flute, 2 oboes, 2 bassoons, 2 horns in C *alto* and F, 2 trumpets, kettledrums and strings.

Haydn may have dedicated these last three Symphonies to Monseigneur le Comte d'Ogny in Paris, and he may have sent them to Schloß Wallerstein in Bavaria, but he always had in mind his own orchestra at Eszterháza: there were certainly two flutes not only in Paris but also at Wallerstein; at Eszterháza there was one flute only, and so for one Haydn wrote. There were no clarinets at Eszterháza either in this period, so there are no clarinets in Symphonies Nos. 88–92. Another speciality at Eszterháza were the C *alto* horns which took the place of trumpets in festive works with kettledrums. But Haydn must have known that C *alto* horns were (and are) extremely difficult to play and that they were probably unknown in Paris (or London). It is typical that the authentic Le Duc edition, based on the autograph, simply dropped the word 'alto' and so did Longman & Broderip in their authentic edition of 1791. So we have a fine point here: when Haydn played the work at Eszterháza he used high horns and simply omitted the trumpet parts; in London we know that he used the trumpet parts (because they are included in the authentic print 'as performed at M^r. Salomons [*sic*] conçert Hanover Square'), but what did he do with the horns? Did they really play in C *alto*? Life for an eighteenth-century musician was nothing but an endless series of compromises ...

There is an interesting formal device in the first movement. Haydn must have pondered the problem of uniting the slow introduction more closely to the body of the movement. Here he does so by the simplest, most direct but also most effective (because easily audible) means: the music of bars 5/8 of the introduction, Adagio, speeded up to Allegro assai, becomes the main theme of the quick section. The movement as a whole has the brilliance for which Haydn's C major festive symphonies are known, but it lacks the trenchant power of No. 82's beginning. No. 90 is more ceremonious and has something of the cool reserve that we noted in No. 89.

The slow movement is much in the same restrained vein: even the big section in F minor is more of a formal device than a sense of self-identification with the sombre key as in Symphony No. 49 or the Quartet, Op. 20, No. 5. The coda (bars 120ff.), with its rich woodwind scoring, is beautiful in its quiet dignity: one notes the *pp* which suddenly enters at bar 128 to underline the surprise modulation to D flat major.

There is once again, as in No. 82's Menuet, something very French about this movement: gone are the stamping peasants of No. 88; here is a glittering ball at the Château de Versailles in the last season it would ever know. It is extraordinary that Haydn could imagine another civilization without ever having experienced it at first-hand. If we sense the bluest sky in the world when hearing Haydn's music for the King of Naples (Concertos Nos. I–V), with Symphony No. 90, Haydn has with the same genius entered Louis XVI's artificial, brilliant and extravagant court, flourishing while France lay in the grip of starvation.

The Finale is one of Haydn's fast-moving, monothematic movements in sonata form. When the movement appears to have come to a close at bar 167, there follows a rest of four bars and the movement suddenly continues in the flattened supertonic (D flat), rather the way, nowadays, popular melodies are pushed up a semi-tone towards the middle. The ensuing coda is enormous (bars 168, counting the rests, through 241) and full of drollery; but it is much more the Haydn we know, though without the usual amount of warmth. Possibly for that reason, the jokes appear more ironical than witty.

SYMPHONY NO. 91 IN E FLAT (1788)

Scoring: 1 flute, 2 oboes, 2 bassoons, 2 horns and strings.

E flat is a favourite key with most composers, and Haydn was no exception: he, too, appreciated its mellowness, the rich sonority that wind instruments assume when in that key, and the curious effect whereby the strings lose their edge. The very introduction of No. 91 shows how much the key influenced the composition, as it did at the same juncture in No. 84. This expansive and generous music went right out of Haydn's head by 1791: he could not remember it when asking Frau von Genzinger to send the work to London and had to quote the beginning of the fast section. In a similar way, Mozart forgot the whole 'Haffner' Symphony and was astonished at how good it was when his father sent it back to Vienna six months later.

The main theme of the first movement's Allegro assai is constructed in double counterpoint at the octave, whereby the second part of the theme is the top and bottom lines reversed. Haydn keeps adding extra voices to his theme: when the dominant is reached, the first violin has a new voice (bars 57ff.) and soon the flute and oboe as well. There is a sequential second subject and a long closing episode to set off the contrapuntal austerity of the main theme. In the development, this subject is given yet another extra voice (bars 128ff.), first in the oboe and then in the flute. We now have the main subject, itself in double counterpoint, with a variety of countersubjects, and finally, at the end of the movement (bars 253ff.), there is the supreme contrapuntal feat of combining them all simultaneously in a five-voiced display: countersubject I in the flute, oboe I and violin I; countersubject II in the viola; top voice of the theme in oboe II and violin II; bottom voice in bassoons, 'cellos and basses. *Deo Matematica*.

The dancing quality of the Andante is immediately apparent. The movement appears to be a normal theme and variations, with the usual droll effects (the bassoon solo; the 'minore' section, and so forth); but we are not prepared for the riotous series of trills just before the end, where the whole orchestra seems to have gone mad.

In the third movement, marked (oddly) 'Un poco Allegretto', we notice the beautiful lead-back to the return of the 'A' section of the Menuet proper: a long dominant pedal point, with delicate bassoon colouring. The Trio has strong elements of the waltz; in the second section, there is a series of very original *fz decrescendi*, first in the horns, then in the oboes: Haydn will return to this little bizarrerie with added zest in the Trio of No. 92.

The Finale has a gay melody over a chattering second violin part, later transferred to the 'cellos. Except for a tiny second subject at bars 55ff., the whole movement is in the secure grasp of this main theme: Haydn detaches the first six notes and uses them as accompaniment (bars 77ff.), then he uses just the fifth and sixth notes (e.g. at 94 and 99) and spins these two notes out to produce a whole passage in the middle of the development (bars 107ff.). A winning conclusion to a bright, warm-hearted Symphony.

SYMPHONY NO. 92 IN G ('OXFORD'; 1789)

Scoring: 1 flute, 2 oboes, 2 bassoons, 2 horns, 2 trumpets, timpani and strings.

On the occasion of the first performance of *The Creation* in Italy, which took place at Bergamo in 1809, the libretto contained notes on the composer and his works by 'G. S. M.', who was none other than the famous operatic composer, Giovanni Simone (Johann Simon) Mayr, the conductor, since 1802, of Santa Maria Maggiore at Bergamo. Mayr, a careful student of Haydn, used (translated) part of an article in the *AMZ*,[1] and we read: 'Non hanno questi *Allegri* tavolta neppure un *tema*, e sembrano di cominciare in mezzo; e nulladimeno trovasi in essi ad onta di tutta la leggerezza una fluidità, un ordine, che annunziano sempre la mano maestra.' And it *is* very often the case that 'these *Allegri* sometimes do not even have a theme and seem to begin in the middle'.

The quick movement of No. 92/I 'begins in the middle' and is off-tonic, moreover; who does not think of the Quartet, Op. 50, No. 6/I? Once again, it would not have been considered correct to start the Symphony with this non-theme in the non-tonic. Thus the slow introduction, which is in its own right of an extraordinary profundity and loveliness, with a wandering middle part for the violoncello. Its intense chromaticism as the music progresses underlines the late-summery stillness that, as the Symphony moves into its slow movement, becomes autumn. On 14 July 1789, two things happened: the Bastille fell and, by a curious stroke of fate, Mozart's *Le nozze di Figaro* arrived at Eszterháza. As the ordered and serene life of the *ancien régime* began to disintegrate, Haydn was preparing Mozart's revolutionary opera for performance and was penning this very Symphony, a tribute to all that was gracious and beautiful in pre-revolutionary Europe.

The off-tonic first theme does not settle into G major until the first tutti, when the trumpets and kettledrums – which although authentic, may have been a later addition: they are missing in the autograph and authentic first edition by Le Duc, Paris, but are included in the MS. parts Haydn sent to Wallerstein – also make their first appearance.

---

1 See also *Haydn in England 1791–1795*, p. 511. The *AMZ* review by Zelter (not Rochlitz, as on p. 511) may be found, translated, in *Haydn: the Years of 'The Creation' 1796–1800*, pp. 592ff.

As this extraordinary movement progress, we sense the justice of Mayr/Zelter, namely that 'just the same, you find in them [the fragmented themes], despite all their lightness, a fluidity, a sense of order, that mark the master's hand.' Haydn's inventiveness with this very small subject (four bars, to be exact) is boundless. As is often the case when Haydn's first subject is small in size, we are given a fully developed second subject: this was also true of No. 86/I. The enormous contrapuntal possibilities of the first subject are revealed to us by Haydn *le grand presdigitateur* during the development section: the first subject with the grace-note figure of the second, the first subject in cancrizans with itself, in inversion with itself, as a canon in several parts. It is in the great contrapuntal tradition of Flanders, Italy, Saxony and Vienna.

This is the second slow movement (Adagio) in which Haydn introduces the trumpets and timpani. The theme is of the kind we came to know as a hymn tune in the last few years of Haydn's life; and there is once again, as there was in No. 88/II and in No. 92's slow introduction, a separate 'cello line. Formally, the movement is organized as follows: the big 'A' section is worked out *a-a'* (in other words instead of a double bar, Haydn has written out, and at the same time embellished, the repeat) and then *b-b'-a''* (the final *a''* being differently embellished). During all this, the trumpets and timpani are silent. Now, as 'B' bursts upon us, with G minor, they enter. The first of what will be many wind band solos greet us in the middle of this 'B' section (bars 55ff.). 'A' now returns, with its *a-b-a* pattern, but without the repeats and still further varied. The coda brings us a very long wind-band solo, the longest Haydn ever wrote in a symphonic slow movement thus far, which contains a staggeringly modern sounding series of parallel six chords (bar 104) and ends in a long pedal-point 'apotheosis' such as we have described in connection with No. 87's slow movement.

The Menuet is on the same large symphonic scale as that of No. 86, and with a large middle, or 'development' section. It is also a very serious movement, and not only because of its frequent excurions into the minor: the heart jumps, but not for joy. The Trio takes over the syncopated *forzato-decrescendo* device that we noticed in No. 91's Trio, but here it is still further extended and the syncopated pattern is made more complex. It, too, is a serious, even dedicated movement.

The Finale is, if it were possible, even more dazzling than that of No. 88. It begins with a bizarre effect, the theme in the first violins over nothing except bare octaves in the violoncello (later editors put in harmony here, but the autograph and other authentic sources make Haydn's bold intentions perfectly clear). There is also an extended second subject. Never has Haydn showed such ingenuity as in the contrapuntal extension of his thematic material in the development. Nothing seems too much for him to attempt. Finally, after all this daring and highly chromatic experimentation, we find ourselves in C major and second subject: suddenly the trumpets (which are C trumpets) enter with delightful effect: later Johann Strauss was to show the same sensitive awareness of the trumpet's colour in a *piano* context. When the second subject returns in the recapitulation, Haydn gives a new accompaniment to the second horn, whose player must display not only agility in octave jumping but also display his 'stopped' note C sharp.[1]

---

1 Grosvenor Cooper and L. B. Meyer, in their book *The Rhythmic Structure of Music*, Chicago & London, 1960 (pp. 27 f.), write of this movement: 'The witty and somewhat impertinent – almost brusque – character of this theme is in large part a result of the durational disproportion among the units of the main rhythmic group. The extended anacrusis leads one to expect a longer final unit. Not only is the accent too short, in relation to the upbeat group, but the weak afterbeat is even shorter. The second motive seems to begin too soon, interrupting, as it were, the natural duration of the initial motive. Thus each group embodies in itself a kind of composed accelerando, each unity of the grouping being shorter than the one which precedes it. And this quickening of the pace is carried through into the last two measures, where the amphibrach groupings come twice as fast.'

Haydn was quite right to pick this Symphony for the concert to celebrate his Oxford degree in July 1791, for it artlessly presents the greatest contrapuntal mind since J. S. Bach, embedded within the popular classical style, which with this work achieved a peak of matchless perfection.

The First Series of Quartets for Johann Tost
(Opp. 54 and 55; *c.* 1787–8; III:57–62)

These Quartets comprise six works, in G, C, and E (Op. 54), and in A, F minor and B flat (Op. 55).

Principal sources: (1) Fragmentary autograph sketches (first drafts) of Op. 54, No. 1 (Preussische Staatsbibliothek, Berlin, Mus. ms. autogr. Jos. Haydn 4; no title; 1st movt., bars 1–64 of 2nd, bars 39–68 of 3rd and 1–131 of Finale; watermarks: 'VA', 'REAL', three crescents of decreasing size; ornamental figure) and No. 2 (same library, Mus. ms. autogr. Jos. Haydn 5; same watermarks; containing from bar 37 of 2nd movt. to end of work. These first drafts contain practically no dynamic and very few phrasing marks and were obviously *aides-memoire*: in some cases, whole lines of semiquavers are simply indicated by ♪~~~♪.

The autographs are therefore of little help in solving the tremendous textual problems of these works, brought about because we have no really authentic sources. (2) Printed parts by Sieber, Paris, announced on 13 June 1789 in the *Journal de la Librairie*; although Haydn composed the works as a set of six, the same procedure as in Opp. 71/74 obtained, namely that the publisher, in this case Sieber, who received the engraving copy from Tost himself, issued the works in two sets of three works each, 'Oeuvre 54' and '55', in which form they have come down to posterity; Sieber's sequence of Op. 54 is Nos. 3, 1, 2, and of Op. 55, Nos. 2, 3, 1 (in the traditional order, which we have followed). There are inexplicable additions to this print, possibly performance notes by Tost, which are often self-contradictory and must be treated with the greatest caution. Copy in the Bibliothèque Nationale, Paris. (3) Printed parts by Longman & Broderip, London, entered at Stationers' Hall in two sets, Op. 57 and 61, on 7 July 1789 and 12 March 1790. Textually the most reliable source, the MS. was probably sent by Haydn to the Professional Concert as part of their agreement, and the print specifically lists 'Performed at the Professional Concert Hanover-Square 1789 [1790]'. Copy in British Museum, London. Compared to (2), this source has a striking paucity of dynamic marks, etc. Did Haydn revise the work (copy) for Tost? In the order Op. 54, Nos. 2, 1, 3; Op. 55, 2, 3, 1. (4) Anonymous printed parts which were sold by Artaria and announced on 1 July 1789 (first three, Op. 59, *Wiener Zeitung*) and 13 January 1790 (second three, Op. 60, ditto), in the order that we know today (Hoboken, curiously, reverses Op. 54, Nos. 1 and 2). We do not know from which source Artaria received its engraving source (see Chronicle, 22 September 1788, *infra*, p. 709), not Haydn at any rate. Copy in the Burgenländisches Landesmuseum, Eisenstadt (*ex coll.* Landon).
Critical editions: Complete Quartets, Verlag Doblinger (Landon, 1975), in preparation. *Joseph Haydn Werke*, in preparation. As we have said before, there are nearly insoluble textual problems in these works, and the student has two possibilities: (a) to play the works in the almost dynamicless Longman & Broderip edition, or (b) to try to effect a compromise, using some of the increased dynamic language of (2) and (4).

OPUS 54, NO. I

We have seen in Op. 50 that Haydn assimilated some aspects of the Mozartian style without losing his (Haydn's) own identity in the process. Much of same basic problems occur in the present works. It might be said that the panache, the outwardly brilliant sound, and the overall poise of this G major work, which has always been extremely popular among quartet players and audience alike, owe something to Mozart, as do the slithering chromatic lines, perhaps:

Likewise the sudden slide into a minor I_4^6 progression (bar 20, accented on off beat to draw attention to itself) is vaguely Mozartian. Yet the whole is not simply a copy of the younger man's style, and the repeated quavers, the figures such as

are completely characteristic of Haydn. Might one speak, here, of a spiritual assimilation? Similarly, the delicate shape of the Allegretto movement, with its gliding *portato* accompaniment and the chaste melody, have a faintly Mozartian flavour. But as the movement progresses, and the violin ascends to dizzy heights, we recognize typical music written at Eszterháza for Johann Tost (bars 17f., 85f.). The progression at bars 34ff., with those wonderfully characteristic viola entrances, shows the sense of harmonic adventure with which all these sets are informed, and by the time Minuet/Trio and Finale unfold, we must strive to remember the fleeting Mozartian influence, so powerful has become Haydn's own style. The vivacious Finale, especially (which has clear thematic links with the Trio), is in Haydn's best 'whirling' style, with excursions into the minor, stuttering lead-backs using the first three notes of the theme, and all Haydn's other devices exploited to the full. The ending, in the highest register for all instruments, is destined to encourage an immediate encore of the Finale.

OPUS 54, NO. 2

Here we have one of the most original constructions in Haydn's quartets. If No. 1 might be thought to have been influenced from outside, the structure of No. 2 is wholly a product of Haydn's own development as an artist. 'It is,' wrote Cecil Gray,

> entirely personal to Haydn in every movement and none ... could for one moment be ascribed to Mozart by any one with the slightest pretensions to a feeling for style – to say nothing of the underlying thought. In so far as Haydn was the forerunner of any one, it is of Beethoven, not Mozart. That is the real ancestry ... Mozart actually stands somewhat apart from both his great predecessor and his great successor. His is rounded, complete, and consummated, the perfection and final flowering of the eighteenth century; Haydn is essentially the precursor of the nineteenth and sometimes ... of the twentieth. And while it would have been impossible for Mozart to have written the present work, one can quite easily imagine it to have been written by Beethoven in his early, or even early middle period. [op. cit., vol. 2 (1933), p. 12]

If we examine Haydn's later quartets, we find that C major often awakens in his genius a massive style, almost symphonic. This is certainly true of this bold opening movement, and also of the beginning of Op. 74, No. 1 (1793) and, of course, Op. 76, No. 3 ('Emperor'). The more we study these twelve 'Tost' Quartets, the more they begin to have certain similarities that mark them apart from Haydn's slightly earlier works in the form. Again we have the first violin's ascent to dizzy heights (*d''''* in bars 77f., *c''''* in bars 218f.), the same sense of breadth (formal, too), the daring modulations (from C to A flat without a break in bars 11ff.), the use of silence – all are characteristic for the works of this period.

The second movement is one of those sustained adagio movements (in the favourite 3/4) at which Haydn excels. It is in C minor and is chiefly remarkable for the freedom of form, almost fantasia-like, with which it is constructed. The first eight bars move with expressive slow crotchets, almost like a Baroque movement, but from bars 9 to the end of the movement, Haydn gives the first violin a series of *Primas*-like arabesques that flutter over the music's basic pulse in an effective and exotic manner. Tovey (543) thinks this 'wild, florid counterpoint' should be played *per figuram retardationis*, as in Op. 20, No. 5. The Minuet was, apparently, popular at Eszterháza, for it was incorporated into a musical clock, with chirping ornaments that anyone who plays the quartet version could not possibly imagine. It is a bold, forceful work, harking back to the opening movement's style and also to the first violin's great range upwards (*c''''* just before the end). The C minor Trio has always startled people. 'Nothing', writes Cecil Gray,

> could be more remarkable for imaginative daring and originality than these sombre and menacing strains which break in so rudely upon the polished and courtly conventions of the form, like a *sansculotte* forcing his way into an aristocratic salon. [op. cit., p. 14]

The Finale has the same astonishing originality, as did the last movement of Symphony No. 67. The Quartet's starts with an Adagio, beginning with another poetic eight bars which on first hearing would be considered the main theme, but quite unexpectedly at bar 9, 'the great tune' begins: with a ravishingly beautiful accompaniment in the lower strings, the first violin has a theme which looks forward across ten long years of time to 'Mit Würd' und Hoheit' ('In native worth') from *The Creation*. It is itself a theme of great nobility, the music is bathed in the radiant sonority cast by the 'cello who soars up from his lowest C below the bass clef to *e''* in measured, slurred groups of quavers. It appears that we are to have an entire slow movement along these glorious lines, but no: Haydn had ended his slow movement on a half-close to prepare for the minuet, and repeating the device the music after 56 bars draws to a similar half-close. The last thing one would expect now occurs: Haydn begins one of his racy and racing Presto movements in characteristic 2/4, with the whole bars of rest that we remember from the first movement. But it, too grinds to a sudden halt, and to complete our confusion, the beautiful Adagio begins again, and with one of his greatest melodic inspirations again ringing in our ears, this unique Quartet draws to its *pianissimo* close.

Op. 54, No. 2, has enjoyed a special place of prominence among quartet audiences, who have always intuitively recognized its flash of genius.

OPUS 54, NO. 3

E major, as noted many times in this biography, calls forth a special intensity in Haydn – here what might be called a powerful lyricism, couched in the new, fast Allegro (barred C). A very unusual effect is that after seven bars a long tonic pedal point is introduced, just as if we are at the end of the movement, not the beginning. As the movement progresses we see that this pedal point is one of its central features, for it appears at the end of the exposition (dominant); in broken octaves in the 'cello, first in D major in the middle of the development (bars 81ff.); then shortly thereafter in C sharp (used here as the dominant of F sharp minor); and yet again in its long-held form at the very end of the development (G sharp, acting as V of C sharp minor); from which pivot we jump without further ado into the recapitulation. Thereafter, in the recapitulation, the pedal is used three more times. Now the effect of all these pedal notes which, it will be seen, appear with untoward frequence, is to give a fundamental stability and base to the music. Probably the new 'double' tempo allowed for such effects more readily than the old moderato movements. Another 'fingerprint' which assumes an ever increasing role in Haydn's quartet (not symphonic) language: the use of triplets. We have seen that syncopation has always, from the 1760s, been part and parcel of Haydn's style. This use of triplets is not unknown in earlier Haydn, of course, and one may see it in the first movements of Op. 20, No. 2 (1772), Op. 20, No. 4 (in exposed fashion: typical of that forward-looking work), and in other chamber music; but it is not until Op. 50, No. 1, that these chains of triplets become a real fingerprint by their very numerical preponderance in the overall scheme – in the exposition, triplets dominate 24 of the 60 bars, and they continue throughout in more or less this profusion. Again, these triplets always serve a formal purpose. In Op. 54, No. 3, we have noticed that the theme is 'intensely lyrical'; that it moves in crotchets with only occasional linking quavers; and that the music is, literally, grounded by many pedal points. The triplets act as a contrast and also to accelerate the music's otherwise quiet pulse. They are used, however, only in fourteen of the exposition's fifty-eight bars and with the same numerical frequence in the rest of the Allegro. (Compare the triplets in Op. 50, No. 1: the different numerical proportion of the triplets is carefully calculated.) In Op. 55, No. 1's opening Allegro, *alla breve*, we again find the 'fingerprint' triplets in twenty-four of the exposition's sixty-four bars, but to anticipate that movement for a moment, the triplets' growth is a result of the principal theme:

If we may imagine that Johann Tost's style of playing influenced this music, he must have been a specialist in the *per figuram retardationis* performance of intricate, highly ornamented movements of this kind (see also Op. 54, No. 2's second movement), where we even have figurations in hemidemisemiquavers (which means, in 3/4 time, Largo cantabile, that Haydn can cram forty notes for the violin I in bars 28 and 30). As a result, the music almost approaches the concerto, though it is in variation form. As so often, the concerto is also referred to in the formal cadences with trills (though not so obviously as in the symphonies of the late 1770s and early 1780s).

After a Minuet punctuated with the Lombardian rhythm (or Scottish snap), which is of course Hungarian in origin as far as Haydn is concerned, the Finale is another sample of the swift concluding mixture of sonata and rondo. But if we look at it carefully, we will discover an astonishing link with the first movement which can be perceived at once aurally: that ubiquitous pedal point. And to make this reference perfectly plain, the pedal point is introduced right at the outset and (as in the first movement) immediately repeated at bars 9ff. The fact that the first violin does not enter until bar 10 draws special attention to the beginning's structure. The pedal point also begins the development and is used in that section no less than three times. Thus the Quartet achieves a hidden unity by this predominance of the pedal point.

Although consistently praised by the scholars (Tovey, p. 544: 'No. 3 [E] is one of Haydn's greatest works, and should be better known'), this has never been one of the popular quartets. We would say that it is a fine work but we cannot concur with the late Professor Tovey in placing it among the very greatest.

OPUS 55, NO. I

Of the first movement we have written briefly. The internal link between the various sections of the main theme, and between it and the second theme, have been singled out by critics, including Cecil Gray.[1] The links are easily audible because they are

rhythmic, being (a) the use of triplets and (b) the use of the following figure: ♩. ♫♪

which, when it is used to usher in the second subject, is given a *fz* to make the relationship even clearer.

The second movement is one of those great, sustained adagios for which Haydn was now famous. If the first violin predominates in these lyrical adagios, it is in the nature of the music's structure, but the careful listener and reader will see that, on the contrary, all four instruments have prominent and beautiful parts. In fact the first violin does not enter until bar 9. Although it is sustained music, Haydn keeps it from being staid by a number of rhythmic shifts: syncopations, accented, at bars 20f.; demisemiquaver cadenza for the first violin (bars 28f.) which turn into a quite unexpected unison in *forte* in the same fast pace. The 'cello is given characteristic arpeggios which cut through the texture: the first time to lead into the restatement of the main theme at bar 36, the second time *with* the main theme (bar 40).

If the beginning of the Minuet has that sturdy emphasis on each crotchet, and that

2 + 2 + 2 division of slurs in the first violin ♩♩ ♩♩ ♩♩ , which combine to produce

the typical sound of a Haydn minuet, there seems little doubt that the phrase

derives from the third movement of Mozart's Quartet, K.387:

And can it be an accident that the Finale of our A major Quartet, which begins as if it were a normal rondo, has in its theme the following progression:

That in itself is just one more tribute to Haydn's young admirer, but what about that unprecedented double fugato that suddenly breaks into bar 60? We are still with K.387 and its elaborate contrapuntal development in the Finale.

It is a great final movement, as fine in its way as that of K.387.

OPUS 55, NO. 2

This Quartet opens with one of Haydn's new specialities, a double variation movement in alternating F minor and F major. The F minor melody is not tragic but of a quiet, melancholic beauty which grows on the listener. The F major foil is one of Haydn's most sweetly Italianate tunes and is constructed upon the skeletal image of that in F minor:

---

1 Op. cit., vol. 6 (1937), pp. 14f.

[Andante o più tosto Allegretto]

etc.

For all its exquisite beauty, the movement seems long in performance, and even Sir Donald Tovey suggested making a cut, whereby 'at the second (i.e. last) variation of the major theme, [we] omit the unvaried first statement of its first eight bars, and begin it immediately with the fresh tone of the 'cello. This would lose nothing, and would save the movement from dragging' (op. cit., p. 544).

The second movement (F minor, *alla breve*) is original, gruff and has an astounding modulation from F minor, followed by $2\frac{3}{4}$ bars of silence, and the main theme in G flat (bar 19). The gruppetto ♫♩ – another Haydn 'fingerprint', by the way, also its abbreviation ∞ as used in the slow movement (see musical example, *supra*) – is of central importance here. The long rest comes in the development to mark an equally bold jump, from A flat to A major (bars 84ff.). After following the music's bold impetuosity, one is rather surprised to see it ending in F major; but this is now Haydn's way, and in F major we remain (except for the Trio).

It is said that this was the Quartet Haydn gave to the British publisher who was visiting Eszterháza. Haydn was shaving with bad razors and exclaimed, 'I'd give my best quartet for a pair of good razors'. Bland, thinking this manna from Eszterháza, raced back to his *Gasthaus* and presented Haydn with two English razors. In return, he received this new Quartet. The story (Pohl II, 235) is probably apocryphal, but Bland really was at Eszterháza, as we shall see, and certainly took away the autograph of *Arianna a Naxos* and a contract for the lovely flute trios (piano, flute, 'cello). If Bland was the astute man one believes he was, he will have relished the Minuet of the 'Razor' Quartet, which is one of the most original Haydn ever wrote in a quartet. It starts out as a duet between violin I and viola; it then turns into a trio (violin I, violin II, 'cello) with the identical music differently apportioned, and finally all four instruments play together. The second part is like a development and the music never returns at all to the pattern of the beginning. In other words this is a *durchkomponiertes Menuett*, and nothing quite like it would ever appear again in Haydn's quartets. The Finale, on the other hand, is a more conventional display of Haydn's talents in a typical six-eight *Kehraus*, but as we might expect there are endless details to delight, not least the bouncing octaves with grace notes (bars 43f., 99f.) which look forward to later Haydn.

OPUS 55, NO. 3

The suave opening theme of the fast 3/4 Vivace assai is one of those unisons which break into four-part harmony immediately thereafter and are also organized *p* (unison), *f* (harmony). It is a closely knit movement in which it can be demonstrated that all the thematic material is interrelated. The most striking part is the curious second subject (bars 45ff.) –

– which has something slightly ominous about it, also when it is (in the development, bars 100ff.) first played in its original form and then given with the melody above. The recapitulation continues the development – Haydn was obviously experimenting with the possibilities of *durchkomponierte* movements at this period – even to the point where the theme of the second subject is first given normally and then the melody inverted

One cannot escape the suspicion that these technical innovations are in part aides to a slightly flagging inspiration; nor does the rest of the work – good, but not great, Haydn – fulfil the expectations aroused by Op. 54, Nos. 1 and 2. It is probably no accident that Op. 55 *in toto* has never achieved the public appeal of its immediate numerical predecessors.[1]

Piano Trios for Vienna and London Nos. 20–30
(XV:7–17; 1785–90)

Principal sources: No. 20: (1) Autograph, formerly Thomas G. Odling, London, sold by Sotheby in the Spring of 1977 to antiquarian bookseller Hassfurther, Vienna. It is signed and dated 1785 (and marked 'Fine Laus Deo'). Watermarks: chain lines *c.* 3 cm. apart; three crescents of decreasing size, 'REAL' and 'CS' (1st and 3rd *Bögen*); 2nd *Bögen*: 'GF', crescents and 'REAL', chain lines 2.2 cm. apart. On page one at the bottom Haydn wrote out, presumably for the engraver, the three principal ornaments used: *tr*: ✱ and ∾ . (2) Nos. 19–21 printed in an authentic edition in parts by Artaria & Co., Vienna, pl. no. 75, announced in the *Wiener Zeitung* on 26 April 1786. Copy in Gesellschaft der Musikfreunde, Vienna. Dedicated to Countess Witzay (Viczay). 'Oeuvre 40me.'

No. 21: Artaria print.

No. 22: (1) Autograph, Preussische Staatsbibliothek, Berlin, Mus. ms. autogr. Jos. Haydn 41, signed and dated 1785 (end marked 'Fine Laus Deo'). Watermarks: three crescents of decreasing size, 'REAL', 'CS'. (2) MS. parts sent by Haydn to Forster in 1785 together with Nos. 17 and 23, marked on parts '2d. Recueil 28 Oct. 1785' (perhaps date sent by Haydn?), arrived in London on 26 December 1785. British Museum, Egerton 2379. (3) Forster's ed. ('Op. 42': Nos. 23, 22, 17). Copy: British Museum.

No. 23: as in sources (2) and (3) of No. 22. A second authentic print is that of Hoffmeister, Vienna, pl. no. 33, 1786. Copy: Gesellschaft der Musikfreunde, Vienna.

Nos. 24–6: Authentic first edition by Artaria & Co., Vienna, pl. no. 239, 'Oeuvre 57^{m[e]}', announ-ced in the *Wiener Zeitung* on 1 July 1789. Copy in Gesellschaft der Musikfreunde, Vienna.

No. 27: (1) Authentic first edition by Artaria & Co., Vienna, pl. no. 327, 'Oeuvre 61', Copy in Gesellschaft der Musikfreunde, Vienna, October 1790. (2) Authentic edition by Longman & Broderip, 1792 'as performed by Master Hummel at Mr. Salomon's Concerts'. Copy in British Museum.

No. 28: (1) Authentic edition by John Bland, London in his series 'Le tout ensemble', No. 16, 1790. Copy in British Museum. With the note: 'Advertisement. This & the Two following Trios were wrote at the particular request of the Publisher when he was with Mr. Haydn last [1789], at which time he settled Connection with him, Messrs. Hoffmeister, Kozeluch, Mozart, Vanhall &c. &c. whose Works will come out in this manner with all possible expedition: they are absolute property and Enter'd as such; J. Bland thinks this sufficient notice to other Publishers not to pirate the same.' (2) Authentic edition by Artaria & Co., Vienna, Oeuvre 63, pl. no. 330. Copy in Gesellschaft der Musikfreunde, Vienna. Artaria issued Nos. 28 and 29 in reverse order; we follow Bland's order.

No. 29: as in No. 28. Bland series, No. 13. Artaria op. 62, pl. no. 329.

No. 30: as in No. 28. One copy of Bland's print (series, No. 14) with Haydn's signature, obviously made when the composer was in England, was sold by Leo Liepmannsohn, Verst. Kat. 52 (1928), item 250. Artaria's edition is not authentic and was not issued until 1792 (*Wiener Zeitung*, 22 September).

1 Literature: Apart from the references in the standard literature (for which consult Hoboken), see Sondheimer, op. cit. for all these works. Tovey, op. cit., pp. 543f. Gray, op. cit., vols. 6 (1937) and 8 (1939). Barrett-Ayres, pp. 228ff.

Haydn's works 1785–1790

An extensive sketch of the development section (1st movt.) was sold by G. P. Romer (Hertford) – see his catalogue 86, item 49. Now owned by Baroness Schey. Of these flute trios, we would also mention an interesting MS. (which we used) of No. 29 in the Gesellschaft der Musikfreunde, from the collection of Archduke Rudolph, dated 1790, which in fact turns out to be a copy of the Artaria print.

Critical editions: Complete Piano Trios, Verlag Doblinger, Vienna and Munich, 1968 *et seq.* (these 'middle' trios completed in publication by 1976). *Joseph Haydn Werke*, Reihe XVII, Band 2 (Wolfgang Stockmeier), 1976.

Although these piano trios were all written either in response to a commission or speculatively for possible publication by Viennese (Artaria) and London (Forster, Bland) music publishers, one can see Haydn becoming more and more interested in the form, which (as we have said earlier) he treated in the then convention of 'sonatas for the pianoforte, with an accompaniment of a violin & violoncello'. Gradually they almost entirely eclipsed Haydn's interest in the piano sonata which, except for three isolated works of this period and the series of three composed in England for Therese Jansen-Bartolozzi, gradually fades out of Haydn's life. The variety, charm and intellectual vigour of these piano trios of the 1780s belies the small form in which they were deliberately written. Some are in the old trio sonata form, with opening slow movement (No. 20); some adapt this form by having only two movements, an opening adagio and a concluding fast movement (Nos. 22, 26); and some have an opening allegro and a concluding quick movement (Nos. 21 and 24, finishing with a 'Tempo di Menuetto'; No. 23, finishing with an even faster movement, Presto assai). From the above notes, the formal variety can be observed to be infinite.

Of course, they were deliberately designed for the cultivated amateur, such as Haydn's neighbour, Countess Vizcay; but though they are not very difficult technically, he never wrote 'down' to these amateurs, known and unknown. As we progress to the end of the decade, a certain melancholy seems to creep into the music – as it did in the notturni, symphonies (No. 92) and quartets (Op. 64). The works in minor key all end in the major, as was now Haydn's standard practice, but *within* the works in major, we encounter whole development sections of a seriousness and *tristesse* which one would never expect from the main subjects. This is especially the case with the beautiful and popular Flute Trios of 1790. In No. 28, the sprightly theme

hardly prepares us for the long minor passage in the development, using fragments of the second and first subjects. The second movement in D minor continues this same atmosphere of quiet melancholy: it shows Haydn's appreciation of this aspect of the *flauto traverso*, too, and this ambivalence is a typical eighteenth-century trait. The flute was always a pastoral intrument, associated with shepherds and enchanted gardens, but somehow, in the second part of the century, it also took on overtones of that *tristezza* which is actually as much a part of the *settecento* as its courtly formality. And the same procedure occurs in Trio No. 30, where the perky dotted opening theme hardly leads us to expect the dramatic development section, where Haydn relishes the newly found bass sonority of his fortepiano.

Haydn had no time to write piano trios during his first visit to London, but when he returned in 1794 he again took up this form and carried it to a new level of depth and beauty.

Piano Sonatas for Vienna and Leipzig Nos. 57–59 (XVI:47–49; 1788–90); smaller piano music: Fantasia in C (XVII:4; 1789), and VI Variations (XVII:5; 1790)

Principal sources: Sonata No. 57 in F. Haydn took the second and third movements from a much earlier Sonata (No. 19), transposed them into F and added a new opening movement. Authentic first edition: Artaria & Co., pl. no. 190, 'Oeuvre 55', announced in the *Wiener Zeitung* on 12 July 1788.

No. 58 in C. Authentic first edition, Breitkopf & Härtel, as first number of 'Musikalisches Pot-Pourri', September 1789.

No. 59 in E flat. (1) Autograph, completed on '1 Juny 790' and signed 'Fine Laus Deo', Stadtbibliothek, Vienna, MH 4177/c. Watermarks: bow-and-arrow, three crescents of decreasing size, letters 'A M', from mill of Andrea Mattizzoli, northern Italy. The dedication on the autograph reads: 'Sonata per il Forte-piano Composta per la stimatissima Signora Anna de Jerlischek', about whom *vide infra*, p. 738. (2) MS. copy, Parisian private possession, signed by Haydn 'Sonate del Jos: Haydn mpria 7^{tia} Martz 791' (from a photograph kindly supplied by Dr A. van Hoboken). (3) Authentic printed edition, Artaria & Co., Vienna, pl. no. 352, announced in the *Wiener Zeitung* on 31 August 1791. Copies of

Artaria editions for Nos. 57 and 59: Gesellschaft der Musikfreunde, Vienna. Breitkopf edition of No. 58: Stadtbibliothek, Leipzig.

Critical editions: Breitkopf & Härtel *Joseph Haydns Werke*, Serie XIV, Bd. 3 (Karl Päsler, 1919). *Wiener Urtextausgabe* (Complete Sonatas, vol. 3) (Christa Landon, 1964). *Joseph Haydn Werke*, Complete Sonatas, vol. 3 (G. Feder, 1973; also reprinted by Henle Verlag).

Fantasia in C (XVII:4): authentic first edition by Artaria & Co., Vienna, pl. no. 250, announced in the *Wiener Zeitung* on 5 September 1789. Copies in Gesellschaft der Musikfreunde, Vienna, and Burgenländisches Landesmuseum, Eisenstadt.

VI Variations in C (XVII:5): authentic first edition by Artaria & Co., Vienna, pl. no. 250, announced in the *Wiener Zeitung* on 9 February 1791. Copy in Gesellschaft der Musikfreunde, Vienna.

Critical editions: Henle Verlag, Munich-Duisburg (Sonja Gerlach, 1970). *Wiener Urtextausgabe*, Vienna (Franz Eibner, 1975).

Sonata No. 57, put together from a pretty E minor Sonata of the 1760s with a new opening movement, is patently a work for Haydn's pupils. Its first movement is so uninspired that one wonders why Haydn bothered to publish it at this late date, but he probably felt that the Sonata in E minor, with its opening slow movement, needed to be brought up to date in some fashion; hence the new first Moderato.

Sonata No. 58 is quite another affair. Its opening, marked Andante con espressione, is of the highest improvisatory order, with a wonderful sense of freedom. Haydn composed it for Breitkopf & Härtel, as will be related in the Chronicle (p. 719), and he seems to have taken especial pains for what was probably his first commissioned work for Germany. The first thing that strikes us is the careful attention to dynamic marks, here found in profusion. The use of *pp* shows that Haydn was becoming ever more conscious of the special tonal characteristics of the fortepiano as opposed to the harpsichord. If, as we think, many of the previous sonatas (which have crescendos, and so on) were written with an English spinet-form piano in mind, surely No. 58 and all the other works from now on, were composed with a grand fortepiano in mind.

The 'A' section occupies 26 bars and is in the usual two parts. 'B' is in C minor, with a frequent exploitation of the piano's lower range (Haydn's new and exciting tonal discovery), e.g. bars 34–6, 45f. 'A' returns, endlessly varied and with the same delight in the piano's lower range (bars 73f.). This is music for the piano totally different than any Haydn had written before. If we had thought, listening to the Sonata up to this point, that we were confronted with a slow opening movement in (say) A-B-A form, we underestimate Haydn's ability to surprise also on the formal level. At the end of A' we find B', also in C minor, but with the tension and speed increasing as we move first into regular semiquavers for the accompaniment, then semiquaver sextuplets. The third statement of A is a kind of coda.

The Finale is a huge and powerfully developed rondo which looks forward to the kind of piano writing normally associated with the London period: octaves in the right hand, Clementi-like doublings in the left –

– here is music that does not in the least sound like Mozart. Nor does the tense section in C minor (bars 122ff.) which, if anything, is an uncanny foretaste of Beethoven.

With this brilliant work, Haydn established an entirely new piano style, and one which he would cultivate with great success in England.

Sonata No. 59, dedicated to Prince Esterházy's housekeeper and later Johann Tost's wife, was really written for the delicate hands of Frau von Genzinger, whose pianistic abilities must have been, judging from this Sonata, considerable. There is the same world of difference between this and the final E flat Sonata of 1794 for Therese Jansen, as there is between the Op. 64 Quartets of 1790 and the Opp. 71/74 Quartets of 1793. In this Sonata, there is a sense of leisure, of unlimited time, which the experiences of Haydn's first *Großstadt* would change for ever. There is even a certain old-fashioned quality, for instance in the Baroque sequences that open the development section. But

the most striking part of this movement originates in the figure ⁊♩♩♩ | ♩ at the end

of the exposition. In the development Haydn takes this 'rhythmic lead' and gives us a passage of remarkable tension (bars 108ff.), once again exploiting the lowest range of the piano.

Haydn wrote the first movement round the last two, which were already known to Maria Anna von Genzinger; but this is no potboiler for Artaria in the manner of Sonata No. 57, and this slow movement is one of exceptional depth and beauty. At the beginning of the second section, there is a rhapsodic and intense passage with rolling semiquaver sextuplets in the right hand that is almost Schubertian (B flat minor). In another technical device which Haydn first used to a large extent in the Finale of Sonata No. 33 (1771), the left hand crosses the right. Frau von Genzinger could not negotiate this passage and it is presumed Haydn had to rewrite it for her; or he taught her how to play it when he next went to Vienna.

The Finale, marked 'Tempo di Minuet' (Haydn's spelling), has a fine passage in E flat minor, which Frau von Genzinger will have found difficult (six flats). It too has a sense of slow time, of a leisurely growth (seen in the gradual incorporation of triplets instead of even quavers, for instance), of a certain way of life that was surely much slower than that which Haydn was about to enter.

The Fantasia in C is a brilliant showpiece and Haydn's tribute to C. P. E. Bach, whose fantasias were famous and much admired. It is in the new fast tempo–fast metre, in this case Presto 3/8, and is a work of vast proportions (423 bars) which is, however, not long in duration because of the speed with which the music flashes past us. Haydn experiments in numerous ways. One of the most astonishing is his use of what Beethoven would have called 'ritmo di tre battute'. This occurs as follows. The basic beat of the music is extended to cover three bars at a time, *viz*.

(and the right hand pursues a melodic pattern which makes it quite clear that this is Haydn's intention). This group of three bars occurs no less than four times in a row. Later Haydn extends it to four × four bars, then shortens it to four × two bars. Another innovation of a different nature is Haydn's exploitation of the piano's sonority. He dashes down a series of semiquavers and arrives at the following (l.h.)

The first three bars are marked 'tenuto in tanto finchè non si sente più il sono'. Holding the *e* until the sound dies away entirely is, of course, easier on Haydn's fortepiano of the 1780s than on our large instruments, but the effect can be made by judicious gradation of tone (i.e., not hitting the *e* too heavily). The effect is to introduce the surprise modulation to F. The next time Haydn uses this device, he has moved to low *f* sharp (a note, in the lower octave, above the lowest note of which the piano was then capable): 'tenuto come prima' and then the *g* (as before, *mutatis mutandis*).

The pretty little set of six variations that Haydn composed in haste just before he left for England require no special comment. Ingenious as they are, we know that the greatest variations Haydn ever wrote for piano – the *Andante con variazioni* (Sonata) – are fast approaching. With so much else to choose from, we shall not concern ourselves in any detail with these *opere minori*.

'Deutschlands Klage' (XXVIb:1; 1786); Cantata, 'Arianna a Naxos' (XXVIb:2); and Cantata, 'Miseri noi' (XXIVa:7)

'Deutschlands Klage auf den Tod des Großen Friedrichs Borußens König' is the title of the only known extant source of this work, now in the Preussische Staatsbibliothek, Berlin (Mus. ms. 9940). We have seen that Carl Franz played it at a concert in Nuremberg in 1788. In the *Museum für Künstler* . . ., edited by J. G. Mensel, Mannheim 1788 (p. 100), this Cantata is praised as a 'Meisterstück rührender Harmonie'. Pohl suggests (II, 222) that two former Esterházy artists, Constanza Valdesturla (soprano) and Carl Franz (baryton) performed it at a Gewandhaus Concert in Leipzig on 4 February 1788. The Berlin source gives us only the soprano and bass line, with the text of course, but without the crucial baryton solo. The text begins 'Er ist nicht mehr! Tön traurend Bariton!' The music, in 3/4 time, has no tempo in this section but probably Adagio is meant. The melody has something of the Masonic E flat touch in it (*Die Zauberflöte*). There is a middle section in A flat (Andantino, 2/4) and a return to the first section. More, in view of the work's incomplete state, cannot be said at this time.

Arianna a Naxos. As a subject, the story of Ariadne has always fascinated composers, from the Renaissance (Monteverdi) to the present day (Richard Strauss). Haydn's autograph, said to have been dated 1789, was last seen at the auction of Puttick & Simpson (sale of the Joseph Warren Collection). There are, however, two authentic printed editions:

Principal sources: (1) Authentic printed score by Artaria & Co., Vienna, pl. no. 316, announced on 21 August 1790 in the *Wiener Zeitung* (Artaria first assigned the number 283 to this work, and some copies still have it; 283 was then given to Mozart's Quintet in C, K.515). Copy: Gesellschaft der Musikfreunde, Vienna. (2) Authentic printed score, published by Haydn (signed by him) and later distributed by Bland, announced in the *Morning Herald* on 6 June 1791. Copy in the British Museum.

Critical edition: Haydn-Mozart Presse 197 (M. Flothius, 1968).

If Haydn had happened to score this dramatic work for a large orchestra – such as he would do with the *Scena di Berenice* (1795) – this Cantata would have been an ideal concert piece for a singer making a guest appearance with an orchestra.[1] Rossini who, when he was in Vienna, studied Haydn's operas at some private collector's (Aloys Fuchs?) and thought them dreadful, said to Ferdinand Hiller[2] that apart from the oratorios, *Arianna* 'is my favourite vocal work [of Haydn]; especially the Adagio is very beautiful.' This was, as we have said, one of the few vocal works of the pre-*Creation* era that was circulated in MS. all over Italy.

It is composed in a way similar to *Berenice*:

(1) Accompanied recitative, Largo e sostenuto: 'Teseo mio ben'. E flat.
(2) Aria (Largo) 'Dove sei, mio bel tesoro', B flat, with a wonderfully expressive melody (this is the 'Adagio' to which Rossini refers) – broken off, leading to
(3) Recitative, 'ma, a chi parla?', leading (with two tempo changes, Andante and Adagio) to
(4) Aria (Larghetto), 'ah che morir vorrei', F major, broken off and leading to
(5) Aria (Presto), 'Misera abbandonata', F minor (complete aria).

It is interesting that, as in *Berenice*, Haydn used a scheme of progressive tonality, beginning in E flat and ending in F minor (*Berenice*: D major to F minor). The recitatives are handled with Haydn's usual detailed attention to declamation, expression and his grasp of large vocal forms (total length: 368 bars). We cannot imagine for whom he originally composed this work in 1789, and speculation along these lines is idle The voice is a kind of mezzo-soprano with high notes (much like Celia's original role in *La fedeltà premiata*). The final Aria is in Haydn's preferred key of F minor, which he had used, of course, for *Sturm und Drang* music (1768, 1772) but also in serious vocal parts of this period – e.g. in *L'infedeltà delusa* (1773) and in the powerful *scena* for tenor in Traetta's *Ifigenia in Tauride*, 'Ah! tu non senti, amico' (1786), which ends in a big F minor Aria. There are other examples as well.

CANTATA, 'MISERI NOI' (XXIVa:7)

This Cantata is scored for soprano solo, 1 flute (a second flute was added by Haydn when he was in England), 2 oboes, 2 bassoons, 2 horns and strings.

Principal sources: (1) Score on 'small post paper' by an EH copyist, signed by Haydn 'Cantata' 'del giuseppe Haydn mpria', Library of Congress, Washington, D.C., ML 96, H 36 H, Case. Breaks off after bar 163. (2) MS. score from the Martorell Collection, Library of Congress (vol. 94). *Critical edition*: Diletto Musicale 17, Verlag Doblinger, Vienna-Munich (Landon, 1960); also pocket score Stp. 161. Lists watermarks etc.

This is one of those many vocal works that Haydn took to England, performed there, and usually enriched by adding the occasional instrument that he did not have in Hungary – in this case a second flute. It must have been composed in or before 1790. We have no clue if this was an insertion scene for one of the Eszterháza operas, as seems likely, nor do we know for whom it could have otherwise been composed. The fact that an Italian score exists in the pre-London state (i.e. with one flute) suggests that one of the Esterháza singers took it back to Italy: the watermarks of the Martorell MS. suggest that the score is of Neapolitan origin (there are similar watermarks on the large autograph collection of Cimarosa opera and religious scores in the Library of

1 The Library of Congress owns an old MS. from the Martorell Collection with strings instead of piano; MI505.AI. vol. 94.
2 *Aus dem Tonleben unserer Zeit*, vol. II (1867), p. 30.

Congress). The 'small post paper' score was used for laying out a print of the music ('one line', 'two lines'); but no edition before our own has ever been discovered.

This is Haydn's most important piece in this form (apart from the large scenes in his operas, such as Celia's in Atto II° of *La fedeltà premiata*, 'Ah, come il core'). It is constructed as follows:

(1) Long orchestral introduction (Adagio), leading to

(2) Entrance of soprano and recitativo accompagnato (with various changes of tempo), leading to

(3) Slow section (Largo), 'Sentomi intorno' – a kind of recitative mixed with 'arioso', leading to the

(4) Slow Aria (Largo assai), 'Funesto orror di morte', which turns into Allegro moderato, 'Già la fatal sua sorte'.

The point that strikes the modern listener is the curious way in which the text is treated: the scene describes a city devastated, its walls a smoking ruin. The music that describes this is stately but by no means tragic (beginning). The most interesting section is the slow 'section' (as we called it), with its rich divided violas. Here, in the violins, we have strong reminiscences of Mozart's Symphony in G minor, slow movement (the part that haunted Haydn all his life: he used it touchingly in the last part of *The Seasons*: see *Haydn: the Late Years 1801–1809*, pp. 180f.):

Similarly, the slow section of the Aria has a rather serene E flat music that seems to our twentieth-century ears at odd variance with the grim text, 'Funesto orror di morte'. The concluding quick section develops a markedly nervous sense of pace, with a whole variety of *fz* and, especially, *ff*. A real sense of drama is in that sinister music at bars 133ff., which for the first time really does describe 'Funesto orror di morte'. There follows a series of bravura passages for this dramatic soprano part with the coloratura that was taken for granted for any tessitura in those days. It turns out to be musically a highly effective Cantata, if we do not expect something else from the words. In that respect, the music presages Orfeo's Aria in the last act of *L'anima del filosofo* (1791). If Haydn was ruthless with his Italian colleagues' music at Eszterháza, his own operas are in many respects (especially in a work like this) more Italian than the Italians'.

The first performance in modern times took place in connection with the series 'The unknown Haydn' which we gave for the B.B.C. in 1958: Jennifer Vyvyan (soprano) was accompanied by the London Symphony Orchestra, conducted by Charles Mackerras.

Insertion Arias 1785–1790 (XXIVb:7–19; XXXII:1)

Since the principal sources of the insertion arias are no longer contained in the EH materials of the operas for which they were written, we give a brief list here *omitting* those sources which do appear in the EH parts and which will be listed in their proper place. With a few exceptions, all these arias have been edited by us for the Haydn-Mozart Presse (score, piano score, parts); the exceptions are: (1) 'Dica pure chi vuol dire' (XXIVb:8) for Anfossi's *Il geloso in cimento* (1785); (2) 'La mia pace, oh Dio' (XXIVb:19) for Gassmann's *L'amore artigiano* (1790); and (3) a fragmentary Aria

(XXIVb:16*bis*), of which neither the vocal part nor the text has survived, in the same work by Gassmann.

'Signor, voi sapete' (sop., fl., 2 ob., 2 bsn., 2 hn., str.), Aria di Rosina (XXIVb:7) in Pasquale Anfossi's *Il matrimonio per inganno* (1785).
Further sources: (1) Score from Haydn's library, EH, Budapest, Ms. mus. I. 158. (2) Score from Aloys Fuchs's Coll., Göttweig Abbey. (3) First (authentic?) edition by Artaria, pl. no. 101, 1787 as 'Raccolta d'Arie favorite No. 1'. For voice and piano. Gesellschaft der Musikfreunde, Vienna.

'Dica pure chi vuol dire' (sop., 2 ob., 2 bsn., 2 hn., str.), Aria (for ?) (XXIVb:8) in Pasquale Anfossi's *Il geloso in cimento* (1785).
Further source: First (authentic?) edition by Artaria, ibid., 'No. 2'.

'Sono Alcina' (sop., fl., 2 ob., 2 bsn., 2 hn., str.), Aria di Alcina (XXIVb:9) in Giuseppe Gazzaniga's *L'isola d'Alcina* (1786).
Further source: Autograph, Captain Rudolph Nydahl, Stockholm, signed and dated 1786.

'Ah, tu non senti, amico' (Rec.) & 'Qual destra omicida' (Aria), *Scena di Oreste* (XXIVb:10) for tenor, fl., 2 ob., 2 bsn., 2 hn., str. in Tommaso Traetta's *Ifigenia in Tauride* (1786).
Further sources: (1) Sketch to Rec., Pierpont Morgan Library, New York. (2) Autogaph, EH, Budapest (from Haydn's legacy), Ms. mus. I. 11, signed and dated 1786 and marked at end, 'Fine Laus Deo'.

'Un cor si tenero' (bass, 2 ob., 2 hn., str.), Aria di Corradino (XXIVb:11) in Francesco Bianchi's *Il disertore* (1787).
Further source: Autograph, EH, Budapest (from Haydn's legacy), Ms. mus. I. 12, signed and dated 1787 and marked at end, 'Fine Laus Deo'.

'Vada adagio, Signorina' (sop., 2 ob., 2 bsn., 2 hn., str.), Aria di Cardellina (XXIVb:12) in Pietro Guglielmi's *La quaquera spiritosa* (1787).
Further source: Authentic MS. score from the Esterházy circle, Princely Fürstenberg Archives, Donaueschingen.

'Chi vive amante' (sop., fl., 2 ob., 2 bsn., 2 hn., str.), Aria di Erissena (XXIVb:13) in Francesco Bianchi's *Alessandro nell'Indie* (1787).
Further source: Autograph, Stadtbibliothek, Vienna, MH 6390/c, signed 'Aria # 3' and dated 1787 and with no final remarks at end.
Further critical edition: Musikwissenschaftlicher Verlag, Leipzig (Alfred Orel, 1937).

'Se tu mi sprezzi, ingrata' (tenor, 2 ob., bsn., 2 hn., str.), Aria del Cavaliere (XXIVb:14) in Giuseppe Sarti's *I finti eredi* (1788).
Further sources: (1) Autograph, EH, Budapest (from Haydn's legacy), Ms. mus. I. 13, signed and dated 1788 with no final remarks at end. (2) MS.

score, Preussische Staatsbibliothek as No. 16 in a score of Cimarosa's *Il marito disperato*. (3) MS. score, Gymnasialbibliothek, Zittau: 'Cavatina I di Haydn' with different orchestration (Hoboken, vol. II, p. 214: we have not seen this source). (4) MS. score, Conservatoire de Musique, Brussels (we have not seen this source).

'Infelice sventurata' (sop., 2 ob., 2 bsn., 2 hn., str.), Aria di Beatrice (XXIVb:15) in Domenico Cimarosa's *I due supposti conti* (1789).
Further sources: (1) Autograph, EH, Budapest (from Haydn's legacy), Ms. mus. I. 14, signed and dated 1789 and with 'Fine Laus Deo' at end. (2) Two MS. scores from the Esterházy circle, Österreichische Nationalbibliothek S.M. 9840 (from the 'Kaiserliche Sammlung'). (3) MS. score, Conservatoire de Musique, Brussels (we have not seen this source).

'Da che penso a maritarmi' (tenor, fl., 2 ob., 2 bsn., 2 hn., str.), Aria di Titta (XXIVb:16) in Florian Leopold Gassmann's *L'amore artigiano* (1790).
Further source: Autograph, EH, Budapest (from Haydn's legacy), Ms. mus. I. 15, signed and dated 1790; at end 'Laus Deo'.

Text? Insertion Aria (Haydn?) in *L'amore artigiano* (XXIVb:16*bis*; 1790). *Vide infra*, p. 733.

'La mia pace, oh Dio' (sop., 2 ob., 2 bsn., 2 hn., str.), Aria di Costanza (XXIVb:19) in Gassmann's *L'amore artigiano* (1790).
Only known source: Autograph, Campori Collection, Biblioteca Estense, Modena, with title 'Aria [red crayon: 25, *vide infra*, p.650]. In Nomine Domini di me giuseppe Haydn mpria 790'; at end: 'Fini[s] Laus Deo.' The watermarks (bow-and-arrow, 'AM', 'REAL', crescents) = those of the Aria di Titta.

'Il meglio mio carattere' (sop., fl., 2 ob., 2 bsn., 2 hn., str.), Aria di Merlina (XXIVb:17) in Domenico Cimarosa's *L'impresario in angustie* (1790).
Only known source: MS. score by Johann Elssler, Silverstolpe Collection, Näs Castle, Sweden.

'La moglie quando è buona' (sop., fl., 2 ob., 2 bsn., 2 hn., str.), Aria di Giannina (XXIVb:18) in Domenico Cimarosa's *Giannina e Bernardone* (1790).
Further sources: (1) Score by Anonymous 11 (Esterházy copyist), from Haydn's legacy, EH, Budapest, Ms. mus. I. 155. (2) MS. score from the Aloys Fuchs Coll., Göttweig Abbey. (3) Two authentic scores by Esterházy copyists, Österreichische Nationalbibliothek (from the 'Kaiserliche Sammlung'): S.M. 9837 is a copy by Anon. 63.

648

Music written for the anonymous pasticcio *La Circe* (1789; XXXII:1):

Scena (Pedrillo, bass; fl., 2 ob., str.), 'Son due ore che giro'. Autograph in the material (see Chronicle). First edition, with recording (Joseph Réti, Hungarian State Concert Orchestra, cond. Erwin Lukács; Qualiton LPM 1561), Bartha-Somfai, suppl. vol., 1960.

Aria di Lindora, 'Son pietosa' (sop., fl., 2 ob., 2 bsn., 2 hn., str.).
Further sources: (1) MS. score by an Esterházy copyist, Göttweig Abbey (*ex. coll.* Aloys Fuchs). (2) MS. score by ditto, Silverstolpe Coll., Näs Castle, Sweden. (3) Authentic MS. score by an English copyist, Burgenländisches Landesmuseum (*ex. coll.* Landon), given by Haydn to Caecilia Maria Barthélémon. (4) MS. piano-vocal score by Antonio Polzelli (?), Fitzwilliam Museum, Cambridge.
Critical edition: Verlag Doblinger, Diletto Musicale 19 (Landon, 1959).

Terzetto (Teodora, Brunoro, Corrado; fl., 2 ob., 2 bsn., 2 hn., str.), 'Levatevi presto'.
Further sources: (1) MS. score from Johann Traeg's office, *ex. coll.* Aloys Fuchs, Göttweig Abbey. (2) MS. score by Anonymous 63, Hochschule Graz, cat. 40640. (3) Arranged for piano and shortened 'per me Pietro Polzelli', EH, Budapest, Ms. mus. I. 150/a. Other arrangements (as in Donaueschingen, Fürstenberg Archives) are not listed. See Hoboken XVI:Es1, and vol. II, pp. 592f. Unpublished.

Three of these arias are known to have been composed for Haydn's mistress, Luigia Polzelli ('Signor, voi sapete'; 'Chi vive amante'; 'Il meglio mio carattere'), and probably some of the others, about which we now lack precise information, were for her as well. She had a kind of soubrette voice, and Haydn wrote very characteristic music for her – light, ironic, charming. Sometimes her arias are in the same tempo throughout (Aria di Erissena, 'Chi vive amante'); but usually Haydn starts in a slow tempo and then finishes in a six-eight 'parlando' fast tempo, and this pattern can be found in other soprano arias too, such as the delightful 'Vada adagio, Signorina' which we found at Donaueschingen Castle in 1957 and which proved to be an uproarious success at the Salzburg Festival, 1959 (Rita Streich, Camerata Accademica conducted by Bernhard Paumgartner). It was as a result of this performance that the Haydn-Mozart Presse decided to print the whole series.

'Infelice sventurata' is a wonderfully dramatic piece for a big voice like that of the late Maria Callas; the work is in two parts, a slow introduction and a final allegro in the new quick metre (barred C) which contains what must be an entirely fortuitous quotation of Mozart's G minor Symphony:

Giannina's Aria, 'La moglie quando è buona', which sounds like a Polzelli piece (the cast for this Cimarosa opera is not known), is a slice of high comedy: 'Gelosi maritati a me sentite: le moglie mai ristrette non lasciate' is the beginning of the section marked Allegro assai, in barred C, which contains the delightful doggerel

– 'la fortuna del geloso con la luna sempre va' (the jealous one's fortunes follow the moon's progress). One cannot escape the feeling that Haydn's sympathy was peculiarly attuned to this ironic side of *opera buffa*.

'Ah, tu non senti, amico' is the beginning of a splendid and dramatic tenor scene for the tragic *opera seria* by Traetta, *Ifigenia in Tauride* – then a much admired work on a libretto by Marco Coltellini (Vienna, 1763), who wrote the book for *L'infedeltà delusa.* The F minor Aria 'Qual destra' is in the grand *seria* tradition. 'Se tu mi sprezzi, ingrata' is in what one might call Haydn's 'shining' tenor style (Poco adagio, barred C), with great innate nobility, as indeed befits the protagonist ('Cavaliere'). The third tenor Aria is a witty *buffo* piece, 'Da che penso a maritarmi', for one of the Prince's old favourites, Gassmann's *L'amore artigiano* which Haydn revived in 1790 to cheer up Prince Nicolaus, crushed by his wife's death. Haydn wrote three new arias for the occasion, of which one ('La mia pace'), with a lovely Adagio opening and an Allegro conclusion, was recently discovered in the interesting Campori Collection in the Biblioteca Estense, Modena (from which same collection an unknown Beethoven letter to Countess Guicciardi also emerged). 'La mia pace' is not yet published.

Haydn had a special affinity with the bass voice, as we know, and 'Un cor si tenero' is a beautiful bass aria for one of Bianchi's greatest operatic successes, *Il disertore*, given at Eszterháza in 1787.

The most curious case of Haydn's 'massive intervention' occurs in the *pasticcio* opera, *La Circe*, for which Haydn wrote a number of pieces (more than in Bartha-Somfai or Hoboken; *vide infra*, pp. 714f.). Why, in the middle of all his other activities, did he take the trouble almost to rewrite completely this silly *pasticcio*? Obviously he had a strong artistic conscience and as he began to work on the opera, he became interested. The pieces that have survived intact are listed above. In Pedrillo's *scena* we have 'magic' music which sounds like the great scene from the end of *Armida*, but here with a different setting. Pedrillo is outside the impenetrable castle. To weirdly syncopated music (bars 40ff.), 'sorte il cinese' (the Chinaman appears). The appearance of the Turk (bars 77ff.) suggests 'Turkish' music in A minor (as in Mozart's famous Sonata, K.331). A pretty girl ('Oh, che bella ragazza') arrives from the castle in D major, Allegretto, 2/4, and with a suitably attractive melody.

Haydn's Aria for Lindora (Polzelli?) is one of his most seductively beautiful, in the favourite key of E major (Andante – Allegro di molto), with the ironic text ('e pur semplicetta a tutto si crede') to which Haydn was instinctively drawn. But the most astonishing operation in *La Circe* is the stupendous ensemble piece which has come down to us complete in two sources only, one in Göttweig and one in Graz. This large-scale Terzetto, which comprises no less than 545 bars, could grace any of the late Haydn operas. It begins in a fast (Allegro con brio) 6/8 and switches tempo for a final *Vivace assai* with a fine C minor motif:

The text calls for this unusual music in the minor:

a 3

Ma quel rumor io sento,
Un qualche strano evento
Tempo che accaderà.
Via presto su partiamo,
E tutto nascondiamo
Con gran celerità.

A critical edition by the present writer is in preparation by the University of Cardiff Press.

There are two insertion arias for which we can assign neither the opera to which they belonged, nor any other date (beyond the very general one, *c.* 1780–90). They are 'Tornate pur, mia bella cara' and 'Via, state bonino', for tenor and soprano respectively.

'Tornate pur, mia bella cara' (ten., fl., 2 ob., 2 bsn., 2 hn., str.) (XXIVb:22).
Sources: MS. score from the Johann Traeg office, Österreichische Nationalbibliothek, S. m. 9848 and two 19th-century copies in score, one by Aloys Fuchs (now Preussische Staatsbibliothek, Berlin) and a copy the Fuchs score by Pohl (Gesellschaft der Musikfreunde, Vienna).

'Via, state bonino' (sop., fl., 2 ob., 2 bsn., 2 hn., str.) (XXIVb:23).
Source: MS. score by an Esterházy copyist from the Collection of Aloys Fuchs, Göttweig Abbey (Pohl's copy of that source in the Gesellschaft der Musikfreunde, Vienna).

Both of these delightful arias are unpublished. As soon as we have at our disposal *all* the Esterházy libretti – and we have good reason to believe that ninety per cent of them still survive in a hitherto unknown collection – we shall undoubtedly identify these two and possibly other single vocal works as well ('Pietà di me', 'Miseri noi', to name but two candidates). The tenor aria has that wonderful *cantilena* which Haydn often gives his tenors in Adagio settings (this one has a quicker ending), while the soprano aria is in that pert, soubrette style of which Haydn was such a master (having an available mistress with whom, as it were, to practise constantly).

The thread on which these insertion arias survive is often desperately thin (one source), or has broken entirely. If we look at the gaps in the extant Eszterháza operas, it is entirely possible that another dozen insertion arias of Haydn are lost. We must be glad that so many have survived.

These insertion arias are, of course, typical *pièces d'occasion*, but as Mozart said of Haydn, 'even in the most unimportant trifle [*Posse*] you can see the hand of the master.'[1] Haydn had no *need* to compose a large terzetto for a *pasticcio* that, he must have known, would soon disappear from the boards of the Esterházy Theatre for ever, burying with it all the extra music he had composed for it; or to write all those fetching soprano arias *apart* from those for *la* Polzelli (ça va sans dire ...). The presence of all these favours to the singers reveals a very endearing side to Haydn's generous nature.

Pieces for Musical Clock (*Flötenuhr*)
(XIX:16, etc.)

Haydn was attracted to the mechanical aspects of music making, and wrote a vast number of little pieces for the musical clocks that Pater Niemecz built. In *Haydn in England 1791–1795* (pp. 201f.), we have explained that there remains considerable confusion about the dating of these pieces. For one thing, there was no 1772 clock. The autograph of the pretty fugue which, incredibly, Niemecz managed to incorporate in his clock, is dated 1789 and is reproduced here in its entirety. It will serve as our musical example. Another source, in the Gesellschaft der Musikfreunde in Vienna, also gives 1789 as the date for this work and others: 'Acht Laufwerck Sonaten Komponiert von Herrn Kapellmeister Joseph Haydn, und in die Walze gesetzt von Primitiv Niemecz Bibliothekar zu Esterhas 1789 in December' – which also places the clock's date in the Christmas period of 1789 (perhaps a present for Prince Nicolaus, who was addicted to clocks of all kinds?). This discovery means that XIX:1–6, 7, 8, 9, 10, 11, 12–15 and 16

---

1 *Wiener Schriftsteller und Künstler Lexikon ...*, Vienna 1793, p. 59.

A piece for musical clock, 1789, in Haydn's autograph; one of a series of small works written for a clock constructed by Pater Primitivus Niemecz (Prince Esterházy's librarian), this example is in the form of a fugue. The notes 1 and 2 at the end (on separate staves) are in Niemecz's hand; these are simplifications of bars 8ff. and 20ff., respectively. Haydn signs the MS. 'laus Deo. Jos: Haydn mpria $\overline{789}$', and adds the suggestion 'NB So oft als d[as] Thema komt muß beÿ jedweder Halbe Notte folgender halber Mordant komm[en] [musical example] zum Ex: bey der ersten Note [space] diese Stelle kommt 16 mahl.' ('Whenever the theme appears, the following half mordent [example] must be placed on each minim, e.g. on the first note [space] this passage occurs 16 times.')

must be redated 1789, not 1772. The clock in question is still extant: it is owned by descendants of the Gassmann family, and in 1932 German Parlophon issued an enchanting 10-inch record of its music which is greatly prized by collectors (we owe an acetate copy to the kindness of our old friend and collaborator of a quarter of a century, Karlheinz Füssl).

Many of the autographs of these *Flötenuhr* pieces have survived, as a result of which the clock's execution of them is of the utmost importance (several aspects were pointed out by us in *SYM*, 1955, pp. 138, 155, 156n., 162n.), *viz.* that the grace notes of Symphony No. 85/Trio are *long*; that a trill extending of several bars does not need to end with a 'suffix'; and how Haydn's *tr* may be executed in a fast 3/4 tempo (the crossed turn as ♫ is also neatly performed by the clock). Since the clocks were in

the nature of *settecento* gramophone records, Haydn often adapted his most popular pieces for them: 'La ragazza col vecchione' (Buonafede's scene in Act I of *Il mondo della luna*; XIX:1); Symphony No. 53/II (XIX:3); Baryton Trio No. 82/III (XIX:5); Baryton Trio No. 76/III (XIX:6, known in the Teubner family, who own the clock, as 'Kaffeeklatsch'); String Quartet, Op. 54, No. 2/III (XIX:9).

Like the insertion arias, the fact that Haydn took the trouble to compose (arrange) these pieces for musical clock reveals him in a sympathetic light. And not only did he write them down with evident zest, he knew the clock's mechanical problems and made *ossia* suggestions to Pater Niemecz in case his principal version should prove too difficult (see our facsimile).

There is a fine edition of all these pieces edited by the late Ernst Fritz Schmid (Bärenreiter Verlag, Kassel, for Nagels Musik Archiv, Hanover 1931, revised 1954). For a gramophone record of a newly discovered clock, see *Addenda* in *Haydn: the Late Years 1801–1809*.

Notturni for the King of Naples,
completed 1790 (II:25–32)

Professor Makoto Ohmiya has now edited all the Notturni for *Joseph Haydn Werke* (Reihe VII, 1973) and has made impeccable recordings of them[1] as well. In the course of his researches, he came to the conclusion that Haydn must have written these works in two series, as follows:

FIRST SET OF NOTTURNI (1788–90)

Notturno I (II:25). *Source*: Score by Anon. 11 from Haydn's library, now EH, Budapest, Ms. mus. I. 142. 'Notturno I^{mo}' (2 lire, 2 clar., 2 hn., 2 va., 'basso').

Notturno II (II:26). *Source*: Autograph, followed on pages 8ff. by a copyist, from Haydn's library, now EH, Budapest, Ms. mus. I. 44a. 'Notturno 2do' (2 lire, 2 clar., 2 hn., 2 va., 'basso').

---

1 Japanese Columbia OX-10110-11-N. See our review in *HJB* IX, 391. Another critical edition of the music, scores and parts, was prepared by us in Verlag Doblinger's Diletto Musicale series (48, 1959; the others prepared 1960 *et seq.*; also miniature scores). Professor Ohmiya's article, 'New Order for the "Lyra-Notturni" of Joseph Haydn', in *Tone & Meditation*, Tokyo 1969, pp. 67ff.

Notturno III (II:32). *Source*: Authentic score by an Esterházy copyist, with corrections that Haydn made when re-scoring the work for London, Bibliotheca Musashino Academiae Musicae, Tokyo (AM 109). 'Notturno 3^{zo}' (2 lire, 2 clar., 2 hn., 2 va., 'Basso'; rescored[1] by Haydn for 2 fl. instead of lire), 2 v. (instead of clar.) and 'Violoncello', 'ContraBaßo'. *Facsimile*: First page of music in Landon, *Das kleine Haydnbuch*, p. 83. *Further critical editions* of Notturno III and IV: Musikwissenschaftlicher Verlag (Schmid, 1936).

Notturno IV (II:31). *Source*: Autograph, formerly owned by Christopher Papendiek,[1] now the property of Dr Grumbacher in Basel. 'Notturno in C a 2 Lire, 2 Clarinetti 2 Viole 2 Corni Violoncello di me giuseppe Haydn 7̄9̄0̄ per la Sua Maestà il Re di Napoli'. At end: 'Fine laus Deo'. Sketch to 1st movt.: Preussische Staatsbibliothek, Berlin, Mus. ms. autogr. Jos. Haydn 22 (watermarks: bow-and-arrow, 'A M' [Andrea Mattizzoli], 3 slim crescents of decreasing size, ditto with 'REAL'). For London MS. see footnote below.

Notturno V (II:29). *Source*: MS. parts from Haydn's legacy, EH, Budapest, Ms. mus. I. 106. 'Notturno 5to à Du[e] Violini, Flauto et Oboa, Due Corni, Due Viola con Violoncello, o Basso' [commas, except last, added]. There is no source of the original version with lire and clarinets. C. F. Pohl made a copy of this work for his friend Johannes Brahms in the winter of 1870–1 (Gesellschaft der Musikfreunde, Vienna).

Notturno VI (II:30). *Source*: MS. score by Anonymous 30 of the first two movements (Finale is lost entirely), from Haydn's library, now EH, Budapest, Ms. mus. I. 143. 'Notturno 6to' (2 lire, 2 clar., 2 hn., 2 va., 'basso'). *Further critical edition*: Music Press, New York (Edvard Fendler).

SECOND SET OF NOTTURNI (1790?)

Notturno I (Hoboken *deest*): presumed lost.

Notturno II (II:28). *Source*: MS. parts from Haydn's library, now EH, Budapest, Ms. mus. I. 107. 'Notturno in F a Due Violini, Flauto et Oboè, Due Corni, Due Viola con Violonzello [*sic*] et Basso' [commas added]. For London MS. see footnote. No source of the original version with lire and clarinets exists, and perhaps instead of the latter there were *a priori* violins.

Notturno III (II:27). *Source*: Autograph from Haydn's library, now EH, Budapest, Ms. mus. I. 44[b]. 'Notturno 3^{zo}'. Originally scored for 2 lire, 2 hn., 2 v., 2 va., vc., Haydn later changed the lire to fl. & ob., added a new double bass part and a whole slow introduction (for London, on British paper with British watermark). Facsimile of first page of added introduction in *Haydn in England 1791–1795*, p. 454. In the King's Library (British Museum) there are authentic parts of II:31, II:28 and II:27, each with a new separate double bass part.

We have seen that Haydn created a new and successful hybrid form in the Concertos for the King of Naples. In these enchanting Notturni, he continued along the same lines except, of course, for the fact that the concerto elements had to retreat into the background. Haydn obviously found this new kind of enlarged chamber music stimulating, and he thought enough of these works to play many of them in the Haydn-Salomon concerts of 1791, with the lira parts given to two flutes, or flute and oboe, the clarinet parts given to violins, and a new double pass part composed at least in four cases (II:27, 28, 31, 32). There is an almost unbelievable variety in these works, from meltingly beautiful slow introductions (especially that to II:26) to racy final rondos. In one work (II:25) there is an amusing opening march, most unmilitary as always with Haydn. In another (II:29) there is even a full-scale fugue as a last movement. The 'openness' of the scoring is a delight, and the two violas give a richness to the string section that reminds us of Mozart's Quintets. One of the richest of the opening movements is that in F major (II:28), where Haydn expands the form to symphonic proportions but always relishes the chamber-musical sound of his score. There is also something of that special '1790' style in this music which reaches its glorious and melancholic climax in that unique set of Quartets, Op. 64. In 1790 Haydn was lonely and isolated in the summery stillness of that last season (though no one could guess that) for Eszterháza. His mood is mirrored in his letters to Frau von

1 For Haydn's London revisions and Christoph Papendiek, see *Haydn in England 1791–1795*, pp. 453ff.

Genzinger; it is also clearly reflected in the music of this last season. Perhaps the most striking example of this summery melancholy is found in the third Notturno of the second set, of which the middle Adagio is possibly the greatest single movement of all the Notturni. In the central section, in C minor, we seem to be with Haydn in the garden of Eszterháza on a hot summer's afternoon, watching the slow passing of huge white clouds above the yellow and green of the castle. The Prince is in Vienna, on his last journey as it turned out, the castle is half closed, and the garden is empty. A profound sadness overcomes Haydn, which wells out of this marvellous Adagio in its measured quavers, the interweaving parts slowly moving in a modulation that seems to foretell Brahms. It is a magic moment which we all are privileged to share with this lonely man who filled this music of 1790 with a special mood which he never quite recaptured after his life became so very different.

The second Series of Quartets for Johann Tost
(Op. 64, 1790; III:63–68)

The six Quartets in this set are: No. 1 in C, No. 2 in B minor, No. 3 in B flat, No. 4 in G, No. 5 ('The Lark') in D, No. 6 in E flat.

THE SOURCES

Autographs: No. 1, British Museum, signed and dated 1790; at end 'Fine Laus Deo': 'Quartetto 1mo in C'. No. 2, Gregor Piatigorsky (†): 'Quartetto 2do in H minore'; at end 'Fine Laus Deo. Photograph: Library of Congress, Washington. No. 3, Rychenberg-Stiftung, Winterthur: 'Quartetto 3^{zo} in b fa'; at end 'Fine. Laus Deo'. No. 4's autograph is lost. No. 5, Bibliotheca Musashino Academiae Musicae, Tokyo. We used the photograph owned by the Antiquariat Hans Schneider, Tutzing, which he very kindly placed at our disposal. 'Quartetto 6to in D'. At end 'Fine Laus Deo'. No. 6, Library of Congress, Washington, D.C.: 'Quartetto 5. in Es'. At end, 'Fine Laus Deo.' All the autographs begin with 'In Nomine Domini'. It will be seen that the order of the last two works is reversed in Haydn's original numbering. Since Hoboken has adopted yet another order, we present the evidence of the authentic sources' various orders in a table at the end of this section.
Authentic first edition: Magazin de Musique (Koželuch), Vienna, announced on 23 February 1791 in the *Wiener Zeitung*. 'Composés et dediés a Monsieur Jean Tost ... Oeuvre 65.' Copy: Gesellschaft der Musikfreunde, Vienna.
Authentic British edition: John Bland, London, announced in the *Morning Herald* on 10 June 1791: 'Three Quartets ... composed by Giuseppe Haydn, and performed under his direction at M^r. Salomon's concert, the Festino Rooms Hanover Square. Set I [II]. Op. 65.' Copy: British Museum.

·ORDER OF SOURCES						
Today's order	1	2	3	4	5	6
Haydn's autograph	1	2	3	4	6	5
Magazin de Musique	1	2	3	4	5	6
Bland	3	6	5	4	1	2
Hoboken sequence	3	6	5	4	1	2
Hoboken cat. no. III:	65	68	67	66	63	64

It will be seen that the 'tradition' order is that of the first (Viennese) edition and that Hoboken's is the same as Bland's.
Critical editions: Complete Quartets, Verlag Doblinger (Landon, prepared 1973–4). *Joseph Haydn Werke*, Reihe XII, Band 5 (Georg Feder and Isidor Saslav), in preparation.

Op. 64 is perhaps Haydn's greatest single achievement of the period – six flawless masterpieces which, in our opinion, can be compared in unity of purpose, perfection of execution and profundity of spirit only with Op. 20. To give Op. 64 its due would require a detailed analysis beyond the limits of this present volume, and we will restrict our discussion to a few remarks on certain details.

OPUS 64, NO. 1

In cut time (Hoboken's Catalogue is generally wrong, even as late as Op. 77 in this respect), the opening Allegro moderato continues the new tradition of fast metre. This does not, however, necessarily mean that the music itself is fast; on the contrary, there is a sense of epicurean relish with which this wonderful music moves slowly forward. We note the (by now) usual shift into triplets, the use of *bariolage* (bars 45ff.), the use of the first violin's high register (bars 126f.) – these are technical devices which have become normal procedure. The ways in which Haydn holds this discursive movement tightly together are many and varied: the little figure at bar 3 –  – the central part of the material just before the exposition; instead of (bar 2) being introduced by ♪♩♩ it is now introduced by the triplet figure ♪♪♪ | ♩ ♩ ♩ ♩ (bars 54f., 55f.). The recapitulation turns into a kind of coda at the same time. When the material which was at the end of the exposition reappears (bars 128ff.) Haydn introduces a startling new modulation (bars 133ff.) into A flat and D flat (which is never reached in root position). What happens afterwards is part of that great 1790 style: a wave of melancholy, which is expressed in this long digression into flat keys and then C minor, shows us what this new style is like.

The Minuet is placed second rather than third and although in C major, it has that yearning quality that permeates so much of Op. 64. The Trio uses the same thematic material and reveals it, as it were, in another facet: C minor. The third movement is an Allegretto scherzando, whose initial theme is sufficiently original and rhythmically forceful to be able to dominate the whole movement: ♪ | ♫ ♪ ♫ ♪ | ♫♫♫ | . In the course of this movement, the mood moves from the quiet satisfaction of the beginning to such a passage as that of bars 89ff., where the violins move in shifting suspensions, that reminds us of the 'Emperor' Quartet's slow movement:

[Cf. Op. 76, No. 3/III, bars 100ff.]
This passage occurs again (bars 115ff.) and brings the music to a close.

The pert theme of the Finale –

– also undergoes a transformation which is even more startling because of its seeming innocence. After the double bar, the music that just occurred is repeated in a different layout (dominant seventh of C major), whereupon we hear this:

The imitation continues its rather sinister way up the score and leads to a passage of great contrapuntal brilliance which is largely in minor keys. A more complete transformation could hardly be imagined. The Quartet ends very softly.

OPUS 64, NO. 2

The music begins in D major but by the end of bar two we are in B minor: Haydn repeats a tonal ambivalence that he had also used in his previous B minor Quartet from Op. 33 (No. 1). This Allegro spiritoso is outwardly the most serious of any movement in the set. It is interesting to see Haydn reaching back to his *Sturm und Drang* days for effects which this intense and stern music unconsciously called forth: the wide skips in the melodic material called for *fz* accents on each minim (bars 98–100), and the syncopations and *fz* accents of bars 47ff. remind us of the 1772 style – also the great brevity of the movement (108 bars: No. 1 = 174 bars; No. 5 = 179 bars). The rhythmic acceleration is remarkable: bars 28ff. read (in skeleton)

We also note the new use of the violin's highest register, especially at the end.

When we studied photographs of the autograph at the hospitable Music Division of the Library of Congress, we thought that this must be the most beautiful adagio movement Haydn ever wrote, and for sheer loveliness what music in the world can compare with it? Its peculiarly hypnotic quality comes from its remote key, perhaps (B major), but even more because of its undulating inner voices. The chain trills with which the theme (in a lower register) is provided when it enters again at bars 52ff. are moving beyond words. Gradually we may note how Haydn builds up the music by shifting from quaver inner voices to semiquavers (bars 69 to the end). The *g* natural in the final cadence (bar 91) is Haydn's last twist of the emotional knife.

The Minuet is more like a scherzo with curiously Beethovenian *fz* under that characteristic appoggiatura figure. The Trio is the kind of *Ländler* in which Joseph Lanner would excel a generation later, and is a very Austrian movement. Both Minuet and Finale start in B minor, but the Trio and the end of this Finale are in B major. We note Hungarian (Gypsy) patterns ♪ ♪. ⅄ ♪♪ ⅄ ♪♪ ⅄ and even ♪, ♪, the dramatic use of silence and the witty ending, *pp*, at a dizzy altitude (now almost to be expected in every work).

OPUS 64, NO. 3

Haydn finds some brilliantly original device with which to capture our attention in every movement, and here it is the following, captivating rhythm which makes its first appearance for solo 'cello in bar 8: ♪♫ ♪♫ ♪♫ (an old favourite: cf. Symphony No. 35, first movement), with which Haydn provides moments of humour, drama and surprise. It even manages to insert itself into the *pp* ending.

The slow movement uses the favourite form A(major)–B(minor)–A(major; varied), which we noticed in Symphony No. 92's Adagio and elsewhere. It is another example of Haydn's new found lyrical gifts, with that constant companion of these slow movements, melancholy, not the anguished desperation of a Mozart but (if the simile be permitted) like an early autumn mist that tells us that summer is over.

After a rhythmically compact Minuet, we have a most original Trio (theme in syncopations, then the melody over a chattering 'cello), all in the gay mood of the first movement. The characteristic rhythm of that movement turns out to furnish the basis for the Finale's opening melody. The device to grip our imagination in this Allegro con spirito appears three times, and as Cecil Gray says, 'suddenly the pace slackens and the music stops dead on a reiterated chord followed by a magical harmonic passage' (vol. 7 [1938], p. 18) which is easily identified by the following skeletal plan:

Every time this appealing passage appears (bars 41ff., 97ff., 168ff.) it is harmonized differently and unexpectedly.

OPUS 64, NO. 4

In the middle of the sunny Allegro con brio, with its kaleidoscopic rhythmic variety, we find a stone guest in the form of a syncopated little section in D minor (bars 23ff.), the unsettling mood of which the next tutti (27ff.) does not entirely dissipate. The closing material both here and later is 'sopra una corda', an effect to which Haydn will have increasing recourse. The prominent series of semiquavers in the accompaniment

nourishes (a) the wonderfully dramatic development, in which this pattern propels us with dashing rapidity through a whole series of minor keys (typical) and (b) the accompaniment of the rapturously beautiful slow movement, which though separated from the Allegro by the Minuet (with another Viennese Trio, whose pizzicato accompaniment looks forward to the Trio of Op. 76, No. 1), places the semiquavers so prominently *throughout* the movement that their origin is obvious. It is in the A(major)–B(minor)–A(major; varied) form for which Haydn had such an aptitude, and ends *pp*. In the large-scale Finale, we note the great contrapuntal treatment of the main theme in the development section; and that this part, as is often now the case, is the most serious section of the movement concerned and also the one in which the keys are mostly minor and Haydn's contrapuntal skill is displayed at its most breathtaking (cf. 'Oxford' Symphony's Finale at the same place.

OPUS 64, NO. 5 ('THE LARK')

This Quartet is so well known that analysis is practically superfluous. The entrance of the first violin in its Tost register (high, that is) gave the work its name. Connoisseurs will be interested to follow yet another of Haydn's accelerations by means of triplet quavers (first use: bars 50ff.). In the development and recapitulation they gradually usurp the other rhythms for a long period; but when the main theme enters for the last time in a kind of coda (bars 142ff.) the triplets suddenly disappear, leaving the music to move quietly with even quaver accompaniment (which the theme did not originally have). The slow movement is another thoughtful Adagio in Haydn's usual three parts with a 'B' section in minor. The Trio is also in the minor. The Finale is perhaps the first example of the perpetuum mobile which Haydn was to cultivate with such success (Symphony No. 94's Finale, etc.), and would seem to have been a virtuoso vehicle for Tost. There is a fascinating fugato section in D minor, which adds weight to this celebrated Finale, which Haydn (no doubt rightly) calculated would create a furore in the Hanover Square Rooms.

OPUS 64, NO. 6

The key of E flat calls forth, as usual, the lyrical side of Haydn's nature. The central part of this movement is the development, as usual the most serious and weighty, with contrapuntal texture. The most arresting page is, however, when Haydn seizes on this motif (with ♪♪♪♪ accompaniment): ♩ ♪♪♩♩ (bars 67–83) which lead into a statement of the main subject in G flat. 'Above and underneath a ghostly, chattering little staccato figure', writes Cecil Gray (vol. 3 [1934], p. 14), 'which continues unbroken on the second violin for no fewer than 17 bars, the other three instruments hold mysterious colloquy with one another. This is pure Beethoven, and not merely early Beethoven either, but Beethoven in full and characteristic maturity.'

The last of the slow movements in this set is no less glorious than any other. It is denser in texture, with Haydn's weaving quaver inner parts, than some of the others, with a very complex emotional ambiguity which defies positive identification. The middle section sounds almost Schubertian: the music lurches into semiquaver accompaniment, and the first violin has a melody which recalls the opera house. It is a stark contrast, in its hammering repetitions, to the suave movement of its flanking 'A' parts.

And what a Minuet: one cannot decide what is more striking, the powerful theme

or the ♪♪♪♪ ♪𝄽 | ♪♪♪♪ ♪𝄽 | rhythm of the middle parts. In the Library of Congress autograph there are *two* trios rather than the one given in the pre-Doblinger scores. They are both very Viennese, and the one known up to now carries Tost up to Paganini-like heights (*e* flat′′′′).

The whirlwind of a Finale is in Haydn's modern style, with long passages of contrapuntal erudition that, as it were, fly past us at top speed. The unison passage at bars 148ff. opens up the whole world of Beethoven and his Razumovsky Quartet players sounding 'like a miniature orchestra'. This is another of Haydn's now perfected fusions of popular style and monumental contrapuntal erudition, which would from this point become one of the fixed poles of the Viennese classical style.

The Farewell Song, 'Trachten will ich nicht auf Erden'
(14 December 1790; XXVIa:39)

This was a private song and Haydn never published it. When the autograph was in private hands in New York, we were permitted to take a photograph: it is signed 'In Nomine Domini' and 'Joseph Haydn mpria den 14ten. 10^{bris} $\overline{790}$.' We do not know for whom he wrote it, but we rather suspect that Frau von Genzinger was the recipient.

It was the day before Haydn left for England – the greatest adventure of his life. In those days, travelling was difficult and dangerous, and Haydn, that eve before he left, probably addressed a private prayer to Our Lady to protect him. After all, the French Revolution was in progress, and no one could see how it would end, or with which consequences for Austria, England and Joseph Haydn. On the 14th, as we shall see, he dined with Mozart and Salomon ('bey einem fröhlichen Mahl'). Then he sat down and wrote this solemn little song, Adagio, in his favourite key of E major: unsentimental, with deep and quiet emotion. In an uncanny way, it looks forward to the greatest vocal work composed in England, the *Scena di Berenice*. Haydn's Song (a) was transformed into (b), which is even in the same key and shines with the same inner light:

CHAPTER TEN

The Third Haydn School

HAYDN'S NEW POPULAR STYLE was widely imitated, by his pupils and by the now very numerous *seguaci* all over Europe. Now the imitation of a masterpiece for study purposes is not in itself a bad thing, and we remember our own composition teacher at Boston, Hugo Norden, making his pupils choose a work they liked (we chose Samuel Barber's Overture to *A School for Scandal*) and then compose their own piece using the formal, modulatory and harmonic principles of the model. The trouble with the Haydn *seguaci* was that they sold their products and thus adulterated the original. This was particularly true of Ignaz Pleyel, Haydn's star pupil. In Cramer's *Magazin der Musik* for 1787 we read, in a letter from Italy dated January, that Pleyel and Joseph Martin Kraus ('from Stockholm') are there:

> As one hears, Herr Pleyel has been made Capellmeister at Strasbourg at a salary of 1000 Rthl. He composed sundry beautiful piano sonatas which one expects here impatiently. His pleasant melody therein is not so difficult as Clementi's or Mozart's witchcraft; he is more faithful to nature, without violating the rules of composition. [*Magazin der Musik* 1787, p. 1379]

Sometimes the *seguace* literally copied all the traits of a Haydn work. In the Parish Church at Grodzisk in Poznania (Poland), a Symphony in D by one Pietrowski was recently discovered and published as Volume II of the series, *Symfonie polskie*. Haydn's music was admired in this remote Parish Church: on one of the Grodzisk scores, someone has written 'Haydn is a very good composer', and so it is no surprise to find Symphony No. 70 as the model for Pietrowski's *Sinfonia in D*:

Haydn (1) is the beginning of Symphony No. 70, Haydn (2) its continuation; Pietrowski (1) and (2) are the copies, while Pietrowski (3) is the copy of Haydn (3), the beginning of the Finale of Symphony No. 70. Haydn's movement contained that awesome triple fugue in D minor, and the Finale ended with the initial violin figure being repeated, the second time *pp*, and then thundered out by the whole orchestra. Pietrowski has his (rather mild) fugato in F and turns into the tonic major at bar 142. And of course Pietrowski ends his Symphony with the opening violin figure played twice *pp* and then with big closing tutti chords.

Other *seguaci* were more subtle. One of Haydn's interesting pupils, and a man intimately connected with the first performances of *The Creation*, was Paul Wranizky. In 1790 he composed a big C major Symphony with trumpets and drums in which there are strong overtones of Haydn's Symphony No. 82, but it is the general style, not the actual music, that is copied.[1] The Finale of Wranizky's Symphony follows Haydn's interest in folk-music, and one of the folk-tunes used in the movement is known as a Czech Christmas carol and a Hungarian dance melody; there is also *verbunkos* (recruiting) music in it.

The curious thing that happened almost immediately was that many of these *seguaci* became more successful with the general public than did Haydn. The reason for that extraordinary state of affairs was that the symphonies, trios, piano sonatas and quartets that men such as Pleyel composed were easier to digest than Haydn's: almost a 'poor man's Haydn', that is, with all the originalities, eccentricities, contrapuntal complexities and bizarre elements watered down or removed. The principal models were now Haydn's symphonies, quartets, sonatas and trios of the 1780s, and the *seguaci* proceeded to found what we have termed 'The Third Haydn School' (the preceding one has been discussed earlier in this volume, and the 'Fourth Haydn School' is the subject of *Haydn in England 1791–1795*, pp. 506ff.). At the time, their products achieved an instant popularity but it was not a lasting one. The *Gentleman's Magazine* said in 1809, their 'airy productions, more suited to the indolence of some, and the weak musical capacity of others, seemed to supplant the original in public esteem'; but within a few years Pleyel's music began to disappear from the scene along with all the other *seguaci* compositions.

Nevertheless, this widespread popularity of, say, his pupil Pleyel's works must have 'vexed' Haydn (to use Pohl's words in the Grove I article on Pleyel) and certainly, as we have said, caused great confusion in a metropolis like Paris, where the *seguaci*'s

1 The Symphony is entitled: 'Joy of the Hungarian Nation When her Laws and Freedoms were Restored under Emperor and King Joseph II, on the 28th Day of the Month of Circumcision of the Year 1790. A Grand Symphony Consisting of Three Pieces. I. The Nation's First Expression of Joy and its Dissemination. II. The Pleasant Sensibilities of the Estates of the Realm and the Unity Restored Among Them. III. The Joy of the Community on the Occasion of the Holy Crown's Return.' Joseph II encountered resistance on the part of the Hungarian Estates to his reforms, e.g. the introduction of German as the official language, the curtailment of the Counties' self-government, and especially that he did not have himself crowned as Hungarian King and even removed the ancient crown itself to Vienna. In 1790, many of these reforms were rescinded and the crown was sent back to Buda.

works were published by the dozen under Haydn's name. In a biography of Haydn we can do no more than discuss the problem briefly – one day, perhaps someone will devote a monograph to the subject, which it well deserves, both for its intrinsic interest and as a phenomenon that never repeated itself with any other composer to that extent – and to that end we have chosen two of the most characteristic men of this Third Haydn School: Adalbert Gyrowetz and a man who had the misfortune to be named Joseph Hayda.

In the summer of 1783, a young man sat in his room in the beautiful Bohemian Castle of Chlumetz (Chlumec), and 'there he wrote his first compositions, taking the symphonies of Joseph Haydn as his models, in the imitation of which he was fortunately so successful that he made an honourable name for himself in the world.' The young man was Adalbert Gyrowetz, and was at that time secretary to Count von Fünfkirchen, who then owned Schloß Chlumetz (it was later the property of Beethoven's Prince Kinsky). Later Gyrowetz wrote his entertaining autobiography in the third person, from which we shall now follow the young man's career (he was born in 1763 and was just twenty as he started to become a *seguace* of Haydn). When he returned to Chlumetz years later, he remembered that

> ... he was often carried away by his feelings when he was composing, so that he began to weep and openly to sob; people in the castle heard him and ran to his room to enquire fearfully if anything was wrong. ...
>
> As far as elegant music was concerned, Pleyel's quartets were very *en vogue*, and so were the symphonies of Dittersdorf, Hofmeister, sonatas by Koželuch, Maschek, &c. ... Gyrowetz now organized some good letters of recommendation for Vienna and ... travelled there. When he had arrived he was presented at the house of Herr Hofrat von Käß [Keeß] who was recognized as the first friend of music and dilettante in Vienna, and who gave society concerts at his house twice a week at which the leading virtuosi who were in Vienna and the first composers such as Joseph Haydn, Mozart, Dittersdorf, Hofmeister, Albrechtsberger, Giarnovichi [Giornovichj] and so on, appeared. – Mozart generally played the fortepiano and Giarnovichi, in those days the most celebrated violin virtuoso, usually gave a concerto; the lady of the house sang. ... The best hearted of them seemed to be Mozart; he looked at Gyrowetz, who was then very young, with such a sympathetic glance as if he wanted to say: 'Poor, young thing! You are about to start on your career and await with fear and trembling the fate in store for you.' – His expression made a very great impression on the soul of the young Gyrowetz, whose heart was won from that very instant. Haydn laughed rather archly, Dittersdorf was serious, Albrechtsberger seemed to be entirely indifferent, Giarnovichi as a Dalmatian was rather sinister but nonetheless good-hearted ... He [Gyrowetz] sold his first six symphonies to ... Prince Kražalkoviz [Grassalkovics] ... The Prince had these six symphonies played in a concert where his highness Prince Esterházy ... was invited. Prince Esterházy wanted to own the symphonies ... Prince Kražalkoviz at once had them prepared by a good copyist and presented them in a handsome binding to Prince Esterházy, who often had them played by his large orchestra and was delighted with them; the orchestra was led by a certain Jost [Tost]. [Gyrowetz went to Italy, where he composed concertos for the King of Naples, and then on to France. In 1788–9 he composed a second set of six quartets which he dedicated to Haydn. He arrived in Paris as the Revolution broke out.] The leading artists of the Grand Opéra were invited [to a concert at which two of Gyrowetz's] symphonies were performed with the best results and powerful applause. When Gyrowetz then laid out the music of a third one in G, they looked at him with an inquiring gaze, almost suspiciously and

asked, significantly, if this composition were really his. When he answered in the affirmative, they asked to see the score and when they had examined it bar for bar and saw that everything agreed and was correct, they began to congratulate Gyrowetz, telling him that this Symphony was already engraved and was a 'favorite-pièce' in all theatres and concerts, under Joseph Haydn's name. Gyrowetz was naturally astonished asked how such a thing were possible and who would dare to issue his work in Paris under a strange name. They answered Gyrowetz that it was a great honour to have his symphonies taken for Haydn's, and that Herr Schlesinger [*recte*: Sieber] was the publisher.

Gyrowetz thereupon betook himself at once to the music publisher, Herr Schlesinger, to find out how things stood and heard from him that a German violin virtuoso named Tost came from Vienna to Paris and brought with him three symphonies which he sold to [Sieber] as Haydn's and so it came about that these three symphonies were also engraved under Haydn's name. Tost was music director at the *Kapelle* of his highness Prince Esterházy, and after the Prince had acquired the symphonies by Gyrowetz, Herr Tost had them copied and brought them to Paris ...   [*Selbstbiographie*, ed. Einstein, pp. 105f., 9–13, 59f.]

Gyrowetz had a good memory – he was a very old man when he wrote his autobiography – and most of the facts are substantially correct. Schlesinger (Beethoven's publisher) was Sieber and he had in fact published three symphonies under Haydn's name which Johann Tost had brought with him: Haydn's No. 88 and 89 (which Tost had every right to sell) and Gyrowetz's Symphony in G which begins as follows:

Sieber's edition was entitled *Simphonie Périodique* No. 20 (plate no. 361) and was soon (c. 1793) reprinted by Forster in London. Larsen imagined that this was the Gyrowetz Symphony (see *HUB*, 115) in question, but in those days no sources under Gyrowetz's name could be located. Subsequently the present writer was able to find no less then four sources under Gyrowetz's name, three in Czechoslovakian MSS. (see Landon, *Supplement*, 29) and one which Dr Fritz Kaiser located in the *Catalogue / des / Diverses Musiques* of the Order of Teutonic Knights in Freudenthal (Silesia), now in the Central Archives of the Order at Vienna.

Here we have a graphic instance of how the *seguaci* were published under the master's name. The pretty G major Symphony is indeed a blueprint of a Haydn symphony, and Gyrowetz flooded the market with Haydnesque quartets, piano trios, symphonies, serenades, and so on.[1] Interesting though many of these works are, and professionally though they are fashioned, there is a strange kind of Achilles heel in their emotional structure. Indeed it is almost impossible to believe the emotional strain under which these serene and seemingly unproblematic works were composed (see Gyrowetz's remarks above). If we examine, for instance, Gyrowetz's Symphony in E flat which has been revived in recent years in Prague,

1 See the present writer's list in *MGG*, vol. 5, article 'Gyrowetz'.

we note this fatal flaw in the development section of the first movement, which works into a first-rate sequence in C minor over a marching bass line in quavers. But just when a rather Mozartian lead-back with clarinets starts, as we think, to propel us to the recapitulation, Gyrowetz breaks off in a fatuous series

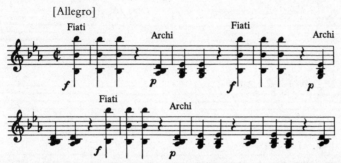

which completely dispels the development's continuity. It is the kind of thing that appears frequently in Gyrowetz's works, and it is astonishing to us that music of this emotional emptiness – not only Gyrowetz but Pleyel's later works are full of such voids – should have achieved such total and, relatively speaking, lasting popularity. Gyrowetz and Pleyel were played well into Beethoven's middle period, i.e. the period of the Vienna Congress. It took a time for the English, for example, who were Gyrowetz's agreeable hosts in the years 1790–2, to realize the thin content behind the professional veneer of his music.[1] We can only marvel how long it actually took.

Another case of a Haydn *seguace* is almost too fantastic to be true: he was an organist and composer by the name of Joseph Hayda (or Heyda), and not only is his name ominously similar but he turns out to have been a passionate admirer of both Joseph and Michael Haydn's music. Since at least one beautiful work has enthralled audiences but has turned out to be the indubitable product of Joseph Hayda, a few words about him will be welcome.

In a book entitled *Denksteine* by August Schmidt (Vienna, 1848, p. 2n.) we read the following description of Hayda:

> Hayda was one of the finest organists of his time, especially praised for his improvisations on the organ: at the age of sixty and more he often played for hours at a time without tiring; with eagerly youthful energy, with the full and undiminished force of his adult powers, he sought a seemingly unimportant motif and wrote a fugue on it in such a way that the great contrapuntist Albrechtsberger often listened with admiration; while the artist, forgetting everything about him, enchanted and drowned in a sea of notes of his own making, played with the tears running down his furrowed cheeks for pure joy. He entertained a particularly devoted admiration for the two great Haydns, and he was proud that his family name differed from that of the two worshipped brothers only through a single letter. Although the two Haydns filled his heart with devotion, the Salzburg brother Michael was his Messiah in the church style, which he considered the highest and most unapproachable. Hayda died in Vienna at a ripe old age, before the arrival of the present [nineteenth] century.

Hayda was organist at the parish church of the Trinity Order in Vienna. In the *Verzeichnisz über sämtliches Musick-Personal* of 1783, he is listed as 'Joseph Haida'

---

1 See a criticism quoted in *Haydn in England 1791–1795*, p. 64.

The autograph dedication of Joseph Hayda's *Litaniae de B.V.M.* and note on the 'Violino' part of the 'Mater amabilis'. This note reads: 'NB dieses Mater amab: welches hier stehet, ist vergessen ge[cancelled] worden in Prim und Secund einzutragen / Wan es können alle geigen komt viel besser heraus. aber nur piano wie es halt steht' ('NB this Mater amab: which is found here was forgotten and should be inserted in the first and second [violins] / if all the violins can play it, it will sound much better. but only *piano*, as it says').

'Organist', his earlier salary having been previously 112 fl. 40 xr. and now (as a result of the Josephinian reforms) reduced to 53 fl. Some years ago, the present writer issued a fine *Litaniae de Beata Maria Virgine* which was attributed to Joseph Haydn, Michael Haydn and Joseph Hayda. The Graz source (source B of our edition) appears to be an authentic Hayda manuscript and the dedication 'Sacrificium ad Honorem SS. Trinitatis. / o : a : m : d : g : et B : V : M : / Joseph Heyda. 776' is certainly autograph, as is the long German remark quoted in the description of the source (preface, p. 3) in our edition. Hayda (or as he spelled his name, Heyda) was a member of the Trinity Order and the Graz manuscript comes from the local seat of that very order. There are several interesting church works by Hayda in manuscript, also in the Esterházy Archives at Eisenstadt (apart from the Litany, where 'Hayda' was changed [when?] to 'Haydn') ; in the National Library of Prague, and elsewhere. We hope that someone will devote a monograph to this interesting contemporary and *seguace* of the Haydns, whose arrival on the twentieth century scene was the result of a curious misattribution: but apart from that, the *Litaniae de Beata Maria Virgine* or (Graz source) *Litaniae Lauretanae* is a beautiful and impressive work which should not be condemned to oblivion because it can no longer be considered a work by Joseph Haydn.[1]

---

1 Otto Biba, 'Die Wiener Kirchenmusik um 1783', in *Beiträge zur Musikgeschichte des 18. Jahrhunderts*, Eisenstadt 1971, p. 37. Our edition of the *Litaniae* as Joseph Haydn, Verlag Doblinger 10.002, 1959. August Schmidt, *Denksteine*, pp. 2f. (n.).

CHAPTER ELEVEN

Chronicle 1785–1790

Chronicle 1785

ITALIAN OPERAS 1785
This year 89 performances are registered (Harich in *HJB* I, 64):

Giuseppe Sarti: I contratempi.
Libretto: Printed by Siess in Oedenburg (no copy survives) and 100 copies bound by Facci in Vienna (his bill: 17 May 1784). Proposed cast, EH, Budapest, Secr. Prot. III. 137:

Carlotta	Mad. Specioli.
Frasconio	S. Mandini.
Cleone	Mons. Negri. [Left 22 August 1784]
Pulcherio	M. Muratti [*sic*].
[EH perf. material: 'Filiberto']	
Pettina [Bettina]	Mad. Polzelli.
Lucinda	Mad. Valdesturla.
Gianastasio	Mons. Dichtler.

Travaglia's proposal for the costumes, 8 June 1784, EH, Budapest, Fasc. 799. Secr. Prot. II. 97. First performance: April 1785, repeated twice and then removed from the boards. Eszterháza performance material: Schellinger's bill (A.M. XVII. 1186) lists 194 *Bögen* vocal parts and 192 *Bögen* orchestral material'. The score (apparently from Wenzel Sukowaty's office in Vienna, where it was performed on 26 April 1784) and the orchestral parts (signed at one point '$\overline{784}$' [V. I] and 'Esterhaz') by Schellinger and Anon. 14, 32, 63, 64 are in EH, Budapest, Ms. Mus. OE–30. The libretto was by Nunziato Porta. Apart from the usual transpositions and cuts, Haydn made the following changes: Atto I°, Sc. 6: oboes (doubling the violins almost throughout) changed to be less 'schematic'. Atto II°, Sc. 5: Bettina's Aria (Polzelli), 'Dica pure che vuol dire' was cancelled and a new Aria substituted, of which we have the *incipit* from the parts (Bartha-Somfai, 286) and the first lines (Anon. 63: 'N^{ro} 15 / Aria / Son pietosa'), but not the vocal part; nor has the score survived. Haydn's authorship cannot at present be established. Note that the original (discarded) text was used by Haydn on another occasion, as an insertion aria in Anfossi's *Il geloso in cimento*. Atto III° was not given; although it is included in the score, it was omitted in the parts. Bartha Somfai, 117, 284–6. Harich in *HJB* I, 59f.

Niccolò Zingarelli: Montezuma. Dramma per musica. Da rappresentarsi nel teatro di S. A. il Sig. Principe Regnante d'Esterhasi. La primavera dell'anno 1785. In Oedenburgo, Nella stamperia di Giuseppe Siess.
Libretto: 250 copies ordered. Copy: EH, Eisenstadt.
Cast:

Montezuma	Sigr. Braghetti.
Teutile	Sigr. Bianchi.
Leisinga [Lisinga]	Mlle. Delicatti [*sic*].
Hernando Cortes	Sigr. Specioli.
Pilpatol	Sigr. Dichtler.
Quagozinga	Mad. Bologna.

Siess's bill (May 1785, sent Feb. 1786): A.M. 4021. Travaglia's proposal for the decorations, 30 April 1785, EH, Budapest, Fasc. 799, Secr. Prot. 1785. I. 15: Bartha-Somfai give extracts: '... In the 1st act: view through a practicable temple, then a part of the residence ... A practicable rise with a view over the city of Mexico ...'. In keeping with the Eszterháza policy of reducing costs, decorations from Haydn's *La fedeltà premiata*, *Orlando Paladino* and *Armida* were used for *Montezuma*. First performance: 5 June (three perf. in all), repeated in July (one) and August (two). Eszterháza performance material: EH, Budapest, Ms. Mus. OE-98. Score (from Italy) and the local orchestral parts (by Schellinger and Anon. 14) have survived. Haydn's changes were as follows (the usual cuts and transpositions are not listed). Leisinga's Aria 'So che non cangio stato' was cut and an insertion aria substituted of which only orchestral parts have survived – see Bartha-Somfai 291 for *incipit*: add *g* to first note (octave). No. 3 (Sc. 2), Montezuma's Aria 'Cara fiamma' was cut and a new aria for Braghetti (his name on the parts) substituted – *incipit* in Bartha-Somfai 292. Haydn's authorship of the first aria cannot be established; of the second it is most unlikely (that aria appears to have originated elsewhere). No. 4 Recit. acc. & Aria (Sop.: our notes [1958] have Leisinga, Bartha-Somfai give Quagozinga) 'Ah che in un mar d'affanni' was cut and a new aria substituted (only orchestral parts survive: *incipit* in Bartha-Somfai, 292); Haydn's authorship cannot be established. No. 6, Teutile's Aria (originally for castrato sop.), 'Di fieri sdegni armato' (C major, 4/4) was cut and a new aria substituted (2 ob., 2 hn, str.), not in Bartha-Somfai. *Incipit* from our notes, 1958:

(only orch. parts survive; Haydn's authorship cannot be established). Sc. 10: for the original aria, a duet was substituted, 'Cara, con quelle lagrime', from (it would seem) another opera. Atto II°, Sc. 4, Leisinga's Aria 'Mi scordo lo scempio' was cancelled and a new aria substituted (only orchestral parts survive):

Haydn's authorship very unlikely. Atto III°: except for one accompanied recitative, all the *figuraliter* numbers were cancelled or substitute arias inserted; we agree that none of these insertions appears to be by Haydn. Sc. 4: Cortes's Aria 'Basta il mio brando solo' cancelled and a new aria substituted (*incipit*: Bartha-Somfai, 293). Sc. 4: Montezuma's Aria 'Nel lasciarvi' cancelled and a new aria substituted (*incipit*: Bartha-Somfai, 293). Quagozinga's Aria 'Ombre dolenti' cancelled and a new aria substituted (*incipit*: Bartha-Somfai, 294). The final chorus seems to be a substitution, too (copyist: Anon. 66). Harich, *Musikgeschichte*, 57. Bartha-Somfai, 125f., 290–4. Harich in *HJB* I, 61.

Pasquale Anfossi: Il matrimonio per inganno. Dramma giocoso per musica da rappresentarsi nel teatro di S. A. il Sig. Principe Regnante d'Estherasi [*sic*]. L'estate dell'anno 1785. In Oedenburgo, nella stamperia di Giussepe [*sic*] Siess.

Libretto: 250 copies ordered (Siess's bill, June 1785, EH, Budapest A.M. 64. 4021). Copies: Österreichische Nationalbibliothek, Theatersammlung 621 754 A; Országos Széchényi Könyvtár, Sign. 206.879. There are no singers listed. We add them from Nunziato Porta's proposed casting (EH, Eisenstadt):

	Attori
Giannina, figlia di Don Fabrizio	Mad. Specioli.
Florindo, giovine [*sic*] di spirito	Mons. Braghetti.
Don Fabrizio, padre di Giannina	Mons. Moratti.
Giulietta	Mlle. Delicatti [*sic*]
Valerio, giovine [*sic*] sciocco ...	Mons. Specioli.
Rosina, cameriera ...	Mad. Polzelli.
Don Volpone, notaro ...	Mons. Bianchi.
Servitori, suonatori che non parlano.	

First performance, after two days of double rehearsals: 3 July (five perf. in all), repeated in August (two), in 1786 and in 1788 – a total of 28 performances and a great success. Eszterháza performance material: Ms. Mus. OE-43. The score (from Italy) and the local orchestral material by Schellinger, with Anon. 14 and 32. Apart from the usual cuts and transpositions, Haydn's changes were: Atto I°, Sc. 4. Giulietta's Aria 'Ah che voi nel petto' was cancelled and a new aria with a slightly varied text, 'Ah' per voi nel mio petto' (*incipit* of first part of aria in Bartha-Somfai, 295; second part:

Since as usual the score of this insertion was removed and the vocal parts of the opera have not survived, Haydn's authorship cannot be determined. Sc. 8: using the original text, Haydn wrote a new aria for

Rosina (Polzelli), 'Signor, voi sapete' (XXIVb:7) – *vide supra*, p. 648. Both the cancelled Anfossi and the new Haydn setting are included in the EH material. Atto II°, Sc. 11: after the libretto had been printed, Haydn inserted a big *scena* for Giannina (*incipit*: Bartha-Somfai, 296; add 'Allegro assai' to first *incipit*; after vocal entrance, add following *incipit* for next section:

and after 'Andante sostenuto' *incipit*, add following *incipit* for closing section:

– there is no evidence of Haydn's authorship).
Harich, *Musikgeschichte*, 57. Bartha-Somfai, 126, 294–6.

Matthias Stabinger: Le astuzie di Bettina. Dramma giocoso per musica da rappresentarsi nel teatro di S. A. il sig. Principe regnante d'esterhasi l'autunno del anno 1785. [angel] – In Oedenburgo, Nella stamperia di Giussepe [*sic*] Siess.
Libretto: 150 copies ordered (Siess's bill, October 1785, EH, Budapest A.M. 64. 4021). Copies: Conservatorio di Musica Santa Cecilia, Rome, Carvalhaes Coll., Vol. 6. Országos Széchényi Könyvtár, Sign. 203. 604. There are no singers listed. We add them from Nunziato Porta's proposed casting (EH, Eisenstadt):

Personaggi

Bettina, donna di governo . . .	Mad. Nencini.
Giannino, suo nipote . . .	Mons. Nencini.
Il Barone di Lagodoro . . .	Mons. Bianchi.
Rosetta, cameriera del Barone . . .	Mlle. Delicatti [*sic*]
Pasquino, servitore di Giannino	Mons. Braghetti.
D. Pacomio, Maestro di Scuola . . .	Mons. Morelli.
La Contessa di Belfiore	Mad. Polzelli.
D. Martino, Maggiordomo della Contessa	Mons. Dichtler.

La Scena si finge in Trieste.
La Musica è del Sig. Maestro Mattia Stabinger.

First performance: October (four perf. in all), repeated in 1786. Eszterháza performance material: Ms. Mus. OE–31. Extant: Atto I° of the score (from Milan), V. II (2 copies) of the whole opera and fragments of the vocal parts. One of Bettina's insertion arias is marked 'Allegretto Fatto da Santi Nencini' (Nencini and his wife, Palmira Sassi, were engaged in August 1785). The parts were copied by Schellinger and Anon. 30 and 14. Apart from the usual cuts and speeding up of tempi (Atto I, Sc. 7: Giannino's Aria 'In quell'occhio ladroncello', Haydn changed 'Andante' to 'Allegro' and 'Allegro' to 'Allegro assai', and cut bars 58–96 [most of the original 'Andante' part]), Haydn's changes were rather minor. Harich, *Musikgeschichte*, 57. Bartha-Somfai, 126f., 296f. Harich in *HJB* I, 61f.

Six operas from earlier seasons were repeated:
Haydn's *La vera costanza*: April (four), May (four), June (four), July (one), August (three), October (one) and in 1786. Although we must list the work as a reprise, since it was reconstructed (after the fire) from some earlier sources, Haydn composed at least a substantial part for this important revival. *Vide supra*, pp. 526ff.
Bologna's *L'isola di Calipso*: April (three), May (three), June (two), July (one), August (one), September (one), and in 1786–90. Margherita Delicati made her début in this opera, taking Valdesturla's place. In a costume proposal by Porta of 12 May 1785 (EH, Eisenstadt, Baucassa), we read, 'Since Your Highness ordered a new costume to be made for Mad. Delicati . . .'. Harich in *HJB* I, 61.
Haydn's *Armida*: May (five), June (two), July (two), September (two), October (six), and in 1786–8.
Sarti's *La Didone abbandonata*: May (three), June (two) and July (one).
Anfossi's *Il geloso in cimento*: July (one), August (one), September (three), November (six) and in 1787. Since most, if not all, of the work's original performance material was destroyed in the 1779 fire, new material had to be copied. This new material (EH, Budapest, Ms. Mus. OE–37) did not include Atto I° of the score (Viennese origin), on which may be seen evidence of the fire; the rest of the score is lost. The new parts are dated in part 1785 (V. I 'Primo' part) and were copied by Schellinger and Anon. 11 and 14.

Fragmentary vocal parts, some of the 1778 performance (copied by Joseph Elssler, who died in 1782), and some of 1785 (Schellinger and Anon. 10), have survived. Haydn's changes, apart from cuts and transpositions, included the following: Atto II°, No. 11: Haydn added an insertion aria which has survived only incomplete (no vocal part etc.); *incipit* in Bartha-Somfai, 298; the composer cannot be determined. No. 16. Haydn added his own insertion aria, 'Dica pure chi vuol dire' (XXIVb:8) – *vide supra*, p.648 ; it was added before the copyists began their work, i.e. it was decided upon beforehand and was not a later addition. The whole orchestral material is present, which means that using Artaria's piano score, the aria may now be reconstructed entirely; Haydn made corrections in the parts after the Artaria printed had appeared – some of these are on a large scale (24 new bars added: see Bartha-Somfai, 299, for the interesting details); Haydn later cut the aria. No. 17: Haydn added an insertion aria here after the parts had been copied (*incipit*: Bartha-Somfai, 300); only the V. I has survived. Bartha-Somfai, 297–300.

Bianchi's *La villanella rapita*: August (one), September (five), October (one) and in 1786–7.

The season this year ran from April to the beginning of November (six performances in that month). Harich in *HJB* I, 62ff.

MARIONETTE THEATRE 1785

No performances registered for this year

THE GERMAN THEATRICAL TROUPE 1785

This was Diwald's last season at Eszterháza: the list of his members was given for the 1784 season (*supra*, p. 483), and at that time we also noted his undated correspondence of this period. There is no further news of the troupe's constitution or of their repertoire for this, their last season.

This year also saw the beginning of the regular operatic season at Pressburg, sponsored by Count Johann Nepomuk Erdödy and managed by Hubert Kumpf. Many of the operas given were those of the Eszterháza repertoire, including Haydn's *La fedeltà premiata* (1785), *La vera costanza* (1786), *Orlando Paladino* (1786) and *Armida* (1786). A complete list of the Pressburg productions in numerical order is included in an 'Anhang' to the libretto of Salieri's *Axur* for the Pressburg performance of 1788 (Országos Széchényi Könyvtár, Mus. Th. 2874–b), with the entire theatrical personnel (including orchestra) as well.[1] Haydn's operas were given in German, translated by Franz Xaver Giržick (himself a baritone; born at Prague in 1760). The orchestra there was smaller than that at Eszterháza, but included two clarinets (necessary for one of their first productions in 1785, Mozart's *Entführung*).

Haydn was in Vienna in January, and had apparently sold twelve of his latest minuets (IX:8) to Torricella, who announced them on 12 and 15 January in the *Wiener Zeitung* ('ganz neu und sehr schön'). They had been performed at the Casino in the Trattnerhof, and in the event they were printed not by the nearly bankrupt Torrricella but by Artaria.

On 15 January, as we have seen, Mozart played his six new quartets (K.387 etc.) to Haydn, and the last three again for Haydn and Leopold Mozart on 12 February. (For Haydn to be so often in Vienna was a special luxury, made possible by the fact that the operatic season in Hungary did not start till April.) On 2 February he was back in Eszterháza (see his letter quoted *supra*, p. 505) but returned to Vienna for his initiation at the Lodge 'Zur wahren Eintracht'.

---

1 In the *Hochgräflich-Erdödyscher Theaterallmanach auf das Jahr 1788*. Herausgegeben von Johann Nep. Schüller ... Pressburg [1788], the precise dates when the Haydn operas were performed are given, viz.: *La fedeltà premiata*: première 3 June 1785, repeated 6 June, 1 July, 1 August, 7 October and 9 December. *La vera costanza*: première 30 January 1786, repeated 6 February, 28 April, 28 August. In 1786 *La fedeltà premiata* was repeated on 21 February and on 8 June 1787. *Orlando Paladino*: première on 22 May 1786, repeated on 5 June, 2 October, and on 26 January and 20 July 1787. *Armida*: première on 3 November, repeated on 6 Nov., 1 Dec. *La fedeltà premiata* had the longest success, followed by *La vera costanza*.

In an 'Anhang' to this delightful little *Allmanach*, which seems to exist in only one copy (Stadtbibliothek, Vienna, 94718 G), there are two fold-out extracts of music, a Duet from *Orlando Paladino* 'Dein allerliebstes Gesichtelein', i.e. No. 16, 'Quel tuo visetto amabile'; and an 'Arietta' from *La vera costanza* (both listed as 'by Hayden'), 'Ich habe kein Vermögen, bin arm erzogen', i.e. No. 6 'Io son poverina'. (These interesting early editions not listed in Hoboken.)

On 15 March, Michael Ignatz Stadlmann, I. R. Lute and Violin Maker, furnished 'a bundle of the best Italian fifth' (*Quinten*) strings,[1] 'as ordered by H. von Haydn', and four G-strings.

On 18 March 1785 the *Wiener Blättchen* wrote:

> Tomorrow on St Joseph's Day, Herr Willmann will give a grand musical academy in the I. R. National Theatre [Burgtheater], in which will be given Haydn's Opera, l'Isola disabitata, a grand new work not yet heard here, the only one [*sic*] that this favourite composer set to Italian words, and for which two years ago he received the well-known magnificent present from His Royal Apostolic Spanish Majesty. Here given for the first time.
>
> [Hoboken Vol. II, p. 395. Pohl II, 100]

According to Pohl, it was the violoncello virtuoso of that name who put on the concert.

A friend of Haydn's brother Michael in Salzburg, P. Werigand Rettensteiner, came to visit Joseph in Eszterháza and was presented with the new edition by Boßler of the Sonatas Nos. 54–56 (XI:40–42), on which Rettensteiner wrote: 'Following 3 Sonatas were given to me as a present by Herr Joseph Haydn at Esterhasz on 3rd June 1785 at an entertaining conversation of one hour, and they were played by him' (Rettensteiner's copy now at the Monastery of Michaelbeuern, *Land* Salzburg. H. Unverricht in Larsen *Festskrift*, 296).

Only one letter has survived of the correspondence between Joseph and Michael Haydn. Did they exchange music? In a letter to Sebastian Winter, *valet-de chambre* at Donaueschingen (and a former servant of the Mozarts), of 3 January 1785, Michael discusses sending some of his works to Donaueschingen and says he will send news if something of his turns up(!), or of 'the Viennese Heyden' (Michael signs himself 'Heyden' in this letter), 'but as far as I am concerned, there is not much to hope for, because of my age, and my course is run.' In the same years as this rather paranoic letter was sent, Michael composed one of his greatest compositions, the Serenade in D with its enormous slow movement in D minor (Andante con variazioni, with trumpets and drums, lasting some thirteen minutes). Did he send a copy to Eszterháza? And who arranged for Michael's three symphonies to be published with Artaria about this time? Joseph? Mozart? Michael tended to retreat into the friendly cellar of St Peter's, drink his wine with a few cronies, and forget the outside world: his is a curious story of a man with enormous talents who wasted them on provincial Salzburg.

We do not know if Haydn took the time to see his *La fedeltà premiata* performed in Pressburg – probably not. In the *Preßburger Zeitung* of 15 June we read, in an article about the new Erdödy Theatre,

> The applause of estimable connoisseurs continues to pursue them as before. Recently the opera *Die belohnte Treue* was twice performed to the satisfaction and admiration of all who heard it. The music is by Herr Hayden, that Hungarian Orpheus who will remain for all time an object of veneration for all friends of music. [*HJB* VIII, 274f., in Eugene Hartzell's translation.]

On 1 September, Mozart wrote the famous letter of dedication to Haydn, accompanying the Artaria first edition of his Quartets (K.387, 421, 428,458, 464, 465):

---

1 EH, Budapest, A.M. XVIII.1212. Valkó II, 602. In this summary bill, he notes 7 July a bundle of E, 19th ditto a bundle of E, 17 September ditto a bundle of E, and 19 Nov. a bundle of E. Total 15 fl. 20 xr., countersigned by Haydn. A bundle cost 3 fl., the four G-strings 20 xr.

[To Haydn from W. A. Mozart. *Italian 'Tu' form*]
To my dear friend Haydn:

A father, having resolved to send his sons into the great world, finds it advisable to entrust them to the protection and guidance of a highly celebrated man, the more so since this man, by a stroke of luck, is his best friend. – Here, then, celebrated man and my dearest friend, are my six sons. – Truly, they are the fruit of a long and laborious effort, but the hope, strengthened by several of my friends, that this effort would, at least in some small measure, be rewarded, encourages and comforts me that one day, these children may be a source of consolation to me. – You yourself, dearest friend, during your last sojourn in this capital, expressed to me your satisfaction with these works. – This, your approval, encourages me more than anything else, and thus I entrust them to your care, and hope that they are not wholly unworthy of your favour. – Do but receive them kindly, and be their father, guide, and friend! From this moment I cede to you all my rights over them: I pray you to be indulgent to their mistakes, which a father's partial eye may have overlooked, and despite this, to cloak them in the mantle of your generosity which they value so highly. From the bottom of my heart I am, dearest friend,

Your most sincere friend,
W. A. Mozart

Vienna, 1st September 1785.   [CCLN, 49f.]

In October, Haydn had a remarkable visitor, General Francisco de Miranda, the Venezuelan revolutionist and friend of Washington and Hamilton in America. In his Diary, he writes (26 October 1785):

... the famous Hayden [*sic*], for whom I was carrying letters, accompanied me directly and showed me the whole of the Palace ... The theatre which performs the whole year round costs him [the Prince] 30,000 florins a year, and the actors' salaries are for life – in the evening went to the opera, saw the Prince, his niece, and his mistress, vulgar woman ... the representation cold – the orchestra twenty-four instruments, Hayden played the harpsichord [*el clave*]. ...

[Two days later, 28 October, we read:] The next day early Hayden came and we went together in a coach sent by the Prince to see the garden ... talked a lot about music with Hayden, and he agreed with me about the merit of Boccherini ...   [*Viajes Diarios 1750–1785*, Caracas, 1929, vol. 1, p. 435]

Two letters to Artaria concern the publication of Haydn's new piano trios:

[To Artaria & Co., Vienna. *German*]

Estoras, 26th November 1785.

Dearest Friend!

Please let me know, by the Monday dispatch of the Princely Hussars, if my Sonatas[1] are already engraved, and when you intend to give them to the Countess Witzey;[2] the reason why I would very much like to know is that, before my departure, which will be in a fortnight at the latest, I want to pay a visit to the Countess at her estate; I only waited for the first proofs of the Sonatas, in order to correct them, for there is a mistake that needs to be set right. Therefore please write me once more on next Monday. I would also ask you to send me a copy of the last *Lieder* on this occasion; I shall pay for it with thanks. I am, most respectfully.

Your wholly obedient servant,
Haydn.

1 Piano Trios Nos. 19–21 (XV:6–8), which Artaria published as Op. 40 the following Spring.
2 Marianne Witzey (Viczay), *née* Countess Grassalkovics de Gydrak.

[Address:]   Monsieur
         Monsieur d'Artaria et
         Compag
                à
                  Vienne.

Please expedite.
[Artaria's clerk notes: 'Haydn / Esterhass 26th Nov. 1785 / answered 6th Dec.']
[CCLN, 50f.]

[To Artaria & Co., Vienna. *German*]

Estoras, 10th December 1785.

Mon tres cher Amy!

Day before yesterday I received the pianoforte Sonatas,[1] and was greatly astounded to have to see such bad engraving, and so many glaring errors in all the parts, especially in the pianoforte part. I was at first so furious that I wanted to return the money to you and send the score of the Sonatas instantly to Herr Hummel[2] in Berlin; for the sections which are occasionally illegible, and the passages omitted or badly spaced, will bring little honour to me and little profit to you. Everyone who buys them will curse the engraver and have to stop playing, especially on page 8, and on the first page of the 3rd Divertimento,[3] page 15, where the ⬜ marked in red are especially badly laid out, and this seems to be the result of misguided space saving. I would rather pay for two new plates out of my own pocket than see such confusion.

Even a professional would have to study before disentangling this passage, and then where would the dilettante be? Four notes are missing on page 18, and in the last line the engraver was too lazy to write out the whole of the bass part: such abbreviations[4] and signs are all very well in the viola part of symphonies, but not in pianoforte parts. Moreover, most of the natural signs are so small, and occasionally so close to the note, that you can barely see them: one such case is found on page 18, at the end of the uppermost stave. There are prodigiously many wrong notes and omitted notes. On pages 6 and 8 most of the following signs ∾ are wrongly placed, for they ought not to be put directly over the note but over the neighbouring dot, in this way: ▱ (page 6, bar 4). All the way through, the dots ought to be further away from the notes, so that the sign ∾ comes directly over the dot. And on this very page, in the second stave, you should put instead of the sign *tr*: the following: ↛ , for the first one, as the engraver has done it, means a trill, whilst mine is a half mordent.[5] If, therefore, the Herr Engraver doesn't know signs of this sort, he should inform himself by studying the masters, and not follow his own stupid ideas. In the 2nd Sonata he even forgot the tempo at the beginning, where the clef is. A whole bar is missing in the violin part, too. I spent the whole of yesterday and half of today in correcting, and yet I have only glanced over them.

Now, my good friend, see to it that everything is corrected, for otherwise little honour will accrue to either of us. By the way, I hope to see you personally and am, meanwhile, most respectfully,

         Your wholly obedient servant,
         Joseph Haydn.   [CCLN, 51f.]

1 Trio Sonatas, see previous letter.
2 Hummel, the celebrated music publisher, whose name often occurs in Haydn's letters of this period.
3 Divertimento, another name for Sonata (i.e. Trio).
4 'Schlender', literally 'lounger', 'dawdler'. Probably the engraver put // or 'col basso', as Haydn would have written it in the score. Since Artaria published parts, the abbreviations would be meaningless.
5 We have seen that on the autograph of the D major Trio No. 20, Haydn wrote out the principal ornaments for the engraver's benefit.

It transpires that Artaria actually had the Trios engraved again. He wrote to Bernhard Schott in Mainz, for on 3 January 1786 we find Schott writing to the Canon J. G. Batton, 'Artaria asked me to repair the ruined piano trios for the Countess Witzay. So I shall have them engraved speedily' (Hoboken, vol. I, p. 688).

Chronicle 1786

ITALIAN OPERAS 1786

This year 125 performances are registered, a record for Eszterháza (Harich in *HJB* I, 64):

Niccolò Zingarelli: ALSINDA. Dramma per musica da rappresentarsi nel teatro di S. A. il sig. principe regnante NICCOLÓ ESTERHASI DE GALANTHA L'ANNO 1786 [angel with harp & wreath on cloud] IN OEDENBURGO, Nella STAMPERIA DI GIUSEPPE SIESS.

Personaggi

Alsinda	Mdme. Bologna
Zelmira	Mdme. Nencini
Singeo	Mons. Morelli
Livango	Mons. Dictler [*sic*]
Parmene	Mons. Braghetti
Scilace	Mons. Nencini

Libretto: Copy (in Italian & German) in the Carvalhaes Collection (Vol. 7), Biblioteca, Conservatorio di Musica Santa Cecilia, Rome. Siess's bill of 28 February 1786: EH, Budapest, A.M. 64.4019. There is also a 'Piano dimostrativo' listing the proposed singers as in the libretto. First performance: 1 March (after three stage rehearsals on 26, 27, 38 February), repeated on 5, 9, 14, 19 and 23 March, 11 and 20 April, 6 June, 13 July, 20 August, 22 October and, for the last time, on 26 November. There are documents showing that *Alsinda* was given as a marionette opera. Eszterháza performance material: Schellinger's bill (A.M. 18.1211) lists 171 *Bögen* of vocal parts and 139 *Bögen* of instrumental parts. The score, the orchestral parts (lacking Ob. II) and most of the vocal parts (all the numbers and the recitative booklet for Alsinda) are in EH, Budapest, Ms. Mus. OE–97. The score of this *opera seria* comes, apparently, from Milan. The local copyists were Schellinger and Anon. 11. Apart from the usual cuts and transpositions, Haydn made no additions (arias). Bartha-Somfai 131,300–2. Harich in *HJB* I,65.

Domenico Cimarosa: La ballerina amante dramma giocoso per musica da rappresentarsi nel teatro di S. A. il sig. principe regnante niccoló Esterhasi de Galantha. L'anno 1786. In Oedenburgho Nella stamperia di Gussepe [*sic*] Siess.

Madama Rubiconda ...	Mdme Nencini.
Don Totomaglio ...	Sigr. Bianchi.
Cavalier Bireno ...	Sigr. Braghetti.
Betta Locandiera ...	Mdme. Polcelli [*sic*].
Franchiglione ...	Sig. Dictler [*sic*].
Ortensia ...	Mdme. Delicati.
Mazzacogna Vetturino ...	Sigr. Nencini.
Don Petronio ...	Sigr. Morelli.

Libretto: Copy (in Italian and with a German translation of the plot) in the Theatersammlung (621.754-A. Th.Slg.), Österreichische Nationalbibliothek, Vienna. Siess's bill of 30 March 1786 (EH, Budapest, A.M. 64.4018) is for the third *Bogen* of the libretto 'which had to be reprinted because of the aria that was sent afterwards.' There is also a 'Piano dimostrativo' listing the proposed singers as in the libretto. First performance: 2 April (double rehearsal on 1 April), repeated on 2, 4, 16, 18 and 25 April, with a last perf. on 21 May. Eszterháza performance material: Schellinger's bill (A.M. 18.1211) lists 194 *Bögen* vocal parts and 219 *Bögen* instrumental material. There has survived, as Ms. Mus. OE–54, the score (from Italy), the complete orchestral material, all the complete vocal numbers and the recit. booklets of Mazzacogna and 'Monsieur Franchiglione'; the local copyists were Schellinger, Anon. 14 and Anon. 10. Apart from cuts and transpositions, Haydn added an aria in Atto II°, Sc. 3, 'No. 12' of the score (which, as usual, is missing): 'Se il mio core non comprendi' (a vocal part has survived). It is not by Haydn, but it would seem to be the reason for the libretto's having to be reprinted. Bartha-Somfai, 131, 320–4. Harich in *HJB* I, 65.

Domenico Cimarosa: Chi dell'altrui si veste presto si spoglia. Dramma giocoso in due atti. Da rappresentarsi nel teatro di S. A. il Sig. Principe Regnante Niccolò Esterhasi de Galantha l'anno 1786. In Oedenburgo, nella stamperia di Giuseppe Siess.

Libretto: Printed in an edition of 250 copies (none survives); Barbara Pfundtner bound 150 of them. Siess's bill in A.M. 64.4017, dated 30 April 1786. The 'Piano dimostrativo' lists the cast as follows:

Palmira Nencini	Ninetta
Delicati	Baronessa Stellidaura
Polzelli	Mirandolina
Braghetti	Putifare
Bianchi	Martuffo
Morelli	Gian Fabrizio
Dichtler	Gabbamondo

First performance: 2 May (after two rehearsals), repeated only on 4 May and 16 May. Eszterháza performance material: Schellinger's bill (A.M. 18.1211) lists 189 *Bögen* vocal parts and 222 *Bögen* instrumental material. EH, Budapest, Ms. Mus. OE–56 includes the score (from Italy), and the complete orchestral material (vocal parts are wanting), copied by Schellinger and Anon. 11 and 13. On the inner cover of the score, the note by Haydn, 'distributed [unreadable] of Dec. 785'. Apart from cuts and transpositions, Haydn added an aria in Atto II°, Sc. 5 (whose? *incipit* in Bartha-Somfai, 305) and cut the whole of the third act. Harich, *Musikgeschichte*, 58. Bartha-Somfai, 131f., 304–6. Harich in *HJB* I, 65.

Tommaso Traetta: Ifigenia in Tauride. Dramma per musica in tre atti. Da rappresentarsi nel teatro di S. A. il Sig. Principe Regnante Niccolò Esterhasi de Galantha, l'anno 1786. In Oedenburgo, nella stamperia di Giuseppe Siess.

Libretto: 200 copies of the Italian and 300 copies of a German libretto (separate); of the Italian, EH Eisenstadt has a copy. The 'Piano dimostrativo' lists the cast as follows:

Matilde Bologna (Iffigenia[*sic*])
Marg. Delicati (Pilade)
Braghetti (Oreste)
Nencini (Toante).

Siess's bill, 30 June 1786: A.M. 64.4016, with a note 'the same in German'. First performance: 4 July (rehearsals on 26 & 28 June, 1 July; general rehearsal on 3 July); further rehearsals on 19, 21, 22 (double rehearsal), 24 and 25 July – a very difficult piece, obviously. There were 30 Grenadier 'supers' involved, also six boys and six girls, to which two more boys and two more girls were later added. At one point there were 54 'supers' on the stage, the organization of which made great difficulties for Porta, the theatre manager. But the Prince liked it and in a costume bill (EH, Eisenstadt, Baucassa 1786) by Porta, it is said that two more performances, on 26 and 27 July, were especially ordered by the Prince. There was a Turkish ballet, danced by three girls and two boys, which also required further rehearsals. Eszterháza performance material: Schellinger's bill (A.M. 18.1211) lists 168 *Bögen* vocal and 189 *Bögen* instrumental parts. EH, Budapest, Ms. Mus. OE–36 includes the whole score but none of the parts (score from Vienna). Apart from cuts and transpositions, Haydn added his great insertion *scena* for Oreste, 'Ah, tu non senti, amico' (XXIVb:10), Atto I°, Sc. 1. In Sc. 5, Oreste's Aria 'Oh Dio, dov'è la morte' was cancelled and another one substituted. Bartha-Somfai give the opening *incipit* (309); here is the second section (composer?):

Haydn made very extensive cuts in this work; whole numbers (choruses) had to be omitted. Harich, *Musikgeschichte*, 58. Bartha-Somfai, 132, 307–10.

Luigi Caruso: L'albergatrice vivace.

Libretto: No copy survives of the 250 printed, Siess's bill (30 September for delivery in July): A.M. 64.4015. The 'Piano dimostrativo' gives the cast:

Palmira Nencini (Barberina) [was actually sung by Barbara Sassi: *vide infra*]
M. Delicati (Belinda)
L. Polzelli (Marinetta)
Braghetti (Le Blanc)
Nencini (Pericco)
Bianchi (Bartolo)
Morelli (Micheluccio)

First performance: 6 August (rehearsals: 2, 4, 5 August), repeated on 8 and 15 August, 5, 12, 26 September, 15 October and 7 November. Eszterháza performance material: Schellinger's bill (A.M. 18.1211) lists 192 *Bögen* vocal and 189 *Bögen* instrumental parts. Ms. Mus. OE–58 (EH, Budapest) includes

Atto I° only of the (Venetian) score and fragmentary material, copied (dated 1786) by Schellinger and Anon. 11 and 14. Barberina's vocal part is marked by Haydn 'M. Barbara Sassi'. Apart from cuts, Haydn made very few changes in what Bartha-Somfai rightly call the strikingly taut and concise score. Bartha-Somfai, 132f., 310f. Harich in *HJB* I, 66.

Vincenzo Righini: L'incontro inaspettato. Die unvermuthete Zusammenkunft. Commedia per musica di Nunziato Porta. Da rappresentarsi nel teatro di S. A. il Sig. Principe Regnante Niccolò Esterhasi de Galantha. L'anno 1786.

> Aurora ... Mdme [Matilde] Bologna
> Irene ... Mdme Nencini
> Rosina ... Mdme. Polzelli
> Lindoro ... Sigr. Braghetti
> Gradasso ... Sigr. Nencini
> Barone ... Sigr. Bianchi
> Cardone ... Sigr. Morelli
> Pirolino ... Sigr. Dictler [*sic*]

Libretto: Porta ordered 124 copies of the Italian libretto from Kurzbeck in Vienna (Michael Chmelik, the director submitted a bill for them on 10 March 1785)[1] and had Siess print the title page and the cast for the Eszterháza performance. Copy: Gesellschaft der Musikfreunde, Vienna. The Opera had been given at Vienna in 1785 (therefore there were already libretti available at Kurzbeck's). First performance: 1 October (after three stage rehearsals – on 25, 27 and 29 September – and a dress rehearsal on 30 Sept.), repeated only on 3 and 19 October, Eszterháza performance material: Schellinger's bill lists 189 *Bögen* of vocal and 222 *Bögen* of instrumental material. EH, Budapest, Ms. Mus. OE–83 includes the score by the Wenzel Sukowaty office in Vienna (missing in part, from Sc. 11 of Atto II° to end) and the incomplete orchestral parts; the vocal parts are lost. Apart from cuts and transpositions, Haydn cancelled Gradasso's Aria, 'Se sapesti' (Atto I°, Sc. 3) and added another which we already met in Gassmann's *L'amore artigiano* (*incipit*: Bartha-Somfai, 186), but using the original text. Haydn's authorship is unlikely. Bartha-Somfai, 133f., 186, 311–4.

Giuseppe Sarti: Idalide. Dramma per musica. Da rappresentarsi nel teatro di S. A. il Sig. Principe Regnante Niccolò Esterhasi de Galantha. L'anno 1786. – In Oedenburgo, nella stamperia di Giuseppe Siess. Libretto: 250 copies (none survives) with a German translation of the plot. The cast may be reconstructed by a 'Piano dimostrativo':

> Bologna (Idalide)
> P. Nencini (Alcilae)
> Braghetti (Enrico)
> Nencini (Palmoro)
> Bianchi (Ataliba)
> Dichtler (Ismaro).

First performance: 24 October, repeated on the 26th; 2, 12 and 19 Nov., 21 Dec., and in 1787. In the above mentioned 'Piano' (A.M. 3996), the work is, curiously, listed: 'Idalide o sia vergine del Sole opera seria a 6 persone di Haydn' (Porta). Eszterháza performance material: Schellinger's bill (A.M. 13.1211) lists 185 *Bögen* vocal and 178 *Bögen* instrumental parts. EH, Budapest, Ms. Mus. OE–91 contains the complete score, the orchestral parts (lacking Horn II) and two booklets of vocal parts. The score is of Italian origin. The parts were copied by Schellinger and Anon. 10 (with the date 1786). Apart from cuts, Haydn found the work to have no overture and added one (composer? *incipit*: Bartha-Somfai, 314). Harich, *Musikgeschichte*, 59. Bartha-Somfai, 134f., 314f. Harich in *HJB* I, 68.

Domenico Cimarosa: I due baroni di Rocca azzurra.
Libretto: if one was printed, none has survived. First performance: 6 Dec. (St Nicholas), repeated on 10 and 19 Dec. and in 1787. The cast may be reconstructed from a 'Piano dimostrativo' (which is incomplete and was not followed: Ripamonti left at the beginning of July):

> Ripamonti (Laura)
> Delicati (Sandrina)
> Bianchi (Demofonte)
> Morelli (Baron Jotaro [*sic*])
> Dichtler (Franchetto)

1 A.M. 64.4020: including the binding 25 fl. '12 copies bound in fine green paper with gold borders, each at 10 Xr. 2[fl.]'. Siess's bill of 30 Sept. 1786, A.M. 64.4015, sends Porta the bill, which reads *inter alia* 'Anno 1786, in the month of July: an opera libretto called L'Albergatrice vivace, of 4¾ Bögen, of which 250 copies were printed, a Bögen as agreed at 5 fl. makes 23 fl. 45 xr. More in September: a title page for a Viennese opera, together with the cast list, tit: <u>die unvermuthete Zusammenkunft</u> 1 [fl.] 15 [xr.] Suma 25 fl. Oedenburg, 20th Sept. 1786' countersigned by Porta 'Director vidi' and Siess's receipt of 23 Feb. 1787. Facsimile of both documents in Bartha-Somfai, 6 and 7 (text, with mistakes, on 134).

The actual vocal parts (EH) read, however, *Madama* (Haydn: 'M^d Sassi / Ripamonti'); *Sandra* (Haydn: 'M. Delicati'); *Demofonte* (Haydn: 'Bianchi'); *Barone* (Haydn: 'Morelli') and *Franchetto* (Haydn: 'Dichtler'). Eszterháza performance material: Schellinger's bill (A.M. 18.1211) lists ('I due Paroni') 189 *Bögen* of vocal and 224 *Bögen* of instrumental parts. EH, Budapest, Ms. Mus. OE–55 includes the complete score, incomplete orchestral parts and most of the vocal parts (listed above). Sandra's booklet for the recit. is wanting. The score lists all the actual performers at Eszterháza: Madama was Sassi (the rest as in the 'Piano'). The parts were copied by Schellinger (with dates: 14 and 18 Nov. 1786) with Anon. 10, 11 and 73. Apart from cuts, Haydn made no major changes in this score. Bartha-Somfai, 135, 315–7. Harich in *HJB* I, 68; *HJB* VII, 32, n. 11.

Nine operas from earlier seasons were repeated:
Stabinger's *Le astuzie di Bettina*: 3 and 21 March, 6 April, 30 May, 27 June, 6 July, 3 August, 28 November and 14 December.
Bianchi's *La villanella rapita*: 7 March, 9 April, 9 May, 15 June, 11 and 23 July, 10 and 24 August, 10 Oct., 14 Nov. and 3 Dec., and in 1787.
Haydn's *La vera costanza*: 12 and 18 March, 7 May and 29 July.
Anfossi's *Il geloso in cimento*: 16 March, 23 April, 11 May, 18 July, 1 and 17 August, 29 Oct., 9, 16 and 23 Nov., and in 1787.
Bologna's *L'isola di Calipso abbandonata*: 26 March, 18 May, 22 and 27 August, 3, 19, 21 and 28 Sept., 31 Oct., and in 1787–90.
Haydn's *Armida*: 30 March, 14 May, 11 and 20 June, 16 July, 8 October, 30 Nov., and in 1787–8.
Sarti's *Giulio Sabino*: 27 and 30 April, 25 May, 4 June, 15 August, 10 and 17 Sept., 12 Oct., 17 Dec., and in 1787.
Anfossi's *Il matrimonio per inganno*: 23 and 28 May, 1, 8, 13 and 22 June, 2, 9, 30 and 30 July, 4, 14 and 24 Sept., 5 and 17 Oct., 21 Nov., 12 Dec., and in 1788.
Gazzaniga's *L'isola d'Alcina*: 18 and 25 June. For this revival, Haydn composed (Atto I^o, Sc. 5) a new insertion aria, 'Sono Alcina' (XXIVb:9), of which the autograph has survived. In the EH material two autograph violin parts (I & II) have survived, as well as the beginning of a vocal-bass line particella (bars 1–37 of vocal part written, not the bass line). Facsimile: 23 of Bartha-Somfai. Literature of this and other revivals: Bartha-Somfai, 306f., Harich in *HJB* I, 68–70. Watermarks of Haydn's autograph parts: 'cs', three crescents of declining size.

MARIONETTE THEATRE 1786

Zingarelli's *Alsinda* also given with marionettes. Harich in *HJB* I, 65.

THE GERMAN THEATRICAL TROUPE 1786

The new theatrical troupe – Diwald's had left at the end of 1785 – was Johann Mayer. According to his contract with Prince Nicolaus of 23 May 1785 (A.T. 50), he undertook to perform plays, ballets, German operattas and a puppet opera (is this the explanation of *Alsinda* in the marionette theatre?) between Easter and the end of 1786. In a subsequent letter Mayer informed the Prince that, apart from himself, his company contained seventeen members; the dancers formed their own *corps de ballet* of eight members. Here is Mayer's list (taken, like all this information, from Horányi, pp. 131ff.; German, pp. 135ff.):

Male comedians: Myself: first fathers, first heroes, character parts. H. Anton Hornung: first lovers, young character and comic parts. H. Matthias Mayer: second lovers. H. Lang: second fathers, second character parts. H. Paul Hornung: secondary parts, especially those of low comedy. H. Harr: Jews, secondary parts. H. Lorenz: prompter. A boy actor.
Actresses: my wife: first mothers in tragedies and comedies. My sister, Mad. Ditelmeyer: leading ladies. Mad. Therese Mayer: first soubrettes. Nanette Hornung: second soubrettes. My daughter: performs.
In the ballet: H. Anton Hornung: serious dancer, ballet master. H. Matthias Mayer: comic dancer, ballet master. Both are good and each does ballet in his own fashion. H. Paul Hornung, H. Lange: supernumeraries. The boy dances. Mad. Therese Mayer: *prima ballerina*. Mlle Nanette Hornung, *seconda ballerina*. My daughter dances.

Mayer adds that four of his group are singers and the others, while not being professionals, can sing too. He agrees to add one more heroine to Mad. Ditelmeyer and to engage some other actors and a good *danseuse*. He enclosed a letter of praise from Temesvár. There is no record of their repertoire at Eszterháza in 1786, but the next year they were included in the Gotha *Theater-Kalender*.

On 28 January, Boßler issued the following announcement in the Frankfurt *Staats-Ristretto* (Unverricht in Larsen *Festskrift*, 291f.):

Announcement

Newly [*ganz neu*] appeared in the Boßler Music Publishing House at Speier:
Joseph Haydn 3 Piano Sonatas with an accompaniment for a *violin* and *violoncello*
op. 40 with a very accurate silhouette of Herr Haydn 2 fl. 24 kr.

[Copies: HCRL, Seitenstetten Monastery, Munich Univ. Library. Title page
reproduced here: see pl. 27. These were the piano trios of which two were by
Pleyel and one by Haydn himself, No. 18 (XV:5). Haydn had, as we see, sold them
not only to Forster but also to his friend Boßler.]

Two documents from the Esterházy Archives[1] inform us (1) that 'the coachman of
Capellmeister Haydn has entered the hospital here and is to receive the necessary
medicaments. Eszterház, 17 March 1786. Nicolaus Fürst Esterhazy' and (2)
'Commission ... Capellmeister Haydn is to receive in *lieu* of a new winter uniform
170 Fl. and then for a new summer uniform 170 Fl., together that is 340 Fl.', signed by
Prince Nicolaus at Esterház, 17 May 1786, and the receipt by Haydn, which only
mentions cash received for a summer uniform 170 Fl.

Haydn made a flying trip to Pressburg, as the following letter reports:

[To Nanette Peyer, Pressburg.[2] *German*]

Estoras, 5th May 1786.

Dearest Nanette!

I cannot tell you how happy I am that I shall be seeing you soon. Would you
kindly ask His Grace the Count[3] if he would be good enough to send his carriage
for me on this coming Thursday the 11th inst. as far as Fraunkürchen,[4] where I
shall arrive on Friday the 12th at 9 o'clock at the latest, having left Estoras at 5 in
the morning with my own horses. I would then go on to Pressburg with the
Count's carriage and arrive there between 1 and 2. I must tell you in advance,
however, that I can't stay there more than 24 hours. Hoping to embrace you soon,
I am, with the greatest esteem,

Your most obedient servant,
Joseph Haydn.

P.S. I respectfully kiss the hands
of the Count and Countess.

[On the outside is the following note in another hand: 'dt. 5 et accept 7ᵗ. May 1786/
Jos Hayden (*sic*)'.]   [CCLN, 52f.]

In a pathetic letter, Johann Schellinger petitions the Prince to help him. 'Although
through no fault of mine I have had to endure a grave illness, as Your Highness
knows'. He asks the Prince to take over the expenses of the illness, 'for my whole
monthly salary has to go in the baths, food and small things' and he presented the bills
to the amount of 32f. 10xr. 'It is hard for me to pay it all'. Prince Nicolaus promptly
paid the sum (signed 23 July 1786): Harich in *HJB* IV, 99f.

In an announcement in the *Preßburger Zeitung* of 29 July 1786, Ignaz Pleyel offers
twelve new quartets by subscription, lamenting bitterly that pirated reprints and
'mangled editions' of his works had robbed him of his legitimate profits. Opp. 3 and 4
of his Quartets were made without his knowledge from MS. copies, and this has
determined him to become his own publisher: which, of course, he did, and with great
success.

1 A.M. 64.3993; 18.1205–1206. Valkó II, 602f.
2 See pp. 487, 505.
3 Apponyi.
4 Frauenkirchen, a pilgrimage town in Burgenland, about midway between Eszterháza and Pressburg.

On 17 August Frederick The Great died at Sans-Souci, and in his memory Haydn composed the Cantata which has been discussed *supra*, p. 645.

This was also the year in which Haydn signed a large contract with William Forster, which reads as follows:

[Contract with William Forster, London. *French*. Only the signature in Haydn's hand]

[1786: exact date not known]

D[1]

I acknowledge to have received of *Monsieur* Guillaume Forster, merchant and music publisher, domiciled in the Strand at London, the sum of seventy pounds Sterling for 20[2] Symphonies, Sonatas, and other pieces of music composed by me, as enumerated below, the beginnings of which are as follows:

No. 1 a Symphony for various instruments which begins thus:[3]

[6 Divertimenti] for 2 *Flûtes traversieres* and Violoncello, which begin as follows:[4]

---

1 This 'D', which may mean 'Document', was probably added when the paper was used as evidence against Longman and Broderip. On the reverse side of this contract is a note, 'Haydns subjects', and D/Forster agt Longman & an[r] – This Paper Writing was shewn to Jos. Haydn at the time of his exam[n]'. in this Court before [me?] Ja Eyre'. This curious note refers to the suit between the two London publishers which must have taken place in about 1794, when Haydn was in England. Longman had imported the Artaria prints of the very pieces which Haydn had sold to Forster under exclusive contract. No more details of this suit are known. See letter of 28 February 1788 and the correspondence with Artaria of this period; also *Haydn in England 1791–1795*, p. 119.

2 The figure 'o' is almost illegible.

3 Symphonies 74, 70, 76, 77, 78, 81, Overture to *Armida*, Symphony 80.

4 These six Divertimenti (IV:6–11) are partly based on pieces from Haydn's earlier (1777) opera, *Il mondo della luna*.

First Set of three Sonatas for the Harpsichord, with Accompaniment of a Violin [and Violoncello]:[1]

Second Set of three different Sonatas for the Harpsichord, with Accompaniment of a Violin [and Violoncello]:[2]

1 Trios Nos. 18 (XV:5) and XV:3–4; the last two are actually by Haydn's pupil Pleyel.
2 Trios Nos. 22 (XV:9), 17 (XV:2) and 23 (XV:10).

And I certify and declare to the whole world that I sold the said Symphonies, Sonatas and other pieces to said *Monsieur* Guillaum Forster, and that I sent him the manuscripts on the following dates, *viz.*:

The six Sonatas for two *Flûtes traversieres* and Violoncello on 31st May 1784.

The Symphonies listed above as Nos. 1 and 2 through *Monsieur le General* de Jerningham[1] on 19th June 1784.

The Symphonies Nos. 4, 5 and 6 together with the aforementioned First Set of 3 Sonatas for the Harpsichord on 25th October 1784.

The Symphonies listed above as Nos. 7, 8 and 9 on 8th November 1784.

And the afore-mentioned Second Set of 3 Sonatas for the Harpsichord on 28th October 1785.

I further certify and declare that he has paid me the price we agreed upon, and that this sum of seventy pounds Sterling has been paid to me in full by letters of exchange on Vienna which he sent me for this purpose (with the exception of the fee for the two Symphonies Nos. 1 and 2, which fee was paid on my behalf to *Monsieur le General* de Jerningham,[1] then in London).

And I further certify and declare that the said Guillaum Forster is the sole proprietor of the said works, that I sold them to him as such, and that I cede and transfer to him all my rights and covenants thereto. In witness of which I have set my signature to this document at Esterhaz, this [not filled in] 1786.

> Giuseppe Haydn [m.p.]ria, *Maestro*
> *di capella di S: Alt: S: il principe*
> *Estorhazy.*

[CCLN, 53–5]

The bill which Schellinger submitted for the year's copying is scarcely believable:

Conto

What was copied from 1st [not 13] January 1786 to the end of December 1786 for the princely theatre, and delivered, as agreed, the Bogen for vocal parts à 7 xr., the instruments 5 xr.

Opera	Vocal parts 7 xr.	Instruments à 5 xr.
La ballerina Amante	194	219
Alsinda	171	139
Chi d'altrui si veste	189	222
Julio[!] Sabino	48	
L'albergatrice	192	189
Matrimonio pr. ing	9	29
L'isola d'Alcina	196	178
Iffigenia[!]	168	189
L'incontro inaspettato	189	222
Geloso in cimento	19	28
Idalide	185	178
I due Paroni [!]	189	224
Soma	1,749	1,817

Soma 335 Fl. 28 xr.
di 15 Decembri 1786   Joan Schilling [*sic*] Theatre copyist

The above total of operas copied has been carefully examined by me, the undersigned, and found to be correct.

> Josephus Haydn mpria
> Capell Meister

Estoras, 29 Dec. 1786.[2]
[A.M. XVIII.1211. Valkó II, 602 with wrong date, '13' Dec., also wrong in Bartha-Somfai 136f. and Bartha 155f.]

---

1 General Charles Jerningham, English Ambassador to the Court of Vienna. See also letter of 20 September 1787. It was he who provided the connection between Forster and Haydn.
2 The operas with only a small number of 'Bögen' are revivals for which only single insertion arias, etc. were needed in addition to material already there.

We would remind the reader that this was the year in which Haydn, incredibly, found time to compose the Five Concertos for the King of Naples; Symphonies Nos. 82, 84 and 86; to begin *The Seven Words*; and to compose some insertion arias.

Mozart's *Le nozze di Figaro* was first performed at Vienna on 1 May, but Haydn was not able to hear it until 8 January 1790. See also *Don Giovanni*'s première at Prague (October 1787), and the subsequent Viennese performances (Chronicle, *infra*, p. 700).

Chronicle 1787

ITALIAN OPERAS 1787

This year 98 performances are registered (Harich in *HJB* I, 77).

Pasquale Anfossi: Il sordo e l'avaro. Dramma giocoso per musica. Da rappresentarsi nel teatro di S. A. il Sig. Principe Regnante Nicolò Esterhasi de Galantha l'anno 1787. Vienna, Presso Franc. Antonio Kroyss.
Libretto: 500 copies ordered (none survives). Kroys's [*recte*] bill: 18 Feb. 1787 (EH, Eisenstadt). Cast (source not given in Harich, *Musikgeschichte*, 59) included Palmira Sassi, M. Delicati, Polzelli (female singers) and Morelli, Bianchi and Nencini (males). First performance: end of Feb., after three rehearsals; repeated in Feb. (once), March (one) and May (two). Eszterháza performance material: Schellinger's bill (A.M. 18.1220) lists 287 *Bögen* of vocal and 194 *Bögen* of instrumental parts, also some later additions (*vide infra*, p. 702). Nothing survives of this opera in EH. Bartha-Somfai 138, 317f. Harich in *HJB* I, 72f.

Francesco Bianchi: Il disertore. Dramma per musica in tre atti. In Oedenburg, nella stamperia di Giuseppe Siess

Personaggi:	
Ormondo, che commando un Corpo di Truppe . . .	Signor *Nencini*.
Gualtieri, Ospite in Casa di Belinda . . .	Signor *Braghetti*.
Adelina, promessa sposa di Gualtieri . . .	Madame *Bologna*.
Belinda.	Madame *Delicati*.
Corradino, Uffiziale . . .	Signor *Bianchi*.
Beraldo, amante occulto di Adelina.	Signor *Dictler* [*sic*]

Libretto: copy in Országos Széchényi Könyvtár, Sign. 160.858. In a Baucassa-Rechnung of March 1787 (EH, Eisenstadt), N. Porta is listed as the author, but as all the Italian sources list Bartolommeo Benincasa, Porta was clearly responsible only for the local additions and changes. See Bianchi's première in Teatro di S. Benedetto, Carnovale 1785, Venice (with Banti as Adelina and Pacchierotti as Gualtieri): Library of Congress copy of libretto, ML48, S978. In EH libretto, 'Berardo' for (*recte*) 'Beraldo'. First performance: end of April, repeated in May (three), June (two) and in 1788 and 1789. Eszterháza performance material: Schellinger's bill (A.M. 18.1220) lists 194 *Bögen* vocal and 239 *Bögen* instrumental parts. EH, Budapest, Ms. Mus. OE–45, includes the complete score (from Venice, copied by Coradino) and fragmentary vocal and orchestral material (partly dated 1 April 1787), copied by Schellinger, Anon. 10, 11 and 73. Apart from cuts and transpositions down, Haydn made the following major changes. Corradino, originally a castrato, was now given to Bianchi, a baritone (low tenor), whose parts Haydn wrote in the bass clef (*vide infra*). Atto II°, Sc. 4, Corradino's Aria, 'Un cor si tenero in petto' was cancelled and Haydn wrote a new insertion aria of his own composition (XXIVb:11) for Bianchi. Bartha-Somfai fail to understand that Bianchi did not sing the rest of his part in falsetto but two octaves lower (or one, depending on the situation: hence the transpositions of his part, e.g. Atto I°, Sc. 2, from F to E flat). Conte Perrucchetto, created by Bianchi in Haydn's *La fedeltà premiata*, was also written in the bass clef. Atto III°, Sc. 1 cut. Otherwise, Haydn seems to have respected this work, which may have been one of the reasons why his high opinion of Bianchi is also reflected in English sources (*Haydn in England 1791–1795*, p. 281). Harich, *Musikgeschichte*, 59f. Bartha-Somfai, 138f., 318–20. Harich in *HJB* I, 73.

Pietro Guglielmi: La Quaquera [Quakera] spiritosa. Dramma giocoso per musica. In Oedenburgo, Presso Giuseppe Siess. 1787.
Libretto: no copy survives. The cast may be reconstructed from EH material (score), Budapest:

Vertunna: Nencini [Palmira Sassi]	D. Matusio: Braghetti, crossed out and Dichtler substituted.
Cardellina: Sassi [Barbara Sassi]	Conte: Moratti [Libretto 1783: 'Il conte D. Bucefalo']
Robinetta: Polcelli [*sic*]	Kolibacco: Dichtler, crossed out and Bianchi substituted.
Tognino: Nencini [Santi Nencini]	

[Textbook consulted: 'La Quakera spiritosa ... Napoli MDCCLXXXIII', Library of Congress.] First performance: 3 June (preceded by five rehearsals: in a tailor's bill in EH, Eisenstadt, five Gypsy 'supers' are listed, apart from the singers); repeated in June (four times in all), July (three), August (two), September (two) and 1788. Eszterháza performance material: Schellinger's bill (A.M. 18.1220) lists 282 *Bögen* of vocal and 245 *Bögen* of instrumental parts. EH, Budapest, Ms. Mus. OE–19 includes the complete score (Italian origin), the orchestral parts and some of the vocal material, copied by Schellinger, Anon 11 and 73.

Apart from minor cuts and transpositions, Haydn's major changes included cutting entirely the whole part of Ciletta (necessitating other changes because of keys no longer matching). Atto I°, sinfonia: main theme cut in recapitulation(!). Sc. 10, Cardellina's Aria, 'Vada adagio, Signorina', was cancelled and Haydn wrote his own replacement (same text: XXIVb:12). The score and orchestral material were later removed except for a vocal-basso part in Haydn's autograph (facsimile: Bartha-Somfai, No. 26); we discovered the only extant (authentic) source at Donaueschingen Castle in 1957. Atto II°, Sc. 3: Polzelli's Aria 'Compatisca il genitore' was transposed from B flat to G, and the necessary parts copied by the young Johann Elssler, who makes his first appearance in EH material here insofar as he is not identical with Anon. 48. Sc. 5: Aria of Matusio, 'Senti, che ho fretta' ('Aria N 18') was removed from all parts including the (otherwise complete) *particella* for vocal soloists; was this a Haydn insertion? Haydn followed an old cut in his score made before it arrived in Hungary: Atto III° was cancelled. Harich, *Musikgeschichte*, 59. Bartha-Somfai, 139f., 320–4. Harich in *HJB* I, 73f.

Francesco Bianchi: Alessandro nell'Indie. Dramma per musica da rappresentarsi nel teatro di S. A. il Sig. Principe Regnante Nicolò Eszterhasi de Galantha. L'anno 1787. Vienna, Presso Franc. Antonio Kroyss.

Libretto: Kroys's bill of 30 June 1787 in EH, Budapest, A.M. 64.4013. No copy survives. First performance: 26 July (total: two perf.), preceded by seven stage rehearsals and a dress rehearsal, involving 'supers' of eight boys and 38 Grenadiers. Repeated in August (one), with an inexplicable rehearsal on 8 October (no perf. attached), and then continued only in 1788. Eszterháza performance material: Schellinger's bill (A.M. 18.1220) lists 189 *Bögen* of vocal and 198 *Bögen* of instrumental parts, and EH, Budapest, Ms. Mus. OE–44 includes the complete score (Coradino, Venice) with the EH cast:

Poro: Braghetti
Alessandro: Nencini [Santi Nencini]
Cleofide: Bologna
Gandarte: Delicati
Erissena: Polcelli [*sic*]
Timagene: Dichtler

Of the local parts, the orchestral material lacks V. I and Basso, and of the three parts for two trumpets and timpani (not in the score!) probably only the timpani were actually used (there were no trumpets in Haydn's band in 1787). The vocal parts are very fragmentary. These EH parts copied by Schellinger and Anon. 10 and 73. Apart from cuts and transpositions downwards, Haydn cancelled Erissena's (Polzelli) Aria, 'Chi vive amanti' in Atto I°, Sc. 5 and composed a new one (XXIVb:13). The autograph score was removed, but the parts are still present (Schellinger). Sc. 10: to Bianchi's orchestration of str. only, Haydn added (or caused to be added) 2 ob., 2 bsn. and 2 hn. (parts: Schellinger). Atto III°, Sc. 6, Aria (Poro), 'Dov'è – s'affretti per me la morte' is an addition, of which the composer's name and date have been scratched out (legible '... 177[?]') of the score; the role of the score (Poro) is the same. Perhaps this is a later addition of Bianchi himself (*incipit*: Bartha-Somfai, 327). Harich *Musikgeschichte*, 59. Bartha-Somfai, 140, 324–7. Harich in *HJB* I, 74.

Giovanni Paisiello: Le gare generose.
Libretto: Bill by Joseph Facci in Vienna of 20 August 1787: EH, Budapest, A.M. 64.4012. No copy survives. A Viennese perf. took place on 1 Sept. 1786, and perhaps Facci simply reprinted the Viennese textbook, with or without title variants, for EH. Of the cast, EH's musical material lists only Miss Meri: *vide infra*. First performance: September (total: three), preceded by three stage rehearsals and a dress rehearsal; repeated in November (two) and in 1788, 1789 and 1790. Eszterháza performance material: Schellinger's bill (A.M. 18.1220) lists 274 *Bögen* of vocal and 282 *Bögen* of instrumental parts. EH, Budapest, Mrs. Mus. OE–23 includes the Viennese theatre copyist Wenzel Sukowaty's copy of the score (now incomplete), fragmentary vocal parts and complete orch. material by Schellinger with Anon. 10, 11 and 73. On Rec. booklet for Miss Meri, Haydn has written 'per la Sᵗᵃ Saßi / 12 augusti' (date *not* by Schellinger), i.e. when the vocal parts were distributed. Haydn made only very minor changes in this successful work (no insertions). Bartha-Somfai, 140f., 327f. Harich in *HJB* I, 74.

Nine operas from earlier seasons were repeated:
Cimarosa's *I due baroni di Rocca azzurra*: February (one) and March (one).
Bologna's *L'isola di Calipso*: February (one), April (two), October (six), November (one), and in 1788, 1789 and 1790.

Sarti's *Idalide*: March (one), July (two), September (one).

Anfossi's *Il geloso in cimento*: March (one), April (two), May (three), June (one), July (one), August (one), September (three), October (four), November (one).

Haydn's *Armida*: March (one), May (one), June (one), July (two), and in 1788.

Anfossi's *I viaggiatori felici*: March (two), April (three), May (two), June (two), August (three), September (two), and in 1788.

Bianchi's *La villanella rapita*: March (one), April (two), May (two), June (one), July (three), August (one), September (one).

Sarti's *Giulio Sabino*: April (one) and June (one).

Cimarosa's *L'italiana in Londra*: August (two), November (one) and in 1788. Literature of revivals: Harich in *HJB* I, 75ff. For some of these revivals, Schellinger copied a (small) amount of new material: *I viaggiatori felici* and *L'italiana in Londra* (see Chronicle, *infra*, p. 702), probably insertion arias or transposed numbers for new singers.

MARIONETTE THEATRE 1787, 1788, 1789, 1790

There is no further record of any performances being given in this once popular little theatre. On the contrary, the costumes and decorations were taken to the nearby village of Széplak and stored there in a princely warehouse.[1]

THE GERMAN THEATRICAL TROUPE 1787

We are informed of the Lasser Troupe's constitution by the *Theater-Kalender auf das Jahr 1788* (pp. 214–6) of Gotha which, of course, always refers to the previous year.

Esterhazy [*sic*]

Entrepreneur Herr Lasser. Regisseur, Herr Nuth. Actresses. Mad. König, heroines, naive girls: sings. Mad. Meyer, all first soubrettes; *prima ballerina*. Mad. Müllner, first heroines in comedies and tragedies, soubrettes; sings and dances. Mlle Repke, principal *prima ballerina*. Madam Schulze, secondary roles. Mad. Teller, all the decorous and serious roles, Orsinas, Bardonias, etc. Mad. Unger, all principal tender and comic mothers, character parts. Actors. Herr Brera, secondary parts for old women, tender fathers, soldiers. Herr von Crenzin, all principal tender and moody fathers, old soldiers, character parts. Hr. Erdmann, some fathers; pedants. Hr. Gieseke: all first lovers in comedies and tragedies, Germanized Frenchman [*Deutschfranzosen*], eccentric lovers [*Karakterliebhaber*]. Hr. König, secondary lovers, comic peasants; dances. Hr. Löffler, prompter, also plays some pedants and old women. Hr. Mayer [*sic*], comic servants, easy-going fellows [*lockere Bursche*]; is the ballet master. – Herr Müllner, secondary roles, Jews. Hr. Nuth, all characters requiring decorum and dignity; kings, noble fathers, old people, also angry old soldiers, heroes. Hr. Schulze, comic old women, pedants, confidants. – New plays: *Der vernünftige Narr*, comedy. *Räuschen*, comedy. *Heyrath durch Irrthum*, comedy. *Verstand und Leichtsinn*, comedy. *Liebreiche Stiefmütter*, comedy. *Stille Wasser sind betrüglich*, comedy. *Nachschrift*, comedy. *Johann von Schwaben*, tragedy. *Adelheid von Salisbury*, tragedy. *Schwarze Mann*, tragedy. *Schauspielschule*, comedy. *Mädchen und den ganzen Kram*, comedy. *Verlobung*, comedy. *Neue Emma*, comedy. *Jeder reutet sein Steckenpferd*, comedy. *Wind für Wind*, comedy. *Was ists?* comedy. *Der Schreiner*, comedy. *Die Drossel*, comedy. *Liebhaber ohne Namen*, comedy. *Die eingebildeten Philosophen* [Paisiello's *I filosofi immaginari*], Singspiel. *Die Feldmühle*, comedy. *Liebe von Ungefähr*, comedy. *Armuth und Liebe*, comedy. *Athelstan* [*Athelston?*], tragedy. *Die Brille*, comedy. *So zieht man dem Betrüger die Larve ab*, comedy. *Muttersöhnchen auf der Galeere*, comedy. *Dagobert*, tragedy. When the Prince left Esterházy [*sic*] to go to Vienna at the beginning of December, this Company went to play for the winter at Passau, which theatre was actually taken over by Herr Lasser. . . . The permission to play at Esterhazy [*sic*] for the year 1788 has been given to Herr Mayer, director at Pressburg.

Johann Lasser was at Linz when he heard that Mayer was to be engaged at Pressburg for the 1787 season, and wrote at once offering his services to Prince Nicolaus (A.T. 43), followed on 4 January by another (A.T. 44), in which Lasser tells of his company's plans and provisional constitution. The letter shows that Prince Nicolaus had insisted on having actor Nuth and actress Teller, and Lasser was not sure if he could engage Mlle Repke as principal *prima ballerina*. The contract (A.T. 54) was signed on 8 January, in which (apart from the usual clauses), Lasser's Troupe agrees to perform the ballet parts in those operas of the Italian company when required.[2]

From the list of plays given, we can see that the theatrical standard had dropped considerably from the days when Carl Wahr was in command: now, we find no Shakespeare, no Goethe, no Lessing, no Schiller, in fact a very provincial and second-rate repertoire. Perhaps we may see in this the first signs that Prince Nicolaus was growing old and taking less of a personal interest in theatrical matters.

---

1 Information from Dr Janos Harich in Eisenstadt, May 1977.
2 There are slight discrepancies between the list of performers in this contract and the perhaps later list for Gotha. Horányi, 134f.

During the Christmas vacation of 1786–87, Haydn was lured to Graz, probably at the instigation of Carl Chorus, the oboe player and former member of the Esterházy band, who now lived in the Styrian capital. In the *Preßburger Zeitung* of 2 January 1788, we read that the musicians at Graz followed Vienna's example in establishing a society for widows and orphans of musicians, which 'is to Hrn. Karl Chorus's honour'. About Haydn's visit there, we may read in the *Grazer litterarisch-ökonomisches Wochenblatt* No. 25 (20 June 1787):

[The report begins with a reprint of the Eszterháza article by Weber which we mentioned when it first appeared in January 1782: *supra*, pp. 462f. The article then continues:] Recently in the month of January Graz also had the inestimable pleasure of harbouring this excellent artist within its walls; one was at great pains to entertain him according to his merits; all rallied round him and vied with one another to make his short stay very pleasant. Among other things a musical academy was given in his honour at the Rheinerhof: he himself conducted, and only his works were performed. Everything that man could call pleasant, joined to the deepest art; all that was original, beautiful, surprising and exciting could be heard in those heavenly melodies to the full. It was all worthy of the creative spirit of the great Haiden; only he sometimes outdid himself. A friend of the muses composed a poem on this occasion, which I insert here.

Freu dich des Glücks, um das dich Kön'ge neiden
   O Vaterstadt, die du als Gast
Den mit Unsterblichkeit geschmückten Haiden
   In deinem Schooß bewirthet hast.

Er ists, durch dessen Himmel süsse Tönne
   Das Herz im Wonnenmeere schwebt!
Aus Welten schwang'rer Brust, so manche Thräne
   Vom holden Mädchen Auge bebt.

Er dessen Ruhm, der Deutschlands Stolz erhebet,
   Sich schnell durch Europa schwang,
Und selbst dem Neid, der stäts Verläumdung webet,
   Ein unwillkührlichs Lob entzwang.

Sanft eingewiegt von seinen Harmonien
   Vergißt der Franzmann Tanz und Scherz,
Und in dem Reiche süsser Phantasien
   Wallt froh sein Wonne trunknes Herz.

Der stillen Wehemuth süsse Thränen flüssen
   Vom Aug des edlen Britten hin,
Er hält von seiner Kunst dahin gerissen,
   Für einen zweyten Hendel* ihn.

---

* [original footnote:] Ein Deutscher, der sich in England durch seine Musik Composition so sehr auszeichnete, daß ihn die Engländer in der Westminster bei den Königen begruben, und ihm eine Ehrensäule setzten.

The footnote, about Handel, reads: 'A German who excelled himself with his musical compositions in England to the extent that the English buried him in Westminster [Abbey] with the kings and put up a monument in his honour.' Haydn lived in Sackstraße No. 1 (now renamed). See also *Grätzer Magazin*, 1787; Winkler's *Chronologische Geschichte*. Haydn was also in contact with the monks of Rein Abbey near Judendorf. Kalchberg's poem also printed in his *Vermischte Gedichte*, Graz 1793, pp. 221–4. Cornelius Preiss, 'Die Beziehungen Josef Haydn's zu Graz', in *Urania Almanach* 1920, pp. 51f. We have to thank our old friend, Harald Egger (born in Graz, now Vienna), who organized this material for us from his friends in Graz. See also *HJB* VIII, 190 (music in Graz, *PZ*, 2 Jan. 1788).

Der Stolz Italiens selbst unterlieget
　Der Deutschen Kunst, die ist den Geist
Durch Sphären Thon in süsse Träume wieget,
　Ist mächtig strömend mit sich reißt.

Ja dort, wo unterdrückte Menschheit ächzet,
　Entfällt durch seinen Zauberton
Der Dolch, der stets nach Blut der Kezer lechzet,
　Der Faust der Inquisizion.

Ihn ruffen Europens Nationen
　In ihren Schooß um reichen Gold,
Doch er zu groß, um fremder Macht zu frohnen,
　Liebt Deutschland mehr als fremdes Gold.

Sey stolz o Vaterland! dem Strom der Zeiten
　Trozt mehr sein Ruhm, als Erz und Stein,
Er wird, wenn gleich Jahrhunderte vergleiten,
　Bekannt der späten Nachwelt seyn.

Joh. v. Kalchberg.

For the coming Carnival season, Artaria announced Haydn's latest *Six Allemandes* (for orchestra: IX:9) on 3 January in the *Wiener Zeitung*. At the end of the month (29 January), a correspondent from Vienna sent a letter to Cramer's *Magazin der Musik* (pp. 1273f.):

> ... Our good, dear Pleyel, as you know, is in Straßburg and is very successful there; in particular, the Parisians pay a great deal for his compositions; he will be a great success there, even more than in Italy. His unforgettable teacher Haydn has been here for some weeks. The day before yesterday I heard three divine new Symphonies[1] of his which he wrote for Paris ... Mozart set off a few weeks ago on a trip to Prague, Berlin and, it is said, even to London. I hope it all works out to his pleasure and satisfaction. He is the finest, most perfect piano player I ever heard; a pity, however, that in his artful and really beautiful way of composing [*Satz*], to be a new creator, he aims too high, as a result of which sensitivity and heart gain but little; his new Quartets for 2 violins, viola and bass that he dedicated to Haydn are really too strongly seasoned – and which palate can stand that for long. Forgive the metaphor from the cookery book. ...　A★★.

One small detail of history comes to life in a receipt for the musicians' salaries on a single sheet, where all the musicians signed the receipt for their money. In the monthly list for February 1787, with Haydn as No. 1 (Capel[l-]meister) and Schellinger as the last (No. 37, Coupista), we find that as No. 5 there is an entry for [female singer] 'and her husband Polceli'; as No. 19 'd[itt]° with N°. 5 Polceli'. Haydn signed for both these entries in his own hand, 'Polzelli' ...[2] A delightful vignette of a *ménage à trois* (*quatre*?).

1 One of the 'Paris' set (Nos. 82–7).
2 Facsimile 8 in Bartha-Somfai: A.M. 938 (Haydn's triple signature, incredibly, not even noted by the authors). The list includes, as singers, Matilde Bologna, Palmira Sassi[marr. Nencini], Barbara Sassi, Luigia Polzelli, Margherita Delicati, Leopold Dichtler, Santi Nencini, Bartolomeo Morelli, Prospero Braghetti, Benedetto Bianchi, Vitus Ung(e)richt and Christian Specht. Violins: Tomasini, Grisi, Tost, Purgsteiner, Polzelli, Leopold Hirsch (includes violas). 'Cellos: Kraft, Bertoja. Violone (double bass): Johann Dietzl. Horns: Oliva, Pauer, Chiesa, Nickl, Joseph Dietzl. Oboists: Franz Czerwenka, Mayr. Flute: Zacharias Hirsch. Bassoons: Schiringer, Pe(c)zival, Jos. Czerwenka [about the confusion of Franz and Joseph Czerwenka, *vide supra*, p. 70], Steiner. 'Guateroba': Porta. Copyist: Schellinger (the names are in the usual confusion, the signatures usually being different from the scribe's previous spelling). For the final list of musicians included in this volume, see Chronicle, Sept. 1790 (*infra*, p. 749).

On 7 February, the *Preßburger Zeitung*[1] announced that on Saturday (10 February) the Erdödy Theatre, under the direction of Herr Kumpf,

> will perform a grand comic opera entitled 'Roland der Pfalzgraf' [*Orlando Paladino*] in three acts. – The music is by Hr. Jos. Haiden [*sic*] ... and is a real masterpiece. [*HJB* VIII, 188]

The following letters to Artaria have been preserved:

[To Artaria & Co., Vienna. *German*]

Estoras, 11th February 1787.

Mon tres cher Amy!

This is to report that I have arranged 4 of the Sonatas[2] as quartets, and have completed them; you will receive the whole work this coming Friday. Meanwhile you can give the first violin part[3] of the first four Sonatas to the engraver, just as it stands, because there was no need to change anything. You will receive the Quartet[4] a week from tomorrow. Please don't forget my portraits.[5] Should you not find any safe and convenient opportunity in the *Herrschaft* mansion, please send them next Monday by the diligence to the following address in Oedenburg:

> A Monsieur
> Mons. Baumgartner, Princely Estorházi House-Master
> à
> Oedenburg

from whom I shall have them collected by my own carriage. In any event you can dispatch it under my name, or inform the conductor about it verbally.

Meanwhile I am, most respectfully,

> Your most obedient servant,
> Joseph Haydn.

[Address:] Monsieur
Monsieur d'Artaria et Comp.
à
Vienne.

[CCLN, 56]

Estoras, 14th February 1787.

Mon tres cher Amy!

I enclose herewith all four altered parts,[6] and hope that the copyist will understand me well, and especially that he will do all the parts in the right order, that is, as proper quartets. If there should arise any doubt about certain passages, the copyist should let me know about them at once, so that I can help him in time. All 4 parts, that is, each Sonata in which there are changes, must be written out anew.

As soon as proofs of the Sonatas (both as quartets and for full band) can be made, please send me the first copy, so that I can correct it. The content[7] of the

---

1 *PZ* 5 of 17 January also prints Kumpf's letter in which he praises Haydn's *La fedeltà premiata* (*HJB* VIII, 187f.).
2 The Oratorio, *The Seven Words*.
3 Of the orchestral version, which Artaria also issued.
4 One of Op. 50, which Artaria was preparing to publish.
5 See *supra*, pp. 447f.
6 Of *The Seven Words* (see previous letter). Obviously Haydn took the four principal string parts of the orchestral version and adapted them to make the quartets.
7 Haydn means the actual words of the Saviour (see letter of 8 April 1787), which were prefaced to each Sonata.

Sonatas expressed in music is also enclosed herewith, and it must be printed in the quartet version as well.

The Quartet[1] will follow soon. The opera rehearsals here detain me. Meanwhile I am, most respectfully,

Your most obedient servant,
Joseph Haydn.

P.S. Please buy 7 copies of the enclosed sheet of 'Bemerkungen und Erinnerungen' at Herr von Tratnern[2] and send them to me here. I shall pay for it with thanks.

[No address; Artaria's clerk notes: 'Joseph Haydn 1787/Esterhatz 14. February/ ans'd 17 ditto.']

[CCLN, 57]

Estoras, 27th February 1787.

Mon tres cher Amy!
Many thanks for the portraits you sent me, which arrived safely the day before yesterday; please have the kindness to let me know what I owe you for the frames.

But now, my dear friend, as to the letter from Paris that you sent me,[3] I must frankly tell you that after due consideration, I cannot agree to it, for the following reasons: first, because by so doing I would terribly offend the gentlemen from Cadiz, who after all are responsible for my having written the Sonatas, and who paid me for them; secondly, the French gentlemen would be even more offended if I accepted payment for a work which was to be published in three weeks, from which work you, my good friend, certainly stand to derive the greatest possible profit, the more so since it can be sold as a whole as well as in quartet form.

Another thing: yesterday I received a letter from Herr von Jacoby,[4] Royal Prussian Minister, in which he wrote the following: WHAT ARE THE CIRCUMSTANCES OF SOME PIECES OF YOURS WHICH HERR ARTARIA INTENDS TO SEND TO THE KING AT BERLIN? I WOULD LIKE TO HAVE AN EXPLANATION FROM YOURSELF, AND THEREFORE BEG YOU TO GIVE ME ONE.

I hope that you do not perhaps intend to dedicate these Sonatas[5] to His Majesty, either as quartets or for full band, because that would be contrary to all common sense; but I believe that you must mean the new Quartets, which I highly approve of, if this is what you intend to do.

Please let me know about this, to allay my suspicions; I wouldn't want you thereby to disgust me altogether, for I have always been your sincere friend and will remain so.

Your most obedient servant,
Joseph Haydn.

[Address:]   Monsieur
                Monsieur d'Artaria
                        et Compagnie
                                a
                        Vienne.
[Artaria's clerk notes: 'Haydn 1787./ Esterhatz 27 February']

[CCLN, 57f.]

---

1 From Op. 50.
2 A Viennese bookseller and publisher; *recte*: (Johann Thomas) Trattnern.
3 From the Concert Spirituel, who must have offered to print the work or perform it from MS. parts.
4 Konstantin von Jacobi (Jacoby), Prussian Minister to the Court at Vienna, was also on good terms with the Mozarts. See Leopold's letter of 21 February 1785 (Deutsch-Paumgartner, *Leopold Mozarts Briefe an seine Tochter*, Salzburg 1936, p. 72).
5 *The Seven Words.*

Estoras, 7th March 1787.

Dearest Friend!

I have no objections to any of the negotiations you propose to undertake because of the Sonatas,[1] but motives of policy prevent my agreeing to the letter from the *Concert Spirituel*.[2] If you wish to make an offer in your name, I shall be quite satisfied. I approve of your holding back the engraving, and quite see the substantial and advantageous profits[3] you will thereby gain. I am sincerely delighted for your sake, for I know that you will not be stingy with me on other occasions. Herr von Jacobi [*sic*] only wanted to know what work it was that you intended to dedicate to the King of Prussia, and I wrote to him that I believed it would be quartets.

I send you herewith the first movement of the 3rd Quartet;[4] you will receive the others one of the next days. I am pressed for time.

Your wholly obedient servant,
Joseph Haydn.

[No address.]   [CCLN, 58f.]

On 26 March there was an important performance of *The Seven Words* at the Palais Auersperg (head of the family was Prince Johann Adam Joseph, 1721–95) in the Josephstadt suburb – the palace is still one of Vienna's great landmarks – which was attended by Count Zinzendorf, in a box together with the Kinsky, Rothenhan and Buquoi families:

... Le soir chez le P^ce Adam Auersperg <u>au Concert</u> de Hayden sur les 7. paroles de notre Seigneur sur la croix. La seconde du Paradis, la derniere du dernier soupir me parut bien exprimée.   [Olleson, 48; Pohl II, 215]

Haydn now (successfully) offered *The Seven Words* and other works to William Forster:

---

1 *The Seven Words*.
2 See previous letter.
3 We now know that Artaria was authorized to sell MS. copies in advance of the printed parts. One letter offering such a MS. has survived: see Gustav Bereths, *Die Musikpflege am kurtrierischen Hofe zu Koblenz-Ehrenbreitstein*, Mainz 1964, pp. 200ff. The original, in French, may be consulted in H. Unverricht, *Joseph Haydn Werke* IV, kritischer Bericht, p. 23. MS. Staatsarchiv Koblenz, Abt. 1c Nr. 946 (fol. 249f.). It is addressed to the Elector of Trier (Trèves):

> Your Electoral Grace! We have just acquired a brand new work of music, a piece of instrumental music scored for [list follows] ... It consists of 7 Sonatas, each one fitted to the 7 Last Words of Jesus on the Cross, then the Earthquake. We cannot sing more clearly the praises of this really sublime, truly lyrical work than by naming its author, Joseph Haydn. The price of this valuable piece in manuscript is 8 ducats. If it pleases Your Electoral Highness to acquire this work, we will send it to you or deliver it according to your instructions, and would ask you to reserve it for us so that it does not come into the danger of appearing in public. We take the liberty at this time further to offer new works, with which we are plentifully supplied ... Artaria & Comp. Vienna, 21st February 1788.

The first performance in Kurtrier was on 1 April 1790 (Bereths, 200). The next day, they performed Haydn's *Stabat Mater* (Bereths, 301), also done in 1787. 291ff. In thirty-two programmes of Electoral Court concerts Jan. 1783–Jan. 1792, not a single work by Haydn of any kind was performed. There were Symphonies by Rosetti, Lang, Philidor, J. C. Bach (Symphony for double orchestra in two programmes, another symphony, presumably also J. C.), Mozart Symphony (in two different concerts), Aria from *Idomeneo* and piano Concerto, Pleyel (5 symphonies), Zimmermann (two symphonies on one programme, 4 Nov. 1784, one the Sinfonia 'Echo'), works by Wallerstein composers (Concerto a due Corni by Rosetti, played by Palsa and Türnschmidt [sic]), works by Beecke, arias etc. by Cimarosa, Paisiello, Sarti, Cherubini, Piccinni, etc., a 'Sinfonie' (prob. Overture) by Gluck, Vincenzo Righini (who also conducted himself, receiving a golden snuff-box and 40 Carolinen), Pichl, Gyrowetz (Sinfonia Concertante). Among the chamber music concerts (pages 215f.) one Haydn Quartet figures against two by Hofstetter ('Op. 3' composer) and quintets, quartets and a septet by Pleyel. Among the Arias is a 'Favoritarie' by Haydn (perhaps 'Ah come il core', issued by Artaria in 1782). As a matter of historical accuracy, Clemens Wenzeslaus was Elector at this period (1768–1802).

The important thing about this document is that it shows that *The Seven Words* did penetrate courts where the music of Haydn's pupils and *seguaci* were clearly much more popular than the model. Most of the contemporary MSS., insofar as they are not authentic sources prepared by Haydn, are ones sold by Artaria & Co.: a list in Unverricht (kritischer Bericht).
4 From Op. 50.

[To William Forster, London. *German*]

Estoras, 8th April 1787.

Monsieur!

After a long silence I must at last enquire after your health, and at the same time report that the following new works may be had of me, *viz.*: 6 elegant Symphonies;[1] a big pianoforte Concerto;[2] 3 small pianoforte Divertimenti for beginners, with violins and bass[3]; a Sonata for pianoforte alone.[4]

A brand new work, consisting of purely instrumental music divided in 7 Sonatas, each Sonata lasting 7 or 8 minutes, together with an opening Introduction and concluding with a *Terremoto*, or Earthquake. These Sonatas are written around, and composed according to, the Words which Christ our Saviour spoke on the Cross, and are entitled *The Seven Words*.

The first Word: Pater, dimitte illis, quia nesciunt, quid faciunt.
The 2nd — hodie mecum eris in Paradiso.
The 3rd — Mulier, Ecce filius tuus.
The 4th — Deus meus, Deus meus, ut dereliquisti me?
The 5th — Sitio.
The 6th — Consummatum est.
The 7th — In manus tuas commendo Spiritum meum.

The conclusion follows immediately afterwards, i.e., The Earthquake.

Each Sonata, or rather each setting of the text, is expressed only by instrumental music, but in such a way that it creates the most profound impression even on the most inexperienced listener. The whole work lasts a little more than one hour, but there is a bit of a pause after each Sonata so that one can contemplate the following text. As far as the copying goes, all the Sonatas together require a little more space than one of my symphonies, and the whole work would take about 37 sheets. Item: I have, moreover, 3 brand new and charming Notturni[5] with violin *obligato* – but not at all difficult – flute, violoncello, 2 violins ripieno, 2 hunting horns, viola and contrabasso. If you want anything of all these works, please be good enough to let me know at your earliest convenience, and also the fee you propose to give me. The 7 Sonatas are already copied, neatly and clearly, on small-sized music paper for mailing [*klein(es) Post Papier*]. Hoping for an answer I am, with esteem,

Your wholly obedient servant,
Joseph Haydn.

Please answer in French.

I hope to see you personally at the end of the year, but since I haven't heard from Herr Cramer[6] up to now, I shall accept an engagement to go to Naples this Winter.[7] But I am much obliged to you for your kind offer to put me up.

---

1 The six 'Paris' Symphonies (Nos. 82–87), written in 1785 and 1786 for the *Concert de la Loge Olympique*. Forster took only these and *The Seven Words*.
2 The famous D major Concerto, known as 'Op. 37', Hoboken XVIII:11.
3 Probably earlier works: Haydn wrote numerous Divertimenti and Concertini for this combination of instruments, mostly about 1760.
4 Possibly the piano Sonata No. 58 in C (XVI:48).
5 This description is not clear: Haydn may refer to the Divertimenti which Artaria had issued as Op. XXXI (Hoboken X: 12, 3, 5, 1, 4, 2) for flute, two violins, viola, bass and two horns; or (and this seems more likely) he may mean arrangements of some of the Concertos for 2 lire, 2 violins, 2 violas, 'cello (bass) and 2 horns which Haydn had composed for Ferdinand IV, King of Naples, in 1786.
6 Wilhelm Cramer, born in Mannheim, came to London and made a considerable reputation for himself as leader, solo violinist and impresario. He almost succeeded in persuading Haydn to come to London at this time.
7 The afore-mentioned Concertos had evidently so delighted Ferdinand that he had invited Haydn to come to Naples.

[Envelope:]   To Mr. Will. Forster, Musical-Instrument-Maker
to the Prince of Wales, N. 348, Strand.

[CCLN, 59–61]

[The letter is written on 3 pp.; the 4th is blank: no envelope is bound in with the letter at present, but Pohl (*H in L*, p. 356) quotes the above address: perhaps at that time the envelope was still extant.]

While Haydn was away from Vienna, Mozart's doctor, Sigmund Barisani – his father had been the Archbishop's personal physician in Salzburg and a friend of the Mozarts –, wrote in the composer's commonplace-book, dated 14 April 1787.[1] In it are the words,

Wenn deine Kunst, in der dir nur
Ein Bach, ein Joseph Hayden gleicht . . .

It was not yet common to link Haydn, Mozart and (C. P. E.?) Bach.

At Eszterháza, Haydn's correspondence continued:

[To Haydn from Friedrich Wilhelm II, King of Prussia. *German*]
His Majesty, King of Prussia, &c., &c. is sensible of the mark of respect which *Herr Kapellmeister* Haydn, in sending him six new Symphonies[2], again wishes to show to His Serene Majesty. They have especially pleased him, and there is no doubt that His Majesty has always appreciated *Herr Kapellmeister* Haydn's works, and will appreciate them at all times. To provide concrete assurance of the same, he sends him the enclosed ring as a mark of His Majesty's satisfaction and of the favour in which he holds him.

F. Wilhelm.

Potsdam, 21st April 1787.   [CCLN, 61]

[To Artaria & Co., Vienna. *German*]

Estoras, 26th April 1787.

Dearest Friend!
Thank you many times for the unexpected 12 ducats – a proof of your friendship, mine, and your efforts on my behalf. I hope to earn the same often by my diligence, especially if, as a true friend and honest man, you will candidly tell me who it was that offered you my new Symphonies;[3] I swear to you on my honour not to say a word about it; but as such a theft can be disastrous to me in the future, and might thereafter cause damage to you, too, your conscience should dictate to you to tell me the truth of the matter, so that I can discover this dangerous embezzlement in time: I assure you that I shall be eternally grateful to you. I therefore await with distress a speedy reply, and then I shall explain further about the Symphonies. I am, most respectfully,

Your most obedient servant,
Joseph Haydn.

[No address: Artaria's clerk notes: 'Haydn from Esterhaz/ 26 Apl 1787/ ans'd 27 ditto'.]

[CCLN, 61]

---

1 Deutsch *Dokumente*, 255. By 'Bach' presumably C. P. E. is meant.
2 The 'Paris' Symphonies (Nos. 82–87). For some curious reason Dies, and every later biography, substituted the word 'Quartets' for 'Symphonies', and it was Hoboken who first discovered the correct text, as printed in the *Wiener Zeitung* on 6 June 1787; see Hoboken, p. 408.
3 The 'Paris' Symphonies (Nos. 82–87). As the next letter shows, Artaria must have been offered other symphonies, already known.

[To Artaria & Co., Vienna. *German*]

Estoras, 2nd May 1787.

Nobly born,
Most highly respected Sir!

I was most delighted to hear of the falsehood concerning my Symphonies. I daily expect a letter from Paris: as soon as I receive the permission, you alone shall have the right to them. I enclose a letter from Wallerstein.[1] I would like to know, one day, who this Ludwig is,[2] but there's no hurry about it. In the next mail you will hear of a present which I received quite unexpectedly from a great man.[3] Meanwhile I am, most respectfully,

Your wholly obedient servant,
Joseph Haydn.

P.S. A young Viennese composer by the name of Joseph Eybler[4] has composed 3 pianoforte Sonatas, not at all badly written, and has asked me to recommend them to you for engraving and publication. The young man is very promising, plays the pianoforte well, and knows a great deal about composition. If you wish to examine these works further, in order to guard yourself against loss, you can discuss the details with him personally. He lives on the Hoher Markt in the Juden Gässl in the Lagenhof No. 500, 2nd floor, at Herr Höbert's, silvermaster.
[No address]   [CCLN, 62]

[To Joseph Eybler, Vienna. *German*]

Estoras, 2nd May 1787.

Well born,
Most highly respected Sir!

I never received your first letter. The second, however – which is not dated –, I read with pleasure, and have sent a letter in today's mail to Herr Artaria, suggesting to him as warmly as possible (for you certainly deserve it) that he agree with your wish. In case you do not hear about this from Herr Artaria, be good enough to go and see him personally, and then he will discuss the details with you. I consider it my obligation to serve you in any way I can, and am, with great esteem,

Your most obedient servant,
Josephus Haydn [m.p] ria.
[No address on the other side of the sheet.]   [CCLN, 62f.]

[To Artaria & Co., Vienna. *German*]

Estoras, 19th May 1787.

Most worthy Friend!

This is to inform you that I have already finished the 4th Quartet,[5] and will certainly send it next Friday. Now here is something important I have to tell you: you know that I received a beautiful ring from His Majesty, the King of Prussia. I feel deeply in His Majesty's debt because of this present, and for my part I can think of no better and more fitting way to show my thankfulness to His Majesty (and also in the eyes of the whole world) than by dedicating these 6 Quartets to him; but you won't be satisfied with that, because you will want to dedicate the

---

1 From someone in the service of Prince Oettingen-Wallerstein, with whom Haydn was in contact.
2 The man who offered Artaria some of Haydn's symphonies (see previous letter).
3 The ring from Friedrich Wilhelm II (see letter of 21 April).
4 Joseph Eybler (1765–1846) was later Court *Kapellmeister* in Vienna. See also next letter.
5 From Op. 50.

works yourself, and to someone else. But to make amends for this loss, I promise to give you other pieces free of charge. Let me know what you have to say to this. Perhaps we can both be satisfied. In haste,

> Your most obedient
> Joseph Haydn.

[Address:]   Monsieur
                  Monsieur d'Artaria et
                  Compag
                       à
                  Vienne.
[Artaria's clerk notes: 'Haydn, Giuseppe/ Esterhase/ 19 Mag /87'.]

[CCLN, 63]

An interesting little list, of the 'supers' who participated in the operas being given by Haydn for the month of May, has survived:

Il sordo e l'avaro	12 supers, performed once.
Il geloso in cimento	12 supers, five boys, three perf.
Armida	4 girls, 38 supers, 8 assistants, 1 perf.
I viaggiatori felici	12 supers, two perf.
La villanella rapita	6 girls, 12 supers, 4 boys, 2 perf.
Il disertore	36 supers, 8 assistants, 3 perf.

[Also rehearsals for *La Quaquera spiritosa*. EH, Eisenstadt. Harich in *HJB* I, 72f.]

Haydn's correspondence continues:

[To Artaria & Co., Vienna. *German*]

Estoras, 10th June 1787.

Dearest Friend!
        Since I shall complete the 5th Quartet this week, I assure you that you shall receive both Quartets in good order by a week from tomorrow, and finally the 6th in a short time.
        I read in the paper today that my *Seven Words* is already at the engraver's. Please send me only one single copy. I understand that we shall soon have the honour of seeing you here: this would give me great pleasure.
        Meanwhile I remain, most respectfully,

> Your wholly obedient servant,
> Josephus Haydn.

[CCLN, 63f.]

[To Artaria & Co., Vienna. *German*]
Nobly born,
Most highly respected Sir!
        I have revised and corrected the *Seven Words*, not only for full band but also for quartet and piano score; but I cannot send it today with the Hussars because the parcel is too large, and so I shall send you everything, together with the 4th and 5th Quartets,[1] on Sunday at the latest, with the widowed Princess von Liechtenstein,[2] or Count von Lamberg.[3] I am sorry that the Berliners have anticipated you, but you are to blame for it yourself, for they did not receive it from me.[4] As for the

---

1 From Op. 50.
2 Leopoldine, Princess von Liechtenstein (*née* Countess Sternfeld), Princess Marie Hermenegild's mother.
3 Count von Lamberg, Prince Esterházy's nephew.
4 It is not quite clear to which work (or works) Haydn refers. The passage may refer to Hummel's first set of the Paris Symphonies, which he brought out in the same month (December 1787) as did Artaria; it seems unlikely, however, that Hummel would have announced the works half a year before he issued them. *The Seven Words* cannot be meant either, because Hummel's edition of that work did not appear until after Artaria's.

dedication of the Quartets to His Majesty, the King of Prussia, I should prefer that you have it drawn up yourself by some intelligent person in Vienna, but brief and to the point. The Minister, Herr von Jacoby,[1] could assist you best of all. You can ask him in my name, too, and I shall write to the worthy gentleman myself this coming Thursday.

Meanwhile you can announce the Quartets on your own subscription.

If you want to have the first 3 Symphonies[2] from me, please let me know. Meanwhile I am, most respectfully,

Your wholly obedient servant,
Joseph Haydn.

Estoras, 21st June 1787

[No address; Artaria's clerk notes: 'Haydn Giuseppe/ die Esterhazi/ 21st June 87 / ans'd 5th July'.]

[CCLN, 64]

[To Artaria & Co., Vienna. *German*]

Estoras, 23rd June 1787.

Dearest Friend!

I send you the proofs of *The Seven Words* in all 3 forms.[3] *Inter alia* I compliment you on the piano score, which is very good and has been prepared with the greatest care. I should be happy if you could place the word 'Fr—lim'[4] of the 3rd Sonata in the first violin part of the version for full band, just as I have indicated it in the quartet version. I enclose the fourth Quartet,[5] you will quite certainly receive the 5th this coming week.

I am, as always,
Your most obedient servant,
Haydn.

N.B. The last movement, *il Terremoto*, is not engraved in the viola part at all.

[No address: Artaria's clerk notes: 'Haydn Giuseppe/ Esterhaze 23rd June/ 87/ ans'd 5th July'.]

[CCLN, 65]

[To William Forster, London. *French*]
Monsieur!

I enclose the music composed after the Seven Last Words which Jesus Christ spoke on the Cross; I leave it to your judgement to send me what you think I deserve for it.

I hope perhaps to have the pleasure of seeing you this Winter; meanwhile I am, *Monsieur*, respectfully,

Your most humble and obedient servant,
Joseph Haydn [m.p.] ria.

Estoras, 28th June 1787.

[No address on the letter (it was sent with the Oratorio in one parcel); the blank reverse side contains the date of arrival in London: 'July 16th/p'.] [CCLN, 65f.]

---

1 See *supra*, p. 689.
2 Of the 'Paris' set: see letter of 2 August 1787. Artaria published them in sets of three each, as Opp. 51 and 52.
3 See previous letters.
4 It is unclear what Haydn means here: the Words which preface the third Sonata are 'Mulier, Ecce filius tuus', nor does 'Fr—lim' stand for these words in French or German.
5 From Op. 50.

[To Artaria & Co., Vienna. *German*]

Estoras, 12th July 1787.

Well born,
Most highly respected Sir!

I send you herewith the 6th Quartet.[1] Lack of time prevented my writing down the 5th up to now, but I have composed it meanwhile. I would have gladly sent you the Quartet version of *The Seven Words*, but there was no opportunity yet; I hope, however, to find one soon.

I shall bring you the [first three of the 'Paris'] Symphonies myself after St Anne's Day [26 July]. Meanwhile I am, most respectfully,

Your most obedient servant,
Joseph Haydn.

[No address; Artaria's clerk notes: 'Haydn Giuseppe/ Esterhaze 12th July/87'.]

[CCLN, 66]

[To John Gallini,[2] London. *Italian*]

Estoras, 19th July 1787.

... I acknowledge to have received your letter dated the 26th of last June and then, when I thought to have heard of your offers, you request once more to know my terms. So I tell you this: that I promise and commit myself to write a new opera and to assist at your concerts in Hanover Square, and my final demand for this is £500 stirling [*sic*] and a free benefit concert. And in giving me that sum within a limited time, I shall be entirely at your service during the contract. If, on the other hand, you can agree with Mr. Cramer[3] and his Associates that between you the sum of £500 shall be made up, I will write a new opera for you, assist at your concerts in Hanover Square, and I will compose for Mr. Cramer and his Associates six pieces of instrumental music, and in that case, each of you must give me a free benefit; so that if you choose to have me alone, I ask £500 and only one free benefit. If, on the other hand, with Cramer &c., the same sum of £500 and two benefits, i.e. one from you and another from Mr. Cramer and his Associates. If you come to an agreement with each other for this sum, I am ready to comply with your request, and as soon as it is settled, I oblige myself by these presents to execute the commission, and give you authority to announce my arrival in the public newspapers. I desire nothing more at present than the pleasure of knowing you personally, as I have hitherto by reputation, and look forward to putting my modest talents at your disposal. ...

Giuseppe Haydn.

[From the English translation in Sotheby, Wilkinson & Hodge's Catalogue No. 569, of 1905; CCLN, 66f.]

[To Georg Anton Kreusser,[4] *Kapellmeister* to the Kurfürst von Mainz. *German*]

Estoras, 28th July 1787.

Nobly born,
Most highly respected Sir,

I take the liberty of asking you to be good enough to deliver in my humble name the two Symphonies[5] herewith enclosed to your gracious Prince and Serene

---

1 From Op. 50.
2 Gallini, impresario and director of the Italian opera, later commissioned Haydn to write *L'anima del filosofo*, in 1791.
3 Wilhelm Cramer, see *supra*, p. 691.
4 Kreusser was a well-known composer; his Symphonies and other works were widely circulated in manuscript and printed editions (e.g. Hummel). Adolf Sandberger, who first published the letter, thought the letter might have been addressed to Johann Michael Schmid (or Schmidt), but he was a very old man in 1787 (if in fact he was still alive), and Kreusser was undoubtedly the recipient.
5 Either two of the 'Paris' Symphonies (Sandberger's and Larsen's opinion) or Symphonies Nos. 88 and 89 (1787) (Hoboken's opinion). In view of the fact that Haydn was offering the 'Paris' Symphonies to many publishers and individuals at this time, we consider Sandberger's and Larsen's suggestion the more plausible of the two.

Highness; and as he recently wanted to know the costs of all the music I sent him up to now, I beg to inform His Highness that the copying charges were 50 gulden, and for my underserving self I humbly suggest one hundred Taler. If this demand should seem in any way exorbitant to your most gracious Prince, I won't demand a Kreutzer.[1] I deem myself fortunate to enjoy the privilege of having His Highness condescend to listen to my humble efforts.

I commend these two Symphonies to your profound insight; and with the hopes that they will be performed in a manner commensurate with the same, I am, Sir, with profound respect,

Your wholly obedient servant,
Josephus Haydn [m.] pria.

[No envelope extant]   [CCLN, 67f.]

[To Artaria & Co., Vienna. *German*]

Estoras, 2nd August 1787.

Well born,
Most highly respected Sir!

Last time I forgot to indicate the order of the Symphonies,[2] which should be engraved as follows: the Symphony in A Number 1, in Bb No. 2, in g [minor] No. 3, in Eb No. 4, in D No. 5, in C No. 6.

You can print the first 3 in 3 months, as you have promised, but if at all possible I would ask you to wait a little with the last 3.

You must tell the person to whom you will give the Symphonies for copying emphatically not to pass them on.

Now may I ask you, if it is possible, to have the piano score of *The Seven Words* copied for one of my special-friends; I promise you on my honour that you will not suffer the least damage because of it. I shall pay for the copying at once. Please send me the portraits of Morichelli and Salieri.[3] Meanwhile I remain, most respectfully,

Your most obedient servant,
Jos: Haydn.

[Address:]   Monsieur
             Monsieur d'Artaria et
             Compag.
                       à
                  Vienne.

[Artaria's clerk notes: 'Haydn Giuseppe/ Esterhaze 2 Agt/87'.]

[CCLN, 68f.]

[To William Forster, London. *French*]
Monsieur,

I hope that you will have received my last letter [28 June], and the music of *The Seven Words*. I would like to inform you that I have composed six Quartets and six Symphonies,[4] which I have not yet given to anyone. If you would like

---

1 The smallest unit of currency.
2 The 'Paris' Symphonies. The suggested order is possibly that in which they were written, i.e. 87, 85, 83, 84, 86, 82; 87 and 83 are dated 1785 on the autographs, 84, 86 and 82, 1786; the complete MS. of 85 has not survived.
3 The famous soprano, Anna Morichelli, who later sang in Haydn's benefit concert in London (May 1795), and the Court *Capellmeister* Antonio Salieri (1750–1825), both of whose portraits (engraved, as had been Haydn's by Mansfeld) Artaria had published.
4 Quartets, Op. 50, and the 'Paris' Symphonies. Forster took them both.

them, be good enough to let me know it at your earliest convenience. I will give you all twelve pieces for twenty-five guineas. I am, with all possible esteem,

Your most humble servant,
Joseph Haydn.

Estoras, 8th August 1787.

[Address:] [postal stamp 'Au[g] 25', the date of arrival in London]
To Mr Forster Musical
Instrument-Macker, to the
Prince of Wales.
N^{ro} 346 [*sic*]   a
in the Strand
London.   [CCLN, 69]

Domenico Cimarosa was in Vienna at this time. Emperor Joseph II writes to the Austrian Ambassador at St Petersburg, Ludwig, Count Cobenzl from Augarten (suburb of Vienna with the famous gardens) on 24 September:

[To Count Cobenzl. *German*]
Dear Count Cobenzl! The bearer of this letter is Kapellenmeister [*sic*] Cimarosa, who has asked me to provide a letter to you.
Since this man really knows a great deal about music and I think moreover that he would please a small party even singing at the clavier, I recommend him to you so that you will give him such support as he requires.

Joseph m. p.[1]

In 1787, Cimarosa was invited to take Sarti's place at St Petersburg. *En route*, he stopped at Vienna, where Joseph II kept him for 24 days and asked him repeatedly to sing at court. From there Cimarosa went to Poland, arriving in St Petersburg on 3 December. Can Cimarosa have followed Sarti's footsteps and gone to Eszterháza? *L'italiana in Londra* had been revived and there was actually a performance of it in November. (Fanny's Aria, 'Venite, o amanti, al placido' is one of the *settecento*'s great lyrical inspirations, of a melting beauty that makes one wonder why Cimarosa is not more popular.) And as for the Emperor, it is one more piece of evidence that shows his true appreciation of these Italian composers and his lack of understanding for Haydn and Mozart.

We continue with Haydn's voluminous correspondence:

[To Artaria & Co., Vienna. *German*]

Estoras, 16th September 1787.

Nobly born,
Most highly respected Sir!
Because no safe opportunity presented itself, I could not send the enclosed Quartet[2] before. Now, thank God! I am glad that I finished them at last.
Please send the proofs of the first [Quartets] of the series for correction as soon as possible.
I am, most respectfully,

Your wholly obedient servant,
Joseph Haydn [m.] pria.

[No address]   [CCLN, 69]

---

1 *Joseph II und Graf Ludwig Cobenzl. Ihr Briefwechsel* (ed. A. Beer and J. von Fiedler), Band II (1785–1790), Vienna 1901, pp. 201f. *Enciclopedia dello spettacolo* III, 765ff. (Adelmo Damerini).
2 The fifth of Op. 50.

[To William Forster, London. *French*]
Monsieur!

I received your letter with much pleasure. I would inform you that I have received five guineas from *Mons. le General* Jerningham,[1] but you must see yourself that for music such as that of *The Seven Words* I deserve more; you could give me at least five guineas more.[2] Meanwhile I send you the six Quartets,[3] for which you will be kind enough to send me twenty guineas as soon as possible, as stipulated in the contract. I shall not fail to send you the six Symphonies[4] at the first opportunity. I await the favour of your early reply, and remain with all possible esteem, *Monsieur*,

Your most humble and obedient servant
Joseph Haydn [m.p.] ria.

Estoras, 20th September 1787.   [CCLN, 70]

[No address, since the letter was sent with the Quartets in a parcel; on the other side of the sheet, Forster or one of his clerks has written: 'with Haydn's 4^tos [quartettos] Op. 44', the opus number under which Forster published them.]

[To Artaria & Co., Vienna. *German*]

Estoras, 7th October 1787.

Mon tres cher amy,

I shall send you the Quartets,[5] at the very first opportunity, and I shall be playing through them today; I cannot send them in the mail bag. I was astonished at your penultimate letter concerning the theft of the Quartets.[6] I assure you on my honour that they were not copied by my copyist,[7] who is a most honest fellow, whereas your copyist is a rascal, for he offered mine 8 gold ducats this Winter if he would give him *The Seven Words*. I am sorry not to be in Vienna myself so as to have him arrested: My plan would be to make Herr Lausch appear before Herr von Augusti, the mayor, and make him confess from whom he received the Quartets. Herr von Augusti is an old friend of mine and will certainly help you in this matter, as he did once before in just such an affair. Although you have everything copied on your own premises, you may be swindled all the same, because the rascals put a piece of paper *a parte* under the music, and thus by degrees they secretly copy the part they have in front of them. I am sorry that this misfortune happened to you. In future I shall take the precaution of sending my own copyist up to you. I am, most respectfully,

Your wholly obedient servant,
Haydn.

---

1 See *supra*, p. 682.
2 Forster seems to have paid Haydn the additional five guineas; in the firm's account book is the note: 'July 1787. Rec^d of Haydn M.S.S. of the Crucifixion published with title of "Passion". Ten guineas was paid for this instrumental piece; and the Postage cost fifteen Shillings' (Sandys and Forster, *The History of the Violin*, London 1864, p. 310).
3 Op. 50.
4 The 'Paris' Symphonies.
5 The proofs of Op. 50.
6 L. Lausch, a well-known Viennese music copyist who sold MS. copies of the newest works of Haydn, Mozart, etc., seems to have bribed someone to get the Quartets (Op. 50) which Artaria was in the process of publishing. Apparently Artaria felt that the sale of these copies, even though in MS., was detrimental to his business. In a letter to Artaria of 18 August 1788, Haydn's old friend Dittersdorf offers some new quartets, and adds in a P.S. 'I must add that no one has the quartets (not like the Hayden Quartets you printed, which not only the Prince here, but various other people had bought long before in MS. copies, on subscription, for 6 # [ducats]) ...' (Artaria-Botstiber, p. 43).
7 Probably Johann or Joseph Elssler Jr.

[Address:]   Monsieur
        Monsieur d'Artaria et
       Compag
          a
         Vienne.
[Artaria's clerk notes: 'Haydn Giuseppe/ Esterhaze 7th Oct/ 1787 ans'd 25th Oct.']
[CCLN, 70f.]

Once again, Joseph II went out of his way to help an operatic composer. This time it was Martin y Soler (the author of *Una cosa rara*), also *en route* to Russia:

[Joseph II to Count Ludwig Cobenzl, St Petersburg]
    Vienne 22 Oct. 1787 [recommending] un nommé Martin qui se rend aussi à Pétersbourg. Il s'est signalé ici par trois jolis opera qui ont eu du succés. Il n'est pas aussi bouffon que Cimarosa, mais sa composition n'est moins agréable. . . .
[Correspondence, *op. cit.* II, 212]

Haydn took a cash payment instead of his two uniforms, summer and winter, and so did Luigi Tomasini and others (Haydn's sum amounted to twice 170 fl., Tomasini's twice 75, which again shows what a splendid piece of tailoring Haydn's must have been).[1]

On 29 October 1787, Mozart's *Don Giovanni* was given for the first time, at Prague (and repeated there several times). It was later, in 1788, given in Vienna (the exact dates from 7 May to 15 December in Deutsch, *Dokumente*, 275), and then never again in Vienna in Mozart's lifetime. Therefore, the famous story of Haydn at a party after a performance, defending Mozart,[2] meant that Haydn must have received special leave to hear the work in May 1788 (when, in fact there was opera at Eszterháza only for eleven days in that month).

On 10 November Friedrich Benda (in the service of the King of Prussia) wrote from Potsdam to Prince Nicolaus, enclosing the piano score and libretto of *Medea*, with the hope that it might be performed in Eszterháza. The letter[3] began, after the usual address, 'Your princely highness is used to hearing nothing but masterpieces from your all-famous Kapellmeister Haydn.' But the Prince was not interested in German-speaking melodramas or operas – nor had he the singers for them – and nothing came of Benda's offer.

On 15 November the old Gluck died in Vienna. Haydn had respected him, known him, and conducted his *Orfeo* at Eszterháza; but the two men had never been close.

The correspondence with Artaria continues:

[To Artaria & Co., Vienna. *German*]

                     Estoras, 22nd November 1787.

Nobly born,
Most highly respected Sir!
    I regret that it was not till today that I had a safe opportunity by which I could return to you the corrected Quartets and Symphonies.[4]

1 A.M. XVIII.1234, Eszterhaz, 28 Oct. 1787. Valkó II, 604.
2 *Haydn: the Years of 'The Creation' 1796–1800*, p. 337. Deutsch, *Dokumente* 275.
3 Valkó I, 657. Bartha-Somfai, 143. No answer from Nicolaus has yet been discovered, though it is probable that he wrote one.
4 Op. 50 and the 'Paris' Symphonies.

Concerning the lie of Herr Bartolozzi, or rather the true cavalier of Verona,[1] I don't know whether I should laugh or be angry, since I am grateful to the Lord when I am able to complete my works once in my handwriting; these are boastful and wild imaginings, and such falsifications attempt to belittle my credit. In the end I won't publish anything at all. Meanwhile I am, Sir, most respectfully,

Your wholly obedient servant,
Josephus Haydn.

[Address:]   Monsieur
          Monsieur Artaria et
          Compag.
               à
               Vienne.
Together with a parcel of music

[Artaria's clerk notes: 'Haydn di / Esterhaze 2 (*recte*: 22) Nov./1787'.]

[CCLN, 71f.]

Estoras, 27th November 1787.
Nobly born,
Most highly respected Sir!

You will forgive me, good Sir, that I have been unable to answer you sooner, for want of a good opportunity. You want me to give you a certificate [*Attest*] for the 6 Quartets: I enclose it herewith. It is not true, however, that I gave a separate certificate to Herr Forster, giving him the sole rights to these works; but it is true that I sent one to him after the Quartets had already been engraved. It's your own fault, because you could have sent the Quartets to Herr Langmann[2] 3 months ago, and at the same time given him the sole rights. But your having held them back derives from your own great selfishness: no one can blame me for attempting to secure some profit for myself, after the pieces have been engraved: for I am not properly recompensed for my works, and have a greater right to get this profit than the other dealers. Therefore you will see that the contracts between us are more carefully drawn up, and that I am sufficiently remunerated. If you lose GENERALLY because of this, however, I shall find a way to compensate you in another way. Meanwhile I remain, with the greatest esteem, Sir,

Your most obedient servant,
Joseph Haydn.

[Artaria's clerk notes: 'Haydn Giuseppe / Esterhaze 27th Nov./1787'.]

[CCLN, 72f.]

Schellinger's yearly copying bill was countersigned by Haydn on 1 December (see table overleaf).

---

1 Probably Gaetano Bartolozzi, the well-known artist and engraver, who lived in London and with whom Haydn later became friends when he came to England. The clause 'des sicheren Cavaliers aus Verona' may be a paraphrase of some play or *Singspiel* (a translation of Shakespeare's *Two Gentlemen of Verona*?). Bartolozzi must have informed Artaria of Forster's forthcoming edition of the new Quartets (see next letter), and said that Haydn had sent a second autograph to London. Forster had received parts, of course.
2 Longman & Broderip, Artaria's London associates, later published many of Haydn's late pianoforte trios, etc.

[Schellinger's bill for copying:]

[The vocal parts at 7 xr., the instrumental parts at 5 xr. per *Bogen*]

Operas	Vocal parts at 7 xr.	Instr. at 5 xr.
L'avaro	287	194
Il disertore	194	239
La quaquera	282	245
Gare generose	274	282
Italiana in londra repaired	49	29
Viaggiatori felici repaired	28	27
L'avaro repaired	9	14
Alessandro in india	189	198
	1,312	1,228

Makes 153 Fl. 4 xr.
Makes 102 Fl. 20 xr.
di 1 Dec. 1787
Id est 255 Fl. 24 xr.
Above-listed 2,540 *Bögen* have been carefully examined by me the undersigned and found to be correct.

Estoras, 1 Decembris 1787   Josephus Haydn mpria
                                               Capell Meister.

[Prince Nicolaus's order for payment follows. A.M. 18.1220. Valkó II, 604; Bartha-Somfai, 142; Bartha, 184]

We close the Chronicle (except for a short list of works and two reviews) for this year with the famous letter that Haydn wrote about Mozart:

[To Franz Roth (Rott),[1] *Oberverpflegs-Verwalter*, Prague. *German*]

December 1787[2]

... You ask me for an *opera buffa*. Most willingly, if you want to have one of my vocal compositions for yourself alone. But if you intend to produce it on the stage at Prague, in that case I cannot comply with your wish, because all my operas are far too closely connected with our personal circle (Esterház, in Hungary), and moreover they would not produce the proper effect, which I calculated in accordance with the locality. It would be quite another matter if I were to have the great good fortune to compose a brand new libretto for your theatre. But even then I should be risking a good deal, for scarcely any man can brook comparison with the great Mozart.

If I could only impress on the soul of every friend of music, and on high personages in particular, how inimitable are Mozart's works, how profound, how musically intelligent, how extraordinarily sensitive! (for this is how I understand them, how I feel them) – why then the nations would vie with each other to possess such a jewel within their frontiers. Prague should hold him fast – but should reward him, too; for without this, the history of great geniuses is sad indeed, and gives but little encouragement to posterity to further exertions; and unfortunately this is why so many promising intellects fall by the wayside. It enrages me to think that this incomparable Mozart is not yet engaged by some imperial or royal court! Forgive me if I lose my head: but I love the man so dearly. I am, &c.

Joseph Hayden [*sic*].

N.S. My respectful compliments to the Prague Orchestra and all the virtuosi there.   [CCLN, 73f.]

1 Roth (or more probably Rott, as in Dlabacz) held concerts several times a year in his house in Prague. See Schönfeld, *Jahrbuch der Tonkunst von Wien und Prag*, 1796, p. 140; Dlabacz, *Künstler-Lexicon für Böhmen*, Prague 1815, II, 597.
2 The letter, first printed in Niemetschek's *Mozart* (Prague 1798, pp. 51f.) and later that year in the *Allgemeine Musikalische Zeitung*, is not dated more exactly. The autograph has not survived.

The principal compositions of this year were Symphonies No. 88 and 89, and the Quartets, Opp. 54/55 (which were perhaps begun in 1787 and completed in 1788). Two criticisms from Cramer's *Magazin der Musik* deserve quotation: the first concerns a Le Duc (Paris) edition of three Haydn piano sonatas – Nos. 35 (XVI:43), 34 (33) and an arrangement of the very early *Divertimento a Sei* (II:11) as a piano sonata (the arrangement doubtful: XVI:15):

> *Trois Sonates pour le Clavecin ou Piano-Forte par Giuseppe Hayden. Oeuvre XLI & V de Clavecin. à Paris [Le Duc]* ... Although these Sonatas are written in a good style, there is in them a certain character that remains constant in each piece and which leads the reviewer to doubt if they are really from Haydn's pen, even if they belong, after due consideration, to the best Sonatas for the harpsichord or piano forte; they may have been published wrongly under his name, and yet there are many thoughts and turns of phrase in them which seem to suggest that they can only be by Haydn. Haydn then might have given his admirers three excellent sonatas with the present collection, which have but one single mistake: that one remembers still finer products of his genius which have the advantage that by this contrast one remembers them vividly. The Sonatas are easier than their predecessors, and since their composer perhaps took special pains to make them easy, their flights of fancy are somewhat fettered. The first one in A flat major pleases us the most. The opening *moderato* is constructed out of modest emotions of youthful joy, in which every strain contributes to the work's beauty. In the second in D major, the Adagio in D minor is a fine melody and requires an especially warm heart in performance. The last in C major is short and contains at the end a little Aria with five easy variations of which the first four are on the upper part and the fifth on the bass part.   Pgl. [1787, pp. 1287f.]

The second review concerns Piano Trios Nos. 22, 17 and 23 (XV:9, 2, 10) in Hummel's edition:

> *Trois Sonates pour le Clavecin ou Piano-Forte accompagnées d'un Violon & Violoncello obligées, composées par Mr. Joseph Haydn. Oeuvre XXVII. Chez J. J. Hummel. Prix F. 3* ... Among the many excellent compositions of this great man for the keyboard [*Flügel*] and for other instruments, these three Sonatas take pride of place. The opening Adagio of the first in A major has an indescribable charm and forms an admirable contrast to the ensuing Vivace. In the Allegro of the second in F major the abridgement of the rhythm in the sixth bar surprises the listener and may be too sudden for some. The theme of the final Adagio with four variations gains greatly in originality by expanding the rhythm in the seventh bar. The most beautiful Sonata among these beauties is surely the third in E flat, which contains the highest flights of Haydn's fancy. It is more difficult to play than the others. If the hoard of composers who write for the piano with the accompaniment of a violin or other instrument *ad libitum* could hear these Sonatas well played, should they not, or at least some of them, be ashamed of their crossbreed products? But what can you expect of people who are afraid of working, or don't know how to work!   [1787, pp. 1310f.]

That which slightly confused the first reviewer was the mixture of Haydn's music of 1755–60 with works of the early or middle 1770s, all of which now sounded old-fashioned. When the critic encountered a Haydn work of the 1780s (which except for Piano Trio No. 17 the next three are), he felt more at home; and even the earlier No. 17 was sufficiently 'modern' in spirit not to disturb him. Not having any idea of the real chronology, the critics imagined that both sets must be the latest products of Haydn's pen and understandably felt confused.

Chronicle 1788

ITALIAN OPERAS 1788

This year 108 performances are registered (Harich in *HJB* I, 83).

Domenico Cimarosa: Giunio Bruto. Dramma tragico per musica. In Oedenburgo Presso Giuseppe Siess. 1787.

Attori

Giunio Bruto, Console	[Nencini]
Tito, suo Figlio	[Braghetti]
Tullia, figlia de Rè Tarquinio	[Bologna]
Aronte, Ambassatore di Porsenna, Rè de' Toscani	[Dichtler]
Marzia, Dama Romana, amica di Tullia	[Sassi]
Procolo, Tribuno militare	[Bianchi]

Libretto: copy in Országos Széchényi Könyvtár, Sign. IM. 1269. No list of the cast was printed (ours is taken from the EH, Budapest, score). First performance: 2 February (preceded by five stage rehearsals), repeated on 6 and 7 February. Schellinger's bill (A.M. 18.1240) lists 167 *Bögen* of vocal and 239 *Bögen* instrumental parts. Eszterháza performance material: EH, Budapest, Ms. Mus. OE–51 contains the complete score (from Genoa, 1786), the complete orchestral material and fragmentary vocal parts, copied by Schellinger with Anon. 10, 11 and 73. The inside cover of the score lists (in Porta's hand) the members of the cast, and Aronte's recit. booklet is marked 'Dichtler Leopoldus'. Apart from cuts, Haydn's editing activities were minimal. Harich, *Musikgeschichte*, 60. Bartha-Somfai, 144f., 329–31. Harich in *HJB* I, 78.

Giuseppe Sarti: I finti eredi. Dramma giocoso.
Libretto: Joseph Facci's bill of 21 Nov. 1787 (A.M. 64.4011) shows that a libretto existed; Bartha-Somfai (145) suggest that Facci may have delivered copies of the Viennese libretto for the performance of 1786. Cast from the EH, Budapest, vocal parts:

Giannina: Sassi. D. Isabella: Nencini [*née* Palmira Sassi]. Cavaliere: Dichtler. D. Grifagno: Bianchi.

First performance: 9 March (after two stage rehearsals and a dress rehearsal), repeated in March (three more), April (one), May (one), June (three), August (one), October (two), November (one), and in 1789–90. Eszterháza performance material: Schellinger's bill (A.M. 18.1240) lists 189 *Bögen* of vocal and 236 *Bögen* of instrumental parts. Ms. Mus. OE–89 contains a complete score (from the Viennese copying house of Wenzel Sukowaty), the orchestral material and fragments of the vocal parts copied by Schellinger with Anon. 10, 11 and 73. Apart from cuts, Haydn cut the parts for clarinets and trumpets (not being available). Atto I°, Sc. 3: in a brilliant piece of research, Bartha-Somfai have shown conclusively that the cancelled Aria of the Cavaliere, 'Signorina, a dirvi il vero', was replaced by Haydn's insertion Aria, 'Se tu mi sprezzi, ingrata' (XXIVb:14), of which the score (autograph) and parts were removed from the material for other use. The autograph bears, in Schellinger's hand, 'N 3' (the place of the missing aria). Atto II°, Sc. 10, Haydn cancelled the original Aria by the Marchese (No. 17), and substituted a new one (*incipit*: Bartha-Somfai, 333; in bar 3 for 'sf' read 'forz'), of which the authorship cannot be established (copyists are local). Sc. 17, Haydn added yet a third Aria (this time for Giannina), of which the vocal part is missing: *incipit* in Bartha-Somfai, 334. Bartha-Somfai, 145, 331–4. Harich in *HJB* I, 79.

Vincenzo Fabrizi: I due castellani burlati. Dramma giocoso.
Libretto: none exists and it is not known if one was printed (no bills survive). First performance: 6 July (preceded by the usual three stage rehearsals), repeated in July (two more), September (one), October (one), Nov. (two), Dec. (one), and in 1789. Eszterháza performance material: Schellinger's bill (A.M. 18.1240) lists 187 *Bögen* of vocal and 194 *Bögen* of instrumental parts, of which nothing whatever has survived. Bartha-Somfai, 146, 336.

Alessio Prati: La vendetta di Nino. Melodramma tragico per musica. Da rappresentarsi nel teatro di S. A. il Signor Principe Esterhasi. In Oedenburgo, Presso Giuseppe Siess. 1788.
Libretto: no copy exists. First performance: 1 August (total: six), Sept. (three), Nov. (two), Dec. (one) and in 1789. Eszterháza performance material: Schellinger's bill (A.M. 18.1240) lists 192 *Bögen* of vocal and 258 *Bögen* of instrumental parts. EH, Budapest, owns the score (no cat. no.: Bartha-Somfai, Anhang d), which was ordered from Florence (Porta's statement of 10 August 1788, submitted and approved Jan. 1789: A.M. 18.1241) and cost 24 Fl. The other material no longer exists. Haydn wrote a cadenza for oboe solo and Semiramide in Atto I°, Sc. 1, Aria 'Se palpitar degg'io con cento larve' (*incipit*: Bartha-Somfai, 373). Because the parts are wanting, and he always removed his own insertion aria scores from the conducting score, we cannot establish whether he composed any, but one is certain: Atto I, Sc. 9, Seleuco's Aria is removed from the score. Harich, *Musikgeschichte*, 60. Bartha-Somfai, 146f., 373f.

Ferdinando Bertoni: Orfeo ed Euridice. Azione Teatrale per musica. Da rappresentarsi nel teatro di S. A. il Sig. Principe Esterhasi. – In Oedenburgo, Presso Giuseppe Siess. – 1788. [No names of cast in EH]. Libretto: copy in Országos Széchényi Könyvtár, Sign. 182.000. First performance: September (two in all), repeated in 1789. Eszterháza performance material: In Porta's statement of 10 Aug. 1788 (*supra*) we find 'Orfeo stampa in Venezia, per lire 36' (Bertoni's score was in fact printed at Venice), which was Schellinger's source (his bill, A.M. 18.1240, lists 69 *Bögen* of vocal and 187 *Bögen* of instrumental parts, all of which have disappeared completely). Harich, *Musikgeschichte*, 60. Bartha-Somfai, 147, 336. Harich in *HJB* I, 80.

Domenico Cimarosa: Il marito disperato. Dramma giocoso per musica. Da rappresentarsi nel teatro di S. A. il Sig. Principe Esterhasi. – In Oedenburgo, Presso Giuseppe Siess. 1788. Libretto: no copy survives. The cast may be reconstructed from a note on the inside cover of the EH (Budapest) score:

> [Porta?] Gismonda: La Benvenuti
> Valerio: de Paoli
> Conte: Moratti
> Corbellone (Corbolone): il Nencini
> Eugenie: La Nencini
> Dorina: La Sassi
> Marchese: Bianchi

First performance: October, repeated in November (three). It required four previous stage rehearsals. Eszterháza performance material: Schellinger's bill (A.M. 18.1240) lists 186 *Bögen* of vocal and 198 *Bögen* of instrumental parts. Ms. Mus. OE–48 contains the complete score (of Italian origin), the orchestral parts and fragments of the vocal parts copied by Schellinger with Anon. 10, 11 and 12. V. II was first marked 'Sig. Tost' (left March 1788), later 'Attilio' (Grisi): a similar state in V. II of *La quaquera spiritosa*, which was played in 1787 ('Sig. Tost') and in 1788 (red crayon: 'Oliva'). Apart from cuts, Haydn's editing was minimal. Harich, *Musikgeschichte*, 60. Bartha-Somfai, 148, 336f. Harich in *HJB* I, 80.

Giovanni Paisiello: IL TAMBURO NOTTURNO. DRAMMA GIOCOSO da rappresentarsi nel teatro di S. A. il sig. principe Esterhasi [two rabbits] – IN OEDENBURGO. Presso Giuseppe Siess – 1788. [No names of cast in EH]. Libretto: Biblioteca, Conservatorio di Santa Cecilia, Rome, Carvalhaes Coll., vol. 9. Bill from Siess for libretto: A.M. 18.1247 'and in the month of February Anno 1789 an opera libretto was made with $4\frac{1}{2}$ *Bögen*, entitl. Il Tamburo Notturno, of which 250 printed, 1 *Bögen* a 5 Fl. makes 21 Fl. 15 xr. . . .'. First performance: December (total of two, preceded by six stage rehearsals), reappeared in 1789 & 1790. Eszterháza performance material: Schellinger's bill (A.M. 18.1240) lists only 69 *Bögen* of vocal and 29 *Bögen* of instrumental parts – apparently just to fill out a set of parts which Porta managed to purchase: all has disappeared. Bartha-Somfai, 152, 338. Harich in *HJB* I, 80.

Eight operas from earlier seasons were repeated.
Bianchi's *Il disertore*: Rehearsal (Jan.), Feb. (one), March (two), April (two), May (one), June (one) and 1789.
Paisiello's *Le gare generose*: Rehearsal (Feb.), Feb. (one), March (one), April (one), May (two), June (two), September (three), October (one), Nov. (two), Dec. (one), and in 1789–90.
Cimarosa's *L'italiana in Londra*: February (three), March (one), April (two) and July (one).
Anfossi's *I viaggiatori felici*: February (one), April (one) and June (one).
Bianchi's *Alessandro nell'Indie*: February (one), March (one), April (two), May (two) and June (two).
Guglielmi's *La quaquera spiritosa*: March (one), May (two) and June (one).
Haydn's *Armida*: Rehearsal (March), March (one), April (one), June (one) and Nov. (one).
Paisiello's *La contadina di spirito* (*Il marchese villano*): April (one), May (one), June (one), Dec. (one), and in 1789. The 1777 material perished in the 1779 fire, and new score and parts had to be made for the revival. If a new libretto was printed, none has survived. The score was ordered from Vienna (contained in the oft-cited Porta statement of 10 Aug. 1788) and cost 25 Fl. Under the third of its alternative titles, *Il matrimonio inaspettato* (the fourth: *Il marchese Tulipano* was not used in EH) – Schellinger included in his bill (A.M. 18.1240) with 179 *Bögen* of vocal and 189 *Bögen* of instrumental parts. Ms. Mus. OE–25 contains the score (copied by Wenzel Sukowaty) but none of the parts. Apart from cuts (including choruses and arias), it cannot be determined whether Haydn added insertion arias or not (if his own, they would be missing in the score anyway). Bartha-Somfai, 145f., 334f. Harich in *HJB* I, 82f. In general, Harich in *HJB* I, 80ff.
Bologna's *L'isola di Calipso*: May (one), June (one), July (one) and Nov. (one), also in 1789–1790.
Anfossi's *Il matrimonio per inganno*: September (one), October (one) and for the last time in November.

THE GERMAN THEATRICAL TROUPE 1788

Lasser had left Hungary and gone to Passau and then to Graz. His place was taken by the Mayer Troupe once again, which however did not begin at Eszterháza until Easter and continued to the end of 1788 (contract: A.T. 51). At the beginning of 1788 their constitution was as follows (A.T. 53):

Names of actors	Parts
Johann Mayer, directeur:	fathers and character roles
Hornung:	lovers; is a dancer
Math. Mayer:	servants and peasants; is a dancer
Kunst:	lovers; is a dancer
Ferrary:	servants, character roles; is a dancer
Hart:	friends, 2nd lovers; is a dancer
Horschfeld:	fathers
Hübner:	understudy; secondary roles; supernumerary
Löfler or another:	announcer; wardrobe-attendant
Actresses	
Mayer or Titelmayer:	mothers and other leading parts
Mad. Kunst:	leading heroines
Mad. Mayer:	young girls; dances
Mad. Hornung:	heroines; dances
Josepha Mayer:	young girls; dances
Mad. Hart:	understudy; dances
Heiline:	understudy; supernumerary

[Horanyi, German, 140f., English, 136–8]

Our Chronicle opens with a letter from Haydn to the agent of a German prince:

[To Ferdinand Müller von Müllegg,[1] Vienna. *German*]

Estoras, 3rd February 1788.

Nobly born,
Most highly respected Herr von Müller!

The appreciation which His Highness the Prince von Oettingen has shown for my modest compositions is of the greatest possible value to me, and I only regret that at present I cannot have the great pleasure of writing the 3 Symphonies that are demanded, because I now have to compose 6 Notturni for His Majesty the King of Naples[2] and a new opera[3] for my gracious Prince. But when these works are finished, I shall make every effort to compose the 3 Symphonies, for which I do not presume to set a price, but beg to leave this entirely to the discretion of His Most Serene Highness the Prince. For the oratorio,[4] which I recently improved by adding two new choruses, I beg to ask 16 ducats, five of which I must pay the copyist. Should I be fortunate enough to receive the gracious approval of some of these proposals, I shall then await further commands. Meanwhile I am, Sir, in profound submission,

Your most obedient servant,
Joseph Haydn.

[CCLN, 74f.]

---

1 Ferdinand Müller von und zu Müllegg (*c.* 1758–1824) was an ardent amateur musician and, among other things, Prince Oettingen-Wallerstein's Court Agent in Vienna. On 16 January the Prince had written to von Müller concerning the oratorio and 3 new Symphonies, which (said the Prince) 'no one should own except me'. See letter of *c.* 17 October 1789 (p. 727). This and the following notes are based largely on Diemand, 'Joseph Haydn und der Wallersteiner Hof' (*Zeitschrift des historischen Vereins für Schwaben und Neuburg*, Band 45 [1920–1922], pp. 31ff.).
2 Ferdinand IV. Haydn delivered the Notturni in 1790, when Ferdinand was visiting his royal relatives in Vienna, in 1790.
3 This is possibly a white lie, because Haydn wrote his last opera for the Prince in 1784 (*Armida*).
4 The oratorio was *Il ritorno di Tobia* (1774–75): the score is still preserved in the Oettingen-Wallerstein Archives, Harburg Castle.

The following correspondence is with Haydn's publishers:

[To Artaria & Co., Vienna. *German*]
Nobly born,
Most highly respected Sir!
    Please don't take it amiss that through lack of time I couldn't write to you myself recently[1] about the Oratorio. Should the Oratorio be copied already (which I trust is the case), please give it to our porter, from whom I shall receive it safely. Send him the bill for the copying costs at the same time, which I shall repay at the first available opportunity. By the way, I am very much obliged to you for the excellent cheese you sent me, and also for the sausages, for which I am your debtor; but I shall not fail to return the obligation, when an opportunity offers.
    Please also send me C. P. Emanuel Bach's last two pianoforte works.[2] Meanwhile I remain, Sir, most respectfully,

Your most obedient servant,
Joseph Haydn.

Estoras, 16th February 1788.
[Address:]   Monsieur
        Monsieur d'Artaria et Compag
                    a
                Vienne.
    Please expedite.   [CCLN, 75f.]

[To William Forster, London. *German*]

Estoras, 28th February 1788.

My very dear *Mons*: Forster!
    Don't be angry at me that you have disagreeableness with Herr Langmann.[3] I shall make it up to you another time. It's not my fault but the usurious practices of Herr Artaria. This much I can promise you: that as long as I live neither Artaria nor Langmann shall have anything from me, directly or indirectly. I am too honest and straightforward to want to hurt your feelings or to damage you. But you certainly must realize that whoever wants to have the exclusive rights for 6 new pieces of mine must pay more than 20 guineas. In fact I have recently signed a contract with someone who pays me 100 and more guineas for each 6 works. I shall write you more about this another time. Meanwhile I am, with great respect,

Your wholly obedient servant,
Joseph Haydn.

[Address:] [postal stamp 'M[a]r 15', the date of arrival in London]
            To Mr Forster Musical
        Instrument-Macker to the Prince
        of Wales. N^{ro} 348 in the Strand.
                        a
                    London.

[CCLN, 76]

---

1 Haydn got his brother, Johann, who was a tenor in the Esterházy choir, to write. The letter (Stadtbibliothek, Vienna, cat. 69610) reads: 'Nobly born and highly respected Sir, At the request of my brother, *Cappell Meister* Haydn, I take the liberty of asking you to send me *The Seven Words* for the pianoforte, in his arrangement; you should give it, marked with my address, to Herr Rosenbaum, Prince Esterházy's porter. My brother will see to the payment, and he has permitted me in the future to ask in his name for those pieces which I require. He will confirm this when he pays you his next visit. Hoping to receive the piece soon, I remain, Sir, &c. Johann Haydn. Eisenstadt, 9th December 1787.'

2 C. P. E. Bach, who died in December 1788, published only one work with Artaria: Six Sonatas for Harpsichord (pl. no. 181). Haydn, however, probably referred to the recent German editions of the 5th and 6th collections of *Clavier-Sonaten* (1785 and 1787 – Wotquenne 59 and 61), or the *Sechs neue Sonatinen*, 1787 (Wotquenne 63).

3 *Recte*: Longman (& Broderip).

In May, when there were opera performances at Eszterháza for only eleven days of the month, Haydn managed (as we have said above) to escape for a day or two to Vienna in order to hear *Don Giovanni*. On the 15th, Haydn received his 170 gulden as cash payment in lieu of his new summer uniform.[1] On the 22nd he wrote to Artaria:

[To Artaria & Co., Vienna. *German*]

Estoras, 22nd May 1788.

Dearest Friend!

I would be unjust and ungrateful if I were to throw away your friendship so boorishly. I shall never forget that you gave me preference over many, though I well know that I occasionally deserved it more than the others; as soon as my present affairs are completed, you shall have some of my works, as before. If you were to write me before your departure, so that I could answer it in time, I should be pleased for a number of reasons. My time is too short today. I am, as always, most respectfully,

Your wholly obedient servant,
Josephus Haydn.
[CCLN, 76f.]

In 1784, Franz Anton von Weber (later the father of the composer Carl Maria) came to Vienna with his sons Fritz and Edmund, aged twenty-three and eighteen, to find a good music teacher for them. Haydn was chosen and accepted the two young men as pupils; Haydn's fee was 150 ducats each. In 1788, Franz Anton came to fetch his two sons. Fritz had been engaged as violinist in the Esterházy orchestra on 1 April (he left again in September). When Edmund, of whom Haydn was particularly fond, had to leave, the teacher wrote the following lines in the pupil's commonplace-book:

Fürchte Gott – Liebe deinen Nächsten – und Deinen
Meister Joseph Haydn so Dich von Hertzen lieb hat.
Estoras den 22 May 788.[2]

We next hear of Haydn in the following letters to Artaria:

[To Artaria & Co., Vienna. *German*]

Estoras, 10th August 1788.

Well born,
Most highly respected Sir!

My manifold affairs have prevented me from writing my long-overdue answer to your last letter. I repeat that it will always be a pleasure to supply you with my works. Since I am now in a position where I need a little money, I propose to write for you, by the end of December, either 3 new Quartets or 3 new pianoforte Sonatas with accompaniment of a violin and violoncello. I would ask you, for your part, to send me an *a conto* of 25 gold ducats next Wednesday by our outgoing Hussars. You can leave the letter and the money with our porter Wednesday morning. Meanwhile the present letter should serve as your security.

---

1 EH, Budapest, A.M. 18.1235: Eszterház. Valkó II, 604.
2 Weber information from Pohl II, 203f. Franz Anton, having settled his sons in Haydn's care, then married again (he had been a widower for some years): the pretty young Genovefa von Brenner, then seventeen, from Bavaria, who had been sent to Vienna to study music. They were married on 20 August 1785, and their children included Carl Maria. Pohl received photographs of Edmund's commonplace-book through the courtesy of Johannes Brahms.

You shall have the receipt on the coming Monday. Of course it is understood that I shall then complete the other 3 Quartets, or pianoforte Sonatas, so that the edition will comprise half-a-dozen, as usual. NB. – For 6 Quartets the previous sum of one hundred ducats, for 6 pianoforte Sonatas 300 fl. In the hope of a favourable answer, I am Sir, most respectfully,

> Your most obedient servant,
> Josephus Haydn.

[Address:]   Monsieur
        Monsieur d'Artaria et Compag
            à
               Vienne.

[CCLN, 77]

[To Artaria & Co., Vienna. *German*]

Estoras, 17th August 1788.

Well born,
Most highly respected Sir!
     Many thanks for the 25 ducats which you sent me. The zeal I shall bestow on the 3 pianoforte Sonatas[1] with accompaniment of a violin and violoncello which you want, shall be a guarantee of my wish to retain your friendship in the future. Meanwhile I am, Sir, most respectfully,

> Your most obedient servant,
> Josephus Haydn.

[CCLN, 77f.]

A letter dated 29 August from Haydn to Artaria is known to us only from a mention in a Parisian antiquarian bookseller's catalogue of 1887. The correspondence continues:

[To Artaria & Co., Vienna. *German*]

Estoras, 22nd September 1788.

Monsieur
et mon tres cher Amy!
     A few days ago I was told that you, my dear Sir, were supposed to have purchased from Herr Tost[2] my very newest 6 Quartets and 2 new Symphonies. Since I would like to know, for various reasons, if this is true or not, I would ask you to let me know on the next postday. I remain, Sir, most respectfully,

> Your most obedient servant,
> Joseph Haydn.

[Address:]   Monsieur
        Monsieur d'Artaria et compag:
            a
               Vienne.

[CCLN, 78]

---

1 Nos. 24–26 of the chronological list: Artaria published them in July 1789 as Op. 57 (pl. no. 239).
2 Johann Tost went on a journey to Paris about this time, taking with him the 6 Quartets, Opp. 54 and 55, and two new Symphonies, Nos. 88 and 89. Tost, when he returned to Vienna in 1789 or 1790, married a rich wife and became a well-known merchant (*Grosshandlungs-Gremialist*) and patron of chamber music. Both Haydn and Mozart wrote some of their loveliest works for him. See Larsen, p. 114 n. 56, and Hoboken's address in *Das Archiv für Photogramme* (brochure published by the Österreichische Nationalbibliothek, Vienna 1958, pp. 37f.), for the most recent research on the subject, also *supra*, pp. 81f.

[To Artaria & Co., Vienna. *German*]

Estoras, 26th October 1788.

Well born,
Most highly respected Sir!

In order to compose your 3 pianoforte Sonatas particularly well, I had to buy a new fortepiano. Now since no doubt you have long since realized that scholars are sometimes short of money – and that is my situation at present – I should like to ask you, Sir, if you would be kind enough to pay 31 gold ducats to the organ and instrument-maker Wenzl Schanz, who lives on the Leimgruben at the Blauen Schif[f] N°· 22; which 31 ducats I shall repay to you, with thanks, by the end of January of the coming year 1789. To convince you that I shall keep my word, I have enclosed a small promissory note which I have recalled today. But should you have any doubts of my integrity, I shall send you on the next post-day a bond for a thousand Gulden signed by my Prince himself. I don't like to be in debt to tradesmen, and – thank God! – I am free of such burdens; but since great people keep me waiting so long for payment, things have come to a standstill. Meanwhile this letter should be your security, and shall be valid in any court. I will pay off the interest in cash.[1] Confident that you will not refuse my request I wrote to the organ-builder, who will quite certainly come to get his money.

Please excuse this liberty: it is bestowed on a man who is grateful, and will ever remain

Your most obedient servant,
Joseph Haydn
Capell Meister.

P.S. I shall have the pleasure of seeing you in Vienna towards the end of December.
[Address:]   Monsieur
           Monsieur d'Artaria et
           Compag.

           à
           Vienne.
[Artaria's clerk notes: 'Heydn [*sic*] Giuseppe/Esterhaze 26th Oct/1788/ ans'd 30th ditto'.]

[CCLN, 79]

[To Artaria & Co., Vienna. *German*]

Estoras, 16th November 1788.

Well born,
Most highly respected Sir!

Many thanks for the correct payment which you made in my name to Herr Schanz. I shall keep my word punctually, not only as to the repayment but also as to the 3 new Sonatas, of which one and one-half are already completed. Meanwhile I remain, respectfully,

Your most obedient servant,
Joseph Haydn.

[Address 'as always' – note on Pohl's MS. copy, the earliest preserved source.]

[CCLN, 80]

---

1 Haydn writes 'mit Notten ersetzen', which may mean either 'in [bank] notes', i.e. cash, or 'with music'.

Schellinger's bill for opera copying reads as follows

Conto
What was copied for the princely theatre from 1st [not 13] January 1788 to December 1788, the vocal parts à 7 xr., the instrumental à 5 xr. as per agreement

Operas	Bögen	
	Vocal parts	Instrumental
il Giunio Pruto [*sic*]	167	239
I finti Eredi	189	236
Matrimonio inaspettato	179	189
Orfeo	69	187
I due Castellani	187	194
Vendetta di Nino	192	258
Le Gare Generose repaired	9	36
Il Marito disperato	186	198
Il tamburo notturno	69	29
Soma...	1,247	1,566

Joan Schilling [*sic*] Copista di Theatro
di 1 Decbris 1788

Id est 275 F. 39 xr.

I the undersigned have carefully examined the above sum and found it to be correct.
Estoras, 29 December 1788   Joseph Haydn
                                                                     Capell Meister

[Prince Nicolaus's order for payment signed Kismartonii (Eisenstadt), 20 Jan. 1789]
[EH Budapest, A.M. 18.1240. Valkó II, 605. Bartha-Somfai, 150. Bartha, 197 – all with '13 January' instead of (*recte*) '1st January']

Our closing section for the Chronicle 1788 is a curious little biography of Haydn published in the *Allmanach* [*sic*] *der k. k. National-Schaubühne auf das Jahr 1788 von F. C. Kunz. Wien, gedruckt und zu finden bey Gerold*:[1]

Joseph Haidn [Beethoven's usual spelling!] ... a small sketch of this declared favourite of composers, for his friends.

Joseph Haydn was born in Vienna about the year 1730. In his earliest childhood he already showed an exceptional taste and love for music as well as rare gifts for it. His parents thought it would be good to have him educated in a Jesuit college, and there he found sufficient possibilities of cultivating his favourite art. The progress that he made during his stay in that college was so rapid that before he had learned the first rules of harmony, he was already composing symphonies, trios, sonatas &c., in which the rising sun of his shining genius could be observed. Although these works lacked the regularity and consistency that come only as the fruits of maturity, from each piece that he wrote there exuded a natural lilt and a flowering of inspiration which, when channelled into its proper course, and its too florid branches trimmed[!], looked forward to the results that we know. The fruitfulness of his genius made such an impression on all his friends that they advised him seriously to let his pen rest for a while and to concentrate on his studies of counterpoint without which no composer, no matter how great his genius be, can be correct. Haydn followed their advice and in a short period he became,

1 For printed works we do not usually list the library from which we took our text (or xerox), but in this case, the book is rare and other scholars may wish to consult it: Stadtbibliothek, Vienna, G 14747, pp. 112ff. The very rare Pressburg *Theater Almanach* exists (never complete in one library) in the Stadtbibliothek; in the Országos Széchényi Könyvtár (also in the archives of the late Erwin Major, who owned the only known engraving of a Haydn opera as performed on the Pressburg stage: the last scene of Atto II⁰ in *Armida*, from the *Almanach* 1787; Major showed this to us in 1958, when we were in Budapest; in the O.S.K. copy, the engraving is missing; it is also reproduced in *Magyar Salon*, 1890, of which we have not been able to locate a copy). The *Portfeuille* quoted in *Haydn in England 1791–1795*, p. 189, is in Göttweig Abbey.

through diligent and constant application, a complete master of the harmonies in their fixed rules. The fame which his compositions reaped soon awakened a whole swarm of jealous colleagues who sought to blacken his reputation. One accused him of writing music that was too volatile, unimportant and wild. One accused him of founding a new musical school, of introducing a kind of new music never before experienced; but they were soon reduced to silence and paid tribute to the truth.[1] It was Haydn to whom was reserved the refining of music in Germany, of bringing it to the culmination of perfection; and in every way he made himself a model of originality, repentance [*Reuheit*] and beautiful sòng. I don't mean by that statement that because of a pleasant melody and a sweet song he laid aside the fugue. There are fugues to excess in his works. But in his hands they never degenerate into mere pedantry, are never heavy but are set against the pleasantest inspirations of fantasy, a most charming wit [*Laune*], and a surging of riotous variety. About seventeen or eighteen years ago [i.e. 1770 or 1771] his *Stabat Mater* was first heard in Vienna [*recte*: 1767]; many of his enemies were present, listened carefully to it, and admitted the composer's success about which they had so long doubted. Haydn has composed various operas which have been given in Vienna, Dresden, Berlin and in the private theatre of Prince von Esterhaz, where he is Kapellmeister. The salary which he receives annually from the Prince makes his situation sufficiently pleasant for his spirit to enjoy that freedom necessary to develop all its ideas. Nature and long experience enable him to write with ease that which would be the hardest exertion for a normal composer; for him it is only a joke; a relaxation. It is to this ease that one must ascribe the great quantity of music in all genres which, if they be added together, outpace the complete works of any other composer except Handel. The universality of Haydn's genius can be seen in no other way as clearly as through the large demand for his works that obtains in all of Europe. His music is not just fashionable; one expects it with enthusiasm. He receives continually commissions from France, England, Russia, Holland and Spain, also from individuals and music publishers. [The report ends with a wrong description of the circumstances surrounding the 'Farewell' Symphony: here it is said that the musicians resigned because they fell out with the 'house officers', etc.]

Chronicle 1789

ITALIAN OPERAS 1789

This year 92 performances are registered (Harich in *HJB* I, 87). The season began at the end of February and concluded on the Prince's name-day, 6 December. The Prince was, it seems, away in July, in which month there was only one performance (*La Circe*).

Domenico Cimarosa: I due supposti conti.
Libretto: none extant. Possibly copies of the Vienna libretto (first perf. 12 May 1789; copy in Biblioteca, Cons. di Musica S. Cecilia, Rome, Carvalhaes Coll., vol. 9) were ordered, with a changed title page and new cast list (?). First performance: end of February, repeated in March (two), April (one), May (two) and for the last time in October. Eszterháza performance material: Schellinger's bill (A.M. 19.1262) lists 196 *Bögen* of vocal and 210 *Bögen* of instrumental parts. MS. Mus. OE–52 (EH Budapest) includes the complete score (copied by one 'Preta' in Milan), and the incomplete vocal and complete orchestral parts (V. I, 1st part, lacks Atto II°) copied by Schellinger with Anon. 11 and 12. Apart from the usual cuts and ordinary transpositions, Haydn transposed (from A to G) and rewrote the Aria for Laura (Lauretta) in Atto I° 'Se voi foste un cavaliere', which necessitated his writing eight pages in score (facsimile of first page as No. 27 in Bartha-Somfai); Haydn also subtly changed even the theme. In Atto II°, Sc. 5: Beatrice's Rec.

---

1 These thoughts are surely taken from the (in)famous article of 1784 in the *European Magazine* (*supra*, pp. 496f.). H.C.R.L.

('Misera me') and Aria ('Infelice sventurata') were cancelled and Haydn wrote a new insertion aria on the same text (XXIVb:15); we have the autograph (discussed on p. 648), marked 'No. 14' (its place in the opera), an autograph *particella* for voice and b.c. (facsimile of first page in Bartha-Somfai, No. 28), and the original parts (bsn. wanting) by Schellinger and Anon. 12. We suspect that the part of Lauretta, with its characteristic transposition downwards, was composed for Polzelli, the dramatic new Aria for Bologna, Sassi-Nencini or Barbara Sassi. On the reverse side of Schellinger's copy of one of the vocal parts is the Haydn autograph *particella* of 'Sono Alcina' (*supra* p. 648f.). Bartha-Somfai, 153, 338–41. Harich in *HJB* I, 85.

Pasquale Anfossi: Le gelosie fortunate. Dramma giocoso da rappresentarsi nel teatro di S. A. il Sig. Principe Esterhasi de Galantha. L'anno 1789. In Oedenburgo, Presso Giuseppe Siess.
Libretto: no copy survives. Siess's bill (A.M. 18.1247) 'In the month of June, an opera libretto entit. Le Gelosie, with 4½ Bogen, of which 250 were printed. 1 Bogen a 5 Fl., makes 22 Fl. 30 xr.' First performance: middle of May (total: two), repeated in July (two) and in August (three). Eszterháza performance material: Schellinger's bill (A.M. 19.1262) lists 189 *Bögen* of vocal and 196 *Bögen* of instrumental material. EH, Budapest, Ms. Mus. OE–40 contains the complete score (from Vienna), nearly complete orchestral parts (V. I, 1st part, missing)' but no vocal parts at all (copyists: Schellinger with Anon. 12 and 30); on 1st part of V. II 'Sig. Attilo' (Grisi, who had now firmly taken Tost's place). Apart from cuts, Haydn added an insertion aria for Riccardo in Atto I°, Sc. 11; it was taken from Bianchi's *Alessandro nell'Indie* in the EH version (1787), 'Or che il Cielo a me ti rende', and must have been a popular number Atto II°, Sc. 4 (Giro) arrived from Vienna with Mozart's insertion aria, K.541, 'Un baccio di mano' (the EH copy of the score, obviously from the lost autograph, is now the work's principal source), marked 'del Sig: Wolf: Mozart'. Haydn cut it! In Sc. 13, Haydn removed the Aria 'Allor ch'io pazzo' and substituted another (composer unknown: *incipit* in Bartha-Somfai, 342). Harich *Musikgeschichte*, 61. Bartha-Somfai, 153f., 341–3. Harich in *HJB* I, 85.

Domenico Cimarosa: Il pittore Parigino. Dramma per musica in due atti. Da rappresentarsi nel teatro di S. A. il Sig. Principe Esterhasi de Galantha. In Oedenburgo, Presso Giuseppe Siess. 1789.
Libretto: no copy survives. Siess's bill (A.M. 18.1247) 'In the month of June, an opera libretto entit. Il pittore Parigino, with 4 Bogen, 250 were printed, 1 Bogen a 5 Fl: makes 20 Fl.' First performance: beginning of June (total: four), repeated in August (one), Sept. (three), Nov. (two) and in 1790. Eszterháza performance material: Schellinger's bill (A.M. 19.1212) lists 191 *Bögen* of vocal and 189 *Bögen* of instrumental parts. Ms. Mus. OE–13 includes the complete score from the office of Wenzel Sukowaty, Vienna, almost complete vocal parts and nearly complete orchestral parts (lacking V. I, 1st part, and 'Basso'), copied by Schellinger with Anon. 10, 11, 12, 30 and 61. Apart from cuts, Haydn cancelled Broccardo's Aria 'La cara padroncina s'accente Dottorina' and added a new one, 'Quel amabile visetto' (*incipit* in Bartha-Somfai, 343) in Atto I°, Sc. 6; the composer is unknown but might be Haydn. Atto II°, Sc. 6. Instead of the Duetto Monsieur-Barone 'Presto finiamola', Haydn added a Cavatina by Martin y Soler dated 1789. In Sc. 14, Haydn inserted an accompagnato 'Ohime! ch'innanzi agli occhi' and aria 'Penso che per morire ci vuol tre cose' (E flat, 4/4) which (our notes of 1958 say) are 'obviously not Haydn'. Cimarosa's Sc. was for Frasonio, the EH insertion for the Barone. Harich, *Musikgeschichte*, 61. Bartha-Somfai, 154, 343–5. Harich in *HJB* I, 85.

Pasticcio: La Circe ossia L'isola incantata. Dramma per musica, da rappresentarsi nel teatro di S. A. il sig. Principe Esterhasi – 1789. In Oedenburgo, Presso Giuseppe Siess.

Attori
Circe Maga.
Lindora, sua Damigella.
Teodoro, Capitan di Vacello.
Corado, suo compagno di Viaggio.
Brunoro, servo di Circe.
Pedrillo, Schiavo di Teodoro.
Una Fata.

La Scene si finge in un'Isola.

Le Decorazzioni sono tutte nuove d'invenzzione,
e direzzione del Sig. Pietro Travaglie [sic]
Pittore Teatrale di S. A.

Libretto: Siess printed 250 copies, of which one has survived in EH, Eisenstadt (photograph: H.C.R.L.). First performance: July, repeated in August (six), September (one), October (two), Nov. (one), Dec. (one) and in 1790. Eszterháza performance material: Schellinger's bill (A.M. 19.1212) lists 187 *Bögen* of vocal and 198 *Bögen* of instrumental parts. EH, Budapest, MS. Mus. OE–57 contains the score (with many gaps for material removed), which consists of Johann Gottlieb Naumann's *Ipocondriaco*, an unknown *buffo* opera (*La Circe*) which is positively not identical with Cimarosa's work of that title (despite the EH attribution in the catalogue of 1806 by Hummel [*HJB* IX, 104]) and a third section composed or put together by Haydn himself (Hoboken assigns this section the number XXXII:1). It is also not derived from *La Maga Circe, Commedia in Musica* (Anfossi: libretto for Monza, 1790, in Rome, Bib. di S. Cecilia, Carvalhaes 32/11). Cimarosa's *La Circe*: libretto for Milan, Carnival 1783. Library of Congress s 2005, with figures: Circe – Ulisse – Prisco – Canente – Subino – Clerinto. We are concerned with the part Haydn put together at Eszterháza. Haydn made the following major additions and subtractions: Atto I°, Overture (Naumann), heavily cut by Haydn. Sc. 2 (Anonymous), Lindora's Aria 'Quasi in tutte le ragazze naturale è la magia' edited and shortened by Haydn, necessitating an autograph for bars 41–53 (two pages, sewn over orig.): *incipit* Bartha-Somfai, 347. Sc. 3, Duetto Corrado-Teodoro 'Qual cambiamento è questo' is by Naumann, followed by Naumann's storm music. Sc. 4, a huge cut in the recit. by Haydn required Schellinger to copy the first three bars of a new page. Sc. 5 (the score's marking) = Sc. 6 of libretto. Teodoro's Aria 'Dal campo dell'onore' (*incipit* Bartha-Somfai, 348, add lower octave to first two notes and *sf* to bar 3, 3rd note): score removed, only parts. Composer? Sc. 6 (libretto 7) begins with a Cavatina for Circe missing in the score but in the parts (missing in Bartha-Somfai):

The vocal part is missing, but the text (the beginning of which easily fits the Andantino's melody) is

> Io son capriccioseta
> E sol mi piace quello
> E tale il mio cervello
> E non gli so che far.
> [etc.]

Sc. 7 (8), Circe's Aria, 'Il cor ch'io serbo in petto', cut in the score, appears in the libretto and therefore Haydn provided a substitute which was later removed in the score and parts. Sc. 8 (9), Corado's Aria 'Benedette sian le Donne' is by Naumann. The next scene in the score was cut, so that the score's Sc. 10 is also the libretto's. This fine *scena*, discussed above (p. 650) was published by Bartha-Somfai. Haydn's autograph, dated 1789, still exists because he could not do anything else with this piece, so closely is it connected with the progress of the opera itself. (He could use the other, removed, pieces in concert.) Atto II° Sc. 2, Corado's D major Aria was cancelled and another, 'V'e la sala al primo ingresso' in E flat, substituted (transposed): Bartha-Somfai say only one V. II part survives, but there is also a bass part as a result of which one may give at least those *incipits*. No. 12 (Cavatina) begins

Sc. 4, La Fata's Aria is also an insertion (No. 14), 'Plachi il destin tiranno l'ingiusto suo rigore' (probably for soprano?), of which we may give the *incipits* of the two sections from the 'Basso' part:

Allegro vivace

Sc. 5, No. 15 can be identified from the surviving 'Basso' part as Haydn's insertion aria, 'Son pietosa, son bonina' for Lindora (perhaps Polzelli?). Sc. 6 is for Pedrillo, and the Aria which follows – the score of the whole second act, except the Finale, is missing – may be a Haydn insertion (No. 17): 'Fra il timor, e la speranza',

Sc. 8, No. 18, is the Terzetto, 'Levatevi presto' (Teodoro, Corado, Brunoro). Before closing, we must add that our central 'Circe' part of the opera, to which EH forces (Porta?) added the role of Pedrillo, is also not identical with Astaritta's *La Circe* (performed at this period in Prague). Harich, *Musikgeschichte*, 61. Bartha-Somfai, 154f., 345–53. Harich in *HJB* I, 86.

Pietro Guglielmi: Le vicende d'amore. Dramma in musica a cinque voci. Da rappresentarsi nel teatro di S. A. il Signore Principe regnante Niccola Eszterházy [*sic*]. Vienna, presso la società tipografica. Libretto: no copy extant. Bill from the società (successor to Kurzbeck), Vienna, 20 Sept. 1789 (A.M. 18.1249). First performance: October (total: three), repeated in Nov. (two) and in 1790. Eszterháza performance material: Schellinger's bill (A.M. 19.1262) lists 197 *Bögen* of vocal and 196 *Bögen* of instrumental parts. EH, Budapest, Ms. Mus. OE–72 includes only the score, purchased in Vienna. Apart from cuts, Haydn inserted two arias for Don Alonso (a tenor): Atto I°, Sc. 7 (Bartha-Somfai found that the last page of the cancelled score was exactly the same, and in the same key, as the substitution: a mystery), and Atto II° Sc. 4 – *incipits* in Bartha-Somfai, 353f. Text of the first, 'Per questa mano bella' (also used by Mozart as a bass aria, K.612), of the second 'Pensa che l'hai tradita'. Haydn made a small but characteristic harmonic 'improvement' (for as such he would have considered it) in Atto II°, Sc. 6, Aria (Elvira), 'Questo core a te donai', bar 25 (score fol. 269v.), changing Guglielmi's pattern of A^6 – F sharp^6 – B minor to A^6 – D – F sharp^6 – B minor. Harich, *Musikgeschichte*, 61. Bartha-Somfai, 154f., 353–5. Harich in *HJB* I, 86.

Vincenzo Martin y Soler: L'arbore di Diana. Dramma giocoso in due atti. [Following is covered over by a new printed sheet: Da rappresentarsi per l'arrivo di Sua Altezza Reale Maria Teresa Archiduchessa d'Austria: sposa del Principe Antonio de Sassonia. In Vienna presso Giuseppe Nob. de Kurzbek, stampatore di S. M. I. R.] [new sheet reads:] Da rappresentarsi nel teatro di S. A. il Signore Principe regnante Niccolò Esterhazy. Vienna, presso la Società Tipografica. Libretto: the Viennese libretto (for 1 Oct. 1787) exists in several copies, the adapted one for Eszterháza in none. Cast (from the extant vocal parts of EH material):

> Endimione: Brizzi [Prizzi]
> Britomarte, ninfa: Benvenuti
> Diana: Bologna
> Clizia: Sig^ra Polcelli [Haydn's autograph]
> Silvio: Braghetti
> Doristo: Nencini

First performance: middle of November (total: four), repeated on Prince's name-day (6 Dec.) and in 1790. Eszterháza performance material: Porta purchased the score and vocal parts in Vienna (EH, Budapest, A.M. 19.1251, dated 7 Dec. 1789: 'La Partitura dell'Arbore di Diana: 30 Fl. Le Parti de' Cantanti della suddetta Opera 36 Fl. 44 xr.'). Schellinger's bill (A.M. 19.1262) therefore lists only 249 *Bögen* of orchestral parts. EH, Budapest, Ms. Mus. OE–6 contains the entire material (score and all parts). The clarinets and trumpets of the original score were not even copied from the Sukowaty score; the other parts (orch.) by Schellinger with Anon. 11 and 12. Haydn himself noted the date when the vocal parts were distributed on Polzelli's (and Benvenuti's) parts: '16. Ott. 1789'. Apart from cutting three small sections (a cadenza, the middle part [17 bars] of an aria and a long secco), Haydn made no changes in this successful and charming music. Harich, *Musikgeschichte*, 61 (also mentioning a German-language libretto, Vienna 1788, which EH owned). Bartha-Somfai, 155, 354f. Harich in *HJB* I, 86.

Nine operas from earlier seasons were repeated:

Prati's *La vendetta di Nino*: March (four), April (two), May (two), August (one), September (three), October (one).

Paisiello's *Il tamburo notturno*: March (one), April (two), October (one), November (one), and in 1790.

Bianchi's *Il disertore*: March (one), April (one), May (one), July (one), October (two).

Paisiello's *Le gare generose*: March (one), May (one), June (one), September (one), October (one), November (one), and in 1790.

Bologna's *L'isola di Calipso*: March (one), April (two), September (one), and in 1790.

Bertoni's *Orfeo ed Euridice*: March (two).

Fabrizi's *I due castellani*: April (two), October (one), November (one), December (one).

Paisiello's *La contadina di spirito*: May (one).

Sarti's *I finti eredi*: June (one), August (one), September (three), October (one), and in 1790. Haydn seems to have added an insertion aria for the 1789 revival, because Schellinger includes 'Finti Eredi repaired' on his annual bill. Literature: Harich in *HJB* I, 87.

THE GERMAN THEATRICAL TROUPE 1789

We have no information regarding the constitution and repertoire of the Mayer Troupe during their stay at Eszterháza this year.

Our Chronicle opens with Porta's 'consegnation' for various operas:

Consegnation Eisenstadt 6ª Jan. 1789
Axur Re d'Ormus [Salieri]: 30 Fl.
La Vendetta di Nino, fatta copiare in Firenze per il prezzo F. 24
Per il porto . . .
Orfeo stampa in Venezia, per lire 36 Fanno . . . 7. 12
La Contadina di spirito, fatta Copiare in Vienna per . . . 25 [Fl.]
L'Albergatrice [Caruso]: 22 Fl. 30 xr.
10 Agosto 1788 /Somma 108 Fl. 42 xr.

[Prince Nicolaus's order for payment,   Porta mp.
Eisenstadt, 7 Jan. 1789.]   Josephus Haydn mpria
                          [EH, Budapest, A.M. 18.1241. Valkó II, 606]

Our next references to Haydn are found in his correspondence:

[To Artaria & Co., Vienna. *German*]

Estoras, 8th March 1789.

Well born,
Most highly respected Sir!
     The abrupt decision of my Prince to leave Vienna, which he hates, caused my hasty departure for Estoras, and prevented my being able to take leave of the greater number of my friends; I hope that you, too, will therefore forgive me. On the day of my departure I was seized with such a violent catarrh that for three whole weeks I was of no use to anyone, but now – thank God! – I feel better. I promise to send the 3rd Sonata[1] in a week, and enclose herewith the two signatures you requested. As to the other works – some of which I have finished – I shall inform you another time. Meanwhile I am, dear Sir, most respectfully,
                          Your most obedient servant,
                          Josephus Haydn.

[No address; Artaria's clerk notes: 'Heydn Giuseppe/Esterhaze 8. Marzo/1789'.]
                          [CCLN, 80]

---

1 The last of the three pianoforte Trios: see *supra*, p. 642, No. 26 (XV:13).

[To Johann Traeg,[1] Vienna. *German*]

Estoras, 8th March 1789.

Well born,
Most highly respected Sir!

This is to inform you that the new pianoforte Sonata which Herr Breitkopf requested[2] shall be finished by the coming week. You will therefore be good enough to let me know to whom I should address the sonata, and who shall pay me the 10 ducats upon delivery of the same. I hope to receive a satisfactory reply and am, most respectfully,

Your most obedient servant,
Josephus Haydn [m.p] ria.
Capell Meister von
Fürst Esterhazy.

P.S.: You need only leave your letter at the porter's in the Prince's mansion; a carriage leaves almost daily.
[Address:]

Dem Wohl Edlen Herrn Johann
Traeg Musicalien Händler zu
zustellen.[3]
auf den Hohen Marck[t] in
N^{ro} 423 in   Wienn.
4^{tn} Stock   [CCLN, 8of.]

[To Joseph Eybler,[4] Vienna. *German*]

Estoras, 22nd March 1789.

Dearest *Mons.* Eybler!

Thank you so much for all your good wishes: I return them all to you with my whole heart. I was pleased to hear of the good reception of your Symphony and regret that I could not be there as an eye- and ear-witness, but I hope to hear it in Vienna. Now, my dear friend, I would ask you to write 3 new Dance Minuets for me, but including a Trio with each one. I shall tell you the reason for my request myself, by and by; meanwhile I can only say that these 3 Minuets are intended for one of my best friends, and that you must not give them to anyone else beforehand, much less have them performed. *Sed hoc inter nos.*

You can tell Herr Humel[5] that 2 of my Symphonies, which I composed for Herr Tost,[6] will soon appear in print. The other two, however, will not appear for

---

1 Johann Traeg, one of Vienna's busiest copyists, later became a music publisher.
2 Christoph Gottlob Breitkopf had made a journey to Austria in the autumn of 1786, and had intended to visit Haydn in Eszterháza; the composer happened to come to Vienna in December, however, and Breitkopf met him there. On 10 January 1789, Breitkopf wrote a letter to Haydn. The letter no longer exists, but we can quote a summary of it (Hase, pp. 3f.) Breitkopf writes that 'he would like to have a new pianoforte Sonata, one which has never before been printed, to include in a collection of various pieces of music which he [Breitkopf] is putting together. As a recommendation for the whole undertaking, he would like to have an original composition by Haydn, even if it is only one movement. Haydn can choose his own fee, and the Sonata must be in his hands by March at the latest, because he intends to start the publication in that month ... He asks if Haydn would not do him the honour of giving his firm other compositions, and if so, would [Haydn] not write six pianoforte Sonatas; he can choose his own fee for these works, too.' Haydn chose the Sonata No. 58 in C which, however, he could not send until 5th April (see letter, *infra*). The Sonata was published as the first number of 'Musikalischer Pot-Pourri'. In all these dealings, Traeg acted as the go-between.
3 'To be delivered to . . .' etc.
4 See *supra*, p. 693, and *infra*, p. 743.
5 Hummel, the Berlin music publisher.
6 Symphonies Nos. 88 and 89: see *supra*, p. 709.

a few years. Please excuse this hasty note, but this is the 10th letter I have to mail. Meanwhile I am, most respectfully,

> Your most sincere friend and servant,
> Jos: Haydn.

Please send my affectionate[1] greetings to the 2 great men, Mozart and Albrechtsberger.

[Address:]   Monsieur
Monsieur Joseph Eybler
    Maitre de la Musique
in der Kohlmesser
gasse N^r: 668 im   a
2^{tn} Stock   Vienne.

> [CCLN, 81f.]

[To Artaria & Co., Vienna. *German*]

> Estoras, 29th March 1789.

Mon très cher ami!

I send you herewith the 3rd Sonata,[2] which I have rewritten with variations, to suit your taste. Please hurry the engraving of all 3 as best you can, because many people are anxiously awaiting the publication. In my leisure hours I have completed a new *Capriccio*[3] for the pianoforte which, from its taste, singularity and careful execution cannot but fail to be received with approbation from professional and non-professional alike. It's only one piece, rather long, but not all too difficult; since I always give you the preference in my works, I now offer it to you for 24 ducats: the price is rather high, but I assure you a profit on it; since in any case I am your debtor, you can deduct the sum from the debt. In awaiting your opinion, I remain, most respectfully,

> Your most obedient servant,
> Joseph Haydn.

[Address:]   Monsieur
Monsieur d'Artaria et
    Compag
   With a roll of music
          Vienne.

[Artaria's clerk notes: 'Heydn Giuseppe / Esterhaze 29.Marzo/1789/ans'd 2 Apl.'.]

> [CCLN, 82f.]

A princely decree dated 'Eszterhaz den 4ten April 1789' resolved 'that Herr Kapellmeister Haydn is to receive, in addition to his previous *Convention* [contract] 1 pig' – one more little gesture to keep Haydn (or in this case Frau Haydn) content.[4]

---

1 'Küssen Sie stat meiner'.
2 Pianoforte Trio see *supra*, p. 642, No. 26 (XV:13).
3 The *Fantasia* in C, which Artaria published as Op. 58 (pl. No. 250) in September; an advance copy was sent to Haydn two months earlier (see letter of 5th July 1789).
4 EH, Budapest, *Eisenstädter Commissions Prothocol* 2489, item 1679. Valkó II, 605.

Haydn's correspondence continues:

[To Christoph Gottlob Breitkopf, Leipzig. *German*]

Estoras, 5th April 1789.

Well born,
Most highly respected Sir!

Through Herr Traeg[1] I am sending you the new pianoforte Sonata, fully hoping that it will meet with the musical world's approbation. I have received the 10 ♯ [ducats] in good order, for which I thank you. As for the other demands in your letter, I cannot accommodate you because I am simply overloaded with work. I would only ask for a clean engraving, and that you send me a few copies. Meanwhile I remain, most respectfully,

Your most obedient servant,
Joseph Haydn.

I would ask you at your convenience to send me a few English engravings, but beautiful ones, for I am a great admirer of them; I shall repay you gratefully by something of my work.

[CCLN 83f.]

[To Jean-Georges Sieber, Paris. *German*]

Estoras, 5th April 1789.

Monsieur!

I am very surprised not to have received a letter from you, because (as Herr Tost[2] wrote to me a long time ago) you are supposed to have purchased 4 Symphonies and 6 pianoforte Sonatas for one hundred Louis d'or: as far as I am concerned, I regret being bound to Herr Tost for the 4 Symphonies, because he still owes me 300 f [Gulden] for the 4 pieces. If you will take over this debt of 300 f, I guarantee to compose these four Symphonies for you; but Herr Tost has no rights at all to the six pianoforte Sonatas, and has thus swindled you; you can claim your damages in Vienna. Now I would ask you to tell me candidly just how, and in what fashion, Herr Tost behaved in Paris. Did he have an *Amour* there? And did he also sell you the 6 quartets, and for what sum? Item, will the Quartet and the 2 Symphonies be engraved and soon appear? Please let me know all this as soon as possible. Meanwhile I remain, most respectfully,

Your wholly obedient servant,
Josephus Haydn.

[Address:]   Monsieur Sieber
Marchand de la Musique,
Paris.

[CCLN, 84f.]

---

1 See the commentary on Haydn's letter to Traeg of 8 March, 1789. The passage in the present letter concerning 'the other demands' may be explained as follows: we have seen that Breitkopf wanted Haydn to write six new Sonatas. Haydn seems to have told Traeg that he would do so, and that the price would be 60 ducats; if pianoforte Trios, his price would be 80 ducats, but this time he would give them to Breitkopf for only 70. Breitkopf thereupon announced the six pianoforte Sonatas in February 1789 on a subscription basis, and wrote to Haydn in March reminding him of the works. As it happened, the response to the subscription was not very promising, and Breitkopf subsequently (June 1789) asked Haydn to send two rather than six Sonatas, which would be included in further numbers of the 'Pot-Pourri'. But nothing came of this new plan, either. (Hase, pp. 4ff.)

2 With this letter, the *affaire* Tost, to which Haydn had previously referred in a letter to Artaria (see letter of 22 September 1788), becomes even more mysterious. Tost had with him Symphonies Nos. 88, 89 and six Quartets (known as Opp. 54 and 55). Haydn never denied Tost's rights to these works, and obviously expected Tost to sell them, as the end of the present letter shows. But how the two Symphonies suddenly became four is most unclear. Perhaps Haydn intended to write two more for Tost. (See also the passing reference to the four works in the letter of 22 March, *supra*.) In 1788 and 1789, Haydn did in fact compose three new Symphonies (Nos. 90–92), but he dedicated them to the Comte d'Ogny in Paris, and they were patently intended for the *Concert de la Loge Olympique*, for which he had written the 'Paris' Symphonies. The *affaire* Tost is further complicated by the fact that Tost seems to have sold Sieber a Gyrowetz Symphony under Haydn's name (Symphony in G: see Larsen, *HUB*, p. 115 and Landon, *SYM*, p. 3). The six Sonatas are possibly Nos. 34, 53 and 35 (XVI:33, 34 and 43) together with 54–56 (XVI:40–42); three, however, may have been Nos. 32, 29 and 31 (XVI:44–46), earlier works which Artaria issued as Op. 54 about this time.

[To Artaria & Co., Vienna. *German*]

Estoras, 6th April 1789.

Well born,
Most highly respected Sir!

I enclose the two security receipts which you asked for, and also the *Capriccio*,[1] with the solemn promise that no other soul shall receive it from my hands. I am sorry that the work involved does not allow me to reduce the price of 24 ducats by a single Kreutzer. I would ask you only that the Sonatas[2] and the *Capriccio* be neatly and legibly engraved.

Please expedite at once the enclosed letter to Herr Sieber,[3] the Parisian publisher: it concerns his best interests.

Meanwhile I remain, most respectfully,

Your most obedient servant,
Joseph Haydn.

Please answer in the German language.

[Address:]   Monsieur
                Monsieur d'Artaria et
                Compag   à
                            Vienne.

Please expedite.

[Artaria's clerk notes: 'Heydn Giuseppe / Esterhaze 6 April/1789/ (ans'd) 18th June'.]   [CCLN, 85]

We now arrive at a new turning-point in Haydn's life: his friendship with Maria Anna von Genzinger. Since his correspondence with her is of great importance in our knowledge of Haydn's life and thoughts, a few words about the Genzinger family may be welcome. We quote the introduction to CCLN (1959):

> Her husband, Peter Leopold von Genzinger, was a popular 'Ladies' Doctor', whom the Empress Maria Theresa had raised to the nobility in 1780; in 1792, he became Rector of the Vienna *Hochschule*. For many years before that, he had been Physician in Ordinary to Prince Nicolaus Esterházy, in which capacity Haydn must have become friendly with him. Genzinger's wife, Maria Anna Sabina (1750–93) was the daughter of Joseph von Kayser, Prince Batthyáni's Court Councillor, and Maria Anna, *née* von Hackher zu Hart, an old Austrian aristocratic family. She seems to have married Genzinger about 1772 and subsequently bore him five children, three boys and two girls. Her musical education must have been exceptional, for she was able to read full orchestral scores and transcribe them for the pianoforte. The Genzingers gave soirées to which Vienna's musical élite, including Mozart, was invited.
>
> The correspondence began with a letter to Haydn (her German, incidentally, is several grades more appalling, orthographically, than Haydn's). In the course of the next half dozen letters, it becomes apparent that Haydn was very much attracted to the charming and cultivated 'gnädige Frau'. Theodor von Karajan (who edited the correspondence for the first time in 1861) found someone still living – an acquaintance of Leopold von Sonnleithner – who reported as follows: 'Haydn seems to have cherished not only respect for the artistic abilities of this

1 The *Fantasia* in C: see *supra*, p. 718.
2 The piano Trios: see *supra*, p. 709.
3 The previous letter (5 April).

lady, but also more tender feelings. Their contemporaries knew nothing of such
an emotion being returned, however, and Frau von Genzinger's well-disposed
attitude towards Haydn seems to have been based purely on friendly attention and
on her respect for his artistic position.'

Haydn was now frequently in an entirely different *milieu* than that in which he had
been forced to live when he first came to Eisenstadt in 1761 – the other musicians and
the 'house officers', higher servants, in a word. His music had now brought him in
touch with the bourgeoisie and even on equal social terms with the lower aristocracy
such as the Genzingers. What were these Austrian women like? Fortunately we have
an interesting contemporary report[1] by N. William Wraxall written when he was on
the Continent in the 1770s. About Austrian women he writes:

> . . . The Austrian ladies are by no means deficient in external accomplish-
> ments, mental and personal: they are in general elegant, graceful, and pleasing;
> but they rarely possess a cultivated mind. The principal reading of a woman of
> quality, is such as tends to pervert and contract, rather than to enlarge and improve
> her understanding. Holy legends, lives of female saints and devotees, masses, and
> homilies, constitute her chief information. She knows little of Madame de
> Sevigné, and less of Racine, Molière, or Fontenelle. If she has perused the works of
> Cervantes, of Crebillon, and of Le Sage, she has done much. With Saint Theresa
> and Saint Catharine of Sienna, she is familiar.
> This want of improvement is universal, and the necessary result of their
> confined education. Young women of condition are all sent to a convent, either at
> Prague, at Presburg, or at Vienna. There they are taught to sing hymns to the
> Virgin, and to tell their beads devoutly. Of history, poetry, and polite letters, they
> imbibe no tincture; and the spirit, if not the precepts of their religion, set bounds
> to any liberal enquiries, by the detestation that they inspire for heretics, and
> heretical productions. Women of fashion rarely stir out in a morning, except to
> hear mass, or on particular occasions. They usually take a cup of coffee or
> chocolate when they rise; and they either remain afterwards invisible in their own
> apartments, in a state of the greatest undress, or devote the hours before dinner to
> the occupation of the toilet. Few of them admit visits from men at that time of the
> day, which is sacred to indolence, affected to devotion, or reserved for private
> concerns of a domestic nature. . . . The reserve of the Austrian women, so
> unpleasant on first acquaintance, imperceptibly wears off, and gives place to their
> natural character. Their conversation, if not improving, is rarely deficient in spirit,
> vivacity, and animation. But a learned woman, so common with us, is a thing
> totally unknown at Vienna. . . . The women of condition are noble in their
> deportment, and have an air of dignity. I think that in general their persons are on
> a larger scale than with us, and that there are more fine forms, than pretty figures:
> their hair and teeth are commonly good, particularly the latter, to which the
> dryness of the air and climate contribute. If there be room for criticism, it is about
> the neck. Nature seems to have been lavish of that attribute of beauty, only in Italy
> and in Greece; while in other European countries she dispenses it with a more
> sparing hand: there are in Vienna itself many charming exceptions to the remark.
> Rouge is universally worn by married and unmarried women of fashion; but they
> use it in general with moderation, as well as taste: girls of fifteen wear it as much as
> persons of thirty. . . .

---

1 *Memoirs of the Courts of Berlin, Dresden, Warsaw, and Vienna, in the years 1777, 1778, and 1779,* 2 vols. London 1800 (2nd ed.), vol. II, pp.
240ff.

The superstition of an Austrian woman, however characteristic, habitual, and excessive, is by no means inconsistent or incompatible with gallantry: she sins, prays, confesses, and begins anew; but she never omits her masses, not even for her lover. Few of them touch meat either on the Friday or Saturday of every week, or during the whole period of Lent, and they confess frequently; if not from principle, yet from habit or from fear. The marriage ring is seldom worn or kept, as its loss would be ominous in their estimation, and presage misfortune. In order to avoid so great a calamity, they are generally sent to a celebrated chapel of the Virgin, at Maria Zell in Styria; a shrine where I am assured there are more gold rings, than the Carthaginian General found on the field of Cannae. Very little of the exterior of devotion is nevertheless visible among women of condition: it interrupts no pleasures of society or conversation; it neither mixes with their discourse, nor tinges their manners: they reserve it for the altar, or the confessor. I ought likewise to add, that there are not a few, who entertain much more liberal and expanded ideas of the Deity and of Religion, than the Catholic Faith usually inspires, particularly at Vienna.

Within two years Haydn would be in England, where he soon met many English ladies, and had an opportunity – which as a connoisseur of female beauty he will certainly not have missed – to compare the female sex of the two nations. Perhaps the difference is revealed at its most graphic in the following 'card' in the personal column of *The Times* on Monday, 14 July 1794:

The lady who met a Gentleman on Horseback on Tuesday Evening, about Nine o'Clock, and who walked his horse by the side of her, till he got into Oxford-street, where he dismounted, and crossed over to New Bond-street, and wanted to walk home with her, till she put him in mind not to leave his horse with strangers, but to go home and call upon her on Wednesday at ten. Presents her compliments to him, hopes he did not suffer by the fatigue of his walk to her house, and for the generosity of his conduct, and being a man of his word, she begs when he next makes an appointment he will be not be so much before his time, but if he has any regard for his word or honour as a man, he will explain himself, by a Letter directed to L. J. No. 8, New Bond-street, and if he is not afraid of being known, will mention where she may direct to him.

Even allowing for the deplorable state of Austrian newspapers at this period, and although it is clear that Austrian women had many enticing sides to their nature, a letter such as the one just quoted simply could not have been written in Vienna. There is a bold and (dare we use the word any more?) liberated spirit in those lines which reveal strikingly those qualities in British women that Haydn will have found fascinating and irresistible.

[To Haydn from Maria Anna von Genzinger. *German*][1]

† † †

Most respected Herr v. Hayden,

With your kind permission, I take the liberty of sending you a pianoforte arrangement of the beautiful Andante from your so admirable composition. I made this arrangement from the score quite by myself, without the least help from my teacher; please be good enough to correct any mistakes you may find in it. I hope that you are enjoying perfect health, and I wish for nothing more than to see

1 The letter begins with the three-fold sign of the Cross.

you soon again in Vienna, so that I may demonstrate still further the esteem in which I hold you. I remain, in true friendship,

Your obedient servant,
Maria Anna *Noble v.* Gennzinger

My husband and children also *née Noble v.* Kayser.
ask me to send you their
kindest regards.
Vienna, 10th June 1789.   [CCLN, 85f.]

[To Maria Anna von Genzinger, Vienna. *German*]
Nobly born and gracious Lady!

In all my previous correspondence, nothing delighted me more than the surprise of seeing such a lovely handwriting, and reading so many kind expressions; but even more I admired the enclosure – the excellent arrangement of the Adagio, which is correct enough to be engraved by any publisher. I would like to know only whether Your Grace arranged the Adagio from the score, or whether you took the amazing trouble of first putting it into score from the parts and only then arranging it for the pianoforte; if the latter, such an attention would be too flattering to me, for I really don't deserve it.

Best and kindest Frau v. Gennsinger! [*sic*] I only await a hint from you as to how and in what fashion I can possibly be of service to Your Grace. Meanwhile I return the Adagio, and very much hope to receive from Your Grace some demands on my modest talents; I am, with sincere esteem and respect,

Your Grace's
most obedient servant,
Josephus Haydn [m.p] ria.

Estoras, 14th June 1789.

N.S. Please present my respectful compliments
to your husband.   [CCLN, 86]

On 1 July Artaria announced publication of the Three Piano Trios Nos. 24–26 (XV:11–13). Two contemporary reviews may be quoted here:

For a long time no sonatas have appeared which could rival the superior qualities of these three. *In toto* they distinguish themselves greatly by the well-known originality of their composer. The working-out is excellent, and largely in a serious manner. Herr Haydn, especially in the middle movement in C major on p. 26 [Trio 26/II], shows how attractive a common theme can be made by masterly development. It is more the frequent modulations to remote keys – where many accidentals, often double sharps and flats occur – than any innately difficult passages or those requiring great technical ability, which these sonatas require from an untrained hand. But if one cannot immediately play them at sight, one will be very richly rewarded for the effort. For if played nicely in all the parts and performed with the proper expression, they provide the greatest enjoyment which this kind of music can produce.

[*Allgemeine deutsche Bibliothek*, vol. CXVII, Stück 1, 1790]

The original style of the composer, his beautiful modulations and his wealth of ideas are too well known to require anything further on our part for the recommendation of these works here announced. Neither the principal [piano] part, nor the accompanying parts, are encumbered with difficulties such as would require especially trained players for these sonatas. The violin part only once, in the Andante of the last (also the second) Sonata, exceed *c'''* and even these seemingly difficult passages lie very well in the hand for untrained players.

[*Musikalische Real-Zeitung* (1789, No. 36, p. 280)]

Another letter to Artaria follows:

[To Artaria & Co., Vienna. *German*]

Estoras, 5th July 1789.

Well born,
Most highly respected Sir!

Thank you very much for the 3 Sonatas and the *Fantasia*[1] which you sent to me; I only regret that, here and there, some mistakes have crept in, which can no longer be corrected, because the works are already circulated and on sale. It is always painful for me that not a single work of mine that you have published is free from errors. Formerly you always sent me the first copy, before publication, and you acted wisely; I could not use the single copies of the Sonatas you sent me as samples, because I didn't want to soil them and was also afraid of having to do without them for such a long time, or perhaps of losing them altogether, which is always irritating to an author. As to my debt of 39 fl., I ask you to be patient a little longer; I have hopes of collecting a debt of seven years' standing from the Archduke of Milan, and would then gratefully repay you in cash. Meanwhile please be good enough to send me 3 copies of the Sonatas, 3 of the *Fantasia*, likewise a copy of *The Seven Words* in piano score, and a copy of the new Quartets.[2]

Now I would like to know the truth about something: that is, from whom you procured the 2 new Symphonies[3] which you recently announced – whether you purchased them from Herr Tost or whether you got them already engraved from Herr Sieber in Paris. If you purchased them from Herr Tost, I beg you to furnish me at once with an *a parte* written assurance of the fact, because I am told that Herr Tost pretends I sold these 2 Symphonies to you and thereby caused him a great loss.

Hoping for a speedy reply I am, Sir, most respectfully,

Your most obedient servant,
Josephus Haydn.

[No address]   [CCLN, 86f.]

There follows a bill from the printer Joseph Siess in Oedenburg:

List of printing work ordered by Herr Nunziato Porta, Director of the Theatre in the Princely Castle Eszterház and executed & delivered by me, *viz.* Anno 1789 in the month of February, an opera libretto was printed and delivered with 4¼ Bogen, entitl:

Il Tamburo Notturno,
of which 250 were printed, 1 Bogen à 5 Fl. makes .... 21 Fl. 15 xr.
In the month of June, an opera libretto entitl:
Le Gelosie,
with 4½ Bogen, of which 250 were printed, 1 Bogen
à 5 Fl. makes .... 22 Fl. 30 xr.

1 See *supra*, p. 718.
2 Op. 50 or Op. 54/55.
3 Nos. 88 and 89.

In the month of June, an opera libretto entitl:
Il Pittore Parigino,
with 4 Bogen, 250 were printed, 1 Bogen à 5 Fl.,
makes .... 20 Fl.
_____
Suma: 63 Fl. 45 xr.

Oedenburg, 6th July 1789.   Joseph Siess, Printer
[A.M. 18.1247. Valkó II, 606.]

By an extraordinary quirk of fate, the score of Mozart's *Le nozze di Figaro*, with the vocal parts, arrived at Eisenstadt (*en route* to Haydn) on 14 July 1789:

Nota.
The following was purchased by me on the written orders of Kapellmeister Haydn for the princely theatre:
Score of Gelosie Fortunate .... 30 Fl.
Score Pittor Parigino .... 30 Fl.
Score le Nozze di Figaro .... 30 Fl.
Vocal parts for that opera.................................... 30 Fl.
_____
Suma ...   120 Fl.
Porta mp.

[Haydn's hand:]
Id est 120 Fl.
Josephus Haydn mpria
Eisenstadt, 14 July 1789.   [A.M. 18.1245. Valkó II, 605f.]

When Haydn realized the full implications of the French Revolution, he was already in England. He was not for the Revolution, and if he had an opinion, it was probably that of the famous *graffito* which we recently saw in the old Fort Charlotte above Nassau: 'Only Evil lies under 1789'.

Haydn's correspondence continues with another letter to Sieber in Paris:

[To Jean-Georges Sieber, Paris. *German*]

Estoras, 27th July 1789.

Monsieur!
[Contents of the first part of the letter: Haydn discusses publication of the four Symphonies (see letter of 5th April 1789) and two Sonatas (probably pianoforte Trios), and describes his correspondence with Artaria on the subject. He agrees][1] to compose [the Symphonies], and this present letter should serve to protect your interests in any court. On the other hand, I beg you to convince Herr Tost as well, and in order to deprive him of all his other claims to these 4 Symphonies, please send me your authentic signature of contract so that my interests are protected. Thus you are protected for your part, and I am for mine, while Herr Tost will be reduced to silence for ever. I hope to receive the favour of an early reply. Meanwhile I am, most respectfully,

Your most obedient servant,
Josephus Haydn.
[CCLN, 87f.]

The autograph of the next letter was recently discovered (see *HJB* VII, 308f., where we first published it complete in German):

1 Summary from Maggs Brothers' Catalogue No. 320 (1914), item 328.

[To Jean-Georges Sieber, Paris. *German*]

Estoras, 28th August 1789.

Nobly born,
Most Respectful Sir!
    Since I am now quite certain that I can do these four Symphonies for you, most noble Sir, I shall make every possible effort to finish them one after another and to send them. You need have no doubts as to the care I shall take, for I shall not forget my reputation. N.B.: one of these four Symphonies shall be called a National Symphony.
    Meanwhile I am with every respect

Monsieur
Your
most obedient s^t
Josephus Haydn mpria

[Other side:]   Monsieur
[Post office: 'Vienne']
[Parisian postman: 'Rue S^t honoré']
Monsieur Sieber
Marchand de la Musique
tres Rennomé
a
Paris

[CCLN, 88; incomplete; from autograph, Pierpont Morgan Library, New York.]

The next letter deals with the welcome cash substitute for the new uniform:

[To Prince Nicolaus Esterházy. *German*]

[Eszterháza, beginning of October 1789]
Most Serene Highness and Noble Prince of the Holy Roman Empire, Gracious and dread Lord!
    The undersigned, together with all the members of the Princely band, make the following humble request to your illustrious and Serene Highness: that Your Highness graciously allow them to receive the value of their summer uniforms in cash, as was the case in previous years, instead of receiving the actual uniforms; for they are all in possession of several brand new summer uniforms which they have saved. Commending ourselves in profound submissiveness,

Your Illustrious and Serene Highness'
humble and obedient servant,
Joseph Hayden, *Kapellmeister*,
and all the other princely chamber musicians.[1]

[The file contains the following note as an answer:]
On the 10th inst., His Highness granted the suppliants' request that they be paid cash instead of the new summer uniforms which would have had to have been made, the payment to take place at the time the uniforms would have been delivered, *viz.*: the *Herr Capellmeister* one hundred and fifty Gulden, and the other musicians seventy-five Gulden each.
    Datum ex Commissione Celsissimi Principatus Eszterháziani Kissmartonii 12 Octobris 1789.

Paulus Eötvös *Praeses*
Franciscus Gáll mp. *Act.*
[CCLN, 88f.]

1 The whole letter is a copy written by a Princely clerk.

The following correspondence takes us to the beginning of December. In November, as we have seen, the London music publisher John Bland came to stay with Haydn in Eszterháza and ordered *inter alia* the three Flute Trios (with piano) which have always proved to be among Haydn's most popular chamber music.

[To Ferdinand Müller von Müllegg, Vienna. *German*]

Estoras [*c.* 17th October 1789[1]].

Nobly born,

Most highly respected Herr von Müller!

At last I can deliver to you, Sir, the 3 Symphonies for His Serene Highness, the most gracious Prince Oettingen von Wallerstein. I beg you sincerely to forgive the delayed delivery, but you, Sir, must see for yourself how difficult it is (when one serves a master who even at an advanced age has an insatiable appetite for music) to keep one's word. I intended day after day to satisfy the most kind Prince von Wallerstein, but my many daily duties prevented me against my will from doing so. A week from today, at the latest, I shall take the liberty of sending 12 brand new Dance Minuets with 12 Trios for this wonderful celebration.[2]

Now I would humbly ask you to tell the Princely *Kapellmeister* there that these 3 Symphonies, because of their many particular effects, should be rehearsed at least once, carefully and with special concentration, before they are performed.

Meanwhile I am, Sir, most respectfully,

Your most obedient servant,
Josephus Haydn.

[CCLN, 89f.]

[To Haydn from Maria Anna von Genzinger. *German*]

Vienna, 29th October 1789.

† † †

Most respected Herr v. Hayden,

I hope that you will have safely received my letter of 15th September together with the 1st movement of the Symphony (the Andante of which I sent you some months ago), and now here is the last movement, too, which I have arranged for the pianoforte as best I could; I only hope that it pleases you, and I entreat you to correct at your leisure any mistakes that you may find – a service which I shall always accept from you, dear Herr v. Hayden, with the utmost gratitude. Please be good enough to let me know whether you received my letter of 15th September together with the movement, and if it suits your taste, which would delight me; for I am very uneasy and concerned whether you have received them safely, or if perhaps it has not met with your approval. I hope you enjoy the best of health, which I would be very happy to hear, and commending myself to your further friendship and remembrance, I remain your devoted friend and servant,

Maria Anna *Noble v.* Gennzinger
née Noble v. Kayser

My husband also sends you his compliments. [CCLN, 90]

1 On 21 October von Müller writes to the Prince that he 'will send to His Highness the 3 requested Symphonies, which the composer Herr Josef Haydn finally, and after repeated requests, delivered; I shall place it on the next mail-coach.' Haydn's undated letter must have been written shortly before. The Symphonies are Nos. 90–92, and the copies are still extant in the Oettingen-Wallerstein Archives at Harburg Castle. Haydn actually wrote the works for the Comte d'Ogny in Paris: see *supra*, p. 594.
2 Prince Krafft Ernst's (second) marriage celebrations.

[To Maria Anna von Genzinger, Vienna. *German*]
Nobly born and gracious Lady!

I beg your forgiveness a million times for the long delay in returning your laborious and admirable work: when my apartments were cleaned, which occurred just after receiving the first movement, my copyist mislaid it among the mass of other music, and just recently I was fortunate enough to find it in an old opera score. Dearest and best Frau von Gennziger! [*sic*] Don't be angry at a man who values you above everything else; I should be inconsolable if this delay was responsible for my losing even a fraction of your favour (of which I am so proud).

These two movements are fully as admirably arranged as the first. I do admire the trouble and patience which Your Grace spends on my modest talents, and on the other hand I assure you that, in my frequent depressed moods, nothing cheers me so much as the flattering conviction that your memories of me are pleasant; for which favour I kiss your hands a thousand times and remain, with sincere esteem,

Your Grace's
most obedient servant,

Estoras, 7th November 1789.   Joseph Haydn [m.p.] ria.

P.S. My respectful compliments to your husband and the whole family. I shall soon claim permission to wait on you.   [CCLN, 90f.]

[To Haydn from Maria Anna Genzinger. *German*]

Vienna, 12th November 1789.

† † †

Most respected Herr v. Hayden,

I am quite incapable of expressing adequately the pleasure I felt on reading your kind letter of the 9th [*sic*]. How well am I rewarded for my pains when I see your satisfaction! I would wish nothing more ardently than to have more time (which my many household affairs do not allow), for then I would certainly devote many hours to music, my most agreeable and favourite of occupations. You must not take it amiss, dear Herr v. Haydn, that I bother you once again with a letter (but I could not miss the chance of informing you of the safe arrival of your letter): I look forward with the greatest pleasure to the happy day when I shall see you in Vienna. I commend myself to your further friendship and remembrance, and remain as always

Your most devoted friend and servant,
[no signature].

My husband and children also send you their compliments. The bearer of this letter is a jeweller here, his name is Siebert and he's a trustworthy man.

[CCLN, 91]

[To Artaria & Co., Vienna. *German*]

Estoras, 15th November 1789.

Well born,
Most highly respected Sir!

Since you have often shown me various kindnesses, and since I really am your debtor, you may be assured that at all times you shall have the preference for my works. I have various new pieces which I shall tell you about when – and this will be soon – I arrive in Vienna. Last week Mr. Bland, an Englishman, was here to see me and wanted to purchase various pieces from me; but on your account he did not receive a single note.[1] Hoping to see you soon, I am, Sir, most respectfully,

Your wholly obedient servant,
Josephus Haydn.

[Address:] Monsieur
Monsieur Artaria et Compag.
à
Vienne.   [CCLN, 91f.]

[To Maria Anna von Genzinger, Vienna. *German*]
Estoras, 18th November 1789.
Nobly born and gracious Lady!

The letter which I received through the jeweller Sibert gave me still another proof of your excellent heart, for Your Grace, instead of rebuking me for my recent remissness, gave me renewed proof of your friendship, and this, combined with such great indulgence, kindness and special attention, quite astonished me; in return I kiss Your Grace's hands a thousand times. If my modest talents enable me, even in small measure, to return so many compliments, I venture to offer you a little musical vegetable pot; indeed, I do not find too much that is fragrant in this *pot-pourri*, but perhaps the publisher may rectify this fault in future editions.[2] If the arrangement of the Symphony in it is yours, Oh! then I shall be doubly pleased with the publisher; if not, I dare to ask Your Grace to have one of the Symphonies you arranged copied at your leisure and sent to me, when I shall then deliver it forthwith to the publisher at Leipzig to be engraved.

I am happy to have found an opportunity which, I trust, will lead to few more delightful lines from you. Meanwhile I am, in lifelong respect,

Your Grace's
sincere friend and obedient
servant,
Josephus Haydn [m.p] ria.

My sincere compliments to your husband
and the whole family.   [CCLN, 92]

[To Ferdinand Müller von Müllegg, Vienna. *German*]
Nobly born,
Most highly respected Herr von Müller!

According to our arrangement, I should have sent scores of the Symphonies[3] and not copies of the parts. But because I suffered almost all Summer from the

---

1 This is, of course, not true. John Bland, the well-known London music publisher, supposedly took with him the autographs of the 'Razor' Quartet (from Op. 55) and the Cantata *Arianna a Naxos*. See *supra*, p. 640, and note to the letter of 11 January 1790.
2 Breitkopf's 'Musikalischer Pot-Pourri', the first volume of which included Haydn's piano Sonata No. 58 and a pianoforte arrangement of Symphony No. 79 in F. See also *supra*, p. 719.
3 Nos. 90–92 (see the previous correspondence with von Müller). The Prince seems to have objected to Haydn's having sent parts rather than the scores. Haydn's answer at first satisfied the Prince, for he asks von Müller '. . . to write to Haiden [*sic*] and ask him if he can take it upon himself to write 3 new Symphonies and bring them here in score . . .'. Haydn apparently had no time for this new commission, although the Prince repeatedly asked von Müller about it. Subsequently the Prince seems to have heard that he was by no means the sole owner of Nos. 90–92 (the autographs of which, beautifully written, Haydn dedicated to the Comte d'Ogny in Paris). On 9th December 1789, von Müller tries to convince the Prince of Haydn's innocence; in fact von Keeß, whom the Prince suspected as having the Symphonies, did own them (the copies are now in the Thurn und Taxis Library at Regensburg). Von Müller writes: 'He [Haydn] wrote 3 new Parthyen [Symphonies] some time ago and published them, too, and these will be the ones that Herr von Kees owns, for I am convinced that he [Haydn] will not give the works he wrote specially for you to anyone else, as is stipulated.' The '3 new Parthyen' von Müller refers to are probably Symphonies from the Paris set, though he may mean Nos. 76–78 or 79–81. Concerning von Keeß, a famous Viennese patron of music, see *supra*, p. 663.

most terrible pains in my eyes, I was unfortunately quite incapable of writing a clean score, and thus was forced to have these 3 illegible Symphonies (of which the enclosed, the best of the three, can serve as a sample) copied in my room by one of my composition pupils, and then to have the parts made by several copyists (so that the works would not be stolen). Any connoisseur can judge from the enclosed illegible score what the others are like; this time it is not my fault, for since my youth I have been accustomed to write very neat scores. If, however, there are any wrong notes in the Symphonies I sent, I would ask the *Concertmeister* there to inform me of them at once in a letter, so that I can send him the exact corrections. Therefore I would ask His Serene Highness the Prince humbly to excuse me: but if His Highness nevertheless insists on the scores, I shall of course dutifully deliver them (but it will be very hard for me, because I am still not free of the pains in my eyes). The most gracious Prince's approbation of these 3 Symphonies is a source of great encouragement to me, and will remain so to the last days of my life. I would like to have a portrait of His Highness, but only a silhouette, for I am a great collector of leading personalities.

My dear Herr Müller (our long-standing acquaintance makes me bold enough to suggest this form of address), you will be kind enough to excuse me to the gracious Prince, on account of the true reasons given above.

I remain, noble Sir, with every esteem,

Your most obedient servant,
Esterhaz, 29th November 1789.   Joseph Haydn.

I did not receive your letter till yesterday,
because it was addressed to Eisenstadt instead
of to Esterhaz.   [CCLN, 93f.]

It was in December 1789 that Haydn wrote a series of works for the new musical clock which Prince Nicolaus's librarian, Pater Niemecz, ingeniously put together (*vide supra*, pp. 651 ff.).

We now have Schellinger's yearly copying bill:

Conto
What was copied for the princely theatre from 1 January 1789 through this whole year, the vocal parts à 7 xr., the instrumental à 5 xr. as per agreement

Operas	Bögen	
	Vocal parts	Instrumental
I due supposti conti	196	210
Le Gelosie fortunate	189	196
Il Pittore Parigino	191	189
Finti Eredi repaired	—	9
La Circe	187	198
Le Vicende d'Amore	197	196
l'arbore di Diana	—	249
	960	1,247

Id est 215 Fl. 55 xr.   Joan Schilling [*sic*] fürstl Theat. copist di 30 Decbris 1789

The above-listed sum for the copying has been carefully examined by me the undersigned and found to be correct.

Josephus Haydn
Capell Meister

Esterhaz, 30 Dec. 1789

[A.M. 19.1252. Valkó II, 607f.]

Conto

Delle Partiture, e parti da me Sottoscritto comprate e prodotte nel corrente Anno 1789 come d'alla dimostrazione del Sign. M[aest]ro Haydn a dimostrato

	[Fl.]	[xr.]
La Partitura dell'Arbore di Diana	30	
Le parti de Cantanti della Sudetta Opera	36	44
La Partitura dell'Opera Le Vicende d'Amore	30	
Diversi Altri pezzi di Musica, e parti da inserirsi in diversi Spartiti per l'importo di	36	16

Total[e]: 133 Fl.

7 Dec. 1789   Porta

[Haydn's hand:] Io Giuseppe Haydn mpria confermo l'istessa Soma per 133 Fl.

[A.M. 19.1251. Valkó II, 608]

Haydn's last document is signed Esterhaz, 30 December 1789. On that day he left for Vienna, for on the last day of the old year, Mozart invited him and Puchberg to a rehearsal of the new Opera, *Così fan tutte*. In Mozart's letter to Puchberg written a few days before, we read:

> ... Tomorrow on account of the appointment there can be nothing at our house, – I have too much work, – if you see Zisler anyway, please tell him – Thursday [31 Dec.], however, I invite you (but just you alone) to come at 10 o'clock in the morning to me, for a small opera rehearsal; – only you and Haydn are invited. – Then *a viva voce* I'll tell you about all the cabals of Salieri, which however all fell into the water – adieu
>
> Always Your
> thankful friend and [Masonic] brother
> W. A. Mozart

[Puchberg: 'sent 300 fl.']

[Mozart, *Briefe und Aufzeichnungen*, IV, 100]

Chronicle 1790
ITALIAN OPERAS 1790

This year 61 performances are registered (Harich in *HJB* I, 91). The season began in the middle of February and concluded immediately before the Prince's death on 28 September.

Giovanni Paisiello: Il barbiere di Siviglia. [Following is covered over by a new printed sheet: Dramma giocoso in quattro atti da rappresentarsi nel teatro di corte l'anno 1783. In Vienna presso Giuseppe Nob. de Kurzbek.] [new sheet reads'] Da rappresentarsi nel teatro di S. A. il Signore Principe Regnante Niccolò Esterhazy. Vienna, presso la Società Tipografica.
Libretto: the Viennese libretto (for 13 August 1783) exists in several copies,[1] the adapted one for Eszterháza in none. Cast (from the extant vocal parts of EH material): Rosina, Benvenuti; Figaro, Amici. First performance: 9 May (after four stage rehearsals), repeated twice more in May and in June (four) and July (two). Eszterháza performance material: Ms. Mus. OE–5. Score from the office of Wenzel Sukowaty, Vienna, complete orchestral and fragmentary vocal parts copied by Schellinger with Anon. 10a, 11, 12 and ? (unidentified). V. I, 1st part, dated 1790. Apart from a few very minor cuts within numbers, and the omission in Atto I° of Figaro's Aria 'Scorsi già molti paesi', and in Atto II° of Rosina's Aria 'Già ride primavera', Haydn presented this great Paisiello masterpiece as its composer conceived it. Harich, *Musikgeschichte*, 62. Bartha-Somfai, 161, 355–5. Harich in *HJB* I, 88.

Domenico Cimarosa: (a) L'impresario in angustie. Farsa in uno atto[,] da rappresentarsi nel teatro di S. A. il Signore Principe Regnante Nicolò Eszterhazy de Galantha. L'anno 1790. In Oedenburgo, Presso Clara Siessin. 1790.
Libretto: EH, Eisenstadt. Eszterháza performance material: Ms. Mus. OE–50. Score of Italian origin, nearly complete orchestral and incomplete vocal parts copied by Schellinger with Anon. 10, 11, 12 and

1 EH, Eisenstadt, etc.

61. V. I, 1st part, lacks Atto II° (= *Il credulo*) V. II (2nd part) and Fl. I missing. The vocal parts give us most of the cast:

> Doralba: Sra Benvenuti
> Merlina: S. Polzelli
> D. Crisobolo: [Haydn's hand:] S. Majeroni
> Gelindo: Braghetti
> Fiordispina: Zecchielli
> Campanello: De Paoli.

Many individual numbers were removed from the score and their presence is known only by a forgotten duplicate part or by some other accident (or not at all). Haydn's revision – apart from cuts – included: Sc. 4. The original Aria, 'Il meglio mio carattere', cancelled and for Polzelli (Merlina) Haydn composed a witty new insertion (XXIVb:17), of which the EH score now contains nothing (removed for concert purposes). Thereafter Haydn wrote (autograph) 12 pp. of secco recit. for four scenes (numbers), of which most of the arias are now missing entirely. Sc. 5 is the missing bass aria (Perizionio); Sc. 6 the missing soprano aria (Fiordispina); Sc. 7 the missing Terzetto – all are now completely missing. In Sc. 7 (Finale) Haydn changed the ending and added 25 bars of his own (six pages of autograph), replacing 8 of Cimarosa.

(b) Il credulo [Atto II°]. In the EH material (same cat. no.), Haydn removed Sc. 5 from the score with Norina's Aria 'La donna ch'è amante' (a new composition by someone?), also Sc. 7, D. Astrolabio's Aria 'Ecco già'. Sc. 12, Catapazio's Aria 'Cara mia sposa amata', is an insertion (MS. of Italian origin).
Libretto: Il credulo. Farsa per musica da rappresentarsi nel teatro di S. A. il Signore Principe Regnante Niccolò Eszterhazy. In Oedenburgo, Presso Clara Siessin. 1790. – [no copy extant].
The two works were played together, as acts one and two. First (and only) performance: 6 June, preceded by two stage rehearsals and a dress rehearsal. Harich, *Musikgeschichte*, 62. Bartha-Somfai, 161, 356–62. Harich in *HJB* I, 88.

Giovanni Paisiello: L'amor contrastato. Commedia per musica da rappresentarsi nel teatro di S. A. il Signore Principe Regnante Nicolò Eszterhazy de Galantha. L'anno 1790. In Oedenburgo, Presso Clara Siessin. 1790.
Libretto: no copy extant. First performance: 13 July (preceded by four stage rehearsals), repeated three times in July. EH material lost. Bartha-Somfai 161f., 362. Harich in *HJB* I, 88.

For the next three premières, Harich (*HJB* I, 91f.) provides the following information. Until just before the death of the Prince on 28 September, opera performances continued at Eszterháza. Proof of this comes from a document by Director Nunziato Porta, 'Specification über die Grenadier-Mannschaft, welche bei denen Oppern [*sic*] in Proben als Staben und Gehülfen gewest sind.' In that document, Porta lists the 'supers' who took part (mostly the princely Grenadiers and their children) in one rehearsal and six performances in August, and two performances in September. The data listed in Porta's *Specification* agree completely with the lists drawn up by the hairdresser, seamstress and cobbler, and show that eight performances in this period certainly occurred. Porta lists one of these operas, performed three times in August and once in September, as requiring nineteen Grenadiers, a number never required in any of the other operas (premières or revivals). This work is called 'X'. 'Y' required eighteen Grenadiers for one August and two September performances. 'Z' required thirteen 'supers' for one performance in August. The suggestion that these were three new works is strengthened by the fact that there were no performances in the first half of August. Examination of the Budapest materials (H.C.R.L.) showed that there are only three works which could have been performed, i.e. with materials that were complete and have survived: Cimarosa's *Giannina e Bernardone*, Mozart's *Le nozze di Figaro* and Salieri's *Axur*. The material for Paisiello's *Il re Teodoro in Venezia* was not quite ready (horn II was incomplete when news of the Prince's death reached Eszterháza, and Schellinger never finished it), although the singers had started to learn it. We shall therefore list 'X', 'Y' and 'Z', though the exact order of these works three cannot be determined.

Domenico Cimarosa: Giannina e Bernardone.
Libretto: none survives (if one was printed); probably copies of the Vienna (Sept. 1784) libretto were ordered. First performance: August 1790. Eszterháza performance material: Ms. Mus. OE–49. Cast included: Bernardone – Majeroni; Aurora – Benvenuti; D. Orlando – Amici. Score from the office of Wenzel Sukowaty in Vienna; some of the vocal parts came from Italy and some were locally copied by Schellinger and Anon. 61; all the orchestral parts are local copies by those two and Anon. 11. V. I, 1st part, dated (Schellinger) 1790. Apart from cuts, Haydn's changes include some additions in tempi, transpositions downwards, and in Sc. 10 of Atto I° a new insertion aria for Giannina, 'La moglie quando è buona' (XXIVb:18); score and parts were removed from the score (but the one violin part remaining – Haydn usually took only one copy of each part, leaving the duplicates – permitted the identification). Sc. 13, Giannina's Aria 'Non son schiava' was cancelled and replaced by a new one (composer?): *incipit,*

Bartha-Somfai, 364. Sc. 16, Bernardone's Aria 'Son imbrogliato' was cancelled (together with the previous ending of the secco), and a new insertion added: composer? (*incipit*, Bartha-Somfai, 365). Atto II°, Sc. 7, Giannina's Aria 'Voi sapete, o caro amico' was cancelled and a new aria substituted (score missing, parts present; *incipit* Bartha-Somfai, 365). Bartha-Somfai 163, 363–5. Harich in *HJB* I, 91f.

Wolfgang Amadeus Mozart: Le nozze di Figaro. Libretto: none survives (if one was printed); probably copies of the Vienna libretto (1 May 1786, 1789) were ordered. Of the cast, we know that 'Il Conte' was sung by 'Sig' De Paoli'. First performance: August 1790. Haydn must have rewritten the clarinets (when soli) into other instruments, but he apparently found a second flute (part extant). The trumpets were omitted. Eszterháza performance material: Ms. Mus. OK.11. This includes Atti III° and IV° (rest missing) of the score from Wenzel Sukowaty's office in Vienna. Our reconstruction of the 1790 performance (several dates '1790' on parts) is greatly hampered by the fact that these parts were used for a German-language performance under Hummel in Eisenstadt in the early 19th cent. Of the 1790 parts, copied by Schellinger and Anon. 12, there are V. I (2 pts.), V. II (dup. missing), Va., Fl. I and II, Ob. I, Bsn., Hn. I. The vocal parts were purchased from Vienna (*supra*, p. 725). That Haydn managed to organize a second flute is also seen in the parts to *Axur* (*infra*). Harich has seen documents in which the Prince himself requested that Mozart's Opera be performed (*Musikgeschichte*, 62). Bartha-Somfai, 163, 366–8. Harich in *HJB* I, 91f.

After examining all the available evidence, we suggest that the possible performance of *Figaro* in 1790 was in the nature of a 'trial performance': this would explain the fact that there are no traces of Haydn's usual 'editing' on the extant parts. The fact that there is no general bill for Schellinger's copying activities in 1790 removes what would have been conclusive evidence that all the parts were actually made. Travaglia's proposal for decorations and costumes was submitted on 8 August 1789 (CCLN 98, from document in EH, Budapest).

Antonio Salieri: Axur, rè d'Ormus. Libretto: only a German-language textbook (Ofen und Pest [Budapest], 1790]) survived in EH (copy in Eisenstadt). Probably copies of the Vienna libretto (1788) were reprinted. Cast unknown. Eszterháza performance material: Ms. Mus. OE–1. Score by the Sukowaty office, also a single V. I part (given an Esterházy' title by Schellinger). Vocal and orchestral material copied by Schellinger with Anon. 10 and 12. Orchestral parts include 2 fl., 2 ob., 2 bsn., 2 hns., timp., 'Tamburo grande e Trommel[!] e piatti'. V. II, 2nd pt., missing. Atto IV°, Sc.'1, Duetto Biseroma-Axur 'Non borbotta, parla schietto', with the preceding secco, was cut by Haydn. Harich, *Musikgeschichte*, 63. Bartha-Somfai, 163, 368f.

Nine operas from earlier seasons were repeated.
Martin y Soler's *L'arbore di Diana*: February (two), March (three), April (one).
Sarti's *I finti eredi*: February (one).
Cimarosa's *Il pittore Parigino*: February (one), April (two), May (one), June (two), July (one).
Pasticcio *La Circe*: February (one), March (one), June (one), July (one).
Paisiello's *Le gare generose*: March (one).
Paisiello's *Il tamburo notturno*: March (one).
Guglielmi's *Le vicende d'amore*: March (two), April (five), June (two).
Gassmann's *L'amore artigiano*: March (one), April (three), May (two), June (two). Some new copies of the libretto were ordered from Vienna: L'amore artigiano. Dramma giocoso in due atti. Da rappresentarsi nel teatro di S. A. il Signor Principe Regnante Niccolò Eszterhazy. Vienna, presso la Società Tipografica. [no copy survives]. For this revival Haydn, according to his letter to Maria Anna von Genzinger of 14 March (*infra*, p. 739), composed three new arias. Two of these are now known, the third perhaps identified. EH, Budapest, Ms. Mus. OE–17 (see 1777 Chronicle): Atto I°, Sc. 5, Titta's Aria 'Da che penso a maritarmi' was replaced with Haydn's own setting (XXIVb:16), of which the autograph is dated 1790. Sc. 11, Giannino's Aria 'Occhietti cari del mio tesoro' was at first sung, then drastically cut (bars 50–99!) and then replaced by a new insertion (no vocal part extant but text presumably identical; composer?): *incipit*, Bartha-Somfai, 184: add the following second section –

This number is designated XXIVb:16 *bis* in Hoboken's Catalogue, but there are other possibilities for the missing third Haydn insertion aria. The next is Atto II°, Sc. 6, Rosina's Aria. Gassmann's text was 'Ti ho voluto sempre bene'. Apparently for the 1790 revival, a new aria with the text 'Son ragazza di buon core' was added: score (Anon. 10) is on oblong Italian paper with watermarks 'AM', bow-and-arow, vertical chain lines, three crescents of declining size and 'REAL'. *Incipit* in Bartha-Somfai, 185: add 'a mezza voce' as dynamic mark and add (a) entrance of Rosina and (b) the second section

Son ra-gaz-za di buon co-re, son con-

The insertion is scored for strings. No composer is indicated. Sc. 12, Titta's Aria 'Se sapeste che bestia che sono' was replaced by an insertion with the same text in 1790 (it was sung in Gassmann's version previously): *Particella* for voice and b. c. (watermarks: bow-and-arrow, three crescents as before) and parts, copied by Schellinger and Anon. 12. This insertion was also used in Righini's *L'incontro inaspettato* of 1786 (q.v.). Composer? Sc. 14, Angiolina's Aria 'Lo voglio giovanotto' was cancelled in 1790 and replaced by another insertion, of which score and parts (2 ob., bsn., 2 hn., str.) were removed (the places of their removal in the parts show the work's orchestration). This Aria was 'No. 23' and for alto: the number is important because it enabled us to identify the second known insertion aria for this work, *viz.*: Sc. 17, score reads 'Volti Presto. Muta Scena e siegue subito Cavatina Costanza' and the indication '25' in red crayon added. The autograph of Haydn's insertion, 'La mia pace, oh Dio' (XXIVb:19), is marked '25' in red crayon. *Vide supra*, p. 648. As will be seen, identification of the missing third aria is rather more complicated than at first appears, and there are several possibilities. Harich, *Musikgeschichte*, 63. Bartha-Somfai, 161, 182–7. Harich in *HJB* I, 90.

Bologna's *L'isola di Calipso*: April (one). Literature: Harich in *HJB* I, 91.

OPERAS IN A FINAL STATE OF PREPARATION

Giovanni Paisiello: *Il rè Teodoro in Venezia*. Libretto: EH (Eisenstadt) owns a copy of the Vienna libretto (Joseph Edlen von Kurzbek[!], 1784, in two languages) and probably a set had been ordered. Eszterháza performance material: EH, Budapest, MS. Mus. OE–3. Score and most of the vocal parts were from the office of Wenzel Sukowaty, Vienna, who was (we repeat) the official copyist for the Vienna court theatres. Cast listed on EH vocal parts: Taddeo, Majeroni. Sandrino, Brizzi [Prizzi]. Schellinger and Anon. 12 copied the orchestral parts and the (few) missing vocal parts; the parts are occasionally dated 1790. Schellinger was working on the last part, Corno 2do, when news of the Prince's death reached the Castle; the part was never completed (it breaks off after the 'Introduzione'). Haydn cut the chorus in Atto I^o, Sc. 4, and made three cuts in Sc. 14 of Atto II°, Duetto Lisetta-Taddeo 'Cosa far pensi, o figlia'. It is interesting to note that when the clarinets were soli, Haydn wrote 'flauti' on the score; this is undoubtedly his usual solution in *Figaro*, too. Harich, *Musikgeschichte*, 63. Bartha-Somfai, 366.

Grétry's *Riccardo*. The score is the Italian version (EH, Budapest: Ms. Mus. OE–8) and is of Italian origin. Apparently they had just started copying the vocal parts – these were always prepared before the orchestral parts so that the singers could begin to learn their roles – when news of the Prince's death arrived. Anon. 10 was working on the part of Riccardo (for Atto II°) and had finished four sheets. There are no traces of Haydn's editing in the score. Bartha-Somfai, 369. Libretto: EH, Eisenstadt, owns the German libretto (trans. by Stephanie the Younger), Vienna 1787.

Antonio Salieri: *La grotta di Trofonio*. Libretto: EH, Eisenstadt, owns a German translation, Cologne 1787. Only the score (EH, Budapest: Ms. Mus. OE–2) by Wenzel Sukowaty (with a reference to the Vienna performance of 1785) survives, but Haydn had not yet started editing the work.

THE GERMAN THEATRICAL TROUPE 1790

The Mayer Troupe was still in residence, but when the season abruptly closed in October 1790, only Mayer, Madame Ditelmayer, Hornung and Hart remained of the group listed at the beginning of the 1788 season. The final list of the company, 5 October 1790 (A.T. 60), included Anton Hornung, Leopold Hart, Karl Augenstein, Heinrich and Josepha Zunger, Karl Medastini, Franz Bürger, Leopold and Julianna Haim, Josepha Bittam and Zaverius Max. Their repertoire is not known to us. Horányi, 138.

During his winter stay in Vienna in January 1790, Haydn had his first opportunity of hearing *Le nozze di Figaro*: when it had been given in 1786, he had been at Eszterháza the whole time, and its performances in 1789 took place when he was away from Vienna. He probably heard it twice, on 8 January and 1 February; that he did hear it is made clear in his letter to Frau von Genzinger of 9 February.[1]

Having heard what was presumably a piano rehearsal of *Così fan tutte* with the singers, Mozart now took Haydn to the orchestral-vocal rehearsals, but before we list the documents, a letter to Haydn's publisher must claim our notice:

[To Artaria & Co., Vienna. *German*]

[Vienna] From my home,
11th January 1790.

Nobly born,
Most highly respected Sir!

I had hoped, in vain, to see you here day before yesterday morning, so that I could show you various pieces of music; but you won't have been able to come because of your many affairs. This is to inform you that this very day I received a letter from *Mon*. Bland in London, wherein he asks me for pianoforte Sonatas with accompaniment of a violin and violoncello.[2] But this time I give you the preference and so I herewith inform you that you can have the first Sonata from me any time, the 2nd in a fortnight, and the third by the end of carnival time— each, as usual, for 10 ducats. Will you be good enough to let me have your decision by tomorrow morning?—A couple of lines will do. But in order to cancel my debt to you, you must also accept the 12 new and most splendid Minuets with 12 Trios, for 12 ducats.[3] Hoping to receive the favour of your reply, I am, Sir, most respectfully,

Your wholly obedient servant,
Josephus Haydn.

[Address:]   Monsieur
          Monsieur d'Artaria
              et Compag.
                  a
              Son Logis.

[Artaria's clerk notes: "Haydn Giuseppe / di qui"] [CCLN, 94f.]

[W. A. Mozart to Michael Puchberg, Vienna. *German*]

[Vienna, 20 January 1790]
... If you can and would trust me with another 100 fl., I would very much be your debtor. –

Tomorrow is the first orchestral rehearsal in the theatre – Haydn will go with me – if your affairs allow of it, and if you perhaps would like to attend the

---

1 Performances of *Figaro*: Deutsch, *Dokumente*, 238. Pohl II, 238.
2 It is not quite clear which three Trios are meant here: either No. 27 in A flat, and Nos. 28 and 29 (with flute instead of violin), or Nos. 28–30 (the latter also with flute). In view of the fact that Artaria published Nos. 27–29 in 1790, but No. 30 two years later, it would seem that this letter refers to the former three. Haydn sold Nos. 28–30 to Bland, but not No. 27, which he later asked Genzinger to send him to London. Bland published the Trios with the following note: "This & the Two following Trios were wrote at the particular request of the Publisher when he was with Mr. Haydn in Novr. last [1789] ... J. Bland thinks this sufficient notice to other Publishers not to pirate the same." Bland must have received the first work (No. 28) early in 1790, the second (No. 29) about June—he entered it at Stationers' Hall on June 28th—and the third (No. 30) probably on 12th July: an envelope large enough to contain a Trio, addressed in Haydn's hand to Bland, and containing someone's (Bland's?) note "Haydn 12 July 90", has been discovered; the owners, J. A. Stargardt of Marburg/Lahn, kindly permitted us to study this envelope. See also Hoboken, p. 701. Artaria accepted Haydn's offer, and Haydn signed a receipt in two (or three?) almost identical copies, dated Vienna, 13th January 1790. He received 35 Gulden for the Trios, and Artaria was to be the sole owner.
3 Artaria did not publish these Dances.

rehearsal, you need only have the goodness to come to me tomorrow morning at 10 o'clock, and we will all go together.

Your most sincere friend
20th January 1790 W. A. Mozart
[Puchberg: 'eodem sent the 100 fl.']

The actual performances, some of which Haydn obviously attended, took place on 26, 28 and 30 January (the others took place after he had left for Hungary).[1]

[To Maria Anna von Genzinger, Vienna. *German*]
Dear, kind Frau von Gennzinger!
    This is to tell your Grace that all the arrangements for the little quartet party we agreed to have this coming Friday are completed. Herr von Häring[2] considered himself fortunate to be able to assist me on this occasion, the more so when I told him of the attention and all the other kind favours I had received from Your Grace. Now I hope only to receive a small measure of approbation. Your Grace shouldn't forget to invite the Pater Professor.[3]
    Meanwhile I kiss your hands and am, most respectfully,
Your Grace's
sincere and most obedient servant,
Josephus Haydn.

[Vienna] From my home, 23rd January 1790.
[Address:]   Madame
            Madame de Gennzinger
            Noble de Kayser
            a
                Son Logis.   [CCLN, 95]

The quartet party took place on 29 January (perhaps with the new Quartets, Opp. 54/55, or Mozart's new K.575 or the Clarinet Quintet, K.581).
    On 31 January Haydn collected some of his players' salary:

    Receipt
    that I the undersigned, and on behalf of the following musicians, have received our monthly salary for January, *viz*. Nencini, Mayer, Steiner, Lendway, and Schellinger, correctly and in cash, for which this is the receipt.
    Vienna, 31 January 1790.   Josephus Haydn
                                                    Capell Meister
                                        [A.M. 19.1264. Valkó II, 608]

Haydn was now called back to Hungary, which gave rise to the most amusing, sad, witty and self-revealing correspondence of his career:

[To Maria Anna von Genzinger, Vienna. *German*]
Noble and kindest Frau von Gennzinger!
    I was most flattered to receive yesterday Your Grace's most recent invitation that I should spend the evening with you today, but painful as it is, I must tell you

---

1 Cast: Fiordiligi – Adriana Ferraresi del Bene; Dorabella – Louise Villeneuve; Despina – Dorotea Bussani; Guglielmo – Francesco Benucci; Ferrando – Vincenzio Calvesi; Don Alfonso – Francesco Bussani. Ferraresi also sang Susanna in *Figaro*, Caterina Cavalieri the Countess. Deutsch, *Dokumente*, 308.
2 Johann Baptist von Häring (or possibly Herring), a Viennese banker whose violin playing was highly esteemed. See Nohl, p. 112.
3 Probably from the neighbouring *Schotten* (Scottish) Monastery.

that I cannot even thank you personally for all the kind favours I have received
from you; I regret this very much, and from the bottom of my heart I wish you,
not only tonight but for ever and ever, the most agreeable and happy of
gatherings. Mine are over—tomorrow I return to dreary solitude. May God only
grant me good health, but I fear the contrary, for I am far from well today. God
bless your Grace—your dear husband—and all your sweet children. I kiss your
hands once more and am as always, now and my whole life

Your Grace's
obedient servant,
Joseph Haydn.

[Vienna]   From my home, 3rd February 1790.
[Address:]   Madame
        Madame Noble de
        Gennzinger Noble de
        Kayser
              a
            Son Logis.   [CCLN, 96]

[To Maria Anna von Genzinger, Vienna. *German*]
Nobly born,
Most highly respected and kindest Frau von Gennzinger,
    Well, here I sit in my wilderness—forsaken—like a poor waif—almost
without any human society—melancholy—full of the memories of past glorious
days—yes! past alas!—and who knows when these days shall return again? Those
wonderful parties? Where the whole circle is one heart, one soul—all these
beautiful musical evenings—which can only be remembered, and not described—
where are all these enthusiastic moments?—all gone—and gone for a long time.
Your Grace mustn't be surprised that I haven't written up to now to thank you. I
found everything at home in confusion, and for 3 days I didn't know if I was
Capell-master or *Capell*-servant. Nothing could console me, my whole house was
in confusion, my pianoforte which I usually love so much was perverse and
disobedient, it irritated rather than calmed me, I could only sleep very little, even
my dreams persecuted me; and then, just when I was happily dreaming that I was
listening to the opera, *Le nozze di Figaro*,[1] that horrible North wind woke me and
almost blew my nightcap off my head; I lost 20 lbs. in weight in 3 days, for the
good Viennese food I had in me disappeared on the journey; alas! alas! I thought
to myself as I was eating in the mess here, instead of that delicious slice of beef, a
chunk of a cow 50 years old; instead of a ragout with little dumplings, an old sheep
with carrots; instead of a Bohemian pheasant, a leathery joint; instead of those
fine and delicate oranges, a *Dschabl* or so-called *gross Sallat* [*sic*]; instead of pastry,
dry apple-fritters and hazelnuts—and that's what I have to eat. Alas! alas! I
thought to myself, if I could only have a little bit of what I couldn't eat up in
Vienna. —Here in Estoras no one asks me: Would you like some chocolate, with
milk or without? Will you take some coffee, black, or with cream? What may I
offer you, my dear Haydn? Would you like a vanilla or a pineapple[2] ice? If I only
had a good piece of Parmesan cheese, especially in Lent, so that I could more easily
swallow those black dumplings and noodles; just today I told our porter here to
send me a couple of pounds.

---

1 *Vide supra.*

2 'Ananas'; this Brazilian word (meaning pineapple) was used in Austrian dialect to refer to strawberries, and only gradually came to be
used in its correct meaning.

Forgive me, kindest and most gracious lady, for filling the very first letter with such stupid nonsense, and for killing time with such a wretched scrawl, but you must forgive a man whom the Viennese terribly spoiled. I am gradually getting used to country life, however, and yesterday I studied for the first time, and quite Haydnish, too. Your Grace will certainly have been more industrious than I. The pleasing Adagio from the Quartet has, I hope, by now received its true expression from your fair fingers. My good friend *Fräulein* Peperl[1] will (I hope) be reminded of her teacher by singing the Cantata[2] frequently; she should remember to have a distinct articulation and a correct vocal production, for it would be a crime if so beautiful a voice were to remain hidden in her breast; so therefore I ask her to smile frequently, lest I be disappointed in her. Likewise I advise *Mons.* François[3] to cultivate his musical talents; even when he sings in his dressing-gown, he does very nicely. I shall often send him some new things to encourage him. Meanwhile I again kiss your hands for all your kind favours, and am, as always, most respectfully,

Your Grace's
most sincere and wholly obedient
servant,
Josephus Haydn.

Estoras, 9th February 1790.
N.S. Please present my respectful compliments to Your Grace's husband, and also my compliments to *Mons.* Hofmeister Junior, to Fräulein Nanette and the whole Hacker family.[4]   [CCLN, 96–8]

On 20 February, Emperor Joseph II died, to be succeeded by his brother, Leopold, Grand Duke of Tuscany. Leopold and his wife, Maria Ludovica, were equally ambivalent about Mozart's music (the 'porcheria tedesca' remark supposedly made by the Empress after the première of Mozart's *La clemenza di Tito* in Prague in 1791 puts her in rather special class for Mozart lovers). Five days later, Princess Maria Elisabeth, Esterházy's wife, died at Eisenstadt. It is believed that Haydn wrote, for this occasion (if it was not for the death of Prince Nicolaus himself), the solemn *Libera me* which the present writer found in a pile of old music in the organ loft of the Parish Church St Martin (now Cathedral) in Eisenstadt. The piece was so hurriedly prepared – probably Haydn could not be present and sent the work to be played by the local Esterházy forces in his absence; hence, too, the small orchestra, strings only – that Haydn himself wrote the principal parts, leaving Schellinger to prepare the duplicates and also the strings, which double the voices. In its *stilo antico* organization, with the connecting Gregorian chant ('cues' for which were noted on the tenor part), this *Responsorium ad absolutionem* shows that curious interest that all the great composers of this period had in preserving the 'Palestrina' style (as they might have called it). The work has strong stylistic and even thematic relations to the Offertorium 'Non nobis, Domine', which is discussed in another volume.[5] We believe that the first performance since 1790 was given at Llandaff Cathedral (Cardiff) in a concert that we devised in the Autumn of 1971.

---

1 Peperl (Josepha) and François (Franz), then sixteen and fifteen; the eldest children of Maria Anna.
2 *Arianna a Naxos* (see letter of 14 March, *infra*).
3 See note 2.
4 Hofmeister was the family tutor in foreign languages (see letter of 13 May); Fräulein Nanette is Maria Anna de Gerlischek (or Jerlischek) who married Johann Tost (Hoboken, p. 775). Maria Anna's mother was *née* Hackher zu Hart.
5 See our article, 'Haydn's newly discovered *Responsorium ad absolutionem*, "Libera me, Domine"', in *HJB* IV (1968), pp. 140ff. Offertorium: *Haydn: the Years of 'The Creation' 1796–1800*, pp. 77ff.

[To Maria Anna von Genzinger, Vienna. *German*]

Estoras, 14th March 1790.

Nobly born,

Most esteemed and kindest Frau von Gennzinger!

I ask Your Grace's forgiveness a million times for having so long delayed the answer to your kind 2 letters. This is not negligence (a sin from which Heaven will preserve me as long as I live) but is because of the many things I have to do for my most gracious Prince in his present melancholy condition. The death of his wife so crushed the Prince that we had to use every means in our power to pull His Highness out of this depression, and thus the first 3 days I arranged enlarged chamber music every evening with no singing; but the poor Prince, during the concert of the first evening, became so depressed when he heard my Favourite Adagio in D that we had quite a time to brighten his mood with the other pieces.

On the 4th day we had an opera, on the 5th a comedy [play], and then our theatre daily as usual. Meanwhile I ordered them to prepare the old opera *L'amor Artigiano* by Gasman, because the Prince had said to me recently that he would like to see it: I wrote 3 new arias for it,[1] which I shall be sending Your Grace shortly, not because of their beauty but to show Your Grace how diligent I am. Your Grace shall receive the promised Symphony[2] during the month of April, but in time so that it can be produced at the Kees Concert.

Meanwhile I respectfully kiss Your Grace's hands for the Zwieback you sent me, which however I did not receive till last Tuesday; but it came at just the right moment, for I had just eaten up the last of the previous lot. I am delighted that my favourite *Arianna* [Cantata] is well received at the Schottenhof, but I do recommend *Fräulein* Peperl to articulate the words clearly, especially the passage "chi tanto amai". I take the liberty of sending you my best wishes for your approaching name-day,[3] and ask you at the same time to retain me in your favour, and to consider me on every occasion as your own, though unworthy, teacher.

I also take the liberty of informing you that the language teacher can come here any day, his journey will be paid for here, and he can travel either by the diligence or by some other carriage, the schedules of which may be found daily in the Madschakerhof.[4]

I shall return the box for the Zwieback to Your Grace at the first opportunity.

Since I am sure that Your Grace takes an interest in all my doings (far more, in fact, than I deserve), I should like to tell Your Grace that last week I received a present of a charming gold snuff-box, weighing the value of 34 ducats, from Prince Oetting von Wallerstein,[5] together with an invitation to pay him a visit at his expense sometime this year; His Highness is specially desirous of making my personal acquaintance (a pleasant encouragement for my drooping spirits). Whether I shall make up my mind to go is another question.

---

1 At least two of these 'insertion' arias have survived: 'Da che penso a maritarmi' (for tenor, in E flat), and 'La mia pace' (for soprano, in B flat).

2 Haydn did not then compose this symphony, though he later refers to it; perhaps it turned into one of the Salomon Symphonies (No. 93?) – see letter of 2 March 1792 (*Haydn in England 1791–1795*, pp. 140–1).

3 Haydn must have confused the data, because the Feast of the Ascension of the Virgin Mary (and Maria Anna's name-day) occur on 15 August (see letter of that date, *infra*).

4 A Viennese tavern, connected with the Monastery of Göttweig.

5 For Symphonies Nos. 90–92; see the previous correspondence with von Müller. On 9 February, von Müller wrote to Prince Krafft Ernst: '...je lui ai écrit, pourqu'il m'assigne une personne, à qui je pouvais confier la Tabattière d'or avec les 50 Ducats, affin qu'ils lui parviennent...et lui ai proposé de faire un tour à Wallerstein au frais de Votre Altesse, qui souhaiteroit faire la connoissance personelle...' (L. Schiedermair, 'Die Blütezeit der Öttingen-Wallerstein' schen Hofkapelle', *Recueil de la Société Internationale de Musique*, 91 ème Année, Livr. I, Oct. – Dec. 1907, p. 106).

Do please forgive this hasty letter; I am, with every possible esteem, as always
Your Grace's
sincere and obedient servant,
Josephus Haydn.

N.S. My respectful compliments to Your Grace's
husband and the whole Hacker family.

I have just lost my faithful and
honest coachman; he died on
the 25th of last month.

[CCLN, 98–100]

Haydn had not forgotten his obligations to Artaria, and on 6 May he sent them the
second Piano Trio (of what was apparently the three works Nos. 27, 29 and 28, in that
order; Bland's order of 28 and 29 is the one adopted by us in the chronological list), i.e.
No. 29:

[To Artaria & Co., Vienna. *German*]

Estoras, 6th May 1790.

Mon tres cher amj!
I send you herewith the 2nd Clavier Sonata – the 3rd will follow shortly.
Joseph Haydn mpria

[on   other   side,   [not in CCLN; autograph in
Artaria's   note: the   Campori   Collection,
'Haydn / 6 maggio']   Biblioteca Estense, Modena]

Our next letter is Haydn's to Frau von Genzinger:

[To Maria Anna von Genzinger, Vienna. *German*]

Estoras, 13th May 1790.

Nobly born,
Gracious and kindest Frau von Gennzinger!
I was astonished to see from your kind letter that Your Grace did not receive
my last letter, in which I mentioned that our landlord had engaged a French
teacher, who came by chance to Estoras, and so I at once made my excuses not
only to Your Grace but also to Herr Hofmeister.[1] My dear benefactress, this is not
the first time that some of my letters, and also those of many others, have gone
astray, inasmuch as our letter-bag, on its way to Oedenburg, is always opened by
the house-master there (in order to put the letters into it), as a result of which
mistakes and other disagreeable occurrences have often arisen: for greater security
in the future, however, and to put a stop to this disgraceful curiosity, henceforth I
shall enclose all my letters in an extra envelope addressed to our porter, Herr
Pointner.[2] This occurrence makes me the more unhappy because Your Grace

---

1 See *supra*, p. 738.
2 This is the place, perhaps, to mention a charming little letter (undated) which accompanied a pretty *Directoire* fan; both are owned by
the Pierpont Morgan Library, New York, which allowed us to publish all their Haydn letters in *HJB* VII, 307ff.; there the fan and the
letter are reproduced in facsimile, and the letter is transcribed in its original German. It reads

    Dearest Madame Pointner
    I thank you heartily for the help you have given me during my illness. Please accept this trifle as a sign that I appreciate you,
respect you, and remain
                              Your sincere fr[iend] and st
                              Joseph Haydn *mpria*

Perhaps Haydn wrote the letter after the second London journey, when he was frequently ill (e.g. after finishing *The Creation* in 1798).

might blame me for my negligence, from which Heaven defend me! Anyway, these curious people, male or female, cannot have discovered anything improper in this letter, or in any of the others either. And now, my dear benefactress, when shall I have the inexpressible happiness of seeing Your Grace in Estoras? Since business doesn't permit me to go to Vienna, I console myself with the thought that I shall quite surely kiss your hands here this summer. In which flattering thought, meanwhile, I am, most respectfully,

> Your Grace's
> most sincere and obedient servant,
> Josephus Haydn [m.p] ria.

My respectful compliments to
Your Grace's husband and the whole family.   [CCLN, 100f.]

In the next letters to Frau von Genzinger we hear of Haydn's increasing frustration with Esterháza. Altogether, this is a different Haydn from the one we met at the beginning of this volume. His circle of friends is different, his interest broader, and he has outgrown Eszterháza and the restricted life of a provincial opera *Capellmeister*; he had also outgrown *la* Polzelli, whose charms, such as they were, were obviously of a strong but rather limited character.

[To Maria Anna von Genzinger, Vienna. *German*]

Estoras, 30th May 1790.

Nobly born,
Most highly esteemed and kindest Frau von Gennzinger!

I was just at Oedenburg when I received your last welcome letter, whence I had gone to enquire about the lost letter: the house-master there swore by all that is holy that he had seen no letter in my hand-writing at that time, and so this letter must have gone astray in Estoras. Be that as it may, this curiosity can do me no harm, much less Your Grace, for the whole contents of the letter were partly about my opera, *La vera costanza*, which was performed at the new theatre in the Landstrasse,[1] and partly about the French teacher who was to have come to Estoras. Your Grace need have no fear, therefore, either about the past or about the future, for my friendship and the esteem in which I hold Your Grace (tender as they are) will never be reprehensible, because I always have in mind my respect for Your Grace's profound virtue, which not only I, but all who know Your Grace, must admire. Therefore I beg Your Grace not to be frightened away from consoling me occasionally by your pleasant letters, for they comfort me in my wilderness, and are highly necessary for my heart, which is so often deeply hurt. Oh! If only I could be with Your Grace for a quarter of an hour, to pour forth all my troubles to you, and to hear all your comforting words. I have to put up with many annoyances from the Court here which, however, I must accept in silence. The only consolation left to me is that I am—thank God!—well, and eagerly disposed to work; I am only sorry that despite this eagerness, Your Grace has had to wait so long for the promised Symphony, but this time it's simply bare necessity which is responsible, arising from my circumstances here and the present rise in the cost of living. Your Grace therefore mustn't be angry at your Haydn who, often as his Prince absents himself from Estoras, cannot go to Vienna even for 24 hours; it's scarcely credible, and yet the refusal is always couched in such polite terms, so

---

1 Written in 1778 for Vienna, where intrigue prevented its being given; the first performance took place in Esterháza in the Spring of 1779. The theatre in the Landstrasse – then a suburb of Vienna (now the 3rd District) – had been opened in 1790. See Gustav Gugitz, *Alt-Wiener Thespiskarren*, Vienna 1925, pp. 235-237, 382f.

polite in fact that I just don't have the heart to insist on receiving the permission. Oh well! As God pleases! This time will also pass away, and the day come when I shall have the inexpressible pleasure of sitting beside Your Grace at the pianoforte, hearing Mozart's masterpieces, and kissing your hands for so many wonderful things. With this hope, I am,

Your Grace's
most sincere and humble servant,
Josephus Haydn.

My respectful compliments to Your Grace's
husband and the whole family, likewise to
the Hackers and the P. Professor. [CCLN, 101f.]

[To Maria Anna von Genzinger, Vienna. *German*]

Estoras, 6th June 1790.

Nobly born,
Most esteemed and kindest Frau von Gennzinger!

I am terribly sorry that Your Grace was so long in receiving my last letter, but the previous week none of the Hussars was dispatched from Estoras, so it's not my fault that the letter reached you so late.

Between ourselves! I must inform Your Grace that our *Mademoiselle* Nanette[1] has commissioned me to compose a new pianoforte Sonata for you, but which no one else can own. I esteem myself fortunate to have received such a command. I shall deliver the Sonata to Your Grace in a fortnight at the latest. This *Mademoiselle* Nanette promised to pay me for the work, but you can easily imagine that I shall refuse it now or any other time: the best reward for me will always be to hear that I have in some measure received your approbation. Meanwhile I am, most respectfully,

Your Grace's
most obedient servant,
Jos: Haydn.
[CCLN, 102f.]

Haydn's next letter is to a merchant on the subject of Haydn's pupil F. C. Magnus, who published Three Trios (2 v., vc.) as Op. I with Hummel in Berlin-Amsterdam. Haydn's extracts of Fux's *Gradus ad Parnassum* in Magnus's copy has survived and is in the Esterházy Collection, Budapest.[2]

[To Friedrich Jakob van der Nüll,[3] Vienna. *German*]

Estoras, 7th June 1790.

Nobly born,
Most highly respected Sir!

One of my pupils, by the name of Magnus, a poor but well-educated and well-bred young man from Livonia, to whom I give composition lessons free of

---

1 Nanette was Maria Anna de Gerlischeck; see letter of 9 February, *supra*. The Sonata was to be No. 59 in E flat, and Haydn began it on 1 June (autograph now Vienna, Stadtbibliothek).
2 Cari Johannson, *J. J. & B. Hummel: Music-Publishing and Thematic Catalogues*, Stockholm 1972, vol. I, p. 103; pl. no. 803, announced in the *Berlinische Nachtrichten* of 14 April 1792. EH, Budapest, Ha. I. 10. 'Elementarbuch der verschiedenen Gattungen des Contrapunkts. Aus den grösseren Werken des Kappm. Fux, von Joseph Haydn zusammengezogen. Esterhazy 22 7tbr. [Sept.] 1789. F. C. Magnus'.
3 Friedrich Jakob van der Nüll, a wholesale merchant and a partner in the firm of Ignaz von Schwab; Haydn usually refers to him as 'von' rather than 'van' der Nüll. His house was on the Michaelerplatz. See Caroline Pichler, *Denkwürdigkeiten aus meinem Leben*, a new edition (E. K. Blümml), Munich 1914, I, pp. 545f. Van der Nüll was a passionate admirer and 'amateur' of music; he subscribed to Haydn's *Creation*, for example. See also letter of 25 March 1796: *Haydn: the Years of 'The Creation' 1796–1800*, p. 96.

charge because of his extraordinary diligence, has at last, through my insistent intervention, received a cheque from his father in the amount of [not filled in]. No one hereabouts can or will accept this cheque, and since I have long been convinced of your inborn love for your fellow men, I come to you with the humble request, please, if at all possible, to help the poor young man in this instance. Our porter, Herr Pointner, who is a trustworthy man, will deliver this cheque to you, good Sir, and you can entrust him with the money without any risk at all.

Hoping that you will fulfil my wish to encourage this poor young man in his industry, I am, Sir, with all possible esteem,

Your wholly obedient and humble servant,
Joseph Haydn.

N.S. My respectful compliments to all the gentlemen who live in the Häring[1] house; as for the ladies, I respectfully kiss their hands with all the musical tenderness I have been capable of expressing throughout my life. [CCLN, 103f.]

Haydn's various letters now begin to give us, for the first time, a detailed picture of his intimate thoughts, and also something of his lively personality (which we knew, as it were, only through his music).

[Certificate for Joseph Eybler. *German.* Only the place, date, signature and title in Haydn's hand]

I the undersigned cannot fail to give the bearer of these lines, Herr JOSEPH EYBLER, the certificate which he humbly requested of me, and which should wholly reflect his outstanding talents and the diligence he has hitherto shown in the field of music. He possesses not only all the musical and theoretical knowledge necessary to pass with distinction the most difficult examination of any musical judge; but as a practical musician he is a highly respectable pianoforte player and violinist, and as such can win the approval of any connoisseur. In view of the former, he can fill the post of a *Kapellmeister* with distinction, and in view of the latter, he can be a useful member of any chamber music concert.

As far as his knowledge of COMPOSITION is concerned, I think that I can give no higher recommendation than if I say that he is a pupil of the justly celebrated Herr Albrechtsberger.[2] Equipped with all these abilities, he lacks nothing more than a generous Prince who will give him the position wherein he can further develop and demonstrate his talents, in which capacity the undersigned hopes soon to be able to congratulate him.

Josephus Haydn [m.] pria,
Fürst: Esterhazischer
Capell Meister.

[CCLN, 104]

Esterhaz, 8th June 1790.

[To Maria Anna von Genzinger, Vienna. *German*]

Estoras, 20th June 1790.

Nobly born,
Most esteemed and kindest Frau von Gennzinger!

I have taken the liberty of sending Your Grace a brand new pianoforte Sonata with accompaniment of a flute or violin, not as anything remarkable, but simply a

---

1 Häring (Herring), probably the banker and amateur violinist mentioned in the letter of 23 January 1790.
2 Mozart also wrote a letter of recommendation for Eybler (30 May 1790).

trifle to amuse you in moments of utmost boredom.[1] I would only ask you to have it copied as soon as possible and then to send it back to me. The day before yesterday I delivered the new Sonata[2] to *Mademoiselle* Nanette, my patroness; I had hoped that she would express a wish to hear me play this Sonata, but up to now I have not received any such order, and for this reason I also do not know whether Your Grace will receive this Sonata in today's mail or not. This Sonata is in E flat, brand new, and was written especially for Your Grace to be hers forever, but it is a curious coincidence that the last movement is the very same Minuet and Trio which Your Grace asked me for in your last letter. This Sonata was destined for Your Grace a year ago, and only the Adagio is quite new, and I especially recommend this movement to your attention, for it contains many things which I shall analyze for Your Grace when the time comes; it is rather difficult but full of feeling. It's a pity, however, that Your Grace has not one of Schantz's[3] fortepianos, for Your Grace could then produce twice the effect.

N.B. *Mademoiselle* Nanette must know nothing of the fact that this Sonata was already half completed, for otherwise she might get the wrong impression of me, and this might be very disadvantageous for me, since I must be very careful not to lose her favour. Meanwhile I consider myself fortunate to be at least the means of providing her with some amusement; especially since the sacrifice is made for your sake, dearest Frau von Gennzinger. Oh! how I wish that I could only play this Sonata to you a few times; I could then reconcile my staying for a while in this wilderness. I have so much to say to Your Grace, and so many things to tell you about which are destined for Your Grace alone and no one else: but what cannot be new will, I hope to God, come to pass this Winter; almost half the time has already elapsed. Meanwhile I console myself patiently, and am content that I have the inestimable privilege of subscribing myself

Your Grace's
most sincere and obedient friend
and servant,
Josephus Haydn [m.p] ria.

My respectful compliments to your
husband and all the family, I kiss
Your Grace 1000 times—on the hands. [CCLN, 104f.]

[To Maria Anna von Genzinger, Vienna. *German*]

Estoras, 27th June 1790.

Nobly born,
Highly esteemed and kindest Frau von Genzinger!

Your Grace will certainly have received the new pianoforte Sonata, but if not, you will perhaps receive it along with my letter. 3 days ago I had to play this Sonata at *Mademoiselle* Nanette's in the presence of my gracious Prince. At first I rather doubted, because of its difficulty, whether I would receive any applause, but was soon convinced of the contrary, inasmuch as I was given a gold tobacco-box as a present from [her] own hand. Now I only hope that Your Grace will be satisfied with it, so that I may earn the increased approval of my benefactress; and for this reason I would ask Your Grace to tell her, if not personally, then at least through your husband, that I could not conceal my delight at her generosity, the more so since I am sure that Your Grace shares my pleasure at all the benefits

---

1 A pianoforte Trio: from the presence of the flute we can deduce that it was either Trio No. 28, 29 or 30; if it was really 'brand new', it was probably No. 30, which Haydn seems to have sent to Bland at this time. See also *supra*, p. 735.
2 Pianoforte Sonata No. 59: see *supra*, p. 644.
3 Wenzel Schanz: see also letters of 26 October and 16 November 1788.

conferred on me. It's only a pity that Your Grace doesn't own a Schantz fortepiano, on which everything is better expressed. I thought that Your Grace might turn over your still tolerable harpsichord [*Flügl*] to *Fräulein* Peperl, and buy a new one for yourself. Your beautiful hands and their facility of execution deserve this and much more. I know I ought to have composed this Sonata in accordance with the capabilities of your piano [*Claviers*], but I found this impossible because I was no longer accustomed to it.

Again I find that I am forced to remain here. Your Grace can imagine how much I lose by having to do so. It really is sad always to be a slave, but Providence wills it so. I'm a poor creature! Always plagued by hard work, very few hours of recreation, and friends? What am I saying? One true one? There aren't any true friends any more – one lady friend? Oh yes! There might be one. But she's far away from me. Oh well! I have my thoughts. God bless you, and may you never forget me! Meanwhile I kiss Your Grace's hands 1000 times, and am as always, most respectfully,

Your Grace's
sincere and most obedient servant,
Josephus Haydn.

My respectful compliments to your husband
and all the family.
Please forgive my bad handwriting today: I am suffering a little from pains in my eyes.   [CCLN, 106]

[To Maria Anna von Genzinger, Vienna. *German*]

Estoras, 4th July 1790.

Nobly born,
Kindest Frau von Genzinger!

I have just received your letter, and this very moment the mail goes out. I am simply delighted that my Prince intends to give Your Grace a new fortepiano, all the more so since I am in some measure responsible for it: I constantly implored *Mademoiselle* Nanette to persuade your husband to buy one for Your Grace, and now the purchase depends entirely on Your Grace and simply consists in Your Grace choosing one to fit your touch and suit your fancy. It is quite true that my friend Herr Walther[1] is very celebrated, and that every year I receive the greatest civility from that gentleman, but between ourselves, and speaking frankly, sometimes there is not more than one instrument in ten which you could really describe as good, and apart from that they are very expensive. I know Herr von Nikl's fortepiano: it's excellent, but too heavy for Your Grace's hand, and one can't play everything on it with the necessary delicacy. Therefore I should like Your Grace to try one made by Herr Schanz, his fortepianos are particularly light in touch and the mechanism very agreeable. A good fortepiano is absolutely necessary for Your Grace, and my Sonata will gain double its effect by it.

Meanwhile I kiss Your Grace's hands for exercising the caution I suggested with regard to *Mademoiselle* Nanette. It's a pity that the little gold box she gave me, and had used herself, is so tarnished, but perhaps I can have it polished up in Vienna. As yet I haven't received any order to buy a fortepiano. I fear that they will deliver one to Your Grace's house, which will be beautiful outside but will have a stiff action within. Your husband should refer them to me, and say that I

---

1 Anton Walther (Walter), a Viennese pianoforte builder whose instruments were particular favourites of Mozart's.

consider Herr Schanz at present to be the best pianoforte maker; I shall then arrange everything else. In great haste I am

> Your Grace's
> most obedient servant,
> Jos: Haydn.

[CCLN, 107]

Now that Joseph II was dead, some of the truth about the weird circle of musicians with which he surrounded himself at court began to come out. In a letter from Vienna, the *Musikalische Korrespondenz der teutschen Filharmonischen Gesellschaft* (vol. I) which Haydn's friend Boßler published in Speyer reported that in the chamber music concerts at the Viennese court under Joseph II, the works of Haydn, Mozart, Koželuch and Pleyel were deliberately excluded through the manipulations of the *valet-de-chambre* Strack and the violinist Franz Kreibich (Kreybich). No doubt their devious operations coincided with Joseph's taste, so everyone was satisfied.

Maria Anna Genzinger's next letter to Haydn (they have been preserved in her own drafts, which she kept with Haydn's answer) reads:

[To Haydn from Maria Anna von Genzinger. *German*]

Vienna, 11th July 1790.

✝ ✝ ✝

Most respected Herr v. Haydn,

I duly received your letter of 4th July, and leave it entirely to you to choose me an excellent fortepiano, for *Mademoiselle* [Nanette], as soon as she arrives here, will give you the commission to purchase one in the Prince's name. I am also quite willing (since you think it best) to purchase one from Herr Schanz, but I would prefer that you try it out yourself before I take it, because I don't really know enough about it and might perhaps choose one that is not really good.

I like the Sonata very much, but there is one thing which I wish could be changed (if by so doing it does not detract from the beauty of the piece), and that is the passage in the second part of the Adagio, where the hands cross over; I am not used to this and thus find it hard to do, and so please let me know how this could be altered.

I shall return the other Sonata [Trio] in a few days, it too is very beautiful. But I should like to ask one thing, and that is about the Symphony you promised me, which you agreed you would write just for me and no one else, and to which I look forward so very much: I hope that it hasn't been displaced by the Sonata. I know I shouldn't bother you any more, especially since you have just gone to such pains for me, but the great pleasure I have in all your delightful compositions will not allow it to be otherwise.

By the way, I hope that you are well; as for myself, I have not yet quite recovered from my catarrh, and the day before yesterday I began taking a cure of soda water with milk; I hope, God willing, that I shall soon feel its good effects. I must close now, and remain with much veneration,

> Your sincere friend,
> Maria Ana [*sic*] Noble *v*. Gennzinger,
> *née Noble v*. Kayser.

My family all send you their best wishes.   [CCLN, 107f.]

Lasser, who would have liked to return to Eszterháza with his players, wrote a long letter to Prince Nicolaus from Graz, in which (writes Horányi) 'he suggested a sweeping reorganization of the theatrical life at Eszterháza'. The details are printed in Horányi's most useful book,[1] but since nothing ever came of them, we may pass over them here, and continue with Haydn's correspondence.

[To Joseph Züsser, Receiver-general of the Princely Cashier's Office, Eisenstadt. *German*]

Esterház, 31st July 1790.

Well born,
Most highly respected Herr Züsser!
    I do not doubt that you have long since received, through Herr Kaufmann,[2] the commission concerning a newly engaged female singer by the name of Melo,[3] who will get a yearly salary of 1,000 Fl. beginning on 1st July, but who did not receive her monthly wage along with the money sent here. Therefore please give her monthly wage to the bearer of this letter, our chief-baker-mistress [*Frau Beckermeisterin*]. With my compliments to your family I am, most respectfully,
                                            Your most obedient servant,
                                                    Joseph Haydn.
[Address:] Monsieur de Züsser Receveur
        general de S: Altesse Monseig[neur]
        le Prince Esterhàzy
                à
                        Eisenstadt.
[In the hand of the chief baker-mistress: 'Received 83 Gulden A.M. Tauber']
                                                    [CCLN, 108f.]

[To Maria Anna von Genzinger, Vienna. *German*]
                                        [Estoras 15th August 1790][4]
Nobly born,
Kindest Frau von Gennzinger!
    It would have been my duty to have written to you last week in answer to Your Grace's letter, but I had been thinking of this day for a long time, and had gone to all sorts of pains to think out just how and what I was to wish for Your Grace today; and thus a week went past and now, when my wishes should have taken some form, my small intellect comes to a standstill and (ashamed of itself) doesn't know what to say at all. Why? Because I could not fulfil those musical hopes which Your Grace certainly had the right to expect today at her own home. If only Your Grace knew and could see how troubled my heart is about this, you would certainly feel pity and indulgence for me: the poor, long-expected Symphony has haunted my imagination ever since it was commissioned, but (unfortunately) the pressure of urgent business has hitherto prevented its being born. The hope, however, of your kindly lenity towards me for this delay, and the happier time, now approaching, when my promise can be more easily fulfilled, will help soon to make my wish reality. Among all the many hundred congratulations you will have received yesterday and today, mine will perhaps appear to be an insignificant interloper: I say perhaps, because it would be vain of me to think that Your Grace couldn't find anything better to wish for. So you see,

---

1 Pp. 135f., based on EH, A.T. 55.
2 Kaufmann was Princely Secretary ('Hochfürstl. Esterházischer Sekretär').
3 Teresa Melo.
4 The letter, though undated, was obviously written on Maria Anna's name-day, 15 August (the Virgin Mary's Ascension Day).

kindest and most gracious lady, that I cannot wish you anything at all on your name-day, because my wishes are too feeble and therefore unproductive! I – now I must wish something too, for myself: your kind indulgence, your continuing friendship and your goodness which is so important to me: this is what I most want. If you still have room for one more wish, then mine should change and become identical with your own, for I am sure that none other remains, except that I always wish to be allowed to subscribe myself

Your Grace's

most sincere friend and servant,

Josephus Haydn [m.p] ria.

My respectful compliments to your husband
and the whole family.
On the day after tomorrow I expect an answer about the fortepiano;
Your Grace shall then receive the alteration in the Adagio.

[CCLN, 109f.]

About this time, Haydn was also bothered by widespread repairs in the music house.[1]

On 19 September there was a famous triple marriage at the Viennese court: Archduchess Marie Clementine married the Crown Prince Francis of Naples (proxy: Archduke Carl); the Neapolitan Princess Maria Teresa married Archduke Francis (later Emperor); and the Neapolitan Princess Ludovica Louisa married Ferdinand, Grand Duke of Tuscany. King Ferdinand IV of Naples was also there, and when Haydn came to Vienna, he met the King just before he set out for England (*vide infra*, p. 753). At a concert in the Redoutensaal, given the day of the marriage during the public banquet, Salieri conducted and a Haydn symphony, which the King knew and hummed,[2] was played.

The opera performances were suddenly stopped after two evenings in September. The reason was that the Prince, perhaps feeling ill and in need of expert medical help, went to Vienna. On the 28th, 'after a short illness, in his 76th year' (*Wiener Zeitung*) he died. Now it is quite clear that his successor, Prince Anton, had planned to dismiss the entire orchestra and the players, which were astronomically expensive, as soon as his father died. Within two days, they were all given notice, and their last salaries paid. The shock must have been incredible. Only the wind band (*Feldharmonie*) was retained for the hunt and other ceremonies, and Haydn was touchingly remembered in Prince Nicolaus's will, receiving a pension for life of 1,000 gulden *per annum* (and, in the event of his death, half to his widow); Luigi Tomasini received a life pension of 400 gulden and Leopold Dichtler – the faithful singer – a pension of 300 gulden. Haydn and Tomasini were retained in their respective official capacities but were free to accept engagements elsewhere; they were given a yearly salary of 400 gulden in addition to their pensions. The theatrical company under Johann Mayer received a 'special gratuity' of 200 gulden as indemnity for being dismissed without notice. On 30 September Mayer and Madame Dietelmeyer received the final 100 gulden salary for

---

1 'Repairs in the halls of the music building ... Your Highness allowed princely Capellmeister Haydn to have a stucco flooring in the back room ... The room measures 7½ square *Klaffter*, stucco flooring à 24 xr.: 3 Gulden 24 xr. ... In the music building are 43 stoves which need repairing: to be packed properly, well coated with loam, for each stove 12 xr. ... for princely Capellmeister Haydn a new ... domed stove ...'. EH, Budapest, fasc. 799, Prot. Com. 1790, p. 503. Valkó I, 657.
2 Pohl II, 245.

the Troupe. Mayer, who later became a member of the Vienna Court Theatre, tried in 1795 to collect 1,300 gulden, the Troupe's salary for the last three months of 1790.[1]

The musicians were given their salaries for the month of September – presumably on 1 October. This document of a great ensemble – for Haydn's operatic and orchestral company must have been one of the greatest in Europe at that time – is reproduced in facsimile in Somfai, 106. Capellmeister 'Haidn', the singers Bologna, Sassi, 'Polcelli', Benvenuti, Zecchielli, Melo, Braghetti, Prizzi, de Paoli, Martinelli, Majeroni, Amici, Ung(e)richt and Specht; violinists Tomasini, Grisi, 'Purcksteiner', Hirsch, Fux, Oliva, 'Polcelli'; 'cellists Kraft and Tauber; violonist (double bass) Johann Dietzl; horn players Oliva, Pauer, Nickl and Joseph Dietzl; oboists Czerwenka and Mayer; flautist Hirsch; bassoonists Czerwenka, Peczival and Steiner (Peczival being the timpani player); the 'Garderobba' manager Porta; and copyist Schellinger – they appear before us for the last time. They went all over Europe. Four of the singers, according to the *Preßburger Zeitung* of 25 December, were engaged 'on trial' by the Vienna Theatre; the others returned to Italy and to their modest careers. Many of the musicians in the orchestra went to Vienna, and we encounter them again in the later volumes of this biography.

Haydn fled to Vienna. He went away so quickly that he left many important papers and scores behind in his frantic desire to escape the Eszterháza prison. Before we follow Haydn's life in Vienna, we must close the chapter of the Rococo castle in which Haydn had spent a quarter of a century.

It was left to the house officers and became, at best, a glorified hunting lodge. Later the Esterházys used it as a storage centre for furniture that was not needed. In 1870, the Opera House was demolished. The park ceased to exist, all the temples and Chinese pavilions disappeared. The clocks that Prince Nicolaus loved were given away or lost. The castle now stood empty for most of the year. During the Second World War, it was first occupied by German officers, and we hear of a Kafka-like concert that was given by members of the Vienna Philharmonic in 1945, just as the Red Army reached Hungary:

> In the middle of February I was informed by the *Reichsstatthalterei* that the Schneiderhahn Quartet was to prepare itself for a concert in a place that was not more specifically designated. We received in our passports visas for the then autonomous Slovakia; a military car fetched us, but started to drive us, curiously, southwards, until we arrived at the Hungarian border near Oedenburg. Despite the wrong visa we were admitted to Hungary and arrived at Kapuvár, Headquarters of *Herresgruppe Süd* and General Wohler. From there we were ordered to a 'front concert' at Eszterháza Castle a few miles away.
> ... We played by candlelight before officers and men. At the request of the General there were Mozart's 'Hunt' Quartet, the slow movement of Schubert's 'Death and the Maiden' and Haydn's 'Emperor' Quartet on the programme... While we peacefully played, the Russians had already crossed the Danube south of Budapest, and afterwards, at an evening meal with a group of officers, we drank the obligatory toast to the Führer's health.
> [Otto Strasser, *Und dafür wird man noch bezahlt: Mein Leben mit den Wiener Philharmonikern*, Vienna-Berlin 1974, p. 216]

The Russians came to Eszterháza. They needed a place for a hospital for their wounded and convalescent. The furniture, paintings, musical instruments were

---

1 EH, Budapest, A.T. 60. Horányi, 138.

dragged out to the garden and placed in a huge pile, then set on fire. That evening, people in Oedenburg could see the sky aglow with the red from the fire's reflection. In the smoking ruins, one of the former Esterházy employees found the neck of a violin . . .

We were there in 1958, when the Hungarian authorities had started to restore the buildings. On the walls were the usual Red Army slogans. 'Comrade Officers! We men encourage you in your fight against Nazi-Fascist oppressors . . .'. In the autumn of 1959, Eszterháza Castle was reopened to the public with a series of concerts. Every year since then a few more rooms have been lovingly restored. That it survived at all is one of the miracles of post-war Europe.[1]

Haydn took rooms with Johann Nepomuk Hamberger, a government official ('Registrator') who lived on the Wasserkunst-Bastei (entrance from the Seilerstätte). In terms of present-day Vienna, this means that Haydn's quarters overlooked what is now the Stadtpark (and was then the so-called Glacis). A year later Haydn described Hamberger as 'a very good friend of mine, a man of tall stature . . . my wife's landlord'. It was here that Haydn taught Beethoven in 1792–3.[2]

It was probably in these rooms that Haydn completed his Quartets, Op. 64, and the remaining Notturni for the King of Naples. As we consider these last products of the Eszterháza years, we might think of the words written by the great German lexicographer, E. L. Gerber, in his *Historisch-Biographisches Lexikon der Tonkünstler* (Breitkopf & Härtel, 1790, columns 699ff.):

> When we speak of Josef Haydn, we think of one of our greatest men; great in small things and even greater in large; the pride of our age. Always rich and inexhaustible; forever new and surprising, forever noble and great, even when he seems to laugh. He gave to our instrumental music, and in particular to quartets and symphonies, a perfection that never before existed. Everything speaks when he sets his orchestra in motion. Every subsidiary part, in other composers an unimportant accompaniment, is often a major principal voice in his hands. Every harmonic device, be it even from the Gothic age of the grey contrapuntalists, is at his disposal. But instead of its former stiffness, it takes on a pleasing shape as soon as he prepares it for our ears. He has the great art of appearing already known in his movements. Through it, despite all contrapuntal tricks that are found therein, he is popular and attractive for every amateur. His themes bear the stamp throughout of an original genius, and render their maker unmistakable among thousands to the attentive listener. Frequently, however, he seems to have only written casual notes on his music paper. But what a change these notes, which seemed at first so undistinguished, take under his masterly hands. One is carried away! Alternating anxiety and joy over the development and solution of his grand ideas grip the listener and he forgets himself entirely. The young and beautiful of the fair sex as the contrapuntalist who has grown grey with all his scores hear his works with delight and approval. Proof enough how much nature and art are at his fingertips.

---

1 Description of the fire from Dr Janos Harich, who talked to several former Esterházy employees afterwards. He himself had visited the Castle in 1945 to examine the contents; at that time he saw the now destroyed portrait of Haydn in blue and gold uniform by J. B. Grundmann. Pohl II, 243.
2 T. von Karajan, *Haydn in London*, Vienna 1861, p. 15. Haydn's description of Hamberger: his letter from London, 13 Oct. 1791 (CCLN 119f., *Haydn in England 1791–1795*, pp. 105f. – wrongly in the latter volume as 'Hamburger'); Haydn's letters from London often give us information about these final weeks, i.e. Haydn's haste in leaving Hungary in a letter to Polzelli of 22 May 1791, CCLN 136, *H. in E.* 166). Haydn's house number was 992 (later Seilerstätte, house no. 15).

His first quartets, which became known about the year 1760, already made a general sensation. One laughed and was amused, on the one hand, over the extraordinary naiveté and cheerfulness than predominated in them, but in other parts of the Continent they cried about music being reduced to comic triviality [*Tändeleyen*] and about shocking parallel octaves ... but one soon got used, despite all the cries of protest, to that style, and soon it was even imitated. ... [speaks of *seguaci* and especially Reichardt].

Meanwhile his great genius drove Haydn from one level of perfection to another; until about the year 1780 he reached, in his church and theatrical pieces, the highest degree of excellence and of celebrity in the art of composing.

From Dies we learn that 'Count Graschalkowiz' (*sc.* Prince Grassalkovics) offered Haydn a position as *Kapellmeister*, but Haydn 'showed his attachment to his Prince and refused, and an unusual occurrence provided him with the occasion to persuade Prince Anton to reverse his decision and to re-engage the whole wind-band section of the dismissed orchestra' (Dies, 119). Apparently this was for the Coronation festivities of Leopold II at Pressburg, where on 15 November the joint wind bands of Esterházy and Grassalkovics played with such success that they were persuaded to make a guest appearance at the Tonkünstler-Societät concert in April 1791 (with a work for twenty-one wind instruments by Druschetzky).[1]

Meanwhile, Johann Peter Salomon, who had often tried to lure Haydn away from Hungary to England, was in Cologne on his annual tour of the Continent to recruit singers for his coming concert season in London, when he read in the newspapers of Prince Esterházy's death. He immediately set off for Vienna and one evening a visitor was announced, and in walked Salomon with the (later) famous words, 'I am Salomon of London and have come to fetch you. Tomorrow we will arrange an *accord*.'[2] Haydn also had an understanding (as we shall shortly see) to go to Naples at the invitation of Ferdinand IV – the composer thought he might have become a celebrated opera composer if he had gone to Italy. But Salomon was a persuasive gentleman and Haydn obviously liked him from the first. Haydn said to Salomon, according to Dies (81), 'If my Prince approves of the idea, I will follow you to London.' Prince Anton was a generous patron and willingly gave his permission. Haydn had always written to Salomon in previous years, when the latter had pressed him to come to England, that he could not break his word to Prince Nicolaus (we have seen that this 'word' was given after the Prince had twice rebuilt Haydn's little house in Eisenstadt). Now, however, there was no reason not to go, but difficulties there certainly were. We read in a contemporary source:

Never would Salomon have been able to lure Herr Hayden [*sic*], that great and inimitable genius, away from the quiet atmosphere of his homely and modest existence; and persuaded him to seek – under whatever pretext – permission from

---

1 Pohl II, 242.

2 This version is from *Orpheus, Musikalisches Taschenbuch*, 1841; the play on words with 'accord' and the whole dramatic scene were often related later in life by their recipient. In Dies (80) the similar words, 'Ich bin Salomon aus London und komme, Sie abzuholen; morgen werden wir einen Akkord schließen.' In Griesinger (21f.), we read that Gallini had gone to Italy to recruit singers for the opera, while Salomon, who was ending his trip to Germany for that purpose [and also to engage musicians for his concerts, presumably] 'hastened to Vienna. Towards evening someone knocked at Haydn's door; Salomon walked in, and his first words were, 'Make yourself ready to travel. In a fortnight we shall go together to London.' Haydn began by resisting the proposal. He pointed out his ignorance of the English language and his inexperience in travelling.' All this was brushed aside. 'It was agreed that Haydn should receive 3,000 gulden for an opera and 100 gulden for each piece he conducted in twenty concerts. Haydn was thus covered up to 5,000 gulden, and this sum was to be deposited in the Viennese bank of Fries & Co. by Gallini [the entrepeneur of the Opera] as soon as Haydn should set foot on English soil. This foresight was not superfluous, for without it Haydn ... would not have been paid for his *Orfeo ed Euridice*, because its performance was not permitted in the theatre ...'.

his then Prince, Anton Esterhazy, for leave of absence, were it not for your happy letter to General Jerningham (the British Ambassador), which to the general astonishment of this city, worked miracles. Everyone who knew the philosophical character of this first of virtuosi were astonished at this unexpected decision. What thanks, on the part our musical world, are your due, my dear friend, for your recent visit to Vienna and for this wonderful, fortunate letter.
[*Musikalische Korrespondenz der teutschen Filharmonischen Gesellschaft* 1791, No. 7. Pohl II, 246, thinks that John Bland must have written the letter.]

On 8 December, Salomon had signed the 'accord' with Haydn and was able to write to England and insert a notice to that effect in the *Morning Chronicle*. Meanwhile it appears that plans were afoot to ask both Mozart and Haydn to compose music for the forthcoming coronation ceremonies in Prague; but Haydn (who was already in England when the invitation came) refused: 'Wo Mozart ist, kann sich Haydn nicht zeigen' ('Where Mozart is, Haydn cannot show himself'). The two men were constantly together. Abbé Stadler reports:

that Beethoven, although a great admirer of Mozart, was not himself sufficiently advanced to excite much of Mozart's attention, but that Haydn and Mozart were like Brothers. Mozart delighted in Haydn's writing and owned repeatedly that he was much indebted to him in forming his style. Stadler said that on his first arrival at Vienna and becoming acquainted with Haydn's work, Mozart naturally changed his manner of composing.

Haydn was not a great Pianoforte player (his best instrument the Violin) – but he delighted in hearing Mozart play the pianoforte. Haydn owned Mozart's superiority and said, 'he was a *God* in Music'. (Stadler exclaimed to me 'Mozart est *unique*; il etoit universel et savoit *tout*'). Mozart and Haydn frequently played together with Stadler in Mozart's Quintettos; particularly mentioned the 5th in D major, singing the Bass part,

the one in C major and still more that in G minor.

Although Mozart was indebted to Haydn yet he added so much of his own genius in the formation of his style – that the *mélange* became his own. Stadler once asked him how he contrived to write everything he wished in so exquisite and perfect a manner – and Mozart simply answered – 'Je ne peux pas écrire *autrement*' – The Abbé added that at 8 years Mozart was already well versed in all the rules of Musical Grammar and that his Genius was such as to render it easy for him to excel in all styles just as he pleased.

The work quoted is, of course, Mozart's great String Quintet, K.593, composed in December: the performances to which Stadler refers must have been the first. It is thought Mozart wrote it (like the others of its genre during this period) for the now rich Johann Tost. Among its many beauties – that incredible place in the slow movement (bars 53ff.), when Mozart's spirit seems to soar into the blazing light of the future – Haydn will not have failed to notice how Mozart brings back, towards the end of the first movement, the material of the Larghetto introduction with which the work ended. (Using material from the introduction later in the work is one of the many innovations of the noble Symphony in C minor by J. M. Kraus; there, the introduction returns in the *slow* movement; a similar use of the slow introduction later in the movement may be noted in Kraus's characteristic Overture to *Olympie* [*Olympia*, Stockholm 1792].) Of course, Haydn's attentive mind put this innovation to his own spectacular use in the first movement of the 'Drum Roll' Symphony No. 103 (London, 1795).[1]

A last letter to Artaria, before the final stages of the journey's preparations began, may be quoted at this point:

[To Artaria & Co., Vienna. *German*]
I the undersigned promise and swear to deliver the 6 new *Variazioni*[2] for the pianoforte to Herr Artaria one week from today.
Vienna, 22nd November 1790.

> Joseph Haydn
> *Capellmeister.*

[CCLN, 110]

Haydn went to pay his respects to the King of Naples and to deliver the Notturni. Griesinger relates:

Shortly before his departure, Haydn brought to King Ferdinand of Naples, who was in Vienna at that time, several works he had commissioned. 'The day after tomorrow we will perform them', said the King. 'I am eternally sorry,' answered Haydn, 'that I cannot be present, for the day after tomorrow I leave for England'. 'What? and you promised me to come to Naples!' The King left the room rather indignantly and did not return for one hour. Haydn had to promise him again to go to Naples when he returned from England. He received a letter of introduction to Prince Castelcicala, the King's envoy in London, and the King sent after him [Haydn] a valuable snuffbox.   [Griesinger 23]

Haydn was given letters to take to England, and he thought it provident to secure some letters of introduction himself. Those which (as far as they have survived) Haydn took with him have been quoted in *Haydn in England 1791–1795*, (pp. 27f., 35). We may now proceed to one that Haydn arranged to be sent on his behalf.

One of the men in England to whom Haydn wanted a formal letter of introduction was the Austrian Ambassador to the Court of St James, Johann Philipp Count Stadion. Haydn discovered that Baron van Swieten was in correspondence with the Count and persuaded the Baron to write the following letter:

Haydn[3] n'a certainement pas besoin de vous être recommandé par moi, Monsieur le Comte. Les rares talens vous sont connus, et doivent lui amirer la meilleure reception de votre part. Cependant comme il desire de[4] vous être presenté par moi, je saisis avec compressement l'occasion de me rappeler à votre prevenir. J'aurois bien mieux aimé vous l'amener moi même pour jouir de toutes les belles choses en musique qu'on vous prépare pour cet hyver, et partout de la

---

1 Salomon's announcement: *Haydn in England 1791–1795*, p. 30. Prague invitation: Griesinger, 56. Stadler to Vincent Novello in *A Mozart Pilgrimage* (travel diaries of Vincent Novello and his wife Mary, 1829), pp. 170ff. For a brilliant essay on K.593, see Charles Rosen, *The Classical Style*, pp. 283ff. 'Drum Roll' Symphony: see *H. in E.*, pp. 594ff.
2 Artaria, hearing of Haydn's imminent journey to London, must have feared that he would not find the time to finish the *Variazioni*, for which Artaria had presumably contracted and paid. The above receipt exists in two autograph copies, with minor differences (the second one has an abbreviated date and no 'Capellmeister'). The Variations (Hoboken XVII:5) appeared early in 1791.
3 Perhaps at first 'Hayden'.
4 'de' inserted with a caret.

grande commémoration annuelle[1] de Handel mon idole, mais je dois encore rester enchainé à ma galere, et qui primer[2] rames sans cesse contre vents et marée. J'ay l'honneur d'etre avec une considération tres distinguée Monsieur le Comte

Votre tres humble et tres
obeissante Serviteur
Swieten

Vienna le 14 dec: 1790[3]

Griesinger (22) reports on the last meal that Salomon, Mozart and Haydn had together:

> Mozart said, at a merry meal with Salomon, to Haydn: 'You won't stand it for long and will soon return, for you aren't young any more.' 'But I am still vigorous and in good health,' answered Haydn....

It was at this meal that Salomon arranged for Mozart to come to England when Haydn returned (Pohl II, 250), and on similar terms as those for Haydn. From Dies we learn further, that

> Especially Mozart took pains to say, 'Papa!' (as he usually called him), 'You have had no education for the great world, and you speak too few languages'. – – 'Oh!' replied Haydn, 'my language is understood all over the world!' [The travellers fixed their departure] and left on December 15, 179[0] ... Mozart, that day, never left his friend Haydn. He dined with him, and at the moment of parting, he said, 'We are probably saying our last adieu in this life.' Tears welled in both their eyes. Haydn was deeply moved, for he applied Mozart's words to himself, and the possibility never occurred to him that the thread of Mozart's life could be cut by the inexorable Parcae [Fates] the very next year.
>
> [Dies, 81f., 83f.]

Haydn and Salomon went first to Munich, where Haydn met the composer Christian Cannabich (Griesinger, 23; Dies, 84). Next they went to Wallerstein Castle as guests of Prince Krafft Ernst von Oettingen-Wallerstein; there Haydn appears to have conducted (at least) Symphony No. 92, which he had sent the prince a few years earlier. (On examining the MS. parts of the Wallerstein source – it is now in Harburg Castle – we found Haydn's characteristic addition of *fz* on a violin part which was not, as far as can be determined, part of the original set Haydn sent.) There was no

---

1 'annuelle' inserted with a caret.

2 Unclear: 'priser'?

3 Haus-, Hof- und Staatsarchiv, Vienna, Dépôt Stadion Bündel 57, fol. 33. Swieten kept up a regular correspondence with Stadion. While Haydn was still in London, we read in Swieten's answer to a letter Stadion wrote him (lost) as follows: '18 April 1792 ... C'est une bien belle nouvelle que le retour de Haydn, que vous annoncez. Je n'oisois plus espérer de le revoir ici d'après l'exemple de tant d'artistes, qu'on n'a jamais pu engager à quitter Londres lorsqu'ils y avoient réussi. Je ne doutois pas que notre compatriote n'eut un succès bien marqué, mais je ne suis pas moins charmé d'apprendre, qu'on ait apprécés [d'une maniere distinguée] et senti sons talens vraiment rares; l'economie ne se trouve pas communément à coté du génie, et à cet egard notre bon Haydn, sans cependant donner dans aucun excès, a fait ses preuves depuis longtems, et toujours il y a en défaut de calcul dans son ménage.' [] = caret insertion. Bündel 57, fol. 112, 113. Later letters deal with a recipe for mock turtle soup, about procuring music for the I. R. library (Handel). Refers to the Arnold edition owned by Prince Lichnowsky (15 Jan. 1793, fol. 332, 333). The present owner of the 'Dépôt', Countess Gabriele Mensdorff-Pouilly, Fürstenfeld (Styria) kindly allowed us the freedom of this vitally important collection. See also the valuable book by Hellmuth Rössler, *Graf Johann Philipp Stadion*, 2 vols., Vienna-Munich 1966.

There was much more unofficial contact between London and Vienna (and vice versa) than is realized. In a letter from Vienna of 18 Jan. 1791 to Stadion, we read, 'Count Harsch Haye in the Staats Kanzley and the others want to know how things are going for Clement, a very young virtuoso on the violin, in London and if he is making his fortune there, I would be glad of your kind answer on this point.' About Clement, see *Haydn in England 1791–1795*, p. 85 and *passim*. In another letter from Vienna of 16 March 1791, we read, 'is the artist Hickel not yet in London? He will bring Your Well Born Self a letter from me.... haven't you heard any more of the violinist Clement? How is it going with Hayden [*sic*]?' Bündel 57 of the Archives.

time to tarry, however, and Haydn had to promise to come again for a longer stay.[1]
From Wallerstein, the route was to Bonn. Dies (84f.) reports:

> In Bonn, the capital, he was surprised in more ways than one. He arrived there
> on a Saturday and intended to rest during the following day.
> Salomon [a native of Bonn] took Haydn on Sunday to the court chapel to hear
> Mass. Hardly had they entered the church and found a good place, when the High
> Mass began. The first sounds announced a work of Haydn's. Our Haydn
> presumed this to be a flattering coincidence, but it was pleasant for him to hear his
> own work. Towards the end of Mass, someone approached and invited him to go
> into the oratory, where he was awaited. Haydn went and was no little astonished
> to see that the Elector Maximilian had summoned him, took him at once by the
> hand, and presented him to his musicians with the words, 'Now may I present to
> you the Haydn you admire so much.' The Elector gave them time to become
> acquainted and then, to show Haydn persuasive proof of his esteem, invited him to
> his own table. Haydn was no little embarrassed by this unexpected invitation, for
> he and Salomon had arranged to have a small *dîner* served in their rooms, and it
> was already too late to make a change. So Haydn had to make his excuses, which
> the Elector kindly accepted. Haydn then took his leave and returned to his
> quarters where he was surprised by unexpected evidence of the Elector's good
> will. His little *dîner* was transformed by the Elector's quiet order into a large one
> for twelve, and the ablest of the musicians were invited to it.

From Bonn the travellers proceeded to Calais, and from there, Haydn sent his first
letter of the trip to Maria Anna von Genzinger:

[To Maria Anna von Genzinger, Vienna. *German*]

Calais, 31st December 1790.

Nobly born,
Most highly respected Frau von Gennzinger!
    The recent bad weather and the continual downpour of rain were responsible
for my having just arrived (as I write this letter to you) at Calais this evening.
Tomorrow morning at 7 we cross the sea to London. I promised Your Grace to
write from Brussels, but I could not stay there more than an hour. I am well, thank
God! though I am somewhat thinner, owing to fatigue, irregular sleep, and eating
and drinking so many different things. In a few days I shall describe my journey in
more detail to Your Grace, but I must beg you to excuse me today. I hope to God

---

1 The Prince of Oettingen-Wallerstein wrote to his agent Müller in an undated letter (Archives, Wallerstein Castle): '...That your
elder brother received the present for Haidn [*sic*], he told me himself. But I am curious to know if Haydn was satisfied with it, and
whether he has decided to send me some new symphonies together with the scores. He was here recently, but only passed through in
haste, but he wants to stay longer on his return trip from England; altogether I would ask you, my dear Court Agent, that you, with
your usual punctiliousness, send me everything by Haidn which appears in print or in copies, especially those Parthien [= Symphonies]
which Herr von Kees owns. And that I would like a catalogue, with a list of prices, first of all Haidn operas, oratorios, cantatas, arias and
church music...'. Ludwig Schiedermair, 'Die Blütezeit der Oetting-Wallerstein'schen Hofkapelle', in *Recueil de la Société Internationale
de Musique*, 9ième Année, Livr. 1 (Oct.–Dec. 1907, p. 106).

that Your Grace, your husband and the whole family are well. I am, most respectfully,

Your Grace's
most obedient servant,
Jos: Haydn.

[Address:]   Madame
Madame Noble de Gennzinger
née Noble de Kayser
à
Vienne.

[CCLN, 110f.]

On New Year's Day, 1791, Haydn set forth across the Channel for England and the greatest adventure of his life.

[Hirschbach im Waldviertel, 31 August 1977]

Appendix

Framery's 'Notice sur Joseph Haydn',
Paris 1810

INTRODUCTION

As it happens, Framery's *Notice* hardly concerns us after Haydn left Eszterháza in 1790, and the extracts we have taken from it are therefore divided between those given in *Haydn: the Early Years 1732–1765* and those given here. The reason for Framery's concentration on the years up to 1791 is surely that his principal source of information for these anecdotes was Ignaz Pleyel, who (as we have seen) was Haydn's pupil from 1772 to 1777 or thereabouts, and whose name figures in some of the stories reprinted below. On the face of it, many of the stories seem absurd and not worth perpetuating, e.g. the one in which (after the fire of 1776 at Eisenstadt) Haydn wrings his hands over the loss of *Armida*, the only source of which perished in the flames. Pleyel has secretly copied it, however, and is able to save the day. *Armida* was composed in 1784, and the fire of 1776 (or the one at Eszterháza in 1779) cannot have touched it; but if, as we have proposed, one substitutes *La vera costanza* (1778?) for *Armida*, the story begins to take shape. It is the same with others: there are too many points that ring true, such as the description of 'un vieillard sourd et infirme qui jouait du basson', who turns out – from documentation listed *supra* (p. 72) – to have been Johann Hinterberger. This description is part of the incredible story of the 'Farewell' Symphony, here related in a new and interesting way. In the main text, we have followed the official accounts of Dies, Griesinger and Neukomm; but suppose it really happened as Pleyel related to Framery? Perhaps Haydn, still a princely employee when relating his life to Dies and Griesinger, would have 'softened' the story a little. The vignette of a sulky Prince Nicolaus 'at the back of his box', refusing to applaud a new Haydn symphony, is in any case worth retaining, if only for the illuminating remark that Haydn's new symphonies were usually first played in the entre'actes of plays, and a 'runner' was sent up to the princely box to inform His Highness of the coming event. There are similarly instructive details in all these stories, not least the entertaining and rather touching story of Sarti coming to Eszterháza (which Framery will have had, not from Pleyel, who had already left Eszterháza when the event took place in 1784, but from one of Sarti's many friends or pupils, such as Cherubini, who of course settled in Paris after having studied with Sarti). Even the (on the face of it) wildly improbable story of Haydn and Joseph II, with Gassmann as the intriguing villain, may have had some basis in fact. We believe this biography has shown sufficiently clearly that many similar anecdotes may clothe, however exotically, a kernel of truth and should not be dismissed out of hand. In this light we present these extracts from Framery, with (at the end, p. 763) notes which we have tried to keep as brief as possible.

[p. 14] ...

C'est chez le prince Nicolas d'Esthérazy [*sic*] qu'Haydn a composé la plupart de ses plus beaux ouvrages; c'est pour lui qu'il a fait presque toutes ses symphonies, genre dans lequel, avant ni depuis, aucun autre ne l'a égalé; supérieur à tous dans la musique instrumentale, c'est lui qui le premier imagina, pour les petits concerts particuliers du prince, ces luttes si piquantes où quatre instrumens seuls s'efforcent tour à tour de déployer toute leur habileté; compositions que les Français nomment quatuor.[1] Ceux [p. 15] d'Haydn ont été fréquemment imités depuis, mais n'en sont pas moins restés

---

1 [Original footnote:] Les Allemands les nomment en leur langue *quartetten* et les Italiens, dans la leur, *quartetti*; mots qui au pluriel, dans les deux langues, signifient *morceaux à quâtre parties*: les Français, dont le langage musical, qui a tant besoin de réforme, est une bigarrure de latin, de grec, d'italien et de français, se servent du mot latin *quatuor*, qui signifie simplement *quatre*, et par conséquent ne rend pas l'idée qu'on prétend exprimer.

inimitables. C'est encore pour plaire à son protecteur qu'il a travaillé si souvent pour un instrument que celui-ci aimait de prédilection, qui n'est pas d'usage en France, et qu'on nomme *baryton*.

Les talens du maître, ses attentions, ses complaisances, bien senties par celui qui en était l'objet, les avait unis l'un à l'autre d'un attachement qui s'étendit au-delà de leur vie. Le prince d'ailleurs possédait au nombre de ses grandes qualités une extrême bonté; cependant, en sa qualité d'homme, il était sujet de temps à autre à des accès d'humeur noire qui le rendaient pendant plusieurs jours insupportable à toute sa maison; tant qu'ils duraient il ne recevait personne, aucun de ses officiers n'osait en approcher: une seule chose pouvait le tirer de cet état; c'était une nouvelle symphonie de son maître de chapelle, qui produisait sur ses organes le même effet que la harpe de David sur ceux de Saül.

Un jour qu'un accès de cette nature, plus violent qu'à l'ordinaire, le tourmentait aussi depuis plus longtemps, chacun se réunit auprès du maître pour l'engager à employer le moyen, dont l'efficacité était bien connue : Haydn compose une symphonie en consé- [p. 16]quence, et met tous ses soins à ce qu'elle produise le plus grand effet. Au premier jour du spectacle, dans l'entr'acte, après que le maître, selon l'usage, eut envoyé dire au prince qu'il allait lui faire entendre une symphonie nouvelle, l'orchestre se mit en devoir de l'exécuter. Le premier morceau, d'un mouvement vif, commence et se termine avec beaucoup d'éclat: Haydn s'attend à recevoir du prince les applaudissemens qu'il a coutume de lui prodiguer ... Il n'entend rien. Pour les provoquer il se tourne vers la loge du prince, dont les regards froids et distraits annoncent l'indifférence la plus parfaite: le maître en est piqué, mais dissimule; il attend son auditeur à l'Andante: on sait que tous ceux de ce compositeur sont délicieux; celui-là est un des plus charmans ... Pas un coup de main; le prince reste muet et immobile; Haydn a peine à dévorer son dépit. Le Menuet, si ingénieusement varié, aura-t-il un meilleur sort? L'infortuné n'ose plus l'espérer; cependant il jette encore un regard furtif vers le prince, qui, toujours silencieux, loin de paraître donner aucune attention à ce qu'on exécute pour lui, affecte de se retirer au fond de sa loge. A ce moment la fureur du maître éclate; dans sa rage il veut briser son violon, déchirer partition et parties: on s'y oppose; mais le final de la [p. 17] symphonie s'exécute sans qu'il y prenne la moindre part.[1]

De toute la nuit suivante il ne put trouver un instant de sommeil; il se lève de très-bonne heure, dresse une pétition, et se présente chez le prince aussitôt qu'il apprend qu'il y est jour. 'Etes-vous fou? lui dit un chambellan; vous savez que quand il est de cette humeur il ne reçoit personne, et il vous recevrait moins que tout autre, car, je ne sais pourquoi, il est furieux contre vous. – C'est précisément à cause de cela, dit le maître, que je désire lui être annoncé.' Un valet de chambre s'acquitte de cette commission. 'Que me veut-il? dit le prince: je n'ai que faire à lui; s'il a quelque

chose à me faire savoir qu'il me l'écrive.' Le valet de chambre vient rendre cette réponse. 'Je n'ai point à lui écrire, dit Haydn; il faut absolument que je lui parle. – Hé bien, qu'il entre donc, puisqu'il le veut; mais il verra comment je le recevrai.' La colère éclatait dans ses yeux, enflammait toute sa figure quand Haydn fut introduit; celui-ci, calme, déterminé, entend avec le plus grand sang-froid les reproches mêlés d'injures dont on l'accable; il n'y répond qu'en présentant, de l'air le plus respectueux, l'écrit par lequel il ne *demande pas*, mais il *donne* sa démission. Le prince, qui ne s'attendait pas à cet [p. 18] acte de vigueur, est frappé d'étonnement; mais il le dissimule; autant par dépit que par un reste d'accès, il signe sur-le-champ la pétition, et la démission est acceptée.

Aussitôt que le maître fut rentré il chargea M. Pleyel,[2] son élève, de faire assembler l'orchestre; il raconte mot à mot à ceux qui le composaient ce qui vient de se passer: sa conduite est généralement approuvée; on s'emporte contre ce seigneur, qu'on accuse de traiter durement ses vassaux, et d'ignorer comment on doit en agir avec des artistes; les têtes se montent, s'échauffent; tous, à la réserve de deux, veulent prendre à l'instant le même parti que leur chef, qui s'efforce en vain de les calmer par ses observations; on rédige une adresse par laquelle l'orchestre en corps donne sa démission, et, sans désemparer, elle est signée par tous les instrumentistes, excepté par un vieillard sourd et infirme qui jouait du basson,[3] et par un autre des plus médiocres parmi les seconds violons de l'orchestre.[4] Sur-le-champ l'adresse fut envoyée au prince, qui, n'étant pas encore guéri de son attaque, et irrité de ce qu'il regardait comme un complot, accepta sans hésiter la démission générale, même en y comprenant les deux malheureux par qui la demande n'avait pas été signée. L'orchestre, dans son engagement avec le prince, ne pouvait [p. 19] quitter son service ni en être renvoyé qu'après l'expiration d'une année à compter du jour de la notification; mais celui-ci leur fit dire qu'ils étaient libres de s'en aller quand ils voudraient, et que l'année entière leur serait payée comme s'ils avaient achevé leur service: il fut convenu qu'ils ne resteraient plus que huit jours.

Ce peu de temps suffit pour apporter beaucoup de calme dans les esprits de part et d'autre; si d'un côté la crise, qui avait momentanément altéré le caractère naturel du prince, s'était apaisée par le seul effet de sa durée, de l'autre Haydn se repentait d'avoir obéi trop inconsidérément à des mouvemens d'amour-propre, de n'avoir pas eu assez d'égard à l'état de maladie dans lequel son prince se trouvait alors; il réfléchit d'ailleurs que malgré sa réputation, dont il ne connaissait pas toute l'étendue, il lui serait difficile de trouver une maison souveraine où il fût aussi chéri, aussi considéré qu'il l'était à Esthérazy: de leur côté les artistes de l'orchestre ne paraissaient plus aussi certains que le seul crédit de leur chef pût leur procurer à tous des places aussi avantageuses que celles qu'ils allaient quitter; ils ne pensaient plus au prince que pour le regretter et faire son éloge; ce paiement même d'une année qu'ils n'avaient pas remplie, attribué d'abord à l'effet [p. 20] du dépit, était alors regardé par eux comme un acte de générosité qui le leur rendait plus cher. Dans ces circonstances Haydn, qui s'en occupait, s'avisa d'un expédient assez bizarre, qui a laissé des traces dans ses œuvres, et qui mérite d'être raconté.

Le jour fixé pour le départ il va trouver le prince, et lui dit qu'avant de le quitter son orchestre et lui désiraient lui donner une dernière marque de leur reconnaissance pour toutes ses bontés passées, en exécutant devant lui une symphonie nouvelle qu'il avait composée exprès pour cette circonstance: le prince y consent avec joie, et même avec attendrissement. La salle est éclairée comme en un jour de concert; chacun prend sa place accoutumée, et la symphonie[5] commence.

Le premier morceau, d'un style très-brillant, d'un mouvement vif et gai, semblable pour la forme au début de la plupart des symphonies, mais moins étendu, fait entendre tous les instrumens marchant ensemble; suit un récit de violon exécuté par Haydn seul, qui conduisait l'orchestre, et après lequel il se lève, renferme tranquillement son violon dans l'étui, le met sur son épaule, et s'en va. Le prince, étonné, s'inquiète; il craint qu'il ne soit arrivé au maître quelque chose de fâcheux; il envoie avec beaucoup d'empressement savoir la cause d'un [p. 21] départ si extraordinaire au milieu d'une symphonie: Haydn charge le messager de remercier le prince de cette preuve d'intérêt, de le prier de ne point s'alarmer, et d'entendre le reste de l'exécution. Elle continue.

Le chef des seconds violons joue un récit seul, comme l'avait fait le premier, serre ensuite son instrument, se lève et s'en va, suivi de toute sa bande; après lui et successivement le premier des hautbois, des flûtes, des clarinettes, des cors, des bassons, chacun après son récit, se retire de la même manière, dont le prince comprit fort bien l'intention, jusqu'à ce qu'enfin il ne reste plus dans l'orchestre que les deux pauvres hères qui n'avaient pas signé l'adresse, et qui terminent la symphonie par un lamentable duo.

Le souverain d'Esthérazy, dont la bonté naturelle avait vaincu la fierté, le cœur gonflé, se précipite dans la salle où s'était rassemblé l'orchestre, et, les yeux pleins de larmes: 'Mes amis, leur crie-t-il, mes vieux amis! est-ce ainsi que vous m'abandonnez! Et pourquoi m'abandonnez-vous? Comme votre prince, vous sentez que je ne puis vous demander grâce; je sens également qu'en votre noble qualité d'artistes vous ne pouvez pas non plus me la demander: n'y aurait-il pas moyen de tout concilier, et de faire comme s'il ne s'était rien passé de part [p. 22] et d'autre?' La réponse du maître et de tout son monde fut de tomber aux genoux du prince, qui le reçut dans ses bras, et tout fut à jamais oublié.

Les fonctions de maître de chapelle, que Haydn reprit de ce moment, ne se bornent pas à composer de la musique; il est encore chargé de diriger celle de tout autre auteur dont l'exécution lui est demandée, soit pour le théâtre, soit pour les concerts, et à former et conduire des compagnies italiennes d'Opéras bouffons et sérieux. Haydn

avait fait souvent représenter par ces dernières le *Giulio Sabino* de Sarti, l'un des maîtres dont il faisait le plus de cas, sans doute parce que le style énergique et noble de ce compositeur avait le plus d'analogie avec la nature de son talent; et cet ouvrage, l'un des meilleurs et des plus vigoureux de Sarti, était aussi l'un de ceux auxquels Haydn donnait la préférence.

Appelé un jour dans une cour du nord pour écrire des opéras, Sarti se trouva passer assez près d'Esthérazy pour se détourner de route, curieux de voir un homme que ses nombreux ouvrages, et particulièrement ses symphonies, avaient rendu célèbre dans toute l'Europe; il désirait lui demander et lui offrir une mutuelle amitié. Il arrive sur la fin du jour au palais du prince; c'est à [p. 23] l'illustre Haydn qu'il désire parler. 'Pour le moment, lui dit-on, cela est impossible; le maître conduit l'opéra qui va commencer, car le prince vient d'entrer dans sa loge. – Ne pourrais-je au moins trouver place dans un coin de la salle? – Oh, sans difficulté; nous avons ordre d'y placer avec distinction tous les étrangers. – Quel est l'opéra que l'on chante? – C'est l'*Armida*, celui des ouvrages du maître qu'il affectionne le plus.' Ce fut un nouvel aiguillon pour Sarti, qui ne connaissait d'Haydn aucun ouvrage dramatique; il désira d'être placé le plus près possible de l'orchestre, et il l'obtint. Pendant tout le premier acte, la beauté des morceaux qui se succédaient l'étonna, le ravit, le mit dans l'enchantement; il les applaudit avec transport: mais vers la fin du second il ne se possède plus; dans une sorte de délire il se lève, franchit les banquettes qui le séparaient de l'orchestre, sans la permission de ceux qui les occupaient, saute au cou du maître surpris... 'C'est Sarti qui t'embrasse, lui crie-t-il, Sarti qui voulait voir le grand Haydn, admirer ses beaux ouvrages, mais qui n'espérait pas en admirer un aussi beau!' Le prince, qui du fond de sa loge voit ce mouvement extraordinaire et désordonné, mais qui n'a pu rien entendre, s'effraie, pousse un cri. 'Qu'est-ce donc? [p. 24] qu'y a-t-il, et qu'est-il arrivé? – C'est *Giulio Sabino*, répond à haute voix Haydn, saisi du même enthousiasme, c'est Giulio Sabino, c'est l'auteur de cette superbe musique, c'est Sarti qui vient voir son bon ami Joseph!' Et ces deux grands hommes, ces deux amis, qui se voyaient pour la première fois, se jurèrent en s'embrassant une amitié comparable à l'estime qu'ils avaient l'un pour l'autre.[6]

Ce mouvement exalté de Sarti pour l'opéra d'Armide devait être sincère, car c'est véritablement le plus beau des ouvrages dramatiques d'Haydn; cependant, loin de s'en faire un titre de gloire aux yeux des nations, et d'en permettre la publication comme il permettait celle de toutes ses autres œuvres, son Armide était pour lui comme un trésor dont il se réservait la jouissance à lui seul: cette sorte d'avarice fut sur le point d'être cruellement punie.

Il n'avait qu'un seul manuscrit de cette partition; toutes les fois qu'il faisait exécuter l'ouvrage il le remettait au copiste, qui en distribuait les parties, et qui lui rendait le tout le lendemain matin. Un jour M. Pleyel, le plus chéri de ses élèves, désirant admirer de plus près cet ouvrage, et en étudier les beautés de détail, le pria de lui permettre d'en tirer une copie pour son usage particulier: Haydn le refusa; les plus vives instances [p. 25] furent inutiles; il ne consentit pas même à ce que son élève et son ami pût en prendre lecture et l'examinât sous ses yeux. Après avoir laissé passer assez de temps pour que sa demande fût oubliée, M. Pleyel proposa au copiste une somme de vingt-cinq ducats, à la condition de lui faire une copie de cette partition, ce qui lui serait facile dans les heures pendant lesquelles elle restait entre ses mains. Cet homme, qui connaissait assez la loyauté de M. Pleyel pour être sûr qu'il n'abuserait pas de sa confiance, ébranlé d'ailleurs par l'appât de la somme, se laissa séduire, et comme on représentait souvent cet ouvrage, la copie en fut faite et livrée avant la fin de la saison.

Dans un des intervalles où les spectacles étaient suspendus à la cour du prince pour faire place à d'autres amusemens, Haydn, dont la présence lui était alors moins nécessaire, fut chargé par lui d'une mission qui l'obligea de faire un voyage de plusieurs semaines à quelque distance d'Esthérazy. Pendant ce temps, par l'imprudence d'un domestique, le feu prit à une maison de la ville d'Eisenstadt, principale résidence de la cour, dans le quartier de celle qu'habitait Haydn, et qui lui appartenait. On sait quels ravages font les incendies dans ces contrées où les maisons sont presque toutes en bois, et les secours [p. 26] assez mal organisés; quoique celle où le feu avait commencé ne fût pas contiguë à celle de notre maître de chapelle, la flamme ne tarda pas à l'atteindre, et, comme elle était alors inhabitée, la maison, les meubles, les hardes, le linge, les bijoux, en un mot tout ce que possédait le maître, tout ce que son économie avait pu acquérir depuis qu'il jouissait de sa place, fut en peu d'heures dévoré par le feu.[7]

Lorsque le prince apprit à Esthérazy le malheur arrivé à sa ville d'Eisenstadt, son premier soin fut de s'informer de la maison d'Haydn; il sut qu'elle n'était plus qu'un monceau de cendres. Sur-le-champ il donne l'ordre qu'on en bâtisse une autre sur le même terrain, et enjoint à tout son monde de cacher autant que possible à son cher Haydn ce fâcheux événement; puis il mande M. Pleyel et lui dit:

'Personne ne connaissait mieux que vous la forme extérieure et la distribution intérieure de la maison du maître, dont vous êtes le digne élève; je vous charge d'aller à Eisenstadt présider à la construction de celle qui va la remplacer: apportez tous vos soins à ce qu'il ne s'y trouve pas la plus légère différence. Mais ce n'est pas assez; vous devez avoir présens à la mémoire tous ses meubles, qui n'existent plus; faites en faire d'autres [p. 27] absolument semblables, et n'y épargnez rien; remplacez de même son linge de table, de corps, celui de sa femme, tous les ustensiles de son ménage, en nombre égal autant que possible, mais plutôt plus que moins: les fonds ne vous manqueront pas. Il est bien juste que je fasse quelque chose pour l'homme d'un

mérite si rare qui se consacre tout entier à mes plaisirs!'

M. Pleyel exécuta de point en point les ordres du prince avec tout le zèle de la reconnaissance et de l'amitié. La mission d'Haydn fut prolongée de quelques jours pour donner aux ouvriers le temps de tout terminer; enfin il arrive. Il avait appris en route l'événement d'Eisenstadt, et il en était désolé. 'Perdre en un jour, disait-il, le fruit de plusieurs années d'économie et de privations! Où trouverai-je de quoi faire bâtir une autre maison, acheter d'autres meubles, me remonter en linge, en hardes? Et quand je pourrais tout réparer, ce ne serait pas les mêmes choses que j'ai perdues; j'étais attaché à leurs formes; je les avais fait faire selon mon goût. Je vais donc pendant plusieurs années manquer de tout ce dont je jouissais avec délices?' Il va demander au prince la permission de partir de suite pour Eisenstadt, afin de voir par lui-même l'effet de son désastre: les travaux n'étant pas [p. 28] encore achevés, cette permission lui est refusée sans lui en dire aucune raison. Il s'en indigne; il accuse son patron de caprice, de tyrannie, de cruauté; il se propose de s'échapper furtivement: cependant la semaine suivante il reçoit cette permission si désirée; il part avec son élève Pleyel.

En arrivant à la ville, dans le quartier où fut sa maison, il voit une foule d'ouvriers occupés à reconstruire celles que l'incendie avait détruites; puis il en aperçoit une isolée de droite et de gauche, debout au milieu des décombres, et sans aucun dommage...

'Mais, Pleyel, voilà ma maison! On prétendait qu'elle avait été brûlée de fond en comble... C'est bien elle; je reconnais mes fenêtres, le mur de mon petit jardin; c'est bien là ma porte qu'on a fraîchement repeinte! (Et il s'en approche avec une violente palpitation de cœur.) J'en ai justement la clef, que j'avais prise à tout hasard. (Il l'essaie; elle ne tourne pas.) – C'est que vous la tenez mal, mon maître; vous tremblez; donnez la moi. (Et il y substitue adroitement la clef de la serrure nouvelle; il ouvre; ils entrent.) – Ce sont bien là tous mes meubles, qu'on a même entretenus avec soin pendant mon absence, car ils me paraissent plus frais que quand je les ai quittés. (Il court à ses armoires.) Voilà bien mon linge; j'en trouve [p. 29] le compte; plus que le compte!... Mais, Pleyel, tout ce linge est neuf! Qu'est-ce donc que cela veut dire?'

L'élève n'y peut tenir plus longtemps, et, en embrassant son maître, il lui avoue que sa maison a été rebâtie aux frais du prince; que tout ce qu'elle contient est neuf et le résultat de ses bienfaits. Dans le transport de sa joie le maître à son tour serre dans ses bras son élève, et sa figure est inondée de larmes. Après qu'il eut joui rapidement de sa nouvelle propriété dans toute son étendue, il se hâte de reprendre le chemin d'Esthérazy, pour épancher aux genoux de son souverain l'effusion de reconnaissance dont son cœur était oppressé. Si jusque là il avait eu pour lui un attachement sincère et tendre, on juge combien ce sentiment fut augmenté par une générosité si grande, exercée aussi délicatement.

Après s'être ainsi soulagé, Haydn retomba dans une tristesse profonde qui ne faisait qu'augmenter chaque jour, et qui commencait même à compromettre sa santé. M. Pleyel s'en aperçut. 'Maître, lui dit-il, qu'est-ce donc qui vous tourmente? Si la perte de votre maison et de vos effets n'avait pas été si noblement, si promptement réparée, je concevrais le chagrin dont vous semblez affecté; mais je vous vois plus riche que jamais, puisqu'une maison toute neuve, et un mobilier [p. 30] qui n'a pas encore servi remplacent avantageusement ceux que le temps avait altérés: de quoi pouvez-vous donc vous plaindre? – Mon ami, répond le maître, tout ce que je possédais, tout ce que l'incendie a détruit a pu m'être rendu par la bonté du prince, même dans un meilleur état qu'auparavant; mais ni lui, ni aucune puissance humaine ne pourrait me faire retrouver l'objet que je chérissais le plus, et dont la perte m'est plus sensible que n'aurait pu l'être celle de tout le reste: cet objet irréparable, et dont je déplore la privation, (t'avouerai-je ma faiblesse, cher ami!) c'est mon Armide,[8] dont la partition complète, la seule qui existait au monde, était enfermée dans mon cabinet qui a été brûlé.'

A ce nom d'Armide un mouvement de joie si vif éclata sur le visage de l'élève, que le maître en fut offensé. 'Qu'est-ce donc, M. Pleyel! lui dit-il; est-ce ainsi que vous partagez ma peine? Vous en paraissez tout joyeux. – Je le suis infiniment, mon maître, puisque je puis rendre un moment de bonheur à celui dont je tiens tout le mien. Vous rappelez-vous le jour où vous me priai de me laisser prendre une copie de ce bel ouvrage? Vous me le refusâtes; mais je l'ai eue par adresse: au moyen de quelques ducats j'ai séduit votre copiste, qui m'en [p. 31] a fait une autre sans votre aveu; je l'ai chez moi; je prends souvent un grand plaisir à la lire; mais j'en ai plus encore à vous l'offrir. Me pardonnez-vous cette supercherie? – Si je te la pardonne! Elle me rend la vie et la tranquillité.' En effet, dès qu'il revit cette partition tant aimée, sa gaîté, sa santé revinrent, et M. Pleyel, son élève, lui devint plus cher que jamais.

Leur mutuel attachement se manifesta dans toutes les circonstances, non seulement pendant le long espace de temps qu'ils vécurent ensemble, mais même après que le besoin de prendre un état et de voler de ses propres ailes eut obligé l'élève à s'éloigner de son maître chéri.

Voulant mettre à profit les excellentes leçons qu'il en avait reçues, il s'attacha particulièrement à composer des sonates de clavecin, dont le mérite est bien connu. Il y avait déjà quelque temps qu'ils étaient séparés lorsque l'élève envoya au maître, comme prémices de son talent, deux de ces sonates, composées à Strasbourg, qu'il habitait alors, et où elles avaient eu beaucoup de succès.

Ce cadeau, qui n'était que l'hommage de la reconnaissance, eut un effet qui aurait pu brouiller ensemble deux hommes moins faits pour s'estimer et pour s'aimer. Quelque temps après qu'Haydn

l'eut reçu un marchand de [p. 32] musique de Londres, dont le nom, je crois, est Forster, lui demanda par écrit *trois sonates nouvelles de sa composition*, en lui déterminant le prix qu'il lui en voulait donner, et à la condition de les lui faire passer tout de suite: le maître, alors occupé d'un grand ouvrage, ne voulut pas l'interrompre pour cette bagatelle; mais, désirant ne pas renoncer non plus au prix avantageux qui lui était offert, il envoya au marchand, avec *une* sonate qu'il venait de composer, les *deux* dont son élève l'avait gratifié, qu'il ne se fit pas scrupule de donner comme de lui, persuadé que M. Pleyel n'en ferait jamais d'autre usage.[9]

A peu près dans le même temps un des associés de la maison Longmann et Broderip, autres marchands de musique de Londres, passant à Strasbourg, y entendit plusieurs ouvrages de la composition de M. Pleyel, dont la réputation commençait à s'étendre, et notamment les deux sonates qu'il avait faites pour Haydn; il en parut charmé, fit l'acquisition de quelques-unes de ses productions, et désira faire également celle des deux sonates.

'Non, dit cet auteur, je les ai composées pour mon maître, et les remerciemens qu'il m'en a faits sont le seul prix que j'en veuille retirer. – Permettez au moins, dit Longmann, que, pour votre [p. 33] gloire, elles soient publiées sous votre nom.'

Il insista si fort, que M. Pleyel y consentit, bien loin de se douter qu'Haydn en avait disposé pour son propre compte.

L'œuvre d'Haydn et celui de Pleyel parurent à Londres à peu près dans le même temps; mais le premier acquéreur, étonné de ce que la maison Longmann avait osé publier sous le nom de Pleyel deux sonates qu'il tenait d'Haydn même, et qui, dans son opinion, ne pouvaient être que de lui, intenta un procès à ces négocians, qui de leur côté n'étaient pas moins surpris que l'on donnât sous le nom d'Haydn deux sonates faites par M. Pleyel, à Strasbourg, à la connaissance de toute la ville: ils répondirent donc à l'assignation par une assignation semblable. On sait avec quelle sévérité s'exécutent en Angleterre les lois sur les contrefaçons, les plagiats, et autres supercheries que se permettent quelquefois les marchands de musique ou de livres; tout ce qu'il y avait d'amateurs à Londres s'intéressait à cette affaire, et ne savait quel jugement en porter.

Sur ces entrefaites, et pendant que le procès s'instruisait, notre maître de chapelle, ayant obtenu un congé de son prince, vint à Londres, où le vœu de ces mêmes amateurs l'appelait depuis longtemps; en arrivant il fut informé de cette contestation dont il était [p. 34] l'objet, et, se rappelant qu'en effet les deux sonates en question étaient de son élève, il ne laissait pas que d'être embarrassé. Peu de temps après, par un hasard assez singulier, M. Pleyel eut la curiosité de voir la ville de Londres, sans savoir que son ancien maître y fût aussi; dès qu'il l'apprit il s'empressa d'aller lui faire visite. L'affaire s'éclaircit entr'eux; mais, ne voulant pas se nuire l'un à l'autre, ils ne savaient ce qu'ils devaient répondre aux juges devant lesquels les intéressés, profitant de leur réunion dans cette ville, les avaient fait mander: ils ne trouvèrent rien de mieux à dire que la simple vérité, qui en effet, dans presque toutes les occasions, nous sert mieux que le plus adroit mensonge. Les juges et les marchands eux-mêmes reconnurent la bonne foi des deux auteurs: au lieu d'un jugement, qui eût été ruineux, on fit un accommodement. Haydn en fut quitte pour les frais, qui à la vérité sont énormes à Londres, et il donna trois sonates nouvelles de sa composition à chacun des deux éditeurs.

Haydn resta maître de chapelle du prince Nicolas d'Esthérazy tant que celui-ci vécut; à sa mort il en conserva le titre et même les émolumens, qui, suivant l'usage du pays, consistaient partie en nature, partie en pension annuelle: telle fut la disposition testa- [p. 35] mentaire de ce prince, à la famille duquel il continua de rester attaché, mais sans être assujetti à aucune fonction.

On a lieu de s'étonner qu'un aussi grand homme, qui jouissait d'une si haute réputation, qui n'avait pas de rivaux pour la musique in-strumentale, n'ait pas été appelé comme maître de chapelle à la tête de la musique de l'empereur; la surprise redouble en songeant que cet empereur était Joseph II, le souverain le plus éclairé de son temps, le plus ami des arts, le plus vraiment philosophe. Il est vrai qu'Haydn, beaucoup plus occupé de son art que de sa fortune, satisfait de son sort, et trop modeste pour croire que son talent en méritât un autre plus brillant, était incapable de faire les démarches, les sollicitations nécessaires pour obtenir une place plus distinguée. Mais, dira-t-on, ce n'était pas non plus à lui à la demander; l'empereur devait le connaître assez pour se faire un titre de gloire d'être le premier à la lui offrir: c'est aussi ce que Joseph II se proposait de faire pendant un séjour qu'Haydn fit à Vienne; voici ce qui l'en empêcha.

Le maître de chapelle de l'empereur, qui l'est aussi de la cathédrale, était alors un nommé *Gasman*,[10] homme d'un talent au dessous du médiocre, mais aussi habile [p. 36] en intrigue qu'il l'était peu dans son art, d'un caractère jaloux, bas courtisan, souple, adroit, et d'autant plus dangereux qu'il cachait tous ces vices sous l'apparence de la bonhommie et de la simplicité; c'est à lui que l'empereur confia le projet de lui adjoindre Haydn comme maître de chapelle. Gasman, qui n'aurait eu rien tant à craindre qu'une pareille association, se garda d'en rien témoigner; il répondit avec l'air de la franchise:

'Sire, je suis fort lié avec Haydn, et j'aimerais mieux l'avoir pour adjoint que tout autre; mais je crois devoir éclairer Votre Majesté sur la nature de son talent. Il est certain que ce compositeur jouit d'une grande réputation, et qu'il la mérite à quelques égards, sinon du côté de l'imagination, dont il est entièrement dé-pourvu, du moins pour l'adresse avec laquelle il sait s'emparer des idées des autres, les fondre et

les déguiser de manière à ce qu'il est difficile de les reconnaître, à moins d'être initié dans les mystères de l'art; il est à l'affût de toutes les nouveautés qui paraissent; on n'en exécute pas une qu'il ne prenne des notes sur tous les morceaux qu'il entend, pour peu qu'il espère en tirer quelque parti. Mais, afin que Votre Majesté ne puisse croire que je lui en impose, j'offre de lui en donner la preuve [p. 37] incessamment: on doit sous peu de jours représenter à la cour un opéra nouveau d'un compositeur de beaucoup de mérite; si Votre Majesté l'approuve, j'y inviterai Haydn, que je placerai en face de sa loge, et elle pourra juger la conduite de ce maître pendant l'exécution de l'opéra.'

L'empereur y consentit.

En effet, Gasman alla très-cérémonieusement inviter Haydn à cette représentation, en lui faisant même valoir l'avantage d'y être placé vis-à-vis l'empereur, qu'il désirait voir. Le soir ils s'y rendirent ensemble.

Un peu avant l'ouverture Gasman, cherchant dans sa poche:

'Ah, que je suis étourdi! s'écria t-il; j'ai oublié chez moi mon agenda musical et mes lunettes; et justement l'empereur m'a ordonné de prendre note des morceaux les plus saillans de l'opéra qu'on va exécuter, pour les lui faire copier séparément, et les placer dans ses concerts; en auriez-vous un? – Oui, dit Haydn, j'en porte toujours avec moi quand je suis en voyage (ce que Gasman savait très-bien) pour y écrire les pensées fugitives qui m'assiégent lorsque je marche seul. – Hé bien, dit le traître, faites-moi le plaisir d'y inscrire les thèmes de tous les morceaux que je vous indiquerai.'

Haydn s'y prêta volontiers. [p. 38] A chaque morceau de marque, à chaque passage, à chaque idée piquante et qui avait un caractère d'originalité, ce qui se rencontra souvent dans l'ouvrage, Gasman ne manqua pas de presser le genou de son compagnon, signe convenu entr'eux, et le trop confiant Haydn d'écrire soigneusement sur son agenda sa condamnation et sa honte, au moins aux yeux de l'empereur. Ce monarque, qui les examinait attentivement, incapable de soup-çonner un stratagème aussi odieux, perdit dès lors le désir de prendre à son service un homme qui, d'après ce qu'il avait cru voir, s'enrichissait aussi impudemment des idées des autres.

Comment un prince du mérite de Joseph II put-il tomber dans un pareil piége? Les souverains, à vérité, ne peuvent tout voir, tout juger par eux-mêmes, et ils feraient fort mal de s'en rapporter à eux seuls dans les choses où ils n'ont pas de connaissances approfondies; mais ils doivent être extrêmement sévères dans le choix de ceux qu'ils chargent de juger pour eux. Sous le rapport des arts, l'exclusion d'Haydn est une tache dans le règne de ce monarque célèbre; on ne l'excuserait pas par le peu d'importance de l'objet; dans un empire bien gouverné il n'est aucune partie indifférente, et certes ce ne sont pas les beaux-arts que [p. 39] doit dédaigner un souverain qui veut arriver avec gloire à la postérité : ce n'était donc pas un Gasman, c'était l'Europe entière qu'il fallait consulter sur Haydn. Comment l'empereur a-t-il pu croire, sur la foi d'un musicien qui, pour être à lui, n'en était pas plus remarquable, que celui qui jouissait d'une si universelle renommée n'était qu'un misérable plagiaire ? Que de voix intéressées n'eussent pas divulgué ses larcins s'il en eût été coupable ! Et s'il n'avait eu que les idées d'autrui, où en aurait-il trouvé assez pour composer de si nombreux ouvrages ? car peu de musiciens furent jamais aussi féconds. Si l'on veut additionner ce qu'il en a écrit de plus ou moins considérables, on en trouvera huit cent quatre-vingt-deux; en voici l'aperçu d'après son propre catalogue. . . .

NOTES

1 The Symphony cannot, of course, be identified; but chronologically it might have been one of the other 1772 works, *viz.* Nos. 46 or 47.

2 Pleyel's name here figures for the first time; he was Haydn's pupil in 1772, and this suggests that the story undoubtedly has some basis in fact – a crisis of some sort would seem to have occurred in 1772.

3 Johann Hinterberger (see Introduction).

4 Perhaps Joseph Purksteiner (Burgsteiner), who was paid 16 fl. monthly as against Tomasini's 40 fl. 12½ xr. and Blaschek's 25 fl.

5 Symphony No. 45 ('Farewell'); the scoring, of course, did not include 'flûtes' or 'clarinettes' and the 'lamentable duo' did not consist of the bassoon player and second violinist who had not signed the petition, but of two solo violins (Haydn and Tomasini).

6 Both Sarti's *Giulio Sabino* and Haydn's *Armida* were in the repertoire in 1784 at Eszterháza. For this visit and for some documents concerning Sarti, see pp. 482ff.

7 Since Pleyel was involved, the fire referred to must have been the one at Eisenstadt in 1776 (not 1768). The story of the Prince *secretly* rebuilding and refurnishing Haydn's house may after all be true; at any rate Haydn's thankfulness has been noted *passim* in this volume.

8 We believe Pleyel now confuses the Eisenstadt fire of 1776 with the Eszterháza fire of 1779; in the latter conflagration, *La vera costanza*'s autograph score seems to have perished. See *supra*, pp. 528ff.

9 The essence of this story, in Framery's version, has been quoted *supra*, pp. 378f.

10 Florian Leopold Gassmann, whose operas were appreciated also at Eszterháza.

Index

GENERAL INDEX

Principal references are shown in bold type; references to artists, engravers etc. in captions to the plates are indicated parenthetically, e.g. (*pl. 5*). In documents cited in the text, variant forms (and misspellings) of proper and place names are frequently found; such variations and alternatives are shown in parenthesis, e.g. 'Bauer (Pauer)' etc., as appropriate. The following lists are placed after the general index: compositions by Haydn; doubtful and spurious works attributed to Haydn; plays, operas and other works for the stage; insertion arias by composers other than Haydn. For abbreviations of musical instruments, see p. 19.

Abel, C. F. (composer) 595, 603
Abert, Hermann 338, 393n., 516n., 531
Aberdeen (University) 389n.
Abingdon, Willoughby Bertie, Earl of (Lord) 586, 595, 598
Abraham, Gerald 247n.
Abrams, Miss 451
Achau 114
Acton, Harold 622
Adamberger, Valentin (singer) 16, 489
Adani, Mariella (singer) 524
Adeste fideles (hymn) 288
Adler, Edition (music publishers) 525, 624
Admont Abbey 317n.
Agricola, J. F. 65: *La citella (zitella) ingannata* 65
Ahnsjö, C. H. 527, 544
Aisenreiter (bassoon player and corporal) 87
Akademie Kammerchor (Vienna) 232n., 236n., 555
Aland, H. J. W. von 504
Alba, José Alvarez of Toledo, Duke of 598
Alberman, Eva 30
Albert, Prince (Duke) of Sachsen-Teschen 14, 28n., 114, 122, 133, 135, 152, 163, 172, 177, 185, 187, 191f., 197, 447, *pl. 12*
Alberti bass 584
Albrechtsberger, J. G. 273, 316, 554, 560, 572, 663, 718, 743; brother 316n. concerto for harp and orchestra 572
Alencé, Elisabeth d' (married d'Ogny) 592
Alexandrian Library 603
Allgemeine deutsche Bibliothek 131, 341, 723
Allgemeine Musikalische Zeitung (AMZ) 629, 633, 702n.
Allgemeine Theaterzeitung 502
Alloja, Vincenzo (*pl. 34*)
Almac[k]'s (London club) 421
Almanach musical 159, 341, 346n.
Almeida, Antonio de 255n., 271n., 566n.
Alram, Anna (actress) 439
Alram, Franz (actor) 439
Alram, Joseph (actor) 439
Alsólendva (Esterházy estate) 32n.
Alt-Aussee 228n.
Altenburg Abbey 23
Altmann, Wilhelm 570
Alva, Luigi 524, 535, 537
Alxinger, J. B. von 502
Amati, Antonio (Antony) 90
Amati, Hieronymus 90
Amati, Nicolaus 90
Ameling, Elly 544
America, Haydn's music in (18th century) 33, 255, 401
Amici, Giuseppe 54, 731f., 749
Amsterdam 318, 320, 344, 562, 565, 571, 614, 742
Anderson, Emily 268n.
Andre (Esterházy grenadier) 64
André, J. J. 265n., 346, 376, 569f., 585
Anfossi, Pasquale 39f., 45, 47ff., 52f., 56f., 59ff., 63, 72, 408,

411f., 415, 417, 422, 424, 436f., 439, 452, 459, 466n., 470, 472, 480f., 484ff., 488, 499, 528f., 551, 553, 647f., 668, 669f., 678, 683, 685, 705, 713f.;
WORKS:
Gli amanti 55;
'Azione drammatica per musica' (title unknown) 55;
Il curioso indiscreto 47, 50, 53, 57, 60, **459f.**, 466n., 472, 485;
'Deh frenate' 459; 'Gaurdate che figura' 459;
La finta giardiniera 50, 53, 55, 57, 62f., 72, **424**, 470, 484;
'Appena mi vedon' 424; 'Geme la tortorella' 72; 'Noi donne poverine' 424; 'Si promette facilmente' 424; 'Vorrei punirti' 424, 470;
La forza delle donne 49, 53, 55, 57, 59, **422**, 484;
Le gelosie fortunate **713**, 724f., 730; 'Allor ch'io pazzo' 713;
Il geloso in cimento 49, 51, **408**, 417, 486, 647f., 668, **670f.**, 678, 682, 685, 694;
Isabella e Rodrigo o sia La costanza in amore 50, 53, 55, 57, 61, 63, **436f.**, 452, 484; 'Non ama la vita' 436; 'Saper bramante' 436;
La Maga Circe 714;
Il matrimonio per inganno 48, 50, 52, 55f., 60, 63, 648, **669f.**, 678, 682, 705; 'Ah, che voi' 669; 'Signor voi sapete' 670;
La Metilde ritrovata (L'incognita perseguitata) 49ff., 57, 61ff., **415**, 418, 484, 553;
Il sordo e l'avaro 48, 50, 52, 55, 60f., **683**, 694, 702;
Lo sposo disperato **459**, 466n., 484;
La vera costanza 45, 411f., 528f.;
I viaggiatori felici 47, 50, 52, 57, 60f., **480f.**, 485, 488, 499, 685, 694, 702, 705; 'Dove mai' 481; 'Voi pergoletti amori' 481;
Anonymous compositions:
Concerto de cors de chasse 79;
'La gentille et jeune Lisette' (folk tune) 608;
'Nachtwächtermelodie' 280f., 312, 350;
'Nichts Irdisch ewig gewehrt' (folk tune) 281;
'Trinche vaine star' (Aria) 254;
see also list of insertion arias, p. 799
Anonymous copyists:
—(No. 2) 243, 246, 394;—(No. 3) 245, 395;—(Nos. 4-9) 395;—(No. 10) 402, 459, 469, 544, 671, 675, 678, 683f., 704f., 713, 733f.;—(No. 10a) 731;—(No. 11) 648, 653, 670, 675f., 683f.,·704f., 712f., 715, 731;—(No. 12) 414, 705, 712f., 715, 731, 733f.;—(No. 13) 482, 676;—(No. 14) 402, 481f., 668ff., 675;—(No. 15) 402;—(No. 16) 402;—(No. 23) 415, 417f., 425, 534;—(No. 27) 423;—(No. 28) 423;—(No. 30) 425, 482, 537, 615, 654, 670, 713;—(No. 31) 425;—(No. 32) 425, 481f., 668f.;—(No. 33) 425;—(No. 40) 458;—(No. 46) 469;—(No. 47) 459;—(No. 48; Johann Elssler?) 238, 253n., 460f., 534, 537, 544, 604;—(No. 58) 472;—(No. 61) 713, 732;—(No. 63) 263, 544, 557n., 614, 615, 648f., 668;—(No. 64) 668;—(No. 66) 669;—(No. 73) 683f., 704
Anselm, Herr (Freemason) 506
Anselmo, Petro 90
Antal, Dora 259
Anton, Prince (of Saxony) 715
Antoni, Caspar 245

767

Index

INDEX OF COMPOSITIONS BY HAYDN
(HOBOKEN REFERENCES IN PARENTHESES)

TE DEUM:
—for Prince Nicolaus Esterházy (XXIIIc:1) 79;
—for Empress Marie Therese (XXIIIc:2) 291
Terzetto 'Pietà di me' (XXVb:5) 301, 358n., **604f.**, 651
TRIOS 130, 132, 141, 161, 174, 283, 354, 474, 711;
(a) for baryton, va. and vc. (listed by Hoboken numbers which conform with those given in *HV*, 1805) 134, 140f., 148, 154, 318, 347, **349ff.**, 760;
—(XI:2) 350, 352;—(XI:5) 350;—(XI:18) 118n.;—(XI:21-31) 126n.;—(XI:23) 118n.;—(XI:24) 118n., 126n., 349;—(XI:29) 350;—(XI:33) 351;—(XI:35) 280f., 350;—(XI:36) 351;—(XI:37) 350;—(XI:38) 345, 350;—(XI:40) 242f., 345, 351;—(XI:41) 141, 242f.;—(XI:42) 141, 349;—(XI:43) 349, 351;—(XI:52) 285, 350-2;—(XI:54-6) 351;—(XI:57-62) 353n.;—(XI:57) 242f., 349;—(XI:58) 351;—(XI:61) 348;—(XI:64) 350;—(XI:67) 351;—(XI:68, 69) 242f.;—(XI:70) 354;—(XI:71) 351;—(XI:73-96) 174, 176;—(XI:74-6; published by Boßler in version for v., va., vc., as Op. 32) 475n.;—(XI:75) 351;—(XI:76) 350f., 652;—(XI:77) 351;—(XI:78) 352;—(XI:79) 242f., 349;—(XI:81) 351f.;—(XI:82; 'Das alte Weib') 350, **352f.**, 652;—(XI:85) 352;—(XI:94) 351;—(XI:97) 350f., 353, 586;—(XI:101) 351, 475;—(XI:103) 350, 475, 583;—(XI:105) 174, 583;—(XI:106) 174, 242f., 349;—(XI:108) 475;—(XI:109) 228, **351**, 353;—(XI:110) 350;—(XI:111, 112) 475n;—(XI:114) 351, 475;—(XI:123, 124) 475;
(b) for fl. or v, v. II and vc. (IV:6-11; Forster, Op. 38; Traeg, Op. 100) 353, 450n., 559, **585f.**, **680f.**;
—(IV:6, 7) 680;—(IV:8) 586, 681;—(IV:9) 350, 586, 681;—(IV:10) 586, 681;—(IV:11) 681;
(c) for 2 fl. and vc. ('London'; IV:1-4) 242f., 586;
(d) for cor., v., vc., see Divertimentos: *Divertimento a tre* (IV:5);
(e) for pf., v., vc. (some with fl. instead of v.; arranged as in the chronological Doblinger edition) 345, 360, 549;
—Nos. 5, 14 (XV:1, f1) 272;—Nos. 17-19 (XV:2, 5, 6) **583**;—No. 17 (XV:2) 350, 379n., 450n., 681, 703;—No. 18 (XV:5) 378-80, 450n., 679, 681, *pl*. 27;—No. 19 (XV:6) 37, 673ff.;—Nos. 20-30 (XV:7-17) **641f.**;—No. 20 (XV:7) 37, 242f., 673ff.;—No. 21 (XV:8) 37, 673ff.;—No. 22 (XV:9) 242f., 379n., 450n., 583, 681;—No. 23 (XV:10) 379n., 450n., 583, 681, 703; contemporary criticism 703, 723f.;—Nos. 24, 25 (XV:11, 12) 709f., 720, 723f.;—No. 26 (XV:13) 709f., 716, 720, 723f.;—No. 27 (XV:14) 735, 740;—Nos. 28, 29 (XV:16, 15) 727, 735, 740, 743f.;—No. 30 (XV:17) 727, 735, 743f.;—No. 39 ('Gypsy Rondo'; XV:25) 281f.;—No. 45 (XV:29) 584;

(f) for v., va., vc.;
arrangement of Piano Sonatas Nos. 54-6 (XVI:40-2), published by Hoffmeister 585;
(g) for 2 v. and vc.;
—(V:FI, 19, D2, 18, 15, 16; Chevardière, Paris) 590

VARIATIONS (cemb. or pf.):
—in C (XVII:5) 342, 643, 645;—in D (XVII:7) 337;—in D (XVII:8) 350, 352; see also *Andante con variazioni*; *Arietta con variazioni*
Vol(c)ks Lied (*Volkslied*), see 'Gott erhalte'

DOUBTFUL AND SPURIOUS WORKS
ATTRIBUTED TO JOSEPH HAYDN
(correct authors, as far as can be established, are shown in parentheses)

Aria (Cantata), 'Aime [Oime], dove m'ascondo' (*Fra i due litiganti*; XXIVa:Es1;=G. Sarti) 12, 471
Cassatio in F (II:F3;=Joseph Purksteiner) and—(II:G3; =Purksteiner) 77
Concerto for cor. and orchestra (VIId:4; author?) 80, 357
Divertimento (IID:20 = II:Es7; = Pankraz Huber) 405
Litaniae de B.V.M. (XXIIIc:C2;=Joseph Hayda) 666f.
Minuets (unidentified; = Joseph Eybler) 380, 717
MUSIC FOR THE STAGE:—Shakespeare's *King Lear* (Ia:9;=G. W. Stegmann) 204
OPERAS:
    Calipso (= Luigi Bologna) 473;
    Genovefen I-IV (pasticci; marionette operas; XXIXa:5 and *deest*) 36, 208, 211, 395f., 402, 403, 404, 406, 485;
    Die reisende Ceres (Hoboken *deest*) 18, 522
OVERTURES:
    —*Die Feuersbrunst* (XXIXb:A;=Ignaz Pleyel, see index of works by Haydn: Operas;

—*L'infedeltà delusa* (3rd movement of concert version; Ia:1; = Ignaz Pleyel), see index of works by Haydn: Operas
QUARTETS:
    —Op. 3 (III:13-18; = Roman Hoffstetter) 315, 380, 477, 591
SYMPHONIES (listed as in Hoboken Group I, starting with the key of C and ending in B [B flat]):
    —I:Es1 (= Herffert) 169;
    —I:Es6 (= Franz Aspelmayer or P. van Maldere) 405;
    —I:Es11 (= Theodor von Schacht) 608;
    —I:Es15 (= Anton Zimmermann) 539n.;
    —I:G3 (= Adalbert Gyrowetz) 663f., 719n.;
    —I:A6 (= Carlos d'Ordoñez) 389;
see also a group of spurious works published together with Symphony No. 30 (FI = Franz Dussek; CI5 = ?; G8 = J. M. Haydn; EI = J. M. Haydn; B8 = ?) 309
TRIOS:
    —Op. 40, Nos. 1, 2 (Forster; XV:3, 4; = Ignaz Pleyel) 378-80, 450n., 679, 681, **763f.**, *pl. 27*

LIST OF PLAYS, OPERAS AND OTHER WORKS
FOR THE STAGE

The works, listed alphabetically by title, are each identified by author or composer and classified by types. The abbreviations used are : B – ballet; MO – marionette opera; O – opera; OR – oratorio; P – play; PA – pantomime; S – *Singspiel*; SC – *scena*. In cases where the author or composer is unknown or not named in the context, appropriate references are given; in all other cases see general index under name of author or composer, and for works by Haydn under separate index of compositions.

Abramo (Mysliwecek), OR
Acide e Galatea (Haydn), O
Achilles und Daira (Schmalögger), B
Adelheid von Salisbury, P   685
Adelheid von Siegmar (Gebler), P
Adelheit von Ponthieu (Seipp, after St. Marc), P
Adelson und Salvini (Seipp), P   96f.
Albert I (Weisse, from the French), P   396
Albergatrice vivace, L' (Caruso), O
Alceste (Gluck), O
Alceste (Ordoñez), MO
Alcide al Bivio (Hasse), O
Alessandro il Grande (pasticcio; Haydn), O
Alessandro nell'Indie (Bianchi), O
Alexander (Gluck), O
Alle haben recht, P   98
Alle irren sich, P   98
Alsinda (Zingarelli), O
Amalie oder die Leidenschaften (Biwanki), P   97, 185
Amanti, Gli (Anfossi), O
Americano, L' (Piccinni), O
Amor contrastato, L' (Paisiello), O
Amor costante, L' (Cimarosa), O
Amor costante, L' (Gazzaniga), O
Amore artigiano, L' (Gassmann), O
Amore et musica, L' (di Capua), O
Amore in musica, L' (Piccinni), O
Amor senza malizia, L' (Ottani), O
Amor(e) soldato, L' (Felici), O
Andromaco (Paisiello), O
Arbore di Diana, L' (Martini), O
Arcifanfano, rè de' matti (Dittersdorf), O
Argwöhnische Liebhaber, Der (Schletter), P
Arlequin als Todtengerippe (Bienfait and Christ[e]l), PA   94
Arlequin der Hausdieb (Bienfait and Christ[e]l), PA   94
Armida (Gazzaniga), O
Armida (Haydn), O
Armuth und Liebe, P   685
Arnaud, P   94, 97
Arist oder der ehrliche Mann (Wahr), P   96
Arria (Klinger), P   396
Ascanio in Alba (Mozart), O
Assedio di Gibilterra, L', MO   28n., 65f., 470, 472, 478, 484
Assedio di Gibilterra, L' (Guglielmi), O
Astratto, L' (Piccinni), O
Astuzie di Bettina, L' (Stabinger), O
Athelstan (Leonhardi), P   685
Avaro deluso, L' (Paisiello), O
Axur (Salieri), O
'*Azione drammatica per musica*' (Anfossi), O (?)

Barone di Rocca antica, Il (Dittersdorf), O
Ballerina amante, La (Cimarosa), O
Barbiere di Siviglia, Il (Paisiello), O
Barbier von Sevilien (Beaumarchais), P
Barnwell (Lillo), P
Batterie, Die (Ayrenhoff), P
Bediente, Nebenbuhler seines Herrn, Der (André), P   95, 97
Bekanntschaft im Bade, Die (Stephanie Jr.), P   97

Bekanntschaft auf der Redoute, Die, P   97
Bellandra, P   409
Bernadons Reise in die Hölle (Kurz-Bernadon), P
Besuch nach dem Tode, Der, P   483
Bestrafte Rachbegierde, Die (Bader; Haydn), MO
Betrogene Philosoph, Der, P   210
Betrogene Vormund, Der, P   97
Betschwester, Die (Gellert), P
Bettelstudent, Der (Weidmann), P   94, 96, 98
Bettler, Der (Bock), P   95f.
Betulia liberata (Gassmann), OR
Blutschwitzende Jesus, Der (Eberlin), OR
Brille, Die, P   685
Buona figliuola, La (Piccinni), O
Bürger, Der (Bodmer?, Marinelli?), P   96
Bürgerliche Dame, Die (Hafner), P
Burlie, Diener, Vater und Schwiegervater, P   95

Cadi dupré, Le (?; Gluck), O   28n.
Calipso abbandonata, La (Bologna), O
Canterina, La (Haydn), O
Cantico dei tre fanciulle (Hasse), OR
Cavaliere errante, Il (Traetta), O
Chi delle altrui si veste, presto si spoglia (Cimarosa), O
Christmas Oratorio (Bach), OR
Circe, La (Astaritta), O
Circe, La (Cimarosa), O
Circe, La (pasticcio; Haydn), O
Citella ingannata, La (Agricola), O   65
Clavigo (Goethe), P
Clementine oder das Testament (Gebler?), P   95, 97, 209
Clemenza di Tito, La (Mozart), O
Combattimento fra Tancredi e Clorinda (Monteverdi), SC
Contadina in corte, La; Contadina ingentilità, La (Sacchini?; Piccinni?), O
Contadina fedele, La (Dittersdorf), O
Contadina di spirito, La (Paisiello), O
Contratempi, I (Sarti), O
Convitato di pietra ossia il dissoluto (Righini), O
Convito, Il (Cimarosa), O
Così fan tutte (Mozart), O
Creation, The (van Swieten; Haydn), OR
Credulo, Il (Cimarosa), O
Curioso indiscreto, Il (Anfossi), O

Dagobert, König der Franken (Babo), P   685
Dankbare Sohn, Der (Engel), P   94
Dankbare Tochter, Die (Hartmann), P   96
Darf man seine Frau lieben? (Gebler), P   95
Debora e Sisara (Guglielmi), O
Demofoonte (Pauersbach), MO
Derby (Crenzin), P   97
Deserteur, Der (Monsigny?; Sedaine), S   95
Deserteur aus Kindesliebe, Der (Stephanie Sen.), P
Dido (Bader; Haydn), O
Didone abbandonata, La (Sarti), O
Diener, Nebenbuhler . . . see *Bediente* . . .
Discordia fortunata, La see *L'avaro*
Diesmal hat der Mann den Willen (Ordoñez), S

798

INSERTION ARIAS ETC.
COMPOSED FOR OR USED IN OPERAS PERFORMED AT ESZTERHÁZA
(for arias known, or suspected, to be by Haydn, see separate index of compositions, p. 789)

The following list is subdivided into: (a) anonymous and otherwise unidentified insertions or borrowings, arranged alphabetically under name of composer of opera concerned (see general index under name of composer of opera); and (b) arias the text of which is known, listed alphabetically with name of composer of insertion given in parentheses (see general index under name of composer of insertion, where known; and, in the case of anonymous insertions, see principal reference, in bold type, under name of composer of opera concerned; for arias used in the pasticcio *La Circe*, see pp. 713f.).

(a) Anonymous and unidentified arias etc.:
—in Anfossi's *Il geloso in cimento*; *Le gelosie fortunate*;
—in Astaritta's *Il Francese bizzarro*;
—in Cimarosa' *Chi dell'altrui si veste, presto si spoglia*; *Giannina e Bernadone*;
—in Gassmann's *L'amore artigiano*;
—(Bonaga) in Guglielmi's *Il ratto della sposa*;
—in Piccinni's *La schiava riconosciuta*;
—in Righini's *L'incontro inaspettato*;
—in Sarti's *I finti eredi*; *Le gelosie villane*;
Overture to Sarti's *Idalide*;
—for Leiringa, Cortes, Montezuma, Quagozinga and Montezuma (anon.) and chorus (anon.) in Zingarelli's *Montezuma*

(b) Arias etc. (with composer where known), listed alphabetically):
—'Amor tristarello' (Bologna) in Traetta's *Il cavaliere errante* and Righini's *Il convitato di pietra*;
—'A per voi nell'mio petto' (anon.) in Anfossi's *Il matrimonio per inganno*;
—'Benedette sian' (Naumann) in *La Circe* (pasticcio);
—'Cara con quelle lagrime' (anon.) in Zingarelli's *Montezuma*;
—'Cara mia sposa' (anon.) in Cimarosa's *Il credulo*;
—'Cavatina' (Soler) in Cimarosa's *Il pittore Parigino*;
—'Che contento, che piacere' (anon.) in Cimarosa's *L'italiana in Londra*;
—'Compatite miei Signore' (Storace) in Sarti's *Fra i due litiganti il terzo gode*;
—'Dal campo' (anon.) in *La Circe* (pasticcio) 714;
—'Damerini cari e belli' (Bologna) in Cimarosa's *Il falegname*;
—'Dov'è si affretti per me la morte' (anon.) in Bianchi's *Alessandro nell'Indie*;
—'È tanto il furore' (anon.) in Righini's *La vedova scaltra*;
—'Fra l'affanno' (anon.) in Cimarosa's *Il falegname*;
—'Guardate che figura' (anon.) in Anfossi's *Il curioso indiscreto*;

—'Imperate o zittellucce' (Bonaga) in Guglielmi's *Il ratto della sposa*;
—'In amor ci vuol finezza' (Soler) in Sarti's *Fra i due litiganti il terzo gode*;
—Infelice sventurata' (anon.) in Paisello's *L'avaro deluso*;
—'La donna a bella rosa somiglia' (Naumann) in Anfossi's *La finta giardiniera*;
—'Non ti muove' (Bonaga) in Guglielmi's *Il ratto della sposa*;
—'Odio furor dispetto' (Jomelli) in Righini's *Il convitato di pietra*;
—'Ohime! ch'innanzi agli occhi' (Recit.) and 'Penso che per morire' (anon.) in Cimarosa's *Il pittore Parigino*;
—'Or che il cielo' (Bianchi) in Anfossi's *Le gelosie fortunate*;
—Overture (Naumann) to *La Circe* (pasticcio);
—'Pensa che l'hai tradita' (anon.) in Guglielmi's *Le vicende d'amore*;
—'Penso che per morire', see 'Ohime!' above;
—'Per questa mano' (anon.) in Guglielmi's *Le vicende d'amore*;
—'Pietà d'un sventurato' (anon.) in Traetta's *Ifigenia in Tauride*;
—'Qual cambiamento' (Naumann) in *La Circe* (pasticcio);
—'Quant'è vezzosa (anon.) in Piccinni's *La schiava riconosciuta*;
—'Quasi in tutte le ragazze' (anon.) in *La Circe* (pasticcio);
—'Questo core' (anon.) in Guglielmi's *Le vicende d'amore*;
—Scena di Giulietta (anon.) in Anfossi's *Il matrimonio per inganno*;
—'Se il mio core' (anon.) in Cimarosa's *La ballerina amante*;
—'Se sapeste che' (anon.) in Gassmann's *L'amore artigiano* and Righini's *L'incontro inaspettato*;
—'Se voi sapete' (Bonaga) in Guglielmi's *Il ratto della sposa*;
—'Tira, tira' (anon.) in Righini's *Il convitato di pietra*;
—'Tutti schiavi' (anon.) in Righini's *La vedova scaltra*;
—'Un baccio di mano' (Mozart) in Anfossi's *Le gelosie fortunate*;
—'Viva, viva li sposi' (Righini) in Guglielmi's *Il ratto della sposa*